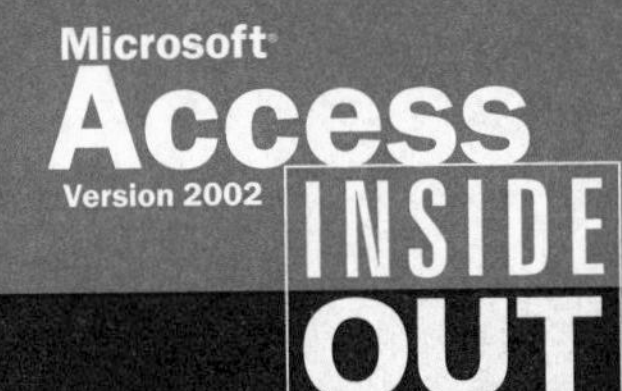

Third-Party Utilities, Demos, and Trials

All the third-party add-ins on this CD have been tested for use with Access Version 2002. You get full details on each tool—including a full description, application size, system requirements, and installation instructions.

Includes:

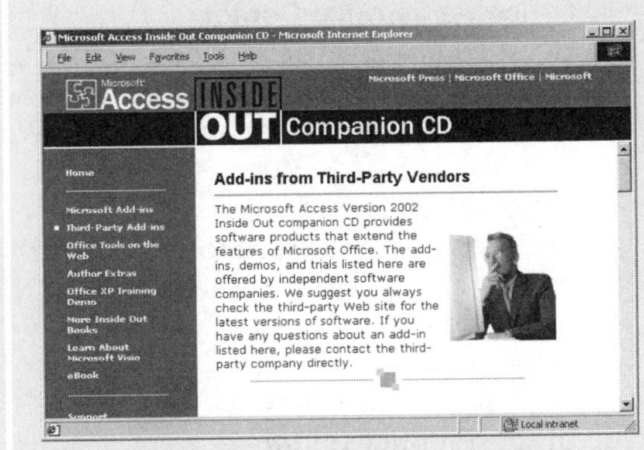

- **Rich Fisher's Find And Replace**—search and replace in Access tables, queries, forms, reports, macros, and code.
- **J Mueller's cJAM**—organize workgroups, authorize user access, and manage various data sources with this security-management and user account-management tool.
- **HiSoftware's metaPackager™**—encapsulate your files in *pure* XML so they're easy to index and manage.
- **GlobeSoft's MultiNetworkManager**—connect to multiple networks the easy way.
- **FMS Total Access Analyzer**—uncover detailed information on each object in your database, get extensive cross-references on where and how each object is used, and see more than 100 types of errors and suggestions to fix and improve your database.
- **FMS Total Access Statistics**—get the stats on your data, including weighted averages, percentiles, t-tests, frequency distributions, confidence intervals, correlations, regressions, crosstabs, ANOVA, Chi-Square, non-parametrics, test value probability calculator, and much more!
- **Database Creations Inventory Manager**—simplify the work of managing your inventory with logical, user friendly forms and great reports. Keep track of your inventory or integrate into your own sales or purchase order system.
- **Database Creations Report Manager**—categorize, maintain, and print reports in a few easy steps. Users can select from multiple criteria options and date ranges to create any number of variations of the same report.
- **Database Creations Search Manager**—call a search interface from any form to filter the form, or call the search interface to modify the row source for any combo or list box.

Microsoft Access Version 2002 INSIDE OUT

Office Tools on the Web

Here you'll find ready links to the most helpful and informative online resources for Office XP, direct from Microsoft. Find out exactly how each site can help you get your work done—then click and go!

Office Assistance Center
Get help using Office products with articles, tips, and monthly spotlights. Learn more about working with documents, data, and graphics; using e-mail and collaboration features; creating presentations and Web pages; and using everyday time-savers.

Office eServices
Use these Web services to get the most from Office. Learn how to store and share files on the Web; build and host Web sites; find communication services, language translation, learning and reference, and online postage resources; tune up your computer; and much more!

Office Product Updates
Obtain recommended and critical updates to enhance your Office XP experience.

Office Download Center
Download updates, add-ins, viewers, and more from the Office Download Center. Use the online search tool to find the utilities to help you work faster and smarter.

Design Gallery Live
Pick out clip art or photos for your Office project from this huge royalty-free selection. New items are constantly added to meet your needs. The advanced search facility makes finding the right artwork quick and easy.

Microsoft Office Template Gallery
Instead of starting from scratch, download a template from Template Gallery. From calendars to business cards, marketing material, and legal documents, Template Gallery offers hundreds of professionally authored and formatted documents for Microsoft Office.

Online Troubleshooters
Microsoft has developed Office XP online troubleshooters to help you solve problems on the fly. Access them using the links on the CD—and get the diagnostic and problem-solving information you need.

Microsoft® Access Version 2002 INSIDE OUT

Author Extras

Here's where your Inside Out author went the extra mile: great sample files on CD for you to take apart and study! They're an excellent way to make the examples used inside the book come to life on your PC. The sample files illustrate a number of Access features in action and can help you jump-start your own projects.

- **Sample Access databases**—get hands-on experience with the techniques used in the book by studying and manipulating a variety of sample databases.
- **Sample add-ins**—add extra functionality to Access with add-ins for design schemes, menu manager, renaming, and more.
- **Sample code**—examine the code used in the chapters and use it to create your own add-ins and shortcuts.

More Inside Out Books

The Inside Out series from Microsoft Press delivers comprehensive reference on Windows XP and the Office XP suite of applications. On this CD, you'll find sample chapters from the companion titles listed below, along with details about the entire line of books:

- Microsoft Windows XP Inside Out
- Microsoft Office XP Inside Out
- Microsoft FrontPage® Version 2002 Inside Out
- Microsoft Outlook Version 2002 Inside Out
- Microsoft Excel Version 2002 Inside Out
- Microsoft Word Version 2002 Inside Out
- Microsoft Visio Version 2002 Inside Out

Microsoft® **Access** Version 2002 **INSIDE OUT**

Complete Microsoft Press eBook

You get the entire MICROSOFT ACCESS VERSION 2002 INSIDE OUT book on CD—along with sample chapters from other INSIDE OUT books—as searchable electronic books. These Microsoft Press eBooks install quickly and easily on your computer (see System Requirements for details) and enable rapid full-text search.

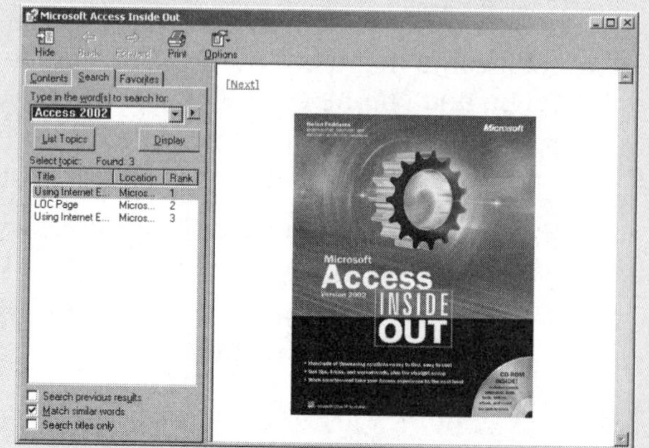

Features:

- Super-fast HTML full-text search
- Full-size graphics and screen shots
- Copy, paste, and *print* functions
- Bookmarking capabilities
- A saved history of every file viewed during a session

CD Minimum System Requirements

- Microsoft Windows 95 or later operating system (including Windows 98, Windows Millennium Edition, Windows NT® 4.0 with Service Pack 3 or higher, Windows 2000, and Windows XP)
- 266-MHz or higher Pentium-compatible CPU
- 64 megabytes (MB) RAM
- 8X CD-ROM drive or faster
- 46 MB of free hard disk space (to install the eBook and interactive tutorials)
- 800 x 600 with high color (16-bit) display settings
- Microsoft Windows–compatible sound card and speakers
- Microsoft Internet Explorer 4.1 or higher
- Microsoft Mouse or compatible pointing device

NOTE

System Requirements may be higher for the add-ins available on the CD. Individual add-in system requirements are specified on the CD. An Internet connection is necessary to access the hyperlinks in the Office Tools on the Web section. Connect time charges may apply.

Helen Feddema
Expert author, columnist, and database-application developer

Microsoft

Microsoft® Access Version 2002 INSIDE OUT

- Hundreds of timesaving solutions—easy to find, easy to use!
- Get tips, tricks, and workarounds, plus the straight scoop
- Work smarter—and take your Access experience to the next level

® Microsoft Office XP Application

PUBLISHED BY
Microsoft Press
A Division of Microsoft Corporation
One Microsoft Way
Redmond, Washington 98052-6399

Library of Congress Cataloging-in-Publication Data
Feddema, Helen Bell.
Microsoft Access Version 2002 Inside Out / Helen Feddema.
p. cm.
Includes index.
ISBN 0-7356-1283-8
1. Microsoft Access. 2. Database management. I. Title.

QA76.9.D3 F437 2001
005.75'65--dc21 2001042743

Printed and bound in the United States of America.

1 2 3 4 5 6 7 8 9 QWT 7 6 5 4 3 2

Distributed in Canada by Penguin Books Canada Limited.

A CIP catalogue record for this book is available from the British Library.

Microsoft Press books are available through booksellers and distributors worldwide. For further information about international editions, contact your local Microsoft Corporation office or contact Microsoft Press International directly at fax (425) 936-7329. Visit our Web site at www.microsoft.com/mspress. Send comments to *mspinput@microsoft.com.*

Acquisitions Editor: Kong Cheung
Series Editor: Sandra Haynes

Body Part No. X08-06079

To Woody Leonhard, for all his help over the years.

Contents At A Glance

Table of Contents

Chapter 2
Overview of Basic Access Features 27

Chapter 3
Introduction to Database Design 55

Chapter 7
Using Reports to Print Data 233

Chapter 8
Using Design Tools 301

Part 3
Queries and Recordsets 337

Chapter 9
Using Queries to Select Data 339

Chapter 10
Using Action Queries 395

Part 4
Customizing Access 493

Chapter 13
Customizing Access Toolbars and Menus (Command Bars) 495

Chapter 14
Using Macros 545

Chapter 15
Using Add-Ins to Expand Access Functionality 571

Acknowledgments

Many thanks to my agent, Claudette Moore, and to Microsoft Press lead editor, Sandra Haynes, for helping coordinate the complex process of writing this book; to Susan Harkins, for writing Chapters 8–11 when time was short; and to Jean Ross, Dail Magee, Jim Fuchs, Marzena Makuta, Julie Xiao, Brian Johnson, and Robert Lyon for testing the code.

My thanks also to Jennifer Harris, Rebecca McKay, Kathy Murray, Ina Chang, Shawn Peck, Barbara Levy, Marilyn Orozco, Rob Nance, and Bill Teel for your help in producing this book (which often included long nights and weekends to meet the tight deadlines).

We'd Like to Hear from You!

Our goal at Microsoft Press is to create books that help you find the information you need to get the most out of your software.

The INSIDE OUT series was created with you in mind. As part of an effort to ensure that we're creating the best, most useful books we can, we talked to our customers and asked them to tell us what they need from a Microsoft Press series. Help us continue to help you. Let us know what you like about this book and what we can do to make it better. When you write, please include the title and author of this book in your e-mail, as well as your name and contact information. We look forward to hearing from you.

How to Reach Us

E-mail: nsideout@microsoft.com
Mail: Inside Out Series Editor
Microsoft Press
One Microsoft Way
Redmond, WA 98052

Note: Unfortunately, we can't provide support for any software problems you might experience. Please go to http://support.microsoft.com *for help with any software issues.*

Conventions and Features Used in This Book

This book uses special text and design conventions to make it easier for you to find the information you need.

Text Conventions

Convention	Meaning
Abbreviated menu commands	For your convenience, this book uses abbreviated menu commands. For example, "Choose Tools, Track Changes, Highlight Changes" means that you should click the Tools menu, point to Track Changes, and select the Highlight Changes command.
Boldface type	**Boldface** type is used to indicate text that you enter or type.
Initial Capital Letters	The first letters of the names of menus, dialog boxes, dialog box elements, and commands are capitalized. Example: the Save As dialog box.
Italicized type	*Italicized* type is used to indicate new terms.
Plus sign (+) in text	Keyboard shortcuts are indicated by a plus sign (+) separating two key names. For example, Ctrl+Alt+Delete means that you press the Ctrl, Alt, and Delete keys at the same time.

Design Conventions

newfeature!

This text identifies a new or significantly updated feature in this version of the software.

InsideOut

These are the book's signature tips. In these tips, you'll get the straight scoop on what's going on with the software—inside information on why a feature works the way it does. You'll also find handy workarounds to different software problems.

tip Tips provide helpful hints, timesaving tricks, or alternative procedures related to the task being discussed.

Troubleshooting

Look for these sidebars to find solutions to common problems you might encounter. Troubleshooting sidebars appear next to related information in the chapters. You can also use the Troubleshooting Topics index at the back of the book to look up problems by topic.

Cross-references point you to other locations in the book that offer additional information on the topic being discussed.

This icon indicates sample files or text found on the companion CD.

caution Cautions identify potential problems that you should look out for when you're completing a task or problems that you must address before you can complete a task.

note Notes offer additional information related to the task being discussed.

Sidebar

The sidebars sprinkled throughout these chapters provide ancillary information on the topic being discussed. Go to sidebars to learn more about the technology or a feature.

Part 1

Access Fundamentals

Chapter 1

newfeature!

Exploring What's New in Access 2002

Whether you're a new user of Microsoft Access or an experienced Access database developer, you'll find a number of solid improvements in Access 2002. With an eye toward enhancements both in form and function, the changes in Access make working with the interface more intuitive than ever; extend the reach of your data by giving you new options for displaying, reporting, and publishing; and provide more programming control over the functionality and appearance of the databases you create.

As you'll see, Microsoft Access 2002 includes many new features, fixes, improvements, and other significant additions to functionality. This chapter provides a brief overview of these new and improved features. These features will be covered in more detail in their respective chapters.

Office-Wide Changes

Some new features in Access 2002 are not specific to Access. Instead, they are implementations of new features in Microsoft Office XP. Many of the improvements in Office XP are geared toward improving the user interface—making the features easier to get to than in prior versions—and extending the overall functionality of the applications so that you can use them together more intuitively, with less duplication of effort. Those benefits, along with features that help users recover from system crashes and preserve important files, will make your work with Access easier as well.

Task Panes

Access 2002 replaces the earlier Startup dialog box with the new Office-wide task pane feature, and it's a welcome change. When you open Access, the Access task pane appears on the right side of the Access window, with the New File mode selected. The task pane displays a list of files you've worked with recently, to make it easy to reopen a database. The task pane also serves as a search pane when you click the Search button on the Access toolbar, and it lists available items to paste when you select the Clipboard mode by choosing Edit, Office Clipboard. Whatever task pane mode is selected, you can continue working in the Access window while you select the options you need from the task pane.

You can also create a new database, data access page, or project; create a database from a template; and (a brand-new option in Access 2002) create a database that is a copy of an existing database, to save you the trouble of importing numerous objects into the new database. Figure 1-1 shows the Access 2002 task pane as it appears when you open Access.

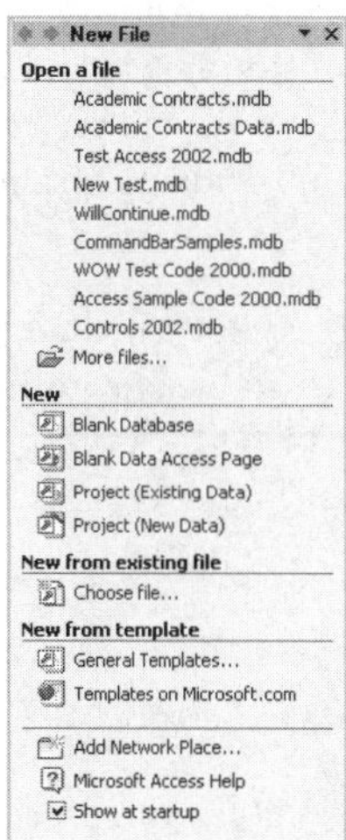

Figure 1-1. The task pane offers choices for opening or creating databases when Access is opened.

See Chapter 2, "Overview of Basic Access Features," for more details on the new Access task pane.

Smart Tags

Smart tags are a new feature in Office XP that do just what their name implies—they provide tags with links that lead to more information about a specific person, company, place, or thing. They provide a "smart" use of data by allowing you to share information when you're working with Microsoft Word, Microsoft Excel, and Microsoft Internet Explorer. Access 2002 doesn't support smart tags directly, but you can use the tags in Word or Excel data that you import to or export from Access database tables.

note For more information about using smart tags with Office XP applications, see *Microsoft Office XP Inside Out* (Microsoft Press, 2001), *Microsoft Excel 2002 Inside Out* (Microsoft Press, 2001), or *Microsoft Word 2002 Inside Out* (Microsoft Press, 2001).

Speech Recognition

Access now supports speech recognition for both voice dictation and command and control operations, allowing users to dictate text and navigate Access menus by using speech and voice commands. Speech recognition could be a wonderful boon to users who have difficulty using a keyboard or mouse—or for those users who simply want to cut down on unnecessary keystrokes.

For best results with speech recognition and dictation, you need a high-quality microphone. You should also be prepared to spend considerable time "training" the speech recognition software to understand your tone and phraseology. The effectiveness and functionality of speech recognition are sure to increase in subsequent versions of Office; for now, however, it's something worth trying if you ever find yourself with the time to experiment.

note Speech recognition is not available in Design view for tables, queries, or diagrams in Access projects (ADP files).

Access Changes

Access has always been a great database system. As it has evolved, it has gained even more functionality, including new import and export formats, database replication, data access pages, and, most recently, PivotTables and PivotCharts.

Access users will be pleased to see that Access now supports multiple Undo and Redo commands—a long-awaited feature. With enhanced PivotTables and brand-new PivotCharts, users can analyze their data from different perspectives in either tabular or graphical format.

For Access programmers, the new *Printer* object and *Printers* collection make working with printers in code much easier. Access projects are now easier to work with, and Access now supports Extensible Markup Language (XML) as an import and export format.

Data access pages are easier to design, and a new banded report format allows data levels to be expanded or collapsed. A Save To Data Access Page selection for forms lets you quickly create a data access page from an Access form.

These changes and many others make Access even more powerful and easier to use. The sections that follow take a closer look at the changes and improvements specific to Access 2002.

New Database Format

Access 2002 offers a new database format designed to better handle new properties and features, including some that might be available in future versions of Access. If you don't need to share a database with other users who are running earlier versions of Access, you can convert an existing database to the new format, or you can create a new database in Access 2002 format, which will let you use great new features such as PivotCharts.

The new database format is not the default format for new databases in Access 2002. Unless you manually change the Default File Format setting on the Advanced tab of the Options dialog box, new databases will be created in Access 2000 format. Figure 1-2 shows the Advanced tab of the Options dialog box with the default Access 2000 selection in the Default File Format box.

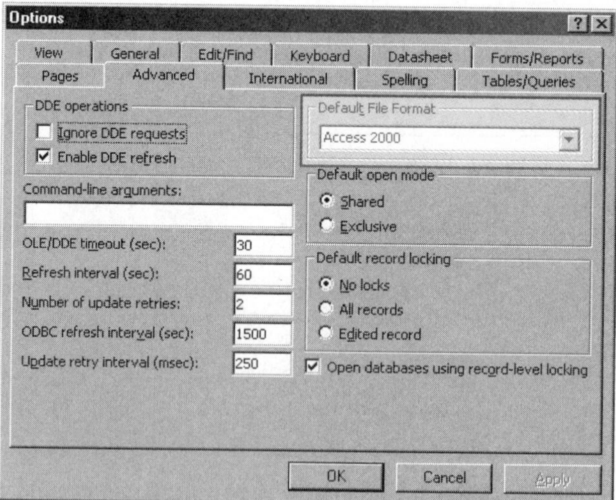

Figure 1-2. The Access 2000 format is still the default selection for new databases.

The database format is displayed in a database's title bar, in parentheses after the database name, as shown in Figure 1-3.

Figure 1-3. The Access 2002 database format is indicated in a database's title bar.

For more information about working with databases in different Access versions, see Appendix A, "Setup and Installation."

Improvements to Compact And Repair

The Compact And Repair utility has two components (which were separate utilities prior to Access 2000). The Compact component reduces database size by removing temporary objects, sometimes resulting in an amazing reduction of size—as much as 90 percent compaction. The Repair component repairs some database problems.

The Compact And Repair utility has been improved so that it is able to repair databases containing broken forms and reports more frequently than before. Additionally, it appears that some earlier version databases with corrupted forms or reports are repaired when they are converted to Access 2002 format, even without using Compact And Repair.

For more information on working with the Compact And Repair database utility, see Chapter 15, "Using Add-Ins to Expand Access Functionality."

Better Handling of Broken References

Access 2002 handles broken references better than earlier versions do, and it provides more informative error messages when references to code libraries can't be found. This makes it easier to correct broken references. If a back-end table is moved or renamed, however, you'll still get the *Could not find file* message. When you convert a database from an earlier version of Access, generally any references to Microsoft components (such as DAO, Word, or Outlook) will automatically be upgraded to the correct version. But if you have references set to non-Microsoft products, they might not be upgraded. Figure 1-4 shows the error message for a missing reference to the Find And Replace MDE file in a database converted from Access 97. (Find And Replace is an Access add-in.)

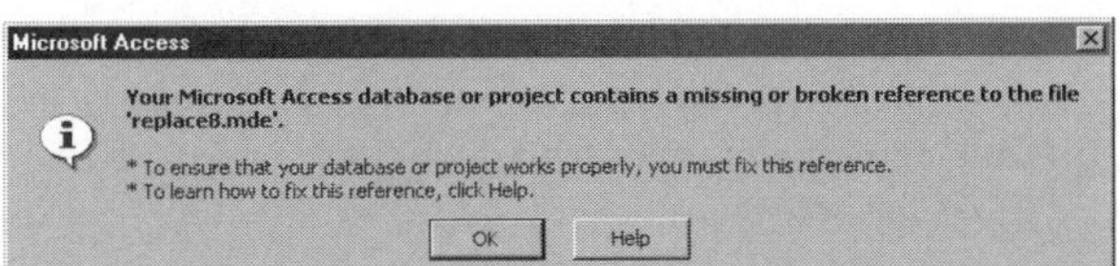

Figure 1-4. This error message offers details about a missing reference in a converted database.

Multiple Undo and Redo

Support for multiple Undo and Redo commands is a long-awaited Access feature now available in Design view for database (MDB) tables and queries; Access project (ADP) views, stored procedures, and functions; and forms, reports, data access pages, macros, and modules. The Design toolbars of most Access database objects now have drop-down Undo and Redo action lists. The Undo and Redo lists for tables, queries, forms, reports, and macros work just like their familiar counterparts in Microsoft Word.

In modules, the Undo/Redo functionality is slightly different: Undo and Redo buttons are available but not action lists, so to undo multiple actions, you simply click the Undo button repeatedly. Figure 1-5 shows the Undo list for an Access form in Design view.

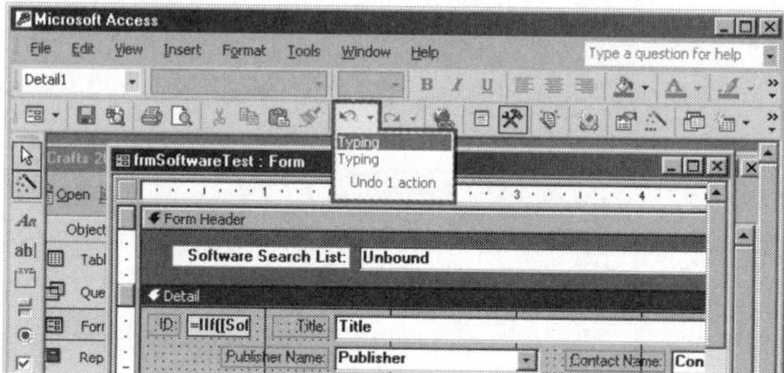

Figure 1-5. You can open the Undo drop-down list in an Access form in Design view.

The new multiple Undo/Redo functionality has some limitations. For example, the list of items that can be undone isn't saved when you switch between views for MDB tables, ADP views, ADP stored procedures, ADP functions, and data access pages. (This limitation is not surprising, given that these are quite different types of objects.) Linked tables don't have Undo functionality because their structures can't be modified—instead, they must be modified in their native databases. And Undo doesn't work in PivotTables (although it does work—at least for some actions—in PivotCharts).

> **note** Undo functionality has not changed for Datasheet and Form views; they have only a single-level Undo for changes to data.

PivotChart and PivotTable Views

Access 2002 forms have two new views, PivotChart and PivotTable, that enable you to look at your data in new ways. PivotCharts and PivotTables give you the flexibility to dynamically change the way your data is summarized and displayed by moving rows and columns and rearranging various elements on a form. As soon as you make the change, the PivotChart or PivotTable is redrawn, showing a new view of your data.

Access 2002 provides a wizard to help you design these views, although PivotTables and PivotCharts are quite easy to create without a wizard, so it isn't needed as much as for some other database objects. PivotTables are actually Excel objects embedded in Access forms, so some of the tools on the PivotTable and PivotChart toolbars resemble their Excel counterparts. Figure 1-6 shows a PivotTable listing the number of orders for products by country and salesperson.

For more information on PivotCharts and PivotTables, see Chapter 12, "Using PivotTables and PivotCharts to Analyze Data."

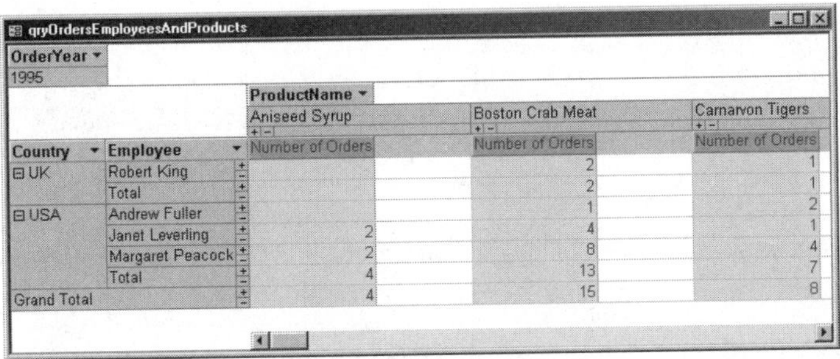

qryOrdersEmployeesAndProducts

OrderYear: 1995

Country	Employee	Aniseed Syrup: Number of Orders	Boston Crab Meat: Number of Orders	Carnarvon Tigers: Number of Orders
UK	Robert King		2	1
	Total		2	1
USA	Andrew Fuller		1	2
	Janet Leverling	2	4	1
	Margaret Peacock	2	8	4
	Total	4	13	7
Grand Total		4	15	8

Figure 1-6. This PivotTable displays orders by country and salesperson and allows users to swap rows and columns if desired.

New Form and Control Events

While Access was already rich in form and control events, Access 2002 has a number of new events for forms and reports, which give Access programmers more control over the appearance of reports (in print preview) and make it possible to run code from even more user actions than before.

Table 1-1 describes the new events available for forms. Many of these events apply only to PivotTable or PivotChart views.

note When the event name used in the properties sheet differs from the event name used in code (and listed in the Object Browser), Tables 1-1 and 1-2 list the code version of the event name in parentheses after the properties sheet version.

Table 1-1. New form events

Event	Description
OnUndo	Occurs when a user undoes all edits to a form
OnMouseWheel (MouseWheel)	Occurs when the user rolls the mouse wheel in Form, Datasheet, PivotTable, or PivotChart view
BeforeScreenTip	Occurs before a ScreenTip is displayed for an element in a PivotTable or PivotChart
OnCmdEnabled (CommandEnabled)	Occurs when an Office Web component determines whether the specified command is enabled
OnCmdChecked (CommandChecked)	Occurs when an Office Web component determines whether the specified command is checked
OnCmdBeforeExecute (CommandBeforeExecute)	Occurs before a specified command is executed
OnCmdExecute (CommandExecute)	Occurs after a specified command is executed
OnDataChange (DataChange)	Occurs when certain properties are changed or when certain methods are executed in PivotTable view
OnDataSetChange (DataSetChange)	Occurs when the data set changes in a data-bound PivotTable
OnPivotTableChange (PivotTableChange)	Occurs when the specified PivotTable field, field set, or total is added or deleted
OnSelectionChange (SelectionChange)	Occurs when the user makes a new selection in a PivotTable or PivotChart
OnViewChange (ViewChange)	Occurs when the specified PivotTable or PivotChart view is redrawn
OnConnect	Occurs when a PivotTable connects to a data source
OnDisconnect	Occurs when a PivotTable disconnects from a data source
BeforeQuery	Occurs when a PivotTable queries its data source

Table 1-1. *(continued)*

Event	Description
OnQuery (*Query*)	Occurs when a PivotTable query becomes necessary
AfterLayout	Occurs after all charts in a PivotChart have been laid out, but before they have been rendered
BeforeRender	Occurs before any object in a PivotChart has been rendered
AfterRender	Occurs after the specified object in a PivotChart has been rendered
AfterFinalRender	Occurs after all elements in a PivotChart have been rendered

Controls have two new events that work similarly to form events of the same name. (See Table 1-2).

Table 1-2. New control events

Event	Description
OnDirty (*Dirty*)	Occurs when data in a control is changed
OnUndo	Occurs when a user undoes changes to data in a control

New Form and Report Properties and Methods

Access offers several new properties and methods that give you increased control over the appearance and function of the forms and reports you create. These new capabilities include the following:

- You can now create a custom icon on the taskbar for forms and reports as well as for the application itself (replacing the standard form and report icons). To create a custom icon for forms and reports, choose Tools, Startup to open the Startup dialog box, select an icon file, and check the Use As Form And Report Icon check box, as shown in Figure 1-7. Both the application and its forms and reports will use this custom icon on the taskbar.

note You might have to close the database (or a form or report) and then reopen it to display the new icon. This is particularly likely when you're changing back to the standard icon from a custom icon.

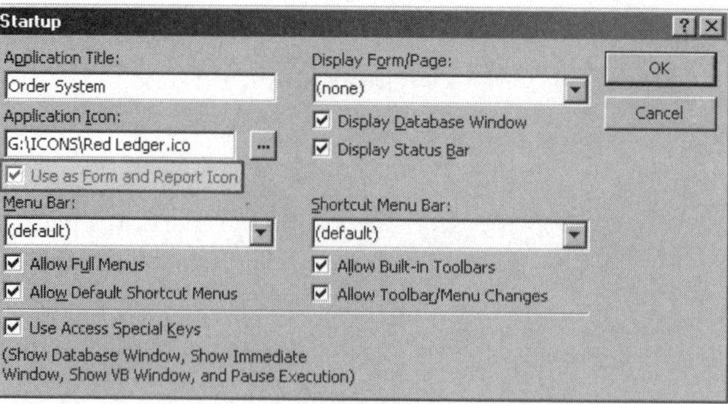

Figure 1-7. You can specify that the application icon should also be used for forms and reports displayed on the taskbar.

- A number of properties previously available only for forms are now also available for reports: *Modal*, *PopUp*, *BorderStyle*, *AutoResize*, *AutoCenter*, *MinMaxButtons*, *CloseButton*, and *ControlBox*. These properties give developers more control over how a report looks in print preview.
- The *OpenReport* method now has a *windowmode* argument that lets you open a report in hidden mode or as an icon (minimized).
- Both forms and reports now have a *Move* method that you can use to move and resize the form or report (like the old *MoveSize* action). This means that you can move or resize a form without first selecting it, which is much more convenient. (*MoveSize* works only on the currently selected object.)

Shortcut Keys and Accessibility

A number of new shortcut keys and accessibility features make Access much easier to use without a mouse. Table 1-3 lists these shortcut keys.

Table 1-3. New Access shortcut keys

Shortcut key	Description
F4	In Design view, opens the properties sheet
F7	When a form or report is open in Design view (with the focus on the Design view window or a properties sheet), takes the user to the code window, open to the form or report code module
Shift+F7	When the focus is on a properties sheet in Design view, moves the focus back to the design area without closing the properties sheet
F8	In a form or report in Design view, opens the field list; in a data access page in Design view, toggles the field list on or off

Table 1-3. *(continued)*

Shortcut key	Description
Ctrl+Right Arrow key or Ctrl+period	Moves to the next view when you're working with tables, queries, forms, reports, pages, views, and stored procedures
Ctrl+Left Arrow key or Ctrl+comma	Moves to the previous view when you're working with tables, queries, forms, reports, pages, views, and stored procedures
Ctrl+Tab	Navigates from a form or report section to a subsection
Enter	In Design view, with a field selected in the field list in a form or report, adds the selected field to the form or report design surface

For more information on working with forms in Design view, see Chapter 5, "Creating Forms for Entering, Editing, and Viewing Data."

Interface Enhancements

Even if you're comfortable with the Access interface and didn't see any need for enhancements, you'll find that the following changes to the user interface in Access 2002 make it easier for you to view your information the way you want to see it and to get the help you need without leaving the Access windows:

- Two new zoom powers, 1000% and 500%, have been added to the Zoom option for Print Preview.
- The Access menu bar now provides an Ask A Question box, where you can quickly enter a word or phrase to search for in Help. The drop-down list displays the previous few questions, so you can ask the same question again if you need to. After entering a word or phrase and pressing Enter, you'll see a list of appropriate Help topics to choose from. Figure 1-8 shows the list of topics provided after the term **PivotTable** is entered.

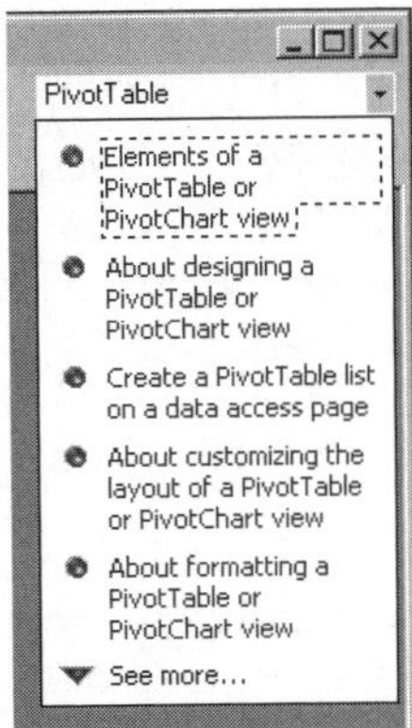

Figure 1-8. Type a phrase into the Ask A Question box to view a list of relevant Help topics.

- You can now open a subform in its own window either by right-clicking the subform and choosing Subform In New Window on the shortcut menu or by selecting the subform and choosing View, Subform In New Window. (These improvements also apply to subreports.) This is not so much a new feature as a restoration of a much-missed feature in earlier versions of Access.

Conversion Error Logging

When you're converting an Access 95, Access 97, or Access 2000 database to either Access 2000 or Access 2002 format, any errors that occur during the conversion are logged to a table. You'll find this table helpful when you need to track down and fix any conversion problems.

Figure 1-9 shows the Conversion Errors table for an Access 97 database converted to Access 2000 format (which, as mentioned, is the default format in Access 2002).

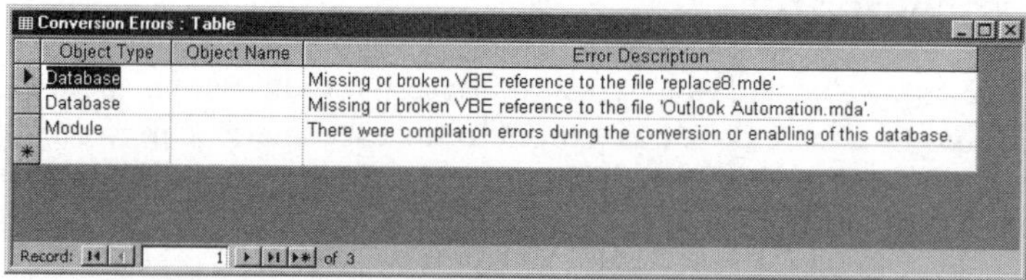

Conversion Errors : Table

Object Type	Object Name	Error Description
Database		Missing or broken VBE reference to the file 'replace8.mde'.
Database		Missing or broken VBE reference to the file 'Outlook Automation.mda'.
Module		There were compilation errors during the conversion or enabling of this database.

Record: 1 of 3

Figure 1-9. The Conversion Errors table helps you find and fix any conversion errors.

Expanded Programmability

Access 2002 provides several new properties and methods that let Access programmers obtain information about database objects, perform housekeeping chores, add or remove items in a list, and more, including the following:

- You can now pass a database password when you open a database programmatically by using the new *bstrPassword* parameter for the *OpenCurrentDatabase* method of the Access *Application* object.
- You can now obtain the *DateCreated* and *DateModified* properties for any Access object by using the new *DateCreated* and *DateModified* properties of the *AccessObject* object. For example, the following expression yields the date on which the frmColors form was last modified:

```
CurrentProject.AllForms("frmColors").DateModified
```

- Combo boxes and list boxes now have *AddItem* and *RemoveItem* methods, making them work more like these controls do on Microsoft Visual Basic and Visual Basic for Applications (VBA) forms. These methods can be used only when a combo box's or list box's *RowSourceType* property is set to Value List.

See Chapter 6, "Working with Form Controls," for an example of code that uses the *AddItem* and *RemoveItem* methods.

- The Access *Application* object now has a *CompactRepair* method to use in code. This method corresponds to the Compact And Repair Database command. (Choose Tools, Database Utilities.)
- The Access *Application* object has a new *ConvertAccessProject* method that you can use to convert an Access project from one Access version to another.
- The Access *Application* object has a new *BrokenReference* property. This is a Boolean property that tells you whether a database has any broken references. (You still have to iterate through the *References* collection to locate and fix any broken references.)
- When a module is edited and saved without compiling, only the changed module is saved, and then the entire project is saved when the project is compiled. This can save a good deal of compile time, particularly in large databases.

Printer Object and *Printers* Collection

The Access object model has a new *Printer* object and a *Printers* collection, making it much easier to work with printers in code than the old *PrtDevMode, PrtDevNames*, and *PrtMip* properties of reports, which were hard to understand and use. The *Printer* object is far more intuitive—it has properties corresponding to the options in the Page Setup dialog box.

The *Printer* object and *Printers* collection let you print reports on a specific printer, using the appropriate paper sizes and trays and special features such as duplexing, without having to first open the report and save it with that printer selected.

The *Printer* object and *Printers* collection are described in more detail in Chapter 20, "Customizing Your Database Using VBA Code."

Better Support of Multilingual Text and Graphics

Access 2002 adds significant new support for meeting the challenges of working in multiple languages, including the following:

- If you install the required fonts, multilingual text (English, Asian, and complex script) is displayed better in tables, forms, and reports.
- You can now output Access objects to Unicode RTF, HTML, text, and Excel file formats, thereby preserving multilingual text.

- A new Spelling tab has been added to the Options dialog box (accessed by choosing Tools, Options), allowing you to select a number of languages and other language-specific options. Figure 1-10 shows the Spelling tab with the Canadian French dictionary language selected.

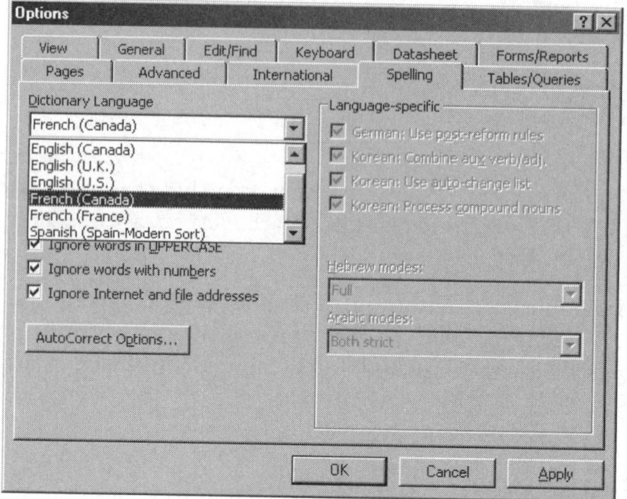

Figure 1-10. The new Spelling tab offers a wide selection of language-related options.

- A new International tab, shown in Figure 1-11, has been added to the Options dialog box, allowing you to select reading directions and other options for complex script languages.

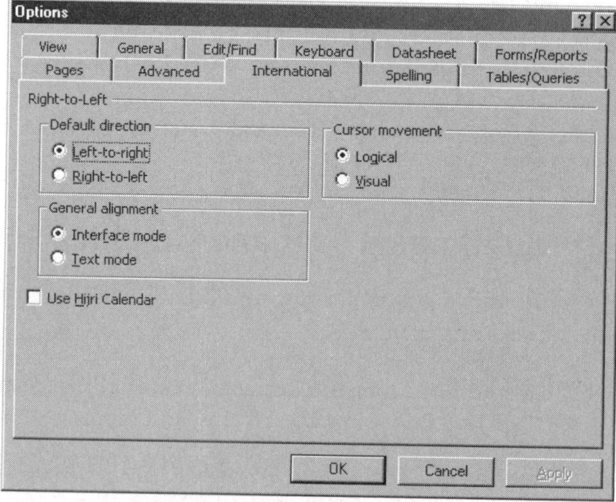

Figure 1-11. The International tab of the Options dialog box provides support for languages with complex scripts.

- Grouped line manipulation has been improved for Asian versions of Access. You can group a set of table-like lines, and then move individual lines by pressing Alt and an arrow key.
- The *IMEMode* property of the *ComboBox*, *ListBox*, and *TextBox* objects is now available to all users at all times, if the supported Input Method Editors (IMEs) are installed. This property allows you to set properties related to various Asian languages, such as kanji conversion, full-pitch or half-pitch hiragana, and katakana.

ADP Project Changes

A number of new features make it easier to work with Access projects, the ADP files that are the Access front end to data in SQL Server tables. Some of these new features include a new version of the Microsoft Database Engine that allows you to work with projects even if you don't have SQL Server, as well as many enhancements to project front ends.

For more information about working with Access projects, see Chapter 19, "Creating Access Projects," and Appendix E, "Upsizing to SQL Server."

SQL Server 2000 Desktop Engine

SQL Server 2000 Desktop Engine (formerly the Microsoft Database Engine, or MSDE) is included with SQL Server 2000 and is provided on the Microsoft Office CD in the MSDE2000 folder. To install MSDE, double-click Setup.exe in this folder. Figure 1-12 shows the folder on the Office CD with Setup.exe selected. With MSDE installed, you can create projects even if you don't have the full version of SQL Server installed.

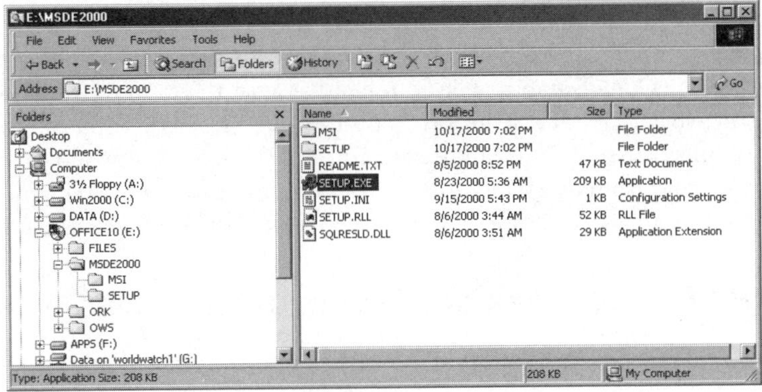

Figure 1-12. You can install MSDE from the MSDE2000 folder on the Office CD.

The SQL Server 2000 Desktop Engine setup includes a new version of the Microsoft Data Access Components (MDAC)—version 2.6. These components help you integrate data from a wide variety of sources and include Microsoft ActiveX Data Objects (ADO), OLE DB, and Open Database Connectivity (ODBC).

For more information about the SQL Server 2000 Desktop Engine and how it compares with SQL Server, see Chapter 3, "Introduction to Database Design."

Running Access Projects Against SQL Server 2000

Access 2002 and SQL Server 2000 work together more tightly than ever before. Here are some of the highlights:

Using SQL Server functions. SQL Server 2000 functions provide the same functionality as Jet parameterized queries. Use functions to replace stored procedures that returned a single result set, or any place a view was used. You can use these functions as record and row sources for forms, reports, data access pages, combo boxes, and other objects.

Extended property support. SQL Server 2000 now provides support for extended properties, letting you set up lookup relationships, validation text, formatting, subdatasheets, and other features of tables, views, and functions, just as with MDB files.

Updatable views. You can now update values in a view or function directly by using a datasheet. Any update that can be performed using an MDB query can now be performed using a SQL Server view or function.

Linked Table Wizard. The Access Linked Table Wizard can now be used to create tables linked to a SQL Server database, an MDB file, or other OLE DB sources.

Copy Database File and Transfer Database support. Access 2002 allows you to attach SQL Server MDF files to your local server. You can now use the Copy Database File command against the current ADP database on a local server to create a copy of the MDF file, so that you can move it to a different server. You can use the Transfer Database command to transfer a database from one server to another, even if you're not working on your local server. To access these commands, choose Tools, Database Utilities.

Running ADP Projects Against All Versions of SQL Server

If you're running an earlier version of SQL Server, you'll also see some changes, as follows:

Batch updates in a form. The new *BatchUpdates* property on the Data tab of a form's properties sheet allows you to tell Access to batch all data entry and send it to the server when the user navigates off the form, closes the form, or chooses Records, Save All Records. You can also create a button that programmatically saves or undoes all records, thereby eliminating the need to create unbound forms that gather all the data and commit changes at one time.

Better input parameter support for functions and stored procedures. You can now specify parameter values for a record source, just as with an MDB-based form or report. For example, if the following SQL statement is used as a report's record source, when the report is run, a parameter dialog box will appear, asking for the *Country* value:

```
SELECT * FROM tblCustomers
    WHERE Country = @ [Enter a country for the Customers report]
```

This new feature gives you more flexibility, eliminating the need to create different record sources with specific filters.

Password security. The new Set Login Password command (choose Tools, Security) allows you to change your logon password for the current logon specified for the ADP connection, without having to log off first.

SQL replication and Security dialog boxes removed. Because of security changes in SQL Server, Access no longer offers SQL replication and security. You must use SQL Server 2000 Enterprise Manager to implement replication and security for your database.

Using Recordsets

You can now use recordsets (sets of records that behave as objects) as row sources for combo boxes and lists, which gives you another option for providing lists of items to select. Additionally, disconnected recordsets can be used for all ADP objects that have *RecordSource* and *RowSource* properties.

XML and Access

Significant XML support has been added to Access, both in the core product and in data access pages. XML extends HTML to deal with structured data from many applications and allows the creation of custom data formats for special situations. Some of the new features are described briefly in this section.

XML Import/Export

You can create XML data or schema documents from Jet or SQL Server structures and data, or you can use XML data or schema documents to import (either programmatically or through the export user interface) data or structure into either SQL Server or Jet.

Import User Interface

The Import dialog box (choose File, Get External Data, Import) now provides an XML Documents selection, which allows you to import schema and data documents into either SQL Server or Jet. Figure 1-13 shows the XML Documents selection.

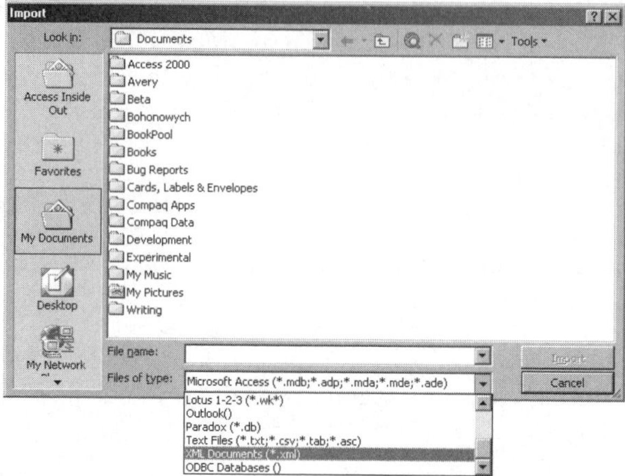

Figure 1-13. You can import an XML document into either SQL Server or Jet.

Export User Interface

The Access table/query/report/form export feature (choose File, Export with a table, query, report, or form selected) now includes an XML Documents Save As Type selection, as shown in Figure 1-14.

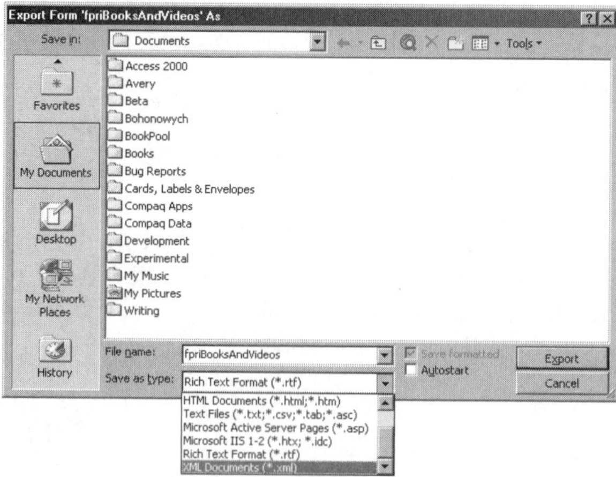

Figure 1-14. You can export an Access database object to an XML document.

XSL Transformations and Presentations

With Extensible Stylesheet Language (XSL), you can create your own style sheets for formatting XML data. You can create your own XSL data transformations for changing the data document format, and you can also create your own presentation formats and add them to the drop-down lists within the Export and Import dialog boxes by adding a metaheader to your XSL document.

Data Access Page Changes

Data access pages give you the means of publishing pages on the Web that work with data in Access or SQL Server databases. Data access pages were first introduced in Access 2000, but they weren't very easy to use. Access 2002 provides many enhancements that make it much easier to create and modify data access pages. In this section, we'll look briefly at each of these enhancements.

See Chapter 18, "Working with Data Access Pages," for more details on the changes to data access pages.

Data Access Page Designer

When you create a new data access page (or open an existing data access page in Design view), you'll find a host of improvements and new features, including the following:

- The Designer now supports multilevel Undo and Redo.
- Microsoft Internet Explorer 5.5 and 6.0 users have both keyboard and mouse multiselect support for applying sizing, horizontal and vertical spacing, alignment, and property settings to data access pages.
- Internet Explorer 5.5 and 6.0 users can also see the control's actual size while they're resizing it. Snap-to-grid support has been improved, and the Size To Fit command sizes the control to the size of its content.
- Multiselect drag-and-drop is now available from the field list.
- Banded (grouped) pages have more functionality, including intuitive drop zones, automatic indenting of group levels, a group-level Properties drop-down option on each group's shortcut menu, and automatic formatting for caption and footer properties.
- Banded pages are updatable. You can control updating by using the group-level properties *AllowAdditions*, *AllowDeletions*, and *AllowEdits*.
- The AutoSum feature makes it easy to create aggregates by selecting a control and clicking AutoSum.

- Controls, sections, group-level properties, and page properties now have shortcut menus.
- You can create customized navigation controls by applying the class name of the control to most HTML element types. For example, you can turn a label into a Next navigation control by appending *MsoNavNext* to the class name of the label.
- The Layout Wizard now supports Tabular, PivotChart, and Spreadsheet options.
- You can now bind the Spreadsheet control to data.
- The Designer now inherits extended properties from both Jet and SQL Server 2000 databases so that lookups are dropped as lookups instead of as static values, and label properties are set appropriately.

Improved Properties Sheet

Data access page properties are now easier to use because of better organization of the properties sheet and several new builders that help you select the appropriate value for a property. You'll find the following enhancements:

- Only relevant properties are shown for each element type. Some unneeded properties have been removed, and a richer set of applicable properties are exposed.
- You can set interior properties of ActiveX controls through the properties sheet.
- The properties sheet supports builders, including Page Connection, Color Picker, and Zoom.
- You can turn on a record selector by right-clicking a section, choosing Group Level Properties on the shortcut menu, and then setting the *RecordSelector* property to *True*. (The default setting is *False*, so the record selector isn't displayed for that group.) The record selector is a vertical band on the left side of the data access page. However, unlike with Access forms, you can't click the record selector to delete a record from a data access page after selecting it because the Delete Record option on the Edit menu is disabled for data access pages.
- All pages use alternate row colors by default, but you can change this setting in the Group Level properties sheet.

Deploying Data Access Pages

Access 2002 includes several new features that make it easier to deploy your data access pages on the Web after you've designed them, as follows:

- Access 2000 data access pages will be converted to Access 2002 format when they're opened in Design view in an Access 2002 database. Solutions created using Access 2000 will still work after you install the new Office Web Components.
- A page-level script notifies the user with appropriate messages when the correct browser or Office Web Components are not present.
- Users can set relative paths to Access databases, although only when the page is opened through the file system, not through HTTP.
- Developers can point all pages in a solution to Office Data Connection (ODC) or Universal Data Link (UDL) files by using the page's *ConnectionFile* property. When the page is loaded, it retrieves the connection file and sets the connection specified in the file. Set the default connection for all new pages on the Pages tab of the Options dialog box, by choosing Tools, Options.
- Developers can set the default pages folder on the Pages tab of the Options dialog box.
- The page's link property is exposed both programmatically and in the Page Properties dialog box in the Database window.
- With the *OfflineCDF*, *OfflineSource*, and *OfflineType* properties, you can build applications that work with SQL Server and Jet replication or XML data files. This feature is fully integrated with the Internet Explorer offline synchronization model.

note See *Microsoft FrontPage 2002 Inside Out* (Microsoft Press, 2001) for more information about deploying Access data on the Web using Microsoft FrontPage. FrontPage has its own set of tools for this purpose, some of them more powerful than the tools in Access.

Other DAP Improvements

There are a few other miscellaneous changes related to data access pages that make them easier to work with, including a Data Access Page selection in the Save As dialog box for forms, some features that allow you to link to XML documents, and a number of Data Source control attributes.

Working Off Line

You can prepare a data access page for offline work by setting a number of page properties, all available through the object model, or by opening the data access page in Internet Explorer and selecting Make Available Offline in the Add Favorite dialog box. For details on working with data access pages off line, see Chapter 18, "Working with Data Access Pages."

Chapter 1

Saving Forms and Reports as Data Access Pages

You can now save forms and reports as data access pages by selecting Data Access Page in the Save As dialog box, as shown in Figure 1-15. Saving a form as a data access page saves a lot of time when you want the page to look just like an existing form. You don't have to design the data access page from scratch; instead, you can create it from a form you've already created.

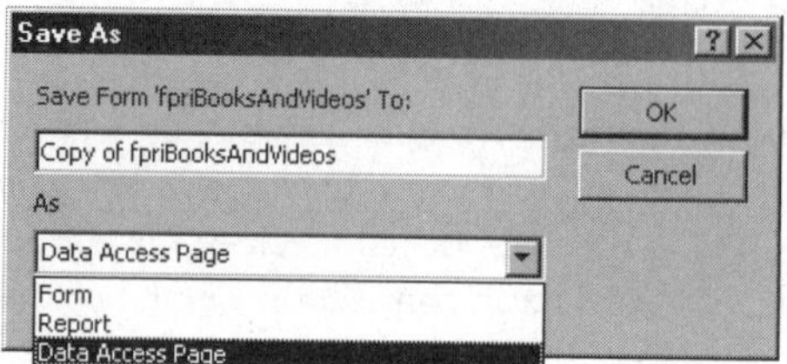

Figure 1-15. You can save a form as a data access page and save the time it takes to design the page from scratch.

Creating an XML Data Document

You can create an XML document or XML data island (XML data embedded in HTML code) from a data access page by using the *ExportXML* method.

Binding Data to an XML Data Document

You can set the properties described in Table 1-4 either on the page's properties sheet or through code at runtime.

Table 1-4. XML data binding properties

Property	Value	Description
XMLLocation	*dscXMLDataEmbedded*	Data appears on the page as a data island.
	dscXMLDataFile	Data is an XML data document.
XMLDataTarget	*dscXMLDataEmbedded*	Sets the ID of the data island.
	dscXMLDataFile	Sets the UNC, URL, or absolute path and name of the XML document.
UseXMLData	*True*	Connection to the live source is dropped and the data access page is bound to the XML source.

Binding to an Arbitrary Recordset

You can now bind data access pages to any arbitrary recordset. Use the *SetRootRecordset* method to bind to disconnected and persisted recordsets.

New Data Source Control Events

The Data Source control is used behind the scenes to bind data access pages to a data source. Unlike other controls, it has no representation in the interface; you program it in VBA code. This control now has several new events that give you more places to respond to user actions.

Table 1-5 lists the new Data Source control events.

Table 1-5. New Data Source control events

Event	Description
AfterDelete	Occurs after a record deletion has been confirmed and the record has actually been deleted, or after the deletion is canceled
AfterInsert	Occurs after a new record is added to the recordset
AfterUpdate	Occurs after a record is updated with changed data or after the record loses focus
BeforeDelete	Occurs before the record is actually deleted
BeforeInsert	Occurs when the first character is entered into a new record, but before the record is actually added to the recordset
BeforeUpdate	Occurs before a record is updated with changed data or before the record loses focus
Dirty	Occurs when the contents of a record change, and before the *BeforeUpdate* event
Focus	Page-level event that occurs when a section receives the focus (as opposed to the *Current* event, a recordset-level event that occurs when the record changes in the underlying recordset)
RecordExit	Occurs after all update events have fired and before the record loses currency

New Data Source Control Constants

Table 1-6 lists the new Data Source control constants. These constants are used to set the Data Source control properties or are returned by its events, enabling you to take different actions in code depending on what choice a user makes in the interface.

Table 1-6. New Data Source control constants

Constant	Description
dscDeleteOK	Indicates that delete operation succeeded
dscDeleteCancel	Indicates that delete operation was canceled through code
dscDeleteUserCancel	Indicates that delete operation was canceled by the user
dscDisplayAlertContinue	Determines whether a custom error message or no error message is displayed
dscDataAlertDisplay	Indicates that standard error dialog box should be displayed
dscRefreshData	Causes the *Refresh* method to refresh the data cache while maintaining the current connection

New Data Source Control Function

The new *EuroConvert* function converts a number to euros or from euros to another currency. You can also use this function to convert a number from one currency to another by using the euro as an intermediate value.

Updating Data Access Pages

Banded data access pages are now updatable, and child recordsets are fully updatable, enabling you to add, modify, and delete records from the child recordsets assigned to each band of data.

The Group Level properties sheet allows you to control whether the child recordsets are updatable by setting the following properties:

- *AllowEdits*
- *AllowAdditions*
- *AllowDeletes*

These properties are set to *False* by default for converted DAPs. DAPs created in the interface have these properties set to *True*.

Chapter 2

Overview of Basic Access Features

Microsoft Access 2002 is a powerful program with a huge collection of tools and features. Although the program interface is fairly easy to figure out and the Help system and built-in wizards make performing basic tasks a bit easier, you'll still have a substantial learning curve to master as you familiarize yourself with the workings of the program. If you're not an experienced Access user, you'll want to read this chapter to get a general overview of Access, learn about the Access interface, and understand the options you have when creating Access databases. These topics will be covered briefly in this chapter; later chapters provide more in-depth coverage.

Uses of Microsoft Access

Microsoft Access is an all-in-one database program that can store data internally or link to data in external sources. The data applications you can create range from simple to sophisticated. You can use Access to create address books or invitation lists or to create a database to house your personal CD collection. With some programming knowledge, you can create single-user applications for small businesses (perhaps linking to Microsoft Outlook, Microsoft Word, or Microsoft Excel), or you can create sophisticated multiuser client-server databases to run on an intranet or the Internet (linked to data stored in Microsoft SQL Server databases).

Access provides excellent design tools for creating forms for entering and editing data and for creating reports that you can use to collect and present that data. Access forms and reports can be connected to local tables, linked to external data sources, or converted to data access pages to display information on the Web or a company intranet. This flexibility allows you to use Access either as an all-in-one database containing both data tables and interface objects or as a front-end database with links to data stored in other sources.

Front-End and Back-End Databases

Access databases are often split into a back-end database, which contains the data tables, and a front-end database, which contains the forms, reports, data access pages, and other interface and supporting components. Splitting a database allows the interface components to be replaced or modified without disturbing the data in the tables.

See Chapter 15, "Using Add-Ins to Expand Access Functionality," for more details on using the Database Splitter utility.

Access is also an excellent prototyping tool. With Access, you can design forms and reports that are bound to Access tables filled with dummy data to show potential users how the final database will look. When the interface design has been finalized, you can connect the forms and reports to real data in another Access database or in a SQL Server database. You can even start with an Access database that stores data internally and then upsize to a SQL Server back end with a user-friendly Access front end when the size of the tables (or the need to connect via the Internet) makes it appropriate to store data in SQL Server tables.

The following sections introduce you to the main Access components, as well as the general tools and utilities you'll use to work with Access databases.

Creating Databases, Data Access Pages, and Projects

When you create an Access database, you have the choice of creating a new database, a data access page, or a project. A database is the right choice when you're working with data on your own computer: An Access database stores data in its own tables, or it links to other Access databases, as well as to Excel worksheets and text files. A data access page is the best choice when you want to work with data in Access or SQL Server databases via the Internet or an intranet, using Microsoft Internet Explorer 5.0 or later. A project is the correct choice if you need to create a large-scale client-server application to work with data in SQL Server tables. Projects store their data in SQL Server tables and use Access forms and reports as an interface (or data access pages when the data is not stored locally).

Projects in Access

Access uses the term *project* in two very different ways. If you choose a project selection when creating a new database, you create an ADP file that contains Access interface objects connected to data stored in a SQL Server database. Chapter 19, "Creating Access Projects," gives more details about this topic.

The other type of project is a Microsoft Visual Basic for Applications (VBA) project. Every Access database (MDB file) has its own VBA project, which can be viewed in the Project Explorer pane of the Visual Basic Editor (VBE) window. An Access VBA project contains the code attached to forms and reports (in the Microsoft Access Class Objects folder), any standard modules in the database (in the Modules folder), and possibly other objects. The database's project has the same name as the database, as shown in Figure 2-1.

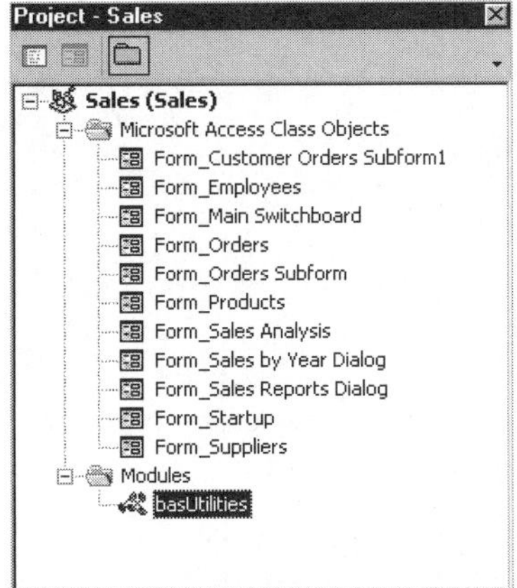

Figure 2-1. An Access database's project has the same name as the database itself.

If you have Microsoft Office XP Developer, you can also create new VBA projects and compile them into COM add-ins, as described in Chapter 21, "Creating Your Own Add-Ins."

An Access database contains a variety of objects in which you can store and manipulate data, such as tables, forms, queries, reports, macros, and modules. (A database won't necessarily contain all these objects.) An Access project, on the other hand, contains only interface objects; the data is stored in tables in an external database, usually a SQL Server database.

The Database Window

newfeature!

When you open (or create) a database in the Access window, a Database window appears within the main Access window. The title bar of the Database window contains the database's name and version. On the left side of the Database window is an Objects bar, from which you can select the type of database objects you want to view. The Database window has its own toolbar, which includes buttons that you can click to perform actions on the selected database object or to change the appearance of the Database window itself. Figure 2-2 shows the Database window, with some of its main features labeled.

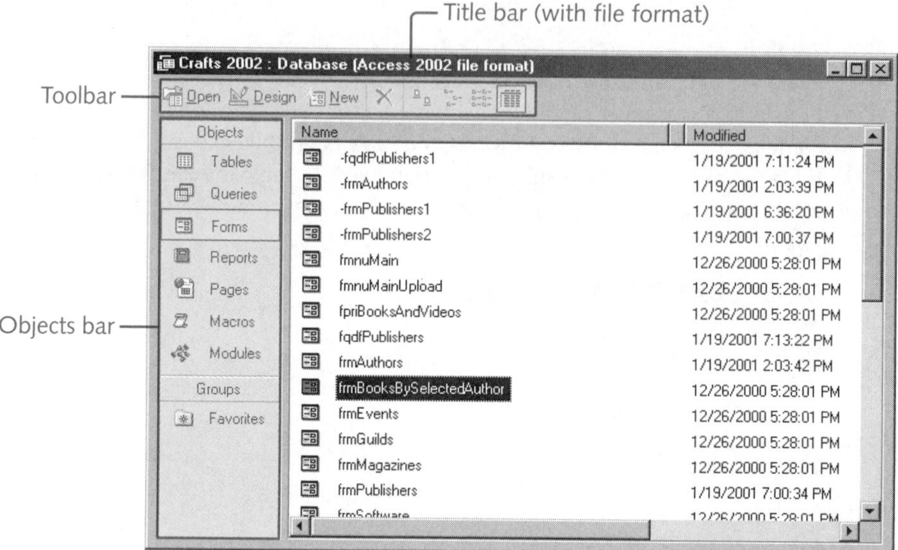

Figure 2-2. The Access Database window allows you to select the types of data objects you want to view.

note The Northwind and the Crafts databases are used throughout this chapter to illustrate database features. Both databases are available on the companion CD.

As an example of how the main database components are interrelated, the diagram in Figure 2-3 illustrates how you might use a form to enter data—in this example, you're entering information about crafts-related books and videos into tables and then filtering that data by queries and printing it in various reports. After you've entered all your information, you can also access the various database components that you have created—reports, queries, and so on—via the database's main menu.

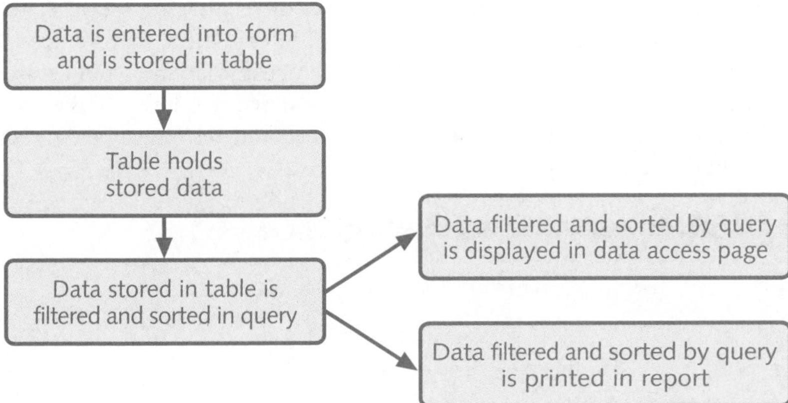

Figure 2-3. After you enter data in a form, you can filter and sort the data by using queries and print the results in reports.

Tables

You can use Access database tables to store data internally or to link to external data. *Local tables* store data in the same database as interface elements (forms and reports). *Linked tables* display data stored in external data sources, such as other Access databases, Excel worksheets, comma-delimited text files, and dBASE files. Figure 2-4 shows several local and linked tables in an Access database. Linked tables are indicated by arrows, and special icons indicate linked dBASE files, Excel worksheets, and text files.

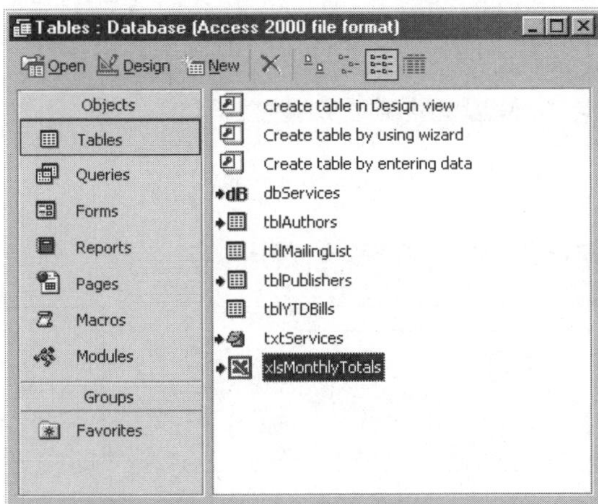

Figure 2-4. A different icon is used to indicate each linked table type—a plain arrow for linked Access tables, the Notepad icon for linked text files, a dB icon for dBASE files, and the Excel icon for linked Excel worksheets.

Database tables consist of rows and fields. A *row* (or record) is a set of related data about a particular subject; a *field* is a category of information. For example, a Customers table would have one row (or record) for each customer and would store information in fields such as Customer ID, Last Name, and Street Address. Different fields can store different types of data, such as numbers, text, and Yes/No values. You create and modify tables in Design view, as shown in Figure 2-5.

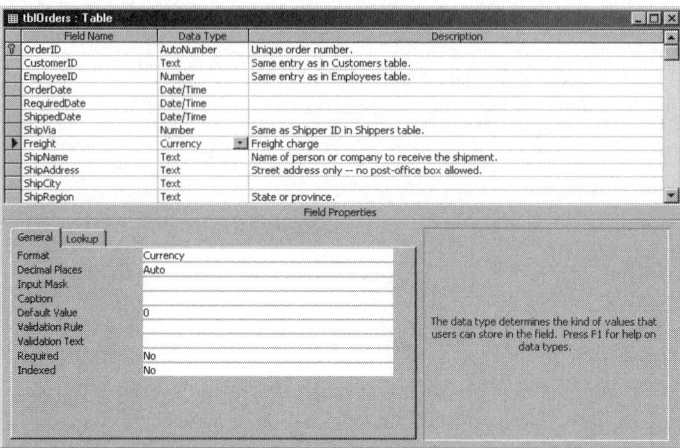

Figure 2-5. You can create and modify Access tables in Design view.

You can enter data directly into a table in Datasheet view (see Figure 2-6), but for ease of use and for data security, it's preferable to use a form as the interface for entering and modifying data. However, it's sometimes convenient to open a table in Datasheet view for a quick edit or a search-and-replace operation.

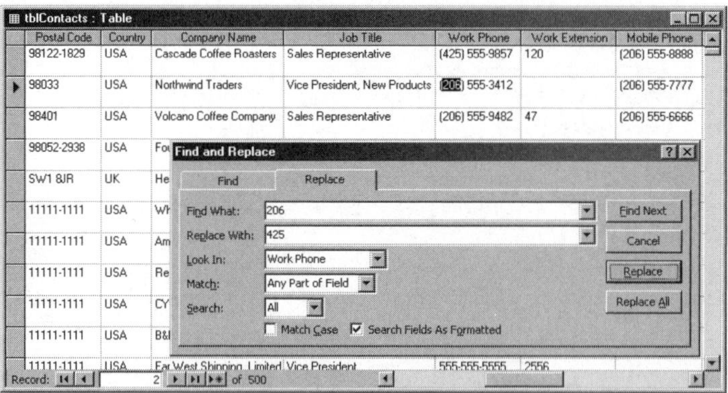

Figure 2-6. You can use Datasheet view to change an area code with Find And Replace.

See Chapter 4, "Creating a Database," for more information about tables and fields.

newfeature!

A database typically contains a number of tables related to one another by key fields. The diagram in Figure 2-7 shows the links between tables in an Access database in the Relationships window. You can print the Relationships window by choosing File, Print Relationships.

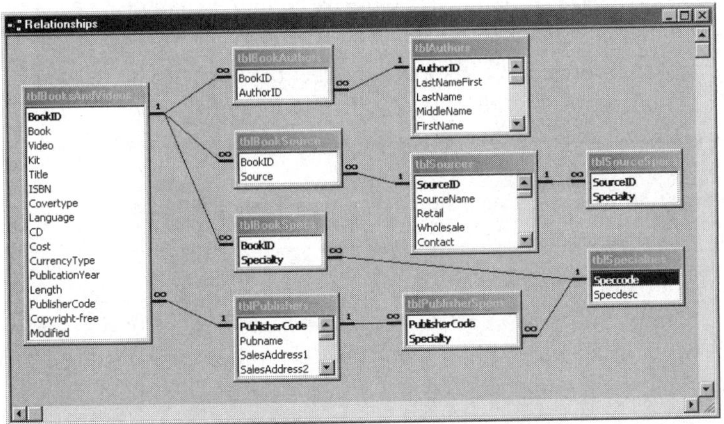

Figure 2-7. The Relationships window shows links between tables in an Access database.

> See Chapter 3, "Introduction to Database Design," for more information about key fields and setting up relationships among tables in a database.

Access projects don't contain tables; instead, they work with tables located in SQL Server databases. See Chapter 19, "Creating Access Projects," for more information about projects.

Queries, Views, and Stored Procedures

You use queries to sort, filter, add, delete, and modify data in your Access databases. For example, to find out how many CDs in your collection were recorded by Record Artist, you use a query to tell Access which data you want to find. Access then displays only those records that list Record Artist as the artist. You'll use primarily two types of queries in your work with Access: *select queries* and *action queries.* Sorting and filtering are done in select queries, whereas the various types of action queries can be used to modify data in tables and create new tables.

> For more information about the different query types, see Part 3, "Queries and Recordsets."

Access projects don't have queries; instead, they have views and stored procedures, which correspond to various types of queries. Views and stored procedures are stored in the SQL Server database, not in the Access project itself.

Views in Access

The word *view* is used in the following two ways in Access:

- Views of a database object, such as a table, form, or query, are selected from the View menu. These views will be discussed in the chapters dealing with specific database objects.
- Views in Access projects correspond to select queries (which are used to return a set of records on the basis of criteria you specify) in Access databases.

For more information about views and stored procedures, see Chapter 19, "Creating Access Projects."

Queries are also commonly used to sort data for reports or data access pages. For example, you might want to display data for only a specific range of dates. Figure 2-8 shows a query in Design view, with criteria that limit the query results to orders placed between June 1 and December 31, 1995.

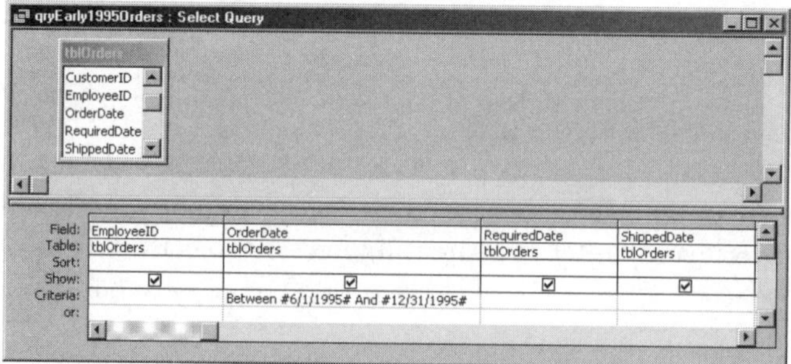

Figure 2-8. This query filters by a date range in Design view.

Figure 2-9 shows the same query in Datasheet view, with only orders in the specified date range displayed.

qryEarly1995Orders : Select Query

Order ID	Customer	Employee	Order Date	Required Date	Ship
10523	Seven Seas Imports	King, Robert	01-Jun-95	29-Jun-95	
10524	Berglunds snabbköp	Davolio, Nancy	01-Jun-95	29-Jun-95	
10525	Bon app'	Davolio, Nancy	02-Jun-95	30-Jun-95	
10526	Wartian Herkku	Peacock, Margaret	05-Jun-95	03-Jul-95	
10527	QUICK-Stop	King, Robert	05-Jun-95	03-Jul-95	
10528	Great Lakes Food Market	Suyama, Michael	06-Jun-95	20-Jun-95	
10529	Maison Dewey	Buchanan, Steven	07-Jun-95	05-Jul-95	
10530	Piccolo und mehr	Leverling, Janet	08-Jun-95	06-Jul-95	
10531	Océano Atlántico Ltda.	King, Robert	08-Jun-95	06-Jul-95	
10532	Eastern Connection	King, Robert	09-Jun-95	07-Jul-95	
10533	Folk och fä HB	Callahan, Laura	12-Jun-95	10-Jul-95	
10534	Lehmanns Marktstand	Callahan, Laura	12-Jun-95	10-Jul-95	
10535	Antonio Moreno Taquería	Peacock, Margaret	13-Jun-95	11-Jul-95	

Record: 1 of 237

Figure 2-9. Here's the same query in Datasheet view.

Forms and Reports

In Access, both databases and projects use forms to enter, edit, and modify data in local or linked tables. Reports are used to preview and print data for distribution. Although you can print an Access form, you're better off using forms for entering and modifying data and using reports for printing data, even if you have to create two database objects instead of one. The design elements needed for a useful and attractive form make for an ugly and not particularly useful report (and vice versa).

Figure 2-10 shows a typical form displaying data from a single record in a table.

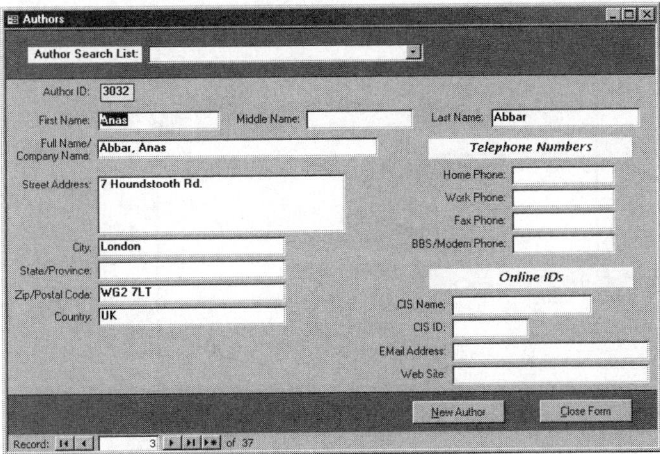

Figure 2-10. This useful form displays a single record's information.

Figure 2-11 depicts a grouped report in Print Preview, showing data from several records in a table.

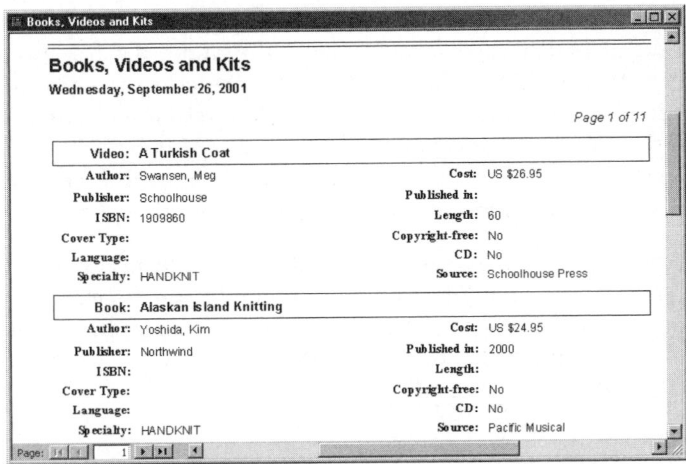

Figure 2-11. This useful report displays information from multiple records.

Both forms and reports use *controls,* which are interface objects that either display data from tables or provide decorative elements. On forms, different types o f controls let users enter data by typing, selecting from a list, or choosing an option from a group of options. Figure 2-12 shows a form in Design view. The Toolbox is used for inserting various types of controls; the field list is used for inserting fields from a table or query; and the properties sheet is used for modifying the properties of a control, a form section, or the entire form.

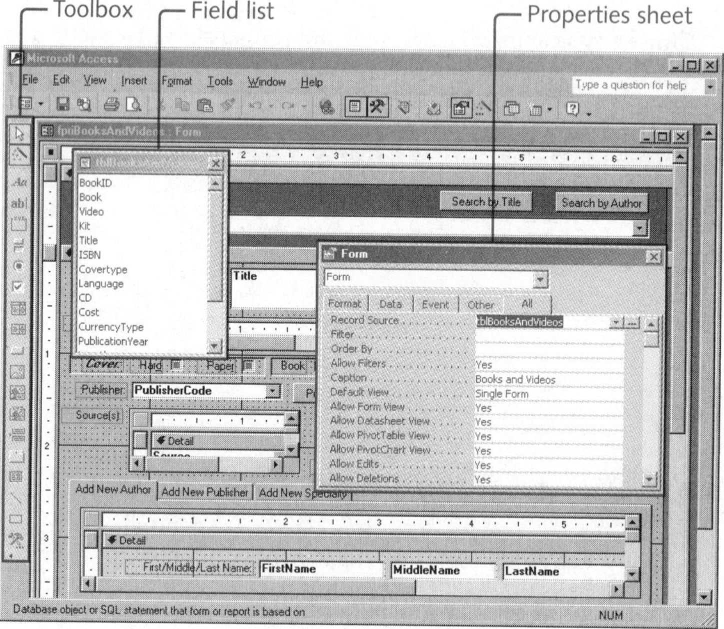

Figure 2-12. Design view offers many tools that you can use as you design your forms.

Figure 2-13 shows a complex form—in this case, the Crafts Books, Videos, And Kits form, which is the main data entry form for the Crafts sample database (available on the companion CD). This form includes text boxes for entering data directly, combo boxes for selecting items from drop-down lists, check boxes for indicating Yes or No choices, and option groups for selecting one of a number of options. It also has a tab control with several tabs, each with an embedded subform, and several command buttons that run event procedures to perform various actions.

You can use command buttons and embedded subforms on forms to quickly access related data. On the Books And Videos form, for example, you can click the Publisher Data button next to the Publisher box to get complete data about the selected publisher, and you can click the Works By Same Author button under the ID box to display a form listing all books by the selected author.

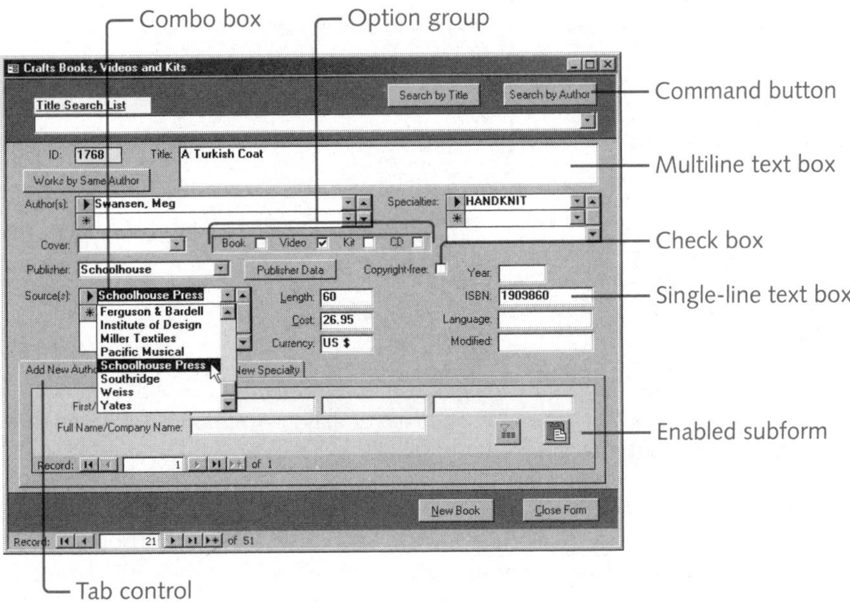

Figure 2-13. This complex form is shown in Form view.

For more information about using various types of controls on forms, see Chapter 6, "Working with Form Controls."

newfeature!

Reports are used to display (or print) data, not to modify data directly, so interactive controls such as combo boxes aren't useful on reports. However, reports do have several special features that don't apply to forms, such as the ability to sum numeric fields both for data groups and for the entire report, which is useful when you're preparing financial reports that contain breakdowns by month or by quarter. Additionally, you have many options for displaying data in reports, including grouped reports, columnar (datasheet) reports, charts, graphs, and—new to Access 2002—PivotTables and PivotCharts.

For more information about creating various types of reports, see Chapter 7, "Using Reports to Print Data."

Macros and Modules

Macros are collections of actions that enable you to perform database tasks using the keyboard or mouse. As the programming language for Access has become more powerful (first with Access Basic and then with VBA), code has largely replaced macros. However, macros are still useful for automating repetitive database tasks. They're also useful for two special purposes: creating database startup routines and creating your own custom hot keys. Figure 2-14 illustrates a macro that performs a number of actions necessary for importing and processing data from a mainframe computer; all you need to do to perform these actions in the correct sequence is run the macro.

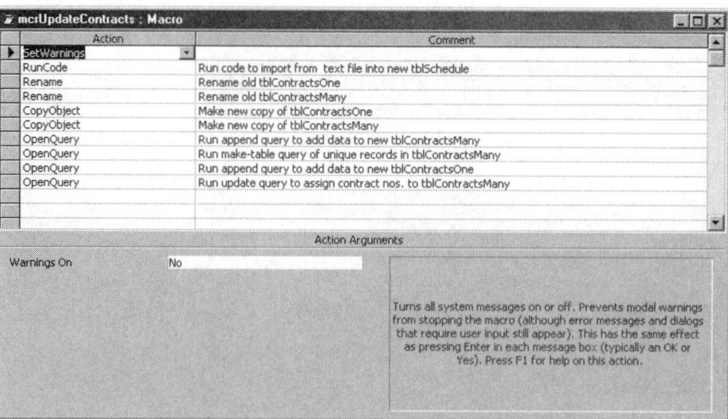

Figure 2-14. This macro runs a sequence of actions to import data from a mainframe computer.

Modules are collections of VBA procedures used to perform database actions. (See Figure 2-15.) Macros also perform database actions, but they have limitations; VBA code allows you to go beyond the boundaries of macro actions and fully automate a sophisticated database application. You can write procedures in stand-alone modules (that is, standard modules) or in modules attached to forms and reports (that is, code behind forms), and you can also define new database objects in class modules. Some programming tasks, such as error handling, require VBA code and cannot be handled with a macro.

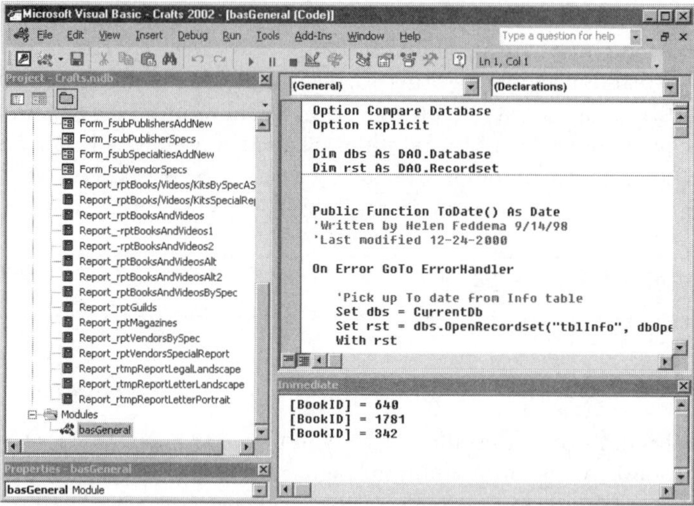

Figure 2-15. The Access Visual Basic Editor (VBE) window shows form and report code modules and a standard module.

For more information about macros, see Chapter 14, "Using Macros." For more information about writing code in modules, see Chapter 20, "Customizing Your Database Using VBA Code."

Data Access Pages

Data access pages are used to work with live data via the Internet or an intranet or with data in the database. When you create a new database, the task pane offers a data access page option that lets you create a stand-alone data access page (one that is not part of a database). However, data access pages can also be components of Access databases, listed in the Pages group of the database's Objects bar.

Data access pages can display data in much the same way as forms. (See Figure 2-16.) They also offer a mode for working with grouped data that resembles a grouped report more than a traditional Access form. Data access pages offer advantages over reports when you need to distribute data over the Internet or by e-mail—users see current data when they open the message, as opposed to the stationary data displayed in a report snapshot.

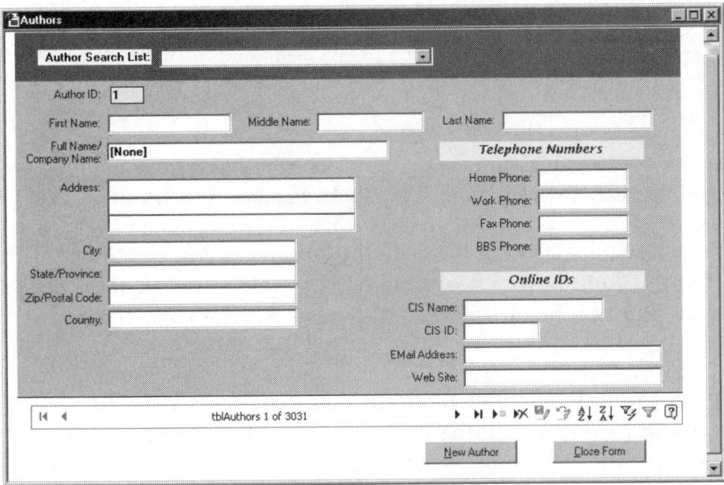

Figure 2-16. This data access page was created from a form.

> **caution** Sending a data access page to someone by e-mail is risky. Unless the recipient has a connection to the appropriate database, the data access page won't be able to display the data.

Using Online Help

newfeature!

Access 2002 includes several ways to get help. One method is to type a question directly into the new Ask A Question box on the right side of the main Access menu bar. (You can type any word or phrase—you don't have to style it as a question.) For example, typing **datasheet** in the Ask A Question box displays a list of topics to choose from, as shown in Figure 2-17. You can select one of the listed topics or click the See More selection at the bottom of the list to display additional topics.

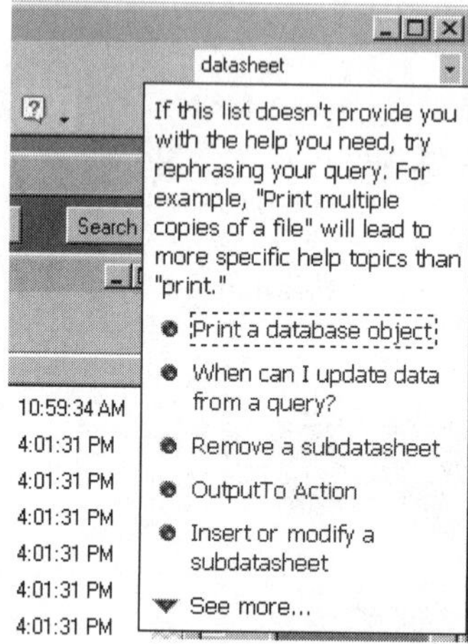

Figure 2-17. You can get help from the Ask A Question box on the Access menu bar.

You can also get help by clicking the Help button on the Access toolbar, which opens an Office Assistant balloon in which you can enter a search phrase. You'll get the same list that the Ask A Question box displayed. (You can open the same balloon by choosing Help, Microsoft Access Help.)

If you prefer not to use the Office Assistant, right-click the Assistant, choose Options from the shortcut menu, and on the Options tab in the Office Assistant dialog box, clear the Use The Office Assistant check box.

After you turn off the Assistant, clicking the Help button or choosing Help from the Help menu will open the Microsoft Access Help window. Double-clicking a book icon in the left pane displays a list of Help topics. You can select a topic to display its contents in the right pane, as shown in Figure 2-18.

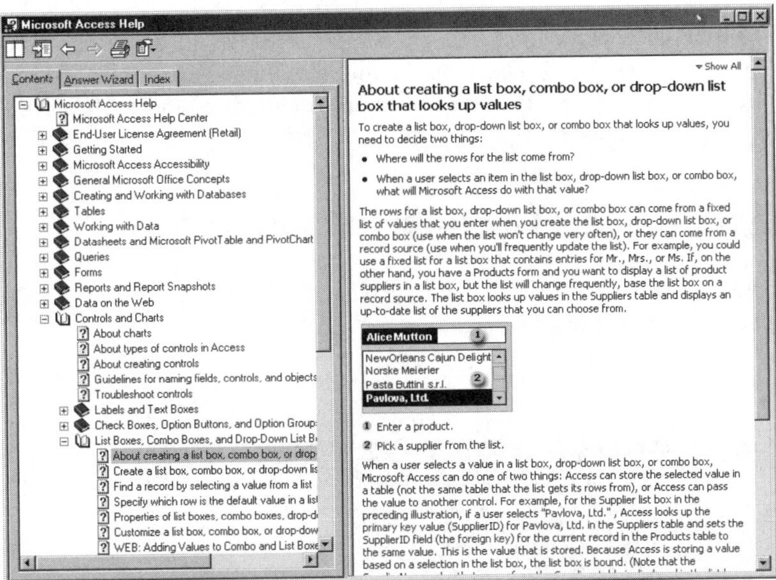

Figure 2-18. Selecting a Help topic displays its contents in the right pane of the Microsoft Access Help window.

newfeature!

You can display definitions for the terms in blue by clicking them, as shown in Figure 2-19. (The definition will appear in green directly following the term you selected.) To display all the definitions in a Help topic, click Show All in the upper right corner of the Help page.

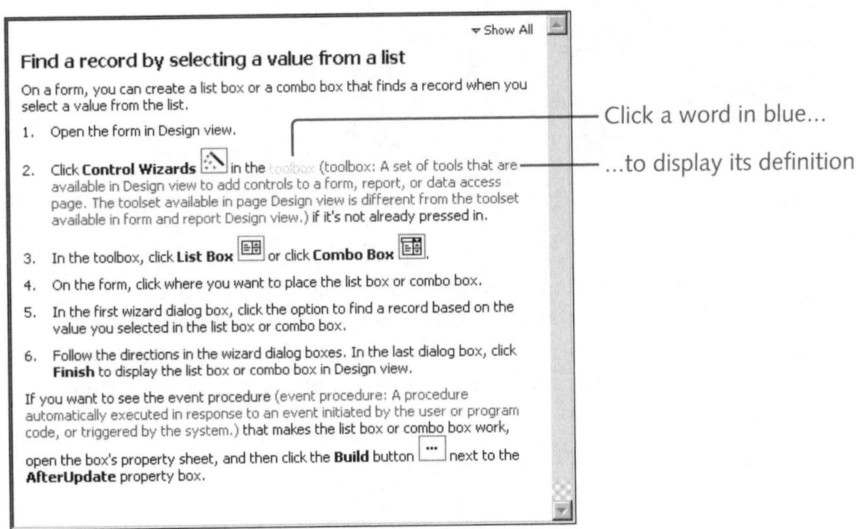

Figure 2-19. Clicking a word displays its definition.

Chapter 2

newfeature!

Some Help topics include the prefix *WEB*. These Help topics aren't part of the Access Help system, but they are available on the Internet. When you select one of these topics, you'll be connected to the Internet (if you aren't already connected), and the appropriate Help topic will appear.

Navigating the Access Interface

newfeature!

When you run Access, you'll see a window like the one shown in Figure 2-20, with a menu bar, a toolbar, and a task pane on the right.

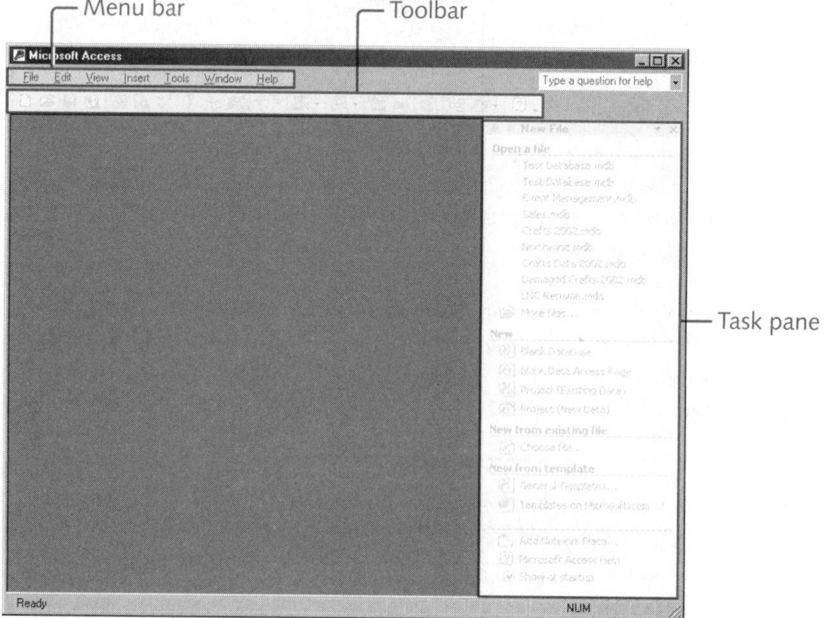

Figure 2-20. The main Access window is the first window you'll see when you start Access.

The menu bar and the toolbar at the top of the Access window are probably familiar to you from other Microsoft Office applications and from Microsoft Windows applications in general. Some of the menu selections and toolbar buttons are found in all Office applications—for example, the File menu and the Cut, Copy, and Paste buttons; others are specific to Access. The main Access toolbar buttons and their functions are described in Table 2-1.

> **tip** If you don't see the task pane, you can open it by right-clicking the gray background of the toolbar and choosing Task Pane from the shortcut menu.

Table 2-1. **Access toolbar buttons**

Toolbar button	Function
New	Creates a new database
Open	Opens an existing database
Save	Saves a database object
Search	Opens the task pane in search mode
Print	Prints a database object
Print Preview	Previews a database object
Spelling	Does a spelling check
Cut	Cuts selected text or object
Copy	Copies selected text or object
Paste	Pastes selected text or object
Undo	Undoes last action
OfficeLinks	Opens OfficeLinks list, with selections for exporting Access data to Microsoft Word or Microsoft Excel
Analyze	Opens a list of options for analyzing the database
Code	Opens selected object's code module
Microsoft Script Editor	Opens the Microsoft Script Editor
Properties	Opens the properties sheet for the selected objects
Relationships	Opens the database Relationships window
New Object	Opens a list of new database objects you can create
Help	Opens a Help window

newfeature!

The task pane—a new feature in Office XP—is implemented somewhat differently in each Office application. In Access, it has three main functions: to give you choices about which database to open or what type of database or project you want to create when you run Access, to serve as a search pane when you click the Search button on the toolbar, and to enable you to view the contents of the Office Clipboard. The task pane you see when you open Access has several areas, which are described in the following sections.

The Open A File Area

If you're running Access 2002 for the first time, you won't see any files in the Open A File area—you'll see only the More Files folder icon, which you can click to browse for a file to open. As you open and close files, Access adds their names to the list, up to a maximum number that you can specify by configuring the Recently Used File List option on the General tab of the Options dialog box. For more information about setting this value, see the section "Choosing Your Access Preferences," on page 46.

The list of recently used files in the task pane is the same as the list at the bottom of the File menu, which is a feature carried over from earlier versions of Access. To open a recently used file, just click the appropriate file name in the list. If you want to work with a file that isn't listed, click More Files and select the file name in the Open dialog box.

The New Area

If you want to create a new file rather than open an existing file, the New area offers several selections. Blank Database creates a new Access database, Blank Data Access Page creates a new data access page, Project (Existing Data) creates a project linked to an existing data source, and Project (New Data) creates a project and a new data source.

With the exception of Blank Database, each of these selections opens a dialog box in which you can make further selections appropriate to that type of object.

See Chapter 3, "Introduction to Database Design," and Chapter 4, "Creating a Database," for more information about Access databases. See Chapter 18, "Working with Data Access Pages," for more information about data access pages, and see Chapter 19, "Creating Access Projects," for more information about projects.

newfeature!

The New From Existing File Area

With the New From Existing File area (new to Access 2002), you can create a new database based on an existing database. The new database is simply a copy of the old database, with a *1* (or a higher number) appended to its name. This selection is useful when you want to create a new database that is similar to an existing database.

The New From Template Area

With the New From Template area, you can create a new database based on one of the database templates included with Access. (You can also download this set of templates from the Microsoft Web site, at *www.microsoft.com.*) Click General Templates to display the Templates dialog box. This dialog box contains two tabs: the General tab for the new database and project selections available under the New area of the task pane, and the Databases tab, which provides a selection of Access database templates. (See Figure 2-21.)

The Access database templates are actually wizards that guide you through the process of setting up a database to suit your needs. Chapter 15, "Using Add-Ins to Expand Access Functionality," takes you through the steps of creating a new database using a database template.

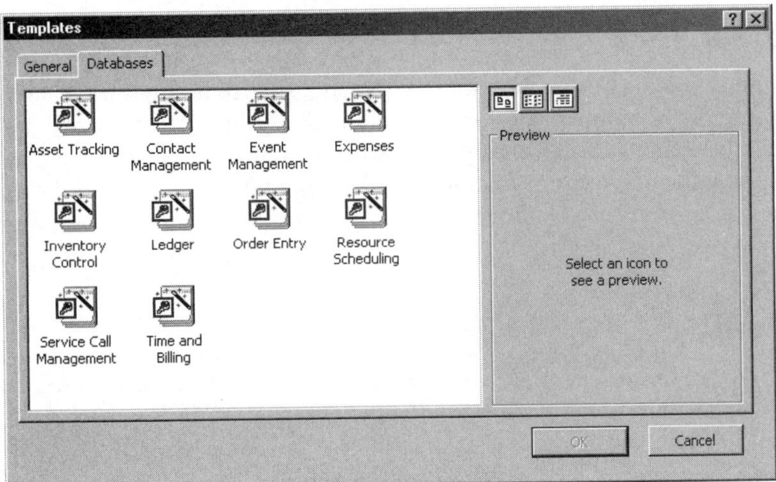

Figure 2-21. You can use database templates to more easily create a new database.

Using Keyboard Shortcuts to Get out of Trouble

Access provides several keyboard shortcuts that come in handy in the following circumstances:

- **Problem:** You need to see the Database window, but it has disappeared.

  Solution: Press F11 to bring the Database window to the front.

- **Problem:** Your code isn't working as expected, and you need to see the results of your *Debug.Print* statements.

  Solution: Press Ctrl+G to open the Immediate window.

- **Problem:** You need a command that isn't on your custom menu bar.

  Solution: Press Ctrl+F11 to toggle between the custom menu bar and the built-in menu bar.

- **Problem:** You need to stop code from executing, or you need to stop retrieving records from a remote table.

  Solution: Press Ctrl+Break to stop VBA code or (in an Access project) to stop Access from retrieving records from the server.

- **Problem:** You want to quickly switch to the VBE window.

  Solution: Press Alt+F11 to open the VBE window.

- **Problem:** You want to open an Access database without running startup code or opening the startup form.

  Solution: In the Windows Explorer pane, open the database by selecting the MDB file and pressing Shift+Enter.

Choosing Your Access Preferences

The Options dialog box, which you open by choosing Tools, Options, enables you to set an impressive number of database options. Generally speaking, you'll be fine if you leave all the settings at their default values, but you might want to change a few settings. The following sections offer a general discussion of the Options dialog box. More detailed discussions of specific options are provided in the chapters dealing with specific database objects.

The View Tab

The Show options on the View tab of the Options dialog box (see Figure 2-22) let you specify which objects will be displayed in the Database window.

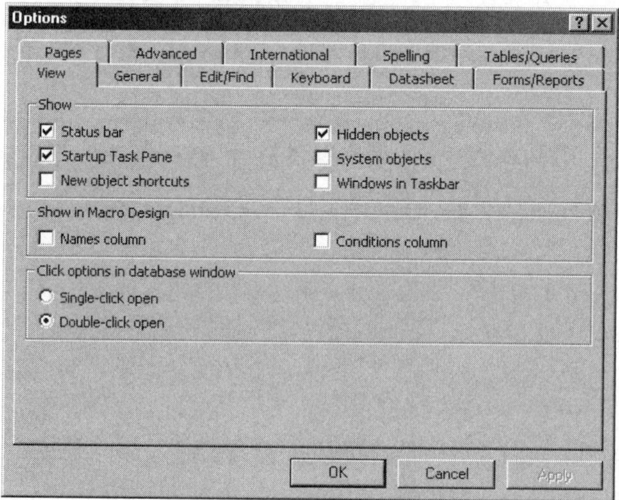

Figure 2-22. The View tab enables you to choose which objects you want to see in the Database window.

newfeature!

You can clear the Startup Task Pane check box if you don't want to see the task pane when you start Access. You can make a similar choice for the new object shortcuts. With the Hidden Objects and System Objects check boxes, you can display or hide hidden tables and system tables. The Windows In Taskbar check box controls whether database objects have their own icons on the Windows taskbar.

Figure 2-23 shows the Database window as it appears when all the options in the Show group are checked.

With the Show In Macro Design group on the View tab, you can specify whether to display the Names and Conditions columns automatically in new macros. With the Click Options In Database Window group, you can specify whether a single click or a double click will open a database object.

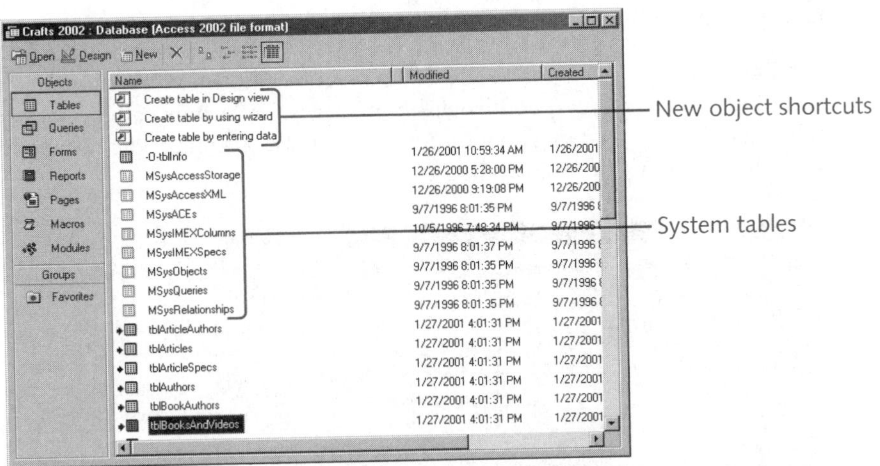

Figure 2-23. This Database window has all the Show options selected.

The General Tab

With the General tab of the Options dialog box, you can set print margins, turn on four-digit year formatting, and set the default database folder and a number of other miscellaneous options. Probably the most useful selection on this page is the Recently Used File List option, which you can configure to display up to nine entries in the list of files to open in the task pane, as shown in Figure 2-24.

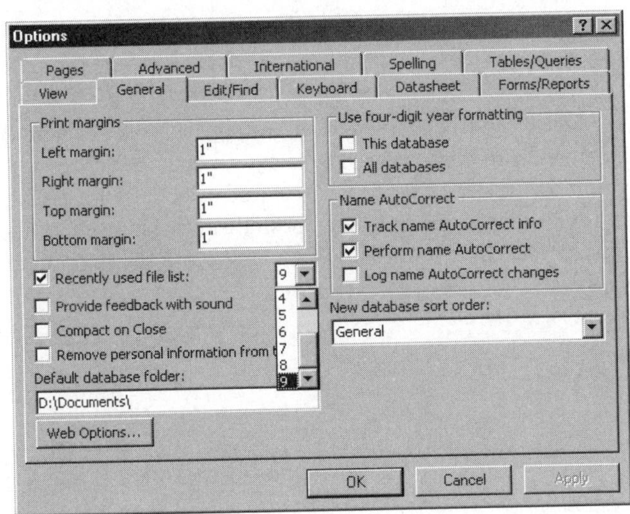

Figure 2-24. The General tab of the Options dialog box allows you to set a number of formatting options.

The Edit/Find Tab

The Edit/Find tab (see Figure 2-25) offers several options for searching in datasheets and allows you to turn off confirmation messages for various database actions, such as deleting objects and running action queries. You can also limit the number of records to be displayed in a drop-down list.

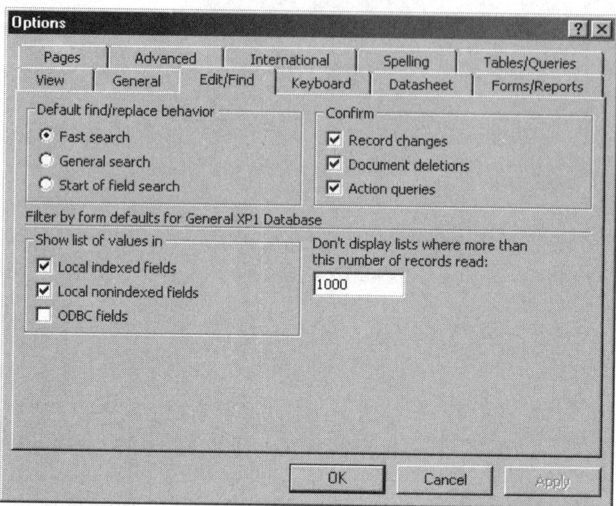

Figure 2-25. With the Edit/Find tab of the Options dialog box, you can specify search behavior in datasheets.

The Keyboard Tab

The Keyboard tab (see Figure 2-26) specifies what happens as you navigate through text boxes on forms or in cells in datasheets. The default behavior is pressing Enter to move the insertion point to the next field or control and select all of the text, but you can change this behavior so that pressing Enter doesn't move the insertion point to the next control or so that the insertion point is positioned before the first character, among other options.

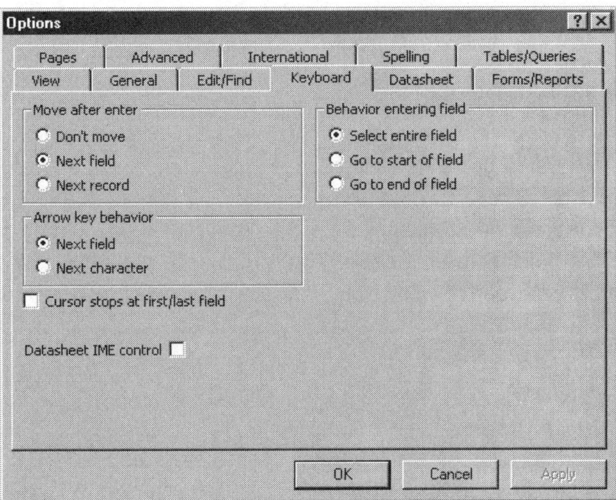

Figure 2-26. The Keyboard tab of the Options dialog box specifies how you navigate text boxes.

The Datasheet Tab

The Datasheet tab (see Figure 2-27) enables you to select the font, color, and size of text displayed in datasheets. You can also change the appearance of table gridlines.

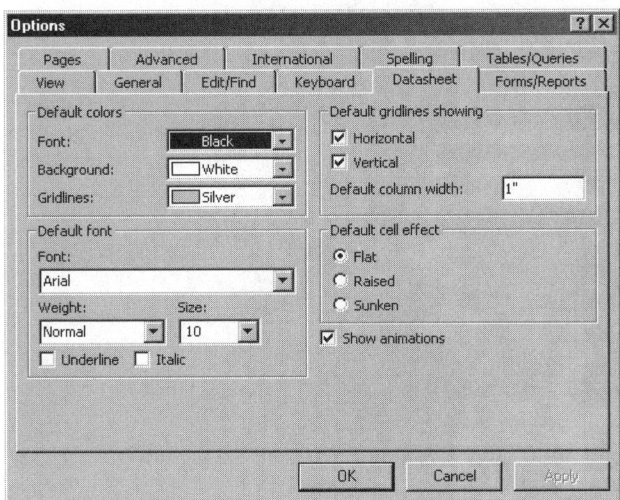

Figure 2-27. With the Datasheet tab of the Options dialog box, you can specify the default formatting for text in datasheets.

Chapter 2

InsideOut

The Datasheet tab of the Options dialog box lets you be very creative (perhaps too creative) with datasheet formatting. You can format the datasheet cells with the Raised special effect, a purple background, and green script text, but generally it's advisable to leave the text black on a flat, white background, in a readable font such as MS Sans Serif or Arial. If users find datasheets hard to read, it's unlikely that they'll know how to change the font, color, or special effect to fix the problem, so it's up to you to make your datasheets readable from the start.

The Forms/Reports Tab

newfeature!

With the Forms/Reports tab (see Figure 2-28), you can configure a few settings related to form design. The Selection Behavior group specifies whether an object must be fully enclosed by a selection box to be selected, or just partially enclosed. The Form Template and Report Template boxes allow you to enter the name of the form and report templates to use when creating new forms or reports. The Always Use Event Procedures check box allows you to bypass the Choose Builder dialog box and go directly to the event procedure from a form, report, or control properties sheet—a real time-saver for developers.

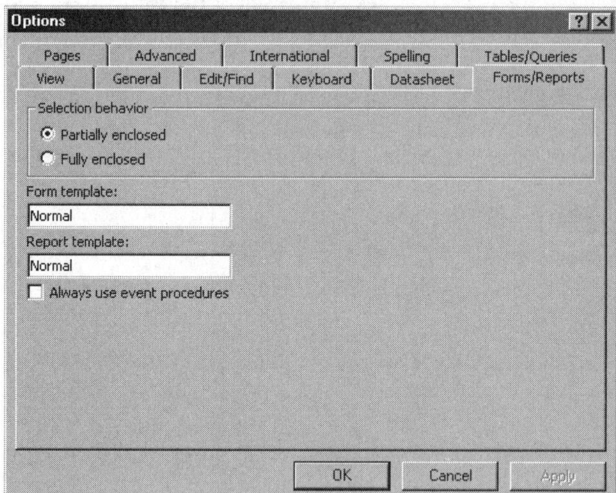

Figure 2-28. With the Forms/Reports tab of the Options dialog box, you can set options related to form design.

The Pages Tab

With the Pages tab, you can set options related to the appearance and storage of data access pages, such as the alternate row color and the caption and footer section styles. (See Figure 2-29.) Unfortunately, the latter two selections offer no Build button or drop-down list of selections; instead, you have to type in the formatting string in a specialized syntax.

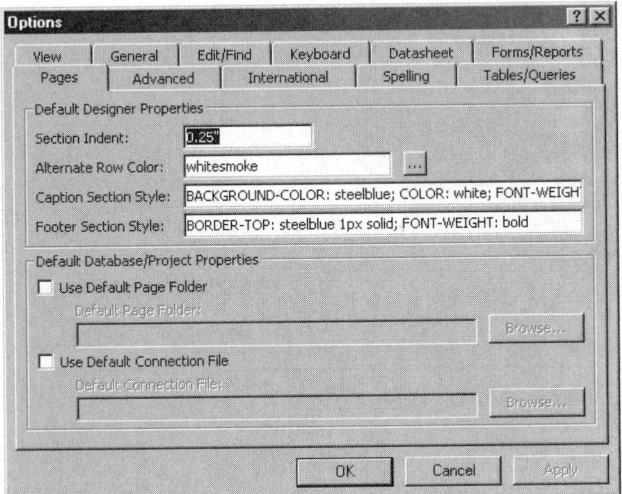

Figure 2-29. With the Pages tab of the Options dialog box, you can change the appearance of data access pages.

The Advanced Tab

You can use the Advanced tab to set a variety of advanced options. (See Figure 2-30.) The only setting you're likely to want to change is the Default File Format, which specifies the format of a new Access database.

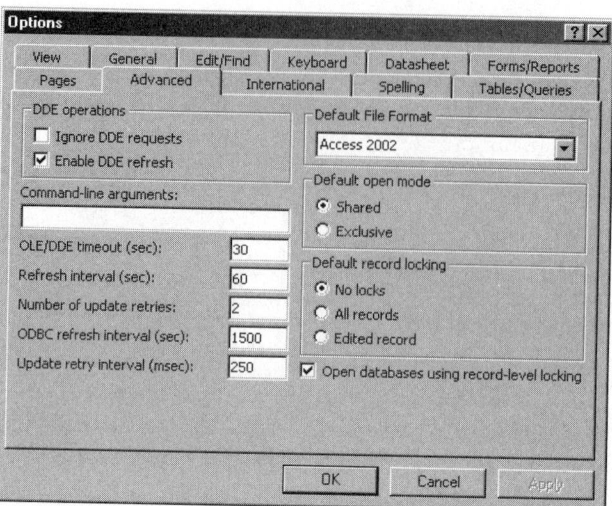

Figure 2-30. WIth the Advanced tab of the Options dialog box, you can set advanced options.

> **tip** **Work with Access 2000 and 2002 together**
>
> If you work in a mixed Access 2000/Access 2002 environment, setting the Default File Format option to Access 2000 will guarantee that any new databases you create will be usable by both Access 2000 and Access 2002 users, although you won't be able to use new features such as PivotTables.

The International Tab

The International tab (see Figure 2-31) enables you to set a number of options useful in non-English versions of Access—for example, options that specify whether fields are displayed left to right (the order familiar in English and European languages) or right to left (the direction familiar to Middle Eastern language users).

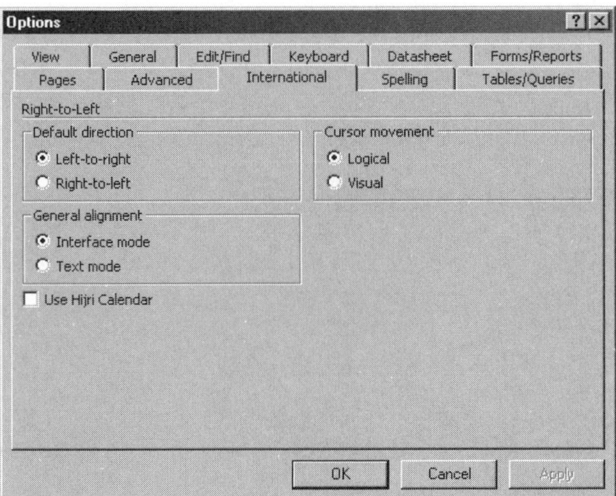

Figure 2-31. Use the International tab of the Options dialog box to set options for non-English versions of Access.

The Spelling Tab

Use the Spelling tab (see Figure 2-32) to set options related to checking spelling. Some of these options are specific to a particular language.

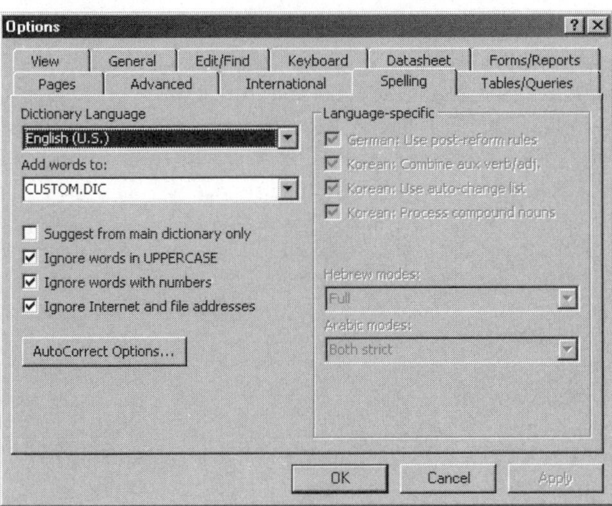

Figure 2-32. You can use the Spelling tab of the Options dialog box to set spelling options.

The Tables/Queries Tab

Use the Tables/Queries tab (see Figure 2-33) to set table-related options. Some of them are rather obscure, such as whether to use SQL Server Compatible Syntax (ANSI 92) and how to use AutoIndex when you're importing or creating a table.

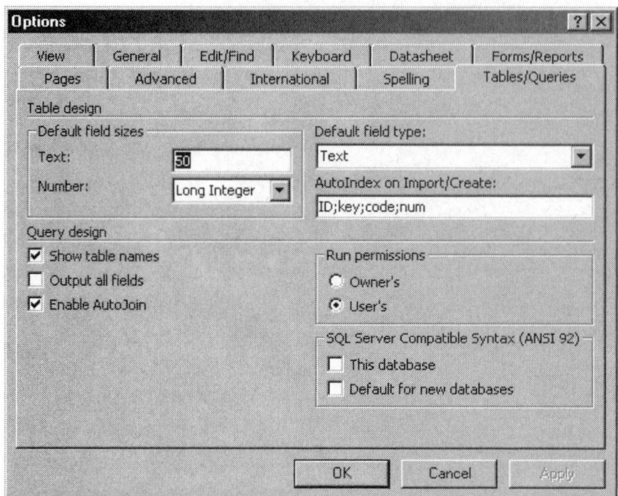

Figure 2-33. You can use the Tables/Queries tab of the Options dialog box to format tables.

Because of Access's tremendous flexibility and the superiority of its design tools, it's suitable for all database tasks, from building a simple home database that takes half an hour to create using the built-in database wizards, to building large, Web-enabled database applications linked to a SQL Server back end and requiring weeks or months of programming. In the following chapters, you'll learn how to create powerful and easy-to-use Access applications that meet your specific needs.

Chapter 3

Introduction to Database Design

Even if you know how to create tables and fields, you'll need more than that knowledge to turn a pile of paper documents, or a set of imported tables, into a useful database. Whether you're creating a small database to store information about your CD collection or developing an enterprise database to run on the Web, attention to design at the beginning will save time later on. Although Microsoft Access lets you change your database structure after you create forms and reports, doing so can be time-consuming. It's best to take some time at the start to analyze your requirements and set up the database tables in the most efficient manner.

This chapter begins with a brief overview of databases. Next, database design is introduced and a design example is presented. The chapter finishes with a review of database terminology, which we'll use throughout the rest of this book.

Overview of Database Concepts

Before you start designing your database, it's important to understand some fundamentals. This section introduces some of the basic concepts of databases.

Database Elements

A *database* is a collection of information stored in an organized manner. Two common database types are *relational databases* and *flat-file databases*. In a relational database such as Access, data can be subdivided into containers called *tables*. Tables organize data into *rows* and *columns*. (Rows are also called *records*, and columns are also called *fields*.) A record contains information about a particular item, such as a customer, while fields identify the category of information, such as the contact name or address. Figure 3-1 shows these database elements.

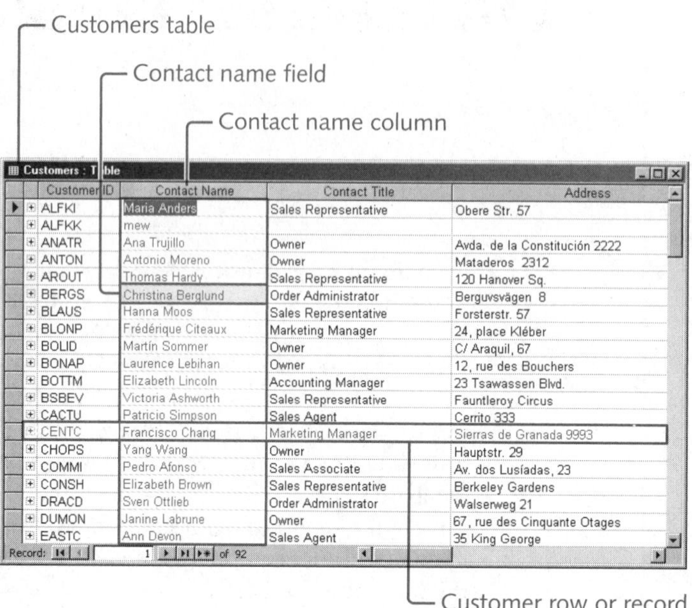

Customer ID	Contact Name	Contact Title	Address
ALFKI	Maria Anders	Sales Representative	Obere Str. 57
ALFKK	mew		
ANATR	Ana Trujillo	Owner	Avda. de la Constitución 2222
ANTON	Antonio Moreno	Owner	Mataderos 2312
AROUT	Thomas Hardy	Sales Representative	120 Hanover Sq.
BERGS	Christina Berglund	Order Administrator	Berguvsvägen 8
BLAUS	Hanna Moos	Sales Representative	Forsterstr. 57
BLONP	Frédérique Citeaux	Marketing Manager	24, place Kléber
BOLID	Martín Sommer	Owner	C/ Araquil, 67
BONAP	Laurence Lebihan	Owner	12, rue des Bouchers
BOTTM	Elizabeth Lincoln	Accounting Manager	23 Tsawassen Blvd.
BSBEV	Victoria Ashworth	Sales Representative	Fauntleroy Circus
CACTU	Patricio Simpson	Sales Agent	Cerrito 333
CENTC	Francisco Chang	Marketing Manager	Sierras de Granada 9993
CHOPS	Yang Wang	Owner	Hauptstr. 29
COMMI	Pedro Afonso	Sales Associate	Av. dos Lusíadas, 23
CONSH	Elizabeth Brown	Sales Representative	Berkeley Gardens
DRACD	Sven Ottlieb	Order Administrator	Walserweg 21
DUMON	Janine Labrune	Owner	67, rue des Cinquante Otages
EASTC	Ann Devon	Sales Agent	35 King George

Figure 3-1. A database table has rows and columns (records and fields).

In a flat-file database, different types of information are not broken out into separate tables but are included in one table. The same data might (and generally does) appear in multiple records in the table. For example, a customer's full name and address might be stored in many records of an Orders table. If that customer's address changes, it must be changed in all those records. Flat-file databases were used in early database systems, and many mainframe databases still have a flat-file format, as do some low-end PC databases intended for personal use, such as DBMaker.

InsideOut

If you need to save an Access table for use in a flat-file database and the format you need isn't available as one of the export formats in the Export Table *tablename* To dialog box, select the Text Files export type, and give the text file the .csv extension (*.csv* stands for comma-delimited). Comma-delimited files can be imported by almost any database program, whether flat-file or relational.

Relationships

In a relational database, you can create relationships between tables. This means, in effect, that two or more tables can share information. Relationships are established by linking a unique field (called a *primary key*) in the first table to a corresponding field (called a *foreign key*) in the second table.

When a field in a table is set as the primary key, each record in the table must have a value in that field and each record's value must be unique. Sometimes a table already has a field with unique data that can be set as the primary key field, such as an EmployeeID field in an Employees table. Otherwise, you can add a field of the *AutoNumber* type to a table and use it as the primary key field, providing a unique ID number for each record in the table. A foreign key field doesn't need to have unique values in its table.

In a one-to-one relationship, a record in one table can have only one related record in the other table. Figure 3-2 shows an example of this type of relationship.

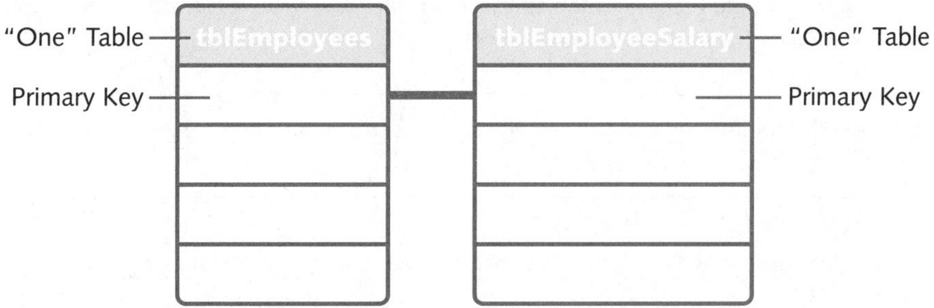

Figure 3-2. The one-to-one relationship shown here links two tables so that one record in tblEmployees matches one record in tblEmployeeSalary.

In a one-to-many relationship, a record in one table can have multiple matching records in another table, as shown in Figure 3-3.

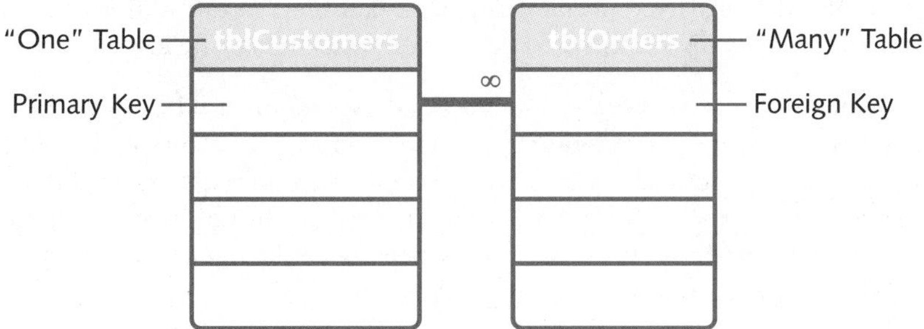

Figure 3-3. In this one-to-many relationship, many records in the tblOrders table match one record in the tblCustomers table.

In a many-to-many relationship, many records in one table can have many matching records in another table. Access doesn't provide an explicit many-to-many relationship type, but a many-to-many relationship can be set up indirectly by using a linking table containing just the key fields of the two tables to be linked, as shown in Figure 3-4.

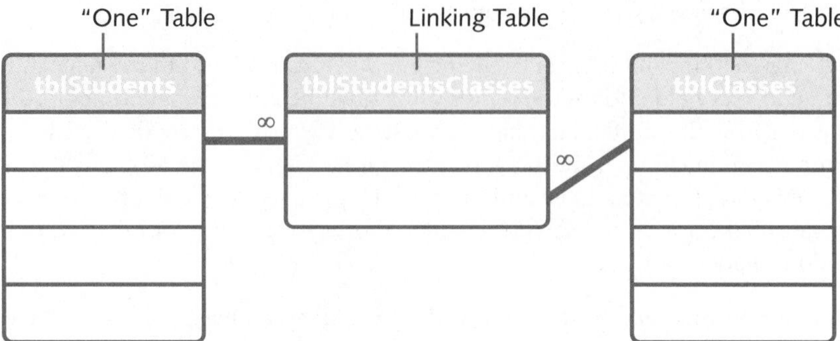

Figure 3-4. A many-to-many relationship allows one record in the tblStudents table to link to multiple records in the tblClasses table, and vice versa, using tblStudentsClasses as an intermediary.

note The 1s and infinity symbols (∞) at the ends of the join lines represent the "one" and "many" sides of a relationship.

For information about creating relationships, see Chapter 4, "Creating a Database."

Avoiding Data Duplication

The primary advantage of relational databases over flat-file databases is that information isn't duplicated in different tables, or in multiple records in a single table. In a proper ly designed relational database with no duplicated data, when you change a customer's address in one table (for example), any table that links to the address information will automatically pick up the updated data through its linking field.

For simple information storage, flat-file databases might still be acceptable, and even when you're working in a relational database, you might need to exchange data with a flat-file database, requiring you to create a table including data from different related tables. But if you're designing an Access database, it should be normalized to avoid duplicate data and to prevent data errors. See "Normalizing and Refining," page 63, for more information about normalizing a database.

For a list of database definitions, see "Database Terminology," page 75.

Database Design Considerations

Before you begin creating a database, it's a good idea to do some planning and preparation. Sometimes when you're creating a database for another person, you're given a vague, high-level description of what the database is supposed to do, without any guidance as to the desired interface or what type of users will be performing what tasks with the database. At other times, you might be given instructions in excruciating detail, accompanied by stacks of hard-copy documents more suitable for pencil and paper work than computer data input.

Sometimes these instructions are based on the requirements of obsolete databases, or even on nondatabase programs such as Microsoft Excel, so the instructions might be difficult—or even impossible—to implement. A typical example is data entered in all uppercase, which might have been the only way data could be entered in some long-ago database from the 1950s, but now just makes the data hard to read.

As a database creator, you need to step back and analyze the database's requirements before starting work. Rather than try to follow vague or inappropriate instructions literally, you need to determine what the database should do and then construct the database in Access so that it does what the users need it to do and is easy for them to work with. The following sections introduce some of the considerations involved in designing a database.

Planning the Database

Before you begin work constructing the Access database, make sure you know what your customer is expecting in response to the following questions:

- What are the overall goals of the database?
- What specific tasks will the database perform?
- How do users want to output information from the database?
- What kinds of users will be working most with the database, and what is their level of comfort with Access and computers in general?
- Are the tasks or procedures to be implemented in the database finalized and working correctly in their current implementation?
- Will all users have Access 2002, or are some using an older version of Access?
- Does the customer prefer a familiar, tried-and-true interface or the newest Access 2002 features?
- Are there any specific Access features the customer wants you to incorporate into the database?

If you're creating a complex database for a customer, be sure to refer to the section "Design Considerations for Large or Complex Databases," page 66.

You don't need to build the database with all the latest features of Access. On the other hand, it would be a mistake to omit a useful feature—for example, a tabbed form created using the tab control—just because the database users don't know enough about Access to request it. Talking with your customer about these issues beforehand will help you plan for a smoother development process.

tip **Be flexible in design**

If users don't like the way you've implemented a feature and it's possible to change the feature to please them, you should try to do so. Things work out a lot better in the long run if you can design database features to work the way users want them to work, rather than spending a lot of time (and generating a lot of negativity) trying to teach users to use features designed your way.

Identifying How the Database Will Be Used

When you're designing a database, you need to consider how the database will be used and how (and where) its data should be stored. There are typically three types of databases: *personal, corporate/networked,* and *Web-enabled.*

note These are not official Access database terms, but we'll use them occasionally in this book.

Personal Databases

A personal database generally stores its data in the same database as the interface objects, instead of placing the data tables in an external database. Personal databases are used to store information such as addresses, phone lists, CD collections, and other personal data. Although flat-file databases can be used for personal data, even a simple name and address database for personal use works better if it's set up as a relational database, with data separated into linked tables.

A personal database isn't necessarily a small or simple database—you might need a large and complex database to manage a personal interest or hobby such as genealogy or Civil War history. The main distinction between a personal and a corporate database (apart from the fact that a personal database is rarely networked) is that you have complete design control over a personal database, and you can spend as much time as you see fit on each database element, without the constraints of a corporate budget or the need to interface with a mainframe database.

Corporate/Networked Databases

A database designed for business use should usually be broken into a *front-end database* (containing the interface elements, such as forms and reports) and a *back-end database* (containing just the data tables). Separating the data from the front end makes it possible to update the database interface without disturbing existing data. It also enables you to place the back end on a server, with separate front ends on individual workstations, which can improve performance to some extent and allows for customized front ends for different users.

A front-end/back-end database isn't the same thing as a client-server database. In a true client-server database, the application needs to be divided into a *client component*, which contains interface objects, and a *server component* (such as Microsoft SQL Server), which stores data and performs data manipulation on a *server* (a central computer used for high-powered data processing and storage of massive amounts of data).

Web-Enabled Databases

An Access front end using data access pages can be connected to an Access or a SQL Server table located on a Web server. This scenario enables users to connect to the database via the Web, either on a corporate intranet or using the Internet. A Web-enabled database is suited for applications whose users are mobile—with Web access, users can log onto the database and view or modify data (with the proper permissions) from anywhere in the world.

Reviewing Data

It's easy to create Access tables and fields—very easy, if you use the Database Wizard or the Table Wizard. Once you get beyond the standard wizard-created tables and fields, however, you need to understand your data to determine how you'll divide the data into fields in the tables.

Before you create your tables, or any other database elements, you should analyze the data you'll be storing. For example, if you're creating a database to store information about your CD music collection, you need to decide whether you want to store only data about the CD number, title, and artist for each CD or whether you also want to include the liner notes, the individual performers, publisher, instruments, language, type of music, and so on. Additionally, you might want to store separate information about title, artist, and other information for each track on a multitrack CD.

If you're creating the database for a customer, you'll need to establish which data elements are important to the customer, to ensure that those elements will be represented by fields in the tables you create, and also to determine how the user wants to input and output the data.

As a rule, it's better to divide your information as finely as possible. This makes your database more flexible and leaves your options open for extracting data in many different ways. As a rule of thumb, if you want to look up a certain type of information later on, it needs to be stored in a separate field. However, even if you don't anticipate looking up specific information, it doesn't hurt to make the data atomic.

For example, suppose that you don't expect to need information about individual performers, so you enter only group names (such as Josh Barnhill's jug band) for the CDs in your CD database. Later, if you want to find all CDs that feature a certain performer (such as Molly Shapiro), you won't be able to retrieve that information for CDs on which that performer sang as a member of the group. But if you enter the names of individual performers as well as groups, you can retrieve information about either groups or performers.

Entering Name and Address Data

Many databases store name and address data, and it's especially important to enter this data in separate fields for each name or address component, rather than entering the complete name in a Name field and the complete address in an Address field. Countless databases have had to be redesigned later because names were entered into a single field instead of being split (at a minimum) into FirstName, MiddleName, and LastName fields (or better still, into Prefix, FirstName, MiddleName, LastName, and Suffix fields). Splitting a name into its components enables you to perform a variety of sorting tasks, including alphabetizing by last name in a report or printing name badges using first names only. And you won't have reports listing names such as Jones Jr., John, because the suffix was put in the same field as the last name.

The same principle applies to addresses: You should split addresses into (at least) Street Address, State/Province, Postal Code, and Country fields, for maximum usefulness. In some cases, you might want to split the street address into several fields, especially if you need to track the physical address and mailing address separately. You can always concatenate the separate address components into a single variable for exporting to Microsoft Word, for example, but it's much harder to extract the separate address components from a single Address field.

tip **Split names and addresses according to Microsoft Outlook**

You can use Microsoft Outlook's system of dividing names and addresses into fields as a guide for your own data strategy. (Open the Check Name and Check Address dialog boxes for a contact in order to see these Outlook fields.) If you expect to transfer Access data to or from Outlook, be sure to use the same country names that Outlook does because otherwise you might find that your U.S. addresses are sorted into two or three country categories, depending on whether the country was entered as U.S.A., U.S., or United States of America.

Designing Tables

Once you have identified the type of database and reviewed the data, you should examine how the information will be stored in the database and determine how it should be split up into tables. For example, you should have one table for each significant category of information to be stored in the database, such as customers, orders, and shippers.

Designing for a New Database

When you're designing a database application from scratch, one approach to use is to first create *unbound forms*—forms that don't display data from tables—as a prototype of the application. Then get feedback from users, and modify the forms until they provide all the features users need to work with their data. Create tables with *fields* to hold all the information displayed on the forms, bind the prototype forms to the tables, and then create the other interface objects needed for modifying and displaying information.

This approach can save a lot of time later on, in contrast to designing tables first and then creating forms bound to the tables. Unbound forms as a design technique are especially suited for clients who don't know exactly what they want or need until they see it. Prototype forms let users (and the developer) think through how they need to interact with the data and are helpful in clarifying what tables are needed, what fields are needed in each table, and what relationships are needed between tables. On the other hand, clients who are more comfortable with abstract concepts are able to analyze their needs and give you a complete list of tables and fields without examining prototype forms.

Designing with Existing Data

When you're designing a database to manage existing data (for example, data stored in an old Access database, in another database format, in Excel worksheets, or in text files), it's generally advisable to first create (or import) the tables to store the data and normalize the tables (if needed), then create queries and forms to modify existing data and enter new data, and last create reports and data access pages for displaying and printing the data. This sequence will ensure that the tables have appropriately normalized relationships (discussed in the next section, "Normalizing and Refining") before you create other database objects referencing the tables.

Normalizing and Refining

Normalization is the process of designing a database so that there's no duplication of data in different tables, other than the linking fields that establish relationships. Although Access is a relational database, no constraints exist that prevent users from setting up Access tables with duplicate data—in effect, using Access as if it were a flat-file database. If you inherit such a database, although it will probably be a tiresome task, it's definitely worthwhile to separate the data into normalized, linked tables so that you won't have to worry about out-of-sync duplicated data in the future. If you're designing a database from scratch, it's easy to set it up correctly from the start.

As an example of the normalization process, let's say that you've been given a list of contacts, in the form of a Word document, in which each contact has one or more addresses, several phone numbers, and one or more e-mail addresses. You might be tempted to create a single table, tblContacts, with fields to hold all the data, including several sets of address fields (say, Home, Business, and Other), perhaps three sets of phone fields (Voice, Fax, Mobile), and a few sets of e-mail address fields. This table is a flat-file table—no doubt, you've seen such tables. In some older (or mainframe) databases, you don't have any other option, but in an Access database, this is poor design, because using fixed sets of fields to store multiple address, phone, and e-mail data for each client limits your options, in addition to wasting database space. If you have two sets of e-mail address fields, you won't be able to enter a third or fourth e-mail address for contacts that have them. If you have three sets of address fields, two sets will be empty for the majority of clients who have only one address.

Because each contact can have many addresses, many phone numbers, and many e-mail addresses, it's best to create separate tables to hold each type of data, linking them by a ContactID field. Using linked tables guarantees that you'll be able to enter all the information you need for each client, and you can retrieve the linked information as needed for forms and reports.

Troubleshooting

How can I export data from normalized tables to an Excel file or a text file?

It's usually a good idea to thoroughly normalize a database using one-to-many and many-to-many relationships to avoid duplicated data while still allowing you to include linked data in queries and SQL statements. But there are some exceptions. If you need to export Access data to a Word table, an Excel worksheet, or a comma-delimited text file for upload to a mainframe database (because these applications don't support relational data), you need to produce a non-normalized table for export—one that contains information from several tables and thus violates normalization by containing duplicate data.

It's rarely desirable to store your data in a non-normalized fashion, even if you need to export a non-normalized table. It's most efficient to store data in normalized tables and then, when you need to export data, create a table incorporating data from several linked tables, using a make-table query. The process of creating a non-normalized table from normalized tables is called *denormalization,* or *flattening*. Figure 3-5 shows a query used to combine data from a number of linked Northwind database tables. This query is in turn used as one of the data sources for the make-table query used to create a flattened data table that will be used to export data from the Northwind database to a Word table, in VBA code.

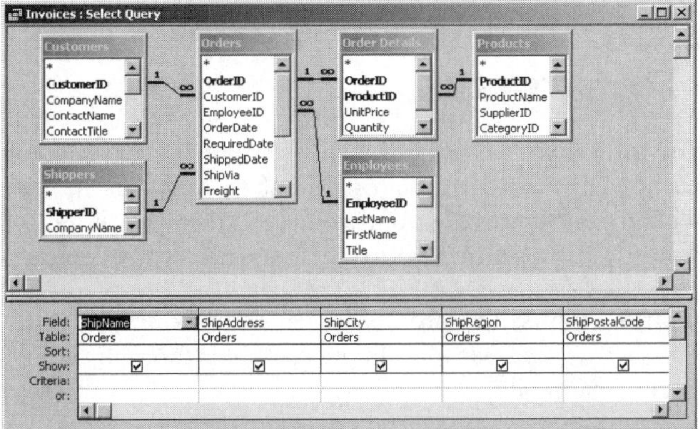

Figure 3-5. A query is used to produce a flattened table for export to Word.

Figure 3-6 shows the same query in Datasheet view—note the repeated data in several fields. The table created by the make-table query would also be suitable for export to an Excel worksheet or a text file for upload to a mainframe.

For more details on this technique, see Chapter 17, "Exporting Data from Access."

Invoices : Select Query

Ship Name	Ship Address	Ship City	Ship Region	Ship Postal Code	Ship Country
Island Trading	Garden House	Cowes	Isle of Wight	PO31 7PJ	UK
Island Trading	Garden House	Cowes	Isle of Wight	PO31 7PJ	UK
Island Trading	Garden House	Cowes	Isle of Wight	PO31 7PJ	UK
Island Trading	Garden House	Cowes	Isle of Wight	PO31 7PJ	UK
Reggiani Caseifici	Strada Provinciale 124	Reggio Emilia		42100	Italy
Reggiani Caseifici	Strada Provinciale 124	Reggio Emilia		42100	Italy
Reggiani Caseifici	Strada Provinciale 124	Reggio Emilia		42100	Italy
Ricardo Adocicados	Av. Copacabana, 267	Rio de Janeiro	RJ	02389-890	Brazil
Ricardo Adocicados	Av. Copacabana, 267	Rio de Janeiro	RJ	02389-890	Brazil
QUICK-Stop	Taucherstraße 10	Cunewalde		01307	Germany
QUICK-Stop	Taucherstraße 10	Cunewalde		01307	Germany
Split Rail Beer & Ale	P.O. Box 555	Lander	WY	82520	USA
Split Rail Beer & Ale	P.O. Box 555	Lander	WY	82520	USA
Lehmanns Marktstand	Magazinweg 7	Frankfurt a.M.		60528	Germany
Lehmanns Marktstand	Magazinweg 7	Frankfurt a.M.		60528	Germany
Lehmanns Marktstand	Magazinweg 7	Frankfurt a.M.		60528	Germany
Lehmanns Marktstand	Magazinweg 7	Frankfurt a.M.		60528	Germany
Folk och fä HB	Åkergatan 24	Bräcke		S-844 67	Sweden
Folk och fä HB	Åkergatan 24	Bräcke		S-844 67	Sweden

Record: 1 of 2155

Figure 3-6. Flattened data generated by a query is used to produce a table for export.

Design Considerations for Large or Complex Databases

Designing a database for a client—especially if the database is large or complex—is a whole different ball game from creating a simple database for yourself. Your development experience will go more smoothly—and your customers are more likely to get the databases they want—if you think about three important considerations up front:

- **A picture is worth a thousand words.** Create a set of prototype, or dummy, forms that you can use to walk the customer through the system before you begin creating it.
- **Choose your tools carefully.** Think about whether the database project will be better served by the SQL Server 2000 Desktop Engine or SQL Server.
- **Divide and conquer your data.** Splitting the database into a front end and a back end creates a system you can easily modify later.

The sections that follow provide more detail on each of these design techniques for large and complicated databases.

Creating an Interface Prototype for User Feedback

If you have a large database project that's not well defined, you can help clarify the client's expectations and test your preliminary database design by creating forms that let the users get a feel for how the database works, without actually writing the code and creating the tables that will ultimately be needed. To do this, create a set of unbound forms as an interface prototype and then demonstrate the prototype to the database users so that they can comment on the form design and functionality before you create the tables, queries, and bound forms. Creating a prototype is a good way to clarify exactly what data needs to be stored in what table and can save you a good deal of time in the long run.

See Chapter 5, "Creating Forms for Entering, Editing, and Viewing Data," for more details on creating forms.

It's easier to change table and field structure in Access than in some older databases. In Access, you can add or delete a field or change a field's data type if necessary. However, it's still preferable to get the table and field structure finalized as much as possible before you begin working on queries, forms, and reports, because changes to table structure generally require changes to queries, forms, and reports that are bound to the tables.

Here are some suggestions for user feedback you might want to gather using dummy forms:

- Can the primary key for a table be an AutoNumber value, or should it be entered manually or selected from a list of existing IDs (such as Employee IDs or Product Numbers)? Generally, it's best to use an existing ID, if it's unique and available for each record.
- If an existing ID code (such as Employee ID) is to be used as the key field, is it a text or numeric value?
- If the customer wants to use an existing code as the key field (say, an employee number or a Social Security number), would it ever happen that a record has to be entered without the code? In that case, you need to use another field—usually an AutoNumber field—as the key field.
- Is data to be entered manually or imported from some other data source, such as a text file generated by a mainframe computer database?
- Should contact names be typed in or selected from a table of contacts displayed in a combo box?
- Should e-mail addresses be typed in or selected from the Outlook Contacts list or a global address book?
- Do you need to store only a fixed set of telephone numbers (say, home and work numbers) or an open-ended list, which would require creating a linked table?
- Do you need to store only a fixed set of addresses for a customer (say, home and work addresses) or an open-ended list, which would require creating a linked table?
- Do you need to duplicate every feature of an old paper form, or can some components be discarded or replaced by computer-specific elements such as combo boxes, now that data entry is done on the computer?
- Could you use some new Access features not present in the old system, such as tabbed forms, PivotTables, or PivotCharts?

Answering these questions will help you set up your tables and fields properly in the first place, minimizing time-consuming modifications later in the development process.

Choosing Access or SQL Server as a Back End

For a small database, especially a single-user database, an all-Access database is fine, but if you're developing a database intended for use by a small workgroup, you can use SQL Server 2000 Desktop Engine (the successor to Microsoft Data Engine [MSDE]) as a data storage back end, linked to a front-end Access project. For more information about Access projects, see Chapter 19, "Creating Access Projects." SQL Server 2000 Desktop Engine uses the same data engine as SQL Server, so a single Access project can be linked to either back end, but there are some differences between the two. Apart from some highly technical differences, these are the two main differences:

newfeature!

- SQL Server 2000 Desktop Engine comes with Access 2002; SQL Server must be purchased separately.
- SQL Server 2000 Desktop Engine has a 2-GB database limit.

In general terms, SQL Server 2000 Desktop Engine has the basic data engine features of SQL Server 2000, but it lacks a user interface, management tools, analysis capabilities, merge replication support, client access licenses, developer libraries, and SQL Server Books Online. It also limits database size and user workload.

SQL Server 2000 Desktop Engine is an excellent choice if you think that at some point in the future your database will need to be moved to full SQL Server—you can develop the Access project with a SQL Server 2000 Desktop Engine back end and then upsize it to SQL Server when necessary, using the Upsizing Wizard. (See Appendix E, "Upsizing to SQL Server," for more information about using the Upsizing Wizard.)

Splitting a Database into Front and Back Ends

Even if you don't need to convert your Access database to a project and give it a SQL Server 2000 Desktop Engine (or SQL Server) back end, you can still split the database into a front end (containing the interface objects) and a back end (containing only the data tables). If you're creating a database for a client, this is generally a good idea, because splitting a database into a front end and a back end makes it easier to swap in a modified interface, without disturbing data entered or modified by the client—all you have to do is send the client a new front-end database.

If tables, forms, reports, and other database objects are all in the same database and you send the client an updated database, their newly entered data will be lost. See Chapter 15, "Using Add-Ins to Expand Access Functionality," for more details on using the Database Splitter utility, which automates the process of splitting a database into a front end and a back end.

Making and Delivering Database Changes

If you have Microsoft Office XP Developer, you can create a distributed version of your Access application, which can be run by users who don't have Access installed. (See Appendix B, "Distributing Access Applications," for more details on preparing a distributed application.) This isn't always the best option, however (and if you don't have the Developer edition of Office XP, it isn't an option at all). If your clients want to modify the database themselves, and all potential users have Access installed, it will save time to just prepare an Access database. Additionally, if you need to be able to make modifications to the database on line, this can be done only if the regular version of Access is installed at the client's location.

tip **Package your application using the Packaging Wizard**

If you have Office XP Developer installed and you want to deliver an Access application that uses regular Access rather than the runtime version of Access, you can use the Packaging Wizard component to package your application, including any ActiveX controls and other components that you need. This option is especially useful if you need to ensure that all the required supporting files are installed with the database.

Design Example: The Crafts Database

The Crafts sample database on the companion CD contains information about books, book authors, videos, magazines, publishers, sources, and other information related to crafts. In a relational database, that means tables have been set up for each of these subjects, as shown in Figure 3-7.

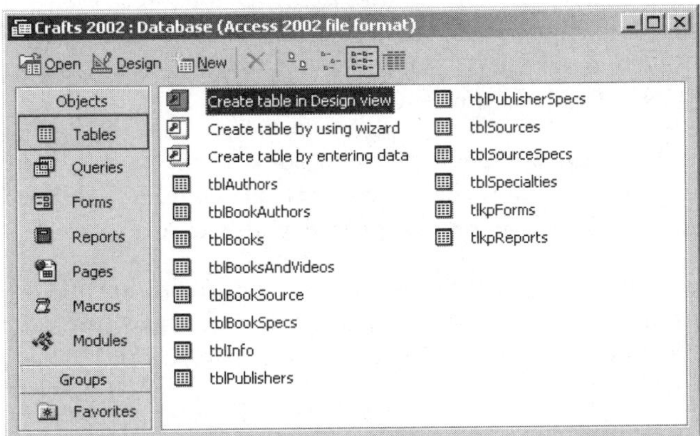

Figure 3-7. Tables in the Crafts database contain information about crafts books, authors, and so on.

How do you know that a particular data category deserves its own table, and not just a field (or set of fields) in an existing table? The primary consideration should be whether the same information might be duplicated in many records. This is clearly the case with publisher data, as one publisher publishes many books. To prevent errors and ensure that the publisher name will always be correct in a book record, it's best to have a separate Publishers table and set up a lookup field in the Books table for selecting a publisher. This is also true of author and source information, but not true of ISBN number (each book, video, and kit has a unique ISBN number), language, or publication date information.

On the other hand, you shouldn't carry this process to ridiculous extremes—the name *John* might occur in many records in the FirstName field of the tblAuthors table, but that doesn't justify setting up a separate table of first names, and selecting first names from a drop-down list.

Information such as ZIP or postal codes and state or province abbreviations can go either way, depending on whether accuracy or ease of use is of primary importance. It's quicker and easier to type NY than to select it from a drop-down list of state abbreviations, but users might enter incorrect data. However, you can ensure accuracy by using a validation rule on the field.

After you've created a table for each database category, your next task is to set up relationships between the various tables.

See Chapter 4, "Creating a Database," for more information about setting up relationships.

Working with the Crafts Sample Database

Throughout this book, I'll use the sample relational database named Crafts (Crafts 2002.mdb on the companion CD) to explore and illustrate various aspects of database development. As a historical note, this database started life in dBASE, then was moved to Paradox, and then to Access 1.0 and up the Access versions since then. I developed the Crafts database to store information about books, videos, and kits related to various crafts, and its original output was in the form of ASCII text files, which were zipped and uploaded to the old Crafts forum on CompuServe.

This was well before the development of the Web, so users had to download and unzip the files to read or print them. Now the same Crafts data could be published directly on a Web page and viewed on line, fully formatted, with graphics.

The Crafts database lends itself well to discussions of normalization and relationships, because it contains many different types of data (authors, books, sources, specialties, publishers) that need to be linked in a variety of one-to-many and many-to-many relationships.

Design Problems and Solutions

If you're creating a database to store information about crafts books, you might start by looking at a book—say, Elizabeth Zimmermann's *Knitting Without Tears*—and creating a Books table with fields to store all the information you can extract from the book. In this starter table, the ISBN field was set as the primary key. Figure 3-8 illustrates such a table, with actual data from this book.

Title	Author	Publisher	PubYear	Cover	Price	Pages	ISBN
Knitting without Tears	Elizabeth Zimmermann	Charles Scribner's Sons	1971	Paperback	$7.95	120	684-13505-1

Figure 3-8. A starter Books table lists data from a single book.

This process seems reasonable, when you look at this record. But (as I know from experience with the Crafts database), this table design won't survive the addition of other book records, or the requirements of normalization. The following list describes some of the problems you might encounter while setting up a relational database, and offers possible solutions. Although the specific examples are from the Crafts database, the problems are typical of those you might encounter while creating any new database or normalizing an existing database.

- **Problem: Books without ISBN numbers.** The ISBN numbering system wasn't adopted until the late 1960s. Therefore, older books won't have an ISBN number, and because the ISBN field has been designated as the key field, you won't be able to add records for these books (because a key field can't be left blank).

  Solution: Use an AutoNumber BookID field instead, so each book will have a unique ID, regardless of whether it has an ISBN.

- **Problem: Author name in one field.** Placing the author's entire name in one field makes it difficult, if not impossible, to print a report listing books by author, last name first.

  Solution: Break the author's name into separate fields for First Name, Middle Name, and Last Name.

- **Problem: Multiple authors.** This table doesn't allow you to list multiple authors for a single book, other than by creating a new record with duplicate data, which would violate normalization, as well as being difficult to work with.

  Solution: Create an Authors table to hold author information, and set up a many-to-many relationship between the Books and Authors tables. The Author field can then be eliminated from the Books table.

- **Problem: Publisher name inconsistency.** Publishers might change their names as the years go by or their names might have a different form. For example, one book might list its publisher as Charles Scribner's Sons and another as Scribners. Even though these are the same publisher, they wouldn't appear in the same Publisher category in a report, which would be incorrect.

  Solution: Set up a separate Publishers table, and then make the Publisher field in the Books table a lookup field so that the publisher name can be selected from a drop-down list. In the Publishers table, enter the full, official name (Charles Scribner's Sons) in one field and the commonly used abbreviation (in this case, Scribners) in another field, for selection in the lookup field's drop-down list. This ensures that all books from this publisher will have the same entry in the Publisher field in the Books table.

- **Problem: Cover type inconsistency.** As with the publisher name, you might encounter problems with reports sorted by Cover because *Paperback* was typed in some fields and just *Paper* in others.

  Solution: There are two solutions for this problem. One is to make the field a lookup field with a value list containing just two values: Hardback and Paperback. The other is to make the field accept an Integer value, selected from an option group, and translate it into Hardback or Paperback for reports.

- **Problem: Currency type inconsistency.** The data type of the Price field is Currency. (Access is smart enough to create a Currency field when you enter an amount preceded by a dollar sign.) This isn't a problem if all your books are published and sold in the United States, but you will have a problem if you also want to enter book prices for other countries.

  Solution: Add a field that identifies the currency type, preferably a lookup field for consistency, and change the data type of the Price field to a Double. This lets you add the appropriate currency symbol (such as a British pound symbol) to the price when you print reports.

- **Problem: What if it's not a book?** As I worked on my Crafts database, I realized that I also needed to add videos, and later kits, to the table, as they were also informational materials related to crafts. Also, some books include CDs, and I needed a way to record this fact. The starter table provides no way to indicate whether an entry is a book, video, or kit or whether it includes a CD.

  Solution: Again, this problem has two possible solutions. The first solution is to add four Yes/No fields, one each for Book, Video, Kit, and CD, to indicate whether a record in the table represents a book, video, or kit (or perhaps some combination of these, such as a book and kit set) and whether it includes a CD. The second solution is to separate Books, Videos, and Kits into three tables. (CDs stay as a Yes/No field, because they exist only as companion CDs for books.) This solution would make it difficult to deal with combination sets, so for the Crafts database, I chose the first solution. The check boxes are bound to separate Yes/No fields, rather than being part of an option group, to allow selection of more than one (for example, for a book/video combination).

- **Problem: Need to add additional information.** The original Books table is fine for entering data that is listed in (or on) the book, but sometimes you need to add information about the book that isn't listed in the book—for example, a source from which the book can be purchased, or the book's crafts specialty, or whether the book contains copyright-free information.

Solution: Add new fields or create additional tables as needed. Specialties and Sources (like Authors) both require a many-to-many relationship to Books, as a book can have multiple specialties or sources, and a specialty or source can have many books.

Figure 3-9 shows, in two views, the finalized tblBooksAndVideos table for the Crafts database. (The *tbl* prefix indicates a table—see Chapter 4, "Creating a Database," for a discussion of using tags to identify database objects.) Notice that the ISBN numbers have an inconsistent format. As is often the case when entering real-world data, the sources weren't consistent in entering the dashes in ISBNs, and the dashes can't be inserted automatically because (unlike Social Security numbers) ISBNs don't have a consistent format.

tblBooksAndVideos : Table

BookID	Book	Video	Kit	CD	Title	ISBN	Cover
335	Yes	No	No	No	Knitting Around	0-942018-00-4	Hardback
336	Yes	No	No	No	Knitting Workshop	0-9420-1800-1	Hardback
338	Yes	No	No	No	Knitting without Tears: Basic Tech	0684135051	Paperback
342	Yes	No	No	No	Knitter's Almanac	0-486-24178-5	Paperback
1768	No	Yes	No	No	A Turkish Coat	1909860	
1769	No	Yes	No	No	Puzzle-Pillow Blanket	1909845	
1779	No	Yes	No	No	Knitting Glossary	1909-850	
1780	No	Yes	No	No	Knitting Workshop	1909-800	
1781	No	Yes	No	No	Aran Winter Coat	1909-803	
1782	No	Yes	No	No	Bog Jacket	19090827	
1783	No	Yes	No	No	Fair Isle Yoke Sweater	1909-801	
1784	No	Yes	No	No	Knitted Dickeys	19090840	
1785	No	Yes	No	No	Mittful of Mittens	1909-806	
1786	No	Yes	No	No	Moccasin Socks	1909-810	
1787	No	Yes	No	No	Moebius Scarf & Vest	1909-828	

Record: 1 of 51

tblBooksAndVideos : Table

Language	Cost	CurrencyType	Publicati	Length	PublisherCode	Copyright-free	Modified
	24.95	US $	1989	191	Schoolhouse	No	5/29/1995
	17.95	US $	1981	183	Schoolhouse	No	5/29/1995
	14.95	US $	1971	120	Scribner's	No	5/29/1995
	4.95	US $	1974	160	Schoolhouse	No	2/27/2001
	26.95	US $		60	Schoolhouse	No	
	21.95	US $		30	Schoolhouse	No	7/19/1995
	69.95	US $		240	Schoolhouse	No	7/19/1995
	95	US $		360	Schoolhouse	No	5/29/1995
	26.95	US $		60	Schoolhouse	No	5/30/1995
	21.95	US $		30	Schoolhouse	No	5/30/1995
	26.95	US $		60	Schoolhouse	No	5/30/1995
	21.95	US $		30	Schoolhouse	No	5/30/1995
	21.95	US $		30	Schoolhouse	No	5/30/1995
	21.95	US $		30	Schoolhouse	No	5/30/1995
	21.95	US $		30	Schoolhouse	No	5/30/1995

Record: 1 of 51

Figure 3-9. The finalized tblBooksAndVideos table omits information stored in linked tables.

Notice too that the Author field from our original Books table has been removed—it isn't needed because the relationship between Authors and Books is handled by the linking table tblBookAuthors, which establishes the many-to-many relationship between Authors and Books. Figure 3-10 shows a portion of the tblAuthors table. The LastNameFirst field in tblAuthors is used to store the author's name in last name first format (the field is automatically filled in when data is entered into the individual name fields on the form for the tblAuthors table) or to store a name that isn't a person's name.

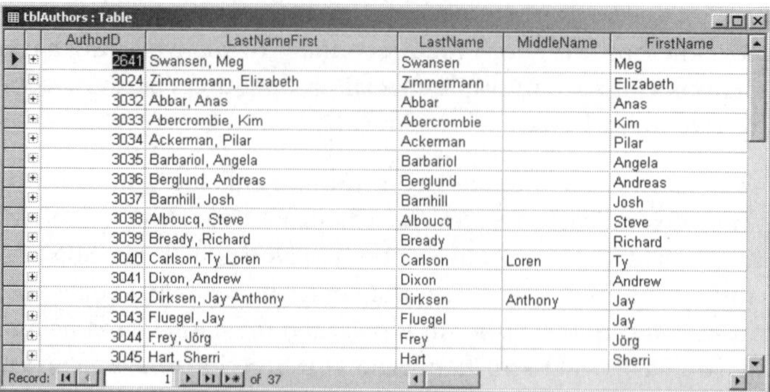

tblAuthors : Table

AuthorID	LastNameFirst	LastName	MiddleName	FirstName
2641	Swansen, Meg	Swansen		Meg
3024	Zimmermann, Elizabeth	Zimmermann		Elizabeth
3032	Abbar, Anas	Abbar		Anas
3033	Abercrombie, Kim	Abercrombie		Kim
3034	Ackerman, Pilar	Ackerman		Pilar
3035	Barbariol, Angela	Barbariol		Angela
3036	Berglund, Andreas	Berglund		Andreas
3037	Barnhill, Josh	Barnhill		Josh
3038	Alboucq, Steve	Alboucq		Steve
3039	Bready, Richard	Bready		Richard
3040	Carlson, Ty Loren	Carlson	Loren	Ty
3041	Dixon, Andrew	Dixon		Andrew
3042	Dirksen, Jay Anthony	Dirksen	Anthony	Jay
3043	Fluegel, Jay	Fluegel		Jay
3044	Frey, Jörg	Frey		Jörg
3045	Hart, Sherri	Hart		Sherri

Record: 1 of 37

Figure 3-10. The first few fields from the tblAuthors table show the author name divided into three fields.

The remainder of the fields in tblAuthors are used to store data about the authors, including address, phone numbers, online IDs, and other such information if it's available. Figure 3-11 shows the tblBookAuthors table, which links tblAuthors to tblBooksAndVideos in a many-to-many relationship, using the two tables' primary keys.

tblBookAuthors : Table

BookID	AuthorID
335	3024
336	3024
338	3024
342	3024
1768	2641
1769	2641
1779	3024
1780	3024
1781	3024
1781	2641
1782	3024
1782	2641
1783	3024

Record: 1 of 58

Figure 3-11. tblBookAuthors links tblAuthors and tblBooksAndVideos in a many-to-many relationship.

Troubleshooting

The database appears to be frozen, but it isn't listed as *Not responding* in the Task window

This puzzling situation can arise when a modal dialog box (such as the Save Changes To The Following Objects dialog box) is hidden behind another window. Press Alt+Tab to locate the modal dialog box, and then close it. This will unfreeze the database.

Figure 3-12 shows the Relationships window, with links set up for the needed one-to-many and many-to-many relationships between database tables. (This figure shows only a representative set of the table relationships in this database, to conserve space.) The 1s and infinity symbols (∞) at the ends of the join lines represent the "one" and "many" sides of one-to-many relationships.

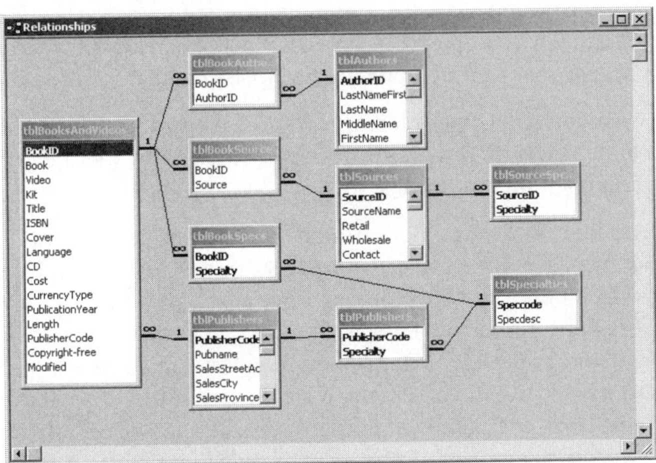

Figure 3-12. The Relationships window for the Crafts database shows one-to-many and many-to-many relationships.

Database Terminology

To complete this chapter, this section provides a list of some of the more important database terms, along with a brief description of each one. Some definitions also include a figure to help explain the term. These terms will appear in later chapters. If you're familiar with basic database terminology, feel free to skim this section and move on to the next chapter.

Application Generally speaking, an application is a program that performs a specific task or set of related tasks, such as Microsoft Word or Access. A *database application* is a complete set of database objects (tables, queries, forms, reports, macros, modules, and data access pages) that are linked so as to automate a task or set of tasks. The main difference between a simple database (containing many of these same objects) and a true database application is in the programming that automates the application to make it easier to use.

Automation Formerly OLE Automation. A Microsoft technology based on the Component Object Model (COM) that allows one application to work with objects belonging to another application.

Automation client An application that works with other applications' objects using Automation.

Automation server An application that lets other applications work with its components through Automation. Since most of the applications included in the current versions of Microsoft Office are both Automation clients and Automation servers, you can easily control these applications programmatically. For example, you can write code to create Word documents from Access, save Outlook tasks to an Access database, and so on.

Bound object An object, such as a form, report, or control, that is bound to data from a table, query, SQL statement, or recordset. Users can add, delete, and edit data in most bound objects.

Client-server application An application divided into a client component, containing an interface that's typically presented to the user, and a server component, which performs some type of processing on a server. For Access, a client-server application generally has SQL Server on the server side, with an Access front end as the client component. Splitting a database into a front end and a back end doesn't make it a true client-server database (see "Front-end/back-end database"). To be considered a true client-server database, a substantial amount of processing needs to be done on the server, such as creating a set of results from a complex query to send back to the client.

Column Database tables are divided into rows and columns. A column contains all the data in the table for a particular field.

Control An interface object on a form—for example, a text box or label.

Database A collection of information stored in an organized manner. An Access database is a collection of database objects (tables, forms, queries, reports, macros, modules, and data access pages) related to a specific topic, stored as a file with an MDB extension. Note that the term *database* might be used differently in other database applications (such as dBASE), typically to reference just a table or a collection of tables.

Database Management System (DBMS) A layer of software that manages the interface to the actual data.

Event Any significant action that can be detected by a system. Example events include clicking a button, moving the mouse, or pressing a key on the keyboard. You can write code to run when an event occurs. This code is called an *event handler* or *event procedure.*

Field A category of information in a database record. For example, in a database table that contains customer information, each record contains information about a single customer. The categories of information in the customer record are fields such as ContactName, ContactTitle, StreetAddress, and so on.

Flat-file database A simple type of database that places related information in a single table. Unlike a relational database, a flat-file database doesn't support relationships to link tables, and thus duplicate data (such as customer names and addresses) is typically stored in multiple tables or in multiple records in the same table.

Foreign key In a one-to-many relationship between tables, the field in the "many" table that links to the primary key field in the "one" table.

Front-end/back-end database Division of a database into a back-end database, containing only the data tables, and a front-end database, containing the interface elements (forms, reports, data access pages, and other supporting components) to allow updating the database's interface without disturbing the data. An Access database that has been split into a front-end/back-end database is not necessarily a client-server database.

Inner join Also called an *equi-join*. A join that combines records from linked tables that have matching values in the linking field in both tables—for example, records in the Customers table and the Orders table that have a CustomerID field equal to 55.

Interface object Database objects (such as forms and reports) that let users view and modify data in tables. Figure 3-13 shows a form and a report from the Northwind sample database.

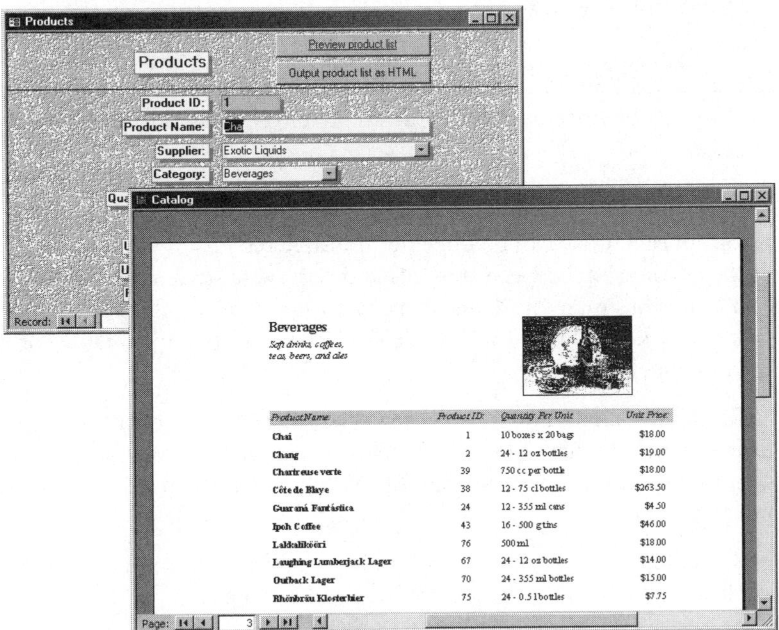

Figure 3-13. A form and report are examples of interface objects in the sample Northwind database.

Join A query operation that combines records from two or more tables. Joins can be inner, outer, or self-joins.

Key field Also called a *primary key.* A table field that uniquely identifies each record, such as a customer ID or a Social Security number.

Linked table A table that links to data stored outside the current Access database, either in another Access database or in some other data source, such as an Excel worksheet or a comma-delimited text file.

Local table A table whose data is stored in the current Access database.

Lookup field A field that displays and stores values from a linked field in another table, generally using a combo box for selecting the value. Figure 3-14 shows a lookup field in the Order Details table in the Northwind database.

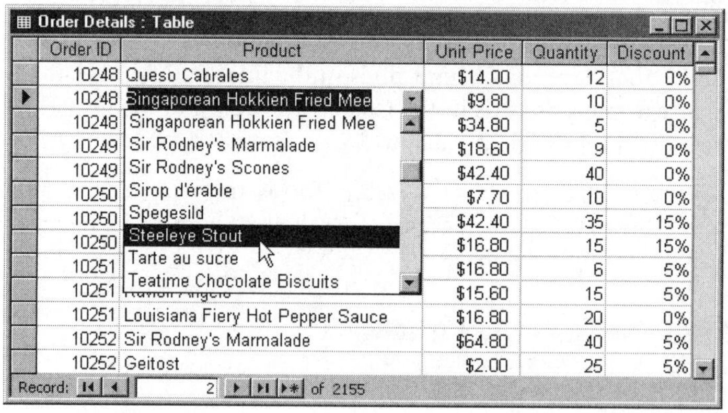

Figure 3-14. A lookup field in the Northwind database is used to select a value from another table.

Many-to-many relationship A relationship between two tables in which a record in each table can be linked to multiple records in another table, such as the relationship between students and classes—a student has many classes, and a class has many students. A many-to-many relationship is set up by linking the key fields in the two tables to be linked to a third table containing only the key fields.

Normalization Designing a database so that there's no duplication of data in different tables, other than linking fields. There are five levels (*normal forms*) of normalization; Access databases generally are normalized to the third normal form.

Object A component of an application, especially as represented in the application's object model for use in Automation code.

Object model A group of objects organized in a logical or hierarchical fashion that lets you work with the objects programmatically. Figure 3-15 shows some of the top-level objects in the Access object model diagram.

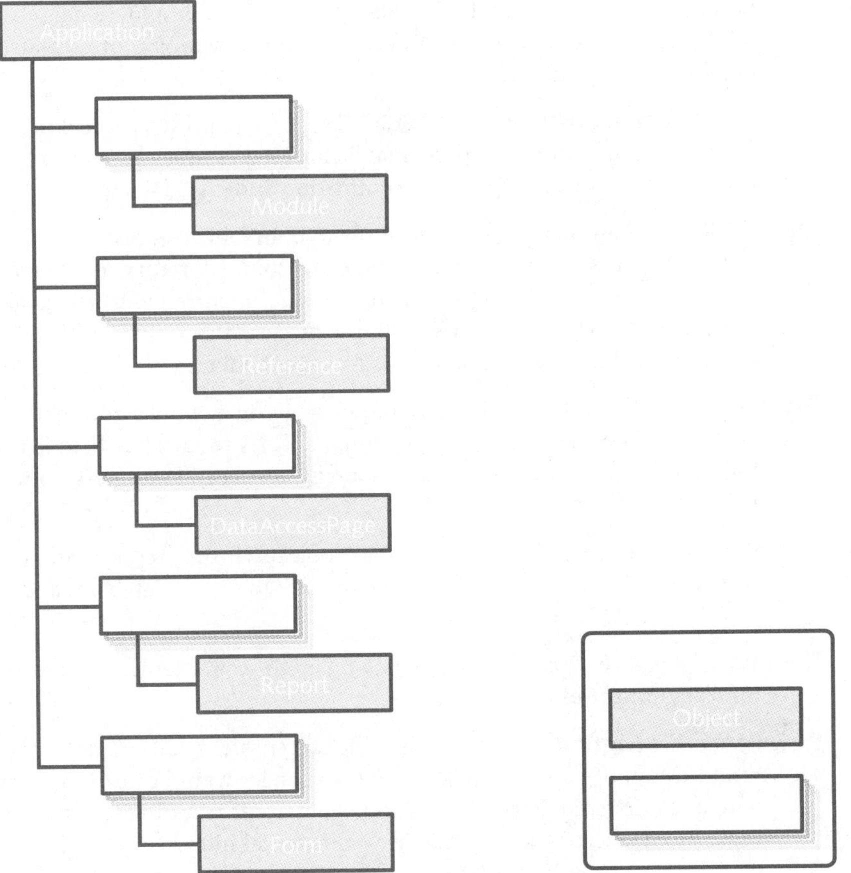

Figure 3-15. The Access object model shows Access components you can work with in Automation code.

OLE DB A technology based on COM for connecting to data in various sources, including nonrelational data stores such as Microsoft Exchange folders.

One-to-many relationship A relationship between two tables in which a single record in the "one" table can be linked to multiple records in the "many" table, such as customers and orders. The tables are linked on the primary key field in the "one" table and the foreign key in the "many" table.

One-to-one relationship A relationship between two tables in which a record in one table can have only one related record in the other table. One-to-one relationships are typically used when certain information needs to be kept more secure than other information, or is only rarely needed on forms or reports. For example, a table of employee name and job description data could be linked one-to-one with a more sensitive employee salary data table.

Open Database Connectivity (ODBC) A standard for connecting to data in various formats. This format is not used as much as it used to be because of the increasing use of Automation and OLE DB.

Outer join A join that returns records from both tables. Access offers two outer join types in the interface: a left outer join will return all the records in the table referenced on the left, and a right outer join will return all the records in the table referenced on the right. Available only in SQL, a full outer join will return all the records from both tables.

Primary key A field containing a unique value for each record, such as a customer ID or a Social Security number. The primary key field is used to link to other tables in one-to-many, many-to-many, and one-to-one relationships.

Project In Access, a collection of database objects (forms, reports, and data access pages) used as a front end to data in SQL Server databases and stored as an ADP file.

Record A set of related data (fields) making up a row in a table—for example, information about a customer.

Referential integrity A set of rules that prevent the addition, deletion, or modification of data in a table when the changes would cause a problem with a relationship. For example, adding an order record without a matching customer record might generate a referential integrity error.

Relational Database Management System (RDBMS) A database management system in which data is organized into tables and relationships can be established between tables.

Row All the information about a particular entry in a table, such as a customer or book.

Self-join A join that returns records based on other records in the same table.

Structured Query Language (SQL) A standardized data query language. As you create a query in Design view, Access automatically creates a corresponding SQL statement. Figure 3-16 shows a query in Design view, along with the corresponding SQL statement in SQL view.

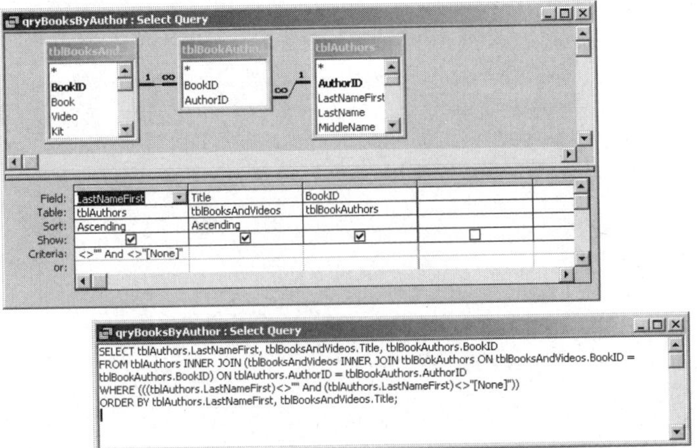

Figure 3-16. Access creates a SQL statement automatically as you design a query in Design view.

Table An Access (or other) database object that contains data. A table is arranged in rows (records) and columns (fields). A Customers table, for example, stores information about customers, one customer per row; customer fields (columns) contain information such as customer ID, contact name, contact title, and address. In Access databases, a table can be local or linked.

Unbound object An object, such as a form or control, that is not bound to data.

Validation rule A rule that defines whether data can be stored in a table field or accepted into a form control.

Visual Basic for Applications (VBA) A subset of the Microsoft Visual Basic programming language used in Microsoft Office and other applications.

Chapter 4

Creating a Database

In this chapter, you'll learn how to create the database you envision—whether that database is small and simple or large and complex. You'll learn how to name your database objects and create and link Access tables with the goal of creating an efficient and effective data management system—either for your own use or to meet your client's database needs.

Naming Database Objects

Using a consistent naming convention for database objects makes your database easier to work with, both when you are dealing with tables, queries, and other database objects in the interface and when you are writing VBA code.

Why Naming Conventions

Why use a naming convention? Basically, using a naming convention for database objects and controls makes your database self-documenting. Every time you see a drop-down list of database objects, each item's tag (prefix) will tell you what kind of object it is. Some dialog boxes offering a choice of objects have separate pages for each type of database object, but others don't. For example, when you select a record source for a form or report, all the tables and all the select queries in the database are listed in a single alphabetical list, so unless you have used a naming convention with distinctive tags for each database object, you won't know whether you are selecting a table or query. Figure 4-1 shows the drop-down list for selecting a record source for a form in the sample Northwind database, which doesn't use a naming convention for database objects.

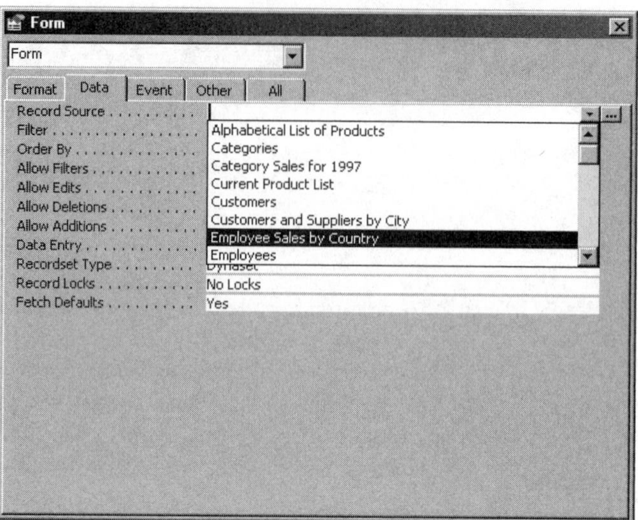

Figure 4-1. Without a naming convention, there is no way to distinguish between tables and queries when selecting a data source for a form or report.

Likewise, when you see a reference to an object, a control, a variable, or a field in VBA code, you'll know what kind of element it is—essential information for understanding what you can do with it, so you won't try to assign a currency value to a date variable, or use the *SetFocus* method on a field, for example.

Naming Restrictions

With Access, you can name database objects (including fields and controls) anything you want. Well, almost anything—there are a few absolute restrictions, as follows:

- Names can't be longer than 64 characters.
- Names can't include a period (.), an exclamation point (!), a grave accent (\`), or square brackets ([]).
- Names can't start with a space.
- Names can't include ASCII controls characters (ASCII characters 0–31).
- In a project, names can't include a double quotation mark (").

It's good to be able to give objects long, descriptive names. (This feature was especially welcome in Access 1.0, when many users were coming to Access from MS-DOS database applications, which limited object names to 8 or 10 characters.) But there are some problems with using spaces or punctuation marks in object names, even though Access allows them. If you give objects, controls, or fields names that contain spaces, Access won't recognize these names as object, field, or control names in expressions, and so you'll have to type brackets around them. (Access will automatically bracket single-word names in VBA code and query expressions, in most cases.) If you use punctuation marks in field names, and you export a table to another application that can't accept specific punctuation characters that Access permits, you will have problems during the export, or afterwards.

You might also want to add the following naming restrictions, to prevent possible problems and make database objects easier to work with:

- Don't use spaces in names. Instead, capitalize the first letter of each included word (LastName), or use the underscore character (Last_Name).
- Don't use any punctuation marks in names, other than the underscore. Most punctuation marks won't cause problems in Access, but if you need to export data to another application, you might have problems because the target application can't handle dashes in field names, for example.
- Avoid naming fields with words that are keywords, property or method names, or built-in functions (such as Name, Date, or Count), as they can cause errors in VBA code.
- Use a naming convention to help you recognize and refer to different object types consistently.

A Simple Naming Convention

Chapter 20, "Customizing Your Database Using VBA Code," goes into detail about naming conventions. You may not want to apply a naming convention throughout a database, but there are great benefits from using even a simple naming convention that just prefixes database object names with a three-letter tag that indicates the object type. Table 4-1 shows a basic list of tags for the six main types of database objects.

Table 4-1. Common tags for database objects

Object	Tag
Form	*frm*
Macro	*mcr*
Module	*mod*
Query (any type)	*qry*
Report	*rpt*
Table	*tbl*

For more detailed information on conventions for naming database objects, see Chapter 20, "Customizing Your Database Using VBA Code."

Creating Tables

Tables are the heart of an Access database—they contain the data that is displayed in forms and data access pages and printed in reports. Each table in Access should store data related to a specific category—for example, you might store customer information in one table, product information in another, and vendor information in another. The data in different tables should be related via linking fields, thereby avoiding duplication and other problems.

See Chapter 3, "Introduction to Database Design," for information on normalizing database tables.

Tables store data in columns and rows. Each column is a single data category, or field, and each row constitutes a record, which contains a collection of field entries related to that record. In addition to creating tables to store and organize data, you will build relationships among tables by linking them on key fields. In this section, you'll learn to create tables both manually and using the Table Wizard.

Using the Table Wizard

Access includes a Table Wizard that helps you create tables easily, especially tables that store certain commonly used types of data. The Table Wizard offers a selection of Business or Personal tables that you can use as is, or modify to suit your needs. You can start the Table Wizard two different ways from the Database window:

- Click Tables and then double-click the Create Table By Using Wizard option, or
- Click Tables, click New, and then select Table Wizard in the New Table dialog box (see Figure 4-2); then click OK.

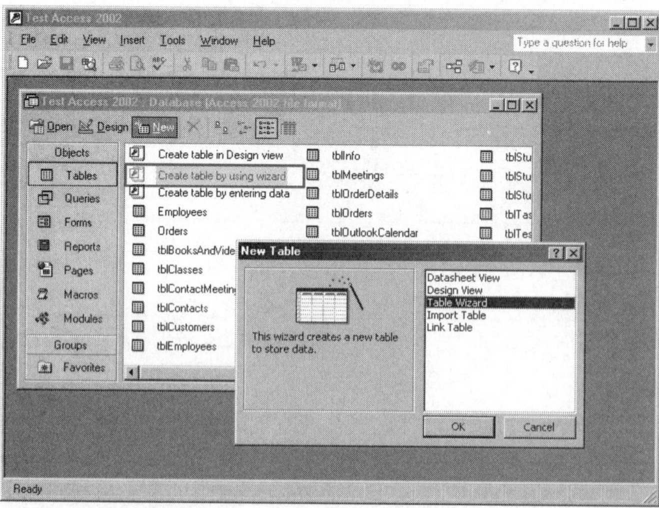

Figure 4-2. Start the New Table Wizard by selecting Table Wizard in the New Table dialog box.

To use the Table Wizard to create a table—in this case, a personal Service Records table, which could be used to record car or truck maintenance—follow these steps:

1. On the first page of the Table Wizard, select the Personal option, and select Service Records in the Sample Tables list.
2. Click the >> button to select all the fields in the Sample Fields list for the table, as shown in Figure 4-3. Click Next.

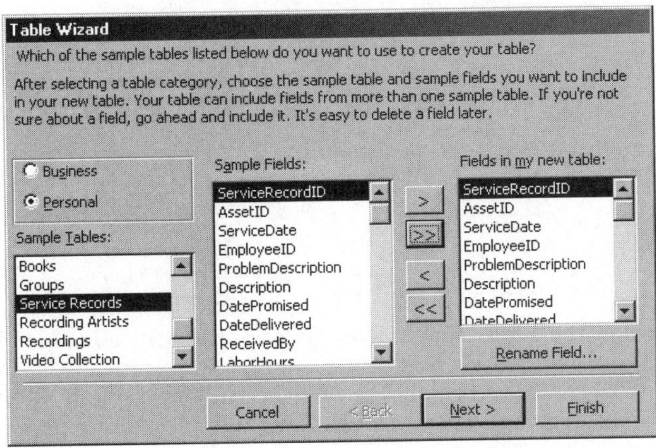

Figure 4-3. Select the personal Service Records table.

3. Name your table, preferably using the *tbl* tag as a prefix, as shown in Figure 4-4.

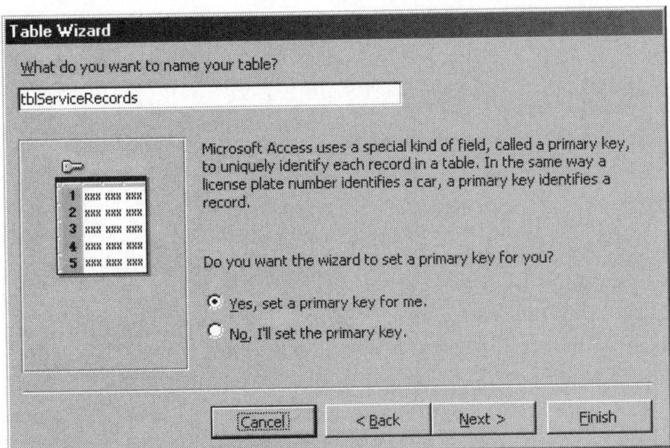

Figure 4-4. Name the new table in the Table Wizard.

4. You have the option of letting Access set the table's primary key (the default) or setting the key manually. Leave the default setting as is so that Access will set the primary key.

5 Click Next to display the next page of the wizard, where you can set links between the new table and existing tables in the database, as shown in Figure 4-5.

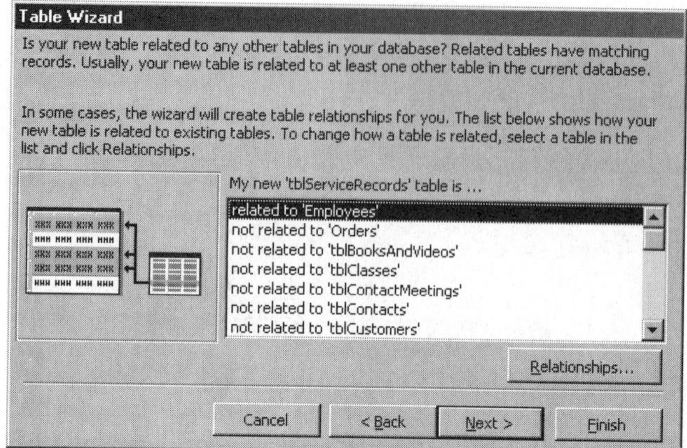

Figure 4-5. The wizard suggests relationships to other tables in the database.

6 If you want to set up a relationship to another table in the database, click the Relationships button to open the Relationships dialog box, and select the appropriate option, as shown in Figure 4-6.

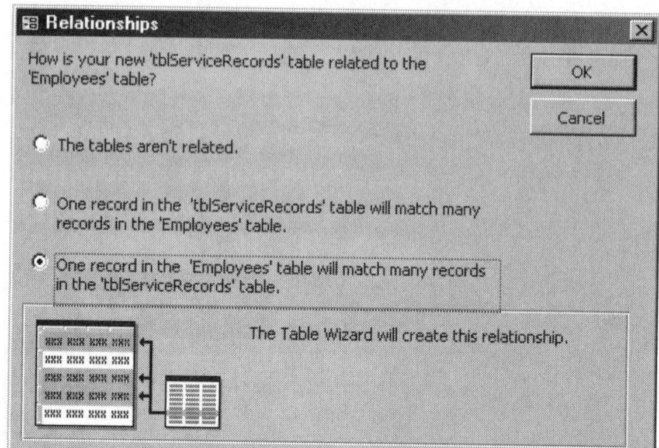

Figure 4-6. Choose the way in which you want Access to create the relationship between the new table and the existing table.

If you select either of the relationship options and click OK, the wizard will create an appropriate linking field (if necessary) and create the relationship.

7 Click Next to display the last page of the wizard, shown in Figure 4-7. This page provides three options: You can open the table in Design view to make further modifications, enter data directly into the table in Datasheet view, or enter data into the table using a form created by the wizard.

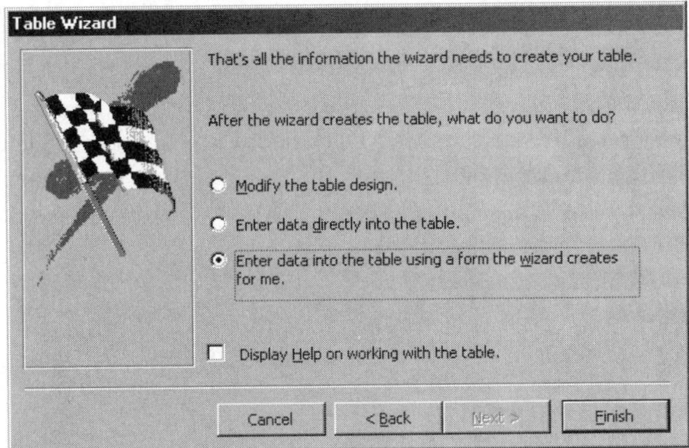

Figure 4-7. On this page, choose to modify the table design or choose a method for entering data into the table.

If you select the third option and click Finish, the wizard creates a form (similar to the form you create by choosing AutoForm from the New Object button's drop-down list) and opens it for editing, as shown in Figure 4-8.

tblServiceRecords
Service Record ID (AutoNumber)
Asset ID
Service Date
Employee ID
Description
Description
Date Promised
Date Delivered
Received By
Labor Hours
Estimated Cost
Actual Cost
Parts Replaced
Record: 1 of 1

Figure 4-8. A form is created by the Table Wizard for entering data into the new table.

Creating Tables Manually

If the database tables you need to create don't quite match the sample tables available in Access, you'll need to create your own. You can create a table manually two different ways, starting in the Database window:

- Click Tables, and then double-click the Create Table In Design View option, or
- Click Tables and click New. When the New Table dialog box appears, as shown in Figure 4-9, select either Datasheet View or Design View and click OK. The new database table is then displayed in the Access work area. Figure 4-10 shows a new table created in Design view.

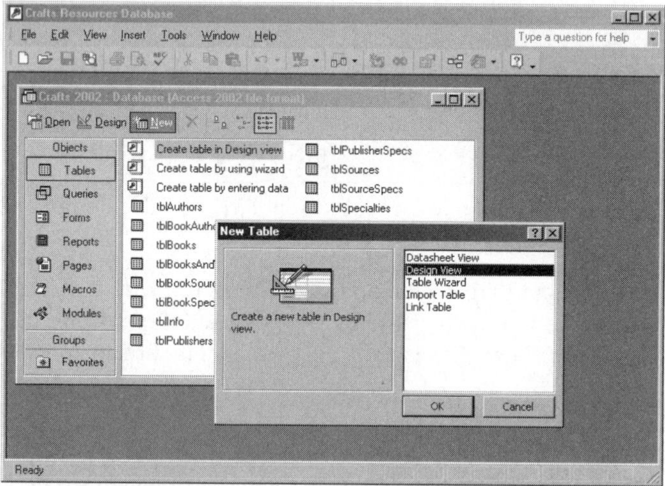

Figure 4-9. Open the New Table dialog box to create a table in Design view.

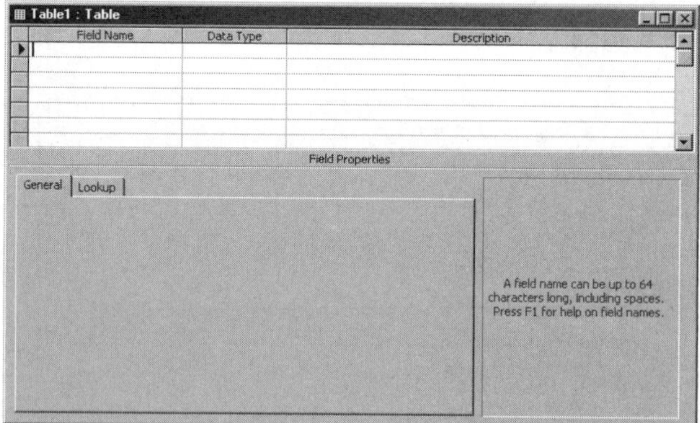

Figure 4-10. Creating a new table in Design view involves naming the fields and choosing their data types.

Troubleshooting

My fields are the wrong data type when I create a table in Datasheet view

When you create a new table in Access, you can choose to create it in Datasheet view or Design view. If you choose to create a table in Datasheet view, you won't be able to select the data type for the fields you create (at least not while in Datasheet view). When you create fields in Datasheet view, Access assigns each field a data type depending on the value you type into that field.

If you type text into a field, it will be a Text field; if you type in a number, it will be a Number field; if you type in a number with a dollar sign, it will be a Currency field; and if you type in a date, it will be a Date field. To create a field using any of the other data types (such as AutoNumber, Memo, or OLE Object), you have to switch to Design view and select the field's data type manually.

It's generally preferable simply to create the table in Design view, where you have all the tools you need to create each field with exactly the right data type. To find out more about setting data types, see the section "Setting Field Data Types" below.

Naming Fields

If you're working in Design view, one of your first tasks is to name your fields. Naming conventions for Access fields are pretty straightforward. See the "Naming Restrictions" section earlier in this chapter for full details on restrictions and recommendations for naming fields—in particular, avoiding spaces and punctuation marks in field names.

To name a field, simply type the field name in the Field Name column for that field, and press Enter or Tab. The selection then moves to the Data Type column.

Setting Field Data Types

In the Data Type column of a table in Design view, you choose the type of data that will be stored in the field. Text is the default data type, but you can choose any one of the types shown in Table 4-2 by clicking the down arrow and choosing the type from the displayed list. When you choose the data type, the options shown in the General tab of the Field Properties section change to allow you to choose specific options for the selected data type.

Table 4-2. **Access field data types**

Data type	Description
Text	Text data, including numbers that don't require calculations. Text can be up to 255 characters in length.
Memo	Longer blocks of text, up to 65,535 characters.
Number	Numeric data that might be used in calculations.
Date/Time	Dates and times.
Currency	Currency (monetary) values. Also used to prevent rounding off during calculations.
AutoNumber	Creates unique sequential (incrementing by 1) or random ID numbers and replication IDs.
Yes/No	Two-valued data, such as Yes/No, True/False. Null values are not allowed.
OLE Object	OLE objects such as Word documents or Excel worksheets. Hyperlinks (either URLs or UNC paths).
Hyperlink	Hyperlinks (either URLs or UNC paths).
Lookup Wizard	Not really a data type. Allows you to select a value for a field from another table or a list of values.

Although choosing the data type you need may be fairly obvious (such as choosing the Text data type for a LastName field), some choices may not be so cut and dried. Should you use Number or Currency for a field that will store monetary values? When is it appropriate to use the AutoNumber data type? The following guidelines will help you determine when to use different data types:

- For storing money values or numeric values in which a high degree of accuracy is required, use the *Currency* data type.
- For storing text up to 255 characters in length or numbers that aren't going to be used in calculations (such as Social Security numbers or phone numbers), use the *Text* data type.
- For storing large amounts of text (more than 255 characters, but fewer than 65,536 characters), use the *Memo* data type.
- For storing whole numbers between –32,768 and 32,767, use the Number data type with Integer selected for the *FieldSize* property.
- For storing longer whole numbers, use the *Number* data type with Long Integer selected for the *FieldSize* property.

- For storing single-precision numbers that might have fractional values, use the *Number* data type with Single selected for the *FieldSize* property.
- For storing double-precision numbers that might have fractional values, use the *Number* data type with Double selected for the *FieldSize* property.
- If you need a unique, incrementing ID number to use as a key field, use the *AutoNumber* data type with Increment selected as the *NewValues* property.
- If you need a unique, random ID number to use as a key field, use the *AutoNumber* data type with Random selected as the *NewValues* property.
- If you need to perform calculations on numbers in a field, use a *Currency* field or a *Number* field with the appropriate field size.
- If you need a globally unique identifier (GUID) for replicated databases, use the *AutoNumber* data type with Replication ID as the *FieldSize* property setting.
- If you need to enter dates in fields, use the *Date/Time* data type.

Choosing Number Data Types

After you assign the Number data type to a field you have created, you have to specify the FieldSize property, which determines the type and size of the numbers that can be entered in the field. You can choose from among the following *FieldSize* choices:

Byte Whole numbers from 0 through 255

Integer Whole numbers from -32,768 through 32,767

Long Integer (default) Whole numbers from -2,147,483,648 through 2,147,483,647

Single Numbers from -3.402823E38 through -1.401298E-45 for negative values and from 1.401298E-45 to 3.402823E38 for positive values

Double Numbers from -1.79769313486231E308 through -4.94065645841247E-324 for negative values and from 4.94065645841247E-324 through 1.79769313486231E308 for positive values

Replication ID Globally unique identifier (GUID), a 16-byte field that is a unique identifier for replication

Decimal Numbers from -10^{38}-1 through 10^{38}-1 (ADP), or from -10^{28}-1 through 10^{28}-1 (MDB)

In VBA (and other programming languages), these are separate data types. When you see an Access field data type described as Double, for instance, this means that it is a Number field with its FieldSize property set to Double.

tip **Describe field contents**

The Description column in Design view is an optional property you can use to describe the field's data. To enter a description, simply click in the property and type the Description text. The description you enter will appear both in Design view and also on the status bar when the user selects the field on a form. When you are working with foreign key fields, for example, you could enter in the Description column the name of the linked table.

Creating Lookup Fields

While you're working in Design view, you can create a lookup field, which enables you to display a list of values from a field in another table. To do this, you use the Lookup Wizard, which is available when you specify the data type for the selected field. To create the lookup field using the Lookup Wizard, follow these steps:

1. Choose the Lookup Wizard data type for a field. The first page of the wizard gives you the option of looking up the values in a table or query or entering them yourself (see Figure 4-11). To create the lookup, click the first option; then click Next.

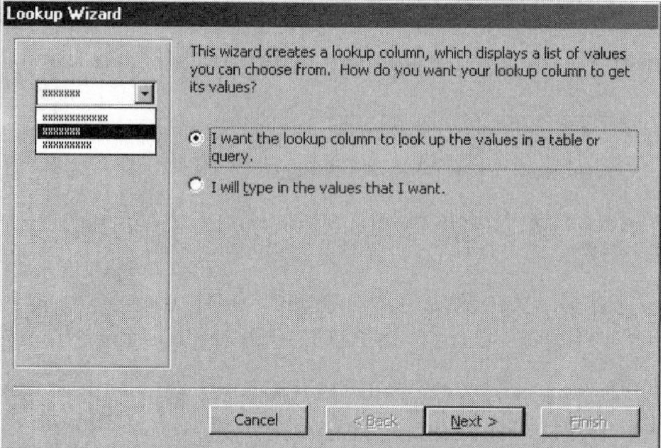

Figure 4-11. The first page of the Lookup Wizard gives you the option of looking up values or entering them manually.

2. Select the table or query that contains the data you want to look up, and click Next.
3. In the Available Fields list, choose the field that contains the values you need to look up (see Figure 4-12). Click the arrow buttons to move the field to the Selected Fields list, and click Next.

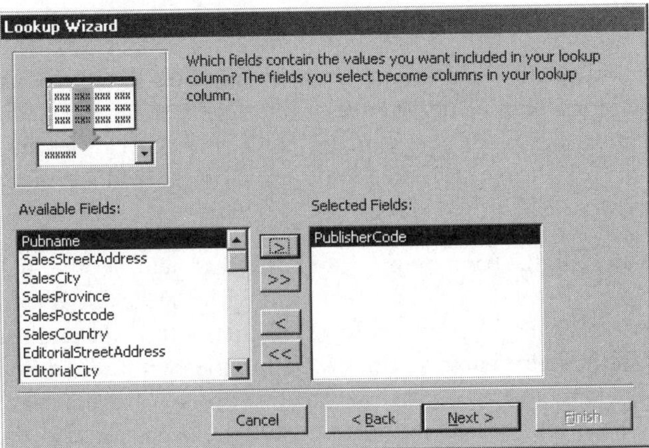

Figure 4-12. Select from the Available Fields list the field you want to use to look up values.

4. If you want to adjust the width of the lookup column, drag the right edge of the column to the desired width; then click Next.
5. On the last page of the wizard, give the lookup column a name. Then click Finish to finish creating the lookup field.
6. A message box appears, telling you that the relationships needs to be saved with the table. Click Yes to complete the operation. Design view is displayed once again, with the lookup information displayed in the Lookup tab of the Field Properties area (see Figure 4-13).

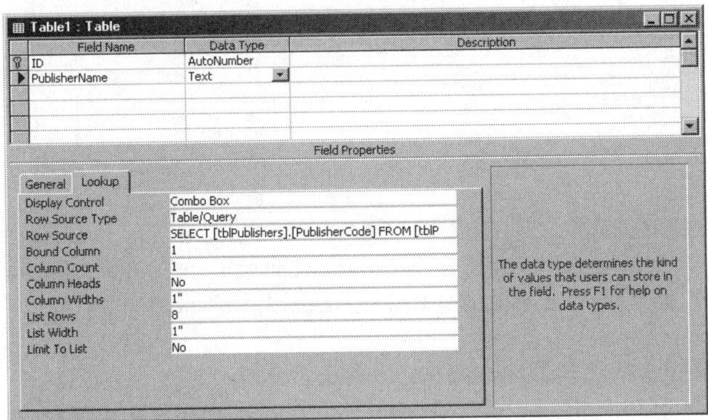

Figure 4-13. After completing the Lookup Wizard, you see the finished lookup field's properties sheet.

Now, when you are working in Datasheet view, you can select a value for this field by picking an item from a drop-down list, which saves time and prevents data-entry errors. When a lookup field is dragged to a form, it appears as a combo box with the lookup table as its row source.

Working with Nulls and Zero-Length Strings

Null is a special value that indicates missing or unknown data. In VBA code, the *Null* keyword is used for a Null value, whereas a *zero-length string* is a string that has zero characters. Primary key fields can't contain Nulls, and you can set the *Required* property to Yes to prevent storage of Nulls in other fields. (A field with Required set to Yes must have an entry; if Required is set to No, the field can contain a Null.)

To prevent a zero-length string being stored in a Text field, set the *AllowZeroLength* property to No. Figure 4-14 shows a Text field with the *Required* property set to No and the *AllowZeroLength* property set to Yes so that both Nulls and zero-length strings can be stored in the field. These settings are appropriate for a field that may have no entry in some records in a table, such as EmailAddress in a contacts table. Initially, when a record has been created and no value has yet been stored in the field, it will contain a Null.

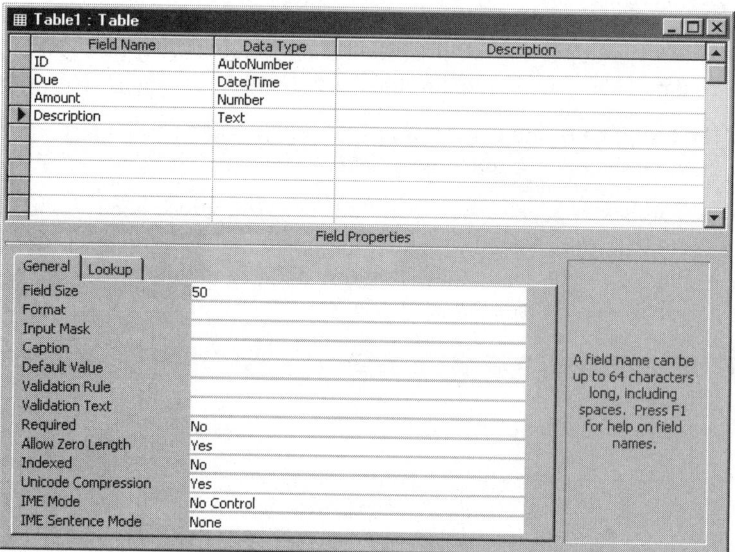

Figure 4-14. Allowing Nulls and zero-length strings in a Text field guarantees that you won't have problems when a record has no data in this field.

When you look at a field in Datasheet view (or in a form), you can't tell the difference between a Null and a zero-length string, but you can use the *IsNull* function to determine whether a field contains a Null value and the *Nz* function to convert Nulls to zero-length strings to avoid problems when storing data in variables.

> **note** If you aren't familiar with VBA code, you may want to return to this code segment after reading Chapter 20, "Customizing Your Database Using VBA Code."

The If...Then portion of the following event procedure displays a message box telling you that a field shown on a form contains a Null. The procedure then uses the *Nz* function to store the contents of the field in a *String* variable to prevent an *Invalid use of Nulls* message when you're attempting to store a Null in a *String* variable. The *String* variable is then displayed in a message box.

```
Private Sub cmdTest_Click()

    Dim strDescription As String

    If IsNull(Me![Description]) Then
        MsgBox "Description contains a Null"
    End If

    strDescription = Nz(Me![Description])
    MsgBox "Description: " & strDescription

End Sub
```

Figure 4-15 shows the test form, with the Test command button that runs the preceding code.

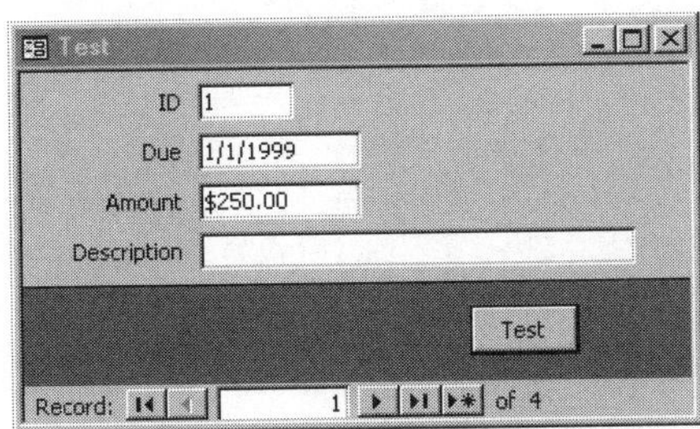

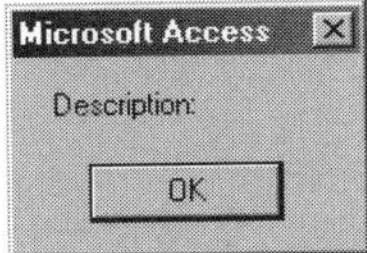

Figure 4-15. The test form tests for Nulls and zero-length strings in a field.

When you're working in VBA code, it's advisable to use the *Nz* function before you store data in variables (especially if there's any chance the data might contain a Null) because the only VBA data type that can accept Nulls is the *Variant* data type.

Setting Validation Rules

If you want to ensure that users can't enter incorrect data in a field, you can set a validation rule for data entry, with a message to be displayed in case the wrong type of data is entered in the field. For example, if you want to ensure that a positive number is entered in a number field, you could create a field validation rule of >0, which specifies that values greater than zero must be entered. Validation rules can be set in tables or in forms, but generally it's better to set them in tables because validation rules set in tables will be inherited by fields placed on forms, and additionally they will work if data is entered directly into a table.

A validation rule that applies to only one field is called a *field validation rule*, and a validation rule that includes conditions on two or more fields in a record is called a *record validation rule*. Both types of rules are specified by the *ValidationRule* property of a field.

You can either type a validation rule directly in the *ValidationRule* property or click the Build button to the right of the property to open the Expression Builder dialog box, where you can easily create a complicated expression by selecting components from lists of database objects, fields, and functions. Figure 4-16 shows a simple expression being created in the Expression Builder—in this case, a validation rule that checks whether the date entered in the Due field is later than tomorrow.

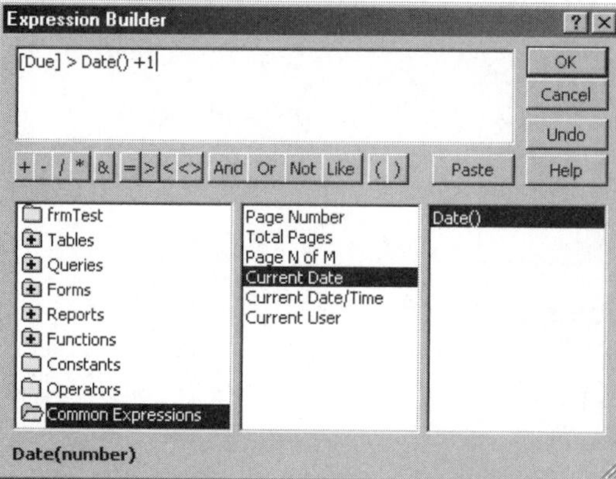

Figure 4-16. You can construct a validation rule in the Expression Builder.

Figure 4-17 shows the validation rule and its validation text on the General tab in the Due field's properties sheet.

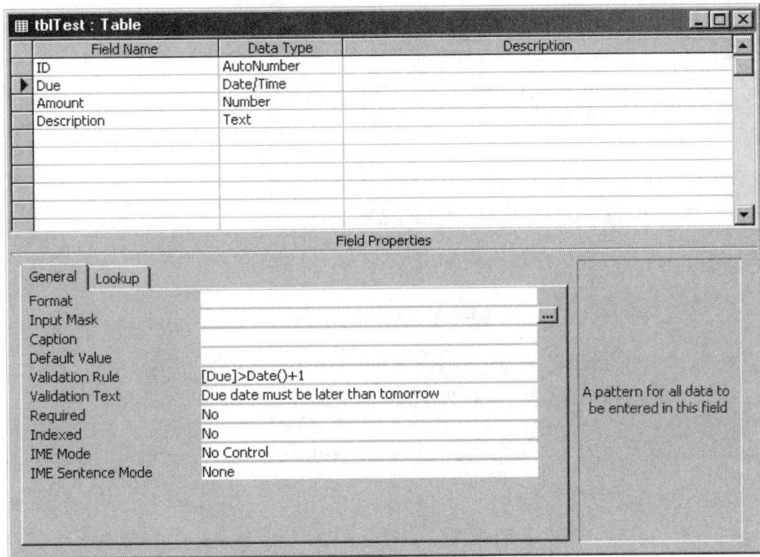

Figure 4-17. Use a validation rule and validation text in a field's properties sheet to enforce and document the field's data requirements.

Creating Input Masks

In addition to validation rules, Access provides another tool you can use to enforce correct data entry: *input masks.* An input mask shows the user a template for data entry and won't accept data that doesn't fit the template. Access provides a list of commonly used input masks that you can select from the Input Mask Wizard, and you can also create your own custom input masks.

To specify an input mask using the Input Mask Wizard, follow these steps:

1. Open a table in Design view, and select a field.
2. In the Field Properties pane, click in the Input Mask property. A Build button appears to the right of the property.

> **tip** To get detailed help on constructing input masks, press F1 while your cursor is in the InputMask property, or type InputMask into the Ask A Question box on the main Access menu.

3. Click the Build button. The Input Mask Wizard starts.
4. On the first page of the wizard, select the appropriate input mask, as shown in Figure 4-18, and then click Next.

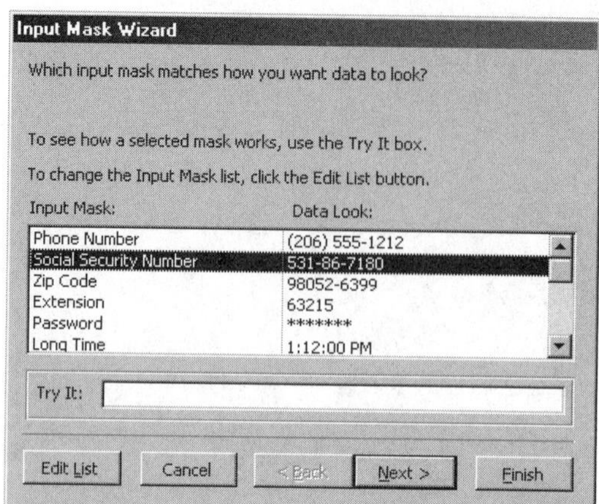

Figure 4-18. Select the Social Security Number input mask for a field.

5 On the next page of the wizard, shown in Figure 4-19, select a different placeholder character if desired. (The underscore is the default placeholder character.) You can also edit the input mask on this screen, if desired, by clicking in the Input Mask box and typing the mask the way you want it to appear. Click Next.

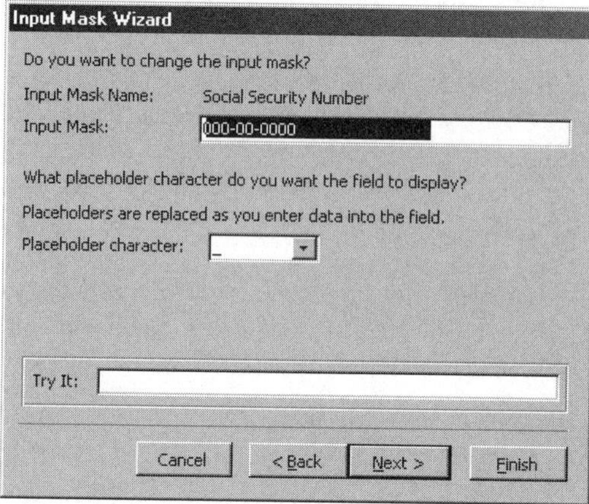

Figure 4-19. Select a placeholder character for the input mask.

6 Now you can specify whether to store the data with or without the symbols in the mask (such as the dashes in Social Security numbers). Make your choice and click Next.

7 On the last page of the wizard, click Finish to write the input mask to the *InputMask* property of the field, as shown in Figure 4-20.

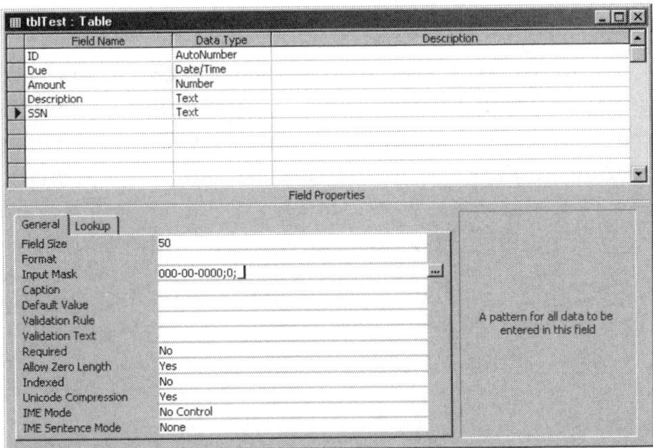

Figure 4-20. View the input mask in the *InputMask* property of the field.

Figure 4-21 shows a table in Datasheet view, with the input mask visible in the SSN field.

tblTest : Table

ID	Due	Amount	Description	SSN
1	1/1/2002	250		___-__-____
2	2/2/2002	100	Best	
3	3/11/2003	0		
4	3/1/2003	20		
(AutoNumber)		0		

Record: 1 of 4

Figure 4-21. An input mask is visible in the SSN field of a table in Datasheet view.

InsideOut

You can't override an input mask—for example, if you get a foreign phone number that doesn't fit the U.S./Canadian phone number format or a foreign ID number that has a different format than a Social Security number. If you need to enter data in a certain format most of the time but occasionally in another format, write code in the *BeforeUpdate* or *AfterUpdate* event of a form control to format the data instead of using an input mask. (See Chapter 5, "Creating Forms for Entering, Editing, and Viewing Data," for additional information on entering data.)

Creating Indexes

You can set an index on a field in an Access table to enable Access to find and sort records faster. Indexes can be set on a single field or on multiple fields; multiple-field indexes are useful when the first field might have duplicate values and you need a value from another field to create a unique key for the table. If you have a primary key field, which is used to relate a table to foreign key fields in other tables, it has a unique index that won't allow Null values in the field, and requires an entry in every record.

You can also index a field so that it allows duplicates—this type of index is often used in a field that might be used for searching or sorting, such as a ZIP Code field. Figure 4-22 shows the available indexing options for a table field.

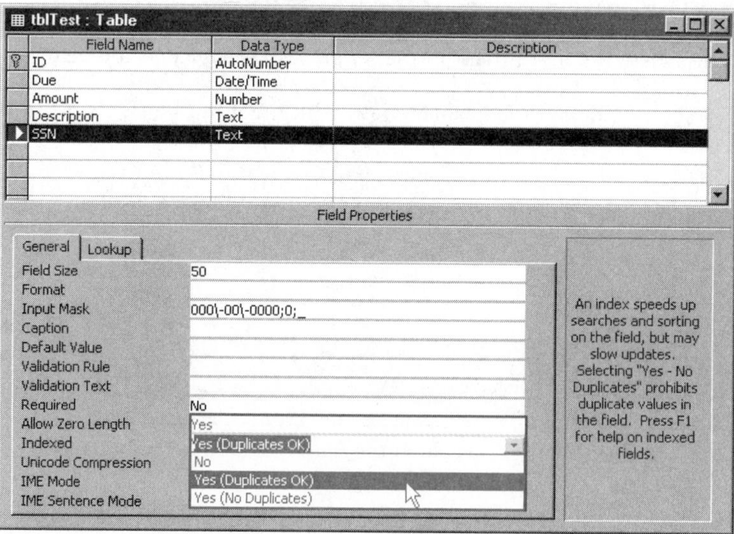

Figure 4-22. Use the available selections for indexing a table field.

> **note** You can't index an OLE Object type field because these fields contain objects—such as Excel worksheets or Word documents—rather than data.

Creating Relationships

Chapter 3, "Introduction to Database Design," included a discussion of normalizing database tables and one-to-one, one-to-many, and many-to-many relationships. These relationships are set up in the Relationships window, by dragging a field from one table to another. When you link two tables, you have a number of options for each relationship, which can be selected in the Edit Relationships dialog box that automatically opens when you link tables.

To test creating various types of relationships, you can create a set of tables as described in Table 4-3 through Table 4-7 below (as a time-saver, these tables can be found in the sample database Test Access 2002.mdb), or you can use your own tables, provided they have appropriate matching fields for setting up the relationships.

Table 4-3. tblStudents—For the "One" Side of a One-to-Many Relationship

Field name	Data type
StudentID	Text (key field)
FirstName	Text
MiddleName	Text
LastName	Text
MatriculationDate	Date/Time
DegreeProgram	Text
GraduationDate	Date/Time

Table 4-4. tblClasses—For the "One" Side of a One-to-Many Relationship

Field name	Data type
ClassNo	Text (key field)
ClassName	Text
Program	Text
Credits	Number (Integer)

Table 4-5. tblStudentCharges—For the "Many" Side of a One-to-Many Relationship

Field name	Data type
StudentID	Text (Indexed, Duplicates OK)
Charge	Currency
Description	Text
ChargeDate	Date/Time
Paid	Yes/No

Table 4-6. **tblStudentIDs—Typical Second Table for a One-to-One Relationship**

Field name	Data type
StudentID	Text (key field)
SSN	Text
MilitaryID	Text
ForeignID	Text

Table 4-7. **tblStudentClasses—Linking Table for a Many-to-Many Relationship Between tblStudents and tblClasses**

Field name	Data type
StudentID	Text (indexed Duplicates OK)
ClassNo	Text (indexed Duplicates OK)
Semester	Text
Year	Text

Creating a One-to-Many Relationship

One-to-many relationships are by far the most common relationships in Access databases. A one-to-many relationship links a table with one record per key field value to another table that may have multiple records for that same value. In the sample table set, tblStudents has one record per StudentID (its key field), while tblStudentCharges has multiple records per StudentID (which will be the foreign key field in the relationship). To set up a one-to-many relationship between these tables, follow the steps below:

1. Open the Relationships window by clicking the Relationships button on the toolbar, or selecting Relationships from the Tools menu.
2. Click the Show Table button in the toolbar to open the Show Table dialog box.
3. Add tblStudents and tblStudentCharges (or two of your own tables with an appropriate matching field).

tip A matching field can have different names in the two tables, but it must be of the same data type, with one exception: An AutoNumber field matches a Number (Long Integer) field.

4 Drag the linking StudentID field from the tblStudents table to the StudentID field of the tblStudentCharges table. The Edit Relationships dialog box opens, as shown in Figure 4-23.

Access detects the appropriate relationship type (One-To-Many) and lists it in the Relationship Type box at the bottom of the Edit Relationships dialog box.

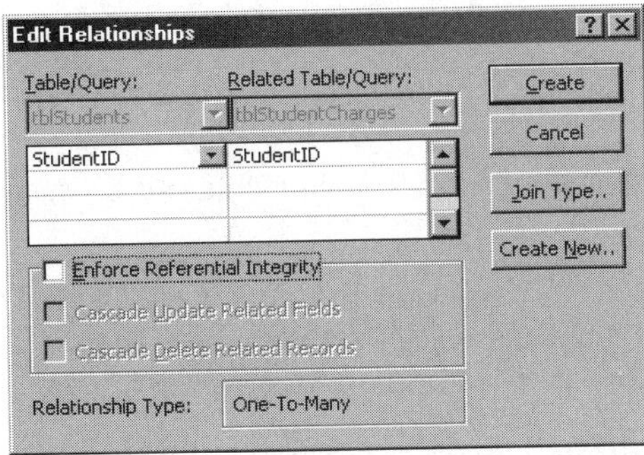

Figure 4-23. The Edit Relationships dialog box lists a one-to-many relationship type when the StudentID field is dragged from tblStudents to tblStudentCharges.

5 Click the Enforce Referential Integrity check box (see the "Selecting Enforce Referential Integrity" section below for details on this option); click the Create button to create the relationship, which appears as a line with a 1 on the "one" side of the linking line, and an infinity symbol on the "many" side, as shown in Figure 4-24.

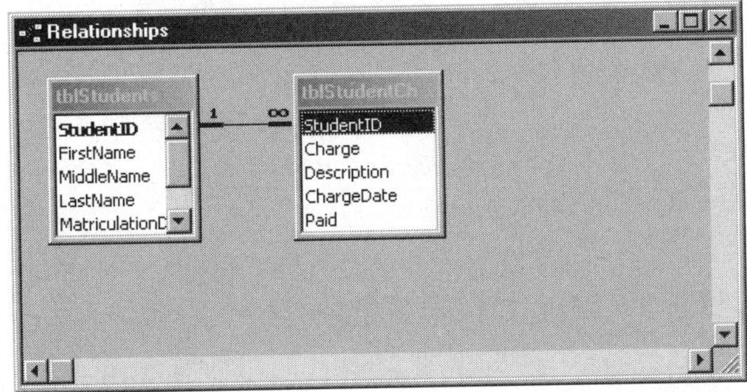

Figure 4-24. A one-to-many relationship in the Relationships window is indicated by the 1 and infinity symbol at the ends of the link.

Creating a One-to-One Relationship

A one-to-one relationship links two tables, each with a key field (so they have only one record per key field value). Typically, two tables are linked in a one-to-one relationship because some of the data is more confidential, or is used less frequently. In the sample table set, tblStudents and tblStudentIDs both have the StudentID field as the key field; tblStudentIDs stores various IDs, and is kept confidential. To set up a one-to-one relationship between these tables (or two suitable tables of your own), follow the steps below:

1. Open the Relationships window and add tblStudents and tblStudentIDs to the diagram.
2. Drag the linking StudentID field from the tblStudents table to the StudentID field of the tblStudentIDs table; the Edit Relationships dialog box opens, with the relationship type listed as One-To-One.
3. Click the Enforce Referential Integrity check box and then click Create to create the relationship, which is indicated by a 1 at each end of the linking line in the Relationships window, as shown in Figure 4-25.

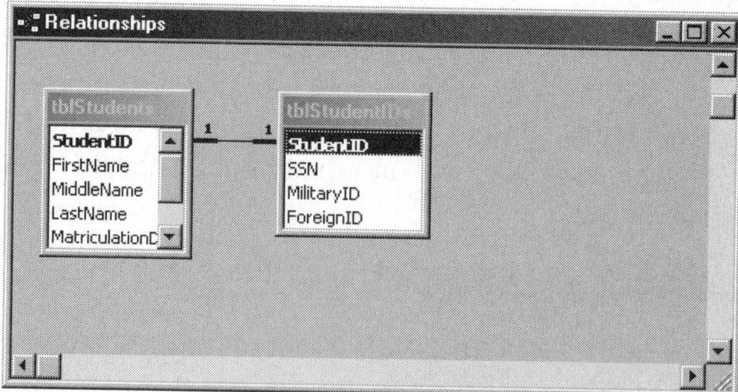

Figure 4-25. A one-to-one relationship is indicated by a 1 at each end of the link in the Relationships window.

Creating a Many-to-Many Relationship

A many-to-many relationship is a pair of one-to-many relationships, with a linking table between the two tables to be linked. The linking table needs only the two fields that are key fields in the two main tables, though it may contain other fields as well. In the sample table set, tblStudentClasses is a linking table that can be used to set up a many-to-many relationship between tblStudents and tblClasses; it contains tblStudentID, the key field of tblStudents, and tblClassNo, the key field of tblClasses. In tblStudentClasses, these fields are not key fields (they will be the foreign keys in the two one-to-many relationships); they are both Indexed, Duplicates OK. Follow the steps below to set up the many-to-many relationship.

1. Open the Relationships window, and add tblStudents, tblClasses, and tblStudentClasses to the diagram (or your own tables with appropriate matching fields).
2. Drag the StudentID field from tblStudentClasses to tblStudents to set up the first of the two one-to-many links that comprise the many-to-many link; as before, select the Enforce Referential Integrity check box and click Create to create the one-to-many relationship.
3. Similarly, drag the ClassNo field from tblStudentClasses to tblClasses to set up the second one-to-many link; select the Enforce Referential Integrity check box and click Create to create this one-to-many relationship. Figure 4-26 shows the finished many-to-many relationship in the Relationships window.

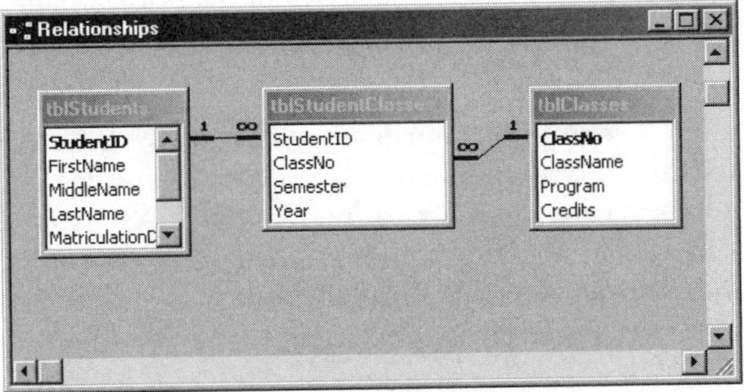

Figure 4-26. A many-to-many relationship consists of two one-to-many relationships with a linking table at the "many" end of both.

After you have set up a relationship in the Relationships window, the link will automatically appear in the Query Design view when you add the linked tables to a query.

Selecting Enforce Referential Integrity

If the Enforce Referential Integrity check box is selected in the Edit Relationships dialog box, Access uses a set of rules to ensure that relationships between records in related tables are valid and that you don't accidentally delete or change related data. To enforce referential integrity, the following requirements must be met:

- The matching field in the primary table must be a primary key or have a unique index.
- The related fields must have the same data type, with two exceptions: an *AutoNumber* field can match a *Long Integer* field, and an *AutoNumber* field with a field size of Replication ID can match a *Number* field with a field size of Replication ID.
- Both tables must be in the same database. For linked tables, you must set the relationship in the original database.

tip It's best to set up relationships and enforce referential integrity as soon as possible after creating tables, to avoid problems with trying to set up a relationship with referential integrity when existing data in the tables conflicts with referential integrity rules.

Rules for Enforcing Referential Integrity

Once you choose to enforce referential integrity in your tables, there are certain things you can and cannot do as you enter data. Here are some ways in which your data entries will be checked for accuracy:

- You can't enter a value in the foreign key field of the related table unless there's a matching value in the primary key of the primary table. For example, you can't enter an order for a Customer ID that doesn't exist in the Customers table.
- You can't delete a record from a primary table if there's a matching record in the related table. For example, you can't delete a Customer record if there's an Order record for that customer, unless you have checked the Cascade Delete Related Records option in the Edit Relationships dialog box. (See the "Selecting Cascade Delete Related Records" section later in this chapter for details on this option.)
- You can't change a primary key value in the primary table if there are matching records in the related table, unless you have checked the Cascade Update Related Fields option in the Edit Relationships dialog box. (See the "Selecting Cascade Update Related Fields" section later in this chapter for details on this option.)

Fixing Referential Integrity Errors

While you're setting up relationships between tables (especially if you're working on tables in an inherited database, in which the data might not have been normalized), you might see an error message similar to the one shown in Figure 4-27 when you try to join two tables in a one-to-many relationship. This error message popped up when I tried to create a link between tblBooksSpecs and tblBooksAndAuthors, in an earlier version of the Crafts database, when the database was being normalized.

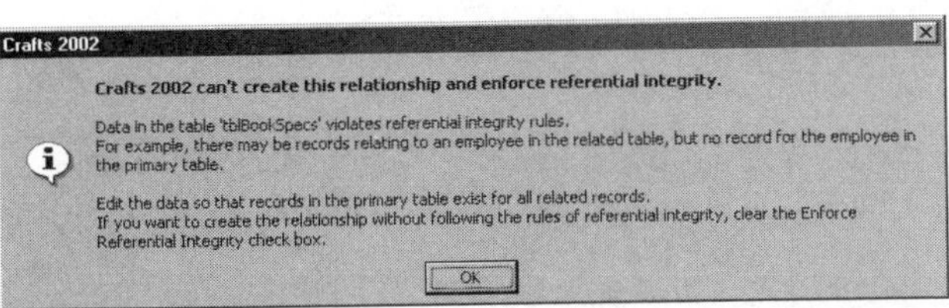

Figure 4-27. An error message indicates that an attempted link between tables violates referential integrity.

This error resulted from records in tblBookSpecs that had a BookID value with no matching record in tblBooksAndVideos. This could happen if a book (and one or more specialties for that book) was entered and then later deleted. Without referential integrity enforced, a deletion such as this can result in orphaned records—records in the "many" table that don't have matching records in the "one" table.

Fortunately, Access includes a handy tool for debugging linking problems: the Find Unmatched Query Wizard query. To fix a referential integrity error, follow these steps, which use a set of test tables from the Test Access 2002.mdb database, containing old Crafts data that violates referential integrity rules.

1. In the Database window, under Objects, click Queries, and then click New on the Database window toolbar.
2. In the New Query dialog box, shown in Figure 4-28, select Find Unmatched Query Wizard and click OK.

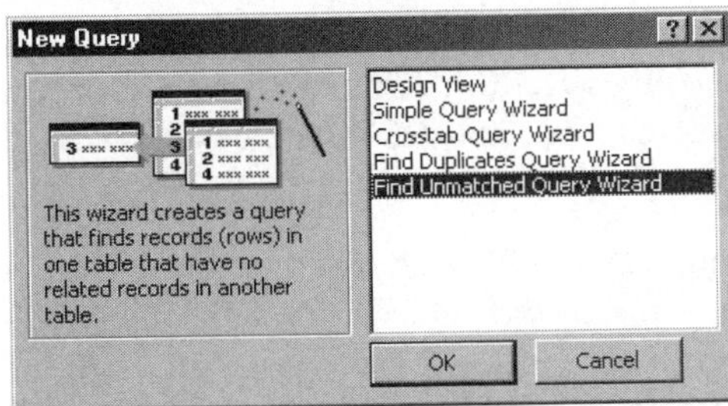

Figure 4-28. Select Find Unmatched Query Wizard to create a new query to track down records causing a referential integrity error.

3. Proceed through the pages of the wizard, selecting first the table that has unmatched data (tblBooksAndVideos is the test table for this purpose), followed by the table that contains the related records (tblPublishers), and then finally the linking field (Pubcode). This last step is shown in Figure 4-29.

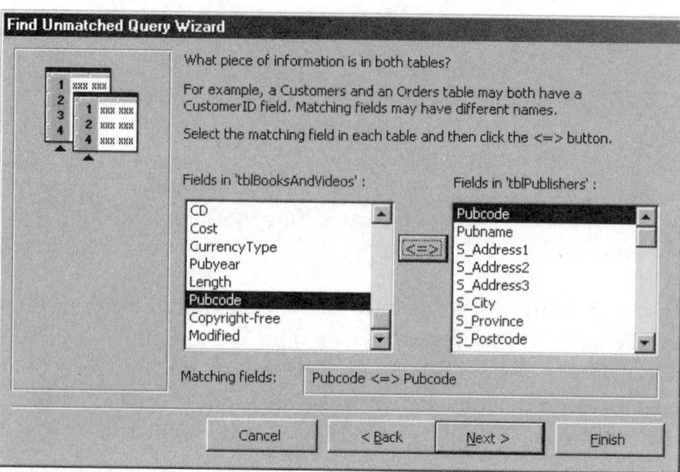

Figure 4-29. Set the linking field for the Find Unmatched Query Wizard on the third page of the wizard.

4 On the next wizard page, select the fields you want to see in the results (ID, Title, and Pubcode).

5 On the final page, either accept or change the suggested query name (it's just a temporary query that will be deleted after the data is cleaned up), and click Finish.

Figure 4-30 shows a typical Find Unmatched query in Datasheet view, listing the Pubcode records in tblBooksAndVideos that don't have matching records in tblPublishers. To fix this problem, select the correct Pubcode value from the tblPublishers table for each record in tblBooksAndVideos (this has already been done in the Crafts database, so that referential integrity could be enforced).

As an example, *Body Blueprint* was a typo (it should have been "Body Blueprints"), so I edited it. Another error was caused by a publisher name that wasn't in tblPublishers; I added Liveright to tblPublishers so it would have a match. I also did a search and replace to replace *Schoolhouse Press* with *Schoolhouse* (the Publisher Code for that entry in tblPublishers). These specific cases are typical of the data errors that will cause the referential integrity error message.

Whatever the cause of the referential integrity error, after either deleting or editing the unmatched records, you should be able to set up a one-to-many relationship between the two tables without triggering the error message.

tblBooksAndVideos Without Matching tblPublishers : Select Query

ID	Title	PubCode
335	Knitting Around	Schoolhouse Press
336	Knitting Workshop	Schoolhouse Press
342	Knitter's Almanac	Schoolhouse Press
1785	Mittful of Mittens	Schoolhouse Press
1787	Moebius Scarf & Vest	Schoolhouse Press
1791	Round-the-Bend Jacket	Schoolhouse Press
1792	Spiral Yoke Sweater	Schoolhouse Press
1793	Swedish Dubbelmossa & Sc	Schoolhouse Press
1852	The Art and Craft of Ribbon V	Body Blueprint
4391	Knit to Fit	Liveright
4660	Bavarian Peplum Jacket	Schoolhouse Press
4662	Catnip Mouse	Schoolhouse Press
4665	Shetland Shawl/Baby Blanke	Schoolhouse Press
4666	Faroe Islands Sweater	Schoolhouse Press
4668	Elizabeth's Pi Shawl	Schoolhouse Press
4669	Round-the-Bend Jacket	Schoolhouse Press
4670	Stonington Shawl	Schoolhouse Press
4672	Cardigan Details	Schoolhouse Press

Record: 1 of 23

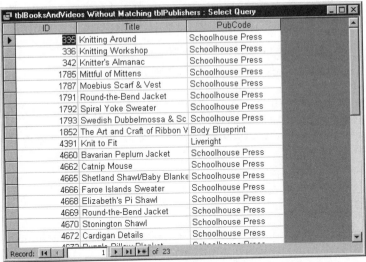

Figure 4-30. When you open the query created by the Find Unmatched Query Wizard in Datasheet view, you can see which records caused the error.

Selecting Cascade Update Related Fields

If referential integrity is enforced, selecting the Cascade Update Related Fields check box in the Edit Relationships dialog box specifies that when you change the primary key of a record in the primary table, Access will change the primary key to the new value in all related records. For example, if a Customer ID is changed in the Customers table, the Customer ID value for all orders for that customer in the Orders table will be changed to match. It's generally a good idea to select this option.

Selecting Cascade Delete Related Records

If referential integrity is enforced, selecting the Cascade Delete Related Records check box in the Edit Relationships dialog box specifies that when you delete a record in the primary table, all the related records in the linked table will also be deleted.

Troubleshooting

I don't want to delete orphaned related records

Checking Cascade Deleted Records in the Edit Relationships dialog box can be dangerous, because in some cases (such as running a delete query), the related records can be deleted without warning. Don't select this option if you don't want to automatically delete linked records. This would be the case if you need to retain these records for archival purposes, or you may want to reassign them to another record in the "one" table.

Specifying Join Type

When you want to create a join between two tables, you are given a number of options for the way in which Access will process queries related to that relationship. You can select and modify the way in which tables are joined by clicking the Join Type button in the Edit Relationships dialog box, or by double-clicking the join line between tables in the Query Designer. The Join Properties dialog box opens, and you can choose one of three options:

- Include only the rows where joined fields in both tables are equal. (This means that there is a record with a matching value in both the tables.)
- Include all the records from the selected table, and only those from the related table in which the joined fields are equal. (This means that records from the selected table will be included even if they don't have a matching value in the linking field.)
- Include all the records from the related table, but only those from the selected table in which the joined fields are equal. (This means that records from the related table will be included even if they don't have a matching value in the linking field.)

These choices are easier to explain in a query, where you can look at the query results, so let's make a simple query in the Test Access 2002 database to see the difference in returned records for the three options.

1. Create a new query in Design view and add tblContacts and tblMeetings to it. A new join line appears, based on the matching ContactID field. Since this join is created in a query, it doesn't have referential integrity enforced.
2. Add ContactID, LastName, MeetingDate and Subject to the query grid, and save the query as qryContactMeetings.

3. Double-click the relationship line to open the Join Properties dialog box as shown in Figure 4-31.

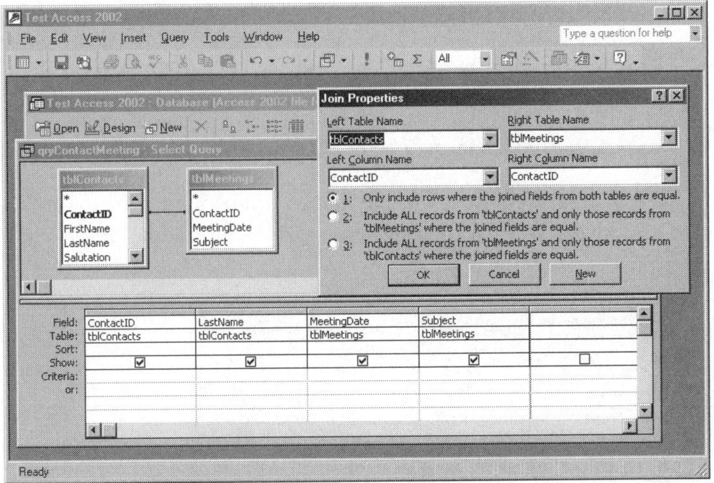

Figure 4-31. Select an option for combining data from two tables in the Join Properties dialog box.

4. Make sure option 1 is selected, which indicates that the query results include only records where the joined fields from both tables are equal, and click OK.
5. Switch to Datasheet view and note that there are four records; these are the records where there is a matching value in the ContactID field in both tblContacts and tblMeetings.
6. Switch back to Design view, open the Join Type dialog box again, select option 2, and then click OK.
7. Switch to Datasheet view and you'll see that there are now 501 records. The extra records represent employees who don't have a matching record in tblMeetings.
8. Finally, switch back to Design view, open the Join Type dialog box, and select option 3; this time, when you switch back to Datasheet view, there are seven records, three of which are meeting records that don't have a matching contact record (this would not be possible if referential integrity was enforced for this relationship).

Which option you choose depends on whether you want to see records from one table that don't have a match in the other table, or only records that have a matching record in both tables.

Working with Database Tools

After you build your tables and create and modify the relationships among them, you may want to analyze your work to make sure that your tables are as well-designed as possible. This section briefly describes tools that can help you do that.

Using the Table Analysis Utilities

Access includes three options on the Analyze submenu of the Tools menu (see Figure 4-32) that are useful for assessing your tables: Table, Performance, and Documenter.

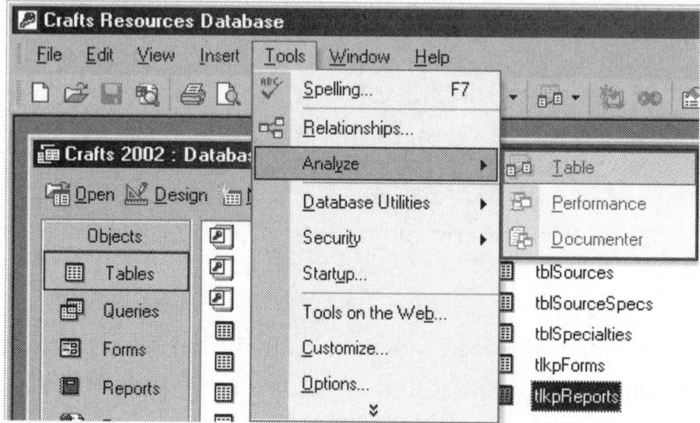

Figure 4-32. You can use the selections on the Analyze submenu to ensure that your tables are designed to function effectively.

The Table option opens the Table Analyzer Wizard, which you can use to split a table containing duplicate data into two or more related tables. This wizard can be helpful when you're normalizing a database. The Performance option opens the Performance Analyzer, which makes suggestions for improving database performance. The Documenter option can be used to produce a report listing tables, table fields, and all their properties.

The Table Analysis utilities are described in more detail in Chapter 15, "Using Add-Ins to Expand Access Functionality."

Part 2

Forms and Reports

Creating Forms for Entering, Editing, and Viewing Data

Microsoft Access forms offer an extremely versatile and easy way to enter, modify, and view data. Unlike Microsoft Visual Basic forms (and Microsoft Office UserForms), Access forms can be bound to data without your writing a line of code, and the data can be obtained from a table, a query, or a SQL statement. In this chapter, you'll learn how to use the rich variety of Access form features to create different types of forms for different purposes.

You can lay out forms in a way that allows you to see a large amount of data—perhaps all the fields in a record—at a glance, using a variety of form controls to simplify entering and selecting values for fields. You can make forms that display several—or many—records at once. Additionally, you can embed subforms in forms, which allows you to work with data from two or more linked tables. And you can write code that responds to form events to perform error trapping or to help automate certain types of data entry.

Working with Form Views

You can open forms in a number of views for entering and editing data, as well as in a view that allows you to modify the form's design. When you open a form from the Forms group in the Database window, you can click the Open button or the Design button on the Database toolbar (or choose Open or Design from the form's shortcut menu). Or you can just double-click the form name in the Database window to open it in Form view to work with its data.

Clicking Design opens a form in Design view, where you can add or delete controls and modify various form properties. Clicking Open opens the form in the form's default view. Figure 5-1 shows the Format tab of the Form properties sheet, with the list of available views dropped down.

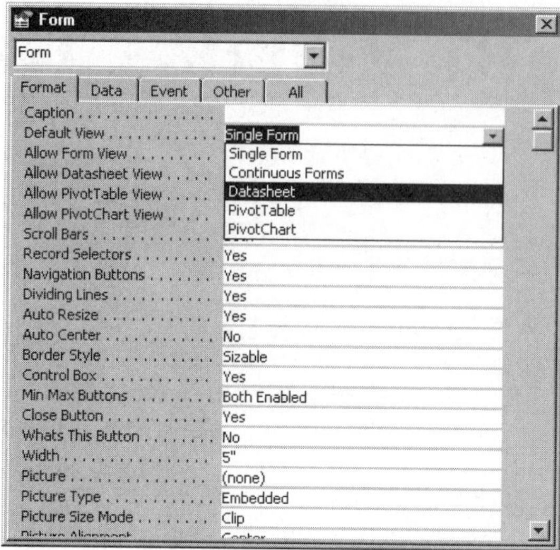

Figure 5-1. You can choose one of several views as a form's default view.

You can set the default view in Design view by selecting one of the following choices for the *Default View* property of the form:

- **Single Form.** Displays one record's data. This is the default view for new forms.
- **Continuous Forms.** Displays several records of data; can be a multirow display.
- **Datasheet.** Displays multiple records of data in a datasheet format (similar to a Microsoft Excel worksheet).

Chapter 5

newfeature!

- **PivotTable.** Displays the form's data as a PivotTable.

newfeature!

- **PivotChart.** Displays the form's data as a PivotChart.

See Chapter 12, "Using PivotTables and PivotCharts to Analyze Data," for more information on the new PivotTable and PivotChart features.

newfeature!

Access 2002 contains four new properties related to form views: *AllowFormView*, *AllowDatasheetView*, *AllowPivotTableView*, and *AllowPivotChartView*. These properties replace the old *ViewsAllowed* property in Access 2000 and earlier, with its more limited choice of Form, Datasheet, or Both. All of these properties are set to Yes by default, and you can adjust these settings as needed. For example, a form that displays name and address data isn't suitable for PivotTable or PivotChart views. To prevent users from switching to these views if they won't display well, simply set the form's *AllowPivotTableView* and *AllowPivotChartView* properties to No.

You can switch among enabled views for a form by using the View selector on the Form (or Form Design) toolbar or by choosing options on the View menu. Depending on whether Single Form or Continuous Forms is the selection for a form's default view, when you open a form from the Database window or switch to Form view by selecting Form on the View selector (or the View menu), you'll get either the Single Form or Continuous Forms view, whichever was selected as the form's default view.

> **note** Continuous Forms is not available as one of the options for switching views, nor does an *AllowContinuousFormsView* property exist for enabling or disabling this view for a form.

Although you can freely switch among enabled views (other than the Continuous Forms view, as mentioned), a form will look best if it is designed with a specific view (or set of views) in mind. For example, a Single Form view can use as much vertical space as is needed to display all the data in a record (possibly using a tab control to divide the data into pages), whereas a form designed to be displayed in Continuous Forms view rarely has more than two rows of controls. Datasheet forms can't display controls such as command buttons or option groups, and each record has a single row, so they are best suited to displaying a few columns of data, with minimal interactivity.

Some examples of these forms from the Crafts database on the companion CD are shown later in the chapter. The fpriBooksAndVideos sample (shown in Figure 5-56 on page 169) is an example of a form that is designed for Single Form view, frmAuthorsContinuous (shown in Figure 5-22 on page 135) is a Continuous Forms form, and frmBooksBySelectedAuthor (shown in Figure 5-60 on page 172) is a Datasheet form.

newfeature!

The PivotTable and PivotChart views work best with data that has been preprocessed in a query to select only the data fields needed for the PivotTable or PivotChart (usually a small subset of the fields in the data source).

After the form's design has been finalized for the view that suits it best, select that view as the default view for the form, and set the *Allow…View* properties to No for the other views to prevent users from accidentally switching to an inappropriate view.

Creating Forms with the Form Wizard

The Form Wizard offers you several choices for creating forms automatically or semi-automatically, which can save you a good deal of time. Remember that you can always fine-tune a wizard-generated form to get exactly the look you want.

When you use the Form Wizard to create your form, you choose one of several pre-packaged form layouts or Design view, which allows you to design the form from scratch. (Don't worry if the variety of choices looks a bit daunting at first. We'll look more closely at each view and layout beginning in the next section.) If you choose the Create Form By Using Wizard selection on the Forms tab of the Database window, you can step through the creation of a form based on a table or query, with the following form layout selections:

- Columnar
- Tabular
- Datasheet
- Justified
- PivotTable
- PivotChart

The other method of selecting a form layout is to click New in the Database window to open the New Form dialog box, which offers the following form layout options:

- Design View
- Form Wizard
- AutoForm: Columnar
- AutoForm: Tabular
- AutoForm: Datasheet
- AutoForm: PivotTable
- AutoForm: PivotChart
- Chart Wizard
- PivotTable Wizard
- Custom Form Wizard

Design View is the do-it-yourself form design choice: A blank form opens in Design view, and you manually place controls on it and set the form's properties as desired. Choosing Form Wizard offers you the form layout selections in the first list; the first three AutoForm selections in the second list create a form in one of the wizard formats with a single click, as though you had stepped through each page of the wizard and accepted all the defaults.

For more information about the PivotTable and PivotChart selections, see Chapter 12, "Using PivotTables and PivotCharts to Analyze Data."

Except for the PivotTable and PivotChart selections, your choices for form design can be categorized as shown in Table 5-1.

Table 5-1. Form views and layouts

Layout selection	Form view	Available from	Description
Columnar	Single Form	Form Wizard, Columnar New Form, AutoForm: Columnar	Controls are arranged in newspaper-style multiple columns. Displays one record at a time.
Datasheet	Datasheet	Form Wizard, Datasheet New Form, AutoForm: Datasheet	A datasheet similar to an Excel worksheet: no header or footer, and some control types aren't visible. Displays multiple records simultaneously.
Free-form (Design view)	Usually Single Form, but can be any other view	New Form, Design View	No controls are automatically placed on the form; you place them where you want them. Displays one record at a time.
Justified	Single Form	Form Wizard, Justified	Labels are placed above text boxes. Controls completely cover the form background. Displays one record at a time.
Tabular	Continuous Forms	Form Wizard, Tabular New Form, AutoForm: Tabular	Labels are column headings in the form header, and other controls are arranged in columns. Displays multiple records simultaneously.
Top-to-Bottom	Single Form	New Object selector, AutoForm	Controls are arranged in a single column from top to bottom. Displays one record at a time.

The following sections describe each of the form layout options in more detail, categorizing the available form designs by the views best suited to them.

Single Form View

The wizard selections described in this section allow you to quickly create a form with a specific layout. You can choose AutoForm (except for the Justified option) to create the new form even more quickly, but you need to step through the wizard to fine-tune the layout. For example, you might need to omit specific fields from the form's record source or select a style for the new form.

Columnar Layout

To create a columnar form in the simplest way, follow these steps:

1. Select the Forms group in the Database window, and click New on the Database window's toolbar to open the New Form dialog box. Select a table or query as the form's data source.

> **tip** If another dialog box opens when you click New, you're probably in another Database window group. Close the dialog box, and click the Forms icon on the Objects bar to go to the Forms group.

2. Select AutoForm: Columnar, as shown in Figure 5-2, and click OK.

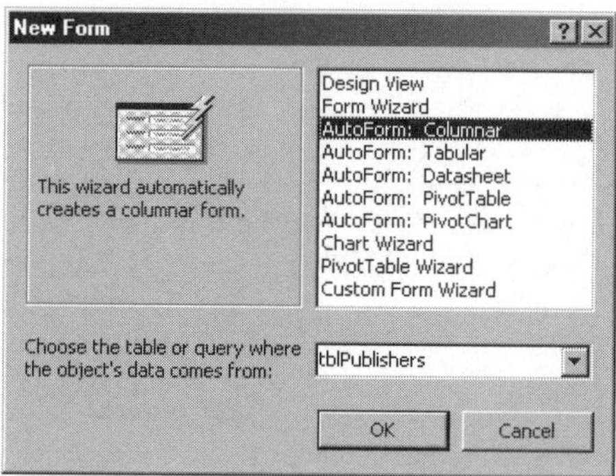

Figure 5-2. Choose AutoForm: Columnar to create a columnar form.

3 The new form opens, as shown in Figure 5-3.

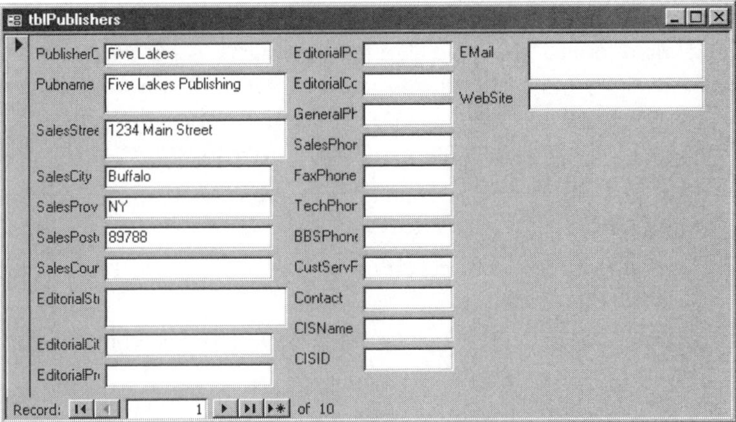

Figure 5-3. The columnar AutoForm has three columns of controls.

The controls are laid out in three columns. Unfortunately, the layout doesn't usually allow enough size to show the entire label captions—you'll have to do some fine-tuning to make a usable form.

See Chapter 6, "Working with Form Controls," and Chapter 8, "Using Design Tools," for more details on resizing and rearranging controls on forms.

Selecting Form Styles

When you use the Form Wizard to create a new form, the wizard uses the format you've selected in the AutoFormat dialog box. If the style of your new form doesn't appeal to you, open the AutoFormat dialog box, and select another style, as shown in Figure 5-4.

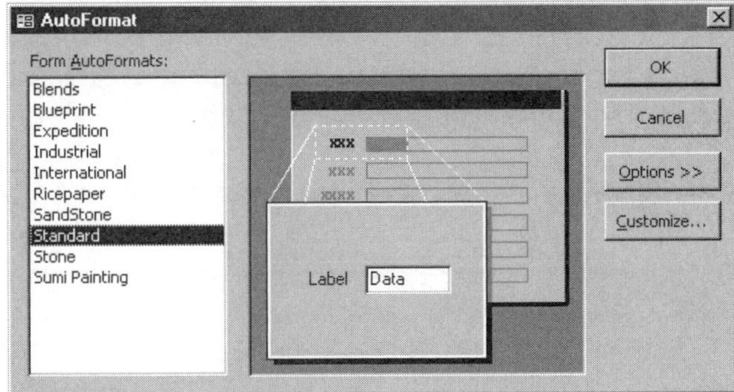

Figure 5-4. You can choose a more suitable format for your form in the AutoFormat dialog box.

(continued)

Selecting Form Styles *(continued)*

The Standard format (shown in Figure 5-3), which has the most conservative appearance, is generally the best choice for business forms. If you want a more extensive choice of conservative color schemes, follow these steps to create your own scheme and save it to one of the named schemes in the AutoFormat dialog box:

1. Change the form's background color, control background, control text color, and control fonts to the colors and style you prefer.
2. Open the AutoFormat dialog box, and select a named format (Stone, for example).
3. Click Customize, select Update 'Stone' With Values From The Form, and click OK. (See Figure 5-5.)

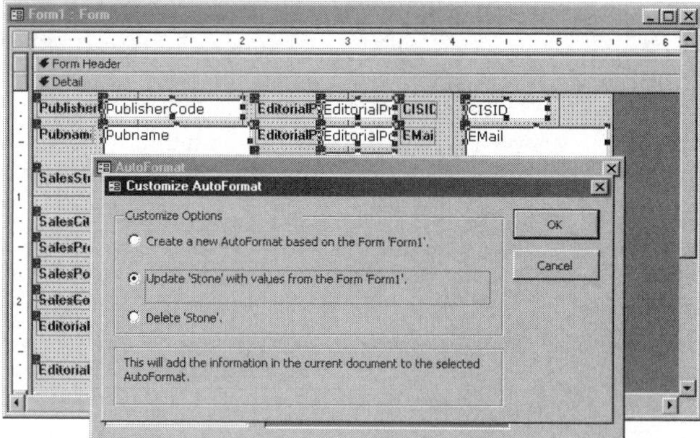

Figure 5-5. You can save a custom format to one of the AutoFormat selections.

Now you can apply your custom color scheme (in this example, a light blue background, bold labels, and Verdana text boxes) to any form by selecting the Stone AutoFormat. Alternatively, you can use the Design Schemes add-in (Design Schemes.mda, available on the companion CD) to apply one of a set of four conservative formats to a form, or create your own custom format in more detail than the Customize AutoFormat dialog box allows.

For more information about the Design Schemes add-in, see Chapter 15, "Using Add-Ins to Expand Access Functionality."

Justified Layout

To create a form with the Justified layout, follow these steps:

1. Double-click the Create Form By Using Wizard selection in the Database window, or click New to open the New Form dialog box.
2. Select the table or query you want to use as the form's data source, select the Form Wizard option, as shown in Figure 5-6, and then click OK.

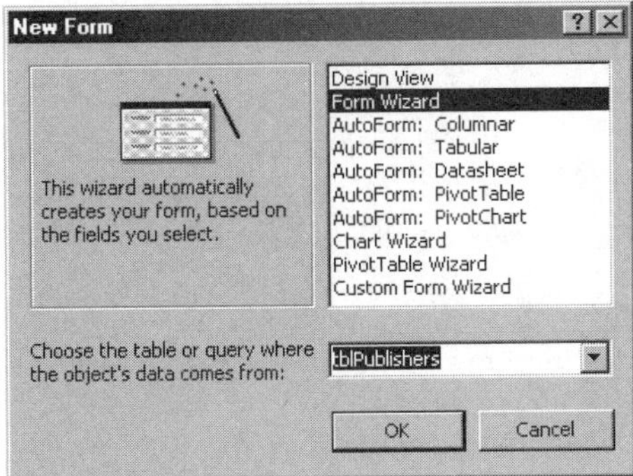

Figure 5-6. Select the Form Wizard in the New Form dialog box to create a form with a Justified layout.

> **note** No AutoForm selection exists for creating a Justified Form.

3. Select the fields you want on the form, as shown in Figure 5-7, and click Next.

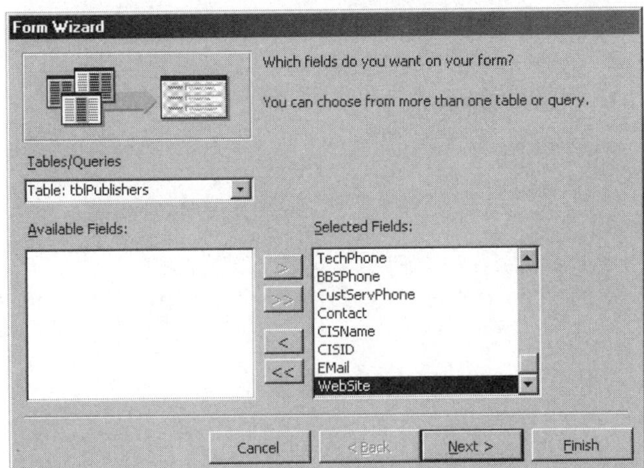

Figure 5-7. The Form Wizard lists available fields for a Justified form.

Chapter 5

4 Select the Justified option, as shown in Figure 5-8. Click Next.

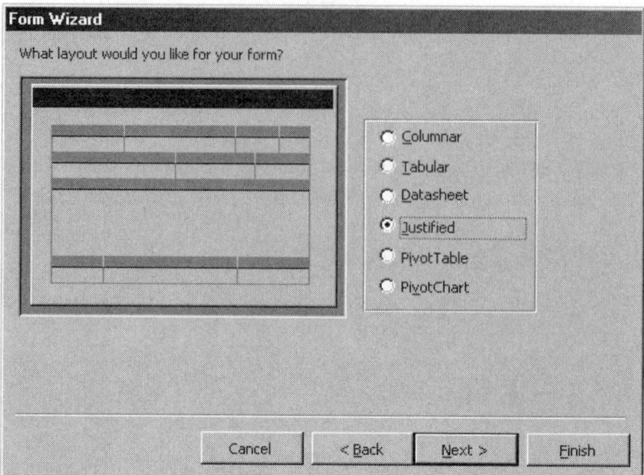

Figure 5-8. Select the Justified option in the Form Wizard for a justified layout.

5 Select a style for the form, as shown in Figure 5-9. Click Next.

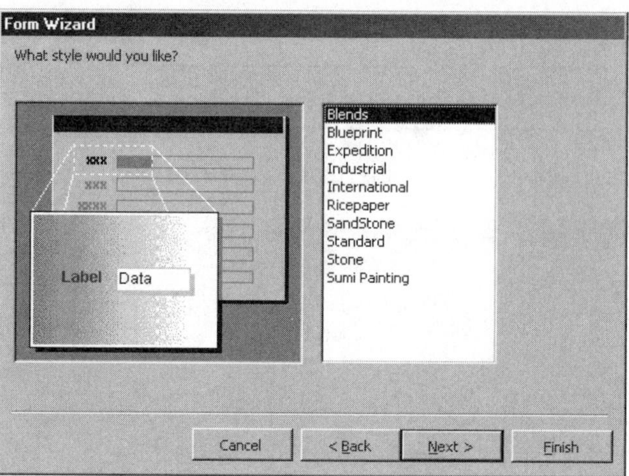

Figure 5-9. You can select from a variety of decorative styles for the form.

6 On the last page of the wizard, give the form a title (caption), as shown in Figure 5-10, and click Finish. The title will also be used as the form's name.

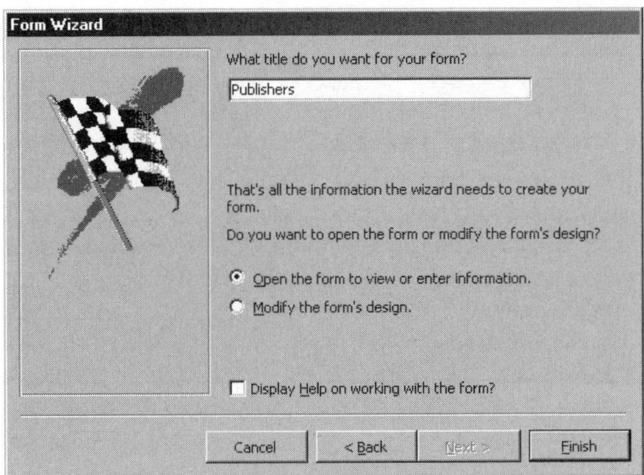

Figure 5-10. Give the form an appropriate title.

If you want to give the form the *frm* tag or some other identifier in accordance with a naming convention, you'll have to do this later by renaming the form in the Database window. See Chapter 4, "Creating a Database," for more details about using a naming convention.

Figure 5-11 shows the finished form, which looks somewhat like a fill-in-the-blanks paper form with labels positioned over the text boxes.

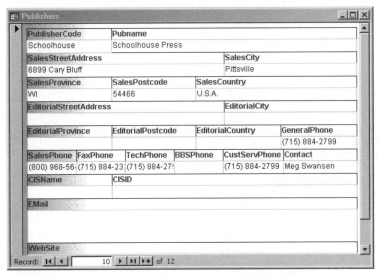

Figure 5-11. The finished Justified form looks like this.

The Justified layout is attractive, but it has one serious drawback: If you find that some of the text boxes are the wrong size, resizing and rearranging the controls to preserve the justified appearance is quite time-consuming.

InsideOut

Suppose you like one of the wizard's layout selections but you want to modify it in some way. For example, you might want the labels in the Justified layout to use a smaller font size. Unfortunately, there's no way to accomplish this in the interface because the wizard code is encrypted and doesn't let you modify its form templates. Unlike Word, Access doesn't allow users to modify the wizard's layout selections. However, there is a workaround: If you want to create a custom form style to apply to your forms, you can use my Design Schemes add-in, which is available on the CD.

Top-to-Bottom Layout

A form created by using the New Object: AutoForm selection has its fields laid out from top to bottom (see Figure 5-12) in a manner that isn't very attractive for general use but makes an effective quick data entry form to use for focused data entry.

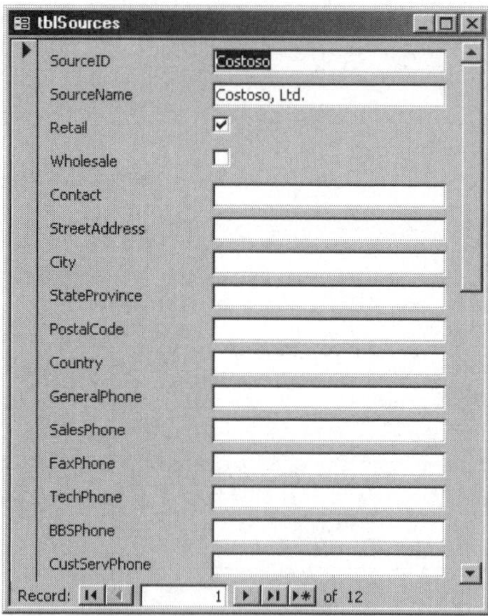

Figure 5-12. This new form was created by using the AutoForm selection.

See the sections "Creating Quick Data Entry Forms," page 142, and "New Record Forms," page 173, for more details about quick data entry forms.

If you create an AutoForm based on a table by highlighting the table on the Tables tab of the Database window and then clicking New Object: AutoForm on the Database Design toolbar (see Figure 5-13), your new form will open in Single Form view.

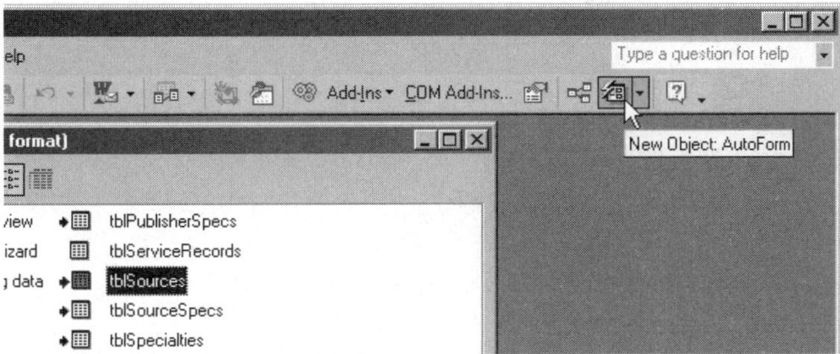

Figure 5-13. You can create a form in Single Form view by clicking the AutoForm selection on the toolbar.

Continuous Forms View

When you need to view or edit only a handful of fields, Continuous Forms view can be an ideal choice because it lets you see several records at the same time. You place controls where you want them, so you have the option of creating a multirow display, unlike Datasheet view, which has one row per record. One of the Form Wizard selections (Tabular Form) creates a single-row form in Continuous Forms view. No Form Wizard selection exists for multirow forms, but you can simply make the detail section taller and rearrange the controls so they form two rows in Continuous Forms view.

Tabular Layout

To create a tabular form while specifying which controls are displayed on the form, follow these steps:

1. Open the New Form dialog box, and select a table for the form's record source.
2. Select Form Wizard, as shown in Figure 5-14, and click OK. (Alternatively, you can double-click Create Form By Using Wizard in the Database window.)

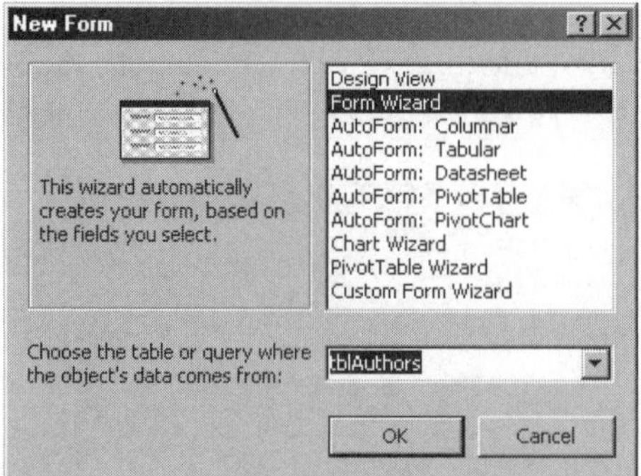

Figure 5-14. Select Form Wizard in the New Form dialog box.

3 On the first page of the Form Wizard, select the fields to use in the tabular form, as shown in Figure 5-15. Bear in mind that you can't use more fields than can be displayed in a single page width. Click Next.

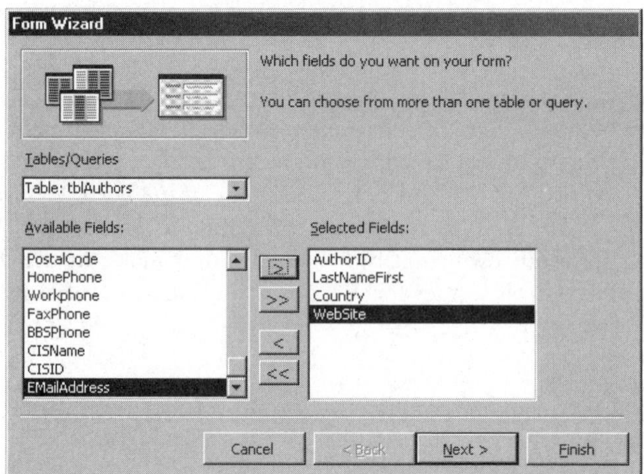

Figure 5-15. Select fields for a tabular form on the first page of the Form Wizard.

4 Select the Tabular layout, as shown in Figure 5-16. Click Next.

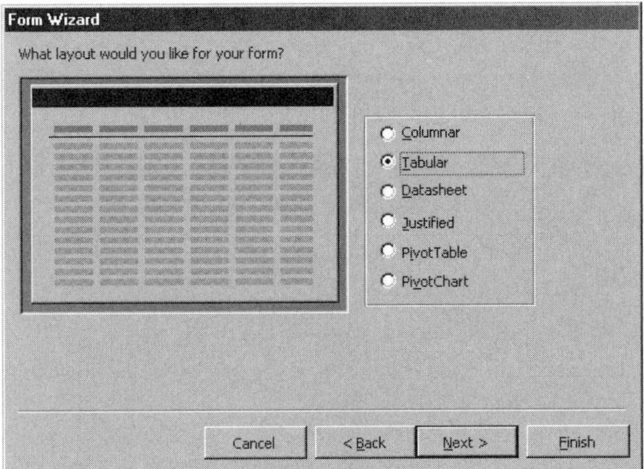

Figure 5-16. Select the Tabular layout for a new form to arrange information in table format.

5 Select a style for the form, as shown in Figure 5-17. Click Next.

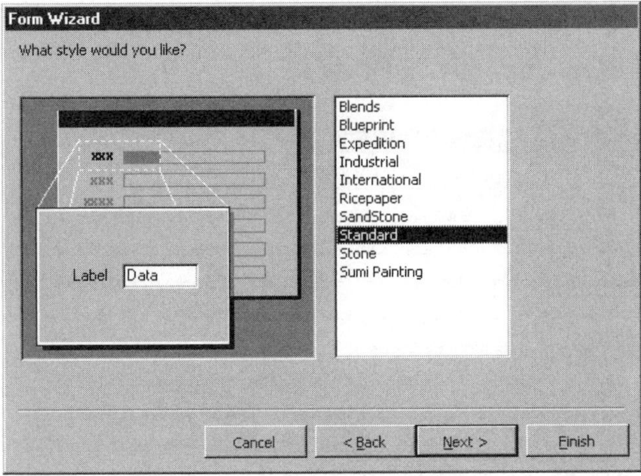

Figure 5-17. Choose from a variety of styles for the new tabular form.

6 Give the form a title, as shown in Figure 5-18. (The title is the caption that appears in the form's title bar and is also used as the form's name.) By default, the form will be opened in Form view, but you can select Modify The Form's Design to open the form in Design view. Click Finish.

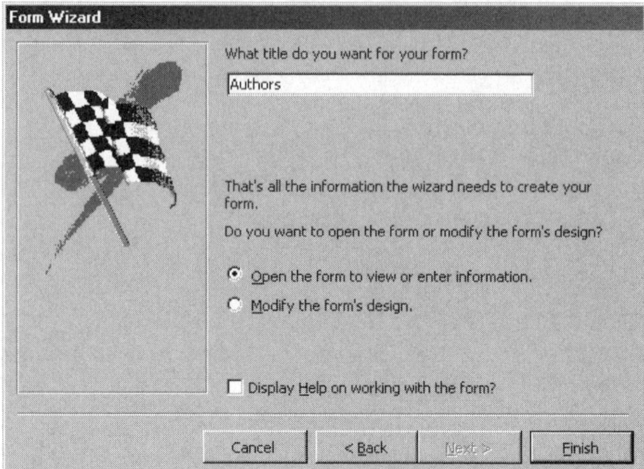

Figure 5-18. Give the form a title on the last page of the Form Wizard.

Figure 5-19 shows the new tabular form.

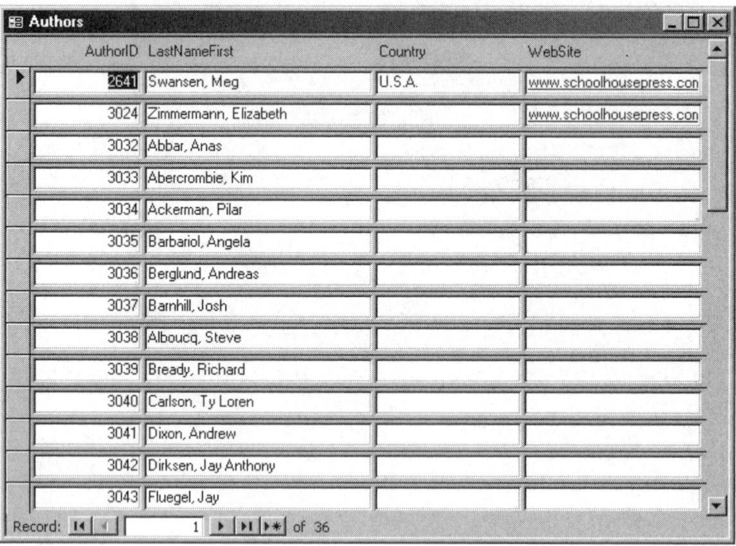
Authors

AuthorID	LastNameFirst	Country	WebSite
2641	Swansen, Meg	U.S.A.	www.schoolhousepress.con
3024	Zimmermann, Elizabeth		www.schoolhousepress.con
3032	Abbar, Anas		
3033	Abercrombie, Kim		
3034	Ackerman, Pilar		
3035	Barbariol, Angela		
3036	Berglund, Andreas		
3037	Barnhill, Josh		
3038	Alboucq, Steve		
3039	Bready, Richard		
3040	Carlson, Ty Loren		
3041	Dixon, Andrew		
3042	Dirksen, Jay Anthony		
3043	Fluegel, Jay		

Record: 1 of 36

Figure 5-19. The finished tabular form looks like this.

Chapter 5

Form Names, Titles, and Captions

Access forms have names (listed in the Database window) and captions (displayed as text in the form's title bar). You can examine and change a form's caption by using the *Caption* property on the All tab of the form's properties sheet, as shown in Figure 5-20. However, you can't change a form's name in its properties sheet (although this is possible with other types of Office forms) because no *Name* property is displayed there.

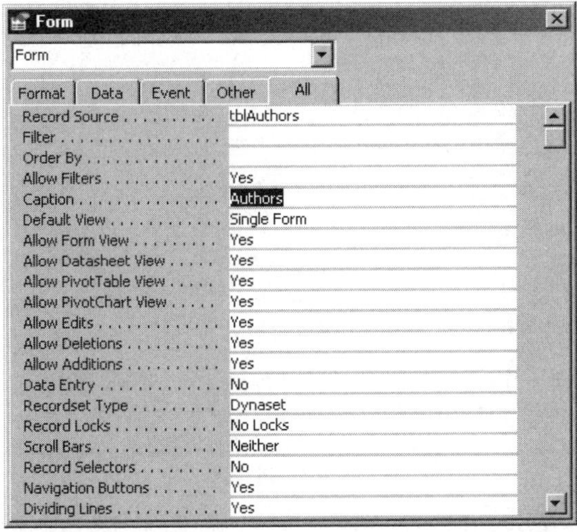

Figure 5-20. A form's *Caption* property is located on the All tab of its properties sheet.

The Access Form Wizard uses the term *title* on the last page of the wizard. This can be confusing because forms don't have a *Title* property. Whatever text you enter as the form's title will be used as both its caption and its name. That presents a problem for users who want to name their database objects in accordance with a naming convention, such as the Leszynski Naming Convention (LNC) discussed in Chapter 20, "Customizing Your Database Using VBA Code."

If you use the LNC naming convention for database objects, a form should generally have a name starting with the *frm* tag. If you give the form the title *frmAuthors* in the Form Wizard, the form's title bar will display *frmAuthors*, which looks strange. If you want Authors as the form's caption and frmAuthors as the form's name, you have to give the form the title Authors in the wizard and then rename it frmAuthors in the Database window, as shown in Figure 5-21. To rename a form in the Database window, select the form name, press F2 to switch to edit mode, edit the name as desired, and press Enter.

(continued)

Form Names, Titles, and Captions *(continued)*

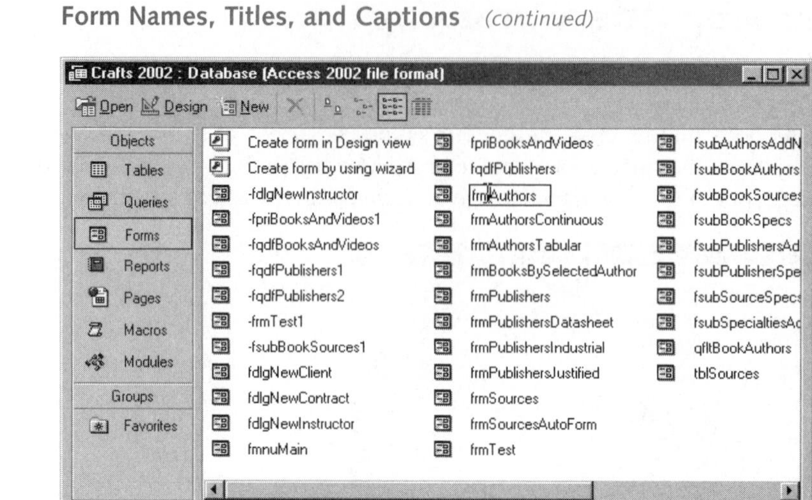

Figure 5-21. You can rename a form in the Database window.

Alternatively, you can give the form the title frmAuthors in the wizard and then change the caption to Authors in the form's properties sheet.

Multirow Continuous Forms Layout

A tabular form has some resemblance to a form in Datasheet view because it is laid out in columns, but a form in Continuous Forms view isn't restricted to a single row of fields per record—you can have several rows of controls in the detail section of a form. A multirow continuous form is a good format choice when you want to display multiple records of data at once but you have more controls than can be displayed in a single row, or you need to use controls that aren't supported in Datasheet view.

For example, if you wanted an Authors form similar to the tabular form shown in Figure 5-19 but with a large Notes control bound to a Memo field, you could create a form in Continuous Forms view, laid out as in Figure 5-22.

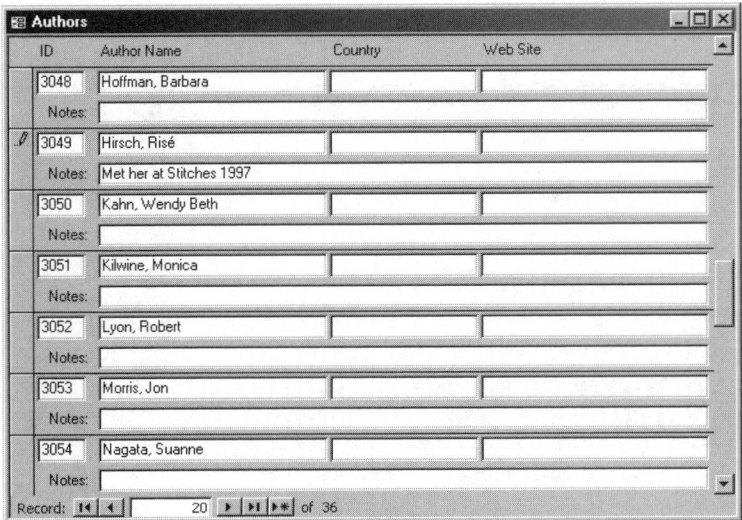

Figure 5-22. Use a form in Continuous Forms view if you need to display more controls than Datasheet view allows.

Datasheet View

The Datasheet view of a form looks like a worksheet, which makes it suitable for displaying columnar data. However, forms in Datasheet view have a number of limitations that you should take into account before selecting this option:

- Command buttons, option groups, and most controls other than text boxes and combo boxes won't appear in the Datasheet view of a form.
- Datasheet forms have no header or footer.
- Datasheet forms can display only a limited number of fields per record (fewer than other form views can display).

Datasheet Form Layout

You create a datasheet form much the same way you create a tabular form; the only difference is that you select the Datasheet option on the layout page of the Form wizard. You can also create a datasheet form by selecting the AutoForm: Datasheet option in the New Form dialog box, but unless your data source has only a few fields, this selection will most likely produce a form with too many narrow columns.

Figure 5-23 shows a datasheet form created by selecting a few fields from tblSources and selecting the Ricepaper style for the form.

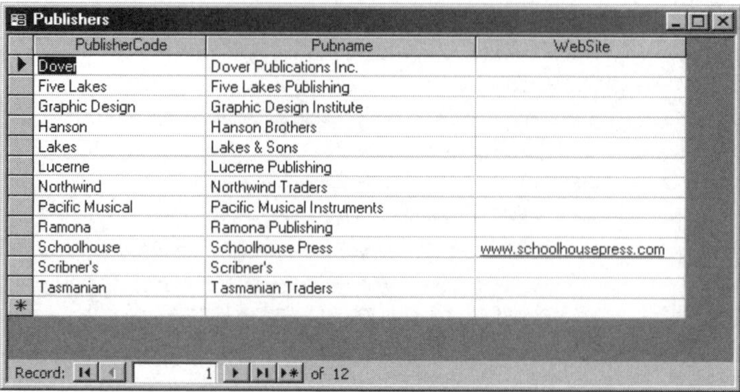

PublisherCode	Pubname	WebSite
Dover	Dover Publications Inc.	
Five Lakes	Five Lakes Publishing	
Graphic Design	Graphic Design Institute	
Hanson	Hanson Brothers	
Lakes	Lakes & Sons	
Lucerne	Lucerne Publishing	
Northwind	Northwind Traders	
Pacific Musical	Pacific Musical Instruments	
Ramona	Ramona Publishing	
Schoolhouse	Schoolhouse Press	www.schoolhousepress.com
Scribner's	Scribner's	
Tasmanian	Tasmanian Traders	

Figure 5-23. A typical datasheet form looks like this.

InsideOut

As you can see in Figure 5-23, there's no visible evidence of the Ricepaper style in the datasheet. No matter what style you select when you're creating the form, the datasheet will appear in whatever style you have selected on the Datasheet tab of the Options dialog box, as shown in Figure 5-24. Unless you change these settings, your datasheet will have black text on a white background. However, if the form can be displayed (and looks good) in both Single Form and Datasheet views, the Ricepaper style will be visible when you switch to Single Form view.

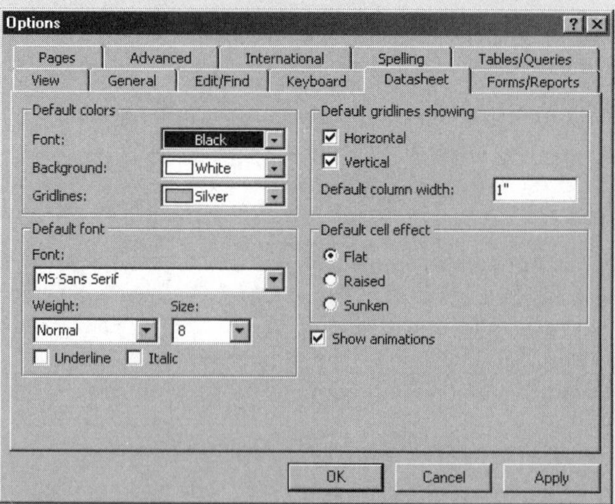

Figure 5-24. You can set datasheet appearance options on the Datasheet tab of the Options dialog box.

The Works By Same Author pop-up form that's discussed in the section "Linked Pop-Up Forms," page 171, is a datasheet form; only a simple form like this is suitable for the Datasheet layout. This form pops up when you click the Works By Same Author command button on the Crafts database's primary form, fpriBooksAndVideos.

Datasheet Subforms

Although a datasheet form is rarely useful, a datasheet subform is often used to display linked data in a datasheet embedded on a main form. The Northwind sample database, for example, uses datasheet subforms on several of its forms. You don't need a header or footer in a subform, so the lack of these elements in a datasheet subform isn't a problem. When using a datasheet subform, you can place any controls needed for form navigation and record selection on the main form. Figure 5-25 shows the Northwind Customer Orders form, which has two datasheet subforms.

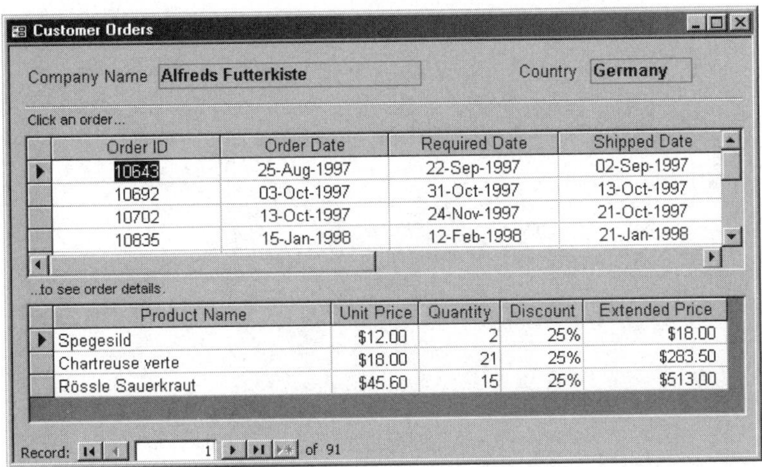

Figure 5-25. This Northwind form has two datasheet subforms.

> **tip** To quickly place a subform on a form, simply open the main form in Design view and drag the form that is to be the subform onto it.

Creating Forms Manually Using Design View

If you need to create a form that isn't laid out like any of the wizard selections discussed in the previous sections, you can create a blank form in Design view and place controls on it just as you like. This method is your best option when none of the available Wizard or AutoForm selections meets your needs, such as when you need to place option groups or subforms on a form or you need a header or footer section with combo boxes or command buttons.

To create a form manually, open the New Form dialog box and select a table or query for the form's record source. Then select Design View (see Figure 5-26) and click OK.

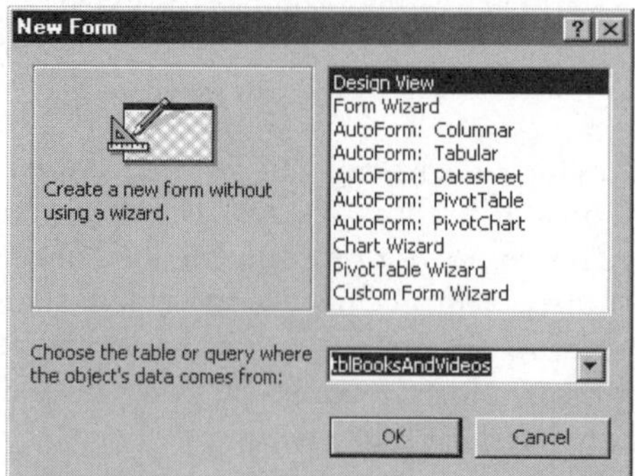

Figure 5-26. If you want to manually place controls on a form, use Design view.

Figure 5-27 shows the new form in Design view.

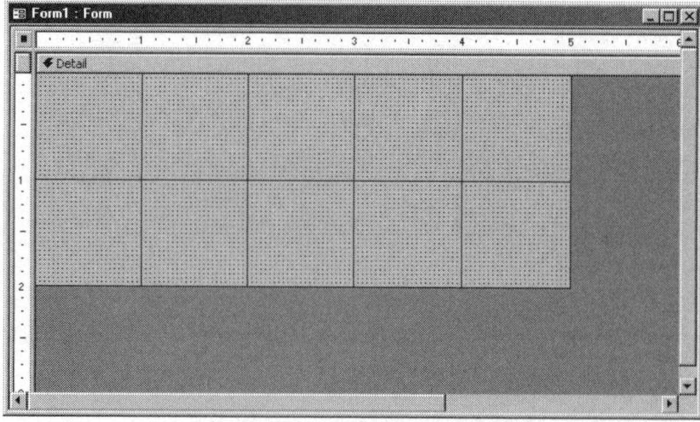

Figure 5-27. A new form in Design view looks like this.

Several toolbar buttons prove very useful when you're working with forms:

- When you're in the Forms group of the Database window, the Open and Design buttons on the Database toolbar allow you to open the selected form in either the default Form view or Design view, as shown in Figure 5-28.

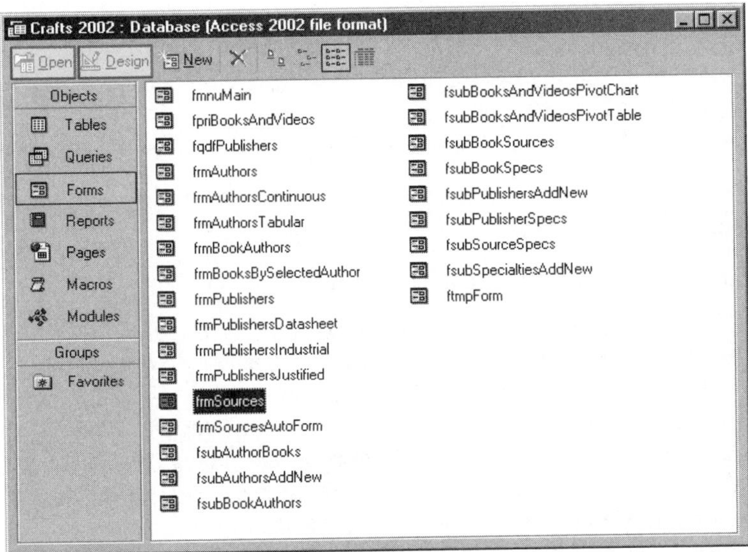

Figure 5-28. You can open the selected form in Form or Design view using Database toolbar buttons.

- When a form is open (in any view), you can switch to another enabled view using the View selector button on the Form View or Form Design toolbar, as shown in Figure 5-29.

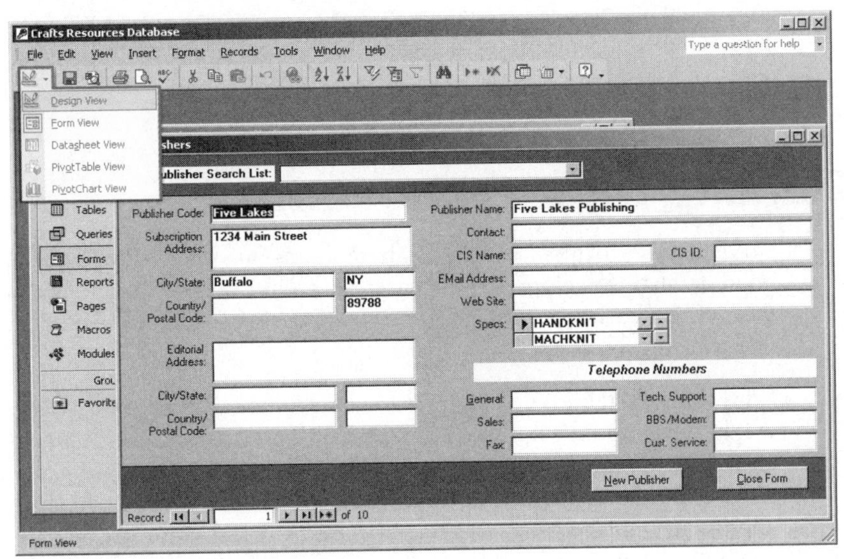

Figure 5-29. You can switch a form to another view using the View selector button on one of the Form toolbars.

note The Form selection on the View selector on the Form Design toolbar switches the form into either Continuous Forms view or Single Form view, depending on which of these views is specified as the form's *DefaultView* property. Datasheet View is a separate selection on the drop-down list.

Troubleshooting

I can't switch to a particular view for a form

By default, all views are enabled for a new form (the *AllowFormView*, *AllowDatasheet-View*, *AllowPivotTableView*, and *AllowPivotChartView* properties are set to Yes). If any of these properties is set to No, that view won't be available for selection on the View selector toolbar button's drop-down list. If a view isn't available, that is probably because the form wasn't designed to display well in that view. If you want to be able to switch to a specific view (for example, Datasheet view), set the *AllowDatasheetView* (or other) property to Yes in the form's properties sheet.

tip It's generally advisable to turn off the record selector and scroll bars for a form (set *RecordSelectors* to No and *ScrollBars* to Neither in the form's properties sheet). Most users don't know the purpose of the record selector (the vertical gray band on the left of a form), and thus it just takes up space without being useful. Scroll bars are needed only when a form is very long or very wide, and generally if a form needs to display a large number of controls, using a Tab control to divide the controls into groups is best, to avoid the necessity of scrolling.

Creating Data Entry Forms

All data entry forms—and all database users—are not created equal. For that reason, good database developers think carefully about the people who will be using their forms to enter data into the database, and design forms to meet the users' needs and preferences.

With some databases, new records are added one at a time, by the same person who will be working with the data later on. For these database users, an easy-to-understand and attractive form is of primary importance. The form should be laid out in a logical fashion (such as grouping name and address components together), and should have appropriate tools to aid in selecting or entering data. Option groups, check boxes and combo boxes are very useful on these forms. We'll call this type of form a standard form.

In other cases, data is entered in large batches by data entry operators and is later reviewed and modified by managers and others. Data entry operators need a form that is designed for quick data entry, which means limiting the use of controls (such as option groups and combo boxes) that require use of the mouse, and arranging controls in a simple (usually top-to-bottom) layout. We'll call this type of form a quick data entry form.

Whether a form is designed for review by managers or for full-time data entry, it should have features that ensure that data entered into the form is accurate. The following sections cover form design strategies that help ensure accurate data entry as well as the use of quick data entry forms for full-time data entry and for entering a new record from a command button on a standard form.

Ensuring Data Accuracy

A standard form has its fields positioned in a logical way so that users have a visual guide to the sequence of data entry. For example, most users are familiar with forms that ask for name, address, city, state, ZIP or Postal code, phone, and e-mail address. It's a logical and familiar progression. Mixing up the order, or introducing new fields in the middle of the sequence (such as adding a Birthdate field just after Address), would be confusing. Replicating a familiar structure that managers or other data entry personnel find comfortable will help make the database easier for users—which is one of your primary goals as a developer.

If you are creating a database for a customer, as you begin the process of interviewing your customer about the goals of the database you are creating, be sure to ask for any paper forms that are currently used to capture the data. By creating standard forms that follow the field sequence in existing paper forms, you'll cut down on the time it takes users to get comfortable with the new process, which should benefit your project.

However, there are some caveats: Replicating a paper form is feasible only when the paper form is itself well-designed. Attempting to duplicate a poorly designed paper form won't lead to a good form design. Additionally, you shouldn't hesitate to use form features (such as combo boxes) that have no analog on paper forms. Selecting a value from a list, rather than typing it in, eliminates the possibility of making a mistake when typing an entry.

For managers, making the standard form layout similar to the layout of a familiar paper form can be helpful. For data entry operators (as discussed earlier), the top-to-bottom layout of a quick data entry form facilitates rapid, interruption-free data entry.

In addition to creating a form that is easy to understand and based on a familiar interface, you can ensure that the form fits the user's needs by including error-trapping features, such as input masks and validation rules. Error trapping helps control the accuracy of data, making sure, for example, that dates are entered in the correct format, that text data is entered in text fields, that numeric values are in the appropriate range, and that numeric data is entered into numeric fields. If data is entered incorrectly, a good form will prompt the user to enter the data in the correct format.

The techniques listed below can make a form easier to use (and reduce errors in the process):

- Default values – Enter the appropriate value (or expression) in the *DefaultValue* property of a field to automatically fill in the field when a new record is created. For example, entering Date() as the *DefaultValue* property of a Date field puts the current date into the field when a new record is created. Entering Now() puts the current date and time into the field, which is useful as a time stamp indicating when the record was created.
- Input masks force data entry to adhere to a specific sequence of letters and/or numbers, such as telephone numbers and Social Security numbers. The Input Mask Wizard has a selection of standard input masks, and you can create your own custom input masks as well. Input masks are particularly useful for IDs, product codes and other such highly structured data.
- Validation rules check data after it is entered, and if data fails the validation test, a message pops up with information telling you what data is valid. For example, entering **>Date+7** into a Date field's *ValidationRule* property pops up an error message if the user enters a date earlier than a week from the current date.
- ControlTip text is the text that displays in a floating yellow box when the mouse cursor is hovered over a control. For example, a txtNotes text box bound to a memo field might have a control tip saying "Parent-teacher quarterly discussion notes." Use this feature sparingly; it can be distracting if overused.

Creating Quick Data Entry Forms

Forms designed for focused data entry (continuous typing of data from paper documents or voice recordings) have significantly different requirements than forms designed for managers or others who primarily review and edit data. In focused data entry form, speed and accuracy of data entry are the prime requirements, and an attractive layout is secondary, if it matters at all. Data entry operators should be able to quickly add, correct, and save records without taking their hands off the keyboard, and error trapping should be as unobtrusive as possible (no modal dialog boxes!)—often just a beep is enough.

Designing a Simple Quick Data Entry Form with the AutoForm Selection

A simple top-to-bottom form layout, with all the controls lined up in a single column, although less than glamorous in appearance than other form layouts, is well suited to quick data entry. To create a simple quick data entry form, follow these steps:

1. Select a table in the Database window. This table will be the form's record source.
2. Click the New Object tool in the Database toolbar to display the drop-down list.
3. Choose AutoForm (see Figure 5-30). Access creates a simple data entry form similar to the one shown in Figure 5-31.

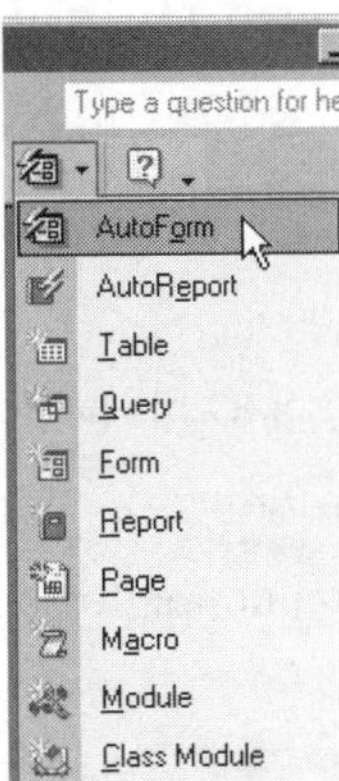

Figure 5-30. You can select AutoForm from the New Object selector's drop-down list to have Access create a simple data-entry form for the selected table.

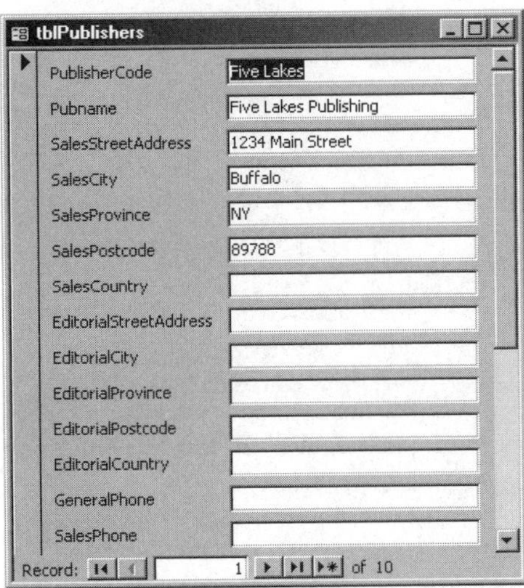

Figure 5-31. The form created with the AutoForm feature isn't fancy, but it's functional for quick data entry.

note The data entry form you create by using the AutoForm selection in the New Object drop-down list doesn't exactly correspond to any of the five AutoForm selections in the New Form dialog box.

Designing a Quick Data Entry Form by Dragging and Dropping Fields

If you want to be selective about the fields you include on your data entry form, you can use the drag-and-drop method to create your quick data entry form. Here are the steps:

1. Select a table in the Database window.
2. Click Forms; then click New. The New Forms dialog box appears.
3. Design View is selected; click OK to create the new form.
4. If the field list is not visible, click the Field List button on the toolbar to display it.
5. Drag the fields you want to use from the field list to the form, as shown in Figure 5-32.

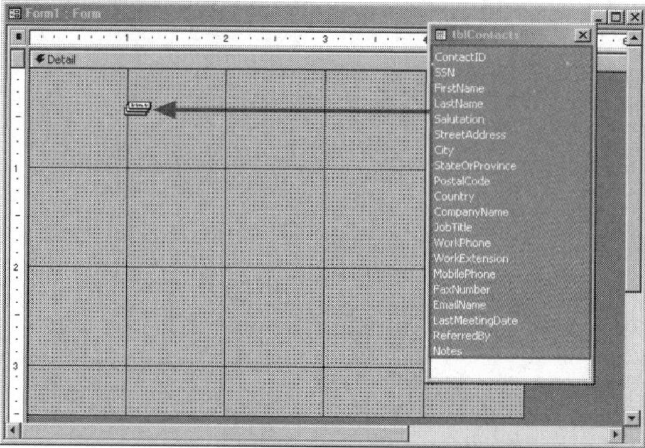

Figure 5-32. You can create a quick data entry form by dragging the fields you want to a form displayed in Design view.

Figure 5-33 shows a standard form from the Crafts sample database, designed primarily for viewing and modifying information, although it could also be used for entering new Publisher records.

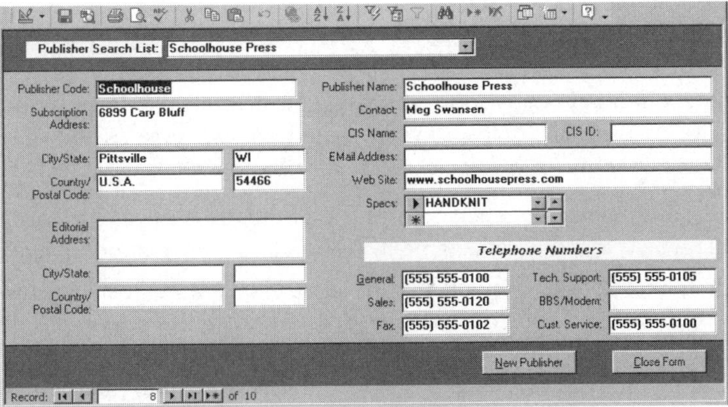

Figure 5-33. The Publishers form is intended primarily for reviewing and modifying data.

Figure 5-34 shows the quick data entry version of this form, designed for rapid entry of multiple data records. Notice that the quick data entry form is streamlined and includes only a selection of fields; it lacks the Specs and Add New Specialty subforms that you'll find on the standard form because this information would most likely be added later and because navigating quickly between a main form and subforms without leaving the keyboard is difficult.

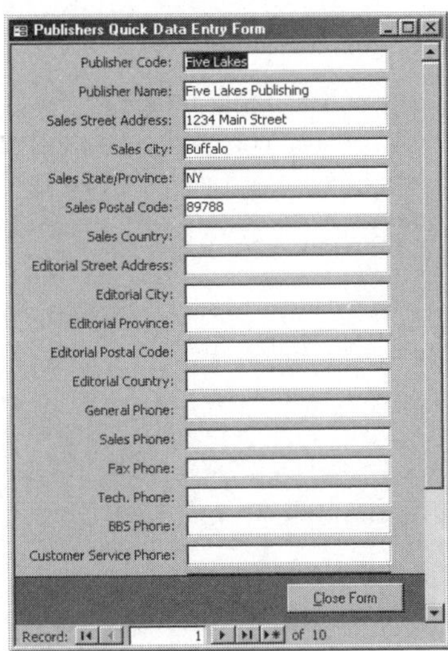

Figure 5-34. The Publishers quick data entry form includes only selected fields and allows users to enter data quickly.

Chapter 5

Creating Effective Quick Data Entry Forms

As you can see, quick data entry forms can help you streamline data entry for the people who will be using the database you create. Here are some additional suggestions for ways you can make your quick data entry forms even more effective:

- Prefill fields with data whenever possible, using default values such as *Date()* for a date field or the most commonly used values for a text or numeric field.
- If a group of records commonly has the same data in a number of fields in a series of records, create a command button or hot key for copying all data (or a subset of data) from the previous record, or copy data from the previous record automatically when a new record is created, using the form's *BeforeInsert* event.
- Use a list box instead of an option group or a combo box for displaying a small number of options.
- If you need a combo box, to select a value from a long list, use its *Dropdown* method to display the list whenever the combo box receives the focus, as shown in this event procedure:

```
Private Sub cboCover_GotFocus()
    Me![cboCover].Dropdown
End Sub
```

- Set the form's *Cycle* property to All Records so that tabbing out of the last control on the form takes the user to a new record. This is the quickest way to start a new record, but it's a good choice only for a quick data entry form—in other form modes, users generally want to stay in one record until they choose to go to another record.
- Avoid using subforms, if possible, because navigating between a subform and the main form is difficult without leaving the keyboard.

tip Use a quick data entry form in partnership with a standard form

A quick data entry form designed specifically for adding new records can serve as an adjunct to a standard form, making it easier to add a complete new record. A quick data entry form to be used for this purpose has its *DataEntry* property set to Yes, so that only the new record being entered is visible. Code on the Click event of a New button on the standard form opens the quick data entry form, and code on the Close button of this form saves the new record and returns to the standard form, with the newly created record selected. (This technique is described in more detail in the "New Record Forms" section of this chapter.)

Giving Your Forms a Consistent Look

Experimenting with various form colors and fonts and trying all the AutoFormat styles is fun, but once you decide which background color, text font, and background style you prefer, it's best to apply that style consistently to all the forms in the database. You don't have to apply the formatting selections manually to each form—you can save your custom style as one of the AutoFormat choices so that you can quickly apply it to other forms.

A consistent color/font scheme gives an application a professional appearance, much like a Web page that uses a Microsoft FrontPage theme. You can use background color (both for forms themselves and for controls on forms) to give the user visual cues about how the form works. For example, you can use one background color for editable forms (or controls) and another color for read-only forms or controls.

Using Form Templates

Whenever you create a new form in Design view without using the Form wizard, the form is based on a form template. Unlike Word templates, which allow you to set up every aspect of a template's appearance—and even much of its functionality, by using macros (Visual Basic for Applications [VBA] *Sub* procedures)—Access templates specify only a few basic form features, such as the background color of form sections and certain control properties. Although Access templates can include VBA code, when you create a new form from the template, the form doesn't inherit any of the code from the template's code module.

Although you can't preload an Access form template with a set of standard controls or include boilerplate code, you can specify the fonts, sizes, or other properties for controls on the new form. You have to import the form or report template into any database in which you want to use it. Because of these limitations, and because the AutoFormat feature now lets you apply one of a set of styles to a form, few Access users take the trouble to create a form template.

However, form templates do offer some advantages over customized AutoFormats. For example, you can specify different colors for the form header, footer, and detail sections. You can also specify properties for various types of controls by placing controls on the template form, setting them as desired, and then choosing Format, Set Control Defaults with the controls selected, as shown in Figure 5-35.

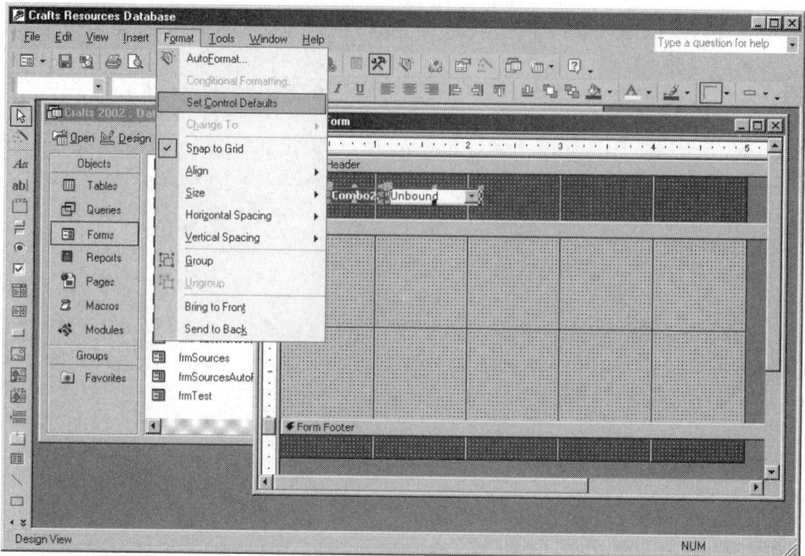

Figure 5-35. You can set control defaults for a form template.

If you do create an Access template and you want to use it when creating a new form in Design view, you must enter the template's name on the Forms/Reports tab of the Options dialog box, as shown in Figure 5-36.

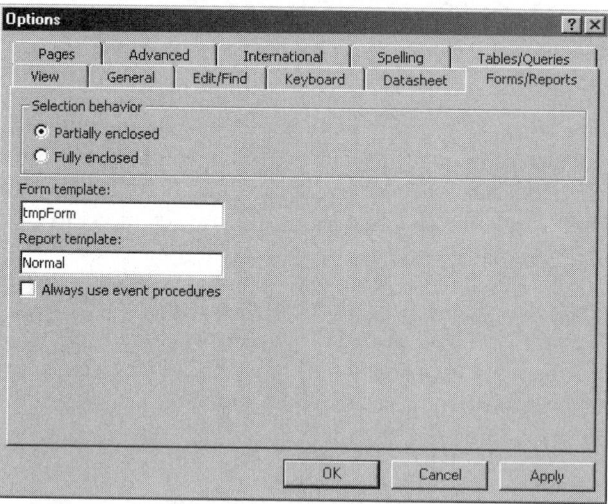

Figure 5-36. Enter your form template's name on the Forms/Reports tab of the Options dialog box.

Now, when you create a new form in Design view, it will have the same header, footer, and detail background colors as the template, and the controls you place on the form will have the default values you set in the template—but only if the template form is available in the current database.

caution The template name that you enter appears on the Forms/Reports tab of the Options dialog box in all databases, but if the named template isn't included in the current database, a new form will use the default Normal template instead.

Using AutoFormat

AutoFormat allows you to apply to your forms the preset format choices already created in Access. You can use AutoFormat styles as they are or you can modify and save them to use again on other projects. The AutoFormat feature is simpler to use than a form template, and it doesn't require you to change any settings in the Options dialog box. Any custom styles you create are available in all your databases, without the need to import any objects into new databases. However, AutoFormat styles don't let you specify different colors for different form sections.

To create and save a custom AutoFormat style, follow these steps:

1. Create a new form in Design view, and set the form's properties as you prefer. For example, choose custom colors for the form's header, footer, and detail sections.
2. If you want to set default control properties, place a control on the form, set its properties as desired, and then highlight it and choose Format, Set Control Defaults.
3. Repeat step 2 as needed for a sample control of each type of control you anticipate using regularly. (Set at least the formats for text boxes, labels, combo boxes, and list boxes.)
4. When the form and its controls have the settings you want, choose Format, AutoFormat to open the AutoFormat dialog box, and select one of the built-in styles that you don't use, as shown in Figure 5-37. You'll overwrite this style with your new, custom version.

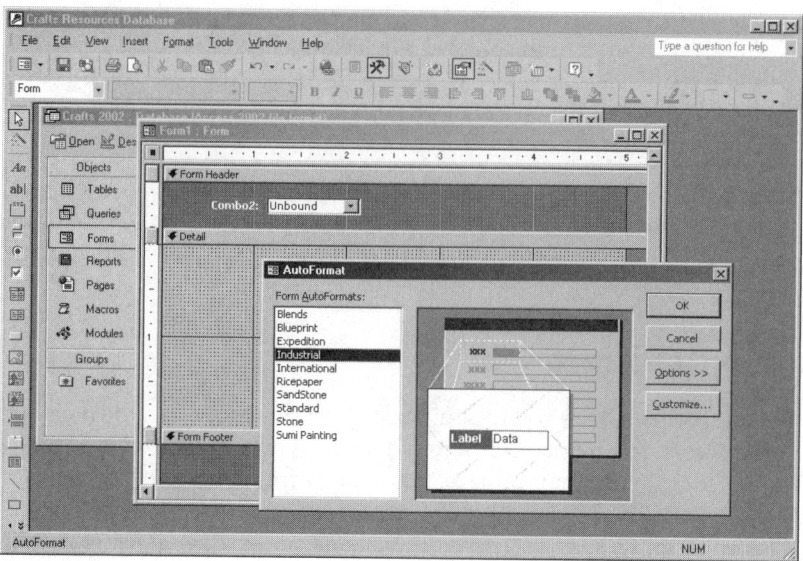

Figure 5-37. Select a built-in style to overwrite with a custom style.

5 Click Customize to open the Customize AutoFormat dialog box, shown in Figure 5-38.

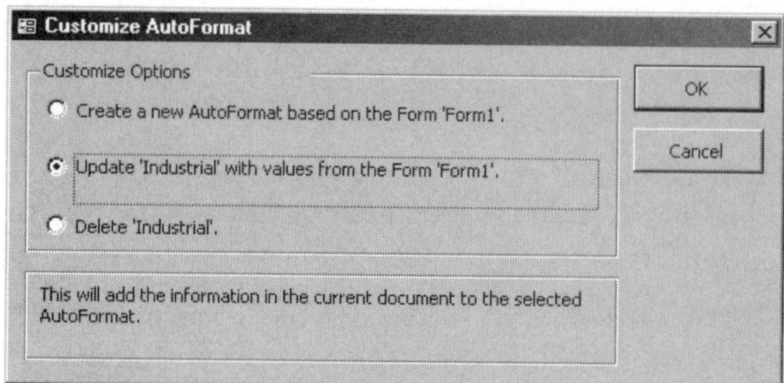

Figure 5-38. Overwrite the built-in style with your custom style.

6 The default selection is to overwrite the selected built-in style with the values from the open form. Click OK to save your format settings to the selected style.

Now, when you apply your custom style to a form, that form will have the colors and control formatting settings you saved to that style. Figure 5-39 shows an example of an applied custom style.

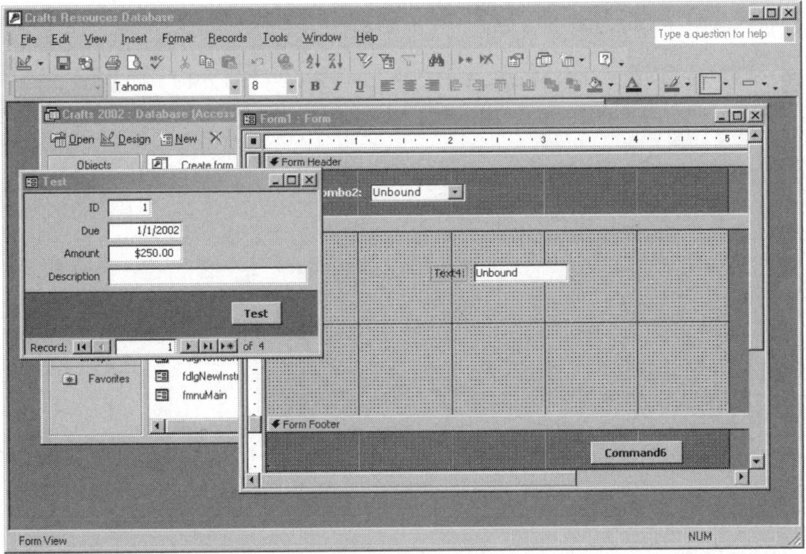

Figure 5-39. The style saved from Form1 as the Industrial AutoFormat style has been applied to the Test form.

Using the Design Schemes Add-In

I originally created the Design Schemes add-in for Access 95, which had no AutoFormat utility. The form template feature in that version was the only option for applying a custom style to newly created forms and did not meet the needs of many advanced users. AutoFormat now offers you control over form section colors and control formats, but you must save your settings to the named style in the AutoFormat dialog box, and you still can't populate new forms with controls or boilerplate event procedures.

Additionally, saved AutoFormats don't allow you to create different types of forms useful for different situations, such as dialog forms, subforms, or forms with a record selector combo box in the header and a Close Form command button in the footer. The Design Schemes add-in allows users to select one of a set of predesigned forms with different sets of form properties. Users can also apply one of four standard (conservative) color schemes to the new form or create a custom color scheme (using the Design Schemes add-in's full selection of control properties).

The Design Schemes add-in is described in detail in Chapter 15, "Using Add-Ins to Expand Access Functionality."

Form Features and Properties

Forms have a great many properties, which are divided into five tabs on a form's properties sheet, as shown in Figure 5-40.

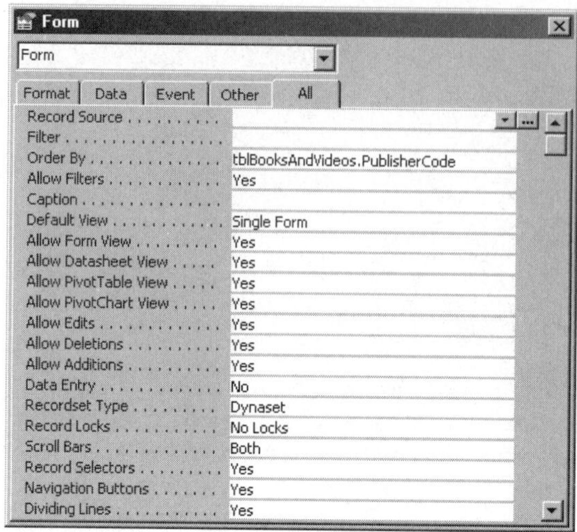

Figure 5-40. A form's properties sheet divides form properties into five tabs.

Three of the tabs (Format, Data, and Other) list subsets of the form's properties. The All tab lists all the form's properties in a single list. The Event tab lists the form's events, which are used for writing VBA code.

newfeature!

The same properties sheet displays the properties of the entire form, a form section, or a control on the form. To open a properties sheet, click the Properties button on the Form Design toolbar (see Figure 5-41), press Alt+Enter, or press F4, which is a new hot key in Access 2002.

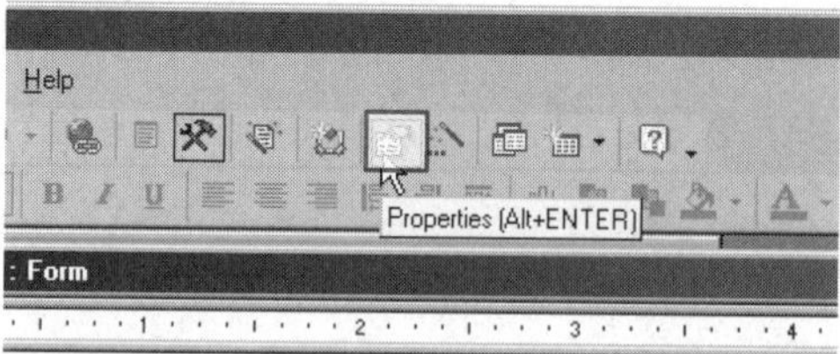

Figure 5-41. You can open a form's properties sheet by clicking the Properties button on the Form Design toolbar.

note You have two other (slower) ways to open the properties sheet: Choose View, Properties, or right-click the form or control and select Properties from the shortcut menu.

Chapter 5

> **tip** In Access 2002, you can open a form's properties sheet in Design view, Form view, and Datasheet view.

Once the properties sheet is open, you can use the following techniques to display the appropriate information:

- To display the form's properties, click the form selector (the gray square in the upper left corner of the form, in Design view), as shown in Figure 5-42. When the form is selected, a smaller black square appears in the middle of the gray square, and the properties sheet's caption is Form.

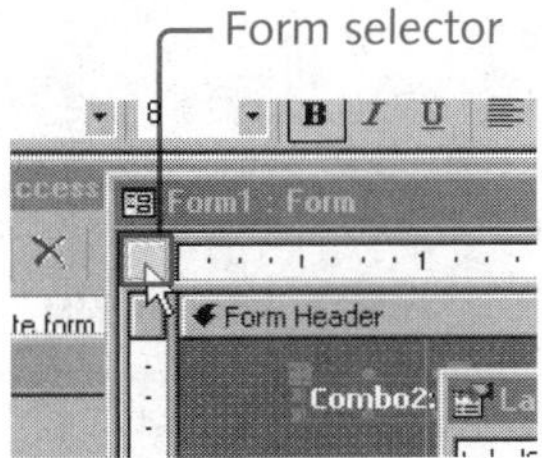

Figure 5-42. You can display form properties in the properties sheet.

- To display the properties of a specific form section, click the section selector (the gray bar over the section). Figure 5-43 shows the form header selector being clicked to display the form header's properties in the properties sheet. The properties sheet's caption is Section: FormHeader (or the appropriate section name).

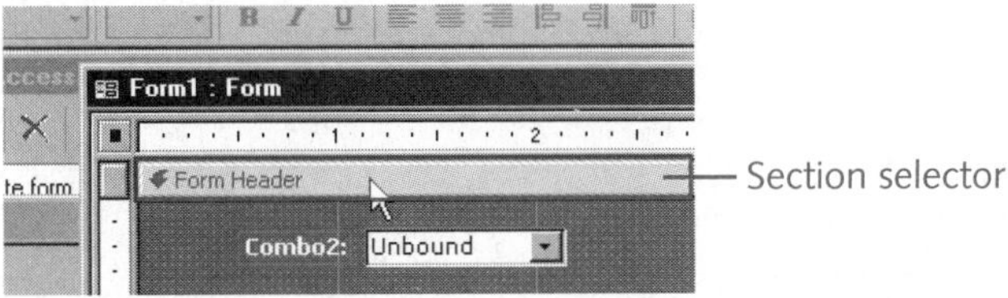

Figure 5-43. You can display form header properties in the properties sheet.

- To display the properties of a control, click the control. The properties sheet's caption displays the control type and control name, such as Text Box: Text4.
- To display the properties of a group of controls, select the controls. The properties sheet's caption becomes Multiple Selection, and only the properties shared by all the controls are available.

Sections and Pages

All forms have a detail section. Forms can also have a form header and form footer or a page header and page footer. Headers and footers are paired sections; you can't have a page header without a page footer, for example, although you can keep a section from being displayed by shrinking it to zero height. To add form header and form footer sections to a form, choose View, Form Header/Footer, as shown in Figure 5-44. The Page Header/Footer option on the same menu toggles a form's page header and page footer sections.

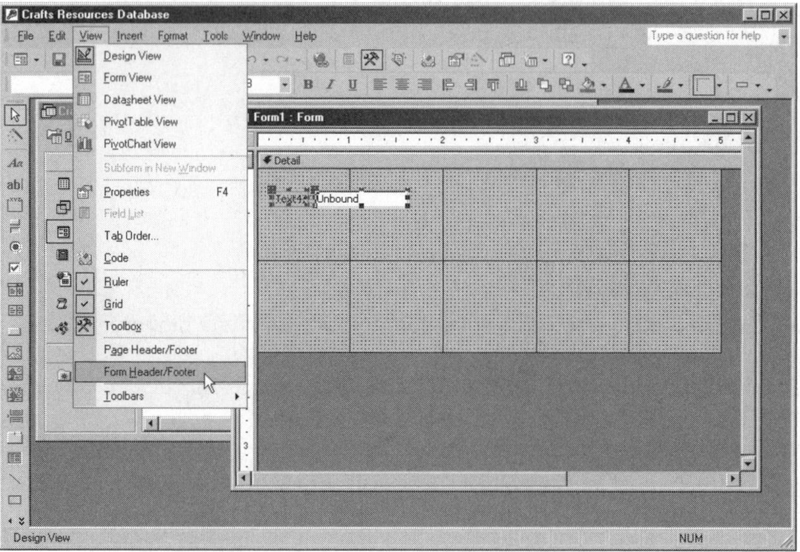

Figure 5-44. You can choose to turn on and off a form's header and footer sections.

> **caution** If you turn off the form header/footer sections, any controls in these sections will be permanently deleted.

Form header and footer sections are quite useful. You can place controls such as record selector combo boxes or command buttons in these sections to perform actions that apply to the entire form. In the earliest versions of Access (before Access 2.0), page headers and footers were also useful when multipage forms were used to display more data than could be displayed at one time. However, multipage forms have not been useful (except for very unusual situations) since the tab control was introduced in Access 2.0, as the Tab control is a more efficient way of displaying large amounts of data on a form.

Figure 5-45 shows the primary form in the Crafts database, shrunk vertically to show only the form header and footer sections. The form header includes a record selector combo box (actually, two combo boxes; only one is visible at a time) and two command buttons, which are used to display one combo box or the other.

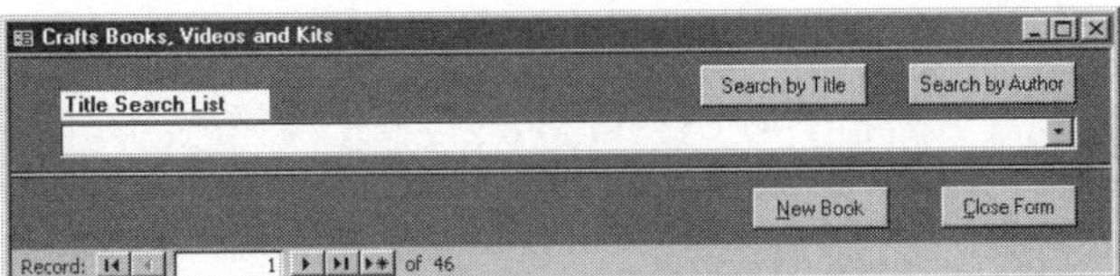

Figure 5-45. Only the header and footer sections of this form are visible.

> **tip** If you shrink a form vertically, its header and footer sections won't shrink; only the detail section shrinks.

The form footer section has two command buttons: one to go to a new record (it could also be used to pop up a New Book form), and another to close the form and return to the main menu. The event procedures attached to the controls in this form's header and footer sections are listed here:

```
Private Sub cboAuthorSearchList_AfterUpdate()

On Error GoTo ErrorHandler

    strSearch = "[BookID] = " & Me![cboAuthorSearchList].Column(2)
    Debug.Print strSearch

    'Find the record that matches the control.
    Me.Requery
    Me.RecordsetClone.FindFirst strSearch
    Me.Bookmark = Me.RecordsetClone.Bookmark

ErrorHandlerExit:
    Exit Sub

ErrorHandler:
    MsgBox "Error No: " & Err.Number & "; Description: " _
        & Err.Description
    Resume ErrorHandlerExit

End Sub

Private Sub cboTitleSearchList_AfterUpdate()

On Error GoTo ErrorHandler

    strSearch = "[BookID] = " & Me![cboTitleSearchList].Column(1)
    Debug.Print strSearch
```

(continued)

```
    'Find the record that matches the control.
    Me.Requery
    Me.RecordsetClone.FindFirst strSearch
    Me.Bookmark = Me.RecordsetClone.Bookmark

ErrorHandlerExit:
    Exit Sub

ErrorHandler:
    MsgBox "Error No: " & Err.Number & "; Description: " _
        & Err.Description
    Resume ErrorHandlerExit

End Sub

Private Sub cmdSearchbyAuthor_Click()

On Error GoTo ErrorHandler

    Me![cboTitleSearchList].Visible = False
    With Me![cboAuthorSearchList]
        .Visible = True
        .SetFocus
        .Dropdown
    End With

ErrorHandlerExit:
    Exit Sub

ErrorHandler:
    MsgBox "Error No: " & Err.Number & "; Description: " _
        & Err.Description
    Resume ErrorHandlerExit

End Sub

Private Sub cmdSearchbyTitle_Click()

On Error GoTo ErrorHandler

    Me![cboAuthorSearchList].Visible = False
    With Me![cboTitleSearchList]
        .Visible = True
        .SetFocus
        .Dropdown
    End With

ErrorHandlerExit:
    Exit Sub
```

```
ErrorHandler:
    MsgBox "Error No: " & Err.Number & "; Description: " _
        & Err.Description
    Resume ErrorHandlerExit

End Sub

Private Sub cmdNew_Click()

On Error GoTo ErrorHandler

    DoCmd.GoToRecord , , acNewRec
    Me![txtTitle].SetFocus

ErrorHandlerExit:
    Exit Sub

ErrorHandler:
    MsgBox "Error No: " & Err.Number & "; Description: " _
        & Err.Description
    Resume ErrorHandlerExit

End Sub

Private Sub cmdClose_Click()

On Error GoTo ErrorHandler

    Dim dbs As Object
    Set dbs = Application.CurrentProject

    If dbs.AllForms("fmnuMain").IsLoaded Then
        Forms![fmnuMain].Visible = True
    Else
        DoCmd.OpenForm "fmnuMain"
    End If

    DoCmd.Close acForm, Me.Name

ErrorHandlerExit:
    Exit Sub

ErrorHandler:
    MsgBox "Error No: " & Err.Number & "; Description: " _
        & Err.Description
    Resume ErrorHandlerExit

End Sub
```

> **See Chapter 20, "Customizing Your Database Using VBA Code," for more information about writing code behind forms procedures.**

Format Properties

The properties displayed on the Format tab of a form's properties sheet are related to the appearance of the form. Some of the more frequently changed properties are described in the following list. In most cases, the remaining properties can be left at their default values.

- ***Caption.*** Use this property to change the text displayed in the form's title bar.
- ***Default View.*** This property offers a selection of available views for the form.
- ***Allow...View.*** Set any of these four properties to No to make the specified view unavailable.
- ***Scroll Bars.*** This property controls which scroll bars will be visible on the form.
- ***Record Selectors.*** This property turns on or off the record selector (the vertical gray bar at the left of the form), which is used to select the entire record. Figure 5-46 shows the record selector.

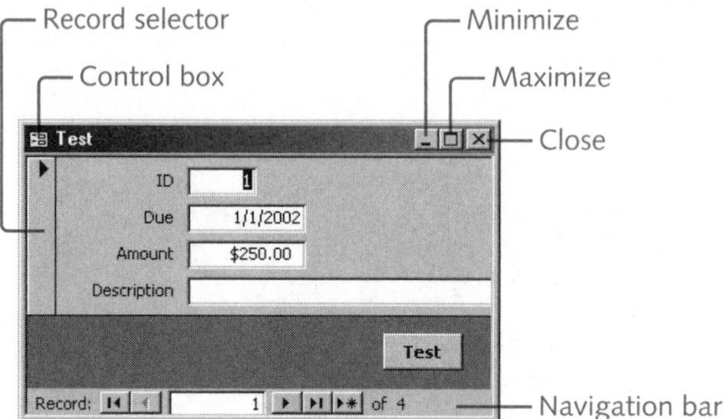

Figure 5-46. This form's record selector is turned on.

Navigation Buttons. This property turns on and off the navigation bar at the bottom of the form.

Control Box, Min/Max Buttons, Close Button, What's This Button. These properties control the small buttons in the upper left and right corners of a form.

> **tip** You can get help for any property by positioning the mouse pointer in the property's current value and pressing F1.

Chapter 5

Data Properties

The following properties are the most frequently used properties on the Data tab of a form's properties sheet:

- ***Record Source.*** This property specifies the table, query, or SQL statement that provides the form's data.
- ***Filter.*** This optional property can contain an expression that specifies a field and a value for filtering the form.
- ***Order By.*** You can add a field or expression to this property to sort the form's records.
- ***Allow.*** You can set these properties to allow or prohibit filters, edits, deletions, or additions.
- ***Data Entry.*** This property specifies whether only the records entered in the current session are visible.

Other Properties

The following properties are the most frequently used properties on the Other tab of a form's properties sheet:

- ***Pop Up.*** When you set this property to Yes, the form will always be on top of other forms.
- ***Modal.*** When you set this property to Yes, users can't do anything else until they close the form. Use this property cautiously—modal forms can drive users crazy.
- ***Cycle.*** For users tabbing through form controls, this property offers a choice of cycling among all records, the current record (generally the best choice), or the current page.
- ***Menu Bar, Toolbar, Shortcut Menu, Shortcut Menu Bar.*** These properties allow you to specify one of four types of custom command bars.

See Chapter 13, "Customizing Access Toolbars and Menus (Command Bars)," for more details on command bars.

- ***Has Module.*** This property specifies whether the form has an attached code module.
- ***Allow Design Changes.*** If All Views is selected, this property allows you to make design changes in all views. This doesn't mean that you can (for example) resize a control in Form view, however; all changes must be made in the properties sheet.

Conditional Formatting

Conditional formatting for form controls is a long-requested feature that was added in Access 2000. This feature lets you apply a specific color, a special effect, or another formatting choice to a control in certain circumstances, by means of a user-friendly dialog box. (You don't have to write code, as you did with Access 97 and earlier.) For example, if you have a txtDue control bound to a Date field and you want the control to have a yellow background if the due date is earlier than today, you can select the control in Design view and choose Format, Conditional Formatting (or right-click the control, and choose Conditional Formatting from the shortcut menu) to open the Conditional Formatting dialog box, as shown in Figure 5-47.

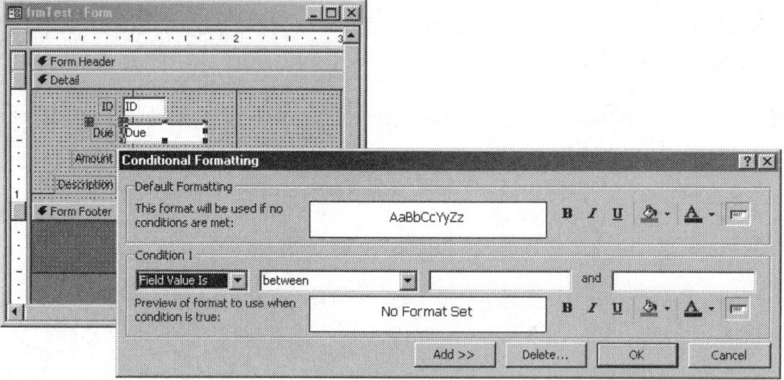

Figure 5-47. The Conditional Formatting dialog box enables you to specify formatting that appears when certain conditions are met.

> **note** You might expect to be able to use the Expression Builder to aid in constructing expressions to use in conditions in the Conditional Formatting dialog box, but unfortunately the Expression Builder is not available in this dialog box.

You can construct up to three conditions for formatting a control. Each condition has three parts: the formatting element, the comparison phrase, and the comparison expression.

The Formatting Element drop-down list provides the following three choices:

- **Field Value Is.** Uses the values in the control as formatting criteria.
- **Expression Is.** Uses an expression as the formatting criterion.
- **Field Has Focus.** Applies the formatting when the control has the focus.

The Comparison Phrase drop-down list provides eight choices:

- Between
- Not Between
- Equal To
- Not Equal To
- Greater Than
- Less Than
- Greater Than Or Equal To
- Less Than Or Equal To

> **caution** Any conditional formatting that you apply to a control won't be preserved when the form is exported to another data format, such as an Excel worksheet. This is understandable because conditional formatting is a feature of Access.

To complete the condition, type a constant value or an expression in the text box. (If you're using either Between or Not Between as the comparison phrase, specify two values or expressions.)

Figure 5-48 shows the Conditional Formatting dialog box with Field Value Is selected for the formatting element, Less Than selected for the comparison operator, and the *Date* function specified for the constant value. A yellow background color and bold formatting are selected as well.

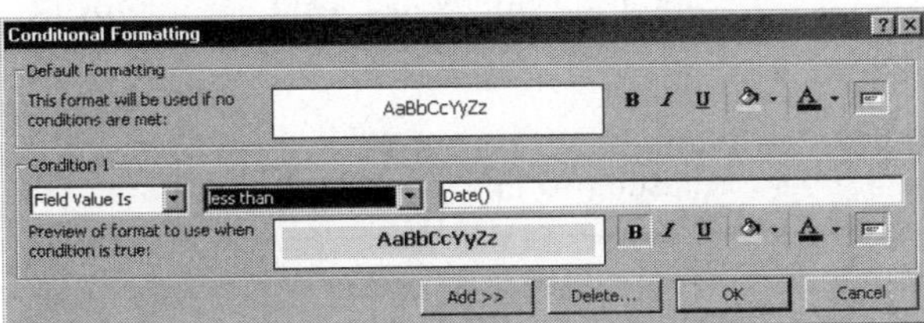

Figure 5-48. The condition in this Conditional Formatting dialog box is complete.

Figure 5-49 shows the sample form in Form view, displaying a record for which the due date is earlier than today.

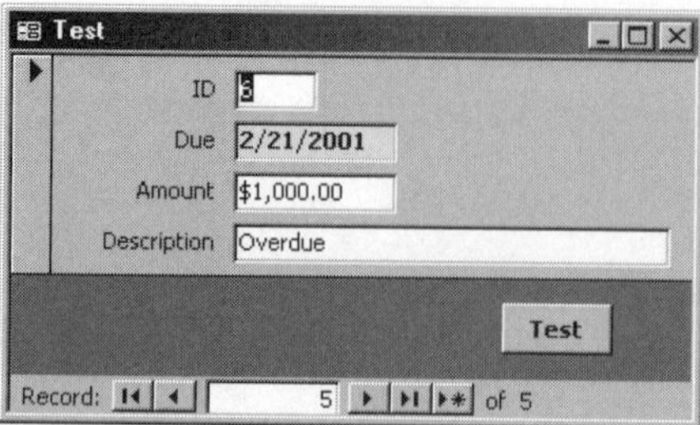

Figure 5-49. The conditional formatting has been applied to this form, shown in Form view.

Sometimes you'll want to clarify which control has the focus by giving the current control a different background color. You can do this by selecting Field Has Focus for the formatting element (the other selections will disappear), as shown in Figure 5-50. You must set the same condition on all controls on the form to get the desired effect (or at least set the condition on all controls that display text, such as text boxes and combo boxes).

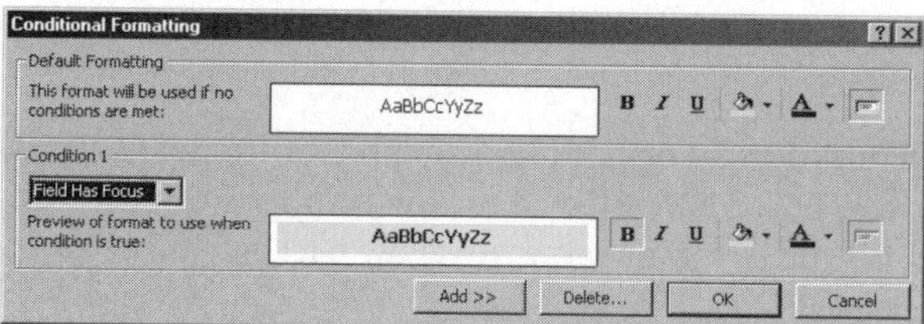

Figure 5-50. You can create a condition to clarify which field has the focus.

> **note** You can't select several controls and apply the same conditional formatting to all of them. You can apply conditional formatting to only one control at a time.

After applying this condition, as you tab from control to control in the form, the current control will appear in boldface and with a yellow background.

Form Record Sources

The data displayed and modified on a form comes from its *record source* (also called a *data source*). When a record source has been specified for a form, that form is called a *bound form.* (Similarly, a bound control displays data from a specific field in the form's data source.) Unlike Visual Basic forms (for example), Access forms can be directly bound to data by simply selecting the data source (usually a table or query) as the form's *Record Source* property. Once you select the record source, all of its fields are available for placement on the form, using the field list.

In addition to selecting a table or query for a form's *Record Source* property, you can also use a SQL statement to get data for a form.

Tables and Queries

Specifying a table or query as a form's record source is easy. If you create the form by using the Form Wizard, you can choose a table or query as the record source for the new form in the New Form dialog box, as shown in Figure 5-51.

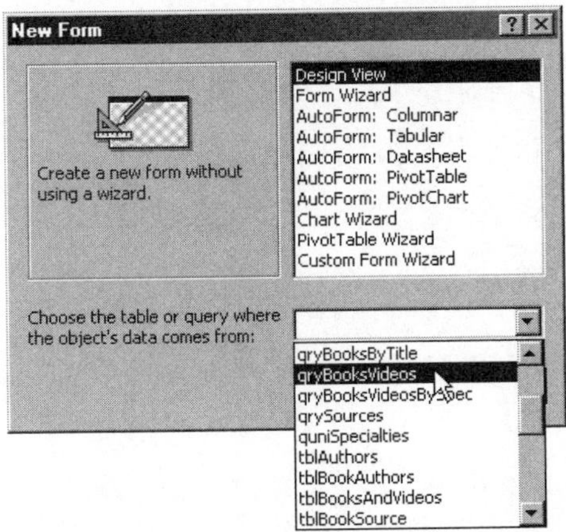

Figure 5-51. Choose a table or query as a form's record source in the New Form dialog box.

SQL Statements

Sometimes you won't have a saved query that does the filtering or sorting you need, and you'll need to create a record source for a form on the fly. You can do this with a SQL statement. (You don't have to be an expert in the SQL language—Access allows you to create SQL statements visually by using the Query Builder.)

For more information on using queries, see Chapter 9, "Using Queries to Select Data."

To create a SQL statement that filters the fpriBooksAndVideos form in the Crafts database for books published in 1980 or later, follow these steps:

1. Open the fpriBooksAndVideos form in Design view.
2. If the properties sheet is not open, open it by pressing F4.
3. Click the Data tab of the properties sheet, and then click the *Record Source* property.
4. Click the Build button, which appears to the right of the property, as shown in Figure 5-52.

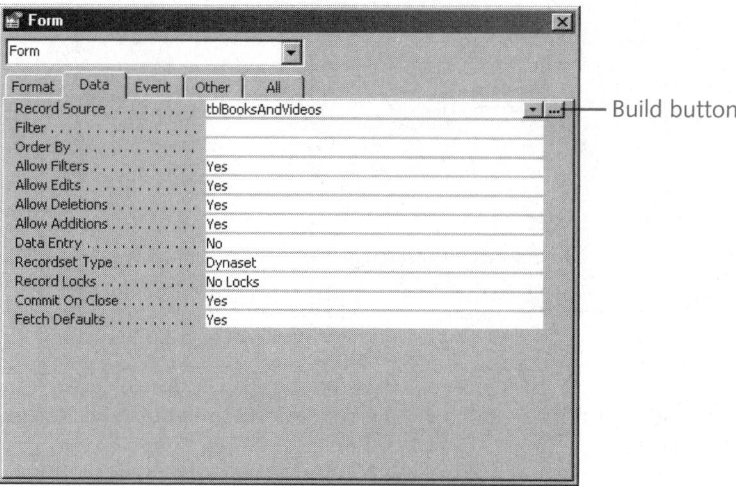

Figure 5-52. Click the Build button to create a SQL statement record source.

5. A message box appears, asking whether you want to create a query based on the table. Click Yes.
6. The Query Builder window opens, much the same as when you create a query, but without the Query Design toolbar.

7 Drag the asterisk from the top of the tblBooksAndVideos field list to the query grid.

8 Drag the PublicationYear field to the query grid, and then clear the Show check box to prevent this field from appearing twice in the recordset.

9 Type **>="1980"** in the Criteria cell for the PublicationYear field. Figure 5-53 shows the completed SQL statement in the Query Builder.

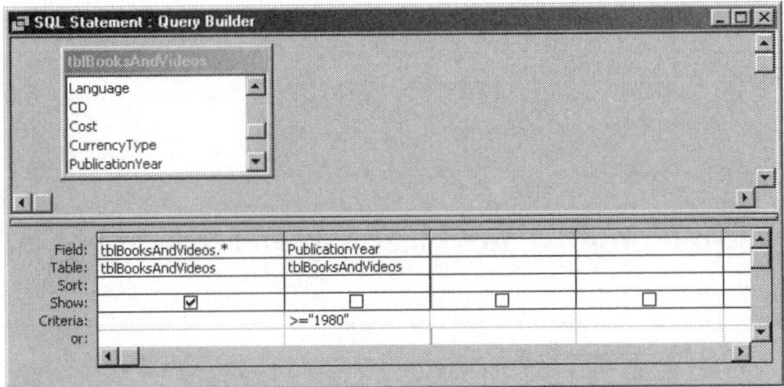

Figure 5-53. The SQL statement looks like this in the Query Builder.

10 Close the Query Builder window, and click Yes in the confirmation message box that appears.

11 The SQL statement now appears as the *Record Source* property for the form, as shown in Figure 5-54.

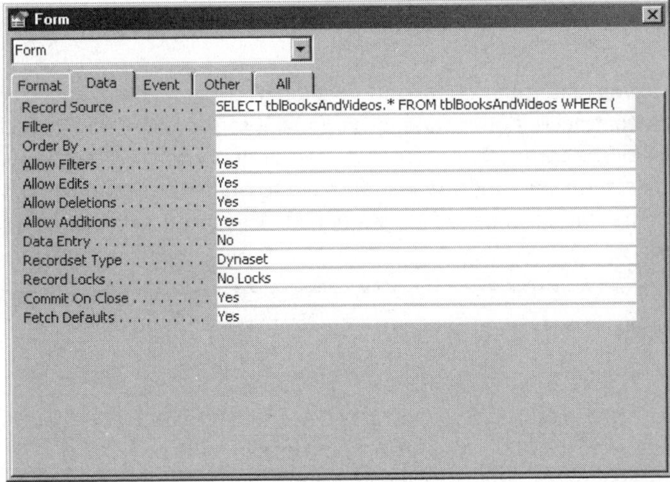

Figure 5-54. The finished SQL statement appears in the *Record Source* property of the form's properties sheet.

If you want to see the entire SQL statement, open the Query Builder again and switch to SQL view. The SQL statement is listed here:

```
SELECT tblBooksAndVideos.*
FROM tblBooksAndVideos
WHERE (((tblBooksAndVideos.PublicationYear)>="1980"));
```

note Access 2002 has a higher limit (32,750 characters) for the size of SQL statements used as record and row sources. If you want to use a database in both Access 2002 and Access 2000, either keep your SQL statement shorter than 2000 characters or use a saved query instead of a SQL statement.

The Books And Videos form will now display only books published in 1980 or later.

Saved Queries vs. SQL Statement Record Sources

You can use either a saved query or a SQL statement as the record source of a form or report. In earlier versions of Access, using saved queries led to some performance improvement, but in Access 2002, you'll find little difference in performance between saved queries and SQL statements. However, if you need to use the same record source for several database objects (such as a form and a report, or several reports), you're better off creating and saving a query rather than creating a SQL statement as the record source of each form or report.

Once you have created the query and selected it as the record source for all the database objects that need it, any changes you make to the query will be picked up automatically by all the forms or reports that use the query as their record source. With SQL statements, on the other hand, you have to open each form or report in turn and make the same changes to the SQL statement. This process is tedious and can also lead to errors.

Recordsets

You can use either Data Access Objects (DAO) or ActiveX Data Objects (ADO) recordsets as record sources for forms, but only in VBA code. The first code sample that follows assigns a DAO recordset to a form; the second code sample assigns an ADO recordset to the same form. Both procedures use the same SQL statement created in the previous example except that the ADO procedure filters for books published in 1980 or later.

```
Public Function ApplyDAORecordset()

    Dim dbs As DAO.Recordset
    Dim rst As DAO.Recordset
    Dim strSQL As String
    Dim frm As Access.Form

    strSQL = "SELECT * FROM tblBooksAndVideos " & _
        "WHERE PublicationYear>='1980';"
    Set dbs = CurrentDb
    Set rst = dbs.OpenRecordset(strSQL, dbOpenDynaset)
    DoCmd.OpenForm "fpriBooksAndVideos"
    Set frm = Forms![fpriBooksAndVideos]
    frm.Recordset = rst

End Function

Public Sub ApplyADORecordset()

    Dim frm As Access.Form
    Dim strSQL As String
    Dim rst As ADODB.Recordset

    strSQL = "SELECT * FROM tblBooksAndVideos " & _
        "WHERE PublicationYear>='1980';"
    DoCmd.OpenForm "fpriBooksAndVideos"
    Set frm = Forms![fpriBooksAndVideos]
    Set rst = New ADODB.Recordset
    rst.Open strSQL, CurrentProject.Connection, adOpenKeyset,
        adLockOptimistic
    Set frm.Recordset = rst

End Sub
```

Using Forms to Display Linked Data

When you have tables with one-to-many or many-to-many relationships, you need a way to display multiple records of linked data in the "many" table for every single record of data in the "one" table. Forms with embedded subforms are ideal for displaying linked data, and embedded datasheet subforms are especially useful for displaying large quantities of linked data.

See Chapter 3, "Introduction to Database Design," for more details on relationships.

Sometimes you might not want the linked data to appear on the main form, but you still want the data to be readily available to the user. You can place on the main form a command button that, when clicked, "pops up" a second form containing the linked data. The following sections discuss both embedded and pop-up forms as well as new record and hyperlinked forms.

Embedded Subforms

One method for displaying linked data on a form is to create a query that includes several (or many) linked tables and then use that query as the form's record source. This is the correct approach if you are creating a PivotTable, PivotChart, grouped data access page, or grouped report because these types of Access objects have their own methods of separating data into groups, and you don't need to—and can't—modify their data. Figure 5-55 shows this kind of query in Design view.

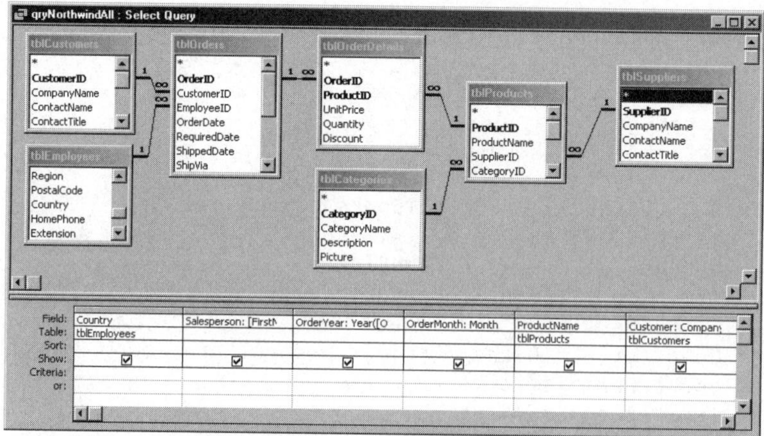

Figure 5-55. This query includes a number of linked tables.

> **The qryNorthwindAll query shown in Figure 5-55 is an example of a query that uses linked tables. This query is used as a data source for PivotTables and PivotCharts in Chapter 18, "Working with Data Access Pages."**

However, in most cases a different approach is preferable for forms intended to display linked data. If you use a query based on linked tables, some of the fields from that query might not be updatable, which can cause problems. Instead of using a single all-in-one query as the form's record source, it is best to bind the main form to the "one" table in a one-to-many relationship and bind one or more subforms to the "many" table (or tables). You don't need to use queries or SQL statements at all (unless you need to filter or sort the data); you can bind the main form and subforms directly to the tables.

Although you can use a subform in Single Form view to display linked data, in general a datasheet subform is more useful. A datasheet subform can display a number of fields in a single row, possibly using a horizontal scroll bar if each linked record has many columns of data.

tip Set the *LinkMasterFields* and *LinkChildFields* properties of the subform control to the linking fields of the "one" and "many" tables to guarantee that, as you move from record to record on the main form, the appropriate linked data is displayed on the subform.

As an alternative to using a subform to display linked data, you can use a table directly in a subform. (Since Access 2000, tables can be selected as source objects for the subform control.) It is generally preferable, however, to use a datasheet subform, which allows you to decide what columns to display in the datasheet, what order to put them in, and what their column headings will be. None of this is possible if you use a table as the subform control's source object.

on the CD **The *fpri* tag indicates that a form is the primary form in the database; the Menu Manager add-in (Menu Manager.mda, available on the companion CD) uses this tag.**

The main form in the Crafts database (see Figure 5-56), fpriBooksAndVideos, has several subforms on it, some linked and some unlinked. (The unlinked subforms are discussed in the section "Using Forms to Display Unlinked Data," page 177.)

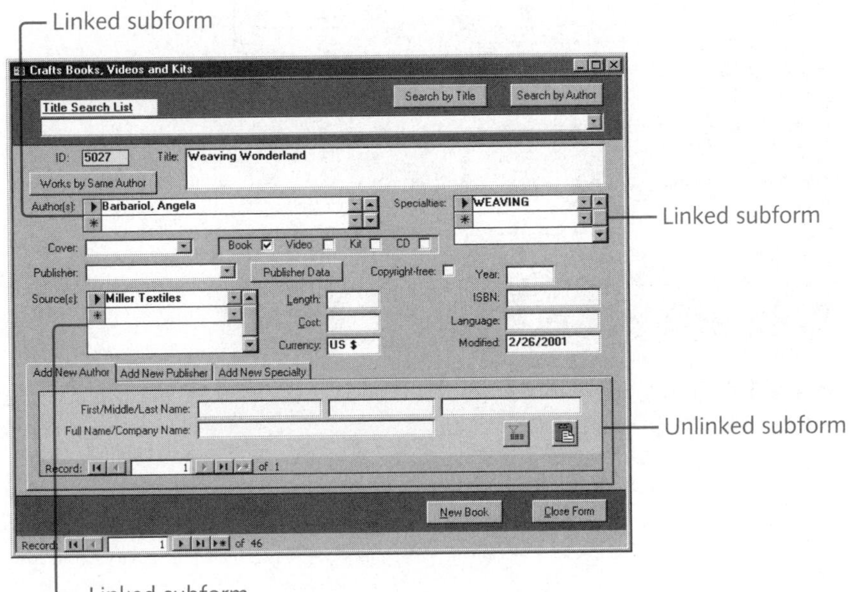

Figure 5-56. The main fpriBooksAndVideos form in the Crafts database has several subforms.

The fpriBooksAndVideos form has three linked subforms: subBookAuthors, subBookSpecs, and subBookSources. Each of these subforms has as its own record source one of the linking tables used to create a many-to-many link. The subBookAuthors subform, for example, is bound to tblBookAuthors, a table that contains only the two linking BookID and AuthorID fields, and thus links tblAuthors and tblBooksAndVideos in a many-to-many relationship. Similarly, the other two subforms are linked to the tblBookSpecs and tblBookSource tables, which are linking tables that set up the tblSpecialties–tblBooksAndVideos and tblSources–tblBooksAndVideos many-to-many relationships.

Each of these subforms has its default view set to Continuous Forms and has only a single control: a combo box bound to the ID field for the linked table (AuthorID, Specialty, or Source). In the case of fsubBookAuthors, the combo box is set to display the author's name, although it is bound to AuthorID. The end result of this setup is a multirow subform with a drop-down list that appears on the selected row for selecting an author, specialty, or source for the book. This allows you to select multiple authors, specialties, and sources for each book. Figure 5-57 shows a second author being selected for a book in the Book Authors subform.

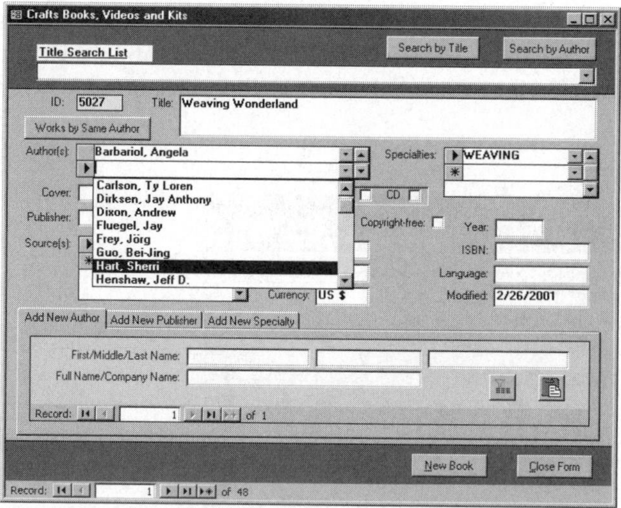

Figure 5-57. The Book Authors subform permits the user to select multiple authors for a book.

tip If you open a form that has a subform and see only a white rectangle where the subform should appear (as in Figure 5-58, where the Book Authors subform is blank), the subform is open in a separate window, possibly hidden behind the main form. Close both the main form and the subform. When you reopen the main form, the subform should appear normally.

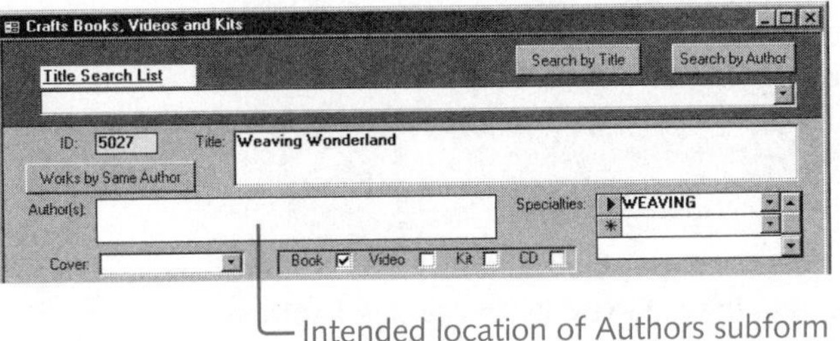

Figure 5-58. The Book Authors subform will appear blank when the subform has been opened separately.

Linked Pop-Up Forms

A *pop-up form* is a form that pops up when you click a command button. Don't confuse pop-up forms with the *PopUp* property (although pop-up forms often have their *PopUp* property set to True). In the Crafts database, the fpriBooksAndVideos form has two command buttons you can use to pop up linked forms. The Works By Same Author command button pops up the frmBooksBySelectedAuthor form, which displays books by the author selected in the top row of the linked Book Authors subform. You create this linkage by using a select query as the pop-up form's record source. Figure 5-59 shows this query in Design view.

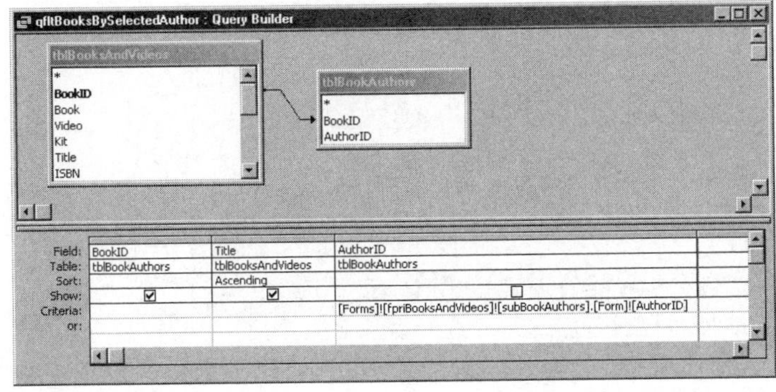

Figure 5-59. This filter query is used as the pop-up form's record source.

In this example, the pop-up form provides more information to allow you to decide whether the author of the current book is the same as the author of some previously entered books. For example, if you encounter a book by Barbara Hoffman on the subject of creating duck decoys, you can click Works By Same Author to pop up the Books By Selected Author form, as shown in Figure 5-60.

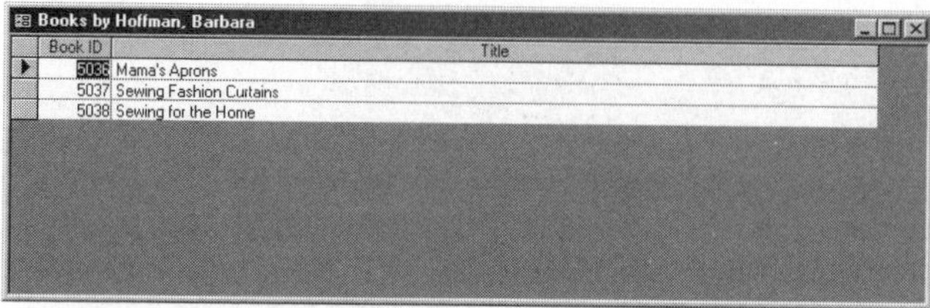

Figure 5-60. The frmBooksBySelectedAuthor pop-up form offers more information about the other books in the database by the selected author.

Since the other books by an author named Barbara Hoffman are all about sewing, it's likely that the current book (about carving duck decoys) is by another Barbara Hoffman, and therefore you should create a new author record for her. The AuthorID AutoNumber field guarantees unique records in tblAuthors, even for authors with the same name. This is necessary because, unlike books, which have ISBNs, authors don't have unique identifiers, and two very different authors can have the same name.

The Publishers pop-up form has a different purpose: It opens the full Publishers form for the selected publisher so that you can verify that this is the correct publisher or add extra information you might get from a book, such as phone numbers, Web site addresses, or a changed address. Figure 5-61 shows the Publishers pop-up form.

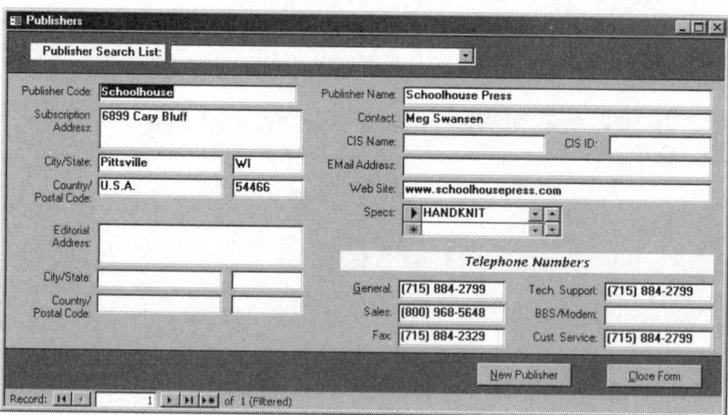

Figure 5-61. The Publishers pop-up form allows you to verify or add information about a selected publisher.

This form is the same one opened from the Other Forms combo box's drop-down list on the Crafts database's main menu (the fmnuMain form). Because the same form is used to work with all the publishers or to display data for only the selected publisher, the filtering for the pop-up form is done in VBA code from the command button's *OnClick* event. This procedure is listed in the following code:

```
Private Sub cmdPublishers_Click()

On Error GoTo ErrorHandler

    Dim strDocName As String
    Dim strLinkCriteria As String

    strDocName = "frmPublishers"

    strLinkCriteria = "[PublisherCode]=" & "'" _
        & Me![cboPublisherCode] & "'"
    DoCmd.OpenForm strDocName, , , strLinkCriteria
    Forms![frmPublishers]![txtCalledFrom] = "Books"

ErrorHandlerExit:
    Exit Sub

ErrorHandler:
    MsgBox "Error No: " & Err.Number & "; Description: " & _
        Err.Description
    Resume ErrorHandlerExit

End Sub
```

New Record Forms

A top-to-bottom layout is often useful for a quick data entry form, a special form used to enter new data, often in a focused data entry situation. A quick data entry form is popped up as an alternative to simply moving to a new record on the main form. A separate data entry form is especially useful when a main form is laid out in a way that organizes the data logically, and perhaps has subforms to display linked or unlinked data. These features make a form more useful for reviewing and editing data, but a plain top-to-bottom control layout is more useful for entering new data efficiently.

See the "Creating Quick Data Entry Forms" section on page 142 for more information on the rationale for these forms.

To create a quick data entry form, select a table on the Tables tab of the Database window and then click the New Object: AutoForm button on the Database Design toolbar. The new form has its fields arranged in a single column from top to bottom. A New Record form needs to have its *Data Entry* property set to Yes so that only the new record shows, and the form needs a Close Form button to close the form and return to the main form. Optionally, you can also add a Cancel button to close the quick data entry form without adding a new record. The New Publisher command button on the main form also needs a line to open the quick data entry form instead of the usual method of moving to a new record on the same form, either by clicking New Record on the navigation bar or by using the *DoCmd.GoToRecord, , acNext* command in a command button's *Click* event procedure.

The controls on the frmPublishers form in the Crafts database are grouped in a way that makes the form more comprehensible for review and editing, but it's definitely easier to enter data quickly in a form that has all its controls laid out top to bottom. Therefore, the New Publisher command button on this form opens fqdfNewPublisher, which is a quick data entry form bound to the tblPublishers table. The New Publisher command button's *OnClick* event procedure is listed here:

```
Private Sub cmdNew_Click()

    DoCmd.OpenForm "fqdfNewPublisher"

End Sub
```

After I created this quick data entry form, I named it fqdfNewPublisher (the *fqdf* tag indicates that it's a quick data entry form) and turned on the form header and footer by choosing View, Form Header/Footer. A New Record form needs only a footer, so I shrank the header down to zero height so that it wouldn't appear. I added two command buttons to the footer: one to close the quick data entry form without saving the new record and one to save the record and return to the main form. These event procedures are listed here:

```
Private Sub cmdCancel_Click()

On Error GoTo ErrorHandler

    DoCmd.SetWarnings False
    If Me.Dirty = True Then
        DoCmd.RunCommand acCmdDeleteRecord
    End If

    DoCmd.Close

ErrorHandlerExit:
    Exit Sub
```

```
ErrorHandler:
    MsgBox "Error No: " & Err.Number & "; Description: " & _
        Err.Description
    Resume ErrorHandlerExit

End Sub

Private Sub cmdSave_Click()

On Error GoTo ErrorHandler

    Dim frm As Access.Form
    Dim strSearch As String

    If IsLoaded("frmPublishers") = False Then
        DoCmd.OpenForm "frmPublishers"
    End If

    Set frm = Forms![frmPublishers]
    If Me.Dirty = True Then
        DoCmd.RunCommand acCmdSaveRecord
    End If

    'Find the Publisher record that matches the control.
    strSearch = "[PublisherCode] = " & Chr$(39) & _
        Me![PublisherCode] & Chr$(39)
    Debug.Print "Search string: " & strSearch

    frm.Requery
    frm.RecordsetClone.FindFirst strSearch
    If frm.RecordsetClone.NoMatch = True Then
        Debug.Print "No match found"
    End If
    frm.Bookmark = frm.RecordsetClone.Bookmark
    frm![cboPublisherSearchList].Requery

    'Close quick data entry form form.
    DoCmd.Close

ErrorHandlerExit:
    Exit Sub

ErrorHandler:
    MsgBox "Error No: " & Err.Number & "; Description: " & _
        Err.Description
    Resume ErrorHandlerExit

End Sub
```

See Chapter 20, "Customizing Your Database Using VBA Code," for more information about working with event procedures.

Figure 5-62 shows the finished quick data entry form. As is typical of these forms, you can't see all the controls at once, so the form has a vertical scroll bar.

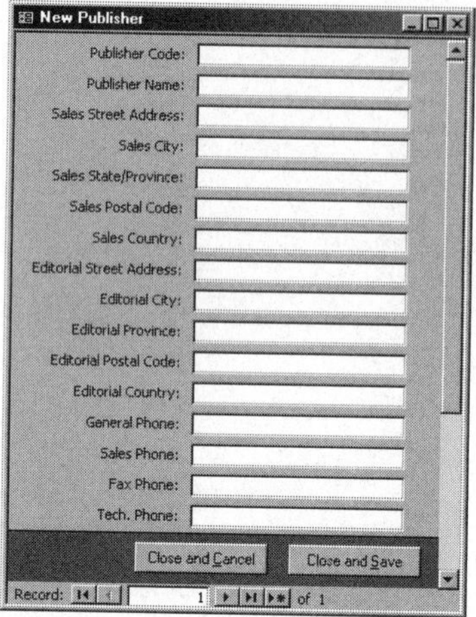

Figure 5-62. When complete, the New Publisher quick data entry form looks like this.

Hyperlinked Forms

You can also open an Access form by using a hyperlink on a command button, but this method simply opens the form without offering you an opportunity to run code. For this reason, it's less useful than using the *OpenForm* method to open a form in VBA code. If you want to open a form using the hyperlink method, click the Build button next to the Hyperlink property of a command button to open the Edit Hyperlink dialog box. Then click the Object In This Database icon on the left side of the dialog box, and select the form (or other database object) from the TreeView control in the center of the dialog box, as shown in Figure 5-63.

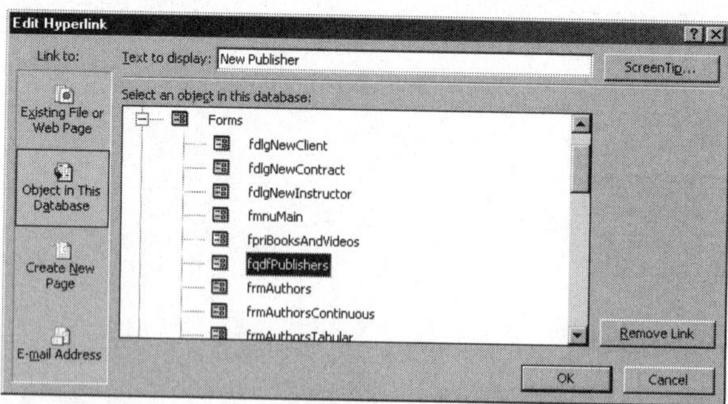

Figure 5-63. The Edit Hyperlink dialog box allows you to open a form by using a hyperlink.

note Although opening forms using hyperlinks has little utility in Access, opening Word documents or Excel worksheets using hyperlinks on command buttons on Access forms can be genuinely useful.

Click OK to save the hyperlink. The properties sheet's *HyperlinkAddress* property will be blank (for a database object), but its *HyperlinkSubAddress* property is filled in with the name of the selected database object, as shown in Figure 5-64.

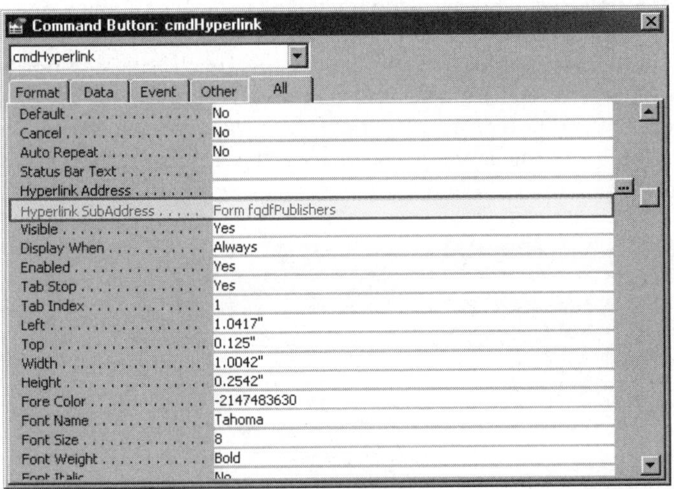

Figure 5-64. You'll find the *HyperlinkSubAddress* property on the properties sheet of a command button.

Using Forms to Display Unlinked Data

Not only can you use subforms to display linked data on forms, but you can also use subforms to display unlinked data. The main fpriBooksAndVideos form in the Crafts database (see Figure 5-56 on page 169) has three unlinked subforms in addition to the linked subforms discussed in the section "Embedded Subforms," page 168. These unlinked subforms are located on the three pages of the tab control at the bottom of the detail section of this form. Figure 5-65 shows the tab control in Design view with one of the subforms on its Add New Author page.

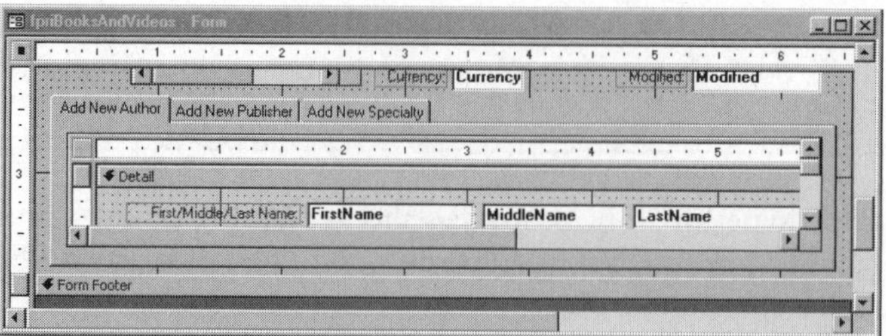

Figure 5-65. This unlinked subform is shown in Design view on a page of a tab control.

You would use these three unlinked subforms to add (respectively) a new author, publisher, or specialty on the fly when you don't need to add full information on the regular form (or when you don't have full data). For example, the fsubAuthorsAddNew subform displays only author name fields, whereas the full frmAuthors form has many other fields as well, as shown in Figure 5-66.

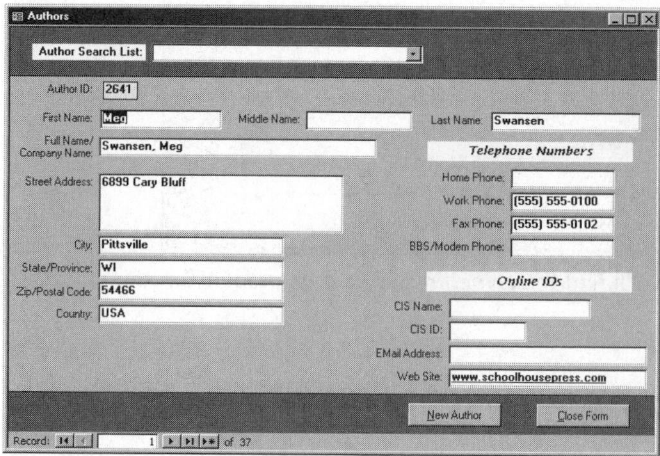

Figure 5-66. The complete Authors form (frmAuthors) looks like this.

In this example, when you're entering books from a stack of books or from a list, you usually don't have any more information about the author than his or her name, so it's handy to be able to quickly enter a new author's name in tblAuthors by using the unlinked Add New Author subform and then have the new name automatically entered in the linked BookAuthors subform. You can always open frmAuthors to fill in missing information later on.

Chapter 6

Working with Form Controls

The purpose of a form is to display data from the table, query, SQL statement, or recordset that is the form's record source. But a blank form won't display any data—you need to place controls on the form to display data from the fields in the form's record source. Sometimes you'll also want to add decorative elements to a form; you use controls for this purpose as well.

Controls are interface elements that are placed on a form (or report). Controls bound to fields (*data-bound controls*) are automatically placed on forms when you use the Form Wizard to create a new form. However, when you create a form using the Design View selection in the New Form dialog box, you have to place all the controls on the form manually. You must always place decorative controls (such as lines and rectangles) on forms manually (although some decorative controls are placed on reports automatically when you create a report using the Report Wizard).

In this chapter, you'll learn about the different types of controls you can place on forms and how to use these controls to display various types of data. You'll learn how to offer users options to select from and how to run Microsoft Visual Basic for Applications (VBA) code associated with particular controls. You'll also learn how to set control properties to make them attractive and easy to use.

Placing Controls on Forms

To begin, you'll need to create a form on which you can place your controls. Choose Insert, Form to open the New Form dialog box. Select Design View from the list of selections, select the table or query containing the data to display on the form, and then click OK. The new, blank, form appears in Design view. You can manually place controls on a form in two ways: by using the Toolbox and by using the field list.

See the "Using the Field List to Place a Control" section on page 186 for more information about using the field list; also see Chapter 5, "Creating Forms for Entering, Editing, and Viewing Data," for information about creating various types of forms.

Fields added to a form from the field list are always inserted as text box controls, with two exceptions: Yes/No fields are inserted as check boxes, and Lookup fields are inserted as combo boxes. If you want to insert text box controls bound to fields, the fastest way is to drag the fields from the field list; otherwise, click the tool icon for the type of control you want to use in the Toolbox and then click the form to insert an unbound control, or drag the field from the field list to insert a bound control of the selected control type. Alternatively, you can click the appropriate tool, click the form to place a control, and then select the control's *Control Source* property from its properties sheet.

For example, if you want to insert a field as a combo box, click the Combo Box tool in the Toolbox and then drag the field from the field list to the form. A combo box bound to the selected field is placed on the form.

Troubleshooting

When I try to select a field for a control's *Control Source* property, there's no drop-down list of fields to select from

If no fields appear in the drop-down list, the form is unbound. To correct this, select a record source for the form, as follows:

1. Click the Form Selector in the upper left corner of the form window.
2. Click the Properties button on the Form Design toolbar to open the properties sheet for the form.
3. Click the Data tab, and choose the name of the table or query you want to bind the form to in the *Record Source* property combo box.

Data-Bound Controls vs. Unbound Controls

Bound controls display data from a field in the form's record source, whereas unbound controls are not linked to data. Some controls can be either bound or unbound (such as text boxes), whereas others are bound only (the bound object frame) or unbound only (labels). Table 6-1 lists some of the most commonly used controls and indicates whether they can be bound or unbound.

Table 6-1. Bound and unbound controls

Control	Bound	Unbound
Label		✓
Text Box	✓	✓
Option Group	✓	✓
Toggle Button	✓	✓
Option Button	✓	✓
Check Box	✓	✓
Combo Box	✓	✓
List Box	✓	✓
Command Button		✓
Image		✓
Unbound Object Frame		✓
Bound Object Frame	✓	
Page Break		✓
Tab Control		✓
Subform/Subreport	✓	✓
Line		✓
Rectangle		✓

Some controls that can be either bound or unbound are genuinely useful in both modes (such as text boxes and combo boxes); others (such as toggle buttons and check boxes) are useful only when bound. See the sections on individual controls for more details about using controls in bound or unbound states.

Using the Toolbox to Place a Control on a Form

To place a control on a form using the Toolbox, click the tool you want to use and click on the form where you want to place the control. You can also click and drag on the form to control the size and position of the control as it is placed on the form. Figure 6-1 shows the various tools available in the Toolbox.

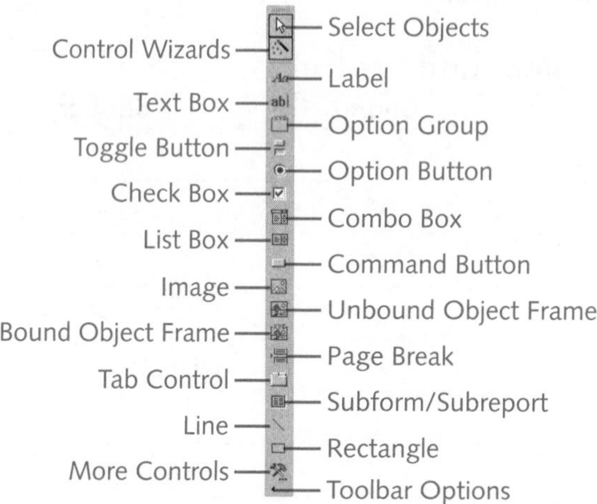

Figure 6-1. The Toolbox contains tools representing the controls that can be added to Access forms in Design view.

Tools and Controls

The buttons you see in the Toolbox are called *tools*. Most of them represent controls you can place on a form or report. To avoid confusion, this book will refer to the control-inserting tools on the Toolbox as *tools* and the controls they place on forms as *controls*. For example, the List Box tool on the Toolbox is used to place a list box control on a form.

The tools in the Toolbox are described in the following list. Some of the tools (Select Objects, Control Wizards, More Controls, and Toolbar Options) aren't used to insert controls; they are tools you use to work with controls or with the Toolbox itself.

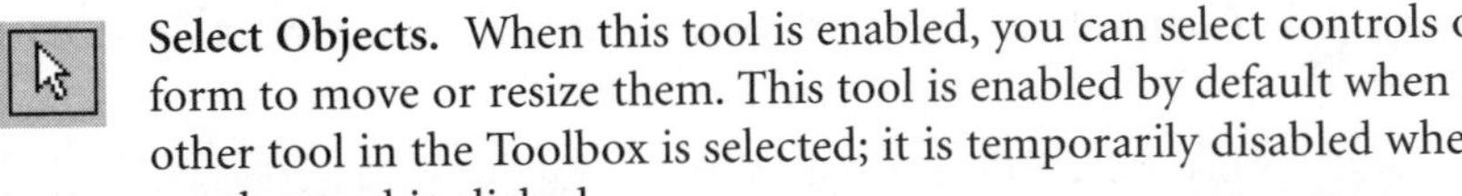

Select Objects. When this tool is enabled, you can select controls on a form to move or resize them. This tool is enabled by default when no other tool in the Toolbox is selected; it is temporarily disabled when another tool is clicked.

Control Wizards. A Control Wizard is a dialog box that guides you through the process of associating data in a table or query with a control or creating a simple event procedure for the control. Clicking this tool enables Control Wizards so that when you select a control to add to the form, the appropriate Control Wizard appears, to guide you through creating the control. The following controls have Control Wizards:

- Combo Box
- Command Button
- Label
- List Box
- Option Group
- Subform/Subreport

Label. Use this control to display descriptive text. Labels are always unbound.

Text Box. This control displays data from a field, the results of an expression, or text entered by the user.

Option Group. This control presents the user with a set of choices, only one of which can be selected at a time.

Toggle Button. When you bind a toggle button to a Yes/No field, the button is up to indicate Yes or down to indicate No.

Option Button. Use this control to indicate a choice. (A black center means that an option is selected.)

Check Box. This control also indicates a choice. (A check mark means that the item is selected.)

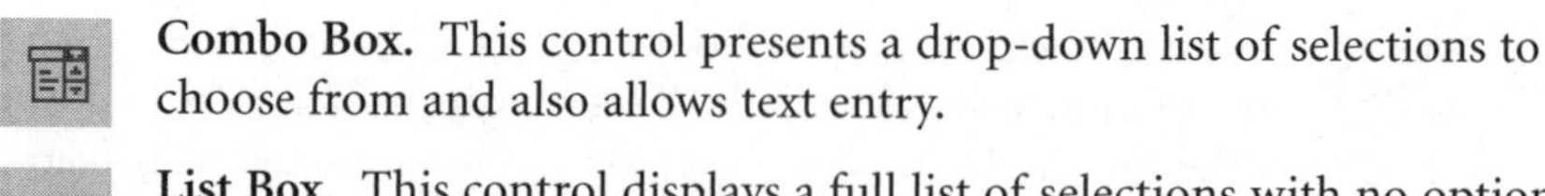

Combo Box. This control presents a drop-down list of selections to choose from and also allows text entry.

List Box. This control displays a full list of selections with no option for manual entry.

Command Button. This control performs an action by running an event procedure or a macro.

Image. This control displays an unbound image (an image that is not stored in an Access table).

Unbound Object Frame. This control displays an unbound OLE object, such as a Microsoft Excel spreadsheet.

Bound Object Frame. This control displays a bound object, such as an image stored in the form's record source.

Page Break. This control indicates a new form page.

Tab Control. This control displays information in groups, each on a tabbed page.

Subform/Subreport. This control displays information from a form, query, or table.

Line. Use this control to add a decorative line to your form.

Rectangle. Use this tool to add a decorative rectangle to your form.

More Controls. Use this tool to open a list of ActiveX controls that you can place on a form.

Toolbar Options. This tool allows you to add or remove Toolbox tools by means of a menu, shown in Figure 6-2.

> **caution** The list that you open with the More Controls tool includes all the ActiveX controls available to any applications on your computer; the list isn't limited to the controls that work on Access forms.

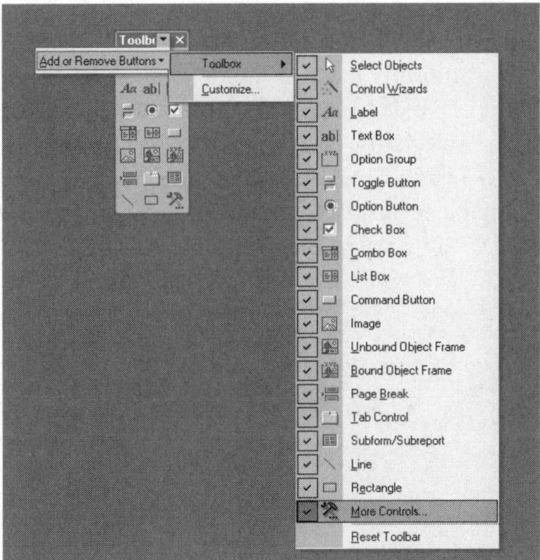

Figure 6-2. You can add or remove Toolbox tools with this menu.

Depending on your screen size and resolution, you might not be able to see all the tools in the Toolbox. If that's the case, a double chevron will appear at the bottom (or right side) of the Toolbox. Click the double chevron to see the missing tools displayed on a submenu as shown in Figure 6-3.

Figure 6-3. A submenu displays extra tools not visible on the Toolbox.

Using the Field List to Place a Control

The field list is a dialog box containing a list of the fields in the table or query that is the form's record source. You can place a control on a form manually by dragging a field from the field list. Access selects the control type based on the field type. As shown in Figure 6-4, the Current field in tblCategories (the table used as the form's record source) is a Yes/No field, so it's placed on the form as a bound check box. (This table is located in the sample Controls 2002 database on the book's CD.)

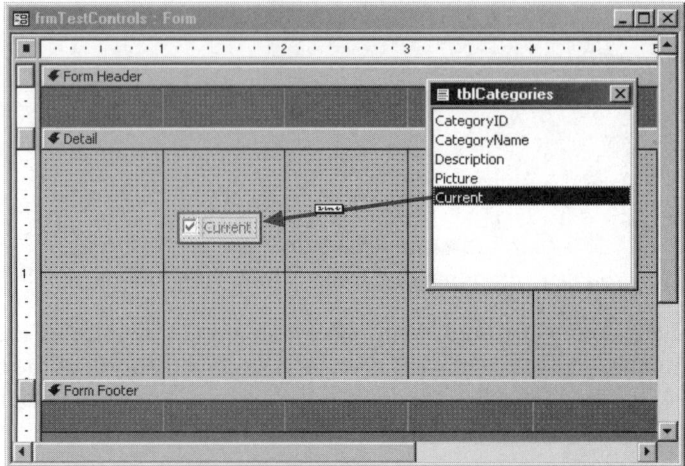

Figure 6-4. You can drag a Yes/No field from the field list to a form to create a bound check box.

tip If the field list isn't visible, press F8 to open it.

caution You can choose the specific control type for a field by clicking the appropriate tool in the Toolbox and then dragging the field from the field list. However, nothing will prevent you from creating an inappropriate control for a field, such as a check box control for a text field. Generally, it's best to let Access select the appropriate control type for fields.

Figure 6-5 shows a form with at least one of each type of control. Some controls appear in two modes: For example, the label control appears as both a stand-alone label and an attached label. Notice that the option button is also displayed in two modes: a stand-alone option button on the right side of the form and a set of option buttons in an option group on the left side of the form (frmTestControls, in the Controls 2002 database).

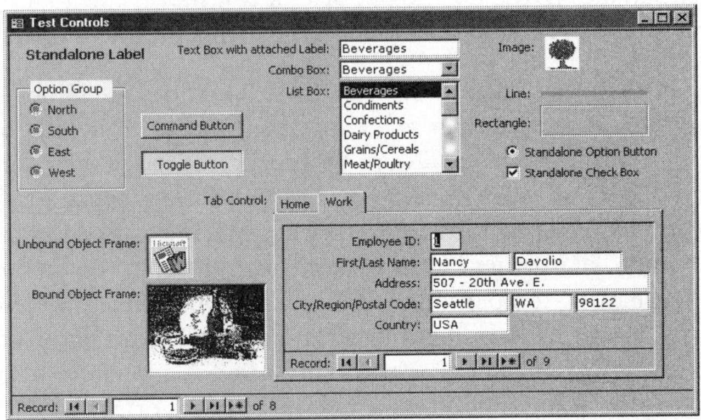

Figure 6-5. This form has at least one of each type of control.

> **tip**
>
> **Drag a group of fields**
>
> To drag all the fields in the field list to a form, double-click the field list's title bar (this highlights all the fields), and then drag the fields to the form as a group. To select more than one (but not all) fields, click the first field, and then use the Ctrl+click hot key to select the other fields (that is, press Ctrl and click to select each individual field). To select a group of contiguous fields, use the Shift+click hot key (that is, click the first field in the group and then press Shift and click on the last field to select all fields between).

> **tip**
>
> If you make a mistake in dragging or resizing a control, press Ctrl+Z immediately to undo the action.

Naming Controls

Before you start placing controls on a form, you should consider how they will be named. When you drag fields to a form, the controls are given, by default, the same names as the fields to which they are bound. For example, if you drag the LastName field to a form, the text box control that appears on the form is also called LastName. If you click a tool in the Toolbox to place a control on a form, the control appears with a name such as Frame4 (the control type with a number appended).

Problems exist with both types of default names. If a text box has the same name as its field (LastName), you might get a circular reference error (see the Troubleshooting sidebar "The control displays *#Error?* or *#Name* when I expect to see the name of the data source or the result of an expression" on page 190 for more solutions for this type of error). If a control is named Frame4, you have no clue as to what the name represents—for example, when you select a control from the drop-down control selector list on the Formatting toolbar in Design view. To avoid these problems, you might want to use the Leszynski Naming Convention (LNC) control name tags to identify controls, as listed in Table 6-2. The LNC tag is used as a prefix to a base name, which is the field name for bound fields and a descriptive word or phrase for unbound controls. Finding the option group used to select a shipper is much easier if the control is named fraShippers rather than Frame4!

For more details about using the LNC, see Chapter 20, "Customizing Your Database Using VBA Code."

Table 6-2. LNC control tags

Control	Tag
Bound Object Frame	*frb*
Check Box	*chk*
Combo Box	*cbo*
Command Button	*cmd*
Custom	*ocx*
Hyperlink	*hlk*
Image	*img*

Control	Tag
Label	*lbl*
Line	*lin*
List Box	*lst*
Option Button	*opt*
Option Group	*fra*
Page (on a tab control)	*pge*
Page Break	*brk*
Rectangle (shape)	*shp*
Subform/Subreport	*sub*
Text Box	*txt*
Toggle Button	*tgl*
Unbound Object Frame	*fru*

Access Control Name Requirements

Access imposes the following restrictions on control names:

- Control names can't be longer than 64 characters.
- Control names can't include a period (.), an exclamation point (!), a grave accent (`), or brackets ([]).
- Control names can't begin with leading spaces.
- Control names can't include ASCII characters 0 through 31 (control characters).
- Control names can't include a double quotation mark (") (for projects).

Apart from these restrictions, you can use any combination of numbers, letters and punctuation marks (including spaces). However, I recommend simplifying control names by following these guidelines:

- Keep control names to 30 characters or fewer.
- Use only letters and numbers; avoid using punctuation marks and spaces.

Shorter names allow easier selection of a control in the drop-down control selector list on the Formatting toolbar, which isn't very wide (see Figure 6-6). Avoiding punctuation marks prevents possible problems when you're working with control names in VBA code.

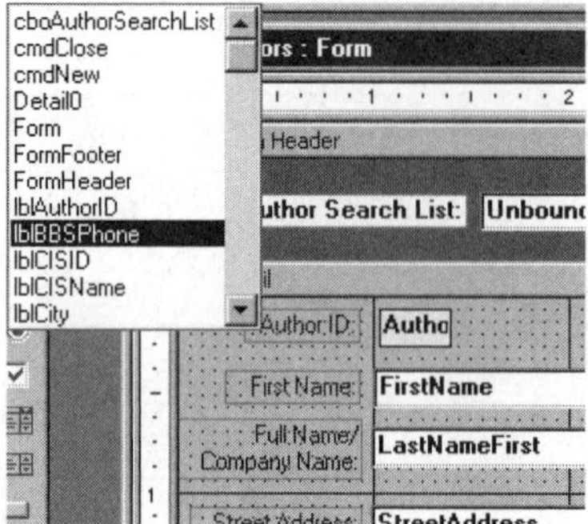

Figure 6-6. Keeping control names short makes it easier to select the appropriate control in the control selector list.

Troubleshooting

The control displays *#Error?* or *#Name* when I expect to see the name of the data source or the result of an expression

There are several possible causes for these errors:

- **Problem:** The field name in the *Control Source* property might be inaccurate, deleted from the table, or renamed.

  Solution: If this is the case, simply reselect a field from the record source, using the field list.

- **Problem:** An expression might have a syntactical error, such as a missing equal sign at the beginning or no brackets surrounding field names.

  Solution: Fix any errors in the expression, using the Expression Builder to make sure the syntax is correct.

- **Problem:** A circular reference error might have occurred because an expression refers to a field that has the same name as the control. Access itself gives bound controls the same names as their fields. If you use the Form Wizard to create a form, you can see this for yourself. For example, Figure 6-7 shows a control named AuthorID bound to the AuthorID field on a form created by the AutoForm: Tabular Wizard. A circular reference error would result if you had an expression including a reference to the Sales field as the control source of a text box named Sales.

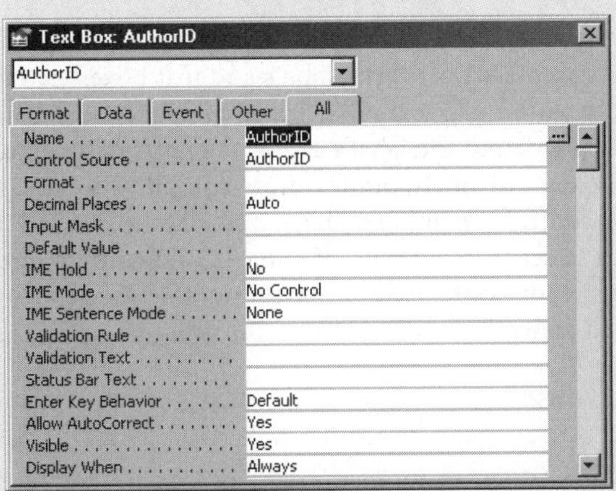

Figure 6-7. This control has the same name as its Control Source field, which could lead to confusion during development.

Solution: The easiest solution is to rename the control with the appropriate tag (for example, txtSales) so that a reference to the field name can't be confused with the control name.

The quickest way to prevent circular reference errors with control names is to run my LNC Renaming COM add-in (described in Chapter 15, "Using Add-Ins to Expand Access Functionality") to rename all controls on a form according to the LNC. Whether you use the LNC Renaming COM add-in to do the renaming or rename the controls on a form manually, using the control tags listed earlier in Table 6-2 will give you the benefits of a naming convention when working with controls.

Commonly Used Controls

Of all the controls you can place on a form, labels and text boxes lead the pack in frequency of use, generally paired as a text box with an attached label. The text box displays data from a single field, and the label's caption describes the data. Some forms might need only text boxes and labels, but for more complex display and selection of data, you can use other controls, such as an image control to display an image, an option group to allow users to select from a group of choices, or a command button to run code. The controls most commonly used on forms are described in this section; and the less commonly used controls are discussed in the following section.

Labels

You can use labels in two ways: as stand-alone labels and as attached labels. Stand-alone labels add descriptive text to a form. For example, you might use a label to identify a group of controls, as shown in the frmAuthors form in Figure 6-8, in which stand-alone labels identify groups of online IDs and telephone numbers. (You can find the frmAuthors form in the Crafts database on the companion CD.)

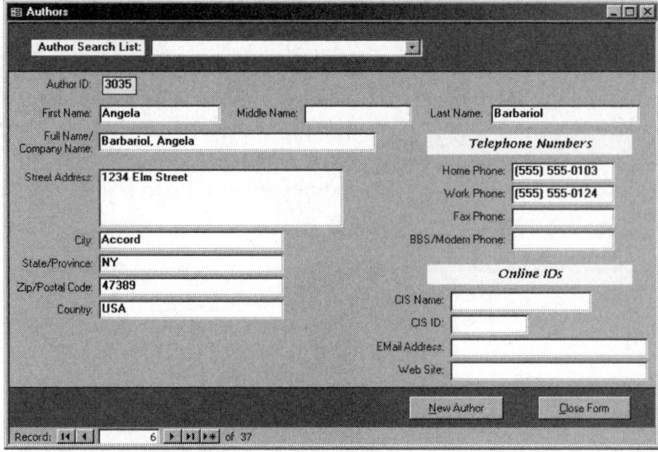

Figure 6-8. On the form shown here, stand-alone labels identify groups of controls containing information about telephone numbers and online IDs.

The frmAuthors form also contains attached labels. An attached label is linked to another control, usually a text box, combo box, or list box. When you move the parent control, the attached label control moves along with it. Each text box control on frmAuthors has an attached label control. By default, when you place a text box, combo box, or list box control on a form, it has an attached label control.

tip **Change label and text box properties in Form view**

You can experiment with changing various properties of labels and text boxes in Form view by setting the form's Allow Design Changes property to All Views. Press Alt+Enter to open the form's properties sheet in Form view. (The F4 hot key works only in Design view.)

Troubleshooting

A label or command button caption containing an ampersand isn't displayed correctly

The ampersand character is used to define a hot key. To make an ampersand appear in Form view, you must use two ampersands, as in the following label:

```
Phones && IDs
```

note **Property names**

In VBA code, property names have no spaces, while in properties sheets they may have spaces. For example, you'll see *Special Effect* in a text box properties sheet, but when referencing this property in VBA code, it is *SpecialEffect*.

Label Format Properties

You can use the *Special Effect* property to give labels and text boxes a variety of styles. Figure 6-9 illustrates the six *Special Effect* selections for labels and text boxes.

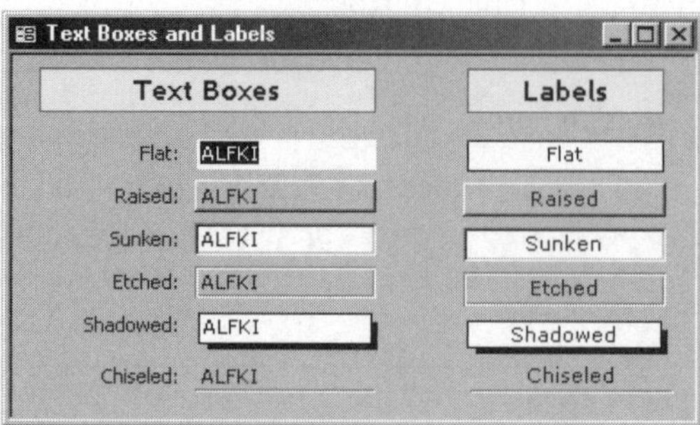

Figure 6-9. You can use the *Special Effect* property to format labels and text boxes in a variety of ways.

The format properties of labels (and text boxes) are interrelated in the following ways:

- If you set a label's *Special Effect* property to Etched or Chiseled, its *Back Style* property will be set to Transparent.
- If a label has any *Special Effect* property setting other than Flat and you set the *Border Width* property to anything other than Hairline, the *Special Effect* property will be set to Flat.
- A label with the Etched or Chiseled *Special Effect* property setting should have its *Border Style* property set to Transparent. If you set this property to Normal, the visual effect of the Etched or Chiseled style will be lost.
- If a label has any *Special Effect* property setting other than Flat and you set the *Border Style* property to anything other than Transparent, the *Special Effect* property will be set to Flat.
- Labels with the Raised *Special Effect* setting should have the *Back Style* property set to Transparent. If you set this property to Normal, the visual effect of the Raised style will be lost.

caution Although the *Border Style* property has many style selections (see Figure 6-10), you probably shouldn't use any of them except Transparent and Solid (unless you're preparing a circus poster).

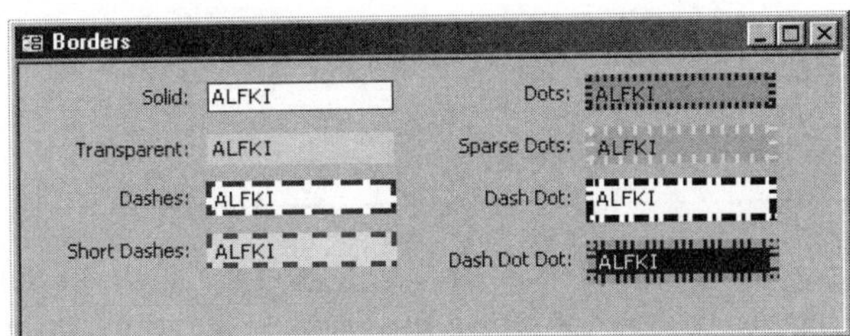

Figure 6-10. Most of the border styles are too busy for everyday use.

Text Boxes

A bound text box control displays data from the field to which it's bound; an unbound text box control can be used to accept a user entry that doesn't need to be saved in a table or (more commonly) to display the results of a calculated expression. For example, the following expression in the *Control Source* property of a text box displays the extended price for that record:

```
=[UnitPrice] * [Quantity]
```

You can dramatically change the appearance of a text box by adjusting the *Border Style*, *Border Width*, and *Special Effect* properties, just as you can modify labels. (See the section "Labels," page 192, for a list of interactions among format properties; see Figure 6-9 for illustrations.) However, just because you can apply a variety of attributes to text boxes doesn't mean you should. Shadowed, etched, or chiseled text boxes with 6-point dashed borders are distracting and give your application an amateurish look. For this reason, you might want to stick to either the Flat or Sunken special effect, white or light-colored backgrounds, and dark hairline borders, at least for business applications.

note When you select multiple controls, only the properties they all share are displayed in the *Multiple Controls* properties sheet. You have to set the other properties in each individual control's properties sheet.

Option Groups

An option group allows you to choose one of a set of alternative choices, such as a shipping method or a choice of Print, Preview, or Save To File. Each alternative is represented by an option button, a check box, or (rarely, and not recommended) a toggle button.

tip When used in an option group, toggle buttons aren't as intuitive to users as option buttons or check boxes so you probably shouldn't use them for this purpose. See the section "Toggle Buttons," page 222, for more details.

The form's user can select only one option in an option group at any time. Using an option group is a little like using the controls on a car radio—you can be tuned to only one station at a time, which is why option buttons are sometimes called radio buttons.

note Although option groups can be unbound, an unbound option group control has little use, since there is no way to respond to a choice—you might as well use a rectangle.

tip **Create option groups that allow non-exclusive multiple choices**

If you want to create a control that looks like an option group but allows multiple choices, surround a group of stand-alone check boxes with a rectangle. In this case, the check boxes are not part of an option group, and each one can be set to Yes or No separately.

Option Buttons

An option button is a small circle with a black dot in the center when selected and no dot when not selected. Within an option group, option buttons represent the choices the user can make. (Only one option button can be selected at a time.) Stand-alone option buttons work like check boxes, representing a Yes/No choice. However, users are less familiar with option buttons used as stand-alone controls, so it's better to use them only within option groups.

Check Boxes

Like option buttons, check boxes represent a Yes/No choice. Check boxes are familiar to users from paper forms, so they are the best choice for stand-alone controls used for Yes/No, True/False, or other binary choices. Check box controls also have a *TripleState* property that cycles an unbound check box control through three states instead of the usual two: Checked (True), Unchecked (False), and Dimmed (Null).

> **caution** Setting *TripleState* to Yes for a bound check box control isn't as useful as it could be because once you've checked a check box, clicking it again just clears it; you can't set the field's value to Null in the interface, nor can you set it to True again.

Combo Boxes

A combo box control has a box at the top for the user to enter text and a drop-down list for selecting an entry. This flexibility gives users a choice of typing in text or clicking a selection in the list. A combo box can be bound to a field in the form's record source; this is the field that's modified when the user makes a selection (or enters text) in the combo box.

Combo boxes also have two special properties for specifying the source of data for the drop-down list: *Row Source Type* and *Row Source*. The *Row Source Type* property of a combo box offers the following three choices, each of which determines the type of data that can be entered in the *Row Source* property:

- **Table/Query.** Lets you use a table or query from the current database (including linked tables) as the *Row Source* value. Using a table or query makes the list dynamic because it will always be up to date as records are added to or deleted from the underlying table.

newfeature!

- **Value List.** Lets you manually enter the list choices as a list of semicolon-separated values typed into the property box, such as **Regular; Preferred; Deluxe.** Value lists are handy if you want your form to present a small number of fixed choices. Value lists are required if you want to use the new *AddItem* and *RemoveItem* methods for combo boxes and text boxes.

> **See the "Paired List Boxes" section on page 210 for more details on using the *AddItem* and *RemoveItem* methods with list boxes.**

- **Field List.** Shows the fields in a table specified in the *Row Source* property. This choice is useful when you need to select a field to set up a query condition.

When you select Table/Query as the row source type and then select a table or query for the row source, only the first column in the table or query will be displayed in the combo box's list unless you change the value of the *Column Count* property to a higher number. This column will also be the bound column (the one whose value is saved to the field specified in the combo box's *Control Source* property) unless you specify a different column in the *Bound Column* property.

Troubleshooting

I can't select a value in a combo box or list box—the computer just beeps when I click on a selection in the drop-down list

If you're unable to select a value in a combo box or list box, check the following:

- Is the control source missing or misspelled?
- Are you using the correct data type? The field selected in the combo box might be the wrong data type for the field to which the combo box is bound. You can't save a text value to a numeric field, for example.

Reselect the appropriate field for the *Control Source* property, and verify that it's the correct data type for the bound column of the combo box or list box.

You have several other options for setting the row sources of combo boxes. You can click the Build button next to the *Row Source* property to open the Query Builder window and create a SQL statement to use as the source of the combo box's list. You can also assign a Data Access Objects (DAO) or ActiveX Data Objects (ADO) recordset in VBA code as a combo box's *Row Source* property.

Troubleshooting

I don't know how to reference data in a specific column of a combo box or list box

To reference a specific column in a combo box's list, use the *Column* property with a number starting at 0. For example, the following expression as a text box's control source would display the value in the second column of a combo box's list:

```
=[cboSelectAuthor].Column(1)
```

Combo boxes have many specialized uses; some of the most common uses are described in the following sections. If you aren't familiar with writing VBA code, you might want to first read Chapter 20, "Customizing Your Database Using VBA Code," and then read these sections.

Troubleshooting

I can't type a new value in a combo box, or the value I type isn't added to the list.

If you can't type a new value into a combo box, the *Limit To List* property is set to Yes. Change it to No.

When you type a value into a combo box, the value isn't automatically added to the drop-down list. You need to write an event procedure for the *NotInList* event to add the item to the list's row source.

See the section "Add-To Combo Boxes," page 202, for details about writing an event procedure to add an item to a list.

Record Selector Combo Boxes

An unbound combo box (see Figure 6-11) is often used as a record selector in the header of a form so that the user can jump to a record by selecting a name or some other distinctive field. The combo box is unbound because it isn't used to modify data; the value selected from its list is simply used in code to go to the selected record.

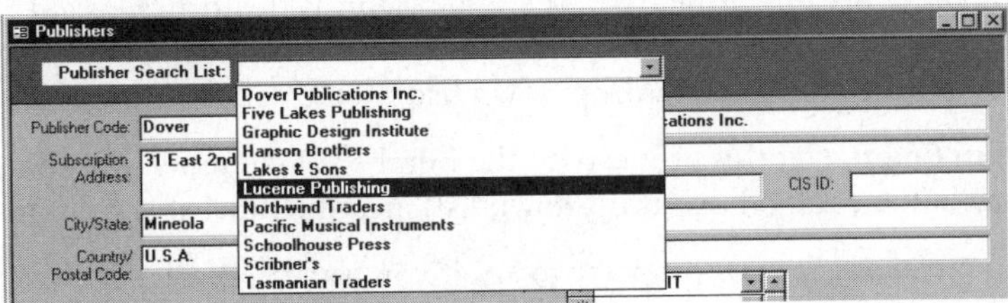

Figure 6-11. This record selector combo box is located in the header of the frmPublishers form in the Crafts database.

The sample Crafts database has a form (frmPublishers) used to enter and edit publisher data. This form has a record selector combo box in its header, to make it easier to select a specific publisher record to edit. Figure 6-12 shows the Publisher Search List combo box's properties sheet.

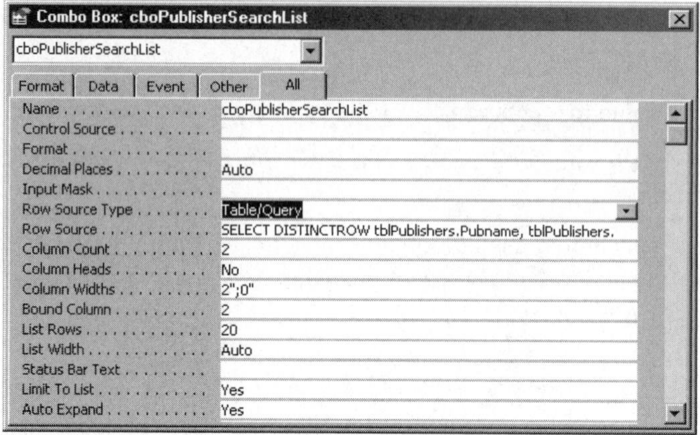

Figure 6-12. You can use the properties sheet of a record selector combo box to specify the combo box's row source and other properties.

Use the following properties to set up a record selector combo box:

- ***Row Source Type.*** Select Table/Query as the *Row Source Type* property because this property needs to be set to the same record source as the form (or to a subset of that record source).
- ***Row Source.*** Set this property to the same value as the form's *Record Source* property or to a query or an SQL statement that contains only the fields needed for the combo box's drop-down list.
- ***Column Count.*** Set this property to the number of columns you want to display in the combo box's drop-down list, including invisible columns.
- ***Column Heads.*** Set this property to Yes if you want to display the names of the fields used in the drop-down list as column headings.

- *Column Widths.* Use this property to set the width of each column in the drop-down list. Set a column to 0 to make it invisible. Often the bound column is made invisible so that the user can make a selection from the list using a more comprehensible field, such as a person's name instead of his or her employee ID.
- *Bound Column.* Use this property to specify which column is the bound column, starting with 1. Although the combo box is unbound, you still have to supply a value for this property because the code in the event procedure will pick up the value of the bound column. Set this property to the number of the column containing the ID field used to select a new record.
- *List Rows.* Use this property to set the number of rows to display in the list.
- *List Width.* Set this property to Auto to make the list the same width as the combo box control. You can set the property to a specific width if you want to make the list wider than the combo box itself. (This is often necessary when multiple columns are displayed in the list.)

The following VBA event procedure is attached to the combo box's *AfterUpdate* event:

```
Private Sub cboPublisherSearchList_AfterUpdate()

On Error GoTo ErrorHandler

    Dim strSearch As String

    strSearch = "[PublisherCode] = " & Chr$(39) & _
        Me![cboPublisherSearchList] & Chr$(39)

    'Find the record that matches the control.
    Me.Requery
    Me.RecordsetClone.FindFirst strSearch
    Me.Bookmark = Me.RecordsetClone.Bookmark

ErrorHandlerExit:
    Exit Sub

ErrorHandler:
    MsgBox "Error No: " & Err.Number & "; Description: " & _
        Err.Description
    Resume ErrorHandlerExit

End Sub
```

The search string used to locate a record by PublisherCode wraps the value from the combo box in single quotation marks (using the *Chr$(39)* function) because this field is a text field. You can omit the quotes when searching for a numeric field, as in the following equivalent line of code from the record selector combo box in frmAuthors, which searches using the AuthorID AutoNumber field:

```
strSearch = "[AuthorID] = " & Me![cboAuthorSearchList]
```

Add-To Combo Boxes

You can use an add-to combo box when you want to let users select from a list of values or add a new value to the list on the fly. If you set a combo box's *Limit To List* property to No, users can save a typed entry in the combo box's bound field if the value isn't found in the list. Those values won't be available for other users to select, however, since they aren't saved in the row source table.

If you want to let users add new entries to the table used as the row source for the combo box's list, use the combo box's *NotInList* event. Make sure that the *Limit To List* property is set to Yes (the default value). The cboCategoryName combo box on the Test Controls form in the Controls 2000 database (on the companion CD) is an add-to combo box, so you can add new categories to tblCategories. Its *NotInList* event procedure is shown here:

```
Private Sub cboCategoryName_NotInList(strNewData As String, _
    intResponse As Integer)
'Set Limit To List property to Yes.

On Error GoTo ErrorHandler

    Dim intResult As Integer
    Dim strTitle As String
    Dim intMsgDialog As Integer
    Dim strMsg1 As String
    Dim strMsg2 As String
    Dim strMsg As String
    Dim cbo As Access.ComboBox
    Dim dbs As DAO.Database
    Dim rst As DAO.Recordset
    Dim strTable As String
    Dim strEntry As String
    Dim strFieldName As String

    'The name of the lookup table
    strTable = "tblCategories"
```

```
    'The type of item to add to the table
    strEntry = "Food category"

    'The field in the lookup table in which the new entry is stored
    strFieldName = "CategoryName"

    'The add-to combo box
    Set cbo = Me![cboCategoryName]

    'Display a message box asking whether the user wants to add
    'a new entry.
    strTitle = strEntry & " not in list"
    intMsgDialog = vbYesNo + vbExclamation + vbDefaultButton1
    strMsg1 = "Do you want to add "
    strMsg2 = " as a new " & strEntry & " entry?"
    strMsg = strMsg1 + strNewData + strMsg2
    intResult = MsgBox(strMsg, intMsgDialog, strTitle)

    If intResult = vbNo Then
        'Cancel adding the new entry to the lookup table.
        intResponse = acDataErrContinue
        cbo.Undo
        Exit Sub
    ElseIf intResult = vbYes Then
        'Add a new record to the lookup table.
        Set dbs = CurrentDb
        Set rst = dbs.OpenRecordset(strTable)
        rst.AddNew
        rst(strFieldName) = strNewData
        rst.Update
        rst.Close

        'Continue without displaying default error message.
        intResponse = acDataErrAdded

     End If

ErrorHandlerExit:
    Exit Sub

ErrorHandler:
    MsgBox "Error No: " & Err.Number & "; Description: " & _
        Err.Description
    Resume ErrorHandlerExit

End Sub
```

> **note** This event procedure makes extensive use of variables, thus facilitating reuse of the code on other forms. After copying the code into the *AfterUpdate* event procedure of an unbound combo box on the new form, all you have to do is set the values of the four variables listed directly under the Declarations section of the procedure (table name, item name, field name, and combo box). The rest of the code needs no alteration.

Figure 6-13 shows the add-to combo box in action. If the user types **Vegetarian** in the text box portion of the combo box and presses Enter, the message box created in the event procedure appears. Clicking Yes adds the new entry to tblCategories; clicking No cancels the addition.

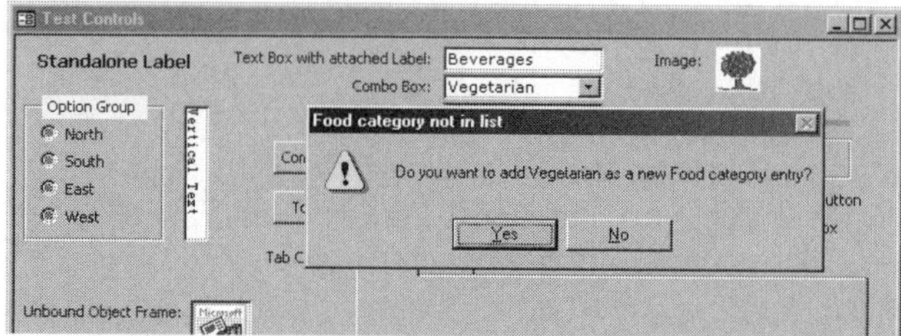

Figure 6-13. This message box pops up from a *NotInList* procedure.

Figure 6-14 shows the new entry at the bottom of the combo box's drop-down list.

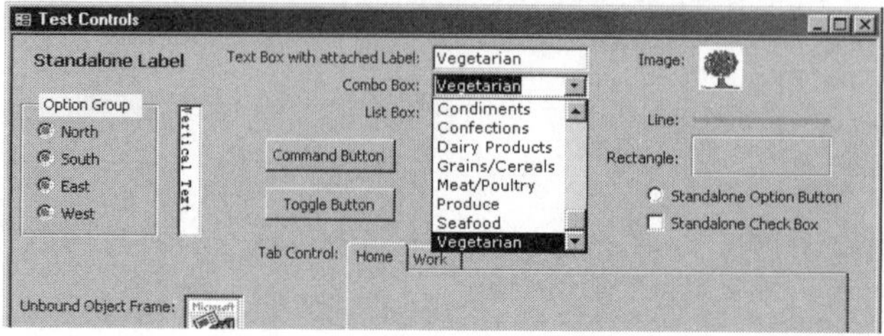

Figure 6-14. A new entry added to an add-to combo box's list looks like this.

> **note** Although a new entry is saved to the form's record source, it might not appear in the drop-down list immediately. To refresh the list, position the insertion point in the combo box, and press F9.

Linked Combo Boxes

Sometimes you need a pair of linked combo boxes to make a selection. For example, you might want to select a sales region in one combo box and then select a salesperson in a second combo box that displays only salespersons in the selected sales region. To demonstrate linked combo boxes, I created a new table (tblSalesRegions) in the Controls 2002 database, and added a SalesRegion field to tblEmployees (a copy of the Northwind Employees table). Then I entered a SalesRegion value for each employee, selecting the values from tblSalesRegions. I then created a form (frmLinkedControls) containing two combo box controls: cboSalesRegion and cboSalesperson.

The row source of cboSalesRegion is set to tblSalesRegions; cboSalesperson's row source is initially set to tblEmployees. To limit cboSalesperson's list to only employees attached to the region selected in cboSalesRegion, I added the following criterion to the Region field in cboSalesperson's *Row Source* SQL statement, as follows:

```
Forms![frmLinkedControls]![cboSalesRegion]
```

I also created an expression to display the employee's full name, last name first, in the column to be displayed in the drop-down list. The complete SQL statement for the combo box's *Row Source* property is shown here:

```
SELECT tblEmployees.EmployeeID, [LastName] & ", " & [FirstName]
AS FullName
FROM tblEmployees
WHERE (((tblEmployees.SalesRegion)=
    Forms!frmLinkedControls![cboSalesRegion]));
```

The first column in the SELECT statement contains EmployeeID, which isn't displayed in the drop-down list. (Its width is set to 0.) The EmployeeID field is the one you'd normally use to work with an employee record in a real application because it's the key field for the table.

One final touch is needed: an *AfterUpdate* event procedure on cboSalesRegion with a statement to set the cboSalesperson value to Null to clear the combo box and a *Requery* statement to repopulate it. This step ensures that cboSalesperson will always be filtered for the correct sales region. This event procedure is shown here:

```
Private Sub cboSalesRegion_AfterUpdate()

    Me![cboSalesperson] = Null
    Me![cboSalesperson].Requery

End Sub
```

Figure 6-15 shows the cboSalesperson combo box, listing employees from the Southeast sales region.

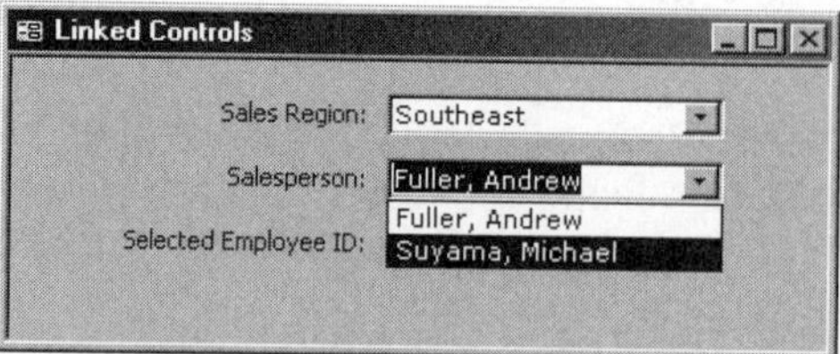

Figure 6-15. The second combo box in a pair of linked combo boxes displays information filtered by the selection in the first combo box.

Display a Bound Column Value in a Combo Box

You can use an unbound text box to display the value of a bound column in a combo box. (This value is often not displayed in the drop-down list.) The syntax requires you to use an equal sign (=) in front of the control name, which is enclosed in brackets. The employee ID of the selected employee is displayed in a locked text box on the form, as shown in Figure 6-16.

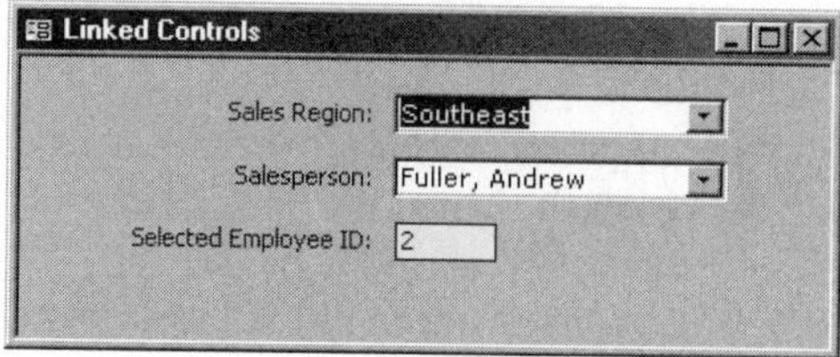

Figure 6-16. This text box displays the employee ID of the employee selected in the Salesperson combo box.

The text box's row source is shown here:

```
=[cboSalesperson]
```

List Boxes

List boxes are similar to combo boxes in that they display a list of items from a table, a value list, or a record source assigned in code. However, list boxes don't offer the opportunity to add a new entry, and they take up more space than combo boxes because they display multiple items at once. Generally speaking, combo boxes are more useful than list boxes for selecting one item from a number of items on a form, but list boxes can be useful for selecting one of a small number of choices or for special purposes such as those discussed in the following sections.

Multiple-Selection List Boxes

When you need to select several entries from a list and perform the same action on all of them, a multiple-selection list box (sometimes called a multiselect list box) is an excellent choice. Multiple-selection list boxes are especially useful on Access forms because Access has an *ItemsSelected* collection that you can use to process just the items selected in the list box.

To create a multiple-selection list box, place a list box on a form and set its *MultiSelect* property to Extended; this allows you to select items by using the Ctrl+click and Shift+click hot keys.

The following example uses the frmMultiSelectListBox form from the Controls 2002 database. Figure 6-17 shows a multiple-selection list box with several items selected; clicking Print Labels runs a procedure that clears the temporary table tblContactsForLabels and then fills it with just the selected records from tblContacts. (You need to save the selected items to a table to use as the report's record source because an *ItemsSelected* collection can't be used directly as a report's record source.)

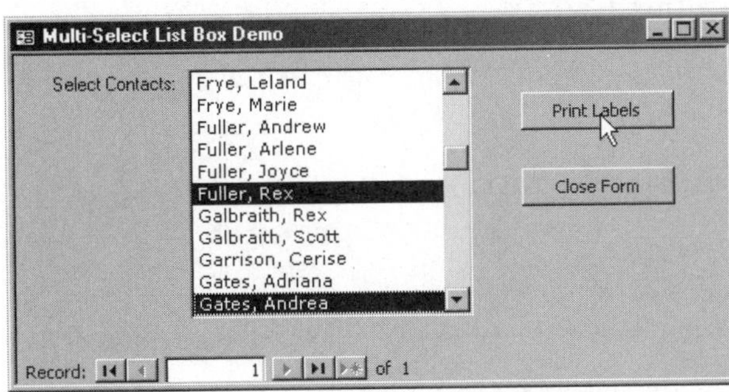

Figure 6-17. This list box has its *MultiSelect* property set to Extended.

The rptContactLabels report (which is bound to tblContactsForLabels) then opens in Print Preview, as shown in Figure 6-18.

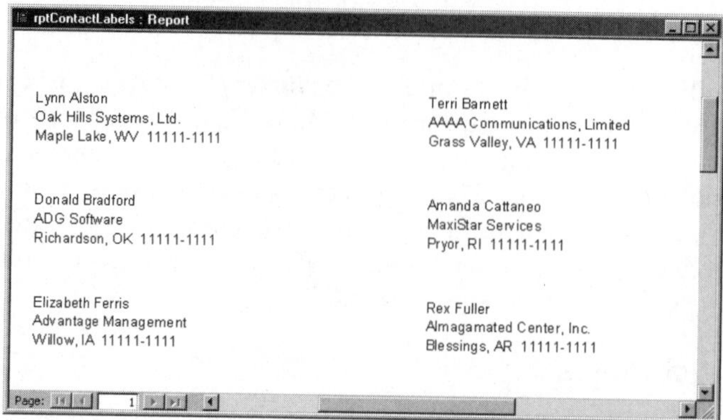

Figure 6-18. This report is based on selections from a multiple-selection list box.

The *Click* event procedure for the cmdPrintLabels command button is shown here:

```
Private Sub cmdPrintLabels_Click()

On Error GoTo ErrorHandler

    Dim lst As Access.ListBox
    Dim strName As String
    Dim strAddress As String
    Dim strJobTitle As String
    Dim strTestFile As String
    Dim varItem As Variant
    Dim intIndex As Integer
    Dim intCount As Integer
    Dim intRow As Integer
    Dim intColumn As Integer
    Dim strTest As String
    Dim i As String
    Dim lngID As Long

    Set lst = Me![lstSelectContacts]

    'Clear old temp table.
    DoCmd.SetWarnings False
    strSQL = "DELETE * from tblContactsForLabels"
    DoCmd.RunSQL strSQL

    'Check that at least one contact has been selected.
    If lst.ItemsSelected.Count = 0 Then
       MsgBox "Please select at least one contact."
       lst.SetFocus
       Exit Sub
    End If
```

```
    For Each varItem In lst.ItemsSelected
        'Check for required address information.
        strTest = Nz(lst.Column(5, varItem))
        Debug.Print "Street address: " & strTest
        If strTest = "" Then
            Debug.Print "Can't send letter -- no street address!"
            Exit Sub
        End If

        strTest = Nz(lst.Column(6, varItem))
        Debug.Print "City: " & strTest
        If strTest = "" Then
            Debug.Print "Can't send letter -- no city!"
            Exit Sub
        End If

        strTest = Nz(lst.Column(8, varItem))
        Debug.Print "Postal code: " & strTest
        If strTest = "" Then
            Debug.Print "Can't send letter -- no postal code!"
            Exit Sub
        End If

        'All information is present; write a record to the temp table.
        lngID = lst.Column(0, varItem)
        Debug.Print "Selected ID: " & lngID
        strSQL = "INSERT INTO tblContactsForLabels (ContactID, 
            & "FirstName, LastName, Salutation, StreetAddress, " _
            & "City, StateOrProvince, " _
            & "PostalCode, Country, CompanyName, JobTitle )" _
            & "SELECT ContactID, FirstName, LastName, Salutation, " _
            & "StreetAddress, City, StateOrProvince, PostalCode, " _
            & "Country, CompanyName, JobTitle FROM tblContacts " _
            & "WHERE ContactID = " & lngID & ";"
        DoCmd.RunSQL strSQL
    Next varItem

    'Print report.
    DoCmd.OpenReport reportname:="rptContactLabels", _
        View:=acViewPreview

ErrorHandlerExit:
    Exit Sub

ErrorHandler:
    MsgBox "Error No: " & Err.Number & "; Description: " & _
        Err.Description
    Resume ErrorHandlerExit

End Sub
```

Paired List Boxes

If you've used the Form Wizard or the Report Wizard, you've seen paired list boxes. Paired list boxes allow the user to select from a number of items in a list and add them to a list of choices. Some users find this method more intuitive than using a multiple-selection list box because all the selected items are displayed together in their own list box. Figure 6-19 shows the first screen of the Report Wizard; the Available Fields list box is loaded with a list of all the fields in the selected table or query. As you select fields, they're removed from that list box and moved to the Selected Fields list box.

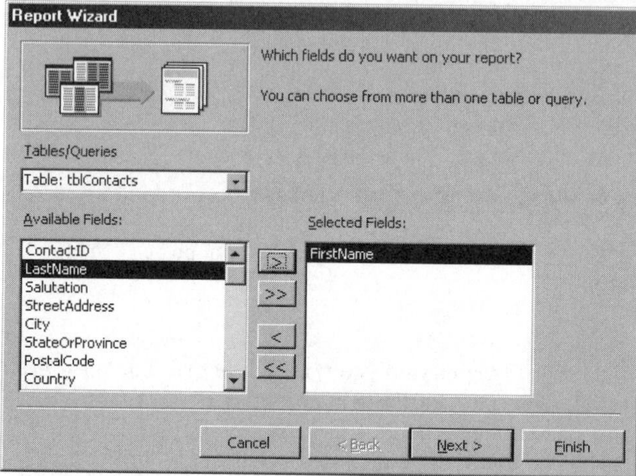

Figure 6-19. These paired list boxes are shown on the first page of the Report Wizard.

Implementation of paired list boxes is easier than ever in Access 2002 because you can use the new *RemoveItem* and *AddItem* methods to streamline the process of moving an item from one list box to another.

To create a set of paired list boxes, follow these steps (the finished form, frmPairedListboxes, is located in the Controls 2002 sample database):

1. Place two list boxes on a form. One will be an Available Items list box, and the other will be a Selected Items list box.
2. Set the *Row Source Type* property for the Available Items list box to Value List.
3. Enter the list values in the *Row Source* property for the Available Items list box by using a semicolon-separated string such as this one:

   ```
   "Beverages";"Condiments";"Confections";"Dairy Products";
   "Grains/Cereals";"Meat/Poultry";"Produce";"Seafood"
   ```

   The Selected Items list box should also have its *Row Source Type* property set to Value List. Leave its *Row Source* property blank.

note The *AddItem* and *RemoveItem* methods work only for value lists.

You can create a set of paired multiple-selection list boxes if you use a table as the row source, but for this example I wanted to use the new *AddItem* and *RemoveItem* methods, and the multiple selection was lost after I tested removing an item from the Available Items list, as a user would do. Because the multiple-selection feature lost its usefulness, I made the paired list boxes on the form shown in Figure 6-20 single-selection list boxes.

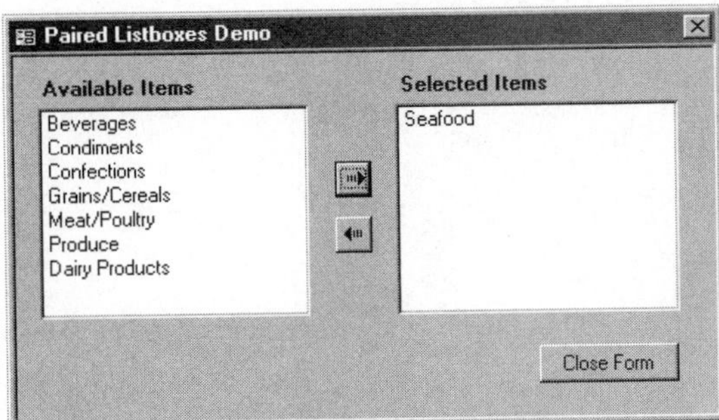

Figure 6-20. This form contains paired list boxes, which use the *AddItem* and *RemoveItem* methods to add or delete list items.

InsideOut

When you use the *AddItem* method to add values to a list box, the values are normally added at the end of the list. Although you can add an item at a particular location (by using its Index number), you won't have a way to sort the list alphabetically. If you need paired list boxes in which the second list is always sorted correctly, you need to use tables or queries as the list box row sources and append and delete queries to add or remove items.

Command Buttons

Typically, you'll use command buttons to run code to perform an action, adding the code to the command button's *Click* event procedure. The command buttons in the paired list boxes form shown in Figure 6-20 run the procedures that remove the selected item from the Available Items list box and add it to the Selected Items list box. These procedures are listed here, along with the variables declared in the form module's Declarations section:

```
Dim lstAvailable As Access.ListBox
Dim lstSelected As Access.ListBox
Dim strItem As String
Dim intItem As Integer
Dim varItem As Variant
Dim intIndex As Integer
Dim intCount As Integer
Dim intRow As Integer
Dim intColumn As Integer

Private Sub cmdAdd_Click()

On Error GoTo ErrorHandler

    Set lstSelected = Me![lstSelectedItemsSingle]
    Set lstAvailable = Me![lstAvailableItemsSingle]

    'Check that at least one item has been selected.
    Debug.Print "Item count: " & lstAvailable.ItemsSelected.Count
    If lstAvailable.ItemsSelected.Count = 0 Then
        MsgBox "Please select an item."
        lstAvailable.SetFocus
        Exit Sub
    End If

    strItem = lstAvailable.Value
    intItem = lstAvailable.ListIndex
```

```
    'Add selected item to Selected Items list.
    lstSelected.AddItem Item:=strItem

    'Delete selected item from Available Items list.
    lstAvailable.RemoveItem Index:=intItem

ErrorHandlerExit:
    Exit Sub

ErrorHandler:
    MsgBox "Error No: " & Err.Number & "; Description: " & _
        Err.Description
    Resume ErrorHandlerExit

End Sub


Private Sub cmdRemove_Click()

On Error GoTo ErrorHandler

    Set lstSelected = Me![lstSelectedItemsSingle]
    Set lstAvailable = Me![lstAvailableItemsSingle]

    'Check that at least one item has been selected.
    If lstSelected.ItemsSelected.Count = 0 Then
        MsgBox "Please select an item"
        lstSelected.SetFocus
        Exit Sub
    End If

    strItem = lstSelected.Value
    intItem = lstSelected.ListIndex

    'Add selected item to Available Items list.
    lstAvailable.AddItem Item:=strItem

    'Delete selected item from Selected Items list.
    lstSelected.RemoveItem Index:=intItem

ErrorHandlerExit:
    Exit Sub

ErrorHandler:
    MsgBox "Error No: " & Err.Number & "; Description: " & _
        Err.Description
    Resume ErrorHandlerExit

End Sub
```

Tabs

Tab controls allow you to manage large quantities of data on a form without crowding controls together or creating a difficult-to-navigate multipage form. You can use a tab control in two ways: to divide the controls from a single record source into groups, displaying one group of controls on each page of the tab control, or to display data from different tables or queries on each page by using subforms, one subform per page of the tab control.

note Properly speaking, the tabs on a Tab control (or any tabbed dialog box) are the protruding bits with captions at the top of each page; however, in ordinary usage, "tab" is often used to reference the entire page. When writing VBA code, you must use Page since each page on a Tab control is a Page object.

The Northwind Employees form uses a tab control with two pages to split data from the Employees table into Company Info and Personal Info groups, as shown in Figure 6-21.

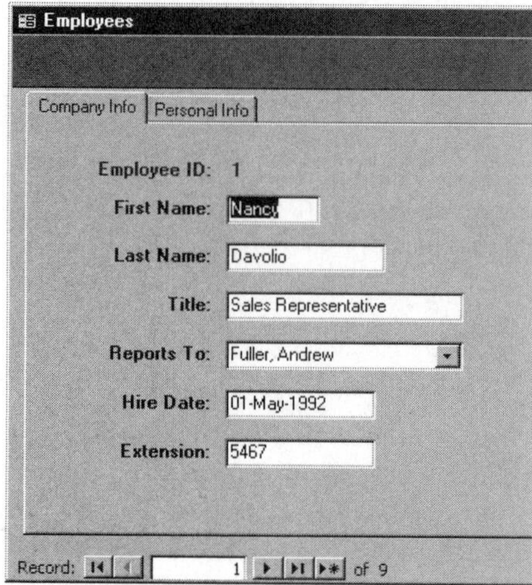

Figure 6-21. The Northwind Employees form uses a tab control to divide employee data into two groups.

When the data for all the pages of a tab control comes from the same record source, all you need to do is place controls bound to fields in the record source on the appropriate pages of the tab control in Design view, as shown in Figure 6-22.

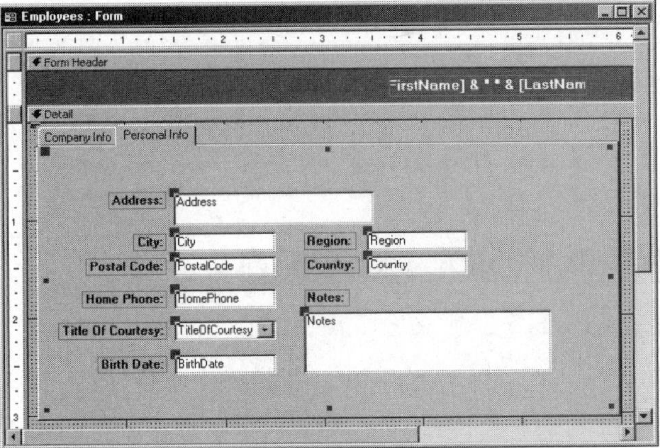

Figure 6-22. These controls (and those on the Company Info page) are bound to fields in the Employees table (the record source for the Northwind Employees form).

You can also use another technique: Place a subform bound to a different record source on each page of the tab control. This technique is illustrated in the fpriBooksAndVideos form in the sample Crafts 2002 database, shown in Figure 6-23. The tab control at the bottom of the detail section of this form has three pages, each of which contains a subform control bound to a different table.

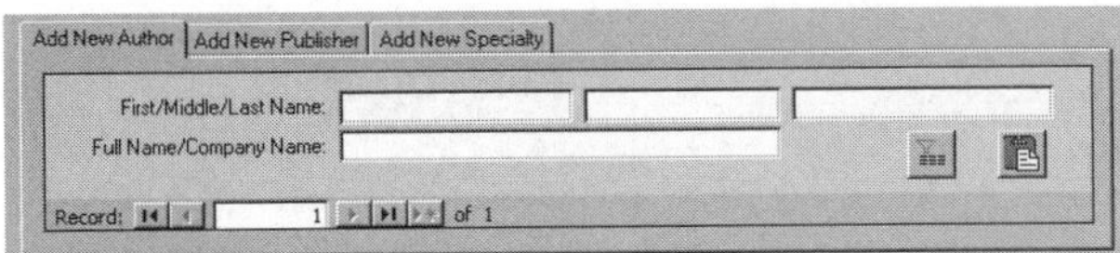

Figure 6-23. This tab control on the Crafts fpriBooksAndVideos form has a subform on each page.

Tab Control Techniques

Working with tab controls can be a little tricky. Here are some special techniques:

- If you want to set the focus on a tab control so that you can move it or resize it, click the blank gray area to the right of the tabs at the top of the tab control.
- If you want to place a control on a specific page of a tab control, click the tab belonging to that page. Black squares will appear around the page, as shown in Figure 6-24.

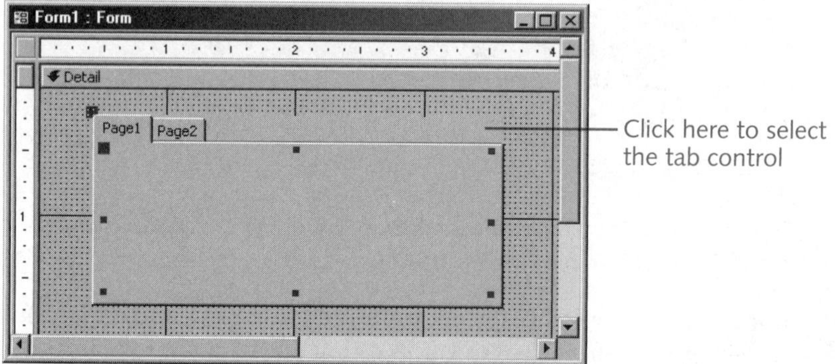

Figure 6-24. Page1 is selected on this tab control.

After clicking the tab, drag a field to the page from the field list. The page turns black when the field is positioned over it, as shown in Figure 6-25.

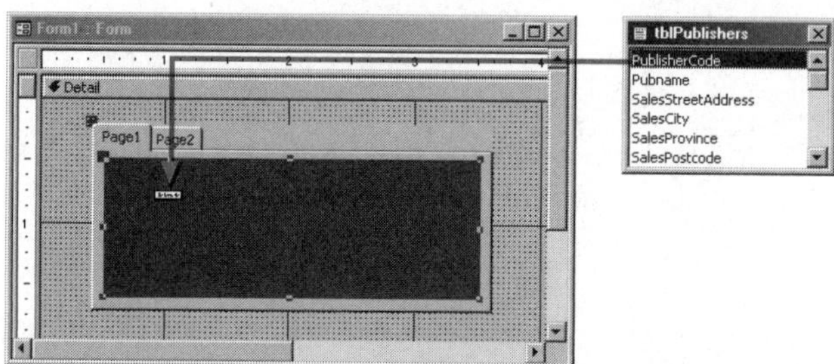

Figure 6-25. You can drag a field to a page of a tab control.

For further details on working with controls, see Chapter 8, "Using Design Tools."

Subforms/Subreports

The subform/subreport control (usually called a subform control when it's used on forms) can display data from a variety of source objects, such as other forms, tables, or queries (or reports, only when this control is placed on a report). Typically, subform controls are used to display data from other forms because a subform whose source object is another form (as opposed to a table or query) gives you more control over what data is displayed and how it's displayed.

Figure 6-26 shows the Source Object drop-down list for a subform control. The list displays forms first (without a prefix), then tables, and then queries.

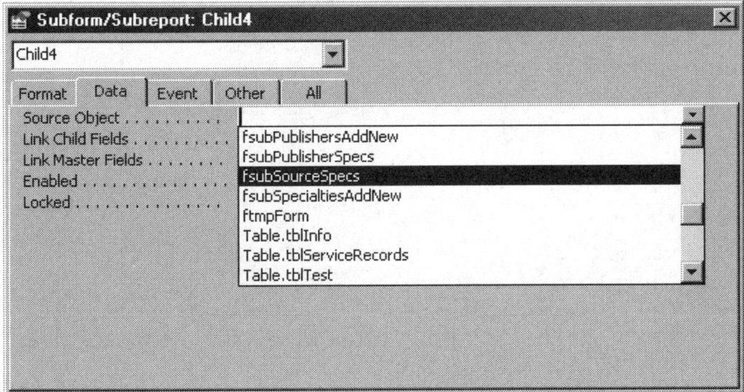

Figure 6-26. You can select a source object for a subform control from the Source Object drop-down list.

note If you use a naming convention and give a distinctive prefix to forms intended for use as subforms, those forms will be easy to identify in the Source Object drop-down list. I use the *fsub* tag for these forms, in accordance with the LNC. See Chapter 20, "Customizing Your Database Using VBA Code," for more information about using a naming convention in Access databases.

Although normally it's best to use subform controls to display forms, in one situation displaying a table might be appropriate: If you want a datasheet-type subform with a working subdatasheet, you must select a table as a subform's source object; a datasheet form used as the source object of a subform control doesn't have the extra column with the plus signs used to open up a subdatasheet displaying data from the linked table. Figure 6-27 shows a form bound to tblEmployees, with a subform control whose source object is tblOrders. You can find this form in the Controls 2002 database. Clicking the plus sign to the left of an order record opens a subdatasheet that shows the order details for that order.

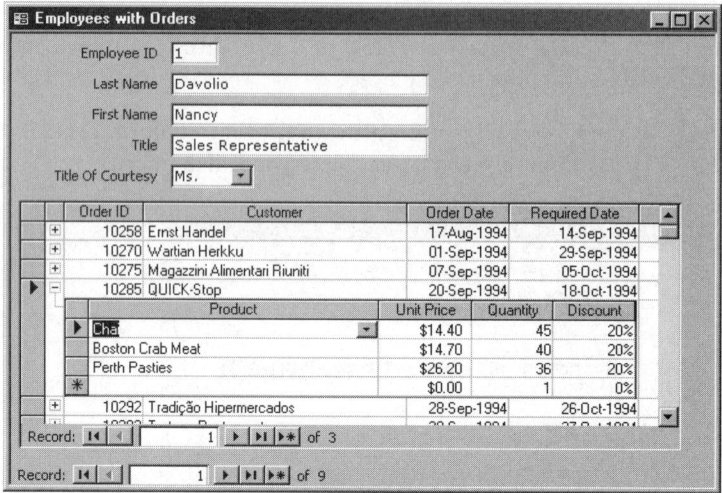

Figure 6-27. This form has a subform bound to a table with a subdatasheet.

> **tip** If you create an AutoForm based on a table that is the "one" side of a one-to-many relationship, use a subform control to place the "many" table on the form.

For more information about using subforms to display both linked and unlinked data on forms, see Chapter 5, "Creating Forms for Entering, Editing, and Viewing Data."

Lines

As the name suggests, you use line controls to place lines on forms, usually to separate areas containing different types of controls. In general, lines are more commonly used on reports than on forms, but they can be useful on forms too, especially to separate controls into groups. A line can be vertical, horizontal, or slanted.

You can apply various special effects to lines, but these effects don't work the same for lines as they do for text boxes and other controls that have the *Special Effect* property. The Flat *Special Effect* property (the default setting) renders the line as an ordinary line. The *Border Width* settings are fairly self-explanatory: The line appears hair-thin if you select the Hairline setting and quite thick if you select the maximum setting of 6 points. You can also select a line color from the regular palette for the *Border Color* property.

As shown in Figure 6-28, the six line controls on the right side of the Lines And Rectangles form all have a *Border Width* of 6 points and a *Border Color* of bright blue; they differ only in the *Special Effect* property. The Raised, Sunken, Etched, Shadowed, and Chiseled lines do not display their *Border Width* or *Border Color* property selection, and therefore, they look exactly the same.

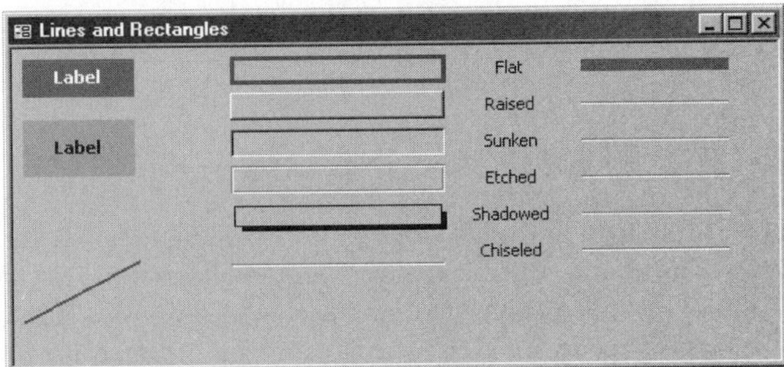

Figure 6-28. This form contains lines and rectangles that display various *Special Effect* settings.

> **caution** Avoid using rectangles with the Raised special effect—a raised rectangle looks just like a command button and will probably confuse users who expect something to happen when they click it.

Rectangles

Rectangles can be solid or transparent, and they have the same *Border Style* and *Special Effect* property selections as lines. However, unlike lines, the six *Special Effect* choices for rectangles all look different, as you can see in Figure 6-28. Prior to Access 2000, it wasn't possible to adjust the margins around a label's caption, so placing a label with a transparent background on top of a solid rectangle was the only way to have text centered in a colored rectangle. Now, however, you can use the *Top Margin* and *Bottom Margin* properties of a label or text box control to manually adjust text to a vertically centered position.

caution If a rectangle has a *Special Effect* property set to anything other than Flat or Shadowed and you set its *Border Width* property to a value wider than Hairline, its *Special Effect* property will change to Flat.

The blue rectangle with the white text in the upper left corner of the form shown in Figure 6-28 is a label within a rectangle; the pink rectangle with black text below is a label with its *Top Margin* and *Bottom Margin* properties set to **0.1"**. Setting the *Left Margin* and *Right Margin* properties isn't necessary; instead, set the *Text Align* property to Centered to center the label text horizontally.

Less Frequently Used Controls

Although the controls described in the previous sections will be the ones you use most often on forms, other controls are available that can be useful for special circumstances, such as when you want to display an image or an Excel worksheet on a form or when you need to create a multipage form. These special controls are described in the following sections.

Images

You can use the image control to display an image on a form. Since this control can't be bound, the image will be the same on every record displayed on a form. You might use this control to place decorative art or a company logo on a form.

Unbound Object Frames

An unbound object frame can display a variety of objects, such as Excel worksheets, Microsoft Word documents, and images. Don't use the unbound object frame to place an image on a form—the image control is better for that. However, if you need to display another type of object on all records of a form, use the unbound object frame.

Bound Object Frames

A bound object frame displays an object (such as a Word document or an image) stored in an OLE Object field in a form's record source. This control displays different content on different records. The Northwind Categories form uses a bound object frame control to display images of the food categories, as shown in Figure 6-29.

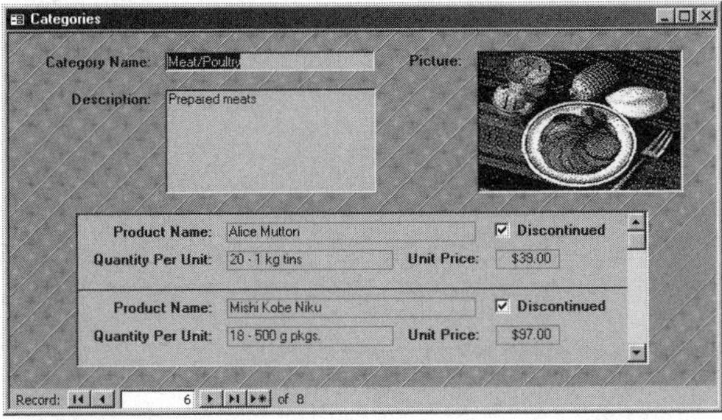

Figure 6-29. A bound object frame control displays an image on the Northwind Categories form.

InsideOut

Storing OLE data in fields in a table can use an enormous amount of space in your database. To save space, consider alternative techniques, such as using hyperlink fields to open Word documents or Excel worksheets or assigning an image field to the *Picture* property of an image control. Refer to the Employees form in the sample Northwind database for an example of this technique. In the Employees form, only the path to the image is stored in the database; the image file itself is retrieved in the form's *Current* event. The files are stored in the \Program Files\Microsoft Office\Office10\Samples folder by default, which means that the code won't work if the images are moved—this potential pitfall should be a consideration when using this technique.

Toggle Buttons

The toggle button control (like a check box or an option button) represents a Yes/No or True/False value. In contrast with those other controls, however, what the different states of the toggle button represent is by no means obvious to users. In addition, the toggle button is likely to be confused with a command button because of its similar appearance.

Although you can painstakingly explain to users that a depressed toggle button control means No and a raised toggle button control means Yes, using a check box control to represent a Yes/No value is much more intuitive—everybody knows what that means.

Page Breaks

The page break control indicates where a new form page begins. In Access 1.0 and 1.1 (before the introduction of an early version of the tab control in Access 2.0), multipage forms were the only way to manage a lot of controls on a form. However, the tab control offers a more elegant (and efficient) way to handle groups of controls, so you should use it instead of the page break control.

See the section "Tabs," page 214, for a discussion of using tab controls to display large amounts of data on a form.

Setting Control Properties

Controls (especially those that display text, such as text box controls) have an enormous number of properties. For the most part, you won't need to change control properties except for those related to size, position, font, and color. See Appendix F, "Control Properties," for a list of the control properties and the controls they apply to. Some properties significant for various types of controls are discussed in this chapter, and the most commonly used properties are described in the next section. For more information about a control property (including some obscure properties not described in detail in this book), position the insertion point in the property box of the properties sheet and press F1 to open context-specific Help.

Commonly Used Properties

As you gain experience working with controls, you'll notice that you use some properties more than others. The following list introduces a number of the most common control properties, with a brief description of their function.

- ***Back Color.*** Sets the control's background color.
- ***Back Style.*** Specifies whether a control is opaque or transparent.
- ***Border Color.*** Sets the color of the control's border.
- ***Border Style.*** Sets the style of the control's border.
- ***Border Width.*** Sets the width of the control's border.
- ***Bottom Margin, Left Margin, Right Margin, Top Margin.*** Set the amount of space between the bottom, left, right, or top edge of the control and the text it displays.
- ***Bound Column.*** Sets the column of a combo box or list box that is bound to a data field.
- ***Caption.*** Sets the text displayed on a control.
- ***Column Count.*** Sets the number of columns in a combo box or list box.
- ***Column Heads.*** Specifies whether to show column headings in a combo box or list box.
- ***Column Widths.*** Sets the width of columns in a combo box or list box.
- ***Control Source.*** Sets the field to which a control is bound.
- ***ControlTip Text.*** Specifies the text displayed in a control's control tip.
- ***Decimal Places.*** Sets the number of decimal places (for a numeric field).
- ***Default Value.*** Sets default value for the field.
- ***Enabled.*** Specifies whether the control is available for use. The control is unavailable if *Enabled* is set to No.

- ***Font Name, Font Size, Font Weight, Font Italic, Font Underline.*** Specify the properties of the font used for text displayed in the control.
- ***Fore Color.*** Sets the color of text displayed in a control.
- ***Format.*** Sets the format to apply to text displayed in a control.
- ***Height, Width.*** Set the width or height of a control.
- ***Hyperlink Address, Hyperlink SubAddress.*** Specify hyperlink address components.
- ***Left, Top.*** Set the left or top position of a control.
- ***Line Spacing.*** Sets the spacing between lines of text displayed in a control.
- ***Option Value.*** Sets the numeric value to save to the option group's bound field when an option button is selected.
- ***Picture.*** Sets the image to display on a control.
- ***Row Source.*** Sets the source of data for rows in a combo box or list box.
- ***Row Source Type.*** Sets the type of row source.
- ***Source Object.*** Sets the source document to display in a subform control.
- ***Special Effect.*** Sets the style for a control (Raised, Sunken, and so on).
- ***Text Align.*** Sets the alignment (Left, Center, Right) of text displayed in a control.
- ***Vertical.*** Controls whether text in a control is displayed vertically.
- ***Visible.*** Controls whether a control is visible.

Working with ActiveX Controls

ActiveX controls supplement the standard controls provided with Access. The DateTimePicker control, for example, pops up a small calendar for selecting a date. Ideally, an ActiveX control should work equally well in all Microsoft Office applications, but that's not always the case; you can't assume that an ActiveX control that works in Microsoft Outlook or Excel will work in Access (or vice versa). Additionally, some ActiveX controls have properties or methods that don't work in all Office applications or that work on Visual Basic forms but not on Office or Access forms. This means that when you want to use an ActiveX control on an Access form, you might have to experiment to find out whether the control works, or which of its properties, methods, and events are functional on an Access form.

InsideOut

If you look up Help for an ActiveX control in the MSDN Library (either using the MSDN CD or online), be aware that as you click links, you might be transported into Help topics that are part of the Visual Basic or Microsoft Visual C++ documentation, leaving you wondering why the code examples look strange and the Help text refers to properties that aren't there when you look at the control's properties sheet on an Access form. Note the Help book listed in the Location column—it usually gives you a clue about the context of the topic. If you aren't in the Office or Microsoft Office XP Developer documentation anymore, be careful! What you read might not apply to using the ActiveX control in Access.

One ActiveX control is included with Access—the Calendar control. The Calendar control is described in the section "Using ActiveX Controls to Add Functionality to Forms," page 228.

Using Controls from Office XP Developer

The Microsoft Office XP Developer edition of Office XP includes a set of ActiveX controls to supplement those provided with Office Premium. Some of these controls can be bound to data, although not by the usual Access method of selecting a data source from a *Record Source*, *Row Source*, or *Control Source* property. Instead, the Office XP Developer controls must be bound to data in VBA code. The Office XP Developer ActiveX controls are listed in Table 6-3, with the data-bound controls indicated by an asterisk.

Table 6-3. Office XP Developer ActiveX controls

Control	Description
*ADO Data Control	Binds to data in a table or other data source. Used to supply data to other controls.
Common Dialog	Displays one of several Microsoft Windows dialog boxes, such as the File Open and Colors dialog boxes.
Chart Control	Displays data in a chart format, similar to an Excel chart.
*Data Report	Used with the Data Report Designer to place fields of data on a report.
*DataCombo	Displays a data-bound combo box.
*DataGrid	Displays a data-bound datasheet.
*DataList	Displays a data-bound list box.
*Hierarchical Flexgrid	Displays data from linked tables, similar to the new subdatasheet feature in Access.
ImageCombo	Similar to a combo box except that you can include images with the list items.
ImageList	Stores a list of images that can be displayed in other controls, such as the TreeView control.
Internet Transfer	Lets you connect to Web sites and FTP sites.

Control	Description
ListView	Displays data as ListItem objects, which can have an associated icon. Can be used to display an expanded view of a TreeView control node.
ProgressBar	Graphically represents the progress of a transaction.
Rich Textbox	Displays rich text, that is, text with color, emphasis, and different fonts.
Slider	Displays a bar with a "thumb" control (similar to a Windows scroll bar). The user moves the thumb to adjust a value.
StatusBar	Displays information about the status of various application components.
SysInfo	Detects system events such as desktop resizing or resolution changes. Can also display operating system or version information.
Tabbed Dialog	Presents several pages of information with tabs for selecting a page.
TabStrip	Displays a strip of tabs used to define multiple pages for a window or dialog box.
ToolBar	Contains a collection of buttons used to create a toolbar for an application.
TreeView	Displays data in a hierarchical tree, like Windows Explorer.
UpDown	Increments or decrements a number. (This control is used in many of the built-in Windows and Office dialog boxes.)
Winsock	Lets you connect to a remote computer using either the UDP or TCP protocol.

tip **Find the controls that will work on Access forms**

To winnow out the ActiveX controls that will actually work in Access from the hundreds of controls listed in the list opened from the More Controls tool in the Toolbox, look for controls that start with the word *Microsoft* and end with the identifier *v. 6.0*, possibly with either the *(OLE DB)* or *(SP4)* qualifier.

In addition to the Calendar control provided with Access itself and the ActiveX controls provided with Office XP Developer, you might be able to purchase third-party ActiveX controls from such vendors as FMS and Database Creations. In purchasing third-party controls, be sure that the vendor has tested the controls with Access; otherwise, you might be disappointed when you try to use the controls on an Access form.

Using ActiveX Controls to Add Functionality to Forms

Whatever the origin of an ActiveX control, you place it on an Access form by selecting it from the list opened from the More Controls tool in the Toolbox or from the Insert ActiveX Control dialog box opened by choosing Tools, Insert ActiveX Control.

Help for ActiveX controls can be hard to find. You might be able to open a Help page for an ActiveX control by right-clicking the control and selecting ControlType Properties from the shortcut menu to open the control's special properties sheet.

Most ActiveX special properties sheets have a Help button, and clicking the Help button might open a Help topic for the control. For the Calendar control, you'll get a Help topic that lists the properties, methods, and events of this control. Whether you will be able to get Help on a particular ActiveX control depends on a number of factors, such as whether you have installed Office XP Developer, or the MSDN Library that comes with Office XP Developer, or HTML Help for another program such as Visual Basic.

An ActiveX control's events might not all appear on the Events tab of the control's properties sheet. For example, the Calendar control's properties sheet lists only four events: *Updated*, *Enter*, *Exit*, *Got Focus*, and *Lost Focus*. Of these events, the *Updated* event looks promising for working with a selection, but it doesn't work in Access—when you click a date on the calendar, the *Enter* and *Got Focus* events fire but not the *Updated* event.

However, the Calendar control actually has many more events than appear in its properties sheet. To view these events, open the VBA window by pressing Alt+F11, select the form on which the Calendar control is inserted in the project list, and then select the Calendar control in the object box (the drop-down list on the left side of the module pane). You'll see a long list of Calendar control events in the procedures/events box (the drop-down list on the right side), as shown in Figure 6-30.

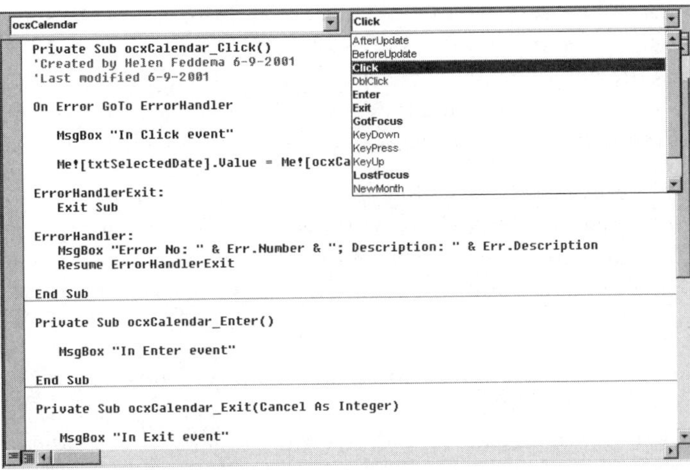

Figure 6-30. The events/procedures list for the Calendar control shows many more events than are listed in the control's properties sheet.

The *Click* event fires when a date is clicked on the calendar. You can use this event to get the value of the selected date and then use the value in code or write it to a text box, as is done in the frmActiveXControls form in the sample Controls 2002 database.

The following *Click* event procedure writes the date selected in the Calendar control to a text box on the form:

```
Private Sub ocxCalendar_Click()

On Error GoTo ErrorHandler

    MsgBox "In Click event"
    Me![txtSelectedDate].Value = Me![ocxCalendar].Value

ErrorHandlerExit:
    Exit Sub

ErrorHandler:
    MsgBox "Error No: " & Err.Number & "; Description: " & _
        Err.Description
    Resume ErrorHandlerExit

End Sub
```

The Calendar control (in some form) has been available for several Access versions; the newer DateTimePicker and MonthView controls (introduced in Office XP Developer) provide several different alternatives for selecting dates. Even if you don't have Office XP Developer, you may be able to use these controls on Access forms, if you have installed Visual Basic 6.0; a number of ActiveX controls are provided with Visual Basic.

The DateTimePicker control (similar in appearance to the controls used to select dates in Outlook) is a compact control that opens a small calendar when its drop-down button is clicked, and collapses to a small text box-like control displaying just the selected date. Because of its small size, this control is ideal for selecting dates on a form with limited available space.

The MonthView control is a large control, similar to the Calendar control except that it lets you display multiple months at once (by setting the MonthColumns property to the number of months to display). On this control, today's date is indicated by a dramatic red circle. Like the Calendar control, most of its events don't show up in its properties sheet, and also like the Calendar control, the Updated event doesn't work, and the Click event does work, as well as two extra control-specific events, DateClick and DateDblClick.

The MonthView control takes up a lot of form real estate, but it may be useful when you want to display a multi-month calendar, and you have room for it on the form. The code listed below uses the DateClick and DateDblClick events to write the start and end dates of a date range to txtStartDate and txtEndDate controls on a form.

tip Because the Click event is fired (as well as the DblClick event) when you double-click a date, select the end date first.

```
Private Sub ocxMonthView_DateClick(ByVal DateClicked As Date)

On Error GoTo ErrorHandler

   Me![txtStartDate].Value = Me![ocxMonthView].Value

ErrorHandlerExit:
   Exit Sub

ErrorHandler:
   MsgBox "Error No: " & Err.Number & "; Description: " & _
       Err.Description
   Resume ErrorHandlerExit

End Sub
```

```
Private Sub ocxMonthView_DateDblClick(ByVal DateDblClicked As Date)

On Error GoTo ErrorHandler

   Me![txtEndDate].Value = Me![ocxMonthView].Value

ErrorHandlerExit:
   Exit Sub

ErrorHandler:
   MsgBox "Error No: " & Err.Number & "; Description: " & _
       Err.Description
   Resume ErrorHandlerExit

End Sub
```

Figure 6-31 shows frmActiveXControls, with the Calendar control at the top left, the MonthView control at the bottom, and the DateTimePicker control on the right side, under text boxes that display the selected date, start date, and end date selected on the Calendar and MonthView controls.

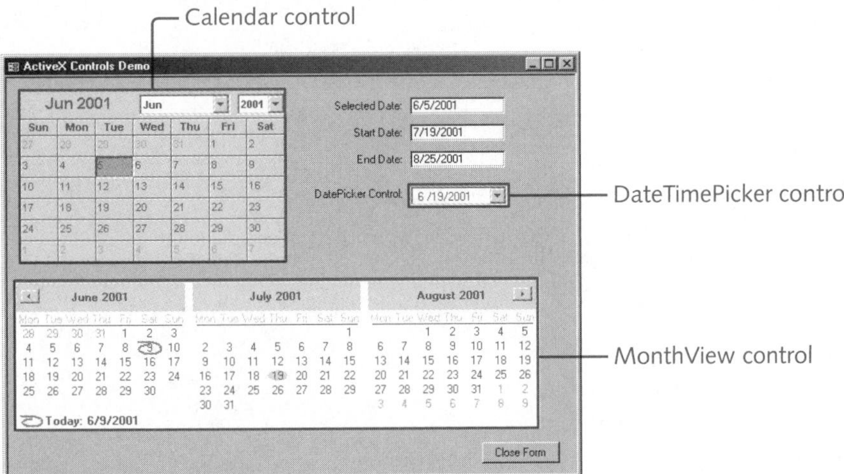

Figure 6-31. frmActiveXControls shows three ActiveX controls used for selecting dates.

Chapter 7

Using Reports to Print Data

After entering data into tables, using forms to make the data entry easier, you'll probably want to print out the data in an organized fashion. Forms are great for reviewing data online, but they are designed primarily for entering and editing data; to print data in an attractive and easy-to-understand fashion, you need to create reports.

Since version 1.0, Microsoft Access has featured a powerful report component capable of producing grouped reports to summarize data—a task that previously required purchasing a third-party reporting tool such as R&R Report Writer or Crystal Reports, which were used to produce reports based on dBASE data. Access reports are optimized for printing data stored in tables, with a number of special features designed to work with multiple records of data.

newfeature!

Access 2002 (unlike Access 1.0) includes several other tools you can use to summarize data—data access pages, PivotTables, and PivotCharts—but reports remain the best all-purpose tool for printing data.

> **tip** If your users will need to work with summarized data in a dynamic manner, you can create a grouped data access page, PivotTable, or PivotChart instead of a report. PivotTables and PivotCharts in particular allow users to rearrange rows and columns of data to get the desired view of the data. See Chapter 18, "Working with Data Access Pages," and Chapter 12, "Using PivotTables and PivotCharts to Analyze Data," for more information on these alternative methods of displaying summarized data.

Reports can display data record by record, as in a name and address or mailing label report, or reports can be grouped by fields significant to users. A *grouped report* (sometimes known as a *banded report*) divides the data into one or more groups, arranged hierarchically, usually suppressing any data that's repeated in the report. For example, a grouped Customers report might group data first by country, then by state/province, and finally by salesperson, to compare sales in different countries and regions. Another grouped report based on the same data could group by salesperson, then by country, and then by state/province, to compare how different salespeople are doing in various countries and regions. Grouped reports are helpful for presenting an overview of data from a specific perspective.

Another common report type is the *summary report*. A summary report, as the name suggests, summarizes data, using a grouping function such as *Sum* or *Count*. Summary reports omit the details and give you just the totals (or counts) of the relevant data, such as total sales by region. Summary reports are often based on crosstab queries, which you can use to manipulate data from different angles to get the results you're interested in.

Because forms and reports have different purposes—forms are designed to display and modify data, whereas reports are designed to print data—you should design reports from the ground up rather than print a form or save a form as a report. Designing a report from scratch lets you optimize the report design for printing and avoid useless or confusing design elements that might be carried over from a form, such as record selector combo boxes or command buttons, which are very useful features on forms, but utterly useless on reports.

To design a report to display data in the most efficient way, you need to be familiar with the controls that work best on reports and with the special report features that let you group, sort, and summarize data in reports. See the "Sorting and Grouping" section later in this chapter for detailed information about grouping, sorting, and summarizing data in reports.

For more details on working with controls, see Chapter 6, "Working with Form Controls." Most of the information in this chapter applies equally to controls on forms and controls on reports.

A well-designed report uses only a few control types and makes only light use of design elements such as color, lines, and rectangles. It might also use special report features such as grouping and summarizing of data or running sums. Interactive controls (such as command buttons and combo boxes) aren't useful on reports and should be omitted.

Printing Forms vs. Printing Reports

Although Access allows users to print forms, when Access forms are printed the format generally isn't as attractive or as useful as a properly designed report. Because of the essential difference in purpose between forms and reports, forms don't print well. Forms are designed to display data one record at a time, or perhaps (for datasheet and continuous forms) several records at a time. Forms display all the data you want to see for each record, and they typically use color (even if it's only a light gray background) and other decorative elements to make it easier to enter, review, and edit data one record at a time. When you print a form, you get page after page of complete data, with colored backgrounds, combo boxes, option groups, and command buttons. These elements are distracting on a printed page and don't have any practical use.

What you usually want in a report is a compact listing or summary of selected data, suitable for review on the printed page. Reports rarely show complete records. Instead, they typically display multiple records per page, often with subtotals or other summary data, grouped by significant fields. Some design elements that are functional on forms (such as combo boxes, option groups, and tab controls) have no function on reports (you can't click a command button on a piece of paper!), and background color on reports makes them hard to read and slow to print.

note Certain design elements work only on reports, such as the *RunningSum* property (used to create running sums), group levels (used to separate data into bands), and the *CanGrow* and *CanShrink* properties of text boxes (used to accommodate text of different sizes). See the section "Neat Report Tricks," page 292, for more information about how to use these special report control properties.

As an example of what happens when you print a form optimized for entering and editing data (and why you shouldn't!), try printing fpriBooksAndVideos (the primary form in the Crafts database on the companion CD). The form header is printed on the first page (although its command buttons and record selector combo boxes are non-functional and confusing when printed on paper), and the footer is printed on the last sheet. The tab control with its subforms isn't printed, which is appropriate (since it, too, is useless on a report), but a large space is printed where the tab control would be. Figure 7-1 shows page 3 of the fpriBooksAndVideos form in print preview.

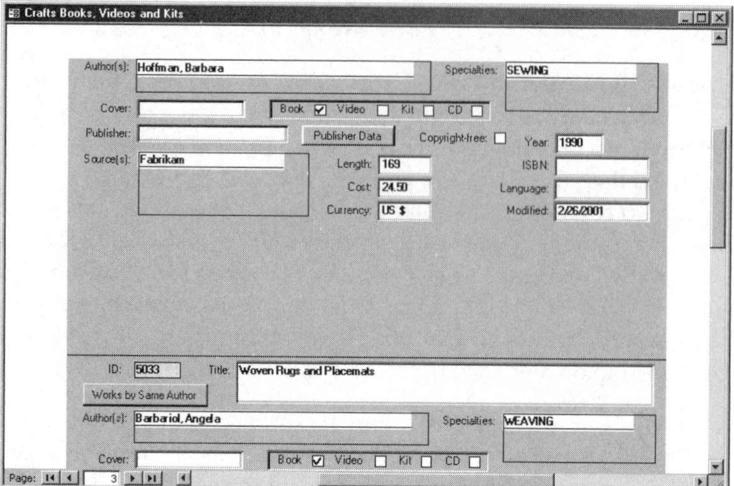

Figure 7-1. The fpriBooksAndVideos form in print preview shows that printing a form is not the best way to review data.

It would be difficult to use a printout of the fpriBooksAndVideos form to review the books and videos in the Crafts database. A printed version of the form is simply page after page of data in no particular order, gray background and all, with some elements missing and no report headers or footers. Furthermore, only the first record of linked data (Authors or Specialties, for example) is displayed for each record.

A properly designed report, on the other hand (such as the rptBooksAndVideos report, described later in this chapter), lists relevant information (usually just a subset of the fields in the data source) grouped by one or more fields (in this report, just the Title field), in a simple black-and-white layout that uses lines or rectangles sparingly so that the report can be printed quickly and is highly readable.

Working with Report Controls

Forms and reports use the same Toolbox, which means that you can place any type of control on a report that you can place on a form by clicking its tool in the Toolbox. Keep in mind, however, that controls designed for on-screen interaction (such as combo boxes, option groups, command buttons, and tab controls) aren't suitable for reports, which you can look at but can't interact with. Check boxes, although you can't select or clear them on reports, are still useful for displaying Yes/No data. Figure 7-2 shows the Toolbox with the controls that work best on reports indicated.

For more information about working with other controls in the Toolbox, see Chapter 6, "Working with Form Controls."

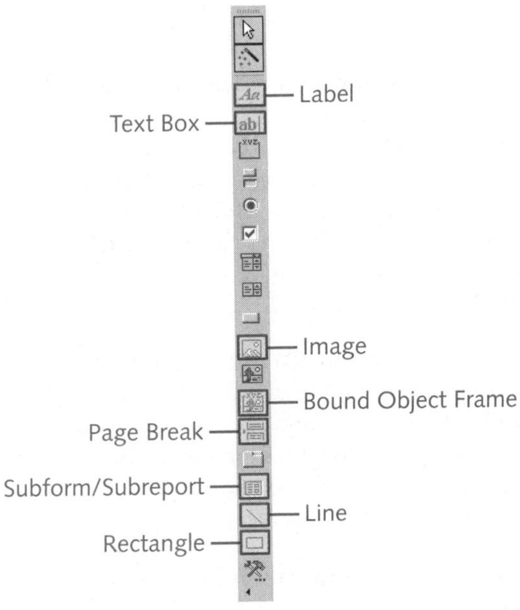

Figure 7-2. The Toolbox contains a number of controls and tools to help you design your reports.

These controls are described in the following list:

- **Label.** Displays descriptive text. Labels are always unbound (that is, they aren't bound to a data field).
- **Text Box.** Displays data from a field or the results of an expression.
- **Image.** Displays an unbound image.
- **Bound Object Frame.** Displays a bound object, such as an image.
- **Page Break.** Indicates a new report page.
- **Subform/Subreport.** Displays information from a form, report, query, or table.
- **Line.** Adds a decorative line.
- **Rectangle.** Inserts a decorative rectangle.

Designing Reports

The look and feel of the reports you design will vary depending on the type of information you want to present. If you're creating a simple report that lists book sales in the southwestern region of the United States, you can use the Report Wizard to create a basic two-column report that lists only regions and sales in a matter of minutes. If you're creating a more complex report that prints a student roster for your graduate program, complete with pertinent transcript subreports within each report, your planning might take several hours as well as the input of a number of people to ensure that the report meets the needs of the users who will read it.

Whether you want to print a report that gives a bare-bones listing of data in a table, a complex grouped report that summarizes data, or a report that displays linked data in subreports, plan to spend some time thinking through what data your report needs to display and how the data should be presented. Planning and foresight will save you editing and revision time later on. As you think about what you want to accomplish with the report you're creating, consider these questions:

- Who will be using this report? What information will users expect to see, and how do they want the information to be laid out?
- What report format is best suited to your needs? For example, will you use multiple columns to present your data? How many columns do you need?
- Does the report need group and/or report subtotals?
- Should the report include all the data in the record source or just summarized data?
- Should you use headings and graphic elements (such as lines and boxes) to help readers understand the report?
- If you're creating the report for a client, do you need to replicate current paper reports your client is used to seeing?

Access has a Report Wizard to aid you in creating reports. The various report types created by the Wizard can save time, and one of the Wizard's selections may be exactly the type of report you need. Sometimes, however, you need a report type the Wizard doesn't create. When that's the case, you can create a report starting with a blank report in Design view, adding controls to the report grid manually, and setting report properties as desired. In the following sections, I'll review several of the questions you should consider when designing reports.

InsideOut

Although you can save a form as a report, this "shortcut" usually ends up taking longer than creating a report from scratch because so much work has to be done to remove elements that work only on forms and to add report-specific components used to group and summarize data. I don't recommend using this method to create a report.

Selecting Report Record Sources

Reports can use the same types of record sources that forms use: tables, queries, SQL statements, and recordsets. You select (or change) a record source for a report the same way you would for a form. For example, if you were designing a simple name and address list report, a table of contact data could be the report's record source. A report that needs to list only a subset of data in a table could be based on a query that selects the output you need; for example, selecting records for the Southeast sales region and the year 2000.

A report that displays only summarized data could be based on a Totals query that uses the *Sum* or *Count* function to present the total dollar amount of sales or the count of orders. Just as for form record sources, SQL statements and recordsets can be used instead of queries as report record sources.

For more details on creating queries, see Chapter 9, "Using Queries to Select Data"; for information on using various types of record sources, see Chapter 5, "Creating Forms for Entering, Editing, and Viewing Data."

Using Grouped Reports

Reports have several features that don't correspond to any form feature: One of them is grouping. A grouped report divides data into bands that correspond to the values in fields that you select for each group level. An example is grouping a name and address report by State and then by LastName. You can have up to ten group levels in a report, but reports rarely need more than three or four levels, and often one group level is all you'll need. The Report Wizard has a Grouped Report selection that you can use to create a grouped report, but before you start the wizard you should create a query to use as the grouped report's record source. This query should contain all the tables you need to obtain the data you want to include in the report, with just the fields needed for the report selected as query columns.

The fields used to create report groups are also fields used for sorting. Even if you don't want to separate your data into distinct groups—and you don't need group headers or footers—you can still use the Sorting and Grouping dialog box to sort the report data as you want. This is especially useful if the report is based directly on a table. You can base several reports on the same table, sorting each by different fields, to produce very different reports from the same data.

For example, to create a report in the Crafts database that lists books and videos, grouped by author, you need a query that contains tblBooksAndVideos, tblBookAuthors, and tblAuthors, as shown in Figure 7-3. These three tables define the many-to-many relationship between books and authors.

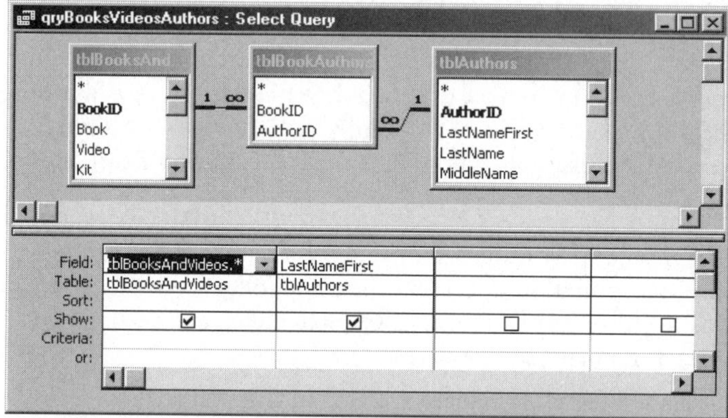

Figure 7-3. You can use this query with three linked tables as a grouped report's record source.

You can also create three-table queries for the Books–Sources and Books–Specialties many-to-many relationships. For an all-in-one report, you can create a query containing all the tables needed for books and videos, authors, sources, and specialties.

For more information about creating queries to select data, see Chapter 9, "Using Queries to Select Data."

Creating Reports with Subreports

Grouped reports require a record source (usually a query) that contains all the information needed to set up the groups. However, you have another way to create a grouped report: by using subreports to display linked data. Just as you can with linked forms, you can select the "one" side of a one-to-many relationship as a report's record source and select the "many" side of the relationship as the record source of another report, and then you can embed the report bound to the "many" table as a subreport on the main report. Because the record source tables are linked on the key field, the subreport will always display the correct records linked to the main report record.

> **tip** You can embed a form in a report as a subreport. As a matter of fact, since Datasheet view is not available for reports, this method is the only way to create a datasheet subreport.

No wizard exists for creating reports with embedded subreports. You have to create such a report yourself in Design view, either by dragging the report you want as the subreport to the main report or by placing a Subform/Subreport control on the report and selecting the report intended to be the subreport as its source object.

For a discussion of various types of reports with embedded subforms and subreports, see "Adding Embedded Subreports and Subforms to Reports," page 273.

Using Wizards and AutoReport to Create Reports

The Report Wizard has several selections for creating reports of different types. To start the Report Wizard, double-click Create Report By Using Wizard on the Reports tab of the Database window. This wizard creates grouped reports in a variety of formats.

See "Grouped Reports," page 245, for more details on working with the Report Wizard.

There are several other ways to create a new report: If you click New at the top of the Database window, the New Report dialog box appears, offering several choices, as shown in Figure 7-4.

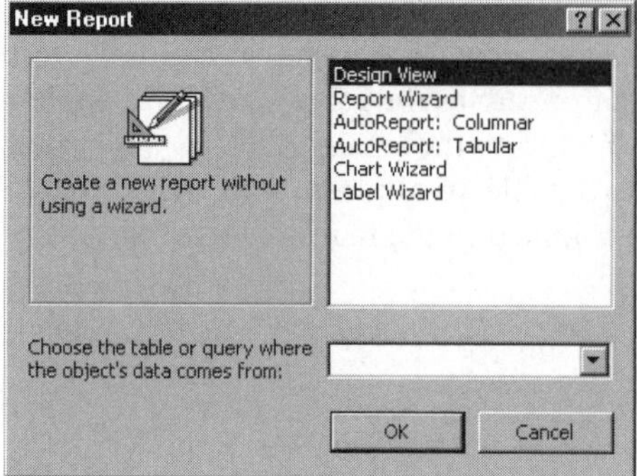

Figure 7-4. The New Report dialog box has selections for creating various types of reports.

In addition, the New Object selector on the Database toolbar offers an AutoReport selection, which creates a not particularly attractive plain columnar report. Table 7-1 lists the available choices for report layouts and indicates where the selection is available. The sections that follow describe how to create reports using these layouts.

Table 7-1. Available report layouts

Layout selection	Available from	Description
Chart	New Report, Chart Wizard	Data from selected fields is charted in a variety of chart formats, using MS Graph.
Columnar	New Report, AutoReport: Columnar	Fields are laid out top to bottom, with visible borders around each text box control.
Crosstab	New Report, Design View	Generates a report based on a previously prepared crosstab query.

Layout selection	Available from	Description
Datasheet	New Report, Design View	Lets you manually create a report with a datasheet subform.
Embedded Subreport	New Report, Design View	One or more embedded subreports are manually placed on the report; the subreports can be linked or unlinked.
Free-Form Report	New Report, Design View	No controls are automatically placed on the report; you can place controls where you want them.
Grouped	Report Wizard, choice of six layouts	Groups data by selected fields, with a choice of indented or left-aligned formats.
Label	New Report, Label Wizard	Data is formatted to be printed on one of a number of commercial labels or according to a custom label format.
Multicolumn	New Report, Design View	Report is manually set up as a multicolumn report in the Page Setup dialog box.
PivotChart	New Report, Design View	Creates a report with an embedded PivotChart subform, formatted to remove interactive elements.
PivotTable	New Report, Design View	Creates a report with an embedded PivotTable subform.
Tabular	New Report, AutoReport: Tabular	Fields are laid out left to right, with column headings.

Creating a Columnar Report Quickly

To create a simple columnar report in the minimum amount of time, select a table or query in the Database window, and then select AutoReport from the New Object selector on the Database toolbar, as shown in Figure 7-5.

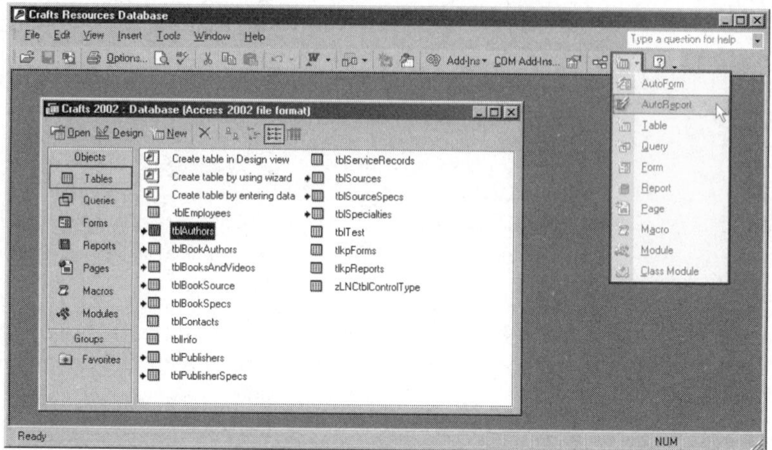

Figure 7-5. The New Object selector lets you create an AutoReport from the Database toolbar.

The report, shown in Figure 7-6, is created automatically. It displays all the fields in the selected table or query, arranged in a single column from top to bottom. You can also create a columnar report from the New Report dialog box, as described in the "Columnar Reports" section on page 256. You'll get exactly the same report whether you use the New Object: AutoReport button or the New Report dialog box selection.

> **tip** A columnar report is a very plain report indeed. Turning it into an attractive report requires considerable work. If you need a quick printout, say for proofreading data, a columnar report is handy; for most purposes, though, you'll probably be better off choosing one of the Report Wizard selections, where you can choose the fields to display on the report and group the data by one or more fields.

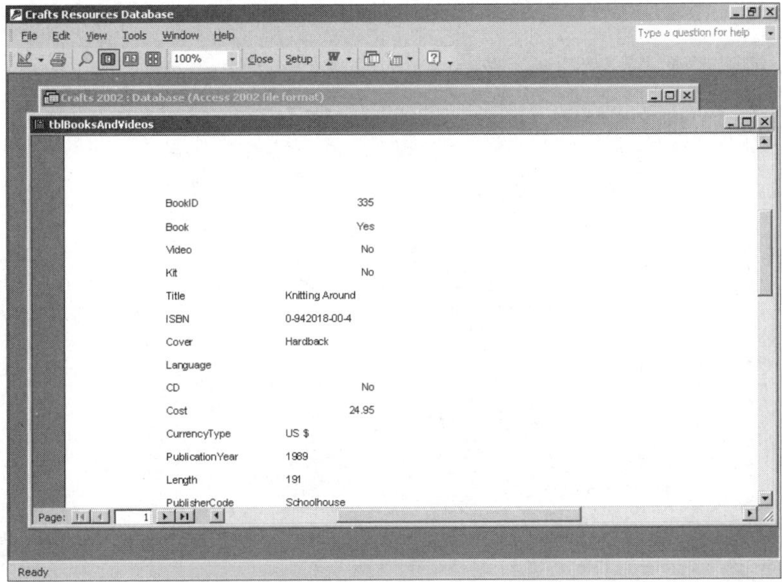

Figure 7-6. Selecting AutoReport creates this report.

Grouped Reports

When you use the Report Wizard to create a grouped report, you have six choices for the report layout. The differences in layout are more a matter of taste than functionality, and all the other wizard selections are the same, so you can identify the layout you prefer by looking at the layout illustration on the wizard screen. Whichever layout you select, you'll probably need to modify it somewhat to create an attractive report.

To create a grouped report, first prepare a query (such as qryBooksVideosAll) containing all the data needed for the report groups, as described in "Using Grouped Reports," page 239. Then follow these steps:

1. Click the Reports tab of the Database window, and click New at the top of the Database window.
2. In the New Report dialog box, select qryBooksVideosAll in the record source drop-down list. Select Report Wizard from the list of report types, and then click OK.

3 Select the fields to place on the report, as shown in Figure 7-7. Click Next.

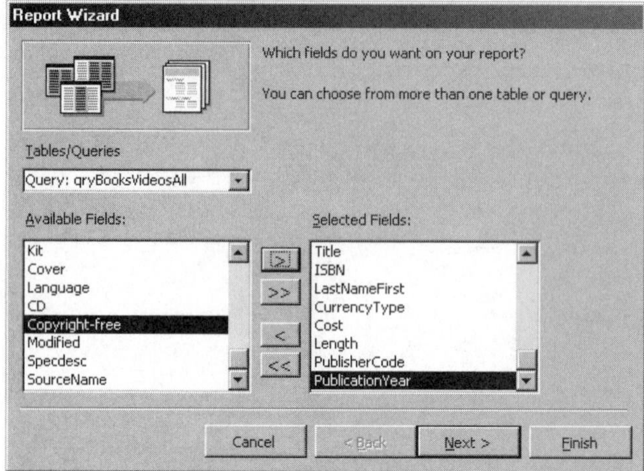

Figure 7-7. The Report Wizard offers a selection of fields for your report.

4 This page of the wizard appears only when the report's record source has two or more tables. Select the table that you want to use as the primary table. In Figure 7-8, tblAuthors is selected as the primary table, so the report's top grouping will be by author name. Click Next.

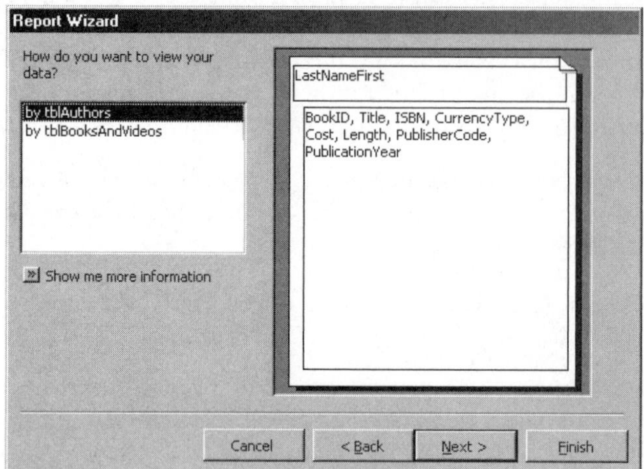

Figure 7-8. If the report's record source has more than one table, use this page of the wizard to select the primary table for the report.

5 Select further grouping levels, if desired. In Figure 7-9, PublisherCode has been added as a group field. The resulting report will be grouped by publisher. Click Next.

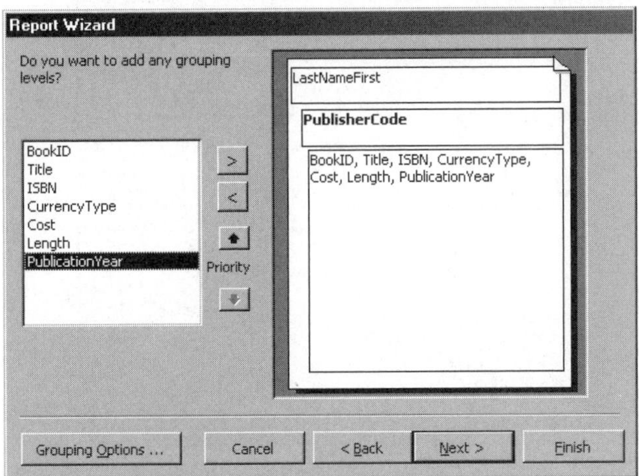

Figure 7-9. Select fields for group levels.

6 Select up to four sort levels. Selecting the sort field Title, as shown in Figure 7-10, will sort the Publisher group by book title. Click Next.

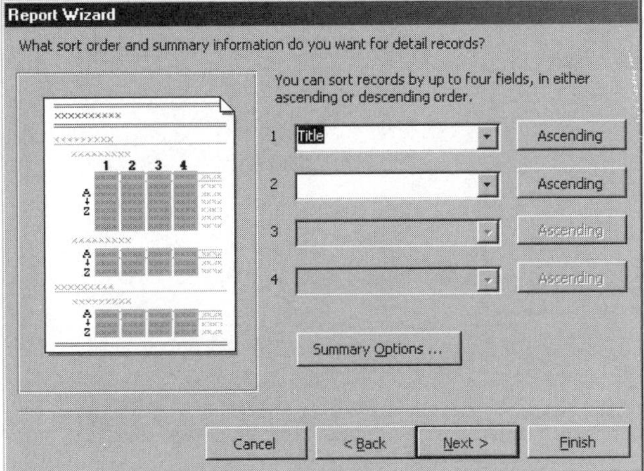

Figure 7-10. Select sort levels.

7 Choose a layout from the Layout option group, as shown in Figure 7-11. You can also format the report for portrait or landscape orientation. Click Next.

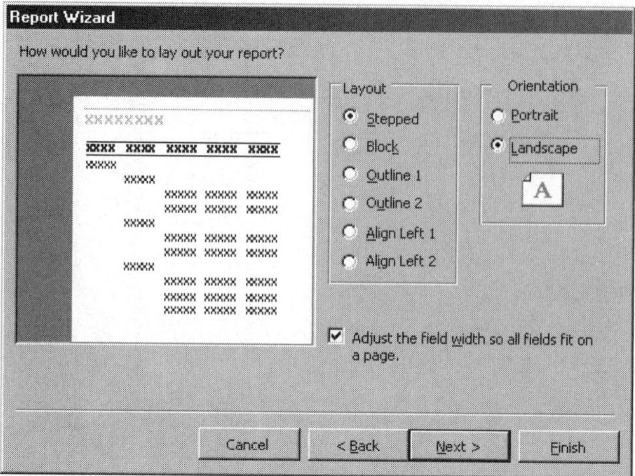

Figure 7-11. In this example, the Stepped layout and landscape orientation have been chosen for the report.

8 Select a style for the report, as shown in Figure 7-12. Click Next.

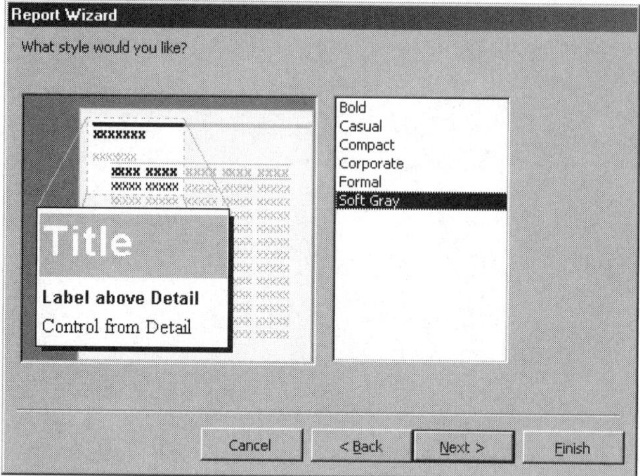

Figure 7-12. Select a report style.

note You can create a style of your own and save it as a named style. The technique is somewhat different from creating custom AutoFormat styles for forms. See "Using AutoFormat," page 284, for more details.

9 Give the report a title, as shown in Figure 7-13. The title is used as the report name, as its caption in print preview, and as a field in the report header. Click Finish.

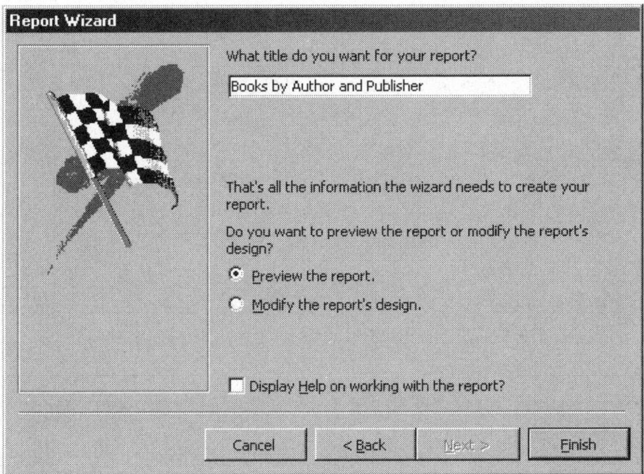

Figure 7-13. Give the report a title on the last page of the wizard.

Figure 7-14 shows the finished report in print preview.

This report is a good start but needs some fine-tuning. None of the standard layouts is ideal, at least to my taste. The Stepped layout takes up an entire column for each group, whereas the Align Left layouts tend to use too many lines and boxes. For a clean, space-saving layout, try selecting the Stepped layout and then moving the group field controls and the first detail control to the left side of the report.

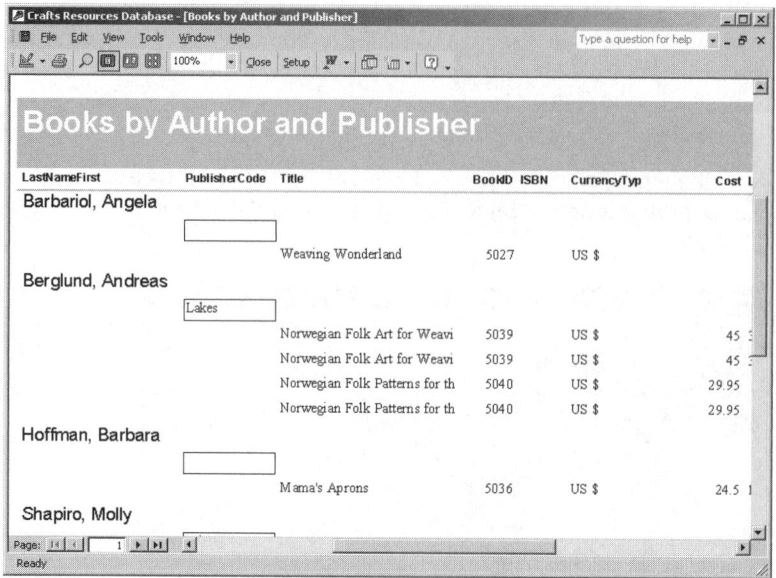

Figure 7-14. The finished report looks like this in print preview.

Troubleshooting

My report breaks in the middle of a group of data

When a grouped report is printed, data that ought to be on a single page is sometimes broken up by a page break so that part of it prints on one page and the rest on the next page.

on the CD To prevent a group from being broken over two pages, open the Sorting And Grouping dialog box (in Design view), and specify Whole Group for the *KeepTogether* property for the group you want to keep together. For example, on rptBooksAndVideos, I wanted all the information on one book to be kept together, so I set *KeepTogether* to Whole Group for the Title group. Now if the information for a specific book title won't fit at the bottom of a page, it will be moved to the beginning of the next page, instead of breaking in the middle of the group.

Troubleshooting

I want to suppress repetitive data in grouped reports

If the same data is repeating over and over in a grouped report, how can you make it print only once per group? For example, in a grouped report with a staggered layout, you generally don't want to have the same data (such as a country name) repeating for every item in the Country group. Fortunately, text boxes on Access reports have a special property that can be used to suppress the printing of repetitive information.

For any text box that might contain repetitive data, set the *HideDuplicates* property to Yes. This allows the first instance of a particular value in the bound field to be printed but suppresses the printing of the same value on following lines in the same section.

on the CD Figure 7-15 shows a simple stepped report based on data in the Crafts database, with the *HideDuplicates* property set to Yes for the txtPublicationYear and Publisher text boxes. (See Figure 7-59 on page 296 for a "before" version of this report, in which the *HideDuplicates* property was left at the default setting No and publisher data repeats.)

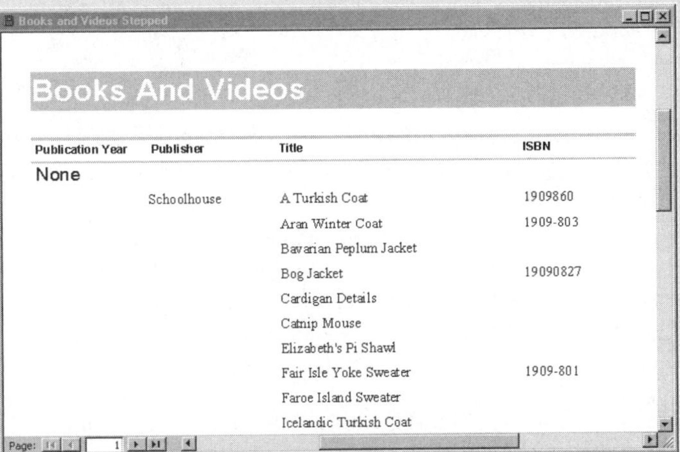

Figure 7-15. A stepped report uses the *HideDuplicates* property to show only the first instance of each value in a group.

Fine-Tuning Reports

You can use a wizard-generated report as is, and a wizard-generated report may be quite adequate for a quick data printout, say for proofreading purposes, as mentioned earlier. But for reports designed to be saved and studied, I recommend making the following changes to give your reports a polished appearance. You won't need to make all of these changes for every report, but you'll usually need to make most of them.

- Remove unnecessary column headings for the group fields — if a field prints in a group header, it doesn't need a column heading, too.
- Adjust the labels and text boxes to the correct width to display their captions or data.
- Change control text alignment as needed, such as setting the *TextAlign* property to Left for a numeric field that's used as an identifier. (By default, Access right-aligns all numeric fields.)
- Use a *ControlSource* expression to combine two or more fields to be displayed in one text box, such as the CurrencyType and Cost fields shown in the Cost column of the report shown in Figure 7-17, which are combined using the following expression:

```
=IIf([Cost]>0,[CurrencyType] & Format([Cost],"#,###.00"))
```

- Format a dollar amount for two decimal points for standard display or zero decimal points to display rounded amounts (or apply the appropriate formatting for other currencies).
- To prevent the user from wondering why a blank appears where data is expected, create an expression to print an informative phrase if data has not been entered into a field. In the example used in the "Using Grouped Reports" section on page 239, the following *ControlSource* expression prints *No publisher entered* if the PublisherCode field is empty:

```
=IIf([PublisherCode],"Publisher: " & [PublisherCode],
 "No publisher entered")
```

- Move column headings as needed to improve the layout in a printed document.
- Set the *HideDuplicates* property to Yes for the detail fields to prevent duplicate data from being printed on a grouped report.
- Set the *CanGrow* property to Yes for the Title control, and also for any controls that can contain more than one line of data, to allow very long text to wrap.
- Set the *CanShrink* property to Yes for all the detail controls, and also for the detail section itself, to avoid blank rows on the report when duplicate data is hidden or the field has no data for a record.
- Set the *KeepTogether* property to Whole Group for a group in the Sorting And Grouping dialog box (as shown in Figure 7-16) so that the group will start on a new page if a page break would otherwise appear in the middle of the group.

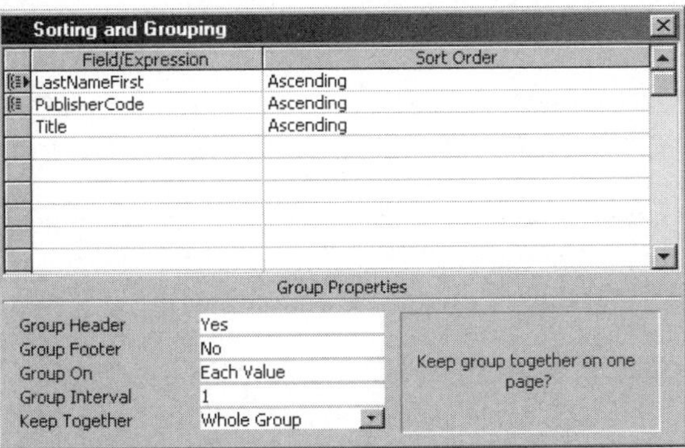

Figure 7-16. Set the *KeepTogether* property to Whole Group to prevent an author group from splitting.

- Set the *RepeatSection* property of header sections to Yes in their properties sheets so that these headers will repeat on the next page if needed.
- If you don't want to start each group on a new page, insert a blank line after a group by setting *GroupFooter* to Yes in the Sorting And Grouping dialog box. No controls are needed in this footer section, although you can add a dividing line if you want.

The third page of the sample report, modified in these ways, is shown in Figure 7-17.

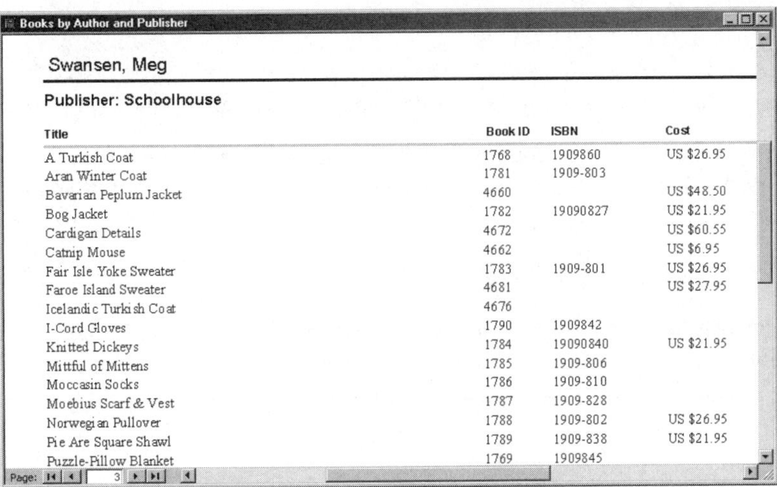

Books by Author and Publisher

Swansen, Meg

Publisher: Schoolhouse

Title	Book ID	ISBN	Cost
A Turkish Coat	1768	1909860	US $26.95
Aran Winter Coat	1781	1909-803	
Bavarian Peplum Jacket	4660		US $48.50
Bog Jacket	1782	19090827	US $21.95
Cardigan Details	4672		US $60.55
Catnip Mouse	4662		US $6.95
Fair Isle Yoke Sweater	1783	1909-801	US $26.95
Faroe Island Sweater	4681		US $27.95
Icelandic Turkish Coat	4676		
I-Cord Gloves	1790	1909842	
Knitted Dickeys	1784	19090840	US $21.95
Mittful of Mittens	1785	1909-806	
Moccasin Socks	1786	1909-810	
Moebius Scarf & Vest	1787	1909-828	
Norwegian Pullover	1788	1909-802	US $26.95
Pie Are Square Shawl	1789	1909-838	US $21.95
Puzzle-Pillow Blanket	1769	1909845	

Page: 3

Figure 7-17. This report is more attractive after fine-tuning.

Changing Report Names, Titles, and Captions

Access reports have names (listed in the Database window) and captions (displayed as text in the report's title bar). Additionally, reports—at least those you create with the Report Wizard—have a Title label control in the report header. You can examine (and change) a report's caption by using the *Caption* property in the report's properties sheet, as shown in Figure 7-18. You can't change a report's name in its properties sheet because no *Name* property is displayed there.

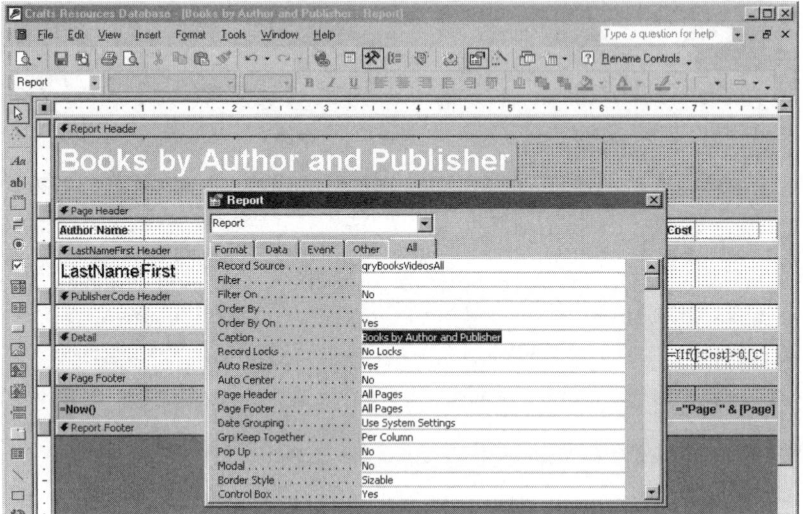

Figure 7-18. You can change a report's caption by changing the *Caption* property.

Reports do have a *Name* property, however. You can print the report name using this property by placing an expression such as the following in the *Control Source* property of a text box:

```
="Report name: " & [Name]
```

A text box listing the report name (say, in the report's page footer) is a handy way of identifying the name of a printed report, in case you need to revise it.

The Report Wizard uses the term "title" on the last page of the wizard. This can be confusing since reports don't have a *Title* property. The text you enter as the report's title will be used as both caption and name. This text will also be displayed in the title label control in the report header. This situation presents a problem for users who want to name their database objects in accordance with a particular naming convention, such as the Leszynski Naming Convention (LNC) discussed in Chapter 20, "Customizing Your Database Using VBA Code." If you use the LNC naming convention for database objects, your report names should start with the *rpt* tag. If you title the report rptBooksByAuthorAndPublisher in the Report Wizard, both the report's title bar (in print preview) and the large title label in the report header will display *rptBooksByAuthorAndPublisher*, which looks strange.

If you want the report's caption to differ from the report's name (which is generally a good idea), you have to give the report a title in the wizard and then rename it in the Database window, as shown in Figure 7-19. To rename a report in the Database window, select the report name and press F2 to switch to edit mode. Edit the name as desired, and press Enter.

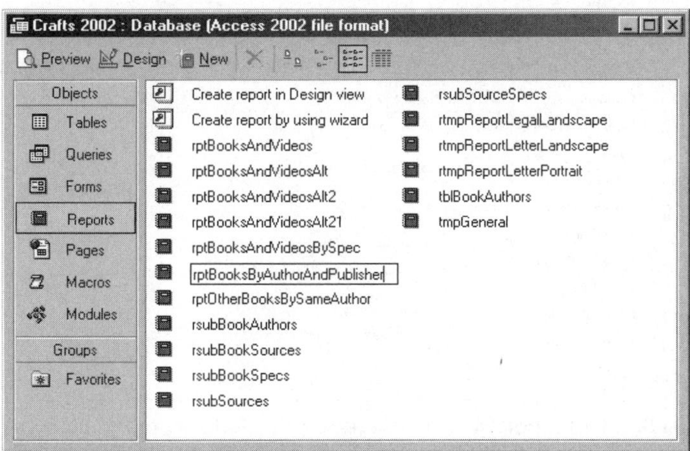

Figure 7-19. You can rename a report in the Database window.

Alternatively, you can give the report the title *rptBooksByAuthorAndPublisher* in the wizard and then change the caption to *Books by Author and Publisher* in the report's properties sheet and in the Title label.

Columnar Reports

Columnar reports, though plain in appearance, are useful for proofreading and checking data; their one-field-per-row layout leaves lots of room for marking corrections. The quickest way to create a columnar report is to click the New Object: AutoReport button on the toolbar, as described in the "Creating a Columnar Report Quickly" section on page 244. However, you can also create a columnar report by following these steps:

1. Click the Reports tab of the Database window, and then click the New button at the top of the Database window.
2. In the New Report dialog box, select a table or query from the record source drop-down list, and then select AutoReport: Columnar from the list of report types.
3. Click OK. The rather ungainly report shown in Figure 7-20 is created.

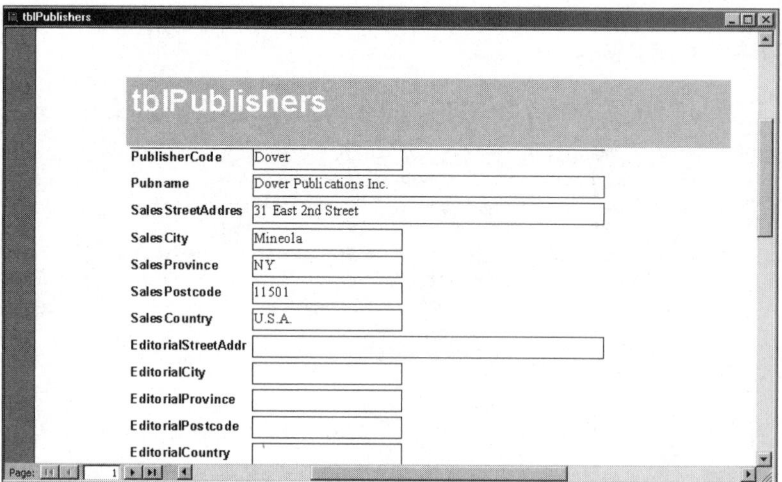

Figure 7-20. This report was created using the AutoReport: Columnar selection.

You can improve this report by adjusting control sizes as needed or by using expressions to concatenate address data, as described in the Troubleshooting sidebar "My Report Has Gaps in Its Data" on page 284.

Tabular Reports

Tabular reports are most useful when you want a report laid out like a worksheet, usually to display financial data.

To create a tabular report, follow these steps:

1. Click the Reports tab of the Database window, and click New at the top of the Database window.
2. In the New Report dialog box, select a table or query in the record source drop-down list, and then select AutoReport: Tabular.

This report type (see Figure 7-21) looks much like the stepped report except that it lacks the group levels.

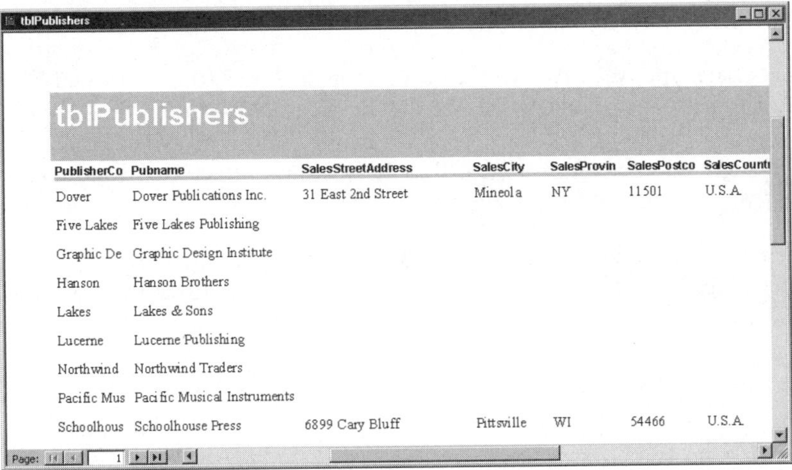

tblPublishers

tblPublishers

PublisherCo	Pubname	SalesStreetAddress	SalesCity	SalesProvin	SalesPostco	SalesCounti
Dover	Dover Publications Inc.	31 East 2nd Street	Mineola	NY	11501	U.S.A.
Five Lakes	Five Lakes Publishing					
Graphic De	Graphic Design Institute					
Hanson	Hanson Brothers					
Lakes	Lakes & Sons					
Lucerne	Lucerne Publishing					
Northwind	Northwind Traders					
Pacific Mus	Pacific Musical Instruments					
Schoolhous	Schoolhouse Press	6899 Cary Bluff	Pittsville	WI	54466	U.S.A.

Page: 1

Figure 7-21. The finished tabular report looks like this.

Although a tabular report somewhat resembles an Excel worksheet, it's significantly more difficult to work with than a worksheet or a datasheet form. This report doesn't have adjustable columns like a worksheet, just text boxes and labels that you must move manually if you want to resize the columns. As is typical of reports created using the Report Wizard, you'll need to resize some labels and text boxes to display all of their captions or data without truncation.

newfeature!

Chart Reports

Chart reports are used when you want to display your data graphically. The MS Graph component used to create Chart reports is showing its age, but it is still useful. However, you may prefer to just create a PivotChart instead. (See the "PivotChart Subreports" section on page 278) for details on this method.)

To create a meaningful chart, you need to select appropriate fields; generally charts are based on queries that preselect data, perhaps from several linked tables. For a pie chart, you need only two fields: one for the series, and one for the data. For example, you have undoubtedly seen a newspaper pie chart that shows government expenditures by department—the dollar amount of expenditures is the data on the pie chart, while the department names are the series.

Other chart types require three fields: one for the series (the horizontal labels), one for the axis (the vertical labels), and one for the data that is summarized. To extend the government expenditures example, a bar graph could have expenditures as data, department names as the series field at the bottom of the chart, and years as the axis field along the left side of the chart.

When creating a report with a chart, you usually won't find all the data you need in a single table, so start by preparing a query that contains the data you want to display in the chart.

For information about creating a query, see Chapter 9, "Using Queries to Select Data."

After you've created the query, follow these steps:

1. Click the Reports tab of the Database window, and then click New at the top of the Database window.
2. In the New Report dialog box, select the query (or a table) that contains the data you want to chart in the record source drop-down list, and then select Chart Wizard.
3. Select the fields to be charted. (See Figure 7-22.) As mentioned, for a pie chart you need only two fields: one for the series and one for the data. Other chart types require three fields: one for the series (the horizontal labels), one for the axis (the vertical labels), and one for the data that is summarized. Click Next.

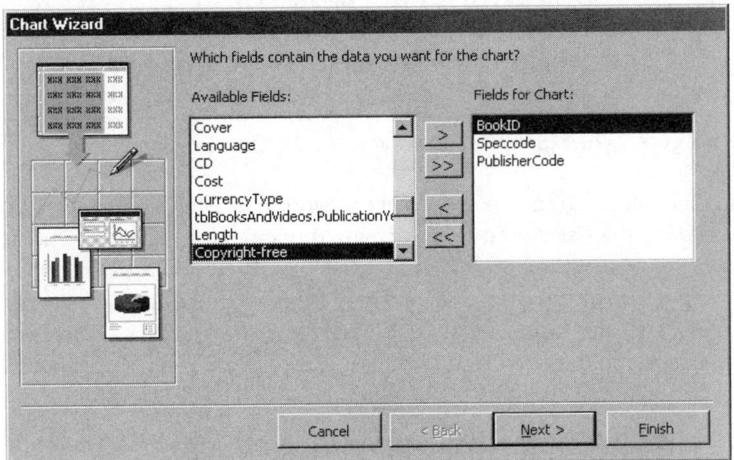

Figure 7-22. Select fields for the chart in the Chart Wizard.

4 Select the chart type. Figure 7-23 shows the 3-D cylinder bar chart selected. Click Next.

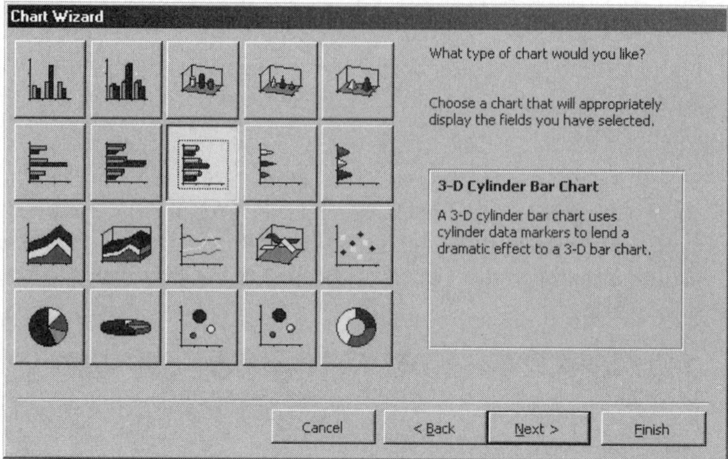

Figure 7-23. Select a chart type for the Chart report.

5 The next page of the wizard allows you to preview the selected chart and adjust the fields used for the chart components as needed. One field is used for the axis (the bottom of the chart), another field is used for the series (the right side of the chart), and a third field is summarized for the data. By default, Access sums numeric data and counts non-numeric data, such as product codes and dates. In Figure 7-24, PublisherCode is the axis, Speccode is the series, and a count of BookID provides the data for the chart.

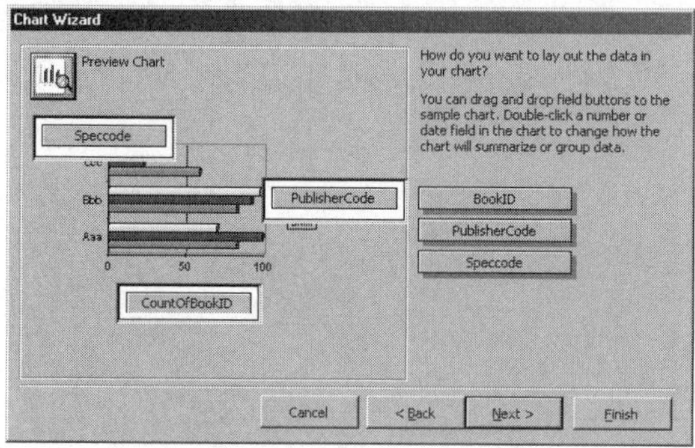

Figure 7-24. The Chart Wizard allows you to preview the selected chart.

Click Preview Chart to preview the chart in a small window. Click Close to close the Sample Preview window. Then click Next.

6 Name the report, as shown in Figure 7-25. The title you enter on this page is used only for the title displayed in the chart; it is not used for the report name or caption. You also have the choice to open the report or modify it in Design view. You'll usually want to select the Modify option because you'll need to resize the chart.

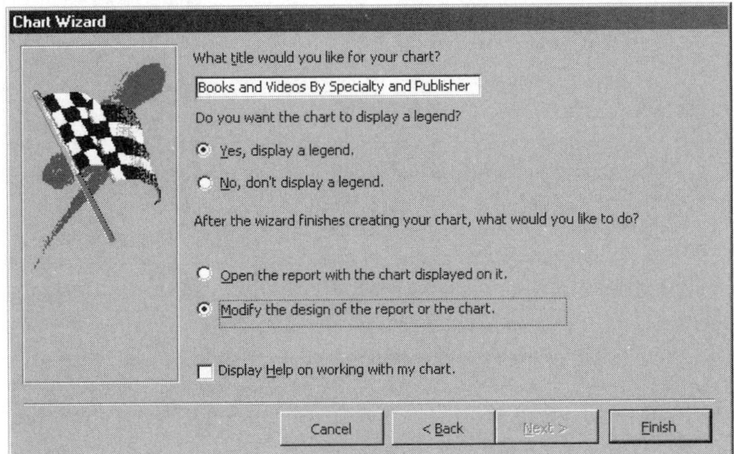

Figure 7-25. The name you give the chart report is not used as a report name or caption.

7 Click Finish. The report opens in Design view, as shown in Figure 7-26. The chart is very small; you'll probably want to resize it.

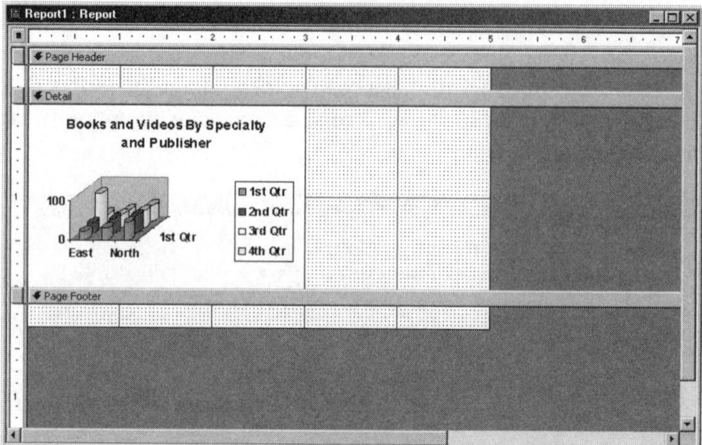

Figure 7-26. The finished Chart report looks like this in Design view.

InsideOut

newfeature!

When you look at a chart report in Design view, you won't see the real data, only dummy data. This is a peculiarity of MS Graph charts. The newer PivotCharts don't have this constraint, so if you find it easier to work with a chart where you can see the real data, PivotCharts are a better choice than Chart reports. See the "PivotChart Subreports" section on page 278 and Chapter 12, "Using PivotTables and PivotCharts to Analyze Data," for more information on creating PivotCharts.

8 Drag the page footer down and the right edge of the report grid out until you get the report size you want, and then stretch the chart diagonally until it fills the report. Figure 7-27 shows the chart in print preview, resized to display its data clearly and named according to the LNC.

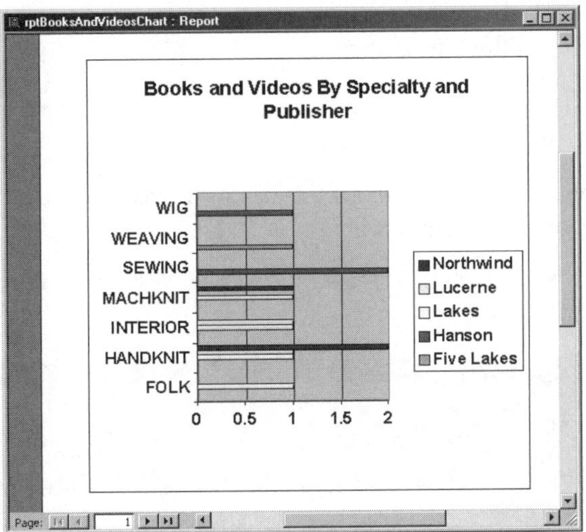

Figure 7-27. The finished chart report has been resized and named according to the LNC.

InsideOut

You might need several runs through the Chart Wizard to get a usable chart. Unlike PivotCharts, MS Graph charts can't be easily adjusted after creation. For this reason, I recommend that you use PivotCharts on reports when you need to display data graphically. (See "PivotChart Subreports," page 278.)

Label Reports

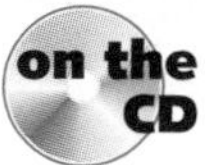

Use the Label Wizard to create mailing labels and other types of labels. The following example creates Avery #5161 mailing labels for the tblAuthors table in the sample Crafts database.

To create a label report, follow these steps:

1. Click the Reports tab of the Database window, and then click New at the top of the Database window.
2. In the New Report dialog box, select tblAuthors as the report's record source and Label Wizard as the report type.
3. Select the label type on the first page of the Label Wizard, as shown in Figure 7-28. Click Next.

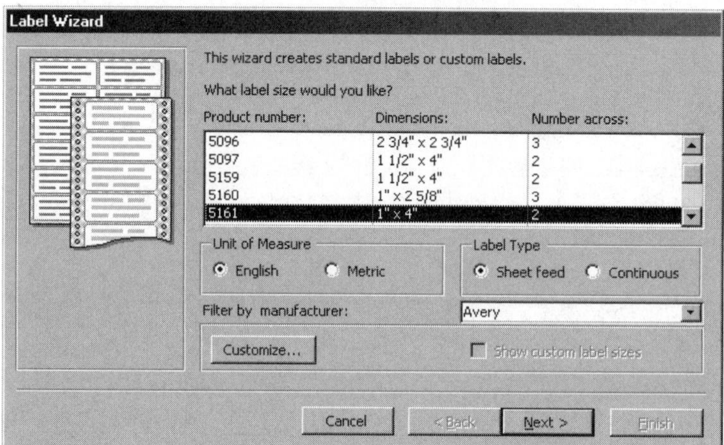

Figure 7-28. Select a label type in the Label Wizard.

4. Select the font to use for the labels, as shown in Figure 7-29. A font size of 8 to 10 points is generally advisable. Click Next.

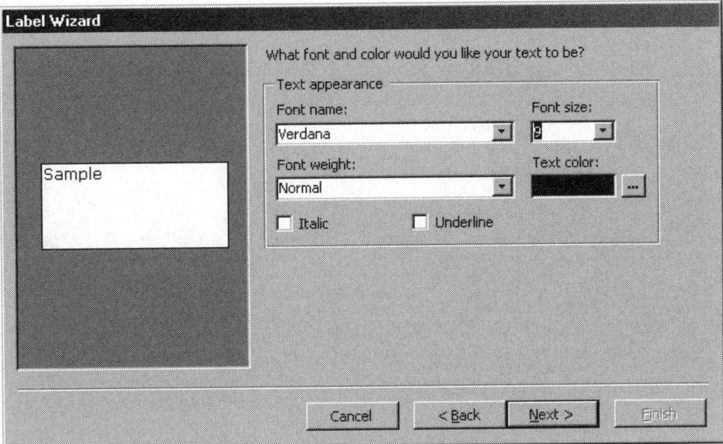

Figure 7-29. Select font characteristics for the labels.

5 Select the name and address components to use on the labels by field, entering punctuation marks as needed and pressing Enter to start a new row. Figure 7-30 shows the completed label layout. Click Next.

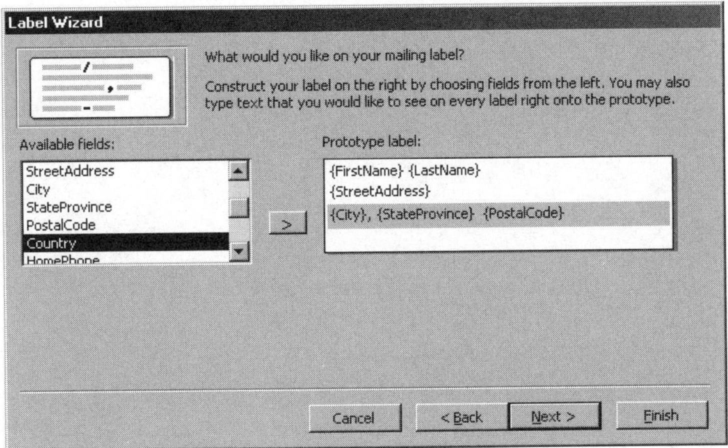

Figure 7-30. Place name and address fields on the label.

6 Sort the labels by one of the fields, as shown in Figure 7-31. Click Next.

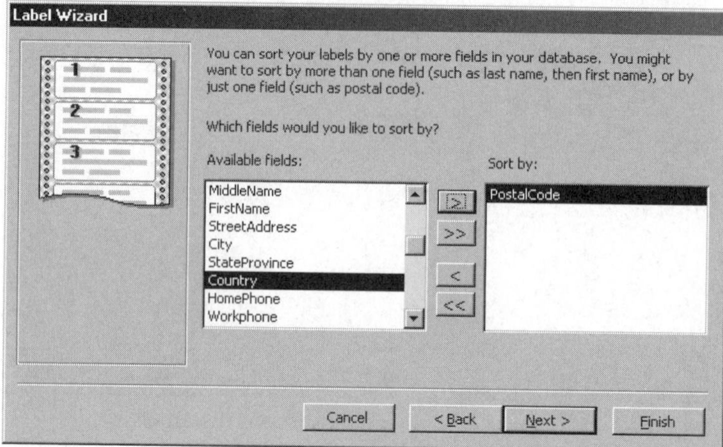

Figure 7-31. Select a field for sorting the labels.

7 Name the Labels report. (See Figure 7-32.) The name entered here is used for the report name and caption. Click Finish.

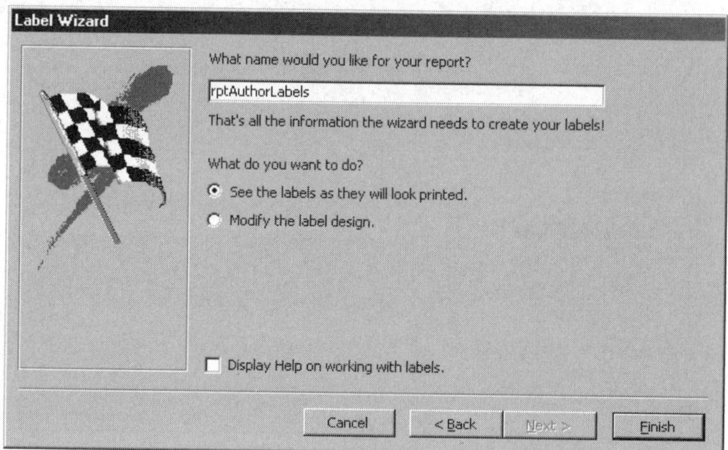

Figure 7-32. Name the Labels report on the last page of the wizard.

> **caution** As of the time of writing, label reports had two serious problems: The labels are the wrong size for the paper and printer, so they have to be manually resized; and most ZIP codes don't print (although United Kingdom postal codes do print).

Creating Reports Manually

In the previous sections, you learned how to use the Report Wizard and the New Report dialog box to generate reports using Access's pre-designed report styles. But not all the reports you create will fit into one of the automated report styles you've seen thus far: Some reports you'll need to create manually. The following sections explain reports you may want to design on your own with Access, including free-form reports, multicolumn reports, and crosstab reports.

Free-Form Reports

A free-form report is one that you put together any way you like. No controls are placed on the report by default; you place controls on the report manually. To create a free-form report, follow these steps. (The same steps are used to start a multicolumn or crosstab report.)

1. Click the Reports tab of the Database window, and click New at the top of the Database window.
2. In the New Report dialog box, select Design View for the report type, and select a table or query as the report's record source, as shown in Figure 7-33.

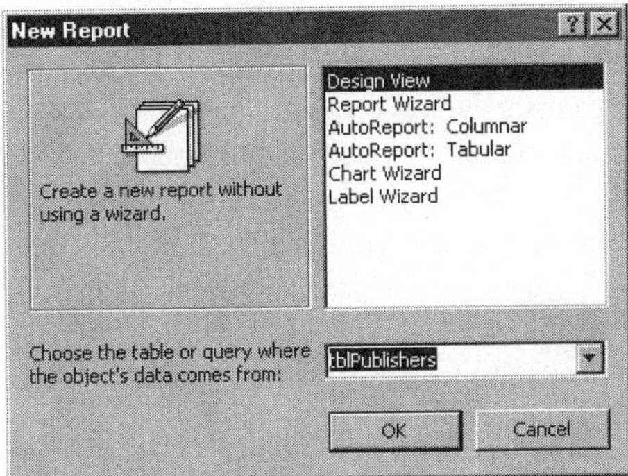

Figure 7-33. Start a free-form report when none of the standard report formats meet your needs.

A blank report opens in Design view. Use the Toolbox to place controls on the report in the layout you want, format them as desired, and then open the Sorting And Grouping dialog box to set up report groups and sort the data as you prefer. See Chapter 6, "Working with Form Controls," for more information on working with controls; controls work much the same on forms and reports.

Multicolumn Reports

Multicolumn reports are useful for displaying data from one or a few fields in a space-saving manner. They are typically used to produce phone directories, lists of product codes, and other such information laid out in several columns. The Crafts Categories report in the sample Crafts database is an example of a multicolumn report.

> **InsideOut**
>
> Access has no wizard for creating a multicolumn report, although one is certainly needed since the settings used to create a multicolumn report in Access are so well hidden that many users don't even realize that it's possible to create such a report.

To create a multicolumn report, follow these steps:

1. Create a blank report bound to the table or record source containing the data you want to put on the report.
2. Choose File, Page Setup to open the Page Setup dialog box, and then click the Columns tab.
3. Enter the number of columns you want in the Number Of Columns box, enter the desired row spacing (to insert vertical space between rows) in the Row Spacing box, and enter column spacing, width, and height in their property boxes. Select one of the two column layout options, and then close the dialog box. Figure 7-34 shows the completed Columns tab.

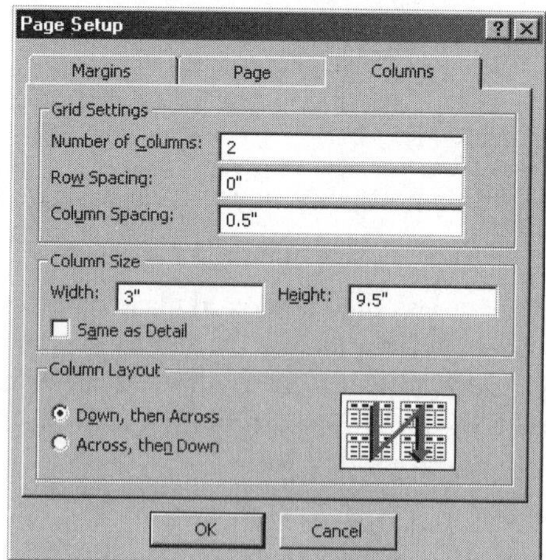

Figure 7-34. Set the column properties for a multicolumn report.

In Design view, a multicolumn report doesn't look different from a standard (single column) report—that is, there's no indication of the column boundaries on the report grid. This means that when you place controls on the report grid, you need to keep them within the boundaries of a single column width. The report header and footer, however, will span the entire report width.

4 Add a label control for the report title in the report header.

Figure 7-35 shows the finished two-column report.

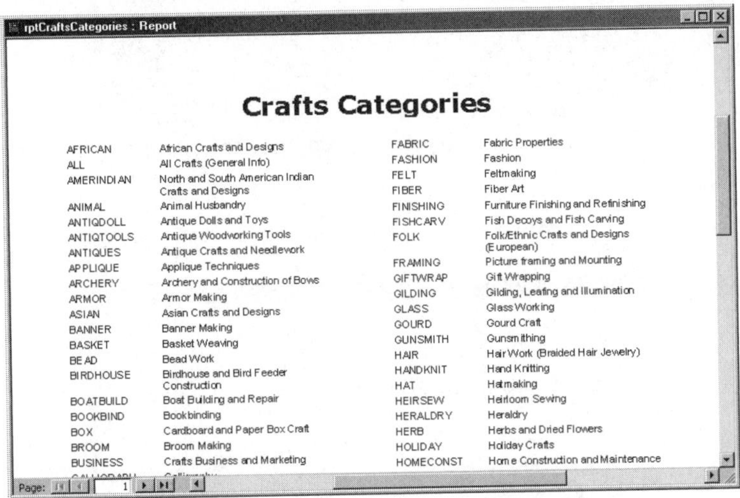

Figure 7-35. The finished two-column report looks like this.

If your report is both grouped and multicolumn, you can choose to start each group in a new column by setting the *NewRowOrCol* property of the group header to Before Section. Figure 7-36 demonstrates this option for a report based on qryBooksVideosSpecs.

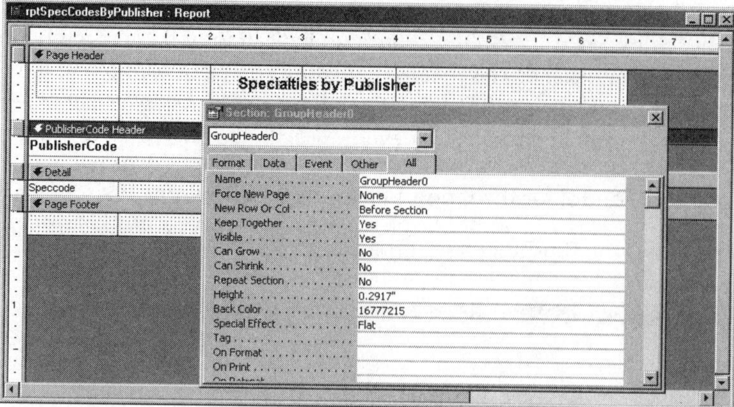

Figure 7-36. You can set a group header's properties to start a new group in a new column.

Figure 7-37 shows the grouped three-column report in print preview.

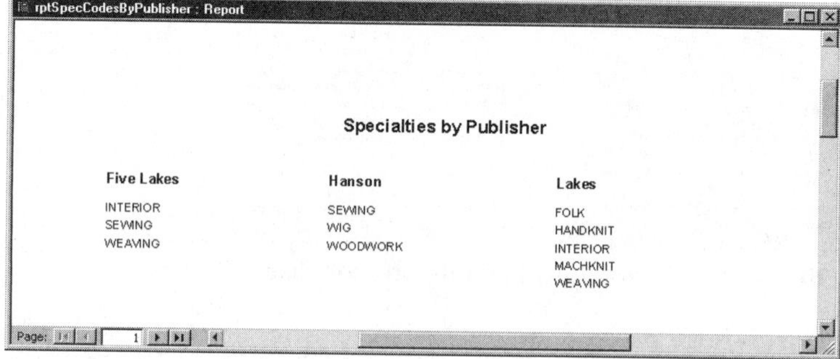

Figure 7-37. A three-column grouped report looks like this in print preview.

Numbering Report Items

A report that lists many items often needs to have the items numbered sequentially so that they can be conveniently referenced. This is especially useful when the items don't have IDs that can be used to identify them. The *RunningSum* property (available only for controls on reports) can be used to dynamically number report detail items, as follows:

1. Place a text box named txtRunningSum at the left side of the report's detail section, with a control source of =1 and the *RunningSum* property set to Over Group (to reset to 1 at the beginning of each group) or Over All (to number continuously throughout the report).
2. If you want a period after the number, add another text box (txtNumber) with a control source, as follows:

```
=[txtRunningSum] & "."
```

Figure 7-38 shows the Books By Year report with consecutive numbers for books in each year group, which are handy for referencing the books.

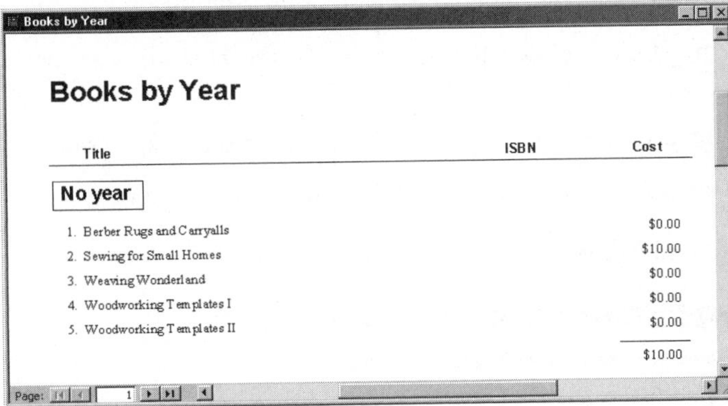

Figure 7-38. Use the *RunningSum* property to create a report with numbered detail items.

Crosstab Reports

If you've created a crosstab query that summarizes data in a useful manner, and you want to print and share the summarized data with other department members, you can generate a crosstab report to print the output of the crosstab query.

To create a crosstab report, follow these steps:

1. Create a crosstab query, as described in Chapter 9, "Using Queries to Select Data."
2. Create a blank report in Design view. Select the crosstab query as the report's record source.
3. Drag all the fields from the field list to the report grid. (If the field list isn't visible, click the Field List button on the toolbar to open it.)
4. Select each label in turn, click Cut on the Edit menu to delete the label and save it to the Clipboard, and then select the form header selector and click Paste on the Edit menu to paste the label into the header section.
5. When you have pasted all the labels into the form header, drag them to appropriate locations for column headings and format them.

   If you want, you can place a line control under the labels used as column headings.
6. Arrange the text boxes under each column heading in the report's detail section.
7. If you want, you can add a large label for a title in the form header.

Figure 7-39 shows the crosstab report in print preview.

rptCrosstab : Report

Books and Videos by Publisher and Specialty

Specialty	Five Lakes	Hanson	Lakes	Lucerne	Northwind
Folk/Ethnic Crafts and Designs (European)			1		
Hand Knitting			1	1	2
Interior Decorating			1	1	
Machine Knitting			1		1
Sewing		2			
Weaving	1				
Wigmaking		1			

Page: 1

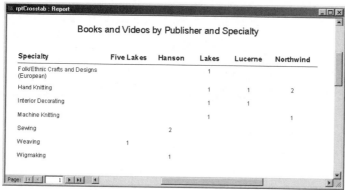

Figure 7-39. The crosstab report in print preview looks like this.

tip **Save time revising your report structure**

If your data is relatively fixed and your columns won't change—for example, if they contain quarterly financial data—a crosstab report is useful. But as you add data to the table underlying a crosstab report, the number of columns may change, so you'll frequently have to revise the report structure. To avoid this problem, use a PivotTable report instead. (See "PivotTable Subreports," page 280.)

Adding Embedded Subreports and Subforms to Reports

The usual way to create a report displaying data from linked tables (described in the section "Using Grouped Reports," page 239) is to create a query based on the linked tables and then use the Report Wizard to create a grouped report. However, you can also create a report that has one or more linked or unlinked subreports, each of which is itself a report. You can also add a subform to a report. You create a report that has a subreport in much the same way that you create a form that has a subform. The main report is linked to the "one" table, and the subreport or subform is linked to the "many" table.

Simulating a Datasheet Subreport with a Datasheet Subform

If you need to display linked data in a datasheet format, a main report containing an embedded datasheet subform is the easiest solution. You can place forms on reports (but not vice versa), so you can create a datasheet form and place it on a report.

Using the Crafts database as an example, follow these steps to create a main report for authors with a linked datasheet subform listing the books by each author:

1. Create a datasheet form based on the two linked tables, tblBooksAndVideos and tblBookAuthors.
2. Save the form with the LNC tag *fsub* to indicate that it's intended for use as a subform.
3. Create a report in Design view based on tblAuthors.

4. Open the Sorting And Grouping dialog box and create an Author group header and footer for the report, using the LastNameFirst field. Set the *KeepTogether* property to Whole Group, as shown in Figure 7-40.

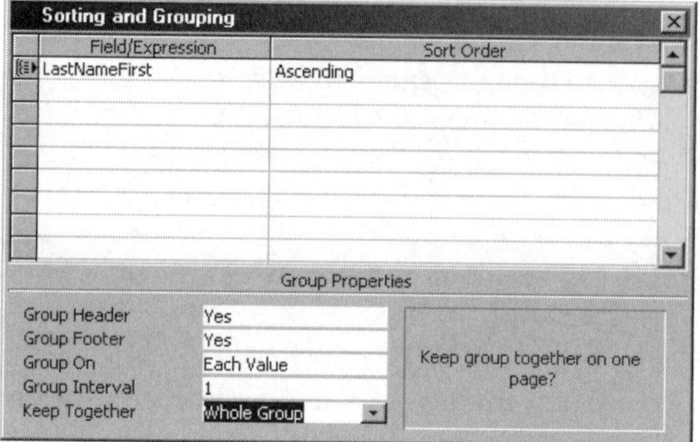

Figure 7-40. Create an Author group by using the LastNameFirst field.

5. Place the LastNameFirst field in the group header, and format it for a large font, including an underline if you want.

6. Add a text box to display the report's caption in the page header section of the report. Set the control source as follows:

```
=[Caption]
```

   This technique ensures that the title displayed on the report will match the report caption.

7. Drag the datasheet subform to the report's detail section.

8. Adjust the size of the subform so that each column's full width is displayed.

9. Set the *ForceNewPage* property of the LastNameFirst group footer to After Section, ensuring that each author's information starts on a new page.

Figure 7-41 shows the Books With Authors report, with the datasheet subform displaying the author's books.

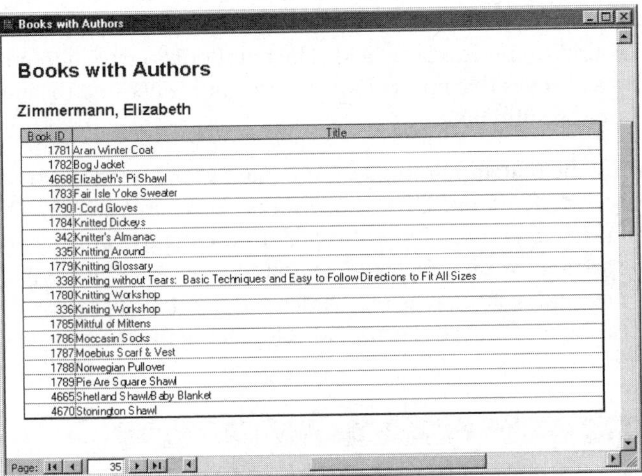

Figure 7-41. This report contains a datasheet subform displaying linked data.

Multiple Subreports

The main table in the Crafts database, tblBooksAndVideos, is linked to three other tables in one-to-many relationships. The standard grouped report format, based on a query that includes all the linked tables, might not be the most useful report format for a report with multiple one-to-many relationships. An alternative is to create one subreport for each linked table, with the main report linked to the "one" table.

In this section, you'll learn how to create a main report for tblBooksAndVideos with three linked subreports for tblAuthors, tblSources, and tblSpecialties. The general principles can be applied to any report that needs to include data from two or more "many" tables linked to a "one" table.

Each of the linked tables needs a simple report with just one control. The data source for each subreport can be just the linking table (the table that links the "one" table to the "many" table) if the linking table contains a field with the data to be displayed in the report. For example, rsubBookSpecs is bound to tblBookSpecs, and it has just one control, a text box bound to the Specialty field. The rsubBookSource subreport is similar, and rsubBookAuthors also has tblAuthors in its record source because the author's name needs to be placed on the subreport.

You can either specify the matching record on the main report using a criterion in the subreport's record source query or SQL statement (as shown in Figure 7-42) or leave the record source unfiltered and link the subreport to the main report by entering the BookID field as the setting for the *LinkChildFields* and *LinkMasterFields* properties of the subreports. The second technique is recommended if you want to use the same subreports on several reports, to avoid errors in referencing the main report by name in the record source criterion.

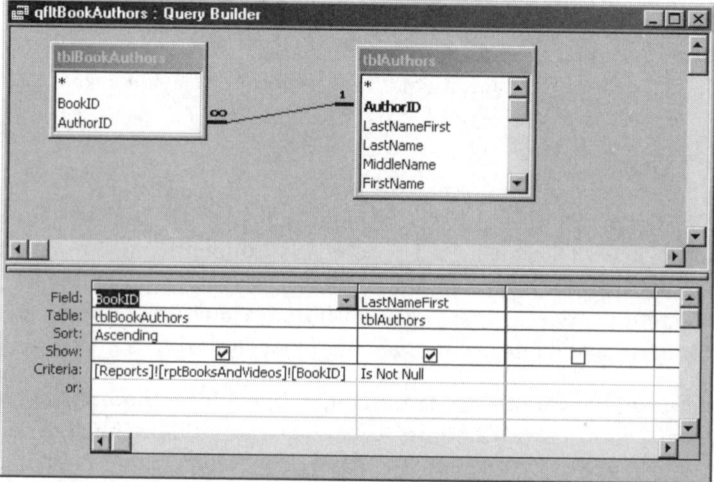

Figure 7-42. A filter query is used as a subreport's record source.

The subreports can be placed wherever they are needed on the main report. In the rptBooksAndVideos report in the Crafts database, rsubBookAuthors is placed in the Title header and rsubBookSource and rsubBookSpecs are placed in the Title footer. Figure 7-43 shows this report in Design view.

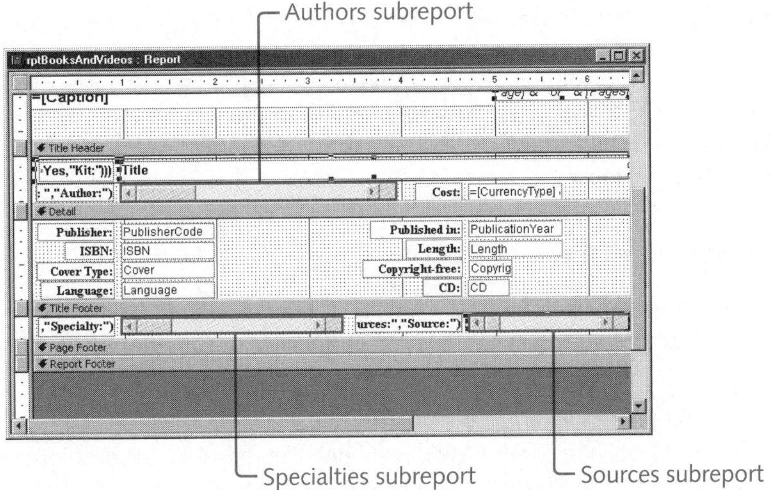

Figure 7-43. The rptBooksAndVideos report is shown here with subreports in Design view.

Figure 7-44 shows the report in print preview, displaying a book with multiple authors and specialties.

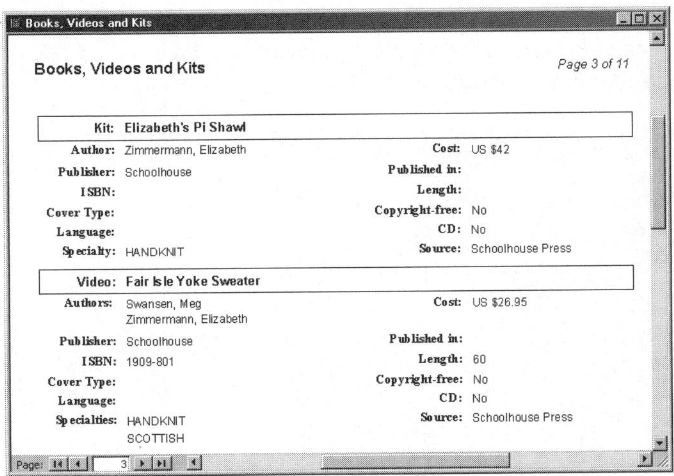

Figure 7-44. The rptBooksAndVideos report is shown here with subreports in print preview.

A report with multiple linked subreports can also be laid out like a worksheet, with the subreports arranged in columnar fashion in the detail section of the report. You can also embed unlinked subforms or subreports in a main report. For example, you might want to display reference data that applies to the entire report. In this case, the unlinked subreport will usually be embedded in the report header or footer, or possibly the page header or footer.

PivotChart Subreports

PivotChart reports are much easier to create and modify than chart reports, so it's preferable to use a PivotChart subform on a report rather than create a chart report.

To create a PivotChart report, follow these steps:

1. Create a PivotChart form. (If you need help creating a PivotChart form, see Chapter 12, "Using PivotTables and PivotCharts to Analyze Data.")
2. Set the form's default view to PivotChart on the form's properties sheet.
3. Clear the Field Button/Drop Zones check box on the Show/Hide tab of the PivotChart's properties sheet. (These interactive elements aren't needed on a printed PivotChart.)
4. Select each axis title in turn, and open the properties sheet. On the Format tab, enter the new caption for each axis, as shown in Figure 7-45. You can also change the font attributes on this tab.

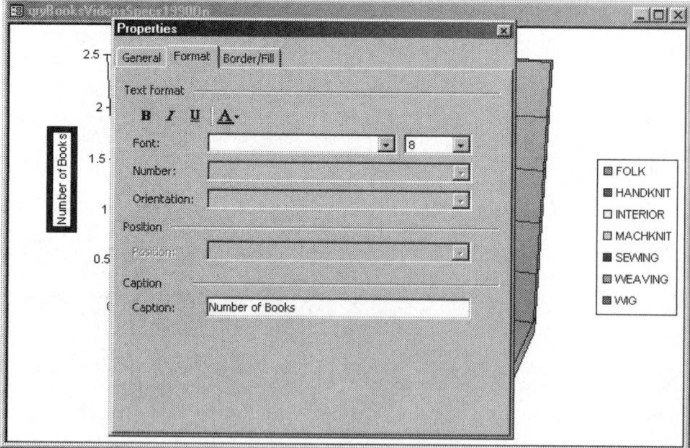

Figure 7-45. Enter axis titles for a PivotChart intended for use on a report.

5. Save the form with the LNC tag *fsub* to indicate that it will be used as a subform.
6. Create a blank unbound report.
7. Drag the subform to the report grid in Design view, as shown in Figure 7-46.

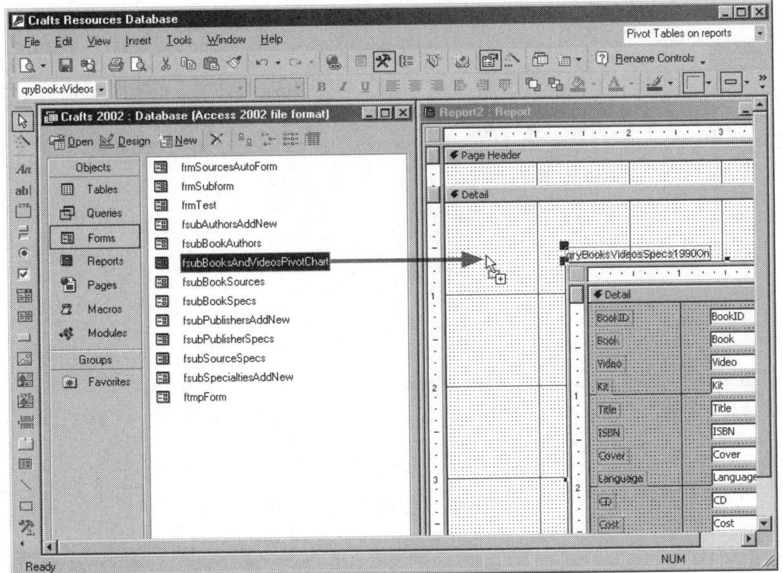

Figure 7-46. Drag the PivotChart subform to a blank report in Design view.

8. Delete the subform's label—you don't need it. If you want, you can add a label with a title for the chart in the report header section.
9. Move and resize the subform control as needed to suitably display the chart.

Figure 7-47 shows the finished report with a PivotChart. PivotChart subforms don't display very well in print preview, but they are perfectly clear when printed.

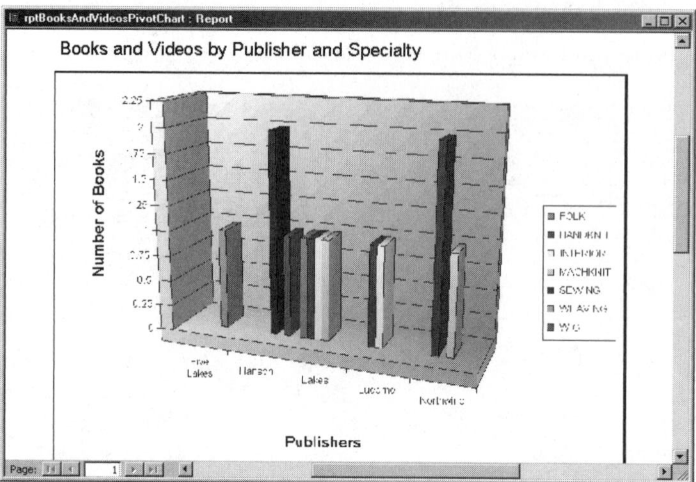

Figure 7-47. The finished PivotChart report in print preview looks like this.

> **tip** **Print a PivotChart form**
>
> Instead of creating a report containing a PivotChart subform, you can simply print the PivotChart form after removing the interactive display elements. This is the only situation I can think of in which printing a form might be useful. However, you can't control the size of the chart when you print it directly from a form—it will be the full height of the page, which might not be the best layout for your purposes.

PivotTable Subreports

You can create a report with an embedded PivotTable by using the same general technique you used with a PivotChart. Even though you can't actually pivot a PivotTable when it is embedded on a report, there's still an advantage to using a PivotTable instead of basing a report on a crosstab query: Using a PivotTable subform on a report ensures that the column headings will always remain accurate after any changes to the data. On the other hand, there is no guarantee that you'll be able to see all the columns. If they extend beyond the width of the report, the extra columns will be cut off.

Figure 7-48 shows a report based on a PivotTable, using the same underlying data used for the crosstab report shown in Figure 7-39.

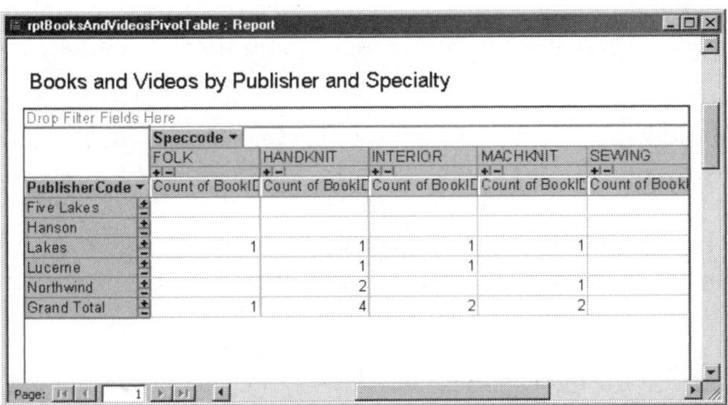

PublisherCode	FOLK Count of BookID	HANDKNIT Count of BookID	INTERIOR Count of BookID	MACHKNIT Count of BookID	SEWING Count of BookID
Five Lakes					
Hanson					
Lakes	1	1	1	1	
Lucerne		1	1		
Northwind		2		1	
Grand Total	1	4	2	2	

Figure 7-48. This report contains a PivotTable subform.

Formatting Reports

Reports generally don't need as much formatting as forms do (that is, if you prefer—as I do—a clean, spare report style), but the Report Wizard does offer you a number of formatting choices. As you can with forms, you can apply a selection of styles to reports by using the AutoFormat selection on the Format menu. You can also create a report template with controls and other features set up the way you want them to be when you create a report in Design view.

Using Report Templates

New reports in Design view are based on the Normal report template, which has a white background and uses the Arial 8-point font for controls. For simple data-checking or review reports, this look might be fine. But in some cases, you might want to customize the report template to go along with the look and feel of other publications in your department. For example, you might want to

- Include your company logo on the report.
- Establish standard formatting for controls in different sections of the report, much as you use different styles for various heading levels in a Microsoft Word template.

- Put controls displaying the page number, report name, or date and time printed in the page footer.
- Use color (sparingly) for emphasis (if you have a color printer)—for example, in a control displaying the report caption or on lines used to separate groups of data.
- Add a line identifying your department name, Web site, phone number, and other information.

You can make your own report templates to use when creating reports by following these steps (remember to substitute colors, fonts, and other formatting elements according to your own preferences):

1. Click the Reports tab of the Database window, and click New at the top of the Database window. In the New Report dialog box, select Design View for the report type, and then click OK. This creates a blank report that you'll use as the basis of your report template.
2. Although leaving the report background white makes it easier to read and quicker to print, you can select a background color if you want (and if you have a color printer), by using the Build button to the right of the *BackColor* property of the report's detail section or other section.
3. Place the controls you plan to use on the report, format them as desired, select them all, and choose Format, Set Control Defaults. This ensures that controls placed on a report made from the template will have the same formatting.
4. Save the blank report with a name such as rtmpReport.
5. Open the Options dialog box (Tools, Options), click the Forms/Reports tab, and enter the new template's name in the Report Template box, as shown in Figure 7-49.

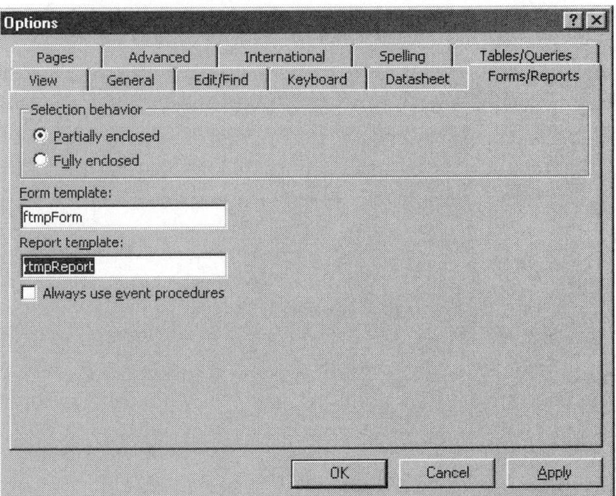

Figure 7-49. Enter the name of a report template on the Forms/Reports tab in the Options dialog box to use that template when creating new reports.

Ways to Use Report Templates

If you enter the name of a report template in the Report template box on the Forms/Reports page of the Options dialog box, new reports will use the properties you set for the controls on the report template and will have the same background color. However, the reports you create won't have any controls on them, nor will they have any code you may have written for the report template.

Design elements such as text boxes, labels, lines, rectangles, and different fonts or sizes for titles won't appear on new reports created from the template. Unlike using a Word template, where text and field codes are carried over to any new document created from the template, when an Access report is created from a template, you get a report with the section background colors you selected for the template—and no controls at all. When you place controls on the new report, they'll have the properties you set with the Format, Set Control Defaults command when you created the report template.

If you want to create new reports already filled with formatted text boxes and controls, perhaps with different fonts and sizes for different report groups, simply copy the report template manually; your new report will then have all the controls and code that you put on the report template.

caution Whichever way you intend to use a report template, you must import it into any database in which you want to use it. If the report template listed in the Options dialog box isn't present in the current database, the default template will be used instead.

Troubleshooting

My report has gaps in its data

Say you created a name and address report with text boxes bound to the fields containing the name and address data, but when the report is printed, big gaps appear between the first name and the last name and between the address components. What can be done to prevent these types of gaps?

To prevent gaps in data, you can create controls with expressions that concatenate components (such as those that compose names and addresses) into a single expression used as the text box's control source. A typical Control Source expression to print a name without gaps is shown here:

```
=[FirstName] & " " & Iif([MiddleName], [MiddleName] & " ", "")
 & [LastName] & " " & [Suffix]
```

To print the City, State, and ZIP line of the address without gaps, use an expression such as the following:

```
=[City] & ", " & [State] & "  " & [Zip]
```

Using AutoFormat

You can use the AutoFormat dialog box (opened by choosing Format, AutoFormat in Design view) to apply a new format to a report. These formats are the same ones that you can select within the Report Wizard.

The AutoFormat feature works somewhat differently with reports than with forms. For example, you can't update one of the built-in styles with your own custom style, as you do with form styles. Although this option is available in the Customize AutoFormat dialog box, you'll get an error message if you select it. However, you can create a new AutoFormat style based on the currently open report, as shown in Figure 7-50. You simply have to use a slightly different technique for report AutoStyles.

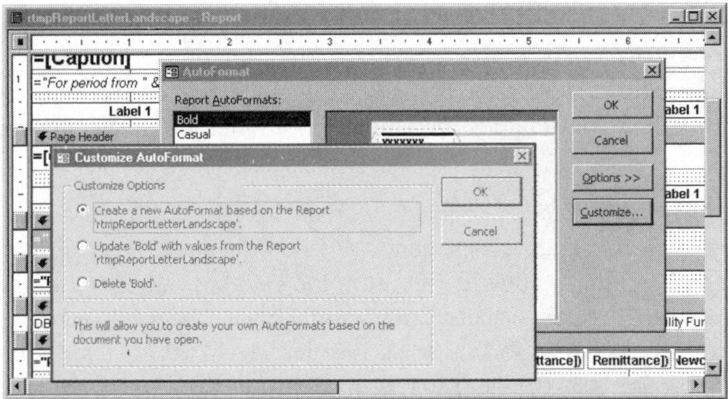

Figure 7-50. You can create a new AutoFormat style from a report.

Clicking OK in the Customize AutoFormat dialog box opens the New Style Name dialog box, shown in Figure 7-51, in which you can enter the name of the new style.

Figure 7-51. Give your new AutoFormat style a name that's easy to remember.

After you save the new style, it will be available, along with the built-in styles, from the AutoFormat dialog box.

Saving Your Report Styles

Being able to create your own styles using the AutoFormat dialog box is not as useful a feature as it might seem because of the limitations on the formatting controlled by the AutoFormat style. Font sizes and styles used for different report elements are not included in saved styles; only a small portion of the original report template's formatting is applied to the new report when you apply a style to it.

If you need to regularly create complex reports, with different fonts for text boxes and labels in different report sections, and perhaps design elements such as lines or rectangles, the best method I've found is the old-fashioned method of simply copying a report template.

To use this method, create a report template with all the controls formatted as you prefer and with the desired graphical elements. When you want to create a new report based on the template, simply copy the report in the Database window, using the standard Windows keyboard shortcuts Ctrl+C and Ctrl+V. (Alternatively, open the report template in Design view, and then choose File, Save As to save it under another name.) Low-tech though it is, this simple technique ensures that everything you put on the report template—text boxes, labels, lines, rectangles, images, and all—will appear on the new report made from the template.

Understanding Report Features and Properties

As you've seen, reports share many of the same properties as forms. In this section, we'll look at a few useful properties unique to reports. You can use report properties to control the way headers and footers are displayed, for example, or to establish report groups, sort report data, choose the column format for report sections, and determine whether you want repetitive data to be hidden or displayed. To get help for any report property, place your insertion point in the property box on the report's properties sheet and press F1 to open context-specific Help.

Report Format Properties

The report format properties that differ from form properties are located on the Format tab of the report properties sheet. These report format properties are described here:

- ***Page Header, Page Footer.*** These properties offer you a choice of All Pages, Not With Rpt Hdr, Not With Rpt Ftr, and Not With Rpt Hdr/Ftr. Choose the appropriate setting to prevent the page header (or footer) from being printed on the same page as the report header (or footer).

- ***Grp Keep Together.*** This property offers you a choice of Per Page or Per Column, allowing you to decide how groups should be kept together.

> **note** Property names in properties sheets can have spaces, but in VBA code they have no spaces. For example, you will see the *Back Color* property in a text box's properties sheet, but in code you'll reference this property as *BackColor*.

Sorting and Grouping

Use the Sorting And Grouping dialog box (View, Sorting And Grouping) to set up report groups, sort report data, and adjust various group properties. (See Figure 7-52.)

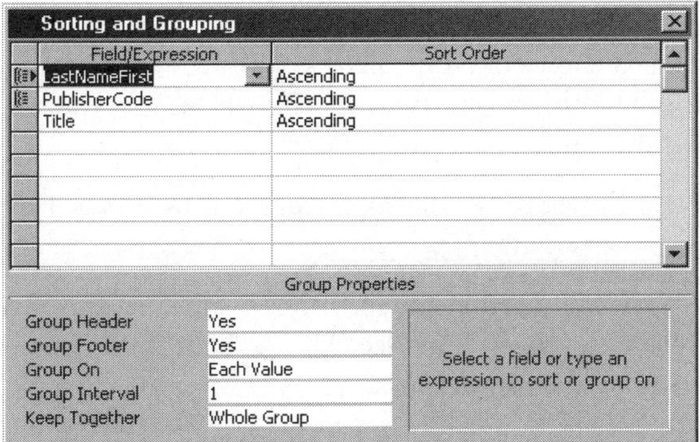

Figure 7-52. You can set group properties by using the Sorting And Grouping dialog box.

The settings shown in Figure 7-52 are for rptBooksByAuthorAndPublisher in the sample Crafts database. There are three group levels, of which LastNameFirst is the top level. The Sort Order column for each group level offers a choice of Ascending (the default) or Descending. Looking at the bottom of the dialog box, you can see the following properties for this group level:

- ***Group Header*** is set to Yes so that the group has a group header section.
- ***Group Footer*** is set to Yes so that the group has a group footer section.
- ***Group On*** is left at the default setting Each Value so that a new group is started with each author.
- ***Group Interval*** is set to 1. You can set this property to another value to start a new group for every five records (or whichever number you choose).
- ***Keep Together*** is set to Whole Group, to keep the LastNameFirst group from being broken up if there isn't enough room for the whole group on a page.

The PublisherCode group level has only a group header, not a footer. All the other properties are left at their defaults. The Title group has neither a header nor a footer; all its properties are left at their defaults. The Title field is used only for sorting.

Report Sections

Reports can have up to ten group levels, but generally two or three are sufficient. Each report section has its own properties sheet, with several significant properties on the Format tab. Each report section has a selection of the following properties (along with other properties shared with forms):

- ***Force New Page.*** Offers a choice of None, Before Section, After Section, and Before & After Section. Use this property to specify where a page break occurs.
- ***New Row Or Col*** Offers a choice of None, Before Section, After Section, and Before & After Section. Use this property to specify where a section break occurs on a multicolumn report.
- ***Keep Together.*** Offers a choice of Yes or No, for preventing a page break within the section.
- ***Visible.*** Allows you to choose whether the section is visible. Set this property to False in VBA code to hide the section. See "Using Section Events for Conditional Formatting of Data in Reports," page 291, for an example.
- ***Can Grow, Can Shrink.*** Offer a choice of Yes or No. These properties specify whether the section can grow or shrink to accommodate data in text boxes that have grown or shrunk.
- ***Repeat Section.*** Offers a choice of Yes or No. If you set this property to Yes, the header section repeats on the next page when the group data is advanced to another page so that every page will have a header.

Troubleshooting

My text boxes don't display all the text

Sometimes long text in text boxes on a report is cut off. You need to expand the text box so that all text will be printed. Text boxes on Access reports have two handy properties (not available on forms) that can be used to make the controls shrink or expand as needed. Setting the *CanGrow* property of a text box to Yes allows it to grow in height so as to accommodate all the text in the field; setting the *CanShrink* property to Yes shrinks the text box vertically to nothing, to prevent a large blank space if a text box has no data.

Report section properties, and the properties of report controls, can be set from VBA code to display or hide information when certain conditions are met, as described in the next two sections. Additionally, you can use the conditional formatting feature of text box controls to set their properties conditionally, as described below in the sidebar "Using Conditional Formatting on a Report Control."

Using Conditional Formatting on a Report Control

As an alternative to writing code for the report's *Format* event, you can use the conditional formatting feature to set conditions for formatting a control in the interface. To make a text box bold and yellow if it has the value 0, follow these steps:

1. Create a report with a text box that you want to format differently in some circumstances. (I created a simple report, based on the tblProducts table in the Northwind sample database, that contains only the ProductName, UnitPrice, and UnitsInStock fields.)
2. Select the text box to be formatted (in this case, txtUnitsInStock), and then choose Format, Conditional Formatting to open the Conditional Formatting dialog box.
3. To make the txtUnitsInStock text box bold and yellow when the value is 0, fill out Condition 1 in the dialog box as shown in Figure 7-53, and click OK to save the condition.

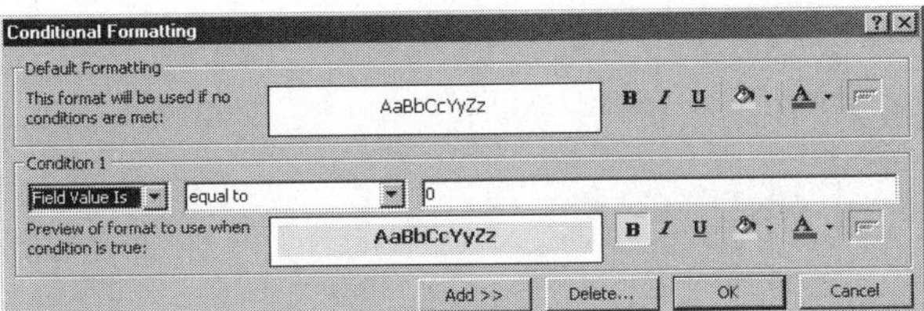

Figure 7-53. Use the Conditional Formatting dialog box to create a condition that changes the color of a text box when its value is 0.

Now the Units In Stock value will be bold and yellow in those rows where it has the value 0.

Conditional formatting works only for controls, not for report sections—to format report sections, you still have to write an event procedure for the *Format* event.

Using Section Properties to Show or Hide Data

Access report sections have three special events—*Format*, *Print*, and *Retreat*—that are useful if you want to apply conditional formatting to your reports (either to individual controls or to entire sections). The *Format* event (the most useful of the three) takes place when the report is formatted but before it is printed. The *Print* event, as you might expect, occurs when the report is printed. The rarely used *Retreat* event occurs when Access returns to a previous report section during formatting, such as when a page break has to be moved to keep a section on one page.

For example, say you have a color printer and you want to make the value of a control named txtSales stand out when it exceeds $10,000. You can write an event procedure for the report's detail section to do the formatting. To make the text in that control larger, bold, and bright red against a yellow background—and additionally (if you want to go over the top to congratulate the best salespeople), to make an image of a large gold star (imgGoldStar) become visible beside txtSales—use the following code in the *Format* event procedure of the report's detail section:

```
Private Sub Detail_Format(Cancel As Integer, FormatCount As Integer)

    If Me![Sales] >= 10000 Then
       Me![txtSales].FontBold = True
       Me![txtSales].FontName = "Arial Black"
       Me![txtSales].FontSize = 12
       Me![txtSales].ForeColor = vbRed
       Me![txtSales].BackColor = vbYellow
       Me![imgGoldStar].Visible = True
    Else
       Me![txtSales].FontBold = False
       Me![txtSales].FontName = "Arial"
       Me![txtSales].FontSize = 9
       Me![txtSales].ForeColor = vbBlack
       Me![txtSales].BackColor = vbWhite
       Me![imgGoldStar].Visible = False
    End If

End Sub
```

Note that the control properties are explicitly returned to their normal state if the $10,000 condition for txtSales is not met; otherwise, the special properties will carry over from the previous item.

Using Section Events for Conditional Formatting of Data in Reports

You can use the *Format* event to hide an entire section of a report if it contains no data to print (or some other condition is met). Setting the entire section's *Visible* property to False is simpler than setting the *CanShrink* property to Yes for all the controls (and the section itself), and it allows you to eliminate an entire group of controls from a report if a certain key field is blank, even if some of the controls contain data (something that you can't do with the *CanShrink* property).

To make an entire group footer section disappear from the report if the txtSchedule control contains a blank value, use the following code:

```
Private Sub GroupFooter3_Format(Cancel As Integer, FormatCount As Integer)

    If Nz(Me![txtSchedule]) <> "" Then
        Me.Section(acGroupLevel2Footer).Visible = True
    Else
        Me.Section(acGroupLevel2Footer).Visible = False
    End If

End Sub
```

The numeric settings and named constants for referencing various report sections are listed in Table 7-2.

Table 7-2. Section numbers and named constants for referencing report sections

Setting	Named constant	Description
0	acDetail	Report detail section
1	acHeader	Report header section
2	acFooter	Report footer section
3	acPageHeader	Report page header section
4	acPageFooter	Report page footer section
5	acGroupLevel1Header	Group level 1 report header section
6	acGroupLevel1Footer	Group level 1 report footer section
7	acGroupLevel2Header	Group level 2 report header section
8	acGroupLevel2Footer	Group level 2 report footer section

If a report has more than two grouping-level sections, they are numbered consecutively beginning with 9.

InsideOut

The section numbers in the report interface don't match either the numeric settings for sections or the section numbers used in the equivalent named constants for various report sections. When referencing a report section in code, don't simply copy the number you see in the properties sheet title bar. Look up the section number or named constant in the Object Browser (or open the *Section* property Help topic from the Section property of the Report object in the Object Browser). Alternatively (for the named constant value only), open the Grouping And Filtering dialog box and count down from the top (starting with 1) to get the correct number for a group header or footer section to use in a named constant such as acGroupLevel2Footer.

Neat Report Tricks

The following sections describe special formatting tricks that use some of the more obscure properties and methods of reports.

Drawing Lines and Circles on Reports

Access has no Circle control type, so if you want to place a circle on a report, you'll find no obvious way to do so. However, you can create a circle using the old MS-DOS methods, functions, and properties that have been carried over into Access VBA. Be forewarned: These techniques are not easy to use, and they can be excruciatingly slow in operation (less so if you have a fast computer). I won't go into detail about the MS-DOS print techniques; refer to Access Help topics for the *Line* and *Circle* methods for details and some examples of how to use these methods.

The *Circle* method is the only way to draw a circle, an arc, or an ellipse on an Access report (unless you want to create the shape in Microsoft Paint and place it in an Image control). The following sample code, running from a report's *Page* event procedure, draws a red quarter-circle on a report:

```
Private Sub Report_Page()

    Me.DrawWidth = 500
    Me.Circle (25, 25), 2000, 255

End Sub
```

Figure 7-54 shows the report with a quarter-circle drawn by the *Circle* method.

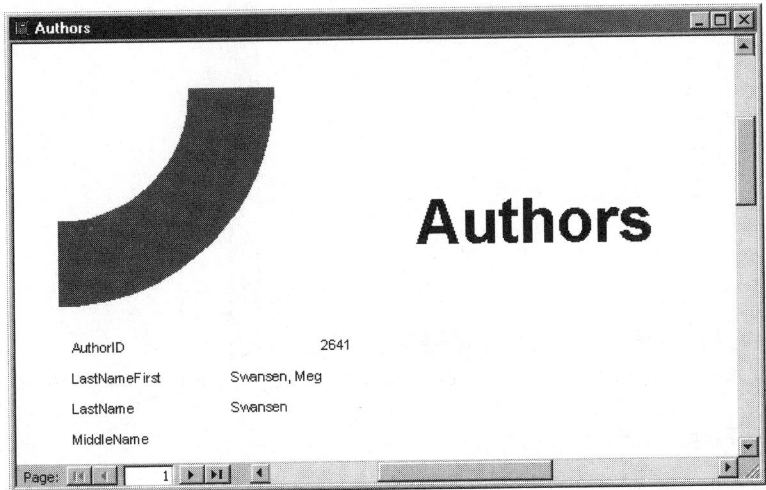

Figure 7-54. You can use the *Circle* method to draw circles (or parts of circles) on your reports.

You can use another MS-DOS print method to place a border around the entire report page, as in the following code, which also runs from the report's *Page* event procedure:

```
Private Sub Report_Page()

    Me.Line (1, 1)-(Me.ScaleWidth, Me.ScaleHeight), , B

End Sub
```

Figure 7-55 shows the report with a border.

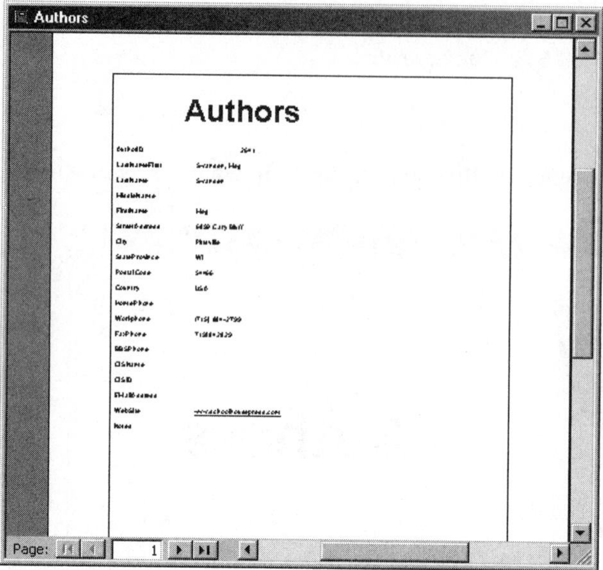

Figure 7-55. The border on this report was drawn by using the *Line* method.

Grouping by First Letter

You can use some of the properties in the Sorting And Grouping dialog box to group records by the first letter of a field, such as the Company or LastName field. (This effect is often used in directory-type reports.) The Northwind database has a report named Alphabetical List of Products that uses this feature. To set up first-letter grouping in a report, you need to enter the grouping field twice in the Sorting And Grouping dialog box, as shown in Figure 7-56. The first entry is grouped on Prefix Characters with a Group Interval of 1 (used to create the big letter for grouping). The second entry is grouped on Each Value (the entire field, used for sorting).

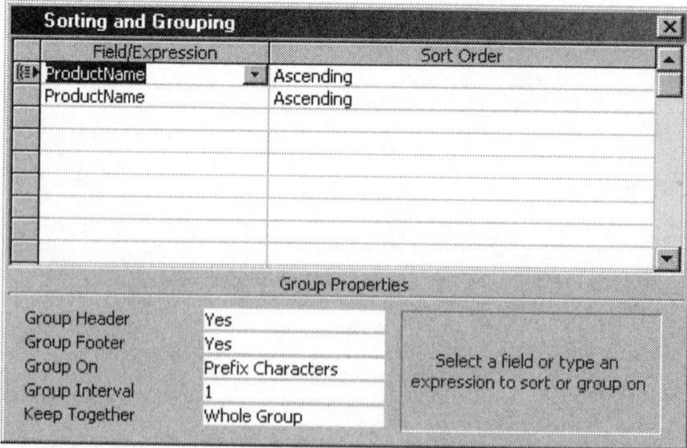

Figure 7-56. You can group a report by prefix characters.

Next, in the report itself you need a text box to display the first letter with the following control source:

```
=Left([ProductName],1)
```

Size the text box appropriately to display the single letter in a large font. Figure 7-57 shows a somewhat modified version of the Northwind report.

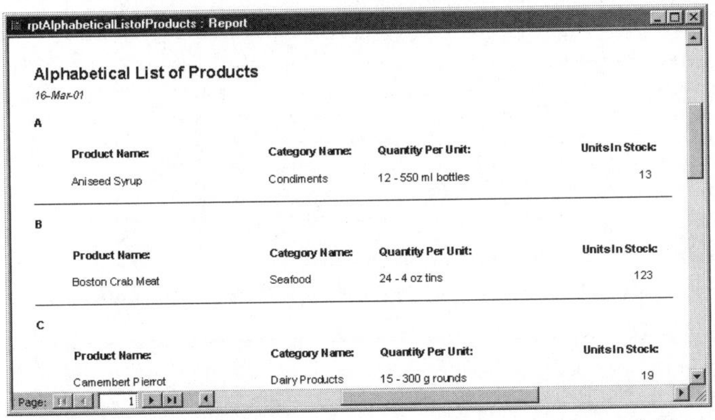

Figure 7-57. This report is grouped by the first letter of the product name.

Alternate-Line Shading

Shading alternating lines on a tabular financial report with many columns of numbers can help you keep track of where you are when you're reading the report. You can create alternate-line shading in VBA code with the obscure *CurrentRecord* property and the *Mod* function. The following code, running from the *Format* event procedure of a report's detail section, makes the detail section's background color white for odd records and light gray for even records:

```
Private Sub Detail_Format(Cancel As Integer, FormatCount As Integer)

    Const vbLightGrey = 12632256

    If Me.CurrentRecord Mod 2 = 0 Then
        Me.Section(acDetail).BackColor = vbLightGrey
    Else
        Me.Section(acDetail).BackColor = vbWhite
    End If

End Sub
```

> **note** The *Mod* operator (short for *modulo,* which you might remember from high school math) divides one number by another and returns the remainder. Dividing even numbers by 2 yields 0 as a remainder, and thus the Mod operator is a handy way to distinguish between odd and even numbers, as in the sample code.

Figure 7-58 shows the Goals By Salesperson report with alternate-line shading.

Goals by Salesperson

Year	Property	Salesperson ID	Jan	Feb	Mar	Apr	May	Jun	Jul	Aug	Sep	Oct	Nov	Dec
1997	FAN	92	1	12	55	66	6	4	34	23	22	2	33	45
1997	GRT	40	25	52	58	50	46	65	28	98	58	45	110	112
1997	GRT	44	25	65	95	85	100	125	150	125	100	85	75	75
1997	NEB	50	45	3	8	78	7	2	44	6	7		8	8
1997	NEB	52	3	34	41	34	8	88	9	9	2	45	8	5
1997	NEB	78	9	56	41	12	22	2	12	12	68	42	58	67
1997	NEB	79	77	12	47	23	3	4	54	52	36	23	44	45
1997	WIL	53	7	45	12	12	23	21	24	25	8	9	3	4
1997	WIL	76	52	45	40	85	75	25	65	87	45	25	125	325
1998	GRN	29	13	2	32	33	22	7	5	55	4	11	32	23
1998	GRN	38	5	45	2	66	12	23	44	56	23	33	9	55
1998	GRN	49	22	9	78	8	33	8	34	54	3	3	45	57
1998	GRN	69	3	45	6	55	2	78	34	5	56	34	45	14
1998	GRN	70	45	34	34	45	33	2	5	66	4	2	66	2
1998	GRN	71	45	56	2	52	45	85	21	55	12	22	11	45
1998	GRT	40	52	54	78	85	100	25	65	36	95	85	32	452
1998	GRT	44	52	45	87	66	25	36	54	25	25	85	85	125
1998	WIL	33	16	43	6	8	3	88	4	8	23	12	2	334
1998	WIL	53	13	23	7	78	77	78	55	88	6	33	11	44
1998	WIL	76	44	75	95	25	65	25	36	56	95	258	41	521
1999	GRT	40	54	52	2	6	66	55	34	9	45	8	4	45

Page: 1

Figure 7-58. Alternate-line shading can make a report easier to read.

Troubleshooting

An *#Error* error message appears on my report in place of the data

If an *#Error* error message is printed in place of field data, as shown in Figure 7-59, there are several possible causes. The bound field's name may have been changed, or the field may have been deleted from the report's record source table or query.

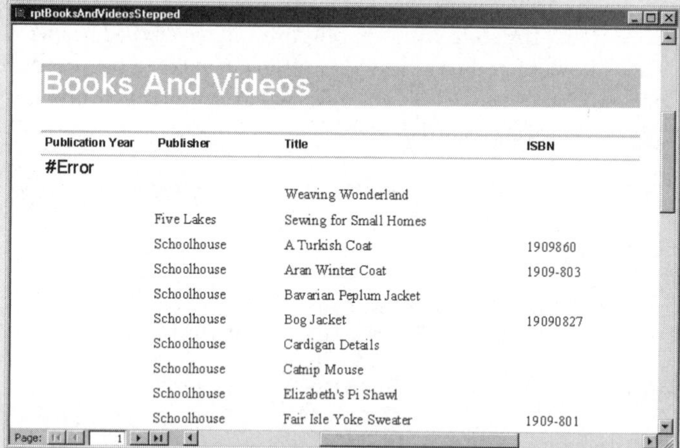

rptBooksAndVideosStepped

Books And Videos

Publication Year	Publisher	Title	ISBN
#Error			
		Weaving Wonderland	
	Five Lakes	Sewing for Small Homes	
	Schoolhouse	A Turkish Coat	1909860
	Schoolhouse	Aran Winter Coat	1909-803
	Schoolhouse	Bavarian Peplum Jacket	
	Schoolhouse	Bog Jacket	19090827
	Schoolhouse	Cardigan Details	
	Schoolhouse	Catnip Mouse	
	Schoolhouse	Elizabeth's Pi Shawl	
	Schoolhouse	Fair Isle Yoke Sweater	1909-801

Page: 1

Figure 7-59. *#Error* is printed on a report instead of data because of a problem with a control or field name.

Placing Totals on Reports

It is delightfully easy to place subtotals and totals on grouped reports. All you have to do is put a text box under the column of figures you want to add and then use an expression such as the following as the text box's control source, where Cost is the field you want to sum. (You can use *Count* instead of *Sum* to get a count of items.)

```
=Sum([Cost])
```

Make sure you reference the field name in the expression, not the control name (the control bound to the Cost field should be named txtCost); otherwise, you might get a reference error. Use the same control source expression in any group footer in which you want a subtotal and the report footer—the only difference is in the name of the control. The correct group subtotal or report total will be displayed in each section.

To get a row total rather than a column total, use an expression such as the following for a text box placed at the right side of the detail section:

```
=[Jan] + [Feb] + [Mar] + [Apr] + [May] + [Jun] + [Jul] + [Aug] +
 [Sep] + [Oct] + [Nov] + [Dec]
```

Another cause of the *#Error* problem is that an expression in the *ControlSource* property references the field name and the text box's name is the same as the field name, causing a circular reference error. Figure 7-60 shows the properties sheet of a text box control illustrating this problem.

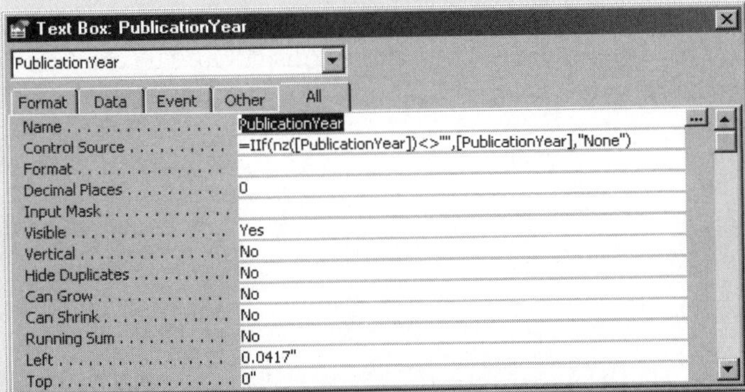

Figure 7-60. When the name of a text box is the same as the name of a field referenced in its *ControlSource* property, a circular reference error results.

If the control source for the text box is a field, fix the problem by reselecting the bound field to make sure that you have the correct spelling, and (if necessary) give the text box a name that is not the same as the field name. In the LNC naming convention, text boxes have the *txt* tag.

Using a Form to Filter Report Records

Several methods are available if you want to filter a report by a specific value in a field, but not always the same value. For example, you might want to filter report data by the month of January one time and by the month of March later. One method you can use to filter a report is a parameter pop-up query. Another method is to use a dialog box popped up from the report's *OnOpen* event. Both methods are useful, but they have their disadvantages.

For more information about filtering by query, see Chapter 9, "Using Queries to Select Data."

The pop-up parameter boxes aren't particularly user-friendly, and it's annoying to have to enter the parameters every time the report runs, especially if you want a report based on the same parameters for a number of successive printings. The dialog box form is modal, and users might be annoyed to find that they can't do anything else while the dialog box is open. A dialog box also requires input every time you run the report.

For filtering reports, consider putting a combo box for selecting a value on the main menu of your database, bound to a table named tblInfo that stores miscellaneous information used throughout the database. Reports that need to be filtered by the selected value have a criterion limiting the appropriate field to the value selected on the main menu.

Using a bound combo box to select the filter value means that the selected value is saved to tblInfo and thus doesn't need to be reselected until you want to filter by a different value. Figure 7-61 shows the cboSpecialty combo box on the main menu of the Crafts database, which is bound to the Specialty field in tblInfo. When the list is opened, both the Speccode and Specdesc fields are displayed. The combo box's bound column contains the Speccode field, which is used for filtering reports.

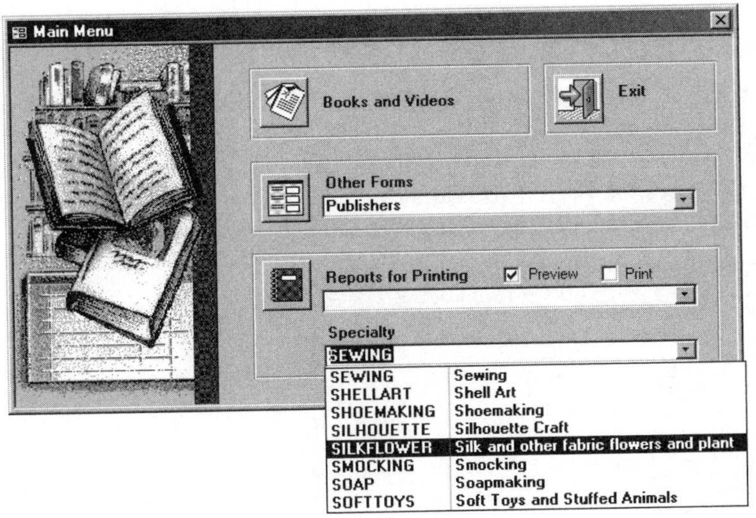

Figure 7-61. Use the cboSpecialty combo box to select a specialty for filtering reports.

Figure 7-62 shows the SQL statement record source for a report filtered by the specialty chosen in cboSpecialty on the main menu.

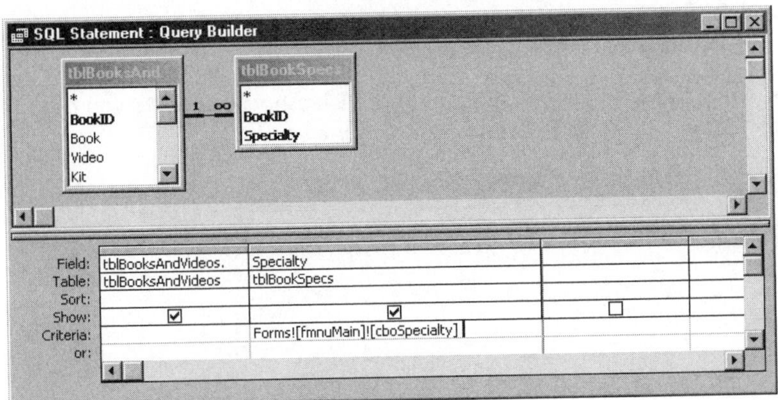

Figure 7-62. This SQL statement filters by a value selected from cboSpecialty.

Exporting Reports Using the Snapshot Utility

One of the selections for exporting a report using File, Export is Snapshot Format (*.snp). Exporting a report to a snapshot (see Figure 7-63) creates a file that you can e-mail or otherwise transfer to another person, who need not have Access as long as she has the Snapshot Viewer. You can download the software from the Microsoft Office download center at *http://office.microsoft.com/downloads.*

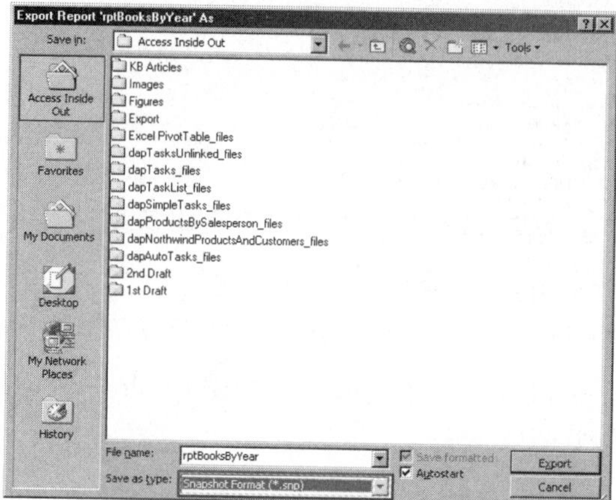

Figure 7-63. You can export a report to snapshot format.

Figure 7-64 shows the report snapshot in the Snapshot Viewer. As you can see, the snapshot looks exactly like the report in print preview.

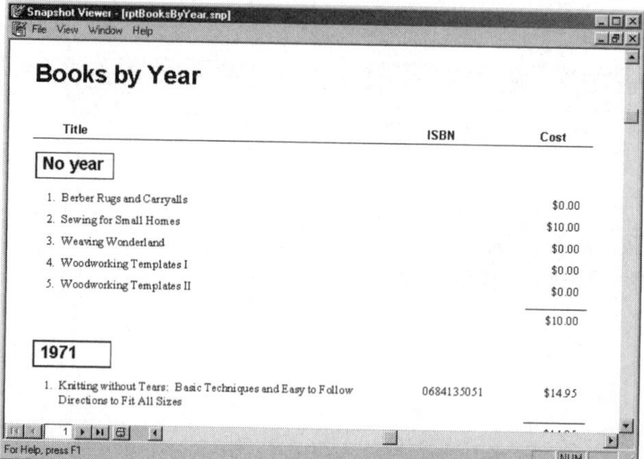

Figure 7-64. A report snapshot opened in the Snapshot Viewer looks just like the original report.

Report snapshots can't be modified. Depending on your point of view, this is either an excellent security feature or an annoyance.

Chapter 8

Using Design Tools

As you learned in earlier chapters, Microsoft Access 2002 provides form and report wizards that automate the process of creating simple reports. You can use the form and report wizards to generate a good first draft of most forms and reports. However, the wizards seldom supply a final solution. Most of the time, you'll need to tweak the results a little. The design environment (Design view) offers a number of tools and formatting options for modifying both forms and reports, including the following:

- The Toolbox
- Selection methods for working with multiple controls
- The grid and the Snap To Grid feature
- Formats for sizing, grouping, and aligning controls

Whether you're new to Access, a power user, or a developer, you'll probably find yourself working in Design view more often than you initially expected. Fortunately, rearranging and grouping controls, adding design elements such as lines and rectangles, inserting unbound and calculated controls, and more can be an efficient use of your time and of the design tools. Just a few enhancements can make a form easier to use or a report more effective.

note Throughout this chapter, you'll work mostly with forms, but remember that you can also apply these techniques to reports. When it comes to controls, keep in mind that the text box is the control of choice for displaying data in reports. You can insert almost any control into a report, but it will probably lose its unique functionality in the report environment. Other than the occasional chart or image control, reports usually contain only text box controls and labels.

Using the Toolbox to Insert Native Controls

Adding new controls to forms will probably be a frequent task. You might need to display the results of an expression (in a calculated control), or you might need to expand your form's functionality as your application grows. (You probably won't add controls to reports quite as often.) The Toolbox offers quick access to native controls. (The term *native controls* refers to the controls that come with Access.) The Toolbox is actually a toolbar that you can toggle on and off by clicking the Toolbox button on the appropriate design toolbar (Form Design, Report Design, or Page Design). In Page Design view, the Toolbox offers more controls than in other design views.

Follow these steps to insert a native control on a form. (You can use the same steps to insert a control on a report or a data access page.)

1. Open a form in Design view by clicking Forms on the Database window's Objects bar and then double-clicking Create Form In Design View. (Alternatively, you can click the New button in the Database window.)
2. If necessary, display the Toolbox by clicking the Toolbox button on the Form Design toolbar or by choosing View, Toolbox.
3. Deselect the Control Wizards tool in the Toolbox to avoid launching a control wizard.
4. Click any control tool in the Toolbox, and then move the mouse pointer toward the form. When the mouse pointer enters the form window, Access will display the crosshair mouse pointer and a small icon that represents the selected control, as shown in Figure 8-1.

   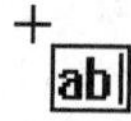

   Figure 8-1. The mouse pointer represents the type of control you clicked in the Toolbox.

5. Click anywhere inside the form (except on another control) to insert a control of the same type that you clicked in the Toolbox.

note The exception to this rule is the label control. When you insert a label control, you do click the form, but Access displays an insertion point, not a blank control. Enter the text you want to display in the label, and Access will adjust the width of the control accordingly. If you click but don't enter anything, Access won't insert a label control. As soon as you click something else, the insertion point disappears.

Using Non-Native Controls

Click the More Controls button in the Toolbox to display a long list of available controls that aren't native to Access. Most of these controls are Microsoft ActiveX controls and are installed by other software. As long as you have a legitimate license for the hosting software, you might be able to use these controls in your Access applications, but this ability can't be taken for granted, because some applications do limit use of controls to only the host software. You should also refer to the host software's licensing information before you distribute a non-native control in an Access application.

If you have the Developer Edition of Microsoft Office XP, you have a set of extra ActiveX controls that will work when used on Access forms. Although these controls don't appear in the Toolbox, they can be located in the More Controls list—scan for controls whose names start with *Microsoft* and end with *version 6.0*, such as the Microsoft Common Dialog Control, version 6.0.

To insert several controls of the same type at one time, follow these steps:

1. First make sure the Control Wizards tool is deselected. Then double-click the control tool that represents the control you're about to insert. (Double-clicking locks the tool to your mouse pointer.)
2. Click inside the form to add a control. Click inside the form a second time to add a second control.
3. Continue clicking inside the form until you insert enough controls. When you've finished, unlock the current tool by clicking the Select Objects tool.

Positioning the Toolbox

As mentioned, the Toolbox is actually a toolbar, which means you can move it around or dock it (attach it to a border). When you first install Access, the Toolbox opens as a floating (undocked) toolbar. Busy or large forms can be a challenge to work with in Design view, and you might want to move the Toolbox to accommodate your form. You can do so simply by clicking the Toolbox's title bar and then dragging the Toolbox to another location. The Toolbox doesn't have a default position, so closing the Toolbox has no effect on its position or state. Access simply remembers where the Toolbox was the last time it was open and returns it to that location.

If the floating Toolbox is in the way, you can move it or dock it in one of two ways:

- Double-click the Toolbox's title bar to return it to its last docked position.
- Drag the Toolbox to any of the four screen borders, and then release it.

To undock the Toolbox, drag the handle—the small raised rectangle at the left end of the docked Toolbox (see Figure 8-2)—away from the docked position, and then release the handle.

Figure 8-2. Drag the Toolbox by its handle to any border, and then release it to dock it.

> **tip** **Resize the Toolbox**
>
> You might find yourself in a tight spot someday—not wanting to dock the Toolbox but unable to arrange it in an out-of-the-way spot. If this happens, you can adjust the size and shape of the Toolbox when it is undocked. Simply position the mouse pointer over any border or corner until Access displays the bidirectional mouse pointer. Use this mouse pointer to adjust the borders as necessary to change the size and shape of the Toolbox.

Using the Grid

When you open a form, report, or data access page in Design view, you'll notice lines and grid points covering the object's background. This is the *grid,* and you'll use these lines and grid points to position controls by aligning controls with a specific point or line.

Adjusting the Grid Points

The grid displays 24 grid points per inch by default. To adjust the distance between the grid points, change the form's *Grid X* and *Grid Y* properties. Reduce the distance between grid points by assigning a value higher than the current property value; increase the distance by entering a lower value.

To alter the distance between grid points, follow these steps:

1. Open a form in Design view by clicking Forms on the Database window's Objects bar and then double-clicking Create Form In Design View.
2. Open the properties sheet, if necessary, by clicking the Properties button on the Form Design toolbar.
3. Locate the *Grid X* property on the Format page in the properties sheet, and then enter a lower value for the current setting. For example, if the setting is 24, enter **12**.
4. Locate the *Grid Y* property, and enter the same value you entered for the *Grid X* property.

   Access will update the grid by increasing the space between each grid point. If you replaced a setting of 24 with 12, you'll see that space double, as shown in Figure 8-3. Originally, there were 24 grid points per inch; now there are only 12.

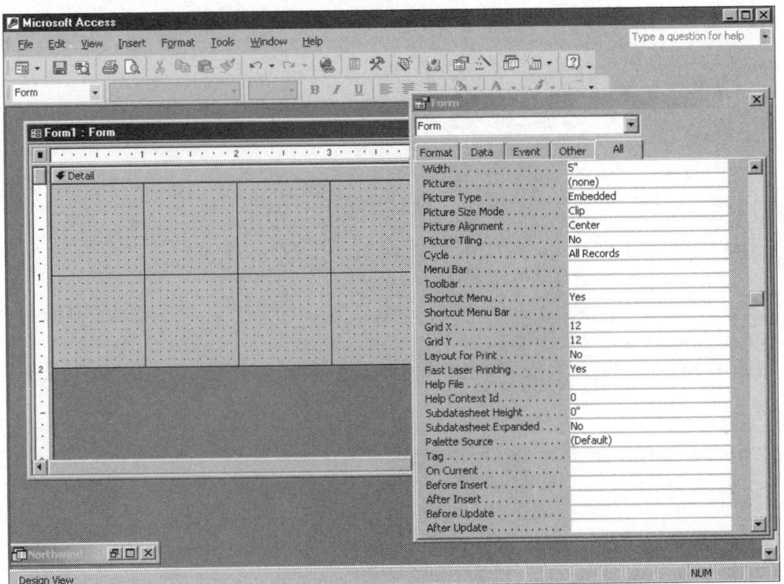

Figure 8-3. In this figure, grid properties are set to the value 12.

note The *Grid X* and *Grid Y* settings don't have to match, but both properties must be a value between 1 and 64. You won't see grid points on a form if you use a setting of 1 or a setting larger than 24, but the setting will still influence the Snap To Grid feature discussed in the next section.

When you've finished working with the grid, clear the Grid option on the View menu to turn it off. The lines and grid points will disappear, as shown in Figure 8-4. To turn the grid back on, simply select the option; the menu item toggles the feature on and off.

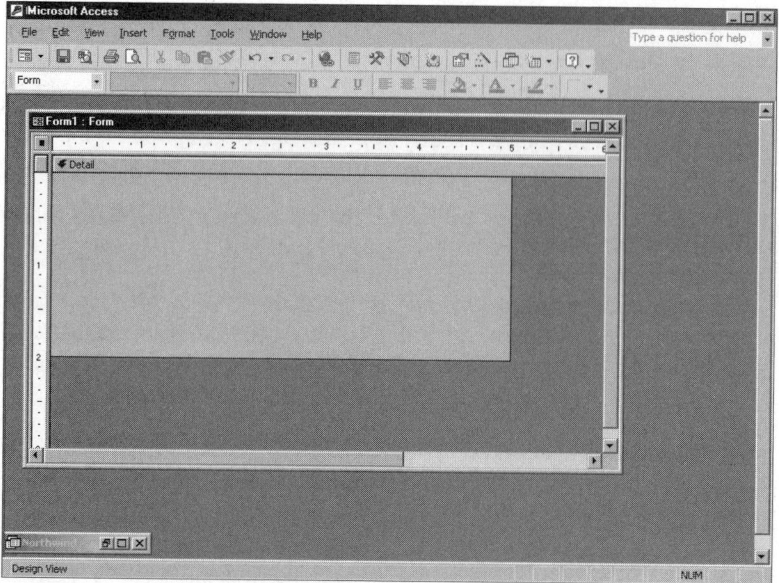

Figure 8-4. Turn off the grid's lines and grid points.

Using Snap To Grid for Control Placement

By default, Access aligns the upper left corner of a control with the nearest grid point or line as you insert the control. That's the Snap To Grid feature in action. When this feature is on, Access won't allow you to position a control's upper left corner between grid points.

Here's a simple example of how Snap To Grid helps you align controls as you insert them:

1. Open a blank form in Design view, or use the one you opened in the last example. (Be sure to toggle on the grid if you use the existing form.)
2. Change the *Grid X* and *Grid Y* properties to 6. The greater the distance between the grid points, the greater the visual impact of Snap To Grid.
3. On the Format menu, make sure Snap To Grid is checked.

4. If the Toolbox isn't open, click the Toolbox tool on the Form Design toolbar. Deselect the Control Wizards tool if it's selected. You don't want to launch any control wizards right now.
5. Next click the Command Button tool, and then click between any two grid points to insert the button.

   Instead of positioning the button exactly where you clicked, Access aligns the control's upper left corner with the grid point or line closest to the spot you clicked.
6. Drag the button around the form a bit. Specifically, try to reposition the button between two grid points. Access simply won't let you; it always aligns the control with the nearest grid point or line.
7. On the Format menu, clear the Snap To Grid option to turn it off.
8. Insert a second command button between two grid points. This time, Access inserts the button exactly where you clicked.
9. Try moving either button. Now Access allows you to drop the button anywhere you want.

tip You can temporarily disable the Snap To Grid feature by holding down the Ctrl key while you move a control.

Selecting Multiple Controls

Regardless of your design task, you'll be working with controls most of the time. That means you'll have to select the controls first. Modifying controls one by one is a real nuisance if you're modifying the same properties or moving or sizing the same controls in the same manner. Here are a few techniques to make selecting (and working with) multiple controls easier and quicker:

- Select nonadjacent controls by clicking a control and then holding down the Shift key as you click remaining controls to add them to the selection.
- Select adjacent controls by clicking anywhere outside a control and dragging the mouse to surround the controls with a temporary rectangle. Access will select all the controls inside the rectangle.
- Select all the controls by choosing Edit, Select All or by pressing Ctrl+A.
- Select a specific area of controls by clicking the horizontal or vertical ruler to select all the controls directly under or to the right of the clicked mark. Alternatively, you can drag the mouse pointer across a selection of the rule to extend a selection.

When dragging to select adjacent controls, you can control the way Access adds partially selected controls. By default, Access will select any control that's inside the rectangle, even if it's only partially selected. This might or might not be what you want. If it isn't, you can change the Selection Behavior setting to Fully Enclosed. When this setting is active, a control must be entirely within the selection rectangle to be included in the resulting multiple control selection. Let's look at a quick example of a form containing several controls, as shown in Figure 8-5.

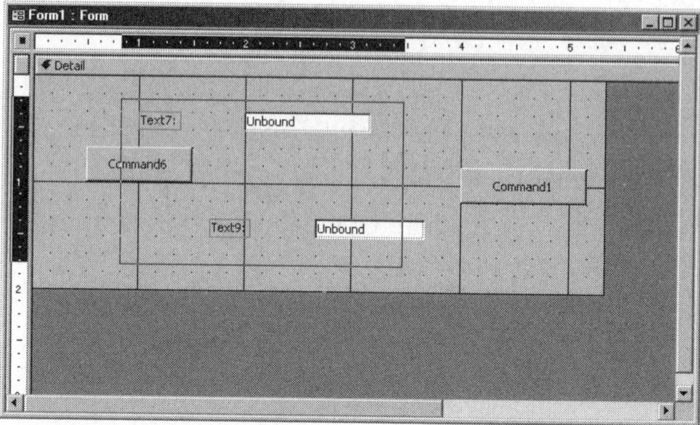

Figure 8-5. The selection rectangle completely encloses some controls while only partially enclosing others.

By default, the selection rectangle shown in Figure 8-5 will select every control it touches or encloses, as indicated by the selection handles shown in Figure 8-6.

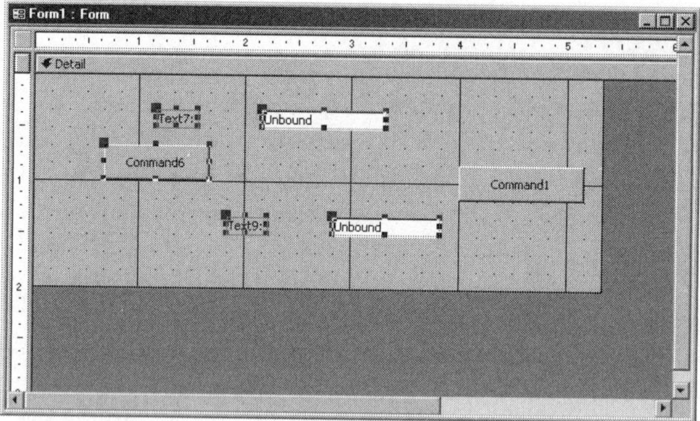

Figure 8-6. The default setting selects controls that are completely or partially enclosed.

You can easily change the setting from its default, Partially Enclosed, to Fully Enclosed. To do so, follow these steps:

1. Choose Tools, Options.
2. Click the Forms/Report tab.
3. In the Selection Behavior section, select Fully Enclosed, and click OK.

Now draw approximately the same selection rectangle as shown in Figure 8-5. This time, however, the selection includes just those controls that are completely enclosed by the rectangle. The one control the rectangle touched but didn't completely surround, Command6, isn't included in the resulting selection, as shown in Figure 8-7. Access considers a *compound control* (a control with an associated label control) completely enclosed if the selection rectangle completely surrounds either component, which explains why Access selects the lower text box control.

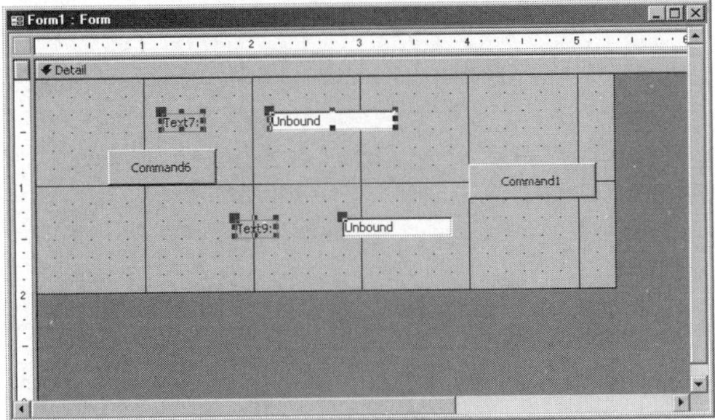

Figure 8-7. The Fully Enclosed option selects only those controls that are completely enclosed in the selection rectangle.

Selecting Most of the Controls

Sometimes the easiest way to select multiple controls is to select all the controls and then deselect the ones you don't want. If you're planning to use most of the controls, this method might result in fewer clicks in the long run.

To put this technique into action, follow these steps:

1. With your form in Design view, choose Edit, Select All, or press Ctrl+A.
2. To deselect a control, hold down the Shift key and click the control you want to deselect. Access will deselect that control while leaving the rest of the selection intact.

tip **Modify a property in multiple controls**

Not only can you move, align, and group multiple controls, but you can also change the properties of more than one control at the same time. Simply select the controls using one of the multiple control selection techniques described in this section. Then click Properties on the Design toolbar. The resulting properties sheet displays a list of properties that are common to all the controls in your multiple selection. When you update a property in the properties sheet, you update that property for each of the selected controls simultaneously.

Sizing, Aligning, and Grouping Controls

Once a control is on your form, you'll want to place it in just the right spot and then adjust its size. The rulers and grid are especially helpful for both aligning and resizing controls. Use the Microsoft Windows drag-and-drop procedure to move controls. In other words, click the control to select it, but don't release the mouse button. The mouse pointer will turn into a small hand, and Access will display handles as shown earlier in Figures 8-6 and 8-7. (The handles are the small black squares around the border of the control.) While holding down the mouse button, drag the control to a new area, and then release the mouse button.

Sizing Controls

Most of the time, you can insert a control close enough to where you want it. You won't have to drag it around the form too much unless you decide to rearrange your controls. A bigger chore is making your controls a consistent size. You can use three methods to size a control:

- Move a control's handles to increase or decrease the control's width and height (the direct route).
- Change the control's *Width* and *Height* properties.
- Use the Size options on the Format menu.

The Direct Route

When you're working with a single control, the easiest way to size it is to select the control and move one of the handles to increase or decrease the size of the control.

To directly manipulate the size of a control, follow these steps:

1. Open any form in Design view, or open a blank form and add a few controls.
2. Select a control, preferably a command button or a text box.

   The selected control displays eight handles, three on each border.
3. Move the mouse pointer over any of the handles.

   The mouse pointer will change into a bidirectional mouse pointer. (As you move the mouse, Access will update the mouse pointer between the bidirectional mouse pointer and the small hand.) The direction of the arrows indicates the direction you can extend or reduce the control.
4. Click any handle. When Access displays the bidirectional arrow, drag the handle in or out to resize the control.

Changing Size Properties

Another sizing method is to change the control's *Height* and *Width* properties. Most of the time, you'll use this method when you have a specific size in mind or you're matching the dimensions of another control. For instance, you could create a group of small icon-size command buttons by changing each button's *Width* and *Height* properties to 0.25", as shown in Figure 8-8.

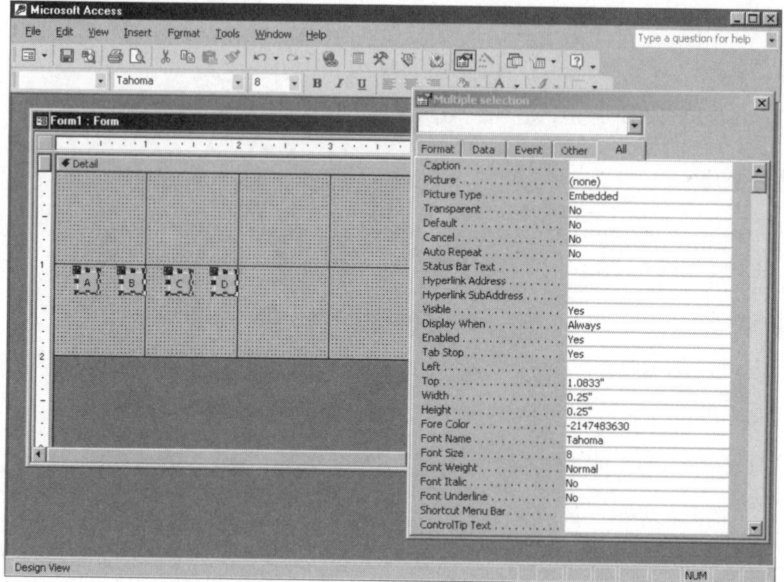

Figure 8-8. Changing the *Width* and *Height* properties to 0.25" makes a small, square tool-type command button.

Adjusting Formatting Options

Access provides two formatting options for sizing controls: To Fit and To Grid. When you want the control to expand or shrink to fit the size of its caption or contents, apply the To Fit option. The To Grid option is similar except that the top and left borders will move to the closest grid point or line. To apply these formats, choose a control or controls and then select the appropriate option from the Format menu.

You can apply the To Fit and To Grid formats to one control or to several controls at the same time. However, some formats apply only to a multiple selection. With two or more controls selected in Design view, choose Format, Size to see the options shown in Figure 8-9.

Figure 8-9. Several size formats are available for controls.

The To Tallest and To Shortest options adjust all selected controls to match (heightwise) the largest or smallest control in the selection. Similarly, To Widest and To Narrowest adjust all the selected controls to match (widthwise) the largest or smallest control in the selection.

To size a multiple selection of controls using the format options, follow these steps:

1. Select two or more controls, as shown in Figure 8-10. As you can see, all the text box controls are different sizes.

Figure 8-10. Each control in this multiple selection is a different size.

2 Choose Format, Size. If you want all the controls to be the same width as the first text box, select To Widest (because the first text box is the widest of the bunch). Figure 8-11 shows that all the selected controls are now the same width.

Figure 8-11. Now the controls are all the same width.

> **tip** **Use the Format Painter to save time**
>
> Sometimes you can size a control faster by using the Format Painter. Just keep in mind that this tool will copy all the source control's formats to the target control. Select the control whose size (and formats) you want to copy, and then click the Format Painter tool on the Formatting toolbar. Next click the control you want to resize. To lock the Format Painter, click it twice. Then click as many controls as you want. To unlock the tool, click it one last time.

Aligning Controls

The term *aligning controls* means lining up the actual control, not aligning the data that the control displays. The points and lines on the grid are helpful for aligning controls. You can also use the horizontal and vertical rulers to line things up just right. However, most of the time you'll be aligning multiple controls. The easiest way to do that is to use the formatting options. Simply select all the controls you want to align, and then assign one of the formatting options shown in Figure 8-12.

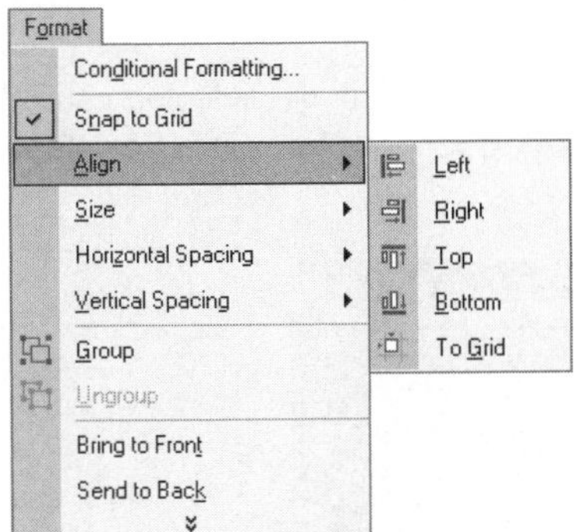

Figure 8-12. Choose one of these format options when aligning multiple controls.

> **tip** **Change text alignment using the Form/Report Formatting toolbar**
>
> The type of data a control displays often determines how the control aligns the data when displayed. By default, controls use General alignment, by which strings are left-justified and numbers are right-justified (most of the time). You can quickly change the text alignment in a control by simply clicking the Center, Align Right, or Align Left text alignment button on the Form/Report Formatting toolbar.

The first four formats are self-explanatory. If you choose the Left option, Access moves all the selected controls to align with the left border of the leftmost control. Right, Top, and Bottom are basically the same: Access aligns all the controls using the most extreme control as the anchor.

To align multiple controls, follow these steps:

1 Select all the controls you want to align. Figure 8-13 shows an example selection.

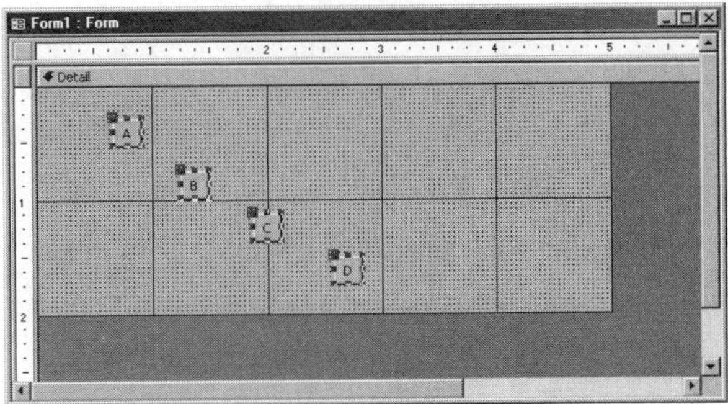

Figure 8-13. When aligning multiple controls, first select the controls you want to align.

2 Choose Format, Align.

3 Choose Left, and Access aligns the left borders of all the selected controls. To align all the controls by their top borders, choose Format, Align, Top. Figure 8-14 shows the results.

Figure 8-14. These controls all have the same top position.

When you work with multiple selections, you don't have to worry about overlapping controls. Access won't position one control on top of another to align it. Instead, Access will position the controls right next to each other. For example, let's say you select the two command buttons shown in Figure 8-15 and assign the Left alignment format.

Figure 8-15. Applying the Left alignment format to the two selected controls would seem to cause them to overlap.

You might expect Access to position the control to the right on top of the far left control, as shown in Figure 8-16, partially blocking the control beneath.

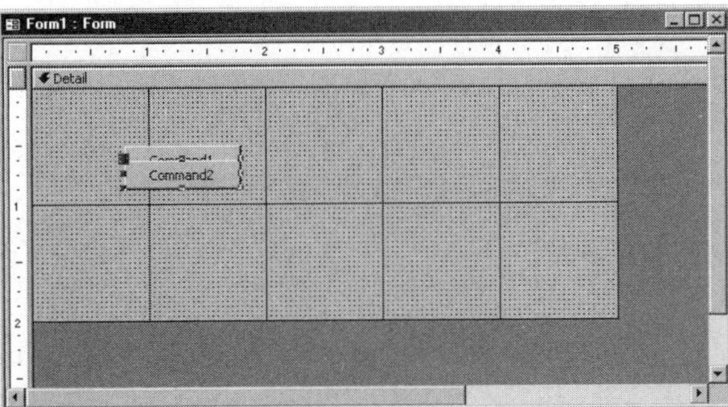

Figure 8-16. You can manually place one control on top of another, partially or totally obscuring the control underneath.

To see how Access solves this potential problem, select both controls, and choose Format, Align, Left. As you can see in Figure 8-17, Access slides the button on the right as far left as possible without obscuring the leftmost button.

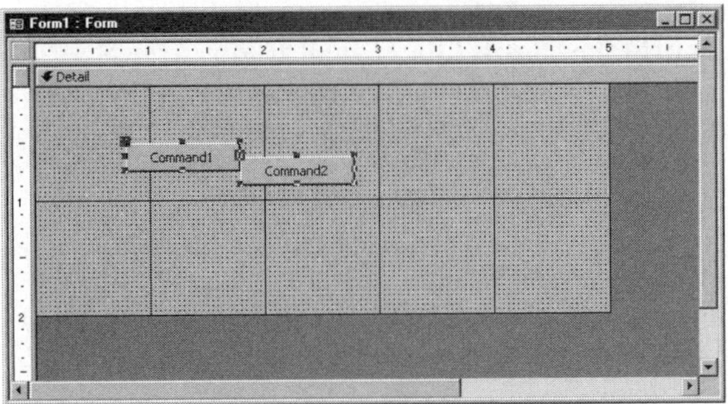

Figure 8-17. Access won't overlap controls.

If you mean to stack one control on another, use drag-and-drop to position the controls. (In fact, some techniques require stacked controls.) Once you have a stack, you can assign the Send To Back or Bring To Front format to one or more controls in that stack. Doing so allows you to quickly rearrange the controls in Design view, with the exception of the List Box and Subform controls. These two controls must always be on top, so you can't assign the Send To Back format to either control.

> **tip** **Select a single control in a stack**
>
> Finding and selecting a single control in a stack of controls can be difficult. You can solve this problem by choosing the control in the Object selector on the Form/Report Formatting toolbar. Or press Tab to cycle through all the controls, and watch the title bar in the properties sheet until the name of the appropriate control appears.

To learn more about selecting multiple controls, see the section "Selecting Multiple Controls," page 307.

The To Grid option will align the top and left borders of an individual control or a multiple selection of controls with the nearest grid point or line. You might want to experiment with this option a bit; the result of applying this format isn't always what you expect.

Using the *Left* and *Top* Properties

In the section "Changing Size Properties," page 312, you learned how to quickly size controls by using the same value for both the *Width* and *Height* properties. You can use this same technique with the *Top* and *Left* properties to align controls. To align controls by their left borders, assign all the controls the same *Left* property value. Likewise, to align controls with the same top position, assign the same *Top* property value. To stack controls, assign them the same *Top* and *Left* property values.

Spacing Controls Evenly

Aligning controls with the same left, right, top, or bottom position is just one alignment possibility. Creating even spacing between each control is another option. For example, the text boxes shown in Figure 8-18 are neatly aligned by their left borders. However, the spacing between the controls isn't uniform.

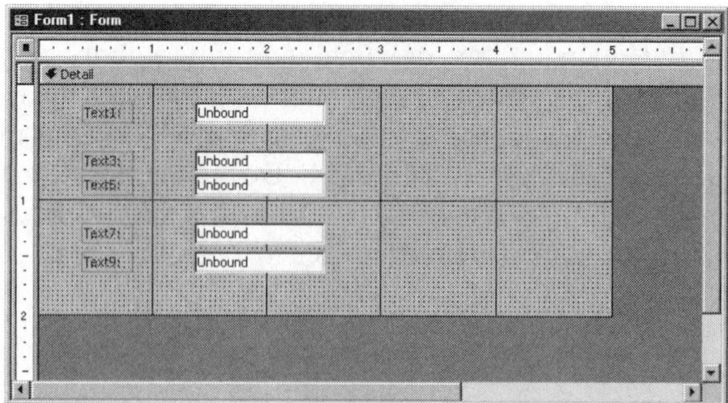

Figure 8-18. These controls are left-aligned, but the space between each control isn't uniform.

You can use the Horizontal Spacing and Vertical Spacing formatting options to easily correct this type of display problem. To evenly distribute the vertical space between the controls, follow these steps:

1. Create a multiple selection by using one of the methods discussed in the section "Selecting Multiple Controls," page 307.
2. Choose Format, Vertical Spacing.
3. Choose Make Equal to evenly distribute the controls. Notice that the top and bottom controls didn't move. Access moves only the controls between the top and bottom controls, as shown in Figure 8-19.

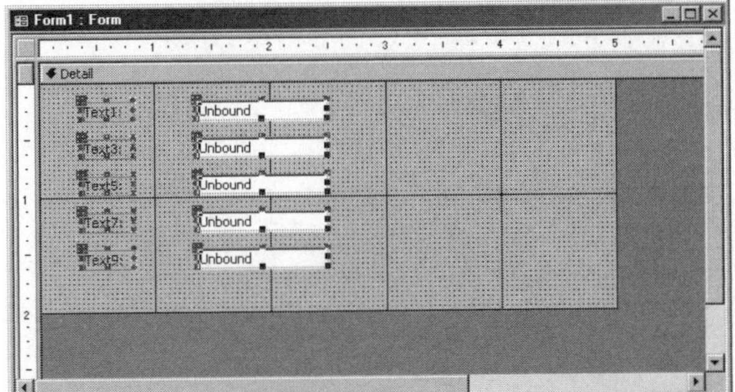

Figure 8-19. After you apply the Make Equal setting to the Vertical Spacing format, the controls are evenly spaced.

Horizontally positioned controls, such as those shown in Figure 8-20, are just as easy to evenly space.

Figure 8-20. These controls are aligned by their top borders, but the space between each control isn't uniform.

To use the Horizontal Spacing format, follow these steps:

1. Create a multiple selection by using one of the methods discussed in the section "Selecting Multiple Controls," page 307.
2. Choose Format, Horizontal Spacing.
3. Select Make Equal to evenly distribute the controls, as shown in Figure 8-21. Access adjusts only the controls between the leftmost and rightmost controls.

Figure 8-21. Applying the Make Equal setting to the Horizontal Spacing format results in evenly spaced controls.

> **tip** **Adjust the spacing between controls**
>
> When the controls are evenly spaced, use the Increase and Decrease options to exercise a bit more influence over the amount of space between each control. When you use these options for vertical alignment, the topmost control doesn't move; for horizontal alignment, the leftmost control doesn't move.

Grouping Controls

Control groups can provide a more flexible solution when you need to size, align, or move multiple controls. However, grouping isn't a direct replacement for working with these controls individually. Grouping creates a type of dependency, or relationship, between the controls.

Within the group, you can adjust individual controls. For instance, you can change the width or height of a control, or you can change property settings for just one control. If you move a control that's part of a defined group, Access will move the remaining controls in that group. For example, if you move one control a half inch to the right, Access will move all the controls in that group a half inch to the right. The following example groups some of the controls shown earlier in Figure 8-21.

To group controls, follow these steps:

1. Select any control that you want to add to the group, and then hold down the Shift key and click the remaining controls. (A group must contain more than one control.)
2. Choose Format, Group. Click the form's background to deselect the group, and then move one of the grouped controls. Access will move all the grouped controls accordingly. While you're working with any control in the group, Access displays a border around the entire group, as shown in Figure 8-22.

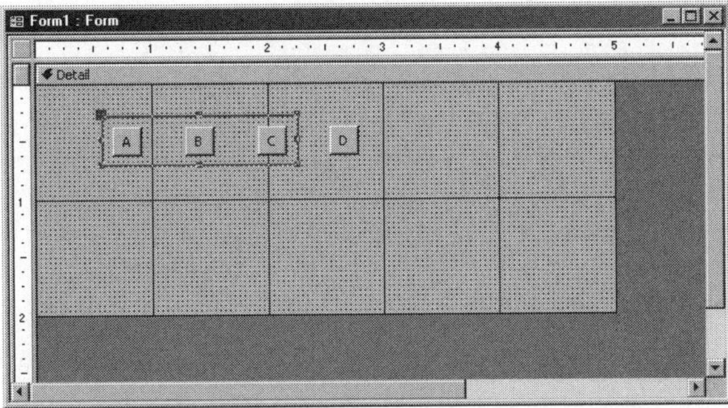

Figure 8-22. Access displays a border around grouped controls.

You can change the dynamics of the group a bit by adjusting this border. Increasing the width or depth of the border will also increase the width or depth of each control. In addition, Access will adjust the position of the controls relative to the new border and the other controls within the group. Figure 8-23 shows the group after the lower right sizing handle was moved down and to the right.

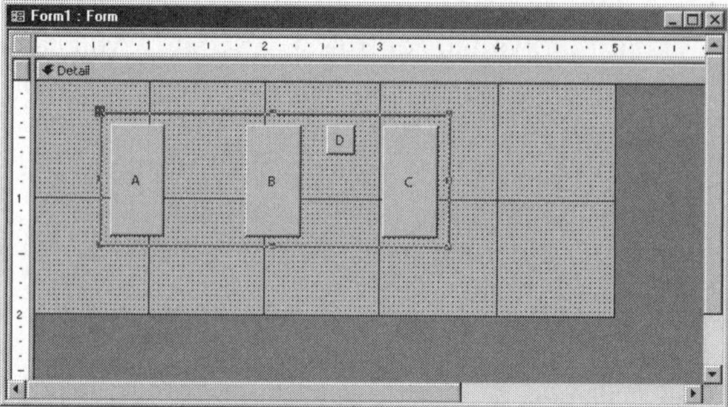

Figure 8-23. You can change the size and position of all the controls in a group by adjusting the group's border.

You can remove a group by selecting any control in the group and choosing Format, Ungroup. You can't add a control to a group by simply moving that control inside the border or, as happened in Figure 8-23, by moving the border to encompass the control. You can move the control, but Access won't recognize it as a member of the group.

> **tip** In Design view, you can press Tab to cycle through all the controls in your form. This cycle also includes the selection borders for any groups.

Working with Attached Labels

By default, Access attaches a label control to each control that displays text (text boxes, combo boxes, and list boxes). The combination (usually a text box with an attached label) is known as a compound control. Whether you're moving, aligning, sizing, or grouping your controls, you'll need to keep these labels in mind. When you position a control for the first time, you'll need to consider the label's placement as well as the control's placement.

For example, let's say you insert a text box control in the upper left corner of a form, as shown in Figure 8-24.

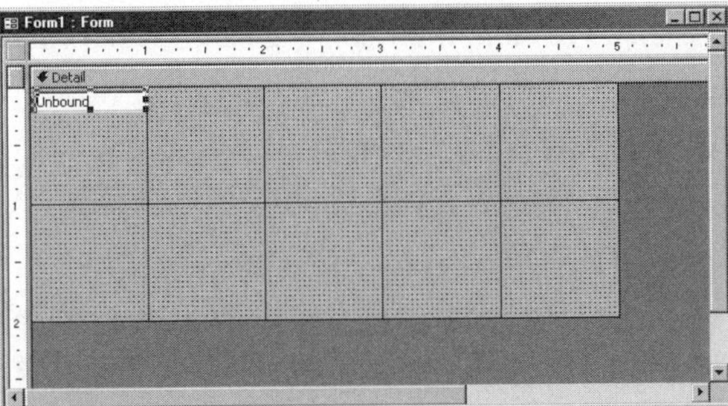

Figure 8-24. If Access can't position the label in the default position, it will hide the label behind the control.

As you can see, the control has no label—or does it? If you move the control, as shown in Figure 8-25, you can see the outline of the label's move handle. Simply click this handle and move the label from its hiding spot behind the text box.

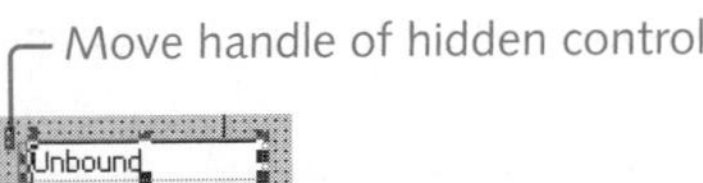

Figure 8-25. To display a control's label, drag the label from behind the control it's attached to.

Moving the Control and Label Separately

When you move a control, the label goes with it (and vice versa). You can use the label or the control's move handle to move either independently of the other, but the components will still be related.

Follow these steps to move one component without the other:

1. Position the mouse pointer over the move handle of one of the components.
2. The mouse pointer changes to an upward-pointing hand, as shown in Figure 8-26.

Figure 8-26. When Access displays the upward-pointing hand mouse pointer, you can drag the label and control independently of each other.

3. Click the handle, and then drag the control or the label to a new position, as shown in Figure 8-27.

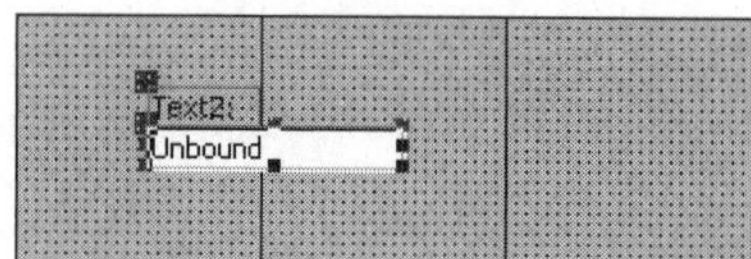

Figure 8-27. The text box is now positioned under the label component.

Troubleshooting

When I try to move attached labels, the controls also move

You can't use the move handle to drag an attached label to a different section of a form or report without taking along the control. You can, however, use the Cut and Paste commands to detach a component from a compound control. Simply click the move handle of the component you want to move, and press Ctrl+X. Select the title bar of the section where you want to position the previously cut control, and press Ctrl+V. Access will paste the component into the upper left corner of the section. As a result of the cut-and-paste procedure, the components will no longer be related to each other.

Omitting the Label

Compound controls are the default, but you can change that, at least for the form you're working in. First select the control in the Toolbox, but don't insert it into the form just yet. Open the properties sheet, and change the *AutoLabel* property to No. Insert your control as you normally would. Access will insert only the control, omitting the label that usually tags along. Access will continue to insert this particular control without its label until you change the *AutoLabel* property back to Yes. You can even save the form and close it. The next time you open the form and insert that particular control type, Access will still omit the label. However, all the other forms in your application will continue to default to compound controls.

tip **Change the default properties for a control**

You can change many default properties for controls. Simply select the appropriate control tool in the Toolbox (note that the properties sheet title bar changes to Default Text Box, or the relevant control type name), and then reconfigure the properties you want to change in the properties sheet. If you want the changes to be permanent, be sure to save your form.

Putting It All Together

So far, this chapter has explained a lot of rules and offered a lot of generic examples of those rules. In this section, you'll put those rules to work by applying much of what you've just learned in a technique for coloring a command button.

If you're an experienced Access user, you know that command buttons come in only one color: gray. However, you're not stuck with dull command buttons. You can trick Access into displaying a command button in any color. In truth, the command button is still gray, but no one will know but you.

This technique uses three components: a command button, a rectangle, and a label control. All you really need is the rectangle to simulate a command button. However, this lone-rectangle approach has a number of limitations: First, Access doesn't include a rectangle in the tab order. Second, you can't assign a default value to a rectangle. Third, the rectangle offers fewer events than a command button offers. Fourth, it's difficult to center the text between the top and bottom margins. If you don't need any of these features, you might just as well use a colored rectangle and give it a *Click* event. Just keep in mind that the pseudo–command button will not have the same functionality that a true command button has.

To create the command button, follow these steps:

1. Open a blank form, open the Toolbox, and deselect the Control Wizards tool if necessary.
2. Insert a command button.
3. Open the properties sheet if necessary, and click the Other tab. Name the command button **cmdColor.**
4. Click the Format tab, and change the *Transparent* property from No to Yes.
5. Click the Event tab, and then click the Builder button to the right of the *OnClick* property.
6. Double-click Code Builder if Access displays the Choose Builder dialog box.
7. In the form's module, create the following procedure. Access supplies the Sub and End Sub statements. (The insertion point should be exactly where it needs to be so that you can type the assignment and MsgBox statements shown in the listing.)

```
Private Sub cmdColor_Click()
    recColor.SpecialEffect = 2
    MsgBox "It worked!"
    recColor.SpecialEffect = 1
End Sub
```

   This procedure simply changes the colored rectangle's *SpecialEffect* property to give the pseudo–command button a just-clicked, or depressed, look. Then the *MsgBox* statement displays a simple message. Finally, the last statement returns the colored rectangle's *SpecialEffect* property to its original state.

8. Choose Debug, Compile to verify that your event procedure has no syntax errors. If Microsoft Visual Basic for Applications (VBA) returns a compilation error, correct the code as necessary. (The error is probably a simple typo.)
9. Return to the form in Design view by closing or minimizing the Visual Basic Editor. Or simply click the appropriate Form icon on the taskbar. (It doesn't matter whether you close the Visual Basic Editor at this point.)

For more information about creating event procedures, see Chapter 20, "Customizing Your Database Using VBA Code."

Now you're ready to add the colored rectangle, which you can do by following these steps:

1. Insert a rectangle anywhere in the form except directly on top of the command button.

   Try to match the command button's approximate size, but don't worry if it isn't exact. Later in this section, you'll use some of the sizing techniques you learned earlier in this chapter to match the size of all three controls.
2. Click the Other tab in the properties sheet, and name the new rectangle **recColor.**
3. Click the Format tab, and then click the Builder button to the right of the *Back Color* property. Select a color from the Color palette (red in this example), and then click OK to return to the properties sheet.
4. Select Raised from the *Special Effect* property.

The next procedure creates the label control. (If you don't need a caption for your pseudo–command button, you can skip this part.)

To create the label, follow these steps:

1. Insert a label control anywhere except on top of one of the other controls. Enter the text **Pseudo** as the label's caption.
2. Choose 12 from the Font Size control, and then click the Bold and Center buttons on the Formatting toolbar.
3. Choose Format, Size, and then choose To Fit. The control will be just large enough to accommodate its text.

At this point, you have three controls, similar to those shown in Figure 8-28, which you can now stack and group.

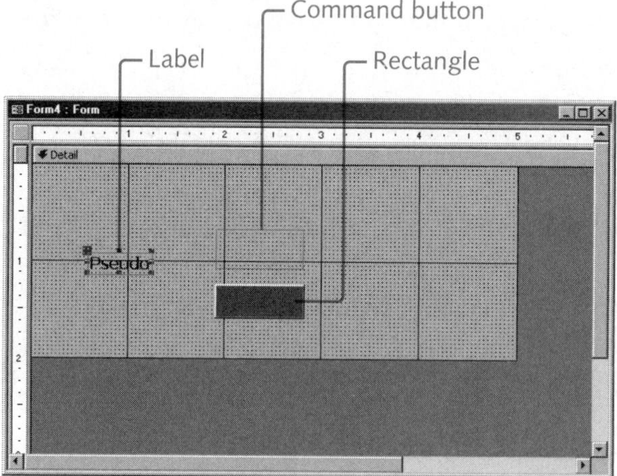

Figure 8-28. You need three components to create a colored command button.

First use any of the single control methods to size the command button. You can change the *Width* and *Height* properties or use the sizing handles. When the command button is the right size, move it to its permanent position. Make any adjustments necessary to position the command button exactly where you want it and make it the size you want before you continue.

You're ready to size the rectangle now. The most precise method is to match the rectangle's *Width* and *Height* properties to the command button's *Width* and *Height* properties. To do so, select the command button (double-click if you need to open the properties sheet), and note the values for both properties. Then click the rectangle control, and enter those values. For example, if the command button were 1 inch wide and 0.25 inch deep, you'd enter **1"** and **0.25"** for recColor's *Width* and *Height* properties. Alternatively, you could create a multiple selection containing both the command button and the rectangle and then use one of the Size formats: To Tallest, To Shortest, To Widest, or To Narrowest. If the rectangle doesn't need to be exact, use the sizing handles. The Snap To Grid feature or the To Grid Size format might be useful here.

Now stack the rectangle on the command button. You can drag the rectangle if exact placement isn't necessary. Just remember that the rectangle should completely cover the command button. Clicking any part of the invisible command button that extends beyond the visible rectangle will trigger the *Click* event, and you probably want to avoid that possibility.

If the precise placement of the command button is important, note the values of the command button's *Top* and *Left* properties and then set the rectangle control's *Top* and *Left* properties to the same values. Doing so automatically aligns the two controls. You can't use the Format Align settings because these options won't allow controls to overlap.

Now your colored command button is functional. On the Form Design toolbar, click View, and then click the pseudo–command button to display the simple message box shown in Figure 8-29.

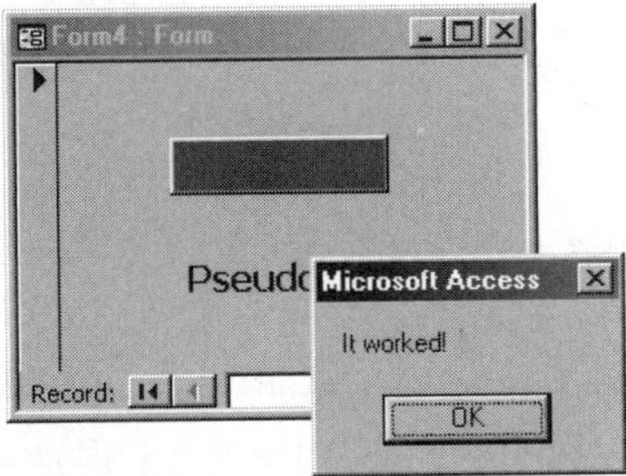

Figure 8-29. Clicking the colored command button displays a simple message box.

Although you could stop now, you probably want the colored command button to display a caption. That's where the label control comes into play. Return to Design view, and drag the label control onto the stacked controls, centering it as best you can. This is another situation in which the Snap To Grid feature and the To Grid formatting option can help. However, there's no direct way to automatically center the label control. You'll just have to rely on a keen eye and the rulers. Remember to reapply the To Fit setting if you change the text. If you don't, the text might appear off-center. If you can't see the label's text, select the label from the Object selector on the Form/Report Formatting toolbar and then choose Format, Bring To Front.

There's one last procedure: You probably want to group the controls. That way, if you have to move the colored command button, you can move all the controls at once.

To create a control group, follow these steps:

1. Click outside the stacked controls, and drag the mouse to create a temporary rectangle around the controls.
2. Choose Format, Group.
3. Save your work, and return to Form view to see the full effect, as shown in Figure 8-30.

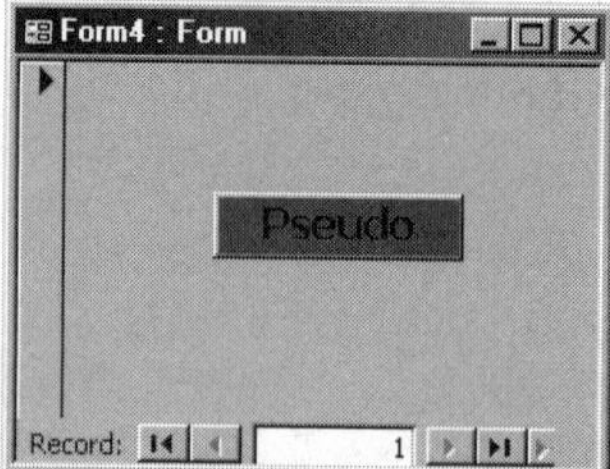

Figure 8-30. Creating this unique command button employs many of the design tools reviewed in this chapter.

> **caution** Don't try to move the group with the group border showing. If you do, you'll move only the individual control you clicked instead of moving the entire group.

Working with ActiveX Controls

At the beginning of this chapter, you learned how to insert native controls into a form or report. ActiveX controls often provide more flexibility and functionality than native controls. In this section, you'll learn how to insert an ActiveX control. You'll also learn a few formatting options for one of the more commonly used controls, the Microsoft Date And Time Picker control (one of the ActiveX controls included with Office XP Developer).

ActiveX controls are in-process Automation components that offer a specialized function. For the purposes of this chapter, it's enough to know that ActiveX controls are non-native controls that you can use in your Access applications. In many cases, using an ActiveX control can save you a lot of work and time because you simply insert the control into your form, set a few properties, and go.

See Chapter 6, "Working with Form Controls," for more details on using ActiveX controls on Access forms.

note The term *in-process* means that the component shares the same address space as the client application—in this case, Access. This way, Windows doesn't have to spend a lot of time managing data and communications between Access and the control, which in turn saves response time. In contrast, an out-of-process component is loaded into its own address space.

Registering an ActiveX Control

Before you can use an ActiveX control, you must register it. Controls that you purchase along with a development package, such as Visual Basic and Office XP Developer, are usually installed and registered when you install the software. Only controls that you acquire independently might need to be registered (as a general rule).

caution Just because an ActiveX control is registered—and appears in the ActiveX Controls list—doesn't mean it will work on an Access form. The control might be intended for use in another program, such as Microsoft Internet Explorer or Visual Basic. And those that do work on Access forms might not have the same functionality as they have in another program.

To register an ActiveX control in Access, follow these steps:

1. With a form open in Design view, choose Tools, ActiveX Controls.
2. The ActiveX Controls dialog box displays currently registered controls, as shown in Figure 8-31.

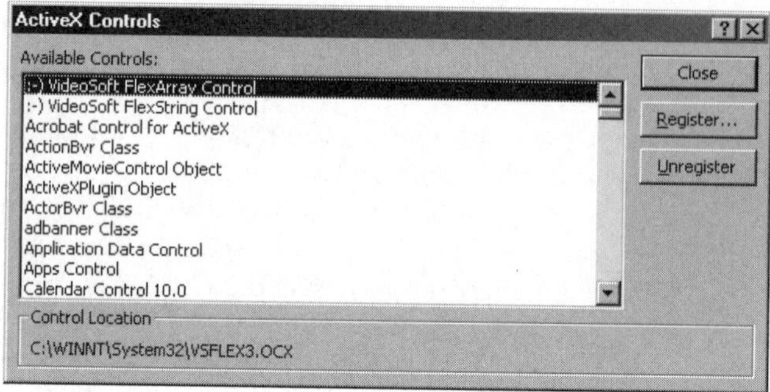

Figure 8-31. You can add registered ActiveX controls to your Access forms using the ActiveX Controls dialog box.

3. Click Register, and locate the control in the Add ActiveX Control dialog box, which is similar to the Open dialog box.
4. When you locate the control, select it and click OK to return to the ActiveX Controls dialog box. Click Close to return to your form.

Generally, if a control is installed on your system and you have a license for the host application, you're free to use that control in your Access applications. This might or might not be true in distributed copies of your application. Always check the host application's licensing information before distributing an ActiveX control. Again, keep in mind that just because the control works in one application doesn't mean it will work well in Access.

InsideOut

You can use a program that comes with Visual Basic, regsvr32.exe, to register ActiveX controls independently of Access.

Inserting an ActiveX Control

After you've registered an ActiveX control, you're just a few clicks away from accessing that control's functionality.

To insert an ActiveX control into a form, follow these steps:

1. Open a form in Design view.
2. Choose Insert, ActiveX Control.

   Access will display a list of the registered controls that are currently available in the Insert ActiveX Control dialog box, shown in Figure 8-32. This dialog box is similar to the ActiveX Control dialog box you use to register controls, but the two dialog boxes aren't interchangeable.

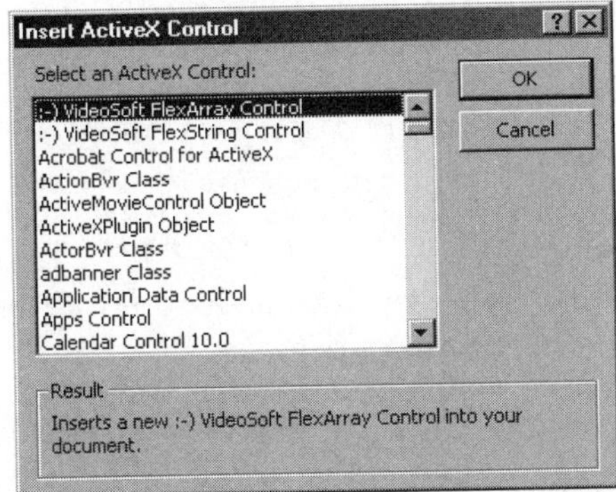

Figure 8-32. Choose an ActiveX control to insert it.

3. Select the control you want to insert from the list, and click OK.

   Access will insert the control into your form. At this point, you can move it, resize it, and modify its properties just as you would with any native control.

Modifying ActiveX Control Properties

ActiveX controls have properties just like native controls. Furthermore, when you select an ActiveX control in Design view, Access displays the control's unique properties in the properties sheet. You can also use the control's custom properties sheet by double-clicking the control. If this doesn't work, right-click the control, choose the *controltype* Object option from the shortcut menu, and then choose Properties. Sometimes the Access properties sheet displays a *Custom* property for these controls. If this is the case, click the Builder button to the right of this property to display the custom properties sheet.

Chapter 8

Unlike native control events, ActiveX control events aren't listed in the properties sheet. They're available only in the form's module. When you insert an ActiveX control, VBA automatically adds the appropriate events to the module, and you can access them from the module's Object and Procedure controls. However, not all events may be functional when an ActiveX control is placed on an Access form (even when you use a control from Office XP Developer).

See Chapter 6, "Working with Form Controls," for more information about working with ActiveX controls on Access forms.

You can bind some ActiveX controls just as you bind native controls: Simply set the control's *Control Source* property to the appropriate field. Not all controls will have this capability; when they don't, the *Control Source* property won't be available.

Using the Date And Time Picker Control to Select Dates

If you've been using Access for a while, you might be familiar with the Calendar control. Another ActiveX control, Microsoft Date And Time Picker, might be a bit easier to work with than the Calendar control. In this section, you'll learn how to insert and modify a date and time picker control. (Microsoft Date And Time Picker comes with Office XP Developer or Visual Basic.) You'll see just how easy this ActiveX control is to use.

A Date And Time Picker control provides an easy-to-use interface for exchanging date and time information between Access and your users. For example, you can use a Date And Time Picker control to prompt a user to enter a date before running a query. Doing so reduces the chance of errors. Users could still select the wrong date, but they don't have to worry about remembering the correct date format, and you don't have to worry about a user making an inappropriate entry.

To insert the Microsoft Date And Time Picker control, follow these steps:

1. Open a blank form in Design view.
2. Choose Insert, ActiveX Control.
3. Select Microsoft Date And Time Picker Control in the Select An ActiveX Control list, and click OK. Access will insert the control, as shown in Figure 8-33.

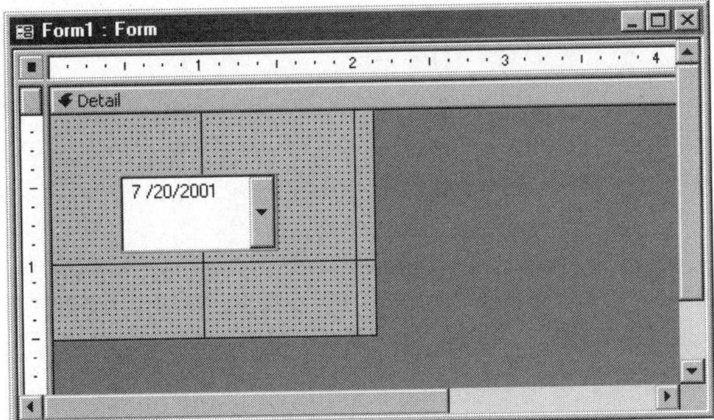

Figure 8-33. Insert a Microsoft Date And Time Picker control into your form.

Click the View selector on the Form Design toolbar to display the form and its new control in Form view. Click the small triangle to the right of the date to display the full calendar shown in Figure 8-34.

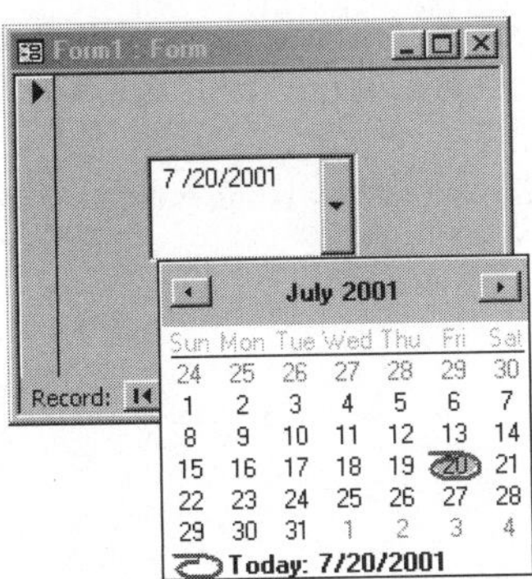

Figure 8-34. Open the control's calendar.

By default, this control is rather high. Unless you are using a very large font, it will look better if you reduce its height to match a standard text box.

Each field displays a date or time component. To update the date stored by the control, use the back and forward arrows to select a month, and click the date you want to select. (The control opens to the current date by default.) If you prefer to use the keyboard, Table 8-1 describes the keystrokes you can use to update the displayed date and, consequently, the control's value.

Table 8-1. Using keystrokes to adjust a Date And Time Picker control

Keystrokes	Description
Arrow keys	Press any arrow key to select a new day. The arrow determines the direction the insertion point moves.
Home and End	These keys select the first and last day, respectively, in the current month.
F4 or Alt+Down Arrow	Use these keys to open the drop-down calendar.
Numbers	With the drop-down calendar closed, enter numbers to update the date. If you enter an invalid date, the control rejects it.
Plus and Minus keys on numeric keypad	With the drop-down calendar closed, use the Plus and Minus keys to increment and decrement the value of the selected date.

As you can see, the Microsoft Date And Time Picker control is definitely much easier to use than the Calendar control if the control's only purpose is to store a date.

See Chapter 6, "Working with Form Controls," for information on getting help when using ActiveX controls.

Part 3

Queries and Recordsets

Chapter 9

Using Queries to Select Data

In Chapter 2, "Overview of Basic Access Features," you learned that queries are used to sort, filter, add, delete, and modify data in Microsoft Access databases. In this chapter, you'll learn how to use queries to request data for forms, reports, and controls when an object relies on specific data rather than on all the data in the underlying table. There are several query types, as follows:

- **Select queries.** These queries retrieve data that meets specific conditions, group records for viewing summary data, and display calculations performed on data fields.
- **Action queries.** These queries modify existing data in some way. You can use action queries to delete, update, and append data or to create a new table.
- **Parameter queries.** These queries prompt you for criteria before running the actual query.
- **Crosstab queries.** These queries summarize data and then group the summarized values into categories.
- **SQL queries.** These queries, which include union, pass-through, and data-definition queries, require specific SQL commands that you must compose in SQL view. (Design view is not available for SQL queries.)

This chapter on selecting data will examine the simpler aspects of working with the select query, which you'll rely on to perform the following tasks:

- Retrieve, sort, and group data
- Limit results
- Evaluate expressions

This chapter also includes discussions of joins and crosstab queries.

An Introduction to the Query Environment

Before diving into an examination of queries, you should be familiar with the query environment, in which you'll encounter the query Design view, the design grid, and the SQL view. This section focuses on these aspects of the query environment.

The Query Design View

Figure 9-1 shows the query Design view, in which you'll identify the tables and queries that you want to include in your query. Notice that the title bar includes the query name and the query type.

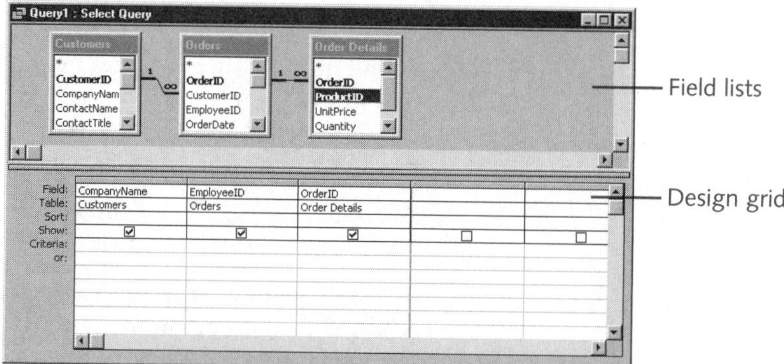

Figure 9-1. You'll create queries in the query Design view.

The upper part of the window displays a field list for each table or query you add to the query. The lower part of the window, known as the design grid, will define the query's fields and accept expressions as criteria for limiting the results of the query.

The SQL View

The query Design view is probably where most of us create and view queries. Access doesn't directly interact with queries, however. Instead, Access must translate the query Design view's version of a query into Jet Structured Query Language (Jet SQL), one of the many versions of SQL.

SQL is a large and varied language, with many versions, but you don't need to know everything about SQL to take advantage of it. Access translates your query into Jet SQL for you. Figure 9-2 shows the SQL view of the query shown in Figure 9-1.

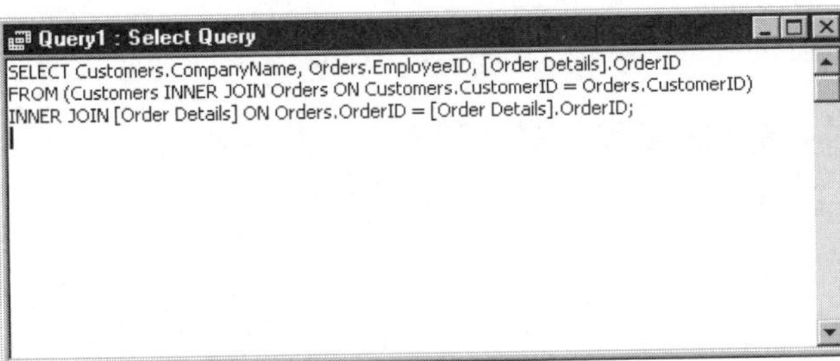

Figure 9-2. The SQL view displays each query's equivalent Jet SQL statement.

Throughout this chapter, you'll see how the elements in the Design view relate to the current query's Jet SQL statement. Knowing SQL can prove advantageous because you can use it to build more powerful queries than those you construct in the design grid.

The Simple Query Wizard

If you're new to queries, you should start your adventure with the Simple Query Wizard. Although the wizard won't limit data, it will retrieve data and evaluate expressions, creating what's known as a "simple" query. For example, you could create a simple phone list for all your customers, but you couldn't limit that list to customers with a particular ZIP code.

To use the Simple Query Wizard to create a phone list for the Northwind customer database (the database that comes with Access), follow these steps:

1. Locate the Northwind.mdb database. By default, it's installed in C:\Program Files\Microsoft Office\Office10\Samples. (If you don't have this database installed, you'll need to install it from your Microsoft Office XP CD-ROM.)
2. Make a copy of the database. (Some of the procedures in this chapter will modify the database, so it's a good idea to make a copy.)

3 Open the copy of the Northwind database.

4 On the Database window's Objects bar, click Queries, and then click New on the Database window toolbar. (Or on the Database toolbar, click the arrow next to the New Object selector, and then click Query.)

5 In the New Query dialog box, double-click Simple Query Wizard. If you get a message stating that this feature isn't currently installed, let Access install it.

6 In the Tables/Queries drop-down list, select Table: Customers.

7 In the Available Fields list, double-click CompanyName, ContactName, ContactTitle, and Phone (in that order) to add these fields to the Selected Fields list, as shown in Figure 9-3. Then click Next.

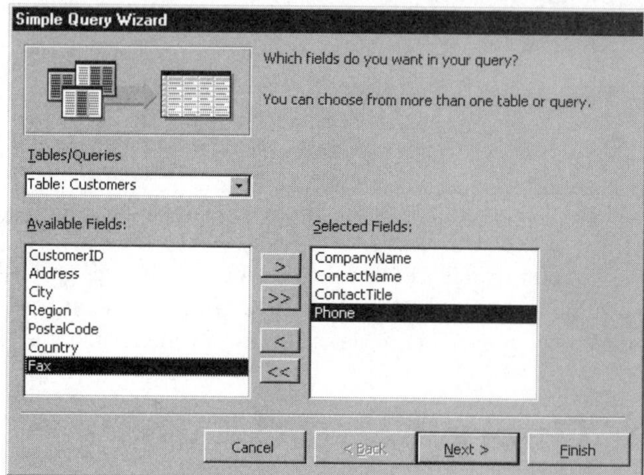

Figure 9-3. Use the Simple Query Wizard to select fields to be included in the query.

8 On the last page of the wizard, name the query **qryPhoneNumbers**, as shown in Figure 9-4, and click Finish.

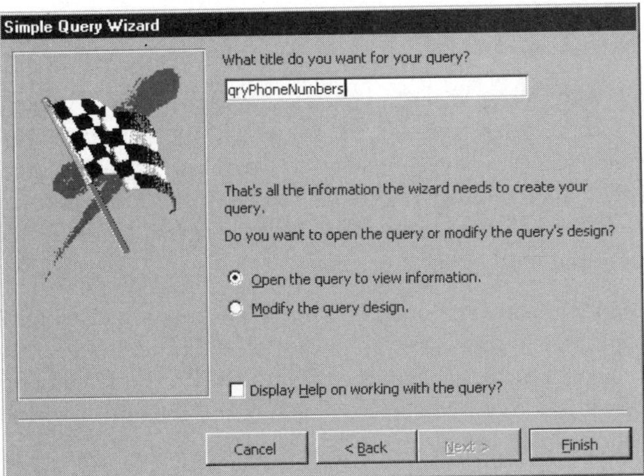

Figure 9-4. Name the query qryPhoneNumbers.

The results of the query, shown in Figure 9-5, contain just the fields specified in the Simple Query Wizard.

qryPhoneNumbers : Select Query

Company Name	Contact Name	Contact Title	Phone
Alfreds Futterkiste	Maria Anders	Sales Representative	030-0074321
Ana Trujillo Emparedados y helados	Ana Trujillo	Owner	(5) 555-4729
Antonio Moreno Taquería	Antonio Moreno	Owner	(5) 555-3932
Around the Horn	Thomas Hardy	Sales Representative	(171) 555-7788
Berglunds snabbköp	Christina Berglund	Order Administrator	0921-12 34 65
Blauer See Delikatessen	Hanna Moos	Sales Representative	0621-08460
Blondel père et fils	Frédérique Citeaux	Marketing Manager	88.60.15.31
Bólido Comidas preparadas	Martín Sommer	Owner	(91) 555 22 82
Bon app'	Laurence Lebihan	Owner	91.24.45.40
Bottom-Dollar Markets	Elizabeth Lincoln	Accounting Manager	(604) 555-4729
B's Beverages	Victoria Ashworth	Sales Representative	(171) 555-1212
Cactus Comidas para llevar	Patricio Simpson	Sales Agent	(1) 135-5555
Centro comercial Moctezuma	Francisco Chang	Marketing Manager	(5) 555-3392
Chop-suey Chinese	Yang Wang	Owner	0452-076545
Comércio Mineiro	Pedro Afonso	Sales Associate	(11) 555-7647
Consolidated Holdings	Elizabeth Brown	Sales Representative	(171) 555-2282
Drachenblut Delikatessen	Sven Ottlieb	Order Administrator	0241-039123
Du monde entier	Janine Labrune	Owner	40.67.88.88
Eastern Connection	Ann Devon	Sales Agent	(171) 555-0297
Ernst Handel	Roland Mendel	Sales Manager	7675-3425

Record: 1 of 91

Figure 9-5. This simple query returns just the specified fields in the Customers table.

Changing Field Order and Column Order

When you work with Access wizards, you select fields from the Available Fields list and move them to the Selected Fields list. The wizard then bases the form, report, or query on the fields you moved to the Selected Fields list, displaying the fields in the same order as they appear in the Selected Fields list. If this order isn't suitable for the new object, select the fields in the Available Fields list in the order in which you want them to appear in the finished form or report.

You can also change the column order in a query by dragging a column to a new location in the design grid. To move a column, click on the column selector (the gray bar at the top of the column) to highlight the column. Then click again on the column and drag it to its new location. While you are dragging the column, a vertical gray line indicates the location where the column will be dropped.

You've seen the results of the wizard's work. Now it's time to go back and review the query in Design view and SQL view. Figure 9-6 shows the query in Design view (click the View button on the Database toolbar), which lists the query's data source—the Customers table—in the upper part of the window and identifies each selected field in the design grid.

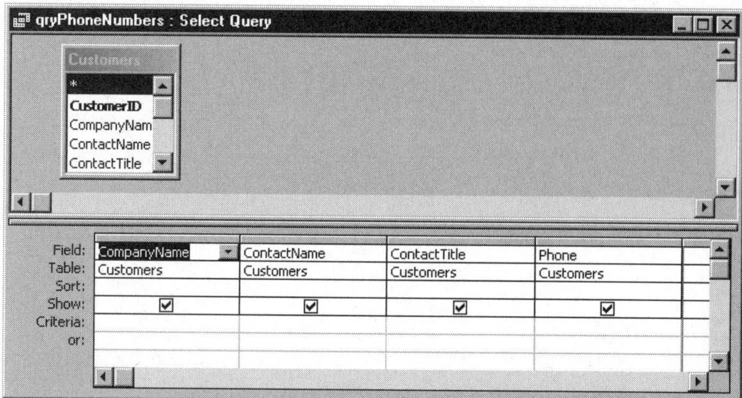

Figure 9-6. The qryPhoneNumbers query displayed in Design view.

note The expression *qry* is the standard tag (prefix) for queries in the Leszynski Naming Convention (LNC). You can use *qry* as the tag for all queries, or you can give each query type its own tab; the tags for the basic database objects are listed in Table 20-4 of Chapter 20, "Customizing Your Database Using VBA Code."

To view the Jet SQL statement for the qryPhoneNumbers query, click the arrow to the right of the View button, and then select SQL View. The SQL view displays the following Jet SQL statement:

```
SELECT Customers.CompanyName, Customers.ContactName,
Customers.ContactTitle, Customers.Phone
FROM Customers;
```

The use of the SELECT clause indicates that this is a select query. The statement then identifies the query's four fields, separating them with commas. The FROM clause identifies the data source (Customers), and the semicolon indicates the end of the statement.

Common SQL Keywords

SQL keywords typically appear in all capital letters. (Operators have only their initial letter capitalized.) The most commonly used SQL keywords are listed here:

- **AS.** Creates a clause that specifies an expression or a value and the field name associated with it (sometimes called an alias).
- **DISTINCTROW.** Excludes duplicate records from the query.
- **FROM.** Creates a clause specifying the table or query from which fields are taken for the query.
- **GROUP BY.** Specifies the field used to group records in a summary or crosstab query.
- **ORDER BY.** Creates a clause that specifies the order in which query records are to be sorted.
- **SELECT.** Creates a clause containing a list of fields to be included in the query.
- **UNION.** Combines two sets of records into a single set.
- **WHERE.** Creates a clause with a condition (or set of conditions) for filtering query records.

Summarizing Data

You can also use the Simple Query Wizard to summarize data—for example, to compute the total of a field. To do so, you must specify a Number field in the query.

To use the Simple Query Wizard to summarize shipping costs, follow these steps:

1. On the Database window's Objects bar, click Queries, and then click New on the Database window toolbar.
2. In the New Query dialog box, double-click Simple Query Wizard.
3. In the Tables/Queries drop-down list, select Table: Orders.
4. In the Available Fields list, double-click CustomerID and Freight to add both fields to the Selected Fields list. Click Next.
5. Select the Summary option, and then click the Summary Options button.
6. In the Summary Options dialog box (see Figure 9-7), select the Sum check box and the Count Records In Orders check box. Click OK, and then click Next.

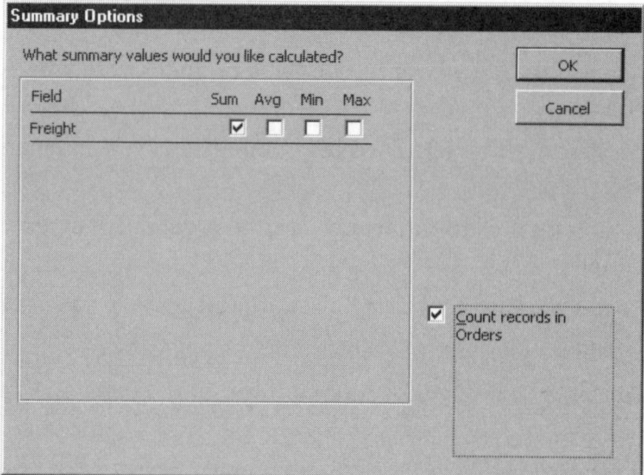

Figure 9-7. Use this dialog box to compute the sum of the Freight field and to count the number of orders in a query.

7. On the final page of the wizard, enter a new name for the query or accept the default, and then click Finish.

The results of the query are shown in Figure 9-8.

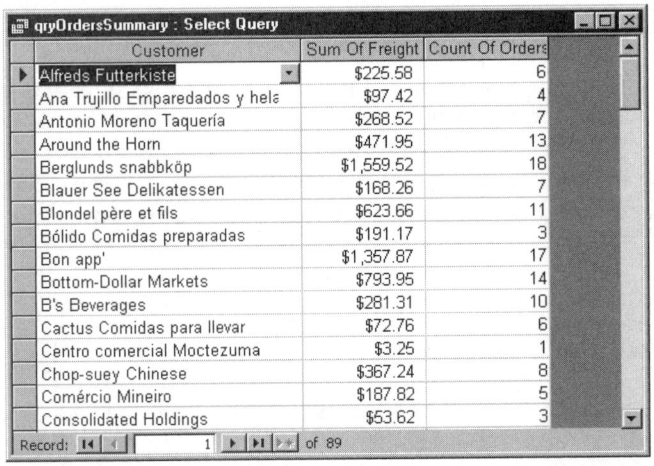

qryOrdersSummary : Select Query

Customer	Sum Of Freight	Count Of Orders
Alfreds Futterkiste	$225.58	6
Ana Trujillo Emparedados y hela	$97.42	4
Antonio Moreno Taquería	$268.52	7
Around the Horn	$471.95	13
Berglunds snabbköp	$1,559.52	18
Blauer See Delikatessen	$168.26	7
Blondel père et fils	$623.66	11
Bólido Comidas preparadas	$191.17	3
Bon app'	$1,357.87	17
Bottom-Dollar Markets	$793.95	14
B's Beverages	$281.31	10
Cactus Comidas para llevar	$72.76	6
Centro comercial Moctezuma	$3.25	1
Chop-suey Chinese	$367.24	8
Comércio Mineiro	$187.82	5
Consolidated Holdings	$53.62	3

Record: 1 of 89

Figure 9-8. The query created with the wizard returns the total freight cost and the total number of orders for each customer.

As you can see, this query returns one record for each customer. The Sum Of Freight field displays the total freight cost for each customer; the Count Of Orders field shows the total number of orders for each customer.

The Jet SQL statement for this query is shown here:

```
SELECT DISTINCTROW Orders.CustomerID, Sum(Orders.Freight)
AS [Sum Of Freight], Count(*) AS [Count Of Orders]
FROM Orders
GROUP BY Orders.CustomerID;
```

This Jet SQL statement is different from the qryPhoneNumbers query shown earlier in this chapter. This time the SELECT statement includes the DISTINCTROW keyword, which returns a unique recordset (excluding duplicates).

The following expression displays the sum of the entries in the Freight field in a field named Sum Of Freight (shown in the AS clause):

```
Sum(Orders.Freight) AS [Sum Of Freight]
```

As before, the FROM clause identifies the data source, but this time it's followed by a GROUP BY clause that groups the records by the entries in the CustomerID field.

Grouping is discussed in more detail in the section "Grouping and Summarizing Records," page 371.)

A lot goes on behind the scenes when you use the Simple Query Wizard. Comparing the Jet SQL statement to the Design view is a good way to familiarize yourself with the logic behind a query.

Retrieving Data

The simplest queries retrieve, group, and organize data, but they don't limit the results or evaluate expressions. You saw two examples of simple queries in the previous sections. Using the Simple Query Wizard might be convenient, but you can create a select query without the wizard. In addition, whether you start with the Simple Query Wizard or build the query from scratch in the query Design view, you can modify a query in a number of ways.

In this section, instead of using a wizard to create the list, let's use the query Design view.

To create the list without using a wizard, follow these steps:

1. On the Database window's Objects bar, click Queries, and then double-click Create Query In Design View.

Troubleshooting

I can't see the Create Query In Design View item in the Database window

If the Create Query In Design View item isn't visible in the Database window, the New Object Shortcuts option might be turned off. (The Create Query In Design View item is one of these shortcuts.) To turn the option back on, choose Tools, Options, and select the New Object Shortcuts check box on the View tab of the Options dialog box.

After you open query Design view, the Show Table dialog box should appear automatically, as shown in Figure 9-9. If the Show Table dialog box isn't displayed, click the Show Table button on the Query Design toolbar.

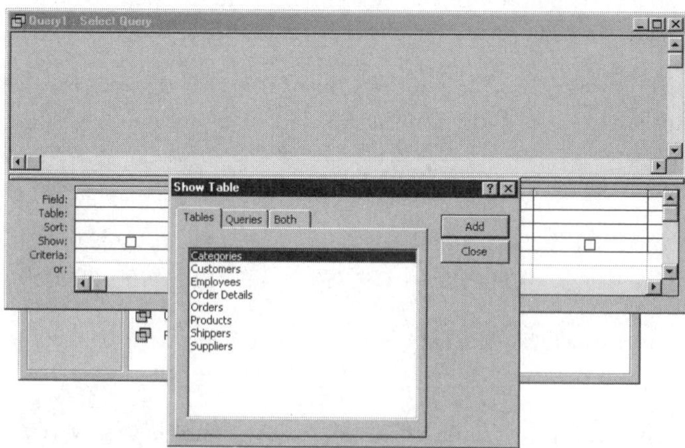

Figure 9-9. When you begin a new query in Design view, the Show Table dialog box is automatically displayed.

2 The Show Table dialog box allows you to identify data sources that you want to add. If the data source is a query instead of a table, click the Queries tab. The Both tab will display both tables and queries. You can also add more than one data source. For this example, add the Customers table, and then click Close.

3 Add the CompanyName, ContactName, ContactTitle, and Phone fields from the Customers table to the design grid, as shown in Figure 9-10.

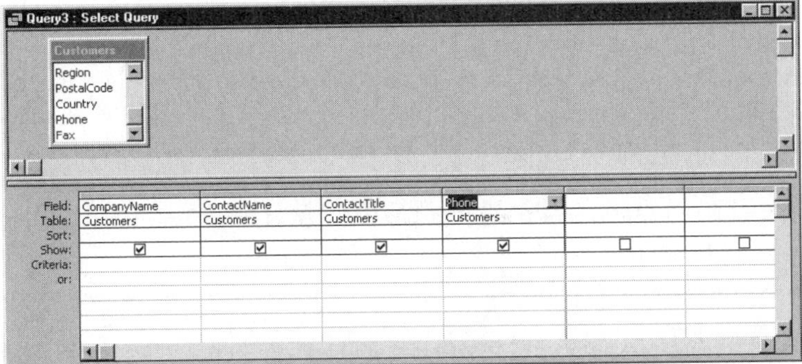

Figure 9-10. The CompanyName, ContactName, ContactTitle, and Phone fields have been added to the design grid.

There are five methods for adding fields to the design grid, as follows:

- Double-click the field in the field list. Access will add the field to the first blank column.
- Drag the field to a column.
- Double-click or drag the asterisk (*) in the field list to add all the fields from a table. The asterisk represents all the fields in the data source.
- In the design grid, choose a field from the Field drop-down list.
- In the design grid, type the field name in a column's Field cell.

When you use either of the last two methods and the query is based on more than one table or query that have a field name in common, choose the appropriate table from the Table drop-down list. (If the Table row isn't displayed, choose View, Table Names.)

Adding Multiple Fields to the Design Grid

You can also select multiple fields in a table and drag them to the design grid. To select a contiguous block, click the first field in the set, hold down the Shift key, and then click the last field in the set. To select a noncontiguous group, hold down the Ctrl key while clicking each field in the field list. Once the desired fields have been selected, drag the group to the design grid. Access will add the fields to the design grid in the same order in which they appear in the field list.

You can also double-click the field list's title bar to highlight all the fields at once, and drag them to the design grid as a block. This method has some advantages over the asterisk method described earlier. If you drag all the fields to the design grid as a block, you can remove a few fields you don't need in the query, and you can add criteria to individual fields. But if you drag the asterisk to the design grid, you won't have to update the query if you add, delete, or change the names of fields in the query's data sources.

4. After you have added the CompanyName, ContactName, ContactTitle, and Phone fields to the design grid, you can specify additional options. Although it's not necessary in this example, you can specify a sort order in a column's Sort field, enter criteria expressions in a column's Criteria or Or cell, and clear the Show check box when you don't want a particular field to appear in the results.
5. To execute the query, on the Query Design toolbar, click the Run button. The results shown earlier in Figure 9-5 should be displayed.

tip **Preload a data source**

Here's a shortcut to preload a new query with a single data source table or query. Before you open query Design view, in the Database window, select the table or query you want to include in the query. Then, on the Database toolbar, click the arrow to the right of the New Object selector, and then click Query. In the New Query dialog box, double-click Design View. The query Design view will open with the selected table or query. You can identify only one data source this way, so if your query is based on more than one table or query, you'll still need to use the Show Table dialog box (by clicking the Show Table button) and select the remaining sources.

Evaluating Expressions with Calculated Fields

In addition to selecting a specific set of records, a query can return the results of expressions for each record. You already had a sneak peek at this capability in the section "Summarizing Data," page 346. You can add calculated fields to almost any query.

When working with a form, you can enter an expression in the *ControlSource* property of a control to create a calculated control. When you're working with a query, you can enter an expression in a Field cell in the design grid. A calculated field, or calculated column, is any field that contains an expression.

The Order Details table offers a good example of using a calculated field. This table contains details for each item in each order. To calculate the extended price of each item, follow these steps:

1 Create a new query in Design view.

2 Add the Order Details table to the query.

3 Add the OrderID and ProductID fields to the design grid.

4 In the Field cell of the third column, enter the following expression (see Figure 9-11):

```
ItemPrice: ([UnitPrice]*[Quantity])-
  ([UnitPrice]*[Quantity]*[Discount])
```

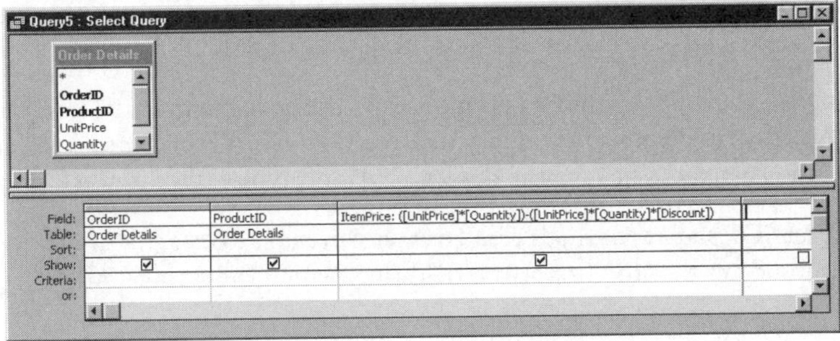

Figure 9-11. Add a calculated ItemPrice field.

5 Run the query. Figure 9-12 shows the extended price for each item.

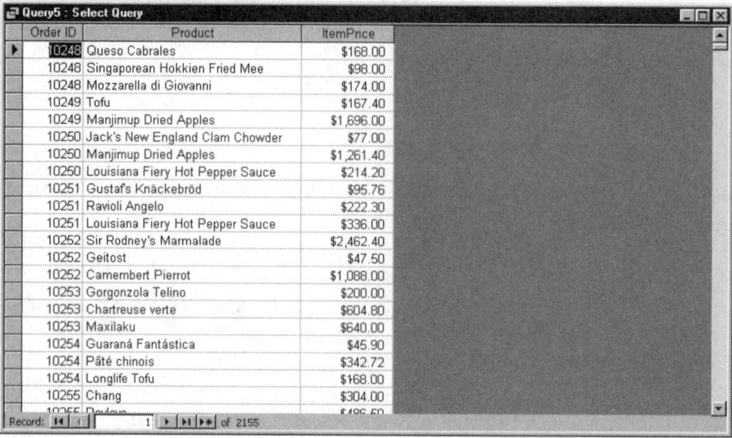

Order ID	Product	ItemPrice
10248	Queso Cabrales	$168.00
10248	Singaporean Hokkien Fried Mee	$98.00
10248	Mozzarella di Giovanni	$174.00
10249	Tofu	$167.40
10249	Manjimup Dried Apples	$1,696.00
10250	Jack's New England Clam Chowder	$77.00
10250	Manjimup Dried Apples	$1,261.40
10250	Louisiana Fiery Hot Pepper Sauce	$214.20
10251	Gustaf's Knäckebröd	$95.76
10251	Ravioli Angelo	$222.30
10251	Louisiana Fiery Hot Pepper Sauce	$336.00
10252	Sir Rodney's Marmalade	$2,462.40
10252	Geitost	$47.50
10252	Camembert Pierrot	$1,088.00
10253	Gorgonzola Telino	$200.00
10253	Chartreuse verte	$604.80
10253	Maxilaku	$640.00
10254	Guaraná Fantástica	$45.90
10254	Pâté chinois	$342.72
10254	Longlife Tofu	$168.00
10255	Chang	$304.00

Figure 9-12. A calculated field evaluates data from specific fields to return a value for each record.

Limiting Data

You're not restricted to evaluating expressions to summarize or otherwise analyze your data. You can also limit the results of your query by specifying criteria expressions. In other words, your query will return only those records that satisfy some condition.

The Criteria cell in the design grid accepts expressions that limit the records returned by the query. You might want to see only customers from a specific state or country. Or perhaps you want to view orders that were taken on a certain day or during a specific week. The reasons for limiting the results of a query are almost limitless.

Suppose you want to find all employees with the last name Fuller. One way to do this in Access is to create a new query in Design view, add the Employees table to the query, add the LastName field to the design grid, and type **Fuller** in the Criteria cell.

The Jet SQL statement that's created is shown here. Notice that it includes an expression that indicates that the LastName field must equal the string "Fuller".

```
SELECT Employees.LastName
FROM Employees
WHERE (((Employees.LastName)="Fuller"));
```

> **tip** **Specify criteria designators**
>
> When you enter a value in the Criteria cell of a query's design grid, enclose it within double quotation marks if it's a string (text) value or pound signs (#) if it's a date. Numeric values don't need a designator. Access will attempt to supply the appropriate designators when you tab away from the Criteria cell after typing in a value or expression, but check to be sure that the designators are correct.

An expression is a statement that contains an operator and at least one operand. (Entering **"Fuller"** in the Criteria cell satisfies this condition; even though you don't explicitly include the equal sign (=) operator, Access just assumes it.) The elements common to expressions are described here:

- **Operators.** The symbols that represent mathematical, comparison, logical, and concatenation tasks. (Table 9-1 contains a list of operators.)
- **Operands.** The values you want the expression to evaluate. Operands come from more than one source, including literal values, identifiers, and functions. The previous example consisted of just one literal, the string "Fuller". Some expressions refer to Access objects by name. When you refer to a field, a form, or a report by name, you're using an identifier. Functions that return a value can also be used as operands in an expression.

Table 9-1. Some operators that can be used in expressions

Arithmetic		Comparison		Logical	
+	Addition	=	Equals	*Or*	Meets any one condition
-	Subtraction	>	Greater than	*And*	Meets all conditions
*	Multiplication	<	Less than	*Not*	Negates argument
/	Division	>=	Greater than or equal to	*Between*	Falls between two extremes and includes the extremes
^	Exponentiation	<=	Less than or equal to		
		<>	Not equal to		
		Is	SQL equivalent to equal sign		
		Like	String matches a pattern		

You can limit records using a number of methods, but most of the time a query that limits data will fall into one of three categories, as follows:

- Restricted by one condition (simplest)
- Restricted by more than one field
- Restricted by one field or another

These three categories don't require much explanation, but creating queries within each category does. Remember that all three categories of queries are created by either a field entry or the results of an expression.

Restricting by One Condition

Perhaps the simplest restrictive query uses a field entry as its criteria. In other words, the criteria expression equals an actual entry, such as the name of a customer or a particular ZIP code. A query of this type can return one or many records, but all the records will have something in common—the contents of one field. The query shown in Figure 9-13 will return only those records in which the UnitPrice entry equals $10.

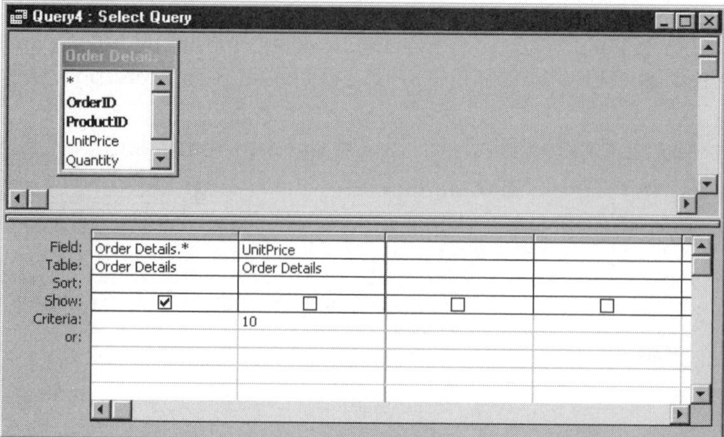

Figure 9-13. The expression in the Criteria row limits the query.

The results of this query are shown in Figure 9-14.

Query4 : Select Query

Order ID	Product	Unit Price	Quantity	Discount
10253	Gorgonzola Telino	$10.00	20	0%
10272	Gorgonzola Telino	$10.00	40	0%
10273	Gorgonzola Telino	$10.00	15	5%
10288	Scottish Longbreads	$10.00	3	10%
10300	Scottish Longbreads	$10.00	20	0%
10303	Scottish Longbreads	$10.00	15	10%
10307	Scottish Longbreads	$10.00	3	0%
10325	Gorgonzola Telino	$10.00	4	0%
10328	Scottish Longbreads	$10.00	10	0%
10334	Scottish Longbreads	$10.00	10	0%
10335	Gorgonzola Telino	$10.00	25	20%
10342	Gorgonzola Telino	$10.00	56	20%
10343	Scottish Longbreads	$10.00	4	5%
10356	Gorgonzola Telino	$10.00	30	0%
10359	Gorgonzola Telino	$10.00	70	5%

Record: 1 of 71

Figure 9-14. The previous query returns only those records in which the UnitPrice field equals $10.

At first, these queries seem similar to the Filter By Selection results available in Datasheet view and Form view, but a query isn't limited by just an actual field entry, which is how the Filter By Selection feature limits its results. Also, you're not limited to the equals comparison operator. For example, the following expression would include all the records in which the UnitPrice field does not equal $10:

```
<>10
```

Similarly, you could look for a range of unit price values using the *Between* and *And* operators. For example, the following expression would return the records shown in Figure 9-15:

```
Between 8 And 10
```

Query4 : Select Query

Order ID	Product	Unit Price	Quantity	Discount
10248	Singaporean Hokkien Fried Mee	$9.80	10	0%
10253	Gorgonzola Telino	$10.00	20	0%
10254	Longlife Tofu	$8.00	21	0%
10259	Sir Rodney's Scones	$8.00	10	0%
10261	Sir Rodney's Scones	$8.00	20	0%
10263	Longlife Tofu	$8.00	36	25%
10272	Gorgonzola Telino	$10.00	40	0%
10273	Gorgonzola Telino	$10.00	15	5%
10287	Spegesild	$9.60	15	15%
10288	Scottish Longbreads	$10.00	3	10%
10289	Aniseed Syrup	$8.00	30	0%
10300	Scottish Longbreads	$10.00	20	0%
10303	Scottish Longbreads	$10.00	15	10%
10307	Scottish Longbreads	$10.00	3	0%
10324	Spegesild	$9.60	30	0%

Record: 1 of 207

Figure 9-15. Here the results are limited to records that have a unit price between $8 and $10 (inclusive of both values).

> **note** The *Between* operator is inclusive, so the results in Figure 9-15 include records that have a unit price of $8 as well as $10.

Restricting by More than One Field

You can express multiple conditions in two ways: You can use the Criteria cells to enter single conditions for each field, or you can enter all the conditions in one Criteria cell using the *And* operator. For instance, both queries shown in Figure 9-16 will return only those records in which the UnitsInStock value is less than 10 and the UnitsOnOrder value equals 0.

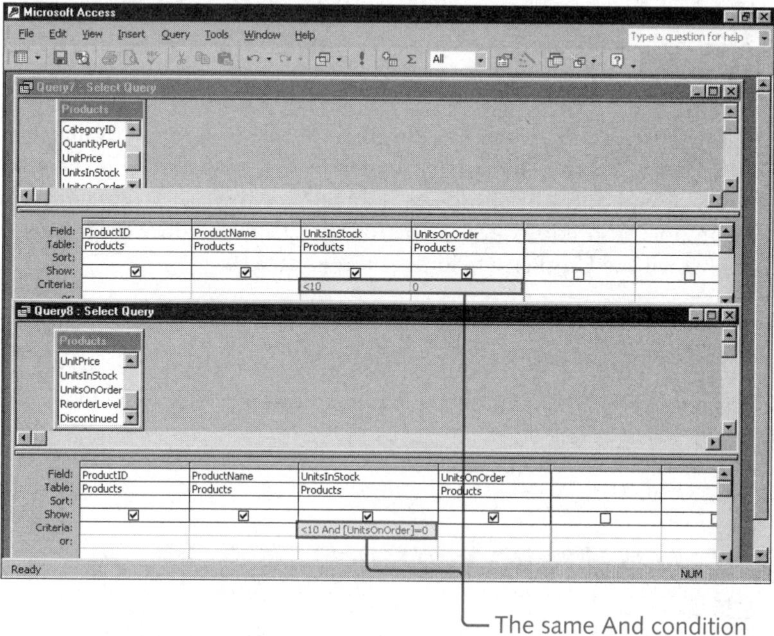

Figure 9-16. These two queries express the same And condition in different ways.

You can prove that the queries are the same by viewing the Jet SQL statement in SQL view. The first query's SQL statement is shown here:

```
SELECT Products.ProductID, Products.ProductsName,
Products.UnitsInStock, Products.UnitsOnOrder
FROM Products
WHERE (((Products.UnitsInStock)<10) And ((Products.UnitsOnOrder)=0));
```

The second query's SQL statement is shown here:

```
SELECT Products.ProductID, Products.ProductName,
Products.UnitsInStock, Products.UnitsOnOrder
FROM Products
WHERE (((Products.UnitsInStock)<10 And [UnitsOnOrder]=0));
```

Although the locations of the parentheses are different in the WHERE clauses, the statements are equivalent.

InsideOut

SQL statements generated by Access often contain extra sets of parentheses (as in the preceding SQL statement). They also typically contain the table names in front of the field name. If you need to copy a SQL statement from SQL view for use in Microsoft Visual Basic for Applications (VBA) code, you can usually strip out the extra sets of parentheses and the table names (including the period) in front of each field name—they generally aren't necessary for the statement to execute properly.

Brackets are needed only for field names that contain spaces; they can be deleted for field names that don't have spaces. If only one data source is used in the query, you can delete the table or query name (and the following period) before field names too.

For example, the preceding SQL statement could be condensed to the following statement:

```
SELECT ProductID, ProductName, UnitsInStock, UnitsOnOrder
FROM Products
WHERE UnitsInStock<10 And UnitsOnOrder=0;
```

To do the cleanup on a large query, copy the SQL statement to Word, where you can use Word's find and replace utility, and then copy the edited statement back into the SQL window.

Restricting by One Field or Another

Records won't always need to meet all conditions. Sometimes a record needs to meet only one condition even if there are several conditions. The example from the previous section returns those records in which the UnitsInStock value is less than $10 *and* the UnitsOnOrder field equals 0. This time, let's return all records that meet one or the other condition rather than both by using the Or cell or the *Or* operator.

Both queries shown in Figure 9-17 return the records shown in Figure 9-18.

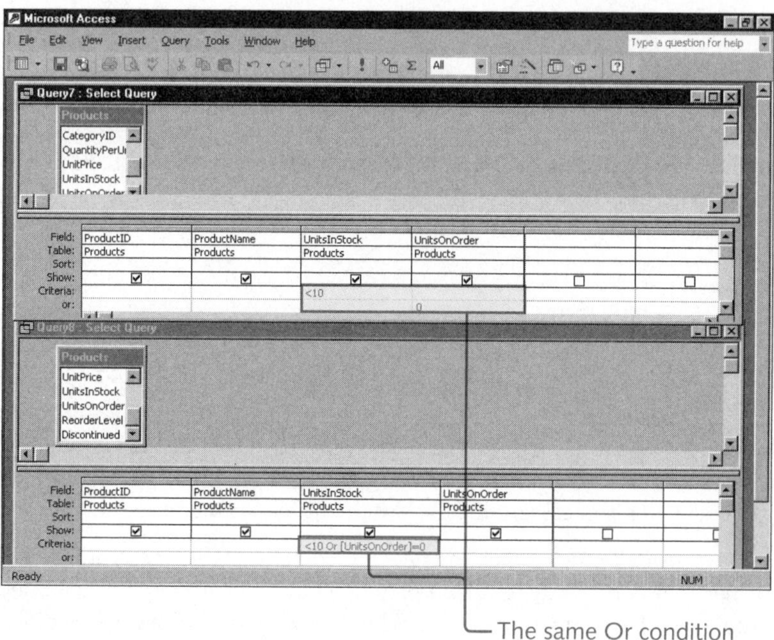

Figure 9-17. These two queries express the same Or condition in different ways.

Query7 : Select Query

Product ID	Product Name	Units In Stock	Units On Order
28	Rössle Sauerkraut	26	0
29	Thüringer Rostbratwurst	0	0
30	Nord-Ost Matjeshering	10	0
31	Gorgonzola Telino	0	70
32	Mascarpone Fabioli	9	40
33	Geitost	112	0
34	Sasquatch Ale	111	0
35	Steeleye Stout	20	0
36	Inlagd Sill	112	0
38	Côte de Blaye	17	0
39	Chartreuse verte	69	0
40	Boston Crab Meat	123	0
41	Jack's New England Clam Chowder	85	0
42	Singaporean Hokkien Fried Mee	26	0
44	Gula Malacca	27	0
45	Røgede sild	5	70
46	Spegesild	95	0

Record: 1 of 67

Figure 9-18. Both Or queries return the same records.

At first glance, you might think a mistake's been made, but the results are correct. (The 0 expression has been moved to the Or cell; the *And* operator has been changed to *Or*.) Only one condition must be met. If you review the records carefully, you'll see that all records whose UnitsInStock value is more than 10 have a UnitsOnOrder value of 0 and all records whose UnitsOnOrder value doesn't equal 0 have a UnitsInStock value of less than 10.

Again, Jet SQL statements prove that the queries are equivalent. The Or cell Jet SQL statement is shown here:

```
SELECT Products.ProductID, Products.ProductName,
Products.UnitsInStock, Products.UnitsOnOrder
FROM Products
WHERE (((Products.UnitsInStock)<10)) Or (((Products.UnitsOnOrder)=0));
```

The *Or* operator criteria Jet SQL statement is shown here:

```
SELECT Products.ProductID, Products.ProductName,
Products.UnitsInStock, Products.UnitsOnOrder
FROM Products
WHERE (((Products.UnitsInStock)<10 Or [UnitsOnOrder]=0));
```

As with the *And* examples in the previous section, the only difference is the parentheses. In some situations, the organization of the parentheses could make a huge difference, but that's not the case with the *And* and *Or* operators.

Understanding the *Or* Operator

Most of the time, returning all the records that meet all conditions (using the *And* operator) doesn't produce any surprises. You want any records that meet all the conditions, regardless of the number of conditions. On the other hand, returning records that meet any of the conditions can be a bit trickier. *Or* criteria don't always return the expected results, so you must be careful when designing queries that use *Or*.

The best way to understand how *Or* criteria work is to look at a couple of examples—one that works and one that doesn't. First review the query shown in Figure 9-19.

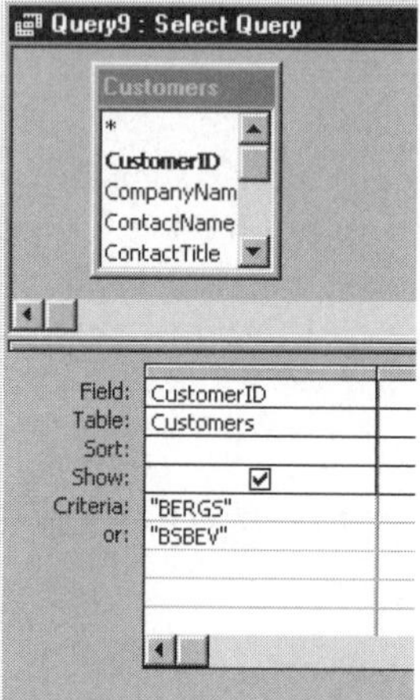

Figure 9-19. The record must match either the expression in the Criteria cell or the condition in the Or cell.

This query returns the records shown in Figure 9-20.

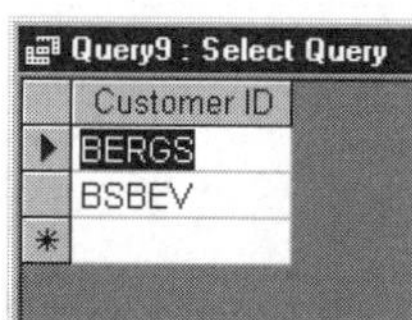

Figure 9-20. This query returns only those records that meet one or the other criterion.

The query has the following Jet SQL statement:

```
SELECT Customers.CustomerID
FROM Customers
WHERE (((Customers.CustomerID)="BERGS")) Or
(((Customers.CustomerID)="BSBEV"));
```

To be included in the results, a record needs to meet only one of the specified conditions. Specifically, the contents of the CustomerID field must equal "BERGS" or "BSBEV". As Access runs the query, it checks the CustomerID field of each record. If the CustomerID field for an entry equals "BERGS", the Criteria expression is true. If the CustomerID field for an entry equals "BSBEV", the *Or* expression is true. If either expression is true, Access includes that record in the results. If both (or all) expressions are false, the record isn't included.

The first four entries in the Customers table aren't included because neither condition is met. Both expressions are false and the records are excluded from the results. When Access evaluates the fifth record, the Criteria expression is true because the CustomerID field equals "BERGS". The *Or* expression is false, but that doesn't matter. Only one expression needs to be true for the record to be included. The next five records fail to meet either condition, and Access excludes those records. The entry for the eleventh record doesn't meet the Criteria expression's condition. However, it does meet the *Or* expression's condition, and Access includes the record in the results.

Now let's muddy the water a bit by adding the *Not* operator, as shown in Figure 9-21.

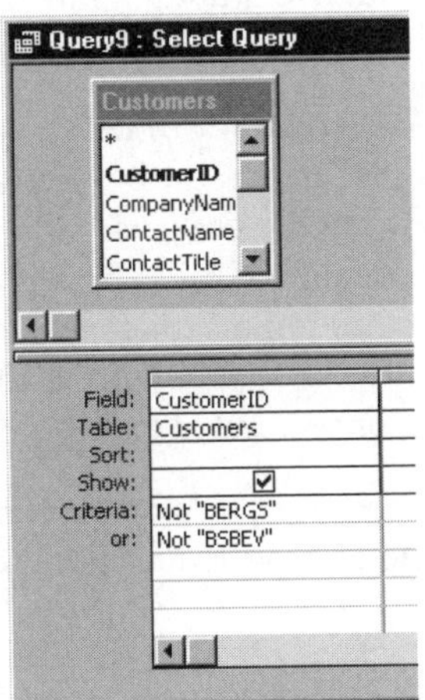

Figure 9-21. The *Not* operator has been added to both expressions.

You might expect this query to return all records except those with entries that match "BERGS" or "BSBEV". Unfortunately, this query doesn't work as expected. It returns all records, as shown in Figure 9-22.

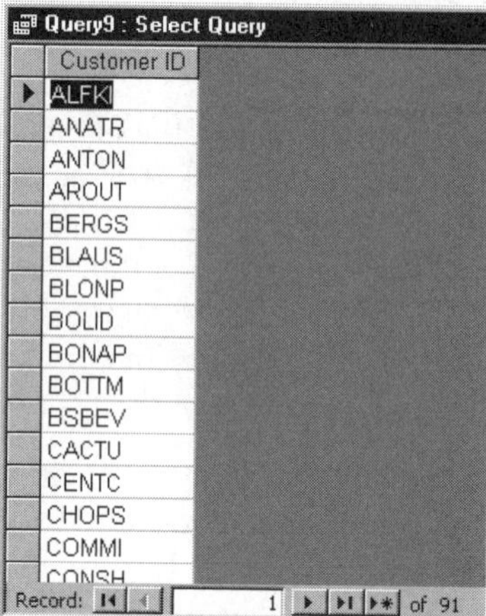

Figure 9-22. This exclusive query doesn't exclude any records.

The problem isn't Access or the query; the problem is your expectation. Don't forget that the expression needs to meet only one condition to be included in the results. Consider the first four records: The CustomerID entry doesn't match "BERGS" or "BSBEV", so both conditions are false. The *Not* operator then negates this value to true. Consequently, all four records are included in the results. (Although only one expression needs to be true, both are true in the case of each of the first four records.)

Now consider the fifth entry, which has a CustomerID equal to "BERGS". When first evaluated, the Criteria expression is true. However, the *Not* operator negates that value to false. So far, so good, right? The problem comes when the Or expression returns false. The *Not* operator then negates it to true. Because one of the expressions is true, Access includes the record in the results. The same situation occurs for the eleventh record, which has a CustomerID equal to "BSBEV". The only difference is that the Or expression is false and the Criteria expression is True, once negated by the *Not* operator.

Take a look at the query's equivalent Jet SQL statement. Each side of the expression includes the *Not* operator, which is the reason for the unexpected results.

```
SELECT Customers.CustomerID
FROM Customers
WHERE ((Not (Customers.CustomerID)="BERGS")) Or
((Not (Customers.CustomerID)="BSBEV"));
```

The solution is to include both conditions in the same expression, as shown in Figure 9-23.

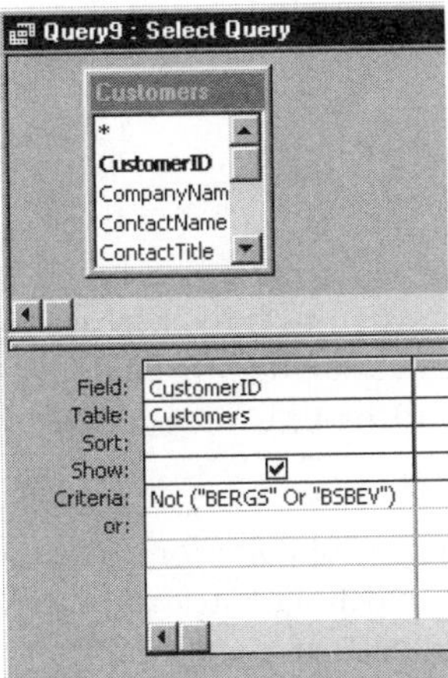

Figure 9-23. Combine both conditions in the same expression.

As shown in Figure 9-24, this query returns the expected records. The difference is that the *Or* operator evaluates both conditions before the *Not* operator has a chance to negate anything.

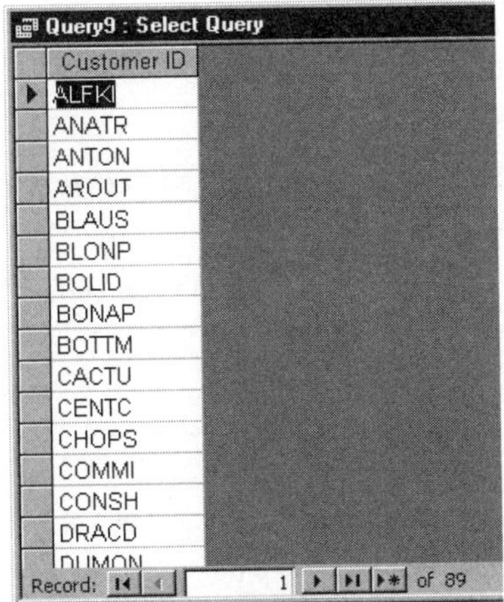

Figure 9-24. The combined Not expression works as expected, and the results don't include CustomerIDs that equal "BERGS" or "BSBEV".

Here's the updated Jet SQL statement:

```
SELECT Customers.CustomerID
FROM Customers
WHERE ((Not ((Customers.CustomerID)="BERGS" Or
(Customers.CustomerID)="BSBEV")));
```

Working with Wildcards

Ever play poker? If so, you know that a wildcard can significantly increase your odds of securing a better hand. The same is true when you're searching through records for specific data. Wildcards minimize your search effort by returning records that fit a profile, rather than matching each condition exactly.

Access supports several wildcard characters; the four most commonly used wildcards are listed in Table 9-2. When searching records for matching entries, you can substitute wildcard characters for literal characters or entire blocks of literal characters. Wildcards make a search more flexible.

Table 9-2. Access wildcard characters

Character	Name	Description
*	Asterisk	Matches any character or block of characters in that position
?	Question mark	Matches any single character in the same position
[]	Brackets	Specifies a range of characters (including numeric values)
!	Exclamation point	Excludes characters from the series specified in []

tip To get information about the more obscure wildcard characters not listed in Table 9-2, type **wildcard** in the Ask A Question box on the main Access menu, and select the "About using wildcard characters" topic.

Table 9-3 shows some search criteria that use wildcard characters and examples of fields that would match. These examples will be discussed throughout this section.

Table 9-3. Search criteria that use wildcard characters

Search criteria	Description	Examples
Like "an*"	Matches any string that begins with "an"	Ana Trujillo Antonio Moreno Ann Devon
Like "*an*"	Matches any string that contains "an", regardless of its position	Maria Anders Ana Trujillo Antonio Moreno
Like "B?l*"	Matches any string that begins with a *b* and has an *l* as its third character	Bólido Comidas preparadas
Like "[A-C]*"	Matches any string that begins with *a*, *b*, or *c*	Ana Trujillo Bernardo Batista Christina Berglund
Like "[A-C,F-H,K-P]*"	Matches any string that begins with *a*, *b*, *c*, *f*, *g*, *h*, *k*, *l*, *m*, *n*, *o*, or *p*	Ana Trujillo Bernardo Batista Christina Berglund Frederique Citeaux
Like "[!A-C,F-H,K]*"	Matches any string that doesn't begin with *a*, *b*, *c*, *f*, *g*, *h*, or *k*	Elizabeth Lincoln Laurence Lebihan Maria Anders
Like "c[a-c]*"	Matches any string that begins with *c* and contains *a*, *b*, or *c* as the second character	Carine Schmitt Carlos Hernandez
Like "c[!a-c]*"	Matches any string that begins with *c* and doesn't contain *a*, *b*, or *c* as the second character	Christina Berglund

Consider the search criterion, which uses the asterisk (*), as shown in Figure 9-25.

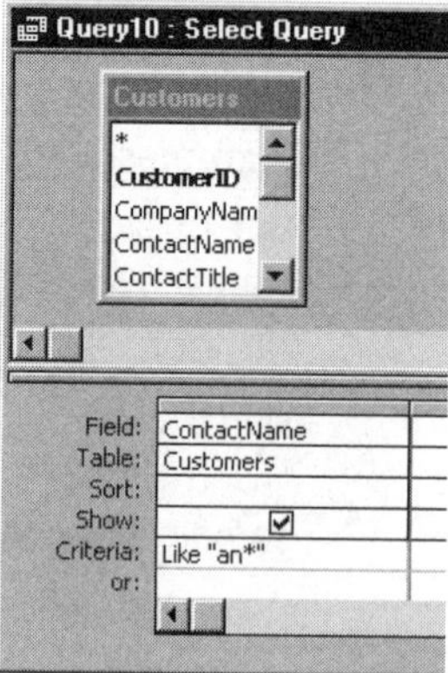

Figure 9-25. Use the * wildcard to match any character.

The simple expression "an" would find only those entries with a ContactName that equaled "an". If you append the * wildcard to the end of the search string, the query matches any entry that begins with "an", as shown in Figure 9-26.

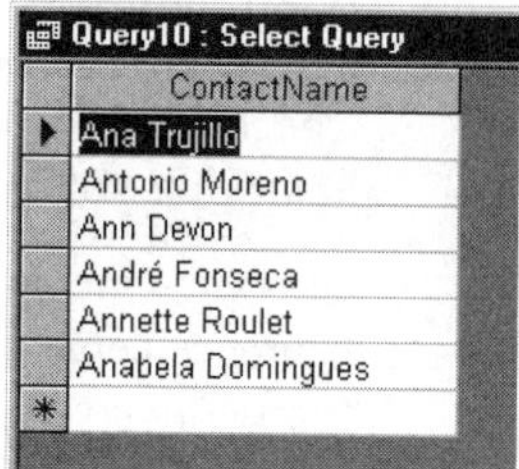

Figure 9-26. Using the "an*" search string, all entries that begin with "an" are returned.

> **note** When you add a wildcard character to a search string, Access automatically inserts the *Like* operator. A search for literal characters doesn't require the *Like* operator.

If you use the "*an*" search string, any entry that contains the string "an" regardless of its position will match. (The "an*" example matched only entries beginning with the string "an".)

As you can see, the position of the * wildcard character is as important as the wildcard itself. The position is even more relevant when you use the question mark (?) as a wildcard. You can replace any character within a search string to represent that one character in only that position. For instance, suppose you don't know how to generate the *ó* character in *Bólido Comidas preparadas* (a customer listed in the Northwind Customers table). You could try the following search criteria:

```
"Bolido Comidas preparadas"
```

This query would return an empty result set, however, because the *o* and *ó* are not equivalent.

The simplest solution might be to use the "B?l*" search criteria. The ? wildcard will match any single character between the letter *B* and the letter *l*. In addition, the * wildcard matches any characters that follow the string B?l.

You might want a bit more flexibility when you're matching a range or series of characters. Perhaps you want to find all the customers whose names begin with the letters *a*, *b*, and *c*. In this case, you'd employ the brackets ([]) and the * wildcard—for example, "[A-C]*".

A series search can include more than one series. For example, you could use the following search expression to match all companies whose names begin with the letters *A*, *B*, *C*, *F*, *G*, *H*, *K*, *L*, *M*, *N*, *O*, and *P*:

```
Like "[A-C,F-H,K-P]*"
```

Each component in the brackets doesn't have to be a series, however. A component can reference a single character. For example, the following expression would match companies whose names begin with the letters *A*, *B*, *C*, *F*, *G*, *H*, or *K*:

```
Like "[A-C,F-H,K]*"
```

Wildcards certainly do add a lot of possibilities, and the exclamation point (!) is no exception. This wildcard allows you to exclude characters within a series. Suppose you want to return all the companies whose names begin with letters other than *A*, *B*, *C*, *F*, *G*, *H*, or *K*. In that case, you'd use the following search expression:

```
Like "[!A-C,F-H,K]*"
```

You can also add a literal character to a series. For instance, the following search expression matches all the names that begin with the letters *Ca* through *Cc*:

```
Like "c[a-c]*"
```

To return names that begin with *C* but don't have *A*, *B*, or *C* as the second character, you could add the exclamation point to the search expression, as shown here:

```
Like "c[!a-c]*"
```

Chapter 11, "Working with Advanced Queries," discusses including wildcard characters in a parameter query.

Sorting Records

The qryPhoneNumbers query created in the section "The Simple Query Wizard," page 341, appears to sort the results by customer, but you haven't directly sorted the query. The Customers table's primary key is the CustomerID field, so Access sorts the records by that field. You can quickly change that order by simply applying a sort order to any field. In this section, we'll look at a few examples.

First open the qryPhoneNumbers query in Design view, click the arrow on the right side of CompanyName's Sort field to display its drop-down list, and then select Descending. On the Database toolbar, click the Run button to view the results shown in Figure 9-27. The list of records is the same as that shown in Figure 9-5 except that the records are reversed. Most sorts can be performed by a simple click, but Access is capable of more.

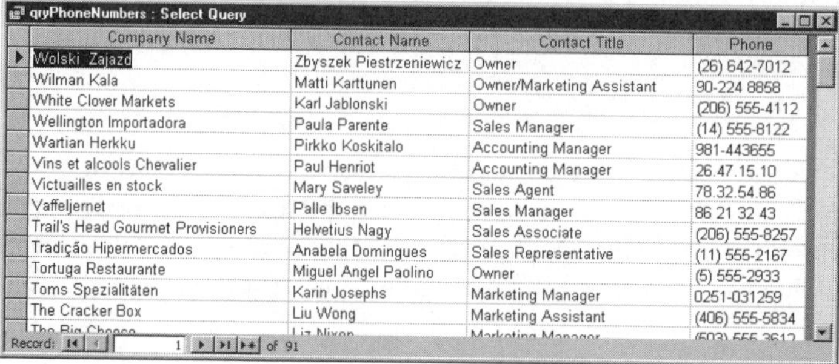

qryPhoneNumbers : Select Query

Company Name	Contact Name	Contact Title	Phone
Wolski Zajazd	Zbyszek Piestrzeniewicz	Owner	(26) 642-7012
Wilman Kala	Matti Karttunen	Owner/Marketing Assistant	90-224 8858
White Clover Markets	Karl Jablonski	Owner	(206) 555-4112
Wellington Importadora	Paula Parente	Sales Manager	(14) 555-8122
Wartian Herkku	Pirkko Koskitalo	Accounting Manager	981-443655
Vins et alcools Chevalier	Paul Henriot	Accounting Manager	26.47.15.10
Victuailles en stock	Mary Saveley	Sales Agent	78.32.54.86
Vaffeljernet	Palle Ibsen	Sales Manager	86 21 32 43
Trail's Head Gourmet Provisioners	Helvetius Nagy	Sales Associate	(206) 555-8257
Tradição Hipermercados	Anabela Domingues	Sales Representative	(11) 555-2167
Tortuga Restaurante	Miguel Angel Paolino	Owner	(5) 555-2933
Toms Spezialitäten	Karin Josephs	Marketing Manager	0251-031259
The Cracker Box	Liu Wong	Marketing Assistant	(406) 555-5834

Record: 1 of 91

Figure 9-27. Sort the phone list in descending order by the CompanyName field.

When you sort by more than one field, Access gives precedence to the leftmost field. As a result, a sort can have unexpected effects, or even no effect. For example, suppose you want the qryPhoneNumbers query to be sorted by the ContactName field in ascending order, and then you'd like the CompanyName field sorted in ascending order. To configure this sorting, you could set the ContactName field's Sort to Ascending, and then set the CompanyName field's Sort to Ascending, as shown in Figure 9-28.

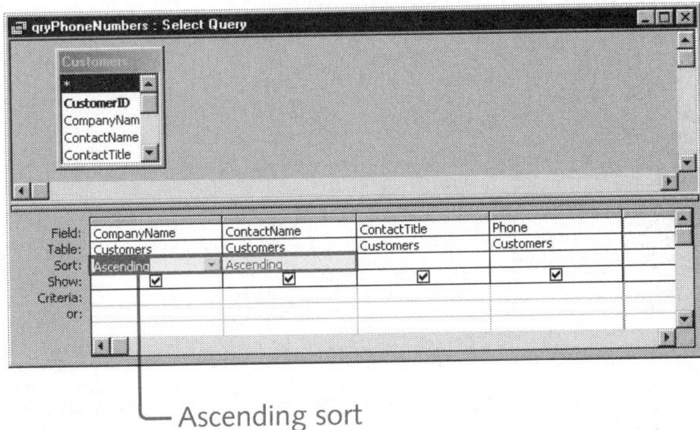

Figure 9-28. Apply an ascending sort to the ContactName and CompanyName fields.

Unfortunately, the results, shown in Figure 9-29, aren't what you expected.

qryPhoneNumbers : Select Query

Company Name	Contact Name	Contact Title	Phone
Alfreds Futterkiste	Maria Anders	Sales Representative	030-0074321
Ana Trujillo Emparedados y helados	Ana Trujillo	Owner	(5) 555-4729
Antonio Moreno Taquería	Antonio Moreno	Owner	(5) 555-3932
Around the Horn	Thomas Hardy	Sales Representative	(171) 555-7788
Berglunds snabbköp	Christina Berglund	Order Administrator	0921-12 34 65
Blauer See Delikatessen	Hanna Moos	Sales Representative	0621-08460
Blondel père et fils	Frédérique Citeaux	Marketing Manager	88.60.15.31
Bólido Comidas preparadas	Martín Sommer	Owner	(91) 555 22 82
Bon app'	Laurence Lebihan	Owner	91.24.45.40
Bottom-Dollar Markets	Elizabeth Lincoln	Accounting Manager	(604) 555-4729
B's Beverages	Victoria Ashworth	Sales Representative	(171) 555-1212
Cactus Comidas para llevar	Patricio Simpson	Sales Agent	(1) 135-5555
Centro comercial Moctezuma	Francisco Chang	Marketing Manager	(5) 555-3392

Record: 1 of 91

Figure 9-29. The previous sort doesn't have the expected result.

Specifically, this query sorts the CompanyName field alphabetically, but the ContactName sort seems to have no effect. Access applied both sorts, just not the way you expected. First Access sorted by the CompanyName field because it's the leftmost field. Then Access sorted by ContactName, but because each CompanyName entry is unique, the sort had no effect.

To solve this sort problem, move the CompanyName field to the right of the ContactName field, as shown in Figure 9-30.

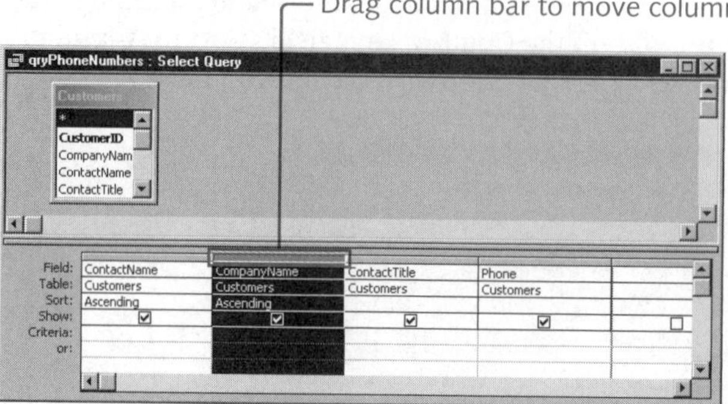

Figure 9-30. Move the CompanyName field to the right of the ContactName field.

tip To move a column in the design grid, first click the column selector (the small horizontal bar at the top of the design grid column) to select the entire column. Next drag the column bar to a new position.

This time Access sorts the records by the ContactName field first and then sorts by the CompanyName, as shown in Figure 9-31.

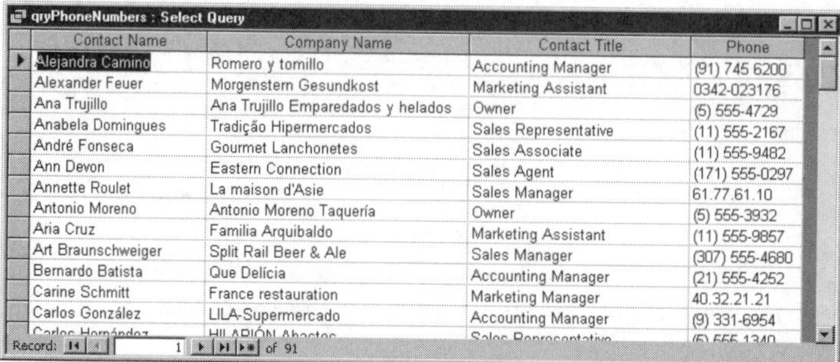

Contact Name	Company Name	Contact Title	Phone
Alejandra Camino	Romero y tomillo	Accounting Manager	(91) 745 6200
Alexander Feuer	Morgenstern Gesundkost	Marketing Assistant	0342-023176
Ana Trujillo	Ana Trujillo Emparedados y helados	Owner	(5) 555-4729
Anabela Domingues	Tradição Hipermercados	Sales Representative	(11) 555-2167
André Fonseca	Gourmet Lanchonetes	Sales Associate	(11) 555-9482
Ann Devon	Eastern Connection	Sales Agent	(171) 555-0297
Annette Roulet	La maison d'Asie	Sales Manager	61.77.61.10
Antonio Moreno	Antonio Moreno Taquería	Owner	(5) 555-3932
Aria Cruz	Familia Arquibaldo	Marketing Assistant	(11) 555-9857
Art Braunschweiger	Split Rail Beer & Ale	Sales Manager	(307) 555-4680
Bernardo Batista	Que Delícia	Accounting Manager	(21) 555-4252
Carine Schmitt	France restauration	Marketing Manager	40.32.21.21
Carlos González	LILA-Supermercado	Accounting Manager	(9) 331-6954

Figure 9-31. Access sorted these records first by the ContactName field.

In this configuration, the CompanyName sort has no effect because the ContactName entries are unique. You could achieve the same results by leaving the structure alone and applying a single ascending sort to the ContactName field.

Troubleshooting

I'm having problems sorting Null values

Records often contain blank fields. Access will list Null values at the beginning of an ascending sort and at the ending of a descending sort. If you don't know whether the data contains Null values, the results might not be what you expect. Plan for Null values by including an *Is Null* or *Is Not Null* expression in the field's Criteria cell for a query. The *Is Null* expression will return only those records that are Null and therefore probably won't be useful in this context. The *Is Not Null* expression will exclude Null fields from the results. Keep in mind that a blank field isn't always the only field that can be considered Null. A field that contains the result of an expression that returns Null is also considered Null. An expression generally returns Null when some component in that expression refers to a Null field (or variables).

See Chapter 4, "Creating a Database," for more details on working with Nulls.

Grouping and Summarizing Records

Groups are typically considered a report function, but you can group records in a query, usually for the purpose of summarizing data. A group is a collection of related records and as such can be beneficial when you're analyzing data. You saw how easy it is to create a group by sorting (in a manner of speaking) in the previous section. However, grouping is usually just a by-product of a sort, not the goal of a sort. Nor is the result considered a group.

Computing Totals for Grouped Records

When you group a set of records, you can also perform calculations based on each group. For example, to create a query that returns the total sales for each employee in the Northwind database, follow these steps:

1. Create a new query in Design view.
2. Add the Orders and Order Details tables to the query.
3. Add the EmployeeID from the Orders table to the design grid.

4 Enter the following expression in the Field cell of the second column:

```
TotalSales: ([UnitPrice]*[Quantity])-
  ([UnitPrice]*[Quantity]*[Discount])
```

(You don't have to enter the brackets; Access will add those for you.)

5 Choose View, Totals. A Total row appears in the design grid.

6 In the EmployeeID field's Total cell, make sure the Group By option is selected.

7 In the TotalSales field's Total cell, select Sum, as shown in Figure 9-32.

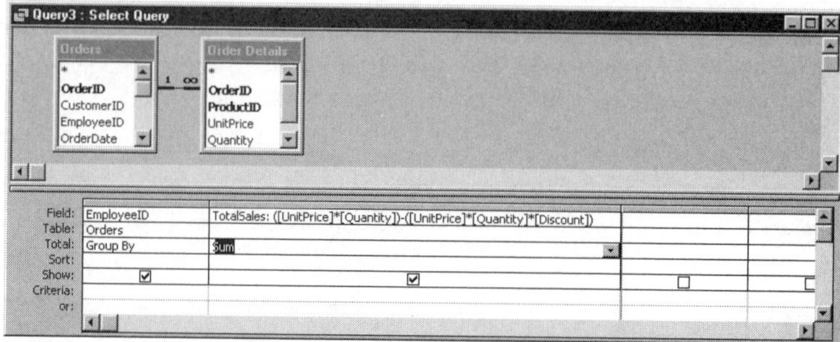

Figure 9-32. Specify Total options for the EmployeeID and TotalSales fields.

8 Run the query to see the results shown in Figure 9-33.

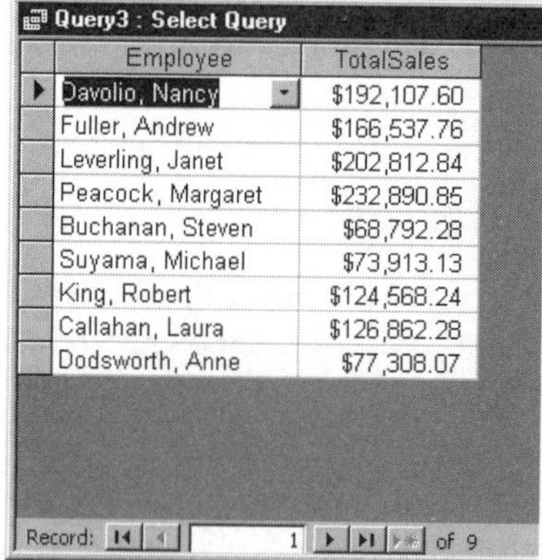

Query3 : Select Query

Employee	TotalSales
Davolio, Nancy	$192,107.60
Fuller, Andrew	$166,537.76
Leverling, Janet	$202,812.84
Peacock, Margaret	$232,890.85
Buchanan, Steven	$68,792.28
Suyama, Michael	$73,913.13
King, Robert	$124,568.24
Callahan, Laura	$126,862.28
Dodsworth, Anne	$77,308.07

Record: 1 of 9

Figure 9-33. The query groups records for each employee and computes the total sales for that employee.

As you can see, the query returns just one record for each entry in the EmployeeID field. In other words, the query returns one record for each employee or salesperson. The *Sum* aggregate function in the TotalSales field sums the values for each group (determined by the Group By aggregate in the Total cell), returning a total sales amount for each employee.

Take a look at the Jet SQL statement for this query, shown here:

```
SELECT Orders.EmployeeID,
Sum(([UnitPrice]*[Quantity])-([UnitPrice]*[Quantity]*[Discount]))
AS TotalSales
FROM Orders
INNER JOIN [Order Details] ON Orders.OrderID = [Order Details].OrderID
GROUP BY Orders.EmployeeID;
```

The TotalSales field displays the results of the expression we entered. The INNER JOIN relates the OrderID field in the Orders and Order Details tables. The GROUP BY clause indicates that the results are to be grouped by the EmployeeID.

You can choose from a number of options and aggregate functions after you display the Total row. As you saw in the previous example, Access defaults to the Group By option. An aggregate function returns information about a set of records, and nine of these twelve options are aggregate functions, as follows:

- ***Sum.*** Totals the values for each group.
- ***Avg.*** Averages the values for each group.
- ***Min.*** Returns the lowest value in each group.
- ***Max.*** Returns the highest value in each group.
- ***Count.*** Returns the number of items in each group (excluding Nulls and blanks).
- ***StDev.*** Returns the standard deviation for each group.
- ***Var.*** Returns the variance for each group.
- ***First.*** Returns the first value in the group.
- ***Last.*** Returns the last value in the group.

The other three options are listed here:

- ***Group By.*** Defines the group by reducing the data to unique entries.
- ***Expression.*** Returns a calculation based on an aggregate function.
- ***Where.*** Specifies search criteria.

note Access sorts the results of a totals query even if you don't specify a sort order. Since Access must group the underlying records, this behavior might seem obvious, but it's easy to miss if you don't realize it's happening. (You don't notice it in Figure 9-33 because Access is sorting by the EmployeeID value [the primary key], which you can't see in the query's results.) Sorting will be apparent only when the query explicitly names a sort order.

Suppose you want to count the number of items in each group. Simply return the query to Design view, select Order Details.OrderID in the Field cell of the third column, and then select Count for the Total field, as shown in Figure 9-34.

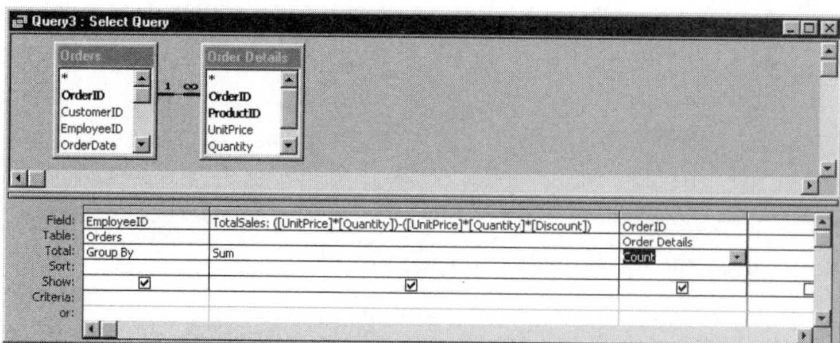

Figure 9-34. This query includes a field to count the number of items in each group.

The results of this query are shown in Figure 9-35.

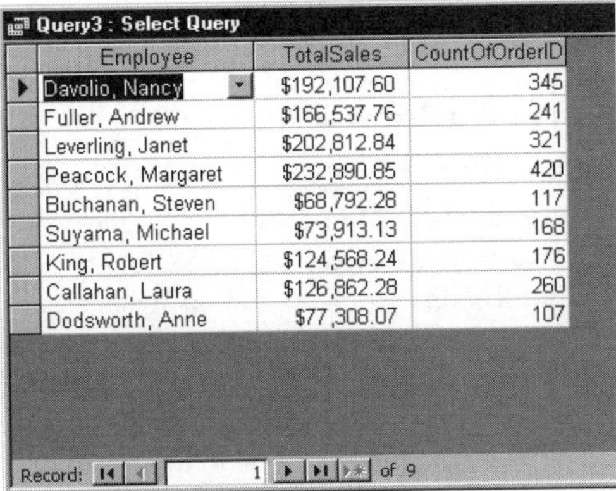

Employee	TotalSales	CountOfOrderID
Davolio, Nancy	$192,107.60	345
Fuller, Andrew	$166,537.76	241
Leverling, Janet	$202,812.84	321
Peacock, Margaret	$232,890.85	420
Buchanan, Steven	$68,792.28	117
Suyama, Michael	$73,913.13	168
King, Robert	$124,568.24	176
Callahan, Laura	$126,862.28	260
Dodsworth, Anne	$77,308.07	107

Figure 9-35. The CountOfOrderID field contains the number of items in each group.

The CountOfOrderID field includes the number of items in each group, which equates to the number of different items sold by each employee (not the quantity of items or the number of orders).

The Jet SQL statement for this updated query is shown here:

```
SELECT Orders.EmployeeID,
Sum(([UnitPrice]*[Quantity])-([UnitPrice]*[Quantity]*[Discount]))
AS TotalSales, Count([Order Details].OrderID) AS CountOfOrderID
FROM Orders INNER JOIN [Order Details]
ON Orders.OrderID = [Order Details].OrderID
GROUP BY Orders.EmployeeID;
```

Notice the *Count* function, as follows:

```
Count([Order Details].OrderID) AS CountOfOrderID
```

This expression counts the number of OrderID entries in each EmployeeID group.

Troubleshooting

My query returns a Cannot group on fields selected with " * " error

Occasionally, a query that groups records will return the error *Cannot group on fields selected with* "*"? If you didn't use the asterisk (*) to specify all the fields, which would be the most obvious problem, the query's *Output All Fields* property is probably set to Yes. Because the Group By option creates groups based on specified fields, you must be careful to add only those fields you want to group or evaluate with a Totals option. When the query's *Output All Fields* property is set to Yes, every field in the data source, not just the ones you added to the design grid, is a group. Consequently, the query results aren't grouped at all. The solution is simple: In query Design view, right-click the query's background, and then select Properties from the shortcut menu to display the Query properties sheet. If the *Output All Fields* property is set to Yes, simply change it to No.

Computing Grand Totals

In the previous example, we summed total sales by employee (groups). But group totals aren't the only summarizing you can do.

Follow these steps to calculate a grand sales total:

1 Create a new query in Design view.

2 Add the Order Details table to the query.

3 Add the following expression to the design grid:

```
TotalSales: ([UnitPrice]*[Quantity])-
  ([UnitPrice]*[Quantity]*[Discount])
```

4 Choose Views, Totals, and then, in the TotalSales field's Total field, select Sum, as shown in Figure 9-36.

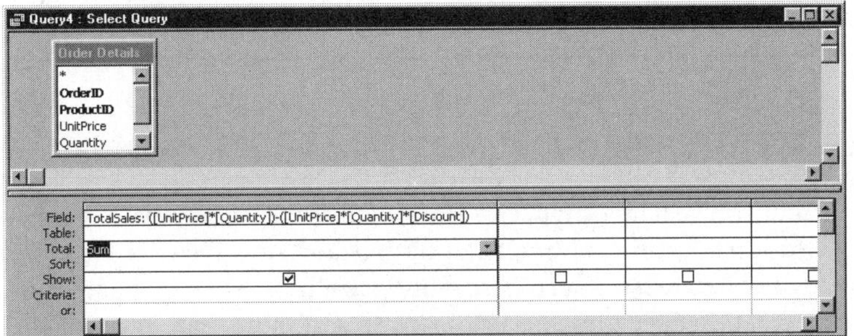

Figure 9-36. This query contains only one field.

5 Run the query to see the results shown in Figure 9-37.

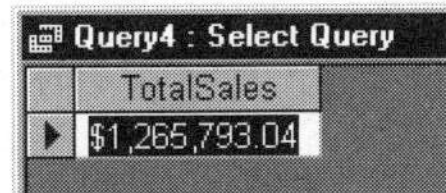

Figure 9-37. This time, the TotalSales field returns just one value: a sales grand total.

This query has a fairly simple Jet SQL statement, shown here:

```
SELECT Sum(([UnitPrice]*[Quantity])-
  ([UnitPrice]*[Quantity]*[Discount]))
AS TotalSales
FROM [Order Details];
```

The query displays just one entry in one field, the results of the following expression:

```
Sum(([UnitPrice]*[Quantity])-([UnitPrice]*[Quantity]*[Discount]))
```

The query calculates the extended price for every item and then totals those results for a grand total.

note Don't be alarmed if Access rearranges the design grid when you run a query, especially if your query contains an aggregate function. Access is just stating your question in the most efficient manner.

Relationships Between Data Sources

Now that you've had a chance to work with some queries, you're ready to advance to the next level. But first you need to understand how relationships affect a query. You've already learned that you can base a query on more than one data source and that a data source can be a table or a query. When you add more than one data source to the Design view, the query inherits any relationships created via the Relationships window. Access represents those relationships by displaying a join line between the related fields, as shown in Figure 9-38.

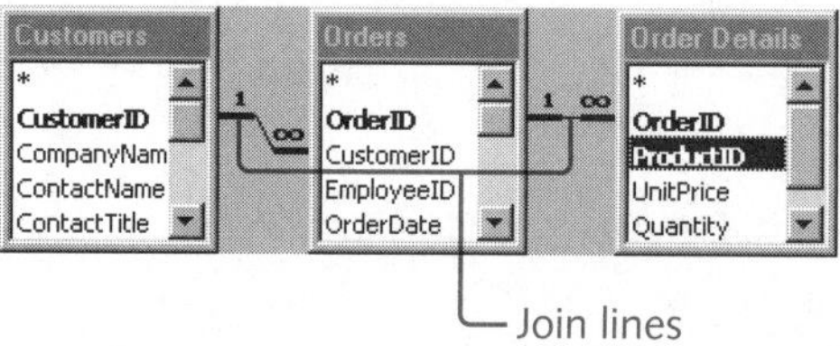

Figure 9-38. Join lines indicating relationships between tables in query Design view.

InsideOut

Access won't update existing queries to reflect changes made to relationships in the query Design view. You'll have to open any existing queries that might be affected by your changes and create the relationship (or relationships) yourself.

Understanding Join Lines

The join line tells a lot about the existing relationship. In Figure 9-38, the join line includes a *1* near the CustomerID field of the Customers table and an infinity symbol (∞) near the CustomerID field of the Orders table. The *1* and the infinity symbol indicate a one-to-many relationship, which means that there can be many orders for any one customer, but only one customer per order. There's also a one-to-many relationship between the Orders table and the Order Details table based on the OrderID field.

This relationship indicates that each order in the Orders table will have one or more detail records in the Order Details table. The presence of the *1* and the infinity symbol is a visual clue that the relationship enforces *referential integrity*—rules that restrict when you can add and delete records. When a relationship is indeterminate, Access displays the join line, but no symbols. You can temporarily sever a relationship (for the current query only) by clicking the join line and pressing Delete.

For more information about types of relationships and referential integrity, see Chapter 4, "Creating a Database."

Access can still define a relationship between two tables even if you haven't created a relationship yourself. By default, Access creates a relationship between two tables in a query if both of the following conditions are true:

Both tables contain a common field of the same name and data type. There is one exception to this rule: You can relate an AutoNumber field to a Long Integer (if the *Field Size* property in both is set to Replication ID). You can manually create a relationship between fields of the same data type—even if their names don't match—by dragging a primary key field from one field list to the related field (foreign key field) in another list. All Access really requires in this case is that the fields be of the same data type. If you want Access to create the relationship automatically, the field names must match.

At least one of the fields is a primary key field. This means that every record in the table has a unique value in this field.

You won't always want Access to automatically create a relationship between tables. To turn off this AutoJoin feature, choose Tools, Options, and then click the Tables/Queries tab and clear the Enable AutoJoin check box. Disabling this feature works only with unrelated tables. Permanent relationships established via the Relationships window will still take precedence in a query.

note Access identifies primary key fields by displaying them in boldface in the field list.

A Cartesian Product

Most multiple-table queries are based on related tables. If tables in a query aren't joined, Access won't know how to associate records. In this case, Access will create a cross (Cartesian) product. That means that Access will join every record in every table. A query based on two unrelated tables—for example, a table with 10 records and another with 20 records—will return 200 records. As a rule, you won't run into this type of query very often.

Self-Join: An Unusual Relationship

A *self-join* combines records from the same table. In other words, you're relating a table to itself. Although not commonly used, a self-join helps you find records that have common values with other records in the same table.

The Northwind Employees table assigns a unique value to each employee by using an AutoNumber field. In addition, the ReportsTo field stores the corresponding manager's AutoNumber value. As a result of this efficient arrangement, you won't need a second table to identify managers. The ReportsTo field displays names, but they're the result of a lookup field, which you need to delete. (You're deleting this feature so you can review a self-join, not because there's anything wrong with the lookup field method of displaying each manager's name.)

> **tip** We'll be modifying a table in the Northwind database in the following example. It would be a good idea to make a copy of the database if you haven't already done so.

To delete the lookup field, follow these steps:

1. In the Database window's Objects bar, click Tables.
2. Select the Employees table, and on the Database window toolbar, click Design. This will open the Employees table in Design view, as shown Figure 9-39.

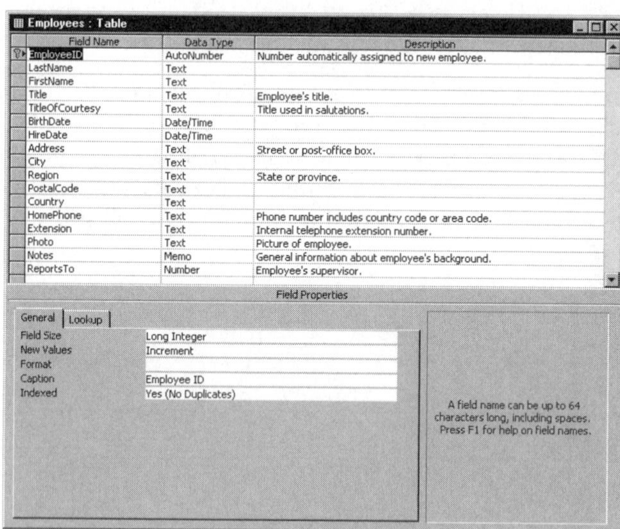

Figure 9-39. The Employees table in Design view.

3. Select the ReportsTo field, and then, in the Field Properties pane, click the Lookup tab.
4. From the list in the *Display Control* property, select Text Box.
5. On the Table Design toolbar, click the arrow to the right of the View button, and select Datasheet View.
6. In the message box asking whether you want to save the table, click Yes.

Take a look at the modified Employees table, shown in Figure 9-40. (Several of the fields that you don't need are hidden.) The ReportsTo field now displays each manager's EmployeeID value.

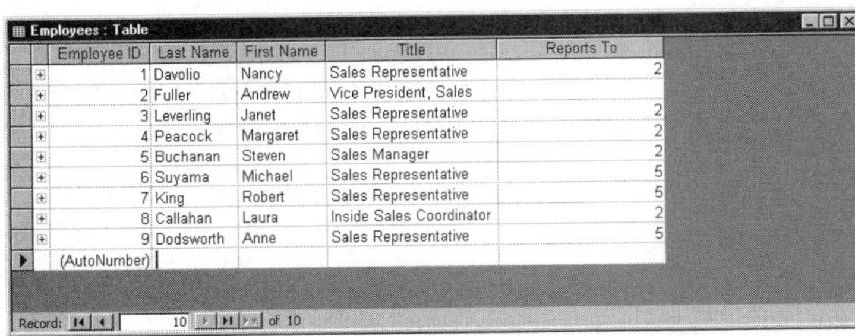

Figure 9-40. After you delete the lookup field, the ReportsTo field identifies the employee's manager by EmployeeID instead of by name.

To create a self-join query that identifies the manager by name instead of by the EmployeeID value, follow these steps:

1. In the Database window's Objects bar, click Tables, and then select the Employees table.
2. On the Database toolbar, click the arrow to the right of the New Object selector, and select Query.
3. In the New Query dialog box, double-click Design View. Access opens the Employees table in query Design view.
4. On the Query Design toolbar, click the Show Table button. In the Show Table dialog box, double-click Employees, and then click Close.

Access adds a second instance of the table and assigns the default name Employees_1, as shown in Figure 9-41.

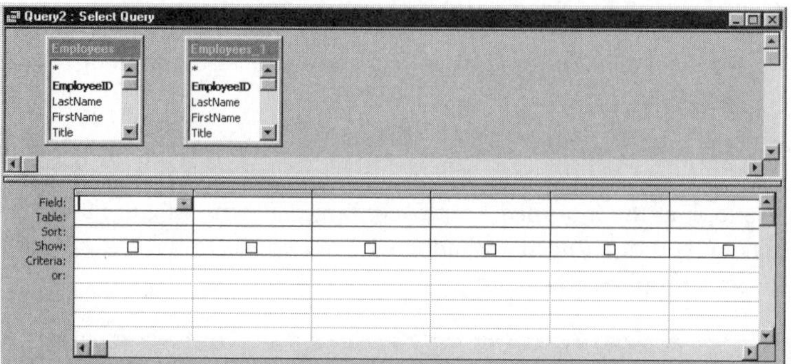

Figure 9-41. Two Employees tables shown in query Design view. Access gives the second instance of the Employees table the name Employees_1.

5 Right-click the Employees_1 table, and choose Properties from the shortcut menu.

6 In the Field List properties sheet, change the *Alias* property from Employees_1 to **Managers**, as shown in Figure 9-42.

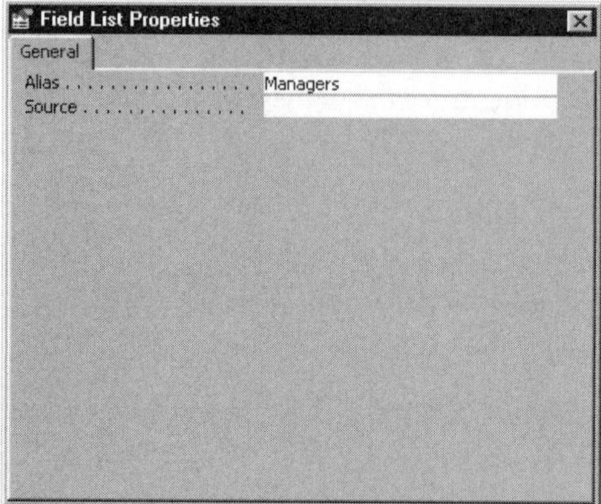

Figure 9-42. Change the *Alias* property for the Employees_1 table.

7 Close the property sheet to return to the query Design view. The Employees_1 field list now displays Managers in the title bar. (Assigning a new alias isn't necessary, but it does cut down on the confusion of working with two almost identically named tables.)

note An alias helps you differentiate between tables in a query without actually modifying the name of the underlying table. Because long table names can be clipped, the *Alias* property also comes in handy when a table has a long name. Assigning a short alias in the query makes each table name easier to read.

8 Now you're ready to create the self-join relationship. Drag the ReportsTo field from the Employees table to the EmployeeID field in the Managers table. A join line appears between these two fields.

9 Add the LastName, FirstName, and Title fields from the Employees table to the design grid.

10 Add a calculated field to the design grid by typing the following expression in the Field cell of the fourth column:

```
Manager: [Managers].[FirstName] & " " & [Managers].[LastName]
```

This expression concatenates the contents of the FirstName and LastName fields with a space in between. When finished, the query Design view should look like Figure 9-43.

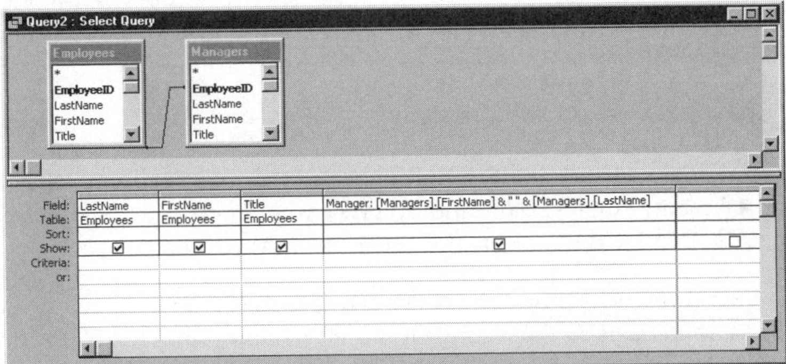

Figure 9-43. Add a calculated field to the self-join query.

11 On the Query Design toolbar, click the Run button to see the results shown in Figure 9-44.

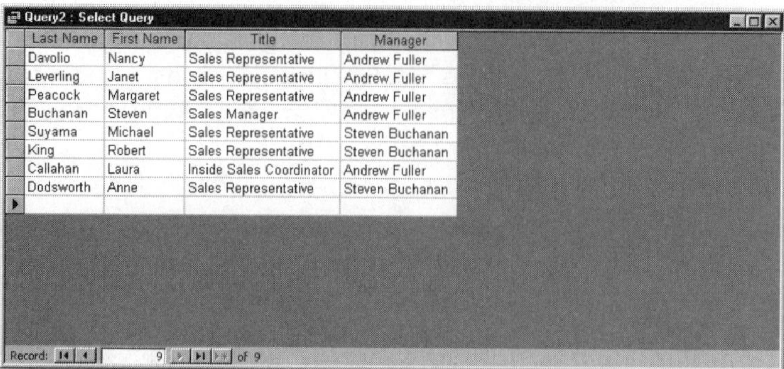

Query2 : Select Query

Last Name	First Name	Title	Manager
Davolio	Nancy	Sales Representative	Andrew Fuller
Leverling	Janet	Sales Representative	Andrew Fuller
Peacock	Margaret	Sales Representative	Andrew Fuller
Buchanan	Steven	Sales Manager	Andrew Fuller
Suyama	Michael	Sales Representative	Steven Buchanan
King	Robert	Sales Representative	Steven Buchanan
Callahan	Laura	Inside Sales Coordinator	Andrew Fuller
Dodsworth	Anne	Sales Representative	Steven Buchanan

Record: 9 of 9

Figure 9-44. The calculated Manager field contains the name of each employee's manager.

There's one problem with the results of this self-join query: Andrew Fuller is not listed in the FirstName and LastName fields. That's because his ReportsTo field is blank, and the default join is an INNER JOIN (the default relationship), which returns only those records in which the values are the same in the related field. You can see this by viewing the query's Jet SQL statement:

```
SELECT Employees.LastName, Employees.FirstName, Employees.Title,
[Managers].[FirstName] & " " & [Managers].[LastName] AS Manager
FROM Employees
INNER JOIN Employees AS Managers
ON Employees.ReportsTo = Managers.EmployeeID;
```

Access defaults to an INNER JOIN. This query displays those records in which the ReportsTo entry matches an EmployeeID entry. Since Andrew Fuller has no ReportsTo entry, the INNER JOIN omits this record from the results.

This query will include Andrew Fuller if you change the join type to a LEFT JOIN. A LEFT JOIN returns all the records in the left table (Employees) of the join operation, but in the right table (Managers), it returns only the records that match the related field.

To change the join type, follow these steps:

1. In Design view, right-click the join line, and choose Join Properties from the shortcut menu.
2. In the Join Properties dialog box, select option 2, as shown in Figure 9-45, and click OK.

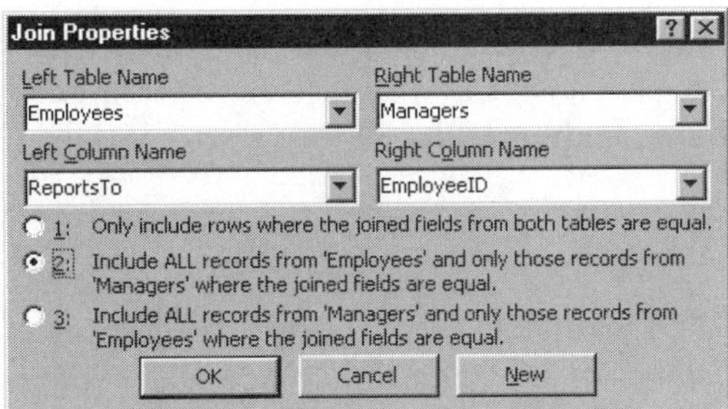

Figure 9-45. Make the join a LEFT JOIN.

3. Click the Run button to display the results shown in Figure 9-46. As you can see, this time the query includes Andrew Fuller, but the Manager field is blank.

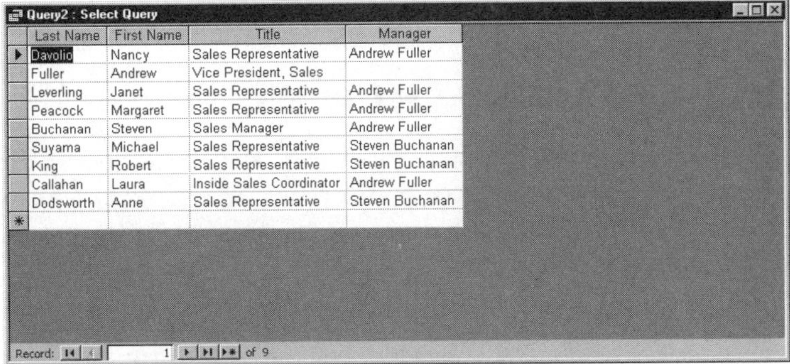

Last Name	First Name	Title	Manager
Davolio	Nancy	Sales Representative	Andrew Fuller
Fuller	Andrew	Vice President, Sales	
Leverling	Janet	Sales Representative	Andrew Fuller
Peacock	Margaret	Sales Representative	Andrew Fuller
Buchanan	Steven	Sales Manager	Andrew Fuller
Suyama	Michael	Sales Representative	Steven Buchanan
King	Robert	Sales Representative	Steven Buchanan
Callahan	Laura	Inside Sales Coordinator	Andrew Fuller
Dodsworth	Anne	Sales Representative	Steven Buchanan

Figure 9-46. This time the query includes Andrew Fuller.

The modified Jet SQL statement is shown here:

```
SELECT Employees.LastName, Employees.FirstName, Employeees.Title,
[Managers].[FirstName] & " " & [Managers].[LastName] AS Manager
FROM Employees
LEFT JOIN Employees AS Managers
ON Employees.ReportsTo = Managers.EmployeeID;
```

The statement is the same as the previous statement, except the type of join is now a LEFT JOIN. The results confirm this, as they display all the records in the Employees table, including the record for Andrew Fuller.

tip **Change a field's name in a query**

In addition to creating an alias for a table, you can create an alias for a field name without affecting the actual field's name in the underlying table. In the design grid, right-click the field in question, and then select Properties from the shortcut menu. In the Field Properties dialog box, enter a new name in the Caption box. The query will display the new *Caption* property as the field's heading in Datasheet view. Any objects you base on this query will display the *Caption* property as the field's heading or label, not the underlying table's field name.

Creating Crosstab Queries

Crosstab queries could be considered the orphan of Access queries because most people tend to ignore them. Crosstab queries are powerful, but they can seem mysterious. This section won't unravel all the mysteries of crosstab queries, but it will give you a good introduction to the subject.

Technically, a crosstab query is a query that groups summarized data by categories. You might consider a crosstab query a more complex way to group and summarize records than the method that was discussed earlier in this chapter in the section "Summarizing Data," page 346. All crosstab queries have the following three components:

- A column heading
- A row heading
- A summary field

The main advantage of a crosstab query is the amount of summarized information it displays in a reasonably compact space. However, crosstab queries have one restriction: They don't allow you to sort the results on a calculated column, which is probably the most likely place for sorting.

Using the Crosstab Query Wizard

The crosstab query example in this section uses the Orders table to total the freight cost per day by country, as shown in Figure 9-47.

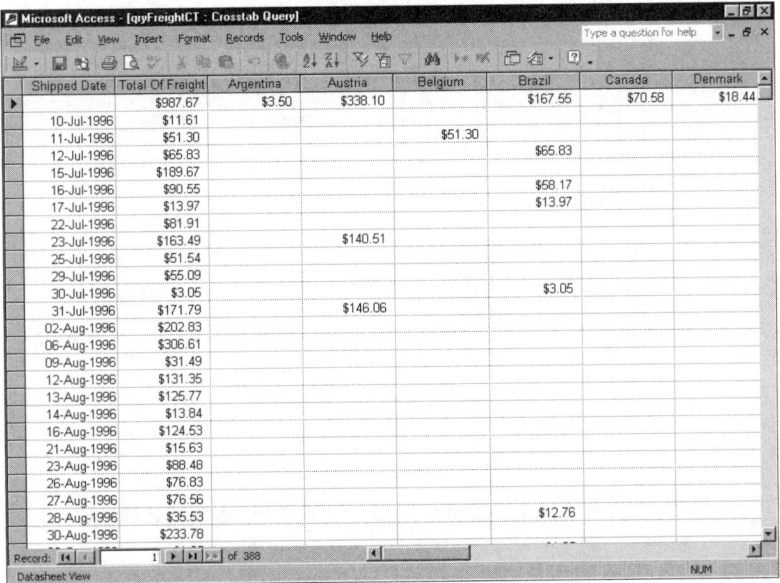

Shipped Date	Total Of Freight	Argentina	Austria	Belgium	Brazil	Canada	Denmark
	$987.67	$3.50	$338.10		$167.55	$70.58	$18.44
10-Jul-1996	$11.61						
11-Jul-1996	$51.30			$51.30			
12-Jul-1996	$65.83				$65.83		
15-Jul-1996	$189.67						
16-Jul-1996	$90.55				$58.17		
17-Jul-1996	$13.97				$13.97		
22-Jul-1996	$81.91						
23-Jul-1996	$163.49		$140.51				
25-Jul-1996	$51.54						
29-Jul-1996	$55.09						
30-Jul-1996	$3.05				$3.05		
31-Jul-1996	$171.79		$146.06				
02-Aug-1996	$202.83						
06-Aug-1996	$306.61						
09-Aug-1996	$31.49						
12-Aug-1996	$131.35						
13-Aug-1996	$125.77						
14-Aug-1996	$13.84						
16-Aug-1996	$124.53						
21-Aug-1996	$15.63						
23-Aug-1996	$88.48						
26-Aug-1996	$76.83						
27-Aug-1996	$76.56						
28-Aug-1996	$35.53				$12.76		
30-Aug-1996	$233.78						

Figure 9-47. The results of a crosstab query created with the Crosstab Query Wizard.

Although the typical crosstab query will usually be based on more than one table, the Crosstab Query Wizard works with only one table. When your results call for more than one table, create a query that includes all the tables, and then specify the query when you run the Crosstab Query Wizard.

To create the freight-summarizing crosstab query, follow these steps:

1. On the Database toolbar, click the arrow to the right of the New Object selector, and then click Query.
2. In the New Query dialog box, double-click Crosstab Query Wizard.

3 On the first page of the wizard, identify the data source for your query. For this example, select Table: Orders, as shown in Figure 9-48, and then click Next.

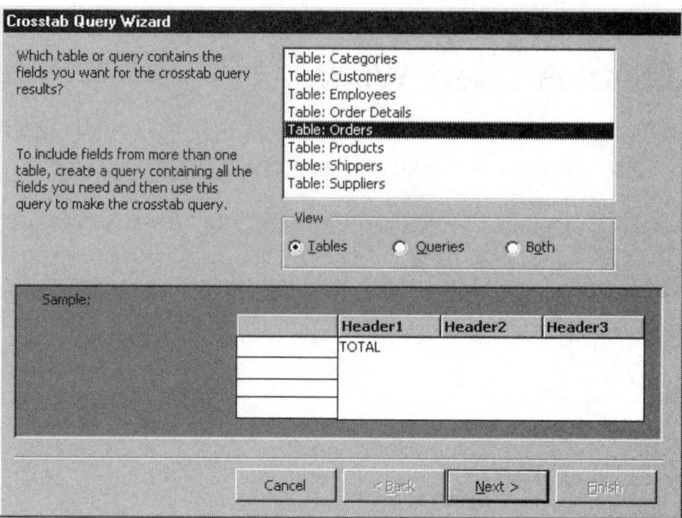

Figure 9-48. Base your crosstab query on the appropriate data source.

4 Identify the field that represents the row heading. In the Available Fields list, double-click ShippedDate to add that field to the Selected Fields list, as shown in Figure 9-49. You can add up to three row heading fields. Click Next.

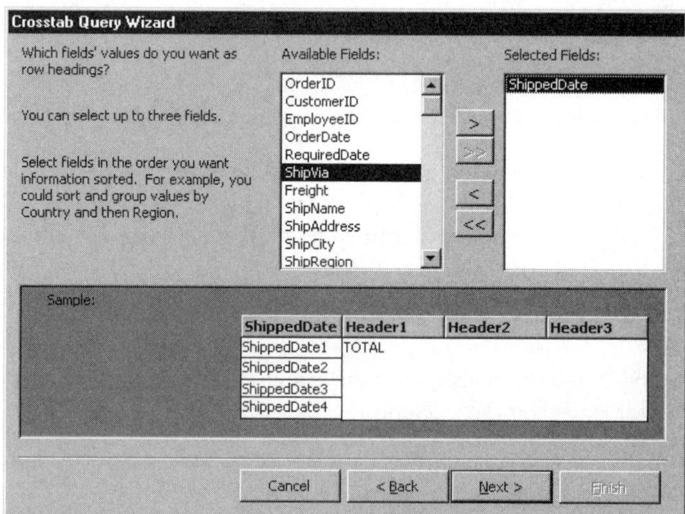

Figure 9-49. Select ShippedDate as the row heading field.

5 Because we're categorizing shipping values by country, select ShipCountry, as shown in Figure 9-50, and then click Next.

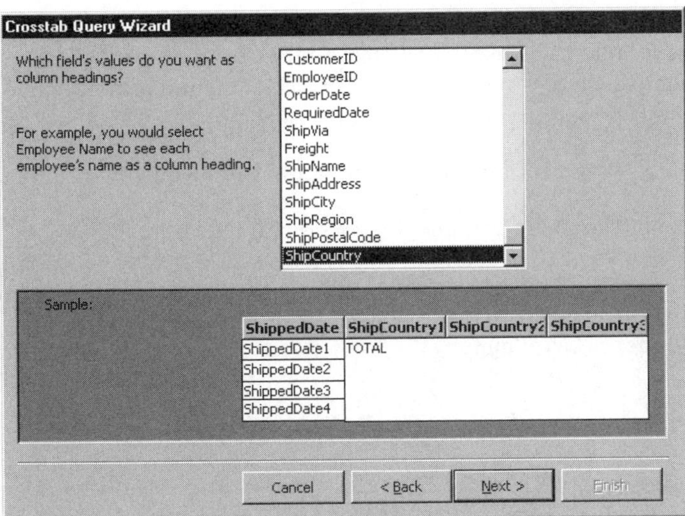

Figure 9-50. Categorize the crosstab query by the ShipCountry field.

6 Identify the value field that you want to summarize by the column heading. In this example, that's the actual freight costs in the Freight field. Click Freight in the Fields list, and then select Sum in the Functions list, as shown in Figure 9-51. Make sure the Yes, Include Row Sums check box is selected, and then click Next.

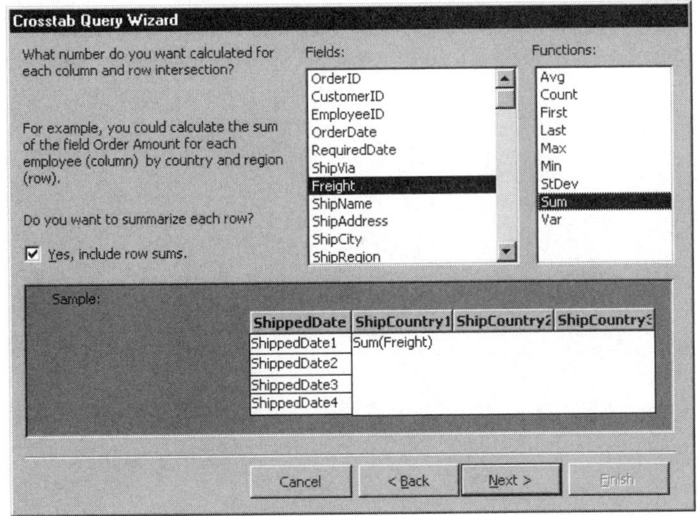

Figure 9-51. Total the Freight entries.

7 On the final page of the wizard, enter a name for the crosstab query or accept the wizard's default name. Click Finish to view the crosstab query shown earlier in Figure 9-47.

The first column in Figure 9-47 displays a list of shipping dates. Freight costs are summed for each day in the next column. The remaining columns summarize the freight costs by country for each shipping day.

The Jet SQL statement for our crosstab query is shown here:

```
TRANSFORM Sum(Orders.Freight) AS SumOfFreight
SELECT Orders.ShippedDate, Sum(Orders.Freight) AS [Total Of Freight]
FROM Orders
GROUP BY Orders.ShippedDate
PIVOT Orders.ShipCountry;
```


Using the *Column Headings* Property to Limit Columns

The crosstab query has a property other queries don't have—the *Column Headings* property. You can use the *Column Headings* property to override the automatic sort order (alphabetic or numeric) of the column headings. This property is particularly useful if you're sorting by months, because the alphabetic sort (Apr, Aug, Dec, and so on) isn't chronological. A quick solution is to enter the months in calendar order (Jan, Feb, Mar, and so on) as the *Column Headings* property. Just be sure the names you use in the *Column Headings* property match the actual month entries in the data source. All you're really doing is restating the column names in the order in which you want them to appear.

You can also use the *Column Headings* property to limit the columns the crosstab query displays. The query results shown in Figure 9-52 display only the USA column.

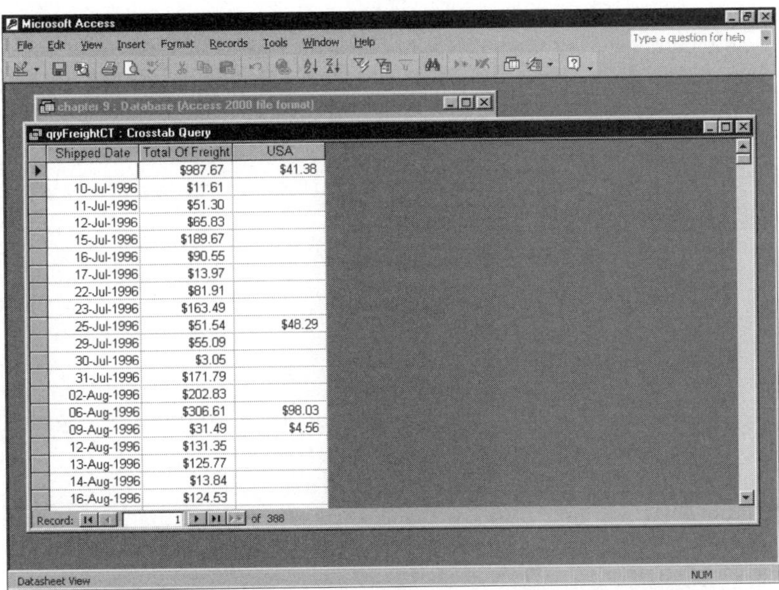

Figure 9-52. USA is the only column this crosstab query displays.

To use the *Column Headings* property to limit the columns displayed, follow these steps:

1. Open the query in Design view.
2. Right-click the blank area to the right of the Orders table, and select Properties from the shortcut menu to display the Query properties sheet. (Make sure the title bar displays Query Properties.)

3. Enter "**USA**" as the *Column Headings* property, as shown in Figure 9-53, and then close the Query properties sheet.

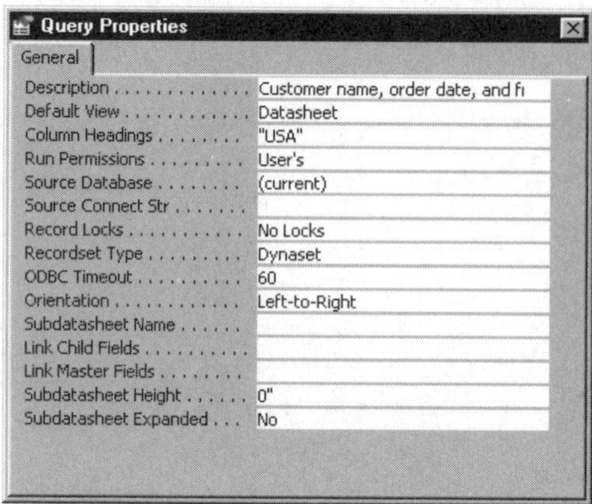
Query Properties
General
Description .... Customer name, order date, and fi
Default View .... Datasheet
Column Headings .... "USA"
Run Permissions .... User's
Source Database .... (current)
Source Connect Str ....
Record Locks .... No Locks
Recordset Type .... Dynaset
ODBC Timeout 60
Orientation .... Left-to-Right
Subdatasheet Name ......
Link Child Fields ....
Link Master Fields ....
Subdatasheet Height ...... 0"
Subdatasheet Expanded ... No

Figure 9-53. Enter "**USA**" as the *Column Headings* property.

4. Run the query.

Compare this limited query's Jet SQL statement to the query's original Jet SQL statement, shown at the end of the previous section:

```
TRANSFORM Sum(Orders.Freight) AS SumOfFreight
SELECT Orders.ShippedDate, Sum(Orders.Freight) AS [Total Of Freight]
FROM Orders
GROUP BY Orders.ShippedDate
PIVOT Orders.ShipCountry In ("USA");
```

Modifying the *Column Headings* property added an *In* operator to the PIVOT clause. As a result, the query returns only the summarized freight values for the records that contain the entry "USA" in the ShipCountry field.

Crosstab Queries vs. PivotTables

Crosstab queries are similar to the PivotTables now supported by Access 2002. Both summarize data using aggregate functions (*Sum*, *Avg*, *Count*, and so on), but PivotTables are more powerful because they can display the detailed data behind those subtotals and grand totals without affecting the groups. PivotTables allow additional column headings, whereas crosstab queries are limited to one. (Crosstab queries allow up to three row headings, but only one column heading.) PivotTables also include crossfoot totals, a testing feature familiar to accounting personnel and some spreadsheet experts. Most of the time, you'll find PivotTables quicker to produce and more flexible than crosstab queries.

See Chapter 12, "Using PivotTables and PivotCharts to Analyze Data" for more technical information about PivotTables.

Optimizing Queries

Queries are a fundamental database tool, and as such, you'll want them to be as efficient as possible. Here are a few guidelines for producing high-performance queries:

- **Avoid using the asterisk (*) method.** A query runs faster if you list all the field names in the design grid.
- **Limit fields.** Include only the fields you really need. If you must include a field (say, for setting a criterion) but you don't need to display the field, clear its Show check box in the design grid.
- **Avoid nested queries.** A nested query is a query based on another query. Most of the time, you can write a nested query as a subquery. Copy the nested query's Jet SQL statement from the SQL window to the Clipboard. Then open the original query in the SQL window, and replace the query reference with the nested query's Jet SQL statement. Be sure to enclose the nested query's statement in parentheses. You might need to tweak things a bit, but most of the time this shortcut works well.
- **Avoid multiple SQL GROUP BY clauses.** A single GROUP BY clause doesn't affect a query's performance, but several GROUP BY clauses in the same query can slow performance.

Chapter 10

Using Action Queries

Select queries (discussed in Chapter 9, "Using Queries to Select Data") retrieve data from tables, possibly filtering the data using expressions to evaluate data in some fields. But when your task is to modify data, you need an action query. In this chapter, you'll learn how to design queries to change the data in a table, including editing records, adding new records, deleting existing records, or creating a brand-new table filled with data.

There are four types of action queries, as follows:

- **Update query.** Replaces existing data.
- **Append query.** Adds new records to an existing table.
- **Delete query.** Removes records from an existing table.
- **Make-table query.** Creates a new table.

The query icon in the Database window identifies the query type.

Protecting Your Data

When you're creating an action query, you'll first want to consider protecting your data. An action query can change data. In most cases, these changes can't be undone, which means that an action query can potentially destroy data. There are two ways to protect your data, one more complex (but more secure) than the other. The quick way is to simply switch to Datasheet view after setting up your action query (and before running it). You'll be able to see the records selected for modification, so you can verify that the query is selecting the right records.

When you're working with a delete, an update, or an append query, for even more assurance that your update won't go wrong, make a copy of the table you want to modify before you run the action query, and then run the query. Open the table with modified data, and verify that the modifications are correct. If the action query doesn't work correctly, delete the modified table, rename the copy using the name of the original table, and then change the query as needed.

There's no need to create a backup table to check the results of running a make-table query. A new table is created each time you run a make-table query, so if the output table isn't right, just modify the query as needed and run it again.

To create a copy of a table, follow these steps:

1. Click the table in the Database window, and press Ctrl+C.
2. Press Ctrl+V. Access will display the Paste Table As dialog box, shown in Figure 10-1.

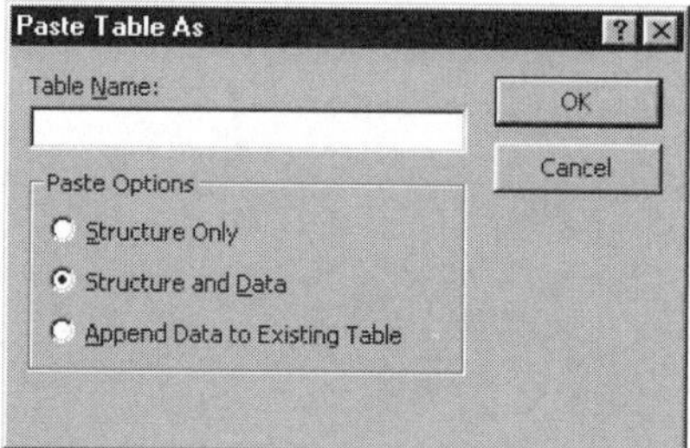

Figure 10-1. Enter a name for your copied table in the Paste Table As dialog box.

3 Enter a name for the copied table. Be sure to enter a new name, such as **Copy of *table***, where *table* is the name of the original table.

4 Choose the Structure And Data option, and then click OK to add the new table to the Database window list. The copied table will be identical to the original, including the data.

caution Many action queries accomplish one-time tasks, so you won't need to save them. If you do save an action query for repeated use, it's important that you run it only at the correct time—running an action query at the wrong time can destroy the integrity of your data. If you're running queries in a specific sequence or at a specified time, you must keep to that schedule; running an action query out of sequence or before or after the set time can be dangerous. For instance, you might use a query to update stock inventory after filling orders at the end of the day. If you run the update query before the orders are actually filled and then run the query again after you've filled the orders, you'd double the amount of inventory subtracted that day. Double-clicking a query will run it, as will opening an action query in Datasheet view. Avoid taking either of these steps unless you mean to run the query.

Changing Data with an Update Query

Entering new records is only one part of maintaining reliable data. Often, you'll need to adjust existing data. Updates are generally made to individual records, but occasionally you might need to modify an entire group of records. Can you imagine making the same change to hundreds or even thousands of records? An update query is the way to go when you're dealing with large groups of records. Update queries allow you to state your change in the form of criteria, and then the query takes care of the entire group.

For example, suppose you want to increase the price of each product listed in the Northwind database by 2 percent. You could spend a lot of time calculating new prices for all 77 products in the Products table and then modify every record yourself. A better idea is to run a query.

note The examples used in this chapter refer to the Northwind database. Because this database ships with Access, you might not want to alter the Northwind files. In these examples, you'll create copies of each table you plan to modify to act as a backup in case the query has unexpected results. After completing each query exercise, you can delete the modified tables and rename the copies with their original names, or you can work with the copies instead of the original tables. Another option is to create a blank database and import the tables.

To run an update query on the Northwind database, follow these steps:

1. Make a copy of the Products table. (See the section "Protecting Your Data," page 396, for details on copying a table.)
2. In the Database window, click Tables on the Objects bar, and select the Products table.
3. Choose Query from the New Object button's drop-down list. (You'll find the New Object button on the Database toolbar.)
4. Double-click Design View in the New Query dialog box, or choose Design View (the default), and click OK.
5. In the Query Design window, drag the UnitPrice field to the design grid.
6. Choose Query, Update Query. The design grid will display an Update To row.
7. Enter the following expression in the UnitPrice field's Update To cell (as shown in Figure 10-2):

```
[UnitPrice]+([UnitPrice]*0.02)
```

note When you create an expression in a text box's *Control Source* property, it must begin with an equal sign. Expressions in queries don't need the equal sign.

Figure 10-2. This expression modifies the existing entry.

This expression evaluates to the original value of UnitPrice plus 2 percent of UnitPrice. Be sure to include the brackets, or Access will interpret the field name as a string and delete the data in the UnitPrice field when you run the query.

8 From the View button's drop-down list, choose Datasheet View to view the results of the query before you actually run it.

Access won't display the new values; it displays only those values that the query will update. In this case, that includes all the values in the UnitPrice field.

9 Return to Design view.

10 Click Run on the Query Design toolbar to update the UnitPrice entry for each record. Access will display the confirmation request shown in Figure 10-3, indicating the number of records your query will update. Click Yes.

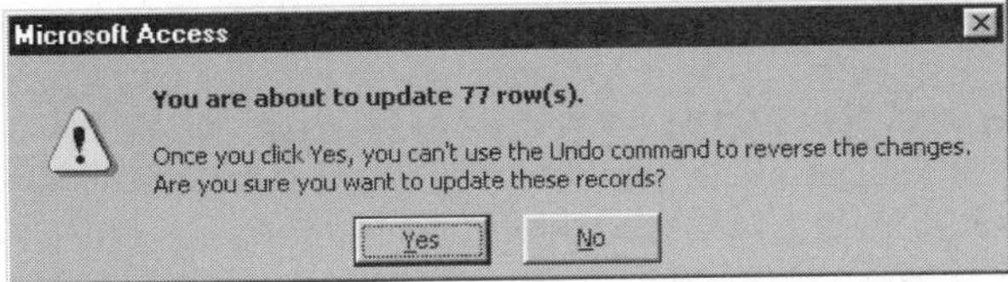

Figure 10-3. Click Yes to update the Products table.

11 Open the Products table, and review the new prices, shown in Figure 10-4. For example, Chai was originally $18 per unit, as shown in the first record of the table. Now, it's $18.36—an increase of 2 percent.

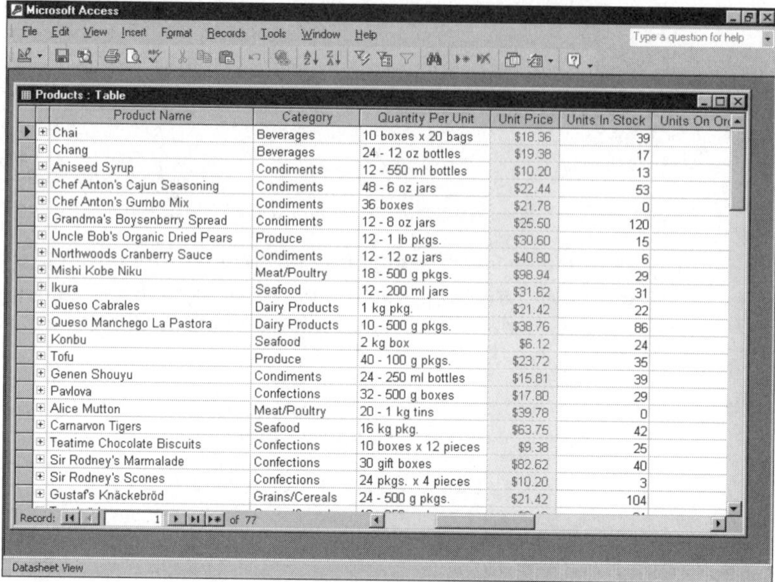

Product Name	Category	Quantity Per Unit	Unit Price	Units In Stock	Units On Or
Chai	Beverages	10 boxes x 20 bags	$18.36	39	
Chang	Beverages	24 - 12 oz bottles	$19.38	17	
Aniseed Syrup	Condiments	12 - 550 ml bottles	$10.20	13	
Chef Anton's Cajun Seasoning	Condiments	48 - 6 oz jars	$22.44	53	
Chef Anton's Gumbo Mix	Condiments	36 boxes	$21.78	0	
Grandma's Boysenberry Spread	Condiments	12 - 8 oz jars	$25.50	120	
Uncle Bob's Organic Dried Pears	Produce	12 - 1 lb pkgs.	$30.60	15	
Northwoods Cranberry Sauce	Condiments	12 - 12 oz jars	$40.80	6	
Mishi Kobe Niku	Meat/Poultry	18 - 500 g pkgs.	$98.94	29	
Ikura	Seafood	12 - 200 ml jars	$31.62	31	
Queso Cabrales	Dairy Products	1 kg pkg.	$21.42	22	
Queso Manchego La Pastora	Dairy Products	10 - 500 g pkgs.	$38.76	86	
Konbu	Seafood	2 kg box	$6.12	24	
Tofu	Produce	40 - 100 g pkgs.	$23.72	35	
Genen Shouyu	Condiments	24 - 250 ml bottles	$15.81	39	
Pavlova	Confections	32 - 500 g boxes	$17.80	29	
Alice Mutton	Meat/Poultry	20 - 1 kg tins	$39.78	0	
Carnarvon Tigers	Seafood	16 kg pkg.	$63.75	42	
Teatime Chocolate Biscuits	Confections	10 boxes x 12 pieces	$9.38	25	
Sir Rodney's Marmalade	Confections	30 gift boxes	$82.62	40	
Sir Rodney's Scones	Confections	24 pkgs. x 4 pieces	$10.20	3	
Gustaf's Knäckebröd	Grains/Cereals	24 - 500 g pkgs.	$21.42	104	

Figure 10-4. The query modified each UnitPrice value.

> **tip** If you want to stop a query after clicking Run, press Ctrl+Break.

Understanding the SQL UPDATE Statement

Update queries use the SQL UPDATE statement to modify data. The UPDATE statement takes the following form:

```
UPDATE table/query
SET col = expression
WHERE criteria;
```

You can update multiple fields in an update query by setting appropriate criteria expressions for each field that needs updating. In this case, the query's SQL statement will have multiple SET clauses, separated by commas.

Let's take a look at the update query's SQL statement from the previous example:

```
UPDATE Products
SET Products.UnitPrice = [UnitPrice]+([UnitPrice]*0.02);
```

The UPDATE keyword is the first clue that you're dealing with a query that modifies existing data. The SET clause identifies the field that the query updates and the field's new value.

Specifying Criteria

Updating data won't always be as clear-cut as in the previous example. Sometimes you need to update some records but not others. For instance, suppose you want to increase the price of only those products that cost less than $20. You can still use an update query, but you have to be specific about which records the query should modify. You do this by adding a criteria expression.

Follow these steps to create a query that contains a criteria expression:

1. Repeats steps 1 through 7 from the example on page 398.
2. Add the following expression to the Criteria cell of the UnitPrice field (as shown in Figure 10-5):

```
<20
```

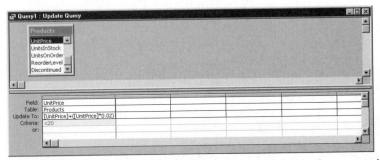

Figure 10-5. The Criteria expression restricts updates to those records in which the unit price is less than $20.

3 Run the query. Click Yes to confirm that you want to update the records.

4 Open the Products table and review the UnitPrice values. Only those items that cost less than $20 have been updated.

As you can see in Figure 10-6, Chef Anton's Cajun Seasoning (the fourth record) is the first record the query didn't update because the UnitPrice value is $22, which is greater than $20.

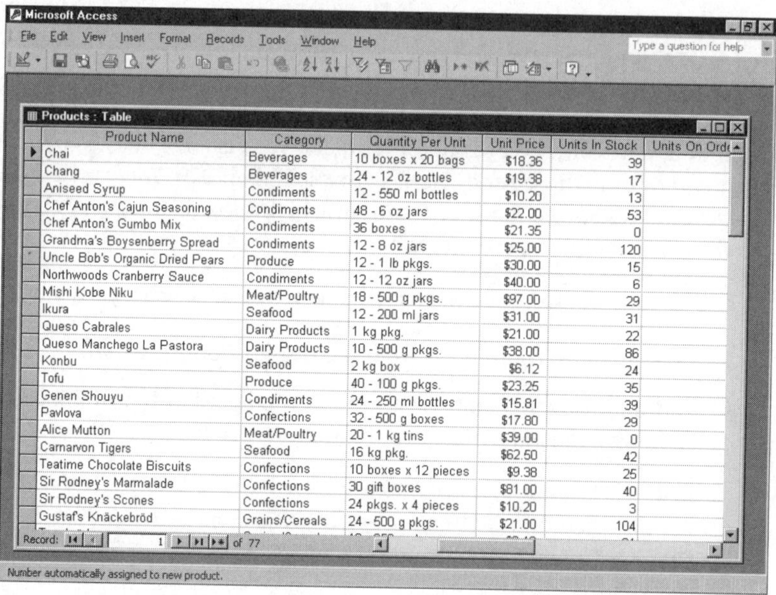

Product Name	Category	Quantity Per Unit	Unit Price	Units In Stock	Units On Ord
Chai	Beverages	10 boxes x 20 bags	$18.36	39	
Chang	Beverages	24 - 12 oz bottles	$19.38	17	
Aniseed Syrup	Condiments	12 - 550 ml bottles	$10.20	13	
Chef Anton's Cajun Seasoning	Condiments	48 - 6 oz jars	$22.00	53	
Chef Anton's Gumbo Mix	Condiments	36 boxes	$21.35	0	
Grandma's Boysenberry Spread	Condiments	12 - 8 oz jars	$25.00	120	
Uncle Bob's Organic Dried Pears	Produce	12 - 1 lb pkgs.	$30.00	15	
Northwoods Cranberry Sauce	Condiments	12 - 12 oz jars	$40.00	6	
Mishi Kobe Niku	Meat/Poultry	18 - 500 g pkgs.	$97.00	29	
Ikura	Seafood	12 - 200 ml jars	$31.00	31	
Queso Cabrales	Dairy Products	1 kg pkg.	$21.00	22	
Queso Manchego La Pastora	Dairy Products	10 - 500 g pkgs.	$38.00	86	
Konbu	Seafood	2 kg box	$6.12	24	
Tofu	Produce	40 - 100 g pkgs.	$23.25	35	
Genen Shouyu	Condiments	24 - 250 ml bottles	$15.81	39	
Pavlova	Confections	32 - 500 g boxes	$17.80	29	
Alice Mutton	Meat/Poultry	20 - 1 kg tins	$39.00	0	
Carnarvon Tigers	Seafood	16 kg pkg.	$62.50	42	
Teatime Chocolate Biscuits	Confections	10 boxes x 12 pieces	$9.38	25	
Sir Rodney's Marmalade	Confections	30 gift boxes	$81.00	40	
Sir Rodney's Scones	Confections	24 pkgs. x 4 pieces	$10.20	3	
Gustaf's Knäckebröd	Grains/Cereals	24 - 500 g pkgs.	$21.00	104	

Figure 10-6. This query modified only some of the UnitPrice values.

Review this query's SQL statement, shown here:

```
UPDATE Products
SET Products.UnitPrice = [UnitPrice]+([UnitPrice]*0.02)
WHERE (((Products.UnitPrice)<20));
```

You can see that this SQL statement is quite similar to our first query's SQL statement. However, this one includes a WHERE clause that restricts the query.

Update queries work just as well with multiple tables. For example, the following SQL statement updates the "many" side of the join based on criteria in the "one" side:

```
UPDATE Orders
INNER JOIN [Order Details]
ON Orders.OrderID = [Order Details].OrderID
SET [Order Details].Discount = 0.1
WHERE Orders.CustomerID = "CHOPS";
```

Specifically, the query states that when the CustomerID value equals "CHOPS", update the Discount value to 0.1 (10 percent).

note You can't create a multiple-table update query if one of the tables in the join is a summary query. For example, including a GROUP BY clause would result in a summary query.

Updating Both Sides of a Relationship

Relationships play a part in the update process, even though this part isn't always readily apparent. In fact, you might not need an update query at all if the correct relationships exist. When updating records in a one-to-many relationship, you typically update many records. However, the perspective changes a bit if you need to change both sides of that relationship.

For instance, let's suppose you want to change a primary key value. Naturally, you'd also need to update all the related records—that is, the foreign key values. You can approach this situation in two ways. You can change the primary key value and then run an update query to modify the related table (foreign key values) accordingly.

The second approach is to create a relationship (if none exists) between the related fields in the Relationships window and select the Enforce Referential Integrity and Cascade Updated Related Fields check boxes in the Edit Relationships dialog box. (See Chapter 4, "Creating a Database," for more details on setting options in the Edit Relationships dialog box.) Access will automatically update the foreign key field in the related table when you change the primary key value. Remember that the cascading updates solution works only when you update the primary and foreign key values. (Keep in mind that you can't update the values in an AutoNumber field.)

For definitions of database terms, see Chapter 3, "Introduction to Database Design."

Adding Data with an Append Query

Adding new data is another job that's typically considered a data entry task, unless you're dealing with large amounts of data. You can use an append query to import data from a foreign source and then append it to an existing table, or you can fill a database with data from another Access database or even a table in the same database. Like select and update queries, append queries can be limited by criteria.

Let's take a look at a simple append query example. To append records from the Employees table to an empty but structurally similar table, follow these steps:

1. Using the method described in the section "Protecting Your Data," page 396, create a copy of the Employees table structure. (Don't copy the data.) Name the copy **EmployeesAppend**.

> **note** In this exercise, you should copy only the Employees table structure, not the data. That's because this table includes a primary key value. Since a primary key field can't contain duplicates, an append query can fail if records with duplicate primary key values are in the target table.

2. Select the Employees table in the Database window, choose Query from the New Object button's drop-down list, and then click OK in the New Query dialog box to open the new query in Design view.
3. Drag the asterisk (*) from the field list to the first Field cell in the design grid.
4. Choose Query, Append Query.
5. In the Append dialog box, choose EmployeesAppend from the Table Name drop-down list, as shown in Figure 10-7, and click OK.

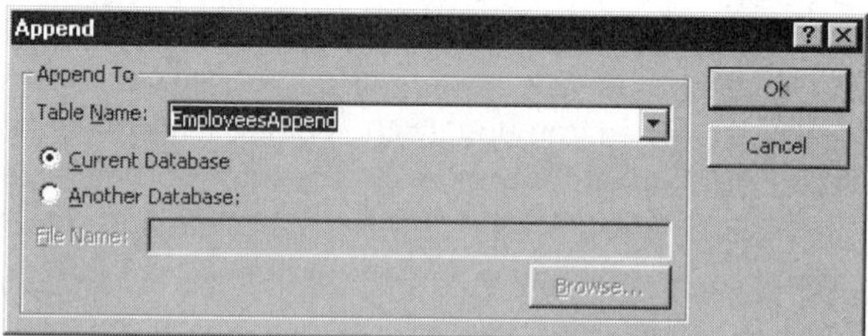

Figure 10-7. Identify the table to which you're appending records.

6 Examine the results before actually running the query. Choose Datasheet View from the View button's drop-down list to preview the results.

7 Return to Design view, and click the Run button on the Query Design toolbar to execute the query. Click Yes in response to the confirmation message shown in Figure 10-8, which indicates the number of records the query will append.

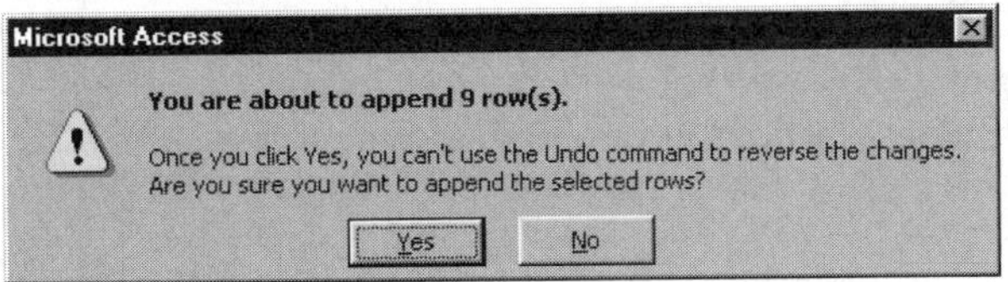

Figure 10-8. Click Yes to append the records.

8 Open the EmployeesAppend table to verify that the query appended the records.

tip **Check your field names in append queries**

Append queries can return a few errors; the cause is usually mismatched fields. An error can occur when the field names in the target table have been changed or when some fields have been deleted. The field names don't have to match in the source table and target table, but the correct field names in the target table must be selected in the Append To cell of each query column. For example, you might want to append from a field named ContactName in one table to a field named Contact in another table. In this case, the query column is named ContactName, and Contact is selected in the Append To cell for this column. Access automatically fills in the Append To cell for fields that have matching names in the source and target tables. For those that don't, you have to select the Append To field manually.

Troubleshooting

I'm getting a Type Conversion error when I try to run an append query

Check that each field in the target table is the same data type as the field in the source table being appended to it. You can't append data from a text field to a numeric field, for example. In some cases, you might need to use a conversion function such as *CInt* or *CStr* to convert field data to another data type in a query column expression to perform a successful append. For more information about conversion functions, type **Conversion Functions** in the Ask A Question box in the Visual Basic Editor window, and select the Conversion Functions Help topic.

Let's take a look at the query's SQL statement, shown here:

```
INSERT INTO EmployeesAppend
SELECT Employees.*
FROM Employees;
```

When appending data to a table with an AutoNumber key field, omit the key field from the design grid. Access will create a new value for this field automatically when the new records are appended to the target table.

The INSERT INTO statement identifies the statement as an append query. Here's the statement in its simplest form:

```
INSERT INTO target
SELECT source;
```

The INSERT INTO statement copies records from one table to another, where *target* refers to a table—directly or by using the IN predicate. The SELECT statement's source is any valid SELECT statement and can include a GROUP BY clause, a join, or a subquery. If you're not appending every field, identify the fields in the SELECT statement instead of using the *table.** syntax.

Appending a Single Row

You can append a single row of data, although this is unusual. In the right circumstances, however, this technique can be extremely useful. For instance, you could use an append query to save control values from an unbound data entry form to a table, letting users add a new record to a table on the fly. The query shown in Figure 10-9 will add a single row to the EmployeesAppend table. The target table's field list isn't visible in the upper pane; simply choose Query, Append Query to view the target table.

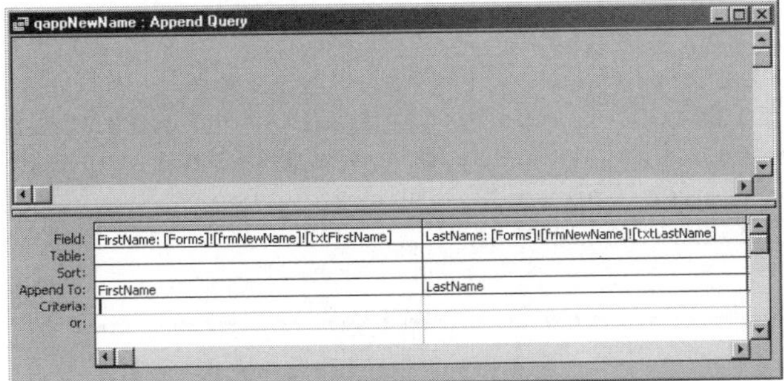

Figure 10-9. An append query can add a single row of specific values to a table.

If you run the query, Access will add a new record and then insert the values Smith and John in the LastName and FirstName fields, as shown in Figure 10-10.

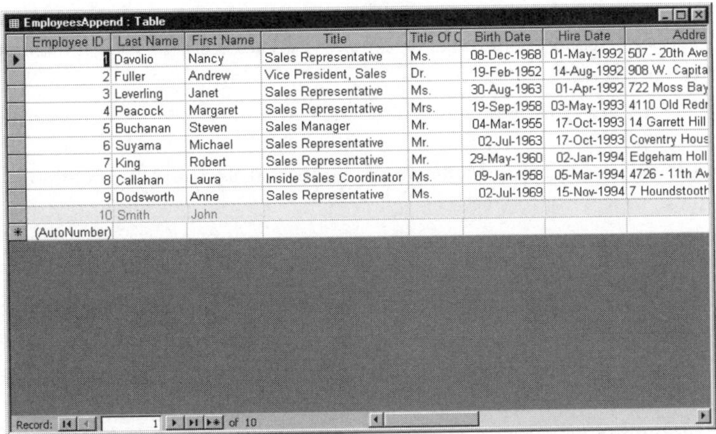
EmployeesAppend : Table

Employee ID	Last Name	First Name	Title	Title Of C	Birth Date	Hire Date	Addre
1	Davolio	Nancy	Sales Representative	Ms.	08-Dec-1968	01-May-1992	507 - 20th Ave
2	Fuller	Andrew	Vice President, Sales	Dr.	19-Feb-1952	14-Aug-1992	908 W. Capita
3	Leverling	Janet	Sales Representative	Ms.	30-Aug-1963	01-Apr-1992	722 Moss Bay
4	Peacock	Margaret	Sales Representative	Mrs.	19-Sep-1958	03-May-1993	4110 Old Redr
5	Buchanan	Steven	Sales Manager	Mr.	04-Mar-1955	17-Oct-1993	14 Garrett Hill
6	Suyama	Michael	Sales Representative	Mr.	02-Jul-1963	17-Oct-1993	Coventry Hous
7	King	Robert	Sales Representative	Mr.	29-May-1960	02-Jan-1994	Edgeham Holl
8	Callahan	Laura	Inside Sales Coordinator	Ms.	09-Jan-1958	05-Mar-1994	4726 - 11th Av
9	Dodsworth	Anne	Sales Representative	Ms.	02-Jul-1969	15-Nov-1994	7 Houndstooth
10	Smith	John					
(AutoNumber)							

Record: 1 of 10

Figure 10-10. The previous query added one row and two field values to the EmployeesAppend table.

The query's intent is a little clearer in its SQL statement, shown here:

```
INSERT INTO EmployeesAppend ( LastName, FirstName )
SELECT [Forms]![frmNewName]![txtFirstName]
AS FirstName, [Forms]![frmNewName]![txtLastName] AS LastName;
```

The INSERT INTO statement identifies the target table and affected fields, while the SELECT statement shows the syntax for picking up data from a control on a form.

Deleting Records with a Delete Query

As you might expect, delete queries remove records from tables. Keep in mind that if you run a delete query, the query will delete the entire record, not just the field you specify in a criteria expression. This will become clearer when we look at a delete query's SQL equivalent later in this section.

Don't Neglect Your Relationships

Relationships are critically important to a delete query. In the sidebar "Updating Both Sides of a Relationship," page 403, you learned how to use a relationship to automatically update foreign key values in the "many" side of that relationship by making a change to the primary key value in the "one" side. The same behavior is possible when you run a delete query—which might or might not be exactly what you want. Using the right tools for the job will make it easier for you to troubleshoot any problems down the road.

To use a simple delete query to delete order records more than four years old based on the current date, follow these steps:

1. Create a copy of the tables you're about to modify. In this case, that would be the Orders and Order Details tables. (Order details are explained a bit later in this section.)
2. Open the Relationships window by clicking Relationships on the Database toolbar. If there's no relationship between the Orders and Order Details tables, you need to create one. Drag OrderID from the Orders field list to the OrderID field in the Order Details field list. In the resulting Edit Relationships dialog box, select Enforce Referential Integrity and Cascade Delete Related Records, as shown in Figure 10-11. Click Create, and then close and save the Relationships window.

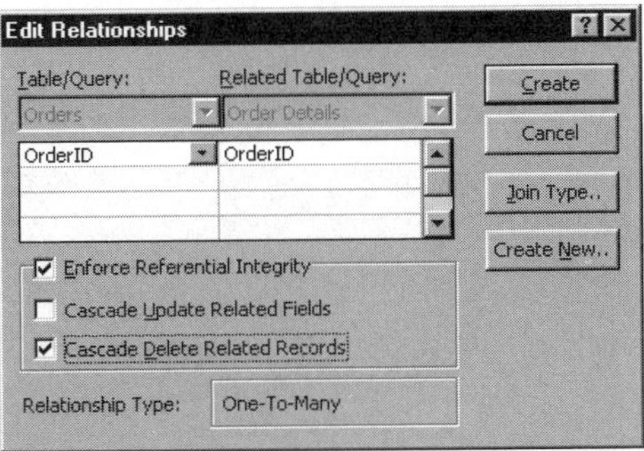

Figure 10-11. Turn on the cascading delete option.

3 In the Database window, click the Orders table, choose Query from the New Object button's drop-down list, and click OK in the New Query dialog box.

4 Drag the Order ID and OrderDate fields to the design grid, and add the following expression to the OrderDate column's Criteria cell (as shown in Figure 10-12):

```
<DateAdd("yyyy",-4,Now())
```

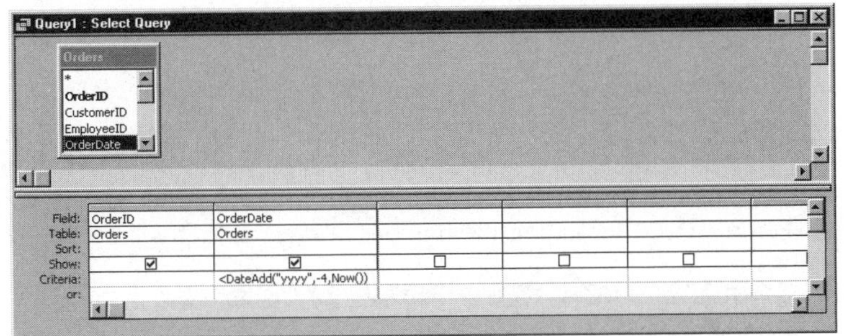

Figure 10-12. The expression limits the query to records that are at least four years old.

> **tip** The *DateAdd* function lets you make calculations on Date/Time fields. To open a Help topic explaining this function, type **DateAdd** in the Ask A Question box in the Visual Basic Editor window, and select the DateAdd Function Help topic.

5 The OrderID field isn't essential to the query, but it's useful in this case. Before running the query, choose Datasheet View from the View button's drop-down list to see the results of the query. Figure 10-13 shows the outcome of the query.

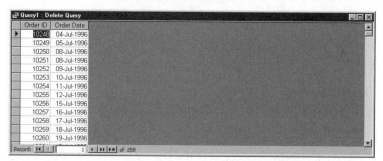

Figure 10-13. Check the query in Datasheet view before you permanently delete the records.

Make a note of the first few and last few order numbers so that you can confirm later that the query actually deleted those records. Don't worry if your order numbers are different from the ones in the figure—the exact orders returned depends on the current date (*Now*). Notice that the record navigation bar displays the number of records the query will delete—in this example, that's 258 records.

6 Return to Design view, and choose Query, Delete Query.

7 Click Run on the Query Design toolbar to execute the query.

8 Click Yes when Access displays the confirmation message shown in Figure 10-14, indicating the number of records that will be deleted.

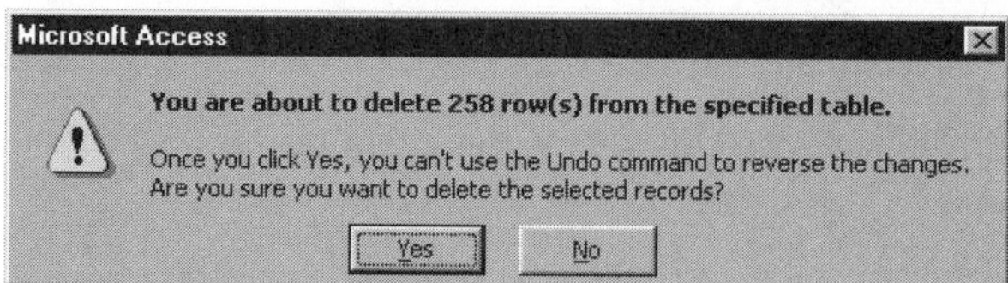

Figure 10-14. Click Yes to run the query.

9 Open the Orders table and confirm that the orders displayed in step 5 were actually deleted from the table.

Remember when I mentioned how important relationships were when running delete queries and you made a copy of the Order Details table? You're about to learn why. Open the Order Details table. As you can see in Figure 10-15, Access deleted all the records related to the orders we just deleted, because the relationship forces cascading deletes.

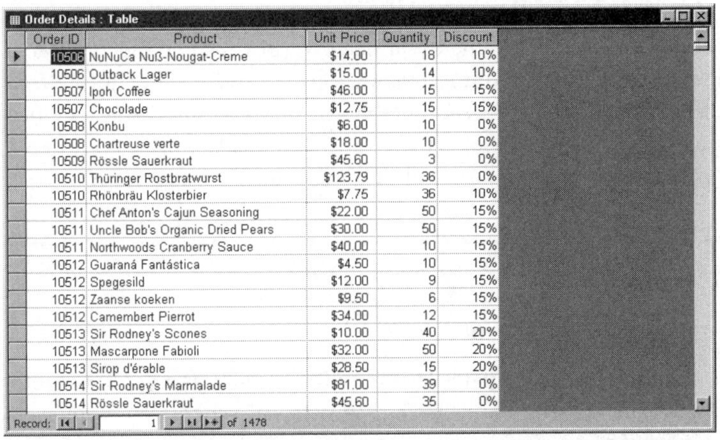

Order Details : Table

Order ID	Product	Unit Price	Quantity	Discount
10506	NuNuCa Nuß-Nougat-Creme	$14.00	18	10%
10506	Outback Lager	$15.00	14	10%
10507	Ipoh Coffee	$46.00	15	15%
10507	Chocolade	$12.75	15	15%
10508	Konbu	$6.00	10	0%
10508	Chartreuse verte	$18.00	10	0%
10509	Rössle Sauerkraut	$45.60	3	0%
10510	Thüringer Rostbratwurst	$123.79	36	0%
10510	Rhönbräu Klosterbier	$7.75	36	10%
10511	Chef Anton's Cajun Seasoning	$22.00	50	15%
10511	Uncle Bob's Organic Dried Pears	$30.00	50	15%
10511	Northwoods Cranberry Sauce	$40.00	10	15%
10512	Guaraná Fantástica	$4.50	10	15%
10512	Spegesild	$12.00	9	15%
10512	Zaanse koeken	$9.50	6	15%
10512	Camembert Pierrot	$34.00	12	15%
10513	Sir Rodney's Scones	$10.00	40	20%
10513	Mascarpone Fabioli	$32.00	50	20%
10513	Sirop d'érable	$28.50	15	20%
10514	Sir Rodney's Marmalade	$81.00	39	0%
10514	Rössle Sauerkraut	$45.60	35	0%

Record: 1 of 1478

Figure 10-15. Records are missing from this table.

Now let's look at the delete query's SQL statement, shown here:

```
DELETE Orders.OrderID, Orders.OrderDate
FROM Orders
WHERE (((Orders.OrderDate)<DateAdd("yyyy",-4,Now())));
```

Notice that the statement identifies only the two fields that we specified in the design grid: OrderID and OrderDate. However, the query deleted the entire record. It makes no difference whether you specify a single field or all the fields in a delete query; the query will delete the entire record, not just the data in the specified fields. This makes the DELETE statement less readable than some of the other SQL statements, but the logic behind the behavior is sound. If you want to delete data from a field rather than deleting an entire record, you should run an update query to update the field to a zero-length string ("") or Null. (See "Changing Data with an Update Query," page 397.)

Creating and Running a Make-Table Query

A make-table query is an action query that creates a new table based on existing data. You can even use criteria to restrict the results. There's one catch: The new table won't contain the original table's primary keys, indexes, or column and table properties (other than the defaults assigned to all tables).

Make-table queries are useful when you need to produce a table of filtered or summarized data. For example, you might want to run a make-table query to save data from a crosstab query based on several tables or queries. Such tables are useful when a complex query slows down performance—you can create a table and then base your forms and reports on that table instead of on the more complex query.

Troubleshooting

Data loses formatting when I export it

Say you export data, but some fields lose their formatting, and you must reformat the data before you can use it again. If this happens to you, chances are you're trying to export the results of a query, not a table, and Access tends to drop important formatting if you try to export the results of a query. The solution is to create a table and export the table instead of the query. This is especially true if you're working with a crosstab query—it's often more efficient to create a table from the crosstab query and work with that instead of working with the crosstab query itself, which can't be updated or exported.

To solve this loss of formatting problem, follow these steps:

1. Create the appropriate query, including any formatting needs.
2. Choose Query, Make Table Query, and enter an appropriate name for the new table.
3. Run the query.
4. Export the table, not the query.

You can learn more about crosstab queries in Chapter 9, "Using Queries to Select Data."

Creating and running a make-table query is remarkably easy. To create a new table for orders shipped by Federal Shipping, follow these steps:

1 In the Database window, choose the Orders table.

2 From the New Object button's drop-down list, choose Query, and click OK in the New Query dialog box.

3 Drag all the fields to the design grid. (Don't use the asterisk [*] if you plan to use criteria expressions to limit records copied to the new table, as shown in the next step.)

See the sidebar "Adding Multiple Fields to the Design Grid" in Chapter 9, "Using Queries to Select Data," for a comparison of dragging the asterisk vs. dragging all the fields to the design grid.

4 Specify appropriate criteria. As shown in Figure 10-16, I added the value 3 to the ShipVia field's Criteria cell. The ShipVia field is really a lookup field; it stores the shipping firm's unique value but displays the firm's name. Lookup fields are explained in Chapter 4, "Creating a Database."

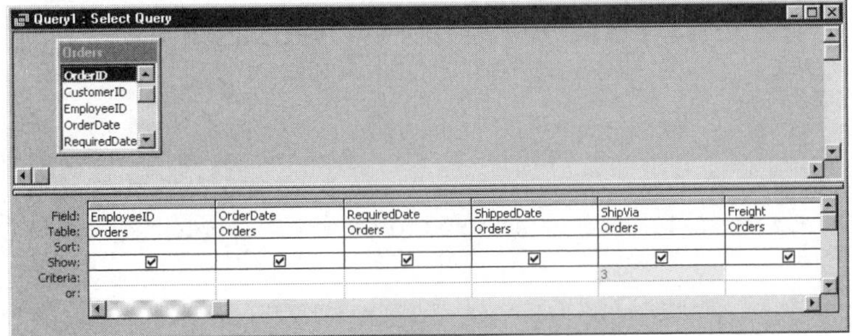

Figure 10-16. Use the make-table query to populate a new table with orders shipped by Federal Shipping.

5 Before running the query, choose Datasheet View from the View button's drop-down list to view the results of the query.

note This step isn't as crucial when you're running a make-table query as it is with other queries because you can simply delete the new table if the query doesn't produce the results you want, but it's still a good idea.

6 Return to Design view, and choose Query, Make-Table Query.

7 Enter a name for the new table in the Make Table dialog box, shown in Figure 10-17, and click OK. I named the new table tblOrdersByFederalShipping.

Figure 10-17. Enter a name for the new table.

You can save the new table in another database by choosing the Another Database option. The Current Database option is the default.

8 On the Query Design toolbar, click Run to create the new table. Access will display the confirmation message shown in Figure 10-18. Click Yes to create the new table.

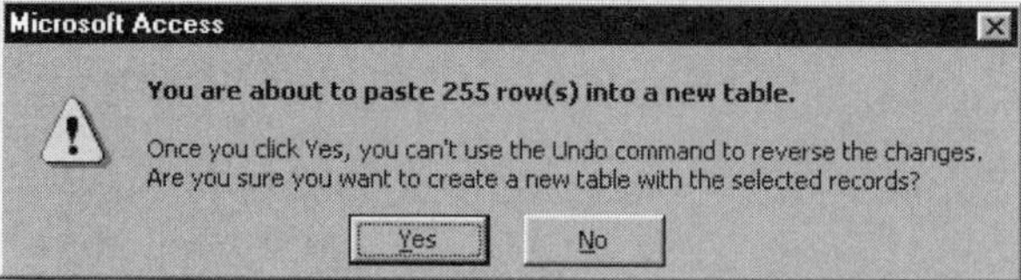

Figure 10-18. Access asks you to confirm your intent to create a new table.

InsideOut

To make it easy to distinguish between tables created by make-table queries and regular tables in the Database window and drop-down lists, I like to use the tag *tmak*. For the make-table queries, I use the tag *qmak*, with the same base name for both the table and the query. Then when I see a table named tmakSpringOrders, I know that it was created by running the query qmakSpringOrders, so I won't waste time modifying table structure—instead, I'll know that I have to modify the make-table query and run it again to re-create the table.

The tags for the database objects are listed in Chapter 4, "Creating a Database."

You can run a make-table query even if the named table already exists, but Access will warn you first, as shown in Figure 10-19.

Figure 10-19. Access warns you when a make-table query attempts to create a table using the name of an existing table.

Clicking Yes will delete the existing table before the query creates the new table. (You'll get this second confirmation message only if there's a table of the same name.)

Here's the make-table query's SQL statement:

```
SELECT Orders.OrderID, Orders.CustomerID, Orders.EmployeeID,
Orders.OrderDate, Orders.RequiredDate, Orders.ShippedDate,
Orders.ShipVia, Orders.Freight, Orders.ShipName,
Orders.ShipAddress, Orders.ShipCity, Orders.ShipRegion,
Orders.ShipPostalCode, Orders.ShipCountry
INTO tblOrdersByFederalShipping
FROM Orders
WHERE (((Orders.ShipVia)=3));
```

This statement looks more complicated than it is because it has so many fields listed in the SELECT clause. The INTO clause is what makes this statement different from a SELECT clause. Because you specified a table name, SQL knows to create a new table instead of returning a recordset.

Troubleshooting

The table created by a make-table query doesn't have the right data type for some fields

You don't have control over the data type of fields in the table produced by a make-table query. If you need the output table to have fields of specific data types, prepare a table in advance, with all the fields set up with the appropriate data types, and then create an append query to append data to the target table.

If you need to create a table of data on a regular basis (say, for export of monthly sales results to an Excel worksheet), you can automate this process by making a backup copy of the target table so that you can make a fresh copy of the target table every time you need to append data to it.

caution A make-table query won't use the underlying table's *Caption* property in the new table. Instead, the query defaults to field names.

Distinguishing Between Updatable and Nonupdatable Queries

All the examples in this chapter have updated table data via queries—updatable queries, to be exact. Sometimes a query isn't updatable (as is the case with some select queries based on multiple tables), which means that changes you make to the datasheet or bound form won't properly update the query's data source.

note You might wonder whether there's any use for nonupdatable queries. The answer is yes, most definitely. Reports can (and often do) use nonupdatable queries based on multiple tables as their record sources, because reports don't update data, they only display it. Also, PivotTables and PivotCharts work fine based on nonupdatable queries. However, for most forms, you'll want to use either a table or an updatable query for a record source so that users can update the data.

Follow these rules for creating and using queries to update data:

- Single-table queries are updatable because there are no relationships to consider. Whether you're working with a select query or an action query, simply specify fields and criteria, and then run the query. The SQL statement in such a query might be as simple as this:

  ```
  SELECT * FROM table WHERE criteria
  ```

  You can make any changes you want to such a recordset. The underlying data source might reject changes on the basis of incorrect data types or data that doesn't meet validation rules, but the query itself won't reject changes or updates.

- A multiple-table query with a one-to-one relationship is updatable.

- A query based on more than one table (or query) utilizes a join to combine data from the tables. Most of the time, the join will create a one-to-many relationship. You can change data on either side of the relationship as long as doing so doesn't violate referential integrity constraints. Subforms are a great way to handle one-to-many relationships, as opposed to basing a form on a multiple-table query. The main form contains the "one" records, and the subform displays related records for the current record in the main form.

See Chapter 5, "Creating Forms for Entering, Editing, and Viewing Data," for a discussion of using subforms to display data from linked tables.)

The following queries are not updatable:

- Crosstab, SQL pass-through, and union queries
- Multiple-table queries based on three or more tables when there is a many-to-one-to-many relationship
- Any multiple-table query based on a many-to-many relationship
- Any query that contains a totals or an aggregate function or that refers to a query or subquery that contains a totals or an aggregate function
- Any query in which the *UniqueValues* property is set to Yes
- Any multiple-table query in which no relationship exists between the tables
- Any query in which the SQL statement includes a GROUP BY clause on the record source

Troubleshooting

An updatable query won't update

Sometimes an otherwise updatable query doesn't update as you might expect. Here are some possible causes:

- You don't have permission to update the underlying table or tables. You should speak to the system administrator to gain the necessary permission.
- The underlying table is read-only. You might be able to alter the table's state yourself, but most likely you'll need permission from the system administrator.
- Another user has a record locked. In this case, you can usually update the data as soon as the record is unlocked.

tip **Know your updatable queries**

You don't have to memorize all the rules for creating an updatable query to know whether the current query is updatable. With the query open in Datasheet view, check the bottom of the datasheet. An updatable query will display a blank row at the bottom, just like a table. If a bound form's navigation button isn't available, or if the navigation button or the New Record command is disabled, you might be dealing with a nonupdatable query. That's not always the case, however—some form properties prevent the user from adding new records. (For example, a form won't be updatable if its *AllowEdits* property is set to No.)

The rules for when a query can be updated vary a little when you're working with an Access project or a data access page, as follows:

- A single table or join must have a primary key constraint, a unique constraint, or a unique index.
- The results shown in a view or returned by a stored procedure that contains a join are read-only by default. You can set the form or page's *UniqueTable* property to a string expression that identifies the join's "many" table.
- You can't update data based on a self-join.

For more details on self-joins, see Chapter 9, "Using Queries to Select Data."

- You can update only the "many" side in a one-to-many relationship.

Using Queries to Archive Data

Archiving data is a hotly debated issue. A developer might feel the need to archive outdated data, but this isn't always necessary. One alternative is to simply flag each record as outdated. The easiest way might be to include a Yes/No field that denotes whether the record is active, and then include criteria in your queries to exclude or include the archived records as needed. Flags are definitely the easiest solution if the amount of data you're flagging doesn't affect performance. Because Access 2002 databases can be up to 2 GB in size, you don't need to be concerned about clearing old records out of the database to accommodate database size limitations, as in years past. (Or, more realistically, if your Access database is approaching 2 GB in size, you should seriously consider upsizing it to a SQL Server back end.)

If you do decide to archive records, you can use the two-query approach: First you run an append query to copy the records to a historical table. Then you run a delete query to remove the records from the active table. Or, if you're copying all the current records, use a make-table query to create the historical table (or an append query to fill it) and then delete all the data from the active table. When dealing with one-to-many relationships, remember to copy and delete related records. As long as the cascading deletes option is on, Access will do the work for you. If that option is off, you'll have to add queries for each related table.

When choosing the two-query approach, you need a historical table for storing the copied records. Usually you can copy the current table by using the method reviewed in the section "Protecting Your Data," page 396. If you do, you'll want to make a few changes to the historical table, as follows:

- If the current table uses an AutoNumber data type to assign a unique value to each record, change that to a Number data type in the historical table.
- You might not need to retain the primary key. Whether you do depends on the existing relationships. Don't delete the primary key if you need to rely on those relationships when searching or retrieving data. If you decide to delete the primary key, be sure to index that field to improve retrieval and search performance.

Another issue is whether to keep the historical records in the current database or a linked database. If archived data is rarely needed, you might even consider storing detached records in a separate back-enddatabase. Simply reattach the tables when they're needed. This approach would certainly take time, but the extra time probably won't be a problem if the archived data is rarely needed.

If archived records are frequently viewed and you're on a network with multiple servers, you might want to consider keeping your historical data on a separate but attached server. Network speed becomes an issue if you intend to archive data on the same server with your current data, because the overall size of the server will have a definite impact on performance. If you're not networked, you might want to consider storing archive data tables in a separate database, either attached or unattached.

Although a larger discussion of archiving is beyond the scope of this chapter, the following guidelines can help you through the process:

- Discuss archiving while you're designing the database. Don't wait until the application is up and running—that's definitely the wrong time to add an archiving feature.
- If possible, flag records instead of copying them to another table.
- When deciding where to store your archived records and whether to keep a live link to those tables, you must consider your network resources—assuming, of course, that your system is networked.

Troubleshooting

My append query doesn't work

If an append query doesn't work or appends the wrong data to the wrong fields, open the query in Design view and do the following :

- Verify that the correct table has been selected as the target table by clicking the Query Type button on the Query Design toolbar. If the target table has been renamed, you'll need to reselect it.
- Make sure that all (and only) the fields with data to be appended are selected in the design grid.
- Verify that the appropriate field in the target table is selected in the Append To cell for each query column. (Reselect the field to ensure that it exists in the target table.)
- For each query column, make sure that the source field and the target field have matching data types.

Chapter 11

Working with Advanced Queries

As you saw in Chapter 9, "Using Queries to Select Data," and Chapter 10, "Using Action Queries," select queries retrieve data and evaluate expressions based on that data, whereas action queries enable you to modify data as needed. In addition to these two important query types, Microsoft Access 2002 includes some advanced queries that enable you to carry out a variety of different tasks. Specifically, this chapter will explore the following types of queries:

- **Parameter queries.** A parameter query can be a select query or an action query. In either case, the query prompts the user for criteria before running.
- **SQL-specific queries.** In the simplest terms, a SQL-specific query is a query you use by running a SQL statement. Technically, all Access queries run SQL statements, but you use the design grid to create most of them. You must write a SQL-specific query in SQL form in the SQL window; the design grid doesn't support SQL-specific queries.

SQL-specific queries include the following:

- **Union.** These queries combine data from tables or queries that have identical structures.
- **Pass-through.** These queries send uninterpreted SQL statements to an ODBC (open database connectivity) database server.
- **Data-definition.** These queries create, delete, and alter tables, and also create indexes in a database.
- **Subquery.** This query is a SQL SELECT statement inside another select query or action query.

In general, specialized queries offer functionality you just can't get using a select query or an action query. In fact, you can't even create a SQL-specific query in the query design window; instead, you must create the SQL string in the SQL window. With the exception of parameter queries, you might not use specialized queries often, but when the need arises, you might find that one of these queries is the only solution. For example, you might use a union query to combine several tables of historical data. Or you might use a few data-definition queries to programmatically create a new table or alter an existing one.

A subquery isn't a type of query in the same sense as the other three advanced query types. Rather, subqueries provide a more efficient structure and often replace multiple nested queries. Be prepared to spend a little time testing, however. Subqueries don't always perform better than nested queries (one query based on the results of another query), and they're harder to work with because you can't create them directly in Design view.

Using Parameter Queries

Select and action queries use specific criteria to limit or restrict the records that the query returns. Parameter queries are more dynamic, prompting you for the criteria before the query is run. For example, you could use one parameter query to view sales totals for different regions, instead of having to write a separate select query for each region.

To create a parameter query, you enter a parameter expression (enclosed in brackets) in the Criteria cell of a query column, instead of entering the specific criteria. When you run the query, Access displays a parameter prompt that contains the text of the parameter expression. After you enter data in response to the prompt, Access uses the data you enter as the query's criteria. The example in this section returns customers based on the country in which they reside.

> **note** The examples in this chapter work with the tables in the Northwind database that comes with Access. If you don't want to actually alter these tables, be sure to work with copies of the tables or a copy of the database. For instructions on how to copy a table, refer to Chapter 10, "Using Action Queries."

To create a parameter query, follow these steps:

1. Select the Customers table in the Database window, and then select Query from the New Object button's drop-down list. The New Query dialog box will appear, with the Design View option highlighted. Click OK in the New Query dialog box.
2. Drag the CompanyName and Country fields to the design grid.
3. In the Country field's Criteria cell, enter the following expression, as shown in Figure 11-1:

   ```
   [Enter a Country]
   ```

   Be sure to include the square brackets.

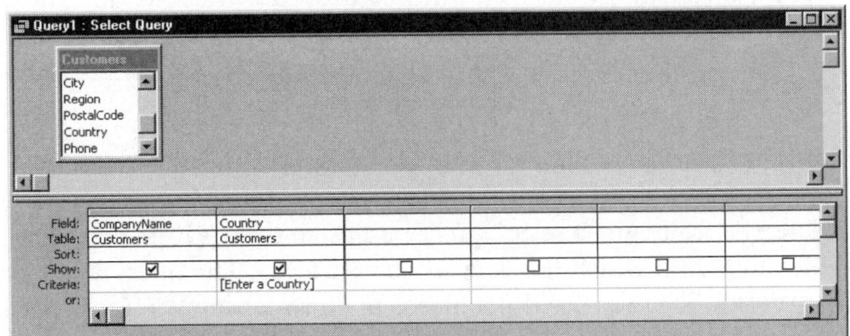

Figure 11-1. Enter a parameter expression in the Country field's Criteria cell.

Chapter 11

4. Click Run on the Query Design toolbar, or choose Datasheet View from the View button's drop-down list. Access will display a parameter prompt.
5. Enter a country name. (The example in Figure 11-2 uses Germany.) Click OK.

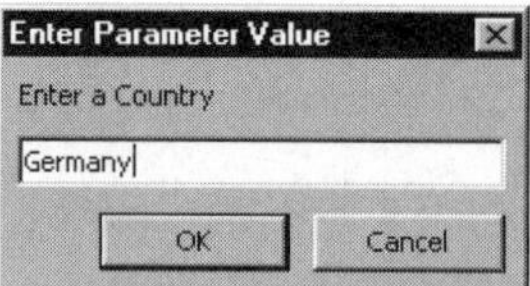

Figure 11-2. Access displays a parameter prompt when you run the parameter query.

The results will include only those records that include the string "Germany" in the Country field, as shown in Figure 11-3.

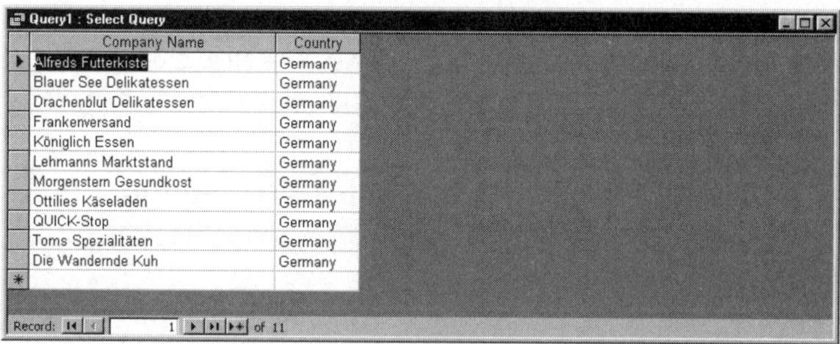

Company Name	Country
Alfreds Futterkiste	Germany
Blauer See Delikatessen	Germany
Drachenblut Delikatessen	Germany
Frankenversand	Germany
Königlich Essen	Germany
Lehmanns Marktstand	Germany
Morgenstern Gesundkost	Germany
Ottilies Käseladen	Germany
QUICK-Stop	Germany
Toms Spezialitäten	Germany
Die Wandernde Kuh	Germany

Figure 11-3. This query returns records for customers in Germany.

Choose SQL View from the View button's drop-down list to view the parameter query's SQL equivalent, shown here:

```
SELECT Customers.CompanyName, Customers.Country
FROM Customers
WHERE (((Customers.Country)=[Enter a country]));
```

This query is really just a select query because it's retrieving data. It specifies the fields and the table from which the data will be retrieved. The query even restricts that data with a WHERE clause. The difference is the form of the WHERE clause. Specifically, *[Enter a country]*, to the right of the equal sign, refers to the parameter expression instead of a literal value.

Troubleshooting

When I run a select query, I'm prompted for a parameter value, but I'm sure I'm not running a parameter query

Sometimes a select query displays an inappropriate parameter prompt when you're not working with a parameter query. This error almost always points to a typo in a field name. To fix the problem, try these solutions:

- Open the query, and make sure that all references to fields are spelled correctly.
- Check any fields you recently renamed at the table level. Renaming can cause a problem in criteria expressions.
- If you still can't find the problem, open the data source, check all the field names, and then recheck your query.

Prompting for Dates

A common use of parameters is to prompt the user for a specific time period. When you need the user to specify a time period, you combine parameter expressions with the *Between* and *And* operators in the following manner:

```
Between [Enter the beginning date] And [Enter the ending date]
```

Access will then prompt you for two dates—the first and the last in the time period in question.

For example, to create a parameter query to view orders required in August 1996, follow these steps:

1. Select the Orders table in the Database window, select Query from the New Object button's drop-down list, choose Design View, and then click OK in the New Query dialog box.
2. Drag the OrderID, CustomerID, EmployeeID, and RequiredDate fields to the design grid.

3 Select the Criteria cell in the RequiredDate column, and enter the following expression (see Figure 11-4):

```
Between [Enter the beginning date] And [Enter ending date]
```

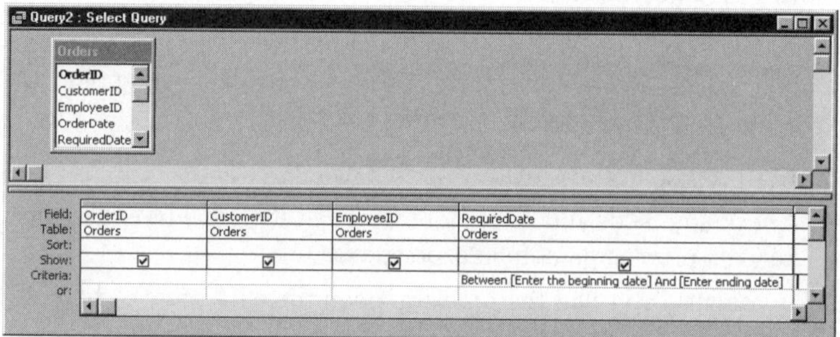

Figure 11-4. Combine operators and parameter expressions to match a specific time period.

4 Click Run, and Access will display the parameter prompt. Enter the date **8/1/96**, as shown in Figure 11-5, and click OK.

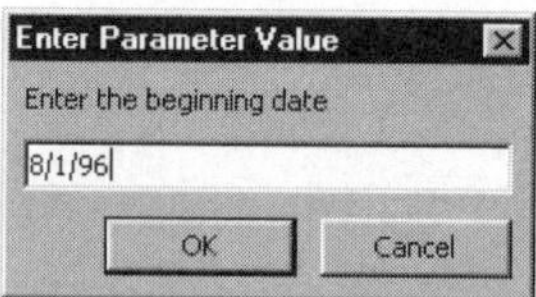

Figure 11-5. Enter the first date in the time period you're matching.

5 When Access displays the second parameter prompt, enter the date **8/31/96**, as shown in Figure 11-6, and then click OK.

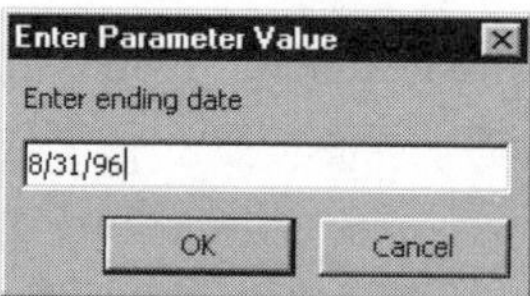

Figure 11-6. Enter the last date in the time period you're searching for.

The results, shown in Figure 11-7, contain only those records with an August 1996 date in the RequiredDate field.

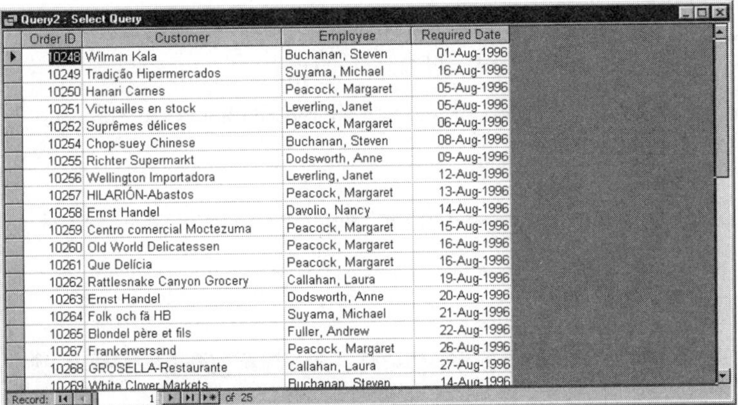

Query2 : Select Query

Order ID	Customer	Employee	Required Date
10248	Wilman Kala	Buchanan, Steven	01-Aug-1996
10249	Tradição Hipermercados	Suyama, Michael	16-Aug-1996
10250	Hanari Carnes	Peacock, Margaret	05-Aug-1996
10251	Victuailles en stock	Leverling, Janet	05-Aug-1996
10252	Suprêmes délices	Peacock, Margaret	06-Aug-1996
10254	Chop-suey Chinese	Buchanan, Steven	08-Aug-1996
10255	Richter Supermarkt	Dodsworth, Anne	09-Aug-1996
10256	Wellington Importadora	Leverling, Janet	12-Aug-1996
10257	HILARIÓN-Abastos	Peacock, Margaret	13-Aug-1996
10258	Ernst Handel	Davolio, Nancy	14-Aug-1996
10259	Centro comercial Moctezuma	Peacock, Margaret	15-Aug-1996
10260	Old World Delicatessen	Peacock, Margaret	16-Aug-1996
10261	Que Delícia	Peacock, Margaret	16-Aug-1996
10262	Rattlesnake Canyon Grocery	Callahan, Laura	19-Aug-1996
10263	Ernst Handel	Dodsworth, Anne	20-Aug-1996
10264	Folk och fä HB	Suyama, Michael	21-Aug-1996
10265	Blondel père et fils	Fuller, Andrew	22-Aug-1996
10267	Frankenversand	Peacock, Margaret	26-Aug-1996
10268	GROSELLA-Restaurante	Callahan, Laura	27-Aug-1996
10269	White Clover Markets	Buchanan, Steven	14-Aug-1996

Record: 1 of 25

Figure 11-7. This parameter query matches only August 1996 dates in the RequiredDate field.

> **tip** Expressions can be long and complex. When you enter an expression in the Criteria cell, press Shift+F2 to open the expression in the Zoom window, where you can view and edit the entire expression. You can also select Build from the shortcut menu to open the Expression Builder for help in constructing the expression with correct syntax.

Setting Data Types

The query in the previous section prompted you for dates. If you enter anything but a valid date, Access might accept your entry and return erroneous data. You can restrict the user from entering invalid data by specifying a parameter's data type. By specifying the valid data types, you help eliminate some data entry problems.

For example, to make sure that employees are keeping up with their orders, follow these steps. If you try to look up the employee's order records but enter incorrect data (such as the wrong employee ID) in response to the employee parameter prompt, you won't get the data you want and you won't know there is a problem.

1. Select the Orders table in the Database window, choose Query from the New Object button's drop-down list, choose Design View, and click OK in the New Query dialog box.
2. Drag the following fields to the design grid: OrderID, CustomerID, EmployeeID, RequiredDate, and ShippedDate.
3. Enter the following expression in the EmployeeID field's Criteria cell:

```
[Enter employee's ID]
```

4. Enter the following expression in the ShippedDate field's Criteria cell, as shown in Figure 11-8:

```
>[RequiredDate]
```

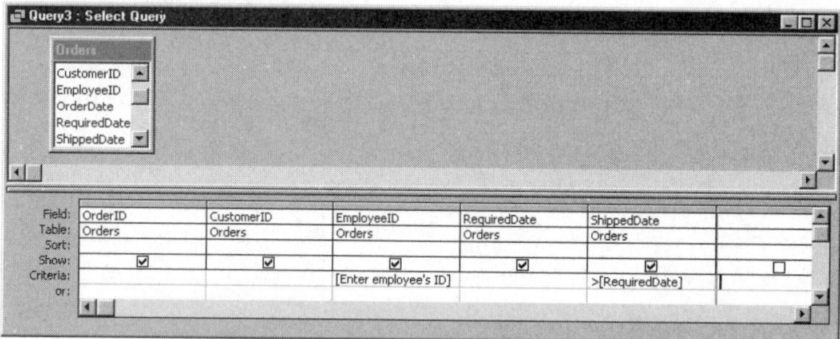

Figure 11-8. This query will prompt users to identify the employee.

5. Click Run, and enter a valid employee identification value in response to the parameter prompt. In this case, enter the value **1**, as shown in Figure 11-9, and click OK.

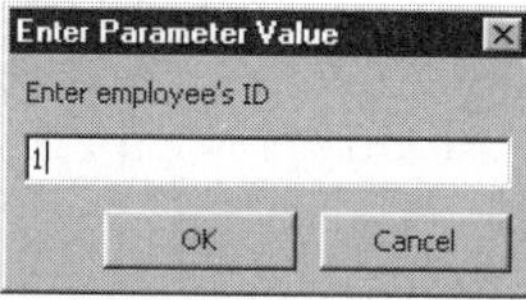

Figure 11-9. Enter a valid employee identification value.

The results, shown in Figure 11-10, include only those records that belong to the employee identified in the earlier prompt. In addition, the results are limited to only those records in which the ShippedDate value is later than the RequiredDate value, meaning that the order was shipped late.

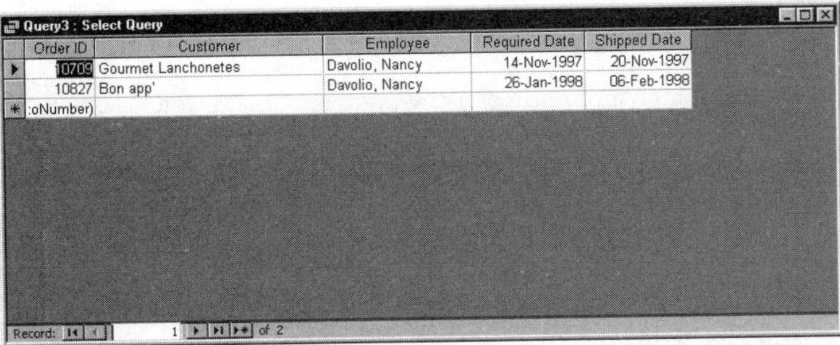

Order ID	Customer	Employee	Required Date	Shipped Date
10709	Gourmet Lanchonetes	Davolio, Nancy	14-Nov-1997	20-Nov-1997
10827	Bon app'	Davolio, Nancy	26-Jan-1998	06-Feb-1998
:oNumber)				

Figure 11-10. The results show records that belong to Nancy Davolio, whose Employee ID is 1.

InsideOut

Many developers avoid using lookup fields because of the confusion they can cause. For instance, in the current example you must enter the employee's EmployeeID value (or primary key value) although the field displays the employee's name. Northwind makes extensive use of the lookup field feature; becoming familiar with the feature can save you a lot of troubleshooting if you should ever acquire a database that uses lookup fields.

Run the query a second time and enter **Nancy Davolio** in response to the query's prompt. This time the query returns an empty result set, but you already know that Nancy Davolio has two late orders from the previous example. (Remember that the EmployeeID field actually contains a numeric value that represents the employee ID, not the employee's name. This field displays each employee's name because it's a lookup field.) You can avoid some data entry errors by setting a parameter's data type. If you limit the parameter to accept only *Byte* values, the query will return an error if you enter anything but the values 1 through 255.

tip You don't have to return to Design view and click Run to rerun the same query. Simply press Shift+F9. If you're running a parameter query, Access will display the parameter prompt.

To set the parameter's data type, follow these steps:

1. In Design view, highlight and copy (by pressing Ctrl+C) the following parameter expression in the EmployeeID's Criteria field:

```
[Enter Employee's ID]
```

2. Choose Query, Parameters.
3. Select the first Parameter field and press Ctrl+V to paste the copied parameter expression.
4. Press Tab, and choose Byte from the Data Type field, as shown in Figure 11-11. Click OK to close the Query Parameters dialog box.

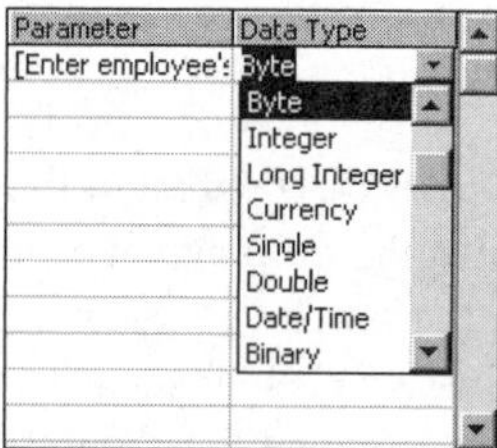

Figure 11-11. Specify a data type for the parameter.

5. Click Run, enter **Nancy Davolio**, and then click OK. This time, Access displays the error message shown in Figure 11-12 in response. The message isn't terribly specific, but it's better than an empty record set and no warning at all.

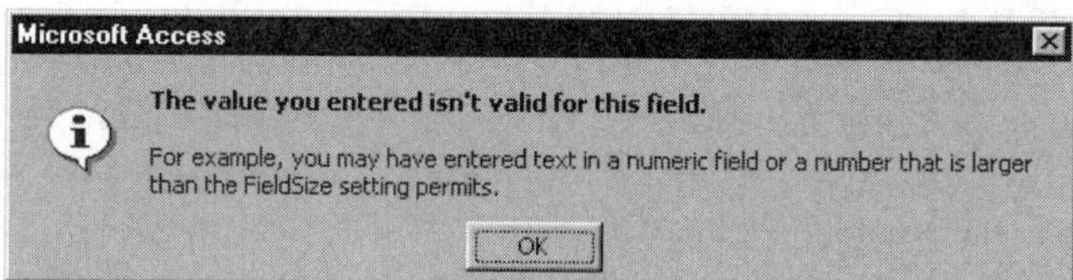

Figure 11-12. Access displays an error message if a parameter isn't the right data type.

Planning for Null Parameters

Parameter queries have one peculiar, unexpected behavior that can be a bit confusing to remedy if you don't understand the cause. You might think that not responding to the parameter would return all the underlying records. After all, by not responding, aren't you eliminating the criteria altogether? Unfortunately, Access doesn't respond the way you might think. Instead of returning all the underlying records, it returns no records. This happens because Access interprets the empty parameter as a Null value. Because the entries in the table aren't Null, they don't match the parameter value, and so they aren't returned.

You can avoid this situation by adding a *Like* operator to the parameter expression in the following form:

```
Like [parameter] & "*"
```

If you enter this parameter, Access tacks on an asterisk (*). The asterisk is a wildcard character that matches other characters. For example, if you enter **London,** Access will search for *London**. If you enter nothing, Access searches for *, which of course, returns all the records. There's one more benefit: You can enter just the first few characters instead of the entire entry. For instance, you could enter **Lon** instead of **London.** Doing so will return all entries that begin with *Lon*, not just London, so this solution might not always be appropriate.

To plan for Null values in a parameter expression, follow these steps:

1. Open the Suppliers table, and delete the city name (London in this example) from the first record's City field. Save this change.
2. Base a query on the Suppliers table, and drag the following fields to the design grid: SupplierID, CompanyName, ContactName, and City.
3. Enter the following expression in the City field's Criteria cell:

   ```
   [Enter City]
   ```

4. Run the query, and enter **New Orleans** at the prompt to return any records in which the City field contains the string "*New Orleans*". (This query should return just one record.)

5 Press Shift+F9 to run the query again. This time, click OK without responding to the prompt. Access will return an empty recordset.

6 Return to Design view, and modify the City's Criteria expression to look like this (see Figure 11-13):

```
Like [Enter City] & "*"
```

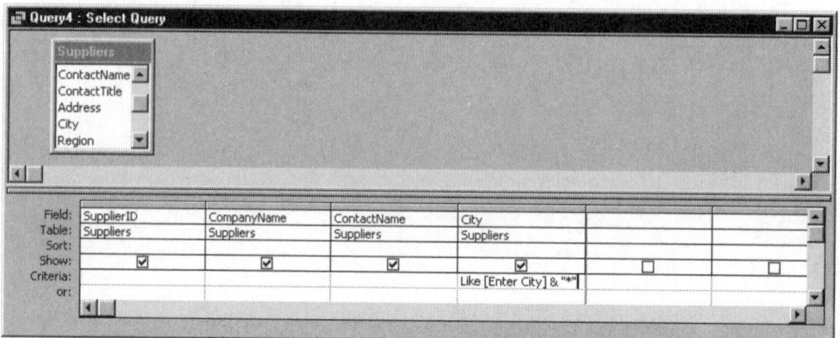

Figure 11-13. Add a *Like* operator to the parameter expression.

7 Run the query again, and click OK instead of entering a parameter value.

This time Access returns all the records. Or does it?

Did you notice that the query didn't return the record with the missing City value? (You deleted London from the first supplier record.) A *Null* parameter, in this context, won't select a Null value. You can remedy this problem quickly enough by adding an *Or* expression in the following form, as shown in Figure 11-14:

```
[parameter] Is Null
```

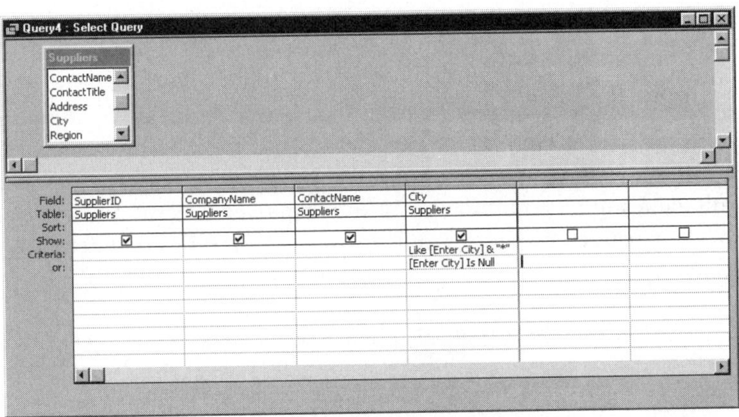

Figure 11-14. An additional parameter expression returns Null values.

Simply open the parameter query in Design view, and add the additional parameter expression to the City field's Or cell. Then run the query again, and click OK without entering a parameter value. This time the query returns all the records, including the first record with the missing City value, as shown in Figure 11-15.

Figure 11-15. After you add the *Is Null* expression, the results include Null values.

An Alternative to a Parameter Query

Earlier you set a parameter's data type to limit the type of data you can enter as that parameter's value. (See the section "Setting Data Types," page 427.) Doing so isn't the same as setting a field's *ValidationRule* property, but these techniques have similar purposes. You can limit parameters only by data type, whereas you can use a validation rule to limit values to a specific range. In the employee ID example, it would be helpful to limit the parameter to accept only those employee IDs that actually exist, but you can't.

For more information about the *ValidationRule* property, see Chapter 4, "Creating a Database."

When restricting the values that a user can enter for a query is critical, you might need another solution. The simplest solution is to replace the parameter query with a form and a nonparameter query. The form offers the user a list of specific choices, usually in a combo box or list box control, and then passes the chosen items to the query. Let's try a simple form and query solution to replace our employee ID example.

For the following example, refer to the Test Access 2002.mdb file on the companion CD.

To create this query, follow these steps:

1. Select the Orders table in the Database window, select Query from the New Object button's drop-down list, make sure that Design View is selected, and click OK in the New Query dialog box.
2. Drag the following fields to the design grid: OrderID, CustomerID, EmployeeID, RequiredDate, and ShippedDate.
3. Enter the following expression in the EmployeeID field's Criteria cell:

```
FindEmployee()
```

> **note** The *FindEmployee* function is discussed a little later in this section.

4. Enter the following expression in the ShippedDate field's Criteria cell (see Figure 11-16):

```
>[RequiredDate]
```

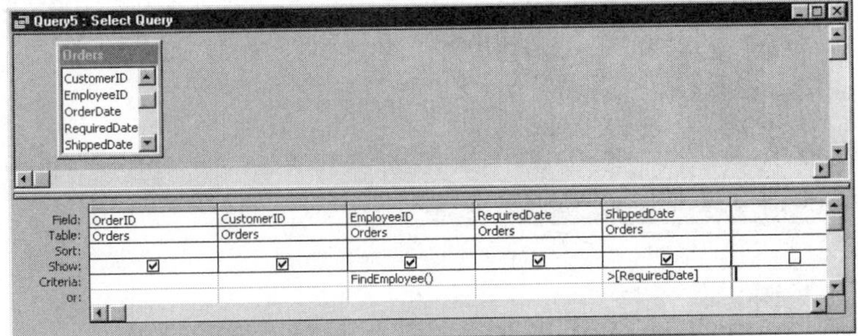

Figure 11-16. This query calls the *FindEmployee* function instead of a parameter expression.

5. Save the query as **qryFindEmployee**, and then close it.

To create the parameter form, follow these steps:

> **note** The following procedure assumes some familiarity with writing code in Microsoft Visual Basic for Applications (VBA). If you aren't familiar with VBA, you might want to first read Chapter 20, "Customizing Your Database Using VBA Code."

1. In the Database window, click Forms in the Objects list, click New on the Database Window toolbar, make sure Design View is selected, and then click OK in the New Form dialog box.
2. Add a list box to the form, and name it **lstFindEmployee**.

3 Enter the following SQL statement as the list box control's *Row Source* property:

```
SELECT DISTINCT Orders.EmployeeID, Employees.LastName,
Employees.FirstName FROM Orders
INNER JOIN Employees ON Orders.EmployeeID=Employees.EmployeeID;
```

This statement displays a unique list of entries from the EmployeeID field in the Orders table and the corresponding last and first names for each of those values. To make it easier to enter the SQL statement (it is long), press Shift+F2 to open the Zoom window. Enter the SQL statement, and then close the window.

4 Change the *Column Count* property to **3**.

5 Enter the Column Widths setting of **0";1";1"**, as shown in Figure 11-17.

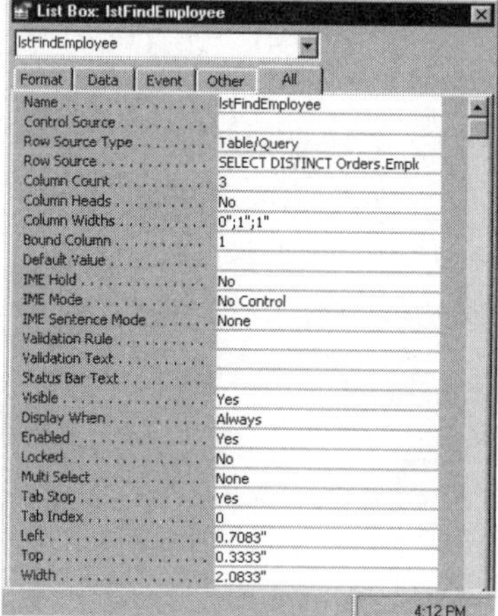

Figure 11-17. The properties sheet shows the list box control's property settings.

This setting hides the EmployeeID field, so all you see is the last and first names.

6 Add two command buttons. Name the first button **cmdFindEmployee** and the second button **cmdCancel**. Set the caption for the first button to **Find Employee** and the caption for the second button to **Cancel**.

7 Save the form as **frmParameterForm**.

8 Launch the Visual Basic Editor (VBE) by clicking Code on the Form Design toolbar or by pressing Alt+F11.

9 If the form's module isn't open, double-click *Form_frmParameterForm* under the Microsoft Access Class Objects mode in the Project Explorer.

10 In the form's module, select cmdFindEmployee in the Object control's drop-down list. You'll find this control to the left, just above the module under the module window's title bar, which you might not be able to see. If this control isn't visible, click the window's Restore button to display the window's title bar.

11 Add the Option Explicit statement, and enter the following VBA statement between the subprocedure's opening and closing statements, as shown in Figure 11-18:

```
DoCmd.OpenQuery "qryFindEmployee"
```

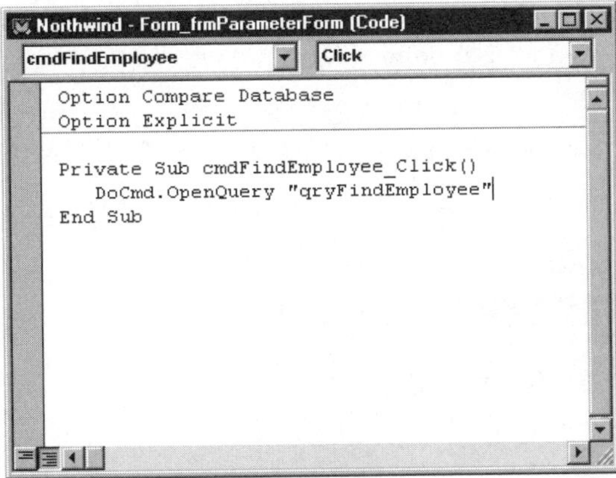

Figure 11-18. Enter the VBA code that runs the query.

This statement will execute the query you just created.

12 Insert a standard module by choosing Insert, Module.

13 Enter the function procedure shown in Figure 11-19.

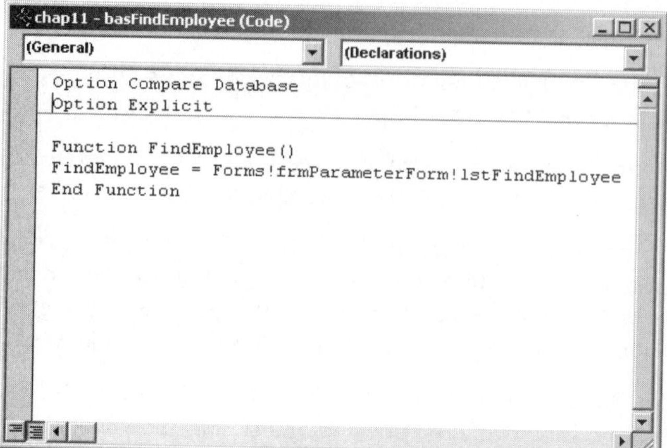

Figure 11-19. This function procedure passes the selected item in the list box to the parameter.

14 Save the module as **basFindEmployee**. The function procedure you just created (also known as a user-defined function) returns the selected item in the list box control.

15 Return to the form in Design view, and click View to display the form.

16 Select the first item, Nancy Davolio, as shown in Figure 11-20, and then click Find Employee to execute qryFindEmployee.

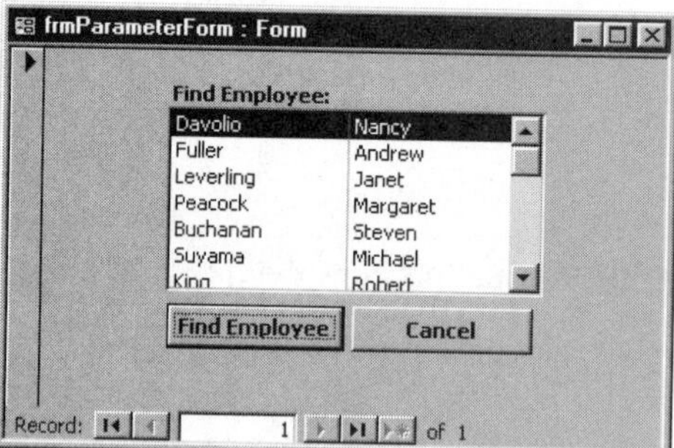

Figure 11-20. Select an item from the list box.

The query then calls the *FindEmployee* function, which equals the selected item in the list box control in frmParameterForm. As a result, the query uses that value as criteria and displays only those records for Nancy Davolio in which the ShippedDate is greater than the RequiredDate. (The results should be identical to those shown earlier in Figure 11-10.)

For additional help in creating this form, see Chapter 5, "Creating Forms for Entering, Editing, and Viewing Data."

As you've seen, setting up the form to limit user input requires quite a bit of additional work. Do the advantages warrant the extra work? More than likely, yes. A user can easily enter an incorrect parameter value or misspell an entry. As a result of this mistake, the parameter query returns erroneous data or no data instead of an error message. Using a parameter form avoids simple typos and prevents user frustration by limiting the user to a list of valid parameters.

Assigning Default Values to a Parameter Query

As you just learned, parameter queries don't warn you when you enter incorrect data in response to a parameter prompt. They have another limitation: You can't assign a default value for the parameter. A default value is useful when you find yourself entering one value more than any other in response to a parameter prompt. You can avoid entering a response at all except on those few occasions when you need a value other than the default. Needing a default value is another good reason for using the alternative described in the previous section. To specify a default value, open the parameter form's module (from the form you created in the last example), and add the following code to the form's *Current* event (where *x* represents the index value of the list item you want to specify as the default parameter value):

```
Private Sub Form_Current()
    Dim ctl As ListBox
    Set ctl = Forms!frmParameterForm!lstFindEmployee
    ctl.DefaultValue = ctl.ItemData(x)
End Sub
```

For instance, if you wanted "Margaret Peacock" to be the default, you'd use the index value 3. (Indexing begins with the value 0.)

InsideOut

If you based a report on a parameter query, you might want to print the parameter values in the report. For example, if the parameter is a date, you could display that date in the report's title or header. To do so, simply add a text box to your report's header or title and specify the parameter by name as the control's *Control Source* using the following form:

```
=Reports![reportname]![parametername]
```

Suppose you want to add the feature to a report named rptDates and the actual parameter is *[Please Enter Date]*. In this case, you'd enter the following expression:

```
=Reports![rptDates]![Please Enter Date]
```

Now suppose that you run the query and enter the date **August 15, 2001**. As a result, the text box that contains the reference to the parameter displays and prints August 15, 2001.

Using Union Queries

A union query combines records from two different tables or queries of identical structure. The only way to create a union query is via the SQL window. Even so, UNION isn't really a SQL statement or clause. It's a special operator used only in SQL statements to combine two recordsets into a single read-only recordset.

The basic syntax for UNION is as follows, where *select1* and *select2* represent two compatible queries. (*Compatible* in this case means that the set of fields returned by the component queries have the same structure.)

```
select1
UNION
select2;
```

The field order for each SELECT statement must be the same because Access matches the fields by their order, not by name.

note OLE object fields aren't allowed in a union query because they contain objects (such as Microsoft Excel worksheets or Microsoft Word documents) rather than data.

Union queries aren't common, but occasionally the need for one does arise. For example, suppose you want to send the same letter to all your customers and employees. If your database is like most, you store employee and customer addresses in different tables. You can use a union query to combine all these addresses.

To use a union query, follow these steps:

1. Click Queries on the Objects list in the Database window, click New on the Database Window toolbar, make sure Design View is selected, and then click OK in the New Query dialog box.
2. Close the Show Table dialog box.
3. Select SQL View from the View button's drop-down list.
4. Enter the appropriate UNION statement, remembering to specify the same fields in the same order for both SELECT statements.

   In this example, this step creates a problem, because there's a discrepancy between the name fields. Specifically, the Employees table has two fields, LastName and FirstName, but the Customers table has only one field, CompanyName. You can't use the following statement because the field names don't match:

   ```
   SELECT LastName, FirstName Address, City, Region,
   PostalCode, Country
   FROM Employees
   UNION SELECT CompanyName, Address, City, Region,
   PostalCode, Country
   FROM Customers;
   ```

Fortunately, concatenating the LastName and FirstName fields, as shown in Figure 11-21, solves the problem.

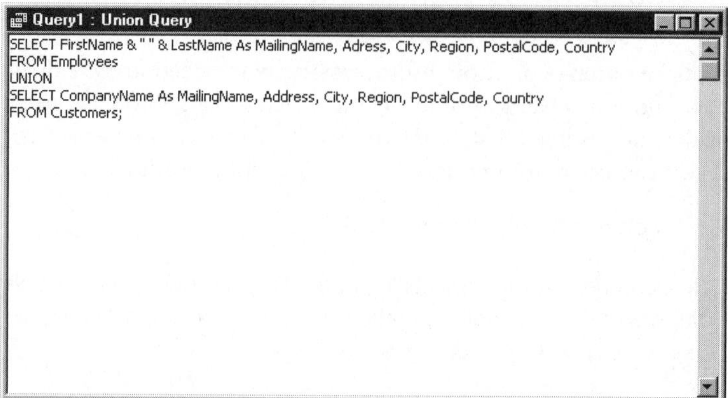

Figure 11-21. The union query in which the field names don't match.

The proper statement lists the same fields: MailingName, Address, City, Region, PostalCost, and Country:

```
SELECT FirstName & " " & LastName As MailingName, Address, City,
Region, PostalCode, Country
FROM Employees
UNION SELECT CompanyName As MailingName, Address, City,
Region, PostalCode, Country
FROM Customers;
```

The Employees table's MailingName field is a combination of the LastName and FirstName fields and the Customers table's MailingName field comes from the CompanyName field, renamed MailingName. The renaming isn't necessary; it's been added for readability. As long as the number of columns in each SELECT is the same and the corresponding columns are the same data type, Access doesn't really care about each column's name. When column names differ, the query uses the name from the first SELECT statement.

5 Run the query to see the results shown in Figure 11-22.

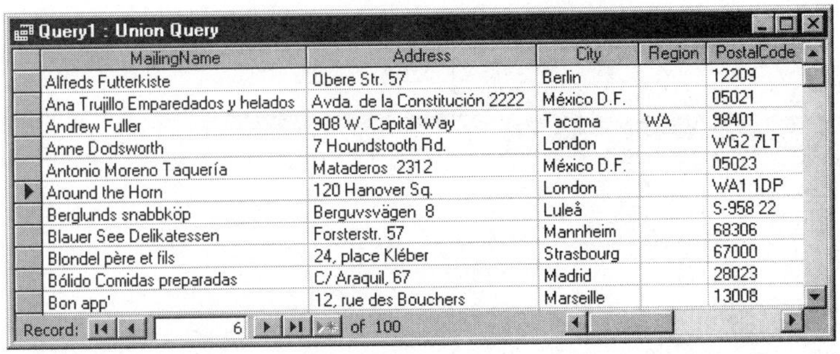

Query1 : Union Query

MailingName	Address	City	Region	PostalCode
Alfreds Futterkiste	Obere Str. 57	Berlin		12209
Ana Trujillo Emparedados y helados	Avda. de la Constitución 2222	México D.F.		05021
Andrew Fuller	908 W. Capital Way	Tacoma	WA	98401
Anne Dodsworth	7 Houndstooth Rd.	London		WG2 7LT
Antonio Moreno Taquería	Mataderos 2312	México D.F.		05023
Around the Horn	120 Hanover Sq.	London		WA1 1DP
Berglunds snabbköp	Berguvsvägen 8	Luleå		S-958 22
Blauer See Delikatessen	Forsterstr. 57	Mannheim		68306
Blondel père et fils	24, place Kléber	Strasbourg		67000
Bólido Comidas preparadas	C/ Araquil, 67	Madrid		28023
Bon app'	12, rue des Bouchers	Marseille		13008

Record: 6 of 100

Figure 11-22. The previous union query returns a combined recordset of names and addresses from the Customers and Employees tables.

One common use for union queries is to add a None or an All option to a combo box's list so that users can return to no selection after making a selection or select to use all the records in an operation (say, selecting records for a report). The combo box or list box with one of these selections should be unbound; otherwise, you could save an inappropriate value in a field.

The union query listed below creates All and None options for a combo box or list box's *RowSource* property. You could display either the CustomerID column, with a blank for the None selection and an asterisk (*) for the All selection, or the text *(All)* and *(None)* for the CompanyName field, depending on your preference. (Both columns are displayed in the sample list box shown in Figure 11-23.) Parentheses are used to force these special entries to the top of the list.

Here's the SELECT statement we'll use:

```
SELECT "" As CustomerID, "(None)" As CompanyName
FROM Customers
UNION SELECT "*" As CustomerID, "(All)" As CompanyName
FROM Customers
UNION SELECT CustomerID, CompanyName
FROM Customers
ORDER BY CustomerID;
```

A list box with this union query as its *RowSource* is shown in Figure 11-23.

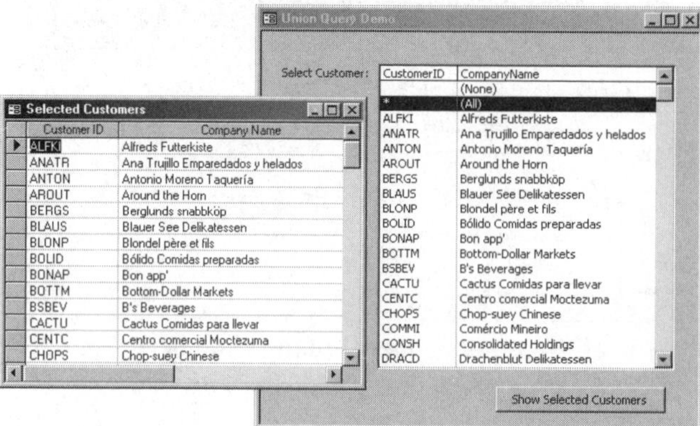

Figure 11-23. This list box displays customers with a (None) selection and an (All) selection created by a union query.

Clicking the Show Selected Customers command button opens (or requeries) a datasheet form based on a query limited to the selection in the list box.

InsideOut

By default, UNION omits duplicate records. To display duplicate records, add the ALL option in the following form:

```
select1
UNION ALL
select2;
```

If you know there are no duplicates and you're working with a large number of records, adding the ALL option can speed up the query a bit because Access is able to skip the comparison step.

Working with Dissimilar Column Types

In Access, it doesn't matter if the field names don't match, but it does matter if the data types aren't compatible. When combining data from two fields in an expression, Access converts the resulting column to a data type that's compatible with all its components. For example, if you combine a Long Integer and an Integer field into a single query field, the resulting column will be a Long Integer. If you combine text and numbers, Access returns a Text column, although it's hard to imagine why you'd want to do this. Think long and hard before you turn a number field into text.

Sorting the Results

As with most SQL recordsets, you can add an ORDER BY clause to a UNION query in the following form, where *field* identifies the field by which you want to sort the resulting recordset:

```
select1
UNION ALL
select2
ORDER BY field;
```

For instance, to sort the example recordset by Country, use the following statement:

```
SELECT FirstName & " " & LastName As MailingName, Address, City,
Region, PostalCode, Country
FROM Employees
UNION SELECT CompanyName As MailingName, Address, City, Region,
PostalCode, Country
FROM Customers
ORDER BY Country;
```

Using Pass-Through Queries

Some data sources don't have a native SQL interface, so the Microsoft Jet database engine translates queries and transforms them into a format your data source can then interpret. However, the Jet interpretation might not be compatible with the data source, so you might need to bypass the Jet interpretation. For this purpose, Access provides SQL pass-through queries, which send uninterpreted SQL statements to a server database—specifically, an ODBC data source. *Uninterpreted* in this case means that Access doesn't perform any kind of syntax check or translation before sending the statement, so you must know the specific SQL dialect that the server database uses.

When using a pass-through query, you work directly with the table on the server instead of creating a link to the table. You'll use pass-through queries to execute stored procedures on the server, join databases on the server, run SQL Data Definition Language (DDL) commands that modify the schema of a server database, and more. But there are trade-offs. For example, a recordset returned by a pass-through query is read-only. You can't use the built-in Access functions or any user-defined functions that you've added to the application.

To create a SQL pass-through query, open a blank query design grid, and choose Query, SQL Specific, Pass-Through. Doing this adds three new properties to the query, so it's important not to bypass this step and go directly to the SQL window. Table 11-1 lists the three pass-through properties.

Table 11-1 Pass-through properties

Property	Description	Default
ODBCConnectStr	Specifies the ODBC connection string	*ODBC;*
ReturnsRecords	Specifies whether the query will return records	*Yes*
LogMessages	Specifies whether Access will log warning and informational messages from the server to a local table	*No*

The *ODBCConnectStr* property has several optional arguments. The default is *ODBC;*, which will prompt you for a connection string each time you run the query. You can avoid this extra step by simply specifying the connection string in the following form:

```
ODBC;DSN=datasource;SERVER=servername;UID=username;PWD=password
```

tip **Use the ODBC Connection String Builder to create the ODBC connection string**

You can use the ODBC Connection String Builder to create the ODBC connection string and thereby create the appropriate property setting. This builder establishes a connection to the SQL database server, displays a series of data source and system options, and then ends the connection after the ODBC connection string is created.

To create a pass-through query, follow these steps:

1. Click Queries on the Objects bar in the Database window, click New on the Database Window toolbar, accept the default Design View, and then click OK in the New Query dialog box.
2. Close the Show Table dialog box without adding any tables or queries.
3. Choose Query, SQL Specific, Pass-Through.
4. Click Properties to display the query's properties sheet, and set the *ODBCConnectStr* property. This property will specify the connection information Access needs to execute the query. Enter the setting yourself, or click Build to glean the necessary information about the server you're connecting to.
5. The *ReturnsRecord* property is set to Yes by default. Change this to No if the query won't return records.
6. Type the query in the SQL Pass-Through Query window. You'll need to review documentation for the SQL database server to which you're connecting for the appropriate statements and syntax. You'll also need to know all the table and field names because Access won't be able to help you with that.
7. Click Run to execute the query. If you don't specify a connection string (see step 4), Access will prompt you for one.

Troubleshooting

I ran a pass-through query as a select query, and now the pass-through query is gone

Although Access will allow you to convert a pass-through query, do so with care. The change is permanent—you can't temporarily change a pass-through query to another query type. If you convert a pass-through query and then run it, you must re-create the pass-through query manually. This is true of all SQL-specific queries—pass-through, data-definition, and union.

Understanding Data-Definition Queries

A data-definition query is a SQL-specific query that contains DDL statements. These statements allow you to create or alter objects in the database. Specifically, data-definition queries create, delete, or alter tables or create indexes in the current database. Each data-definition query consists of just one data-definition statement. Access supports the following statements:

- **CREATE TABLE.** Creates a table.
- **ALTER TABLE.** Adds a new field or constraint to a table.
- **DROP.** Deletes a table or an index from a database, or deletes a field in a table.
- **CREATE INDEX.** Creates an index.

CREATE TABLE

Execute the CREATE TABLE statement when you want to create a new table. For example, the following statement creates a new table named TableOne, with two text fields, FirstName and LastName:

```
CREATE TABLE TableOne (FirstName TEXT, LastName TEXT);
```

Other Ways to Create Tables

In addition to using the CREATE TABLE statement, there are several other ways to create tables in Access, as follows:

- Use the *CopyObject* method of the *DoCmd* object in VBA code to create a new table that's a copy of an existing table.
- Write a make-table query to create a table.
- Append a new *TableDef* to the *TableDefs* collection of the Data Access Objects (DAO) object model in VBA code.

You can add an index by specifying the UNIQUE statement in the following form:

```
CREATE TABLE TableOne (FirstName TEXT,
LastName TEXT UNIQUE (FirstName, LastName));
```

You can specify a primary key for the table using a statement in the following form:

```
CREATE TABLE TableOne (LastName TEXT CONSTRAINT
MyIndex PRIMARY KEY, FirstName TEXT);
```

tip The CREATE TABLE statement won't overwrite an existing table of the same name (unlike a make-table query). If the table already exists, Jet will return an error message to that effect and cancel the task.

ALTER TABLE

SQL's ALTER TABLE statement performs a number of tricks, from renaming a table, to adding and deleting fields, to moving fields. Table 11-2 lists the different tasks you can complete by using ALTER TABLE.

Table 11-2. ALTER TABLE tasks

Task	Query
Rename table	ALTER TABLE *table1* TO *table2*
Add a field	ALTER TABLE *table* ADD *field1 type* [BEFORE *field2*]
Delete a field	ALTER TABLE *table* DROP *field*
Move a field	ALTER TABLE *table* MOVE *field1* [BEFORE *field2*]
Rename a field	ALTER TABLE *table* RENAME *field1* TO *field2*

tip A table must contain at least one field. You can't use the DROP clause to delete a table's last field.

note The following example alters the Northwind Employees table. If you don't want to alter the actual table, work with a copy of the Employees table.

To alter the Employees table, follow these steps:

1. Click Queries in the Objects list in the Database window, click New on the Database Window toolbar, make sure Design View is selected, and then click OK in the New Query dialog box.
2. Close the Show Table dialog box without adding a table or query to the query design window.
3. Choose Query, SQL Specific, and then select Data Definition.
4. In the Data Definition Query window, enter the following statement, as shown in Figure 11-24:

   ```
   ALTER TABLE Employees ADD COLUMN PayRate CURRENCY;
   ```

   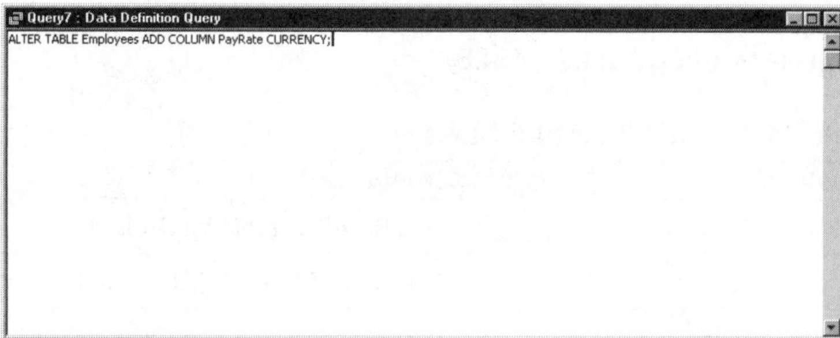

   Figure 11-24. The ALTER TABLE statement will add a new field to the Employees table.

5. Click Run to execute the query.
6. Open the Employees table in Design view to verify that Access added the PayRate field as a *Currency* data type.

DROP

SQL's DROP statement allows you to delete a table or an index. For example, the following statement deletes the index on the LastName field in the Employees table from the Northwind database:

```
DROP INDEX LastName ON Employees;
```

The following statement deletes the Employees table from the Northwind database:

```
DROP TABLE Employees;
```

Be sure to use the DROP TABLE statement sparingly and with caution, because you can't recover the table or its data.

> **tip** To delete a field from a table, use the ALTER TABLE statement.

CREATE INDEX

The last SQL data definition statement is the CREATE INDEX statement. As you might expect, this statement creates an index. In its simplest form, the statement adds an index, as follows:

```
CREATE INDEX index
ON table (field);
```

The resulting index is based on a single field, allows duplicate values, and is not based on a primary key. The index can consist of more than one field: Simply list more than one field, and separate the fields with commas.

To avoid duplicates in an indexed field, add the UNIQUE reserved word in the following form:

```
CREATE UNIQUE INDEX index
ON table (field);
```

The DISALLOW NULL reserved word will require an entry in the field. Simply tack the following qualifier on at the end of the statement:

```
CREATE INDEX index
ON table (field) WITH DISALLOW NULL;
```

To designate the indexed field as a primary key, use the PRIMARY reserved word in the following form:

```
CREATE INDEX index
ON table (field) WITH PRIMARY;
```

InsideOut

There's not much advantage to running a pass-through or data-definition query from the query window. You can just as quickly complete most of these tasks manually, unless you're very familiar with SQL. Most people will use these SQL statements in VBA code to programmatically perform these specific tasks.

Using Subqueries as an Alternative to Multiple Queries

Subqueries are often overlooked because in most cases nested queries are more popular and easier for the SQL novice to create. Any time you base one query on another, you're dealing with a nested query, and often that's the appropriate choice. On the other hand, a nested query can be slow. You might want to try replacing a nested query with a subquery to compare performance. However, subqueries are not necessarily superior to nested queries and can actually slow things down. There's no real tried-and-true rule of thumb you can use for guidance. Being aware that you have an alternative is probably the best guideline.

The next time you're dealing with a nested query, try to rewrite it as a subquery and see whether there's any improvement in performance. Unless you're dealing with a particularly complex set of criteria or a huge amount of data, you probably won't notice much difference, but it's worth a try.

To create a subquery from a nested query, follow these steps:

1. Open the base query in the SQL window, and copy it to the Clipboard.
2. Open the second query in the SQL window, and paste the first SELECT statement into the second. Knowing just where to paste can be a bit of a challenge, but generally you'll position the statement in a WHERE clause.
3. Replace references to the first query in the second query's original SELECT statement.
4. Run the query.

Most of the time, Jet can handle the subquery. When it can't, you can try rewriting the subquery or abandon the effort.

Now let's take a look at a nested query and try rewriting it as a subquery. Suppose you want to find the oldest order in the Northwind Orders table. You also want to identify that order by customer. You can use the *Min* aggregate function to return the oldest order, but the minute you add the Customer field to the mix, you change the dynamics of the group, and the query returns a record for every customer with a different order date.

To solve the problem using a nested query, follow these steps:

1. Create a Totals query on the Orders table by selecting the *Min* summary function in the Total cell of the OrderDate field, as shown in Figure 11-25. Save the query. (In this example, the query is named qryMax1.) If you run the query, you'll see it returns one record with the date 7/4/96.

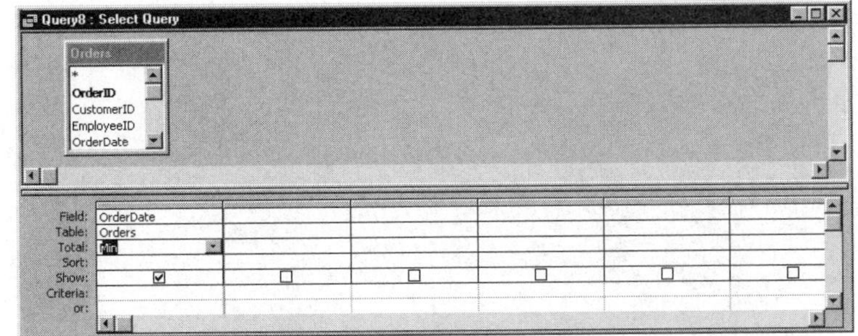

Figure 11-25. Use the *Min* aggregate function to return the oldest order.

For more information about aggregates, see Chapter 9, "Using Queries to Select Data."

2 Base a second query on the first (qryMax1) by selecting qryMax1 in the Database window, selecting Query from the New Object button's drop-down list, and then clicking OK in the New Query dialog box.

3 Click the Show Table button on the Query Design toolbar to open the Show Table dialog box, and add the Orders table to the query design window.

4 Drag the MinOfOrderDate field to the OrderDate field in the Orders field list to create a relationship between the two data sources.

5 Add the CustomerID field from the Orders table and the MinOfOrderDate field from the first query, as shown in Figure 11-26.

Figure 11-26. Base a second query on the first query.

6 Run the query to return the results shown in Figure 11-27. Save the query as **qryMax2**.

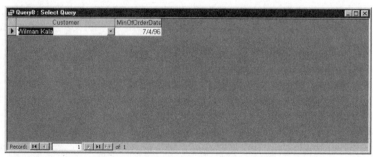

Figure 11-27. The nested query returns the oldest order and the name of the customer who placed it.

Let's review the two SQL statements for both queries. The first (qryMax1) query's statement looks like this:

```
SELECT Min(Orders.OrderDate) AS MinOfOrderDate
FROM Orders;
```

A simple SELECT statement returns the minimum value from the OrderDate field from the Orders table. The second query looks like this:

```
SELECT Orders.CustomerID, qryMax1.MinOfOrderDate
FROM qryMax1
INNER JOIN Orders ON qryMax1.MinOfOrderDate = Orders.OrderDate;
```

This time there are two data sources: qryMax1 and Orders are related on the OrderDate and MinOfOrderDate fields. If the two entries match, the query will return the CustomerID and the OrderDate value for that record.

The alternative subquery looks like this:

```
SELECT Orders.CustomerID, Orders.OrderDate
FROM Orders
WHERE (((Orders.OrderDate) In (SELECT Min(Orders.OrderDate)
As OrderDate FROM Orders)));
```

The WHERE clause replaces the JOIN. Because you're working only with the Orders table, references to qryMax1 need to be restated in terms of the Orders table, as follows:

- Replace *qryMax1.MinOfOrderDate* with *Orders.OrderDate* in the initial SELECT statement.
- Replace *qryMax1* with *Orders* in the FROM clause.
- Replace *INNER JOIN Orders ON qryMax1.MinOfOrderDate = Orders.OrderDate* with the WHERE clause shown in the preceding subquery.

If the transition seems complicated, don't worry. Once you've actually created a subquery from a nested query a few times, you'll get the hang of it.

Chapter 12

Using PivotTables and PivotCharts to Analyze Data

As you know, you can view and modify data in forms, sort and filter data in queries, and print data in reports. But when you look at a form, a query, or a report, you see the results of applying a specific set of filter criteria and sort orders to a specific group of fields—you can't change the field selection, sort orders, or filter criteria in Form view, Datasheet view (for queries), or Print Preview. For example, you might have a report that shows just the current year's sales and groups sales alphabetically by region. This report is just what you need to view the current sales results for the Midwest region, but if you later need to view sales results by salesperson rather than by region, you would have to create a new report, and possibly a new query to use as the report's record source.

newfeature!

PivotTables (a view that summarizes and analyzes data in a datasheet or form, enhanced in Microsoft Access 2002) and PivotCharts (a view that shows a graphical analysis of data in a datasheet or form, new to Access 2002) let you look at your data from many different points of view, without having to create numerous queries and reports to implement different sorts and filters. You can prepare a single query containing the data you want to work with and then do all the filtering, sorting, and cross-tabulating you want directly in the PivotTable or PivotChart. In this chapter, you'll learn how to display your data in flexible and attractive PivotTables and PivotCharts.

You won't see PivotTable or PivotChart groups in the Database window. In Access, these features are implemented as views of various database objects. Tables, queries, and forms have a PivotTable and a PivotChart view, which can be selected from the View menu on the Access menu bar or by using the View selector on the Form View, Design View, or Query Design toolbar. Although several different database objects have PivotTable and PivotChart views, generally forms are used to create them. For convenience, in this chapter, we'll look at just form-based PivotTables and PivotCharts.

Both PivotTables and PivotCharts allow users to rearrange data interactively, right in the PivotTable or PivotChart view. The flexibility of PivotTables and PivotCharts means that the form designer doesn't need to figure out in advance just how users will want to display their data; instead, the designer can concentrate on preparing a set of data for the PivotTable or PivotChart and let users arrange and summarize the data as they prefer, for whatever analysis they want to do at a particular time.

You can create a PivotTable or a PivotChart in a variety of ways in Access 2002, as you'll see later in this chapter. You can switch to PivotTable or PivotChart view from an existing form, create a new form based on a query or table using the PivotTable Wizard, or select the AutoForm: PivotTable selection from the New Form dialog box.

Using PivotTables to Organize Your Data

A PivotTable is an interactive table used to analyze data from different perspectives in tabular form (rows and columns)—an example would be grouping sales data by region, salesperson, and product, a process which is sometimes called "slicing and dicing" your data. PivotTables are ideal for analyzing data from various points of view. A PivotTable presents data in a view that lets users—not just database designers—restructure the data and perform calculations on it. For example, you could examine total sales by salesperson and month or examine the number of items in a particular category sold by salespeople in a specific country from the same PivotTable, without switching to Design view for modifications.

Data displayed in a PivotTable can be analyzed and summarized from different perspectives and at different levels of detail, including cross-tabulation, such as is done in a crosstab query. But unlike a crosstab query, it's easy to swap the position of row and column headings in PivotTable view. The following sections explain the tools and procedures you use to create PivotTables.

> **note** PivotTable view is especially useful for forms, because forms (if designed appropriately) give you more flexibility in switching among views. For example, you could design a form that displays equally well in Form view, PivotTable view, and PivotChart view.

Understanding PivotTables

PivotTables consist of several elements that are used to analyze the data they display in various ways. The most important of these are the row fields (which create the rows of data), the column fields (used to create column headings), and the data fields (which provide the data for the PivotTable). Figure 12-1 shows a typical PivotTable.

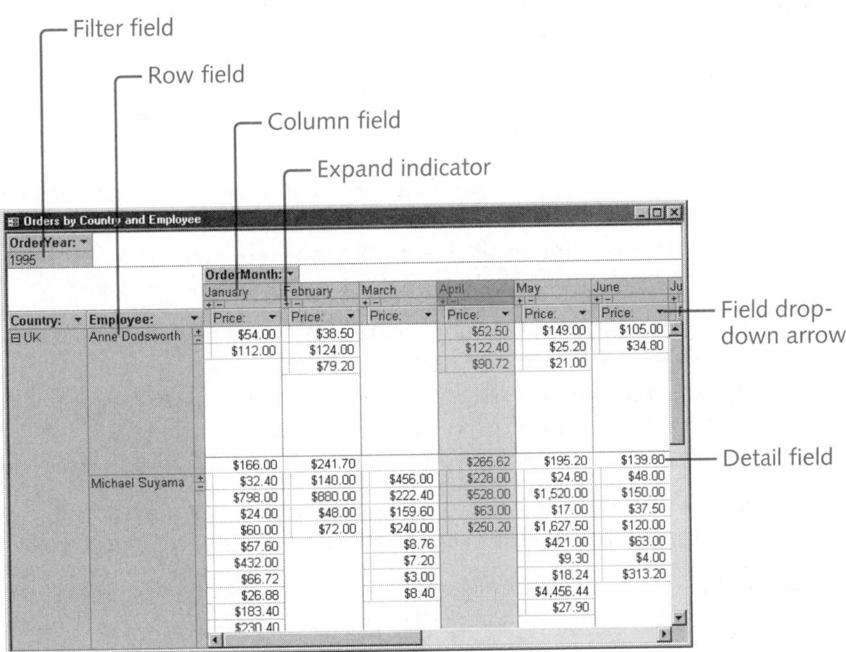

Figure 12-1. A PivotTable lets you select fields for row and column headings and data.

The following list describes these PivotTable elements in more detail:

Field A field corresponds to a column of data; a PivotTable field can summarize multiple rows of a data source such as a table or a query—for example, a salesperson's results for a specific month. A PivotTable has row fields, column fields, data fields, and (optionally) filter fields.

Item An item is a unique value in a field, such as the price of a computer sold by a specific salesperson on a specific date. The cell in the PivotTable where a row and a column intersect generally summarizes the item data for that row and column—for example, summing the sales for a specific computer model by a salesperson on a specific date. If a more detailed level of data is available, it can be displayed by clicking the Expand indicator (+). This PivotTable feature lets users switch between summarized and detailed data whenever they want.

Row field A row field is a field placed in the row area (the left side of a PivotTable). There can be two row fields, an inner row field and an outer row field, representing two levels of grouping, similar to report grouping. (For more information about report grouping, see Chapter 7, "Using Reports to Print Data.") The PivotTable shown in Figure 12-1 has two row fields, the outer one for Country and the inner one for Employee.

Column field A column field is a field placed in the column area (the area across the top of a PivotTable, above the data fields). There can be several columns of summarized data for each column field—for example, Price and Profit columns. The PivotTable shown in Figure 12-1 uses the OrderMonth field for the column field.

Filter field A filter field is a field placed in the filter area (the upper left corner of the PivotTable). Filter fields are used to filter the data displayed in the PivotTable. For example, the PivotTable shown in Figure 12-1 uses the value 1995 from the OrderYear field to display just the 1995 data.

Data field A data field (a field in the data area) contains summarized data from the PivotTable's data source. Data fields usually summarize numeric data using the *Sum* function, but data can also be summarized using the *Count* function—in which case, the detail items are counted. In the PivotTable shown in Figure 12-1, the data is derived from the Price field.

Data area The data area of a PivotTable displays the data fields, usually in summarized form, such as a sum of currency values or a count of employees.

Detail field A detail field displays all the rows from the data source. These are the detail items that are summarized in the data area.

Field drop-down arrow Clicking the arrow to the right of a field displays a drop-down list from which you can select items to display or hide, enabling you to further filter the data.

Drop Zones and Areas

In this chapter, you'll see references to row, column, and data drop zones and also to row, column, and data areas. Drop zones are interactive elements of a PivotTable or PivotChart—dropping a field onto a drop zone tells Access where the data for the corresponding area of the PivotTable or PivotChart comes from. Even when drop zones are turned off (say, in a PivotTable designed to be displayed on a projector), the PivotTable or PivotChart will still have row, column, and data areas.

Exploring the PivotTable Toolbar

PivotTables have their own toolbar, shown in Figure 12-2.

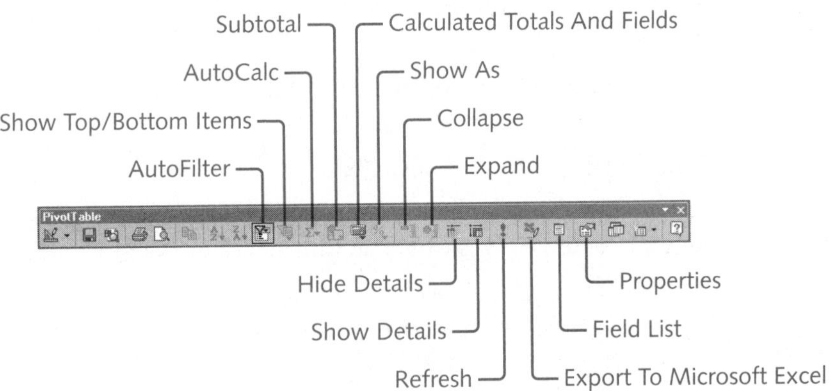

Figure 12-2. The PivotTable toolbar provides special tools for working with PivotTables.

> **tip** If the PivotTable toolbar isn't visible, right-click the gray background of any open toolbar and choose PivotTable on the shortcut menu, or choose View, Toolbars and select PivotTable.

Some of these buttons are probably familiar to you from working with forms and reports. The specialized PivotTable tools are described here:

AutoFilter. Filters fields by selected data items.

Show Top/Bottom Items. Displays only the specified number of top or bottom items in a group, much like a Top Values query.

AutoCalc. Lets you quickly apply a summary function for column subtotals. (*Sum*, *Count*, *Min*, *Max*, and *Average* are the most widely used functions.)

Subtotal. Adds row subtotals.

Calculated Totals And Fields. Lets you add an expression to calculate data.

Show As. Offers a choice of displaying detail values as a variety of percentages.

Collapse. Collapses the inner row fields so that only the outer row fields are visible. (Applies only when the PivotTable contains two row fields.)

Expand. Expands the inner row fields so that both the outer and inner row fields are visible. (Applies only when the PivotTable contains two row fields.)

Hide Details. Hides the detail items. Only the summary results show.

Show Details. Shows the detail items.

Refresh. Refreshes the PivotTable with any changes to the underlying data source.

Export To Microsoft Excel. Exports the PivotTable to Excel.

Field List. Hides or displays the field list.

Properties. Opens the PivotTable properties sheet, which provides a number of settings (some of which aren't available elsewhere) for modifying elements of PivotTables.

PivotTables and PivotCharts can also be displayed on the Web as data access pages and can be viewed and manipulated by users who have the Microsoft Office Web Components installed. See Chapter 18, "Working with Data Access Pages," for more details about using PivotTables and PivotCharts in data access pages.

Creating a Query to Gather PivotTable Data

Like a crosstab query, a PivotTable query needs enough data fields to provide row data (such as employee names or regions), column heading data (such as dates), and of course the data to be summarized in the body of the PivotTable, usually either summed numeric data or counted textual data. If you have the fields you need in the form's record source, you can proceed to set up the PivotTable by dragging fields to the designated portions of the PivotTable.

See Chapter 9, "Using Queries to Select Data," for more information about crosstab queries; see the section "Choosing Fields for the PivotTable," page 467, for more details on adding fields to a PivotTable.

It's rare for a single table to contain all the fields needed for a PivotTable, however. Generally, a PivotTable requires fields from several linked tables. If your form doesn't have all the fields you need to create row headings, column headings, and data, you'll need to first prepare a query containing the data fields you want to work with and then create a new form designed for use in PivotTable view. The PivotTable Wizard (or the AutoForm: PivotTable selection in the New Form dialog box) helps you create such a form, once you've created your query.

A minimum table or query for a data source would contain three fields—say, Customer, OrderDate, and OrderAmount. The Customer field would be the most likely choice for row values and OrderDate the most likely choice for column values, although the two could be swapped. OrderAmount (probably summed) would be the field to use for the values in the PivotTable data area.

Figure 12-3 shows a query based on several tables from the Northwind database (renamed with the *tbl* tag), with calculated fields for the price of each order detail item and the employee name. (You'll find this query saved as qryOrders in the Test Access 2002 sample database on the companion CD.) This query has enough fields in it to allow a variety of PivotTable arrangements, so users can analyze data by company, employee, price, month, and year.

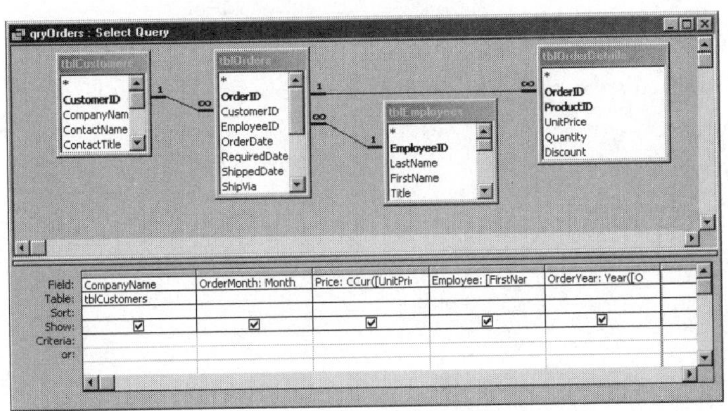

Figure 12-3. A query with several linked tables has plenty of data for a PivotTable.

note Although you can create calculated fields in a PivotTable, it's much easier to create them using the Expression Builder in a query column. See Chapter 4, "Creating a Database," for more details on using the Expression Builder.

This query uses typical formatting expressions in several columns to preprocess data for the PivotTable. Instead of using the OrderDate field directly, date formatting functions are used in two column expressions to create columns with years or months as values. The following expression yields month names to be used as column headings:

```
OrderMonth: MonthName(Month([OrderDate]))
```

The following expression is used to extract year values from OrderDate. This field is useful for filtering the PivotTable.

```
Year([OrderDate])
```

A Price column is created by performing calculations on several other fields, as shown here:

```
Price: CCur([UnitPrice ]*[Quantity]*IIf([Discount]>0,[Discount],1))
```

And last, an Employee column concatenates the FirstName and LastName fields, as shown here:

```
Employee: [FirstName] & " " & [LastName]
```

The finished query displays only the fields you need in the PivotTable.

Creating a Basic PivotTable

Once you have constructed a query containing suitable fields, you can create a new form by using the PivotTable Wizard or by selecting AutoForm: PivotTable in the New Form dialog box. Unlike most other Access wizards, the PivotTable Wizard isn't all that helpful. Basically, the wizard lets you select a data source and (if you want) select fields from the data source.

Switching to PivotTable or PivotChart View in an Existing Access Form

The simplest way to create a PivotTable or PivotChart in Access is to switch to PivotTable view or PivotChart view for an existing Access form. You can do this by choosing View, PivotTable or View, PivotChart, or by selecting PivotTable or PivotChart on the View selector on the Form toolbar.

If the PivotTable or PivotChart view is unavailable, you can open the form's properties sheet and set the Allow PivotTable View or Allow PivotChart View property to Yes. Keep in mind, however, that this property might have been set to No because the form's record source isn't suitable for a PivotTable or PivotChart. In that case, you might need to create a new form to get a useful PivotTable or PivotChart view.

After you switch to PivotTable or PivotChart view, a blank PivotTable or PivotChart layout will appear, with drop zones for dragging row fields, column fields, and filter fields.

After you complete the two wizard pages, you end up with a blank PivotTable and the PivotTable field list, identical to what appears when you switch to PivotTable view for a form or select AutoForm: PivotTable in the New Form dialog box (as described later in this section). Because the PivotTable Wizard doesn't provide any extra help, it's faster to use one of the other techniques for creating a PivotTable.

note When I use the term *PivotTable form*, I don't mean a special type of database object. A PivotTable form is just a standard Access form, but one designed from the start to produce a useful PivotTable view—which isn't always the case if you switch to PivotTable view from an existing form. Forms are often based on a single table, whereas a PivotTable generally needs data from several linked tables.

To conveniently create a PivotTable form, follow these steps:

1. Prepare a query with all (and only) the fields you want to work with in the PivotTable.
2. In the Forms group of the Database window, click the New button, or choose Insert, Form.
3. Select AutoForm: PivotTable from the list.
4. In the New Form dialog box, select the prepared query to use as the PivotTable form's data source from the drop-down list, as shown in Figure 12-4, and then click OK.

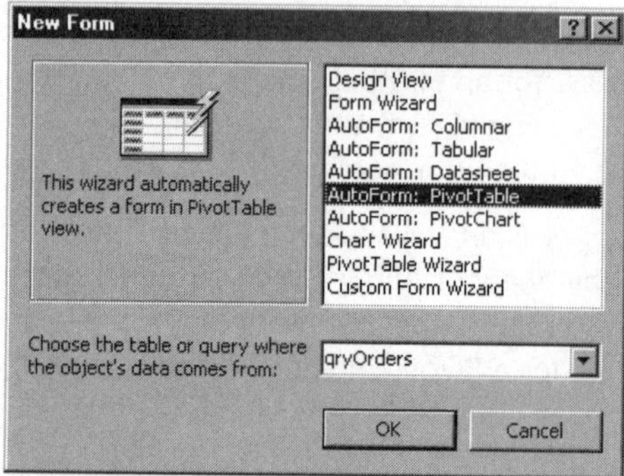

Figure 12-4. Select AutoForm: PivotTable and a query to create a new PivotTable form.

5. A form based on the selected query opens in PivotTable view, as shown in Figure 12-5, with the PivotTable field list visible so that you can select fields for the PivotTable to display.

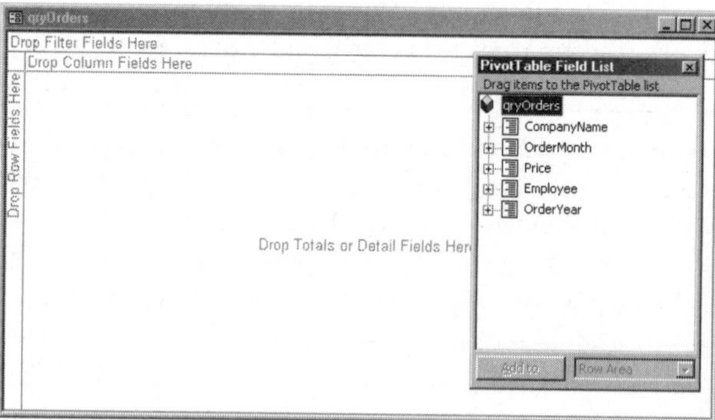

Figure 12-5. A new PivotTable form with the PivotTable field list for selecting fields.

Chapter 12

InsideOut

You can't directly create a PivotTable report, but you can create a form set up for PivotTable view and then save it as a report. The result is not a true PivotTable, however—it's just an image of one (meaning that it's not interactive). This image is basically the same as printing the PivotTable from a form.

Choosing Fields for the PivotTable

The next step is to select the fields to use for row headings, column headings, and data. The PivotTable field list provides a list of all the fields in the form's record source. If you prepared a query in advance, you'll see just a few appropriate fields. (This is one of the advantages of preparing a query for a PivotTable.) Otherwise, you'll see a long list of all the fields in the data source, only a few of which are appropriate for use in a PivotTable.

InsideOut

Lookup fields (such as Customer ID) are listed in the PivotTable field list under the names of the linked fields in the other tables. (For example, Customer ID might be listed as the Customer Name field.) However, when you drag a lookup field to the PivotTable, you'll see the Customer ID field on the grid, not the Customer Name field, which probably isn't what you want, since most likely users will want to see customer names on the PivotTable, not just Customer IDs. (The Customer Name is far more meaningful to a human than the numeric Customer ID field.) To prevent such problems, create a query containing the fields you want to use from each table. Don't rely on picking up a field from another table by using a lookup field.

You need to drag one or more fields to the Row Fields drop zone, another field to the Column Fields drop zone, and a third field to the Totals Or Detail Fields drop zone. (We'll ignore the Filter Fields drop zone for now; its use is optional. You'll learn more about using the Filter Fields drop zone later in this section.)

tip As an alternative to dragging a field from the PivotTable field list to a drop zone, you can select the field and then select the drop zone from the Add To drop-down list at the bottom of the PivotTable field list.

For example, to drag fields to a PivotTable to display data for a text field (CompanyName) in rows, with columns arranging data by months, follow these steps:

In this example, we'll use fields from the sample qryOrders query in the Test Access 2002 sample database on the companion CD, but the same general principles apply to any data source used to provide fields for a PivotTable.

1 Drag a text field containing data you want to see in rows (in this case, CompanyName) from the PivotTable field list to the Row Fields drop zone on the PivotTable, as shown in Figure 12-6.

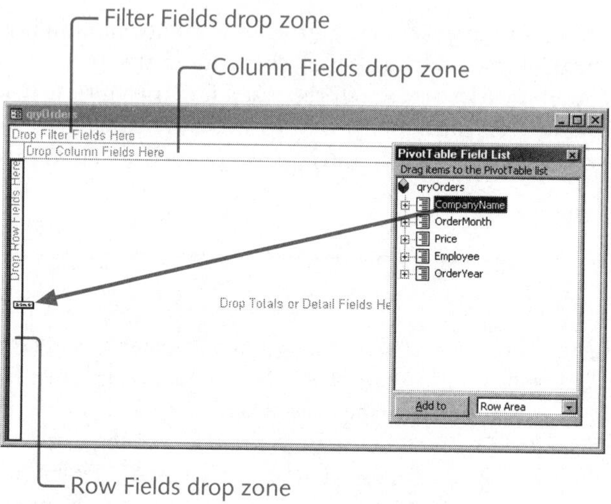

Figure 12-6. Drag a field from the field list to the Row Fields drop zone to use its data for rows in the PivotTable.

tip If the PivotTable field list isn't visible, right-click the PivotTable and choose Field List from the shortcut menu, or press the F8 hot key.

The company names appear along the left side of the PivotTable.

note The drop zone border turns bright blue when the dragged field is positioned correctly for dropping. Fields that have been dragged to the PivotTable appear in boldface in the field list.

2 Drag the text field containing data you want to see in columns (in this case, OrderMonth) from the PivotTable field list to the Column Fields drop zone.

Month columns will appear along the top of the PivotTable, as shown in Figure 12-7.

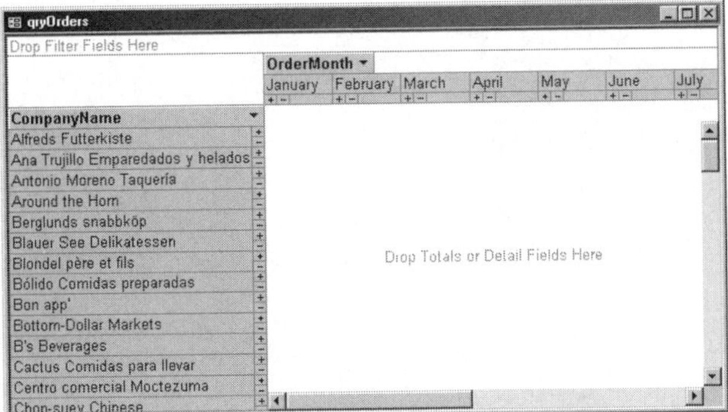

Figure 12-7. The PivotTable now has row and column headings.

3 Drag the field containing data for the PivotTable (in this case, Price) to the Totals Or Detail Fields drop zone. The detail prices appear in the center of the form, in the appropriate rows and columns, as shown in Figure 12-8.

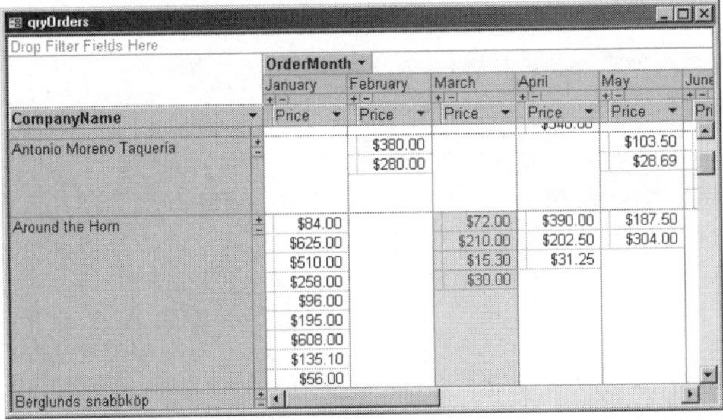

Figure 12-8. Price data now appears in the Detail area of the PivotTable.

4 If you want to filter your PivotTable data, you can drag a field to the Filter Fields drop zone. For example, if you want to see only orders for a specific year, drag the OrderYear field to the Filter Fields drop zone, clear the check boxes for the years you want to exclude on the drop-down list, and then click OK, as shown in Figure 12-9.

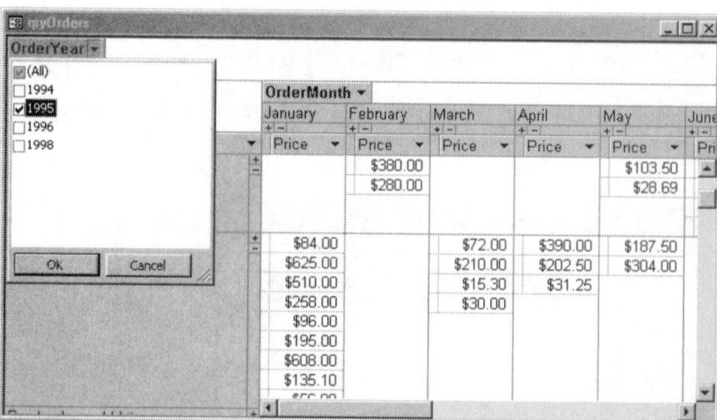

Figure 12-9. Set up a filter condition by deselecting years in the OrderYear drop-down list.

tip You also clear the All check box at the top of the list, and then check the items you want to include in the filter condition.

5 To sum the prices for each row/column combination, click the Price selector over one of the columns (the prices will turn blue to indicate that they're selected), click the AutoCalc button on the PivotTable toolbar, and choose Sum from the drop-down menu, as shown in Figure 12-10.

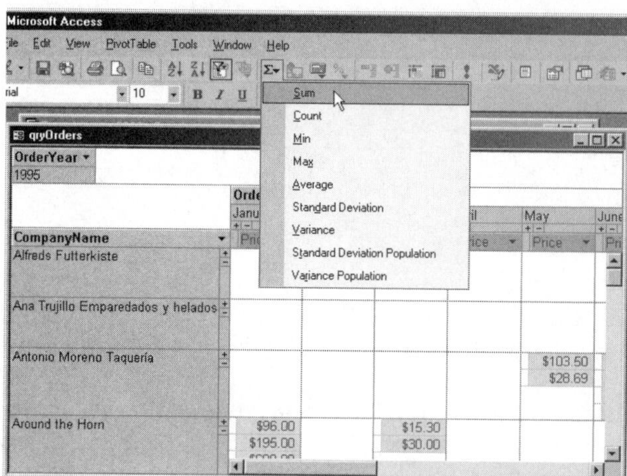

Figure 12-10. Choose Sum from the AutoCalc menu to create a column subtotal for each row of data.

Price subtotals will appear for each row/column combination, as shown in Figure 12-11.

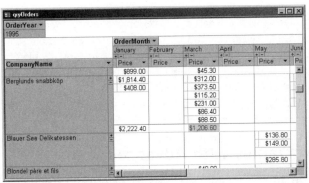

Figure 12-11. The PivotTable now shows a monthly subtotal for each row of data.

6 To show or hide the details for a row, click the tiny plus and minus buttons to the right of the company name in each row. (Click the Hide Details and Show Details buttons on the PivotTable toolbar to hide or show details for the entire PivotTable.)

7 To display more than one summary function, click AutoCalc again and select another function. When details are hidden, the summary type is listed under the top row of column headings (in this case, months). A ScreenTip provides information about a particular summary value when you hover your mouse pointer over it, as illustrated in Figure 12-12, which shows both *Sum* and *Count* summaries of prices.

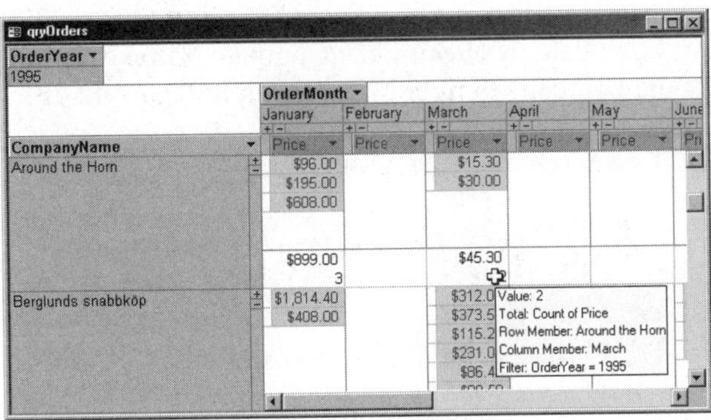

Figure 12-12. A PivotTable shows details of the *Sum* and *Count* summaries of Price in a ScreenTip.

tip To remove a summary row from a PivotTable, right-click the summary value, and choose Remove from the shortcut menu.

8 Scroll to the bottom right of the PivotTable to see a Grand Total row and a Grand Total column.

note PivotTables and PivotCharts are actually Excel objects embedded in Access objects. If you use the PivotTable Wizard or choose the AutoForm: PivotTable selection in the New Form dialog box to create a PivotTable form, an Excel PivotTable object is embedded in an Access form. This might explain why some of the tools on the PivotTable toolbar are similar to Excel tools. However, if you look at PivotTables in Excel 2002, you'll see that they appear rather different from Access 2002 PivotTables.

Fine-Tuning PivotTables with Advanced Tools

You now have a useful PivotTable, but there are several additional ways you can modify it, if needed. You can make stylistic changes by specifying the font, color, and size of the PivotTable components; add captions to explain portions of the PivotTable; and perform advanced filtering and grouping. In this section, we'll look at these and other advanced tools for working with PivotTables.

Filtering PivotTable Data

To filter data by a value in a field, follow these steps:

1. Click the arrow to the right of the field name you want to use for filtering.
2. Select one or more values from the drop-down list.
3. Click OK.

In our example PivotTable, which is filtered by year using a filter field, you can also filter on the CompanyName field by clicking the CompanyName drop-down arrow and selecting a particular company to filter by, as shown in Figure 12-13.

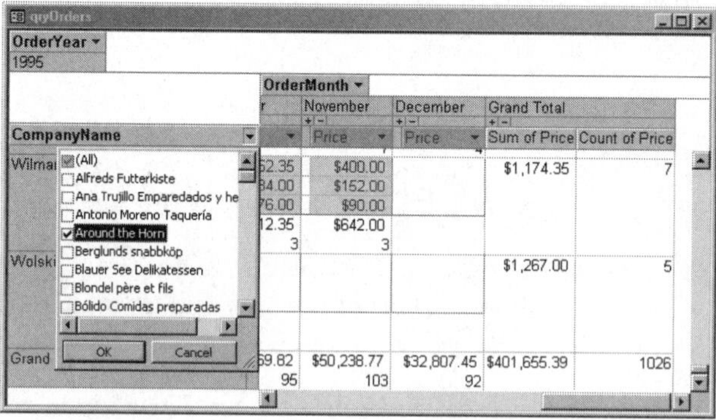

Figure 12-13. You can select a specific company name to filter PivotTable data for just that company.

The filtered PivotTable now contains data for only the company you specified.

Setting PivotTable Properties

In addition to using the PivotTable toolbar buttons to work with PivotTables, you can also click the Properties button to open the PivotTable properties sheet, which contains several tabs, where you can set more options for the PivotTable.

> **note** The PivotTable properties sheet contains a different selection of tabs depending on what element of the PivotTable is selected when the properties sheet is opened.

Formatting a PivotTable On the Format tab of the properties sheet, you can set a number of standard formatting options for the selected PivotTable element, including font, size, and color. To do so, follow these steps:

1. Right-click the element in the PivotTable you want to modify, and choose Properties from the shortcut menu.
2. Click the Format tab, and change the desired options.
3. Close the properties sheet.

For example, to make subtotals bold and bright blue, right-click any subtotal in the PivotTable, open the PivotTable properties sheet, and select the Format tab. Click the Bold button, and then click the down arrow to the right of the Font Color button to open a drop-down list, shown in Figure 12-14, where you can specify the exact shade of blue you want.

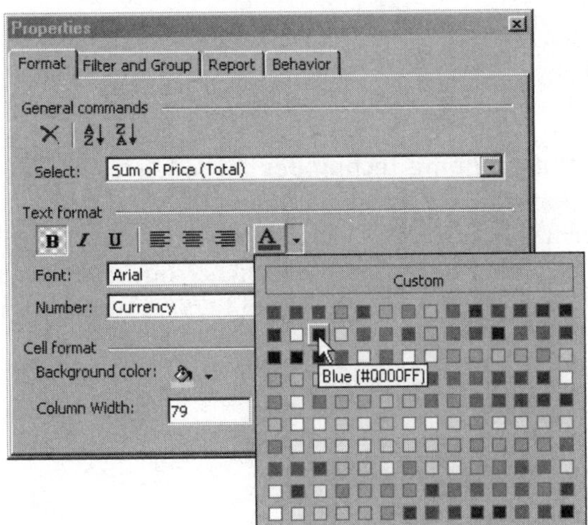

Figure 12-14. You can format PivotTable components using settings on the Format tab of the PivotTable properties sheet.

Modifying PivotTable captions The Captions tab lets you modify the appearance of the row, column, and filter captions (the text that describes the Row, Column, and Filter fields) in the PivotTable. To do so, follow these steps:

1. Right-click the row, column, or filter caption in the PivotTable you want to modify, and choose Properties from the shortcut menu.
2. Click the Captions tab, and change the desired options.
3. Close the properties sheet.

For example, if your field names don't contain spaces (like the CompanyName field in the example) and you want to add spaces to make them more legible, you could select a field and add spaces to its caption, as shown in Figure 12-15.

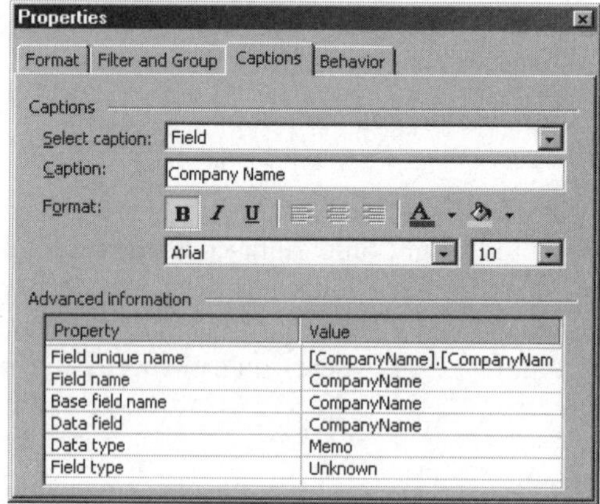

Figure 12-15. You can modify a PivotTable's captions on the Captions tab of the PivotTable properties sheet.

Using advanced filtering and grouping techniques The Filter And Group tab provides more advanced options for filtering and grouping a PivotTable. You can make a PivotTable display the specified number of items at the top or bottom of a list, based on count or percentage, or group items by prefix characters (somewhat like an Access report grouped by the first letter—see Chapter 7, "Using Reports to Print Data"). To do so, follow these steps:

1. Right-click the filter or grouping element in the PivotTable you want to modify, and choose Properties from the shortcut menu.
2. Click the Filter And Group tab, and change the desired options.
3. Close the properties sheet.

Figure 12-16 shows the settings for filtering a PivotTable by the top 10 percent of data.

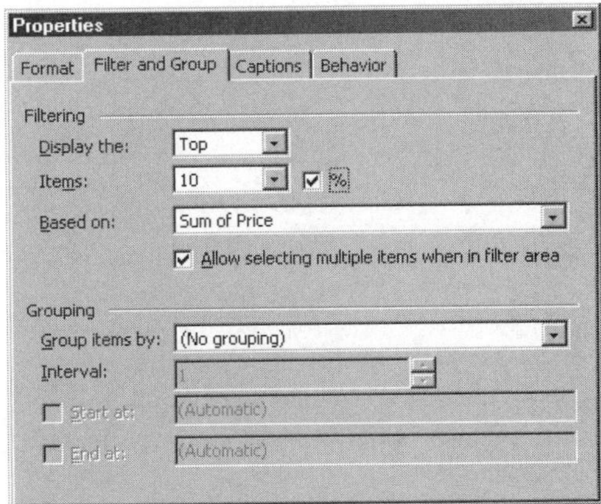

Figure 12-16. You can filter a PivotTable for the top 10 percent of data values using the Filter And Group tab.

Modifying how data is displayed in a PivotTable The Report tab of the PivotTable properties sheet allows you to set generic PivotTable options, such as whether the PivotTable should display empty rows and columns. To do so, follow these steps:

1. Right-click an element in the PivotTable you want to modify, and choose Properties from the shortcut menu.
2. Click the Report tab, and change the desired options.
3. Close the properties sheet.

For instance, choosing the Row Headings option on the Report tab displays the label *Sum of Price* next to the row headings in the example PivotTable, as shown in Figure 12-17. Several other options on this tab let you specify whether empty rows and columns, calculated items, or ScreenTips will be displayed in the PivotTable.

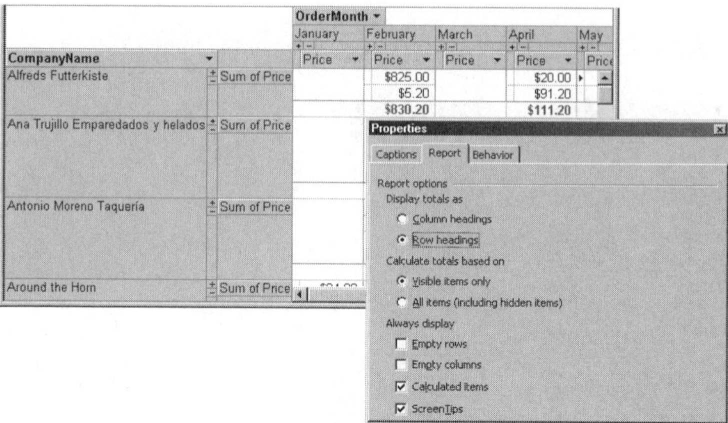

Figure 12-17. You can change how totals are displayed by configuring settings on the Report tab of the PivotTable properties sheet.

The Behavior tab, shown in Figure 12-18, lets you modify some more intricate details of the appearance of the PivotTable, such as whether the Expand indicators are displayed in the PivotTable.

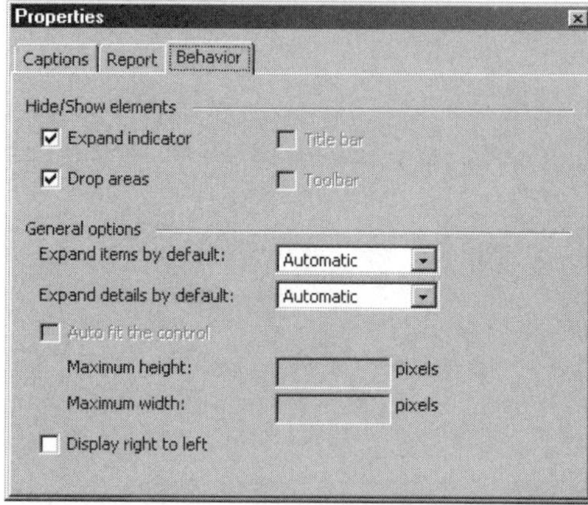

Figure 12-18. You can modify some interactive elements of a PivotTable on the Behavior tab of the properties sheet.

There's no Undo command for PivotTables (unlike for forms, reports, and other Access database objects, which have an Undo button on the toolbar), so if you make a mistake, you have to manually replace or modify the incorrect element. Hopefully, Undo for PivotTables will be added in the next version of Access.

Pivoting a PivotTable

Unlike crosstab queries, PivotTables (as their name implies) can be pivoted—that is, you can swap the vertical and horizontal data simply by dragging the fields to opposite locations. For example, to view the company names in our sample PivotTable as column headings and the months as row headings, all you have to do is drag the CompanyName field to the Column Fields drop zone and the Years field to the Row Fields drop zone. The Months field will accompany the Years field as the new row fields, with Years as the outer field and Months as the inner field. The resulting PivotTable is shown in Figure 12-19.

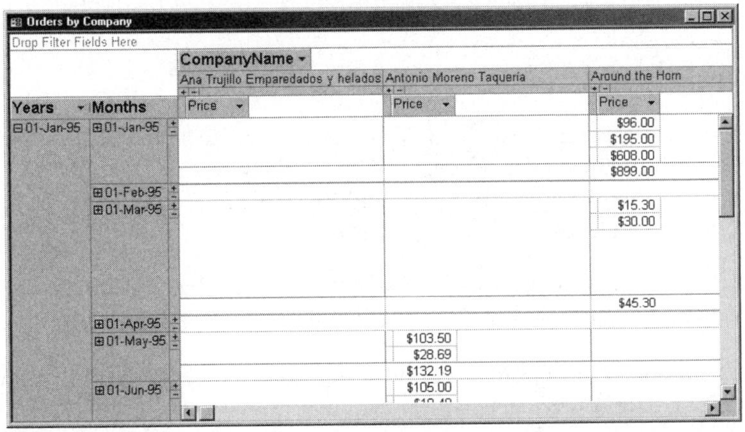

Figure 12-19. A PivotTable lets you swap row and column headings simply by dragging fields.

This flexibility gives PivotTables a great advantage over crosstab queries, as users can manipulate the rows and columns, filter the data, and add subtotals in PivotTable view to analyze data as they prefer.

newfeature!

Using PivotCharts to Display Data Graphically

PivotCharts are new to Access 2002, and they're even easier to use than PivotTables. Although Access 2002 retains the older MS Graph component to provide backward compatibility, you should use the new PivotChart feature for all your charts and graphs, as PivotCharts are both easier to use and more powerful than the older MS Graph charts and graphs.

PivotCharts are even more flexible than PivotTables because of the handy By Row/By Column toolbar button that lets you easily swap the fields used for series and categories, the broad selection of chart types, and the numerous formatting options. Because both PivotTables and PivotCharts are usually views of forms, you can use the same form for a PivotTable and a PivotChart, applying the appropriate formatting in PivotTable and PivotChart view. This flexibility gives PivotCharts a great advantage over the older MS Graph charts—with PivotCharts, users can slice and dice their data in either a tabular or a graphical view, without having to modify the form's design or create multiple forms or reports to get different views of the data.

In this section, you'll learn the basics of creating powerful, easy-to-read PivotCharts.

Understanding PivotCharts

A PivotChart analyzes data visually in a variety of chart formats, such as pie charts or bar graphs, with the flexibility of rearranging the data as desired. Figure 12-20 shows a newly created PivotChart without its field list, with Filter Fields, Data Fields, Series Fields, and Category Fields drop zones.

PivotCharts, like PivotTables, consist of several elements that are used to analyze the data they display in various ways, as described here:

Field. A field is a column of data. A PivotChart field can summarize multiple rows of a data source such as a table or a query—for example, a salesperson's results for a specific month. A PivotChart has series fields, category fields, data fields, and (optionally) filter fields.

Series field. A series field is a field placed in the series area. Series field values are displayed according to the chart type. In a bar graph, for example, the series fields are represented by bar color and the month names are given in the legend, as shown in Figure 12-21.

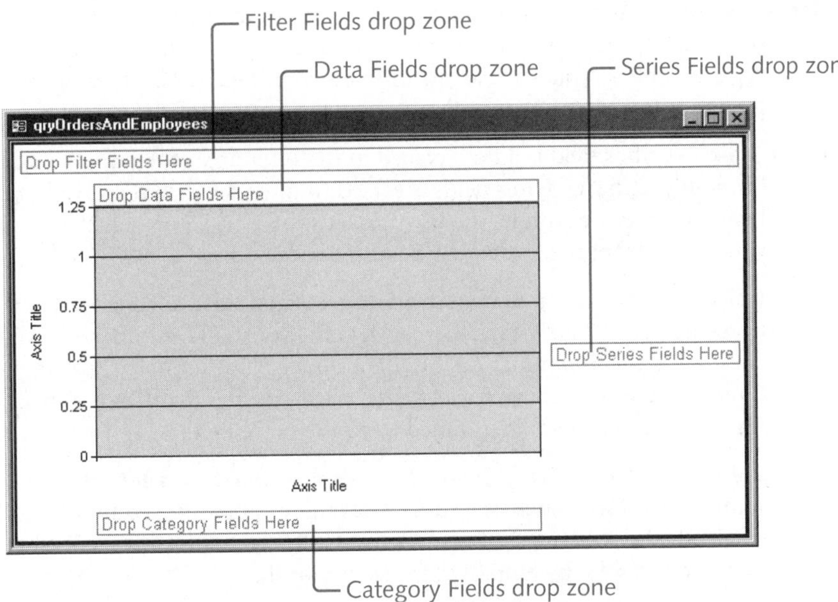

Figure 12-20. A newly created PivotChart has drop zones for filter, data, series, and category fields.

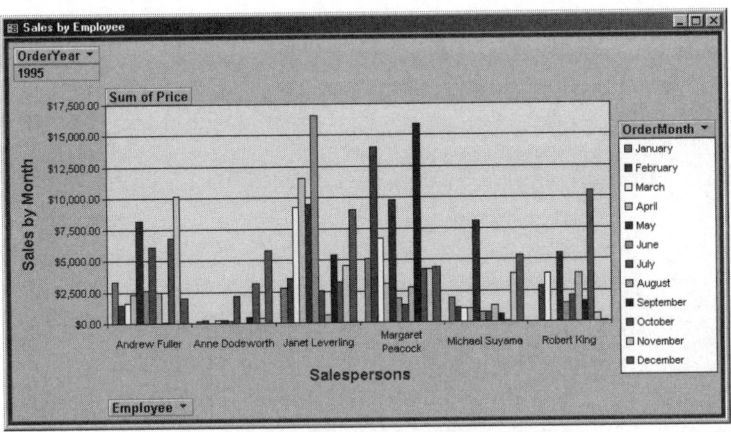

Figure 12-21. The bar graph's legend displays the values in the series field names.

Category field A category field is a field placed in the category area. As with series fields, the exact placement of the category data depends on the chart type. In a bar graph, such as the one shown in Figure 12-21, category values are the Salespersons groups listed along the bottom of the graph.

Filter field A filter field is a field placed in the filter area (the upper left corner of the PivotChart). Filter fields are used to filter the data displayed in the PivotChart. For example, the PivotChart shown in Figure 12-21 uses the value 1995 from the OrderYear field to display only the 1995 data.

Data field A data field (a field in the data area) contains summarized data from the PivotChart's data source. Data fields usually summarize numeric data, using the *Sum* function, but data can also be summarized using the *Count* function to count text or date items. In the PivotChart shown in Figure 12-21, the data is summed from the Price field.

Data area The data area of a PivotChart displays the data fields, usually in summarized form, such as a sum of currency values or a count of employees. In the PivotChart shown in Figure 12-21, the data consists of the bars representing sales by employee for each month.

Field list Clicking the arrow to the right of a field displays a drop-down list from which you can select items to display or hide, enabling you to filter the data—for example, to display data only for specific employees. Figure 12-22 shows the drop-down list for the Employee category field, with only certain employees selected.

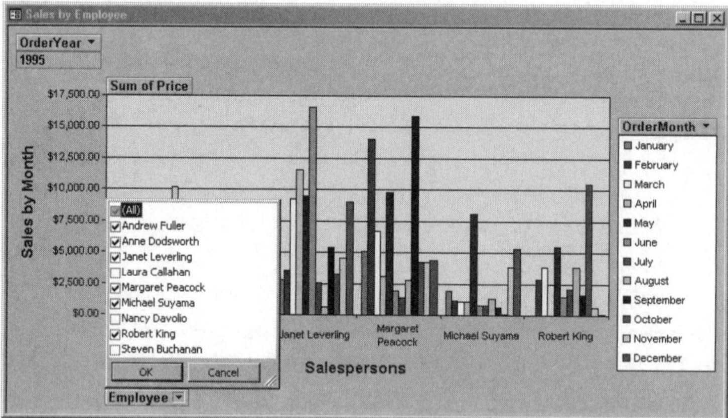

Figure 12-22. You can select check boxes in a field's drop-down list to display only certain data.

note To see the Help topics for PivotCharts, type **PivotChart** in the Ask A Question box on the main menu.

Exploring the PivotChart Toolbar

When a PivotChart is open, a special toolbar is available. The PivotChart toolbar is shown in Figure 12-23.

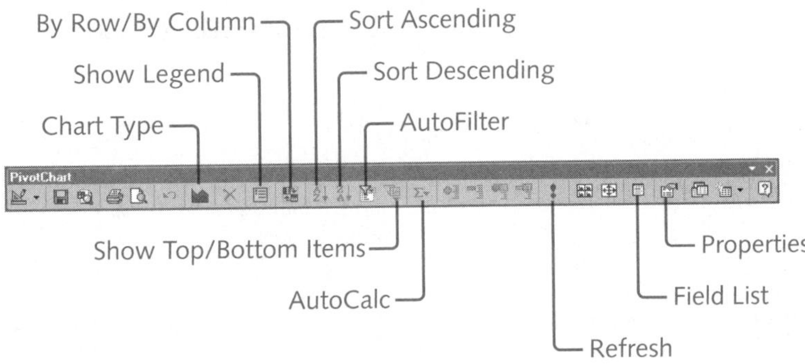

Figure 12-23. The PivotChart toolbar has special tools for working with PivotCharts.

> **tip** If the PivotChart toolbar isn't visible, right-click the gray background of any open toolbar and choose PivotChart on the shortcut menu, or choose View, Toolbars and select PivotChart.

You'll recognize some of the tools on the PivotChart toolbar from working with forms and reports. The specialized buttons for working with PivotCharts are described in the following list. Many of these tools are more useful for PivotTables than for PivotCharts, because they're primarily useful with tabular data, not visual data. The only buttons you're likely to use frequently are the Chart Type, Show Legend, and Field List buttons.

- **Chart Type.** Offers a choice of chart types.
- **Show Legend.** Hides or displays the chart legend.
- **By Row/By Column.** Swaps the series and category fields.
- **Sort Ascending.** Sorts chart data in ascending order.
- **Sort Descending.** Sorts chart data in descending order.
- **AutoFilter.** Filters fields by selected data items.

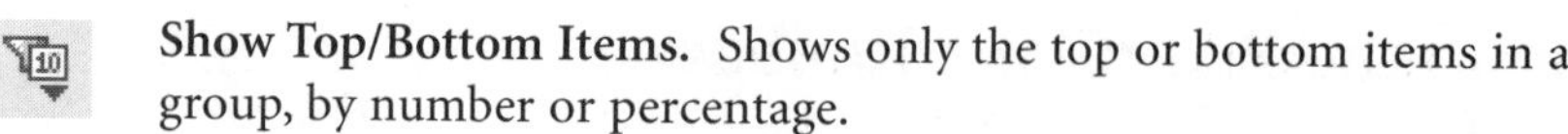

Show Top/Bottom Items. Shows only the top or bottom items in a group, by number or percentage.

AutoCalc. Lets you quickly apply a summary function. (*Sum*, *Count*, *Min*, *Max*, and *Average* are the most widely used.)

Refresh. Refreshes chart data from the chart's record source.

Field List. Displays the Chart field list.

Properties. Displays the PivotChart properties sheet.

> PivotCharts can also be displayed on the Web as data access pages and can be viewed and manipulated by users who have the Microsoft Office Web Components installed. See Chapter 18, "Working with Data Access Pages," for more details about using PivotCharts in data access pages.

Creating a Basic PivotChart

Like PivotTables, PivotCharts are views of forms (and also of tables and queries, although these are less useful). Creating a PivotChart is very similar to creating a PivotTable: You can open an existing form in PivotChart view, you can create a new PivotTable using the PivotChart Wizard, or you can use the AutoForm: PivotChart selection in the New Form dialog box.

As with PivotTables, you'll probably get the best results by using the AutoForm: PivotChart selection in the New Form dialog box to create a new form for the PivotChart. First you should create a query to gather the data that will be used in the chart using the technique described in the section "Creating a Query to Gather PivotTable Data," page 462. (One query can do double duty for a PivotTable and a PivotChart.)

InsideOut

The New Form dialog box includes a Chart Wizard option. You might expect this wizard to create a PivotChart, but it doesn't—instead, it creates an MS Graph chart, an older, noninteractive type of chart. So you might want to leave this wizard alone and create a PivotChart instead.

To create a new PivotChart form based on an existing query, follow these steps:

1. In the Forms group of the Database window, click the New button, or choose Insert, Form.
2. In the New Form dialog box, select AutoForm: PivotChart in the list.
3. Select the prepared query to use as the PivotChart form's data source from the drop-down list, as shown in Figure 12-24, and click OK.

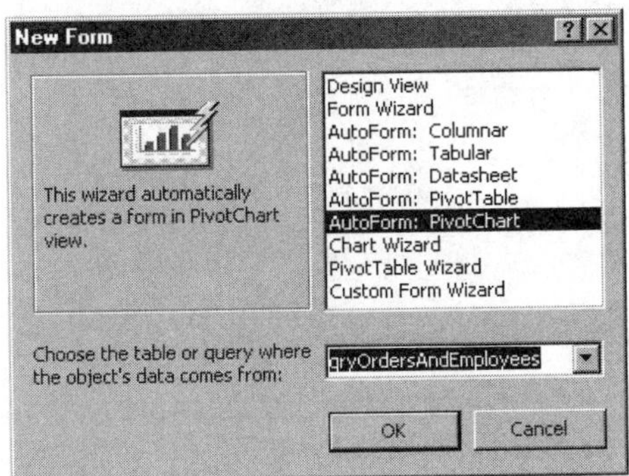

Figure 12-24. Select AutoForm: PivotChart and a query to create a new PivotChart form.

A form based on the selected query opens in PivotChart view, as shown in Figure 12-25, with the Chart field list visible so that you can specify the fields to be displayed in the PivotChart.

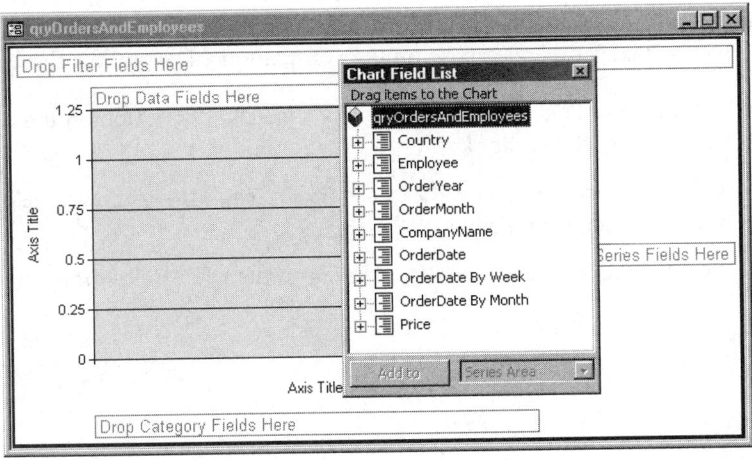

Figure 12-25. A new PivotChart form has a field list for selecting fields.

The requirements for a PivotChart data source are similar to those for a PivotTable data source: You need at least three fields—one category field, one series field, and one data field. (A few one-dimensional chart types, such as the pie and doughnut chart types, need only the category and data fields.) As with PivotTables, it's a good idea to do some preprocessing of your data in a query, so you can use the Expression Builder to create any expressions you want to use. Figure 12-26 shows a query with several calculated fields, intended for use as a PivotChart's data source.

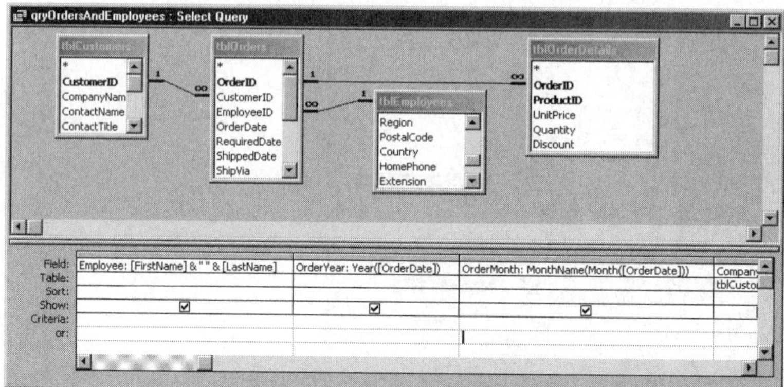

Figure 12-26. You can create a query with several calculated fields for use as the data source for a PivotChart.

Choosing Fields for the PivotChart

To choose fields for a new PivotChart—using as an example the PivotChart based on qryOrdersAndEmployees, shown in Figure 12-25 on page 483 (you'll find this query in the Test Access 2002 sample database on the companion CD)—follow these steps:

1. If the PivotChart field list isn't visible, click the Field List button on the toolbar, or press the F8 hot key.
2. Drag the category field you want to use (in this case, the Employee field) to the Category Fields drop zone.
3. (Optional) Drag the field to use for filtering to the Filter Fields drop zone.

4 (Optional) Click the arrow to the right of the OrderYear field, and select a year in the drop-down list to filter data for that year only—in this case, 1995, as shown in Figure 12-27.

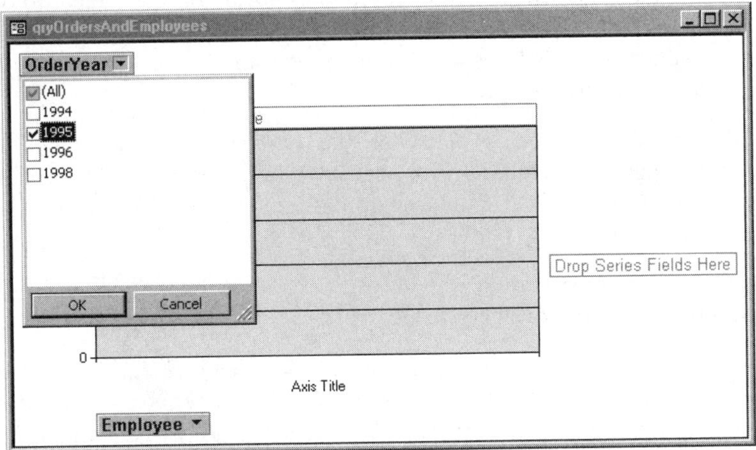

Figure 12-27. Select a year in the OrderYear drop-down list to filter data for that year.

5 Drag an appropriate field, such as the OrderMonth field, to the Series Fields drop zone.

6 Drag the data field (the Price field, in this example) to the Data Fields drop zone.

7 If desired, click the Employee drop-down arrow to filter for selected employees, as shown in Figure 12-28.

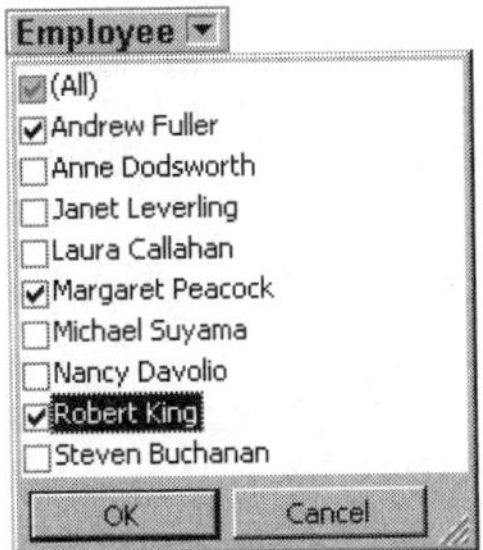

Figure 12-28. Select individual employees in the drop-down list to filter for selected employees.

8. Click the Show Legend button on the toolbar to give the chart a legend explaining the bar colors.
9. To enter a vertical axis title, select the appropriate Axis Title placeholder in the PivotChart, and click the Properties button on the toolbar to open the PivotChart properties sheet. Select the Format tab, enter an appropriate caption, such as **Sales by Month**, in the Caption box, and modify the font, size, and color as desired.
10. Repeat the process in step 9 for the horizontal axis title. (You'll find this completed PivotChart form, titled Monthly Sales By Employee, saved as fpvcMonthlySalesByEmployee in the Test Access 2002 sample database on the companion CD.)

tip **Swap the series and category fields**

You can easily swap the series and category fields by clicking the By Row/By Column button on the PivotChart toolbar. (You'll need to change the series title in the PivotChart properties sheet, to reflect the data in the series area after the swap.)

Fine-Tuning PivotCharts with Advanced Tools

PivotCharts are useful and attractive even if you do no more than select the category, series, and data fields; add titles and a legend; and perhaps change the chart type. However (as with PivotTables), you can set a variety of advanced options to further enhance the appearance of PivotCharts using the PivotChart properties sheet (opened by clicking the Properties button on the PivotChart toolbar). In this section, we'll look at the PivotChart elements you can modify by configuring settings on the PivotChart properties sheet.

note You can't open the PivotChart properties sheet by pressing F4, which is curious, since that technique works for most properties sheets in Access.

Changing the Appearance of the PivotChart and Its Elements

You can change the appearance of the PivotChart's border and add a decorative background fill by setting options on the Border/Fill tab of the PivotChart properties sheet. For example, Figure 12-29 shows the Daybreak style applied as a gradient fill to the Monthly Sales By Employee PivotChart.

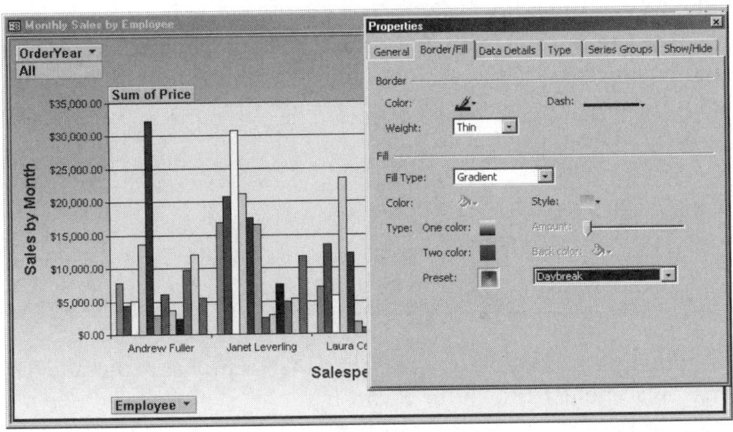

Figure 12-29. The Daybreak gradient fill pattern enhances the appearance of a PivotChart.

> **tip** **Change the border's color and line format**
>
> When you specify a new border style on the Format tab of a PivotChart properties sheet, while the border is selected, it's highlighted with a solid dark blue line. To see the new border with the color and line format you've specified, set the focus on another chart element or close the properties sheet.

The Format tab of the PivotChart properties sheet (available only when a text element—for example, a title—is selected) provides more options for formatting text, such as specifying the font, size, and color for the text. You can also change the caption and the position of the text.

The 3D View tab lets you make minute adjustments to the 3-D properties of the PivotChart. This tab is available only for 3-D chart types (which are found on the Type tab), as you might expect. You can obtain quite dramatic changes in the appearance of a 3-D chart by manipulating the slider controls on this tab.

tip If the properties sheet lacks a 3D View tab, change to a 3-D chart type by clicking the Chart Type button on the PivotChart toolbar.

The General tab includes Undo and Delete buttons, a drop-down list for selecting PivotChart elements, a button for adding titles, and several other buttons for working with multiple charts. Depending on the chart type, other options might be available. For example, if you're working with a pie chart, you can adjust the explosion, angle of first slice, and pie thickness. (If you're not familiar with the terminology on this tab, you can experiment by moving the sliders to change these properties, to see how they change the chart's appearance.)

tip The PivotChart toolbar does include an Undo button, so if you make a change and don't like the results, you can click this button to return to the previous state of the chart. It doesn't undo all actions, but it's very helpful all the same.

The most commonly used option on the General tab is probably the Add Title button, which inserts a placeholder title in the PivotChart.

Figure 12-30 shows the sample pie chart, with an added title and a 50 percent explosion factor.

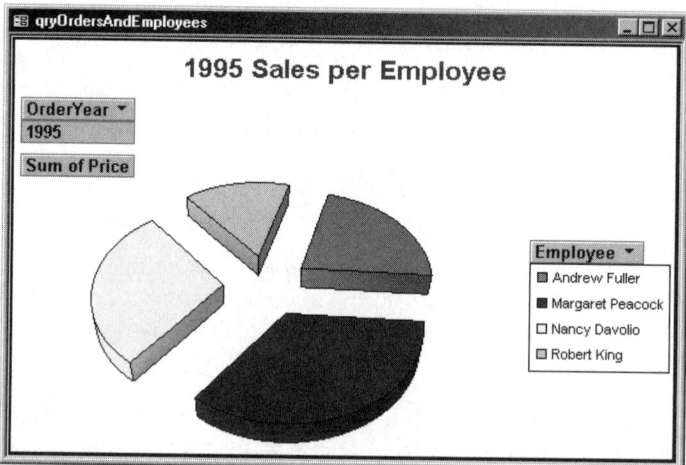

Figure 12-30. You can increase the explosion factor to move the pie slices farther apart.

tip To select an entire chart rather than a chart element, click in the chart background.

Troubleshooting

I see different tabs every time I open the properties sheet

As with some other properties sheets in Access (but perhaps in this case more than most), the tabs you see in the PivotChart properties sheet vary according to what element of the PivotChart is selected, and even the options available on a tab vary according to selection. It can be disconcerting to see the Format tab one time you open the properties sheet and not the next.

For example, if the chart title is selected, you'll see only the General, Format, and Border Fill tabs. If a pie chart is selected, you'll see only the General, Border/Fill, Data Details, Type, 3D View, and Show/Hide tabs, and on the General tab, you'll see Explosion, Angle Of First Slice, and Pie Thickness options. If you want to modify the format of an element such as a chart title, first select the chart title, and then open the properties sheet, and you should see just the tabs you need for working with that chart element.

Changing the Chart Type

You can change the chart type using the Type tab, which provides a list of several chart types. Figure 12-31 shows the sample PivotChart with the SmoothLine choice selected.

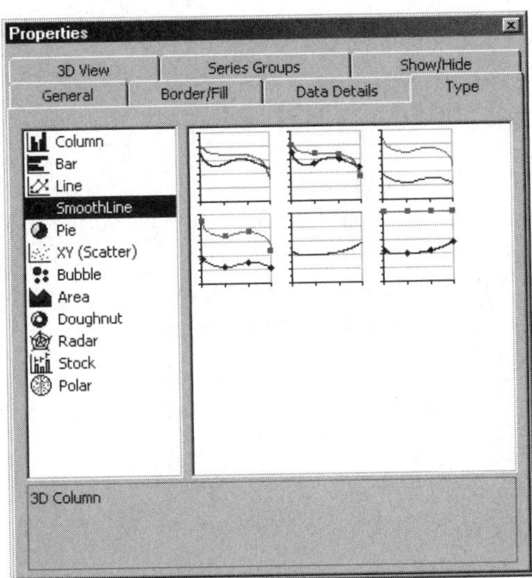

Figure 12-31. You can select a new chart type on the Type tab of the PivotChart properties sheet.

Troubleshooting

My chart doesn't show all my data

Some chart types (in particular, the pie chart and the doughnut chart) are one-dimensional, which means that they use only category data and not series data. If you select one of these chart types and you have both series and category data, one set of data will be ignored.

On the positive side, this means that you don't have to prepare a special data set for these chart types. But if you convert a bar graph to a pie chart, for example, you might find that the pie chart displays the wrong data, perhaps using months rather than salespeople as pie slices. To fix this problem in the new chart, drag the inappropriate category field off the pie chart, press F8 to open the field list, and drag the correct field to the Category Fields drop zone.

Changing How Users Can Interact with a PivotChart

Several tabs of the PivotChart properties sheet let you modify the interactive elements of a PivotChart. The Show/Hide tab lets you turn on or off a number of PivotChart elements. If you don't want users to modify a PivotChart, for example, turn off the appropriate options in the Let Users View area.

It's advisable to turn off ScreenTips and drop zones if the PivotChart will be printed or displayed on a projector screen, because these elements aren't functional in this situation and can be distracting.

Working with Remote Data

If you work with remote data (that is, data outside the current Access database), the Data Details tab lets you set data connection details, if your PivotChart is based on remote data, such as a SQL Server table. (See the online books in Microsoft Developer Network for more infomation about remote data.) The controls on this tab are all disabled for a PivotChart based on a local Access data source.

Pivoting a PivotChart

Unlike the older MS Graph charts, and as you would expect from its name, a PivotChart can be pivoted—that is, you can swap the series and category (vertical and horizontal) data simply by dragging the field buttons to opposite drop zones or by clicking the By Row/By Column button on the PivotChart toolbar.

Sometimes after you select a new chart type, it becomes clear that the series and category fields need to be swapped to make the data easier to understand. For example, after I selected a smooth-line chart type for the sample PivotChart in this chapter, I realized that this chart type needed to display months on the horizontal axis and employees on the vertical axis. I clicked the By Row/By Column button to swap the Employee and OrderMonth field buttons to create a more meaningful smooth-line chart. The result is shown in Figure 12-32.

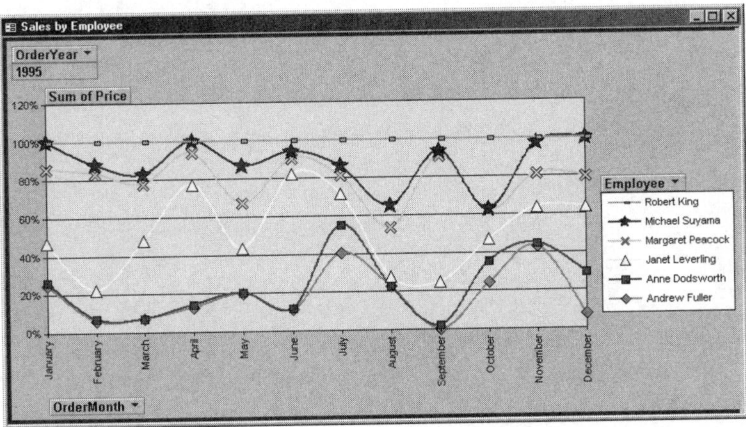

Figure 12-32. After you select a different chart type, you might need to swap the category and series fields to display the data appropriately.

Part 4

Customizing Access

Chapter 13

Customizing Access Toolbars and Menus (Command Bars)

Toolbars and menu bars in some form have been part of Microsoft Access since its earliest versions, but the techniques used to customize them and create new ones have gone through several changes. Early versions of Access used macros to create menus and menu commands. The standard Microsoft Office Customize dialog box and customization through Microsoft Visual Basic for Applications (VBA) code were introduced in Access 97. In Access 2002, you can make certain modifications to menus and toolbars in the user interface, but other command bar modifications can be made only in VBA code.

In this chapter, you'll learn how to customize the built-in Access menus and built-in toolbars using the Customize dialog box, how to create your own custom menus and toolbars, and how to create menus and toolbars in VBA code and add buttons or commands to them, including special toolbar buttons that can only be created in code.

Some Notes on Terminology

Access, like the other Office applications, includes three types of interface objects that offer choices of commands: toolbars with buttons, menu bars with menus offering a list of text selections, and shortcut menus that pop up when you right-click forms or controls. In early versions of Access, menus and toolbars were different types of objects, and menus were created by a special type of macro (menu-macros).

In Access 2002 (and for several earlier versions), however, both menus and toolbars are just two types of command bars. They're created in the interface by using the Customize dialog box or in VBA code by using the *CommandBars* collection and the *CommandBar* object. The very different appearance and functionality of toolbars and menus depends on the properties specified for a command bar and on the types of controls placed on it as buttons or menu commands.

In the Access user interface, the term *toolbar* is often used for both toolbars and menu bars. For example, if you open the properties sheet for the Access menu bar from the Customize dialog box, its title is Toolbar Properties.

The buttons or menu commands you place on command bars can be set to be displayed as images, text, or both. Therefore, you can create menu bars with buttons displaying images, or toolbars with text-only buttons, or even toolbars with menus. The only real difference between toolbars and menu bars in the Access user interface is that menu bars have the Ask A Question box and toolbars don't.

tip **Standardize the user interface**

In the interest of preventing confusion, and to preserve a familiar Office-standard interface for your Access databases, you should stick with using graphics buttons for toolbars, menus for menu bars, and text selections for shortcut menus, with only a few exceptions for special cases.

tip **Add controls to command bars**

You can see special controls such as drop-down lists on built-in Access toolbars. You can add these special controls to command bars only in VBA code; when you drag a command to a command bar in the user interface, it will appear as a standard button or menu command. See the section "Creating Custom Command Bars and Their Controls in Code," page 529, for information about adding special controls to command bars.

Customizing Built-In Access Command Bars

Customizing menus and toolbars in the interface is similar for all Office applications—if you've customized a Microsoft Word or Microsoft Excel toolbar or menu, you're already familiar with the process (although there are slight variations depending on application-specific features). You can use the Customize dialog box to move commands from one menu to another, from one toolbar to another, or even from a menu to a toolbar and vice versa. You can also add new toolbar buttons or menu commands that will execute either built-in commands or macros or functions you have created.

It's easy to rearrange Access menu commands and toolbar buttons to suit your work patterns. Simply place the commands you use most frequently on toolbars, for one-click use.

Follow these steps to make frequently used commands more accessible (thereby saving you a good deal of time as you work in Access databases):

1. Open the Customize dialog box by right-clicking on the gray background of a toolbar and choosing Customize from the shortcut menu.
2. On the toolbar you want to modify, locate the command or button you want to move, and drag it to its new location.

   If you want to move a button or command to a menu, position the button or command over the menu until the menu drops down and then move the command or button to the desired position on the menu. Figure 13-1 shows the Options command being dragged from the bottom of the Tools menu to the Database toolbar, where it becomes a toolbar button that lets you open the Options dialog box with a single click.

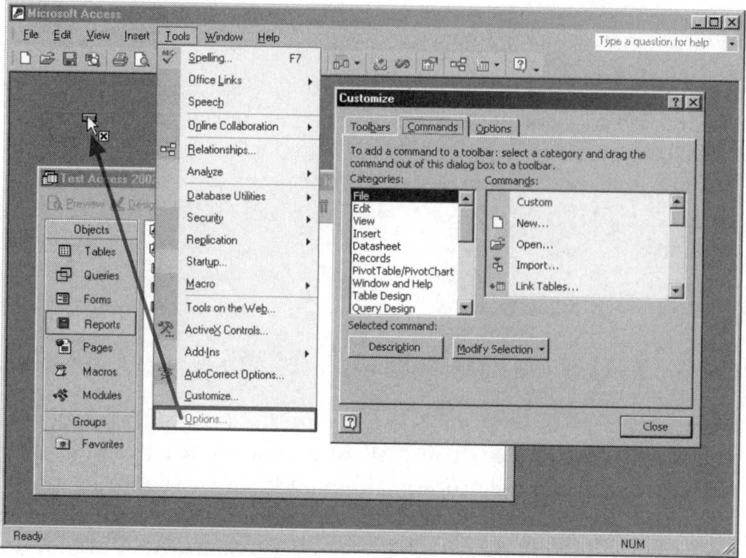

Figure 13-1. Drag the Options command from the bottom of the Tools menu to the Database toolbar so that you can open the Options dialog box with a single click.

> **tip** **Moving and copying buttons and commands**
>
> To move a menu command, an entire menu, or a toolbar button to a new location, drag it from its original location to the new location on another menu or a toolbar. To copy a menu command, an entire menu, or a toolbar button to a new location, press Ctrl and drag the command, menu, or button to its new location.

You can drag the Add-Ins menu to the Database toolbar from its original position on the Tools menu—this change is handy if you use Access add-ins frequently. If you plan to work with COM add-ins, you can drag the COM Add-Ins command (which doesn't appear on any standard menu or toolbar) to a toolbar or menu by selecting it from the Commands list in the Customize dialog box (it's located at the bottom of the Commands list for the Tools category). Figure 13-2 shows the Access Database toolbar with the Options, Add-Ins, and COM Add-Ins buttons added so that you can open these dialog boxes with a single click.

Figure 13-2. This Access Database toolbar has three new commands for opening commonly used dialog boxes.

Placing Custom Commands on Menus and Toolbars

In addition to dragging built-in commands to toolbars and menus, you can add your own functions and macros to toolbars and menus so that you can execute the macros and functions by clicking buttons or selecting menu commands. For example, let's say you've created a macro to run a series of actions needed to import and process data from a mainframe and a function to track down and delete partial records from a table. You can create toolbar buttons to run the macro and the function with a single click.

To create a toolbar button that runs a macro, follow these steps:

1. Open the Customize dialog box by right-clicking the gray background of a toolbar and selecting Customize from the shortcut menu.
2. Click the Commands tab, and then select All Macros in the Categories list.
3. Locate the macro in the Commands list, and drag it to the desired location on the toolbar of your choice, as shown in Figure 13-3.

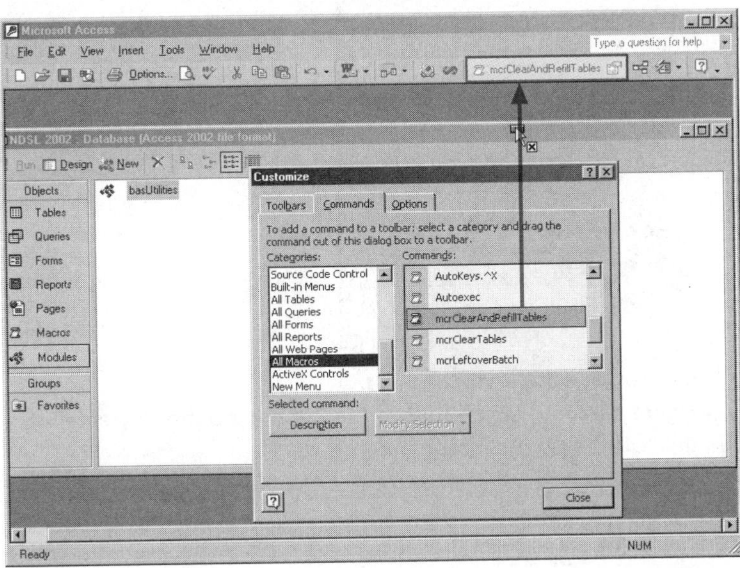

Figure 13-3. Create a toolbar button that runs a macro by dragging the macro to a toolbar.

4. By default, the toolbar button has a small scroll image and the name of the macro. To display an image only, right-click the button to open its shortcut menu, and select Default Style. To give the button a shorter caption, edit the name in the *Name* property shown on the shortcut menu.

The technique for creating a toolbar button to run a function is somewhat more complicated. To place a button that executes a function on a toolbar, follow these steps:

1. Open the Customize dialog box by right-clicking the gray background of a toolbar and selecting Customize from the shortcut menu.
2. Click the Commands tab of the Customize dialog box.
3. Select File in the Categories list.
4. From the Commands list, drag the Custom command to the toolbar, creating a new, blank toolbar button.
5. Right-click the new Custom button, and then select Properties from the shortcut menu to open the control's properties sheet.
6. Type the name of the function in the On Action combo box, preceded by an equal sign, as shown in Figure 13-4.

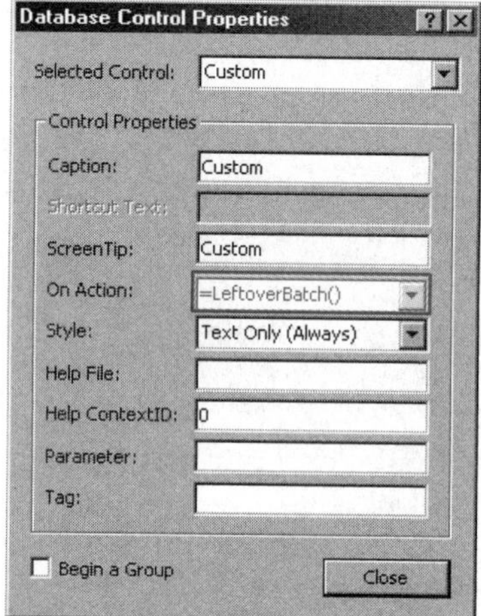

Figure 13-4. Assign a function to a toolbar button by entering its name as the button's *On Action* property.

> **note** The drop-down list for the On Action combo box displays only macros, so you can't use it to select a function.

7. Change the button's name in the Caption text box.
8. Change the text in the ScreenTip box to describe the button's function.
9. Change the button style and any other properties in the properties sheet. (This step is optional.)
10. Click OK to close the properties sheet.

note You can place only functions on toolbar buttons—this technique doesn't work for subroutines.

Figure 13-5 shows two new buttons (one button runs a macro, and the other runs a function) on the Database toolbar, with the ScreenTip for the button that runs the function.

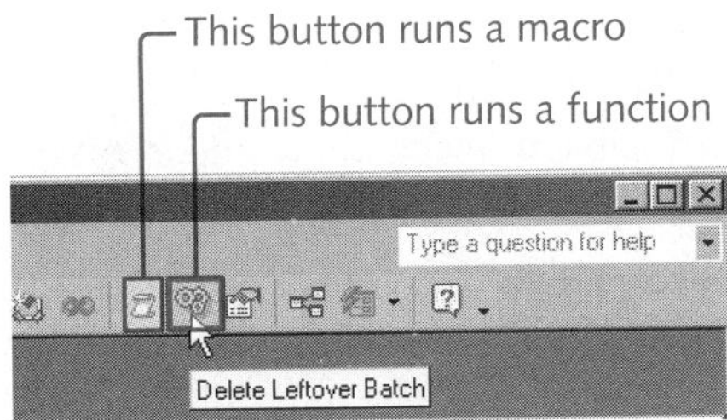

Figure 13-5. One of these toolbar buttons runs a macro; the other runs a function.

Creating Custom Command Bars in the Interface

In addition to moving commands around on built-in toolbars and menus and adding or deleting standard or custom commands, you can create your own custom toolbars, menu bars, and shortcut menus for use in a database. For example, you might have a set of special functions that perform actions related to a form or a set of forms in your database. You can create a custom toolbar with buttons to run these functions, or (if they are specific to a single form) you can place them as commands on a shortcut menu opened by right-clicking the form. A custom toolbar is the way to go if you need to run the custom functions from several different forms. Shortcut menus are preferable for commands specific to an individual form; you can even create a shortcut menu for an individual control on a form.

InsideOut

Although you can create a shortcut menu for a form control, doing so is rarely advisable. Form controls have many events that can be used to trigger procedures (*GotFocus*, *LostFocus*, *BeforeUpdate*, *AfterUpdate*, and others), and in almost all cases, you're better off attaching code to one of these event procedures so that the code will run automatically when the event fires. If you do need to present users with a set of commands that apply to only a single control on a form, you'll have to instruct them to right-click the control to open the shortcut menu, which is much less intuitive than automatically running a procedure when the control is selected (*GotFocus*) or when text in the control is changed (*AfterUpdate*).

Creating Localized and Global Menus and Toolbars

Custom Access toolbars and menus are specific to the database in which they are created. To use a custom toolbar, menu, or shortcut menu in another database, you must import it into that database.

To import toolbars, menus, and shortcut menus into another database, follow these steps:

1. Choose File, Get External Data, Import.
2. Select the database containing the toolbar or menu in the Import dialog box, and click Import.
3. Click the Options button in the Import Objects dialog box, and select the Menus And Toolbars check box, as shown in Figure 13-6. Then click OK.

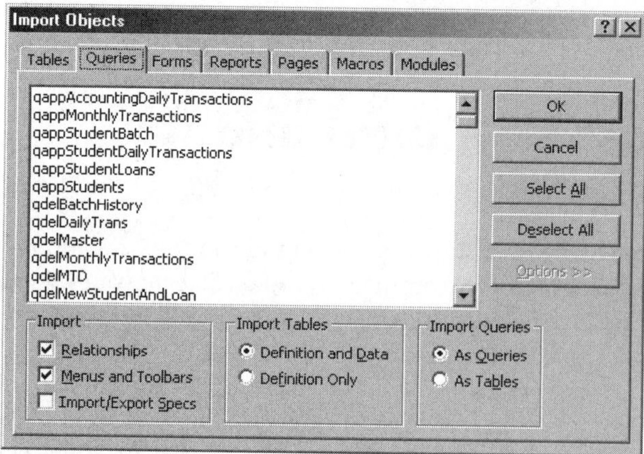

Figure 13-6. You can import your custom toolbars and menus into any other database in which you want to use them.

The custom toolbars and menus you create are local, but Access does provide two global toolbars: the built-in Utility 1 and Utility 2 toolbars. You can customize these toolbars as you want, and they're available to all Access databases in an installation of Access—you don't have to import them into another database.

Troubleshooting

I get a shortcut menu error message when I import a form with an attached shortcut menu

If you import a form with an attached shortcut menu into another database without separately importing the shortcut menu, you'll get an error message (*Microsoft Access can't find the macro "ABC Shortcut Menu")* when you right-click the form. (The word *macro* in this error message must be a holdover from earlier versions of Access, in which menus were created with a special type of macro.)

To fix this problem, import the shortcut menu into the current database. Its name will appear in the *Shortcut Menu* property in the form's properties sheet.

Managing Your Toolbars

Of course, if you keep adding buttons to the built-in toolbars, they'll soon become large and unwieldy. If you don't have a large monitor, tools might drop off the edge of a toolbar, and you'll have to select them from the drop-down list of extra tools on the right (or bottom) of the toolbar. To prevent this inconvenience, and to organize your custom tools into logical groups, you can create custom toolbars or menus.

To create a new toolbar, follow these steps:

1. Open the Customize dialog box by right-clicking the gray background of a toolbar and selecting Customize from the shortcut menu.
2. Click the Toolbars tab, and then click New.
3. Give the new toolbar a name, as shown in Figure 13-7, and click OK to close the New Toolbar dialog box.

Figure 13-7. Give your custom toolbar a name that's logical and easy to remember.

When you click OK, the new toolbar appears. The toolbar is easy to miss. Initially, it's just a small square that might be located outside the Access window, and its title bar is too small to display the full title. A newly created toolbar is shown in Figure 13-8.

Figure 13-8. This newly created Access toolbar isn't too noticeable.

4 To add a button to the toolbar, click the Commands tab of the Customize dialog box, shown in Figure 13-9.

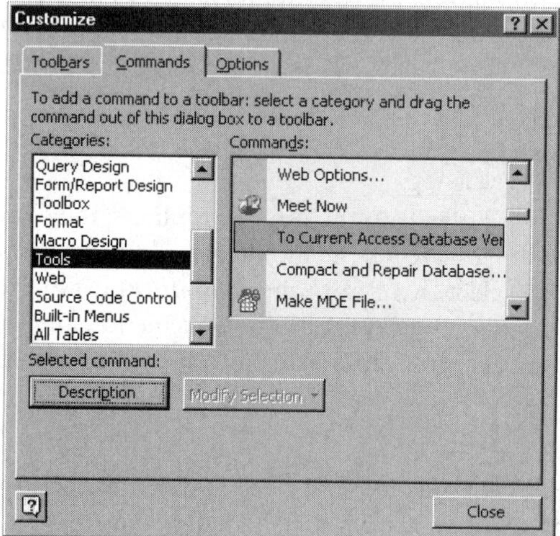

Figure 13-9. Add buttons to your custom toolbars on the Commands tab of the Customize dialog box.

If you're not sure what a command does, select the command, and click the Description button to display a pop-up description, as shown in Figure 13-10.

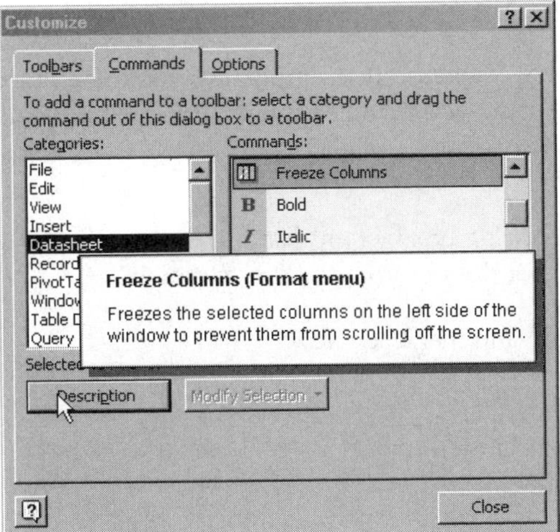

Figure 13-10. Select a command, and click Description to see its pop-up description.

5 Select a category for commands, and then drag the command you want to use from the Commands list to the toolbar. Figure 13-11 shows a formatting command being added to the newly created toolbar. Close the Customize dialog box when you've finished adding commands.

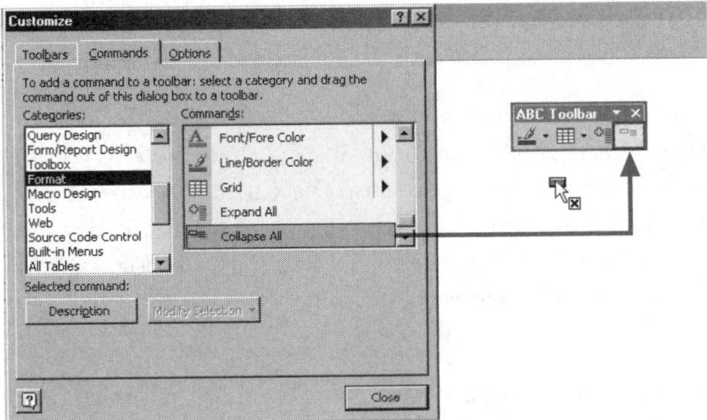

Figure 13-11. Drag a command to a new toolbar.

The default style for toolbar buttons is to display an image only, which is generally desirable. However, if you want a button to display text, or text and an image, right-click the button to open its properties sheet, and select a different style or change the button's caption as described earlier in the section "Placing Custom Commands on Menus and Toolbars."

Creating Custom Menu Bars

By default, Access has one menu bar, called simply the Menu Bar. However, you can create your own menu bars and add menus to them, as described in this section.

To create your own menu bar, follow these steps:

1. Open the Customize dialog box by right-clicking the gray background of a toolbar and selecting Customize from the shortcut menu.
2. Click the Toolbars tab, and then click New.
3. Give the new toolbar a name, and then click OK in the New Toolbar dialog box.
4. Select the new toolbar in the Toolbars list, and click the Properties button to open its properties sheet.

InsideOut

In Access 2002, the built-in menu bar has a default Ask A Question drop-down list. If you create a custom menu, the Ask A Question drop-down list is moved to the custom menu, which is particularly noticeable when the menu is undocked. The Ask A Question drop-down list now appears on the floating menu, and not on the built-in menu, which is probably not what you wanted. If you create more custom menus, the Ask A Question drop-down list remains on the first custom menu. Unlike other menu commands, you can't drag the Ask A Question drop-down list to another menu.

You can remove the Ask A Question drop-down list by right-clicking the list and clearing the Show Ask A Question check box on the shortcut menu. (The Ask A Question drop-down list will disappear when you close the Customize dialog box.) However, this turns off the Ask A Question drop-down list completely. To turn on the Ask A Question drop-down list again, open the Customize dialog box, right-click the list, and select the Show Ask A Question check box on the shortcut menu.

If you have a custom menu docked on the right or left side of the Access window, you won't see the Ask A Question drop-down list when the Customize dialog box is open. To turn this list on or off, first undock the menu so that the list appears.

5. Select Menu Bar from the Type drop-down list. This is the point at which the toolbar becomes a menu bar.
6. You can change other properties for the menu bar in the properties sheet. For example, you can prevent the menu bar from being moved or hidden, or show it on the Toolbars menu. When you have set all the properties you need to set, close the properties sheet.
7. Click the Commands tab of the Customize dialog box.
8. To add a menu to the new menu bar, select New Menu from the bottom of the Categories list and then drag New Menu from the Commands list to the new menu bar, as shown in Figure 13-12.

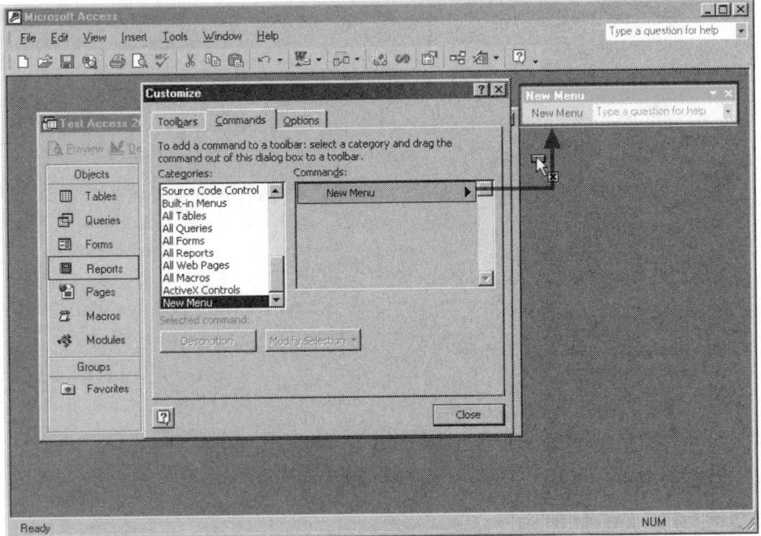

Figure 13-12. Use the New Menu command to add a new menu to a menu bar.

9 Right-click New Menu on the menu bar, and use the shortcut menu to give the new menu a new name, as shown in Figure 13-13.

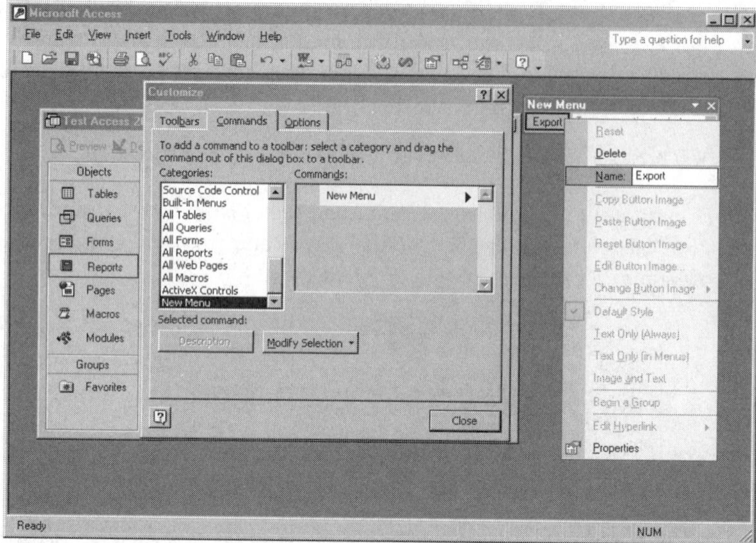

Figure 13-13. Rename a new menu using the shortcut menu.

Now you can add selections to the new menu by dragging commands to it from the Commands list in the Customize dialog box. (The menu will drop down as you drag a command over it.) Figure 13-14 shows a third command being dragged to the Export menu on the ABC Menu menu bar.

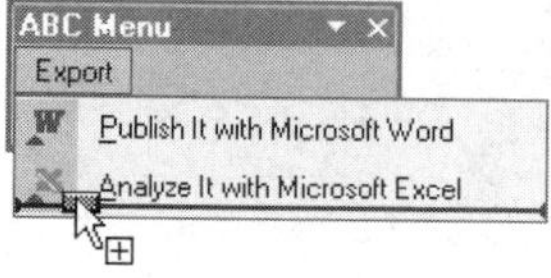

Figure 13-14. Drag a command to a menu on a menu bar.

Set the menu's other properties in its properties sheet, as you would for a toolbar button.

Adding Shortcut Menus

Access also allows you to add shortcut menus to interface objects—primarily forms and form controls—which enables you to create menus that are specific to forms (or reports in print preview) or to individual controls on forms.

To create a shortcut menu, follow these steps:

1. Open the Customize dialog box by right-clicking the gray background of a toolbar and then clicking Customize on the shortcut menu.
2. Click the Toolbars tab, and then click New.
3. Give the new toolbar a name, and then click OK in the New Toolbar dialog box, as shown in Figure 13-15.

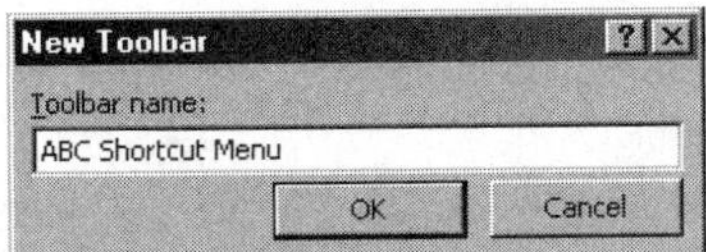

Figure 13-15. Naming a new shortcut menu for a form.

4. Select the new toolbar in the Toolbars list, and then click the Properties button to open its properties sheet.
5. Select Popup from the Type drop-down list.
6. An informative message appears, as shown in Figure 13-16. Click OK to close the message box.

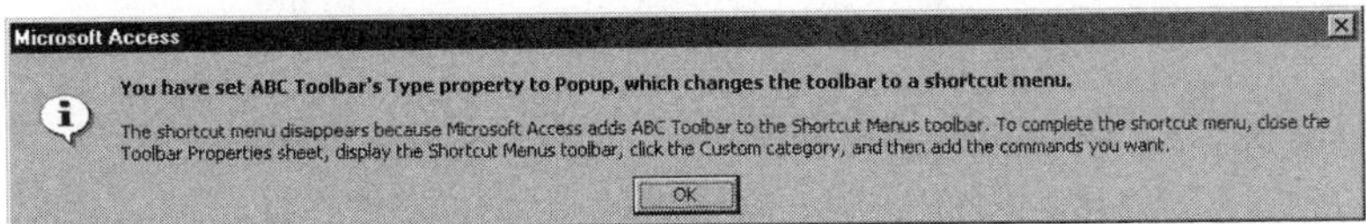

Figure 13-16. A message that includes steps on how to complete your custom shortcut menu appears when you create a shortcut menu.

7. As described in the message box, the next step is to display the menu. To do so, check the check box to the left of Shortcut Menus in the Toolbars list in the Customize dialog box.
8. Click Custom in the Shortcut Menus toolbar that appears. You'll see the new shortcut menu.
9. Drag commands from the Commands tab of the Customize dialog box to the shortcut menu on the Custom menu, as shown in Figure 13-17.

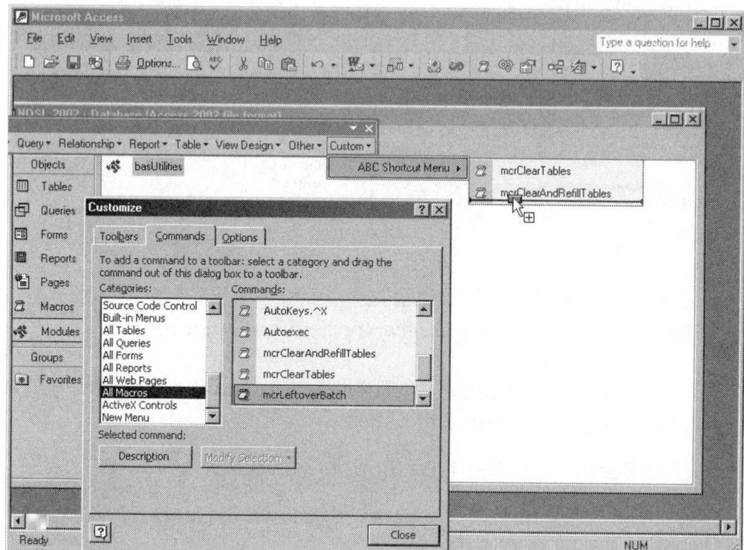

Figure 13-17. Drag a command to a shortcut menu.

> **note** You might have to move the Shortcut Menus toolbar to the left to be able to see enough of your shortcut menu to add commands to it.

Assigning Toolbars, Menus, and Shortcut Menus to Forms and Controls

If a menu bar or toolbar is not assigned to a specific database object, it will be displayed at all times (at least, if it's checked in the Toolbars list in the Customize dialog box). This is desirable if the commands on the toolbar or menu bar can be used from several different forms (or all forms) in the database. Sometimes, however, you might need a toolbar or menu that has commands specific to a particular form, or even a specific control.

An order form, for example, might need a custom toolbar or menu with commands related to checking inventory or current prices for items. In this case, you can create a toolbar or menu and attach it to a form (or rarely, to a report) or to a form control. A form toolbar or menu only appears when the form is open; a report toolbar or menu appears when the report is previewed, and a control shortcut menu appears when the control is right-clicked.

To attach a menu or toolbar to a form or report, follow these steps. (These steps describe attaching a menu or toolbar to a form; the procedure is the same for a report.)

1. Open the form in Design view.
2. Open the form's properties sheet.
3. Click the Other tab in the properties sheet.
4. From the drop-down list for the *Toolbar* (or *Menu Bar*) property, select the toolbar or menu bar you want to attach to the form, as shown in Figure 13-18.

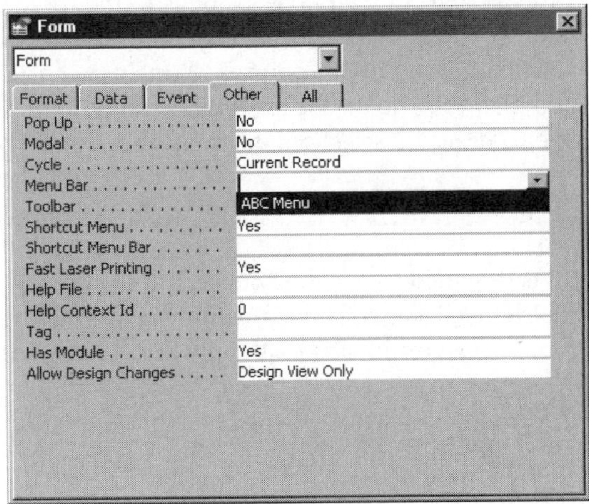

Figure 13-18. Assign a custom menu to a form.

Now the custom menu you selected will be visible in Form view for this form only, as shown in Figure 13-19.

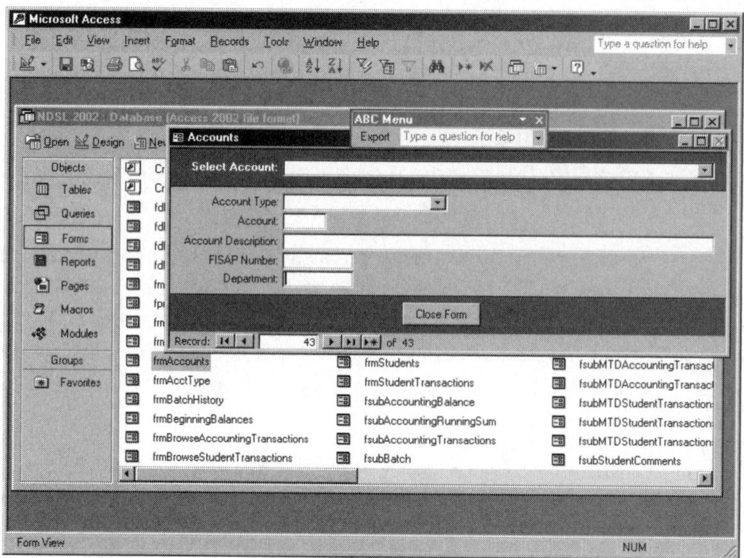

Figure 13-19. This custom form menu is visible in Form view for a specific form.

InsideOut

Although you can attach a toolbar or a menu bar to a form or control, it might not be intuitively apparent that the toolbar (or menu bar) belongs to the form, because a command bar can be either free-floating or docked at one of the edges of the Access window but it can't be docked to the top of a form. A shortcut menu clearly belongs to only one object, however, so you should use shortcut menus rather than toolbars or menu bars when you need to display a selection of commands relevant to only a particular form.

A custom shortcut menu is designed to pop up when a specific object (usually a form or a control on a form) is right-clicked, just like the built-in shortcut menus. Shortcut menus are handy places to assign commands that apply to only a specific form or control, such as checking the current price of an item before finalizing an order or selecting one of a set of filters for form data. Shortcut menus are object-specific, so you must assign your newly created shortcut menu to a database object for it to be useful. As with a menu or toolbar, you assign a shortcut menu to a form by using the *Shortcut Menu Bar* property, shown earlier in Figure 13-18.

To assign a shortcut menu to a specific control on a form, open the properties sheet for the control, and select the shortcut menu from the list in the *Shortcut Menu Bar* property, as shown in Figure 13-20.

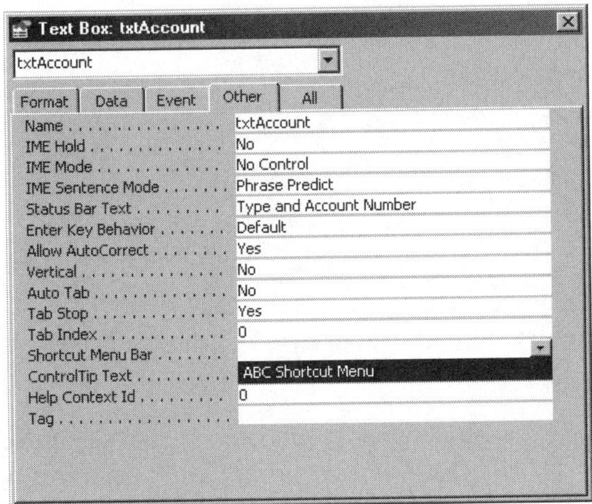

Figure 13-20. Assign a shortcut menu to a control to enhance that control's usefulness.

Now the custom shortcut menu replaces the default shortcut menu for this control when you right-click the control, as shown in Figure 13-21.

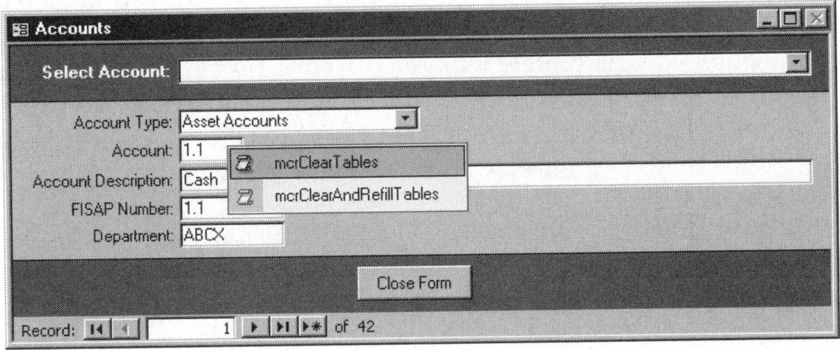

Figure 13-21. The custom shortcut menu for a control replaces the default shortcut menu.

Creating Global Menu Bars and Global Shortcut Menu Bars

You can designate a global menu bar or a global shortcut menu bar in the Startup dialog box. Figure 13-22 shows a database's Startup dialog box, with the ABC Menu designated as the global menu bar and the default selection for the shortcut menu bar.

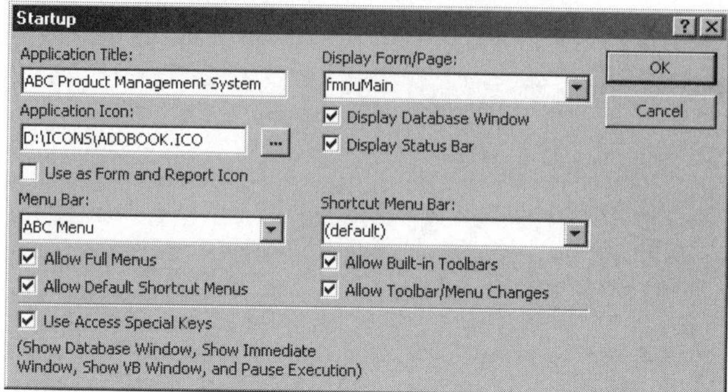

Figure 13-22. Select a custom menu bar for a database in the database's Startup dialog box.

When you're working in code, you can designate a global menu bar or shortcut menu bar by setting the *Menu Bar* or *Shortcut Menu Bar* property of the Access *Application* object to the desired menu bar or shortcut menu.

Working with the Customize Dialog Box

The Customize dialog box is the tool you use when modifying existing toolbars and menus, as well as for creating new ones. In addition to modifying (or creating) entire toolbars or menus, you can modify individual toolbar buttons or menu commands, to get menus and toolbars that work and look as you want. To get started with modifying a toolbar or menu, open the Customize dialog box by right-clicking the background of a menu or toolbar and selecting Customize from the shortcut menu.

The Customize dialog box opens to the Toolbars tab, listing all the toolbars and menus (technically, menu bars) in the current database. Currently active toolbars and menu bars are checked in the Toolbars list. You can check a toolbar to make it active or uncheck a selected toolbar to hide it.

Chapter 13

Troubleshooting

I see too many toolbars

All the Access toolbars and menu bars are shown in the Customize dialog box's Toolbars list, not just the ones that are appropriate for the current view. Unfortunately, this means that you can select completely inappropriate toolbars, such as making the Print Preview toolbar visible in Form Design view.

To see a list of just the toolbars that are appropriate for a specific Access object, use the Toolbars command on the View menu. Figure 13-23 shows the Toolbars list for a report open in Design view.

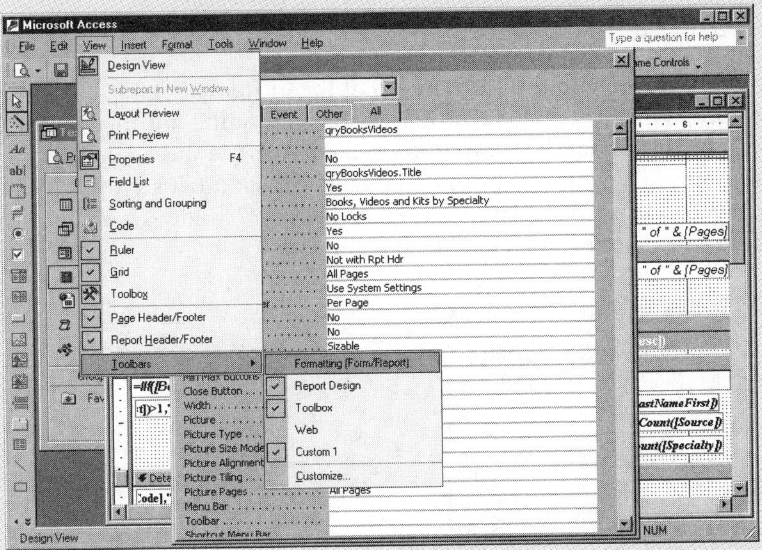

Figure 13-23. These toolbars are appropriate for a report in Design view.

Renaming, Deleting, and Resetting a Toolbar

Use the Rename button on the Toolbars tab of the Customize dialog box to rename a custom toolbar. You can't rename a built-in toolbar; the Rename button is disabled when a built-in toolbar is selected.

Use the Delete button on the Toolbars tab to delete a custom toolbar. You can't delete a built-in toolbar; the Delete button is disabled when a built-in toolbar is selected.

Use the Reset button to reset a built-in toolbar or menu bar to its original settings. You can reset only built-in toolbars; the Reset button is disabled when a custom toolbar is selected.

Changing Toolbar Properties

The Properties button on the Toolbars tab of the Customize dialog box opens the toolbar's properties sheet. This button is enabled for both built-in and custom toolbars and menu bars, but some of the options in the properties sheet aren't available for built-in toolbars. Figure 13-24 shows the built-in Menu Bar's properties sheet. Only the properties related to display, position, and customizability are enabled; you can't change the title or type of this menu bar.

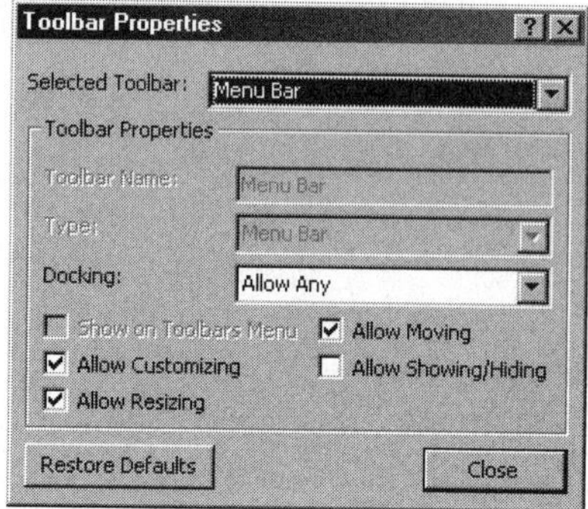

Figure 13-24. The default Access Menu Bar's properties sheet has only a few options enabled.

Figure 13-25 shows the properties sheet for a custom toolbar. All the properties can be changed, including the name and type.

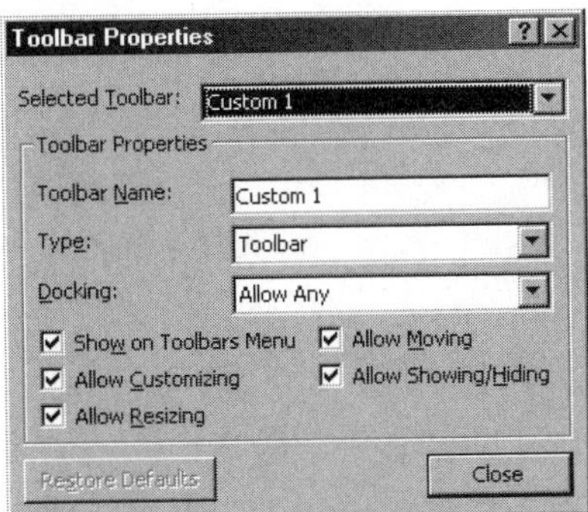

Figure 13-25. The properties sheet of a custom toolbar has more options enabled.

You have three choices in the Type drop-down list, as follows:

newfeature!

- **Menu Bar.** This selection turns the toolbar into a menu bar suitable for displaying drop-down menus. Menu bars also feature the new Ask A Question drop-down list. Menu bars (and their menus) give users more choices than a toolbar with buttons, because each menu offers a list of commands.
- **Toolbar.** This is the default selection—a standard toolbar. Typically, a toolbar contains buttons, each of which executes a single command.
- **Popup.** This selection turns the toolbar into a shortcut menu that pops up when a specific object (such as a form) is right-clicked.

The Docking drop-down list offers the following options for docking the toolbar (fastening it to a side of the Access window as opposed to floating it freely over the window):

- **Allow Any.** The toolbar can be docked to the top, bottom, left, or right of the Access window.
- **Can't Change.** The toolbar can't be moved from its current docked location.
- **No Vertical.** The toolbar can be moved only to another horizontal position (from top to bottom or from bottom to top).
- **No Horizontal.** The toolbar can be moved only to another vertical position (from left to right or from right to left).

The check boxes at the bottom of the Toolbar Properties dialog box allow you to make the following selections:

- **Show On Toolbars Menu.** This selection, which is disabled for built-in toolbars, specifies whether a custom toolbar appears in the list of toolbars on the Toolbars tab of the Customize dialog box or in the list of available toolbars on the Toolbars submenu.
- **Allow Customizing.** If checked, allows you to customize a toolbar by adding or removing buttons.
- **Allow Resizing.** If checked, allows you to resize the toolbar.
- **Allow Moving.** If checked, allows you to move the toolbar.
- **Allow Showing/Hiding.** If checked, allows toggling between showing and hiding the toolbar by checking or unchecking the toolbar in the Toolbars list. If this check box is unchecked, the toolbar's state can't be changed in the Toolbars list.
- **Restore Defaults.** Clicking this button (enabled only for built-in toolbars) restores the toolbar to its default state.

Changing the Appearance and Behavior of Toolbar Buttons

The Modify Selection button on the Commands tab of the Customize dialog box displays a menu of options for altering the appearance or functionality of a toolbar button. (This is the same menu you get by right-clicking the button in Customize mode.) Figure 13-26 shows the menu for a typical toolbar button.

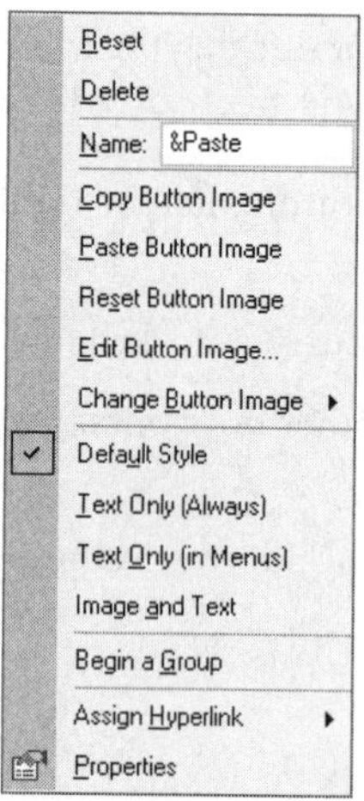

Figure 13-26. This shortcut menu of a toolbar button is shown in Customize mode.

The first group of menu commands includes the Reset command, which restores a button to its original state. However, choosing Reset doesn't restore the original button style if you changed it from the default style to a text style, for example. The Delete command deletes a button from the toolbar.

tip You can delete a button by simply dragging it off the toolbar (with the Customize dialog box open). To restore a deleted button, select the toolbar from which the button was deleted in the Toolbars list, and then click Reset.

The Name command (in a group of its own) lets you change the button's caption. The caption is the text that appears on a text button or the text of a command in a menu.

tip To create a hot key for a command, place an ampersand (&) in front of a letter in the command's name. That letter will be underlined when the command is displayed. Pressing Ctrl and the underlined letter executes the command.

The next section of the submenu has several commands that let you work with the button's image, as follows:

- **Copy Button Image.** Copies the image on the currently selected button to the Clipboard.
- **Paste Button Image.** Pastes a previously copied button image to the currently selected button.
- **Reset Button Image.** Restores the original button image.
- **Edit Button Image.** Opens a Button Editor dialog box, in which you can edit the button's image, as shown in Figure 13-27.

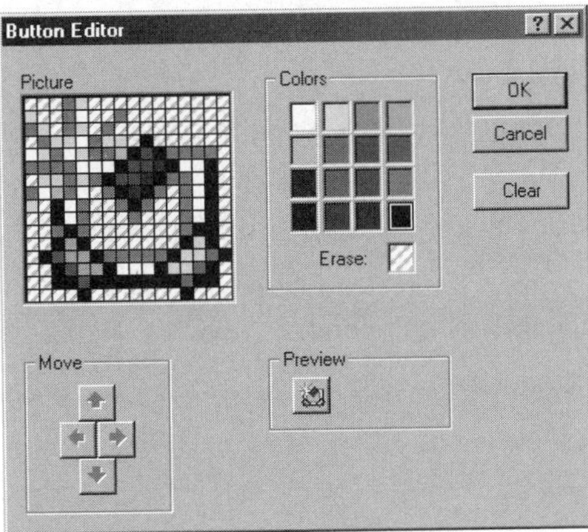

Figure 13-27. Open the Button Editor dialog box to change a button's image.

- **Change Button Image.** Opens a shortcut menu with a limited selection of alternative images you can select for the button, as shown in Figure 13-28.

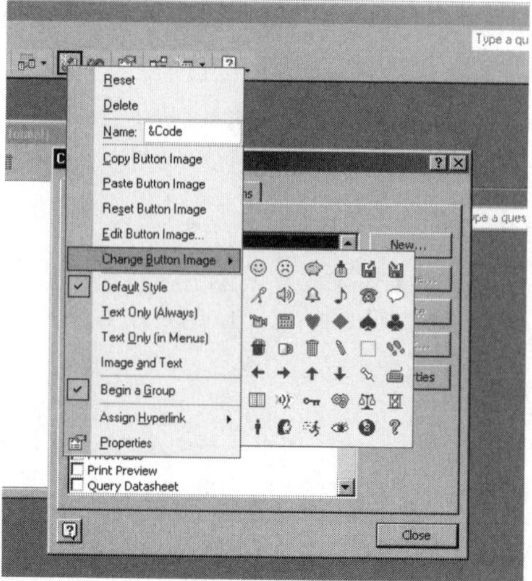

Figure 13-28. Select a new image for a toolbar button.

Copying Button Images from Other Office Applications

You can copy an image from a toolbar button in any Office application and paste it to an Access toolbar button. For example, to copy the E-Mail button image from a button on the Word Standard toolbar to a button on a custom Access toolbar, follow these steps:

1. Open Word and Access, and position their windows so that you can see the toolbars in both applications.
2. In Word, open the Customize dialog box by right-clicking the toolbar background and selecting Customize from the shortcut menu.
3. Open the Customize dialog box in Access in a similar manner.
4. Right-click the E-Mail button on the Word Standard toolbar, and then select Copy Button Image from its shortcut menu, as shown in Figure 13-29.

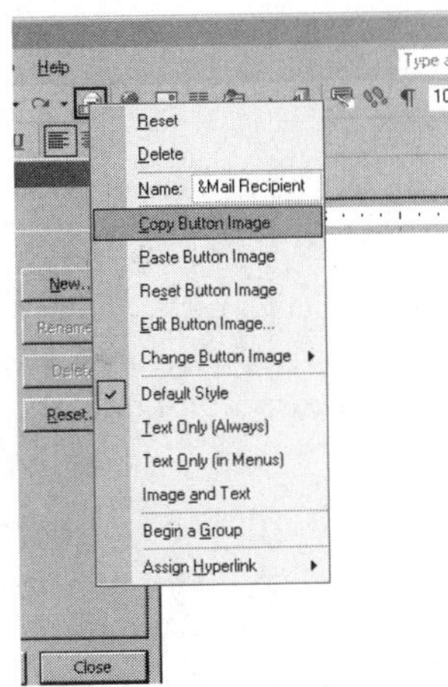

Figure 13-29. Select Copy Button Image from the E-Mail button's shortcut menu to copy a toolbar button's image.

5 In Access, right-click the button whose image you want to replace and then select Paste Button Image from the button's shortcut menu.

The Access button will now have the same image as the Word button, as shown in Figure 13-30.

Figure 13-30. This Access toolbar button has an image pasted from Word.

A much larger palette of button images is available in VBA code. See the section "Creating Custom Command Bars and Their Controls in Code," page 529, for details.

If you want to modify a button's display style, you'll use one of these options:

- **Default Style.** Displays only an image on a toolbar button and an image plus text for a menu command.
- **Text Only (Always).** Makes the button always be displayed as text, both for a menu command and for a toolbar button.
- **Text Only (In Menus).** Makes the button display a text caption for menu commands and an image on toolbar buttons. The Image And Text selection makes the button display a small image and text both on menu commands and on toolbar buttons.
- **Begin A Group (In Its Own Group).** Positions a thin gray divider line on a menu or toolbar to indicate the border of a group of commands. The line is added to the left of the current button on a horizontal toolbar and above the current button on a vertical toolbar.

The Assign Hyperlink submenu contains two commands: Remove Link and Open. Remove Link removes a hyperlink from a button, and Open opens the Assign Hyperlink dialog box, in which you can type in a hyperlink or select one from a list of recently browsed pages, as shown in Figure 13-31. This is an Office-standard dialog box, and some of its selections (such as Create New Document) are not always relevant to Access. In Access, most likely all you'll do is enter (or select) a URL for the hyperlink in the Address box.

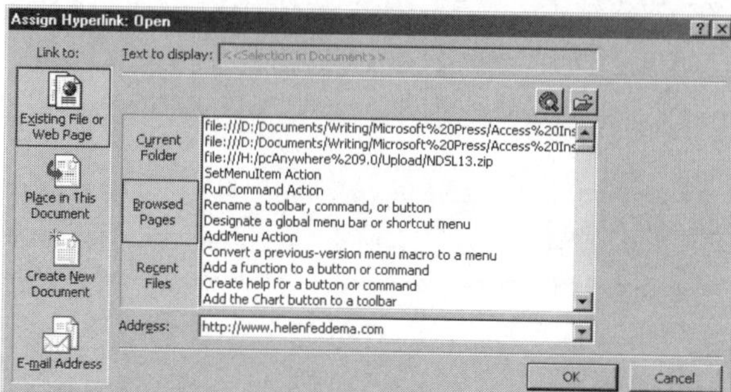

Figure 13-31. You can add a hyperlink to a toolbar button.

The final selection on a toolbar button's menu is Properties, which opens the button's properties sheet, as shown in Figure 13-32.

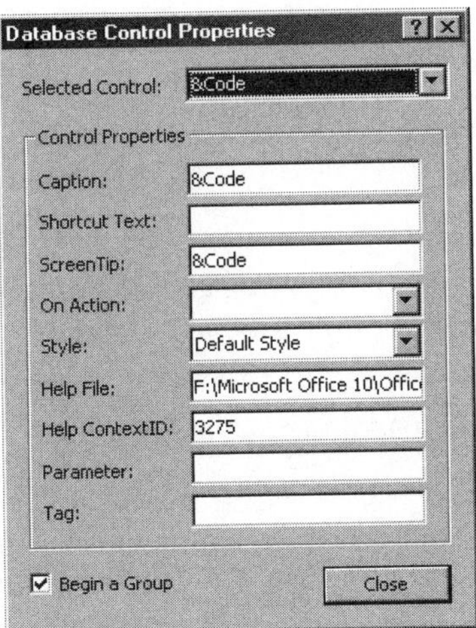

Figure 13-32. You can set advanced properties on the toolbar button's properties sheet.

In this properties sheet, you can set the following advanced properties:

- ***Caption.*** The text displayed on the button itself (if it is a text button) or the text of a menu command. This property corresponds to the Name selection on the button's shortcut menu. You can put an ampersand (&) in front of a letter in the caption to indicate a hot key for the command.
- ***Shortcut Text.*** The text indicating a command's hot key, as displayed next to a menu command.
- ***ScreenTip.*** The text in the floating tip that appears when you position the mouse pointer over the tool. If this property is blank, the caption text is displayed in the ScreenTip.
- ***On Action.*** The macro or VBA function procedure that runs when the button is clicked. For a function, you must use the following syntax:

  ```
  =functionname()
  ```

- ***Style.*** Allows you to choose one of several styles for the button (listed on the button's shortcut menu).

note When you create toolbar and menu bar controls in VBA code, you have several other control type options—including drop-down lists and pop-up buttons—in addition to the CommandBarButton control, which appears as a button on a toolbar or a command on a menu. (When you add a command to a toolbar or menu in the interface, it's always a CommandBarButton control.) See the section "Creating Custom Command Bars and Their Controls in Code," page 529, for more information about these other types of toolbar controls.

- ***Help File.*** Allows you to select a Help file to display when you choose What's This? from the Help menu and click on a toolbar button or menu command.
- ***Help ContextID.*** The context ID of the Help topic specified in the *Help File* property.
- ***Parameter.*** Stores a string that can be used when the command specified in the *On Action* property is run.
- ***Tag.*** Stores an optional string that can be used in an event procedure.

Setting General Toolbar Options

The Options tab of the Customize dialog box (shown in Figure 13-33) allows you to set several properties that relate to all toolbars and menu bars in Office applications.

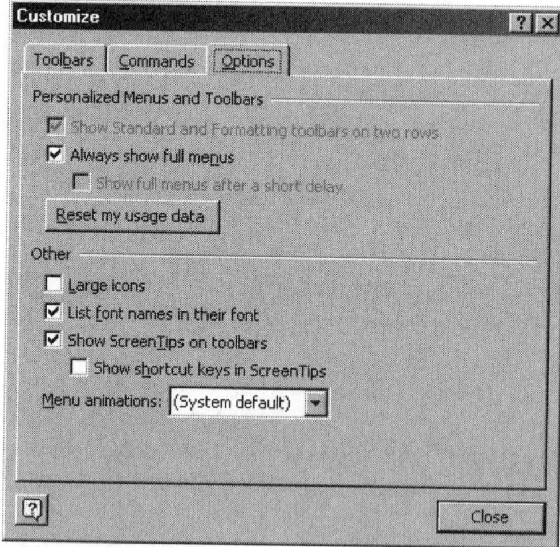

Figure 13-33. You can set general toolbar properties on the Options tab of the Customize dialog box.

caution All the selections on the Options tab of the Customize dialog box affect toolbars in all Office applications, not just in Access.

The Options tab lets you turn off the personalized menus that many users find annoying. The default setting in the Personalized Menus And Toolbars group is for Always Show Full Menus to be cleared, which means that the built-in Access menus will display only the most commonly used commands unless you click the Expand button at the bottom of a menu, as shown in Figure 13-34.

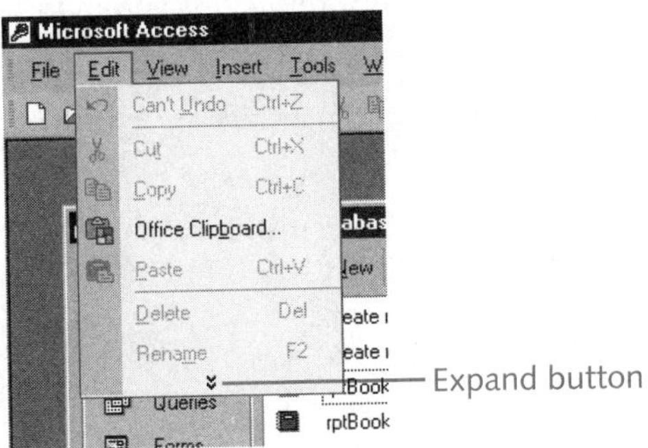

Figure 13-34. You can expand a personalized (contracted) menu by clicking the Expand button.

note If you've turned off personalized menus in Access 2000, you'll notice that the wording of the check box has been switched. In Access 2000, the check box was labeled Menus Show Recently Used Commands First, and you had to clear it to display full menus. In Access 2002, the command is labeled Always Show Full Menus, and you must check it to display full menus, or uncheck it to use personalized menus.

The idea behind personalized menus is that as you work in Office applications, and from time to time expand a menu and select a command, the commands that you use most frequently will remain on your menus, while the commands you rarely or never use will drop off the menus. Access users who like this feature say it makes their menus more compact. Users who dislike it find it annoying to have to expand menus to locate infrequently used commands, or find that they might not be aware of possibly useful commands because they aren't visible on the standard menus.

If you want to see all the menu commands all the time, check the Always Show Full Menus check box. If you don't want to see full menus, uncheck the Show Full Menus check box. This action will enable the Show Full Menus After A Short Delay check box, which offers an intermediate solution: If this secondary check box is checked, menus expand automatically after a short delay. If neither check box is checked, personalized menus don't expand to full menus unless you click the Expand button at the bottom of the menu.

The Reset My Usage Data button clears the personalized menu and toolbar settings so that the default shortened menus are displayed; it doesn't delete any toolbar buttons or change the locations of any toolbar buttons or menu commands you modified by using the Customize dialog box.

tip **Display the commands you want**

You don't have to choose between displaying all the commands on all the menus and toolbars and having a limited selection automatically determined by your usage patterns. You can arrange both menus and toolbars to display exactly the commands you want by using the techniques described in the section "Customizing Built-In Access Command Bars," page 497.

The Other group on the Options tab of the Customize dialog box offers several choices related to toolbar display, as follows:

- **Large Icons.** Makes the toolbar buttons larger.
- **List Font Names In Their Font.** Displays the name of each font in that font in the Fonts drop-down list in Form view and Report Design view, as shown in Figure 13-35.

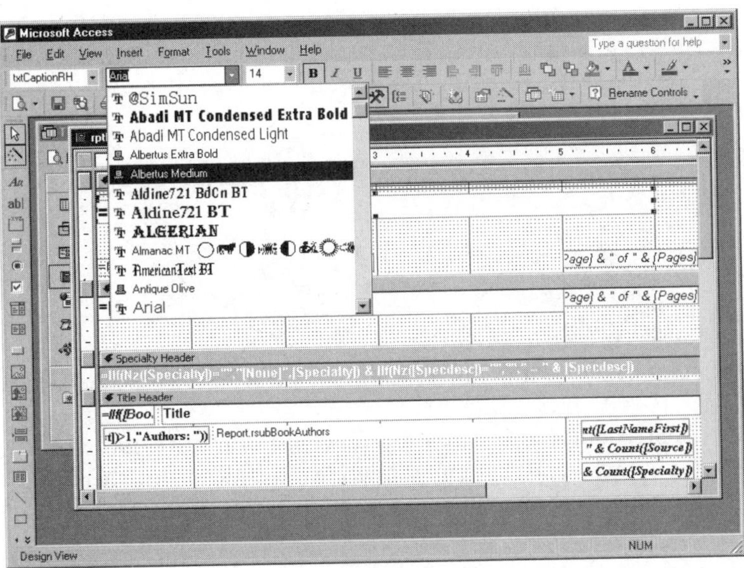

Figure 13-35. In Report Design view, the Fonts list displays the font names in their corresponding fonts.

- **Show ScreenTips On Toolbars.** Enables the floating ScreenTips (also called tool tips or control tips) that appear when you place your mouse pointer over a toolbar button, as shown in Figure 13-36.

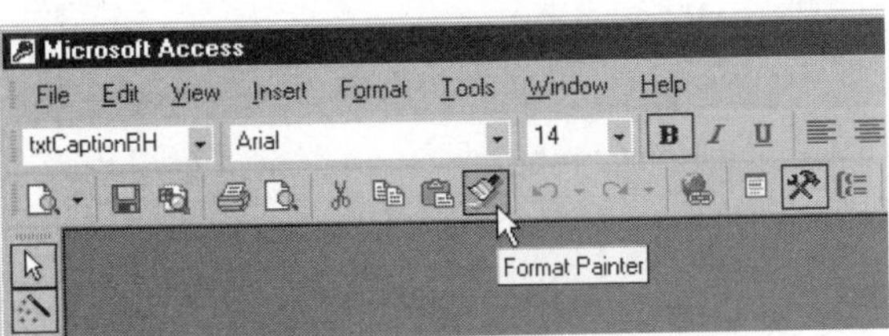

Figure 13-36. This ScreenTip for the Format Painter tool appears when you place your mouse pointer over the corresponding button.

- **Show ScreenTips On Toolbars.** If this check box is checked, the Show Shortcut Keys In ScreenTips check box is enabled. If that secondary check box is also checked, shortcut keys are displayed in ScreenTips, as shown in Figure 13-37.

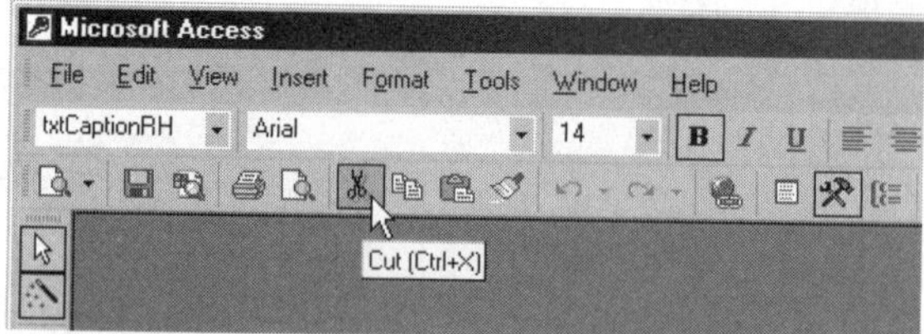

Figure 13-37. The Cut button's ScreenTip includes a shortcut key.

- **Menu Animations.** This drop-down list offers five options, as described in Table 13-1. A fast computer might show little or no difference in menu performance with the different selections; on a slow system, the differences can be quite noticeable.

  If your computer is slow enough to show a noticeable difference between the selections offered in the Menu Animations drop-down list, some of the settings can be quite distracting. In this case, you might want to consider leaving the Menu Animations selection at the default setting.

Table 13-1. Menu animations

Selection	Description
(System default)	Default system setting; generally no animation.
Random	Displays random cycling between different menu styles.
Unfold	Menus unfold from left to right.
Slide	Menus scroll down from top to bottom.
Fade	Menus gradually take form.

The menu animation selections available in VBA code are somewhat different from the selections in the Customize dialog box. You have a choice of None, Random, Unfold, and Slide (the same as the interface selections for Access 2000).

tip **Import toolbars into a database**

When you import objects from another database by choosing File, Get External Data, Import, the Import Objects dialog box doesn't include a Toolbars tab. However, if you click the Options button in this dialog box, a set of extra controls appears on the bottom of the dialog box, including a check box for Menus And Toolbars. If that check box is checked, menus and toolbars will be imported from the selected database into the current database.

Troubleshooting

My toolbar disappeared! (And other toolbar problems)

If some or all of your toolbars have disappeared, open the Customize dialog box and check the ones you want to display. If that doesn't work, make sure that Allow Built-In Toolbars is selected in the database's Startup dialog box. (Choose Tools, Startup to open this dialog box.)

If you can't customize a toolbar, make sure that the Allow Customizing check box in the toolbar's properties sheet is checked. If the Toolbars command on the View menu is dimmed, make sure that the Allow Toolbar/Menu Changes check box is checked in the database's Startup dialog box.

If you can't see all the tools on a docked toolbar, undock it and move it to a row by itself. If you can't see all the buttons on an undocked toolbar, click the More Buttons button at the end of the toolbar to see a list of undisplayed buttons, and perhaps consider splitting the buttons between two toolbars.

If you can't show or hide a toolbar, make sure that the Allow Showing/Hiding check box is checked in the database's Startup dialog box.

Creating Custom Command Bars and Their Controls in Code

The *CommandBars* collection that Access developers use to create custom toolbars and menu bars in VBA is part of the Office object model. Office command bars are used in all the major Office applications. To create a new Access command bar in VBA code, you use the *Add* method of the *CommandBars* collection of the Access *Application* object. To add controls to the new command bar, use the *Add* method of the *Controls* collection of the new toolbar. Both command bars themselves and the controls on them have a great number of properties, but generally you need to set only a few properties to create a useful toolbar or menu bar; the others are fine left at their defaults.

Assigning Images to Toolbar Buttons Using *FaceID*

on the CD

When you create toolbar buttons in VBA code, you assign an image to the toolbar by using the *FaceId* property, which takes a numeric value. You can use any image that has been assigned to any toolbar button in the application (you have several thousand to choose from), but the catch is that you have to know the image's *FaceId* number. Microsoft Office XP Developer 2000 included a function that creates a custom toolbar with all the available images and their numbers. The sample database that included this useful function didn't make it into Office XP Developer, but you can find it on the companion CD, in the modCommandBarCode module of the Test Access 2002 database.

Note that some of the Access databases for this book rely on objects in Microsoft Word 2002. In some cases, the databases use Word to create documents filled with Access data. In other cases, they use the Word System object to get the Documents or Templates path without using the Registry. Because of the references to Word objects, you will need to have Word 2002 installed to use these databases without error.

The function is listed here.

```
Function CBShowButtonFaceIDs(lngIDStart As Long, _
                              lngIDStop As Long)
    ' This procedure creates a toolbar with buttons that
    ' display the images associated with the values starting
    ' at lngIDStart and ending at lngIDStop.

  Dim cbrNewToolbar  As CommandBar
  Dim cmdNewButton  As CommandBarButton
  Dim intCntr     As Integer

    ' If the ShowFaceIds toolbar exists, delete it.
    On Error Resume Next
    Application.CommandBars("ShowFaceIds").Delete

    ' Create a new toolbar.
    Set cbrNewToolbar = Application.CommandBars.Add _
        (Name:="ShowFaceIds", temporary:=True)

    ' Create a new button with an image matching the FaceId
    ' property value indicated by intCntr.
    For intCntr = lngIDStart To lngIDStop
        Set cmdNewButton = _
            cbrNewToolbar.Controls.Add(Type:=msoControlButton)
```

```
        With cmdNewButton
            ' Setting the FaceId property value specifies the
            ' appearance but not the functionality of the button.
            .FaceId = intCntr
            .TooltipText = "FaceId = " & intCntr
        End With
    Next intCntr
    ' Show the images on the toolbar.
    With cbrNewToolbar
        .Width = 600
        .Left = 100
        .Top = 200
        .Visible = True
    End With
End Function
```

When run with the arguments *1, 500*, this function produces the toolbar shown in Figure 13-38. (Be careful not to dock this toolbar. Only a few of its images are visible when the toolbar is docked.)

Figure 13-38. This toolbar displays the specified range of the available button images.

To determine an image's *FaceId* number, hover the mouse pointer over the image on the toolbar; the number will appear in a ScreenTip.

If you aren't familiar with writing VBA code, you might want to read Chapter 20, "Customizing Your Database Using VBA Code," and then return to this section.

The Add method of the *CommandBars* collection of the Application object has the following syntax:

```
Application.CommandBars.Add(Name, Position, MenuBar, Temporary)
```

Table 13-2 lists the *Add* method's parameters.

Table 13-2. The parameters of the *CommandBars* collection's *Add* method

Parameter	Description
Name	(Optional) The name of the new command bar. If this parameter is omitted, the command bar will have a default name of Custom 1 (or some other number).
Position	(Optional) The command bar's position. Set this parameter with one of the msoBarPosition constants listed in Table 13-3.
MenuBar	If *True*, the Access menu bar is replaced by the new command bar. (*False* is the default value.)
Temporary	Set to *True* to make the new command bar temporary (meaning that it will be deleted when Access is closed), Set to False (the default setting) to make the new command bar permanent.

Table 13-3 lists the *Position* parameter's constants.

Table 13-3. The named constants used to set the *Position* parameter of the *Add* method

Named constant	Description
msoBarBottom	The new command bar is positioned at the bottom of the Access window.
msoBarFloating	The new command bar is a floating toolbar.
msoBarLeft	The new command bar is positioned at the left of the Access window.
msoBarMenuBar	The new command bar is a menu bar.
msoBarPopup	The new command bar is a shortcut menu.
msoBarRight	The new command bar is positioned at the right of the Access window.
msoBarTop	The new command bar is positioned at the top of the Access window.

Adding Controls to Command Bars

Because a toolbar without controls isn't very useful, the next step is to add one or more controls to the new toolbar or menu bar. You can use VBA code to add three types of controls to a command bar: CommandBarButton, CommandBarComboBox, and CommandBarPopup. (Only a CommandBarButton control can be added to a command bar in the interface.)

A CommandBarButton control executes a single command. Typically, it's represented as a button on a toolbar or a text command on a menu. The CommandBarComboBox control is a drop-down list of selections, with or without a box in which text can be entered. Built-in Access toolbars contain several such controls, such as the Object, Font, and Size drop-down lists on the Form/Report Formatting toolbar, shown in Figure 13-39.

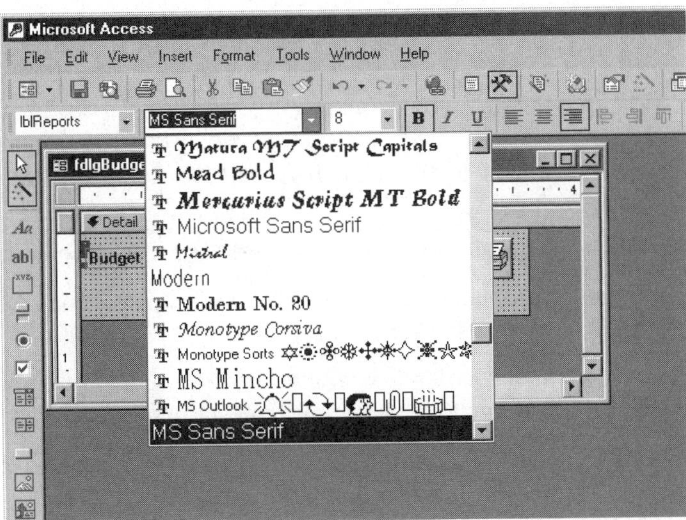

Figure 13-39. A built-in Access toolbar has a CommandBarComboBox control.

The third type of control, the CommandBarPopup control, isn't found on any built-in Access toolbar, but the View selector on the Microsoft Outlook 2000 toolbar is a CommandBarPopup control. This control is a shortcut menu. It combines the features of a command button and a drop-down list but is easier to use because you don't have to click on a tiny drop-down button, as with a combo box control.

To use a pop-up control, click the button on the toolbar, move the mouse pointer down to the command you want to run, and release the mouse button. If you move your mouse pointer away from the list without making a selection, the list closes on its own. This behavior is pleasantly different from the behavior of a drop-down list in an Access combo box, which requires that you either make a selection from the list or press Esc to collapse the list.

Each type of command bar control has several options controlling its appearance and functionality. Some of these options can be set only from VBA code. For the CommandBarComboBox and CommandBarPopup controls, you need to set the list items (or menu selections) in code, as opposed to the simpler CommandBarButton control, which executes a single command.

The syntax for the *Add* method of the *Controls* collection of a command bar is shown here:

```
cbr.Controls.Add(Type, Id, Parameter, Before. Temporary)
```

Table 13-4 describes the *Add* method's parameters.

Table 13-4. The parameters of the *Controls* collection's *Add* method

Parameter	Description
Cbr	A variable representing a specific CommandBar control.
Type	The type of control to add to the command bar; one of the constants in Table 13-5.
Id	(Optional) An integer that specifies a built-in control. If set to 1 or omitted, a blank custom control of the specified type will be added to the command bar.
Parameter	(Optional) For custom controls, can be used to send information to VBA procedures, similar to the Tag property.
Before	(Optional) A number that indicates the control's position on the command bar. If omitted, the control is added at the end.
Temporary	(Optional) True if the control is temporary and will be deleted when Access is closed; False (the default value) if the control is permanent.

Table 13-5 describes the command bar control type constants.

Table 13-5. Command bar control type constants

Constant	Description
msoControlButton	Button
msoControlComboBox	Combo box
msoControlDropdown	Drop-down list
msoControlEdit	Text box
msoControlPopup	Pop-up menu

CommandBarComboBox Variations

Although the *Type* parameter has five selections, only three types of command bar buttons are available in Access: *msoControlComboBox*, *msoControlDropdown*, and *msoControlEdit*. All three selections create CommandBarComboBox controls, with variations in appearance and functionality, as follows:

- A CommandBarComboBox created by using the *msoControlComboBox Type* setting is a control with a drop-down list and a box in which text can be entered.
- A CommandBarComboBox created by using the *msoControlDropdown Type* setting is a control with a drop-down list only.
- A CommandBarComboBox created by using the *msoControlEdit Type* setting is a text box only.

The following code sample creates a custom toolbar with five controls, one for each available type. You add items to the lists of the combo box and drop-down controls by using the *AddItem* method. For the pop-up control, which is itself a type of menu, you must add separate button controls representing the commands on the menu's list.

You'll find this and the following procedures in this chapter in the basCommandBars.bas module of the Test Access 2002 database on the companion CD.

```
Sub CreateTestBar()

    Dim cbrTest As Office.CommandBar
    Dim btnButton As Office.CommandBarButton
    Dim btnComboBox As Office.CommandBarComboBox
    Dim btnDropDown As Office.CommandBarComboBox
    Dim btnTextBox As Office.CommandBarComboBox
    Dim btnPopUp As Office.CommandBarPopup
    Dim btn1 As Office.CommandBarButton
    Dim btn2 As Office.CommandBarButton
    Dim btn3 As Office.CommandBarButton
    Dim btn4 As Office.CommandBarButton

    Set cbrTest = Application.CommandBars.Add(Name:= _
        "Test Toolbar", Position:=msoBarFloating, _
        temporary:=False)
    cbrTest.Enabled = True
    cbrTest.Visible = True

    'Creates a button that beeps when clicked
    Set btnButton = cbrTest.Controls.Add(Type:=msoControlButton)

    With btnButton
        .Style = msoButtonIcon
        .FaceId = 68
        .Caption = "Beep"
        .Style = msoButtonIconAndCaption
        .Tag = "Test Button"
        .OnAction = "mcrBeep"
    End With

    'Creates a combo box in which a beverage can be selected
    ' and saved to a table
    Set btnComboBox = cbrTest.Controls.Add(msoControlComboBox)
```

```
With btnComboBox
    .AddItem "Coffee", 1
    .AddItem "Tea", 2
    .AddItem "Water", 3
    .AddItem "Milk", 4
    .AddItem "Orange Juice", 5
    .Caption = "Select Beverage"
    .Tag = "Test Combo Box"
    .OnAction = "SaveBeverage"
    .Style = msoComboLabel
    .DropDownLines = 8
    .DropDownWidth = 75
End With

'Creates a drop-down list in which an animal can be selected
' and saved to a table
Set btnDropDown = cbrTest.Controls.Add( _
    Type:=msoControlDropdown)

With btnDropDown
    .AddItem "Dog", 1
    .AddItem "Cat", 2
    .AddItem "Parrot", 3
    .AddItem "Kangaroo", 4
    .AddItem "Wildebeest", 5
    .DropDownLines = 8
    .DropDownWidth = 75
    .Style = msoComboLabel
    .Caption = "Select Animal"
    .Tag = "Test Drop-down"
    .OnAction = "SaveAnimal"
End With

'Creates a text box in which a promo can be entered; it is
' picked up when a meeting date is selected in the pop-up
' control.
Set btnTextBox = cbrTest.Controls.Add(Type:=msoControlEdit)

With btnTextBox
    .Caption = "Special Promo"
    .Style = msoComboLabel
    .Text = "10% Off"
End With
```

(continued)

```
    'Creates a pop-up menu for selecting a meeting date; the
    ' meeting date and the promo entered in the text box control
    ' are saved in a table.
    Set btnPopUp = cbrTest.Controls.Add(Type:=msoControlPopup)

    With btnPopUp
        .Caption = "Move Meeting Date"
        .Tag = "Test PopUp"

        Set btn1 = .Controls.Add(Type:=msoControlButton)
        With btn1
            .Caption = "Today"
            .OnAction = "MoveToToday"
            .Style = msoButtonCaption
        End With

        Set btn2 = .Controls.Add(Type:=msoControlButton)
        With btn2
            .Caption = "Tomorrow"
            .OnAction = "MoveToTomorrow"
            .Style = msoButtonCaption
        End With

        Set btn3 = .Controls.Add(Type:=msoControlButton)
        With btn3
            .Caption = "Day after Tomorrow"
            .OnAction = "MoveToDayAfterTomorrow"
            .Style = msoButtonCaption
         End With

         Set btn4 = .Controls.Add(Type:=msoControlButton)
         With btn4
            .Caption = "Next Monday"
            .OnAction = "MoveToNextMonday"
            .Style = msoButtonCaption
        End With

    End With

    cbrTest.Visible = True

End Sub
```

Figure 13-40 shows the toolbar created by this code.

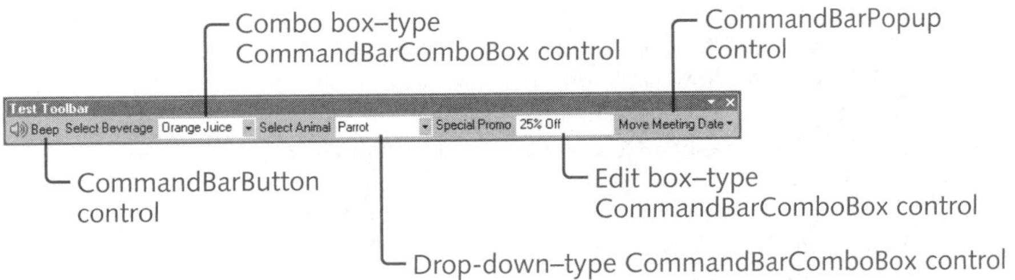

Figure 13-40. This toolbar, created from VBA code, contains several different types of controls.

When a selection is made from the pop-up control, one of several functions runs, writing data to a table (tblInfo) that can be used as a source of lookup information in the database. These functions are listed here:

```
Function MoveToToday()

    Dim strPromo As String
    Dim dbs As DAO.Database
    Dim rst As DAO.Recordset
    Dim cbr As Office.CommandBar
    Dim cbo As Office.CommandBarComboBox

    Set cbr = Application.CommandBars("Test Toolbar")
    Set cbo = cbr.Controls("Special Promo")
    Set dbs = CurrentDb
    Set rst = dbs.OpenRecordset("tblInfo")
    With rst
        .MoveFirst
        .Edit
        ![Promo] = Nz(cbo.Text, "10% Off")
        ![MeetingDate] = Date
        .Update
        .Close
    End With

End Function
```

(continued)

```
Function MoveToTomorrow()

    Dim strPromo As String
    Dim dbs As DAO.Database
    Dim rst As DAO.Recordset
    Dim cbr As Office.CommandBar
    Dim cbo As Office.CommandBarComboBox

    Set cbr = Application.CommandBars("Test Toolbar")
    Set cbo = cbr.Controls("Special Promo")
    Set dbs = CurrentDb
    Set rst = dbs.OpenRecordset("tblInfo")
    With rst
        .MoveFirst
        .Edit
        ![Promo] = Nz(cbo.Text, "10% Off")
        ![MeetingDate] = Date + 1
        .Update
        .Close
    End With

End Function

Function MoveToDayAfterTomorrow()

    Dim strPromo As String
    Dim dbs As DAO.Database
    Dim rst As DAO.Recordset
    Dim cbr As Office.CommandBar
    Dim cbo As Office.CommandBarComboBox

    Set cbr = Application.CommandBars("Test Toolbar")
    Set cbo = cbr.Controls("Special Promo")
    Set dbs = CurrentDb
    Set rst = dbs.OpenRecordset("tblInfo")
    With rst
        .MoveFirst
        .Edit
        ![Promo] = Nz(cbo.Text, "10% Off")
        ![MeetingDate] = Date + 2
        .Update
        .Close
    End With

End Function
```

```
Function MoveToNextMonday()

    Dim strPromo As String
    Dim dbs As DAO.Database
    Dim rst As DAO.Recordset
    Dim dteTest As Date
    Dim cbr As Office.CommandBar
    Dim cbo As Office.CommandBarComboBox

    Set cbr = Application.CommandBars("Test Toolbar")
    Set cbo = cbr.Controls("Special Promo")

    dteTest = Date + 1
    Do While Weekday(dteTest) <> vbMonday
        dteTest = dteTest + 1
        Debug.Print "Testing " & dteTest
    Loop

    Set dbs = CurrentDb
    Set rst = dbs.OpenRecordset("tblInfo")
    With rst
        .MoveFirst
        .Edit
        ![Promo] = Nz(cbo.Text, "10% Off")
        ![MeetingDate] = dteTest
        .Update
        .Close
    End With

End Function
```

InsideOut

For CommandButtonComboBox controls, you have an alternative method of responding to the user's selection (or information entry): You can use the control's *Change* event to execute the procedure specified in the control's *On Action* property. The online help says that to use this technique you must set up a variable for the CommandButtonComboBox control by using the WithEvents keyword in a class module. However, I've found that this is not so (at least in Access). The *OnAction* function fires when a new item is selected in the list, without the need to set up an event handler for the control.

The following functions are run from the *On Action* properties of the combo box control and drop-down list control on the test toolbar:

```
Public Function SaveBeverage()

    Dim strPromo As String
    Dim dbs As DAO.Database
    Dim rst As DAO.Recordset
    Dim cbr As Office.CommandBar
    Dim cbo As Office.CommandBarComboBox

    Set cbr = Application.CommandBars("Test Toolbar")
    Set cbo = cbr.Controls("Select Beverage")
    Set dbs = CurrentDb
    Set rst = dbs.OpenRecordset("tblInfo")
    With rst
        .MoveFirst
        .Edit
        ![Beverage] = Nz(cbo.Text)
        ![MeetingDate] = Date
        .Update
        .Close
    End With

End Function
```

Troubleshooting

My combo box drop-down list doesn't appear in the right place

When you select a toolbar combo box control's drop-down list, the list appears under the caption, not under the box at the top of the list, as shown in Figure 13-41. This is the opposite of the way combo boxes work on Access forms, and if you use combo boxes on both forms and toolbars, this discrepancy will be disconcerting to users. Avoid this problem by using pop-up controls (instead of combo box controls) on toolbars.

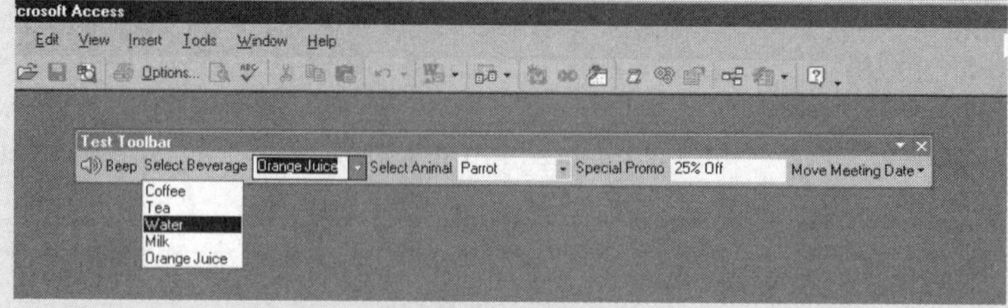

Figure 13-41. This CommandBarComboBox control is shown with its list selected.

```
Public Function SaveAnimal()

    Dim strPromo As String
    Dim dbs As DAO.Database
    Dim rst As DAO.Recordset
    Dim cbr As Office.CommandBar
    Dim cbo As Office.CommandBarComboBox

    Set cbr = Application.CommandBars("Test Toolbar")
    Set cbo = cbr.Controls("Select Animal")
    Set dbs = CurrentDb
    Set rst = dbs.OpenRecordset("tblInfo")
    With rst
        .MoveFirst
        .Edit
        ![Animal] = cbo.Text
        ![MeetingDate] = Date
        .Update
        .Close
    End With

End Function
```

Figure 13-42 shows tblInfo, with information written to its fields from the test toolbar's controls.

Figure 13-42. This Access table is filled with information from selections made in custom toolbar controls.

Chapter 14

Using Macros

Microsoft Access macros offer you a user-friendly way to automate database actions, with a simple Macro Designer interface that lets you select macro actions from a drop-down list. Although macros don't have all the power or functionality of VBA code (see Chapter 20, "Customizing Your Database Using VBA Code," for information about writing code), they're easy to use, and you can get started with database automation using macros if you're not yet ready to learn VBA programming. In addition, macros have some special uses of their own, such as creating custom hot keys or running functions when a database is started—something you can't set in the Startup dialog box.

This chapter shows you how to write simple macros to automate database tasks and gives examples of some special-purpose macros. We won't go into writing complex macros in any detail, because VBA code is more suitable for complex database automation, where you need error handling or logical structures to deal with a variety of conditions. (Macros can handle only very simple conditions, and they don't support error handling.)

Access Macros—Then and Now

In the earliest versions of Access (before Access 2.0), there was no code behind forms. All code had to be written as user-defined functions in standard modules and called from event procedures, usually from the *OnPush* event of command buttons. (The *OnPush* event was replaced by the *OnClick* event in later versions of Access.) But users who didn't want to tackle Access Basic (the dialect of Microsoft Visual Basic used in Access versions earlier than Access 95) had another way to automate Access applications: They could write macros by using the Macro Designer interface and selecting actions from drop-down lists. For beginning to intermediate Access users who weren't yet ready to write code, macros were a useful tool, enabling them to create fairly complex applications without programming.

In Access 2002 (and even in earlier Access versions), however, macros are somewhat of an anachronism. Although Access databases still have macros (with an interface that hasn't changed since Access 1.0), the macros aren't as useful as they once were (with a few exceptions, noted below), for the following reasons:

- In earlier versions of Access, there were some things you could do with macros but not with code (Access Basic or Visual Basic for Applications [VBA]). For example, you could create menus and toolbars only by using macros. Now, however, you can automate every aspect of an Access database with VBA code, and you can do things in VBA code that you can't do with macros. (See "Replacing Macros with VBA Code," page 561, for details.) For example, you can create menus and toolbars using the *CommandBars* collection, as described in Chapter 13, "Customizing Access Toolbars and Menus (Command Bars)."
- Code behind forms (and reports) has made it much easier to run code from form and control events. See Chapter 20, "Customizing Your Database Using VBA Code," for more details on writing event procedures.

Access Macros Compared with Macros in Other Office Applications

Access users who have created Microsoft Word or Microsoft Excel macros might be surprised to find that, unlike macros in all other Microsoft Office applications, Access macros are not automatically saved as VBA code and therefore can't be used as "training" for users who want to move on to writing code. Additionally, Access has no macro recorder (unlike Word and Excel).

If you're trying to write a Word VBA procedure and you don't know the syntax for moving to the end of a Word document, for example, all you have to do is turn on the macro recorder, press the Ctrl+End hot key, stop the recorder, and then open the Visual Basic Editor window and examine the macro you just created, as shown in the following code. You can then cut and paste the line of code from the new macro to your procedure.

```
Sub Macro1()
'
' Macro1 Macro
' Macro recorded 2/23/2001 by Helen Feddema
'
    Selection.EndKey Unit:=wdStory
End Sub
```

Because it has no macro recorder, you can't perform this kind of cut-and-paste operation in Access. However, this doesn't mean that Access macros aren't useful—you can use them for several special tasks, and even do some simple database automation, as long as you're aware of their limitations.

InsideOut

Although you can't record Access macros, the macro recording feature of Word or Excel can be useful when you're writing Access VBA code that uses Automation to work with Word documents or Excel worksheets. You can record a Word or an Excel macro, open the macro in the Visual Basic Editor window, and cut and paste the sequence of recorded actions to your Access VBA code. This technique can save you from spending a lot of time poring through documentation and online Help to find the syntax for a specific Word or Excel action.

Creating Simple Macros

Macros are used to run database actions automatically, as an alternative to performing the actions manually or writing VBA code. Macros are limited in functionality compared with VBA code, but they're also easier to create. Even if you're an expert code writer, you'll find that several special types of macro are still genuinely useful.

Most database users will find an AutoKeys macro useful, to provide a set of custom hot keys. Some databases can use an AutoExec macro because even though you can specify a database's startup form and many other database behaviors in the Startup dialog box, you might need to perform some special tasks when a database is opened. For example, you might want to create a Word or an Excel object for the database to work with, create a lookup table filled with dates calculated from the current date, or set the value of a global variable.

A third special macro type (which doesn't have a name) is a macro that runs a series of functions and/or action queries to automate the import and cleanup of data from an external data source. These three types of special macros are described in the section "Creating Special-Purpose Macros," page 555.

To create a simple macro, follow these steps:

1. In the Database window, click the Macros tab, and then click the New button to open the Macro Designer window.
2. Add actions to the macro by selecting them from the drop-down list in the Action column, as shown in Figure 14-1. When you select an action, its arguments appear in the lower portion of the Macro Designer. Type the values for arguments in the appropriate boxes (or, for some properties, select them from a drop-down list).

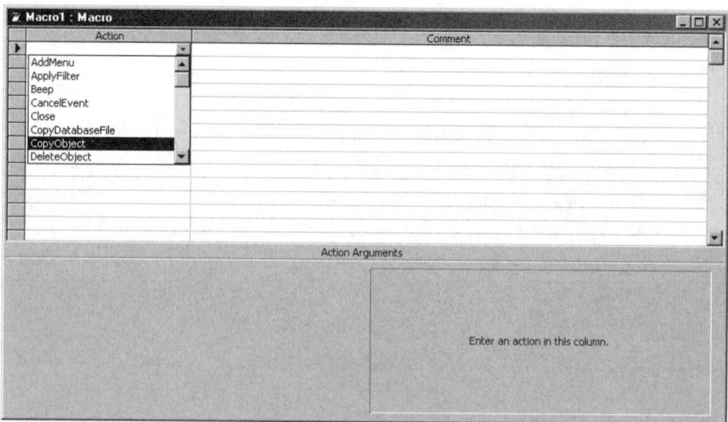

Figure 14-1. Use the Action column to select an action to add to a new macro.

> **tip** To move back and forth between a macro row and its arguments, press the F6 hot key.

3. (Optional) In the Comments column, type a description of what the macro does.
4. Close the Macro Designer window, and type the macro name in the Save As dialog box. The standard naming convention tag for macros is *mcr*. See Chapter 4, "Creating a Database," for more details on using a naming convention.

> **note** Unlike other database objects, macros have only one view: Design view.

By default, each macro has only two columns: Action and Comment. These two columns are all you need to create a simple macro. However, two other columns—Macro Names and Conditions—can be made visible by clicking the appropriate buttons on the Macro Design toolbar, shown in Figure 14-2.

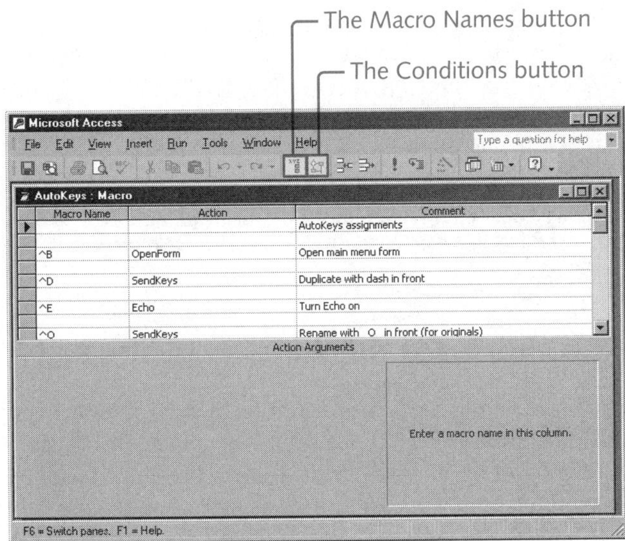

Figure 14-2. The Macro Names and Conditions buttons appear on the Macro Design toolbar.

The Macro Names column is used to enter macro names, which are used when you create a macro group (as opposed to a single macro). (See the sidebar "Macros and Macro Groups," page 551, for more details on macro groups.) The Conditions column is used to enter conditions that must be met before a macro action is run. For example, you could enter a condition specifying that a certain form must be open or that a field must have a certain value. Figure 14-3 shows a portion of the Suppliers macro group from the Northwind sample database, with macro names and a condition for a MsgBox action that displays the message box only if the SupplierID field is Null.

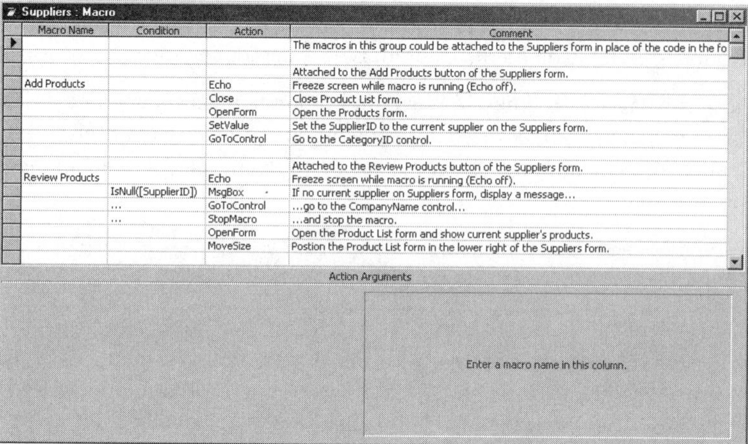

Figure 14-3. A macro group uses macro names to identify individual macros.

A macro condition is the equivalent of a simple *If...Then* construct in code. To use more complex logical structures, such as *Select Case* statements or nested *If...Then* structures, you need to write VBA code. If you need to deal with just one of two alternatives (say, a form that is open or closed), however, a macro condition can handle this situation very well.

See Chapter 20, "Customizing Your Database Using VBA Code," for more details on writing VBA code. See the section "Creating Macro Conditions," page 554, for more details on creating macro conditions.

Setting the Default Columns for the Macro Designer

If you want the Macro Names and Conditions columns to be visible by default in all new macros, select the appropriate check box on the View tab in the Options dialog box shown in Figure 14-4 (choose Tools, Options to open this dialog box). This step will save you time if you often create macro groups or macros with conditions.

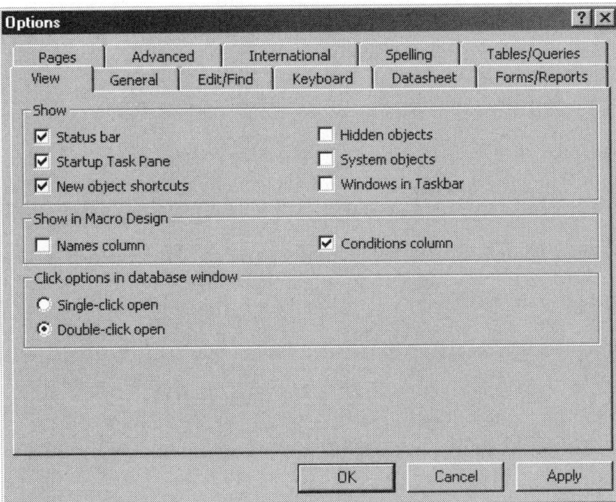

Figure 14-4. You can specify that the Conditions column will be visible by default on the View tab of the Options dialog box.

Macros and Macro Groups

A macro group is not a separate type of database object; it is simply a set of macros, each identified by name in the Macro Names column. Macro groups are created in the Macro Designer, just as single macros are. The only difference is that in a macro group, a group of macro actions is identified by name as belonging together. In earlier versions of Access, a macro group with a set of macros designed to run from various events of a form was often used to automate form events. This use of macro groups has for the most part been superseded by VBA event procedures stored in a form's class module.

The AutoKeys macro, described in the section "Using the AutoKeys Macro Group," page 556, is an example of a macro group.

Commonly Used Macro Actions

Some of the most frequently used macro actions are listed here, with a description of their usage:

- **OpenForm** Opens a form, with the following arguments:
  - *Form Name* The form's name, as it appears in the Database window.
  - *View* A view in which the form will open.
  - *Filter Name* The name of a saved filter or query used to filter form data.
  - *Where Condition* A SQL WHERE clause used to filter form data.
  - *Data Mode* A selection of options for data entry.
  - *Window Mode* How the form window opens (Normal, Hidden, Minimized, and so on).
- **OpenReport** Opens a report, with the following arguments:
  - *Report Name* The report's name, as it appears in the Database window.
  - *View* A view in which the report will open.
  - *Filter Name* The name of a saved filter or query used to filter report data.
  - *Where Condition* A SQL WHERE clause used to filter report data.
- **OpenQuery** Opens a select or crosstab query or runs an action query, with the following arguments:
  - *Query Name* The query's name, as it appears in the Database window.
  - *View* A view in which the query will open, usually Datasheet.
  - *Data Mode* Data entry mode for a select query opened in Datasheet view.
- **Close** Closes the Access window or the active database object window, with the following arguments:
  - *Object Type* The type of database object you want to close.
  - *Object Name* The name of the database object to close.
  - *Save* A flag specifying whether to save the object when closing it. (Possible values are Yes, No, or Prompt.)

- **MsgBox** Displays a message box with information or a warning, with the following arguments:
  - *Message* The text for the message box (up to 255 characters).
  - *Beep* A flag specifying whether to sound a beep when the message box is opened.
  - *Type* The type of message box, with a specific icon. (Possible values are None, Critical, Warning?, Warning! or Information.)
  - *Title* The text displayed in the message box's title bar; if left blank, *Microsoft Access* is displayed.
- **SetValue** Sets the value of a field, control, or property on a form or report, with the following arguments:
  - *Item* The name of the field, control, or property whose value is being set.
  - *Expression* The expression used to set the value. You can click the Build button to the right of the argument to open the Expression Builder to help construct an expression.
- **GoToRecord** Goes to a specific record in an open table, form, or query, with the following arguments:
  - *Object Type* The type of database object that contains the record you want to go to.
  - *Object Name* The name of the database object that contains the record you want to go to.
  - *Record* The record you want to go to; that record will be made the current record. (Possible values are Previous, Next, First, Last Go To, or New.)
  - *Offset* The number of the record to go to (as shown in the Record Number box at the bottom of a form window).

> **tip** To see a Help topic for a macro action and its arguments, position the insertion point in any argument box in the lower portion of the Macro Designer window, and press F1.

Creating Macro Conditions

If you need to run a macro action only if a condition is met—such as a specific form being open—you can create a condition expression in the macro's Condition column. A condition expression must evaluate to True or False; if it's True, the macro action runs; if it's False, the action is skipped. If you need to run one macro action if a condition is True and another if it's False, you need to write two macro rows with different conditions (one the negation of the other).

To write a macro with conditions that will open one form on a weekday and another form on a weekend day, follow these steps. (The two forms referenced in the macro are found in the sample database Test Access 2002.)

1. Click Macros in the Database window's Objects bar, and click New to open a new macro in the Macro Designer.
2. If the Condition column isn't visible, click the Conditions button on the toolbar to make it visible.
3. In the Condition column of the first macro row, enter the following expression:

   ```
   Weekday(Date())=0 Or Weekday(Date())=7
   ```

   (This expression selects Saturday and Sunday only.)
4. Select OpenForm as the macro action, and frmOrdersWeekends as the form name. Leave the other arguments for this action at their default settings.
5. In the Condition column of the second macro row, enter the following expression:

   ```
   Weekday(Date())<>0 And Weekday(Date())<>7
   ```

   (This expression selects weekdays only.)
6. Select OpenForm as the macro action, and frmOrdersWeekdays as the form name, and leave the other arguments at their default settings.
7. Save the macro as mcrOpenOrders.

To test the macro, run it from the Macro Designer by clicking the Run button on the toolbar. If you run the macro on a weekday, frmOrdersWeekdays opens; if you run the macro on a weekend day, frmOrdersWeekends opens.

Troubleshooting

I imported a macro into a database, and when I run it, I get the message *The expression you entered has a function name that* databasename *can't find*

A great many macros use a function named *IsLoaded* to determine whether a form is loaded before running a database action. If you don't have this function in a module in your database, you'll get this error message when you run a macro that uses *IsLoaded*.

The *IsLoaded* function is located in the Utility Functions module in the sample Northwind database. To import it into your current database, follow these steps:

1. Open the database that needs the *IsLoaded* function.
2. Open the Northwind.mdb sample database in another Access window. (It's located in the \Microsoft Office\Office10\Samples folder.)
3. Click the Modules object in the Northwind Database window.
4. Drag the Utility Functions module from Northwind to the other database to create a copy of the module in your database.

The Utility Functions module now contains the *IsLoaded* function, which will be available for use in VBA code and macros in your database.

Creating Special-Purpose Macros

As mentioned earlier in the chapter, from the earliest versions of Access, there have been two macro names reserved for special purposes: The AutoExec macro runs actions when a database is opened, and the AutoKeys macro sets up a group of hot keys to use in a database. New databases don't contain these macros by default, but if you want to run actions when opening a database or set up hot keys, the macros used for these purposes must be named AutoExec (or AutoKeys) for Access to recognize them.

Additionally, there's another type of special-purpose macro that has no reserved name. This macro makes it easier to run a complex series of functions, queries, and macro actions that automate importing data from an external source (such as a text file) and processing the raw imported data as needed to make it more useful in a database. This type of macro is handy if you frequently need to import and process data from an external source.

Using the AutoKeys Macro Group

The AutoKeys macro group is just as useful in Access 2002 as it was in Access 1.0. This macro group specifies actions to run from custom hot keys in an Access database. These hot keys supplement the built-in hot keys with your own hot keys to run actions you need frequently.

Each macro in the AutoKeys macro group corresponds to a letter of the alphabet, preceded by the caret symbol (^), which represents the Ctrl key. For example, after you create a ^A macro in the AutoKeys macro group, you can run the macro by pressing the Ctrl+A hot key. You can use all the letters of the alphabet as macro names in the AutoKeys macro group, but it's generally advisable to avoid hot keys that already have standard uses in Microsoft Windows or Office, such as Ctrl+C and Ctrl+V.

Table 14-1 lists the macros in the AutoKeys macro group that I use in most of my Access databases. Of course, you can create your own hot keys to meet your needs.

Table 14-1. Sample AutoKeys macro group

Macro name	Action	Arguments	Description
^B	OpenForm	Form Name: fmnuMain	Opens the main menu form, named fmnuMain. (You can replace *fmnuMain* with the name of your main menu.) This macro is handy for quickly reopening the main menu when it has been closed accidentally.
^D	SendKeys	Keystrokes: %fa{home} +^{right 2}-{end}	Creates a duplicate of a database object. The new object's name is the same as the original object's but with a dash in front, and you can also append a numeral at the end. Used to create a backup copy of an object. (See Figure 14-5 for an example of this hot key in action.)
^E	Echo	Echo On: Yes	Turns Echo on. Useful when VBA code has stopped abnormally, leaving the screen frozen as a result of Echo being set to False in code.

Macro name	Action	Arguments	Description
^O	SendKeys	Keystrokes: {f2}{home}-O-{enter}{down}	Renames an object in focus by adding an -O- in front of its name. This macro is useful for preserving the original version of a database object before you start making changes.
^Q	SendKeys	Keystrokes: {f2}{home}-?-{enter}{down}	Renames an object by adding a -?- in front of its name. This prefix is used to identify an object that might not be needed anymore but that you're not yet ready to delete.
^R	SendKeys	Keystrokes: {f2}{home}-{enter}{down}	Renames an object by adding a dash in front of its name. This prefix indicates database objects that aren't needed anymore and that can be deleted when you next clean up the database.

Several of these macros are used to rename or copy database objects, which is a way of keeping older versions of objects available by giving them distinctive prefixes. The ^D macro is the one I use most often; it lets me create a series of backup copies of a database object I am working on. If something goes wrong with the object—or if I just decide that I like a previous version better—I can easily revert to an older version of the object. When the object is finalized, I delete all the old versions, which are sorted to the top of the list in the Database window because of the leading dash in the version names.

Many of my AutoKeys macros use the *SendKeys* action to send a series of keystrokes to Access. These macros correspond to the keystrokes you would use to perform the same action in the interface. For example, using the ^D macro is equivalent to the sequence of keystrokes you would have to perform to create a duplicate of the current database object with the new name. When you use this macro, you will see the same Save As dialog box (shown in Figure 14-5) as you would if you performed all the keystrokes.

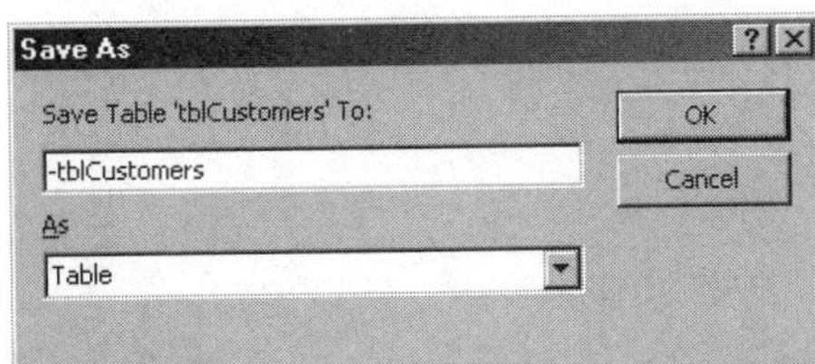

Figure 14-5. Use the ^D macro to make a backup copy of a database object.

> **note** SendKeys isn't used much any more, but it can be useful for creating hot keys in the AutoKeys macro group. There isn't any other way to perform the series of actions in the ^D and ^R hot key macros in this macro group.

Creating an AutoExec Macro

Although the Startup dialog box (opened by choosing Tools, Startup) lets you select a form to open when a database is opened, specify a custom menu for the database, and set various other database options as you prefer, an AutoExec macro is still useful for a few specialized purposes. One of these uses is to turn on global error handling; another is to create a Word, Excel, or other object to use in Automation code.

For example, if you have a function named *OpenWord* that creates a Word object to work with when exporting Access data to Word documents, you could run the function from a RunCode macro action. The same is true for a function (say, *SetErrorTrappingOn*) that turns on global error trapping.

> **note** You can run only functions from the RunCode macro action. If you have a Sub that you need to run from a macro, you'll need to either convert it to a function or call it from within a function.

Using Macros to Automate Importing or Exporting Data

If you need to periodically import data from a text file, reformat the data in a query, and then append the massaged data to a table for use in your database, these actions can be conveniently run from a single macro. To illustrate creating such a macro, we'll use a sample text file typical of data downloaded from a mainframe, with the name and address data in all capital letters, and the entire prospect name in a single field.

> **tip** Before automating a series of actions with a macro, first make sure the actions work properly when performed manually.

Figure 14-6 shows the text file in Notepad.

Figure 14-6. A text file to be imported shows text in all capital letters when opened in Notepad.

To make this data useful in an Access database, some of the name and address data must be converted to proper case (first letter capitalized), and the prospect name must be split into FirstName, MiddleName, and LastName fields.

note The text file used in the following procedure and the sample Test Access 2002 database can be found on the companion CD. This database contains the queries and tables used in the example.

To create the macro to automate importing data from this text file, follow these steps:

1. Open the Test Access 2002 database.
2. Click Macros in the Database window's Objects bar, and click New to open a new macro in the Macro Designer.
3. Select OpenQuery in the Action column's drop-down list, and press F6 to move to the Query Name box.
4. Click the drop-down arrow, and select the qdelProspectsRaw query.
5. On the next macro row, select RunCode as the macro action, and press F6 to move to the Function Name box.
6. Click the Build button to the right of the Function Name box to open the Expression Builder, and double-click the Functions folder to expand it.

7 Click the Test Access 2002 folder to display the functions in this database, click basUtilities and double-click ImportProspects in the list of functions to place it in the Expression box (see Figure 14-7), and then click OK to return to the Macro Designer.

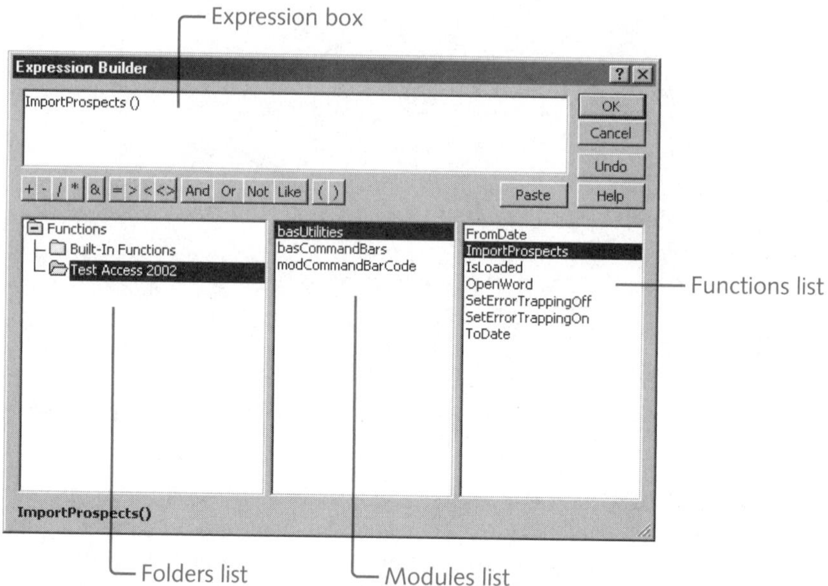

Figure 14-7. The Expression Builder helps you select a function to run from the RunCode macro action.

8 (Optional) In the macro's comments column, enter **Import new prospects from text file**.

9 In the next macro row, select the OpenQuery macro action, and press F6.

10 Click the down arrow, and select qdelProspectsNew.

11 (Optional) Type a description, such as **Clear old prospects table**.

12 In the next macro row, select the OpenQuery action, and select qappProspectsNew as the query name.

13 (Optional) Enter the description **Append new prospects to tblProspectsNew**.

14 In the last macro row of this example, select the MsgBox action, and type **New prospects imported** in the Message box.

15 Save the macro as mcrImportNewProspects.

To test the macro, run it from the Macro Designer by clicking the Run button on the toolbar. You'll see a series of confirmation messages as the macro runs the queries and code. The final table of cleaned-up prospect data is shown in Figure 14-8.

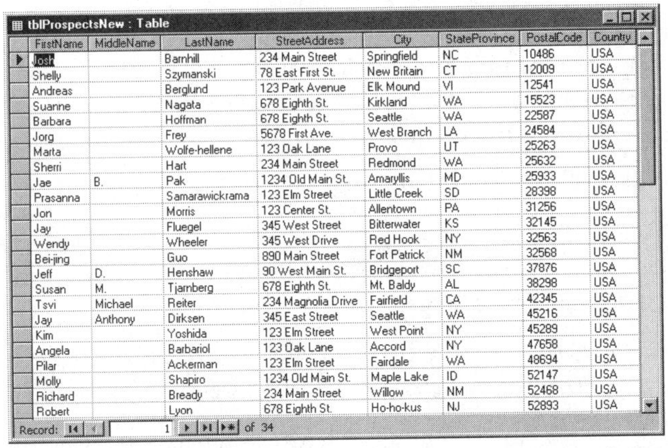

tblProspectsNew : Table

FirstName	MiddleName	LastName	StreetAddress	City	StateProvince	PostalCode	Country
Josh		Barnhill	234 Main Street	Springfield	NC	10486	USA
Shelly		Szymanski	78 East First St.	New Britain	CT	12009	USA
Andreas		Berglund	123 Park Avenue	Elk Mound	VI	12541	USA
Suanne		Nagata	678 Eighth St.	Kirkland	WA	15523	USA
Barbara		Hoffman	678 Eighth St.	Seattle	WA	22587	USA
Jorg		Frey	5678 First Ave.	West Branch	LA	24584	USA
Marta		Wolfe-hellene	123 Oak Lane	Provo	UT	25263	USA
Sherri		Hart	234 Main Street	Redmond	WA	25632	USA
Jae	B.	Pak	1234 Old Main St.	Amaryllis	MD	25933	USA
Prasanna		Samarawickrama	123 Elm Street	Little Creek	SD	28398	USA
Jon		Morris	123 Center St.	Allentown	PA	31256	USA
Jay		Fluegel	345 West Street	Bitterwater	KS	32145	USA
Wendy		Wheeler	345 West Drive	Red Hook	NY	32563	USA
Bei-jing		Guo	890 Main Street	Fort Patrick	NM	32568	USA
Jeff	D.	Henshaw	90 West Main St.	Bridgeport	SC	37876	USA
Susan	M.	Tjarnberg	678 Eighth St.	Mt. Baldy	AL	38298	USA
Tsvi	Michael	Reiter	234 Magnolia Drive	Fairfield	CA	42345	USA
Jay	Anthony	Dirksen	345 East Street	Seattle	WA	45216	USA
Kim		Yoshida	123 Elm Street	West Point	NY	45289	USA
Angela		Barbariol	123 Oak Lane	Accord	NY	47658	USA
Pilar		Ackerman	123 Elm Street	Fairdale	WA	48694	USA
Molly		Shapiro	1234 Old Main St.	Maple Lake	ID	52147	USA
Richard		Bready	234 Main Street	Willow	NM	52468	USA
Robert		Lyon	678 Eighth St.	Ho-ho-kus	NJ	52893	USA

Record: 1 of 34

Figure 14-8. After processing by an append query, the imported data is in proper case, and the name data is split into FirstName, MiddleName, and LastName fields.

In the future, when you need to import and process a new prospects file, you can simply double-click this macro in the Database window to run it.

> **tip** To suppress the confirmation messages while running the macro, insert a new macro row at the beginning of the macro, and select the SetWarnings macro action with a value of No.

Replacing Macros with VBA Code

By now, you might have the impression that macros aren't all that useful in Access 2002. The reasons macros seem to be less useful have more to do with the greatly increased power of VBA code than with any deficiencies in macros. Macros have remained as useful as they were in Access 1.0, but because VBA code has become so much more powerful, macros now appear quite limited in comparison. If you've been using macros since the early days of Access, your old macros will still work—you won't need to convert them to code. But if you're just starting out with Access 2002, there's little reason to use macros to automate a database, much as there's little (if any) reason to learn MS-DOS commands if you're working in Windows 2000 or Windows XP with Office XP.

Comparing Macros with VBA Code

These are some of the specific areas in which VBA code has more functionality than macros:

- Event procedures are part of forms and reports, not separate objects, and so when you import a form or a report into another database, its event procedures are imported with it. Macros are separate objects in the database and must be imported separately.
- VBA provides flexibility in error handling. Macros don't support error handling at all.
- In VBA, you can specify arguments when calling a procedure. Macro arguments are fixed and can't be changed when the macro is run.
- You can't work with Data Access Objects (DAO) recordsets or ActiveX Data Objects (ADO) recordsets in macros, whereas VBA code can handle both.
- Macros don't support complex logical structures such as *Select Case* statements or nested *If…Then* constructs.
- VBA code can be used to work with Word documents, Excel worksheets, and other objects, using Automation code. Macros have no corresponding functionality.
- You can't use macros in Access add-ins.

In addition to these macro limitations, the ease-of-use improvements brought about by the introduction of code behind forms in Access 2.0 and the new methods of creating menus and toolbars using the *CommandBars* collection (introduced in Access 97 and discussed in Chapter 13, "Customizing Access Toolbars and Menus [Command Bars]") make macros less useful and VBA code easier to write and more powerful.

The actions used in writing macros generally correspond to methods used in VBA code, although there are some exceptions. Table 14-2 matches up macro actions with the corresponding DoCmd methods. (Macro actions that are no longer useful but that have been retained for backward compatibility are noted.) If you want to write VBA code to replace your old macros, this table will help you find the right VBA method to use in your code. The next section offers more detail.

In general, macro actions correspond to methods of the *DoCmd* object, a component of the Access object model. The *DoCmd* object doesn't correspond directly to any element of the Access interface; it's simply a way to run a miscellaneous assortment of methods. As Access has evolved from version 1 to version 2002, more and more methods previously run from the *DoCmd* object have changed into methods of objects such as forms and controls. For example, the old GoToControl macro action/*DoCmd* object method has been replaced by the *SetFocus* method of the *Control* object.

Table 14-2. Macro actions and *DoCmd* methods

Macro action	*DoCmd* method	Description	Comments
AddMenu	*AddMenu*	Creates a menu	Although *AddMenu* is still listed as a *DoCmd* method in Access 2002, since Access 97, users have been able to create command bars (menu bars and toolbars) by using the Customize dialog box in the interface or by using the *CommandBars* collection in the Office object model.
ApplyFilter	*ApplyFilter*	Applies a filter to a form or report	
Beep	*Beep*	Sounds a beep	
CancelEvent	*CancelEvent*	Cancels an event	
Close	*Close*	Closes an object, usually a form or report	
newfeature! CopyDatabaseFile	*CopyDatabaseFile*	Copies a database file	
CopyObject	*CopyObject*	Copies a database object, such as a form or report	
DeleteObject	*DeleteObject*	Deletes a database object, such as a form or report	
	DoMenuItem	Runs a menu item	Retained for compatibility with earlier versions of Access. There has not been a DoMenuItem macro action since Access 95. The *RunCommand* method (with one of its numerous constants) supersedes the functionality of the older *DoMenuItem* method.

(continued)

Table 14-2. *(continued)*

Macro action	*DoCmd* method	Description	Comments
Echo	*Echo*	Makes screen updates visible if set to Yes or invisible if set to No	Retained for compatibility with earlier versions of Access. The *Echo* method of the *Application* object is the preferred method.
FindNext	*FindNext*	Finds the next record that meets the criteria specified by the previous FindRecord action	
FindRecord	*FindRecord*	Finds the first record that matches criteria specified in its arguments	
GoToControl	*GoToControl*	Sets the focus on the specified control	Retained for compatibility with earlier versions of Access. Use the *SetFocus* method of an object instead.
GoToPage	*GoToPage*	Goes to a specific page of a form	Although still valid, this method is rarely used, as multipage forms have generally been replaced with multipage tab controls.
GoToRecord	*GoToRecord*	Goes to a specific record on a form	Still valid for moving to specific records on forms (first, last, next, previous), but in VBA code, *GoToRecord* has been generally replaced by the *Find* and *Seek* methods of DAO recordsets or the *Find* and *Seek* methods of ADO recordsets.
Hourglass	*Hourglass*	Toggles the mouse pointer between an hourglass and the regular shapes	

Table 14-2. *(continued)*

Macro action	*DoCmd* method	Description	Comments
Maximize	*Maximize*	Sizes the active window to fill the entire Access window	
Minimize	*Minimize*	Reduces the active window to a small title bar at the bottom of the main Access window	
MoveSize	*MoveSize*	Changes the position and/or size of the active window	Retained for compatibility with earlier versions of Access. Use the new *Move* method of a form or report instead.
MsgBox		Displays a message box	Has no corresponding *DoCmd* method. Use the *MsgBox* function instead.
OpenDataAccessPage	*OpenDataAccessPage*	Opens a data access page	
OpenDiagram	*OpenDiagram*	Opens a database diagram in an Access project	
OpenForm	*OpenForm*	Opens a form	
newfeature! OpenFunction	*OpenFunction*	Opens a user-defined function in a SQL Server database for viewing in Access	
OpenModule	*OpenModule*	Opens a module in Design view	
OpenQuery	*OpenQuery*	Opens a select query, or runs an action query	

(continued)

Table 14-2. *(continued)*

Macro action	*DoCmd* method	Description	Comments
OpenReport	*OpenReport*	Prints a report, or opens it in print preview	
OpenStoredProcedure	*OpenStoredProcedure*	Opens a stored procedure in an Access project	
OpenTable	*OpenTable*	Opens a table	
OpenView	*OpenView*	Opens a view in an Access project	
OutputTo	*OutputTo*	Outputs data in an Access object to one of a number of formats	
PrintOut	*PrintOut*	Prints the active database object	Both the action and the method allow you to specify a page range and the number of copies to print.
Quit	*Quit*	Exits Access	Retained for compatibility with earlier versions of Access. Use the *Application* object's *Quit* method instead.
Rename	*Rename*	Renames a database object	
RepaintObject	*RepaintObject*	Completes pending screen updates for a database object	
Requery	*Requery*	Updates data in a database object	Retained for compatibility with earlier versions of Access. Replaced by the *Requery* method of forms and other objects.

Table 14-2. *(continued)*

Macro action	*DoCmd* method	Description	Comments
Restore	*Restore*	Restores a maximized or minimized window to its previous size	
RunApp		Runs an application	Has no corresponding *DoCmd* method. Use the *Shell* function or the *CreateObject* function to run other applications.
RunCode		Runs a function	Has no corresponding *DoCmd* method. Call the function directly in VBA code.
RunCommand	*RunCommand*	Runs a command	
RunMacro	*RunMacro*	Runs a macro	
RunSQL	*RunSQL*	Runs a SQL statement	
Save	*Save*	Saves a database object	
SelectObject	*SelectObject*	Selects a database object	Because some actions can be performed only on the currently selected object, this action should be run first to ensure that the appropriate object is selected.
SendKeys		Issues one or more keystrokes	Has no corresponding *DoCmd* method. Use the *SendKeys* statement instead.
SendObject	*SendObject*	Sends the specified database object as an e-mail message or as an attachment to an e-mail message	Generally, it's preferable to create a Microsoft Outlook mail message by using the *CreateObject* function and then fill it with Access data and send it by using components of the Outlook object model.

(continued)

Table 14-2. *(continued)*

Macro action	*DoCmd* method	Description	Comments
SetMenuItem	*SetMenuItem*	Sets the state of menu items on a menu bar	Retained for compatibility with menus created using the old menu macro method (prior to Access 97).
SetValue		Sets the value of a control	Has no corresponding *DoCmd* method. You can set the value of a field or control directly in VBA code.
SetWarnings	*SetWarnings*	Toggles on or off warnings about deleting objects or modifying data with action queries	
ShowAllRecords	*ShowAllRecords*	Shows all records (removes a filter)	
ShowToolbar	*ShowToolbar*	Displays or hides a toolbar	
StopAllMacros		Stops all macros	Has no corresponding *DoCmd* method. This action is not needed in VBA code.
StopMacro		Stops the current macro	Has no corresponding *DoCmd* method. This action isn't needed in VBA code.
TransferDatabase	*TransferDatabase*	Exports or imports a database file	
TransferSpreadsheet	*TransferSpreadsheet*	Exports or imports a worksheet file	
newfeature! TransferSQLDatabase	*TransferSQLDatabase*	Exports or imports a SQL Server database file	
TransferText	*TransferText*	Exports or imports a text file	

Converting Macros to VBA Code

You can save a macro and then run the Macro Converter utility to convert it to VBA code, but this utility isn't as helpful as it might be. The Macro Converter simply translates each macro action into the corresponding code (usually a method of the *DoCmd* object), which often leads to inefficient code using obsolete methods such as *GoToControl* with the control name when the *SetFocus* method of the control would be more appropriate.

Even more unfortunate, macros are not converted to the appropriate VBA event procedures, but instead are converted to functions that must in turn be called from event procedures. Additionally, converted macro procedures often use the *CodeContextObject* property, which is used for determining the object in which the code is executing, and which you'll probably never see outside of a converted macro procedure.

Chapter 14

InsideOut

Because of the serious limitations of the Macro Converter, requiring extensive rewriting to turn converted macro code into efficient VBA code, I recommend that you just write VBA code (event procedures and functions) from scratch to replace old macros, using Table 14-2 as a reference to the appropriate VBA methods.

See Chapter 20, "Customizing Your Database Using VBA Code," for more details on writing VBA procedures.

However, if you have an AutoKeys or AutoExec macro, leave them be—these special macros still have uses that can't be duplicated in VBA code.

Chapter 15

Using Add-Ins to Expand Access Functionality

Microsoft Access includes a number of built-in add-in utilities that help you with unfamiliar or complex procedures. Access also lets you extend its capabilities by means of Access add-ins, Component Object Model (COM) add-ins, and Microsoft Visual Basic for Applications (VBA) add-ins created by third-party developers. (See Chapter 21, "Creating Your Own Add-Ins," for more information about creating Access and COM add-ins.) Whether you're creating database tables, queries, forms, or reports or publishing data access pages, these add-ins can help you extend the functionality of Access and the data management systems you create. This chapter explains what each add-in can do for you. At the end of this chapter, you'll also find details on working with the Access Database Wizard to create a database based on a template. Although you won't find the Database Wizard on the Tools, Analyze or Tools, Database Utilities menus, it is an add-in that helps you create a new database from a template, with tables already filled in with standard fields; you can use the wizard to quickly create a variety of sample databases to use to experiment with some of the add-ins included on the companion CD.

An Overview of Add-Ins

An add-in is simply a utility that adds extra functionality to the core Access program. Some add-ins automate or step you through a procedure that you can do manually, and some add brand-new functionality. An add-in might, for example, analyze the relationships in the data tables you create, enable you to use custom commands, or let you quickly rename database objects according to a naming convention. You can use three types of add-ins in Access:

- **Built-in Access add-ins.** These add-ins, which include menu add-ins, wizards, and builders, are designed to add functionality to Access. Some Access add-ins are provided with Access and are available via the menu system. On the Tools menu, for example, you'll find the Analyze, Database Utilities, and Add-Ins submenus, each with its own set of selections. Third-party Access add-ins (such as my LNC Rename add-in, which is described in Chapter 21, "Creating Your Own Add-Ins") can be installed from the Add-Ins menu.
- **COM add-ins.** These add-ins, introduced in Microsoft Office 2000, are Office-wide add-ins (although a COM add-in can be written for just one Office program). Access doesn't come with any COM add-ins (other than one that does housekeeping chores behind the scenes); my LNC Rename COM add-in is an example of a third-party COM add-in. You access the COM add-ins by choosing Tools, COM Add-Ins.
- **VBA add-ins.** These are third-party or custom utilities that help you work with VBA code. They're available only in the Visual Basic Editor, where they have their own Add-In Manager dialog box, which you open by clicking Add-In Manager on the Add-Ins menu in the Visual Basic Editor.

The Office Developer Tools component of Microsoft Office XP Developer offers additional tools and utilities, most of which are designed to be used from the Visual Basic Editor.

note In addition to the add-ins available from various menus, Access also offers a number of wizards that help you create various objects such as forms, reports, controls, and queries, as well as builders that help you select a value for a property. These wizards and builders are covered in the chapters that deal with the particular database objects.

Leading third-party vendors of add-ins include FMS (*http://www.fmsinc.com*) and Database Creations (*http://www.databasecreations.com*). Some of my freeware add-ins are available on the companion CD, and others are available from my Web site, at *http://www.helenfeddema.com*. Rick Fisher's shareware add-in Find And Replace is also available on the companion CD (in the Third Party Add-Ins section) and can also be downloaded from Rick Fisher's Web site at *http://www.RickWorld.com*.

Using Built-In Access Add-Ins

The built-in add-ins on the Analyze and Database Utilities submenus of the Tools menu are part of the standard installation of Access and are available as soon as you install Access.

newfeature!

tip **View all wizards in Access 2002**

To see a list of all the wizards in Access 2002, type **wizards** in the Ask A Question box, and select the Which Wizards Are Installed In Access 2002 Help topic. This topic lists all the Access 2002 wizards and builders and tells you which setup component each one belongs to.

Built-in Access add-ins basically help you do two things: The add-ins available through the Analyze submenu help you analyze and document database components, and those on the Database Utilities submenu have more substantial functionality—they perform housekeeping, repair, and conversion chores. The sections that follow look more closely at all these add-ins.

Using the Add-Ins on the Analyze Submenu

Three of the built-in Access add-ins help ensure that your tables are well designed and well documented. You start an analysis add-in by choosing Tools, Analyze and then selecting one of the following add-ins:

- **Table.** Launches the Table Analyzer Wizard, which walks you through the process of dividing a large, non-normalized data table into separate, linked normalized tables.
- **Performance.** Starts the Performance Analyzer, which evaluates your database and makes suggestions for improving performance.
- **Documenter.** Starts the Documenter, which analyzes the objects in your database and produces an Object Definition report that details each object's attributes.

Troubleshooting

I can't see the wizards I want to work with

If you've installed Office XP using the default selection of Office Components, the add-ins on the Analyze and Database Utilities submenus of the Tools menu should be installed. (They're included in the Typical Wizards component, which is part of the standard Office XP installation.) However, the Add-In Manager, which is needed to install custom Access add-ins, is part of the Additional Wizards component and isn't installed by default.

If you can't see the wizards you want to work with, you can rerun Office XP setup and select either the Typical Wizards or the Additional Wizards component (I recommend selecting both) by following these steps:

1. Close all programs.
2. If you installed Office XP from a CD, insert the CD. If you installed Office XP from a network drive, make sure the drive is available.
3. Open Control Panel, and double-click the Add/Remove Programs icon.
4. Click the Microsoft Office XP selection in the Currently Installed Programs box, and then click the Change button in the highlighted band.
5. On the Maintenance Mode Options page, select the Add Or Remove Features option and click Next.
6. On the Choose Installation Options For All Office Applications And Tools page, expand the Microsoft Access For Windows branch of the feature tree, select Run From My Computer for the Typical Wizards and Additional Wizards selections, and then click Update.
7. A progress bar will indicate that the selected components are being installed, and then you'll see a message stating that Office setup has successfully updated your installation. Click OK to exit setup, and then close the Add/Remove Programs dialog box.

When you next open Access, the extra wizards will be available.

The Table Analyzer Wizard

The Table Analyzer Wizard helps you split a non-normalized table into separate tables, linked by key fields. After splitting the original table into two or more linked tables, the wizard creates a query based on the linked tables and gives it the same name as the table (the table itself is renamed), which ensures that if the table was used as a form, report, or data access page record source, the query will now be the record source.

> **note** To use the Table Analyzer Wizard effectively, you need to understand the principles of data normalization—the wizard isn't a magic wand that will take a mass of non-normalized data and automatically convert it to a set of properly normalized, related tables. For more information about data normalization, see Chapter 3, "Introduction to Database Design."

The Table Analyzer Wizard is a great help for pinpointing data errors that often creep into non-normalized data tables, where information has been typed into the fields rather than being selected from a look-up table.

To use the Table Analyzer Wizard on your database, follow these steps:

1. Choose Tools, Analyze, and then click Table.
2. The Table Analyzer Wizard is launched, and the page shown in Figure 15-1 appears, giving some general information about the problem of duplicate and inconsistent data in tables. Click one of the Show Me An Example buttons if you want to see more information; otherwise, click Next.

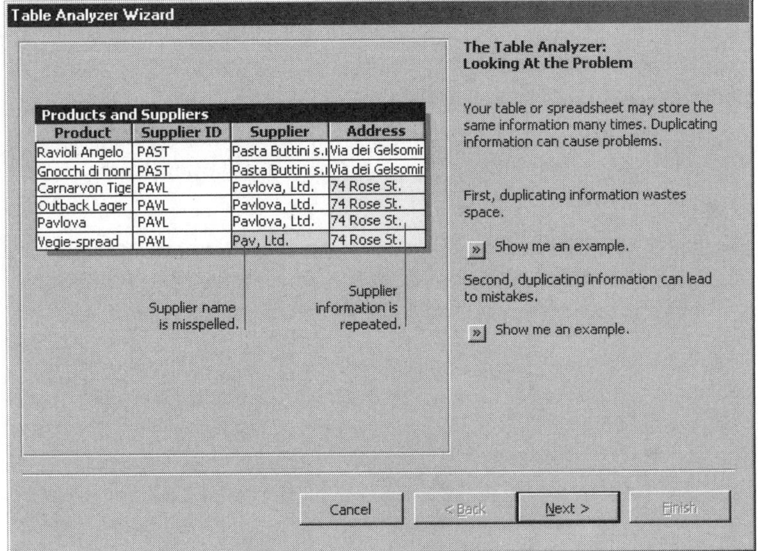

Figure 15-1. The first page of the Table Analyzer Wizard gives an idea of why duplicate information can cause problems.

Why Worry About Duplicate and Inconsistent Data?

Duplicate information wastes space in a database. For instance, in the example shown on the first page of the Table Analyzer Wizard, when the Supplier ID field is present in the table, all the other Supplier information can (and should) be picked up via a link on Supplier ID to the Suppliers table, instead of being duplicated in the Products and Suppliers table. Inconsistent information (such as the misspelled Supplier name highlighted in blue) means that records belonging to a single supplier will be classified incorrectly as belonging to two different suppliers, at least if the supplier name is used for grouping rather than the Supplier ID.

Also, if you make a change to a supplier name in one table, the change won't carry over to the other tables, leading to incorrect data in reports and forms. This type of error won't occur in a normalized database.

3. The next wizard page shows how the sample table used in the wizard can be divided into two linked tables to prevent the duplication of data in the single original table. Click one of the Show Me An Example buttons if you want to learn more; otherwise, click Next.
4. Select the table to be analyzed from a list of available tables in the database. (See Figure 15-2.) By clearing the Show Introductory Pages check box, you can skip the two introductory wizard pages the next time you run this wizard. Click Next.
5. On the next wizard page, you indicate whether you want the wizard to determine which fields are assigned to which tables or whether you want to make those choices yourself. Click Next.

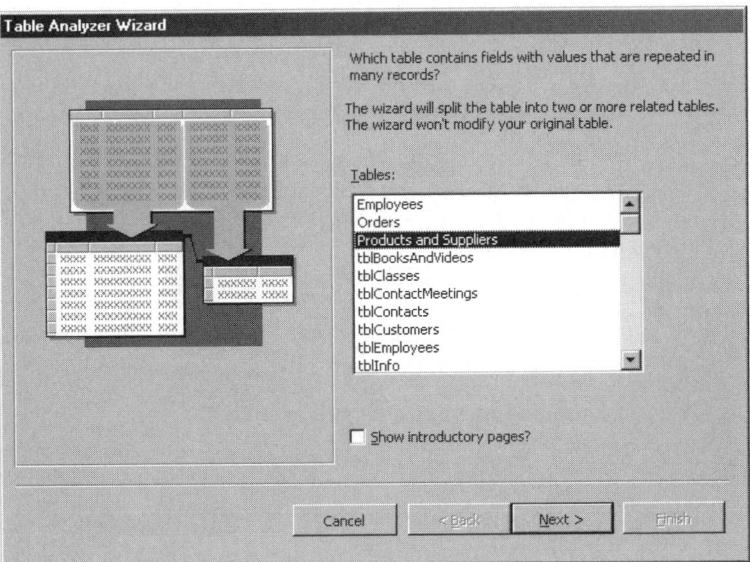

Figure 15-2. Scroll through the Tables list, and select the table you want to analyze.

InsideOut

The Table Analyzer Wizard doesn't always create an optimal set of linked tables—which isn't surprising because the proper division of data depends so much on the nature of the data and what you're going to do with it. You might find that the wizard breaks out addresses and ZIP codes into separate tables, for example, which is rarely appropriate. Another problem area: The wizard generally creates new unique ID fields for tables, even those that already have a suitable unique ID field.

Also, the wizard's practice of renaming the query with the same name as the original table has two problems: It violates any naming convention you might be using (by giving a query the tag used for a table), and it assumes that a query based on linked tables is the most appropriate record source for a form or report. In many cases (particularly for forms), nested subforms, each based on a single table, are a more appropriate interface for displaying and editing data from linked tables.

It's probably best to split a non-normalized table into separate tables and link them appropriately without using this wizard, because the wizard isn't smart enough to do the job right. However, the wizard does a great job of tracking down data errors and inconsistencies, so it's worth using just for that purpose.

6 The wizard will display the proposed new arrangement of linked tables in the Relationships window. (See Figure 15-3.) You can make relationship changes that Access suggests, rename tables, and drag a field from one table to another, as follows:

- To change the relationships or create tables other than those selected by the wizard, drag the fields and/or tables to create the splits and relationships you want. (When you drag all the fields out of a table, the table disappears.)
- To rename a table, select it, click the Rename Table button, and then enter the new table name. I suggest renaming the main data tables with the LNC *tbl* tag and the lookup tables with the *tlkp* tag.

After making the necessary changes, click Next.

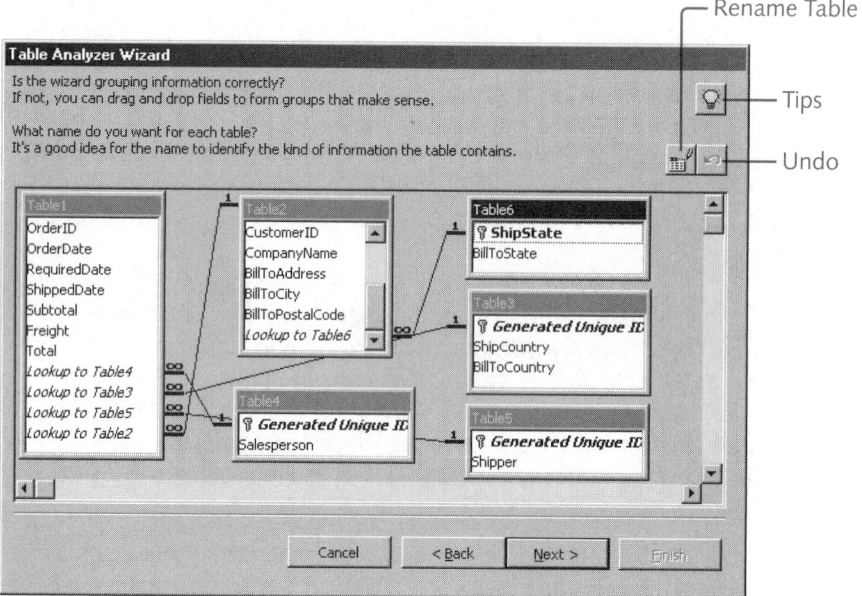

Figure 15-3. The wizard displays the proposed new set of tables and their relationships.

7 The next wizard page asks whether the fields shown in boldface are the appropriate key fields for each table (fields that uniquely identify each record in the table). If any key field isn't appropriate, you can select another field or create a new unique ID field as follows:

- To set an identifier (a field containing unique data) for the new table, select a field and click the Set Unique Identifier button.
- To add a new key for the table, click the table, and then click the Add Generated Key button.
- To see a screen of more detailed information about making changes to the proposed database schema, click the Tips button.
- To undo your last change, click the Undo button.
- After you make any necessary changes, click Next.

For more information about using a naming convention in a database, see Chapter 20, "Customizing Your Database Using VBA Code."

note The Table Analyzer Wizard will check for inconsistent data (spelling errors) only in tables with a Generated Unique ID as the key field.

8 Next, the wizard analyzes the tables for inconsistent data and might display several different pages, depending on the problems found. Figure 15-4 shows a typical page, with two different spellings for entries in the ShipName field. Check the check box for the correct entry, and click Next.

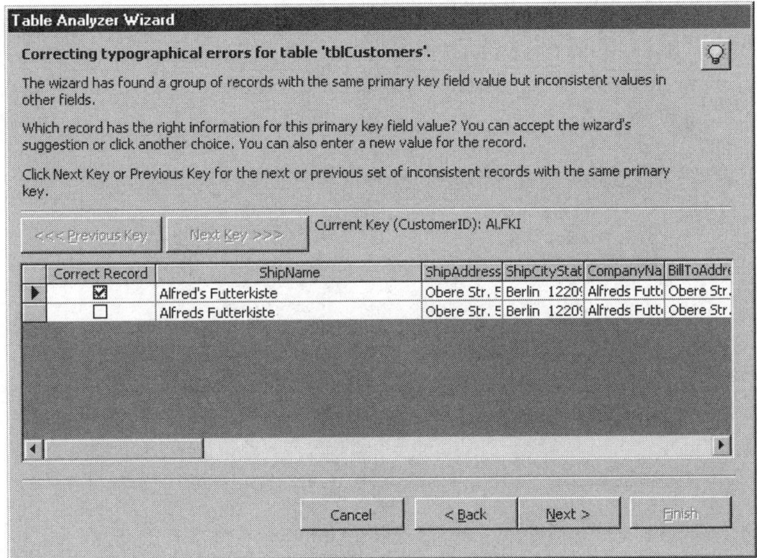

Figure 15-4. The wizard gives you the opportunity to fix typographical errors.

9 The final wizard page (shown in Figure 15-5) gives you the option to create a query based on the linked tables and offers a check box for displaying Help for working with the new tables or query.

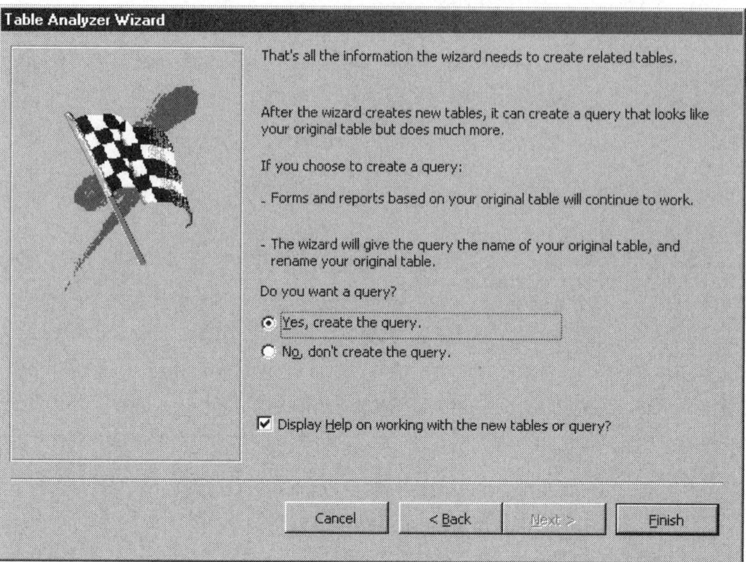

Figure 15-5. The final wizard page asks whether you want to create a query based on the tables it has created.

Figure 15-6 shows the query produced by the Table Analyzer Wizard. (Notice that the query has a misleading *tbl* tag.) You can then make any necessary changes to the query in Design view.

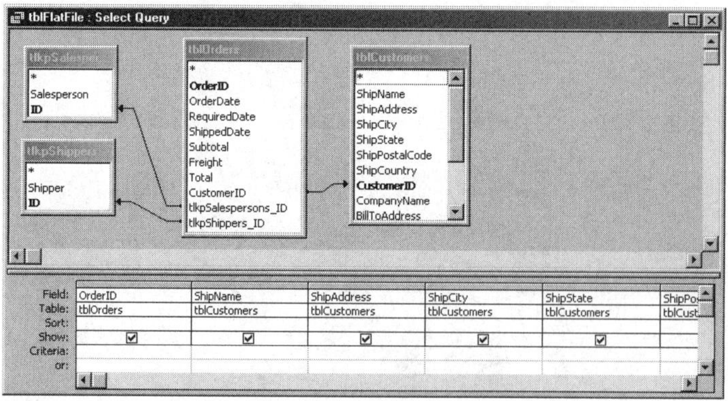

Figure 15-6. The query produced by the wizard links the various tables created from the original table.

Troubleshooting

Even after I use the Table Analyzer Wizard, my tables still need work

Although the Table Analyzer Wizard is a real help when it comes to finding errors and inconsistencies in your data, you'll need to do some of the fine-tuning yourself. You might need to make changes such as these after you use the wizard:

- **Rename key linking fields.** In the example, the foreign key linking fields in tblOrders have names in the form *tablename_ID*, where *tablename* is the name of the table the field links to.

  You can't change these field names in the wizard. If you want to change them (and you probably will), you must do so in the table, in Design view. The changes to the foreign key names will then be picked up in the Relationships window.
- **Finalize relationships.** If the table breakdown goes too far, you might need to fix it. For example, if it creates a separate table for ZIP codes, you'll probably want to move the Zip Code field back to the main table and delete the Zip Codes table.
- **Add links.** If you need to break up a table into two tables (say, to store multiple addresses or phone numbers), split the original table into two linked tables, and set the appropriate field (such as CustomerID) as the foreign key in the "many" table, linked to the primary key in the "one" table.

The Performance Analyzer

The Performance Analyzer evaluates the objects in your database and suggests how the performance of the database might be improved. This tool can make some changes for you automatically, if you choose, or you can make the changes yourself after you exit the tool.

To use the Performance Analyzer on a database of your choice, follow these steps:

1. Choose Tools, Analyze, and then click Performance. You'll see the Performance Analyzer dialog box in Figure 15-7, which is similar to the Access 97 Database window. The dialog box contains tabs for each of the six types of database objects (excluding data access pages), plus a tab for the Current Database and one for All Object Types, which makes it easy to select everything in the database.

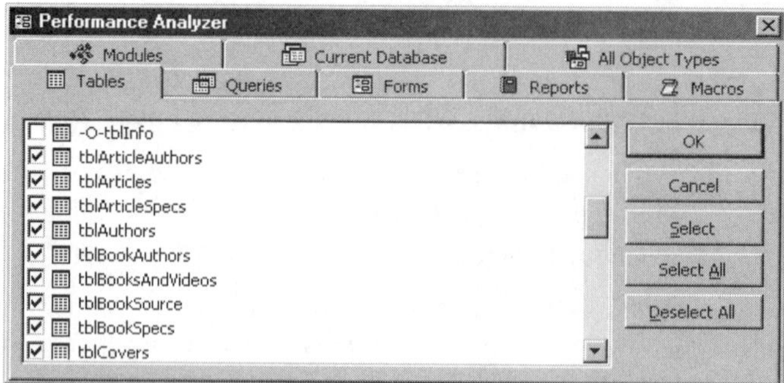

Figure 15-7. The Performance Analyzer dialog box has a tab for each type of database object (except data access pages).

> **caution** Before you run the Performance Analyzer, close any database objects you want to analyze. The Performance Analyzer skips any open objects.

Chapter 15

2 Click the items you want to include in the analysis. If you want to select all objects in the database, click the All Object Types tab, click Select All, and click OK. The Performance Analyzer evaluates the items you selected and displays the findings (as shown in Figure 15-8).

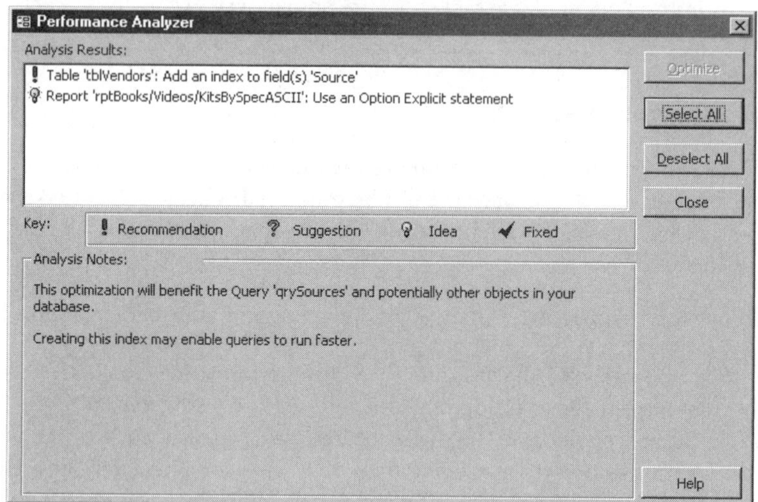

Figure 15-8. The Performance Analyzer makes suggestions for improving database performance.

3. The Performance Analyzer provides three kinds of advice, as follows:
   - **Recommendations.** These are marked with a red exclamation point and point out ways that your database can be optimized.
   - **Suggestions.** These are indicated by a question mark and provide suggestions for improving performance.
   - **Ideas.** These are marked with a light bulb symbol and offer additional tips for enhancing performance.
4. To make a change, select the item, and click Optimize. The symbol for the item will change to a blue check mark, indicating that it has been fixed.

Even if you think your database is performing well, it's still worthwhile to run the Performance Analyzer to see whether it finds anything you missed.

The Documenter

It's a good idea to print the design attributes of the objects in your database because if disaster strikes and you need to re-create some or all of your database, a printout will provide a useful roadmap. A Documenter printout of field names is also useful when you're writing VBA code that references table fields. The Documenter is an add-in that evaluates the objects in your database and produces a report of the design characteristics of each selected object, such as table fields and their properties. You can print the report or save it to a file, depending on your preference and needs.

To use the Documenter in any database, follow these steps:

1. Choose Tools, Analyze, and then click Documenter. The Documenter dialog box will appear, as shown in Figure 15-9.

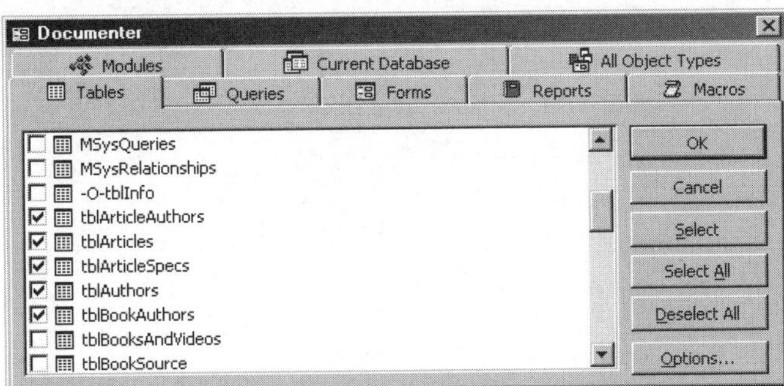

Figure 15-9. The Documenter dialog box has a tab for each type of database object (except data access pages).

Chapter 15

2 On the Tables tab, click the objects you want to document. (If you want to select all database objects, click the All Object Types tab, and click Select All.)

3 Click the Options button. The Print Table Definition dialog box will appear (as shown in Figure 15-10), allowing you to specify attributes of the selected object type you want to document. Select the options you want to print, and then click OK to close the dialog box.

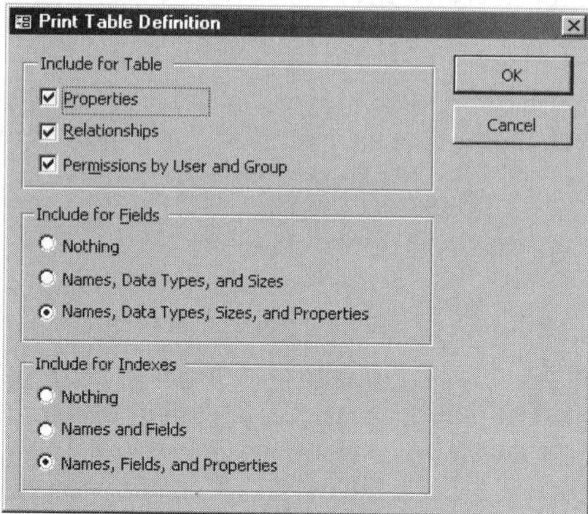

Figure 15-10. The Documenter has several options for documenting tables.

4 Click OK in the Documenter dialog box. You'll see messages about various database objects being analyzed in the status bar, and then an Object Definition report will open in print preview (as shown in Figure 15-11), listing the requested information about the selected database objects.

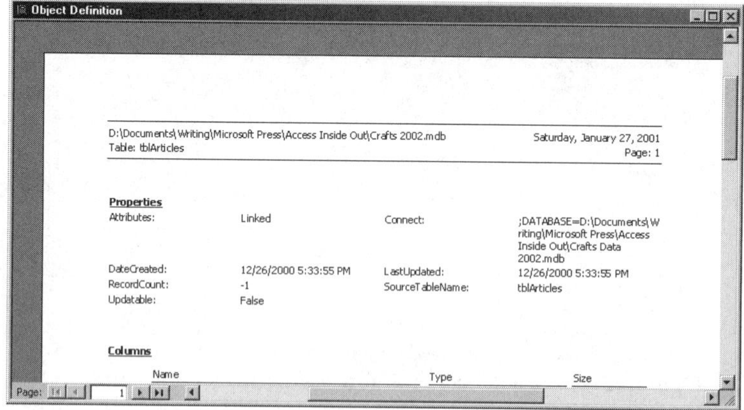

Figure 15-11. The Documenter creates an Object Definition report.

Using the Add-Ins on the Database Utilities Submenu

The add-ins on the Database Utilities submenu of the Tools menu provide various utilities to manipulate your database. Figure 15-12 shows the selections on the Database Utilities submenu.

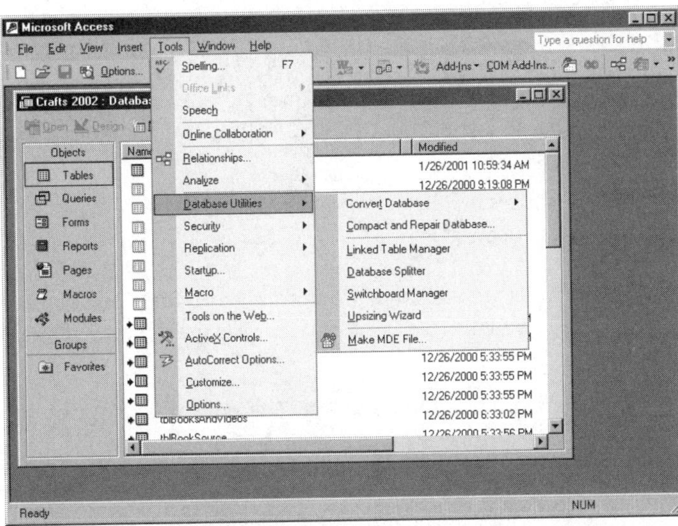

Figure 15-12. The Database Utilities submenu of the Tools menu offers a choice of add-ins.

The Convert Database Utility

The Convert Database utility was introduced in Access 2000. Before that version, there was no way to save a database in an earlier database format. Access 2000 lets you convert an Access 2000 format database to Access 97 format, and Access 2002 lets you convert an Access 2002 database to Access 97 or Access 2000 format or convert an Access 2000 database to Access 97 or Access 2002 format.

Converting from new to old The following steps show a typical sequence of error messages and reparative actions you'd need to take (in Access 97) after opening an Access 97 database created by converting an Access 2002 database to Access 97 format:

1. Open the converted database in Access 97. Figure 15-13 shows a typical error message resulting from an incorrect reference. Access 97 needs a reference to DAO 3.51, and the converted database had a reference to a higher version of DAO (such as 3.60).

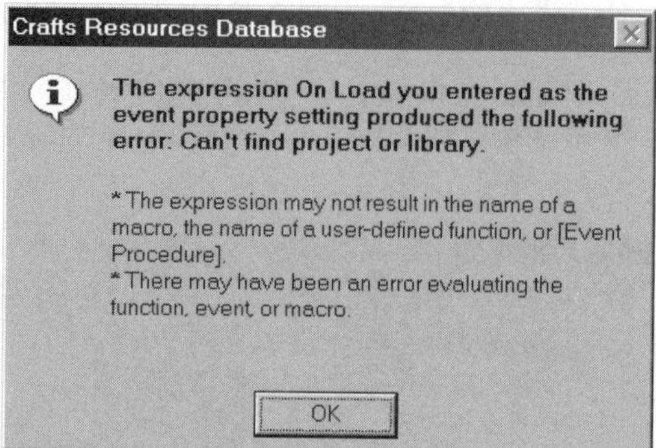

Figure 15-13. This message results from a missing reference when a converted database is opened.

2 Click OK. Another message will appear, informing you that the database has been converted and advising you to compile it. This message will appear even if no errors occurred.

3 Open a module, and compile the database. The error message *Compile Error: Can't find project or library* will appear, giving more specific information about the error. Click OK to close the error message.

4 You can examine the cause of the error by displaying the References dialog box (shown in Figure 15-14). To open this dialog box, press Alt+F11 to display the Visual Basic Editor, and then choose Tools, References.

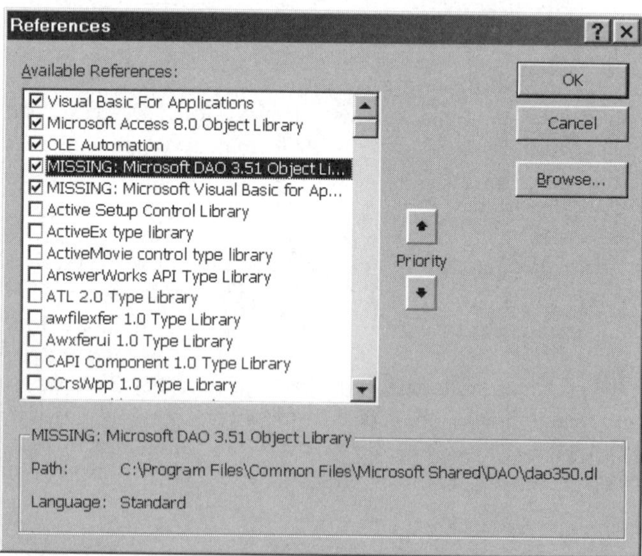

Figure 15-14. Two items are marked *MISSING* in the References dialog box.

In this example, the two references marked MISSING are the problem. You can simply clear the Microsoft Visual Basic For Applications item marked MISSING because there's already a checked item for the current version of this library (the Visual Basic For Applications item at the top of the list). The Microsoft DAO 3.51 Object Library item marked MISSING should also be cleared, but in this case you need to select the appropriate item as well. To do so, close the dialog box, reopen it, and check Microsoft DAO 3.51 Object Library.

5. Click OK to close the References dialog box. The code will compile, and the database will be ready for use in Access 97.

Converting from old to new To convert an older Access database to Access 2002 or Access 2000 format (whichever one you've selected as the default file format on the Advanced tab of the Options dialog box, available from the Tools menu), you don't use the Convert Database utility. To convert an older database to the current format, follow these steps:

1. Open the database in Access 2002. A dialog box will appear (as shown in Figure 15-15), offering a choice of converting the database to the current version or opening it in read-only mode. Click Convert Database, and click OK.

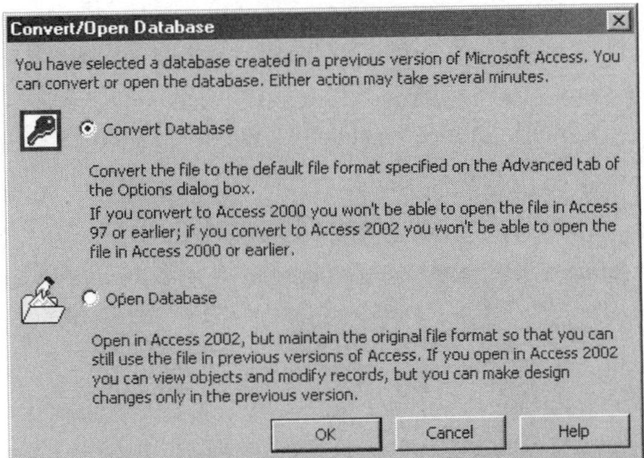

Figure 15-15. This dialog box appears when you try to open an older Access database in Access 2002.

2. A standard File Open dialog box will appear. Select the appropriate folder, enter a name for the converted database, and click Save.

3 If no compilation or conversion problems occur, the database will open in Access 2002 with a message telling you that the new Access 2002 database can't be shared with Access 97 or Access 2000 users. Click OK to close the message.

If compilation problems occur during the conversion, you'll get a different message that reports compilation errors and offers a Help button to click for more information. Click OK to continue.

If conversion errors occur, you'll get a conversion error message, again with a Help button. Click OK to continue, and you'll get the message telling you that the new Access 2002 database can't be shared with Access 97 or Access 2000 users.

Troubleshooting

I'm having conversion problems converting my database to an older format

There are several problems you might experience when you convert a database to an older format. Here are some of the problems and their solutions:

- **Problem:** I can't save a converted database to the name of an existing database. (There's no Overwrite selection when I save the converted database.)

  Solution: Make sure that the name you want to use isn't already in use in the target folder. Rename, move, or delete any existing file with that name.

- **Problem:** I get compile errors in the converted database.

  Solution: Compile the converted database. Generally, that's all you need to do. In some databases, you might need to rewrite some code to take into account changes in the Access object model or other functionality.

- **Problem:** PivotCharts are missing from a database I converted from Access 2002 to an earlier version of Access.

  Solution: PivotCharts are new to Access 2002; you'll have to do without them or replace them with MS Graph charts.

- **Problem:** I get a *Can't find project or library* error when I compile a database converted from a later Access version to an earlier Access version.

  Solution: A reference to an object library hasn't been downgraded to the correct version. This often happens with references to the Microsoft Word or Microsoft Outlook object libraries. To fix this problem, open the References dialog box from the Tools menu in the Visual Basic Editor, clear the references to the Word 10.0 or Outlook 10.0 object library (or any library that's marked *MISSING*), and check the reference for the appropriate version of the object library.

> **note** If any compilation or conversion errors occur, the details are saved in a table named Conversion Errors. Open the table to check out the errors so that you can fix them.

The Compact And Repair Database Utility

The Compact And Repair Database utility runs two add-ins (which were separate selections in earlier versions of Access). One add-in compacts a database by removing temporary objects (usually resulting in a considerable reduction in size), and the other repairs database errors. To start the utility, choose Tools, Database Utilities, and then click Compact And Repair Database.

You'll see a progress bar in the database's status bar, and if the compact and repair process is successful, you'll then be returned to the database. If problems occur, you'll get an error message letting you know what the problem is. Depending on the nature of the problem, you might be able to resolve it; if not, you might have to restore your last backup database.

The Linked Table Manager

The Linked Table Manager helps you fix broken links to back-end tables, which usually result from moving the back-end database to another folder. You open the Linked Table Manager by choosing Tools, Database Utilities and then clicking Linked Table Manager or by clicking Linked Table Manager on the shortcut menu of a linked table.

> **tip** **View table links**
>
> Links to tables in back-end databases are stored as explicit paths; you can see them in the Object Definition report created by the Documenter. For more information about creating an Object Definition report, see the section "The Documenter," page 583.

Because Access lacks a constant that represents the current folder (the folder in which the front-end database is located), you still have to fix broken links even if you move both the front-end and back-end databases to the same folder in a new location.

To fix the broken links, follow these steps:

1. Run the Linked Table Manager, either from the Database Utilities submenu or from a linked table's shortcut menu. The Linked Table Manager dialog box (shown in Figure 15-16) lists all the linked tables, with their stored (now incorrect) paths.

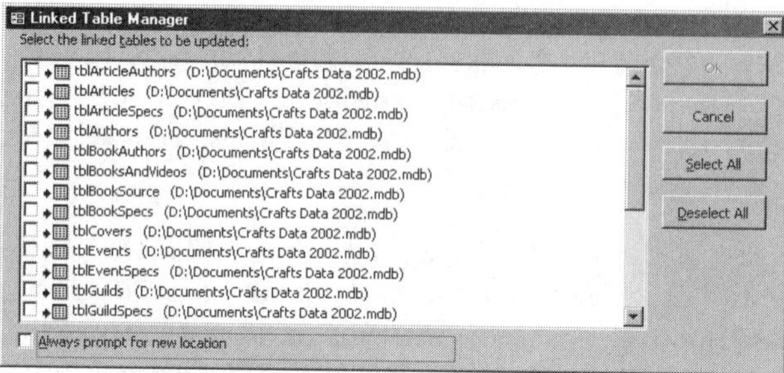

Figure 15-16. The Linked Table Manager dialog box lists incorrect paths for linked tables.

2. Click Select All to select all the tables to refresh. (This is generally what's needed, although you might need to select specific tables if you have two or more back-end databases.) The Always Prompt For New Location check box lets you change the path for a back-end database even if the current link is valid. (Changing the path can be useful if you have several versions of the back-end database in different locations.) Click OK.

3. A standard File Open dialog box will open, in which you can browse for the current location of the back-end database. Select the database, and then click the Open button in the Select New Location Of *tablename* dialog box to refresh the tables.

All links will be refreshed, and you'll see a message confirming this. Click OK to close the message box. Close the Linked Table Manager dialog box, and the linked tables will have the correct links to the database you selected.

tip If you don't have a database with linked tables to experiment with, create one with the Database Splitter, as described in the next section, and then move the back-end database to another folder. This will trigger a "Could not find file" error message when you try to work with data in a linked table in the database, which you can fix using the Linked Table Manager.

Troubleshooting

I can't refresh the link to a certain table

The Linked Table Manager can't refresh links to tables whose names were changed in the back-end database after they were linked (for example, to give them names using LNC tags). If you can't refresh a link to a table, delete the link, and then re-create it by choosing File, Get External Data, and then selecting Link Tables.

The Database Splitter

The Database Splitter is a wizard that automates the process of splitting a database into a front end and a back end. This split makes it easier to make changes to the interface objects without affecting the data.

To start the Database Splitter, follow these steps:

1. Choose Tools, Database Utilities, and then click Database Splitter. The first page of the wizard (shown in Figure 15-17) informs you of the advantages of splitting a database.

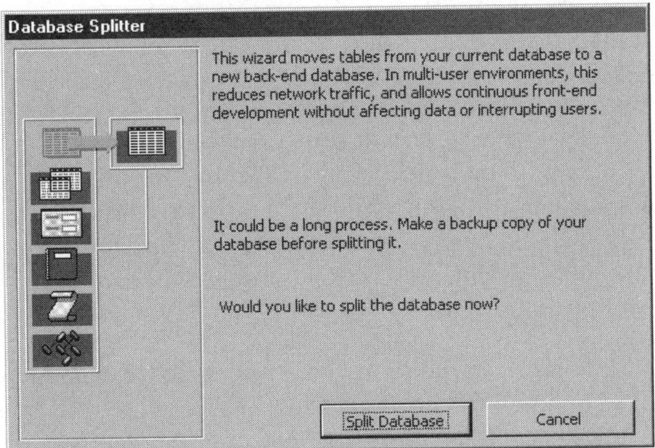

Figure 15-17. The first page of the Database Splitter wizard offers general information about the wizard.

2 Click the Split Database button to start the process.

3 In the Create Back-End Database dialog box, select a location in which to save the back-end database. (By default, the back end has the original database's name with *_be* appended to it.)

4 Click the Split button. The database tables will be moved to the new back end, and a message will appear, telling you that the database was successfully split.

The original database now has links to the tables in the new back-end database, as indicated by arrows to the left of the linked table names in the Database window.

The Switchboard Manager

The Switchboard Manager is a wizard that creates a switchboard (main menu) for a database, with text buttons to run various commands. If you click the Switchboard Manager selection for a database that doesn't already have a switchboard, you'll get the message shown in Figure 15-18.

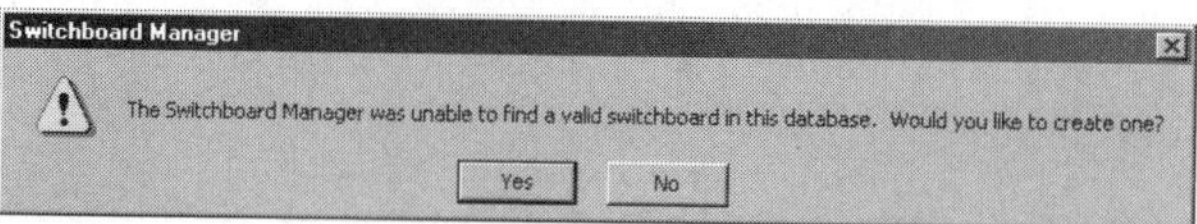

Figure 15-18. A message from the Switchboard Manager indicates that the database doesn't have a switchboard.

You can click Yes to open a dialog box in which you can add new pages to the switchboard or edit existing ones. The switchboard created by the wizard has an old-fashioned appearance. (It hasn't changed significantly since early versions of Access.) It includes a set of buttons, each of which opens a form or a report or performs some other action. You can also create subsidiary menus—say, a Forms menu and a Reports menu, each with its own set of buttons.

The process of adding items to the switchboard is fairly tedious. After you click Yes in the initial message box, the Switchboard Manager dialog box will open, with one Main Switchboard page listed (as shown in Figure 15-19). (If a switchboard page is not listed, you can click New to create a new switchboard.)

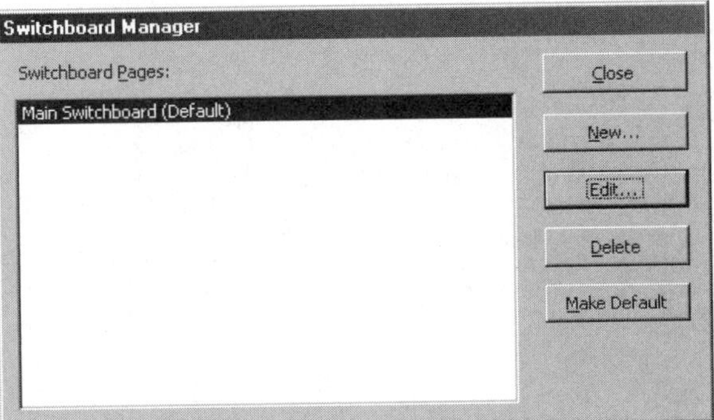

Figure 15-19. The Switchboard Manager lets you set up the default Main Switchboard page.

To add buttons to the Main Switchboard form, follow these steps:

1. Click the Edit button. The Edit Switchboard Page dialog box will appear.
2. Click the New button to open the Edit Switchboard Item dialog box.
3. Enter the text you want to use for the button, and select the command you want to run when the button is clicked. Figure 15-20 shows the dialog box with its fields filled in with data for a button to open a form.

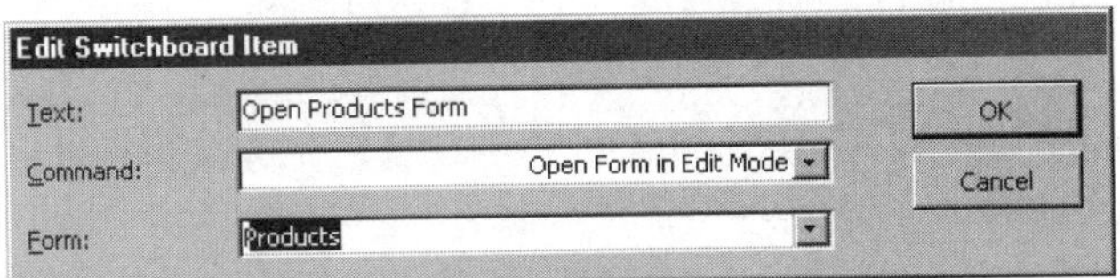

Figure 15-20. You create a button to open a form in the Edit Switchboard Item dialog box.

4. Repeat steps 2 and 3 for each button you want to add to the switchboard. When you finish, you'll have a switchboard like the one shown in Figure 15-21 (which includes buttons for opening three different forms).

The Menu Manager add-in on the companion CD creates a more streamlined all-in-one main menu with drop-down lists of forms and reports to select from and other interface elements that make it easy to work with a database. See the section titled "Creating a Main Menu Using the Menu Manager Add-In" later in this chapter for details.

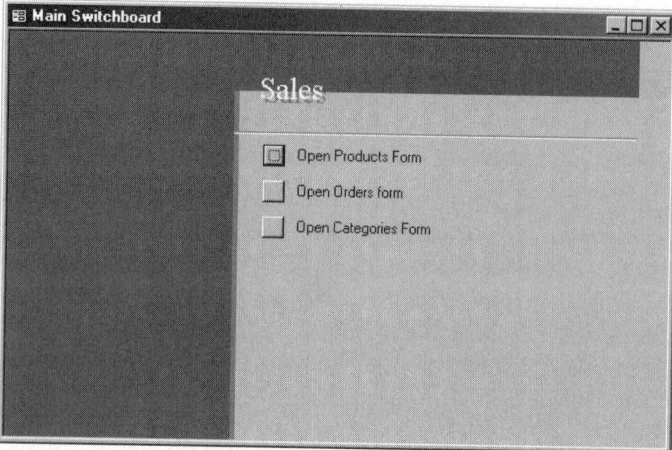

Figure 15-21. The new Main Switchboard form has three buttons for opening forms.

The switchboard form's functionality is based on a Switchboard Items table created by the Switchboard Manager. This table contains information used in a function in the form's class module.

tip **Display the switchboard automatically**

To make the switchboard appear automatically when the database is opened, select the Main Switchboard form (or fmnuMain, if you have renamed it according to the LNC) as the Display Form/Page in the Startup dialog box (choose Tools, Startup).

The Upsizing Wizard

The Upsizing Wizard automates the process of converting an Access database to a Microsoft SQL Server database, with an option to either create a new SQL Server database or use an existing one. You start the wizard by choosing Tools, Database Utilities and then clicking Upsizing Wizard.

For more information about using the Upsizing Wizard, see Appendix E, "Upsizing to SQL Server."

Saving a Database as an MDE File

Saving a database as an MDE file compiles all its modules, removes editable source code, and compacts it. This protects the VBA code from being viewed or edited, while still allowing it to run. Saving a database to MDE is a quick way of securing its code, without the complexity of setting up a secured database. In an MDE file, users can't do the following:

- View, modify, or create forms, reports, or modules in Design view.
- Add, delete, or change references to object libraries or databases.
- Change VBA code.
- Import or export forms, reports, or modules. (However, tables, queries, data access pages, and macros can be imported or exported to non-MDE databases).

To save a file as an MDE file, follow these steps:

1. Choose Tools, Database Utilities, and then click Make MDE File. The Save MDE As dialog box will appear.
2. Navigate to the folder in which you want to save the file, type the file name, and click Save. The default name is the database name with the MDE extension.

> **caution** You can't re-create an MDA file from an MDE file, so be sure to keep a copy of the original MDA file in case you need to edit the database in the future.

Using Office XP Developer Add-Ins

Microsoft Office XP Developer includes a number of advanced add-ins for developers. It includes utilities for working with VBA code, creating file packages for distributing databases you develop, and coordinating development work by several developers, among others. You access these add-ins via the Add-Ins menu of the Visual Basic Editor.

Even if you've installed the Office Developer Tools component of Office XP Developer, you might not see all of the add-ins on the Add-Ins menu because they must be loaded first. You can see the available Visual Basic Editor add-ins in the Add-In Manager dialog box, and for each one, you can set its load properties. For example, if you want to have the Code Commenter And Error Handler Add-In always loaded at startup in the Visual Basic Editor, follow these steps:

1. Display the Visual Basic Editor, if necessary, by pressing Alt+F11.
2. Choose Add-Ins, Add-In Manager. The Add-In Manager dialog box will appear.
3. In the Add-In Manager dialog box, select that add-in, select the Load On Startup check box, and also select the Loaded/Unloaded check box to load the add-in immediately.

If you don't want an add-in to always be loaded because you use it only occasionally (the Packaging Wizard is an example), you can select the Loaded/Unloaded check box to load it for the current session only. Figure 15-22 shows the Add-In Manager dialog box with the Code Commenter And Error Handler and Multi-Code Import/Export add-ins loaded and set to load on startup and the Packaging Wizard loaded for the current session only.

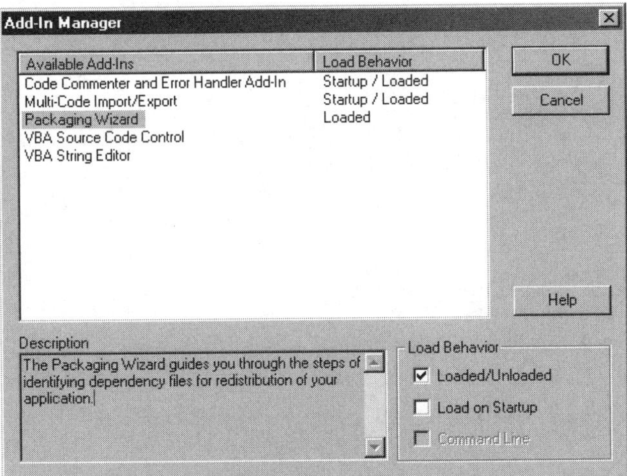

Figure 15-22. The Add-In Manager dialog box lets you set startup and load options for various Visual Basic Editor add-ins.

caution Don't confuse the Add-Ins menu and the Add-In Manager dialog box in the Visual Basic Editor with the similarly named menu and dialog box in the Access window. The menu and dialog box in Access are used to manage Access add-ins, and those in the Visual Basic Editor are used to manage Visual Basic Editor add-ins.

Troubleshooting

I can't find the Code Librarian

The Code Librarian, one of the Office Developer Tools in Office XP Developer, was available from the Add-Ins menu in the Access 2000 Visual Basic Editor. It's now a separate Developer Application, which you can select from the Office XP Developer program group.

newfeature!

Using the Code Commenter And Error Handler Add-In to Enhance Your VBA Code

The Code Commenter And Error Handler add-in combines two separate add-ins: It inserts a comment header section and a standard error handler into procedures using a customizable template (EHT file). To use the Code Commenter And Error Handler add-in, follow these steps:

1 Display the Visual Basic Editor, if necessary, by pressing Alt+F11.

2 In the Visual Basic Editor, choose Add-Ins, Code Commenter And Error Handler Add-In. The dialog box shown in Figure 15-23 will appear.

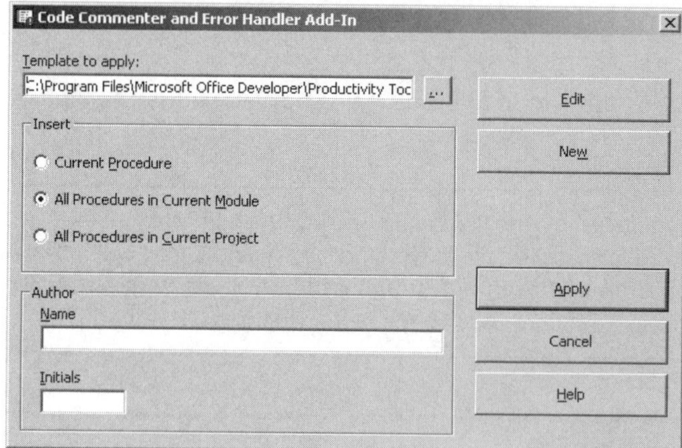

Figure 15-23. The Code Commenter And Error Handler Add-In dialog box lets you add comments and error handlers to VBA code.

3 Specify how you want the template to be applied. You can apply the template to the current procedure only, to all procedures in the current module, or to all procedures in the current project.

4 In the Name and Initials text boxes in the Author section, enter your name and initials as you want them to appear in the comments section of your code.

5 Click Apply. The add-in will apply the template you selected.

Figure 15-24 shows the Comments header block of a procedure after the standard template has been applied.

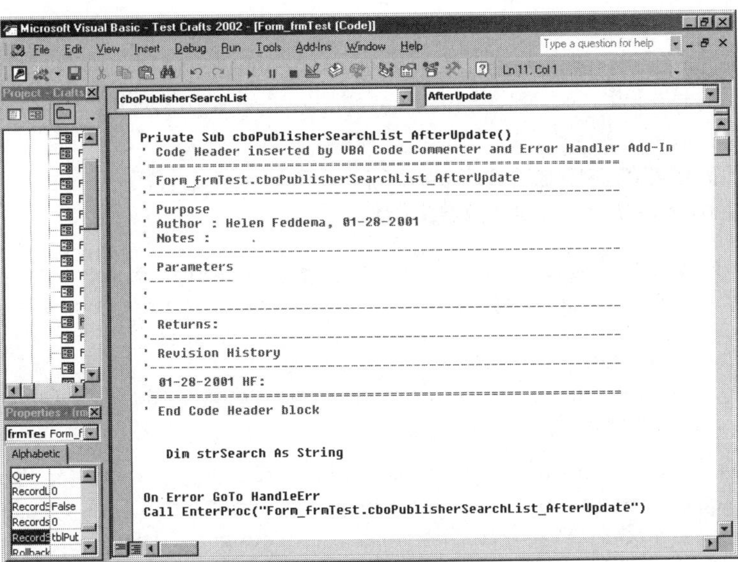

Figure 15-24. This Comments header block was inserted by the Code Commenter And Error Handler add-in.

The error handler inserted by the add-in is shown in Figure 15-25.

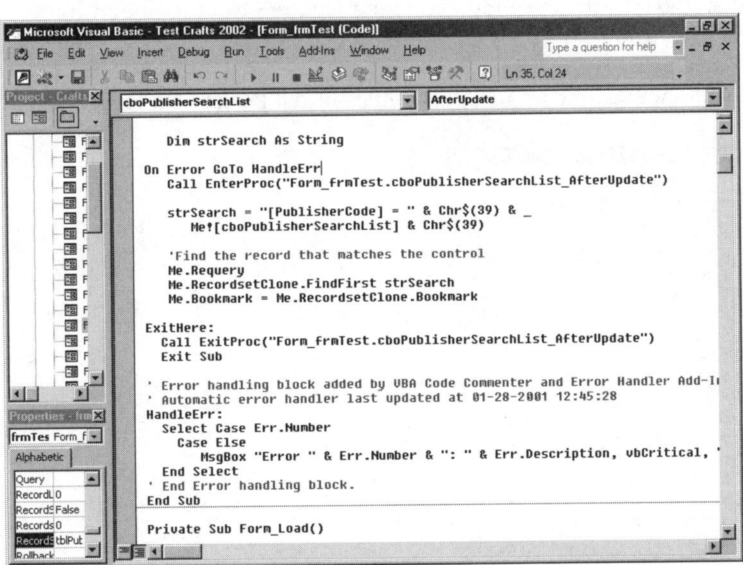

Figure 15-25. This error handler was inserted by the Code Commenter And Error Handler add-in.

Chapter 15

> **note** If a procedure already has an error handler, selecting the Code Commenter And Error Handler add-in will do nothing.

The error handler is in the form of a *Select Case* statement with only *Case Else* filled in. You can insert other *Case* statements as needed to deal with specific errors.

Speeding Up Importing and Exporting Using the Multi-Code Import/Export Add-In

The Multi-Code Import/Export add-in allows you to import or export a number of objects in one pass, which can save a good deal of time. To import objects, follow these steps:

1. On the Add-Ins menu, click Multi-Code Import to open the Multi-Code Import dialog box.
2. Click Browse to open the Select Files To Import dialog box, in which you can select various types of saved code files to import into a VBA project—standard modules (BAS), class modules (CLS), designers (DSR), and UserForms (FRM), although the latter selection is not useful for Access. You can use the standard hot keys to select as many files as you want.
3. Click Open to return to the Multi-Code Import dialog box. The selected files will be listed. You can remove one or more files using the Remove button. When the list accurately represents the files you want to import, click the Import button to start the import.

Figure 15-26 shows some imported modules in the Project Explorer pane.

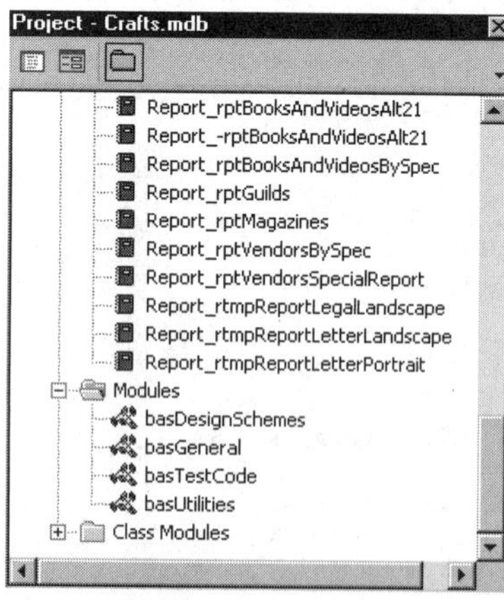

Figure 15-26. Newly imported modules are shown in the Project Explorer pane.

InsideOut

Although Access form and report modules are class modules and they appear in the Select Files To Import dialog box, you can't import them using the Multi-Code Import dialog box. When you import a form or a report in the Access interface, its class module (if any) will also be imported.

To use the Multi-Code Export add-in, follow these steps:

1. On the Add-Ins menu, click Multi-Code Export to open the Multi-Code Export dialog box (shown in Figure 15-27).

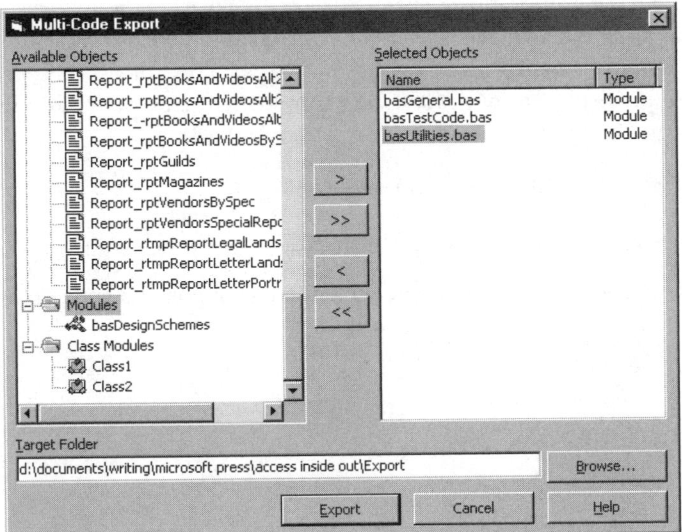

Figure 15-27. You select multiple files to export in the Multi-Code Export dialog box.

2. Select the standard modules or class modules you want to export, and then select a folder to which the files should be saved. Click the Export button to start the export of the selected files. (All the files in the Selected Objects list will be exported.)

note There's little point in exporting Access form or report class modules because they can't be imported—and, in any case, you get the code module along with the form when you import an Access form into another database.

3. The Multi-Code Export Results dialog box will appear, showing you the status of the export and telling you that the export was successful. Click OK to close the dialog box.

Constructing String Expressions Using the VBA String Editor Add-In

The VBA String Editor add-in automatically inserts quotation marks, carriage return constants, and other syntactical elements into strings, which saves you time and reduces errors (such as a missing set of quotation marks). This add-in is useful for constructing strings to be displayed in message boxes or strings to be printed in the Immediate window by *Debug.Print* statements.

To work with this utility, follow these steps:

1. Press Alt+F11 to display the Visual Basic Editor, if needed.
2. Choose Add-Ins, VBA String Editor. The dialog box shown in Figure 15-28 will appear.

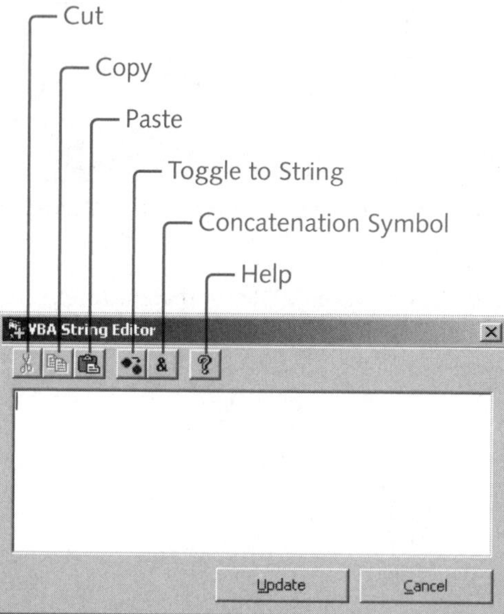

Figure 15-28. The VBA String Editor dialog box offers several toolbar buttons for working with string expressions.

3 Type or paste a string into the dialog box. You might want to use one of the first three buttons on the toolbar (which are standard Cut, Copy, and Paste buttons).

4 Indicate which components of the string are variables by selecting each variable in turn and clicking the Toggle To String button. The variables will appear as blue, boldface text, as shown in Figure 15-29.

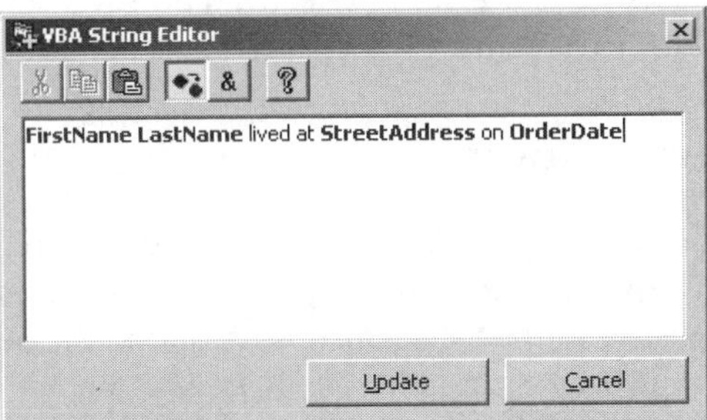

Figure 15-29. The VBA String Editor indicates variables in a string using blue, boldface type.

5 Click the Update button, and the VBA String Editor will add quotation marks as needed. For example, the string

```
FirstName LastName lived at StreetAddress on OrderDate
```

from Figure 15-29 becomes

```
FirstName & " " & LastName  & " lived at " & StreetAddress  & _
    " on "  & OrderDate
```

The VBA String Editor does an excellent job on simple expressions such as this one, but it might not be able to process more complex expressions properly, particularly those that need nested quotes. For example, the editor translates this string:

```
strCriteria = [fldTaskID] = intTaskID And [fldProjectKey] _
    = strProjectKey And [fldTaskConsultant] = strResource
```

into the following string:

```
strCriteria  & " = [fldTaskID] = " & intTaskID _
             & " And [fldProjectKey] = "  & strProjectKey _
             & " And [fldTaskConsultant] = "  & strResource
```

Instead, it should have been translated into the following expression (because the string variables need to be surrounded with quotation marks):

```
strCriteria = "[fldTaskID] = " & intTaskID & " And _
    [fldProjectKey] = '" & strProjectKey & "' And _
    [fldTaskConsultant] = '" & strResource & "'"
```

Even though it might not parse an expression perfectly, the VBA String Editor takes a good deal of the pain out of formatting complex expressions in VBA code.

Other Office XP Developer Tools

Office XP Developer includes a Packaging Wizard, which helps you prepare distributed applications. (This add-in is covered in Appendix B, "Distributing Access Applications.") It also includes Microsoft Visual SourceSafe, which is used to implement source code control and allows multiple developers to work on an application without overwriting each other's work. If you have Visual SourceSafe version 6.0 or later installed, you can use the VBA Source Code Control add-in to help implement source control.

Installing Add-Ins

Application-specific Access add-ins, COM add-ins, and VBA add-ins are installed differently. The following sections explain how to install these different types of add-ins.

Installing an Access Add-In

To install an Access add-in, follow these steps:

1. Copy the add-in's MDA or MDE file to your AddIns folder (typically C:\Documents and Settings\<*username*>\Application Data\Microsoft\AddIns for a stand-alone Office installation in Microsoft Windows 2000 or C:\Windows\Application Data\Microsoft\AddIns for Windows Me).

2 Open an Access database; choose Tools, Add-Ins, and then click Add-In Manager. The Add-In Manager dialog box will open, displaying a list of available add-ins, as shown in Figure 15-30.

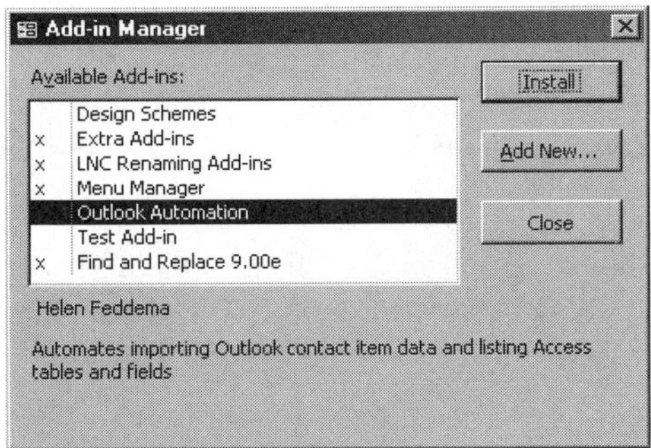

Figure 15-30. You use the Add-In Manager to install an Access add-in.

3 If the add-in you want doesn't appear in the list (perhaps because it's not in the AddIns folder), you can browse for it using the Add New button.

4 Select the add-in, and click the Install button to install it. An "X" will appear next to the add-in's name.

5 Close the Add-In Manager dialog box.

You can unload an Access add-in by selecting the add-in in the Add-In Manager dialog box and clicking the Uninstall button. There are two main reasons for uninstalling an add-in:

- You're developing the add-in, and you need to work on the MDA database.
- You've received a new version of the add-in, and you want to first uninstall the old version before installing the new version (always a good idea).

Installing a COM Add-In

To install a COM add-in, follow these steps:

> **note** If you create a COM add-in's DLL file on your computer, the COM add-in is automatically installed.

1. Copy the add-in's DLL or EXE file to your AddIns folder (typically C:\Documents and Settings\<*username*>\Application Data\Microsoft\AddIns for Windows 2000 or C:\Windows\Application Data\Microsoft\AddIns for Windows Me).
2. Choose Tools, COM Add-Ins to open the COM Add-Ins dialog box (shown in Figure 15-31). If you don't see this COM Add-Ins command, read the sidebar "Placing the COM Add-Ins Command on a Menu or a Toolbar" on the facing page.

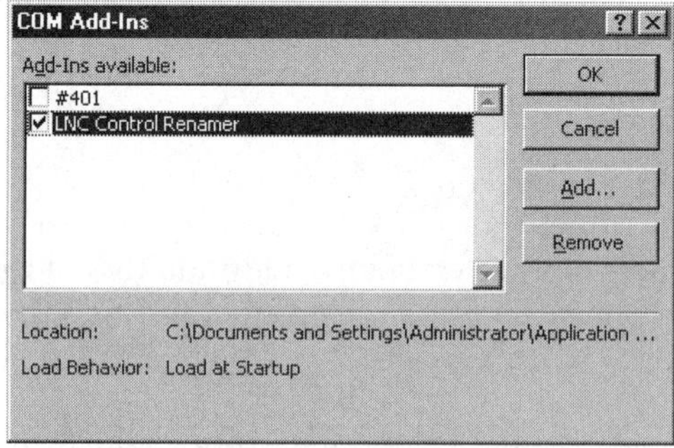

Figure 15-31. In the COM Add-Ins dialog box, select the COM add-in you want to install.

3. Click the Add button to locate the DLL or EXE for the COM add-in.

> **tip** If the COM add-in is in the AddIns folder, it might appear automatically.

4. Check the check box next to the add-in's name in the list of available COM add-ins, and then click OK.

You can unload a COM add-in by clearing the check box next to its name in the COM Add-Ins dialog box.

Placing the COM Add-Ins Command on a Menu or a Toolbar

By default, the COM Add-Ins command isn't available on the Tools menu or elsewhere in the interface. You can manually place it on a menu or a toolbar, however. This procedure is useful if you work with several COM add-ins. To place a button for the COM Add-Ins command on a menu or a toolbar, follow these steps:

1. Right-click the gray background of a toolbar, and then choose Customize on the shortcut menu. The Customize dialog box will appear.
2. On the Commands tab, select Tools in the Categories list.
3. Locate the COM Add-Ins command in the Commands list (it's usually at the bottom of the list), and drag it to the desired location on the menu or toolbar of your choice, as shown in Figure 15-32. (The Tools menu is the logical place for this command, and this book assumes that you'll place the COM Add-Ins command there.)

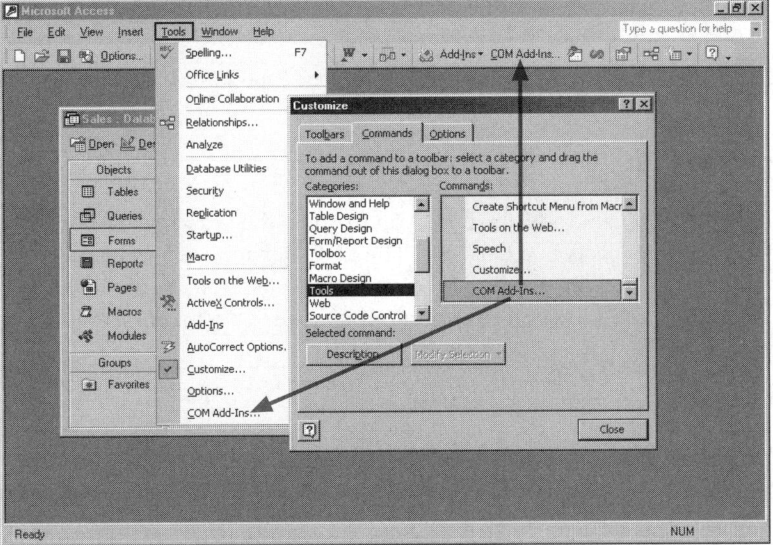

Figure 15-32. You can drag the COM Add-Ins command to a menu or a toolbar to make it more accessible.

Installing a VBA Add-In

You install VBA add-ins by selecting the Developer Tools option when you install Office XP Developer. (For details on installing Office XP Developer, see Appendix B, "Distributing Access Applications.") To change the load or startup behavior of a VBA add-in, open the Add-In Manager dialog box from the Visual Basic Editor's Add-Ins menu, and check either the Loaded/Unloaded or Load On Startup check box, as shown earlier in Figure 15-22.

Using Helen Feddema's Add-Ins

I've written several application-specific add-ins for Access as well as one COM add-in that runs in Access. Chapter 21, "Creating Your Own Add-Ins," describes how I created the LNC Rename Access add-in and the LNC Rename COM add-in. In this section, you'll learn how to use these add-ins and one other in the Access interface.

You can create your own add-ins to save time or add functionality to Access. To find out how, see Chapter 21, "Creating Your Own Add-Ins."

The add-ins referenced in the following sections appear on the companion CD.

Using the LNC Rename Add-In

The LNC Rename add-in allows you to apply the Leszynski Naming Convention (LNC) to existing objects in a database. The LNC Rename add-in includes three menus for renaming database objects and controls on forms and reports plus two builders for renaming an individual control or all controls on a form or report.

See Chapter 20, "Customizing Your Database Using VBA Code," for details on the LNC.

Installing the LNC Rename Add-in

To install the LNC Rename add-in, follow these steps:

1 Copy the LNC Rename.mda file from the companion CD to your AddIns folder (typically C:\Documents and Settings\<*username*>\Application Data\Microsoft\AddIns for a stand-alone Office installation in Windows 2000 or C:\Windows\Application Data\Microsoft\AddIns for Windows Me).

2. Using the Add-In Manager, install the LNC Renaming add-in. (When you load the add-in, Access might warn you that the LNC Rename add-in contains macros—which can carry viruses—and ask whether you want to enable the macros. The macros don't contain viruses, and you must enable the macros for the add-in to work properly.)

Three selections now appear on the Add-In menu (Rename Form Controls, Rename Report Controls, and Rename Database Objects).

Installing Find And Replace

The LNC Rename add-in uses the Find And Replace add-in for some chores (renaming database objects in particular). (Find And Replace is an Access add-in created by Rick Fisher; a 30-day trial version of Find and Replace is included in the Third-Party Add-Ins section of the companion CD.) If you already have Find And Replace version 9.00e installed, you're all set; otherwise, follow these steps to install Find And Replace:

1. Double-click the repl9.exe file on the companion CD to run the WinZip Self-Extractor.
2. Unzip the Find And Replace files to the AddIns folder (C:\Documents and Settings\<*username*>\Application Data\Microsoft\AddIns for Windows 2000 or C:\Windows\Application Data\Microsoft\AddIns for Windows Me).
3. Find And Replace Help opens. You can close it.
4. Using the Add-In Manager, install the Find and Replace 9.00e add-in.

Now you're ready to use the LNC Rename add-in. It will invoke Find And Replace as needed to rename references to database objects.

Rename Database Objects

You can use the Rename Database Objects command to apply the LNC to a database that's totally devoid of a naming convention. The sample database used to demonstrate the LNC Rename add-in is Event Management.mdb. Event Management.mdb is a database created using the Access Database Wizard. Because the wizard doesn't use any naming convention when it creates database objects and controls, the database needs extensive renaming.

To use Rename Database Objects to apply the LNC, follow these steps:

1. On the Add-Ins menu, click Rename Database Objects to open the Choose Database Object form, as shown in Figure 15-33.

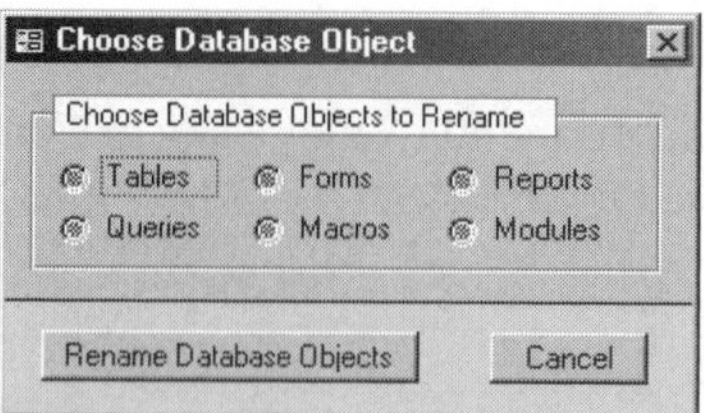

Figure 15-33. On the Choose Database Object form, select the type of database object to rename.

2. Click Tables as the type of database object to rename, and then click the Rename Database Objects button.

tip The majority of references in VBA code will be to tables, so it's advisable to rename tables first and then rename queries, forms, reports, macros, and modules (although in many cases there will be no need to rename macros or modules).

3. The Tables To Rename dialog box (shown in Figure 15-34) will appear, listing all the tables in the database and suggesting new names using standard LNC tags. If you don't want to rename a table, clear its check box in the Use column.

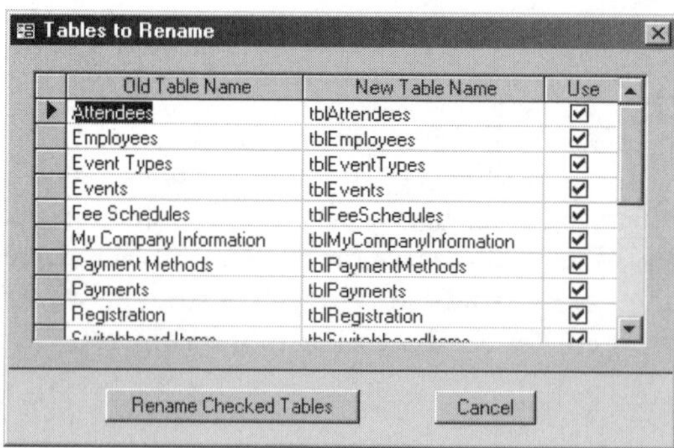

Figure 15-34. The tables in a database are renamed with the LNC *tbl* tag.

4. Click the Rename Checked Tables button. The first time you click the button, Find And Replace will ask you to locate the add-in's help file (Replace9.hlp).

5. Click OK and navigate to the directory to which you extracted the repl9.exe files (C:\Documents and Settings\<*username*>\Application Data\Microsoft\AddIns for Windows 2000 or C:\Windows\Application Data\Microsoft\AddIns for Windows Me), select the Replace9.hlp file, and click Open. A dialog box will be displayed, indicating this is a shareware version of Find And Replace that you can evaluate for 30 days.

6. Click OK. Find And Replace will open, with the information about old and new table names preloaded, and it will proceed to locate all the references to the old object names in the database so you can accept or reject the proposed change. In a database in which the same name has been used for different database objects, be sure to check the context before you accept the proposed changes so you won't, for example, rename a form with the tag for a table (as shown in Figure 15-35).

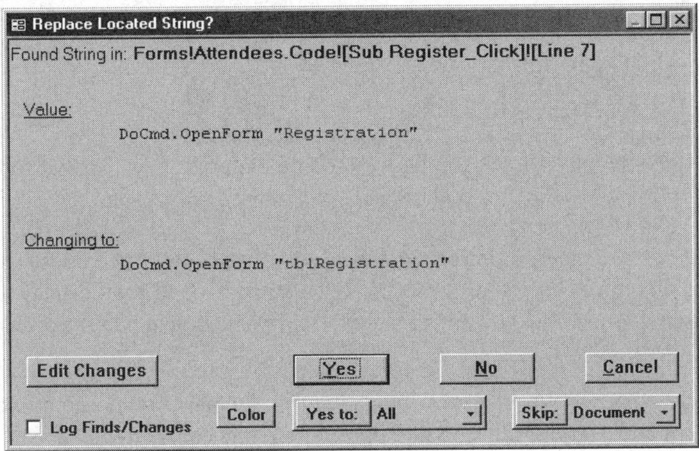

Figure 15-35. Some of the proposed name changes might be inappropriate.

Rename Form Controls and Rename Report Controls

After renaming all the database objects, you can run the Rename Form Controls and Rename Report Controls commands to rename controls on all forms or all reports. To rename controls on all forms, follow these steps:

1. On the Access Add-Ins menu, click Rename Form Controls to open the Forms To Rename dialog box (shown in Figure 15-36). By default, all forms are selected, but if you don't want to rename controls on a specific form, clear its Use check box.

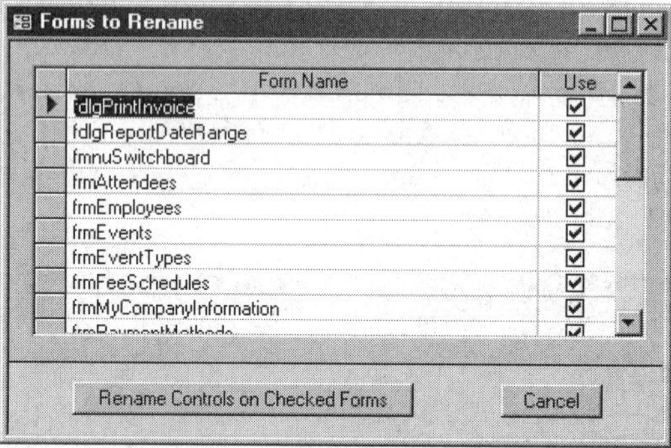

Figure 15-36. In the Forms To Rename dialog box, you select forms whose controls you want to rename.

2. Click the Rename Controls On Checked Forms button. The add-in will proceed to rename all the controls on the selected forms and then display a message asking whether you want to save the original control name to each control's *Tag* property.

   The default button is No, to not save the original control name to the *Tag* property. Generally, this is the appropriate choice. However, if you have some reason to preserve the original control names, click Yes.

3. For each control on the form, you'll see a message box containing the control name, the control source (for bound controls), and the proposed new name, using the LNC tag for that type of object. Click Yes to accept the proposed new name; click No if you want to modify the name. Most of the proposed names will be correct and can be accepted as is, but you might have to type in the correct name in the case of very long descriptive labels or controls with calculated expressions.

4. After all the controls have been processed, you'll get a message asking whether you want to save and close the form. Normally, you can click Yes to save and close the form, but occasionally you might want to review a form before saving it with the renamed controls. In that case, click No to leave the form open in Design view. When all the forms have been processed, you'll see a message stating that all forms have been processed.

The LNC Builders

If you want to rename a single control on a form, you can use the LNC Rename Current Control builder. To do so, follow these steps:

1. On the control's properties sheet, click the Build button next to the control's *Name* property, as shown in Figure 15-37.

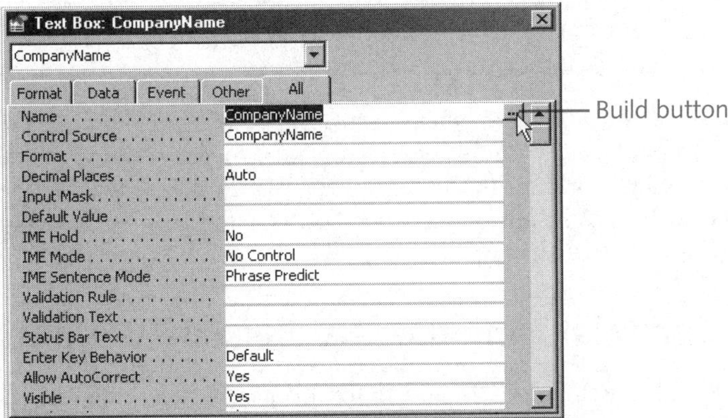

Figure 15-37. To rename a control, click the Build button next to its *Name* property on its properties sheet.

2. The Choose Builder dialog box (shown in Figure 15-38) will open, offering you a choice of LNC Rename Current Control, which renames just the current control, or LNC Rename All Controls, which renames all the controls on the current form or report.

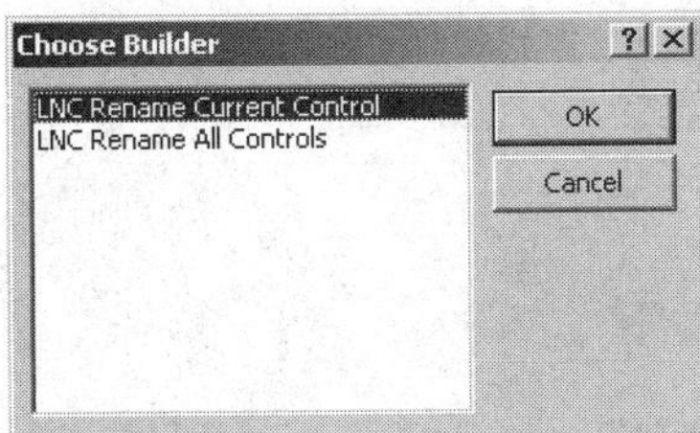

Figure 15-38. The Choose Builder dialog box lists the two LNC builders.

3. Select the LNC Rename Current Control builder, and then click OK. If the name does not use LNC, you'll see a message suggesting the proposed new name using the appropriate LNC tag for the control type.

By default, Access gives a bound control the same name as its field. This can lead to circular reference errors, so it's especially important to rename bound controls in order to avoid confusion with fields of the same name.

See Chapter 6, "Working with Form Controls," for more information about circular reference errors.

To rename all controls on the current form or report, you can use the LNC Rename All Controls builder. To use this builder, open the detail section's properties sheet, and click the Build button next to the *Name* property. In the Choose Builder dialog box, click LNC Rename All Controls and click OK. The builder will display a message suggesting a new name for each control in turn.

Renaming Controls Using the LNC Rename COM Add-In

I wrote the LNC Rename COM add-in to fill a gap between the Rename Form Controls (or Rename Report Controls) commands and the LNC Rename All Controls in the Choose Builder dialog box. The LNC Rename COM add-in renames form controls or report controls on all currently open forms or reports. This add-in places a Rename Controls button on the Form Design and Report Design toolbars for quick access, as shown in Figure 15-39.

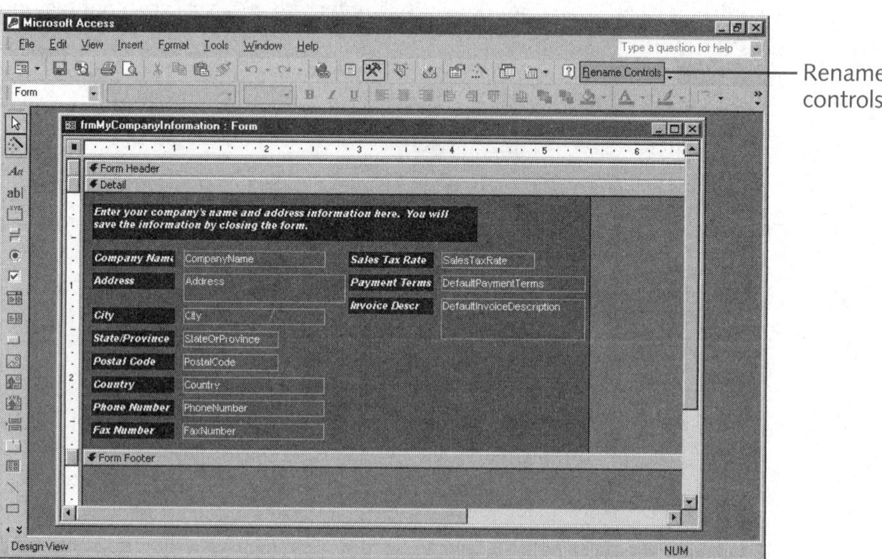

Figure 15-39. The Rename Controls button lets you quickly rename the controls on a form or a report.

You can click the Rename Controls button to cycle through all controls on all open forms or reports, renaming each control, and displaying the same message box as for the Access add-ins. The LNC Rename COM add-in is located on the companion CD and is named LNC Rename.dll. For instructions on how to install it, see the section "Installing a COM Add-In" earlier in this chapter.

Creating a Main Menu Using the Menu Manager Add-In

The Menu Manager add-in creates a main menu for an Access application, with drop-down lists for selecting database objects. It consists of three menu add-ins—one for creating the main menu and two for doing housekeeping chores later on. To install and test the add-in, follow these steps:

1. Copy the Menu Manager.mda add-in included on the companion CD to your AddIns folder (C:\Documents and Settings\<*username*>\Application Data\Microsoft\AddIns for Windows 2000 or C:\Windows\Application Data\Microsoft\AddIns for Windows Me).
2. Open the Test Database.mdb file included on the companion CD. This database contains some Northwind components, with the LNC applied, and a line of code added to the *Close* or *Unload* event of its forms to display the main menu when a form is closed.
3. Click the Tools menu, Add-Ins, and Add-In Manager.
4. Use the Add-In Manager to install the Menu Manager add-in.
5. Click Create Main Menu on the Add-Ins menu.

> **note** The Menu Manager relies on some components of Microsoft Word 2002. If you don't have Word 2002 installed, you will likely get the following error when you try to use the Menu Manager add-in: "Microsoft Access can't find the wizard, or the wizard has not been installed, or there is a syntax error in the Declarations section of a Visual Basic module." To eliminate this error, you will need to install Word 2002.

6. After some processing, the Menu Sidebar Picture Picker dialog box will open. Enter the application title, and select a sidebar picture for the main menu, as shown in Figure 15-40.

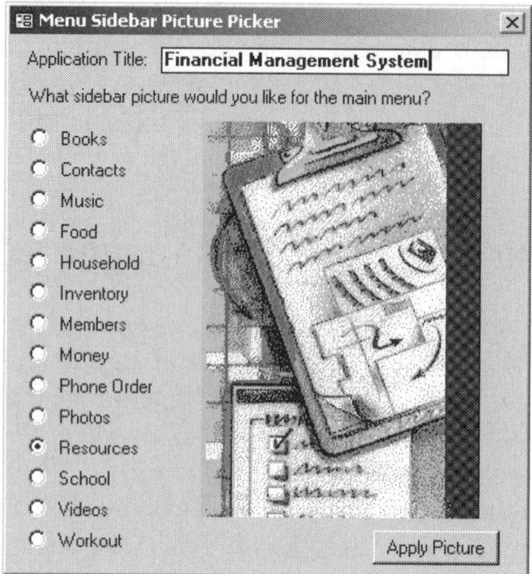

Figure 15-40. Select a sidebar picture for the main menu.

7 Click the Apply Picture button to save the selected picture to the main menu form. A message box will appear, asking whether you want to open the main menu now. Click Yes to open the main menu, as shown in Figure 15-41.

Figure 15-41. The new main menu lets users select forms and reports or create Word letters.

On the main menu, the Orders button opens the application's primary form (which is identified by the *fpri* tag). (The form name can also be hard-coded if you don't want to use this tag.) The other forms in the database are accessed via the Other Forms drop-down list, and the reports are accessed via the Reports drop-down list, as shown in Figure 15-42. Reports are listed by their captions, with a prefix indicating the paper size. These combo boxes are based on lookup tables that the add-in filled with form and report data.

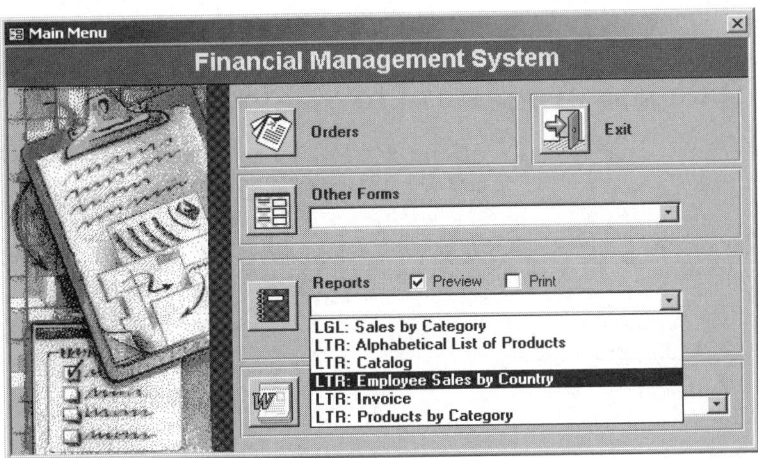

Figure 15-42. Users can select a report from the main menu's Reports drop-down list.

The Word Letters drop-down list lets users select a Word letter to fill with data from Access. Users can select recipients from the Recipients drop-down list. This part of the interface requires some coding to select your Word templates and the specific data you want to export to Word.

After adding or deleting forms or reports, you can refresh the form and report look-up tables by choosing Tools, Add-Ins and then clicking Refresh Lookup Tables.

Using the Database Wizard to Create a Database from a Database Template

When you create a new Access 2002 database, you can use the Database Wizard to create a database based on one of a selection of database templates. A database created from a template is already populated with tables, forms, and possibly other database objects, ready to fill with your data. One set of database templates is provided with Access, and more are available from the Microsoft.com Web site.

Using the Database Templates Provided with Access

To create a new database based on one of the database templates that come with Access, follow these steps:

1 Open Access, and select General Templates in the New From Template section of the task pane, as shown in Figure 15-43.

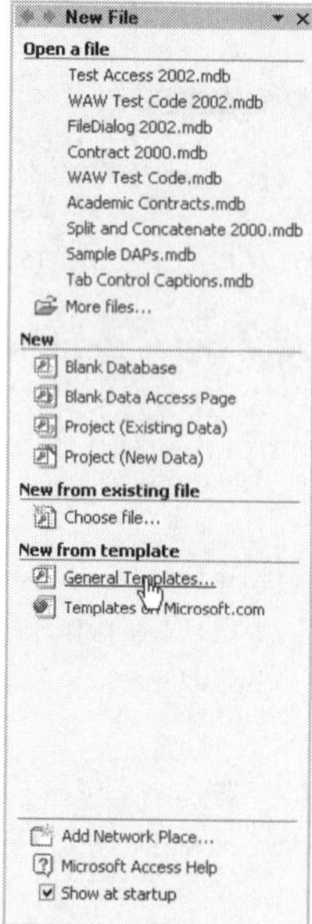

Figure 15-43. Select General Templates in the task pane to open the Templates dialog box.

2 In the Templates dialog box, click the Databases tab. Select one of the templates shown in Figure 15-44 (in this example, Resource Scheduling is selected), and click OK.

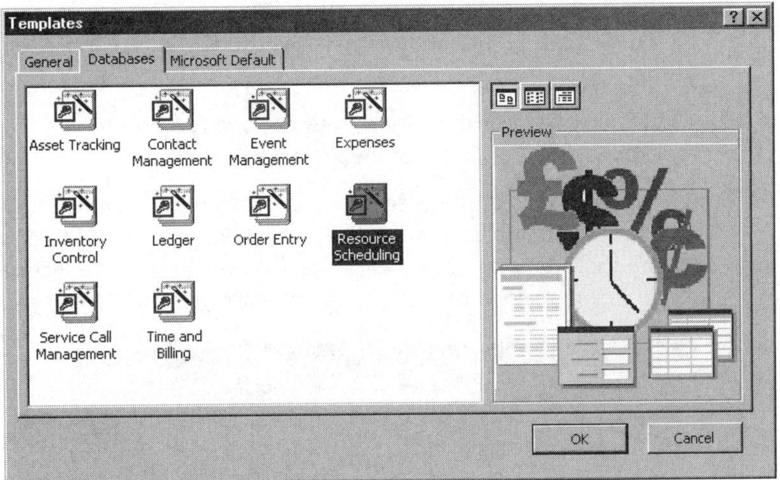

Figure 15-44. You have a selection of database templates to use when creating a new database.

3. A standard File New Database dialog box opens. Type a name for the database, navigate to the folder of your choice, and click Create to create the new database in that folder.
4. The Database Wizard opens. On the first page, the wizard tells you what type of information the database will store. Click Next.
5. The next page of the wizard shows the tables in the database, with the fields for each table. Optional fields are displayed in italics, as shown in Figure 15-45. After you make your optional field selections, click Next.

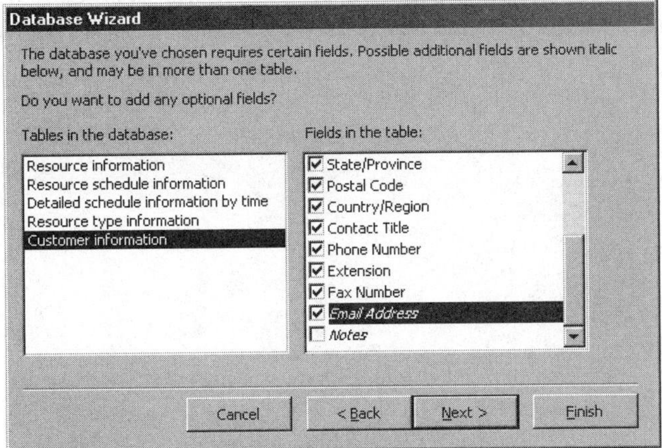

Figure 15-45. You can select optional fields for database tables by checking the italicized field names.

6 On the next page of the wizard, select a style for forms in the database and then click Next. (These are the same selections you see in the AutoFormat dialog box).

7 On the next page of the wizard, select a style for reports and click Next. (The same options are available in the Report Wizard.)

8 On the next page of the wizard, you can give the database a title (which will appear in the database's title bar). If you check the Yes, I'd Like To Include A Picture check box (as shown in Figure 15-46) and click the Picture button, an Insert Picture dialog box will display, in which you can specify an image file.

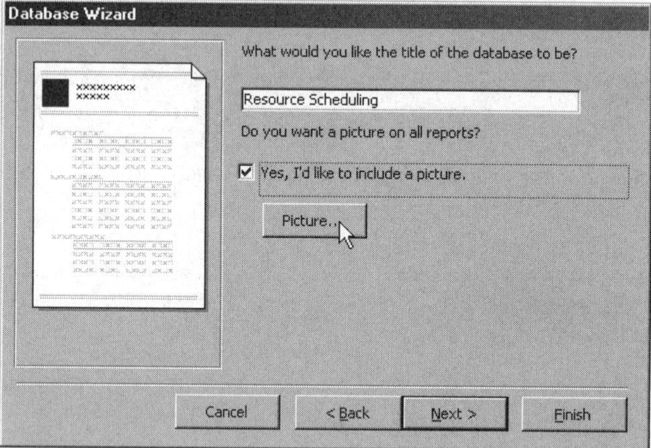

Figure 15-46. Give the new database a title, and (optionally) select an image.

9 The last page of the Database Wizard has two check boxes: one to start the new database immediately and the other to display Help. Click Finish with the Yes, Start The Database check box checked to open the new database.

Figure 15-47 shows the main switchboard of the Resource Scheduling database created from the database template.

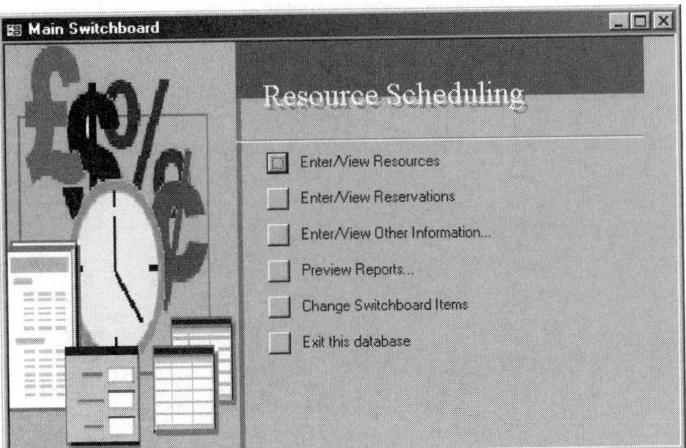

Figure 15-47. The Resource Scheduling database's main switchboard gives you several options for working with resources.

Getting More Database Templates from the Web

More database templates are available in the Microsoft Office Template Gallery on the Microsoft.com Web site. To see what database templates are available (and download the ones you want to try out), follow these steps:

1. If necessary, connect to the Internet.
2. Open Access, and click the Templates On Microsoft.com item in the New From Template section of the task pane. The Microsoft Office Template Gallery Web page opens. (You might first see the Welcome To Office Update Worldwide Web page. If so, click your area on the map, and the Microsoft Office Template Gallery Web page will open.)

3 Enter **access database templates** in the Search For box, and click Go.

4 A page of Access database templates opens, as shown in Figure 15-48. Some of these are the same templates as are available in Access, but others are different. Click a template selection link to start downloading the template.

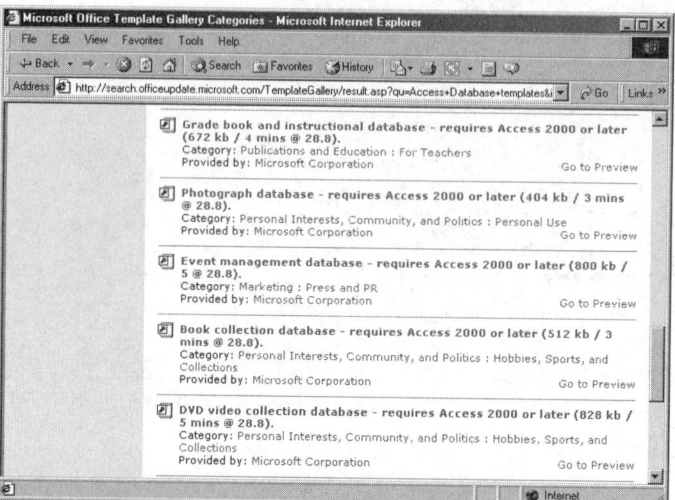

Figure 15-48. More Access database templates are available for download from the Microsoft Office Template Gallery Web page.

Part 5

Importing and Exporting Data

Chapter 16

Importing and Linking Data to Access

You aren't limited to working with Microsoft Access data in an Access database. You can use the power and the sophisticated interface design tools of Access to work with data from a variety of other formats—including Microsoft programs such as Visual FoxPro and Excel and non-Microsoft databases and spreadsheets such as dBASE, Paradox, and Lotus 1-2-3—by importing or linking to Access. And the flexibility doesn't stop there—you can also import text files, XML data and schemas, data files created in an ODBC-compliant database, and even Microsoft Outlook information such as contacts, calendars, and tasks.

This chapter focuses on the methods you use to import and link data to Access. The first part of the chapter shows you how to work within the Access interface to import and link data, and the second half discusses ways to import and link data using Visual Basic for Applications (VBA) coding techniques.

Importing vs. Linking Data

Access gives you two methods of working with data from external sources. When you *import* data, the data is converted from its original format into Access tables that you can work with just like tables you created yourself. Once the external data is imported into an Access table, the data in the new table is local to the Access database and changes made to imported tables won't be carried over to the original files from which the data was imported. In other words, you import data when you need to move data from another file format (such as dBASE) to Access and no longer need to use it in the original program.

If you need to work with data in another file format in Access and you also need to continue working with that same data in the original file format, linking to the data is the right choice. Linking is supported for fewer formats than importing, and some of the selections are read-only, but if you need to modify data in a worksheet both in Access and Excel, for example, you can do this by linking to an Excel worksheet.

As with exporting Access data (discussed in Chapter 17, "Exporting Data from Access"), you can extend built-in importing capabilities in Access by writing VBA code to import data from a variety of programs that support Automation, such as Microsoft Word tables or custom Outlook items.

For more information about the basics of working with Access tables, see Chapter 4, "Creating a Database."

When you *link* data, you insert a link in the current database that displays data from the link's source file in the linked table. The data remains in the source document; only the link is placed in the current file. When you change data in a linked table, the changes are saved in the source file. There are some limitations when you work with linked data, however:

- You can change only the data in a linked table, not the table structure.
- Linked data in files other than Access databases or Excel worksheets is read-only.

Linked tables are indicated by a distinctive icon for each type of data. Figure 16-1 shows linked tables containing dBASE, text, and Excel data in an Access database.

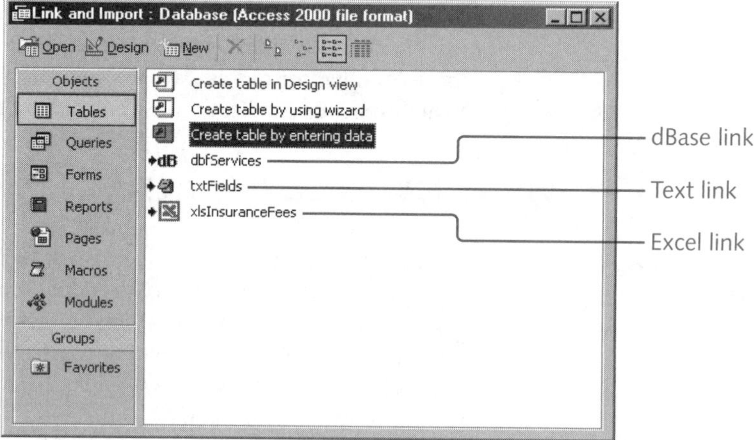

Figure 16-1. These linked tables contain data of various types, indicated by distinctive icons.

Front-End/Back-End Databases

Access databases are often split into a front-end database, which contains interface objects such as forms and reports, and a back-end database, containing only the tables. Linked tables in the front-end database are used to connect to the data in the back-end database. Splitting a database into a front end and a back end makes it easier to update the interface components of a database without disturbing the data.

The Database Splitter (choose Tools, Database Utilities, Database Splitter) automates the chore of splitting an Access database into front-end and back-end databases.

The database splitter utility is described in more detail in Chapter 15, "Using Add-Ins to Expand Access Functionality."

Selecting File Types for Importing and Linking

Access lets you import and link files from a number of applications, which makes it easy to work with data you've already gathered rather than reenter it from scratch. For example, suppose your organization used dBASE to create a donor database back in 1991. Because Access allows you to import data from most major database applications, you can use that data in an Access database that you're currently building. You don't have to reenter the information, and you can create important analyses and reports without a lot of delay or hassle.

You select the type of file you want to import or link by using the Files Of Type drop-down list in the Import dialog box (choose File, Get External Data, Import) or the Link dialog box (choose File, Get External Data, Link Tables). Table 16-1 lists the different file types and their extensions.

note The import options will differ depending on whether you're using the Access interface or VBA code to handle the import or link. To find out more about using VBA code to import or link various file types, see Table 16-2, page 656.

Table 16-1. Supported file types for importing and linking

Data type	Extension(s)
Access databases	MDB, MDA, MDE
Access projects	ADP, ADE
dBASE	DBF
Excel workbooks or worksheets	XLS
Exchange	(Select Exchange folder)
HTML documents	HTM
Lotus 1-2-3 spreadsheets	WK*
Lotus 1-2-3/MS-DOS spreadsheets	WJ*
Outlook	(Select Outlook folder)
Paradox	DB
Text file	TXT, CSV, TAB, ASC
XML documents	XML, XSD
ODBC databases	(Select ODBC data source)

Troubleshooting

The data I need to import doesn't have a selection in the Files Of Type drop-down list in the Import dialog box

If you need to import data from an unsupported file type (such as a Microsoft Works database), you must save the data from that program in one of the formats Access can import. (The dBASE [DBF], Excel [XLS], or delimited text [CSV] formats are good choices for this purpose.) For example, to import data from Works, first export the data to a CSV file, and then import the data from the CSV file into Access.

Importing and Linking Using the Interface

The following sections give step-by-step instructions for importing or linking data in the most widely used formats. You can use the same general techniques to import data from or link to data in the other supported formats.

As mentioned, whether you should import or link data depends on whether you want to permanently move the data to Access and don't need to work with it in the original program in the future or whether you need to continue working with the data in the other program. Depending on the type of data to be imported or linked, the import procedure will differ significantly.

Importing Data from an Access Database

When you import data from another Access database, you're importing a table. If the table you're importing is a local table (a table saved on your computer's hard drive), the import procedure creates a new table, identical to the original one, in the current database. If you import a linked table, you create a new link to the same data source to which the original table was linked.

To import one or more tables from another Access database, follow these steps:

tip **Import a single table or object**

To quickly import a single Access table (or other database object) into the current database, open both databases to the Database window, and simply drag the table from one database to the other. A copy of the object is created in the target database.

1 In the Database window under Tables, click New. The New Table dialog box will appear, as shown in Figure 16-2.

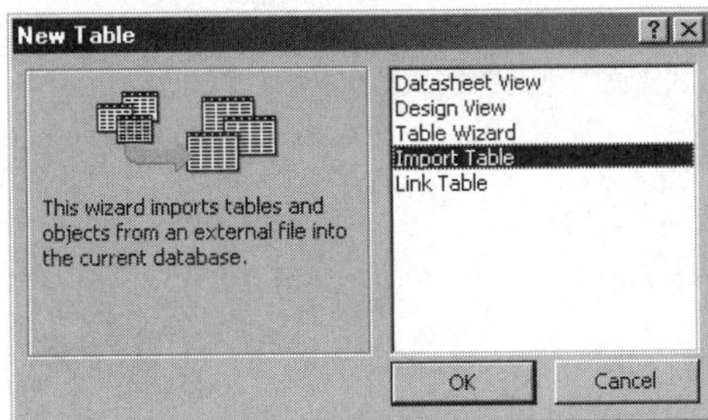

Figure 16-2. You start the import process in the New Table dialog box.

2 Select Import Table and click OK. The Import dialog box will open. (See Figure 16-3.) The Microsoft Access (*.mdb; *.adp; *.mda; *.mde; *.ade) option is the default selection in the Files Of Type drop-down list.

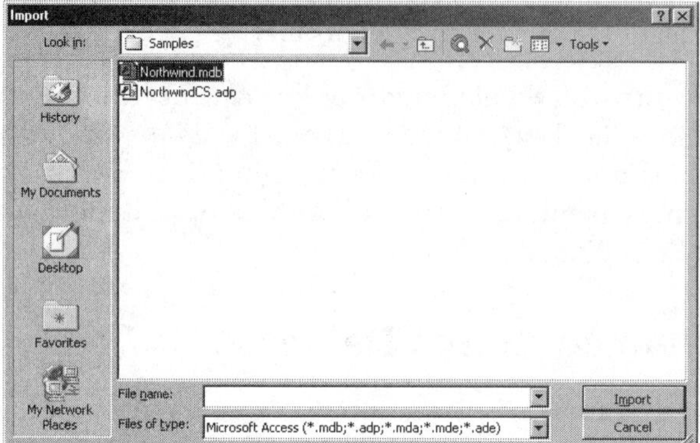

Figure 16-3. The Import dialog box offers a selection of databases for importing.

3 Navigate to the folder in which the target database is located, select the database containing the table or tables you want to import, and click Import. The Import Objects dialog box will open to the Tables tab, as shown in Figure 16-4.

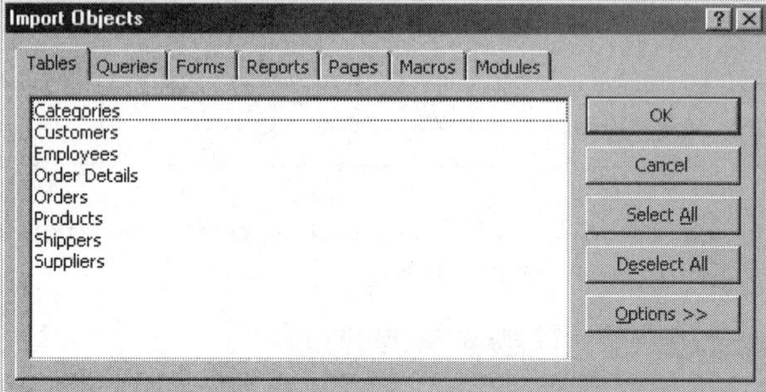

Figure 16-4. The Import Objects dialog box allows you to select the table or tables you want to import.

4 Select the table or tables you want to import, and click OK to complete the process.

tip To select more than one table to import, use the usual Windows hot keys (Ctrl+click and Shift+click), or click Select All to select all the tables at once.

If the table being imported has the same name as a table already in the current database, you won't receive a warning message or a dialog box asking you to confirm that you want to overwrite the existing table. Instead, the imported table will be given a trailing number, starting with *1*. For example, if you import a table named Employees into a database that already has an Employees table, the imported table will be named Employees1. Importing another table named Employees will create an Employees2 table, and so on.

InsideOut

If you want the imported table to replace an identically named table, you can prevent your imported tables from having numbers appended to their names. Before you do the import, rename any tables that have the same names as the tables to be imported—for example, you can give them a leading dash to move them to the top of the Database window. You can then delete the original tables after you verify that the imported tables are OK.

Linking to Data in an Access Database

Linking to data in an Access database enables you to use information stored in another database that you've already created. For example, suppose you want to link your Suppliers database to your overall inventory database so that you can see the latest inventory data and update it as needed. You can link to the Inventory table so that you can update the price or number of items in stock when you order an item from a supplier. Making the changes in a linked table guarantees that the changes are made to the source table—in this case, the Inventory table—so you won't have to worry about updating it separately and possibly having outdated information in the Suppliers database.

To create a link to a table in one of your Access databases, follow these steps:

1. In the Database window under Tables, click New. The New Table dialog box will appear (as shown earlier in Figure 16-2).
2. Select Link Table, and click OK. The Link dialog box will open with Microsoft Access (*.mdb; *.mda; *.mde) as the default selection in the Files Of Type drop-down list, as shown in Figure 16-5.

Figure 16-5. Select a database containing tables to link.

3. Navigate to the folder where the target database is located, and select the database containing the table(s) you want to link.
4. Click Link to open the Link Tables dialog box. (See Figure 16-6.) Unlike the Import Objects dialog box, which you can use to import all sorts of database objects, the Link Tables dialog box has only one tab, Tables. This is because you can link only to tables in another database, not to other database objects. Select the table or tables you want to link to, and then click OK.

Figure 16-6. You select the table or tables you want to link to in the Link Tables dialog box.

Figure 16-7 shows the linked Suppliers table in the Database window. The arrow to the left of the table's icon indicates that it's a linked table.

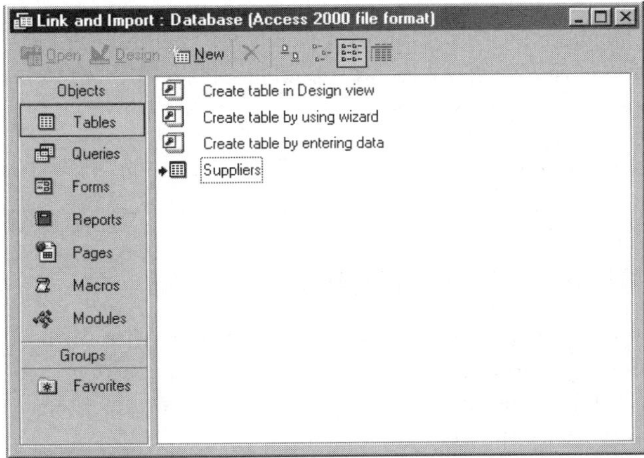

Figure 16-7. The arrow indicates that the Suppliers table is a linked table.

tip

Rename linked tables

You can rename linked tables just as you can rename local tables. Select the table you want to rename and press F2 (or right-click the table name and click Rename), and then edit the table name and press Enter. The linked table (technically, the link) will be renamed in the current Access database, without changing the name of the source table or other file in the source database. Note that if you're working in a multiuser environment, you need to be sure that all users have closed the table before you rename it.

Linking to Databases That Contain Linked Tables

When you look at tables in the Database window, you see arrow icons indicating which tables are linked to external data. When you import a table, however, linked tables in the target database are listed along with local tables in the Import Tables dialog box, without a distinctive icon, so you can't tell which tables in the source are linked. If you import a linked table, you're creating a table that's linked to the original data source, which might not be what you intend.

Access is smart enough to exclude linked tables from the list of tables available for linking in the Link Tables dialog box, so you don't have to worry about linking to a linked table in another database. If you're trying to link to a table in another database and don't see its name listed in the Link Tables dialog box, it might be a linked table.

If you know that the source database contains linked tables, you can either open that database and look at the tables in the Database window to see which ones are linked, or you can use the Documenter in the source database (choose Tools, Analyze, Documenter) to document all the tables in the database for reference when you link to tables in this database. The linked tables are identified on the Attributes line, which will read something like this for a linked table:

```
Attributes:  Linked Connect:  ;Database=D:\NDSL Data.MDB
```


Importing Data from an Excel Worksheet

If you've been tracking data in an Excel worksheet, you can easily import the information into an Access database. You might do this, for example, to incorporate the information you store in an Excel spreadsheet that tracks your spending patterns with the companies in your Suppliers data table.

When you import data from an Excel worksheet using the Access interface, you use the Import Spreadsheet Wizard, which guides you through the import process.

InsideOut

Excel worksheets often contain titles and explanatory text above columns of data or totals below columns of numbers, which might cause unwanted results when you use the imported data in a form or report, and in some cases might even prevent the import entirely. To ensure a clean import, always trim the worksheet to just the data and column headings or prepare a named range that includes only the data cells to import.

To import data from an Excel worksheet, follow these steps:

1. Choose File, Get External Data, Import. The Import dialog box will appear.
2. In the Files Of Type drop-down list, select Microsoft Excel (*.xls), as shown in Figure 16-8.

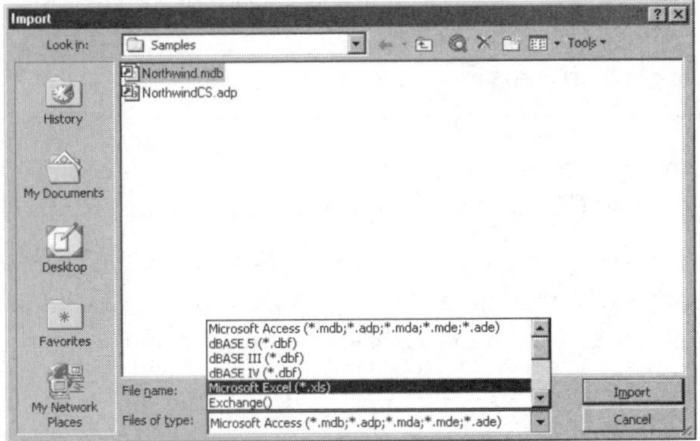

Figure 16-8. You select the import format in the Import dialog box.

3. Navigate to the folder containing the Excel worksheet or workbook you want to import, select the file, and then click Import. The Import Spreadsheet Wizard will launch, offering you a choice of displaying worksheets or named ranges in the selected workbook file, as shown in Figure 16-9.

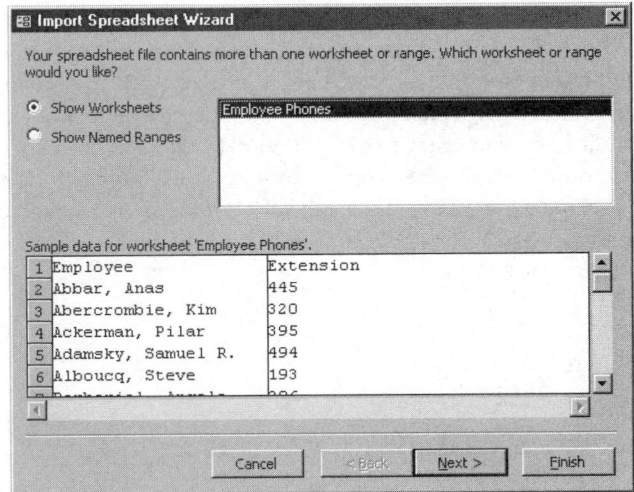

Figure 16-9. The first page of the Import Spreadsheet Wizard lets you choose between displaying worksheets or named ranges in the workbook file.

4 Click the option you want, and then click Next.

note An entire XLS file is a workbook (except in very early versions of Excel), and each workbook contains one or more worksheets. When you select a workbook for importing or linking, you're given a choice of which worksheet in the workbook to import or link to. If you need to import or link to several worksheets from one workbook, you must import or link to each one separately. Each worksheet becomes an imported or a linked table in the Access database.

5 If you want the first row in the spreadsheet to be used as column headings, check the First Row Contains Column Headings check box. Click Next.

6 Access needs to know where you want to store the Excel data. If you want to import the data into a new table, leave In A New Table selected. If you want to add the data to an existing table, click that option and select the table. Click Next.

tip If you haven't prepared an Access table that matches exactly the column headings in the Excel worksheet, select In A New Table because importing to an existing table won't work unless there's an exact match between Excel columns and Access fields.

7 On this page of the wizard, you tell Access how to work with each field you're importing, as shown in Figure 16-10. In the Field Name text box, enter a name for the field. You can select the Do Not Import Field (Skip) check box if you don't want to import the selected field. The Indexed drop-down list lets you specify that you don't want to index the selected field, that you want to index the field and allow duplicate data entries, or that you want to index the field but reject duplicate entries. Excel data types are usually converted to the appropriate Access data type, but if not, you might be able to use the Data Type drop-down list to change the data type of the field. (If the Data Type drop-down list is disabled, only one data type is available for the selected field.) Click Next.

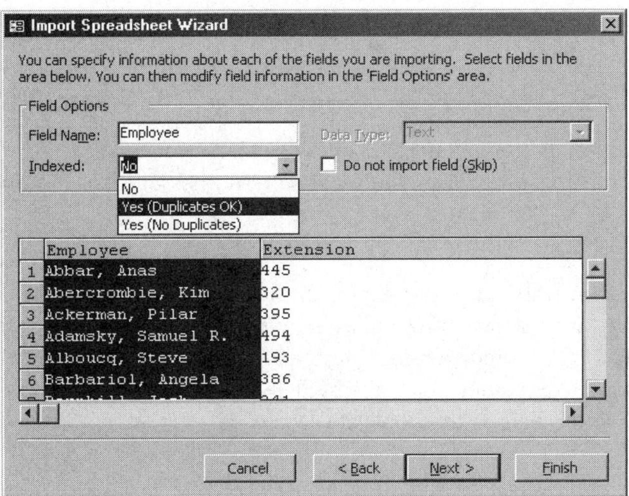

Figure 16-10. You set field options to tell Access how you want to work with incoming data.

8 The wizard lets you make several selections related to setting a primary key, as shown in Figure 16-11. The default setting of Let Access Add Primary Key will add a new AutoNumber field as the primary key. You can also select an existing field as the primary key (select the field from the drop-down list) or opt to have no primary key. Click Next.

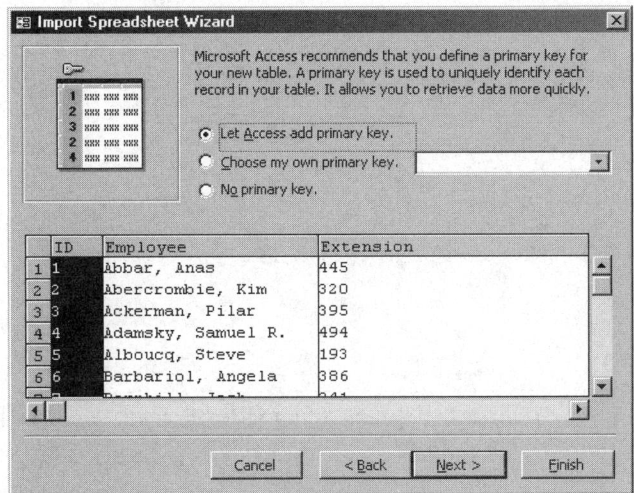

Figure 16-11. You can set a primary key for a table of imported Excel data or choose not to have a primary key.

Troubleshooting

My primary key selection produces an error message

The field you select as the primary key must contain unique data (that is, a different value in every record); otherwise, you'll get an error message like this one:

```
Error creating primary key on field 'EmployeeName'
```

This error might occur because, for example, the same employee name is found in two rows of the Excel worksheet. The simplest way to avoid this problem is to not set a primary key during the import process. Instead, import the data unindexed, and then clean up the duplicate values in Access by deleting duplicate records or by putting a different value in the field in the duplicate record. Then index the key field in the Access table.

9 On the final wizard page, you can specify the name of the new table, as shown in Figure 16-12. The default name is the name of the worksheet. If you want to use a wizard to analyze your imported data or want to open Help, check the appropriate check box. To complete the import, click Finish.

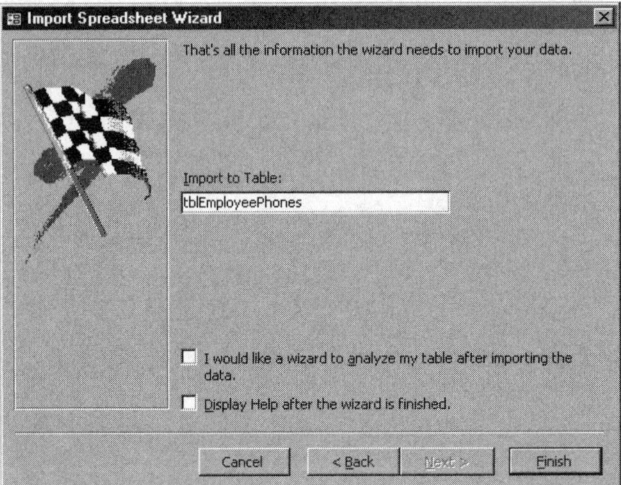

Figure 16-12. You name the table of imported Excel data on the final page of the wizard.

Figure 16-13 shows the new table in Datasheet view.

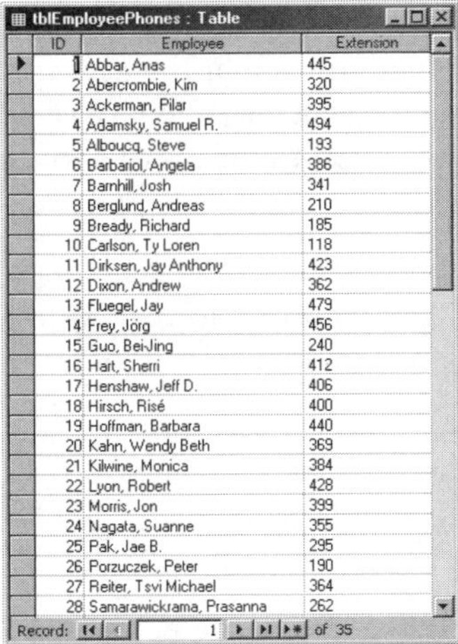

ID	Employee	Extension
1	Abbar, Anas	445
2	Abercrombie, Kim	320
3	Ackerman, Pilar	395
4	Adamsky, Samuel R.	494
5	Alboucq, Steve	193
6	Barbariol, Angela	386
7	Barnhill, Josh	341
8	Berglund, Andreas	210
9	Bready, Richard	185
10	Carlson, Ty Loren	118
11	Dirksen, Jay Anthony	423
12	Dixon, Andrew	362
13	Fluegel, Jay	479
14	Frey, Jörg	456
15	Guo, Bei-Jing	240
16	Hart, Sherri	412
17	Henshaw, Jeff D.	406
18	Hirsch, Risé	400
19	Hoffman, Barbara	440
20	Kahn, Wendy Beth	369
21	Kilwine, Monica	384
22	Lyon, Robert	428
23	Morris, Jon	399
24	Nagata, Suanne	355
25	Pak, Jae B.	295
26	Porzuczek, Peter	190
27	Reiter, Tsvi Michael	364
28	Samarawickrama, Prasanna	262

Figure 16-13. The new table containing data imported from Excel looks like this in Datasheet view.

Using the Table Analyzer

If you're relatively new to creating and working with tables in Access, you might find it helpful to work with the Table Analyzer the first few times you import tables. (Because you can't change the structure of linked tables, the Table Analyzer is useful only for imported tables.) The Table Analyzer is a wizard that walks you through the process of testing and improving the organization and format of your data. To start the Table Analyzer, check the I Would Like A Wizard To Analyze My Table After Importing The Data check box on the last page of the Import Spreadsheet Wizard.

Linking to Data in an Excel Worksheet

You might want to create a link to the data in your Excel worksheet instead of importing the data to your current Access table. Linking ensures that the data in the spreadsheet will reflect any modifications made in your Access table, and vice versa. The process for linking to data in Excel worksheets is similar to the process for importing data from worksheets.

To link an Access table to data in a named range of an Excel worksheet, follow these steps. (Named ranges are useful for selecting only the data for linking or importing, excluding titles, totals, and explanatory material.)

> **note** For more detailed information about working with named ranges in Excel, see *Microsoft Excel Version 2002 Inside Out* (Microsoft Press, 2001).

1. Choose File, Get External Data, Link Tables. The Link dialog box will appear.
2. In the Files Of Type drop-down list, select Microsoft Excel (*.xls).
3. Navigate to the folder containing the Excel workbook you want to link to, select the workbook file, and click Link. The Link Spreadsheet Wizard will launch.
4. Select Show Named Ranges, and then select the named range you want to use. Click Next.
5. Check the First Row Contains Column Headings check box if applicable. There are no options for setting a primary key or index when linking to an Excel worksheet as there are when you're importing. Click Next.
6. Enter the name of the linked table. Click Finish. The imported data will be placed in a linked table.

> **tip** If you want to be able to tell that the new table is linked to Excel data whenever you see its name in a list, prefix the table name with a tag such as *txls*.

Importing Data from Outlook

The Import dialog box has a selection for importing data from Outlook, but importing various types of Outlook data into Access has some limitations, especially if you use custom Outlook items. If you use the interface to import data from Outlook items, you're limited to a fairly small selection of built-in fields. That might be all you need, however, if you don't need to import data from custom fields.

To import data from Outlook, follow these steps:

1. Choose File, Get External Data, Import. The Import dialog box will appear.
2. In the Files Of Type drop-down list, select Outlook().
3. The Import Exchange/Outlook Wizard will start, offering a choice of Address Books and Personal Folders. Expand the Personal Folders selection to see your Outlook folders. Select the folder you want to import data from, as shown in Figure 16-14, and click Next.

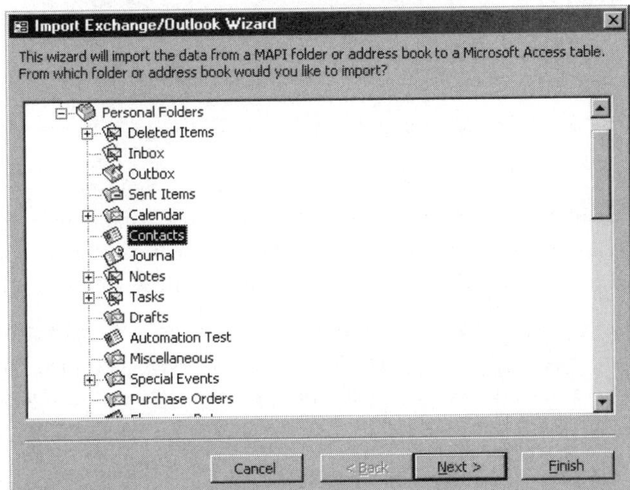

Figure 16-14. In the Import Exchange/Outlook Wizard, you select a folder of Outlook data to import.

4 The wizard lists the fields you can import. In our example, the list displays the Contact fields you can import (which is a subset of all the built-in Contact fields), as shown in Figure 16-15. Leave the In A New Table option selected, and click Next.

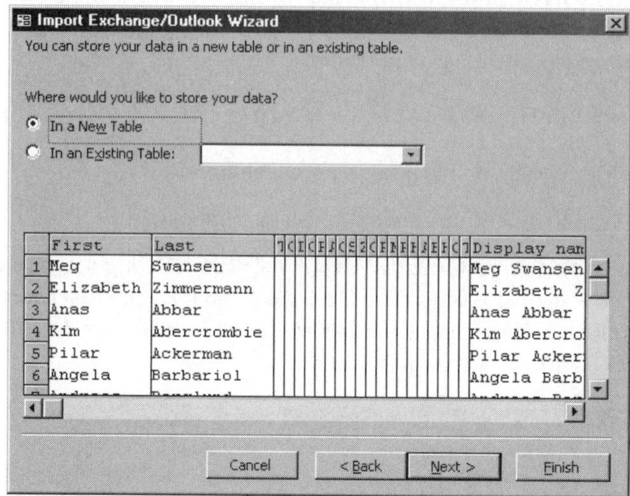

Figure 16-15. A list of fields you can select is displayed in the wizard.

5 You can use the next page of the wizard (shown in Figure 16-16) to select each column in turn and change its data type, and to set an index. Generally, however, it's best to leave these options as is. You can also check the Do Not Import Field (Skip) check box to leave a field out of the import. Click Next.

6 The next page offers the usual import option group of choices related to setting a primary key. For this example, I recommend selecting No Primary Key or letting Access create an AutoNumber primary key because Outlook Contacts don't have a built-in field available in the wizard that contains guaranteed unique data. Click Next.

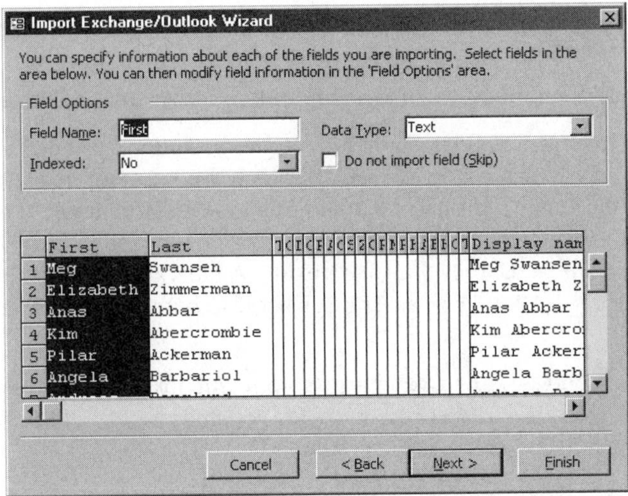

Figure 16-16. You set data type and indexing options for fields on this page of the wizard.

7 On the final wizard page, enter the name of the Access table that will contain the data. You also have the option of checking a check box to open a wizard for analyzing the imported data or checking a check box to open Help. Click Finish to start importing the Outlook contacts into the Access table.

Figure 16-17 shows a portion of the table of imported contacts.

tblOutlookContacts : Table

First	Last	Title	Company	Depart
Meg	Swansen			
Elizabeth	Zimmermann			
Anas	Abbar			
Kim	Abercrombie			
Pilar	Ackerman			
Angela	Barbariol			
Andreas	Berglund			
Josh	Barnhill			
Steve	Alboucq			
Richard	Bready			
Ty	Carlson			
Andrew	Dixon			
Jay	Dirksen			
Jay	Fluegel			

Record: 1 of 37

Figure 16-17. This Access table contains imported Outlook contacts.

The table of imported Outlook contacts will contain the most commonly used name and address fields and will thus be quite useful for most purposes.

Troubleshooting

Important fields are missing when I import Outlook tasks or appointments

If you import tasks or calendar appointments from Outlook using the Import Exchange/Outlook Wizard, several crucial fields will be missing from the table of imported data. Even if you select all the fields available for import, a table of imported tasks will lack the crucial Subject field, and even though it will have Start Date and End Date fields, they will all be blank. A table of imported appointments will fare a little better: It will contain the Subject field but will lack the Start Time and End Time fields.

If you need to import tasks or appointments from Outlook, it's best to skip using the interface and instead use VBA code, which lets you import from all the built-in fields as well as custom fields.

See the section "Importing and Linking Data Using VBA Code," page 654, for a description of using VBA code to import fields.

Linking to Data in Outlook

In addition to helping you import Outlook data into Access tables, the Import Exchange/Outlook Wizard also lets you link to Outlook data. Just choose File, Get External Data, Link Tables to open the Link dialog box, and follow steps 1 through 3 as outlined in the previous section. The Link Exchange/Outlook Wizard doesn't allow you to select fields, so after you select the folder to link to in step 3, the wizard will take you directly to the final wizard page. The final page of the Link Exchange/Outlook Wizard has one check box that's different from the final page of the Import Exchange/Outlook Wizard. This check box gives you the option of having the wizard store your Messaging Application Programming Interface (MAPI) profile name with your linked table. This option is useful if you have multiple Outlook profiles set up, so the link will know which profile to use.

A table of linked Contact data is useful because it contains the most commonly used Contact fields and lets you keep your contacts up to date in both Access and Outlook (as long as you don't use custom fields). You can also run the Mail Merge Wizard to prepare Word letters to send to Outlook contacts using the linked Access table as the data source. (See Chapter 17, "Exporting Data from Access," for more information about using the Mail Merge Wizard.) Linked Tasks and Appointments tables are less useful because of the omission of some crucial fields.

caution In my experience, when you add a new Outlook contact to a Contacts folder that is linked to an Access table, a record for the new contact is also created in the linked table. But the reverse is not the case: Creating a new record in the linked Access Contacts table doesn't create a new Outlook contact item.

Importing Text Data

You can import data from text files into an Access table, but not all text files are suitable for data import. To be useful for importing, the data in a text file must be in delimited or fixed-width format. Delimited text files use a character (typically a comma or tab) to separate data fields and another character (usually a double quotation mark) as a text qualifier. Fixed-width text files arrange data in columns of specific widths, using spaces to pad each field to the required width.

Troubleshooting

I want to import data from a text file that isn't in fixed-width or delimited format

If the data in the text file is in a fairly regular format, you might be able to clean it up in Word before importing. To create a delimited file, use search and replace to ensure that every record ends with a hard carriage return (represented in Word searches as the special character ^*p*) and that fields are separated by an appropriate separator (usually a comma). Also make sure that each text field is enclosed in double quotation marks to prevent problems with quotation marks in the data.

If the text file is closest to the fixed-width format, change to a fixed-width font such as Courier New, and make sure that the columns of data line up, adding or deleting spaces as needed.

After you do the cleanup, save the text file in Plain Text (*.txt) format from Word, giving it the CSV extension for a delimited file or the TXT extension for a fixed-width file. You should then be able to import the file into Access. If you regularly import text files that need cleanup, you can write VBA code to automate the cleanup process, using components of the Word object model.

Comma-Delimited File Import

To import data from a comma-delimited text file, follow these steps:

1. Choose File, Get External Data, Import. The Import dialog box will open.
2. In the Files Of Type drop-down list, select Text Files (*.txt; *.csv; *.tab; *.asc).
3. Navigate to the folder in which the comma-delimited file is located, select the file, and click Import.
4. The Import Text Wizard will open, with the Delimited option preselected, as shown in Figure 16-18. Click Next.

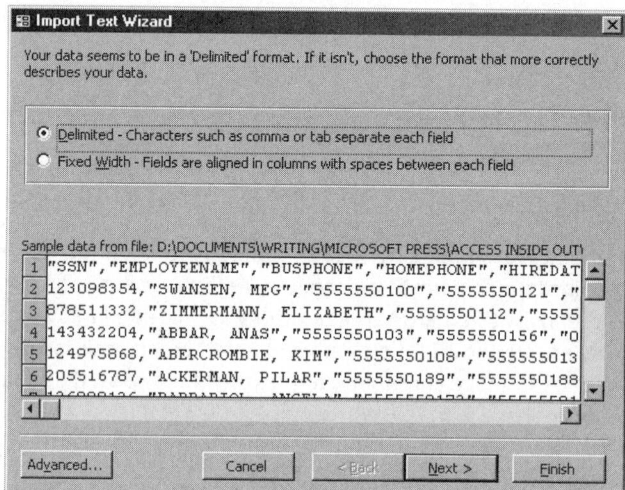

Figure 16-18. The Delimited option is preselected on the first page of the Import Text Wizard.

5. You can designate the first row as field names, and you can choose your delimiter and text qualifier. For this example, use the comma as the delimiter character and the double quotation mark as the text qualifier, as shown in Figure 16-19. You can also change both characters if needed. Click Next.

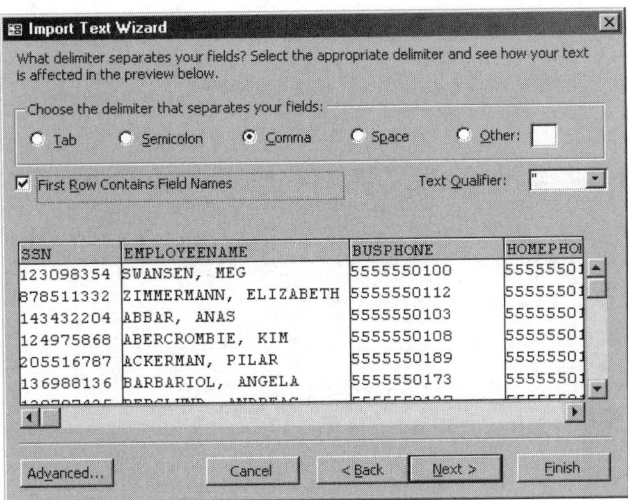

Figure 16-19. Specify the field name and delimiter options.

6 Choose between creating a new table or storing the imported data in an existing table, which has to be prepared in advance with matching field names. (See Figure 16-20.) Click Next.

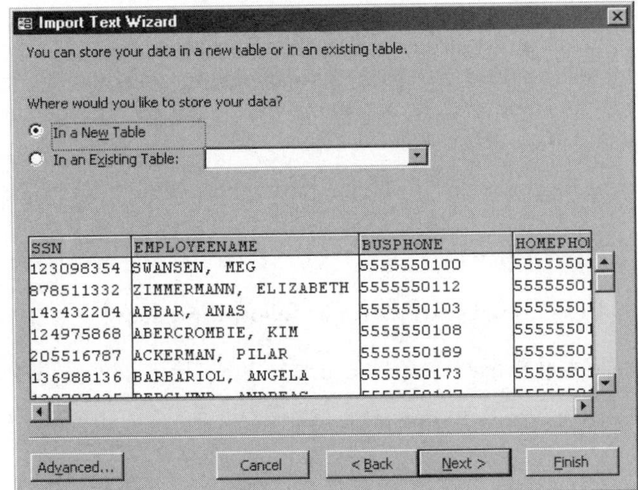

Figure 16-20. Choose to either create a new table or store your data in an existing table.

7 If the text file doesn't have field names in the first row, enter the field names and change the data types as needed by clicking the down arrow and choosing the data type you want from the drop-down list. (See Figure 16-21.) Click Next.

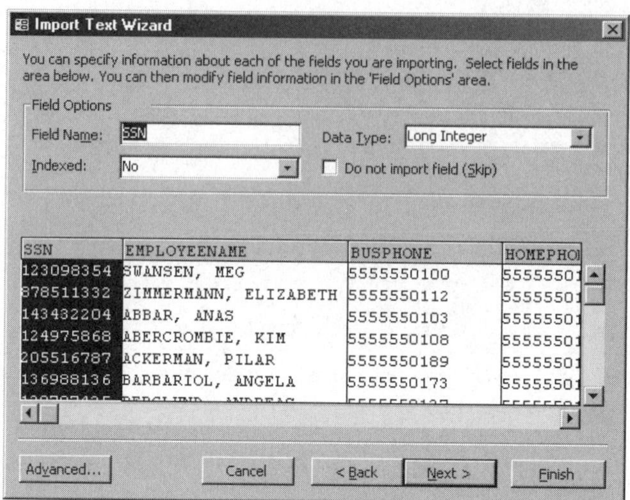

Figure 16-21. Enter field names and specify the data type.

8 Now you need to make choices about the primary key for your table. You can opt to have Access choose the primary key for you, you can select the field to use as a primary key, or you can decide not to use a primary key. Make your choice, and click Next.

9 Type the name you want to assign to the imported table, and click Finish.

Fixed-Width Text File Import

To import data from a fixed-width text file, follow these steps:

1 Choose File, Get External Data, Import. The Import dialog box will open.

2 In the Files Of Type drop-down list, select Text Files (*.txt; *.csv; *.tab; *.asc).

3 Navigate to the folder in which the fixed-width file is located, select the file, and click the Import button.

4. The Import Text Wizard will open with the Fixed Width option preselected. Click Next.
5. Adjust the field breaks if needed by dragging the dividers to the desired location. (See Figure 16-22.) Click Next.

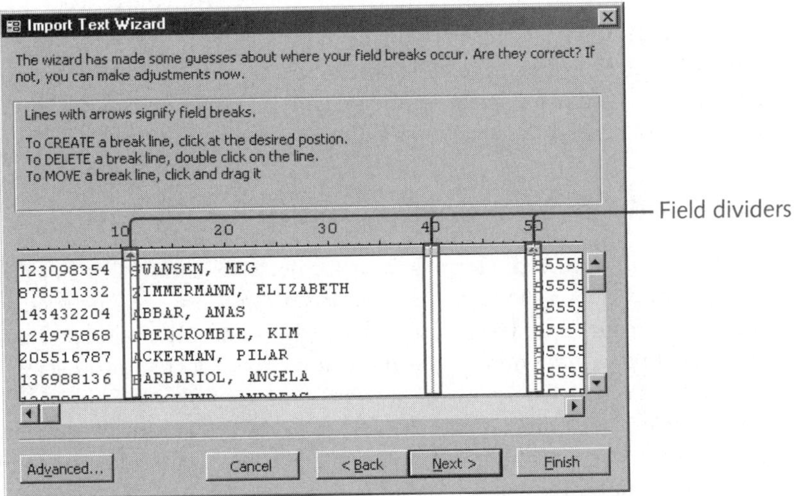

Figure 16-22. The wizard allows you to adjust the field borders for a fixed-width file.

6. Choose between storing the imported data in a new table or in an existing table. As with the other import formats, it's best to select a new table unless you have prepared a table in advance that exactly matches the field names in the text file. Click Next.
7. Name each field. Unlike with some other import types, you don't have the option to use the first row as column headings. Click Next.
8. Set a primary key, and then click Next.
9. Specify the name of the table, and then click Finish.

Linking to Text Data

If you've created a text file containing data that's regularly updated, you can create a link in Access that gives you access to the information but also ensures that the Access data stays current with any updates made to the text file. The process for linking to text files is virtually identical to that for importing from text files. The only difference is that you choose File, Get External Data, Link Tables to start the process. However, working with linked text file tables (both fixed-width and delimited) has limitations. For example, you can't delete or update data in a linked fixed-width table, although you can add new records to the text file.

Importing Data from Non-Microsoft Applications

Years ago, dBASE was the top database for personal computers, but it lost its leading position by delaying the move to Windows. Even though it isn't used much anymore, the dBASE format still has its uses, especially as an output choice when exporting data from an application whose files can't be directly imported into Access (such as Microsoft Works). The following sections give examples of importing several types of non-Microsoft data into Access tables. Linked tables of non-Access data can't be updated, nor can records be added or deleted, but they're useful when you need a table of read-only data for reference purposes.

dBASE

Follow these steps to import data from a dBASE DBF file:

1. Click New on the Tables tab of the Database window, select Import Table in the New Table dialog box, and click OK. The Import dialog box will open.
2. Navigate to the folder containing the dBASE file you want to import, select the file, and then select the appropriate dBASE format from the Files Of Type drop-down list.
3. Click Import to import the file. A dialog box indicating a successful import will appear. Click Close.

> **note** Paradox is another relational database program that was popular in the years before Access really took off. Importing a Paradox file into an Access table is an almost identical process to importing a dBASE file. In the Files Of Type drop-down list in the Import dialog box, select the Paradox (*.db) format, and then click Import. The data will be imported into your Access table.

Lotus 1-2-3

To import data from a Lotus 1-2-3 spreadsheet, follow these steps:

1. On the Tables tab of the Database window, click New. In the New Table dialog box, select Import Table to open the Import dialog box.
2. Navigate to the folder containing the Lotus spreadsheet file you want to import, and select the file. From the Files Of Type drop-down list, select Lotus 1-2-3 (*.wk*).
3. The Import Spreadsheet Wizard will open. It will have fewer selections than for importing Excel worksheets. On the first page, the First Row Contains Column Headings check box is the only option. Check it, and click Next.
4. You can choose to create a new table or store the Lotus data in an existing table. (An existing table must be prepared in advance with matching fields.) Click Next.
5. On this wizard page, you can rename fields (if desired), set an index on a field, or exclude a field from the import. Click Next.
6. Choose your preferred primary key (if desired). You can let Access add a primary key, choose a primary key from the data fields, or choose not to have a primary key. (Figure 16-23 shows the AccountNo field being selected as the primary key field.) Click Next.

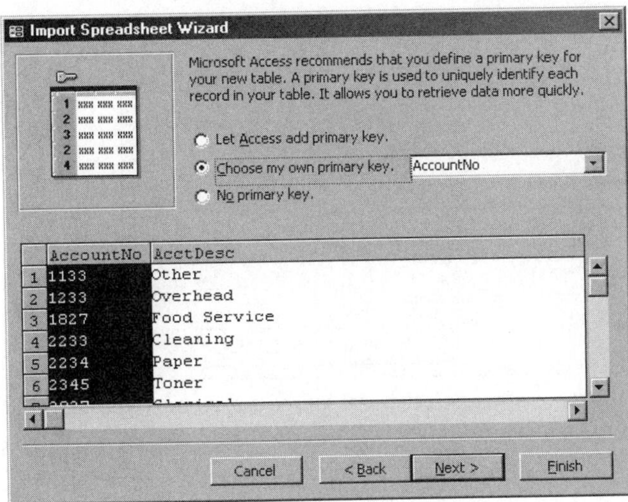

Figure 16-23. Select a primary key for the table.

7. Specify the table's name, and click Finish. The data will be imported as specified.

Chapter 16

Importing and Linking with ODBC

Open Database Connectivity (ODBC) is a data exchange standard that enables you to work with information across a variety of applications and platforms. Many of the choices available through the ODBC selection (dBASE, Excel, and Access) have their own selections in the Import dialog box (where years ago they were available only through ODBC), but you can also import data through ODBC from formats that currently lack their own import formats, such as SQL Server and Visual FoxPro.

tip To link an Access front-end database to tables in a SQL Server back end, you can use the Upsizing Wizard. For information about doing this, see Appendix E, "Upsizing to SQL Server."

Follow these steps to import a table from a SQL Server database:

1. Choose File, Get External Data, Import to open the Import dialog box.
2. In the Files Of Type drop-down list, select ODBC Databases(). The Select Data Source dialog box will open, as shown in Figure 16-24.

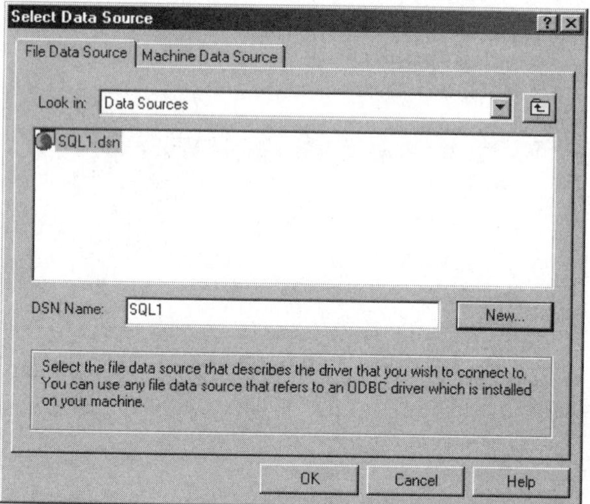

Figure 16-24. In the Select Data Source dialog box, you select an ODBC data source for importing.

3 On the File Data Source tab, select a previously created SQL Server data source file, and click OK.

4 In the Import Objects dialog box (shown in Figure 16-25), select one or more tables to import, and then click OK to start the import.

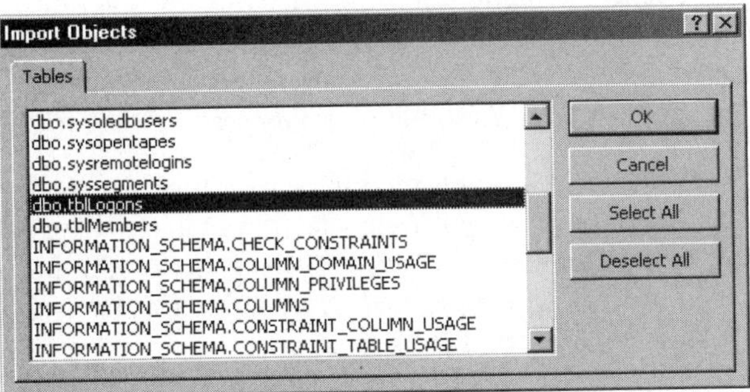

Figure 16-25. In the Import Objects dialog box, you select a SQL Server table to import.

Linking to dBASE and Paradox databases can give you added flexibility—and more data to work with—as you gather, organize, compare, and contrast data that gives you a picture of your business or organization. The process of linking to these formats is virtually identical to that for importing from them; the only difference is that you choose File, Get External Data, Link Tables to start the process. (Lotus spreadsheets don't have the Link option.)

Working with linked dBASE or Paradox files has limitations, however. You can't edit, delete, or update data in a linked dBASE or Paradox file, so this option is useful only if you need a read-only table of data. This might be the case when one or more of the following conditions is true:

- Your old data is archived in dBASE or Paradox files.
- The current data is stored in an Access database.
- You need to see the old data when comparing results over the years.
- You need to modify only current Access data.

Importing and Linking Data Using VBA Code

Now that you understand how to use the Access interface to import and link data, you might want to go beyond the menu selections by writing VBA code to import or link data. VBA, which is included in Office XP, lets you import file types that aren't supported in the Import dialog box. The only requirements for importing data in VBA code are that the source program is an Automation server, and that it contains data.

Although most of the examples in this section deal with importing data, many (but not all) data types support linking as well. Your selection of a named argument when using the *TransferText*, *TransferDatabase*, or *TransferSpreadsheet* method determines whether the data is imported or linked. Using *acLink* as the value for the *TransferType* argument performs a link; using *acImport* performs an import.

See Chapter 20, "Customizing Your Database Using VBA Code," for more information about writing VBA code.

You might be wondering why you'd want to write VBA code to do an import when so many importing options are available through the interface. Maybe you just love writing code. Apart from that, there are two main reasons:

- You need to import data from a format that isn't supported in the interface, such as data in a Word table or custom Outlook contact items.
- You need to do the same import frequently (for example, to import the current month's sales data from an Excel worksheet), and you want to make the import process quick and easy, without having to go through the wizard every time. Running a function from a toolbar button lets you accomplish this goal.

Import/Export Terminology

You'll need to know the following terms to understand importing and linking in Access using VBA:

- **Automation** A technology for exchanging data among applications. An Automation server makes its data available to other applications via its object model; an Automation client works with data made available by Automation servers.
- **Object model** A set of components published by an Automation server that can be accessed through code by Automation clients. These components, or objects, allow the client to communicate with the server application.
- **Enum** Short for *enumeration*. A listing of named constants (with corresponding numeric values) that can be used as (among other things) arguments for functions or methods or as the return values of functions.
- **Method** An action that an object can perform, such as *TransferDatabase* or *CopyObject*.
- **Parameter (or argument)** A piece of information provided to a function or a method.

newfeature!

Access offers three methods for importing data from various types of files to Access: *TransferDatabase*, *TransferSpreadsheet*, and *TransferText*. A fourth method, the new *TransferSQLDatabase* method, is used to copy one SQL Server database to another. For file formats not supported by these methods, you can write Automation code to work with the object model of the application whose data you want to import, and use the Data Access Objects (DAO) object model to store the data in Access tables. Access has three object models: The Access object model represents interface objects, and the DAO and ADO (ActiveX Data Objects) object models represent data in Access databases. The DAO object model is generally more useful for working with Access data.

on the CD The code samples described in this section are available on the companion CD in the basGeneral module of the Link and Import.mdb file.

Choosing Import Methods and Argument Values Based on the Data Source

The VBA method you use when you import or link data will vary depending on the source of the incoming data. Table 16-2 lists the choices for importing or linking data in VBA code.

Table 16-2. Data sources and VBA methods for importing or linking data

Data source	VBA method and argument values to use
Access	*Access.DoCmd.TransferDatabase* method with *acImport* or *acLink* as the *TransferType* parameter and "Microsoft Access" as the *DatabaseType* parameter
dBASE 5	*Access.DoCmd.TransferDatabase* method with *acImport* or *acLink* as the *TransferType* parameter and "dBase 5.0" as the *DatabaseType* parameter
dBASE III	*Access.DoCmd.TransferDatabase* method with *acImport* or *acLink* as the *TransferType* parameter and "dBase III" as the *DatabaseType* parameter
dBASE IV	*Access.DoCmd.TransferDatabase* method with *acImport* or *acLink* as the *TransferType* parameter and "dBase IV" as the *DatabaseType* parameter
Delimited text files	*Access.DoCmd.TransferText* method with *acImportDelim* or *acLinkDelim* as the *TransferType* parameter
Excel 3	*Access.DoCmd.TransferSpreadsheet* method with *acImport* or *acLink* as the *TransferType* parameter and *acSpreadsheetTypeExcel3* as the *SpreadsheetType* parameter
Excel 4	*Access.DoCmd.TransferSpreadsheet* method with *acImport* or *acLink* as the *TransferType* parameter and *acSpreadsheetTypeExcel4* as the *SpreadsheetType* parameter

Data source	VBA method and argument values to use
Excel 5	*Access.DoCmd.TransferSpreadsheet* method with *acImport* or *acLink* as the *TransferType* parameter and *acSpreadsheetTypeExcel5* as the *SpreadsheetType* parameter
Excel 7	*Access.DoCmd.TransferSpreadsheet* method with *acImport* or *acLink* as the *TransferType* parameter and *acSpreadsheetTypeExcel7* as the *SpreadsheetType* parameter
Excel 8	*Access.DoCmd.TransferSpreadsheet* method with *acImport* or *acLink* as the *TransferType* parameter and *acSpreadsheetTypeExcel8* as the *SpreadsheetType* parameter
Excel 9	*Access.DoCmd.TransferSpreadsheet* method with *acImport* or *acLink* as the *TransferType* parameter and *acSpreadsheetTypeExcel9* as the *SpreadsheetType* parameter
Fixed-width text files	*Access.DoCmd.TransferText* method with *acImportFixed* or *acLinkFixed* as the *TransferType* parameter
HTML files	*Access.DoCmd.TransferText* method with *acImportHTML* or *acLinkHTML* as the *TransferType* parameter
Jet 2.*x*	*Access.DoCmd.TransferDatabase* method with *acImport* or *acLink* as the *TransferType* parameter and "Jet 2.x" as the *DatabaseType* parameter
Jet 3.*x*	*Access.DoCmd.TransferDatabase* method with "Jet 3.x" as the *DatabaseType* parameter
Lotus WJ2 (Japanese version only)	*Access.DoCmd.TransferSpreadsheet* method with *acImport* or *acLink* as the *TransferType* parameter and *acSpreadsheetTypeLotusWJ2* as the *SpreadsheetType* parameter
Lotus WK1	*Access.DoCmd.TransferSpreadsheet* method with *acImport* or *acLink* as the *TransferType* parameter and *acSpreadsheetTypeLotusWK1* as the *SpreadsheetType* parameter

(continued)

Table 16-2. *(continued)*

Data source	VBA method and argument values to use
Lotus WK3	*Access.DoCmd.TransferSpreadsheet* method with *acImport* or *acLink* as the *TransferType* parameter and *acSpreadsheetTypeLotusWK3* as the *SpreadsheetType* parameter
Lotus WK4	*Access.DoCmd.TransferSpreadsheet* method with *acImport* or *acLink* as the *TransferType* parameter and *acSpreadsheetTypeLotusWK4* as the *SpreadsheetType* parameter
ODBC databases	*Access.DoCmd.TransferDatabase* method with *acImport* or *acLink* as the *TransferType* parameter and "ODBC Database" as the *DatabaseType* parameter
Paradox 3.*x*	*Access.DoCmd.TransferDatabase* method with *acImport* or *acLink* as the *TransferType* parameter and "Paradox 3.x" as the *DatabaseType* parameter
Paradox 4.*x*	*Access.DoCmd.TransferDatabase* method with *acImport* or *acLink* as the *TransferType* parameter and "Paradox 4.x" as the *DatabaseType* parameter
Paradox 5.*x*	*Access.DoCmd.TransferDatabase* method with *acImport* or *acLink* as the *TransferType* parameter and "Paradox 5.x" as the *DatabaseType* parameter
Paradox 7.*x*	*Access.DoCmd.TransferDatabase* method with *acImport* or *acLink* as the *TransferType* parameter and "Paradox 7.x" as the *DatabaseType* parameter

As you can see in this table, the oddly named (but very useful) *DoCmd* object in the Access object model has several methods that are used to import or link to data. These methods are part of Access VBA, not part of the core VBA feature set. If you've worked with Visual Basic or Excel VBA, they might be new to you.

newfeature!

The *TransferDatabase* method's *DatabaseType* parameter takes a text string, whereas the *TransferSpreadsheet* method's *SpreadsheetType* parameter and the *TransferText* method's *TransferType* parameter both take a named constant from an *enum* (an enumerated list of constants). Access enums are visible in the Object Browser as classes with the *Ac* prefix. Hopefully, the *DataType* parameter will have its own enum in a future version of Access, but for now you have to supply a text string for this parameter.

Importing Data from Another Access Database

One of the easiest ways to add data to your Access database is to simply import it from a table in another Access database. Earlier in this chapter, you learned how to import Access data using the interface. You can perform the same task by creating a function in VBA code.

The following function imports a table named Employees from a copy of the Access Northwind database into a table named tblEmployees in the current database. The function could be run from a toolbar button (see Chapter 13, "Customizing Access Toolbars and Menus [Command Bars]," for details on creating a toolbar button to run a function), or it could be called from another procedure.

```
Function ImportFromAccess()

    DoCmd.TransferDatabase transfertype:=acImport, _
        databasetype:="Microsoft Access", _
        databasename:="D:\Documents\Northwind.mdb", _
        objecttype:=acTable, Source:="Employees", _
        destination:="tblEmployees", structureonly:=False

End Function
```

Troubleshooting

I need to import from another database in the current path, but I don't want to hard-code the path because the database might be moved

You can use the *Split* function (introduced in Access 2000) to get the path of the current database, store it in a *String* variable, and use it with the name of the source database. The following function returns the path of the current database:

```
Function ExtractDBPath() As String

On Error GoTo ErrorHandler

    Dim strFilePath As String
    Dim strFullDBName As String
    Dim strFileName As String
    Dim strFullPath() As String
    Dim strDBName As String
    Dim intUBound As Integer

    'Extract path of current database.
    Set dbs = CurrentDb
    strFullDBName = dbs.Name
    strFullPath = Split(strFullDBName, "\", -1, vbTextCompare)
    intUBound = UBound(strFullPath)
    strDBName = strFullPath(intUBound)
    strFilePath = Mid(dbs.Name, 1, Len(dbs.Name) - Len(strDBName))
    Debug.Print "Database path: " & strFilePath

ErrorHandlerExit:
    Exit Function

ErrorHandler:
    MsgBox "Error No: " & Err.Number & "; Description: " & _
        Err.Description
    Resume ErrorHandlerExit

End Function
```

Alternatively, you can simply use the *CurrentProject.Path* property to get the path of the current database. Just set a variable equal to this property, and use it in your code:

```
strFilePath = CurrentProjectPath
```

Importing Data from an Excel Worksheet

Earlier in this chapter, you learned how to import Excel data by using the Access interface. In the interface, you proceed through the pages of the Import Spreadsheet Wizard to specify how the Excel data is to be placed in the Access table. The following function uses a single line of code to import data—from a worksheet named Employee Phones in an Excel workbook named Employee Phones.xls located in the D:\Documents folder—into a table named tblEmployeePhones in the current database. This function calls the *TransferSpreadsheet* method and supplies as arguments the same information you would enter on the pages of the Import Spreadsheet Wizard if you were importing through the interface.

```
Function ImportFromExcel()

    DoCmd.TransferSpreadsheet transfertype:=acImport, _
        spreadsheettype:=acSpreadsheetTypeExcel7, _
        tablename:="tblEmployeePhones", _
        filename:="D:\Documents\Employee Phones.xls", _
        hasfieldnames:=True

End Function
```

Importing Data from a Text File

Data in text files isn't as easy to import into Access as spreadsheet or database data because it isn't as tightly organized. If the text data is arranged in a fixed-width format (in which all the fields are the same size) or in a delimited format (in which the fields are separated by a special character, such as a comma or a tab), you can import the text in a single line of code using the *TransferText* method. Unlike with other import types, when you call *TransferText*, you must supply the name of an import specification—one that was previously saved during a manual import of the same text file or a file with an identical structure.

See the section "Creating Import Specifications for Recurring Import Tasks," page 674, for details on creating an import specification.

The following function imports data from a fixed-width text file named Members.txt (located in the D:\Documents folder), using an Import Specification named Members Import Specification, into a table named tblMembers. The function could be run from a toolbar button (see Chapter 13, "Customizing Access Toolbars and Menus [Command Bars]," for details on creating a toolbar button to run a function) or called from another procedure.

```
Function ImportFromTextFile()

    DoCmd.TransferText transfertype:=acImportFixed, _
        specificationname:="Members Import Specification", _
        tablename:="tblMembers", _
        filename:="D:\Documents\Members.txt", _
        hasfieldnames:=True

End Function
```

Importing Data from a dBASE Database

dBASE was one of the early powerful database applications available for personal computers running MS-DOS. Over the years, dBASE has gone through several upgrades and has increased in power and efficiency as it has changed to take advantage of growing technologies. Although dBASE isn't as friendly (or, some would say, as intuitive) as Access, you might find yourself with old dBASE data that you want to use in your Access tables, or you might need to work collaboratively with another group that uses dBASE files.

The following function imports data from a dBASE III file named Customer.dbf (located in the D:\Documents folder) into a table named tblNewCustomers in the current database. Note that for dBASE (and other databases that store each table in a separate file), the *Databasename* parameter of the *TransferDatabase* method is set to the file path and the *Source* parameter is set to the file name.

```
Function ImportFromDBase()

    DoCmd.TransferDatabase transfertype:=acImport, _
        databasetype:="dBASE III", _
        databasename:="D:\Documents", _
        objecttype:=acTable, _
        Source:="CUSTOMER.dbf", _
        Destination:="tblNewCustomers", structureonly:=False

End Function
```

Importing Data from Outlook Contacts

If you're like most Outlook users, you're continually gathering new data as you work with Outlook. Each time you add a new contact to your Contacts folder, an e-mail address to your address book, an appointment to your calendar, or a task to your Tasks list, you're updating the MAPI database stored in the Outlook personal folders file (or in Exchange Server folders, if you're on a network).

You can import that Outlook data into Access. Importing data from Outlook requires much more than a single line of code because none of the *Transfer* methods can import Outlook data. To import data from Outlook items (such as contacts), you must write a procedure that works through the Outlook object model to specify the folder that contains the items you want to import. The code must then iterate through the items in that folder, filtering them for item type (because most Outlook folders can contain items of various types), and then the data will be saved to records in an Access table.

The following function from the basGeneral module in the Link and Import.mdb sample database, available on the companion CD, imports data from selected fields of standard Outlook contacts in the default local Contacts folder into a table named tblOutlookContacts in the current database.

```
Function ImportFromOutlook()

    Dim appOutlook As New Outlook.Application
    Dim nms As Outlook.NameSpace
    Dim fld As Outlook.MAPIFolder
    Dim itm As Object
    Dim con As Outlook.ContactItem
    Dim dbs As DAO.Database
    Dim rst As DAO.Recordset
    Dim strTable As String

On Error Resume Next

    'Turn warnings off.
    DoCmd.SetWarnings False

    'Delete old tables.
    DoCmd.DeleteObject objecttype:=acTable, _
        objectname:="tblOutlookContacts"
```

(continued)

```
    'Make a fresh copy of the Access table to be filled with
    'contact data.
    strTable = "tblOutlookContacts"
    DoCmd.CopyObject , newname:=strTable, _
        sourceobjecttype:=acTable, _
        sourceobjectname:="zstblOutlookContacts"

On Error GoTo ErrorHandler

    'Set reference to the default local Outlook Contacts folder.
    Set nms = appOutlook.GetNamespace("MAPI")
    Set fld = nms.GetDefaultFolder(olFolderContacts)
    For Each itm In fld.Items

        'Check whether the item is a contact item.
        If itm.Class = olContact Then
            Set dbs = CurrentDb
            Set rst = dbs.OpenRecordset(strTable, dbOpenTable)
            Debug.Print "Processing " & Nz(itm.FullName) & " item"
            With rst
                .AddNew
                !CustomerID = Nz(itm.CustomerID)
                !FullName = Nz(itm.FullName)
                !Title = Nz(itm.Title)
                !FirstName = Nz(itm.FirstName)
                !MiddleName = Nz(itm.MiddleName)
                !LastName = Nz(itm.LastName)
                !Suffix = Nz(itm.Suffix)
                !NickName = Nz(itm.NickName)
                !CompanyName = Nz(itm.CompanyName)
                !Department = Nz(itm.Department)
                !JobTitle = Nz(itm.JobTitle)
                !BusinessAddress = Nz(itm.BusinessAddress)
                !BusinessAddressStreet = _
                    Nz(itm.BusinessAddressStreet)
                !BusinessAddressPostOfficeBox = _
                    Nz(itm.BusinessAddressPostOfficeBox)
                !BusinessAddressCity = Nz(itm.BusinessAddressCity)
                !BusinessAddressState = _
                    Nz(itm.BusinessAddressState)
                !BusinessAddressPostalCode = _
                    Nz(itm.BusinessAddressPostalCode)
```

```
!BusinessAddressCountry = _
    Nz(itm.BusinessAddressCountry)
!BusinessHomePage = Nz(itm.BusinessHomePage)
!ComputerNetworkName = Nz(itm.ComputerNetworkName)
!FTPSite = Nz(itm.FTPSite)
!HomeAddress = Nz(itm.HomeAddress)
!HomeAddressStreet = Nz(itm.HomeAddressStreet)
!HomeAddressPostOfficeBox = _
    Nz(itm.HomeAddressPostOfficeBox)
!HomeAddressCity = Nz(itm.HomeAddressCity)
!HomeAddressState = Nz(itm.HomeAddressState)
!HomeAddressPostalCode = Nz(itm.HomeAddressPostalCode)
!HomeAddressCountry = Nz(itm.HomeAddressCountry)
!OtherAddress = Nz(itm.OtherAddress)
!OtherAddressStreet = Nz(itm.OtherAddressStreet)
!OtherAddressPostOfficeBox = _
    Nz(itm.OtherAddressPostOfficeBox)
!OtherAddressCity = Nz(itm.OtherAddressCity)
!OtherAddressState = Nz(itm.OtherAddressState)
!OtherAddressPostalCode = _
    Nz(itm.OtherAddressPostalCode)
!OtherAddressCountry = Nz(itm.OtherAddressCountry)
!MailingAddress = Nz(itm.MailingAddress)
!AssistantTelephoneNumber = _
    Nz(itm.AssistantTelephoneNumber)
!BusinessFaxNumber = Nz(itm.BusinessFaxNumber)
!BusinessTelephoneNumber = _
    Nz(itm.BusinessTelephoneNumber)
!Business2TelephoneNumber = _
    Nz(itm.Business2TelephoneNumber)
!CallbackTelephoneNumber = _
    Nz(itm.CallbackTelephoneNumber)
!CarTelephoneNumber = Nz(itm.CarTelephoneNumber)
!CompanyMainTelephoneNumber = _
    Nz(itm.CompanyMainTelephoneNumber)
!HomeFaxNumber = Nz(itm.HomeFaxNumber)
!HomeTelephoneNumber = Nz(itm.HomeTelephoneNumber)
!Home2TelephoneNumber = _
    Nz(itm.Home2TelephoneNumber)
!ISDNNumber = Nz(itm.ISDNNumber)
!MobileTelephoneNumber = _
    Nz(itm.MobileTelephoneNumber)
```

(continued)

```
!OtherFaxNumber = Nz(itm.OtherFaxNumber)
!OtherTelephoneNumber = _
    Nz(itm.OtherTelephoneNumber)
!PagerNumber = Nz(itm.PagerNumber)
!PrimaryTelephoneNumber = _
    Nz(itm.PrimaryTelephoneNumber)
!RadioTelephoneNumber = _
    Nz(itm.RadioTelephoneNumber)
!TTYTDDTelephoneNumber = _
    Nz(itm.TTYTDDTelephoneNumber)
!TelexNumber = Nz(itm.TelexNumber)
!Account = Nz(itm.Account)

'Use 1/1/4501 to indicate a blank date in Outlook.
If itm.Anniversary <> "1/1/4501" Then
    !Anniversary = Nz(itm.Anniversary)
End If
!AssistantName = Nz(itm.AssistantName)
!BillingInformation = Nz(itm.BillingInformation)
If itm.Birthday <> "1/1/4501" Then
    !Birthday = Nz(itm.Birthday)
End If
!Categories = Nz(itm.Categories)
!Children = Nz(itm.Children)
!PersonalHomePage = Nz(itm.PersonalHomePage)
!Email1Address = Nz(itm.Email1Address)
!Email1DisplayName = Nz(itm.Email1DisplayName)
!Email2Address = Nz(itm.Email2Address)
!Email2DisplayName = Nz(itm.Email2DisplayName)
!Email3Address = Nz(itm.Email3Address)
!Email3DisplayName = Nz(itm.Email3DisplayName)

'Use Switch function to convert numeric Gender
'codes in Outlook into text for the Access table.
!Gender = Switch(itm.Gender = 1, "Female", _
     itm.Gender = 2, "Male", itm.Gender = 0, _
     "Unspecified")
!GovernmentIDNumber = Nz(itm.GovernmentIDNumber)
!Hobby = Nz(itm.Hobby)
!Initials = Nz(itm.Initials)
!Language = Nz(itm.Language)
```

```
                !ManagerName = Nz(itm.ManagerName)
                !Body = Nz(itm.Body)
                !OfficeLocation = Nz(itm.OfficeLocation)
                !OrganizationalIDNumber = _
                    Nz(itm.OrganizationalIDNumber)
                !Profession = Nz(itm.Profession)
                !ReferredBy = Nz(itm.ReferredBy)

                'Use Switch function to convert numeric Sensitivity
                'codes in Outlook into text for the Access table.
                !Sensitivity = Switch(itm.Sensitivity = 3, _
                    "Confidential", itm.Sensitivity = 0, _
                    "Normal", itm.Sensitivity = 1, _
                    "Personal", itm.Sensitivity = 2, "Private")
                !Spouse = Nz(itm.Spouse)
                !User1 = Nz(itm.User1)
                !User2 = Nz(itm.User2)
                !User3 = Nz(itm.User3)
                !User4 = Nz(itm.User4)
                !WebPage = Nz(itm.WebPage)
                .Update
            End With
        End If
    Next itm
    rst.Close

    dbs.Close
    MsgBox "All contacts imported!"
    DoCmd.OpenTable strTable

ErrorHandlerExit:
    Exit Function

ErrorHandler:
    MsgBox "Error No: " & Err.Number & "; Description: " & _
         Err.Description
    Resume ErrorHandlerExit

End Function
```

After the function imports the data, a message will tell you that the import has been successful, and when you click OK, the newly filled table will open. The table will contain several useful fields (such as CustomerID and GovernmentIDNumber) that can be imported only using code.

Troubleshooting

I get a message when I try to import Outlook data

If you get the message shown in Figure 16-26 when you try to import Outlook data, select the Allow Access For check box, and specify 10 minutes. This will set 10 minutes as the amount of time to allow for the import process. (You can specify a shorter time period if you have only a few contacts to import.)

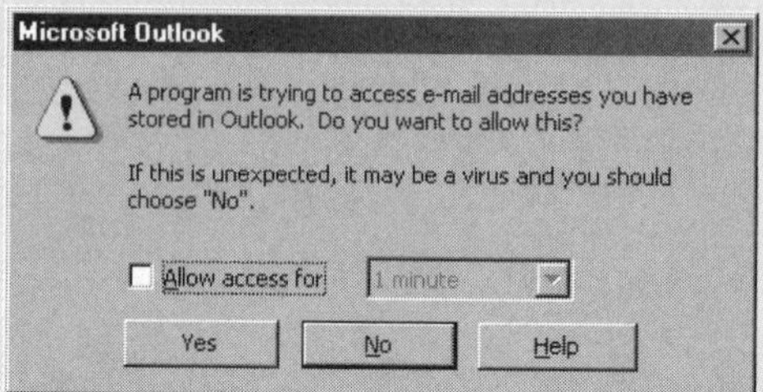

Figure 16-26. A message notifies you that a program is trying to access your Outlook data.

If the import is a lengthy one, the message will pop up again after 10 minutes; you can click the button again to set another period of time.

Importing Data from a Word Table

If you're an experienced Word user, you might be comfortable entering, organizing, and maintaining data lists in Word tables. After all, Word has some basic but functional sorting capabilities, and you can publish your information easily in a form supported seamlessly by a number of applications. Word documents can be opened and printed by all Office users, and users of many non-Microsoft programs as well, whereas Access reports aren't so widely supported for non-Access users.

But what happens if you want to import the data from your Word tables into Access tables? Unfortunately, even though you can store data in a tabular form in Word tables, you can't import data directly from Word tables using the Access interface. You can import Word tables using VBA code, however, by using components of the Word object model.

The following function imports data from a series of tables in a Word document (shown in Figure 16-27) into two Access tables related one-to-many. The Word document organizes the data using styles as well as tables. Each table has a title in Heading 3 style (one of the standard Word styles) indicating the site name, and the table contains a listing of the logon IDs and other information related to that site.

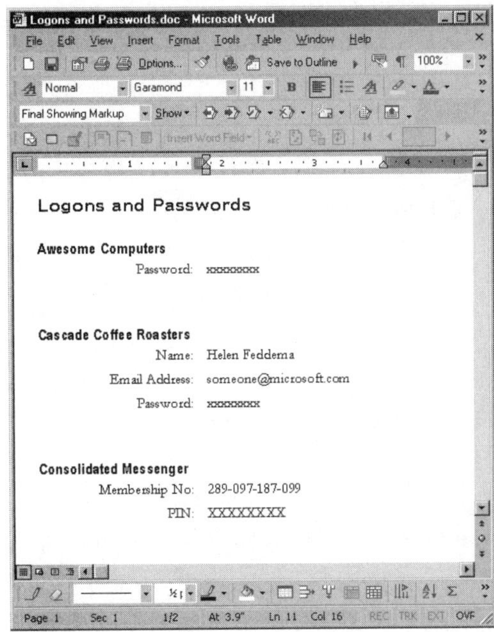

Figure 16-27. This Word document has tables of data to import into Access.

To import this information into the two related Access tables, the site names must be identified, which is done by looking for elements with a Heading 3 style, and written to the SiteName field in tblLogons (the "one" table in the one-to-many relationship). The data in the table rows must be picked up from the table cells and written to tblLogonValues (the "many" table). The tblLogons table has an AutoNumber primary key field used to link records to tblLogonValues as the foreign key field. Each record in each Word table becomes a record in the "many" table. Complex though it might seem, you can do all this in Automation code, using components of the Word object model.

```
Function ImportFromWord()

On Error Resume Next

   Dim strSiteName As String
   Dim strIDName As String
   Dim strIDValue As String
   Dim dbs As DAO.Database
   Dim rstOne As DAO.Recordset
   Dim rstMany As DAO.Recordset
   Dim strDocsDir As String
   Dim lngID As Long
   Dim lngStartRows As Long
   Dim lngRows As Long
   Dim appWord As New Word.Application
   Dim doc As Word.Document
   Dim strDoc As String

   'Delete old tables (if they exist).
   DoCmd.SetWarnings False
   DoCmd.DeleteObject acTable, "tblLogons"
   DoCmd.DeleteObject acTable, "tblLogonValues"

   'Copy fresh tables from backups.
   DoCmd.CopyObject , "tblLogons", acTable, "zstblLogons"
   DoCmd.CopyObject , "tblLogonValues", acTable, "zstblLogonValues"

On Error GoTo ErrorHandlerError

   strDoc = "D:\Documents\Logons and Passwords.doc"
   Set dbs = CurrentDb

   'Set up recordsets based on the empty one and many tables.
   Set rstOne = dbs.OpenRecordset("tblLogons", dbOpenTable)
   Set rstMany = dbs.OpenRecordset("tblLogonValues", dbOpenTable)
   Set doc = appWord.Documents.Open(strDoc)
   appWord.Visible = True
   appWord.Selection.HomeKey Unit:=wdStory

   With appWord.Selection
```

```
NextItem:
      'Pick up site name from Heading 3 style.
      .Find.ClearFormatting
      .Find.Style = ActiveDocument.Styles("Heading 3")
      With .Find
         .Text = ""
         .Replacement.Text = ""
         .Forward = True
         .Wrap = wdFindStop
         .Format = True
      End With
      .Find.Execute
      If .Type = wdSelectionIP Then
         'Selection is an insertion point. Done with the document.
         GoTo ErrorHandlerExit
      End If
      strSiteName = .Text
      Debug.Print "Site name: " & strSiteName
      rstOne.AddNew
      rstOne!SiteName = strSiteName
      lngID = rstOne!ID
      Debug.Print "ID: " & lngID
      rstOne.Update

      'Go to next table.
      .MoveRight Unit:=wdCharacter, Count:=1
      .Goto What:=wdGoToTable, Which:=wdGoToNext, _
         Count:=1, Name:=""

      'Determine how many rows are in the table.
      lngStartRows = .Information(wdMaximumNumberOfRows)
      Debug.Print "Rows in table: " & lngStartRows
      If lngStartRows = -1 Then
         GoTo ErrorHandlerExit
      End If

      'Select current cell.
      .MoveRight Unit:=wdCell
      .MoveLeft Unit:=wdCell
```

(continued)

```
AddValues:
      If .Type = wdSelectionIP Then GoTo NextItem
      .MoveLeft Unit:=wdCharacter, Count:=1, Extend:=wdExtend

      'Save ID name and value to variables.
      strIDName = .Text
      Debug.Print "ID name: " & strIDName
      .MoveRight Unit:=wdCell
      strIDValue = .Text
      Debug.Print "ID value: " & strIDValue

      'Write ID name and value to many table.
      rstMany.AddNew
      rstMany!ID = lngID
      rstMany!ItemName = strIDName
      rstMany!ItemValue = strIDValue
      rstMany.Update

      'Check whether still in table, and go to next heading if not.
      .MoveRight Unit:=wdCell
      lngRows = .Information(wdMaximumNumberOfRows)
      Debug.Print "Start rows: " & lngStartRows & vbCrLf & _
                  "Rows: " & lngRows
      If lngRows = lngStartRows Then
         If .Information(wdWithInTable) = True Then
            'Still in table
            GoTo AddValues
         Else
            'Not in table any more
            GoTo NextItem
         End If
      End If
   End With

ErrorHandlerExit:
   'Close recordsets.
   rstOne.Close
   rstMany.Close
   Exit Function

ErrorHandlerError:
   Resume ErrorHandlerExit

End Function
```

Figure 16-28 shows the two tables of imported Word data.

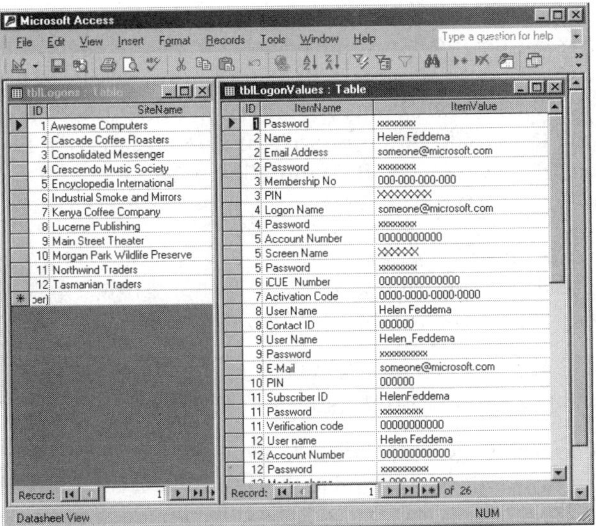

Figure 16-28. These two tables contain linked data imported from Word tables.

Figure 16-29 shows a report listing the data.

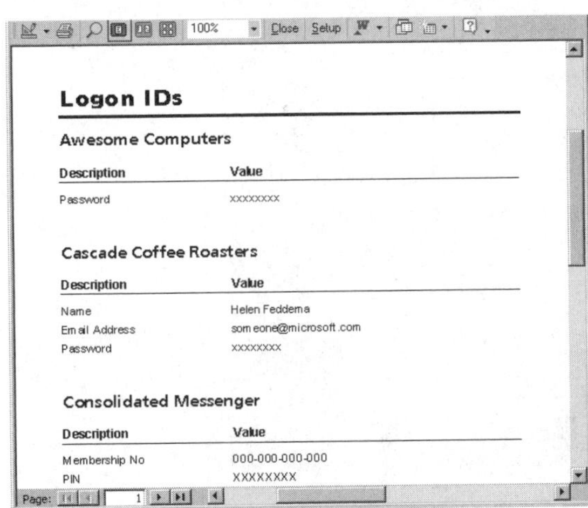

Figure 16-29. This report displays data imported from Word tables.

Creating Import Specifications for Recurring Import Tasks

Let's say you need to do a specific import regularly, such as importing data from an Excel worksheet or a comma-delimited text file on a monthly or quarterly basis. You can save time by saving a specification file for the import. A specification file saves all the options you select manually in the Import Text Wizard or the Import Spreadsheet Wizard. You can apply all the saved options by selecting the specification file from a list that appears when you click Advanced in the Import Text Wizard, or you can call the file by name in a macro or in VBA code.

To create an import specification (generally referred to as a *spec*), you have to step through the appropriate wizard manually and then save your settings to a specification file for future use. You do this by performing the following steps:

1. Follow the instructions for importing a text file outlined in the section "Comma-Delimited File Import," page 646.
2. When you reach the last page of the wizard, name your file—for this example, **CurEmp**. Now before clicking Finish, click Advanced. This will open the CurEmp Import Specification dialog box, shown in Figure 16-30. This dialog box shows all the specifications selected for the current file.

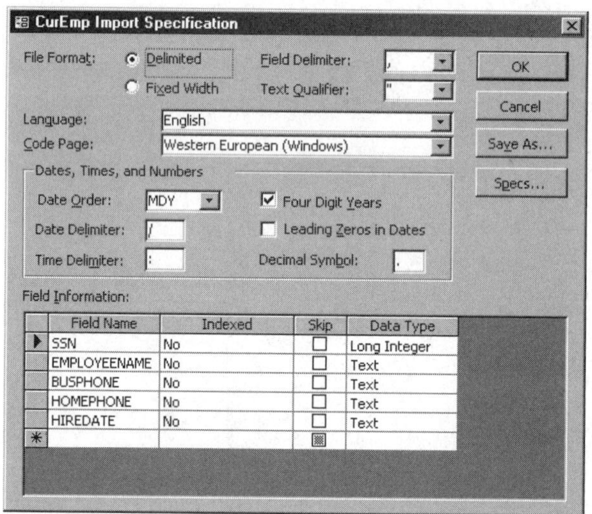

Figure 16-30. The CurEmp Import Specification dialog box shows all the specifications selected for the current file.

3. Click Save As, and enter a name for the spec in the Save Import/Export Specification dialog box, as shown in Figure 16-31.

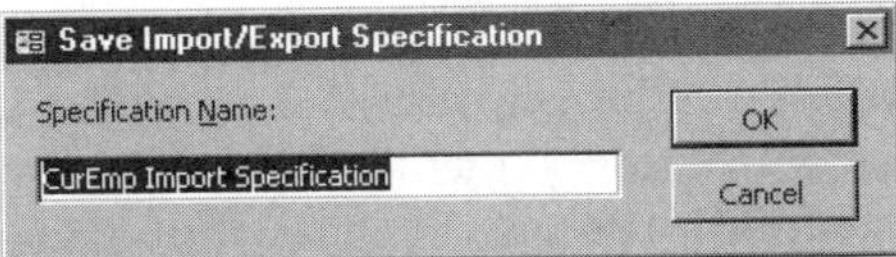

Figure 16-31. Save your import specification with a name that's easy to remember.

4. Close the CurEmp Import Specification dialog box, and click Finish to complete the import.

Now that you've saved the spec, you can use it in the interface, in a macro, or in VBA code, as in the *TransferText* code in the section "Importing Data from a Text File," page 661. To use the spec through the interface, start the Import Wizard with the text file you used to create the CurEmp spec, and click the Advanced button on the first page of the wizard. Click Specs in the CurEmp Import Specification dialog box, and then select CurEmp Import Specification in the Import/Export Specifications dialog box, as shown in Figure 16-32.

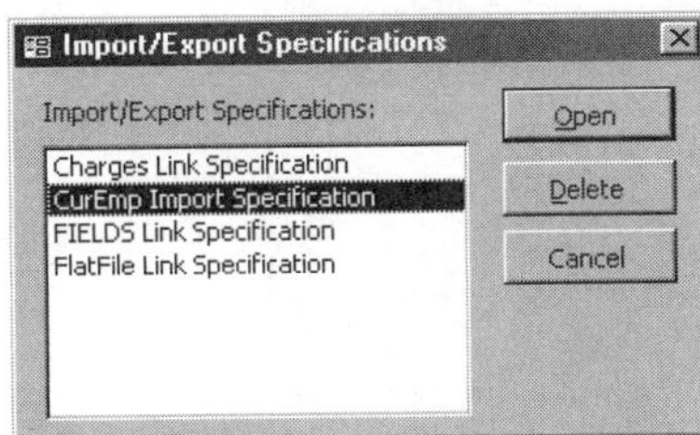

Figure 16-32. Select your saved spec in the Import/Export Specifications dialog box.

InsideOut

Saved specs don't include the name of the Access target table. When you import data using the interface, after you select a saved spec, click Next to go to the last page of the wizard and then enter the table name. In VBA code, the table name is specified as the *tablename* parameter of the *TransferText* method.

Using Queries to Reformat Imported Mainframe Data

When you import data from text files, especially files generated from mainframe databases, the data often needs some processing so that it can be appropriately formatted for use in Access databases. Mainframe databases often lack features (such as input masks in Access tables) that prevent data entry errors and enforce consistency. Also, Access fields have more (or different) data type selections than mainframe databases, so some fields might need to be converted to a different data type, such as dates stored in a mainframe text field.

If you regularly download data to update your files and therefore routinely import text files of identical structure, the best way to massage that data is to import it without attempting to fix it in the Import dialog box (or in the saved spec). Then use a query (or perhaps several queries, depending on how much reworking the data needs) to reformat the data, appending cleaned-up data to another table. Let's look at an example.

The table of raw imported data shown in Figure 16-33 is typical of data downloaded from mainframe databases.

tblCurrentEmployeesRaw : Table

SSN	EMPLOYEENAME	BUSPHONE	HOMEPHONE	HIREDATE
123098354	SWANSEN, MEG	5555550100	5555550121	090181
878511332	ZIMMERMANN, ELIZABETH	5555550112	5555550132	090181
143432204	ABBAR, ANAS	5555550103	5555550156	090195
124975868	ABERCROMBIE, KIM	5555550108	5555550138	090186
205516787	ACKERMAN, PILAR	5555550189	5555550188	010198
136988136	BARBARIOL, ANGELA	5555550173	5555550173	090196
139787425	BERGLUND, ANDREAS	5555550137	5555550140	090184
376774216	BARNHILL, JOSH	5555550122X828	5555550177	090199
110526015	ALBOUCQ, STEVE	5555550175	5555550156	010100
183445006	BREADY, RICHARD	5555550143	5555550144	010198
177381034	CARLSON, TY LOREN	5555550128	5555550129	010195
182711304	DIXON, ANDREW	5555550139	5555550138	090197
264267458	DIRKSEN, JAY ANTHONY	5555550122	5555550123	010100
174576004	FLUEGEL, JAY	5555550188	5555550189	010199
470742224	FREY, JÖRG	5555550149	5555550126	010196
159769505	HART, SHERRI	5555550151	5555550152	010197
197474673	HENSHAW, JEFF D.	5555550153	5555550154	090198
266541854	GUO, BEI-JING	5555550131	5555550132	090198
126605333	HOFFMAN, BARBARA	5555550133	5555550134	090197

Record: 11 of 37

Figure 16-33. This table of raw data imported from a mainframe has formatting problems in several fields.

This table has several formatting problems that need to be dealt with before you store the data in an Access table, as follows:

- The SSN field is a numeric field. It should be a text field, and it needs dashes in the appropriate places.
- The EMPLOYEENAME field contains the employee's entire name. It needs to be broken up into Last Name, First Name, Middle Name, and Suffix fields. This field is also all caps; it needs to be converted to initial caps.
- The BUSPHONE field needs dashes in the phone number and also needs to have the extension parsed out into a separate field.
- The HOMEPHONE field needs dashes in the phone number.
- The HIREDATE field is a text field. It needs to be converted to a Date field.

You can clean up the raw data by taking steps similar to the following. (The Stage1 table and the query that fills it won't be needed if the raw table doesn't need so much cleanup.) You'll find the tables and queries listed in these steps in the Link and Import.mdb database on the companion CD.

1. Create two empty tables to receive the imported data (or just one, if the cleanup is simple) with fields set up with the appropriate Access data types. Copy these tables to make new tables every time the data is downloaded. In this example, the tables to be copied are named zstblCurrentEmployeesStage1 and zstblCurrentEmployees. The *zs* prefix indicates a system table.
2. Run two update queries (or one, if you have cleaner data) to parse and reformat the data as needed. The query qappCurrentEmployeesStage1 appends data from tblCurrentEmployeesRaw to tblCurrentEmployeesStage1 (a copy of zstblCurrentEmployeesStage1), and qappCurrentEmployees appends data from tblCurrentEmployeesStage1 to tblCurrentEmployees.

Parsing out a name field containing up to five components is too complex for a single query. If you need to split a name into that many components, the name parsing should be done in two stages. The first stage (qappCurrentEmployeesStage1) parses out the LastName, FirstNamePlus, and MiddleNamePlus fields; parses the extension out from the BUSPHONE field; and converts the HIREDATE field to a Date field. The output fields are written to tblCurrentEmployeesStage1. The expressions used to parse and format fields in qappCurrentEmployeesStage1 are shown here:

```
FormattedSSN: Format([SSN],"@@@-@@-@@@@")
LastName: Mid([EMPLOYEENAME],1,InStr([EMPLOYEENAME],Chr$(44))-1)
FirstNamePlus: Mid([EMPLOYEENAME],InStr([EMPLOYEENAME],Chr$(44))+2)
MiddleNamePlus: IIf(InStr([FirstNamePlus],Chr$(32))>0,
Mid([FirstNamePlus],InStr([FirstNamePlus],Chr$(32))+1),"")
BusinessPhone: IIf(InStr(UCase([BUSPHONE]),
Chr$(88))-1>0,Mid([BUSPHONE],1,InStr(UCase([BUSPHONE]),
Chr$(88))-1),[BUSPHONE])
Extension: IIf(InStr(UCase([BUSPHONE]),
Chr$(88))-1>0,Mid([BUSPHONE],InStr(UCase([BUSPHONE]),
Chr$(88))+1),"")
FormattedHireDate: CDate(Format([HireDate],"@@\/@@\/@@"))
```

The second query, qappCurrentEmployees, parses out the *FirstName, MiddleName*, and *Suffix* fields, converts all name fields to the proper case (first letter capitalized), and formats the phone number fields with dashes. The expressions used to perform these conversions are shown here:

```
LastNameFirstFormatted: StrConv([LastNameFirst],3)
MiddleName: StrConv(IIf(InStr([MiddleNamePlus],Chr$(32))>0,
Mid([MiddleNamePlus],1,InStr([MiddleNamePlus],Chr$(32))-1),
[MiddleNamePlus]),3)
Suffix: StrConv(IIf(InStr([MiddleNamePlus],Chr$(32))>0,
Mid([MiddleNamePlus],InStr([MiddleNamePlus],Chr$(32))+1),""),3)
LastNameFormatted: StrConv([LastName],3)
FirstName: StrConv(IIf(InStr([FirstNamePlus],Chr$(32))>0,
Mid([FirstNamePlus],1,InStr([FirstNamePlus],Chr$(32))-1),
[FirstNamePlus]),3)
BusinessPhoneFormatted: Format([BusinessPhone],"@@@-@@@-@@@@")
HomePhoneFormatted: Format([HomePhone],"@@@-@@@-@@@@")
```

Figure 16-34 shows the final table with data properly parsed and formatted.

tblCurrentEmployees : Table

SSN	LastNameFirst	LastName	FirstName	MiddleName	BusinessPhone	Extension
108-38-2415	Kahn, Wendy Beth	Kahn	Wendy	Beth	555-555-0144	
110-52-6015	Albouca, Steve	Albouca	Steve		555-555-0175	
123-09-8354	Swansen, Meg	Swansen	Meg		555-555-0100	
124-97-5868	Abercrombie, Kim	Abercrombie	Kim		555-555-0108	
126-60-5333	Hoffman, Barbara	Hoffman	Barbara		555-555-0133	
132-33-1463	Kilwine, Monica	Kilwine	Monica		555-555-0146	45
136-98-8136	Barbariol, Angela	Barbariol	Angela		555-555-0173	
139-78-7425	Berglund, Andreas	Berglund	Andreas		555-555-0137	
143-43-2204	Abbar, Anas	Abbar	Anas		555-555-0103	
158-79-9730	Wheeler, Wendy	Wheeler	Wendy		555-555-0173	
159-76-9505	Hart, Sherri	Hart	Sherri		555-555-0151	
166-38-7235	Morris, Jon	Morris	Jon		555-555-0151	
174-57-6004	Fluegel, Jay	Fluegel	Jay		555-555-0188	
176-62-2507	Yoshida, Kim	Yoshida	Kim		555-555-0177	
177-38-1034	Carlson, Ty Loren	Carlson	Ty	Loren	555-555-0128	
182-71-1304	Dixon, Andrew	Dixon	Andrew		555-555-0139	
183-44-5006	Bready, Richard	Bready	Richard		555-555-0143	

Record: 5 of 37

Figure 16-34. The final table, with data properly parsed and formatted, looks like this.

A sample database (Split and Concatenate 2000) with queries that use various functions to split and concatenate name and address data can be downloaded from the Code Samples page of my Web site, at *http://www.helenfeddema.com*; it's Code Sample #37 in the Access section. This database is also available on the companion CD.

The expressions in the previous queries (qappCurrentEmployeesStage1 and qappCurrentEmployees) use a number of functions to format the data. The following functions are useful for parsing and formatting data:

- *CDate.* Converts text to a date. The text must be recognizable as a date.
- *Chr$.* Returns an ASCII character. Useful for finding or inserting punctuation characters.
- *Format.* Formats a string as specified. Useful for tasks such as inserting dashes and parentheses in social security numbers and phone numbers.
- *InStr.* Finds a character or string within another string. Useful for finding a space or comma in a concatenated name field and for parsing out name components.
- *LCase.* Converts a string to all lowercase.
- *Left.* Returns the specified number of characters, starting at the left side of a string.

- *Mid.* Returns the specified number of characters, starting at the specified point in a string. Used together with *InStr*, this function is useful for parsing out name components.
- *StrConv.* Converts a string to the specified format. If you use 3 for the *Conversion* parameter, this function capitalizes the first character of the text string (sometimes called proper case).
- *UCase.* Converts a string to all uppercase.

After you prepare and test the preformatted tables and the append queries, the final touch is to create a macro or function to run the necessary actions in the correct order. You can run this macro or function whenever you download a new text file from the mainframe. The following function does the import from the text file and then copies the backup tables to tblCurrentEmployeesStage1 and tblCurrentEmployees and runs the two append queries to fill tblCurrentEmployees with properly formatted data. To make this function easier to use, you could run it from a macro or place it on a toolbar as a command button. (See Chapter 13, "Customizing Access Toolbars and Menus [Command Bars]," for more information.)

note Although it isn't necessary to do so, I put the argument names in the procedure to simplify keeping track of the arguments of these complex methods.

```
Function ImportEmployeeData()

On Error Resume Next

    'Turn warnings off.
    DoCmd.SetWarnings False

    'Delete old tables.
    DoCmd.DeleteObject objecttype:=acTable, _
        objectname:="tblCurrentEmployeesRaw"
    DoCmd.DeleteObject objecttype:=acTable, _
        objectname:="tblCurrentEmployeesStage1"
    DoCmd.DeleteObject objecttype:=acTable, _
        objectname:="tblCurrentEmployees"

    'Import data from text file using a saved import spec.
```

```
    DoCmd.TransferText transfertype:=acImportDelim, _
        specificationname:="CurEmp Import Specification", _
        tablename:="tblCurrentEmployeesRaw", _
        filename:="D:\Documents\CurEmp.txt", _
        hasfieldnames:=True

    'Copy blank tables to be filled with data from
    'the imported table.
    DoCmd.CopyObject , newname:="tblCurrentEmployeesStage1", _
        sourceobjecttype:=acTable, _
        sourceobjectname:="zstblCurrentEmployeesStage1"
    DoCmd.CopyObject , newname:="tblCurrentEmployees", _
        sourceobjecttype:=acTable, _
        sourceobjectname:="zstblCurrentEmployees"

    'Run queries to parse and format imported data.
    DoCmd.OpenQuery "qappCurrentEmployeesStage1"
    DoCmd.OpenQuery "qappCurrentEmployees"

End Function
```

Chapter 17

Exporting Data from Access

Throughout this book, you've discovered ways to use Microsoft Access 2002 to manage, maintain, organize, and query data as well as generate reports that help you make the most of your data in a powerful and efficient way. One of Access's strong points is its built-in flexibility; a key aspect of that flexibility is its ability to both accept data from and output data to files that can be used with a variety of programs.

The ability to export data tables from Access to, say, a Microsoft Excel worksheet or a comma-delimited file that can be imported by a mainframe database means that users of widely differing programs can work with your Access data. And by writing Microsoft Visual Basic for Applications (VBA) code using Automation to work with other applications' object models, you can go beyond the menu selections for exporting data—for example, to create Microsoft Outlook contacts or tasks from Access data or to produce an elegantly formatted Microsoft Word report from an Access query that combines data from several tables.

In the previous chapter, you learned about the features that let you bring data into Access through importing and linking. This chapter focuses on the output: exporting data through a variety of means and to a variety of formats. As is true of so many other tasks in Access, you can work with the Access interface or use VBA code when you export data.

Using the Interface vs. Using Code for Exporting

Access gives you the option of exporting data by choosing File, Export and then selecting an export format from a dialog box or by using VBA code. You can also use the Office Links button on the Database toolbar to easily export to three of the most popular formats. These exporting methods differ significantly. Even a beginning Access user can export data using the Export dialog box or Office Links, but using code to export data requires some ability to write VBA code and a basic understanding of the target application's object model.

In the following section, you'll learn how to export data using the interface. In the section "Exporting Data Using VBA Code," page 709, you'll learn how to use coding techniques to export Access objects to different file formats.

Exporting Data Using the Interface

Exporting Access objects using the interface is a fairly simple process. You can choose from two methods. The first is very easy: Just select the item you want to export, specify your export options, and save the file. The second method is an automated process called Office Links that exports objects to Word or Excel for specific uses. This section introduces you to both methods.

tip **Export a single object quickly**

For a really quick export of a single database object to another Access database, open both databases to their Database windows, and simply drag the database object from one Database window to the other. A copy of the object is created in the target database.

Access lets you export any type of database object. Each type of database object has its own selection of export formats (as listed in Table 17-1, page 687).

InsideOut

Unfortunately, you can export some database objects to formats that don't work very well. In most cases, if you think about it, you'll realize why. For example, you can export a form to an Excel worksheet, but Excel doesn't have any built-in capabilities for displaying form controls, so you can't expect to see your form with controls, color scheme, and all in the new worksheet. What you'll see instead is a strangely formatted worksheet, perhaps with overly tall rows and a dark background color that makes the text difficult to read.

The main consideration when you export data from Access to another format is whether you intend to export just the data or export a formatted interface object such as a form or a report. If you're exporting data (by far the most common situation), you select a table or query to export and then select a data format such as another database program, a spreadsheet program, or a delimited text file. (The comma-delimited text file format is a least-common-denominator export file type because it can be imported by almost every type of program.)

If you intend to export a form, report, or data access page to another Access database, you'll have no problems, but exporting any of these objects to other file types can yield surprising—and sometimes unacceptable—results. Data access pages can be exported only to other Access databases or saved as data access pages files. Forms have several export options available in the Export dialog box, but the Excel, HTML, Text File, and Rich Text options don't preserve any of the form's appearance—they simply export the data to a columnar format.

Reports do better than forms for HTML and Rich Text exports (but about the same for Excel and Text File exports—you get only the data). A report exported to HTML format emerges as a set of separate HTM files, one per page, and without the report's formatting, although it does preserve the report layout to some extent. When a report is exported to Rich Text Format (RTF), most of its formatting is preserved, but there are some exceptions, as noted in the section "Using Office Links for Common Exporting Tasks," page 689.

For an alternative method of exporting a report that preserves its appearance well, see the sidebar "Exporting a Report to Adobe PDF Format" on page 690.

If you want to export data using the basic menu selection sequence, follow these steps:

1. In the Database window, click the object type you want to export—for example, Tables or Queries. (These objects work best when exporting data.)
2. On the right side of the Database window, select the name of the table or query that contains the data you want to export.

3 Choose File, Export. The Export dialog box will appear. (See Figure 17-1.)

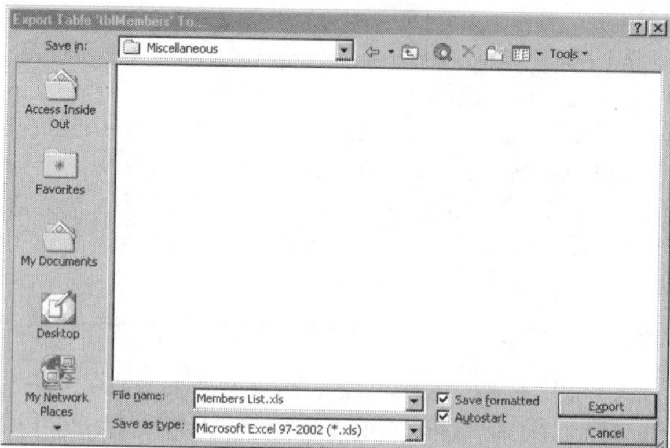

Figure 17-1. You specify export options in the Export dialog box.

> **note** The name of the Export dialog box will vary, depending on the type of database object you've selected to export.

4 Navigate to the folder in which you want to save the exported file.

5 In the Save As Type drop-down list, select the file type to which you want to export the element. Table 17-1 provides an overview of the export file types supported by Access.

6 In the File Name text box, type the name of the file.

7 If you want your data to have the same font when it's exported, check the Save Formatted check box. This check box is available only for selected file formats. The AutoStart check box will become available; check it if you want the newly created file to launch automatically after you export it.

> **note** The Save Formatted check box that's available for some export types preserves the font used in Access. For example, if you're exporting from a query in Datasheet view and the datasheet is formatted as MS Sans Serif 8 pt, if you export to Excel and check the Save Formatted check box, the same font will be used when the data is inserted into the Excel worksheet, rather than the default Excel font. This option doesn't preserve any other formatting.

8 Click Export. Access will save the object in the export format you selected.

Table 17-1. Export choices available through the interface

Data type	Extension(s)
Access databases	MDB, MDA, MDE
Access projects	ADP, ADE
dBASE 5	DBF
dBASE III	DBF
dBASE IV	DBF
HTML documents	HTML, HTM
IIS 1-2	HTX, IDC
Lotus 1-2-3 WJ2	WJ2
Lotus 1-2-3 WK1	WK1
Lotus 1-2-3 WK3	WK3
Microsoft Active Server Pages	ASP
Microsoft Excel 3	XLS
Microsoft Excel 4	XLS
Microsoft Excel 5–7	XLS
Microsoft Excel 97–2002	XLS
Microsoft IIS 1–2	HTM
Microsoft Snapshot	SNP
ODBC databases()	(Select database in the Select Data Source dialog box)
Paradox 3	DB
Paradox 4	DB
Paradox 5	DB
Paradox 7-8	DB
Rich Text Format	RTF
Text files	TXT, CSV, TAB, ASC
Word Merge	TXT
XML documents	XML

note You won't see all of these selections in the Export dialog box at once—each object type has a selection of the export formats listed in Table 17-1.

Generally, you're better off exporting data from a table or query. Forms and reports don't fare well when exported to most formats. There's no export format that preserves the formatting of a form, but there are two export choices that preserve report formatting quite well: RTF preserves most report formatting, and RTF files can be opened in most word processors. Snapshot format preserves all the report's formatting, but the report can't be viewed except by users who have Access (or the Snapshot Viewer) installed.

To export a report in the RTF format, follow these steps:

1. Display the Database window, if necessary.
2. Click the Reports object icon.
3. On the right side of the Database window, select the name of the report you want to export.
4. Choose File, Export. The Export dialog box will appear.
5. Navigate to the folder in which you want to save the exported report.
6. In the Save As Type drop-down list, select the Rich Text file type.
7. In the File Name text box, type the name of the file.
8. Click Export. Access will save the object in the RTF format.

newfeature!

tip If you're in a hurry and want to export data quickly, try using the Office Links feature, which is described in the next section. Office Links automates the export process so that you can merge, publish, or analyze data in Word or Excel.

Using Office Links for Common Exporting Tasks

Office Links is an Access feature that lets you easily export your Access data to other Office applications. Office Links can help you with three common export tasks:

- Merging Access data into a Word document
- Publishing Access data as a Word document
- Analyzing Access data in an Excel spreadsheet

You can display the Office Links options in one of two ways: by choosing Tools, Office Links or by clicking the Office Links button on the Database toolbar (as shown in Figure 17-2).

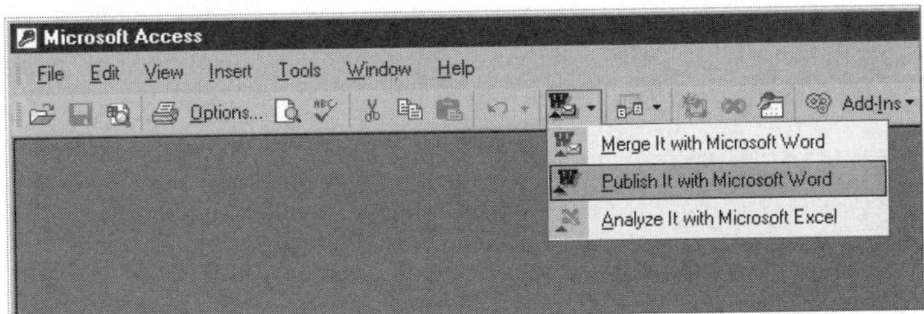

Figure 17-2. You click the Office Links button on the Database toolbar to see the Office Links choices.

Each of the three Office Links choices performs a different task, as follows:

- **Merge It With Microsoft Word.** Starts the Word Mail Merge Wizard, which guides you through the process of merging Access data with a Word document.
- **Publish It With Microsoft Word.** Creates a Word RTF document from your Access data.
- **Analyze It With Microsoft Excel.** Creates an Excel worksheet from your Access data.

note Merge It With Microsoft Word is available only for tables and queries. You can use the other two Office Links choices with tables, queries, forms, and reports.

Exporting a Report to Adobe PDF Format

Although PDF format is not available as an option in the Export dialog box, you can still export a report to the widely used Adobe PDF format—at least if you have the full version of Adobe Acrobat (not just the free Reader). When you install Adobe Acrobat, it creates a new printer selection called Adobe Distiller. To export a report to PDF format, simply open the report, and print it to the Adobe Distiller printer selection. This creates a PDF file that you can then distribute to users.

The PDF version of the report is an exact representation of the report's appearance in Print Preview, and this format has some advantages over the Snapshot format, since the Adobe Acrobat Reader is widely distributed, and most users are likely to have it (which is not always the case with the Snapshot Viewer). The illustration below shows a PivotTable report saved in PDF format using the Adobe Distiller printer installed by Adobe Acrobat 5.0, open in Adobe Acrobat Reader 5.0. As you can see from the illustration, a report exported in PDF format looks exactly like the report in Access.

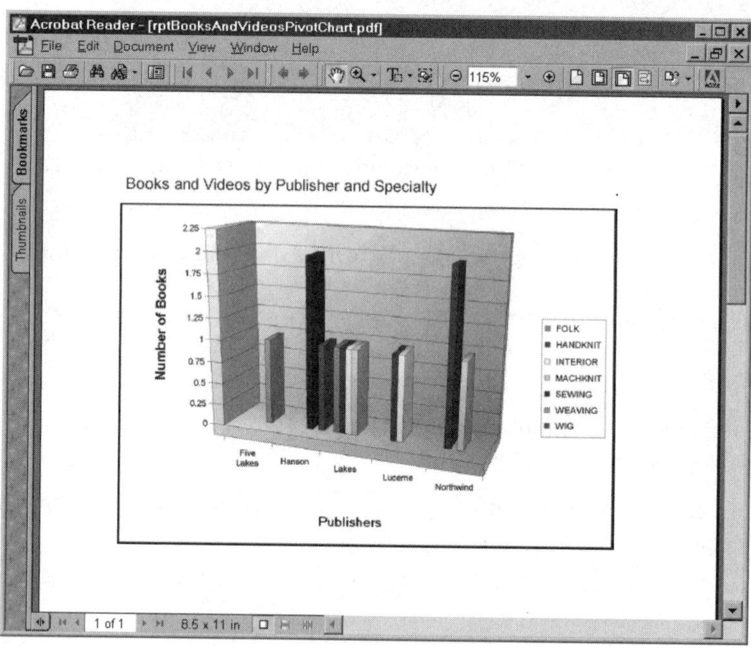

Merging Access Data with a Word Document

If you want to merge Access data with a Word 2002 document and your needs are simple (you don't need filtering or a custom Word template, for example), using Merge It With Microsoft Word is the quickest, easiest approach.

To merge a table of Access contacts to a new, blank Word letter, follow these steps:

1. In the Database window, select a table that contains name and address data.
2. Click the Office Links button, and click Merge It With Microsoft Word. The Microsoft Word Mail Merge Wizard will launch, as shown in Figure 17-3.

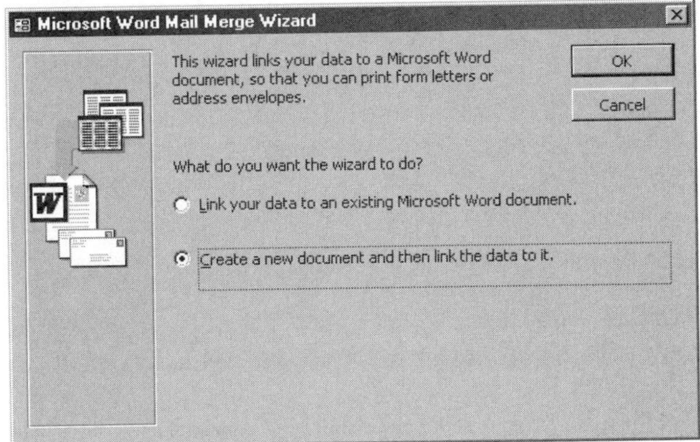

Figure 17-3. The Microsoft Word Mail Merge Wizard starts you on the process of merging Access data with a Word document.

3. On the first page of the wizard, select the Create A New Document And Then Link The Data To It option, and then click OK. A new, blank Word document will open, and the wizard will switch from standard wizard pages to steps in the Word task pane.

4 Click the Letters option to create a new letter, scroll down if necessary, and then click Next: Starting Document at the bottom of the task pane, as shown in Figure 17-4.

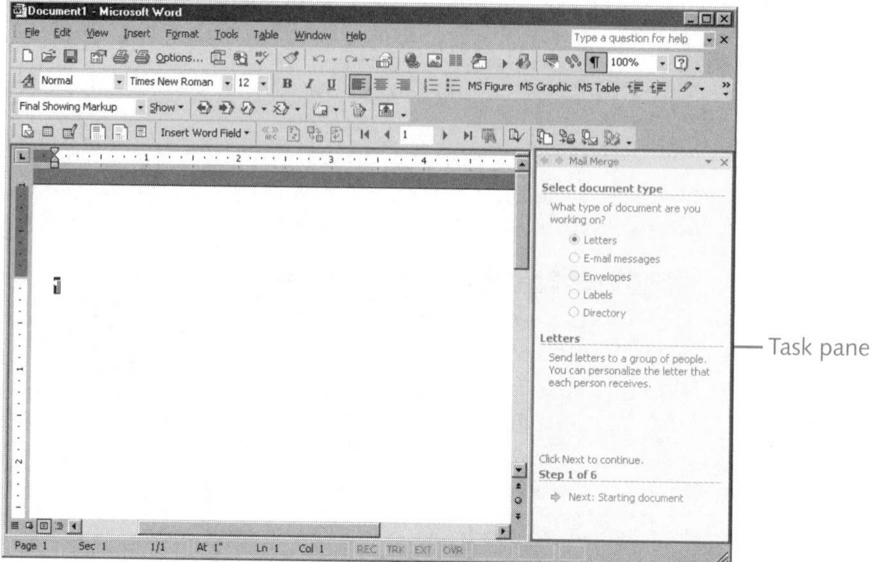

Figure 17-4. In the Word task pane, you specify a document type.

5 Leave the default option selected (Use The Current Document), and click Next: Select Recipients at the bottom of the task pane.

6 Again, leave the default option selected (Use An Existing List), and click Next: Write Your Letter.

7 Compose the text of the letter.

newfeature!

8 You can insert various data components as you go along by clicking in the task pane the item you want to insert (such as Address Block or Greeting Line). You can display additional merge fields by clicking More Items. Figure 17-5 shows a letter with an address block and a first name inserted. Click Next: Preview Your Letters after you finish writing the letter. You might need to scroll down to see where to click.

9 Preview the letter for the first recipient in the data source, as shown in Figure 17-6. Click Next: Complete The Merge.

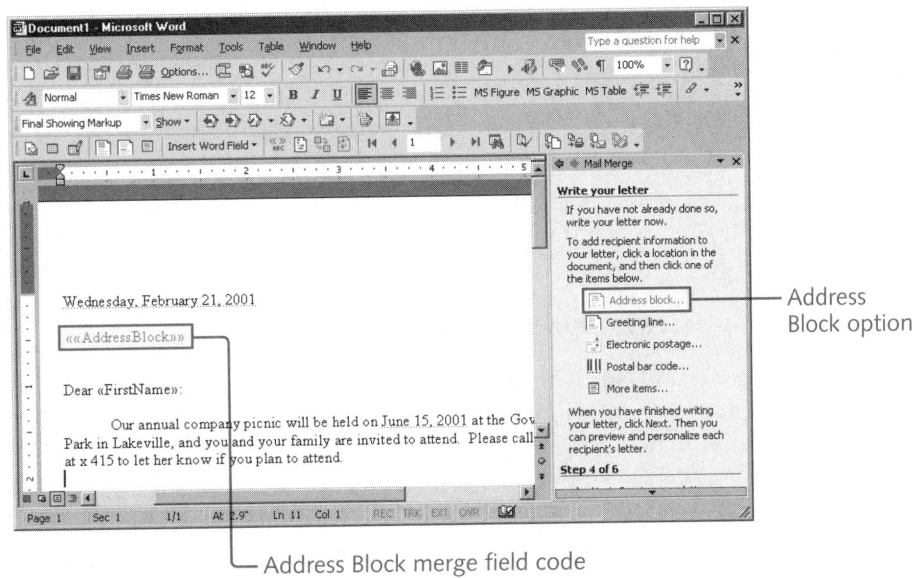

Figure 17-5. You can insert various data components as you compose your letter.

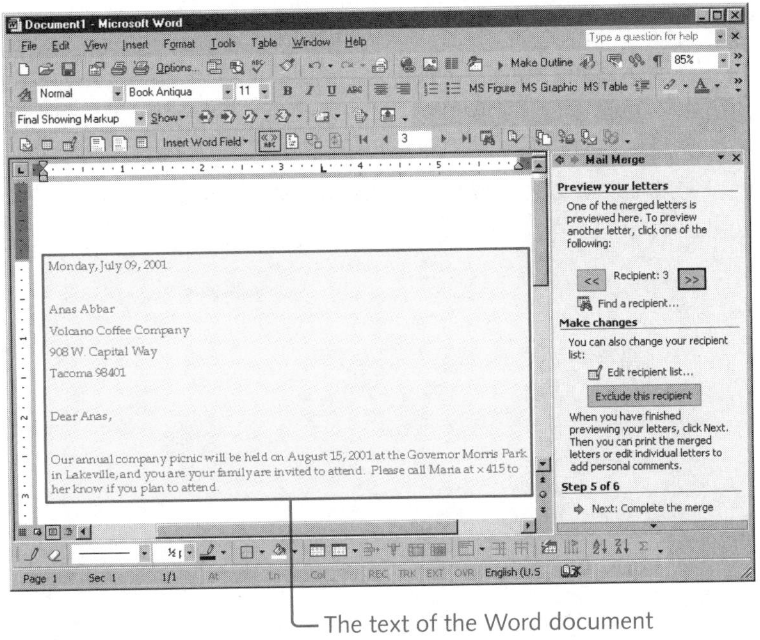

Figure 17-6. You should preview the Word mail merge letter for the first recipient to verify that all of the components appear correctly.

10 In this final step of the wizard, you choose your output. You can click Print to display the Print dialog box and select your print options, or you can click Edit Individual Letters to modify the letters in the Word document before printing.

> **newfeature! note** The Mail Merge Wizard in Word 2002 has been significantly enhanced from the version in Word 2000, bringing all your choices together in an easy-to-follow process that lets you create new data files and documents or work with existing files from various programs.
>
> To find out more about how you can streamline your mail merge tasks with Word 2002, see *Microsoft Word Version 2002 Inside Out* (Microsoft Press, 2001).

Publishing Access Tables in Word Documents

If you're working with an Access table that you want to spruce up and incorporate in a formal report to your board of directors, you can quickly and easily publish the information from Access to Word by using Publish It With Microsoft Word. This Office Links choice lets you go directly from Access into Word and produces a simply formatted but attractive Word table.

To publish an Access table in a Word document, follow these steps:

1. In the Database window, click Tables.
2. Select the table you want to publish in a Word document.
3. Click the Office Links button, and click Publish It With Microsoft Word. Word will launch, and the data will be placed in a default Word table, as shown in Figure 17-7. The default document format is RTF.

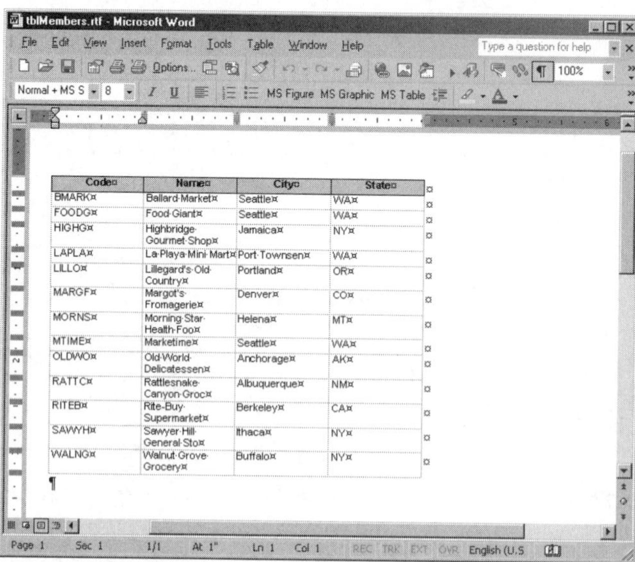

Code	Name	City	State
BMARK	Ballard Market	Seattle	WA
FOODG	Food Giant	Seattle	WA
HIGHG	Highbridge Gourmet Shop	Jamaica	NY
LAPLA	La Playa Mini Mart	Port Townsen	WA
LILLO	Lillegard's Old Country	Portland	OR
MARGF	Margot's Fromagerie	Denver	CO
MORNS	Morning Star Health Foo	Helena	MT
MTIME	Marketime	Seattle	WA
OLDWO	Old World Delicatessen	Anchorage	AK
RATTC	Rattlesnake Canyon Groc	Albuquerque	NM
RITEB	Rite-Buy Supermarket	Berkeley	CA
SAWYH	Sawyer Hill General Sto	Ithaca	NY
WALNG	Walnut Grove Grocery	Buffalo	NY

Figure 17-7. You can use Publish It With Microsoft Word to place an Access table in an RTF document in Word.

Troubleshooting

The default table format doesn't work for me

If you want a different format for the table you've published in Word, you can choose from a number of styles. To modify the format, first select the table by clicking the table selector handle (the small square just outside the upper left corner of the table). The entire table will be highlighted.

Next choose Table, Table AutoFormat. In the Table AutoFormat dialog box, scroll through the various table styles and select the look that best fits your document needs.

Click Apply to reformat your Access table. Don't forget to save the document by pressing Ctrl+S before you exit and return to Access.

Creating an Excel Worksheet from an Access Query

If you want to analyze data in your table or query, you can use Analyze It With Microsoft Excel to export the data to a worksheet. This is a seamless process that simply launches Excel 2002 and pastes the data from the table or query you select into a new worksheet.

Here are the steps:

1. In the Database window, click Tables or Queries.
2. Select the table or query you want to use in the Excel spreadsheet.
3. Click the Office Links selector, and click Analyze It With Microsoft Excel. Excel will launch, and your Access data will be displayed in a new worksheet, as shown in Figure 17-8. You can then format and save the worksheet as you normally would.

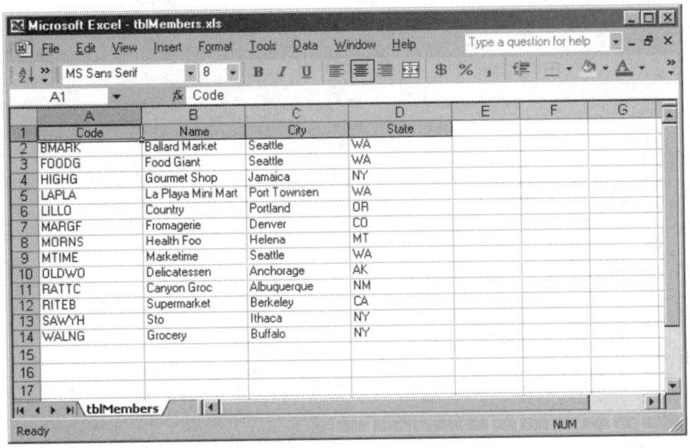
Microsoft Excel - tblMembers.xls
File Edit View Insert Format Tools Data Window Help
Type a question for help
MS Sans Serif
8
A1
Code
Code Name City State
BMARK Ballard Market Seattle WA
FOODG Food Giant Seattle WA
HIGHG Gourmet Shop Jamaica NY
LAPLA La Playa Mini Mart Port Townsen WA
LILLO Country Portland OR
MARGF Fromagerie Denver CO
MORNS Health Foo Helena MT
MTIME Marketime Seattle WA
OLDWO Delicatessen Anchorage AK
RATTC Canyon Groc Albuquerque NM
RITEB Supermarket Berkeley CA
SAWYH Sto Ithaca NY
WALNG Grocery Buffalo NY
tblMembers
Ready
NUM

Figure 17-8. You can create an Excel worksheet from an Access query.

Exporting Forms

You can use two of the Office Links choices—Publish It With Microsoft Word and Analyze It With Microsoft Excel—to publish and analyze form data, but you should first test how these features work before you use them to export forms or reports with lots of data. In some cases (especially for forms), the output is unattractive—you might get something similar to the worksheet shown in Figure 17-9.

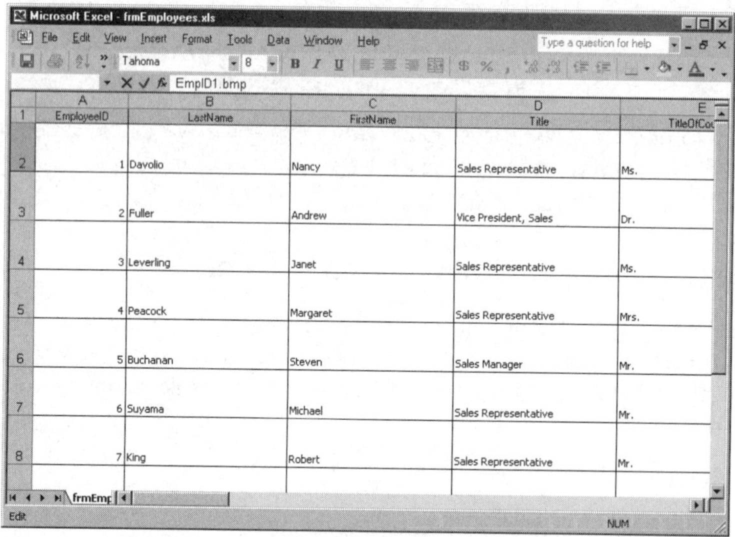

Figure 17-9. An Excel worksheet created from an Access form bears little resemblance to the original form.

As you can see in Figure 17-9, Access exported the data as if it had been exported from a table, but the rows are very tall. You're better off just exporting the data from a table or query and doing any fine-tuning of the document or worksheet in Word or Excel instead of exporting a form.

Exporting Reports

The same caveat applies to using reports with the Office Links choices: Test before you leap. If you export a report (perhaps based on a query that limits results to just a few pages of data) and check what the exported document looks like before you publish that big report you need for the meeting in 15 minutes, you're more likely to be safe than sorry. In my experience, the best choices for exporting reports are RTF and Snapshot. (Actually, the best choice of all, if you have Adobe Acrobat, would be Adobe PDF.) The RTF export isn't perfect, but it gives good results for most reports, as long as they don't use graphics. Snapshot format gives excellent results, but, as mentioned earlier, only users with Access or the Snapshot Viewer installed can read this format.

Although a simple report might fare well when exported to RTF, if you select a complex report (such as the Northwind Catalog report) and click Publish It With Microsoft Word, the Northwind logo, all product graphics, and the decorative lines and rectangles will be missing from the RTF document opened in Word. Each text block will have a tab at the beginning of each line and a hard return at the end. Tabular text will be exported as plain text rather than converted to a Word table. If the report has headers and footers, they won't be converted to Word headers and footers; they'll be included as plain text in the document, with hard page breaks.

One way to make sure that you get an attractive Word report based on your Access data is to take matters into your own hands by using VBA code. You export the data to Word from a table or query, fill a preformatted Word table with the data, and do any other required formatting using components of the Word object model. This approach will give you total control over the appearance of the document. The Word export code sample in the section "Exporting Data Using VBA Code," page 709, illustrates this technique.

newfeature!

Exporting a PivotTable to Excel

As you saw in Chapter 12, "Using PivotTables and PivotCharts to Analyze Data," PivotTables, which were first introduced in Access 2000, have been greatly enhanced in Access 2002. This feature enables you to analyze data from a variety of perspectives. You can even export an Access PivotTable to Excel so that you can analyze the data in a worksheet using Excel's advanced data analysis tools. This is a fairly straightforward process, as follows:

1. In the Database window, click Forms.
2. Open the form with the PivotTable you want to export.

3 Display the PivotTable view by choosing View, PivotTable View.

4 Choose PivotTable, Export To Microsoft Excel. Excel will launch, and the PivotTable will be displayed in a new worksheet, as shown in Figure 17-10.

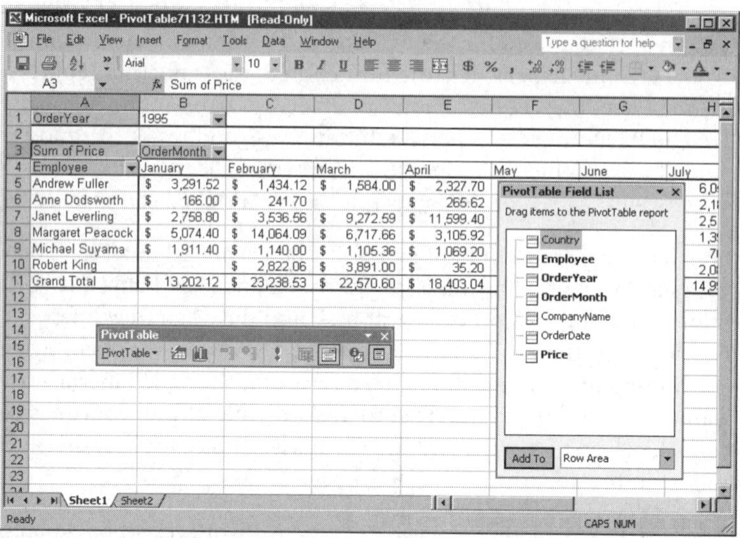

Figure 17-10. This Excel PivotTable was created from an Access PivotTable.

Troubleshooting

My PivotTable is read-only in Excel

The idea behind exporting PivotTables from Access to Excel is to let you analyze the data in the PivotTable using Excel's advanced data analysis tools. Because Excel generates a read-only HTML file when you export a PivotTable from Access, you can't save or modify the Excel PivotTable initially.

If you want to work with the PivotTable in Excel format, you can choose File, Save As and enter a new name for the PivotTable. Select the folder in which you want to store the file, and click Save. Excel will copy the read-only PivotTable into an Excel worksheet, thereby making it editable.

Unfortunately, there's no way to export a PivotChart to Excel. (The PivotChart menu has no Export To Microsoft Excel command.) You can export a form that has a PivotChart view, but you'll just get the usual columns of data in the new Excel worksheet. At that point, you can make a PivotTable with a PivotChart report in Excel, but you're starting from scratch as far as the PivotChart's layout is concerned.

Exporting Database Objects to Other Access Databases

The exporting process in Access doesn't limit you to exporting objects to other programs; you can also export objects to other Access databases. Any database object you create in Access—including tables, queries, forms, reports, macros, and data access pages—can be used in other Access databases.

To export a database object, follow these steps:

1. Display the Database window of the file from which you want to export objects.
2. Select the object type you want to export, and then click the specific item in the displayed list.
3. Choose File, Export, and navigate to the folder containing the database file to which you want to export the object. (See Figure 17-11.)

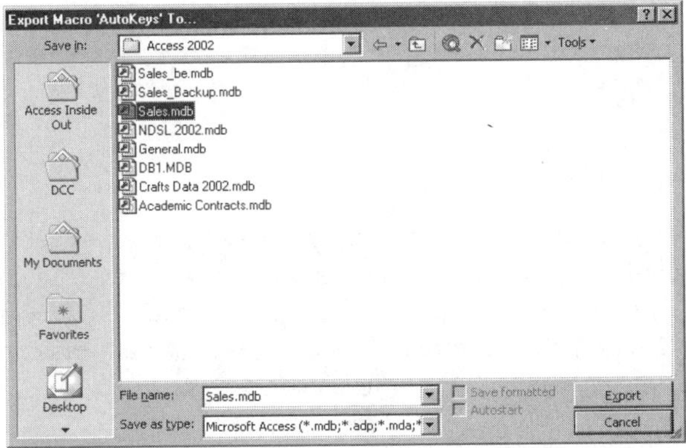

Figure 17-11. You can easily export an object from one Access database to another by choosing File, Export and selecting the target database file.

4. Select the file, and click Export. Access will export the object and add it to the database you selected.

InsideOut

Access doesn't offer an option for exporting custom toolbars and menus to another Access database. However, you can import custom toolbars and menus into an Access database by clicking the Options command button in the Import Objects dialog box and selecting the Menus And Toolbars check box, as shown in Figure 17-12.

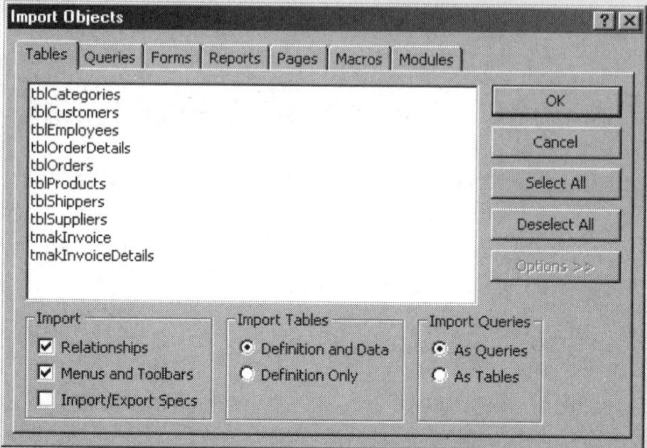

Figure 17-12. Select the Menus And Toolbars check box after clicking the Options button in the Import Objects dialog box to import custom toolbars and menus.

Troubleshooting

newfeature!

I can't export query results to my older Access databases

Suppose you're trying to export a great query you created in Access 2002 to a similar database you created last year using an earlier version of Access—say, Access 97. After you click the Export button, Access will greet you with the following error message: *You can't export database objects (except tables) from the current version of Microsoft Access to earlier versions of Microsoft Access.*

For queries (only), there's a simple workaround for this problem, which is available if you still have the earlier version of Access installed. Open the query in SQL view, and then highlight and copy the SQL statement to the Windows Clipboard by pressing Ctrl+C. Next open the target database in the earlier version of Access, create a new query, paste the SQL statement text into its SQL window by pressing Ctrl+V, and save the query.

Exporting Access Query Results to an Earlier Excel Format

Earlier in this chapter, you learned how to quickly export a table or query to an Excel worksheet using the Analyze It With Microsoft Excel option in Office Links. If you want to export a query to an Excel worksheet using an Excel format that isn't available through Office Links (say, Excel 3 or 4), follow these steps:

1. In the Database window, click Queries.
2. Select the query you want to export.

> **note** When you export a query, you're actually exporting the query results, or the data generated by running the query.

3. Choose File, Export. The Export dialog box will appear.
4. In the Save As Type drop-down list, select the appropriate Excel format.
5. Click the Export button to export the query.

Exporting Data to Text Files

When you export a table or query to a text file, you have the choice of exporting to a delimited file or a fixed-width file. As discussed in Chapter 16, a delimited file is one in which the beginning and end of each data item is marked, or delimited, with a specific separator character—usually a comma, tab, semicolon, or space. A fixed-width file, sometimes also called a positional file, is one in which the fields appear in specific places and are given specific widths for each record field in the file. The fixed-width columns let the database determine where each data field begins and ends.

> **note** Fixed-width text files will be displayed correctly only when a fixed-width font (one whose characters are all the same width, such as Courier New) is used.

To export a table or query to a comma-delimited text file (the most widely used type of text file), follow these the steps:

1. In the Database window, select the table or query.
2. Choose File, Export. The Export dialog box will appear.
3. In the Save As Type drop-down list, select Text Files.
4. Give the new file the CSV extension (*CSV* stands for comma-separated values), and click Export. The Export Text Wizard will open, as shown in Figure 17-13.

tip Files saved with the CSV extension can be opened directly in Excel.

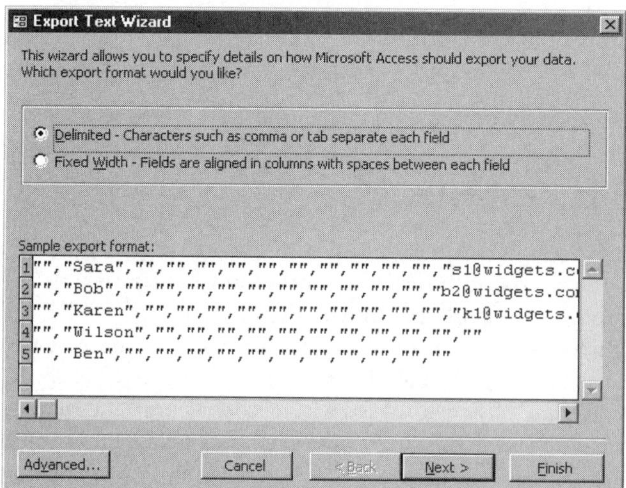

Figure 17-13. The Export Text Wizard helps you export a table or query to a comma-delimited text file.

5. Select Delimited (the default selection), and click Next.
6. Set the delimiter and text qualifier. The default selections of comma and double quotation marks are usually fine. (See Figure 17-14.)

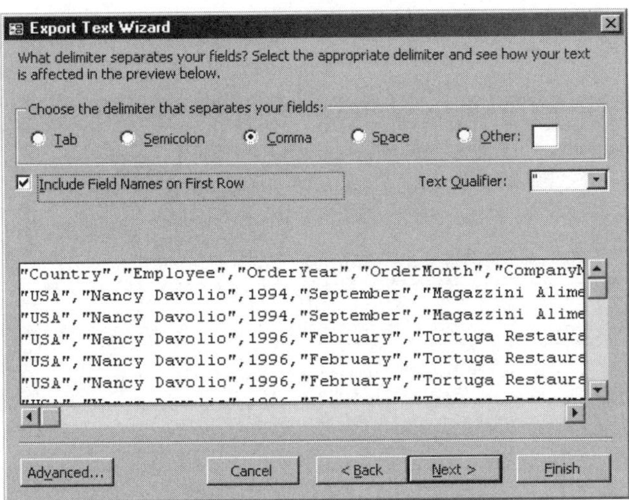

Figure 17-14. The wizard prompts you to select the delimiter to use for separating data items.

7 If you want to include the field names in the exported data, which is generally a good idea, check Include Field Names On First Row, as shown in Figure 17-14. Click Next.

8 If you want, you can change the export file name and path, as shown in Figure 17-15.

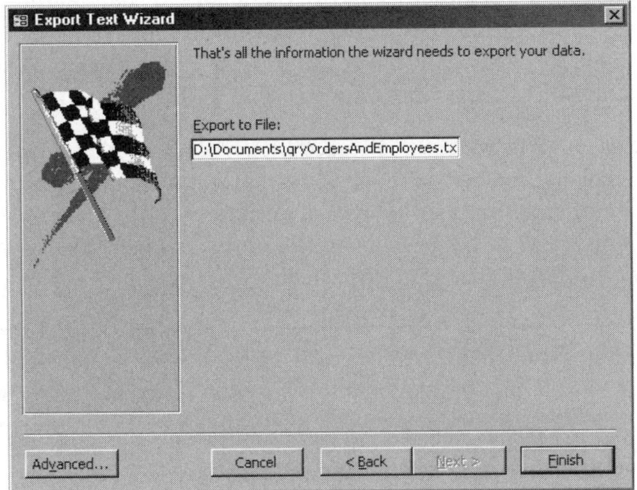

Figure 17-15. You can change the export file name and path on the last page of the wizard.

9 Click Finish to create the text file. Figure 17-16 shows the new text file in WordPad.

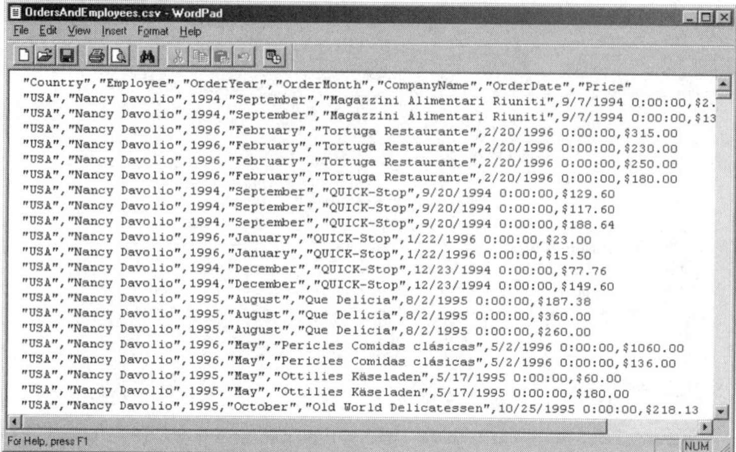

Figure 17-16. The individual data items in each record in the exported text file are separated by commas and enclosed in double quotation marks.

newfeature!

Exporting Data to XML Files

Extensible Markup Language (XML) is gaining popularity as the standard format for data exchange on the Web, although it's less useful for exchanging data among software applications because many applications can't interpret the data in this format correctly. If you export a PivotChart from Access to XML, for example, and then open it in Word or Microsoft Internet Explorer, you'll get a text listing of the data, in XML format (which is a variant of HTML), but you won't see a PivotChart.

If you're able to import XML files in an acceptable manner, Access 2002 lets you export tables, forms, reports, and queries to XML format so that they can be used on the Web and possibly in other software applications. The export options for XML let you opt to save the data only, save the schema in addition to the data, or save the presentation of the data in addition to the data and the schema.

note The *schema* for an XML file is the record of the structure of the data and is saved in a file with an XSD extension. The *presentation* of the data saves the information used to display the data in a spreadsheet format in a file with an XSL extension.

Chapter 17

To export a table or query to XML, follow these steps:

1. In the Database window, select the object you want to export in XML.

> **note** You can export tables, queries, forms, and reports to XML, but you can't create a presentation file of XML data if you export a form or report.

2. Choose File, Export. The Export dialog box will appear.
3. Navigate to the folder in which you want to store the exported file(s).
4. In the Save As Type drop-down list, select XML Documents. The Export XML dialog box will appear, as shown in Figure 17-17.

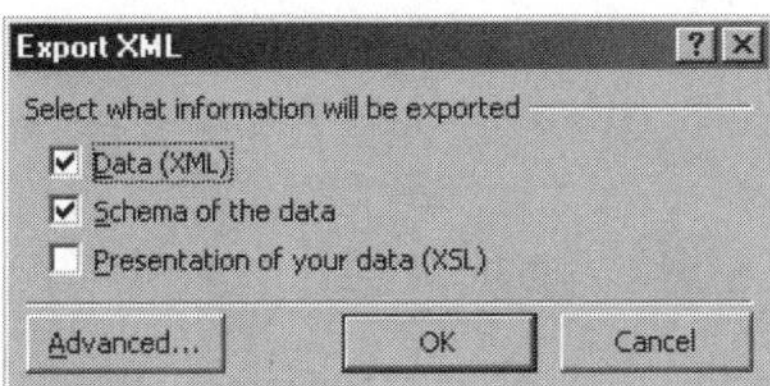

Figure 17-17. When you export an object to XML, you can export the data only, the data and its structure, or the data, its structure, and the way it's presented and linked.

5. Select the export options you want: data only, the schema (data structure) of the exported file, and the presentation of the data (the way in which the data is presented and linked).

   If you want to specify a particular location for the XML data, schema, and presentation files you create, click the Advanced button. Each tab (Data, Schema, and Presentation) includes an option that lets you change the location where the files will be stored.

6. Click OK to export the object to XML in the files you specified. Figure 17-18 shows the resulting XML file opened in Internet Explorer.

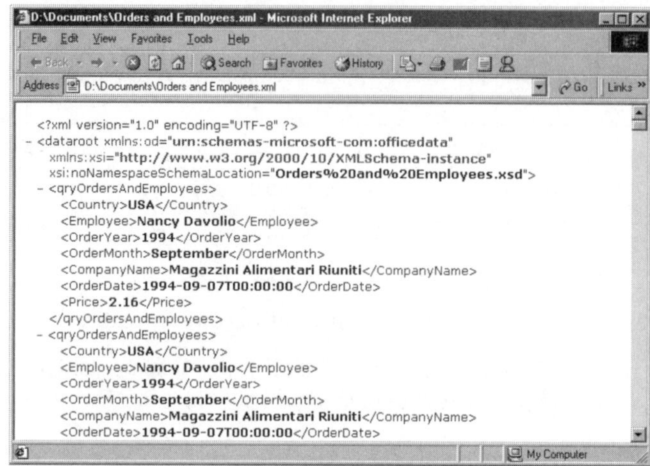

Figure 17-18. This XML file was exported from an Access query.

Exporting Data to Non-Microsoft Applications

In addition to exporting Access data to other Access databases or to Office programs such as Word and Excel, you can also export data to non-Microsoft applications. Databases that were popular before Access 1.0 was released in 1992—such as dBASE and Paradox—are still in use in some businesses. If your company or client uses some of these programs, you'll need some way to trade data with them.

To export a table or query to a non-Microsoft program, follow these steps:

1. In the Database window, select the table or query you want to export.
2. Choose File, Export. The Export dialog box will appear.
3. In the Save As Type drop-down list, select the program and version you want to export to. (Table 17-2 provides a quick overview of supported non-Microsoft export formats.)
4. Navigate to the folder in which you want to store the file.
5. Type the file name you want to assign to the exported file.
6. Click Export to complete the process.

Table 17-2. Export formats for non-Microsoft applications

Application	Versions supported	File format
dBASE	III, IV, 5	DBF
Lotus 1-2-3	WK1, WK3, WJ2	WK1, WK3, WJ2
Paradox	3, 4, 5, 7–8	DB

Exporting to an ODBC Database

Open Database Connectivity (ODBC) is a standard way to share data between databases and programs on various platforms, which extends the reach and potential use of the database objects you create in Access. ODBC isn't used as much as it was in former years, because Automation code lets you work directly with data in many other applications. However, you can still set up an ODBC data source to work with data in an ODBC database from Access. And if you need to export data by using a specific file format that isn't one of the selections in the Export dialog box and that format supports ODBC, you can export a table or query to an ODBC database by following these steps:

1. In the Database window, select the table or query to export, and then choose File, Export. The Export dialog box will appear.
2. In the Save As Type drop-down list, select ODBC Databases. A small Export dialog box will appear with the name of the selected table or query, as shown in Figure 17-19. Verify that this is the object you want to export, and click OK.

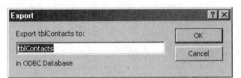

Figure 17-19. This Export dialog box displays the name of the Access table being exported to an ODBC database.

InsideOut

Several of the Machine Data Source selections (dBASE Files, Excel Files, and MS Access Database) have their own export file types. If you want to export to one of these file formats, it's much simpler to just select the format in the Export dialog box instead of working through the ODBC dialog box.

3 In the Select Data Source dialog box, shown in Figure 17-20, select the data source you want to use. (The list of available choices might be different on your system.) Use the Machine Data Source tab to choose a driver that's local to your machine, and use the File Data Source tab to select a file that describes the driver you want to use. Click OK.

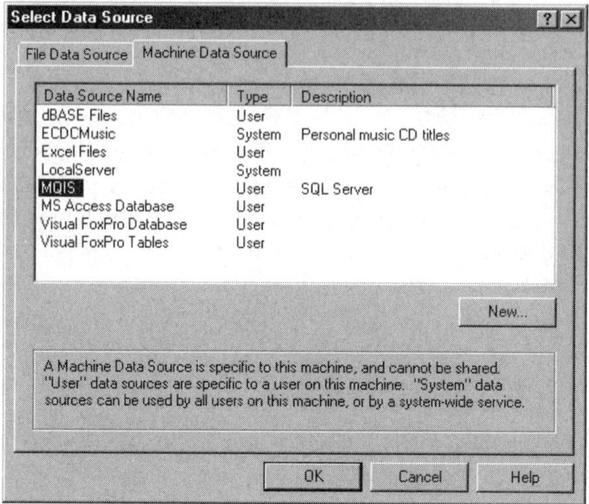

Figure 17-20. In the Select Data Source dialog box, you select a machine source for exporting to an ODBC program.

4 If necessary, log in to the database. Access completes the export without any further messages and exports the selected table or query to the ODBC program.

> **For an alternative method of exporting Access data to SQL Server, see Appendix E, "Upsizing to SQL Server," which describes using the Upsizing Wizard to upsize an Access database to SQL Server.**

Exporting to HTML

If you've created a database object you want to use directly on the Web, you can export the item directly to HTML using Access's export features. Here's how:

1 In the Database window, select the database object you want to export.

2 Choose File, Export. The Export dialog box will open.

3 Navigate to the folder in which you want to store the file.

4 In the Save As Type drop-down list, select HTML Documents. For some export selections, the HTML Output Options dialog box will appear, as shown in Figure 17-21.

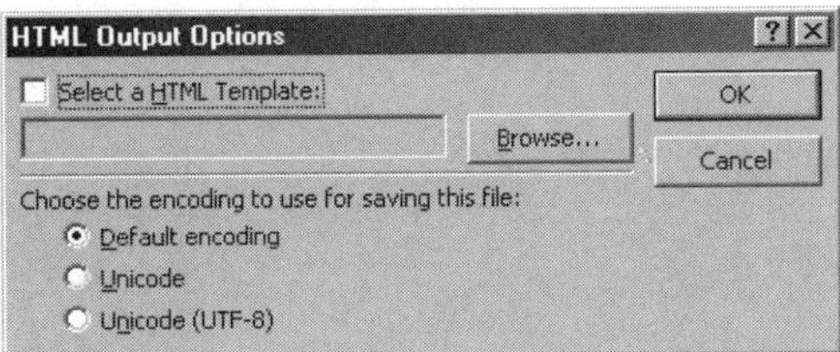

Figure 17-21. When outputting to HTML, you can select an existing HTML template or use the default Access template.

5 If you want to use an existing HTML template, check Select A HTML Template; otherwise, leave Default Encoding selected.

6 Click OK to close the dialog box and export the object in HTML format.

Exporting Data Using VBA Code

Up to now, we've explored various ways to export Access objects to other databases and programs. In the remainder of this chapter, you'll learn how to use VBA code to export to formats that aren't supported in the interface, such as Microsoft Outlook contacts or appointments or a Word document.

For more information about working with VBA in Access, see Chapter 20, "Customizing Your Database Using VBA Code." Also, see the sidebar "Import/Export Terminology" in Chapter 16 for a review of terminology you'll need to know to understand exporting in Access using VBA.

On the companion CD, you'll find the sample database and the VBA code that illustrates the techniques shown in this chapter.

To run this code, follow these steps:

1 On your hard disk, create a folder named Documents. The code assumes that this folder is located on the D drive, so if you locate your folder elsewhere, you need to modify the code before you run it.

2 In the Documents folder, create a folder named Access 2002. Copy the file Export.mdb on the companion CD to the Access 2002 folder.

3 In the Access 2002 folder, create an empty database named General.

4 Copy the file Northwind Invoice.dot to the Templates folder. The exact location of the folder depends on your individual settings and the operating system you run. For example, if you run Windows 2000 Server, the default location is C:\Documents and Settings\<*your id*>\Application Data\Microsoft\Templates.

5 Open the Export database, and open the Visual Basic Editor. You're now ready to run the sample functions by positioning the insertion point inside a function and pressing F5.

Using Transfer Methods to Export

When you export data from Access to other Access databases and applications, you can use the same methods of the Access *DoCmd* object that you use to import data into Access. (See Chapter 16, "Importing and Linking Data to Access," for more information about importing using VBA.) The *TransferDatabase*, *TransferSpreadsheet*, and *TransferText* methods have been available for many Access versions, and the *TransferSQLDatabase* method is new to Access version 2002. (This new method isn't used to export Access data to SQL Server, however, but to copy one SQL Server database to another SQL Server database.) The *Transfer* methods of the *DoCmd* object are listed in Table 17-3.

Table 17-3. Exporting Access data in VBA code

Data type	VBA method to use
Access	*Access.DoCmd.TransferDatabase* method with *acExport* as the *TransferType* parameter and "Microsoft Access" as the *DatabaseType* parameter
dBASE 5	*Access.DoCmd.TransferDatabase* method with *acExport* as the *TransferType* parameter and "dBase 5.0" as the *DatabaseType* parameter
dBASE III	*Access.DoCmd.TransferDatabase* method with *acExport* as the *TransferType* parameter and "dBase III" as the *DatabaseType* parameter
dBASE IV	*Access.DoCmd.TransferDatabase* method with *acExport* as the *TransferType* parameter and "dBase IV" as the *DatabaseType* parameter
Delimited text files	*Access.DoCmd.TransferText* method with *acExportDelim* as the *TransferType* parameter

Data type	VBA method to use
Excel 3	*Access.DoCmd.TransferSpreadsheet* method with *acExport* as the *TransferType* parameter and *acSpreadsheetTypeExcel3* as the *SpreadsheetType* parameter
Excel 4	*Access.DoCmd.TransferSpreadsheet* method with *acExport* as the *TransferType* parameter and *acSpreadsheetTypeExcel4* as the *SpreadsheetType* parameter
Excel 5	*Access.DoCmd.TransferSpreadsheet* method with *acExport* as the *TransferType* parameter and *acSpreadsheetTypeExcel5* as the *SpreadsheetType* parameter
Excel 7	*Access.DoCmd.TransferSpreadsheet* method with *acExport* as the *TransferType* parameter and *acSpreadsheetTypeExcel7* as the *SpreadsheetType* parameter
Excel 8	*Access.DoCmd.TransferSpreadsheet* method with *acExport* as the *TransferType* parameter and *acSpreadsheetTypeExcel8* as the *SpreadsheetType* parameter
Excel 9	*Access.DoCmd.TransferSpreadsheet* method with *acExport* as the *TransferType* parameter and *acSpreadsheetTypeExcel9* as the *SpreadsheetType* parameter
Fixed-width text files	*Access.DoCmd.TransferText* method with *acExportFixed* as the *TransferType* parameter
HTML files	*Access.DoCmd.TransferText* method with *acExportHTML* as the *TransferType* parameter
Jet 2.*x*	*Access.DoCmd.TransferDatabase* method with *acExport* as the *TransferType* parameter and "Jet 2.x" as the *DatabaseType* parameter
Lotus WJ2 (Japanese version only)	*Access.DoCmd.TransferSpreadsheet* method with *acExport* as the *TransferType* parameter and *acSpreadsheetTypeLotusWJ2* as the *SpreadsheetType* parameter
Lotus WK1	*Access.DoCmd.TransferSpreadsheet* method with *acExport* as the *TransferType* parameter and *acSpreadsheetTypeLotusWK1* as the *SpreadsheetType* parameter
Lotus WK3	*Access.DoCmd.TransferSpreadsheet* method with *acExport* as the *TransferType* parameter and *acSpreadsheetTypeLotusWK3* as the *SpreadsheetType* parameter

(continued)

Table 17-3. *(continued)*

Data type	VBA method to use
Lotus WK4	*Access.DoCmd.TransferSpreadsheet* method with *acExport* as the *TransferType* parameter and *acSpreadsheetTypeLotusWK4* as the *SpreadsheetType* parameter
ODBC databases	*Access.DoCmd.TransferDatabase* method with *acExport* as the *TransferType* parameter and "ODBC Database" as the *DatabaseType* parameter
Paradox 3.*x*	*Access.DoCmd.TransferDatabase* method with *acExport* as the *TransferType* parameter and "Paradox 3.x" as the *DatabaseType* parameter
Paradox 4.*x*	*Access.DoCmd.TransferDatabase* method with *acExport* as the *TransferType* parameter and "Paradox 4.x" as the *DatabaseType* parameter
Paradox 5.*x*	*Access.DoCmd.TransferDatabase* method with *acExport* as the *TransferType* parameter and "Paradox 5.x" as the *DatabaseType* parameter
Paradox 7.*x*	*Access.DoCmd.TransferDatabase* method with *acExport* as the *TransferType* parameter and "Paradox 7.x" as the *DatabaseType* parameter
Word Merge	*Access.DoCmd.TransferText* method with *acExportMerge* as the *TransferType* parameter

As with linking and importing, the *TransferDatabase* method's *DatabaseType* parameter takes a text string, whereas the *SpreadsheetType* method's *SpreadsheetType* parameter and the *TransferText* method's *TransferType* parameter both take a named constant from an enum (an enumerated list of constants; Access enums are visible in the Object Browser as classes with the *ac* prefix). Note that the *DatabaseType* parameter does not have a corresponding enum.

Exporting Database Objects to Other Access Databases

You can use the *TransferDatabase* method to export any type of Access database object to another database, with the same limitations as in the interface: Database objects other than tables can be exported only to Access 2002 or Access 2000 databases. Tables can also be exported to Access 97 databases.

The following function exports a table to the General.mdb database (located in the D:\Documents\Access 2002 folder) in structure-only mode. In other words, an empty table is created in the target database, with the same structure as the original table. The function uses the tblMembers table defined in the Export.mdb database, as described at the beginning of this section. You can find this database and the code for this function on the companion CD.

```
Function ExportToAccess()

DoCmd.TransferDatabase transfertype:=acExport, _
    databasetype:="Microsoft Access", _
    databasename:="D:\Documents\Access 2002\General.mdb", _
    ObjectType:=acTable, Source:="tblMembers", _
    Destination:="tblMembers", structureonly:=True
End Function
```

Exporting Data to Excel Worksheets

Depending on how you use Office applications to work with each other, you might routinely need to re-create Excel spreadsheets with updated data that you gather in your Access databases. For example, suppose you use an Access database to track open orders and the employees to whom those orders are assigned for fulfillment. At the end of the week, you publish a report that shows how many orders were fulfilled and lists the number of orders filled per employee. You'd like to summarize the data and export it to a large Excel spreadsheet so that you can analyze it in the context of quarterly and annual data.

The following function exports an Access query named qryOrdersAndEmployees to an Excel 9 workbook named Orders and Employees.xls (located in the D:\Documents folder) using the Access field names as column headings. The Excel worksheet produced by this function could then be used by colleagues who don't have Access or who prefer to analyze data in Excel, using its advanced data analysis tools. Make sure that the query and the location both exist before you run this function.

```
Function ExportToExcel()

DoCmd.TransferSpreadsheet transfertype:=acExport, _
    spreadsheettype:=acSpreadsheetTypeExcel9, _
    tablename:="qryOrdersAndEmployees", _
    filename:="D:\Documents\Orders and Employees.xls", _
    hasfieldnames:=True
End Function
```

Exporting Data to Text Files

As you've seen, text files can be output in two formats: as a delimited file in which data items are separated by a separator character (such as a comma, tab, or space) and as a fixed-width file that stores data in a columnar format in which each data item is stored in the same position in a record and is given the same width. When you export to a file using one of these file types using VBA code, you must use an export specification to define precisely how the text file should be formatted.

Of the two text file export choices, a delimited text file is generally more useful because it can be imported into almost any type of program, including mainframe databases. Fixed-width files are useful when you want a text file with data lined up neatly in columns. And as mentioned earlier in the chapter, fixed-width text files are displayed correctly only when a fixed-width font (such as Courier New) is used.

Creating Export Specifications for Recurring Export Tasks

If you export Access database objects to a text file format on a regular basis, it's helpful to create an export specification to store the options you select, to streamline the export process. It might be part of your weekly routine, for example, to export a comma-delimited text file of all new clients and contacts you made during the previous week. A saved export specification file (often called a spec) can do double duty: It saves time when you're using the interface to export a file, as you can just select the spec by clicking the Advanced button on the first page of the Export Text Wizard instead of selecting all the export options manually, and the same spec can also be used with the *SpecificationName* parameter of the *TransferText* method when you're using VBA code to export.

If you export Access data to a comma-delimited text file, you can then import the data from the text file into a wide range of applications, and the file can be used by colleagues working in a variety of database and spreadsheet programs. To create an export specification for exporting data from an Access table or query to a delimited text file, follow these steps:

1. In the Database window, select the table or query you want to export.
2. Choose File, Export. The Export dialog box will open.
3. In the Save As Type drop-down list, select Text Files.
4. Click Export to open the Export Text Wizard, as shown in Figure 17-22. The default setting is Delimited. Click Next to accept the default.

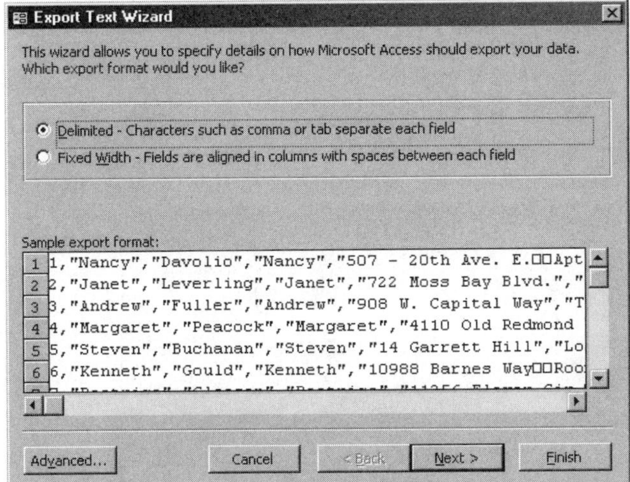

Figure 17-22. Accept the Delimited option on the first page of the Export Text Wizard.

5. Click the Tab option for the delimiter, leave the text qualifier set to a double quotation mark, and then check Include Field Names On First Row, as shown in Figure 17-23.

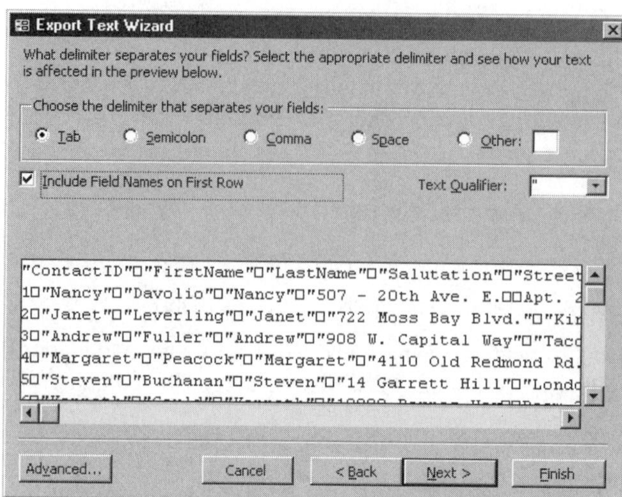

Figure 17-23. Select the options for the export.

6 Click Advanced to open the Export Specification dialog box. (See Figure 17-24.)

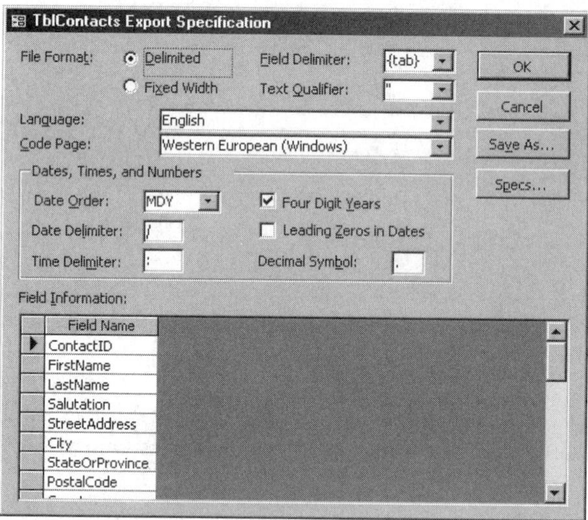

Figure 17-24. Save export settings you use often in the Export Specification dialog box.

7 Make the adjustments you want, click Save As, and enter (or accept) the name of the spec as shown in Figure 17-25.

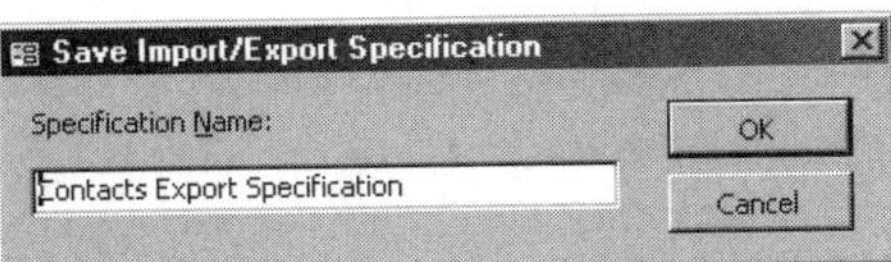

Figure 17-25. Save the export specification with a name of your choice.

8 Click OK to save the spec.

You can now use the spec in code as the setting of the *SpecificationName* parameter of the *TransferText* method or in the interface by selecting it from the dialog box that opens when you click Specs in the Export Specification dialog box.

The following function, which is also included on the companion CD, exports the tblContacts table to a tab-delimited text file named Contacts.csv located in the D:\Documents folder. The function uses the saved export specification "Contacts Export Specification" you just created and includes the Access field names as the first row of the text file. You can run this function after you perform the preparatory steps described at the beginning of this section. The comma-delimited file created by running this function can be opened in Notepad, Word, or Excel or imported into many other programs.

```
Function ExportToTextFile()
DoCmd.TransferText transfertype:=acExportDelim, _
    specificationname:="Contacts Export Specification", _
    tablename:="tblContacts", _
    filename:="D:\Documents\Contacts.csv", _
    hasfieldnames:=True
End Function
```

Exporting Data to dBASE Databases

If you want to create a contacts or members list as a dBASE database to be used by a colleague working in dBASE or perhaps for importing into another database program that has a dBASE import selection, you can do so quickly using a VBA function. The following function exports the tblMembers table to a dBASE IV database named Members.dbf located in the D:\Documents folder. For dBASE (and other databases that store each table in a different file), the database name is set using the *Destination* parameter and the path is set using the *Databasename* parameter. Be sure to complete the preparatory steps, as described at the beginning of this section, before you run this code.

```
Function ExportToDBase()
DoCmd.TransferDatabase transfertype:=acExport, _
    databasetype:="dBASE IV", _
    databasename:="D:\Documents", _
    ObjectType:=acTable, Source:="tblMembers", _
    Destination:="Members.dbf", structureonly:=True
End Function
```

Exporting Data to Outlook Appointments

As when you import from Outlook, you need to understand the Outlook object model to be able to export Access data to Outlook. Since the Outlook object model is hierarchical, you have to work down the object model to the folder you want to populate and then create Outlook items of a specific type, filling them with data from Access records. When you create new Outlook items in VBA code, you start with the Outlook *Application* object, then move down to the *NameSpace* object, then to a specific Outlook folder, and finally to Outlook items in that folder.

The following function creates appointments in the default local Outlook Calendar folder. Note that this function requires references to the Microsoft Outlook 10.0 Object Library and the Microsoft DAO 3.6 Object Library. You can set these references by opening the References dialog box from the Tools menu in the Visual Basic Editor window and then checking those selections, as shown in Figure 17-26.

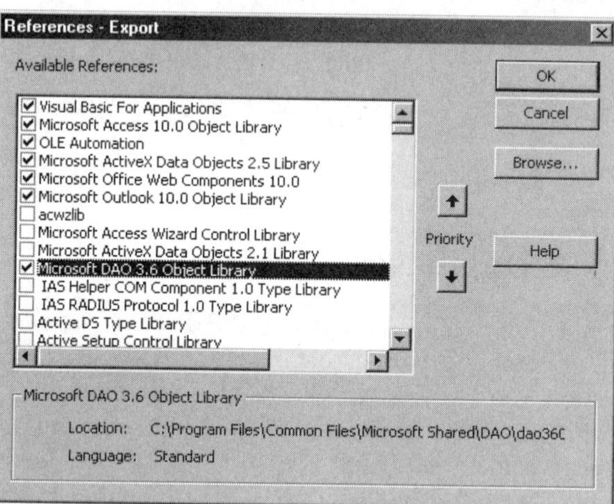

Figure 17-26. You set references to the Outlook and DAO object libraries in the References dialog box.

```
Function ExportToOutlook()

   Dim appOutlook As New Outlook.Application
   Dim nms As Outlook.NameSpace
   Dim fld As Outlook.MAPIFolder
   Dim appt As Outlook.AppointmentItem
   Dim itms As Outlook.Items
   Dim dbs As DAO.Database
   Dim rst As DAO.Recordset
   Dim lngCount As Long
   Dim strStart As String
   Dim strEnd As String

   Set nms = appOutlook.GetNamespace("MAPI")
   Set fld = nms.GetDefaultFolder(olFolderCalendar)
   Set itms = fld.Items

   'Get reference to data table.
   Set dbs = CurrentDb

   'Create recordset based on query.
   Set rst = dbs.OpenRecordset("qryAppointments", dbOpenDynaset)
   rst.MoveLast
   rst.MoveFirst
   lngCount = rst.RecordCount
   Debug.Print lngCount & " appointments to transfer to Outlook"

   'Loop through table, exporting each record to Outlook.
   Do Until rst.EOF
      'Create an appointment item.
      Set appt = itms.Add("IPM.Appointment")
      With appt
        Debug.Print "Exporting " & Nz(rst![Description]) & " record"
        .Subject = Nz(rst![Description])
        .Categories = Nz(rst![ApptType])

        'Concatenate Access date and time fields into a single
        'expression for the Outlook Start and End fields.
        strStart = rst![StartDate] & " " & rst![StartTime]
        strEnd = rst![EndDate] & " " & rst![EndTime]
        .Start = strStart
        .End = strEnd
        .Body = Nz(rst![Notes])
        .Close (olSave)
      End With
      rst.MoveNext
   Loop
   rst.Close

End Function
```

note This function uses the data in the table tblAppointments. Outlook won't accept appointments made in the past, so if the dates in this table are earlier than the date on which you run the code, simply change the dates in the table so that the appointments occur in the future.

When you run this code, you'll get the message shown in Figure 17-27. This message comes from the Object Model Guardian, a security feature that safeguards your Outlook contacts against a possible virus.

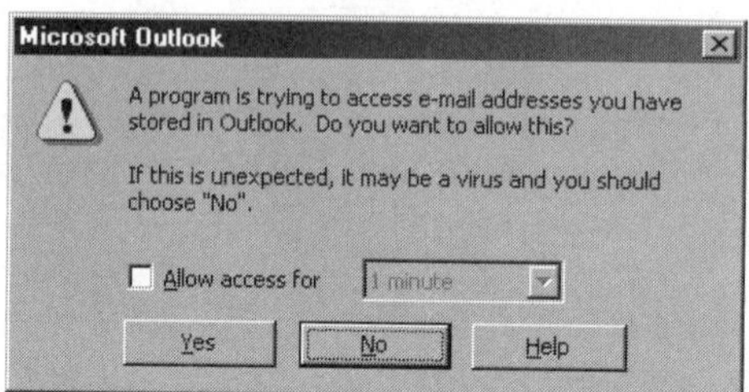

Figure 17-27. This warning message appears when you run the preceding code.

Checking Allow Access For and then selecting 5 Minutes from the drop-down list should give you plenty of time to run the code. Figure 17-28 shows the newly created appointments in the Outlook Calendar.

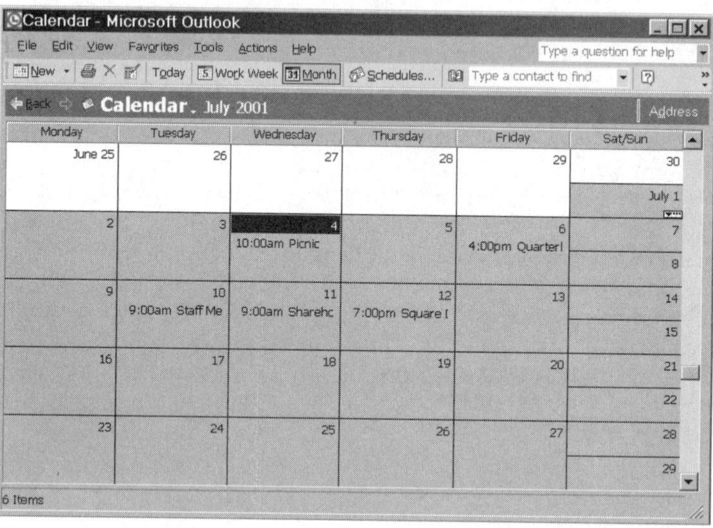

Figure 17-28. These Outlook appointments were created from an Access table.

Exporting Data to Word Tables

> **note** The following example is based on a column I wrote a couple of years ago. The full article is available for download from my Web site, at *http://www.helenfeddema.com/access.htm*. Look for Access Archon article #44.

Since the earliest versions of Access, users have wanted to export a complex Access report to Word, retaining all of its formatting. Unfortunately, there's no quick and easy way to do this, as noted earlier in the discussion of exporting to the Word RTF format. (See the section "Exporting Reports," page 697.) The Northwind Invoice report (see Figure 17-29), for example, doesn't export well to Word (see Figure 17-30). But that doesn't mean it's impossible to export Access data to Word and create a properly formatted invoice filled with the data—it just takes some code-writing skills. Once you have the code written and working, you can do the export with a single click of a toolbar button or by running a macro with a *RunCode* action.

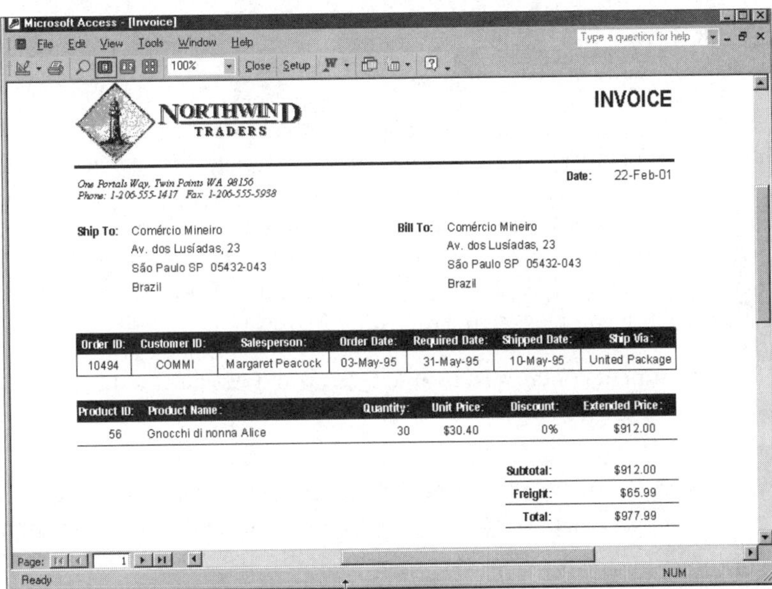

Figure 17-29. The Northwind Invoice report uses graphics and other formatting.

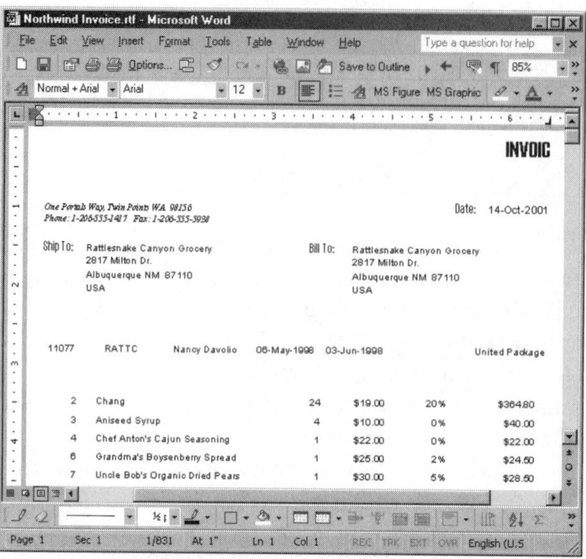

Figure 17-30. When you export the Northwind Invoice report to Word using the RTF selection in the interface, it loses some of its formatting.

Because Word has advanced formatting options, the most efficient technique for exporting an Access report to Word is to create a Word template with as much formatting as possible already built in and then write the Access data to a new document made from the Word template. You can place tabular data into cells of a Word table; other data that you might need in several places in the Word document can be written to Word custom document properties and displayed in the document in *DocProperty* fields. This method has a few advantages over Word Mail Merge:

- Each document contains its own data, so you don't need to have a separate data source open. This helps conserve memory and system resources and prevent sharing violations.
- Once the Word template and Access procedure have been set up, creating a new Word document (or set of documents) from updated data is fast and automatic. You don't need to step through the many pages of the Word Mail Merge Wizard every time you re-create the report.
- When you use this method to create multiple documents (by means of a multiselect list box, for example), you create separate Word documents, not pages in a huge multipage document.

To produce a Word invoice for a specific order based on Northwind data, I created a small dialog form (shown in Figure 17-31) that lets the user select the order number from a drop-down list that also displays the company name and order date. These fields are displayed in text boxes after a selection is made from the combo box.

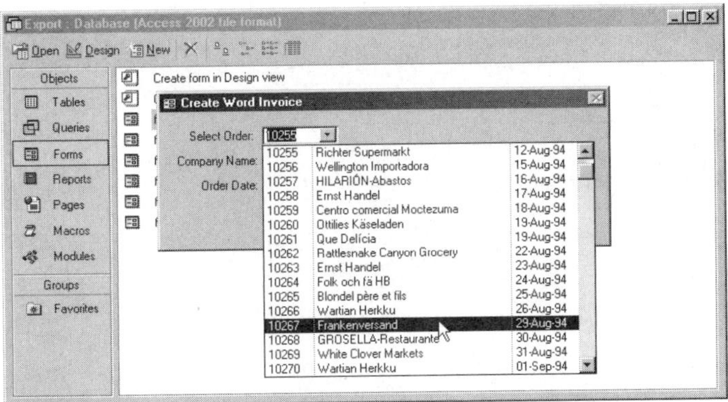

Figure 17-31. You can use this dialog form for selecting an order number to be invoiced.

The following event procedure behind the Create Invoice command button creates the Word invoice for the selected order. Figure 17-32 shows a sample invoice. The procedure is included in the Export.mdb sample code on the companion CD.

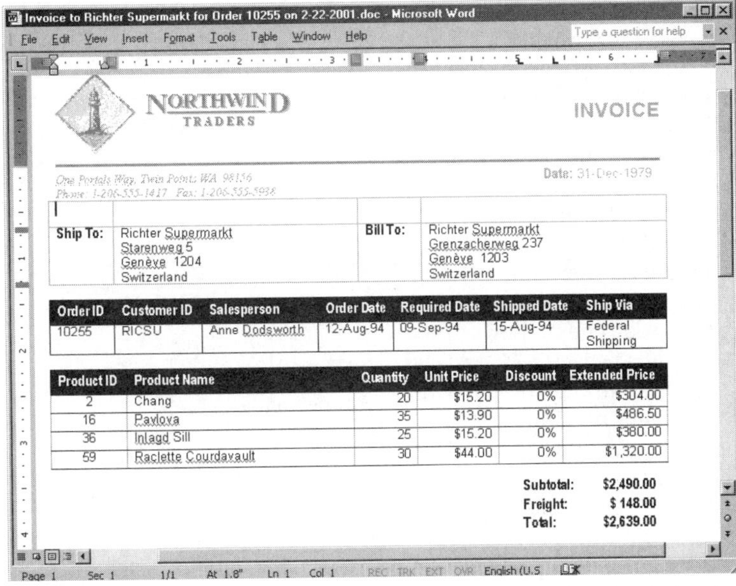

Figure 17-32. This Word invoice was created from Northwind data.

Before you run this code, be sure to perform the preparatory steps as described at the beginning of this section. In addition, the code requires a reference to the Word 10.0 object model. Open the References dialog box from the Tools menu in the Visual Basic Editor window and check the Microsoft Word 10.0 Object Library selection, as shown in Figure 17-33, to make sure the code will compile and run without errors.

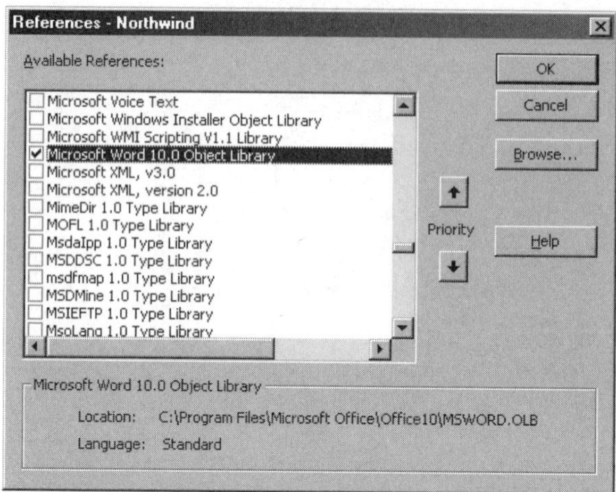

Figure 17-33. You must set a reference to the Word 10.0 object library to run the following code.

```
Private Sub cmdCreateInvoice_Click()
On Error Resume Next

    Dim dbs As DAO.Database
    Dim objDocs As Object
    Dim objWord As Object
    Dim prps As Object
    Dim rst As DAO.Recordset
    Dim blnSaveNameFail As Boolean
    Dim lngOrderID As Long
    Dim strShipName As String
    Dim strShipAddress As String
    Dim strShipCityStateZip As String
    Dim strShipCountry As String
    Dim strCustomerID As String
    Dim strCompanyName As String
    Dim strBillToAddress As String
    Dim strBillToCityStateZip As String
```

```
    Dim strBillToCountry As String
    Dim strSalesperson As String
    Dim dteTodayDate As Date
    Dim dteOrderDate As Date
    Dim dteRequiredDate As Date
    Dim dteShippedDate As Date
    Dim strShipper As String
    Dim curSubtotal As Currency
    Dim curFreight As Currency
    Dim curTotal As Currency
    Dim lngProductID As Long
    Dim strProductName As String
    Dim dblQuantity As Double
    Dim strUnitPrice As String
    Dim strDiscount As String
    Dim strExtendedPrice As String
    Dim strDoc As String
    Dim strDocsPath As String
    Dim strSaveName As String
    Dim strSaveNamePath As String
    Dim strShortDate As String
    Dim strTemplatePath As String
    Dim strTest As String
    Dim strTestFile As String
    Dim strWordTemplate As String
    Dim strMessageTitle As String
    Dim strMessage As String
    Dim intReturn As Integer
    Dim intCount As Integer

    'Create a Word instance to use for the invoice. Uses the existing
    'Word instance if there is one; otherwise, creates a new instance.
    Set objWord = GetObject(, "Word.Application")
    If Err.Number = 429 Then
        'Word isn't running; creating a Word object.
        Set objWord = CreateObject("Word.Application")
        Err.Clear
    End If

'Sets up error handler for the rest of the procedure
On Error GoTo cmdWordInvoice_ClickError
```

(continued)

```
'Run make-table queries to create tables to use for export.
'I use make-table queries instead of select queries because the
'queries have a criterion limiting the Order ID to the one
'selected on the form and such parameter queries can't be used
'in a recordset. Instead, the make-table queries are run to
'create tables that will be used in the recordsets later
'in the code.
DoCmd.SetWarnings False
DoCmd.OpenQuery "qmakInvoice"
DoCmd.OpenQuery "qmakInvoiceDetails"

'Check that there's at least one detail item before
'creating invoice.
intCount = DCount("*", "tmakInvoiceDetails")
Debug.Print "Number of Detail items: " & intCount

If intCount < 1 Then
    MsgBox "No detail items for invoice; canceling"
    Exit Sub
End If

'Create recordset and get needed doc properties for this invoice.
Set dbs = CurrentDb
Set rst = dbs.OpenRecordset("tmakInvoice", dbOpenDynaset)
With rst
    'The Nz function is used to convert any Nulls to zeros or
    'zero-length strings, to prevent problems with exporting
    'to Word.
    lngOrderID = Nz(![OrderID])
    Debug.Print "Order ID: " & lngOrderID
    strShipName = Nz(![ShipName])
    strShipAddress = Nz(![ShipAddress])
    strShipCityStateZip = Nz(![ShipCityStateZip])
    strShipCountry = Nz(![ShipCountry])
    strCompanyName = Nz(![CompanyName])
    strCustomerID = Nz(![CustomerID])
    strCompanyName = Nz(![CompanyName])
    strBillToAddress = Nz(![BillToAddress])
    strBillToCityStateZip = Nz(![BillToCityStateZip])
    strBillToCountry = Nz(![BillToCountry])
    strSalesperson = Nz(![Salesperson])
    dteOrderDate = Nz(![OrderDate])
    dteRequiredDate = Nz(![RequiredDate])
    dteShippedDate = Nz(![ShippedDate])
    strShipper = Nz(![Shipper])
    curSubtotal = Nz(![Subtotal])
    curFreight = Nz(![Freight])
    curTotal = Nz(![Total])
End With
rst.Close
```

```
'The paths for Templates and Documents folders are picked up
'from the File Locations page of the Word Options dialog box.
strDocsPath = objWord.Options.DefaultFilePath(wdDocumentsPath) & "\"
Debug.Print "Docs path: " & strDocsPath
strTemplatePath = _
    objWord.Options.DefaultFilePath(wdUserTemplatesPath) & "\"
strWordTemplate = strTemplatePath & "Northwind Invoice.dot"

'This date string is used in creating the invoice's save name.
strShortDate = Format(Date, "m-d-yyyy")

'This date variable is used to print today's date on the invoice.
'(Unlike a Word date code, it remains stable when the invoice is
'reopened later.)
dteTodayDate = Date

'Check for existence of template in template folder,
'and exit if not found.
strTestFile = Nz(Dir(strWordTemplate))
If strTestFile = "" Then
    MsgBox strWordTemplate & _
        "template not found; can't create letter"
    Exit Sub
End If

Set objDocs = objWord.Documents
objDocs.Add strWordTemplate

'Write information to Word custom document properties from
'previously created variables.
Set prps = objWord.ActiveDocument.CustomDocumentProperties
prps.Item("TodayDate").Value = dteTodayDate
prps.Item("OrderID").Value = lngOrderID
prps.Item("ShipName").Value = strShipName
prps.Item("ShipAddress").Value = strShipAddress
prps.Item("ShipCityStateZip").Value = strShipCityStateZip
prps.Item("ShipCountry").Value = strShipCountry
prps.Item("CompanyName").Value = strCompanyName
prps.Item("CustomerID").Value = strCustomerID
prps.Item("CompanyName").Value = strCompanyName
prps.Item("BillToAddress").Value = strBillToAddress
prps.Item("BillToCityStateZip").Value = strBillToCityStateZip
prps.Item("BillToCountry").Value = strBillToCountry
prps.Item("Salesperson").Value = strSalesperson
prps.Item("OrderDate").Value = dteOrderDate
prps.Item("RequiredDate").Value = dteRequiredDate
prps.Item("ShippedDate").Value = dteShippedDate
```

(continued)

```
prps.Item("Shipper").Value = strShipper
prps.Item("Subtotal").Value = curSubtotal
prps.Item("Freight").Value = curFreight
prps.Item("Total").Value = curTotal

'Highlight the entire Word document and update fields so that
'the data written to the custom doc props is displayed in the
'DocProperty fields.
With objWord
    .Selection.WholeStory
    .Selection.Fields.Update
    .Selection.HomeKey Unit:=6
    .Visible = True
    .Activate
End With

'Go to table to fill with Details data.
With objWord.Selection
    .GoTo What:=wdGoToTable, Which:=wdGoToFirst, Count:=3, _
        Name:=""
    .MoveDown Unit:=wdLine, Count:=1
End With

'Set up recordset of linked Details data to put in table on
'Word invoice.
Set rst = dbs.OpenRecordset("tmakInvoiceDetails", dbOpenDynaset)

'Save Details information to variables.
'Use Format function to apply appropriate formatting to
'Currency and Percent fields.
With rst
    .MoveFirst
    Do While Not .EOF
        lngProductID = Nz(![ProductID])
        Debug.Print "Product ID: " & lngProductID
        strProductName = Nz(![ProductName])
        Debug.Print "Product Name: " & strProductName
        dblQuantity = Nz(![Quantity])
        Debug.Print "Quantity: " & dblQuantity
        strUnitPrice = Format(Nz(![UnitPrice]), "$##.00")
        Debug.Print "Unit price: " & strUnitPrice
        strDiscount = Format(Nz(![Discount]), "0%")
        Debug.Print "Discount: " & strDiscount
        strExtendedPrice = Format(Nz(![ExtendedPrice]), _
            "$#,###.00")
        Debug.Print "Extended price: " & strExtendedPrice
```

```
        'Move through the table, writing values from the
        'variables to cells in the Word table.
        With objWord.Selection
            .TypeText Text:=CStr(lngProductID)
            .MoveRight Unit:=wdCell
            .TypeText Text:=strProductName
            .MoveRight Unit:=wdCell
            .TypeText Text:=CStr(dblQuantity)
            .MoveRight Unit:=wdCell
            .TypeText Text:=strUnitPrice
            .MoveRight Unit:=wdCell
            .TypeText Text:=strDiscount
            .MoveRight Unit:=wdCell
            .TypeText Text:=strExtendedPrice
            .MoveRight Unit:=wdCell
        End With
        .MoveNext
    Loop
    .Close
End With
dbs.Close

'Delete last, empty row.
Selection.SelectRow
Selection.Rows.Delete

'Check for existence of previously saved letter in documents ,
'folder and append an incremented number to save name if found.
strSaveName = "Invoice to " & strCompanyName & " for Order " _
    & lngOrderID & " on " & strShortDate & ".doc"

intCount = 2
blnSaveNameFail = True
Do While blnSaveNameFail
    strSaveNamePath = strDocsPath & strSaveName
    Debug.Print "Proposed save name and path: " _
        & vbCrLf & strSaveNamePath
    strTestFile = Nz(Dir(strSaveNamePath))
    If strTestFile = strSaveName Then

        'Create new save name with incremented number.
        blnSaveNameFail = True
        strSaveName = "Invoice " & CStr(intCount) & _
        " to " & strCompanyName _
        & " for Order " & lngOrderID & " on " & strShortDate & ".doc"
```

(continued)

```
            strSaveNamePath = strDocsPath & strSaveName
            intCount = intCount + 1
        Else
            blnSaveNameFail = False
        End If
    Loop

    'Ask whether user wants to save the document.
    'If you prefer, you can eliminate the prompt and just
    'save the document automatically using the save name.
    strMessageTitle = "Save document?"
     strMessage = "Save this document as " & strSaveName
    intReturn = MsgBox(strMessage, vbYesNoCancel + _
        vbQuestion + vbDefaultButton1, strMessageTitle)

    If intReturn = vbNo Then
        objWord.ActiveDocument.Close SaveChanges:=wdDoNotSaveChanges
        GoTo cmdWordInvoice_ClickExit
    ElseIf intReturn = vbYes Then
        objWord.ActiveDocument.SaveAs strSaveNamePath
    ElseIf intReturn = vbCancel Then
        GoTo cmdWordInvoice_ClickExit
    End If

cmdWordInvoice_ClickExit:
    'Close any open recordset or database, in case code stops because
    'of an error.
    On Error Resume Next
    rst.Close
    On Error Resume Next
    dbs.Close
    Exit Sub

cmdWordInvoice_ClickError:
    MsgBox "Error No: " & Err.Number & "; Description: " & _
        Err.Description
    Resume cmdWordInvoice_ClickExit

End Sub
```


Using Make-Table Queries to Create Flat-File Tables for Export

The *CmdCreateInvoice_Click* routine shown in the previous section uses a select query (shown in Design view in Figure 17-34) to combine data from several Northwind tables into a single query, effectively converting data in linked, normalized tables to a flat-file recordset—something you can't do with any of the standard export selections.

This technique is useful when you need to export data to a program that isn't a relational database. For example, you can use it to create tables of flat-file data to export to another Office application, such as Word, Excel, or Outlook, or for exporting to dBASE files and text files.

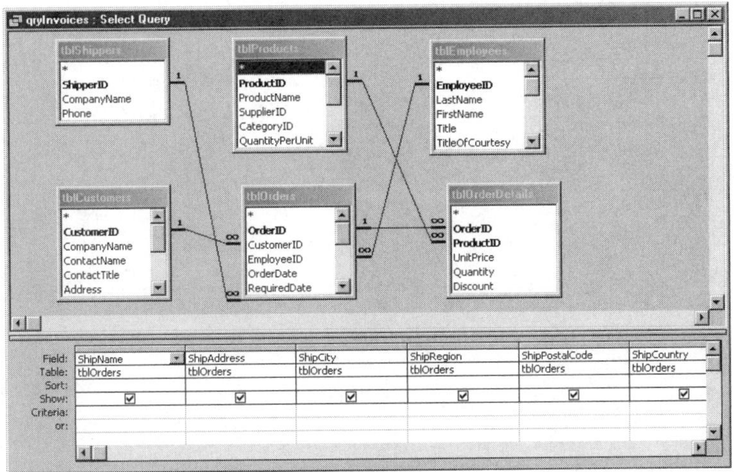

Figure 17-34. This select query combines data from linked, normalized tables into a single flat-file recordset.

A totals query adds up the price of the order details, and two make-table queries produce two temporary tables from the data, one for the body of the invoice and one for the invoice details. Figure 17-35 shows the make-table query that produces the table of data for the body of the invoice.

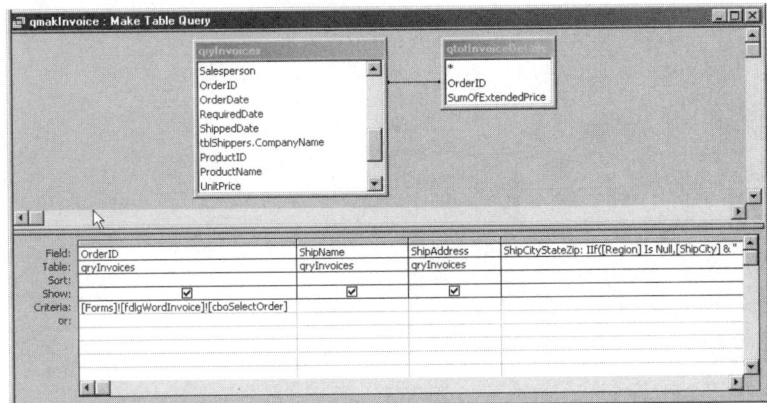

Figure 17-35. This make-table query produces a table used as the source of the invoice body data.

Part 6

Advanced Access Techniques

Chapter 18

Working with Data Access Pages

Access 97 made publishing Microsoft Access data to the Web possible for the first time, but its Web Publishing Wizard wasn't easy to use because it depended on HTML Layout Control to position controls on the page. Access 2000 introduced data access pages, which allow you to put Access data on Web pages with both display and editing capabilities. Data access pages combine the features of a form and a report, so you can use them to view, analyze, and enter data, even if you don't need to publish data to the Web. You can also use data access pages to display data in bands (similar to a grouped report) with options to suppress details if you want a summary view of the data.

For example, you might show customer information in the top-level band, with orders in another band, and order details in a third and lowest band. Depending on which bands are expanded, you could see just customers; customers and their orders; or customers, orders, and order details. In this chapter, we'll take a look at a data access page first, and then we'll discuss how to create a data access page and place Office Web Component controls on it.

note The acronyms used in this chapter are defined in the "Data Access Page Terminology" sidebar later in this chapter.

Understanding Data Access Pages

Unlike other Access components, data access pages are not part of Access databases. The data access page you see inside Access is simply a link to an external DHTML (HTM) file stored on your computer or on a Web server. In addition to this file, the data access page can also have a linked folder of supporting files; if there is such a folder, it must be located in the same folder as the DHTML file to prevent problems when opening the data access page. Figure 18-1 shows a data access page file and its folder in Windows Explorer.

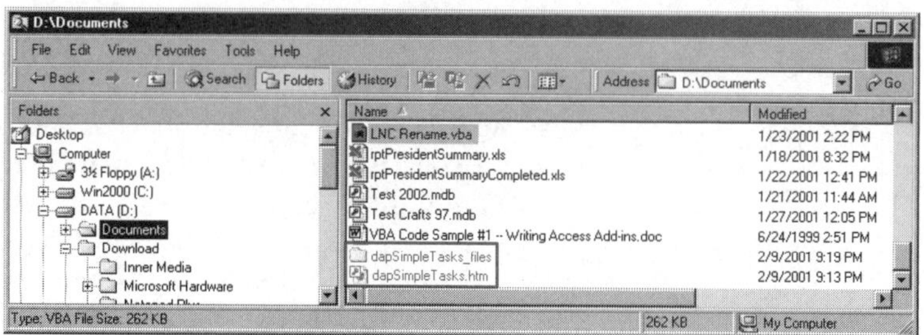

Figure 18-1. A data access page file can have a folder of supporting files.

> **caution** Don't move or delete any of the corresponding HTM files of data access pages. Data access pages are dependent on these files. If you delete or move these files to a new location, Access won't be able to locate them, and you will get an error message when opening the data access page.

A saved data access page exists as a file (and possibly a linked folder) on your computer. You can open a data access page even when Access is closed by double-clicking the HTM file in Windows Explorer on the same computer. The data access page will open in Microsoft Internet Explorer, as shown in Figure 18-2.

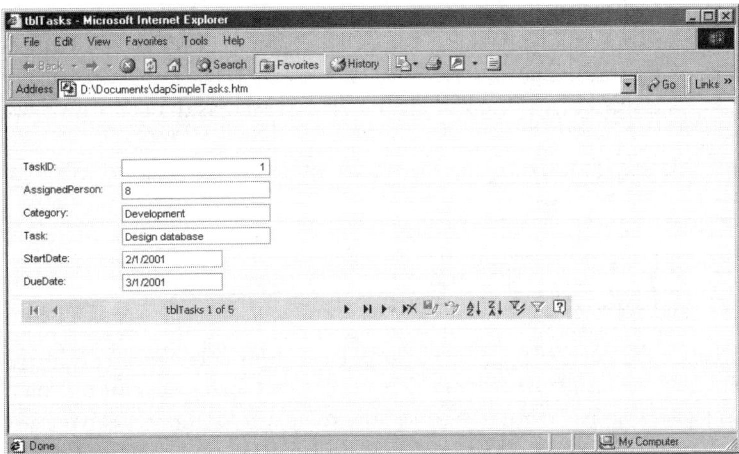

Figure 18-2. Even when Access is closed, you can open a data access page in Internet Explorer.

The Data Access Page Designer introduced in Access 2000 made it much easier to design data access pages and bind them to either Access or Microsoft SQL Server data sources by using DHTML data binding and XML. Once you place a data access page on a Web page, any user with Internet Explorer 5 can access it. For some components, such as spreadsheets or PivotTables, users will also need the Office Web Components, included in Microsoft Office 2000.

> **note** A detailed discussion of DHTML and XML is beyond the scope of this book, but there are many good books on these topics—whether you're a beginner or a more advanced user. Check out *http://mspress.microsoft.com* or your favorite bookstore for a title that fits your needs. For information on working with Web servers, FrontPage, and HTML, see *Microsoft FrontPage Version 2002 Inside Out*, by Jim Buyens (Microsoft Press, 2001).

newfeature!

Access 2002 takes a step forward with data access pages by introducing an enhanced PivotTable component and the new PivotChart component, which allow users to dynamically rearrange data (known as "slicing and dicing") to get just the view they want. The PivotChart component replaces the older, non-interactive MS Graph–based Chart component. (This component is still called Charts in some parts of the interface.)

The Office Spreadsheet component has also been enhanced, so you can now bind spreadsheets to data without programming. The Data Access Page Designer has been enhanced in many ways, including two much-requested features: Multilevel Undo and Redo are now supported, and Access forms can be saved as data access pages.

For a list of the new data access page features, refer to Chapter 1, "Exploring What's New in Access 2002."

Anatomy of a Data Access Page

You can create a data access page by clicking Pages in the database window Objects bar, and clicking the New button, or by clicking the New Object selector on the Access toolbar, and selecting Page. We'll discuss how to create a data access page step-by-step in the next section. Let's take a detailed look at a data access page first. A newly created data access page has a grid where you can place fields and a field list displaying all the tables and queries in the current database. If you select a table or query as the data access page's data source, that table or query's folder is open, and its fields are displayed for choice, as shown in Figure 18-3.

The Access Toolbox, docked on the left of the Access window in Figure 18-3, has several new tools for working with data access pages; their functions are described in the following list:

- **Bound Span.** Inserts a bound span control that makes the page load faster in Page view or in Internet Explorer.
- **Scrolling Text.** Inserts a text box whose text scrolls.
- **Expand.** Expands a sublevel of data on a banded data access page.
- **Record Navigation.** Inserts an ActiveX control that binds the data access page to an Access table or query; works with the Expand control to emulate subdatasheets.
- **Office PivotTable.** Inserts a PivotTable control.
- **Office Chart.** Inserts a PivotChart control.
- **Office Spreadsheet.** Inserts an Office Spreadsheet control.

- **Hyperlink.** Inserts a link to another information resource (text or image).
- **Image Hyperlink.** Inserts an image with an attached hyperlink.
- **Movie.** Inserts a control that plays or displays audio or video content.

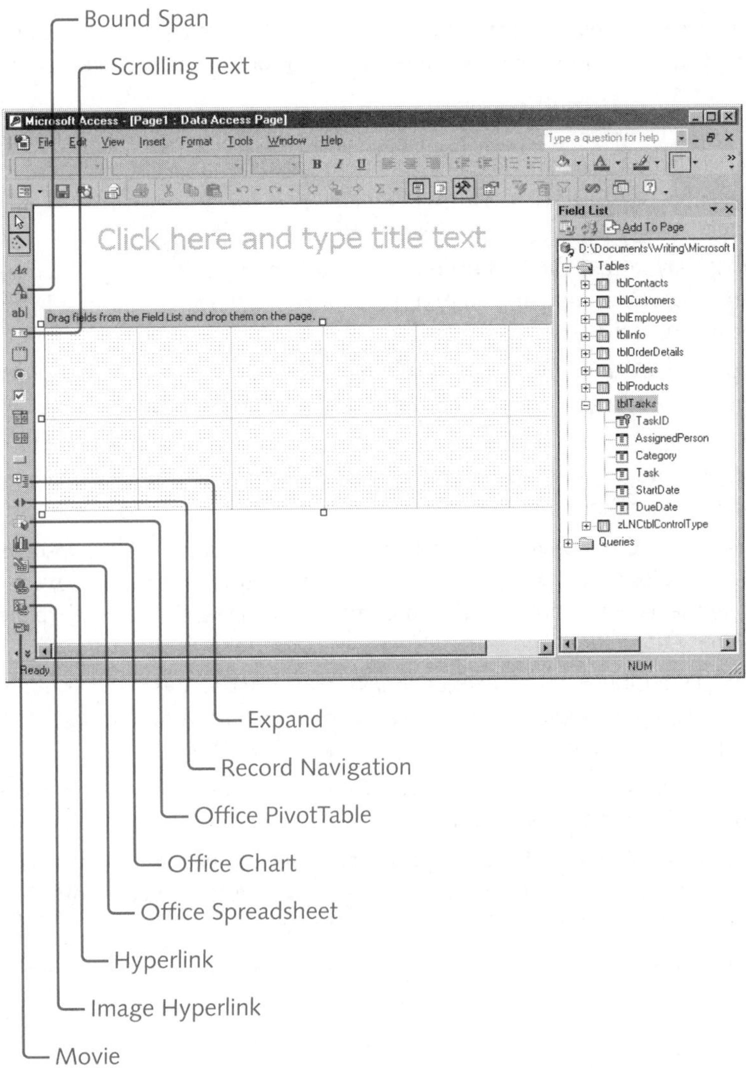

Figure 18-3. The blank Data Access Page Designer contains these tools and a field list.

Data Access Page Terminology

You might never use these terms (or the technologies they represent), but for the sake of completeness, the following list defines terms related to data access pages:

- **Data access page.** Used to display and edit data from an Access or SQL Server database in Internet Explorer 5 (either locally or on a Web page) or in Access.
- **DHTML.** Dynamic Hypertext Markup Language. Makes all HTML elements accessible by using language-independent scripting and other programming languages. With DHTML, you can dynamically change any aspect of a Web page's content.
- **HTML.** Hypertext Markup Language. Based on the older SGML (Standard Generalized Markup Language), HTML describes the structure of a hypertext document, rather than its content.
- **Hypertext.** A segment of text or an image that has a link to another text segment or image (information resources) that you can open by clicking the link.
- **Markup Language.** A language that describes the structure of a document as opposed to its content.
- **Office Web Components**. A set of run-time files (provided as the Msowc.cab file) that allow users without Microsoft Office to use data access pages, spreadsheets, PivotTables, and PivotCharts interactively, in Internet Explorer 5 or later. Office XP includes the Office Web Components.
- **XML.** Extensible Markup Language. Extends HTML to deal with structured data from many applications, and allows the creation of custom data formats for special situations.
- **XSL.** Extensible Stylesheet Language. Allows you to create your own style sheets for formatting XML data.
- **XSLT.** Extensible Stylesheet Language for Transformations. Both a markup and a programming language, XSLT transforms an XML structure into another XML structure, HTML, SQL, or another format.

Creating Data Access Pages

Access 2002 gives you several different choices when creating data access pages. After you start the process by choosing Pages in the database window Objects bar and clicking New, you select the style that fits the data you want to publish to the Web. Unlike the other Access components, in which the New Form (or New Report) dialog box offers you all the available layout selections, data access pages layout choices are divided between two dialog boxes: the New Data Access Page dialog box and the Layout Wizard dialog box, which appears when you drag fields to a new data access page.

Table 18-1 lists all the available options for creating data access pages.

note One selection (Columnar) is available in both dialog boxes; another (Save As Data Access Page) is not available in either dialog box.

Table 18-1. Data access page creation options

Creation option	Available from
Columnar	AutoPage: Columnar selection in the New Data Access Page dialog box; Columnar selection in the Layout Wizard
Tabular	Tabular selection in the Layout Wizard
Banded	Page Wizard selection in the New Data Access Page dialog box
Free-Form	Design View selection in the New Data Access Page dialog box
PivotTable	PivotTable selection in the Layout Wizard
PivotChart	PivotChart selection in the Layout Wizard
Office Spreadsheet	Office Spreadsheet selection in the Layout Wizard
From Existing Web Page	Existing Web page selection in the New Data Access Page dialog box
Saving a Form as a Data Access Page	Choose File, Save As from an open Access form

To create a new data access page, either click Pages in the database window Objects bar and then click the New button, or click the New Object selector and select Page from the drop-down list, as shown in Figure 18-4.

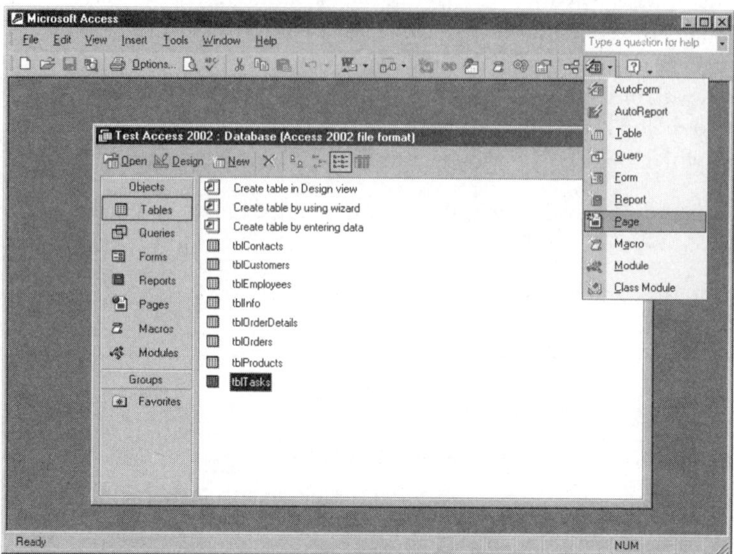

Figure 18-4. You can create a data access page based on a table using the Page item in the New Object selector drop-down list.

The New Data Access Page dialog box opens, as shown in Figure 18-5.

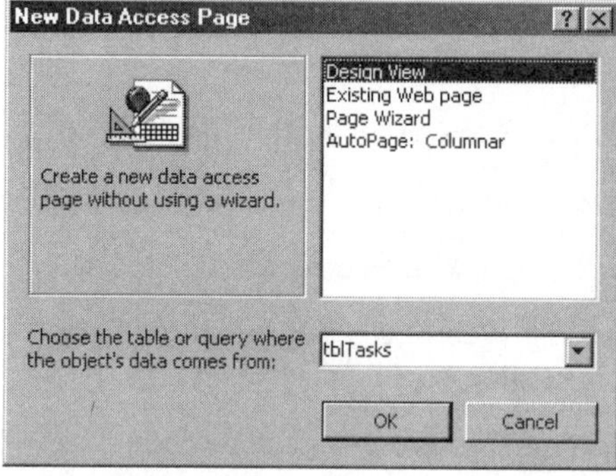

Figure 18-5. You can use the New Data Access Page dialog box to create a data access page.

The New Data Access Page dialog box offers you the following four choices:

- **Design View.** Opens the data access page Designer to a blank page; also gives you access to the Layout Wizard, which contains more data access page layout choices.
- **Existing Web Page.** Opens a saved data access page from its HTM file.
- **Page Wizard.** Starts the Page Wizard, which assists you in creating a banded data access page.
- **AutoPage: Columnar.** Automatically creates a columnar data access page.

As mentioned earlier, the Layout Wizard offers the other choices for creating data access pages. To use this wizard, start a data access page by using the Design View selection in the New Data Access Page dialog box, and then drag a table or query from the field list to the data access page grid. The Layout Wizard opens, as shown in Figure 18-6.

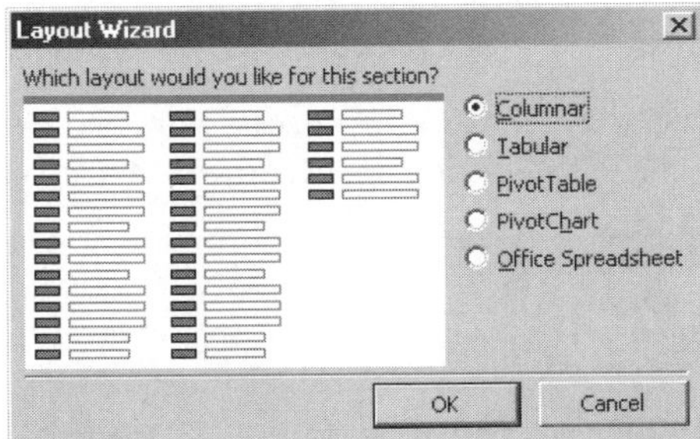

Figure 18-6. You can also create a data access page using the Layout Wizard.

The Layout Wizard offers you the following five choices:

- **Columnar.** The data access page's fields are arranged in a vertical column.
- **Tabular.** The data access page looks like a table, with labels used as column headings.
- **PivotTable.** The data access page has a PivotTable control, with the selected fields used as columns and rows.
- **PivotChart.** The data access page has a PivotChart control, with fields used as series and categories.
- **Office Spreadsheet.** The data access page has an Office Spreadsheet control filled with data from the selected fields.

PivotTables and PivotCharts on Data Access Pages

Although both Access forms and data access pages can host PivotTables and PivotCharts, you create these Office Web controls somewhat differently on forms and data access pages. When you create a new form, the New Form dialog box offers you (among other choices) a choice of AutoForm: PivotTable, AutoForm: PivotChart, and PivotTable Wizard. These selections provide assistance (more in the case of PivotTables) with setting up a form with a PivotTable or PivotChart, as described in Chapter 12, "Using PivotTables and PivotCharts to Analyze Data." The form itself is bound to data, which can be displayed in either PivotTable or PivotChart view.

With data access pages, on the other hand, the New Data Access Page dialog box offers no choices for PivotTables and PivotCharts. You place PivotTables, PivotCharts, and Office Spreadsheets on a data access page by clicking the corresponding tool in the Toolbox, or by dragging a table or query to the data access page design grid and selecting PivotTable, PivotChart or Office Spreadsheet in the Layout Wizard.

Note that you can't create a PivotTable or PivotChart on an Access form and then copy it to a data access page; you must re-create these components on a data access page.

Creating Form-Type Data Access Pages

As mentioned, data access pages combine the features of both forms and reports in one object. However, they are neither a form nor a report. If you want to create a data access page that looks like a form and displays one record of information at a time, you can choose the AutoPage: Columnar option in the New Data Access Page dialog box. This option will help you create a form with fields displayed in a vertical column; the Columnar selection in the Layout Wizard offers you the same choice, but with your choice of fields.

If you want a data access page that looks as much as possible like a regular Access form (perhaps to provide Internet users with a familiar interface), the option to save a form as a data access page is the best way to go. This new option allows you to convert a form into a virtually identical data access page, so users of your applications can review, add, and analyze data in the form over an intranet or the Internet.

To create a columnar data access page, just select the AutoPage: Columnar selection from the New Data Access Page dialog box with a table selected. Figure 18-7 shows a data access page based on tblTasks (see the sidebar "Creating Table Relationships on the Fly in Data Access Pages," page 746) created using this selection.

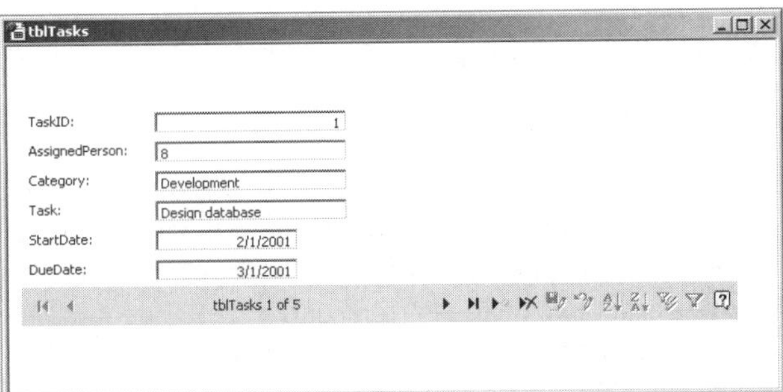

Figure 18-7. This columnar data access page was automatically created from tblTasks.

From Figure 18-7 you can see that the value in the ID field is right-aligned and the field is a little bit too wide. You will probably want to make the TaskID field narrower and left-aligned. To make the text box narrower, switch to Design view, click the TaskID text box so that its sizing handles appear (they are small white squares at the corners and midpoints of the text box), grab the handle on the right side of the text box and drag it inwards until the text box has the correct width. To make its text left-aligned, with the text box selected, click the Align Left button on the toolbar. (These properties can also be set in the text box's properties sheet, which can be opened by clicking the Properties button on the toolbar.)

newfeature!

Working with controls on data access pages is now quite similar to working with controls on forms or reports, so you can generally use the techniques described in Chapter 8, "Using Design Tools," when working with controls on data access pages.

To create a columnar data access page using the Layout Wizard, create a new data access page using the Design View selection in the Data Access Page dialog box, drag a table or query from the field listField list to the data access page's design grid, and then select the Columnar selection from the Layout Wizard. The only difference between the two methods is that the Layout Wizard Columnar selection allows you to select a subset of the fields in a data source, while the New Data Access Page AutoPage: Columnar selection automatically places all the fields in the selected table or query on the data access page.

If you want complete control over the placement of fields on a data access page, select the Design View choice in the New Data Access Page dialog box, and drag fields to the design grid from the Field List, placing them as desired on the data access page design grid.

Creating Table Relationships on the Fly in Data Access Pages

If you preselect a table or query before you create a new data access page, the selected table will be expanded in the Field List, ready for you to drag fields from it to the data access page design grid. However, unlike Access forms and reports, data access pages allow you to drag fields from any table in the current database to the data access page, as long as those fields can be related to the original table.

In the Modified Northwind database available on the companion CD, for example, tblTasks has a field (Assigned Person) that can be related to the Person field in tblPersons. After you drag fields from tblTasks to the design grid, dragging a field from tblPersons to a data access page opens the Layout Wizard first. Choosing a type of data access page and then clicking OK opens the Relationship Wizard (shown in Figure 18-8), which allows you to create a link between the two tables on the fly.

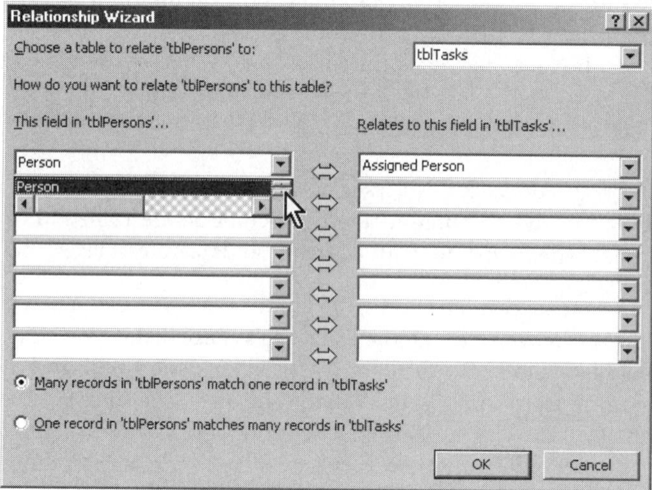

Figure 18-8. You can set up a relationship in the Relationship Wizard after dragging a field from another table to the data access page grid.

Relationships set up in the Relationship Wizard opened from a data access page do not appear in the regular Relationships window or as links when you create queries based on these tables.

newfeature!

Generating Banded Data Access Pages

In Access 2002, you can create a data access page with a hierarchical structure by grouping records on it into specific categories. Grouping records on a data access page is similar to grouping records on a report. To create a banded (also called grouped) data access page, you can either use the Page Wizard selection in the New Data Access Page dialog box, or select the Create Data Access Page By Using Wizard shortcut in the Pages tab of the database window.

To create a banded data access page by using the Page Wizard, follow these steps:

1. Create a query containing all the data you want to display on the data access page. If all the data you need is available in one table, you can use the table as a data source.

Figure 18-9 shows a sample query called qryNorthwindAll based on several Northwind tables. This query is located in the Modified Northwind.mdb database.

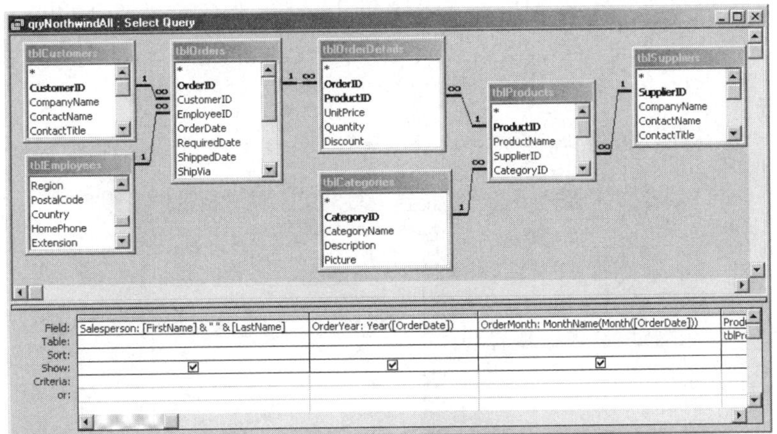

Figure 18-9. This query is intended for use as a data access page data source.

2. Select the table or query to use as the data access page's data source in the database window, click the New Object selector, and select Page from the drop-down list.

   The New Data Access Page dialog box opens with qryNorthwindAll selected.

3. Select the Page Wizard option to start the Page Wizard.

4 Select the fields you want to use on the data access page, as shown in Figure 18-10, and click Next.

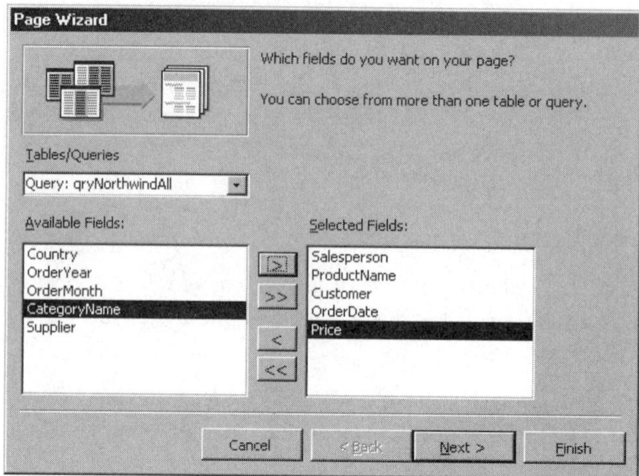

Figure 18-10. The first page of the Page Wizard looks like this.

Selecting Salesperson, ProductName, Customer, OrderDate, and Price allows you to create a banded page using several categories.

5 Select grouping levels, as shown in Figure 18-11. Click Next.

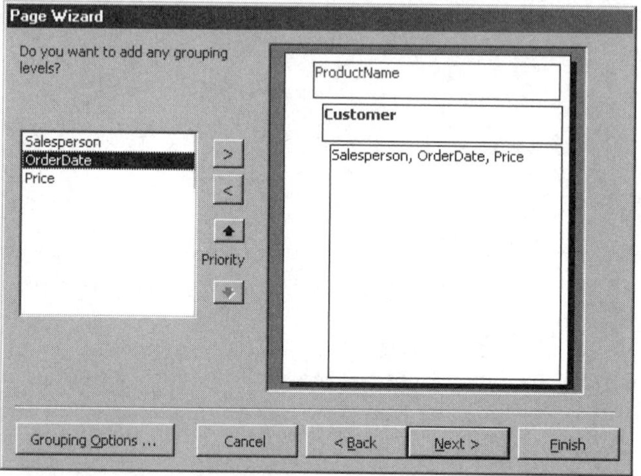

Figure 18-11. Select groups for a banded data access page on the second page of the Page Wizard.

6 Select sort fields for the data access page groups from the drop-down list of the remaining fields in the data source (those not already selected as grouping fields). Note that the sort order is Ascending by default. To sort in descending order, click the Ascending button to the right of a sort field; it will change to Descending.

7 Name your data access page. (See Figure 18-12.)

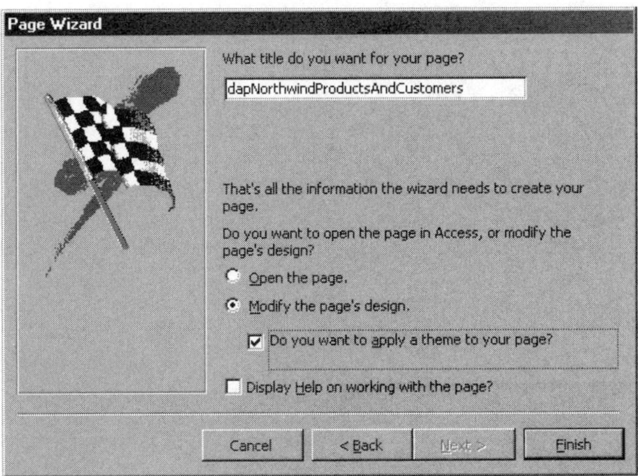

Figure 18-12. The final page of the Page Wizard allows you to specify the page title and other options.

You have several options before finishing the wizard: You can choose to open the page in Page view or Design view, you can select a theme for the page, and you can display Help for working on a data access page. When you've made your selections, click Finish.

note The *dap* tag in the page title is used in the LNC naming convention. (See "Naming Conventions" in Chapter 20, "Customizing Your Database Using VBA Code," for details on using the LNC naming convention.)

If you choose to apply a theme, the Theme dialog box will appear when you click Finish. Figure 18-13 shows the Canvas style. If you click Set Default, the Canvas style will remain the default so that all the data access pages you create in this database will have a consistent appearance.

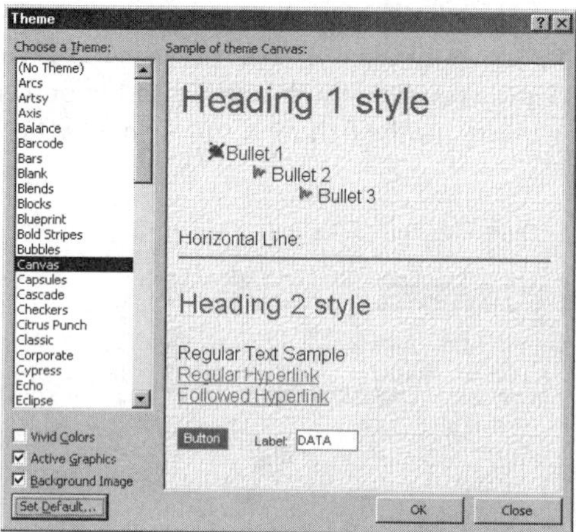

Figure 18-13. You can choose to apply a theme to your data access page.

Figure 18-14 shows the data access page open in Design view with a placeholder at the top where you can enter a title.

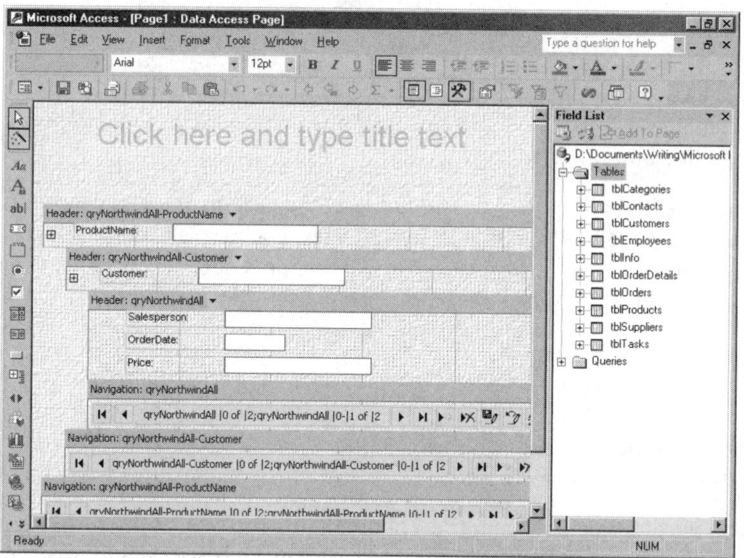

Figure 18-14. The data access page is now banded and includes a field list.

> **tip** Each group level (band) is indented under the band above it. The navigation bars for the bands are at the same indent level as their data, in reverse order.

After you type in the title, you can make changes in Design view. For example, you could add space to the labels and change the size of the controls. When you switch to Page view, the data access page appears with the first product name visible, in collapsed mode, as shown in Figure 18-15.

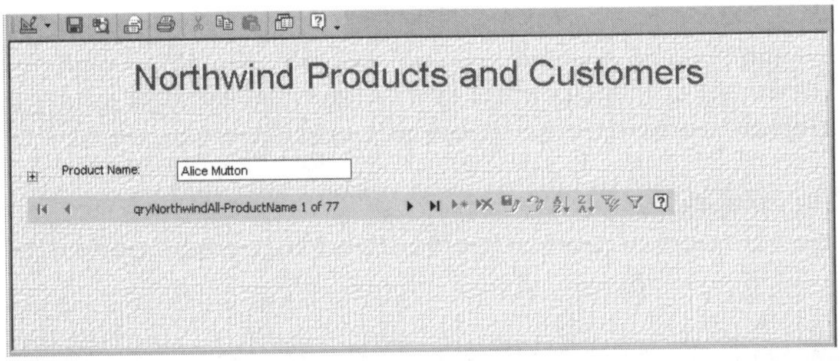

Figure 18-15. The new data access page is collapsed to show the top level only.

If you click the plus sign to the left of the ProductName label, you'll expand the next level, showing the Customer data; clicking the plus sign to the left of the Customer label expands the Detail group, showing the Salesperson, Order Date, and Price data, as shown in Figure 18-16.

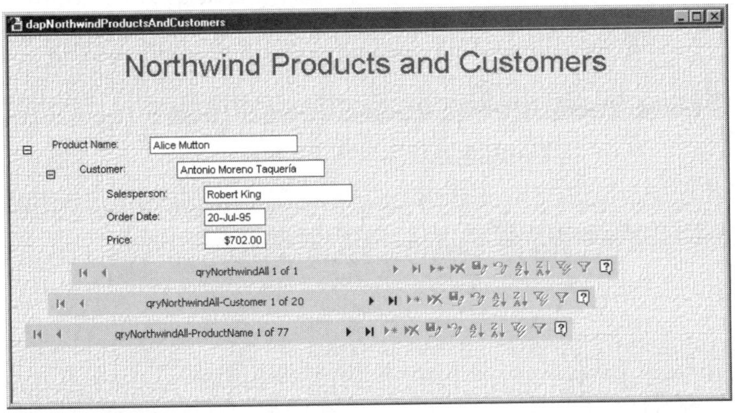

Figure 18-16. In Page view, the new data access page looks like this with all bands of data expanded.

The data access page has three navigation bars that correspond to the Product Name group, the Customer group, and the Detail area. These navigation bars also have buttons for filtering and sorting the data in each group. You can see the number of records in each child group in the navigation bars. For example, the Alice Mutton product has 20 customers and the selected customer (Antonio Moreno Taquería) has one detail record.

Creating Tabular Data Access Pages

If you want to create a table-type data access page, you can also use the tabular layout selection. As the name suggests, a tabular data access page looks like a table, with labels used as column headings. To create a data access page with a table displaying data from selected fields, select Design View in the New Data Access Page dialog box, and then drag a table or query from the field list to the data access page grid. When Access displays the Layout Wizard, select Tabular. Figure 18-17 shows a tabular data access page created by dragging tblTasks to the data access page design grid.

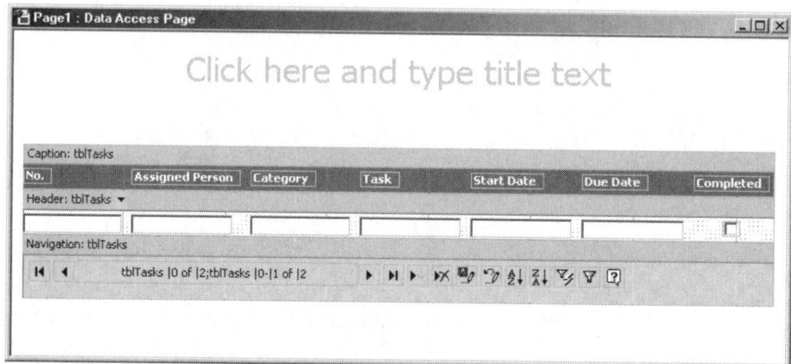

Figure 18-17. This tabular data access page displays all fields from tblTasks.

Figure 18-18 shows the tabular data access page with a title added, in Page view.

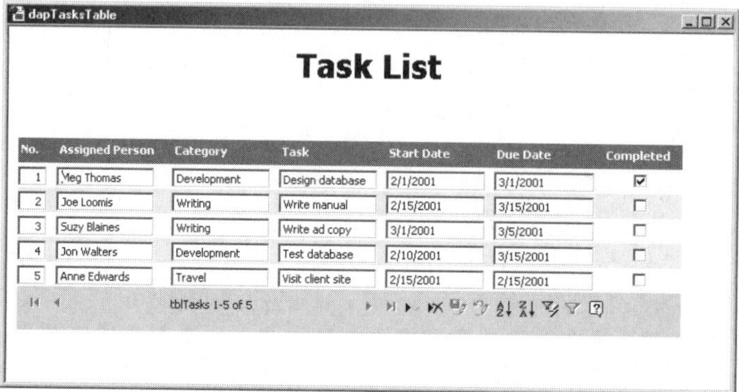

Figure 18-18. The tabular data access page looks like this in Page view.

Chapter 18

Adding PivotTables, PivotCharts, and Spreadsheets to Your Data Access Pages

If you want the viewers of your data access page to be able to dynamically rearrange summarized data on the data access page, use a PivotTable (or a PivotChart if you want to display the data graphically). These selections let users decide for themselves what information they want in rows, and what information in columns, and how they want to analyze or chart it. For example, one user might want to see salespersons' names as rows, and sales by month in columns, while another user might want to see summarized quarterly sales in rows, and salespersons in columns.

With a PivotTable, each user can decide for himself or herself how to arrange the data, without having to switch to Design view and modify the data access page (which in any case might not be possible if the user has only read-only permissions for working with the data access page). Similarly, with PivotCharts users can select different chart and graph types, and swap the data displayed on the horizontal and vertical axes, without the need to redesign the data access page.

For a familiar worksheet look, you can use the Office Spreadsheet. You can create data access pages with any of these three Office Web Components by creating a new data access page in Design view and then placing a PivotTable, PivotChart, or Office Spreadsheet control on the design grid. However, the process of creating these controls and filling them with data is generally simpler if you choose the appropriate selection from the Layout Wizard, which appears when you drag a table or query from the data access page's field list to the design grid.

InsideOut

You can't copy a PivotTable or PivotChart from an Access form to a data access page. If, however, you take the time to create a select query that includes only the data you need in the PivotTable and does some preprocessing of the data using date and string conversion functions, you can use that same query as the data source for a PivotTable on a data access page, thereby saving you a good deal of time when you place a PivotTable control on a data access page. The query qryNorthwindAll, shown in Figure 18-9 on page 747, is such a query.

newfeature!

Creating a PivotTable

A PivotTable is much more flexible in displaying data than a banded data access page. Users can swap the Row and Column fields, add totals, and filter the data on the form to get just the view they want. You can use the same query that you used to create the banded data access page to create a PivotTable data access page.

To do so, follow these steps:

For more details on working with PivotTables, see Chapter 12, "Using PivotTables and PivotCharts to Analyze Data."

1. Click New in the Pages tab of the database window to open the New Data Access Page dialog box, select Design View, and click OK. A blank data access page opens.
2. Place a PivotTable control on the data access page by clicking the PivotTable tool in the Toolbox, and then clicking on the data access page to insert a PivotTable control on the grid, as shown in Figure 18-19. The PivotTable will have its drop zones but won't have any fields selected.

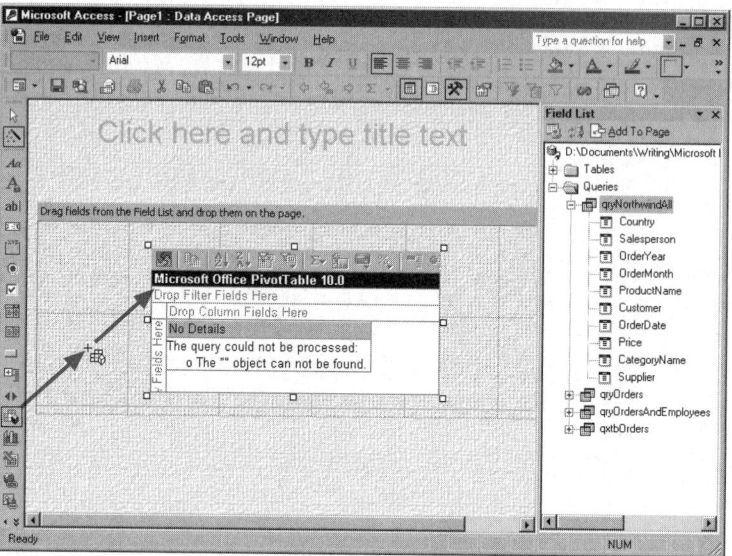

Figure 18-19. Insert a PivotTable control on a new data access page in Design view.

Using Date Functions to Process Date Fields in a Query

When creating a query for use in a PivotTable or PivotChart, you can use several date functions to separate out the data in a Date/Time field into the appropriate time periods, using meaningful words rather than numbers. For example, if you anticipate wanting to display data in months, quarters, or years, you could use the *Year*, *Month*, *MonthName*, and *DatePart* functions to produce properly formatted column headings, using the following query column expressions:

```
OrderYear: Year([OrderDate])
OrderMonth: MonthName(Month([OrderDate]))
OrderQuarter: "Q" & DatePart("q",[OrderDate]) & ", " & Year([OrderDate])
```

These expressions produce the following values (for a sample row):

```
Order Year:  1994
Order Month:  September
Order Quarter:  Q3, 1994
```

These query columns can then be used to create PivotTable columns or rows, or PivotChart series and categories.

3 Alternatively, you can open the Queries folder in the field list, and then drag the qryNorthwindAll query from the field list to the data access page design grid, and then select the PivotTable selection from the Layout Wizard, as shown in Figure 18-20. If you use this method, all the query's fields are placed on the data access page as columns, and you will have to move them to other drop zones, or drag them off the PivotTable, to get the desired layout. The remaining steps assume you created the PivotTable from the Toolbox.

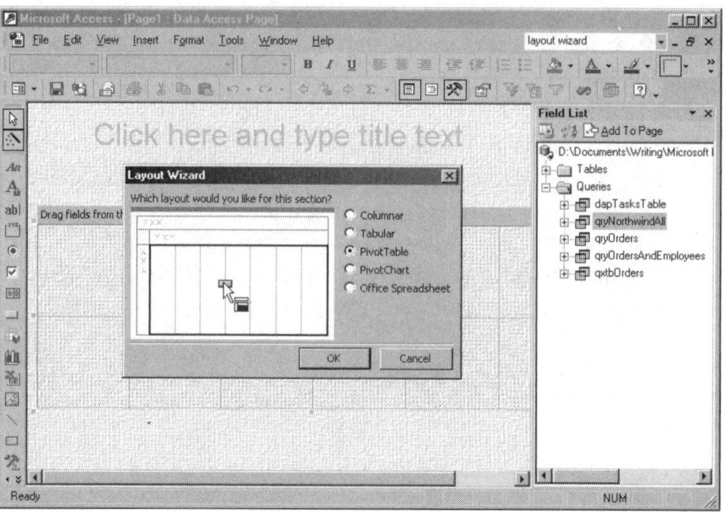

Figure 18-20. Select the PivotTable choice when dragging a query to the data access page design grid.

Troubleshooting

I can't see the drop zones in a newly inserted PivotTable

If the PivotTable's drop zones aren't visible, right-click the PivotTable control, and then choose Commands And Options from the shortcut menu to open the Commands And Options dialog box. Click the Behavior tab and check the Drop Areas check box, as shown in Figure 18-21. You can also turn on the PivotTable's title bar and toolbar on this page.

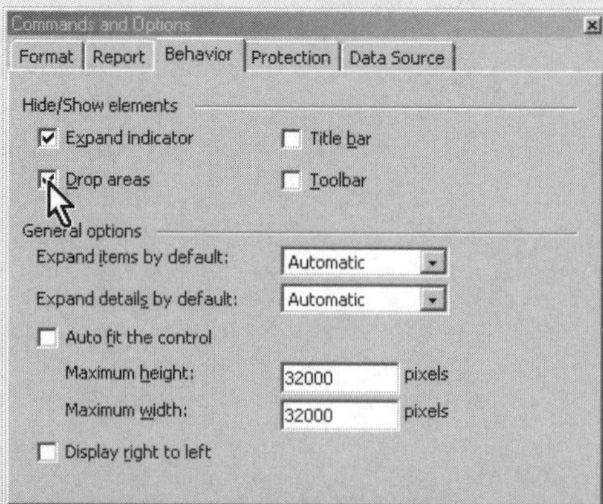

Figure 18-21. Turn on a PivotTable's drop zones in the Commands And Options dialog box.

> **note** PivotTables on data access pages have the Commands And Options dialog box, while PivotTables on other database objects (such as forms) have a properties sheet where you can set options.

4 Use the sizing handles to stretch the PivotTable control to the desired size.

5 Click the Type Title Text area and type in **Product Sales Totals by Salesperson** for the title.

6 If necessary, open the Queries folder in the field list, and open the qryNorthwindAll query so you can see its fields.

7 Drag the ProductName field from the field list to the Row Fields drop zone of the PivotTable control, drag the Salesperson field to the Column Fields drop zone, and then drag the Price field to the Totals/Detail Fields drop zone. Figure 18-22 shows the PivotTable in Design view.

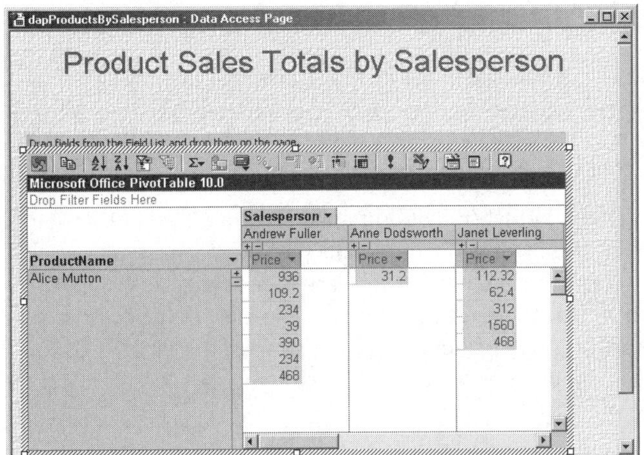

Figure 18-22. The PivotTable data access page looks like this in Design view.

8 Select the Price column and click the AutoCalc button on the PivotTable toolbar (or right-click the selected column and select AutoCalc from its context menu) to add a Sum or Count summary row.

9 Save the data access page as **dapProductsBySalesperson**.

Figure 18-23 shows the data access page in Page view.

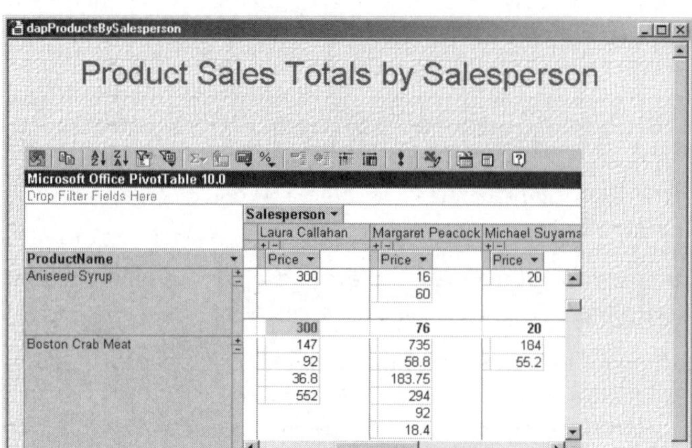

Figure 18-23. The new data access page looks like this in Page view.

Troubleshooting

I can't add a sum to a PivotTable or change the chart type on a PivotChart

Although they look normal (they don't appear dimmed), the AutoSum button and other buttons on the PivotTable and PivotChart toolbars aren't available unless the PivotTable (or PivotChart) control is activated. In data access page Design view, click the control once, and then again. (Don't double-click the control. If you do, the Object Properties dialog box will open.) When you see the PivotTable (or PivotChart) surrounded by a wide, diagonally hatched border, you can use the tools on its toolbar.

You can also swap the Row and Column fields of the PivotTable and add totals. Figure 18-24 shows the same PivotTable with Salesperson as the Row field and ProductName as the Column field.

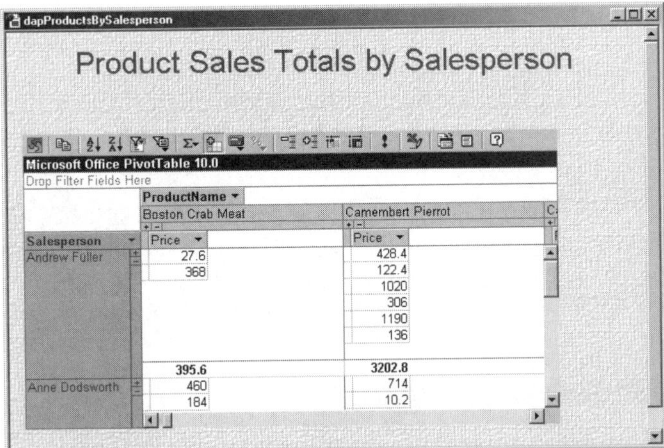

Figure 18-24. The same PivotTable looks like this after you swap rows and columns and add totals.

> **tip** To turn on the PivotTable toolbar, double-click the PivotTable to open its properties sheet and set the *DisplayToolbar* property to True. (Alternatively, right-click the PivotTable control, and then choose Commands And Options from the shortcut menu. Click the Behavior tab and check the Toolbar check box.) The toolbar appears at the top of the PivotTable control; it has only a subset of the controls on the PivotTable toolbar on a form.

newfeature!

Creating a PivotChart

The data access page toolbox doesn't have a PivotChart control. Instead, it has an Office Chart control. In Access 2000, this control put a chart similar to an MS Graph on a form or data access page. In Access 2002, this control places a Microsoft Office Web Component placeholder on a data access page, and you need to select a data source to turn it into a PivotChart. Placing a Chart control on a data access page is primarily useful for creating a PivotChart based on external data, as described in the "Creating a

PivotChart based on an external data source" section later in this chapter. If you want to create a PivotChart based on a local table or query, a much simpler method is available as described in the following procedure:

1. Create a new data access page by using the Design View selection in the New Data Access Page dialog box.
2. In the data access page field list, open the Tables (or Queries) folder, and drag the table or query you want to use for the PivotChart to the data access page's design grid. The Layout Wizard appears. Select the PivotChart option (as shown in Figure 18-25) and click OK to place the PivotChart on the data access page.

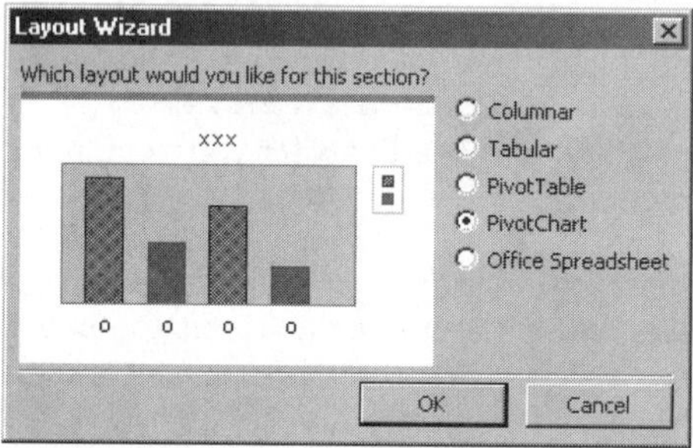

Figure 18-25. Select the PivotChart option on the Layout Wizard when dragging a table or query to a data access page to create a PivotChart.

3. Use the sizing handles of the PivotChart control to resize it as needed.
4. Right-click the PivotChart control and select field list from its context menu to open the PivotChart's field list.
5. Drag one field from the Chart field list to the Category Fields drop zone, another to the Series Fields drop zone, and another to the Data drop zone. If you want to be able to filter the data, drag another field to the Filter Fields drop zone. Figure 18-26 shows the PivotChart with Order Year selected as the Category Field, Salesperson as the Series field, Price as the Data field, and CategoryName as the Filter field.

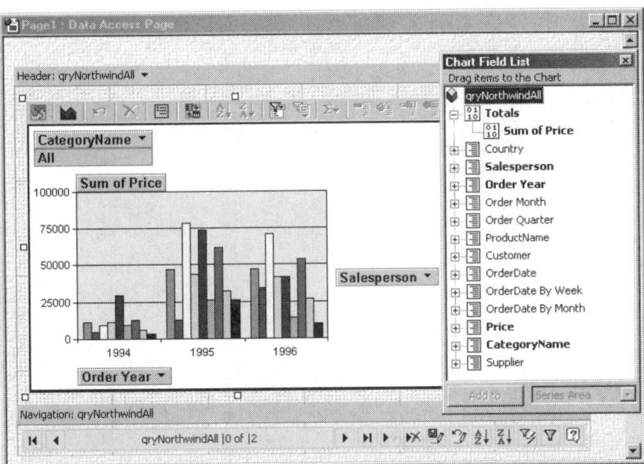

Figure 18-26. This PivotChart in Design view has its Series, Category, Data, and Filter fields filled.

Now that you have the PivotChart set up with the data you want to display on it, you can modify the chart in various ways:

> **tip** **Turn on PivotChart features**
>
> The PivotChart control has its own field list—don't confuse it with the data access page's field list. The PivotChart's field list says Chart Field List in its title bar. If you don't see it, right-click the PivotChart control and select Field List from its shortcut menu. The PivotChart's toolbar and drop zones can also be turned on or off from this shortcut menu.

- To display a legend, click the Show/Hide Legend button on the PivotChart toolbar. (By default, the PivotChart does not have a legend.)
- Select another chart type by clicking the Chart Type button on the PivotChart toolbar, and selecting a chart type, as shown in Figure 18-27.

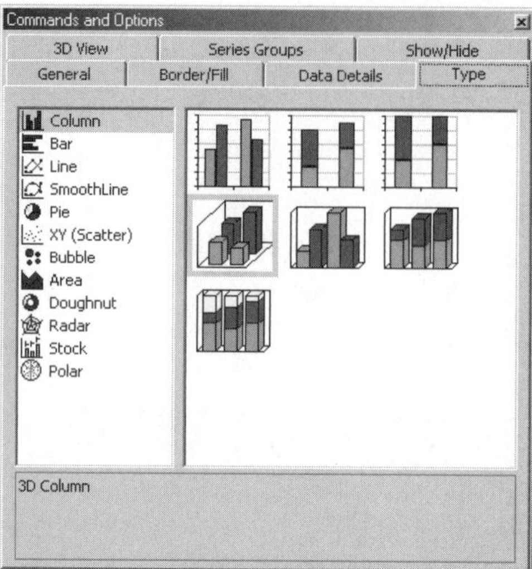

Figure 18-27. You can choose from several chart types for the PivotChart.

Figure 18-28 shows the completed PivotChart in Page view.

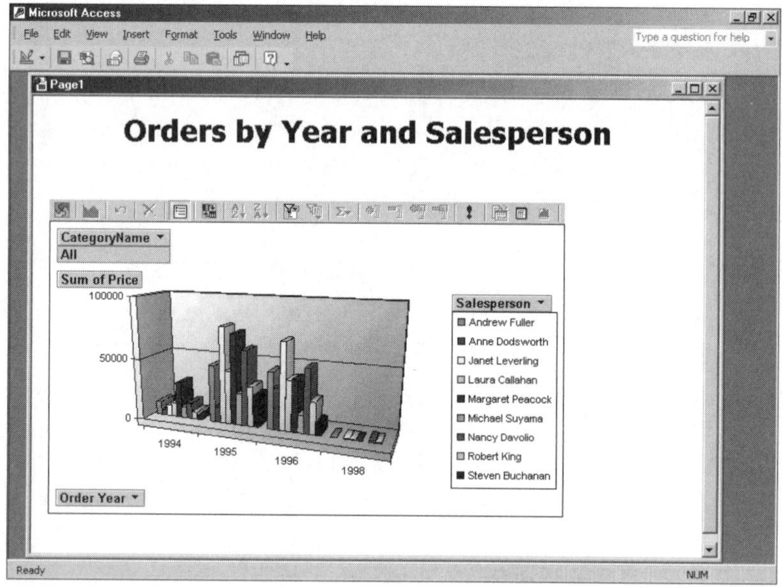

Figure 18-28. The completed PivotChart looks like this in Page view.

You might want to change a few other properties in the PivotChart's properties sheet, although you should leave most of the properties at their default settings. Generally speaking, if the property is familiar from controls on Access forms, or if it starts with "Display," it is safe to change. For example, you can safely change the *FontSize* and *FontStyle* properties, but it's best to leave properties such as *Behavior* and *ClassName* alone.

Creating a PivotChart based on an external data source In addition to creating a PivotChart based on a query or table in the current database, you can also create a PivotChart based on a query or table in an external data source, by setting up an OLEDB connection. To create a PivotChart on a data access page based on a query in another Access database, follow these steps:

1. Create a new data access page by using the Design View selection in the New Data Access Page dialog box.
2. Click the Office Chart tool in the Toolbox to place a Microsoft Office Web Component placeholder on the data access page.
3. Click the placeholder, then click it again, to open the Commands And Options dialog box to the Data Source tab. (Don't double-click the placeholder; doing so will open the regular properties sheet.) Figure 18-29 shows the Data Source tab, with three options for specifying the PivotChart's data source.

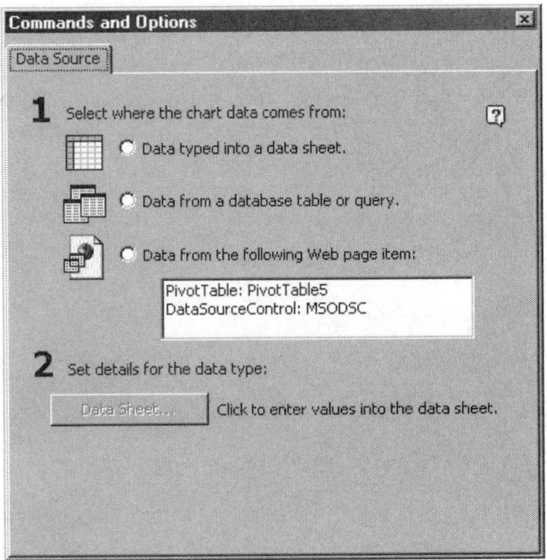

Figure 18-29. You have three choices for selecting a PivotChart's data source.

Data Source Choices for PivotCharts on Data Access Pages

When selecting a data source for a PivotChart control on a data access page, you have three options:

Data Typed Into A Data Sheet This option lets you manually type the data for the PivotChart into a datasheet. When you select this option, the Data Sheet button is enabled. When you click this button, a little datasheet opens so you can fill it in with data.

Data From A Database Table Or Query This option lets you select a table or query in another database as the data source. When you select this option, the Connection button appears on the form, which you can click to set up a connection to the database containing the table or query you want to use as the PivotChart's data source.

Data From The Following Web Page Item This option lets you use the same data as a PivotTable control or Data Source control on the same data access page. When you select this option, the DataSource Details button appears on the form, which you use to select the PivotTable or DataSource control to use as the PivotChart's data source. This is handy if you want to have a PivotTable and a PivotChart displaying the same data on a data access page.

4 To use a query or table as the PivotChart's data source, select the second option on the Data Source tab. The Commands And Options dialog box now has two new tabs, Data Details and Type, and the Connection button appears on the bottom of the Data Source tab, as shown in Figure 18-30.

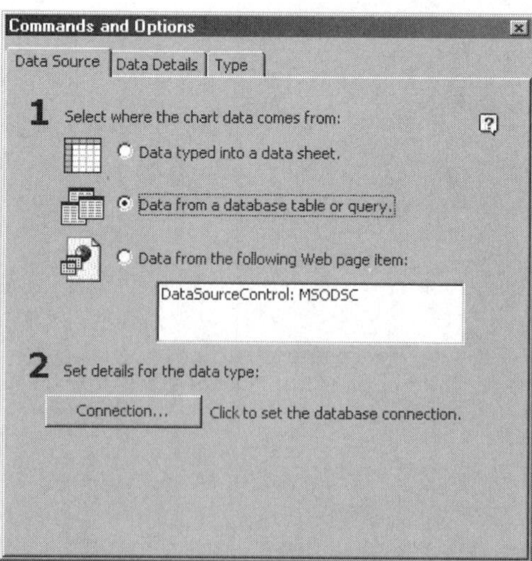

Figure 18-30. Set a connection to a database on the Data Source tab of the Commands And Options dialog box.

5 Click the Connection button to select the database containing the query (or table) you want to use as the PivotChart's data source. For the example, we'll use the qryNorthwindAll query located in the Modified Northwind database, which was prepared in advance with appropriate fields for use in a PivotTable or PivotChart.

6 Click the Edit button on the Data Details tab to open the Select Data Source dialog box, and select the appropriate file type in the drop-down list at the bottom of the dialog box (for the example, I selected Access Databases (*.mdb; *.mde).

7 Navigate to the folder where the database you want to use is located, select the database, and click Open to set the connection.

8 The Select Table dialog box displays, where you can select the table or query from the selected database.

9 After selecting the query or table, you are back on the Data Details tab of the Commands And Options dialog box, with the connection information filled in, as shown in Figure 18-31.

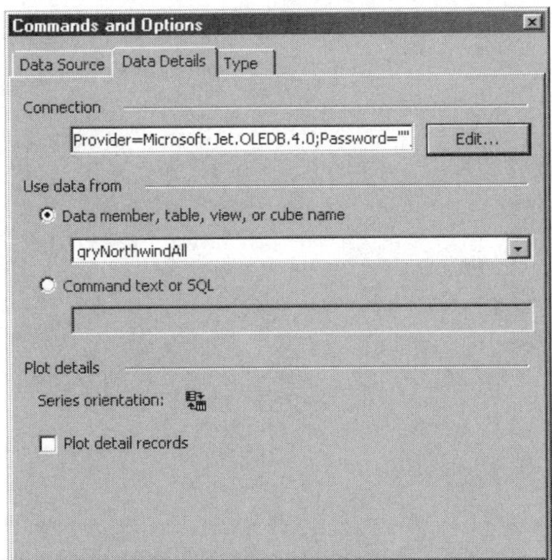

Figure 18-31. After selecting the database and query, the Data Details tab is filled with the necessary connection data.

10 The Microsoft Office Web Component placeholder is gone, replaced by a recognizable PivotChart control. Click the control to activate it (when activated, it has a wide cross-hatched border), and drag the desired fields from the PivotChart's field list to the PivotChart's drop zones.

From now on, the PivotChart control can be modified just as for one based on a local table or query, as described earlier in this chapter.

Adding an Office Spreadsheet Control

The Office Spreadsheet control resembles a Microsoft Excel worksheet, and thus should be familiar to anyone who has worked with Excel. To create an Office Spreadsheet control based on an Access table or query, follow these steps:

1. Create a new, blank data access page using the Design View selection.
2. Drag a table or query to the data access page grid, and then select Office Spreadsheet from the Layout Wizard. The Office Spreadsheet control is preloaded with data from the selected table or query's fields.

> **note** Unlike the PivotTable and PivotChart controls, Office Spreadsheet controls lack drop zones for drag-and-drop field placement. Instead, they display all fields as data columns.

3. Adjust the size of the Spreadsheet control by using its sizing handles. Adjust the column widths by using the Excel double-headed sizing arrows, as shown in Figure 18-32.

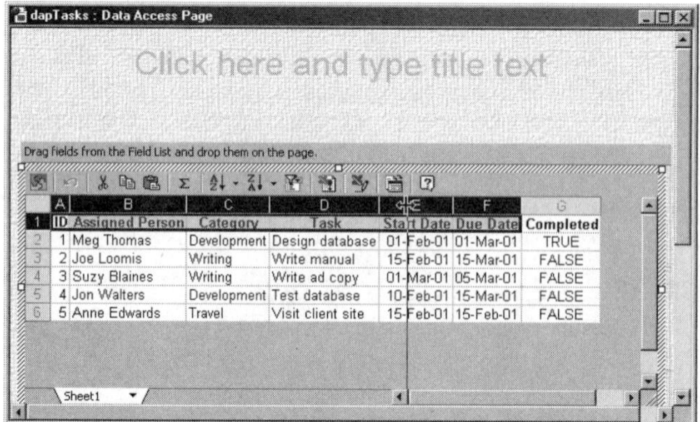

Figure 18-32. You can adjust the column widths of a Spreadsheet control.

> **tip** To get more help on using the Office Spreadsheet control, click the Help button in the spreadsheet toolbar to open the Microsoft Office Spreadsheet Component Help book.

To add a sum to an Office Spreadsheet column, follow these steps:

1. Click a cell in the worksheet, and press Ctrl+End to go to the last cell of the worksheet.
2. Right-click the last row of the worksheet, and select Insert, Rows to insert a row above the last row (no option is available for you to insert a blank row below a selected row).
3. Move down a row and you will see the last row of the worksheet, under the blank row. Right-click the last row and select Cut; then highlight the blank row, right-click it and select Paste.
4. Select the blank cell under the column to be summed, and click the AutoSum button on the Office Spreadsheet control toolbar; a formula appears in the cell, and when you tab away from it, you can see the total amount, as shown in Figure 18-33.

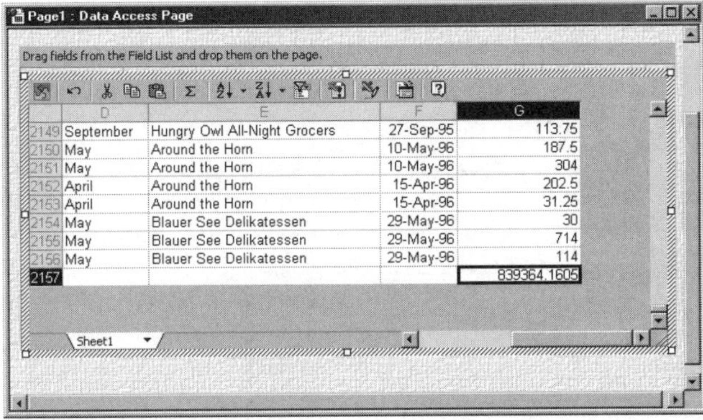

Figure 18-33. You can create a total for a column in an Office Spreadsheet control by clicking the AutoSum button with a blank cell selected.

InsideOut

Because it is more difficult to add a sum to an Office Spreadsheet control than to a PivotTable, and data in an Office Spreadsheet control can't be rearranged dynamically, you will have more flexibility if you use a PivotTable control rather than an Office Spreadsheet control.

Creating an Office Spreadsheet control Bound to an Excel worksheet If you need to display data from an Excel worksheet on a data access page, you can bind the Office Spreadsheet control to data in a worksheet by using the Data Source tab of the Commands And Options dialog box.

To create an Office Spreadsheet control bound to data in an Excel worksheet, follow these steps:

1. Create a new data access page by using the Design View selection in the New Data Access Page dialog box.
2. Click the Office Spreadsheet tool in the Toolbox to place an Office Spreadsheet control on the data access page.
3. Right-click the control to open the Commands And Options dialog box. Click the Data Source tab, where you can set up a connection to a data source (see Figure 18-34).

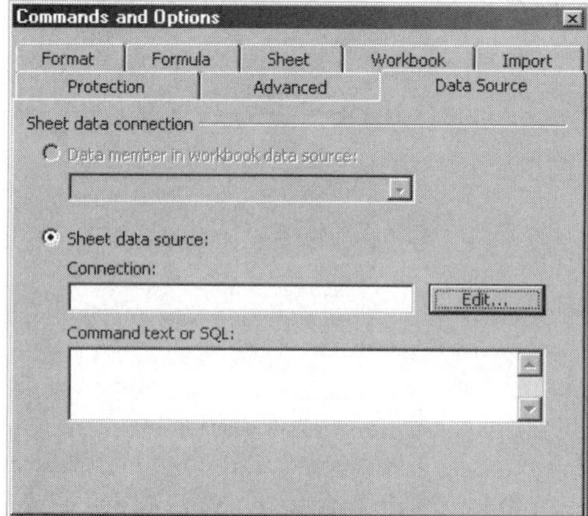

Figure 18-34. The Data Source tab of the Commands And Options dialog box lets you select a worksheet as the data source of an Office Spreadsheet control.

4. Click the Edit button to open the Select Data Source dialog box, and select the Excel Files (*.xls) selection.
5. Navigate to the folder that contains the workbook you want to use, select the workbook, and click Open to bind the control to that workbook.
6. Select the worksheet to use in the Select Table dialog box, and click OK. The connection string appears in the Connection box. If necessary, type the command text or SQL string you want to use to retrieve data from the data source in the Command Text Or SQL box.

   The data from the selected worksheet now appears in the control.

Working with Miscellaneous Data Access Pages

In addition to the data access page types discussed in earlier sections, which are created by selections in the New Data Access Page dialog box or the Layout Wizard that appears when you drag a table or query to the data access page design grid, several other ways are available for you to create data access pages.

Access 2002 allows you to create a data access page by saving a form, a report, a query, or a table in an Access database as a data access page. You can also save tables, views, stored procedures, functions, and forms in an Access project as data access pages. To save an Access form as a data access page, open the form in Form or Design view, choose File, Save As, and then select Data Access Page in the As box.

This new feature works well for simple forms. Figure 18-35 shows a form based on the Northwind Order Details table and the data access page created from it. (Refer to Chapter 5, "Creating Forms for Entering, Editing, and Viewing Data," for a detailed discussion of creating a form based on a table.)

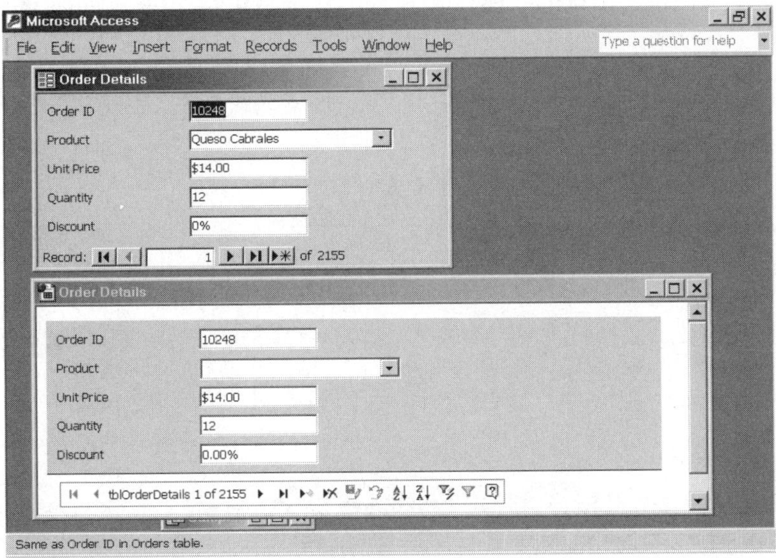

Figure 18-35. The data access page on the bottom was created from the simple form on top.

However, if you try to save a more complex form, such as one with an embedded subform, or a record selector combo box, you may get an error message "Microsoft Access is unable to create the data access page," because Access is unable to save the form as a data access page. You can have the equivalent of a record selector combo box or a subform on a data access page, but you must create these features by using data access page tools. For example, a data access page with a PivotTable can use the Filter field to select records for a single employee, and a banded report can display linked records, much like a subform.

tip Because the design tools in data access pages are less refined than those used with Access forms, it is generally easier to design a form and then save it as a data access page, rather than building a data access page from scratch, at least for a form-type data access page.

Troubleshooting

I get the message *The HTML file associated with this link has been moved, renamed or deleted* when trying to open a data access page

If the saved HTM file for the data access page has been moved or renamed, you can click the Update Link button to search for the current location (or name) of the file; if it has been deleted, though, you will have to re-create it.

And finally, you can open a saved HTM file (for example, a file created in Internet Explorer or FrontPage) as an Access data access page by selecting Existing Web Page from the New Data Access Page dialog box, and then selecting the HTM file for the data access page you want to open from the Locate Web Page dialog box, as shown in Figure 18-36.

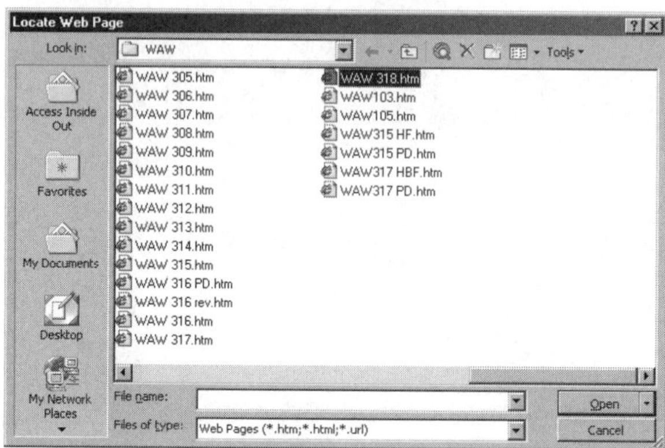

Figure 18-36. You can open a data access page from its HTM file.

Deploying Data Access Pages on the Web

After you create a data access page in Access, and open it on your own computer in Internet Explorer, you might want to place it on your Web page so that other users can look at it, or perhaps modify the data it displays. This is not as easy as you might think, at least for the individual Access user. You may have prepared a data access page, and created a Web site hosted on an ISP, but that's not all you need to publish Access data to the Web. Many ISP-hosted Web sites don't support publishing data from users' databases, and those that do (usually only for more expensive commercial accounts) may have their own restrictions on the type of data that can be placed on the Web site or the software that may be used to place data on the Web page.

If you have a Web site hosted by an ISP, check with your ISP for information on whether (or how) you can publish data from Access databases to your Web site. For example, the ISP may support only Active Server Pages (ASPs) with ActiveX Data Objects (ADO) or Remote Data Objects (RDO), not data access pages, which is not much help if you want to publish a data access page.

On the other hand, if you are a corporate Access user, and your company has its own Web server, possibly with Web folders for publishing data, you can deploy data access pages to the Web using Internet Information Services (IIS) or other high-end tools, which are beyond the scope of this book. The MSDN Online Downloads Web site *(http://msdn.microsoft.com/downloads/)* has information oriented toward large corporations that have their own Web servers and the resources needed to implement two-tier or three-tier databases on the Web, with security, firewalls, and other advanced features.

For more information on publishing data access pages to a Web server, type **Publish Web pages** in the Ask A Question box in Access 2002 and select the Publish Web Pages Help topic.

Chapter 19

Creating Access Projects

Projects were introduced in Microsoft Access 2000; they've been enhanced for easier use in Access 2002. An Access project is a front end to data stored in a SQL Server database. It includes the forms and reports—or, if the application is on the Web, data access pages—that users need to manipulate the data in the SQL Server database. A project has no native tables—just interface objects such as forms, reports, and data access pages, as well as modules. A project has no queries either; the queries you see in a project are interfaces to SQL Server database objects (views, stored procedures, and user-defined functions) that take the place of Access queries.

This chapter focuses on creating and using Access project front ends to data stored in SQL Server databases. Fortunately, you don't have to start from scratch; you can use the same tools to create forms, reports, macros, and other interface objects that you use when you work in an Access database. Throughout this chapter, you'll find references to other chapters where you can review the procedures you need.

When you open a project, you'll see a Database Diagrams group in the Database window, representing a type of object not found in Access databases. Database diagrams, like tables in projects, are actually SQL Server objects, and thus they reside in the SQL Server back-end database. Figure 19-1 depicts the relationship between an Access project and the back-end SQL Server database. Objects in gray are located in the SQL Server database, and those in black are in the Access project front end.

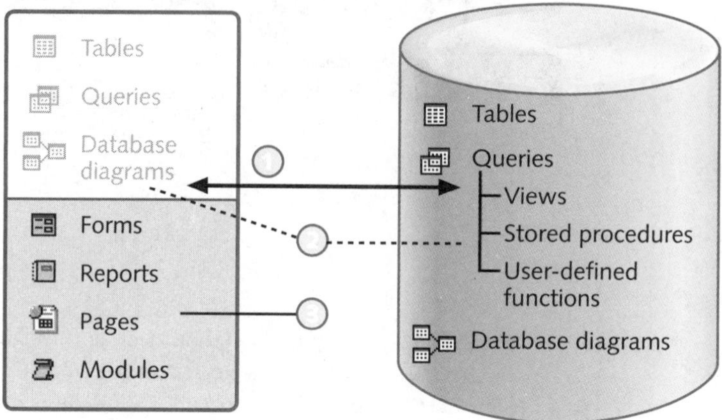

1 Connects the Access project to the SQL Server database

2 Database objects stored in the SQL Server database

3 Database objects stored in the Access project

Figure 19-1. An Access project serves as a front end to a SQL Server back-end database.

> **note** A complete discussion of SQL Server database design and features is beyond the scope of this book. A good book to check out is *Inside Microsoft SQL Server 2000,* by Kalen Delaney, based on the first edition by Ron Soukup (Microsoft Press, 2000), for a discussion of SQL Server.

The Query Designer is somewhat different in Access projects, but it will still be familiar. If you use the SQL Server Upsizing Wizard to migrate the objects in an Access database to a project, most of the views and stored procedures will be created automatically. (See Appendix E, "Upsizing to SQL Server," for more details on using the wizard.)

> **tip** **Download SQL Server Books Online**
>
> SQL Server Books Online documents SQL Server extensively; it's installed with SQL Server 2000. If you don't have SQL Server 2000 installed, you can download this help file from the SQL Server Books Online Web site, at *http://www.microsoft.com/SQL/techinfo/productdoc/2000/books.asp*. Alternatively, you can purchase the SQL Server 2000 180-day trial CD; it also installs this useful information resource for SQL Server.

SQL Server Requirements

To use Access projects, you must have some version of SQL Server installed. This can be a regular installation of SQL Server (Desktop, Standard, or Enterprise) or the SQL Server 2000 Database Engine provided with Microsoft Office XP. To test whether you need to install the SQL Server 2000 Database Engine (which isn't installed automatically with Office XP), choose Help, Sample Databases, Northwind Sample Access Project. (Note: In Office 2000, the corresponding component was called the Microsoft Database Engine [MSDE]. This acronym is still commonly used for the Office XP component.)

If you don't have any edition of SQL Server installed, you'll see the message shown in Figure 19-2.

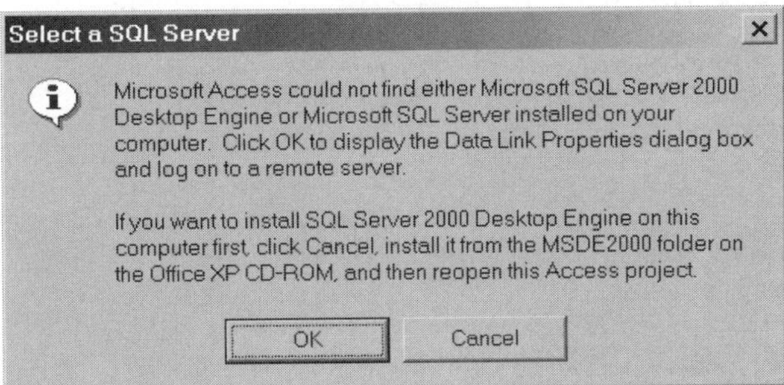

Figure 19-2. A message informs you if you need to install the SQL Server 2000 Database Engine.

If you do have SQL Server installed, you'll get a briefer message (shown in Figure 19-3) asking whether you want to install the NorthwindCS sample database.

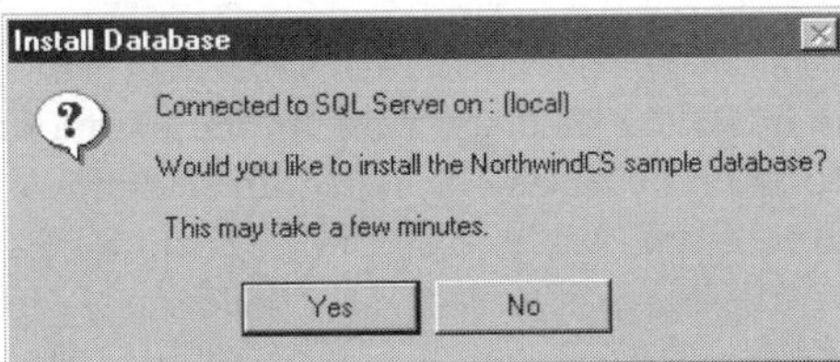

Figure 19-3. A message asks whether you want to install the Northwind project.

To install the SQL Server 2000 Database Engine, insert the Office CD and run SETUP.EXE from the MSDE2000 folder. (If you have Microsoft Office XP Developer, a separate CD contains Microsoft SQL Server 2000 for Microsoft Office XP Developer. Insert that CD, and follow the instructions on screen to install the Personal Edition of SQL Server.)

Access Project Components

You don't have to create a project from scratch to get an idea of what a project looks like. You can simply open the NorthwindCS (*CS* stands for "Client-Server") project provided with Access 2002 by choosing Help, Sample Databases, Northwind Sample Access Project, as mentioned. If you have some version of SQL Server installed and you chose to install the project the first time you opened it, the NorthwindCS project will open much like the equivalent Northwind database, as shown in Figure 19-4.

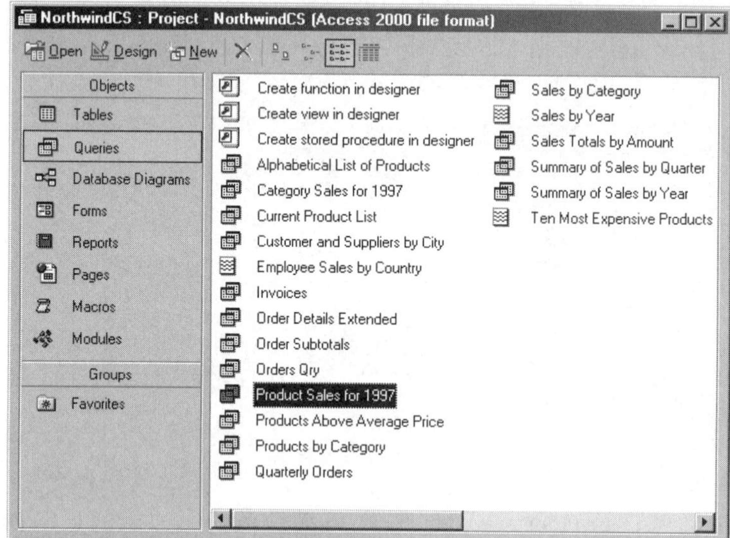

Figure 19-4. Here's the NorthwindCS project window—the project is in Access 2000 format.

As you can see, an Access project and an Access database have similar components except that the project has a new object group named Database Diagrams. Tables and queries of a project, however, differ significantly from their Access database counterparts. Tables, queries, and database diagrams of a project are discussed in the following sections.

Tables

Tables in an Access project look like local tables in an Access database. Although they're actually SQL Server tables, they don't have the arrow icon indicating that they're linked tables. When you open one of the NorthwindCS tables in Design view, it will look different from an Access table; SQL Server uses different field data types than Access. Table 19-1 lists the Access field data types and their SQL Server equivalents.

Table 19-1. Access and SQL Server field data types

Access data type	SQL Server data type
Yes/No	*bit*
Number (Byte)	*tinyint*
Number (Integer)	*smallint*
Number (Long Integer)	*int*
Number (Single)	*real*
(no equivalent)	*bigint*
Number (Double)	*float*
Currency	*money* *smallmoney*
Number (Decimal)	*decimal* *numeric*
Date/Time	*datetime* *smalldatetime*
AutoNumber (Increment)	*int* (with the *Identity* property defined)
Text (n)	*varchar(n)* *nvarchar(n)*
Memo	*text*
OLE Object	*image*
Number (Replication ID) (globally unique identifier [GUID])	*uniqueidentifier* (SQL Server 7 or later)
Hyperlink	*char, nchar, varchar, nvarchar* (with the *Hyperlink* property set to *Yes*)
(no equivalent)	*varbinary*
(no equivalent)	*timestamp*
(no equivalent)	*char* *nchar*
(no equivalent)	*sql_variant*
(no equivalent)	*user-defined*

Figure 19-5 shows the database and project versions of the Northwind Employees table side by side. The field data types have been converted to their SQL Server equivalents, and you can see that some of the field properties displayed on the General tab in the database's field properties sheet are displayed as columns in the project, which makes it easier to review and adjust the properties.

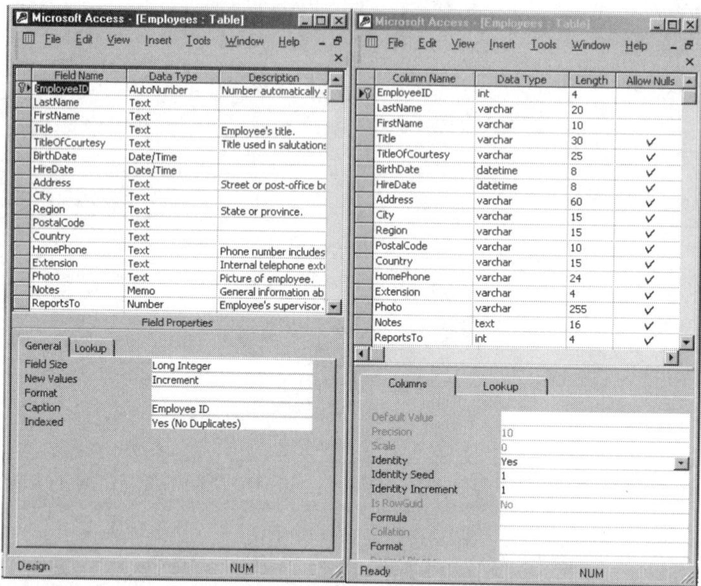

Figure 19-5. The Employees table looks different in the Northwind database (on the left) than it does in the NorthwindCS project (on the right).

Queries

The queries you see on the Queries tab for the project are Access project components that act as interfaces to SQL Server views and stored procedures (and, theoretically, user-defined functions, although there aren't any in the NorthwindCS project). Views are the SQL Server equivalent of Access select queries, and they have the same icon as select queries in an Access database. Stored procedures are roughly equivalent to action queries in an Access database; they have a different icon. (See Figure 19-6.)

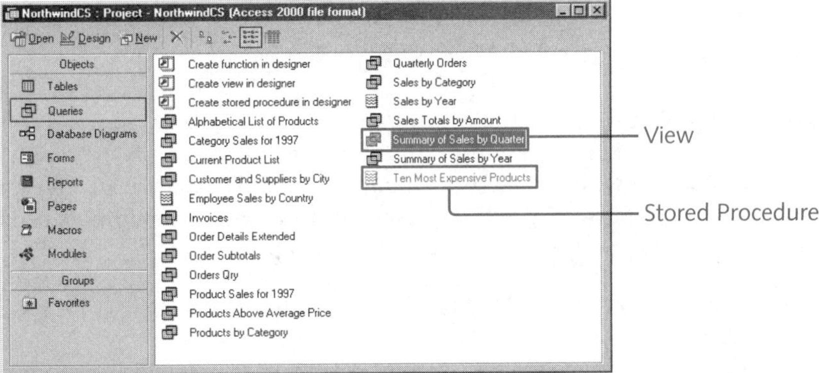

Figure 19-6. Views and stored procedures are listed on the Queries tab for a project.

See the sections "Project Views," page 795, and "Stored Procedures," page 798, for more details on project views.

Database Diagrams

Database diagrams are graphical representations of part or all of a database schema, including tables, columns, and relationships among them. In Access databases, you can have only one Relationships diagram, since there is only a single Relationships window. Projects, however, can have multiple database diagrams, which means that you can create a separate diagram for each set of relationships in the database, instead of putting them all into a single huge diagram. Figure 19-7 shows the Northwind database Relationships diagram.

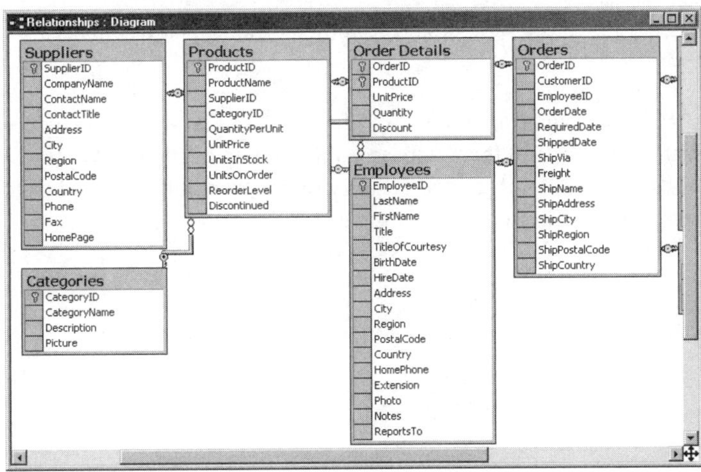

Figure 19-7. The Northwind Relationships database diagram shows links between tables.

Creating a Project File for an Existing SQL Server Back-End Database

To create a project file as a front end for an existing SQL Server database, follow the steps listed below. For this example, the SQL Server back end is the pubs sample database provided with SQL Server. On my system, this database is located in the F:\Microsoft SQL Server\MSSQL\Data folder; the location can differ depending on the version of SQL Server and your computer setup.

1 Click the Project (Existing Data) selection in the New section of the New File task pane.

2 In the File New Database dialog box that appears, give your new project a name, as shown in Figure 19-8, and then click Create. In this example, the project is named Publications.

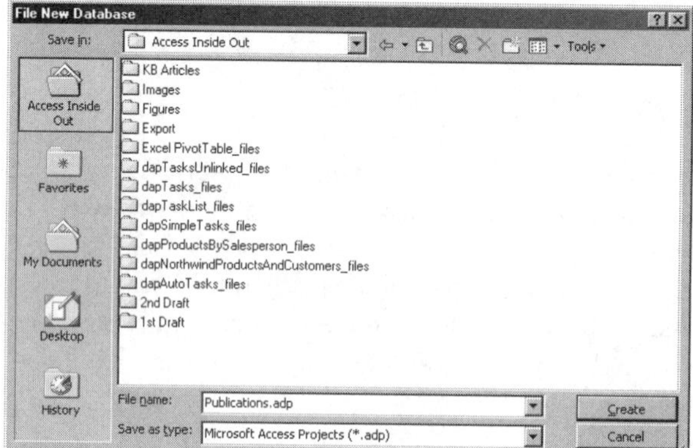

Figure 19-8. Give the new project a name in the File New Database dialog box.

3 In the Data Link Properties dialog box that appears, click the Connection tab and select the server and the database on the server, as shown in Figure 19-9. The Use Windows NT Integrated Security option generally works fine, so you don't need to enter a user name or a password.

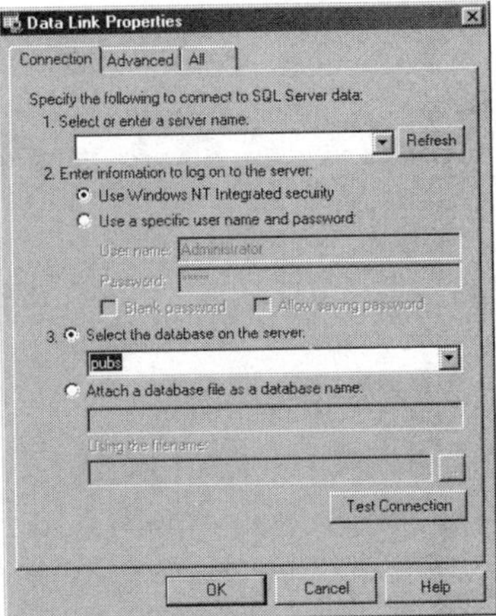

Figure 19-9. You set connection options for the project in the Data Link Properties dialog box.

4 Click the Test Connection button to test the connection to the database. If the connection is good, you'll see a *Test connection succeeded* message.

5 Click OK to open the new project with the SQL Server tables and queries. Figure 19-10 shows the Database window with the tables displayed.

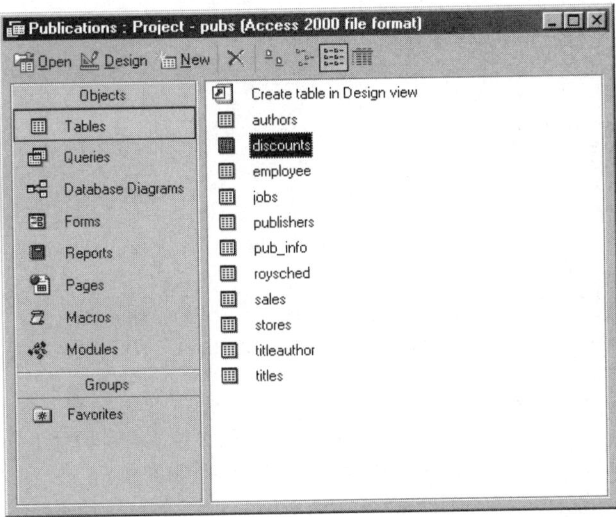

Figure 19-10. Tables from the pubs SQL Server database are listed in a new Access project.

You can now create forms, reports, and other objects using the familiar Access objects and methods, although there are a few special considerations to keep in mind.

See the sections "Using Forms in Access Projects," page 802, and "Using Reports in Access Projects," page 805, for more details on working with forms and reports in projects.

Creating a Project File for a New SQL Server Back-End Database

If you don't have an existing SQL Server back-end database to connect your project to and you want to create a new one for your project as you create the project, follow these steps:

1. Click the Project (New Data) selection in the New section of the New File task pane.
2. In the File New Database dialog box that appears, give the new project a name, as shown in Figure 19-11, and then click Create. In this example, the project is named Tasks.

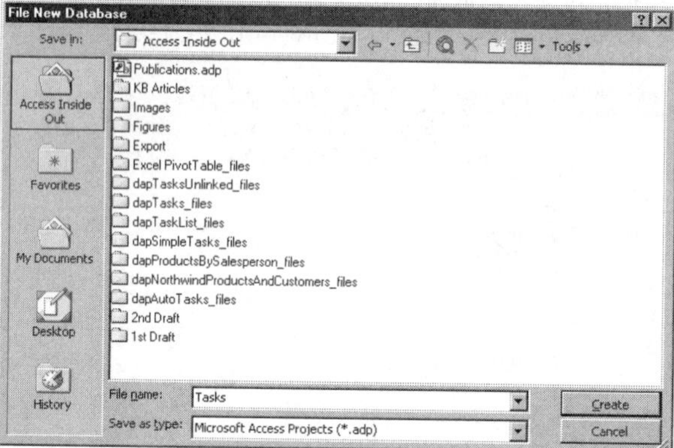

Figure 19-11. Give the new project a name in the File New Database dialog box.

3. The new project will open, and the Microsoft SQL Server Database Wizard will launch. This compact wizard will guide you in creating the new SQL Server database.
4. On the first page of the wizard, shown in Figure 19-12, select the server name (in my case, my computer's name) and select the Use Trusted Connection check box. You can also modify the suggested name for the SQL Server database if you want. Figure 19-12 shows the default project name with *SQL* appended to it.

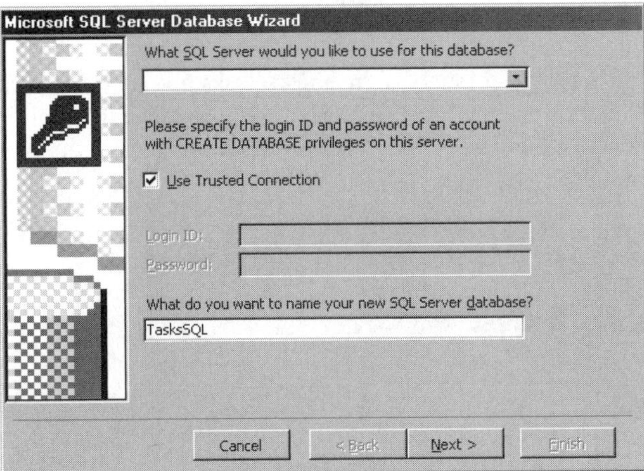

Figure 19-12. The Microsoft SQL Server Database Wizard helps you set up a connection to a SQL Server back-end database.

5 Click Next, and you'll get the second and final page of the wizard, as shown in Figure 19-13.

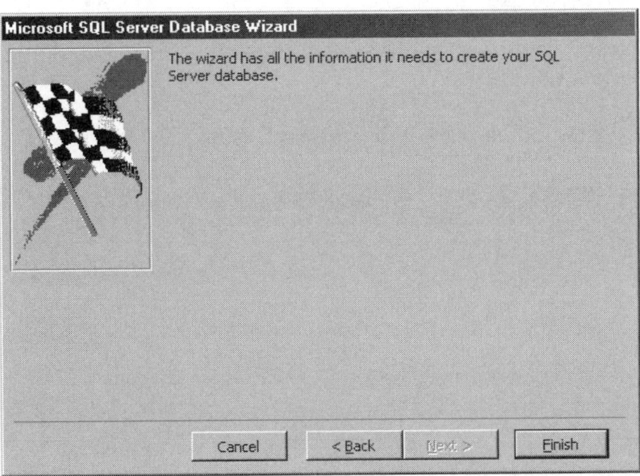

Figure 19-13. The final page of the wizard shows a success message.

6 Click Finish, and you'll see a progress bar while the SQL Server database is being created. The wizard will then return you to the project, where you can create tables, queries, and other database objects, as described in the next few sections.

Creating SQL Server Tables in a Project

To create a table in a project (such as the empty Tasks project we created in the previous section), double-click Create Table In Design View on the Tables tab in the Database window, as shown in Figure 19-14. Alternatively, you can click the New button in the Database window.

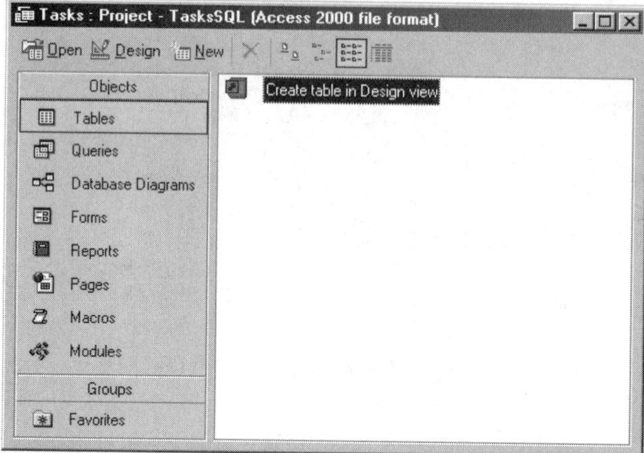

Figure 19-14. You can double-click Create Table In Design View in the Database window to create a new table.

In either case, a new, blank table will open in Design view, as shown in Figure 19-15.

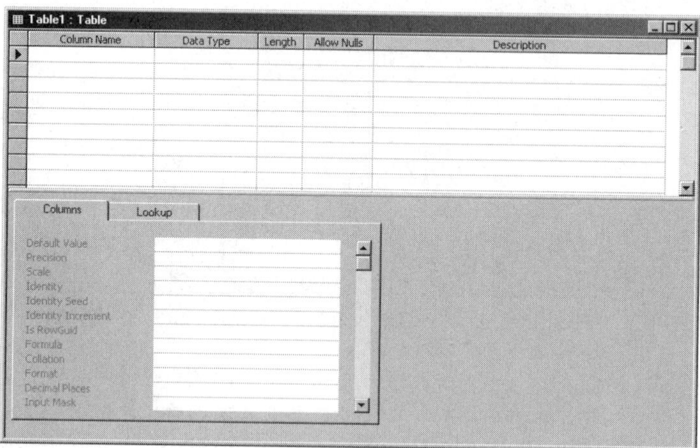

Figure 19-15. A newly created table opens in Design view.

You can add columns (fields) to the table much as you would for an Access table, except that the *Length* and *Allow Nulls* properties are columns in the grid. You need to specify a data type for each column. Table 19-2 lists the SQL Server field data types. (See Table 19-1 for a comparison of Access and SQL Server field data types.)

Table 19-2. SQL Server field data types

SQL Server data type	Description
bigint	Stores whole numbers from –9,223,372,036,854,775,808 through 9,223,372,036,854,775,807.
bit	Stores either a 1 or 0 value; other integer values are interpreted as 1.
char	A fixed-length data type with a maximum of 8000 ANSI characters.
datetime	A date-and-time data type ranging from January 1, 1753, through December 31, 9999, to an accuracy of 3.33 milliseconds.
decimal	An exact data type that holds values from $-10^{38} - 1$ through $10^{38} - 1$. Allows specification of the scale (maximum total number of digits) and precision (maximum number of digits to the right of the decimal point).
float	Stores positive values from approximately 2.23E – 308 through 1.79E + 308 or negative values from approximately –2.23 E – 308 through –1.79E + 308.
image	A variable-length data type that holds a maximum of 2,147,483,647 bytes of binary data. Used to store Binary Large Objects (BLOBs) such as pictures, documents, sounds, and compiled code.
int	Stores whole numbers from –2,147,483,648 through 2,147,483,647.
money	Stores monetary values from –922,337.203,685,477.5808 through 922,337,203,685,477.5807.
*nchar**	A fixed-length data type with a maximum of 4000 Unicode characters.
numeric	An exact data type that holds values from $-10^{38} - 1$ through $10^{38} - 1$. Allows specification of the scale (maximum total number of digits) and precision (maximum number of digits to the right of the decimal point).

(continued)

Table 19-2. *(continued)*

SQL Server data type	Description
nvarchar(n)	A variable-length data type with a maximum of 4000 Unicode characters.
real	Stores positive values from approximately 1.18E – 38 through 3.40E + 38 and negative values from approximately –1.18E – 38 through –3.40E + 38. Zero can also be stored.
smalldatetime	A date-and-time data type ranging from January 1, 1900, through June 6, 2079, to an accuracy of one minute.
smallint	Stores whole numbers from –32,768 through 32,767.
smallmoney	Stores monetary values from –214,748.3648 through 214,748.3647. Rounded up to two decimal places when displayed.
sql_variant	Stores data of several data types, except for text, *ntext*, *image*, *timestamp*, and *sql_variant* types. Used in a column, parameter, variable, or return value of a user-defined function.
text	A variable-length data type with a maximum of 2,147,483,647 characters; the default length is 16.
timestamp	A data type that's automatically updated every time a row is inserted or updated. Values in *timestamp* columns are not *datetime* data, but *binary(8)* or *varbinary(8)*, indicating the sequence of data modifications.
tinyint	Stores whole number from 0 through 255.
uniqueidentifier (SQL Server 7 or later)	A 16-byte GUID.
user-defined	A definition of the type of data that a column can contain, defined by the user with existing system data types. Rules and defaults can be bound only to user-defined data types.
varbinary	A variable-length data type with a maximum of 8000 bytes of binary data.
varchar(n)	A variable-length data type with a maximum of 8000 ANSI characters.

*In an Access project or SQL Server database, the "n" prefix stands for "national." It means that the data type is unicode-enabled. In an Access database, all text columns are unicode-enabled.

Figure 19-16 shows the table with four fields, one of them set as the key field. When you close the new table, you'll be asked to name it. As with naming Access tables, you may want to use the LNC tag *tbl* to identify tables, although this naming convention isn't as widely used for SQL Server tables as for Access tables. In this example, we'll name the table tblTasks.

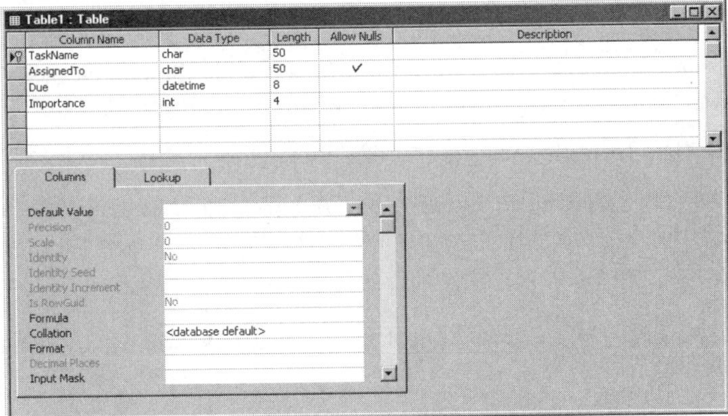

Figure 19-16. A new table has four fields of different data types.

To aid the discussion of setting up relationships between project tables, let's follow the same procedure discussed earlier to create another table named tblPeople. Add to the table two columns: Person and Available. Set both columns' *Data Type* property to char and the *Length* property to 50. Set the Person column as the primary key column.

Column Properties

The column properties for the columns in project tables are set on the Columns tab in the Table Designer, as shown earlier in Figure 19-16. The more commonly used properties are listed here. For information about the more obscure properties, see the "Columns Property Page" Help topic.

- ***Default Value.*** The default value for the column. You can enter this value as text or select it from a drop-down list of global default values.
- ***Precision.*** The maximum number of digits for values in the column.
- ***Scale.*** The maximum number of digits to the right of the decimal point for values in the column.

- ***Identity.*** Specifies whether the column is used as an identity column, with a value of Yes, No, or Yes (Not For Replication).
- ***Identity Seed.*** The seed value of an identity column whose Identity option is set to Yes or Yes (Not For Replication).
- ***Identity Increment.*** The increment value of an identity column whose Identity option is set to Yes or Yes (Not For Replication).
- ***Is RowGuid.*** Specifies whether the column is used by SQL Server as a ROWGUID column. Can be set to Yes only for an identity column.
- ***Formula.*** The formula for a computed column.
- ***Collation.*** The collating sequence that SQL Server applies by default to the column if the column values are used to sort rows of a query result.
- ***Format.*** The display format for the column.
- ***Decimal Places.*** The number of decimal places to use when displaying values in the column.
- ***Input Mask.*** An input mask (or field template) that determines what characters can be entered into a field and optionally supplies literal display characters.
- ***Caption.*** The text in the label attached to text boxes bound to the column.
- ***Indexed.*** Specifies whether there's an index on the column, with a value of No, Yes (duplicates OK), or Yes (no duplicates).
- ***Hyperlink.*** Specifies whether column values can be interpreted as hyperlinks.

The Lookup tab for project columns works the same way as the equivalent feature for Access database table fields.

See Chapter 4, "Creating a Database," for details on creating a lookup field.

Check Constraints

Constraints in an Access project table correspond to validation rules in an Access database table. You set them on the Check Constraints tab in the table properties sheet. Figure 19-17 shows the constraint for the *emp_id* key field of the Employee table in the Publications project we created earlier. The *Constraint* expression corresponds to the database *Validation Rule* property, and the *Validation* text corresponds to the database property of the same name.

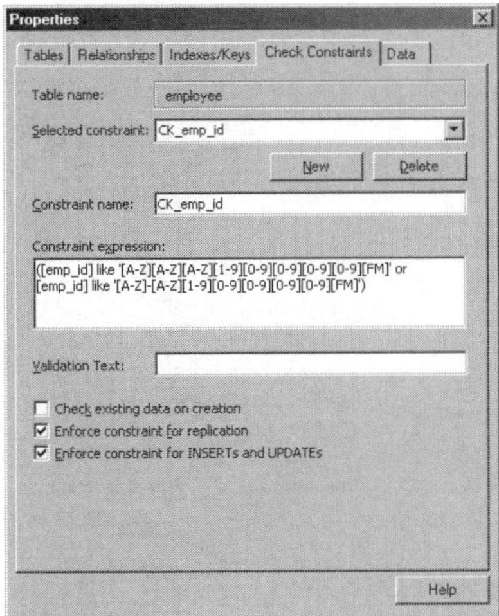

Figure 19-17. A check constraint for a project table field corresponds roughly to a validation rule for an Access table field.

Triggers

Triggers for project tables are a special type of stored procedure. Triggers somewhat resemble event procedures for Access forms, reports, and controls except that they fire when data is modified by an INSERT, an UPDATE, or a DELETE statement. Triggers, like stored procedures, are written in Transact-SQL code.

> **caution** Some of the Access database hot keys don't work in projects (for example, F4 to open a properties sheet and Ctrl+Z to undo an action), and Undo is implemented only for the last action, if it works at all.

Figure 19-18 shows the ALTER trigger for the Employee table in the Publications project. To open this trigger, click the Tables tab in the Database window, right-click the Employee table, and choose Triggers from the context menu. Click Edit in the Triggers For Table Employee dialog box. If you want to create or delete a trigger, click New or Delete in this dialog box.

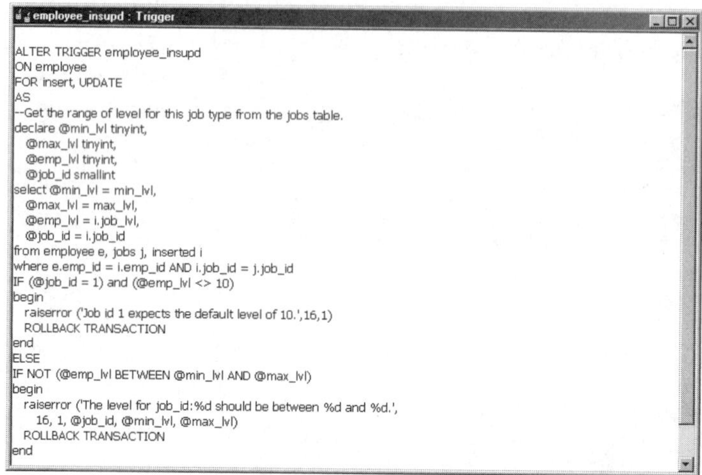

Figure 19-18. The Employee table in the Publications project has an ALTER trigger.

Primary Keys and Indexes

To set a column as a primary key in a project table, select the column, and click the Primary Key button on the Table Design toolbar, as shown in Figure 19-19.

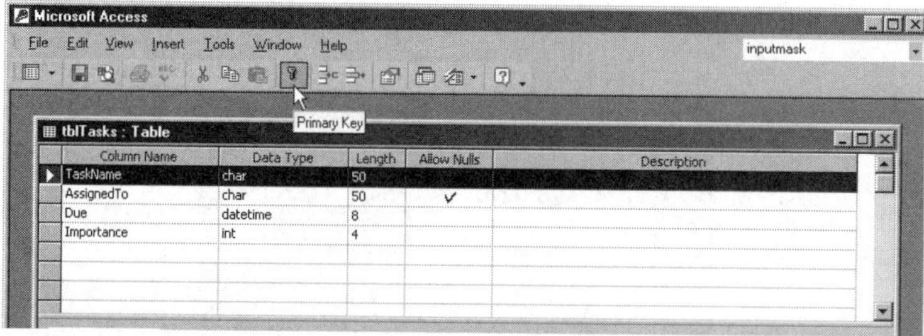

Figure 19-19. Click the Primary Key button on the Table Design toolbar to set a field as the primary key for a project table.

> **note** A field must have its *Allow Nulls* property set to False before you can set it as the primary key field.

To index a column in a project table, select one of the available choices for its *Indexed* property: No, Yes (Duplicates OK), or Yes (No Duplicates). Figure 19-20 shows that you can select an index type for the Due column in the tblTasks table in the Tasks project we created earlier.

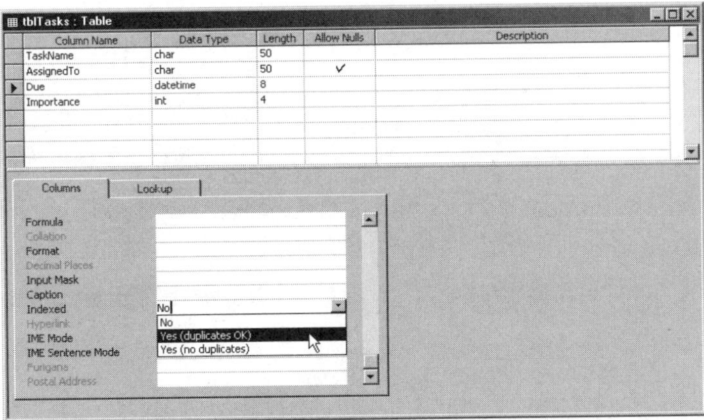

Figure 19-20. You can select an index type for a column in a project table.

Troubleshooting

I opened a project, but I don't see any tables in the Database window, and the project's name has *disconnected* after it

SQL Server might not be set to run when Windows is started. To connect your project to its back-end SQL Server database, select Service Manager from the Microsoft SQL Server program group (or click its icon in the Windows system tray), and click the Start/Continue button to start SQL Server, as shown in Figure 19-21. After you close and reopen the project, it will be connected to its SQL Server back-end database and you can work with the tables and other SQL Server objects.

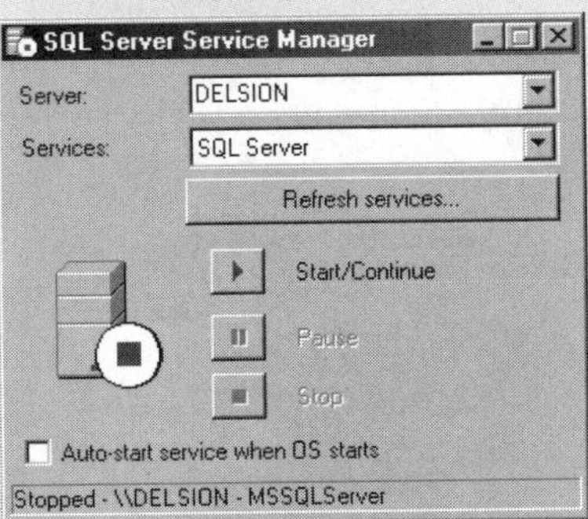

Figure 19-21. Start SQL Server in the SQL Server Service Manager dialog box.

Setting Up Relationships Between Tables

You can create a relationship between tables in a database diagram. The technique is slightly different from the technique used in the Relationships window in an Access database. For this example, we'll use the Tasks project created earlier.

To link two project tables in a database diagram, follow these steps:

1. Click the New button on the Database Diagrams tab in the Database window to create a new, blank database diagram.
2. The new diagram will open with the Add Table dialog box over it. Select tblPeople and tblTasks, and click Add to add them to the diagram, as shown in Figure 19-22. Then close the Add Table dialog box.

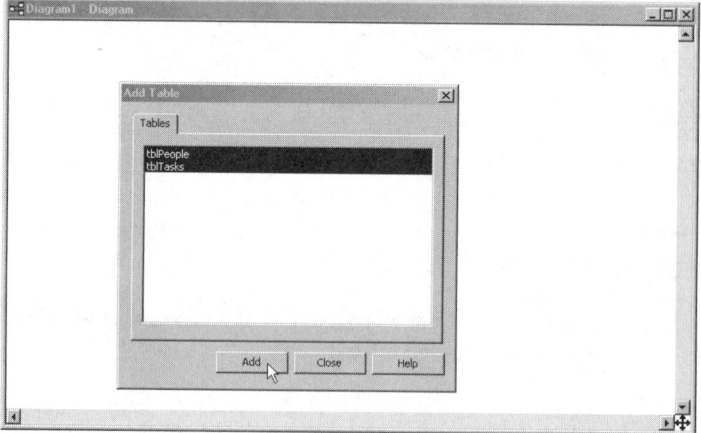

Figure 19-22. You use the Add Table dialog box to add a table to a database diagram.

3. Click the row selector (the gray square to the left of the column name) of the Person column in tblPeople and drag it to the AssignedTo column in tblTasks.
4. In the Create Relationship dialog box that appears, select one or more check boxes, if desired, to verify data or apply referential integrity, as shown in Figure 19-23, and then click OK.

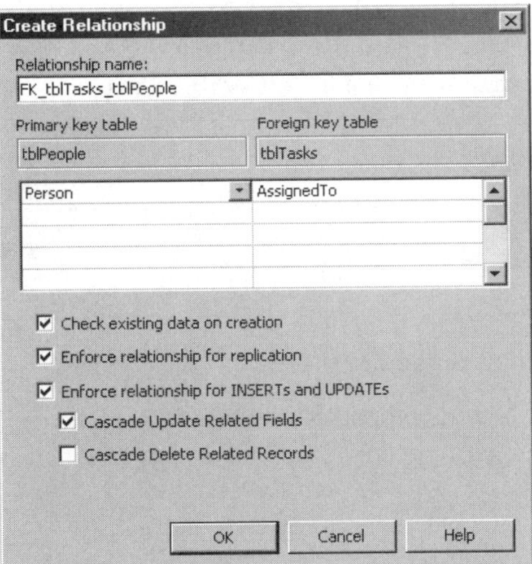

Figure 19-23. You can select relationship options in the Create Relationship dialog box.

5 The tables will appear linked in the database diagram, as shown in Figure 19-24.

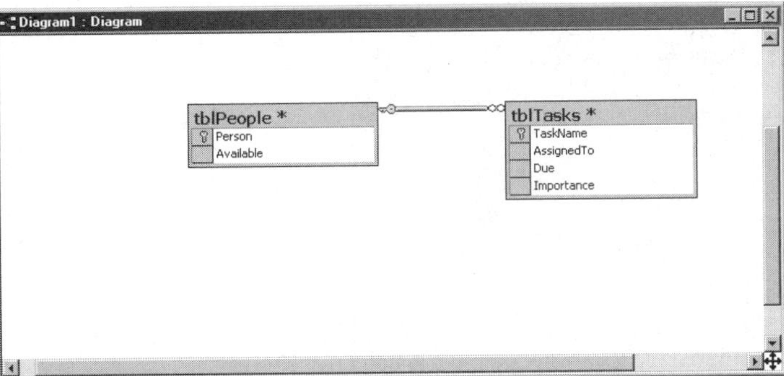

Figure 19-24. Linked tables are displayed in a project database diagram.

> **note** Unlike links in the Access Relationships window, the join lines in a project database diagram aren't attached to the specific linking fields—they're attached only to the table as a whole.

You can also create relationships between project tables on the Relationships tab in the table's properties sheet. To create a relationship between the AssignedTo column of tblTasks and the Person column of tblPeople, follow these steps:

1. Open tblTasks in Design view.

> **note** You must open the table on the foreign side of the relationship to create a relationship in the properties sheet.

2. Press Alt+Enter to open its properties sheet.
3. On the Relationships tab in the properties sheet, click New. A new relationship (FK_tblTasks_tblPeople) will appear in the Relationship name box and the Selected relationship drop-down list, with tblPeople selected as the primary key table and tblTasks selected as the foreign key table.
4. Select Person as the column for the primary key table and AssignedTo as the column for the foreign key table, and select or clear the options at the bottom of the properties sheet, as shown in Figure 19-25.

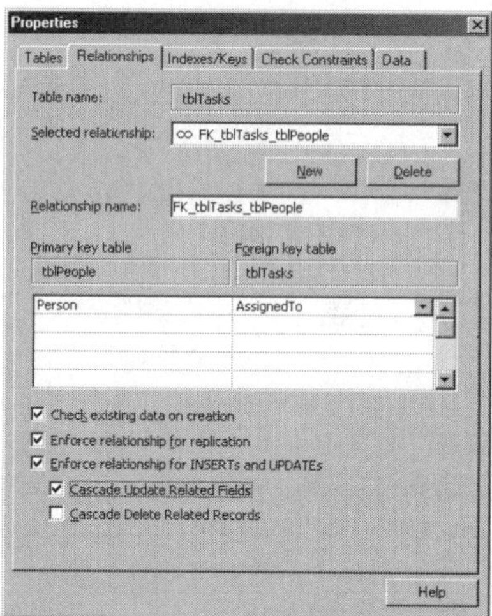

Figure 19-25. You can create a relationship between project tables in the table's properties sheet.

There's no OK button to create the relationship; saving the table saves the new relationship.

Understanding Views, Stored Procedures, and User-Defined Functions

The Queries tab for a project lists views, stored procedures, and user-defined functions. You'll use views to filter and sort data, stored procedures to modify data, and user-defined functions to combine various features of views and other queries into a single query that accepts parameters and returns values. These project components are described in the following sections.

note Views, stored procedures and user-defined functions in projects are generically called queries.

Project Views

A project view is similar to an Access select query in that it selects columns from one or more tables and possibly applies a filter to limit the rows in the view. Unlike Access queries, however, project views can't have parameters. See Chapter 11, "Working with Advanced Queries," for a detailed discussion of parameter queries. Like Totals queries, views can also summarize data. Views are updatable if the user has the appropriate permissions on the underlying table(s).

InsideOut

Don't confuse project views with views in Access databases, such as Design view, Datasheet view, and Form view for forms and Design view and Print Preview for reports. Project views are an entirely different type of object, and it might have been better if they had been given a different name.

Here's an example of the confusion: When you create a new form in an Access database, one of the choices in the New Form dialog box is Design View, which lets you create a new form in Design view. But when you're working in a project, creating a new query, the Design View option in the New Query dialog box lets you design a new view.

To create a view, you can either double-click the Create View In Designer item in the Database window or click New and then select Design View in the New Query dialog box, as shown in Figure 19-26.

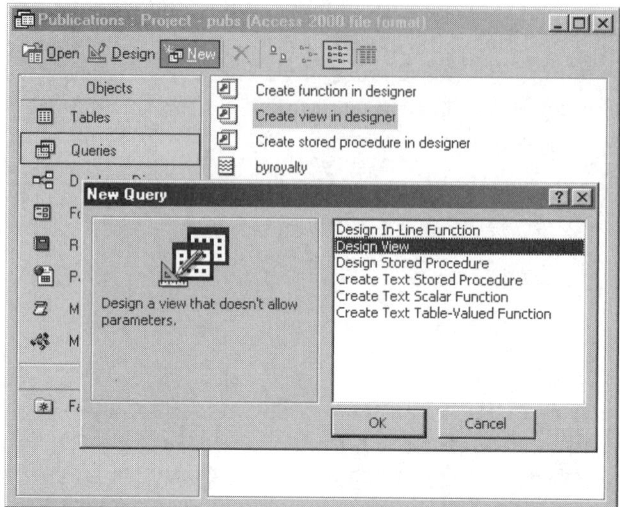

Figure 19-26. You can create a new project view using the New Query dialog box.

In either case, a blank Query Designer window will appear, with the Add Table dialog box open over it. You can select one or more tables, views, or functions to add to the diagram pane of the Query Designer, as shown in Figure 19-27.

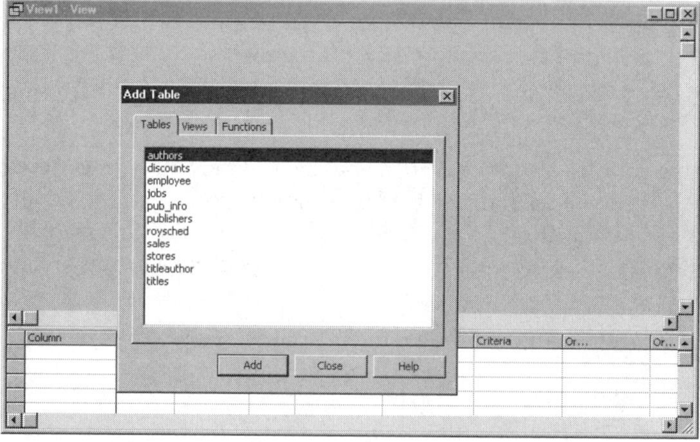

Figure 19-27. You can add tables and other objects to a view using the Add Table dialog box.

When you add tables to the Query designer's Diagram pane (the top pane), any existing links between the tables will be displayed, and you can create new links by clicking a field in one table and then dragging it to the matching field in another table. As with Access queries, links created in a view apply only to the view in which they're created.

The Query Designer interface (which is more sophisticated than the analogous Access Query Designer) displays tables in the Diagram pane and lists the selected fields from the tables in the Grid pane (the bottom pane). The table field lists have check boxes for each field; selecting the check box next to the field adds it to the view and places it on the Grid pane. If you place your mouse pointer over the join between tables, the join type will be displayed in a ScreenTip (also called a ToolTip). Figure 19-28 shows a view with a ScreenTip in the Publications project.

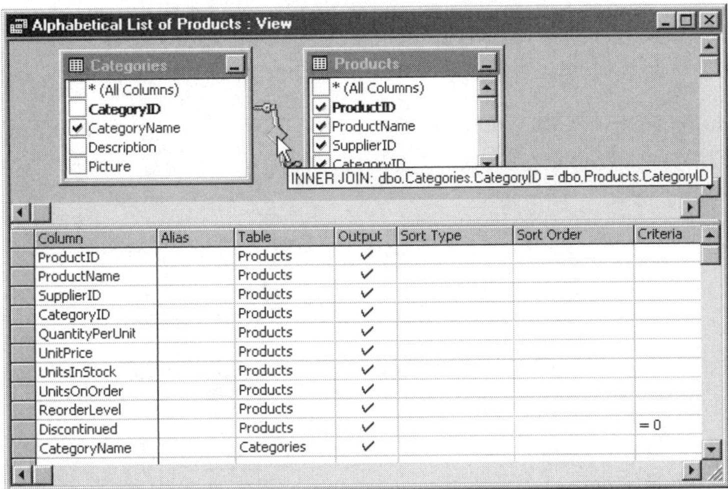

Figure 19-28. You can see join details in a project view that's open with all three panes displayed.

The Query Designer has three panes: the Diagram pane, the Grid pane, and the SQL pane. You can have one, two, or all three panes open at once. The Diagram pane shows the tables, views, or inline functions you're querying; the Grid pane lets you set options for the data columns used in the query; and the SQL pane displays the query's SQL statement. (We'll examine inline functions in the "User-Defined Functions" section on page 800.) Figure 19-29 shows a view in the Publications project, with all three panes visible.

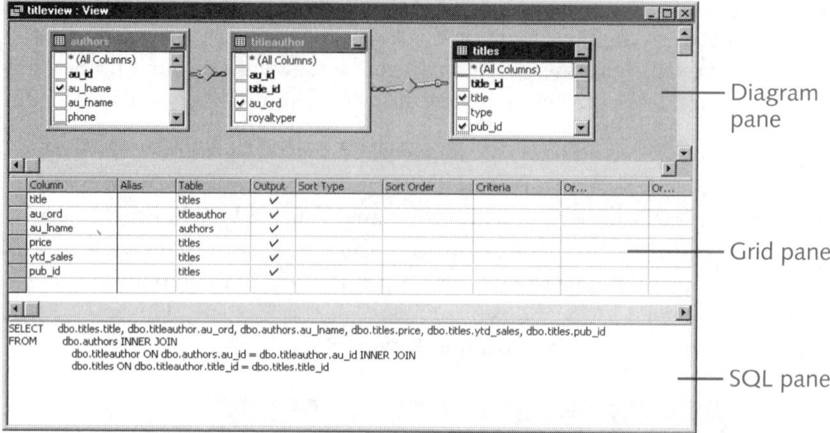

Figure 19-29. A Publications view can have all three panes open in the Query Designer.

To open another pane in the Query Designer, click its corresponding button on the Query Designer toolbar, as shown in Figure 19-30.

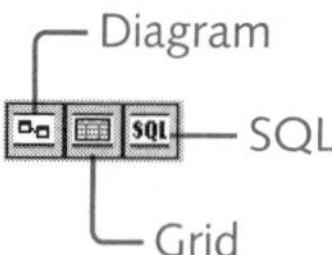

Figure 19-30. The Query Designer toolbar has buttons for opening the Diagram, Grid, and SQL panes.

Stored Procedures

Stored procedures are a cross between queries and procedures. Unlike views, stored procedures can have parameters, and they can handle more complex logic than views. Generally, stored procedures are not updatable, but Access lets you add, delete, and update records on a form bound to a stored procedure if the user has Add, Update, and Delete permissions on the underlying tables.

To create a new stored procedure, double-click the Create Stored Procedure In Designer item in the Database window, or click New and then select Design Stored Procedure in the New Query dialog box, as shown in Figure 19-31.

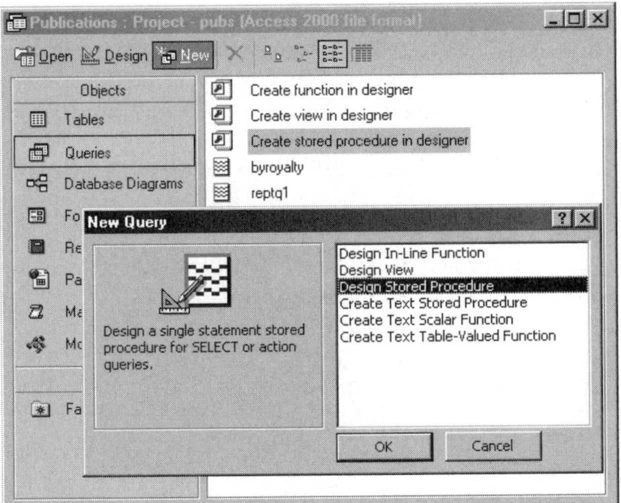

Figure 19-31. You can create a new stored procedure using the New Query dialog box.

In either case, you will get a blank Query Designer window, with the Add Table dialog box open over it. You can select one or more tables, views, or functions to add to the Diagram pane of the Query Designer. Figure 19-32 shows a NorthwindCS stored procedure opened in the Query Designer, with all three panes visible.

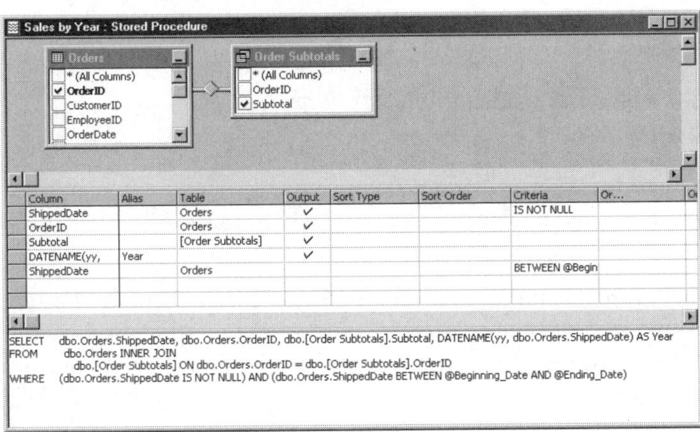

Figure 19-32. You can view a NorthwindCS stored procedure in the Query Designer.

Stored procedures are more powerful than views. They can contain program flow, logic, and queries against the database. They can accept parameters, output parameters, return single or multiple result sets, and return values. You can use a stored procedure for any purpose that you can use a SQL statement for, but with these additional advantages:

- A series of SQL statements can be executed in a single stored procedure.
- Other stored procedures can be referenced within a stored procedure.
- Stored procedures are compiled on the server when they're created, so they run faster than individual SQL statements.

> **note** For more information about writing stored procedures, you might want to look at a book that delves into SQL Server in depth. A good book to check out is *Inside Microsoft SQL Server 2000,* by Kalen Delaney, based on the first edition by Ron Soukup (Microsoft Press, 2000).

User-Defined Functions

User-defined functions combine features of views and queries into a single query that you can pass parameters to, sort, and use to return values. They can be used as record sources for forms, reports, or combo boxes, but not for data access pages. There are three types of user-defined functions, all of which you can graphically create and edit using the Query Designer.

- **Inline function.** Contains a single SELECT statement and returns an updatable table of data. Can be used in the FROM clause of a query.
- **Table-valued function.** Contains one or more SELECT statements and returns a nonupdatable table of data. Can be used in the FROM clause of a query.
- **Scalar function.** Contains one or more SELECT statements and returns a scalar value, such as the *int*, *decimal*, *varchar*, *sql_variant*, or *table* data type. You can use a scalar function anywhere in a query that you can use a column name.

Parameter Queries

A parameter query has a placeholder for a value that's supplied when the query is run. To turn the *reptq1* stored procedure in the Publications project into a parameter query, open the stored procedure in Design view, and type the following expression into the Criteria cell of the pub_id column in the Grid pane of the query:

```
= @Enter_pubid
```

When the query is run, you'll see a dialog box in which you can type the pub_id value, as shown in Figure 19-33.

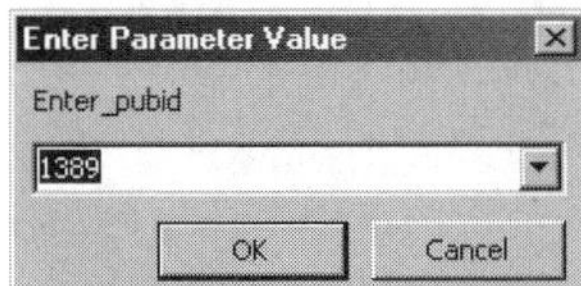

Figure 19-33. A parameter query opens this dialog box.

After you enter a value, click OK. The query will open in Datasheet view, showing only records with the matching pub_id value, as shown in Figure 19-34.

reptq1 : Stored Procedure

pub_id	title_id	price	pubdate
1389	BU1032	$19.99	6/12/1991
1389	BU1111	$11.95	6/9/1991
1389	BU7832	$19.99	6/22/1991
1389	PC1035	$22.95	6/30/1991
1389	PC8888	$20.00	6/12/1994

Record: 1 of 5

Figure 19-34. A stored procedure is filtered by a parameter.

Using Forms in Access Projects

You can base a project form on a database table, just as you can with a database form. For example, if you select the Authors table in the Publications project and click the New Object: AutoForm button on the Database Design toolbar, as shown in Figure 19-35, you'll see a simple form with the fields from the Authors table laid out on it, from top to bottom, as shown in Figure 19-36.

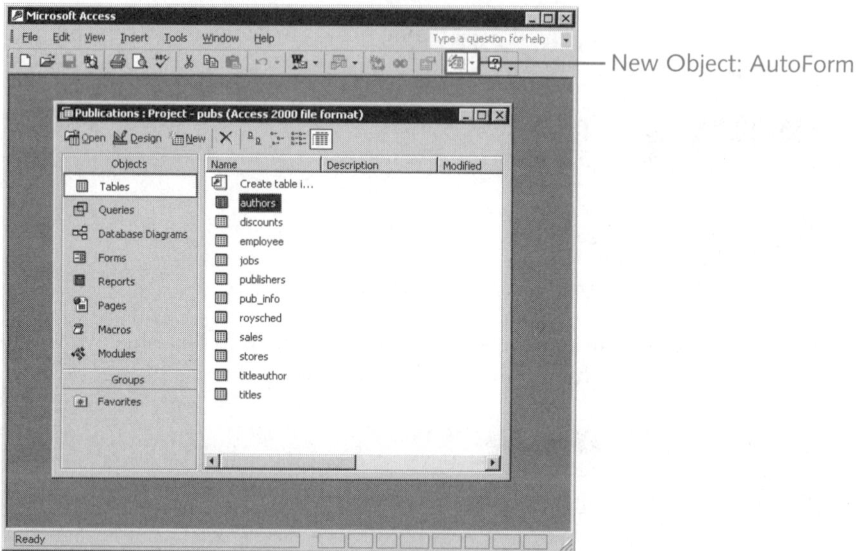

Figure 19-35. You can create an AutoForm for a project table with a single click.

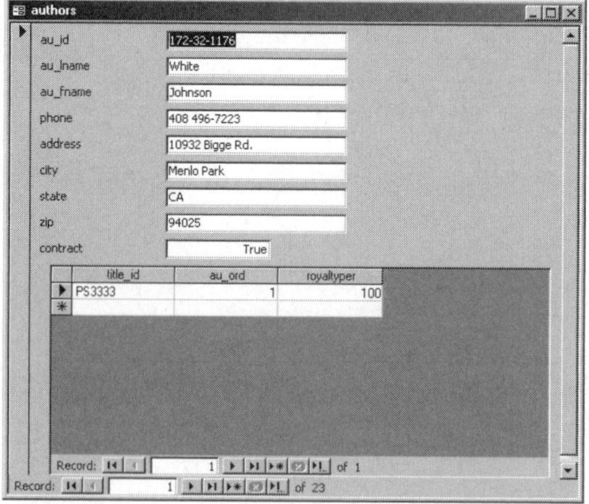

Figure 19-36. An AutoForm based on the Authors table has an embedded subform.

The AutoForm has an embedded subform because the Authors table is linked one-to-many with the Titleauthor table.

You can create other types of forms based on tables using the Form Wizard, just as you can for database tables. Figure 19-37 shows a form based on the Stores table in the Publications project, with the Justified layout and the Ricepaper style.

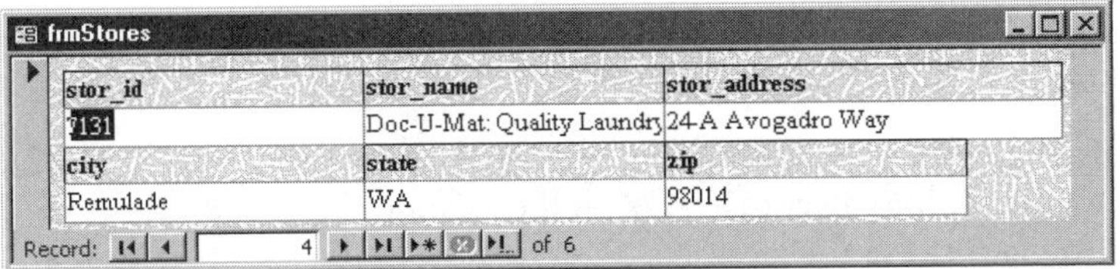

Figure 19-37. This form based on the Stores table uses the Justified layout and the Ricepaper style.

Project Forms vs. Access Forms

Forms in Access projects can be based on tables, views, stored procedures, and Transact-SQL statements that return values. Also, in code only, forms can be bound to ActiveX Data Objects (ADO) recordsets. Although project forms based on tables work pretty much the same as forms based on database tables, when it comes to queries (views and stored procedures), there are some significant differences between database forms and project forms. When a project form is based on a query, it's updatable only if the user has the appropriate permissions (Add, Delete, or Update) for the underlying tables. If the user doesn't have the appropriate permissions, you must write VBA code to do the updating from an unbound form.

newfeature!

New Interface Elements

Forms in Access projects have two new buttons on their navigation bars: Cancel Query and Maximum Record Limit, as shown in Figure 19-38.

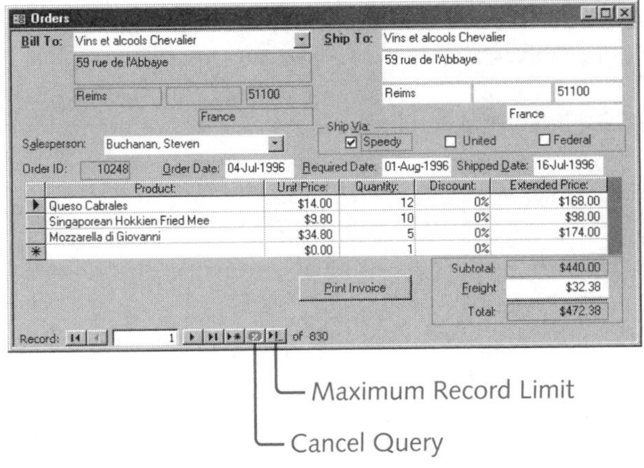

Figure 19-38. An Access project form has two additional buttons on the navigation bar.

All project forms have the Cancel Query button, which is bright red when you initially open a form and the form fetches records from the underlying SQL Server table(s). It changes to gray when all the records have been fetched (or the number of records specified in the form's *Max Records* property has been fetched, whichever is lower). You can click the button while it's red to cancel the downloading of records if the downloading is taking too long.

To globally change the maximum number of records fetched from a SQL Server table, change the Default Max Records value on the Advanced tab in the Options dialog box, as shown in Figure 19-39.

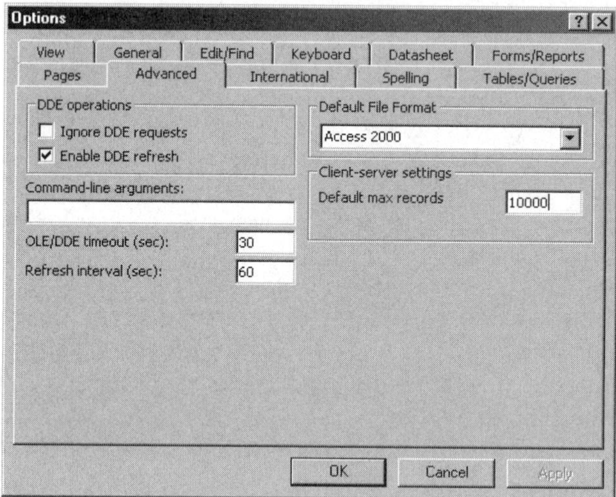

Figure 19-39. You can change the maximum records value in the Options dialog box.

You can also click the Maximum Record Limit button to open a small dialog box (shown in Figure 19-40) in which you can change the *Max Records* property quickly. This button is displayed by default; you can remove it by setting the *Max Rec Button* property to No on the Other tab in the form's properties sheet.

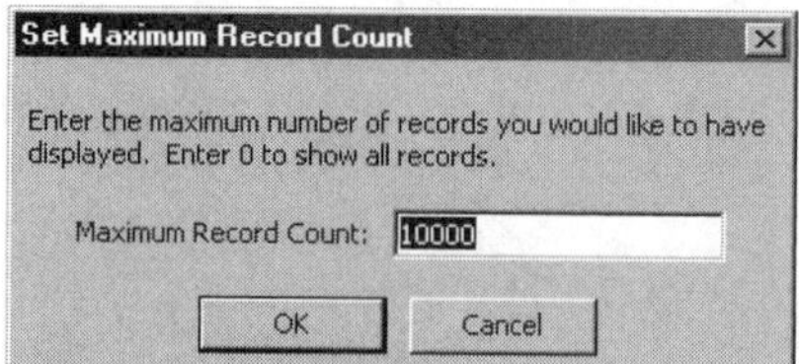

Figure 19-40. You can change the *Max Records* property in the Set Maximum Record Count dialog box.

note Curiously, the *Max Rec Button* property isn't located on the Format tab of the form's properties sheet along with the other buttons that can be turned on and off. Instead, it's on the Other tab.

Using Reports in Access Projects

Reports in Access projects are most efficient if you use views in which only the required columns of data or stored procedures that use parameters and return results are selected. You can use the *Input Parameters* property to supply parameters to a stored procedure that's used as a report's record source, possibly with a form as the interface for entering the values for the parameters.

To illustrate this technique, let's add a combo box on the NorthwindCS main menu to let the user select a company code and then create a simple report based on the Customers table, filtered by the combo box selection.

Follow the steps below to set up the combo box for filtering reports:

1. Choose Help, Sample Databases, Northwind Sample Access Project to open the NorthwindCS project. (The first time you open this project, you will get a message asking if you want to create this project; accept the message and the project will be created automatically.)
2. If the splash screen with the Northwind logo appears, close it.
3. The Northwind main menu should appear next; close it too.
4. In the Database window, click Forms and select the Main Switchboard form; press Ctrl+C to copy the form, and Ctrl+V to paste it to a name such as "Main Switchboard Original" (so you can revert to the original form afterward, if desired).
5. Open the Main Switchboard form in Design view.
6. Drag the bottom of the form down to provide about an inch more room on the form.
7. Click the Combo Box tool in the Toolbox and place a combo box control on the form.
8. Click Cancel to close the Combo Box Wizard.

9 *(Optional)* Adjust the size and font of the combo box and its attached label as desired.

10 Enter "Select a Company:" as the caption of the combo box's label.

11 Open the combo box's properties sheet.

12 Name the combo box cboSelectCompany.

13 Select Customers as the combo box's *Row Source*.

14 Enter 2 for the *Column Count* value.

15 Enter **0.75";2.5"** as the *Column Widths* value.

16 Enter **4"** as the *List Width* value.

Figure 19-41 shows the combo box with its list dropped down to select a company; after the selection is made, only the short company code shows in the combo box.

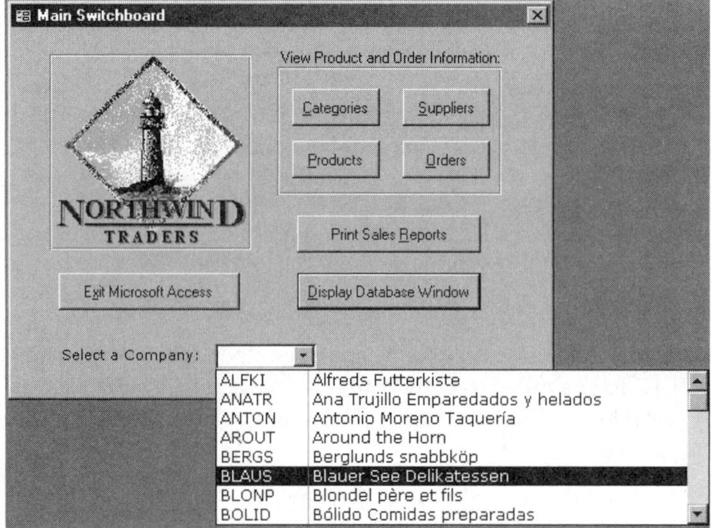

Figure 19-41. Select a company for filtering reports in the Select Company combo box on the Northwind main menu.

Next, follow the steps below to create a simple report to use the company selection made in the combo box on the main menu:

1. Click Reports in the Database window, and click New to open the New Report dialog box.
2. Select Report Wizard as the report type, and select Customers as the data source for the new report; click OK.
3. Proceed through the Report Wizard, setting up the report as desired. (See Chapter 7, "Using Reports to Print Data," for more details on working with the Report Wizard.)
4. *(Optional)* Fine-tune the report's design as desired.
5. Name the report **rptCustomers**. When the report is done, switch it to Design view and open its properties sheet.
6. Set the report's *Input Parameters* property to the following value:

```
CustomerID varchar=Forms![Main Switchboard]![cboSelectCompany]
```

The report is filtered for the selected customer when it's opened, as shown in Figure 19-42. Note, however, that although you see only the group heading for the selected company, all the records are returned.

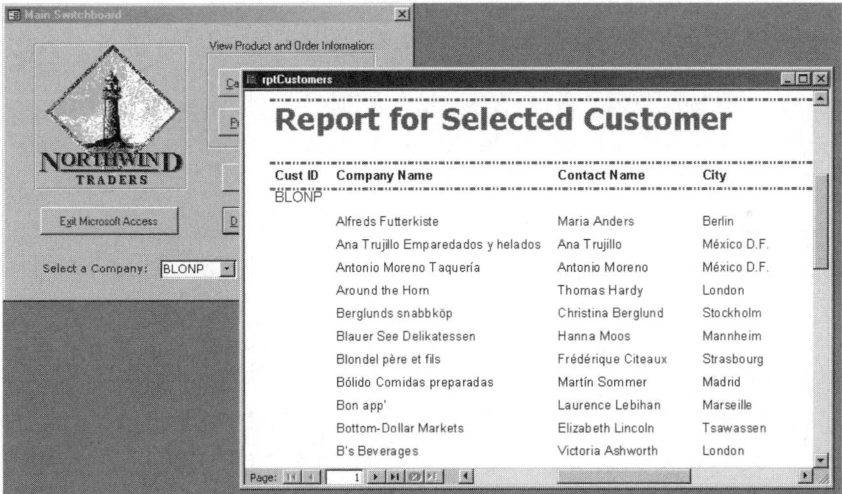

Figure 19-42. A report is filtered by an input parameter picked up from a combo box on a form.

Writing Code in Access Projects

The Data Access Objects (DAO) object model is generally the best choice for writing code in Access databases when you're dealing with data in Access tables. This object model has developed over the years with Access, and it's the most efficient and powerful tool for working with Access data. However, you need the newer ADO object model when you're working with data in SQL Server tables.

You can use both object models in the same project as long as you use the object library prefix to ensure that the object is linked to the correct object library, as shown in the following code segment:

```
Dim dbs as DAO.Database
Dim rstDAO as DAO.Recordset
Dim rstADO as ADODB.Recordset
```

Although each object model has some unique elements—for example, there's no *Database* object in the ADO object model, so you can omit the *DAO* prefix when you declare a *Database* variable—it's good policy to use the object library prefixes so that you're reminded of the type of object you're working with. Using this convention also enables others to read and understand your code.

In a new Access 2000 or Access 2002 database, the ADO object library is selected by default, but the DAO object library isn't. If you're using the DAO object library, you must set a reference to it by opening the References dialog box (choose Tools, References in the Visual Basic Editor window) and selecting Microsoft DAO 3.6 Object Library in the Available References list, as shown in Figure 19-43.

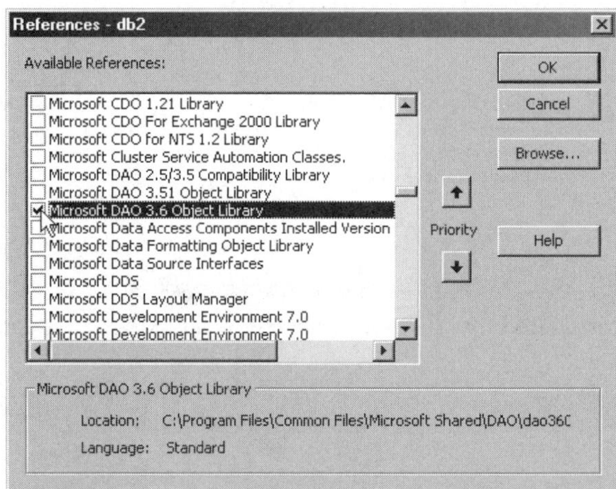

Figure 19-43. You can select the DAO object library reference in the References dialog box so that you can reference its components in code.

Chapter 20

Customizing Your Database Using VBA Code

Although you can create a simple Microsoft Access application without writing a line of code, if you want to create a more sophisticated application, you'll want to learn to write Microsoft Visual Basic for Applications (VBA) code. You can create tables, queries, forms, and reports using the Access interface, with the help of wizards if you want, but an effective application needs more than a bunch of database objects. Many forms and reports, in particular, need some code on their events so that your application's components can interact smoothly with each other.

An Overview of VBA Programming

Access forms, reports, and controls have attached events, and you can write code behind forms to perform actions when the events fire—for example, on closing a form, clicking a command button, or formatting a report. Code behind forms is saved in class modules, one for each form or report that has code.

You can also write code in standard modules that can be called from anywhere in the application, and (starting with Access 97) you can write a special type of class module (not attached to a form or report) that defines a new type of object. Figure 20-1 shows the Project pane of the Visual Basic Editor for the Crafts database, which lists form and report class modules and a standard module.

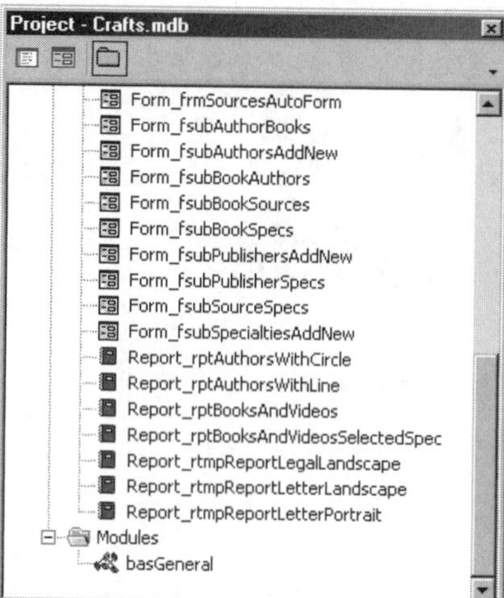

Figure 20-1. Class and standard modules are listed in the Visual Basic Editor Project pane.

Getting to the Code

There are several ways to get to VBA code in Access, depending on whether the code belongs to a form or report or is located in a standard or class module. If you're working on a form or report in Design view, you can open its attached code module by clicking the Code button on the Form Design (or Report Design) toolbar. The Visual Basic Editor opens, displaying the form or report's code module in the code window.

To go directly to a control's procedure, select the control on a form or report in Design view, open the control's properties sheet, and click the Events tab. Click the event that corresponds to the procedure you want to examine or create, and then select *[Event Procedure]* from the drop-down list. Click the event's Build button to open the Visual Basic Editor. The code window displays the form or report module, with the insertion point in the event procedure you selected. If no event procedure exists for the event you selected, a procedure stub that you can fill in with code is created.

For command buttons, there's a shortcut: Right-click the command button, and select Build Event to go directly to the command button's *Click* event. (This is the most frequently used event for command buttons.) You can use the same technique with other controls as well, but the default event procedure (probably *BeforeUpdate*) most likely won't be the one you want to work with.

There are two ways to open a standard or class module: If you're in the Access database, select the Modules group, and double-click the module to open it. If you're in the Visual Basic Editor, open the Modules or Class Modules folder in the Project pane, and double-click the module to open it.

Where Code Resides

Access code is stored in modules, which are collections of declarations, statements, and procedures. Standard modules are stored as separate database objects on the Modules tab in the Database window, and form and report code behind form modules are accessible from their forms or reports or in the Visual Basic Editor window's Microsoft Access Class Objects folder. Access has several types of modules, as follows:

- **Class module (code behind forms).** Contains event procedures for form and report events, form and report section events, and control events. Can also contain functions to be called from event procedures. When you create the first event procedure for a form or report, a class module is created for that form or report.
- **Standard module.** Contains functions and subroutines to be called from form or report event procedures and other procedures.
- **Class module (new object type).** Creates a definition for a custom object. Procedures define the object's methods, and public *Property Let*, *Property Get*, and *Property Set* procedures define the object's properties.

Understanding Functions and Subroutines

Procedures in modules can be either functions or subroutines (commonly abbreviated as *subs*). Functions and subs can take arguments (constants, variables, or expressions), but only functions can return values.

> **tip** If you specify arguments when calling a procedure, statement, or method, you don't need to enclose the arguments within parentheses except when calling functions or methods that return a value.

The following function is from the *basGeneral* module of the Crafts database. I use this function and the similar *FromDate* function in many of my databases. It picks up the value of the *ToDate* field of *tblInfo* for use wherever it's needed in the database—for example, to filter a report by order date.

```
Public Function ToDate() As Date

On Error GoTo ErrorHandler

   'Pick up To date from Info table.
   Set dbs = CurrentDb
   Set rst = dbs.OpenRecordset("tblInfo", dbOpenTable)
   With rst
      .MoveFirst
```

(continued)

```
        ToDate = Nz(![ToDate], "12/31/2002")
        .Close
    End With

ErrorHandlerExit:
    Exit Function

ErrorHandler:
    MsgBox "Error No: " & Err.Number & "; Description: " & Err.Description
    Resume ErrorHandlerExit

End Function
```


on the CD The following subroutine is also from the *basGeneral* module of the Crafts database. It formats the *txtStateProvince* value in all capital letters if the country is U.S.A. It takes three arguments: *strStateProvince*, *strCountry*, and *txt*, which allows it to be called from various event procedures on different forms and controls.

```
Public Sub FormatStateProvince(strStateProvince As String, _
    strCountry As String, txt As Access.TextBox)

On Error GoTo ErrorHandler

    If strStateProvince = "" Then
        Exit Function
    End If

    If strCountry = "U.S.A." Then
        If Len(strStateProvince) = 2 Then
            txt.Value = UCase(strStateProvince)
        End If
    End If

ErrorHandlerExit:
    Exit Function

ErrorHandler:
    MsgBox "Error No: " & Err.Number & "; Description: " & Err.Description
    Resume ErrorHandlerExit

End Sub
```

The following subroutine is the *AfterUpdate* event procedure for the *txtSalesStateProvince* text box control on the *frmPublishers* form. It calls the preceding *FormatStateProvince* sub after setting the three variables needed for the function's arguments.

```
Private Sub txtSalesStateProvince_AfterUpdate()

On Error GoTo ErrorHandler

   strStateProvince = Nz(Me![txtSalesStateProvince].Value)
   strCountry = Nz(Me![txtSalesCountry].Value)
   Set txt = Me![txtSalesStateProvince]
   Call FormatStateProvince(strStateProvince, strCountry, txt)

ErrorHandlerExit:
   Exit Sub

ErrorHandler:
   MsgBox "Error No: " & Err.Number & "; Description: " & Err.Description
   Resume ErrorHandlerExit

End Sub
```


Understanding Variables and Constants

A *variable* is a placeholder for data that can be modified during the execution of code. *Constants* are placeholders for data that can't be changed during the execution of code. Both variables and constants can be declared as specific data types. Although you can declare procedure-level variables or constants anywhere in a procedure, your code will be more readable if you declare them at the beginning of the procedure. Module-level variables and constants are declared in the Declarations section at the top of the module.

Data Typing

It's good practice to declare all variables as specific data types. Doing so conserves memory resources, helps your code run faster, and makes your code easier to read and debug. You should use the Variant data type only if you don't know what type of data will be assigned to the variable or if data of several types might be assigned to the same variable. The most commonly used data types for declaring variables in VBA code are listed in Table 20-1, along with their corresponding Access table field data types.

Chapter 20

Table 20-1. **VBA, DAO, and ADO data types**

Access table field data type	VBA data type	DAO data type	ADO data type
N/A	N/A	dbNumeric*	adNumeric
N/A	N/A	dbTime*	adDBDate
N/A	N/A	dbTimeStamp*	adDBTimeStamp
N/A	N/A	dbVarBinary*	adVarBinary
N/A	N/A	dbBigInt*	adBigInt
N/A	N/A	dbBinary	adBinary
Yes/No	Boolean	dbBoolean	adBoolean
N/A	N/A	dbChar*	adChar
Currency	Currency	dbCurrency	adCurrency
Date/Time	Date	dbDate	adDate
N/A	N/A	dbDecimal*	adDecimal
Number (Field Size: Double)	Double	dbDouble	adDouble
AutoNumber (Field Size: Replication ID)	N/A	dbGUID	adGUID
AutoNumber (Field Size: Long Integer	Long	dbLong	adInteger
Number (Field Size: Long Integer)	Long	dbLong	adInteger
OLE Object	String	dbLongBinary	adLongVarBinary
Memo	String	dbMemo	adLongVarWChar
Hyperlink	String	dbMemo	adLongVarWChar
Number (Field Size: Single)	Single	dbSingle	adSingle
Number (Field Size: Integer)	Integer	dbInteger	adSmallInt
Number (Field Size: Byte)	Byte	dbByte	adUnsignedTinyInt
N/A	Variant	N/A	adVariant
Text	String	dbText	adVarWChar

*ODBCDirect only

Early and Late Binding

When you create code that uses an object exposed by another application's type library, VBA uses a process called *binding* to determine that the object exists and that your code uses the object's methods and properties correctly. VBA supports two kinds of binding: late binding and early binding.

Late binding occurs at runtime and is much slower than early binding because VBA must look up an object and its methods and properties each time it executes a line of code that includes the object. Early binding occurs at compile time, so it's significantly more efficient than late binding.

To take advantage of early binding, you must set a reference to the Automation server's type library (for example, Microsoft DAO 3.60 Object Library) and you must declare object variables as specific data types (for example, *DAO.Recordset*).

If you declare a variable as the generic data type *Object*, late binding occurs. With late binding, an object variable is attached to a specific data type only when the variable is set to an object in the code. Late binding doesn't require a reference to an object library, and thus it's useful when your code has to work with objects (such as Microsoft Word documents or Microsoft Excel worksheets) that might be of different versions, or when you're preparing code that will be imported into other databases, where you don't know what references have been set.

Apart from these special cases, it's generally preferable to use early binding.

Scope and Lifetime of Variables and Constants

All variables have *scope* and *lifetime*. The scope of a variable determines where you can access that variable in your code. A variable's scope can vary from global, where any code in your program can access the variable, to local, where the variable is visible to a single procedure. The lifetime of a variable indicates how long the variable exists in code. A variable can exist the entire time your program is running, or it might exist only while a particular procedure is executing. Depending on how and where a variable is declared, there are three scoping levels:

- **Procedure level.** Variables or constants declared within a procedure. Available only within that procedure.
- **Private module level.** Variables or constants declared Private (or declared without a keyword, which is the same as Private) in the Declarations section of a module. Available only within that module.
- **Public module level.** Variables or constants declared Public in the Declarations section of a module. Available from any module in that project.

Table 20-2 describes the scope and availability of procedures, variables, and constants in different types of modules, depending on how they're declared.

Table 20-2. Scope and lifetime of procedures, variables, and constants

Declaration keywords	Declaration level	Variable scope and lifetime
Public Sub	Module level	Available to all modules in all projects
Public Function	Module level	Available to all modules in all projects
Public Sub	Procedure level	N/A
Public Function	Procedure level	N/A
Private Sub	Module level	Available only in its own module
Private Function	Module level	Available only in its own module
Dim *variable* Private *variable*	Module level	Available only in its own module; retains its value as long as the module is running
Static *variable*	Module level	N/A
Public *variable*	Module level	Available to all procedures in all modules
Dim *variable*	Procedure level	Available only in its own procedure; retains its value as long as the procedure is running
Public *variable*	Procedure level	N/A
Static *variable*	Procedure level	Available only in its own procedure; retains its value as long as the application is running
Const *constant*	Module level	Available only in its own module
Public Const *constant*	Module level (standard modules only)	Available to all procedures in all modules
Const *constant*	Procedure level	Available only in its own procedure

Controlling Data Flow Using VBA Statements

VBA has a number of statements for processing data within procedures, using a variety of logical structures. The most commonly used statements are described in this section.

The *Call* Statement

The *Call* statement is used to execute a sub from another procedure. You can omit the *Call* keyword, but your code will be more comprehensible if you include it. The following subroutine calls another sub to check the validity of a phone number:

note Functions aren't called. Instead, you set a variable (or field, or control) equal to the function to save the return value of the function.

```
Private Sub txtGeneralPhone_BeforeUpdate(Cancel As Integer)

On Error GoTo ErrorHandler

   strCountry = Nz(Me![txtSalesCountry].Value)
   strPhone = Nz(Me![txtGeneralPhone].Value)
   intLength = Len(strPhone)
   Call CheckPhone(strCountry, strPhone, intLength)

ErrorHandlerExit:
   Exit Sub

ErrorHandler:
   MsgBox "Error No: " & Err.Number & "; Description: " & Err.Description
   Resume ErrorHandlerExit

End Sub
```

The *Do While...Loop* Statement

This logical structure repeats a block of statements as long as a condition remains True. When used with the *EOF* property (indicating the end of a recordset), *Do While...Loop* structures are useful for iterating through recordsets, as in the code segment below, which is an extract from a long procedure that takes data from Access tables and writes it to a Word document. (See Chapter 17, "Exporting Data from Access," for the full procedure.)

```
Set rst = dbs.OpenRecordset("tmakInvoiceDetails", dbOpenDynaset)
With rst
   .MoveFirst
   Do While Not .EOF
      lngProductID = Nz(![ProductID])
      Debug.Print "Product ID: " & lngProductID
      strProductName = Nz(![ProductName])
      Debug.Print "Product Name: " & strProductName
      dblQuantity = Nz(![Quantity])
      Debug.Print "Quantity: " & dblQuantity
      strUnitPrice = Format(Nz(![UnitPrice]), "$##.00")
      Debug.Print "Unit price: " & strUnitPrice
      strDiscount = Format(Nz(![Discount]), "0%")
      Debug.Print "Discount: " & strDiscount
      strExtendedPrice = Format(Nz(![ExtendedPrice]), "$#,###.00")
      Debug.Print "Extended price: " & strExtendedPrice

      'Move through the table, writing values from the variables
      'to cells in the Word table.
      With objWord.Selection
         .TypeText Text:=CStr(lngProductID)
         .MoveRight Unit:=wdCell
         .TypeText Text:=strProductName
         .MoveRight Unit:=wdCell
         .TypeText Text:=CStr(dblQuantity)
         .MoveRight Unit:=wdCell
         .TypeText Text:=strUnitPrice
         .MoveRight Unit:=wdCell
         .TypeText Text:=strDiscount
         .MoveRight Unit:=wdCell
         .TypeText Text:=strExtendedPrice
         .MoveRight Unit:=wdCell
      End With
      .MoveNext
   Loop
   .Close
End With
```

The *Do Until...Loop* Statement

The *Do Until...Loop* logical structure runs a block of statements until a condition becomes True. The following procedure exports data from an Access table to a Microsoft Outlook calendar:

```
Private Sub cmdExportDates_Click()

On Error GoTo ErrorHandler

   Dim dbs As Database
   Dim rst As Recordset
   Dim appOutlook As New Outlook.Application
   Dim nms As Outlook.NameSpace
   Dim flds As Outlook.Folders
   Dim fld As Outlook.MAPIFolder
   Dim itm As Object
   Dim lngCount As Long

   Set nms = appOutlook.GetNamespace("MAPI")
   Set fld = nms.Folders("Personal Folders").Folders("Class Dates")

   Set dbs = CurrentDb
   Set rst = dbs.OpenRecordset("tblClassDates", dbOpenDynaset)
   lngCount = rst.RecordCount
   MsgBox lngCount & " records to transfer to Outlook"

   'Loop through table, exporting each record to Outlook.
   Do Until rst.EOF
      Set itm = fld.Items.Add("IPM.Appointment")
      itm.Subject = rst!ClassName
      itm.Start = rst!ClassDate
      itm.Duration = 60
      itm.Close (olSave)
      rst.MoveNext
   Loop

ErrorHandlerExit:
   Exit Sub

ErrorHandler:
   MsgBox "Error No: " & Err.Number & "; Description: " & Err.Description
   Resume ErrorHandlerExit

End Sub
```

The *For...Next* Statement

The *For...Next* statement lets you repeat a block of statements a specific number of times. It's often used with a number derived from counting items, although if the items are members of a collection, you can use the more efficient *For Each...Next* construct instead.

The following code segment sets up a *For...Next* structure to pick up data from a Word table and store it in an Access table. The code uses a Data Access Objects (DAO) recordset and a variable named *lngTableRows*, which holds the number of rows in the Word table.

> **note** You can't use *For Each...Next* with rows in a Word table because there is no collection of table rows in the Word object model.

```
'Pick up data from table cells and store it in the table.
Set sel = appWord.Selection

For lngRow = 0 To lngTableRows - 2
   rst.AddNew
   strName = Nz(sel.Text)
   Debug.Print "Name: " & strName
   If strName = "" Then
      GoTo Done
   Else
      rst![EmployeeName] = strName
   End If
   sel.MoveRight Unit:=wdCell, Count:=1
   strExt = sel.Text
   rst![Extension] = strExt
   sel.MoveRight Unit:=wdCell, Count:=1
   rst.Update
Next lngRow
```

The *For Each...Next* Statement

When you work with members of a collection or elements in an array, you can use the *For Each...Next* construct to iterate through the collection or array, using a variable to stand for a member of the collection. The following code segment uses the *For Each...Next* construct to iterate through the *ItemsSelected* collection of a list box control on an Access form, picking up information to merge into a Word letter:

```
For Each varItem In lst.ItemsSelected
   'Check for required address information.
   strTest = Nz(lst.Column(5, varItem))
   Debug.Print "Street address: " & strTest
   If strTest = "" Then
      MsgBox "Can't send letter -- no street address!"
      Exit Sub
   End If

   strTest = Nz(lst.Column(6, varItem))
   Debug.Print "City: " & strTest
   If strTest = "" Then
      MsgBox "Can't send letter -- no city!"
      Exit Sub
   End If

   strTest = Nz(lst.Column(8, varItem))
   Debug.Print "Postal code: " & strTest
   If strTest = "" Then
      MsgBox "Can't send letter -- no postal code!"
      Exit Sub
   End If

   strName = Nz(lst.Column(2, varItem)) & _
      " " & Nz(lst.Column(3, varItem))
   strJobTitle = Nz(lst.Column(11, varItem))
   If strJobTitle <> "" Then
      strName = strName & vbCrLf & strJobTitle
   End If
   strAddress = Nz(lst.Column(5, varItem)) & vbCrLf & _
      Nz(lst.Column(6, varItem)) & ", " & _
      Nz(lst.Column(7, varItem)) & _
      "  " & Nz(lst.Column(8, varItem))
   Debug.Print "Address: " & strAddress
   strCountry = Nz(lst.Column(9, varItem))
   If strCountry <> "USA" Then
      strAddress = strAddress & vbCrLf & strCountry
   End If

   'Open a new letter based on the selected template.
   appWord.Documents.Add strWordTemplate

   'Write information to Word custom document properties.
   Set prps = appWord.ActiveDocument.CustomDocumentProperties
   prps.Item("Name").Value = strName
   On Error Resume Next
```

(continued)

Chapter 20

```
      prps.Item("Salutation").Value = Nz(lst.Column(4, varItem))
      prps.Item("CompanyName").Value = Nz(lst.Column(10, varItem))
      prps.Item("Address").Value = strAddress
      prps.Item("TodayDate").Value = strLongDate

      'Check for existence of previously saved letter in documents folder,
      'and append an incremented number to save name if found.
      strDocType = appWord.ActiveDocument.BuiltInDocumentProperties(2)
      strSaveName = strDocType & " to " & _
         lst.Column(2, varItem) & " " & lst.Column(3, varItem)
      strSaveName = strSaveName & " on " & strShortDate & ".doc"
      i = 2
      intSaveNameFail = True
      Do While intSaveNameFail
         strSaveNamePath = strDocsPath & strSaveName
         Debug.Print "Proposed save name and path: " _
            & vbCrLf & strSaveNamePath
         strTestFile = Nz(Dir(strSaveNamePath))
         Debug.Print "Test file: " & strTestFile
         If strTestFile = strSaveName Then
            Debug.Print "Save name already used: " & strSaveName

            'Create new save name with incremented number.
            intSaveNameFail = True
            strSaveName = strDocType & " " & CStr(i) & " to " & _
               lst.Column(2, varItem) & " " & lst.Column(3, varItem)
            strSaveName = strSaveName & " on " & strShortDate & ".doc"
            strSaveNamePath = strDocsPath & strSaveName
            Debug.Print "New save name and path: " _
               & vbCrLf & strSaveNamePath
            i = i + 1
         Else
            Debug.Print "Save name not used: " & strSaveName
            intSaveNameFail = False
         End If
      Loop

      'Update fields in Word document and activate document.
      With appWord
         .Selection.WholeStory
         .Selection.Fields.Update
         .Selection.HomeKey Unit:=6
         .ActiveDocument.SaveAs strSaveName
      End With
   Next varItem
```

The *GoTo* Statement

The *GoTo* statement lets you jump directly to a named label in your code. It's typically used in error handlers. For example, when you use the following line at the beginning of a procedure, the code jumps to the *ErrorHandler* label when an error occurs:

```
On Error GoTo ErrorHandler
```

The *If...Then...Else* Statement

An *If...Then...Else* statement lets you run a block of statements if a condition is met, and (optionally) another block of statements if the condition isn't met. You can also add one or more *ElseIf* statements to an *If...Then...Else* statement to run a second (or further) condition test(s) if the first condition isn't met. The following code segment sets a *strAddress* variable to business address components (from an Outlook contact item) if the *intAddressType* variable is equal to 1 and to home address components if the variable is equal to 2:

```
If intAddressType = 1 Then
   strAddress = IIf(![Company] <> strEmpty, ![Company] & vbCrLf, _
   ![Company]) & IIf(![BusinessStreet1] <> strEmpty, _
   ![BusinessStreet1] & vbCrLf, ![BusinessStreet1]) & _
   IIf(![BusinessStreet2] <> strEmpty, ![BusinessStreet2] & _
   vbCrLf, ![BusinessStreet2]) & IIf(![BusinessCity] <> strEmpty, _
   ![BusinessCity] & Chr$(44) & Chr$(32), ![BusinessCity]) & _
   IIf(![BusinessState] <> strEmpty, ![BusinessState] & Chr$(32) _
   & Chr$(32), ![BusinessState]) & ![BusinessPostalCode]
ElseIf intAddressType = 2 Then
   strAddress = IIf(![HomeStreet1] <> strEmpty, ![HomeStreet1] _
   & vbCrLf, ![HomeStreet1]) & IIf(![HomeStreet2] <> strEmpty, _
   ![HomeStreet2] & vbCrLf, ![HomeStreet2]) & IIf(![HomeCity] _
   <> strEmpty, ![HomeCity] & Chr$(44) & Chr$(32), ![HomeCity]) & _
   IIf(![HomeState] <> strEmpty, ![HomeState] & Chr$(32) & Chr$(32), _
   ![HomeState]) & ![HomePostalCode]
End If
```

The *Select Case* Statement

The *Select Case* statement is used to run different blocks of code when an expression might have several different values (more than can conveniently be handled with an *If...Then...Else* statement). As a rule of thumb, if there are more than three possible values, it's best to use a *Select Case* statement.

The following function, from the Menu Manager add-in, uses a *Select Case* statement to deal with the possible values of an option group on an Access form. (The option group is used to select a background picture for a menu form.)

You can find more information about the Menu Manager add-in, which uses this function, in Chapter 15, "Using Add-Ins to Expand Access Functionality."


```
Public Function ChangePicture() As String

On Error GoTo ChangePictureError

   Dim intPicture As Integer
   Dim strPicture As String
   Dim ctlPicture As Control

   Set frm = Screen.ActiveForm
   intPicture = frm![fraPicture]

   Set ctlPicture = frm![imgBackground]

   Select Case intPicture

      Case 1
         strPicture = "imgBooks"

      Case 2
         strPicture = "imgContacts"

      Case 3
         strPicture = "imgMusic"

      Case 4
         strPicture = "imgFood"

      Case 5
         strPicture = "imgHoushold"

      Case 6
         strPicture = "imgInventory"

      Case 7
         strPicture = "imgMembers"

      Case 8
         strPicture = "imgMoney"

      Case 9
         strPicture = "imgPhoneOrders"
```

```
      Case 10
         strPicture = "imgPhotos"

      Case 11
         strPicture = "imgResources"

      Case 12
         strPicture = "imgSchool"

      Case 13
         strPicture = "imgVideos"

      Case 14
         strPicture = "imgWorkout"

   End Select

   ctlPicture.Picture = frm.Controls(strPicture).Picture
   ChangePicture = frm.Controls(strPicture).Picture

ChangePictureExit:
   Exit Function

ChangePictureError:
   MsgBox "Error No: " & Err.Number & "; Description: " & Err.Description
   Resume ChangePictureExit

End Function
```

The *While...Wend* Statement

This statement executes a series of statements while a given condition is *True*. It's rarely used because the *Do...Loop* statement offers more flexibility.

The *With* Statement

The *With* statement (introduced in Access 97) lets you perform a number of operations on an object without repeating the object's name or variable. The following code segment, from an Access form, sets the *Visible* property of a combo box control and calls two of the combo box control's methods:

```
With Me![cboAuthorSearchList]
   .Visible = True
   .SetFocus
   .Dropdown
End With
```

Naming Conventions

Many Access versions ago, two Access developers (Stan Leszynski and Greg Reddick) developed a naming convention for Access objects, based on Charles Simonyi's Hungarian notation for naming objects. The Leszynski-Reddick Naming Convention (L/R) was proposed as a standard to make it easier for developers to understand their own code (especially when returning to it after a significant amount of time had passed), and to understand databases and code developed by others. L/R was introduced in the charter issue of *Smart Access*, in February 1993, and was widely adopted by Access developers and used through Access 95. Since then this naming convention has split into two branches, the Leszynski Naming Convention (LNC) and the Reddick VBA Naming Convention (RVBA), although there's considerable overlap between the two.

Why use a naming convention? Basically, using a naming convention for database objects and controls makes your database self-documenting. Every time you see a drop-down list of database objects, each item's tag will tell you what kind of object it is. Likewise, when you see a reference to an object, control, or field in VBA code, you'll know what kind of element it is—essential information for understanding what you can do with it.

You can call a sub, set a control's value, or assign a variable as a function argument. But if you try to call a control, assign a form name as an Integer argument of a function, or reference the *Height* property of variable, you'll get compile errors or runtime errors in your code. Consistent use of a naming convention prevents these errors, because you'll know from the tag that *frmSales* is a form, *intChildren* is an Integer variable, and *CalcTotals* (since it has no tag) is a procedure name.

Hungarian notation (named after the native country of its originator) uses the following schema for naming objects:

[prefixes][tag]BaseName[Suffix/Qualifier]

Table 20-3 describes each of the schema's components.

Table 20-3. **Hungarian notation components**

Component	Description	Example
Prefix(es)	A lowercase letter that adds more information to the tag.	*p* for Public variable
Tag	A three-letter or four-letter sequence that indicates the object type.	*frm* for Form
BaseName	One or more words describing what the object represents. Each word in the name begins with a capital letter.	*EmployeesBySSN* for a selection of employees sorted by Social Security number
Suffix (RVBA), Qualifier (LNC)	A word that gives more information about the BaseName. Its initial letter is capitalized.	*Max* for the last element in an array

Of these four components, only the tag is required, although most object names consist of a tag and a base name. A stand-alone tag is useful when you're declaring variables in VBA code—for example, *frm* as a variable for a form. You don't have to use all four naming components—using tags alone gives you most of the benefits of a naming convention.

> **note** This book uses the LNC, mainly because it's similar to the original L/R naming convention, which I've used since the earliest versions of Access. Both the LNC and RVBA have branched out from Access objects and Access Basic (later, Access VBA) to cover other VBA dialects as well, and thus they encompass much more than the original Access components. Complete coverage of these naming conventions is beyond the scope of this book, but you can obtain the latest version of the LNC from *http://www.kwery.com* and the latest version of the RVBA convention from *http://www.xoc.net.*

Applying a Naming Convention to a New Database

To apply the LNC to a new database, all you have to do is name each database object, control, variable, and (if desired) field you create using the appropriate tag and base name. (See Tables 20-4 through 20-10, beginning on page 829, for listings of the LNC tags.)

Although it might seem cumbersome at first, the LNC quickly repays the user's effort in implementing it. When all your database objects have been named with the suggested three-letter or four-letter tags, you can tell what kind of object you're looking at whenever you see a list of database objects. Although Access (since Access 2000) generally offers separate tabs for tables and queries in record source drop-down lists or, in some cases, prefaces table names with *Table* and query names with *Query*, all this tells you is whether an object is a table or a query. LNC naming tags give you much more information, allowing you to pinpoint just the relevant objects (for example, select queries or subforms) for selection.

In a database that uses a naming convention, when you create an expression referencing a field or a form control in VBA code or for a query criterion, the object name's tag indicates whether you're referencing a control on a form or the underlying field in the table. Contrast this with a form created by the Form Wizard or a report created by the Report Wizard—Access unhelpfully assigns controls on the form the same names as their fields, which can lead to circular expression errors.

If you use a naming convention, there won't be any confusion between controls and fields, and you can tell at a glance whether a table is a lookup table, a system table, or a linking table or whether a query is an append query, a make-table query, or some other query type.

When you look at your code six months later, it will be considerably more comprehensible—not only to you, but to other developers. And if you work as part of a development team, if all the developers on the team use the same naming convention, you'll all be able to understand each other's code much better than you would otherwise.

You can (and no doubt most users do) add your own extensions to the standard naming convention. I have added the *tmp* tag to indicate a form or report template, the *fpri* tag for the primary form in a database, the *qtot* tag for a Totals query, and the *tmak* tag for a table made by a make-table query, to remind me that if I want to change the table's structure, I have to change the matching *qmak* query, not the table itself.

Although the LNC in its entirety provides tags for many more objects that developers might work with in VBA code, some of these tags (for example, type structures) are of little interest to the average user. All Access users should at least use tags for database objects, controls, and variables; advanced developers will probably want to use tags for other objects, and prefixes and qualifiers as well.

The following tables of tag names follow the LNC, with a few additions of my own. Table 20-4 lists the LNC tags for database objects, Table 20-5 lists field tags, Table 20-6 lists variable tags, Table 20-7 lists control tags, Table 20-8 lists object prefixes, Table 20-9 lists variable scope and lifetime prefixes, and Table 20-10 lists qualifiers.

note The tags and other identifiers in these tables are only a subset of the entire LNC. For the full set of identifiers, see the "LNC for Access" white paper available at *http://www.kwery.com*.

Table 20-4. **LNC database object tags**

Object	Tag
Class module	*cls*
Data access page	*dap*
Form	*frm*
Form (dialog)	*fdlg*
Form (menu)	*fmnu*
Form (message)	*fmsg*
Form (subform)	*fsub*
Macro	*mcr*
Module	*bas*
Query (any type)	*qry*
Query (append)	*qapp*
Query (crosstab)	*qxtb*
Query (data definition)	*qddl*
Query (delete)	*qdel*
Query (form filter)	*qflt*
Query (lookup)	*qlkp*
Query (make-table)	*qmak*
Query (select)	*qry* (or *qsel*)
Query (SQL pass-through)	*qspt*
Query (totals)	*qtot*
Query (union)	*quni*
Query (update)	*qupd*
Report	*rpt*
Report (subreport)	*rsub*
Table	*tbl*
Table (attached dBASE)	*tdbf*
Table (attached Excel)	*txls*
Table (attached FoxPro)	*tfox*

(continued)

Table 20-4. *(continued)*

Object	Tag
Table (attached Lotus)	*twks*
Table (attached ODBC)	*todb*
Table (attached Paradox)	*tpdx*
Table (attached SQL Server)	*tsql*
Table (attached text)	*ttxt*
Table (lookup)	*tlkp*
Table (many-to-many relationship)	*trel*

Table 20-5. LNC table field tags

Object	Tag
Autonumber (random non-sequential)	*idn*
Autonumber (replication ID)	*idr*
Autonumber (sequential)	*ids*
Binary	*bin*
Byte	*byt*
Currency	*cur*
Date/Time	*dtm*
Double	*dbl*
Hyperlink	*hlk*
Integer	*int*
Long	*lng*
Memo	*mem*
OLE	*ole*
Single	*sng*
Text (character)	*chr*
Yes/No (Boolean)	*bln*

Table 20-6. LNC VBA variable tags

Object	Tag
Combo box	*cbo*
Command bar	*cbr*
Control (generic)	*ctl*
Currency	*cur*
Database	*dbs*
Double	*dbl*
Form	*frm*
Integer	*int*
Label	*lbl*
List box	*lst*
Long	*lng*
QueryDef	*qdf*
Report	*rpt*
Single	*sng*
Snapshot	*snp*
String	*str*
Table	*tbl*
Text box	*txt*
Type (user-defined)	*typ*
Variant	*var*

Table 20-7. LNC control tags

Object	Tag
Bound object frame	*frb*
Chart (graph)	*cht*
Check box	*chk*
Combo box	*cbo*
Command button	*cmd*
Custom control (ActiveX control)	*ocx*
Frame	*fra*
Hyperlink	*hlk*
Image	*img*
Label	*lbl*
Line	*lin*
List box	*lst*
Option button	*opt*
Option group	*grp*
Page (tab)	*pge*
Page break	*brk*
Rectangle (shape)	*shp*
Subform/report	*sub*
Text box	*txt*
Toggle button	*tgl*
Unbound object frame	*fru*

Table 20-8. LNC database object prefixes

Object	Tag
Objects that are incomplete, backup copies, or under development	_ or – (In Access 2000 and later, dashes sort to the beginning of the database object list)
Hidden system objects	*zh*
Displayed system objects	*zs*
Programmatically created temporary objects	*zt*
Backup copies of objects, for later copying or reuse	*zz*

Table 20-9. LNC scope and lifetime prefixes

Variable type	Tag
Local variable	[no prefix]
Local static variable	*s*
Module-level variable	*m*
Public variable in a form or report module	*p*
Public variable declared in the Declarations section of a standard module	*g*

Table 20-10. LNC qualifiers

Qualifier	Description
Curr	Current element of a set
Dest	Destination
First	First element of a set
Hold	Hold a value for later reuse
Last	Last element of a set
Max	Maximum item in a set
Min	Minimum item in a set
New	New instance or value
Next	Next element of a set
Old	Prior instance or value
Prev	Previous element of a set
Src	Source
Temp	Temporary value

Table 20-11 lists some sample object and variable names, using prefixes, tags, and qualifiers.

Table 20-11. LNC examples

Object or variable name	Object or variable naming components	Object or variable description
tblCustomers	tag + base name	A table of customer data
qupdSales	tag + base name	A query that updates sales data
fsubInvoiceTotals	tag + base name	A subform that shows invoice totals data
tblCustomersOld	tag + base name + qualifier	A table of old Customers data
intChildren	tag + base name	An Integer variable to hold a value representing the number of children
curSalary	tag + base name	A Currency variable holding a Salary value

Object or variable name	Object or variable naming components	Object or variable description
gcurBaseSalary	prefix + tag + base name	A global Currency variable holding a Salary value
zztblContracts	prefix + tag + base name	A backup Contracts table, for copying and filling with imported data

Applying a Naming Convention to an Existing Database

It's easy to use a naming convention in a new database. It takes just a few seconds to type a three-letter or four-letter tag when you're naming a database object, control, or variable, and the small amount of time you spend will be saved many times over as you proceed to work on the database. However, if you inherit a database that's been created with no naming convention—or, for that matter, if you create database objects using wizards—you have a more burdensome task: applying a naming convention to an existing database.

In short, the problem is that renaming an object (say, a table) doesn't cause the name change to ripple throughout the database, changing Customers to tblCustomers wherever the table is referenced—as a form, report, or query data source; a combo box or list box row source; or in VBA code. You have to track down the changes yourself, renaming all the references to match the new object names, to avoid errors whenever the object whose name you changed is referenced.

I was inspired to write my first add-in, the LNC Rename add-in, after struggling with an inherited database in which the developer had named objects of many different types *Sales*. I had no way of knowing when I encountered *Sales* in the code whether it was a function name, a Currency variable, or a table, form, query, or report. If the variable had been named *curSales*, the table *tblSales*, the form *frmSales*, the query *qrySales*, and the function just *Sales*, there would have been no confusion.

Renaming database objects requires renaming references to them in form and report record sources, combo box control and list box control row sources, report grouping expressions, query fields and expressions, and VBA code—a very time-consuming process. Using a naming convention right from the start eliminates the need to rename objects later on.

Since Access 2000, Access has had a limited ability to propagate name changes: If you select the Name AutoCorrect check boxes on the General tab of the Options dialog box (see Figure 20-2), Access will fix some name references automatically when a form, report, or other object is opened.

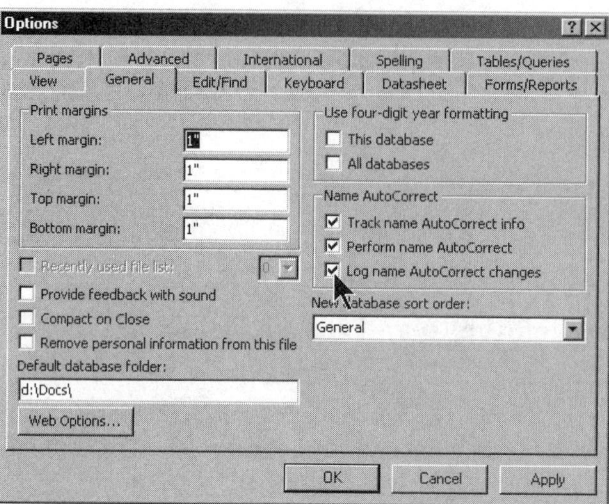

Figure 20-2. Select the Name AutoCorrect check boxes on the General tab in the Options dialog box.

For example, if you rename the Orders form in the sample Northwind database frmOrders and rename the Orders subform fsubOrders (in accordance with the LNC), when you next open frmOrders, it'll display the renamed subform correctly, and if you switch to Design view, you'll see that the subform is displaying fsubOrders. However, recognizing a renamed subform or subreport is only the tip of the iceberg. A search for *Orders Subform* in the Northwind database's VBA code reveals numerous references to the subform's original name, none of which have been changed, and all of which will cause errors when these procedures are run.

Name AutoCorrect doesn't work for references in the following elements:

- VBA code (modules)
- Projects
- Replicated databases
- Data access pages
- Macros
- Desktop shortcuts for specific database objects
- Linked tables

InsideOut

With so many exceptions, the Name AutoCorrect feature isn't always as useful as it could be. When you change a database object, control, field, or variable name, you need to have it changed throughout the database, wherever it occurs. Long before the Name AutoCorrect feature was added to Access, I wrote the LNC Rename add-in, which automatically renames database objects and controls according the LNC. (Variables can easily be renamed using search and replace in modules, so I didn't include them.) This add-in is described in detail in Chapter 15, "Using Add-Ins to Expand Access Functionality."

on the CD The LNC Rename Access add-in (available on the companion CD) ensures that when you rename database objects and controls using the LNC, all of the references to the renamed objects will be changed as well. I also prepared an LNC Rename COM add-in (also on the companion CD) for quick renaming of form and report controls only.

Working with Object Models

An object model is a representation of an application's components, usually in a hierarchical structure, showing the relationships between the application's objects. When you write VBA code to add functionality to an application, you're primarily working with the Access object model, which represents most of the components you work with in the Access interface, such as forms, reports, and controls. The Access object model gives you control over a great many settings and actions via methods such as the *RunCommand* method of the *DoCmd* object. To work with data, however, your application will need to use other object models, such as the Data Access Objects (DAO) object model or the ActiveX Data Objects (ADO) object model.

Properties, Methods, and Events

The objects in an object model might have properties, methods, and events. (Not all objects have all three.) Properties are attributes of an object, such as the *Height* or *Width* properties of a text box control. Methods are actions that can be performed using the object, such as the *Open* method to open a form. (Some people like to think of properties as adjectives and methods as verbs.) Events are things that happen to objects, such as clicking a command button or printing a report, that can be used to trigger actions using event procedures.

Access Object Model

The Access object model represents the Access interface—forms, reports, controls, data access pages, and other Access components. It also has the *DoCmd* object, whose *RunCommand* method is used to run a large number of commands that correspond to actions you can take in the interface. Figure 20-3 shows a high-level view of the Access object model.

Application
Forms (Form)
Reports (Report)
Modules (Module)
References (Reference)
Printers (Printer)
DataAccessPages (DataAccessPage)
Screen
DoCmd
VBE
NewFile
DefaultWebOptions
Assistant
CommandBars
DBEngine
FileSearch
FileDialog
COMAddIns
AnswerWizard
LanguageSettings
CurrentProject
CurrentData
CodeProject
CodeData
Legend
Object and collection
Object only

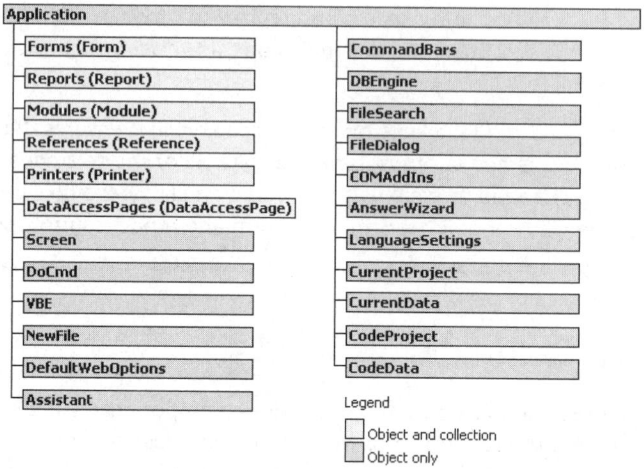

Figure 20-3. A high-level view of the Access object model shows only the main Access objects.

You can view a more detailed diagram of the Access object model in the Access Help facility. To start Access Help, choose Help, Microsoft Access Help. In the left pane of the Access Help window, click the Contents tab to display a list of Help categories (called Help books). To view the Access object model diagram, open the Programming in Visual Basic Reference Help book, and then the Microsoft Access Visual Basic Reference book under it, and select the Microsoft Access Object Model Help topic.

DAO Object Model

The DAO object model has grown up with Access and is still the best object model for working with Access data (as opposed to interface elements such as forms and reports). You can use the DAO object model to work with data in Access tables and to create and manipulate tables and queries programmatically. It also has components you can use to manage security for an Access database. Figure 20-4 shows a high-level view of the DAO object model.

To view the full DAO object model, open the Microsoft Data Access Objects 3.60 (DAO) Help book, and then the Microsoft DAO 3.60 book under it, and then the DAO Objects Reference book under that, and then the DAO Object Model for Microsoft Jet Workspaces Help topic.

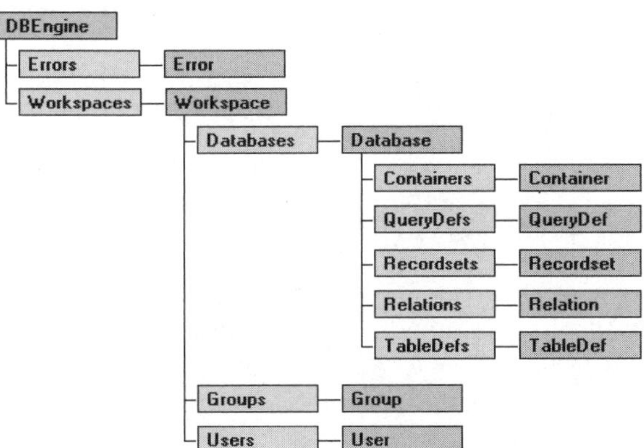

Figure 20-4. A high-level view of the DAO object model shows the main objects only.

ADO Object Model

The ADO object model is the new kid on the block. It has only a few objects and thus has less functionality than the DAO object model for working with Access databases and their data. Unlike with DAO, however, you can use the ADO object model to work with non-Access data (such as SQL Server data or ODBC data sources). If you need to work with data in other formats, you need ADO. Figure 20-5 shows the ADO object model; notice that the objects aren't arranged hierarchically.

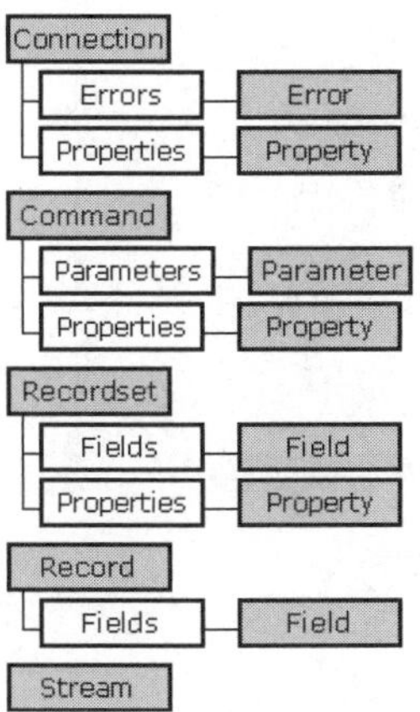

Figure 20-5. The ADO object model isn't hierarchical.

To view the ADO object model in Help, open the Microsoft ActiveX Data Objects (ADO) Help book, and then the Microsoft ADO Programmer's Reference book under it, and then ADO API Reference book under that, and then the ADO Object Model Help topic.

Using the Visual Basic Editor

When you press Alt+F11 or open a code module, the Visual Basic Editor opens. Figure 20-6 shows the Crafts database in the Visual Basic Editor, open to the first event procedure of the fsubPublishersAddNew form. The main features of the Visual Basic Editor window (which is the same in all Microsoft Office applications that support VBA) are described in the following sections.

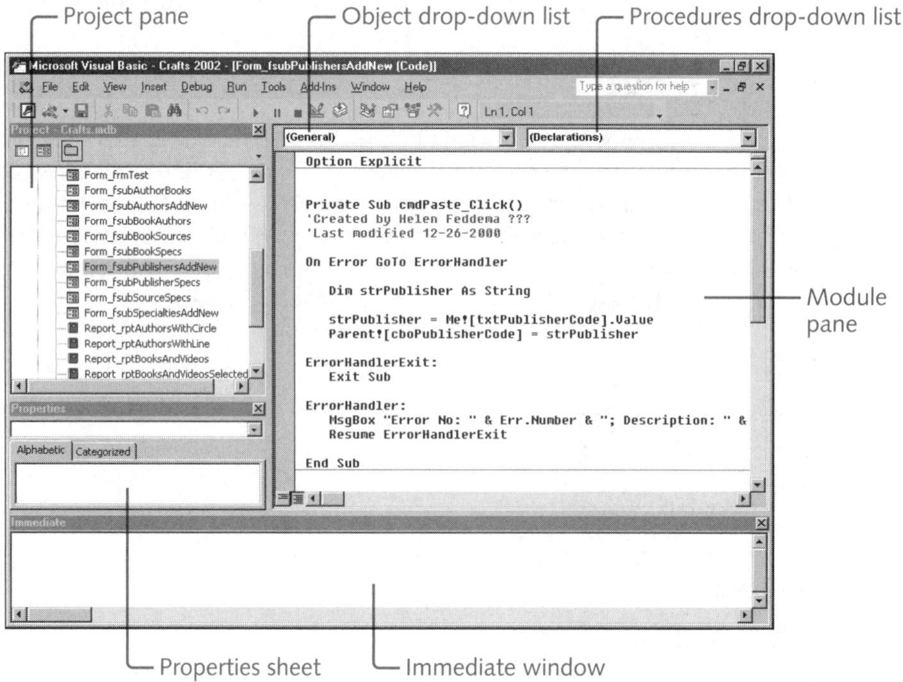

Figure 20-6. Use this window to work on VBA code.

Project Pane

The Project pane (top left in Figure 20-6) is a tree-type display of the modules and other objects in an Access database project. In Access, there are usually only two folders: Microsoft Access Class Objects, which contains form and report class modules, and Modules, which contains standard modules. If you've written class modules to define custom objects, they'll be in a Class Modules folder.

> **note** Access uses the word *project* for two different types of objects, which can cause confusion. A project can be a collection of code in an Access database or a front end to a SQL Server database (an ADP file). Be sure that you don't confuse the two. Microsoft Project uses the word in yet another way.

Properties Sheet

The properties sheet (middle left in Figure 20-6) lists the properties of the selected object. In other Office applications, the properties sheet is genuinely useful for working with UserForms, but because Access has its own forms, the properties sheet has only a few uses in the Visual Basic Editor window, one of which is changing the name of a module.

Code Window

The code window (right side of Figure 20-6) displays the code in the selected module. At the top of the window are two drop-down lists. The Object drop-down list (on the left) lets you select an object that has event procedures for which you can write code. Figure 20-7 shows the list displayed.

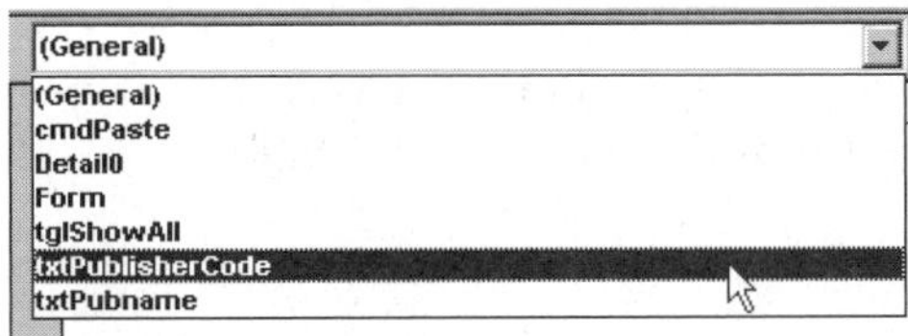

Figure 20-7. You select an object for writing event procedures from the Object drop-down list.

After you've selected an object, the Procedures drop-down list (on the right in Figure 20-6) will list the available event procedures for that object. The events that already have procedures will appear in boldface, as you can see in Figure 20-8. (Here the *Click* event has a procedure.)

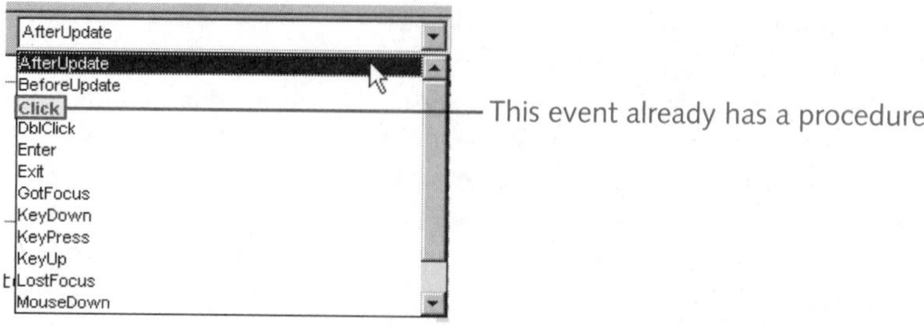

Figure 20-8. The Procedures drop-down list offers a selection of event procedures for the selected object.

When you select a new event procedure, a code stub is inserted into the module, with any arguments needed. The code stub for a text box's *BeforeUpdate* event procedure is shown here:

```
Private Sub txtPublisherCode_BeforeUpdate(Cancel As Integer)

End Sub
```

You can now type in the statements you want to execute when the event fires, between the *Private Sub* and *End Sub* lines.

Object Browser

The Object Browser (shown in Figure 20-9) isn't open by default; you open it by pressing F2 or by clicking the Object Browser button on the toolbar.

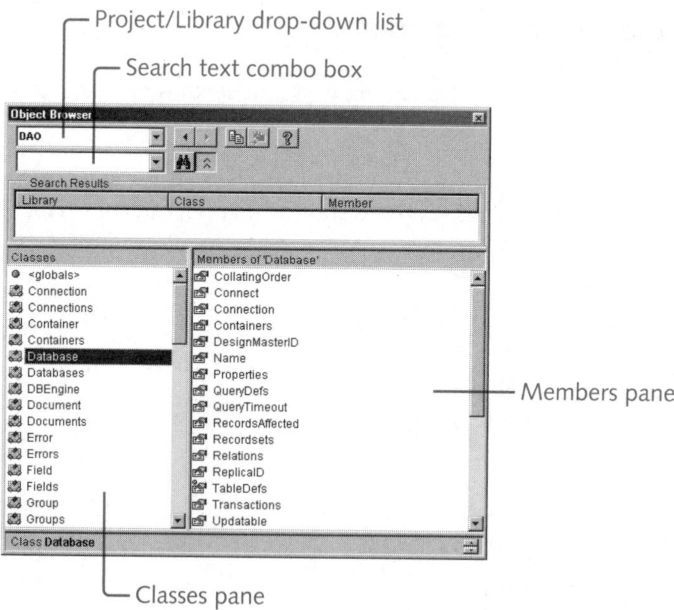

Figure 20-9. The Object Browser lets you select an object library to investigate.

The Project/Library drop-down list at the top left of the Object Browser lets you choose a library to investigate. The Search Text combo box lets you enter text to search for; search results are displayed in the Search Results pane in the middle of the window. The Classes pane displays the classes (objects and enumerations) in the selected library, and the Members pane shows the members of the selected class.

Immediate Window

The Immediate window (the bottom pane in Figure 20-6) shows the text written by *Debug.Print* statements in your code, usually for debugging purposes.

> **tip** **Find Help on a property or method**
>
> To find Help on a property or method, locate it in the Object Browser, and then click the yellow question mark on the Object Browser toolbar to open context-specific Help. This method is generally easier than to trying to find the topic in HTML Help.

Options Dialog Box

When you use the Visual Basic Editor Code window, you can get help from IntelliSense, which in Access modules consists of three features that can be turned on or off in the Visual Basic Editor window's own Options dialog box. (Choose Tools, Options; the Options dialog box will open to the Editor tab, as shown in Figure 20-10.)

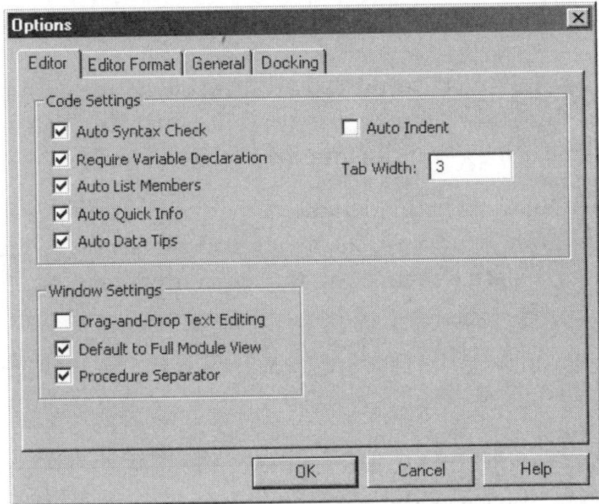

Figure 20-10. The Editor tab of the Options dialog box lets you select code writing options.

The options on the Editor page are as follows:

Code Settings

- **Auto Syntax Check.** Checks syntax after you enter a line of code. This feature can be annoying because you can't leave the incorrect line of code until you fix the error. I recommend leaving this option cleared. (Incorrect syntax will still be highlighted in red.)
- **Require Variable Declaration.** Adds the *Option Explicit* statement to general declarations in any new module so that explicit variable declaration (early binding of variables) is required. Highly recommended.
- **Auto List Members.** Displays a list of available properties, methods, or other language elements available for the statement at the current insertion point.
- **Auto Quick Info.** Displays information about functions and their parameters as you type.
- **Auto Data Tips.** Displays the value of the variable over which your cursor is placed. (Available only in Break mode.)
- **Auto Indent.** Indents all lines of code at the location where the first line of code was tabbed.
- **Tab Width.** Sets the tab width. You can specify between 1 and 32 spaces; the default is 4 spaces.

Window Settings

- **Drag-and-Drop Text Editing.** Lets you drag and drop elements within the current code and from the Code window into the Immediate or Watch windows; works the same as in Word documents.
- **Default To Full Module View.** Sets the default state for new modules to show procedures in the Code window as a single scrollable list or divided into separate procedures. Doesn't change the way currently open modules are viewed.
- **Procedure Separator.** Displays or hides separator bars between procedures in the Code window.

The Editor Format tab of the Options dialog box (shown in Figure 20-11) lets you select the font and color. I suggest leaving the colors as specified and selecting the Fixedsys (Western) font for maximum readability.

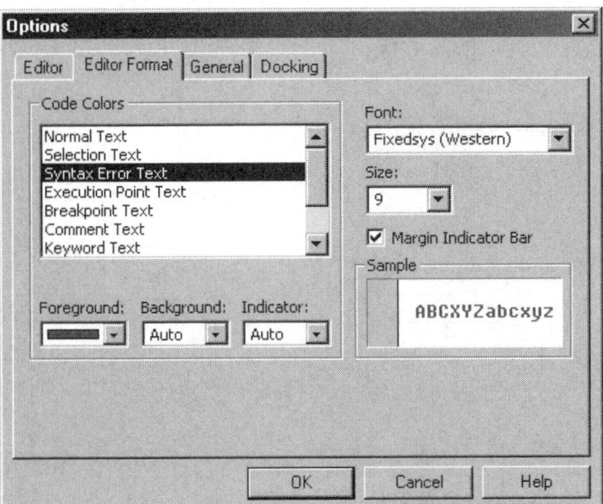

Figure 20-11. The Editor Format tab of the Options dialog box lets you set the font and color for text in the Visual Basic Editor window.

The General tab of the Options dialog box (shown in Figure 20-12) has some options for UserForms (which aren't applicable in Access) and some options for error handling and compilation (which you can generally leave as they are).

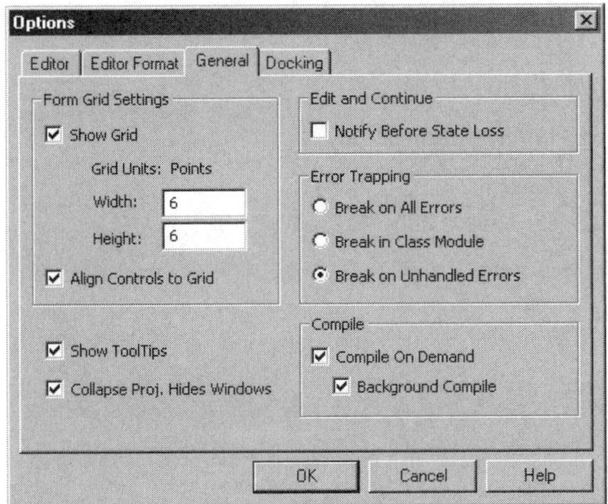

Figure 20-12. The General tab of the Options dialog box provides some error handling and compilation options.

The Docking tab of the Options dialog box (shown in Figure 20-13) lets you specify which of the windows and panes can be docked. A window is docked when it's anchored to the edge of the main application window or to the edge of another docked window within the main application window. A docked window is generally more visible and easier to work with than windows that aren't docked.

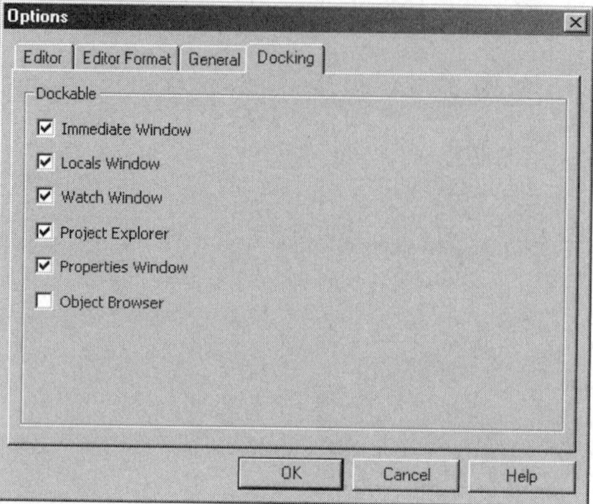

Figure 20-13. Use the Docking tab to dock the windows in the Visual Basic Editor.

Writing Form and Report Event Procedures

To write code for a form, report, form or report section, or form control, open the object's properties sheet, and click the Event tab. All the available events for the selected object will be listed; select *[Event Procedure]* next to an event, as shown in Figure 20-14, to open an existing event procedure or to create a new one.

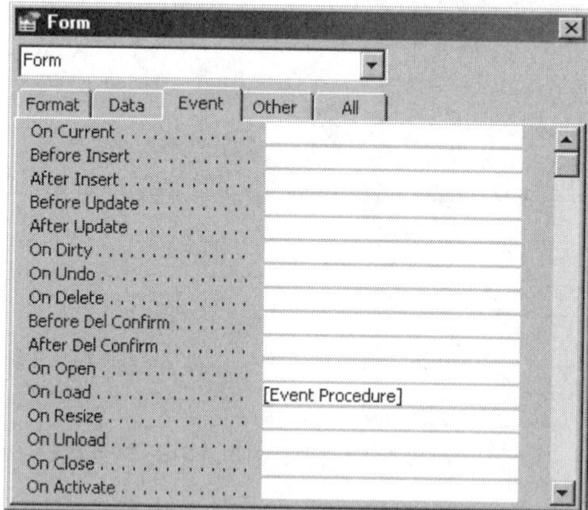

Figure 20-14. The Event tab of the Form properties sheet lists the form's events.

To create a code module for an event, click the Build button next to the event, as shown in Figure 20-15. (The Build button is visible only when you place the focus on that event box.)

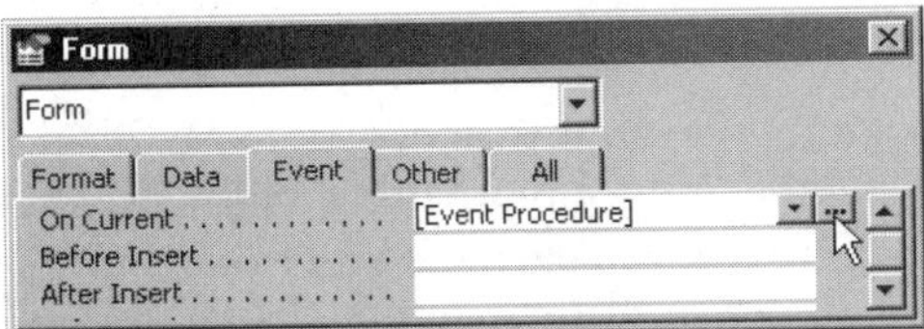

Figure 20-15. Click the Build button to create an event procedure stub.

The Choose Builder dialog box will open; select Code Builder from the list of available builders (as shown in Figure 20-16).

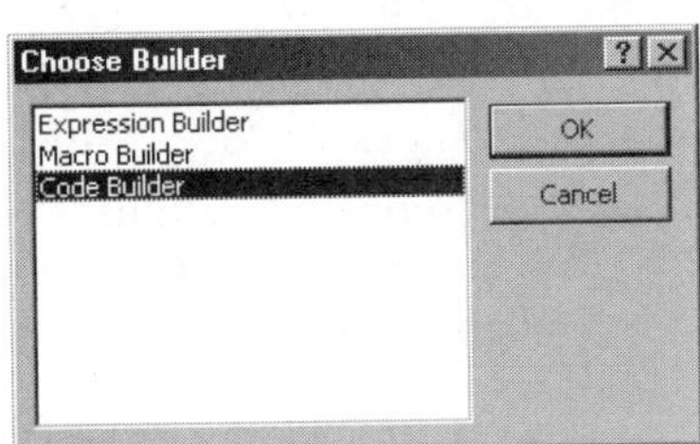

Figure 20-16. The Choose Builder dialog box appears when you create an event procedure.

You can bypass the Choose Builder dialog box and go directly to the code module from the Build button if you check the Always Use Event Procedures check box on the Forms/Reports tab in the Access Options dialog box (as shown in Figure 20-17).

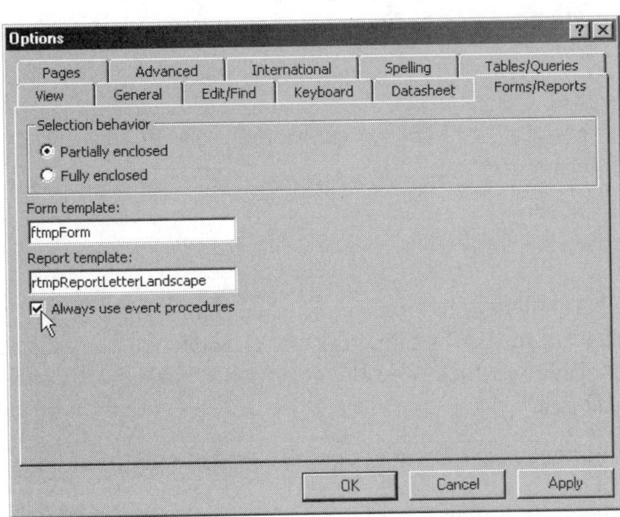

Figure 20-17. Check the Always Use Event Procedures check box to bypass the Choose Builder dialog box when you create event procedures.

Form Events

Forms and form controls have an enormous number of events, but only a few of them are widely used. This section describes the most commonly used form events. For information about other form events, select the form, click the event you want to know more about in the properties sheet, and press F1 to open the event's Help topic.

> **note** A number of events are listed with the *On* prefix on the Event tab in the properties sheet. This prefix isn't part of the event name as it appears in Help or in the Object Browser, and it's not used in the code stub for the event procedure.

- *Current.* Occurs when the focus moves to a new record. This event is useful for making controls visible or invisible, depending on a condition. For datasheet forms, columns can be hidden from this event. The *Current* procedure shown here clears two combo boxes when the user goes to a new record:

```
Private Sub Form_Current()

On Error GoTo ErrorHandler

    Me![cboTitleSearchList] = Null
    Me![cboAuthorSearchList] = Null

ErrorHandlerExit:
   Exit Sub

ErrorHandler:
   MsgBox "Error No: " & Err.Number & "; Description: " & _
      Err.Description
   Resume ErrorHandlerExit

End Sub
```

- *Before Insert.* Occurs when the first data is entered into a new record. This event is useful for automatically filling in certain fields with values, as in the following procedure, which saves the next higher number in a series to be used for an ID field:

```
Private Sub Form_BeforeInsert(Cancel As Integer)

On Error GoTo Form_BeforeInsertError

   Dim lngID As Long

   Me![subGaplessID].Form.Requery
   lngID = Me![subGaplessID].Form![txtMaxID] + 1
```

```
   Me![ID] = lngID
   Me![txtID].Requery

Form_BeforeInsertExit:
   Exit Sub
Form_BeforeInsertError:
   MsgBox "Error No: " & Err.Number & "; Description: " & _
      Err.Description
   Resume Form_BeforeInsertExit

End Sub
```

- *After Insert.* Occurs after a new record is added. Can be used to trigger requerying of another control or a pop-up form. The following event procedure requeries two record search combo boxes:

```
Private Sub Form_AfterInsert()

On Error GoTo ErrorHandler

   Me![cboTitleSearchList].Requery
   Me![cboAuthorSearchList].Requery

ErrorHandlerExit:
   Exit Sub

ErrorHandler:
   MsgBox "Error No: " & Err.Number & "; Description: " & _
      Err.Description
   Resume ErrorHandlerExit

End Sub
```

- *Dirty.* Occurs when the data in a form changes. Useful for making controls visible, such as command buttons to save a new record or to undo changes. Setting the *Dirty* event's *Cancel* argument to *True* wipes out the changes made to the form. Modifying form data from VBA code doesn't trigger this event. The following event procedure gives the user a chance to back out of a change to a form:

```
Private Sub Form_Dirty(Cancel As Integer)

On Error GoTo ErrorHandler

   Dim intResult As Integer

   intResult = MsgBox("Did you mean to make this change?", _
      vbYesNo)
```

(continued)

```
   If intResult = vbNo Then
      Cancel = True
   End If

ErrorHandlerExit:
   Exit Sub

ErrorHandler:
   MsgBox "Error No: " & Err.Number & "; Description: " & _
      Err.Description
   Resume ErrorHandlerExit

End Sub
```


- *Open.* Occurs when a form is opened but before the first record is displayed. The *Open* event procedure listed here opens two other forms in hidden mode so that they can be made visible quickly when various command buttons on the form are clicked:

```
Private Sub Form_Open(Cancel As Integer)

On Error GoTo ErrorHandler

   DoCmd.OpenForm "frmCompanyInformation", , , , , acHidden
   DoCmd.OpenForm "frmPersonalInformation", , , , , acHidden

ErrorHandlerExit:
   Exit Sub

ErrorHandler:
   MsgBox "Error No: " & Err.Number & "; Description: " & _
      Err.Description
   Resume ErrorHandlerExit

End Sub
```

- *Load.* Occurs when a form is opened and its records are displayed. Can be used to size the form to the correct size or set the focus to a specific control, as in the following code sample:

```
Private Sub Form_Load()

On Error GoTo ErrorHandler

   DoCmd.RunCommand acCmdSizeToFitForm
   Me![cboTitleSearchList].SetFocus

ErrorHandlerExit:
   Exit Sub
```

```
ErrorHandler:
   MsgBox "Error No: " & Err.Number & "; Description: " & _
      Err.Description
   Resume ErrorHandlerExit

End Sub
```

- *Close.* Occurs when the form is closed. One typical use is to reopen a main menu form, as in the following procedure:

```
Private Sub cmdClose_Click()

On Error GoTo ErrorHandler

   Dim prj As Object
   Set prj = Application.CurrentProject

   If prj.AllForms("fmnuMain").IsLoaded Then
      Forms![fmnuMain].Visible = True
   Else
      DoCmd.OpenForm "fmnuMain"
   End If

   DoCmd.Close acForm, Me.Name

ErrorHandlerExit:
   Exit Sub

ErrorHandler:
   MsgBox "Error No: " & Err.Number & "; Description: " & _
      Err.Description
   Resume ErrorHandlerExit

End Sub
```

The order of events when a form is opened is shown in Figure 20-18.

Order of events when a form is opened

Figure 20-18. Events occur in a certain order when a form is opened.

The order of events when a form is closed is shown in Figure 20-19.

Order of events when a form is closed

Figure 20-19. Events occur in a certain order when a form is closed.

Report Events

Reports have only a few events. The events of report sections are often used to apply conditional formatting to a group of controls or to display or hide report sections; these events are discussed in section in Chapter 7, "Using Reports to Print Data."

The most commonly used report events are as follows:

- *NoData.* Occurs after a report is formatted but before it's printed, when there's no data to print on the report. This event has a *Cancel* argument that can be used to cancel report printing, as in the following procedure:

```
Private Sub Report_NoData(Cancel As Integer)

On Error GoTo Report_NoDataError

   MsgBox "No records meet the report criteria; _
      canceling report printing"
   Cancel = True

Report_NoDataExit:
   Exit Sub

Report_NoDataError:
   MsgBox Err.Description
   Resume Report_NoDataExit

End Sub
```

- *Open.* Occurs when the report is opened but before it's previewed or printed.

Form Control Events

Controls, like forms, have many events, but only a few are commonly used:

- *Click.* Occurs when you click a control once with the left mouse button. Although this event applies to many controls, it's generally used only with command buttons, which are designed to be clicked. The *Click* event of command buttons is used to run code to perform all sorts of actions, such as in the following procedure on the fpriBooksAndVideos form, which opens a pop-up form listing other books by the same author:

```
Private Sub cmdBooksBySameAuthor_Click()

On Error GoTo ErrorHandler

   DoCmd.OpenForm "frmBooksBySelectedAuthor", acFormDS, _
      acReadOnly
   Forms![frmBooksBySelectedAuthor].Caption = "Books by " & _
      Me![subBookAuthors]![LastNameFirst]

ErrorHandlerExit:
   Exit Sub

ErrorHandler:
   MsgBox "Error No: " & Err.Number & "; Description: " & _
      Err.Description
   Resume ErrorHandlerExit

End Sub
```


InsideOut

The *Click* event for Tab controls doesn't work in Access; use the *Change* event of this control instead, with an *If...Then* or *Select Case* statement to respond to clicks on the tab control's tabs. See the *Change* event code sample later in this section for an example of such a procedure.

- ***DblClick.*** Occurs when you double-click a control with the left mouse button. This event is useful for triggering events from datasheet subforms because command buttons aren't displayed on a datasheet form or subform. The following *DblClick* event procedure opens a form with related information when a cell in a datasheet subform is double-clicked:

```
Private Sub txtLoanNumber_DblClick(Cancel As Integer)

On Error GoTo ErrorHandler

   DoCmd.RunCommand acCmdSaveRecord
   DoCmd.OpenForm "frmStudentLoanDetailsSingle", acNormal

ErrorHandlerExit:
   Exit Sub

ErrorHandler:
   MsgBox "Error No: " & Err.Number & "; Description: " & _
      Err.Description
   Resume ErrorHandlerExit

End Sub
```

- ***AfterUpdate.*** Used to perform an action when the data in a control that contains text (such as a text box, list box, or combo box) is changed. The following procedure runs when a new value is selected in a combo box in a form header; it synchronizes the form with the selected record:

```
Private Sub cboAuthorSearchList_AfterUpdate()

On Error GoTo ErrorHandler

   Dim strSearch As String

   strSearch = "[AuthorID] = " & Me![cboAuthorSearchList]

   'Find the record that matches the control.
   Me.Requery
   Me.RecordsetClone.FindFirst strSearch
   Me.Bookmark = Me.RecordsetClone.Bookmark

ErrorHandlerExit:
   Exit Sub

ErrorHandler:
   MsgBox "Error No: " & Err.Number & "; Description: " & _
      Err.Description
   Resume ErrorHandlerExit

End Sub
```

- ***BeforeUpdate.*** Occurs before changed data in a control is updated. The following event procedure assigns values to several variables and then calls a procedure that checks that the entry in the txtStateProvince text box is only two characters long if the country is U.S.A.:

```
Private Sub txtStateProvince_BeforeUpdate(Cancel As Integer)

On Error GoTo ErrorHandler

   strStateProvince = Nz(Me![txtStateProvince].Value)
   strCountry = Nz(Me![txtCountry].Value)
   Set txt = Me![txtStateProvince]
   Call CheckStateProvince(strStateProvince, strCountry, txt)

ErrorHandlerExit:
   Exit Sub
```

```
ErrorHandler:
   MsgBox "Error No: " & Err.Number & "; Description: " & _
      Err.Description
   Resume ErrorHandlerExit

End Sub
```

- ***Change.*** Occurs when the contents of a text box or the text portion of a combo box changes but before the *BeforeUpdate* event. The *Change* event also occurs when you move to another page in a tab control. The *Change* event doesn't occur when the value in a calculated control changes or when an item is selected in a combo box. The following procedure requeries the appropriate subform when a new page on a tab control is selected:

```
Private Sub tabAddNew_Change()

On Error GoTo ErrorHandler

   Dim pg As Access.Page
   Dim tbc As Access.TabControl
   Dim strPage As String

   Set tbc = Me![tabAddNew]
   Set pg = tbc.Pages(tbc.Value)
   strPage = pg.Name

   Select Case strPage

      Case "pgeAuthors"
         Me![subAuthorsAddNew].Requery

      Case "pgePublishers"
         Me![subPublishersAddNew].Requery

      Case "pgeSpecs"
         Me![subSpecsAddNew].Requery

   End Select

ErrorHandlerExit:
   Exit Sub

ErrorHandler:
   MsgBox "Error No: " & Err.Number & "; Description: " & _
      Err.Description
   Resume ErrorHandlerExit

End Sub
```

Adding Error Handling to Your Code

If your procedures lack error handling, when an error occurs the code will stop executing, an error message will appear, and the user might be left wondering what to do next. Figure 20-20 shows the message that appears when the user tries to save a record with nothing entered in its key field.

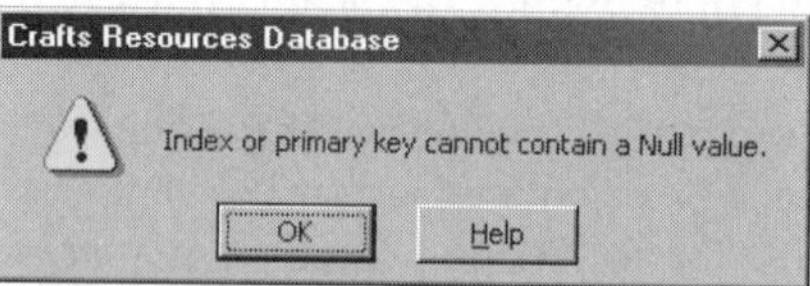

Figure 20-20. A confusing error message appears when the user tries to save a record without a value in its key field.

After clicking OK, the user will be back in the form, at the same spot as before, with no specific information on how to fix the problem. To handle this error in a more informative manner, you can put an error handler into the form's *Close* event. I use the following error handler in my procedures (with the current date):

```
'Created by Helen Feddema 3-25-2001
'Last modified 3-25-2001

On Error GoTo ErrorHandler

⋮

ErrorHandlerExit:
   Exit Sub

ErrorHandler:
   MsgBox "Error No: " & Err.Number & "; Description: " & _
      Err.Description
   Resume ErrorHandlerExit
```

The error handler displays a message box with the error number and description and then exits the procedure. This is cleaner than leaving the user in a halted procedure. For many errors, this is sufficient, but if you want special handling for specific errors, you can use an *If…Then* or *Select Case* statement in the error handler to take a specific action when a specific error occurs.

The *LNCBuilder* function in the LNC Rename add-in (described in Chapter 21, "Creating Your Own Add-Ins") uses a *Select Case* statement in its error handler to handle two specific errors. It also runs two clean-up functions from the *LNCBuilderExit* label before exiting the function, as shown here:

```
LNCBuilderExit:
   'Delete old tables in calling database.
   ClearCurrentSystemTable
   ClearCurrentObjectsTable
   Exit Function

LNCBuilderError:
   'If an option button or a check box is unbound, set
   'fUnbound to True so that the code uses the NA function
   'instead of CS.
   Select Case Err.Number
      Case 2455
         fUnbound = True
         Resume Next
      Case 2465
         MsgBox "You can't rename a single control from the " _
            & "Detail section"
         Resume LNCBuilderExit
      Case Else
         MsgBox "Error No: " & Err.Number & "; Description: " _
            & Err.Description
         Resume LNCBuilderExit
   End Select
```

You can also use error handlers to branch to a different section of code. I often use the following error handler in procedures that work with Word objects using Automation code. The first line of code attempts to assign the global *gappWord* variable to the current instance of Word (to avoid creating multiple Word instances). If Word isn't running, Error 429 occurs and the error handler runs an alternative line of code, setting the *gappWord* variable to a new instance of Word using *CreateObject*.

```
   Set gappWord = GetObject(, "Word.Application")
:
ErrorHandlerExit:
   Set gappWord = Nothing
   Exit Sub

ErrorHandler:
   'Word is not running; open Word with CreateObject.
   If Err.Number = 429 Then
      Set gappWord = CreateObject("Word.Application")
      Resume Next
   Else
      MsgBox "Error No: " & Err.Number & "; Description: "
      Resume ErrorHandlerExit
   End If
```

Using the *References* Collection to Set References Programmatically

If you write code that works with a specific object library, using early binding of variables, and someone else imports that code into a database that lacks a reference to that object library and runs the code, an error will occur. Typically, the error message will be uninformative—for example, the message shown in Figure 20-21 appeared when I tried to close a form after clearing the DAO object library option in the References dialog box (simulating the situation in which code that uses the DAO object model is imported into an Access 2000 or Access 2002 database with the ADO object model checked rather than the DAO object model).

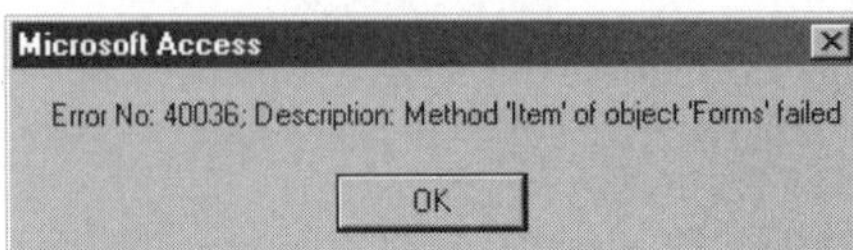

Figure 20-21. An uninformative error message results from a missing object library reference.

Another typical result of a missing object library reference is code that won't compile; when you debug it, a perfectly standard function such as *InStr* or *Mid* (usually one of the string manipulation functions) will be highlighted as the cause of the error. Or you might get the error shown in Figure 20-22 with a DAO object declaration highlighted. This message is reasonably informative, but only to a programmer, not to an end user.

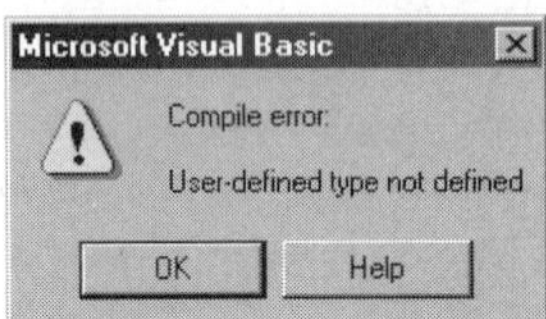

Figure 20-22. A missing object library reference will cause a Compile Error message.

In the Access interface, you can fix problems with missing object library references (after you've identified the cause of the problem) by opening the References dialog box in the Visual Basic Editor window (choose Tools, References) and checking the missing object library. Figure 20-23 shows the DAO object library being checked so that code using its components will compile and run correctly.

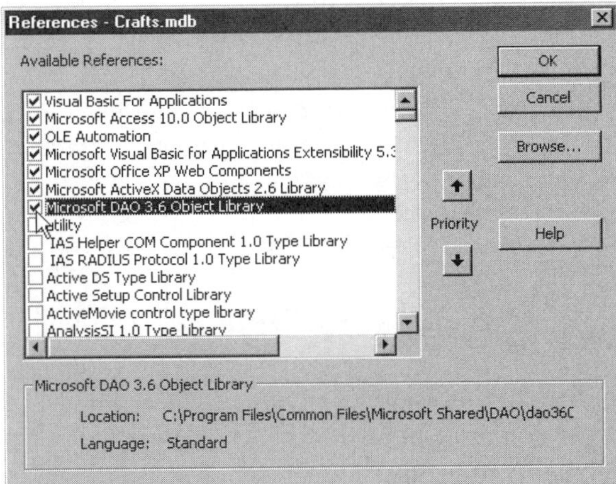

Figure 20-23. You can check the DAO object library reference in the References dialog box to prevent confusion when you reference its components in code.

You can also set references in code, which can be particularly useful for code that will be run on other people's computers, where you can't know which object libraries will be checked.

> **tip** To find the full path and file name of the object library, select its line in the References dialog box and look at the Location line at the bottom of the dialog box.

The following code segment sets a reference to the Microsoft Office XP Web Components object library, which is needed to support PivotTables and PivotCharts. You can run this code from a function that's run when a main menu form is opened or that runs from an AutoExec macro in a database.

```
Dim refs As Access.References

Set refs = Application.References
'The following two lines should be one long line in code.
refs.AddFromFile "C:\Program Files\Common Files
\Microsoft Shared\Web Components\10\OWC10.DLL"
```

caution Unfortunately, if the missing reference you need to supply is the one for the DAO object library, you might not be able to set the reference in code because typically a missing DAO object library reference will prevent code from compiling and running. When I attempted to set a reference to the DAO object library in code after removing it in the interface or using the *Remove* method, I got a *User-defined type not defined* error and the code to add the reference wouldn't run.

newfeature!

Using the *Printer* Object in Code

The new *Printers* collection and *Printer* object in the Access object model address a long-standing need: They let you programmatically select a printer for a report and also change the paper size and orientation.

caution Changing the paper size or orientation of a report doesn't change the report width or the arrangement of controls on the report; only the detail section height is affected when you select a different paper size or orientation. This means that if you select legal landscape paper for a letter-portrait formatted report, it will look very strange indeed.

By using a printer selection combo box powered by the *Printer* object, you let users select any available printer for printing a report without having to open the report, change the printer or other settings, and save and close the report—a great convenience. Although you can't change the dimensions or layout of reports using the *Printer* object, you can at least try different selections until you find the right one for the report you're printing—for example, if you don't know whether the report is designed to be printed portrait or landscape.

Figure 20-24 shows a dialog form with combo boxes for selecting a report for printing, a printer, and the paper size to use; it also has an option group for selecting the orientation. This form is available on the companion CD in the Test Access 2002.mdb database.

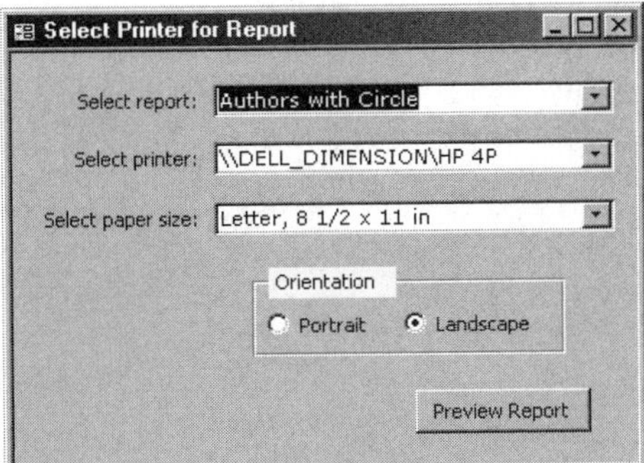

Figure 20-24. The Select Printer For Report dialog box is an example of a form that uses the *Printer* object.

The cboSelectReport combo box has tlkpReports as its row source, which is a table of reports in the database created by the Menu Manager add-in for use as the row source of a report selection combo box on the main menu. The cboSelectPrinter combo box has tlkpPaperSizes as its row source, which is a table listing all the values of the *AcPrintPaperSize* enumeration and is used to set the *PaperSize* property of the *Printer* object.

The cboSelectPrinter combo box is filled with values from the form's *Load* event procedure; the names of the printers in the *Printers* collection are added to the list using the new *AddItem* method of the *Listbox* object. The fraOrientation option group offers two options: Portrait and Landscape. After you select the options you want, you can click the Preview Report button to open the report in Print Preview, with the selected paper size and orientation.

The code for the fdlgSelectPrinter form is shown here:

```
Option Compare Database
Option Explicit

Dim intDefaultPrinter As Integer

Private Sub cmdPrintReport_Click()

On Error GoTo ErrorHandler

   Dim prt As Printer
   Dim strReport As String
```

(continued)

```
   Set prt = Application.Printers(CLng(Me![cboSelectPrinter]))
   strReport = Me![cboSelectReport]
   prt.PaperSize = Me![cboPaperSize]
   prt.Orientation = Me![fraOrientation]
   DoCmd.OpenReport strReport, acViewPreview
   Reports(strReport).Printer = prt

ErrorHandlerExit:
   Exit Sub

ErrorHandler:
   MsgBox "Error No: " & Err.Number & "; Description: " & _
      Err.Description
   Resume ErrorHandlerExit

End Sub

Private Sub Form_Load()

On Error GoTo ErrorHandler

   Dim prt As Access.Printer
   Dim i As Integer
   Dim cboPrinter As Access.ComboBox

   DoCmd.RunCommand acCmdSizeToFitForm
   Set cboPrinter = Me![cboSelectPrinter]
   cboPrinter.RowSource = ""
   i = 0
   For Each prt In Application.Printers
      cboPrinter.AddItem i & ";" & prt.DeviceName
      If prt.DeviceName = Application.Printer.DeviceName Then
         intDefaultPrinter = i
      End If
      i = i + 1
   Next
   cboPrinter = intDefaultPrinter
   Me![cboPaperSize] = 1

ErrorHandlerExit:
   Exit Sub

ErrorHandler:
   MsgBox "Error No: " & Err.Number & "; Description: " & _
      Err.Description
   Resume ErrorHandlerExit

End Sub
```

Chapter 21

Creating Your Own Add-Ins

Add-ins are extensions to applications that provide extra functionality over and above the application's built-in features, such as giving you a choice of formats for a control, a library of code segments, or a way of quickly renaming objects according to a naming convention. You can download Microsoft Office add-ins from the Microsoft Web site, purchase add-ins from third-party vendors, download freeware or shareware add-ins from various Web sites, or create your own add-ins for personal or corporate use.

Application-specific Access add-ins have been available since Microsoft Access 1.0. These add-ins are specifically designed to hook in to Access menus or properties or to run as wizards of various sorts, to aid in the creation of new database objects. Office 2000 introduced a new type of add-in: *COM add-ins*. COM add-ins are an Office feature, and they can be written to support multiple Office applications, unlike application-specific add-ins, which run in only one application.

Creating Access Add-Ins

Application-specific Access add-ins are simply Access library databases—databases saved with the MDA extension. You don't need Microsoft Office XP Developer to create an Access add-in; you can create Access add-ins using core Access functionality. An Access add-in contains a special table with registry information, Microsoft Visual Basic for Applications (VBA) code to provide the add-in's functionality, and possibly tables and/or interface objects such as forms. After creating an add-in, if you want to protect its code, you can save it as an MDE file, which contains only compiled VBA pseudocode, which can't be read.

note Technically, the MDA file that's installed as an Access add-in is a library database containing one or more add-ins of various types. However, the term *add-in* is commonly used to refer to the entire library database, as well as to the add-ins it contains.

Depending on your operating system, add-ins are stored in the C:\Documents and Settings*User Name*\Application Data\Microsoft\AddIns folder (for Windows 2000 and Windows XP, replacing *User Name* with your user name) or in C:\Windows\Application Data\Microsoft\Addins (for Windows Me). You install Access add-ins using the Add-In Manager, which is available from the Tools, Add-Ins menu of a regular Access window.

Access add-ins come in three types, with several subtypes, as follows:

- **Wizards.** A series of forms that guide you through creating a new object. A wizard is invoked when a new object of that type is created. You can write table wizards, query wizards, form wizards, report wizards, and control wizards.
- **Builders.** A single form or dialog box that lets you set properties in Design view of forms and reports. You can write Property Builders and Expression Builders. (Builders are listed in the registry as wizards and are sometimes referred to as wizards.)
- **Menu add-ins.** Called from the Tools menu's Add-Ins submenu; not context-specific.

Creating a Simple Add-In

Creating an add-in is a process that requires some creativity (like writing code in general), and thus it can't easily be reduced to a simple set of steps. However, there are certain requirements and limitations and a number of techniques that will help you create a more useful add-in. This section first introduces some of the basic requirements and processes for creating an add-in and then leads you through the process of creating a simple Property Wizard add-in based on some code developed in a regular Access database. Subsequent sections will go into much greater detail about the more technical aspects of add-in creation. You'll need this information for creating your own add-ins.

The first steps in creating an Access add-in are similar for all types of add-ins: You create a new Access database and save it with the MDA extension rather than the default MDB extension, as shown in Figure 21-1. You have to type in the extension, with the Save As Type All Files (*.*) selection selected, as the Save As Type drop-down list doesn't offer an Add-In (MDA) option.

caution If you leave the default Microsoft Access Databases (*.mdb) selection selected and enter the MDA extension, your new database will actually be saved as *Filename*.mda.mdb, and it won't work as an add-in.

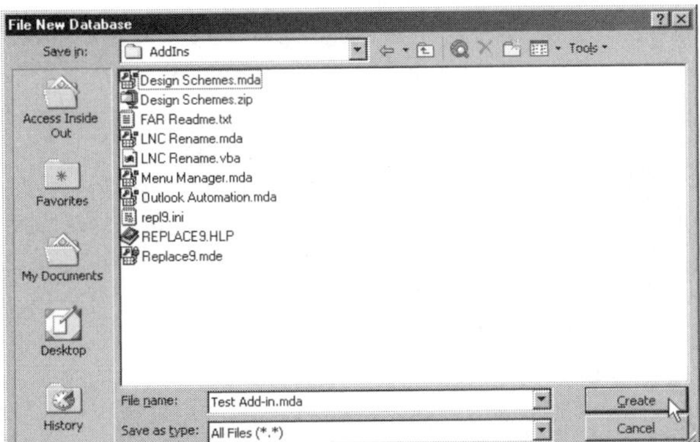

Figure 21-1. You save a new database as an add-in library database, with the MDA extension.

Next you create (or import) the special USysRegInfo system table that stores information to be written to the Windows registry when the add-in is installed. Follow these steps to import a blank USysRegInfo table into a new library database:

1. Choose Tools, Options to open the Options dialog box, and check the System Objects check box on the View tab, as shown in Figure 21-2. Then close the dialog box. (You need to set this option because otherwise the USysRegInfo table won't be visible in the Database window.)

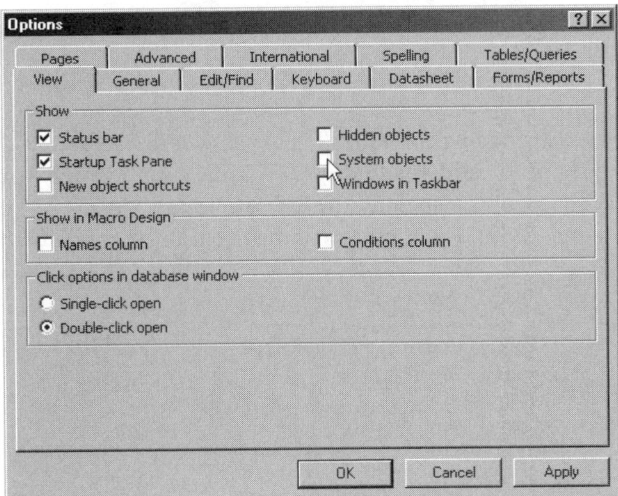

Figure 21-2. Check System Objects on the View tab of the Options dialog box.

2. Choose File, Get External Data, and then click Import to open the Import dialog box. Navigate to the folder in which the Test Access 2002.mdb database is located.

3 Select the Test Access 2002 database, and click Open to open the Import Objects dialog box. Select the USysRegInfo table on the Tables tab, and click OK to import the table into your database.

The USysRegInfo starter table has five rows, with some information filled in. (See Table 21-1 for more details on the meaning of the rows and columns in this table.) You'll need to add specific information for your add-ins and probably more rows—at least if your library database contains more than one add-in. The USysRegInfo table fields are used to create registry entries for the add-in.

Table 21-1. USysRegInfo table fields

Field	Data type	Description
Subkey	Text (255)	The name of the registry subkey where a specific Registry setting is stored. Can be either HKEY_CURRENT_ACCESS_PROFILE or HKEY_LOCAL_MACHINE (plus the path to Office 10).
Type	Number (Long Integer)	The type of entry to create. Can be key (0), string (1), or DWORD (4).
ValName	Text (255)	The name of the registry value.
Value	Text (255)	The value of the registry value.

note Office 10 in the registry corresponds to Office XP in the interface.

The starter USysRegInfo table contains the data shown in Table 21-2. |ACCDIR\ is a reference to the standard Add-Ins folder. If you put your add-ins in another folder (not recommended), you have to enter the full path to the add-in file. For add-ins in the standard folder, only the add-in database name needs to be entered, after the backslash.

Table 21-2. Starter USysRegInfo table

Subkey	Type	ValName	Value
HKEY_CURRENT_ACCESS_PROFILE\	1	Description	
HKEY_CURRENT_ACCESS_PROFILE\	4	Can Edit	1
HKEY_CURRENT_ACCESS_PROFILE\	1	Library	|ACCDIR\
HKEY_CURRENT_ACCESS_PROFILE\	1	Function	
HKEY_CURRENT_ACCESS_PROFILE\	0		

It's generally preferable to use the HKEY_CURRENT_ACCESS_PROFILE key for add-ins because it isn't version-specific; the add-in will be installed in the key for whatever version of Access is in use. If Access user profiles are in use, the add-in's registry keys will be created under that user profile. Otherwise, they'll be created under the HKEY_LOCAL_MACHINE\Software\Microsoft\Office\10.0\Access\ key. If you need to install an add-in for a specific version of Access (say, because it uses a feature not available in other versions), use the HKEY_LOCAL_MACHINE key with the specific version of Access your add-in needs.

Different types of add-ins are stored in different registry keys, so they need different paths in the USysRegInfo table, which correspond to the different keys. Figure 21-3 shows the Registry Editor open to the HKEY_LOCAL_MACHINE_SOFTWARE\Microsoft\Office\10.0\Access\Menu Add-Ins key (where USysRegInfo information is stored when the table specifies the HKEY_CURRENT_ACCESS_PROFILE key, Access user profiles aren't in use, and Office XP is the current version). The Rename &Form Controls menu add-in is selected; this is one of the add-ins included in my LNC Rename add-in, discussed in the section "The LNC Rename Add-In" on page 893. (This add-in renames Access database objects and controls on Access forms and reports according to the Leszynski Naming Convention [LNC].) The Expression and Library keys are filled with information from the USysRegInfo table's Expression and Library columns.

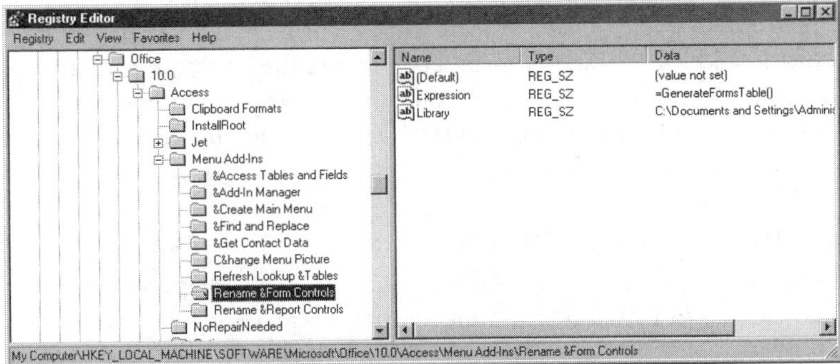

Figure 21-3. The Access Menu Add-Ins entries are shown in the Windows registry.

Wizards and builders are both listed under the various wizard keys in the registry. Notice the LNC Builder and LNC Builder All entries under the Property Wizards key in Figure 21-4.

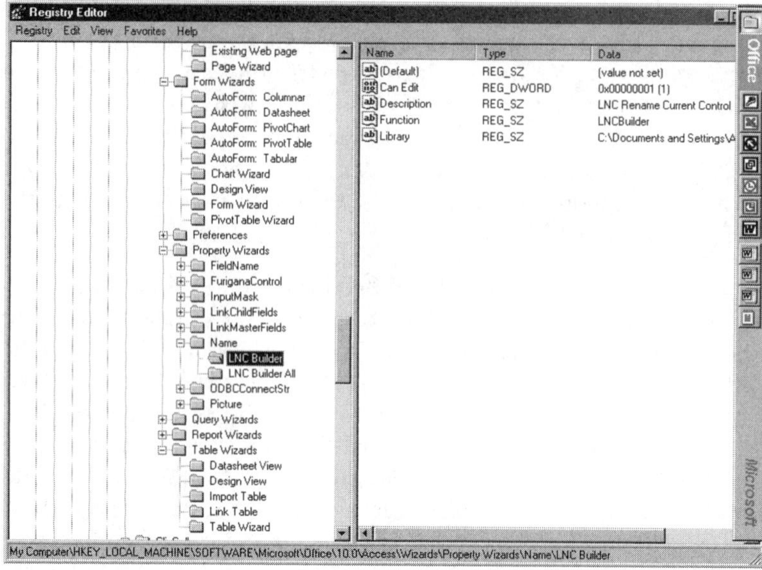

Figure 21-4. Wizards and builders are listed in the Windows registry.

The specific entries needed for each field in the USysRegInfo table will be discussed in the following sections. The requirements differ depending on what type of add-in you're creating. All add-ins need at least three records: one to create the add-in's main subkey, one to add the Library entry, and one to add the Function (or Expression) entry. There are also two optional rows, and you can add even more rows for custom requirements. The five standard USysRegInfo rows are described in Table 21-3, with an explanation of how you need to fill in the rows with specific information for your add-ins.

Table 21-3. Standard USysRegInfo rows

Row number	Type field value	ValName field value	Value field value	Purpose
1	0			Indicates the start of a new add-in.
2	1	Library	|ACCDIR*Add-In Database Name*	|ACCDIR is a placeholder for the standard add-ins folder; you can use a literal path instead. Add-In Database Name is the name and extension of the add-in database.
3	1	Function	*=FunctionName( )*	The name of the add-in's main function.

Chapter 21

Row number	Type field value	ValName field value	Value field value	Purpose
4	1	Description	Add-in description	The text that appears on the Add-Ins menu or in the Choose Builder dialog box.
5	4	Can Edit	0 or 1	Indicates whether the wizard can be invoked for an existing object.

The information that appears in the Add-In Manager dialog box when you install an add-in database comes from fields in the add-in database's properties sheet. The add-in name is the Title field, the description is the Comments field, and the author is the Company field (not the Author field, as you might think). Figure 21-5 shows the LNC Rename add-in's properties sheet, and Figure 21-6 shows the corresponding information for this add-in in the Add-In Manager dialog box.

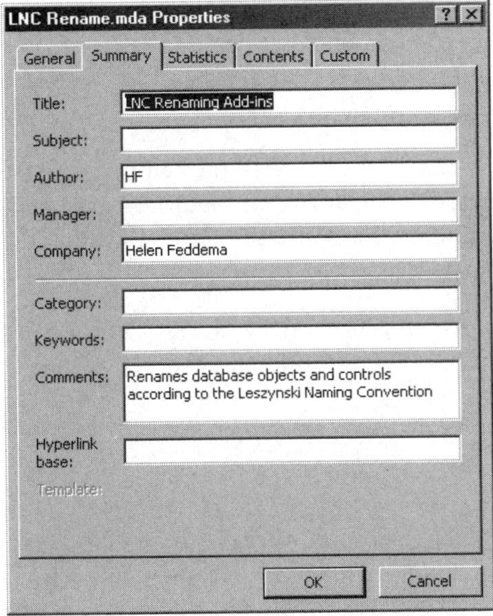

Figure 21-5. Several properties in the LNC Rename add-in database's properties sheet appear when the add-in is selected in the Add-In Manager dialog box.

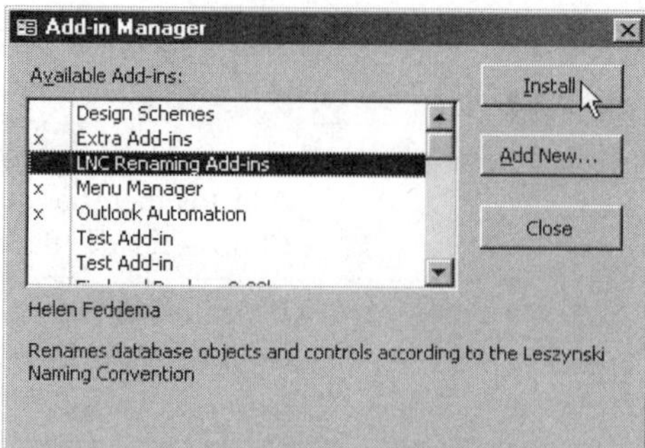

Figure 21-6. Information about the LNC Rename add-in is displayed in the Add-In Manager dialog box.

General Design Considerations

Whether you create a menu add-in, a wizard, or a builder, you need to keep in mind certain considerations while writing the add-in code. When you run an add-in from a regular Access database, the code runs from another database (the add-in library database), and you must take this into account when you reference database objects in code. You can use *CodeDb* to set a reference to the library database and *CurrentDb* to set a reference to the calling database to avoid confusion.

Forms in the add-in library database can be displayed in the calling database (typically as wizard pages). Most add-ins use at least one form, although this isn't a requirement. You can reference tables in the add-in database using the *CodeDb* syntax; these tables are typically used to store standard data needed by the add-in.

Macros and queries shouldn't be used in add-ins. Instead, all of the add-in's functionality should be implemented in public functions that can be run directly from the add-in's modules.

Creating a Simple Wizard

If you find yourself formatting controls, forms, or other database objects in a certain way over and over again and you can't automate the process adequately using any of Access' built-in functionality, this situation calls for an add-in. For example, I like to use locked text box controls to display read-only data (such as AutoNumber fields) or calculated expressions, and I make them light blue, with a flat special effect, to give users a visual cue that they're not standard editable text boxes (which are white, with a sunken special effect).

Similarly, when I place an invisible control on a form or report, I color it yellow, so that I'll know it's an invisible control when I see it in Design view. Changing a standard text box to a locked or an invisible text box requires changing a number of properties and opening the Color Builder, which quickly becomes tedious, so this is a good candidate for creating an add-in.

Tips for Creating Access Wizards

The following tips will help you construct wizards that have a standard Access Wizard look, so users will find them familiar in appearance and easy to use:

- Set the *AutoCenter* property for the forms in your add-in to Yes.
- Turn record selectors off.
- Set scroll bars to Neither.
- Turn navigation buttons off.
- Place the controls used on more than one form in a series of wizard pages in the same position on each form (wizard page).
- Set the *Modal* property for forms to Yes, the *PopUp* property to Yes, and the *BorderStyle* property to Dialog. These settings will ensure that the user can't move to the next page until the current one has been filled in and the Next button has been clicked.

Turning Code into an Add-In

This section describes how to create an add-in database that contains a single add-in, the Lock Wizard (a text box Property Builder, also known as a Control Wizard). You can find this example on the companion CD, in the in the Author Extras section. This add-in needs only a dialog form to let you apply the desired formatting and a few functions to do the formatting.

The first step is to decide what you want the add-in to do: In this case, I needed to write code that would apply one of three sets of properties to a text box (Locked, Invisible, and Unlocked). Because it's easier to debug code in a regular database, when you create an add-in, first write code in a regular Access database to do what you want the add-in to do, and then modify the code as needed until it's working correctly. For this example, I wrote the three functions shown here. (The functions are run from cmdTestControl on frmTest in the Test Access 2002 sample database.)

```
Private Sub cmdTestControl_Click()

   Dim txt As Access.TextBox

   Set txt = Forms![frmEmployees]![txtFirstName]
   'Call NormalControl(txt)
   Call LockControl(txt)
   'Call InvisibleControl(txt)

End Sub
```

(continued)

```
Function LockControl(txt As Access.TextBox)

   txt.Visible = True
   txt.Locked = True
   txt.TabStop = False
   txt.BackColor = vbLightBlue
   txt.BorderStyle = 1
   txt.SpecialEffect = 0

End Function

Function InvisibleControl(txt As Access.TextBox)

   txt.Visible = False
   txt.Locked = False
   txt.TabStop = False
   txt.BackColor = vbYellow
   txt.BorderStyle = 1
   txt.SpecialEffect = 0

End Function

Function NormalControl(txt As Access.TextBox)

   txt.Visible = True
   txt.Locked = False
   txt.TabStop = True
   txt.BackColor = vbWhite
   txt.SpecialEffect = 2

End Function
```

After running each of these functions in turn from the command button on frmEmployees and verifying that each function formats the text box correctly, the next step is to create a new database to use as the library database. You should save this database with the MDA extension in the Add-Ins folder.

Import the starter USysRegInfo table into the library database, as described earlier. Fill in the add-in–specific data for the Control Wizard, as shown in Table 21-4. (Add-in–specific data is indicated by italics in the table.)

Table 21-4. The USysRegInfo table for the Lock Wizard add-in

Subkey	Type	ValName	Value
HKEY_CURRENT_ACCESS_PROFILE *Wizards**Control Wizards**TextBox* *Lock Wizard*	1	Description	*Lock/Unlock Wizard*
HKEY_CURRENT_ACCESS_PROFILE *Wizards**Control Wizards**TextBox* *Lock Wizard*	4	Can Edit	1
HKEY_CURRENT_ACCESS_PROFILE *Wizards**Control Wizards**TextBox* *Lock Wizard*	1	Library	IACCDIR*Lock Wizard.mda*
HKEY_CURRENT_ACCESS_PROFILE *Wizards**Control Wizards**TextBox* *Lock Wizard*	1	Function	*LockWizard*
HKEY_CURRENT_ACCESS_PROFILE *Wizards**Control Wizards**TextBox* *Lock Wizard*	0		

The *LockWizard* function listed on the Function line of the USysRegInfo table is the main function of this add-in; it opens the dialog form that is the add-in's interface. This function uses two standard arguments for a Control Wizard. (See the following sidebar for details.)

Add-In Function Arguments

The main function of a Control Wizard add-in has two required arguments, as follows:

- ***strObjectName.*** Object name (the form or report that contains the control the Wizard acts on).
- ***strCtlName.*** Control name (the control the Wizard acts on).

Property Builders use the same two arguments as Control Wizards, plus one additional argument:

- ***strCurrentValue.*** Current value of the property being modified.

The code module for *LockWizard* declares a number of variables (most of them global variables) in its Declaration section. It also declares some constants for color values that don't have their own named color constants:

```
Option Compare Database
Option Explicit

Dim ctlLabel As Access.Label
Dim ctlTextBox As Access.TextBox
Dim intBackStyle As Integer
Dim intBorderStyle As Integer

'General variables
Global gblnVisible As Boolean
Global gblnLocked As Boolean
Global gblnTabStop As Boolean
Global gfrm As Access.Form

'TextBox variables
Global gintTBSpecialEffect As Integer
Global glngTBBackColor As Long

'Label variables
Global gintLASpecialEffect As Integer
Global gintLATextAlign As Integer
Global glngLABackColor As Long

'Color constants
Public Const vbDarkCyan = 8421376
Public Const vbDarkNavy = 8388608
Public Const vbLightBlue = 16777164
Public Const vbLightGreen = 12639424
Public Const vbLightGrey = 12632256
Public Const vbNavy = 8404992
```

The *LockWizard* function is shown below. (All the variables used in this function are declared in the module's Declarations section.) The *gfrm* global variable is used to reference the active form in the calling database, and the *ctlLabel* and *ctlTextBox* variables are set to the text box with its attached label. (These are the controls whose properties will be changed.) The properties are set in this function, but they won't take effect until the dialog form is closed.

```
Public Function LockWizard(strObjName As String, _
   strCtlName As String)
'Selects a color/special effect scheme for a locked or
'unlocked text box control and its attached label
'Called from a text box's Build dialog box
```

```
On Error GoTo LockWizardError

   DoCmd.OpenForm FormName:="fdlgLockWizard", _
      windowmode:=acDialog
   Set gfrm = Screen.ActiveForm
   Set ctlLabel = gfrm(strCtlName)
   Set ctlTextBox = ctlLabel.Parent
   ctlTextBox.Visible = gblnVisible
   ctlTextBox.Locked = gblnLocked
   ctlTextBox.Enabled = True
   ctlTextBox.TabStop = gblnTabStop
   ctlTextBox.BackColor = glngTBBackColor
   ctlTextBox.BackStyle = 1
   ctlTextBox.SpecialEffect = gintTBSpecialEffect
   ctlTextBox.BorderStyle = intBorderStyle
   ctlLabel.BackStyle = intBackStyle
   ctlLabel.BackColor = glngLABackColor
   ctlLabel.SpecialEffect = gintLASpecialEffect
   ctlLabel.TextAlign = gintLATextAlign

LockWizardExit:
   Exit Function

LockWizardError:
   MsgBox "Error No: " & Err.Number & "; Description: " _
   & Err.Description
   Resume LockWizardExit

End Function
```

All the properties in the *LockWizard* function are set by variables, which were set by the *InitialLockStatus* function, which is called from the dialog form's *Open* event. These properties need to be set so that the function can apply the default properties in case the user closes the dialog box without making a selection.

```
Public Function InitialLockStatus() As Integer
'Sets global variables for Unlocked selection, in case
'no option button is clicked
'Called from Form_Open on fdlgLockWizard

On Error GoTo InitialLockStatusError

   gblnVisible = True
   gblnLocked = True
   gblnTabStop = False
   glngTBBackColor = vbLightBlue
```

(continued)

Chapter 21

```
    gintTBSpecialEffect = 0
    intBackStyle = 0
    glngLABackColor = vbLightGrey
    gintLASpecialEffect = 0
    gintLATextAlign = 3
    intBorderStyle = 1

InitialLockStatusExit:
    Exit Function

InitialLockStatusError:
    MsgBox "Error No: " & Err.Number & "; Description: " _
    & Err.Description
    Resume InitialLockStatusExit

End Function
```


The third and final function in this simple add-in performs the actual formatting changes. The three separate functions that were tested in the regular Access database are used in an *If…ElseIf…End If* statement, with the control variable replaced by global variables that are used to set the text box properties when the dialog form is closed. The *intLockStatus* variable is the value of the option group on the add-in's dialog form.

```
Public Function ChangeLockStatus()
'Applies appropriate properties to selected text box
'Called from fraLockStatus_AfterUpdate on fdlgLockWizard

On Error GoTo ChangeLockStatusError

    Dim intLockStatus As Integer

    Set gfrm = Forms![fdlgLockWizard]
    intLockStatus = gfrm![fraLockStatus]
    Debug.Print "Lock status: " & intLockStatus

    If intLockStatus = 1 Then
       'Locked
       gblnVisible = True
       gblnLocked = True
       gblnTabStop = False
       glngTBBackColor = vbLightBlue
       gintTBSpecialEffect = 0
    ElseIf intLockStatus = 2 Then
```

```
        'Unlocked
        gblnVisible = True
        gblnLocked = False
        gblnTabStop = True
        glngTBBackColor = vbWhite
        gintTBSpecialEffect = 2
    ElseIf intLockStatus = 3 Then
        'Invisible
        gblnVisible = False
        gblnLocked = False
        gblnTabStop = False
        glngTBBackColor = vbYellow
        gintTBSpecialEffect = 0
    End If

ChangeLockStatusExit:
    Exit Function

ChangeLockStatusError:
    MsgBox "Error No: " & Err.Number & "; Description: " _
    & Err.Description
    Resume ChangeLockStatusExit

End Function
```

The final step is to create a form to use as the Property Builder's user interface. I created a small dialog form with an option group for selecting one of the three formatting options. This form is shown in Figure 21-7.

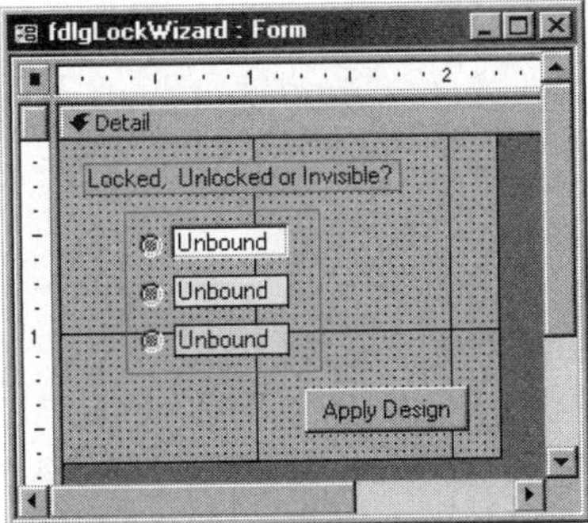

Figure 21-7. The Lock Wizard user interface consists of a simple dialog form.

The code for the dialog form is listed below. Basically, the form events are used to call the code located in the add-in database and to write descriptive text to the unbound text boxes on the form. The event procedures don't handle errors, since all error handling is done in the add-in's functions.

```
Option Compare Database
Option Explicit

Dim ctlTextBox As Access.TextBox
Dim ctlLabel As Access.Label

Private Sub cmdApplyDesign_Click()

   DoCmd.Close acForm, Me.Name, acSaveNo

End Sub

Private Sub Form_Open(Cancel As Integer)

   Me![txtLocked].Value = "Locked"
   Me![txtUnLocked].Value = "Unlocked"
   Me![txtInvisible].Value = "Invisible"

   Call InitialLockStatus

End Sub

Private Sub fraLockStatus_AfterUpdate()

   Call ChangeLockStatus

End Sub
```

tip **Import add-in objects**

You can import the add-in objects from the Lock Wizard Objects.mdb database; it contains the USysRegInfo table, the fdlgLockWizard form, and the basLockWizard code module needed for the add-in. To import these objects, choose File, Get External Data, and click Import.

Putting the Add-In Together

With the USysRegInfo table and the dialog form created and the functions written, all that's left is to enter the add-in's identifying information. To do this, choose File, Database Properties. Enter the add-in's title in the Title field, the author in the Company field (it can be in the Author field too, but the add-in needs it in the Company field), and the description in the Comments field, as shown in Figure 21-8.

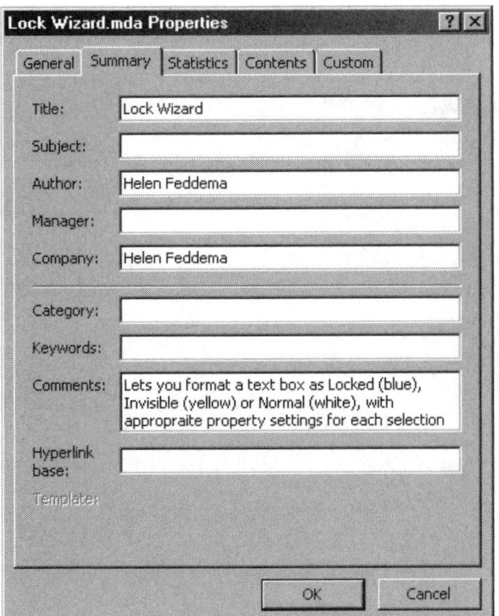

Figure 21-8. Enter the add-in's title, author, and description in its properties sheet.

Open the basLockWizard code module and compile it by selecting Compile from the Debug menu in the Visual Basic Editor. Close the library database after it has compiled successfully.

Finally, you can install and test the add-in. To install this (or any) add-in, follow these steps:

1. Open a regular Access database.
2. Choose Tools, Add-Ins, and click Add-In Manager to open the Add-In Manager dialog box. You should see the Lock Wizard listed as one of the available add-ins.

Troubleshooting

I can't see my add-in in the list of available add-ins in the Add-In Manager dialog box

The most likely reason for this is that the add-in isn't in the standard add-ins folder. You can either move the add-in library database to the standard add-ins folder (C:\Documents and Settings*User Name*\Application Data\Microsoft\AddIns folder for Windows 2000, or C:\Windows\Application Data\Microsoft\Addins for Windows Me) or click the Add button to navigate to its location in another folder.

3. Select the Lock Wizard add-in, and click the Install button, as shown in Figure 21-9. An *X* should appear next to the add-in.

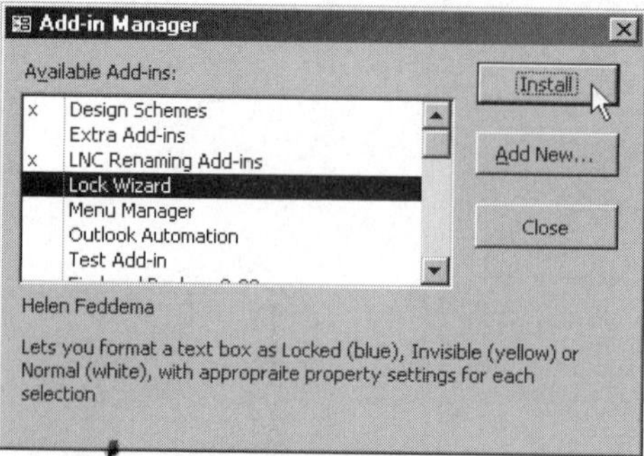

Figure 21-9. Select the add-in, and click the install button to install it in the Add-In Manager dialog box.

4. Click the Close button; the add-in should now be installed.

Chapter 21

To test the add-in, follow these steps:

1. Open a form in Design view, and right-click a text box control.
2. Select Build from the text box's shortcut menu. The Lock Wizard dialog box appears, as shown in Figure 21-10.

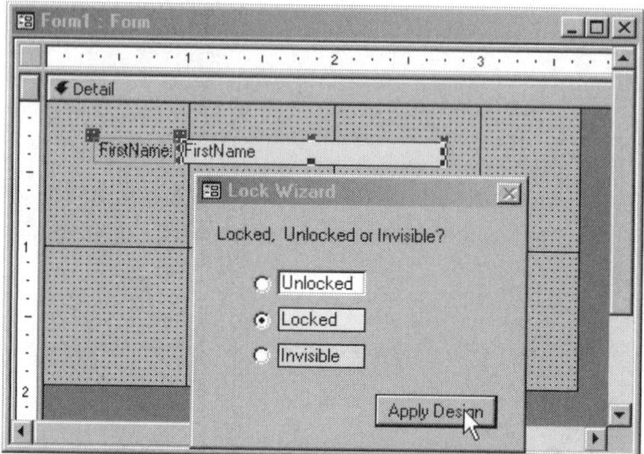

Figure 21-10. Select a formatting option to apply to a text box in the Lock Wizard dialog form.

3. Select the option you want to apply to the control, and click Apply Design.

The text box should now have the appropriate formatting.

Troubleshooting

I get a *This feature is not installed* error message when I try to run the add-in

This none-too-informative error message can result from any number of errors in the add-in's code. Check for problems in the following areas:

- Incorrect syntax (for example, the wrong number or type of arguments) in the main add-in function
- General syntax errors in the add-in code
- Add-in code that isn't compiled

First uninstall the add-in in the Add-In Manager, and close Access. Open the library database, fix any errors, and compile the add-in database. After you reinstall the add-in, it should run properly.

Examining the Text Box Design Wizard

In this section, we'll take an in-depth look at a somewhat more complex add-in. The Extra Add-Ins library database contains two add-ins: a Text Box Control Wizard and a Picture Property Builder.

The Text Box Design Wizard lets you select a design scheme (colors, fonts, and special effects) for a newly inserted text box control to match the color schemes of four of the built-in Access Form Wizard color schemes. I originally wrote this add-in for Access 95; the color schemes have changed in subsequent versions, so some of the schemes in this add-in don't match standard color schemes in Access 2002.

A Control Wizard needs five rows in the USysRegInfo table: the three standard rows, plus a row that contains the add-in's description (the text that appears in the Add-In Manager dialog box) and a Can Edit row where you can specify whether the add-in can be invoked to edit an existing object (in this case, a text box control). If the *Value* property of the CanEdit row is 0, the add-in can be used only with a new control; if it's 1, the add-in can be invoked for an existing control.

The Text Box Design Wizard's rows are listed in Table 21-5. Extra Add-ins.mda is the name of the add-in database containing the sample Text Box Wizard and Picture Picker Property Builder.

Table 21-5. USysRegInfo rows for the Text Box Design Wizard

Subkey	Type	ValName	Value
HKEY_CURRENT_ACCESS_PROFILE *Wizards**Control Wizards**TextBox* *Design Wizard*	0		
HKEY_CURRENT_ACCESS_PROFILE *Wizards**Control Wizards**TextBox* *Design Wizard*	1	Description	*Text Box Design Wizard*
HKEY_CURRENT_ACCESS_PROFILE \Wizards\Control Wizards\TextBox \Design Wizard	4	Can Edit	0
HKEY_CURRENT_ACCESS_PROFILE *Wizards**Control Wizards**TextBox* *Design Wizard*	1	Library	|ACCDIR*Extra Add-ins.mda*
HKEY_CURRENT_ACCESS_PROFILE *Wizards**Control Wizards**TextBox* *Design Wizard*	1	Function	*TextBox DesignWizard*

The italicized text in certain fields is specific to this wizard:

- The Subkey on each row lists the wizard's registry key and subkeys and its name (Design Wizard).
- The Value (in the row with the ValName Description) is the description of the wizard.
- The Can Edit value indicates whether existing text boxes can be edited using the add-in; 1 means they can be edited; 0 means they can't.
- The right side of the Value field (in the row with the Library ValName entry) is the add-in database name (Extra Add-ins.mda). |ACCDIR\ indicates that the library database is located in the default add-ins path (typically C:\Documents and Settings\Administrator\Application Data\Microsoft\AddIns).
- The last row (corresponding to the Function ValName field) is the name of the function that invokes the wizard.

To install the Text Box Design Wizard and the Form Picture Property Builder Wizard, copy the Extra Add-ins.mda database to your add-ins folder, open the Add-In Manager, select Extra Add-Ins from the list of available add-ins, and click the Install button, as shown in Figure 21-11.

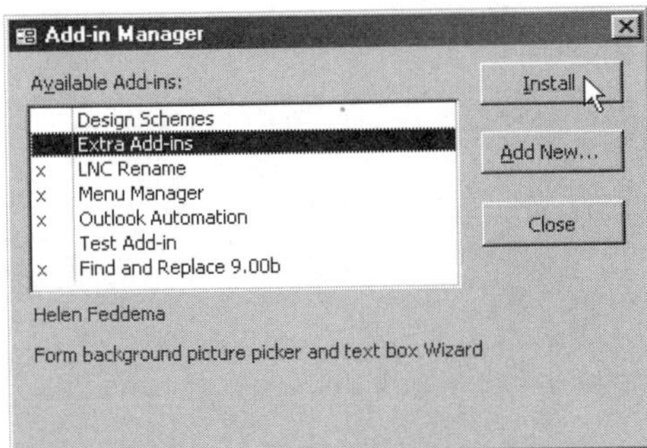

Figure 21-11. You install the Text Box Design Wizard and Form Picture Property Builder using the Add-In Manager dialog box.

See Chapter 15, "Using Add-Ins to Expand Access Functionality," for more details on installing and troubleshooting add-ins.

To use the Text Box Design Wizard, open a form in Design view, and make sure the Wizards button in the Toolbox is selected. Click the Text Box tool, and then click the form to insert a new text box on the form. The Text Box Design Wizard form appears, as shown in Figure 21-12.

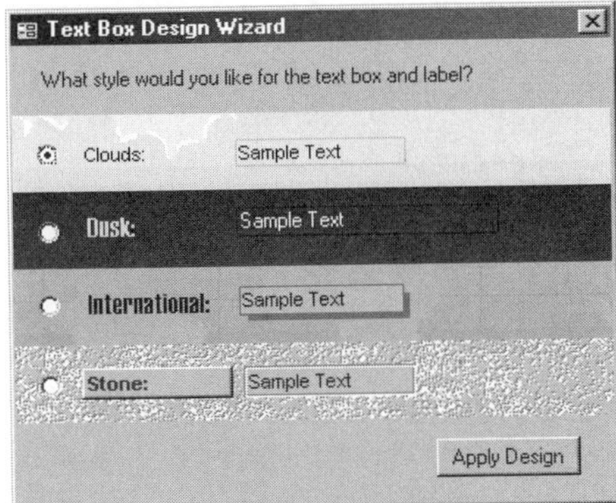

Figure 21-12. The Text Box Design Wizard form offers four design scheme selections.

Each text box design scheme is displayed against the background of the matching form design scheme. (The wizard doesn't change the form's background color.) Selecting the International design scheme applies the appropriate properties to the text box, as shown in Figure 21-13.

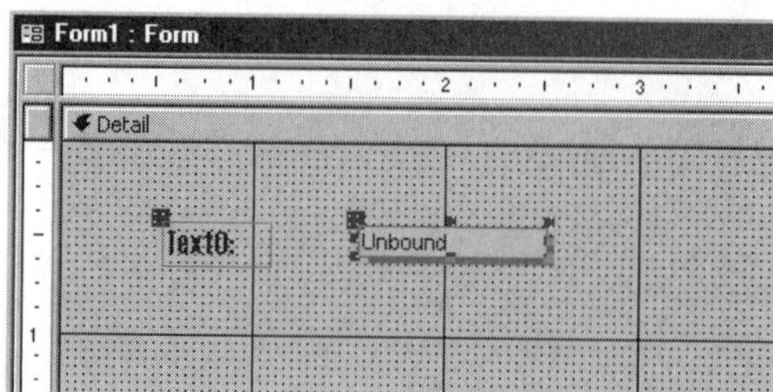

Figure 21-13. A text box formatted with the International design scheme.

VBA Code

The fifth row in Table 21-5 specifies the function to be run when the Text Box Design Wizard is invoked. The *TextBoxDesignWizard* function has the two required arguments for Control Wizards, which represent the form and control. The function opens the wizard form, and the form's *Open* event calls the *InitialColors* function, which saves the default design scheme's values to global variables. These global variables are used in applying the default design scheme to the text box (in case the user simply accepts the default design scheme, thus not triggering the option group's *AfterUpdate* event). If the user selects a design scheme on the form, the option group's *AfterUpdate* event procedure calls the *ChangeDesign* function, which saves the selected design scheme's values to the global variables.

```
Public Function TextBoxDesignWizard(strObjName As String, _
   strCtlName As String) As Variant
'Selects a color/special effect scheme for
'a text box control and its attached label
'The schemes match styles in the Form Wizard.

On Error GoTo TextBoxDesignWizardError

   DoCmd.OpenForm FormName:="fdlgTextBoxDesignWizard", _
   windowmode:=acDialog

   Set frm = Screen.ActiveForm
   Set ctlLabel = frm(strCtlName)
   Set ctlTextBox = ctlLabel.Parent

   'Set the text box design properties.
   With ctlTextBox
      .BackStyle = intTBBackStyle
      .BackColor = lngTBBackColor
      .SpecialEffect = intTBSpecialEffect
      .BorderStyle = intTBBorderStyle
```

```
        .BorderColor = lngTBBorderColor
        .BorderWidth = intTBBorderWidth
        .ForeColor = lngTBForeColor
        .FontName = strTBFontName
        .FontSize = lngTBFontSize
        .FontWeight = intTBFontWeight
        .FontItalic = blnTBFontItalic
        .FontUnderline = blnTBFontUnderline
        .TextAlign = intTBTextAlign
        .Height = intTBHeight
        .Width = 1440
    End With

    'Set the label design properties.
    With ctlLabel
        .BackStyle = intLBBackStyle
        .BackColor = lngLBBackColor
        .SpecialEffect = intLBSpecialEffect
        .BorderStyle = intLBBorderStyle
        .BorderColor = lngLBBorderColor
        .BorderWidth = intLBBorderWidth
        .ForeColor = lngLBForeColor
        .FontName = strLBFontName
        .FontSize = lngLBFontSize
        .FontWeight = intLBFontWeight
        .FontItalic = blnLBFontItalic
        .FontUnderline = blnLBFontUnderline
        .TextAlign = intLBTextAlign
        .Height = intLBHeight
        .Width = 800
    End With

TextBoxDesignWizardExit:
    Exit Function

TextBoxDesignWizardError:
    MsgBox "Error No:  " & Err.Number & "; error message:  " _
    & Err.Description
    Resume TextBoxDesignWizardExit

End Function
```

When the form is closed, the selected design scheme is applied to the text box using the global variables set by either the *InitialColors* function or the *ChangeDesign* function. These functions are shown below.

```
Public Function InitialColors() As Integer

On Error GoTo InitialColorsError

   Set frm = Forms![fdlgTextBoxDesignWizard]
   Set ctlTextBox = frm![txtClouds]
   Set ctlLabel = frm![lblClouds]

   intTBBackStyle = ctlTextBox.BackStyle
   lngTBBackColor = ctlTextBox.BackColor
   intTBSpecialEffect = ctlTextBox.SpecialEffect
   intTBBorderStyle = ctlTextBox.BorderStyle
   lngTBBorderColor = ctlTextBox.BorderColor
   intTBBorderWidth = ctlTextBox.BorderWidth
   lngTBForeColor = ctlTextBox.ForeColor
   strTBFontName = ctlTextBox.FontName
   lngTBFontSize = ctlTextBox.FontSize
   intTBFontWeight = ctlTextBox.FontWeight
   blnTBFontItalic = ctlTextBox.FontItalic
   blnTBFontUnderline = ctlTextBox.FontUnderline
   intTBTextAlign = ctlTextBox.TextAlign
   intTBHeight = 228
   intLBBackStyle = ctlLabel.BackStyle
   lngLBBackColor = ctlLabel.BackColor
   intLBSpecialEffect = ctlLabel.SpecialEffect
   intLBBorderStyle = ctlLabel.BorderStyle
   lngLBBorderColor = ctlLabel.BorderColor
   intLBBorderWidth = ctlLabel.BorderWidth
   lngLBForeColor = ctlLabel.ForeColor
   strLBFontName = ctlLabel.FontName
   lngLBFontSize = ctlLabel.FontSize
   intLBFontWeight = ctlLabel.FontWeight
   blnLBFontItalic = ctlLabel.FontItalic
   blnLBFontUnderline = ctlLabel.FontUnderline
   intLBTextAlign = ctlLabel.TextAlign
   intLBHeight = 240

InitialColorsExit:
   Exit Function

InitialColorsError:
   MsgBox "Error No: " & Err.Number & "; Description: " _
   & Err.Description
   Resume InitialColorsExit

End Function
```

```
Public Function ChangeDesign()

On Error GoTo ChangeDesignError

   Dim intDesign As Integer

   Set frm = Forms![fdlgTextBoxDesignWizard]
   intDesign = frm![grpPicture]

   Select Case intDesign

      Case 1
         Set ctlTextBox = frm![txtClouds]
         Set ctlLabel = frm![lblClouds]
         intTBBackStyle = ctlTextBox.BackStyle
         lngTBBackColor = ctlTextBox.BackColor
         intTBSpecialEffect = ctlTextBox.SpecialEffect
         intTBBorderStyle = ctlTextBox.BorderStyle
         lngTBBorderColor = ctlTextBox.BorderColor
         intTBBorderWidth = ctlTextBox.BorderWidth
         lngTBForeColor = ctlTextBox.ForeColor
         strTBFontName = ctlTextBox.FontName
         lngTBFontSize = ctlTextBox.FontSize
         intTBFontWeight = ctlTextBox.FontWeight
         blnTBFontItalic = ctlTextBox.FontItalic
         blnTBFontUnderline = ctlTextBox.FontUnderline
         intTBTextAlign = ctlTextBox.TextAlign
         intTBHeight = 228
         intLBBackStyle = ctlLabel.BackStyle
         lngLBBackColor = ctlLabel.BackColor
         intLBSpecialEffect = ctlLabel.SpecialEffect
         intLBBorderStyle = ctlLabel.BorderStyle
         lngLBBorderColor = ctlLabel.BorderColor
         intLBBorderWidth = ctlLabel.BorderWidth
         lngLBForeColor = ctlLabel.ForeColor
         strLBFontName = ctlLabel.FontName
         lngLBFontSize = ctlLabel.FontSize
         intLBFontWeight = ctlLabel.FontWeight
         blnLBFontItalic = ctlLabel.FontItalic
         blnLBFontUnderline = ctlLabel.FontUnderline
         intLBTextAlign = ctlLabel.TextAlign
         intLBHeight = 240

      Case 2
         Set ctlTextBox = frm![txtDusk]
         Set ctlLabel = frm![lblDusk]
         intTBBackStyle = ctlTextBox.BackStyle
         lngTBBackColor = ctlTextBox.BackColor
         intTBSpecialEffect = ctlTextBox.SpecialEffect
```

(continued)

```
        intTBBorderStyle = ctlTextBox.BorderStyle
        lngTBBorderColor = ctlTextBox.BorderColor
        intTBBorderWidth = ctlTextBox.BorderWidth
        lngTBForeColor = ctlTextBox.ForeColor
        strTBFontName = ctlTextBox.FontName
        lngTBFontSize = ctlTextBox.FontSize
        intTBFontWeight = ctlTextBox.FontWeight
        blnTBFontItalic = ctlTextBox.FontItalic
        blnTBFontUnderline = ctlTextBox.FontUnderline
        intTBTextAlign = ctlTextBox.TextAlign
        intTBHeight = 228
        intLBBackStyle = ctlLabel.BackStyle
        lngLBBackColor = ctlLabel.BackColor
        intLBSpecialEffect = ctlLabel.SpecialEffect
        intLBBorderStyle = ctlLabel.BorderStyle
        lngLBBorderColor = ctlLabel.BorderColor
        intLBBorderWidth = ctlLabel.BorderWidth
        lngLBForeColor = ctlLabel.ForeColor
        strLBFontName = ctlLabel.FontName
        lngLBFontSize = ctlLabel.FontSize
        intLBFontWeight = ctlLabel.FontWeight
        blnLBFontItalic = ctlLabel.FontItalic
        blnLBFontUnderline = ctlLabel.FontUnderline
        intLBTextAlign = ctlLabel.TextAlign
        intLBHeight = 324

    Case 3
        Set ctlTextBox = frm![txtInternational]
        Set ctlLabel = frm![lblInternational]
        intTBBackStyle = ctlTextBox.BackStyle
        lngTBBackColor = ctlTextBox.BackColor
        intTBSpecialEffect = ctlTextBox.SpecialEffect
        intTBBorderStyle = ctlTextBox.BorderStyle
        lngTBBorderColor = ctlTextBox.BorderColor
        intTBBorderWidth = ctlTextBox.BorderWidth
        lngTBForeColor = ctlTextBox.ForeColor
        strTBFontName = ctlTextBox.FontName
        lngTBFontSize = ctlTextBox.FontSize
        intTBFontWeight = ctlTextBox.FontWeight
        blnTBFontItalic = ctlTextBox.FontItalic
        blnTBFontUnderline = ctlTextBox.FontUnderline
        intTBTextAlign = ctlTextBox.TextAlign
        intTBHeight = 264
        intLBBackStyle = ctlLabel.BackStyle
        lngLBBackColor = ctlLabel.BackColor
        intLBSpecialEffect = ctlLabel.SpecialEffect
        intLBBorderStyle = ctlLabel.BorderStyle
        lngLBBorderColor = ctlLabel.BorderColor
        intLBBorderWidth = ctlLabel.BorderWidth
        lngLBForeColor = ctlLabel.ForeColor
```

```
        strLBFontName = ctlLabel.FontName
        lngLBFontSize = ctlLabel.FontSize
        intLBFontWeight = ctlLabel.FontWeight
        blnLBFontItalic = ctlLabel.FontItalic
        blnLBFontUnderline = ctlLabel.FontUnderline
        intLBTextAlign = ctlLabel.TextAlign
        intLBHeight = 324

      Case 4
        Set ctlTextBox = frm![txtStone]
        Set ctlLabel = frm![lblStone]
        intTBBackStyle = ctlTextBox.BackStyle
        lngTBBackColor = ctlTextBox.BackColor
        intTBSpecialEffect = ctlTextBox.SpecialEffect
        intTBBorderStyle = ctlTextBox.BorderStyle
        lngTBBorderColor = ctlTextBox.BorderColor
        intTBBorderWidth = ctlTextBox.BorderWidth
        lngTBForeColor = ctlTextBox.ForeColor
        strTBFontName = ctlTextBox.FontName
        lngTBFontSize = ctlTextBox.FontSize
        intTBFontWeight = ctlTextBox.FontWeight
        blnTBFontItalic = ctlTextBox.FontItalic
        blnTBFontUnderline = ctlTextBox.FontUnderline
        intTBTextAlign = ctlTextBox.TextAlign
        intTBHeight = 240
        intLBBackStyle = ctlLabel.BackStyle
        lngLBBackColor = ctlLabel.BackColor
        intLBSpecialEffect = ctlLabel.SpecialEffect
        intLBBorderStyle = ctlLabel.BorderStyle
        lngLBBorderColor = ctlLabel.BorderColor
        intLBBorderWidth = ctlLabel.BorderWidth
        lngLBForeColor = ctlLabel.ForeColor
        strLBFontName = ctlLabel.FontName
        lngLBFontSize = ctlLabel.FontSize
        intLBFontWeight = ctlLabel.FontWeight
        blnLBFontItalic = ctlLabel.FontItalic
        blnLBFontUnderline = ctlLabel.FontUnderline
        intLBTextAlign = ctlLabel.TextAlign
        intLBHeight = 240

   End Select

ChangeDesignExit:
   Exit Function

ChangeDesignError:
   MsgBox "Error No: " & Err.Number & "; Description: " _
   & Err.Description
   Resume ChangeDesignExit

End Function
```

Both functions use a set of global variables, which are declared in the code module's Declarations section.

Creating the Picture Picker Property Builder

The Picture Picker Property Builder lets you select an image file to use as a form background picture. Unlike with the built-in MS Picture Builder, you don't have to hunt for the image in the file system, and you can see the image before selecting it. The USysRegInfo table records needed to install this builder are listed in Table 21-6.

Table 21-6. USysRegInfo rows for the Picture Picker Property Builder

Subkey	Type	ValName	Value
HKEY_CURRENT_ACCESS_PROFILE \Wizards\Property Wizards\Picture \Picture Picker	0		
HKEY_CURRENT_ACCESS_PROFILE \Wizards\Property Wizards\Picture \Picture Picker	1	Description	*Picture Picker*
HKEY_CURRENT_ACCESS_PROFILE \Wizards\Property Wizards\Picture \Picture Picker	4	Can Edit	1
HKEY_CURRENT_ACCESS_PROFILE \Wizards\Property Wizards\Picture \Picture Picker	1	Library	|ACCDIR*Extra Add-ins.mda*
HKEY_CURRENT_ACCESS_PROFILE \Wizards\Property Wizards\Picture \Picture Picker	1	Function	*PicturePicker*

You select the Picture Picker by clicking the Build button next to the *Picture* property of a form's properties sheet. Because the *Picture* property has a built-in Property Builder, you'll see a Choose Builder dialog box (shown in Figure 21-14).

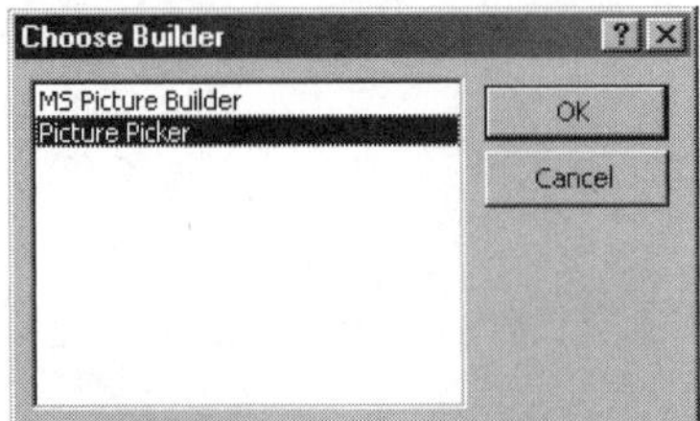

Figure 21-14. The Choose Builder dialog box lets you select a builder.

Select the Picture Picker item to open the wizard form, as shown in Figure 21-15.

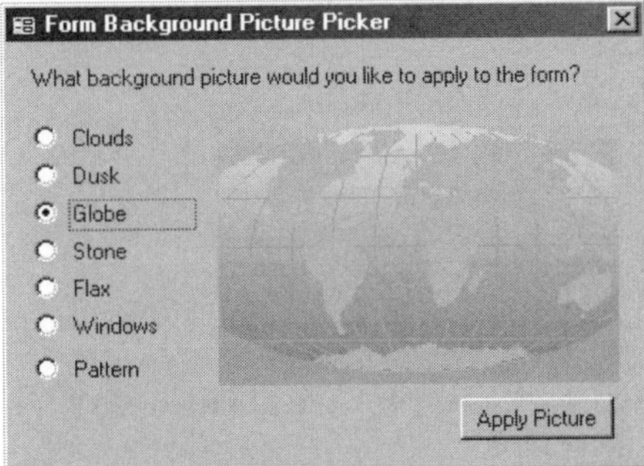

Figure 21-15. The Picture Picker wizard form gives you a choice of background images for a form.

> **note** Some of the background images might not be available in Office XP; they were default selections in Office 95. If you want to substitute your own selections, just modify the image names in the *Select Case intPicture* structure in the *PicturePicker* function.

Figure 21-16 shows a new form with the Globe background image applied using the Picture Picker Property Builder.

Figure 21-16. A form shows the Globe background image.

VBA Code

The Picture Picker Property Builder, like the Text Box Design Wizard, uses a set of global variables. Its main function is the *PicturePicker* function, which has three required arguments; the form name, the control name, and the current property value. The function initializes the *strPicture* global variable with the current value of the *Picture* property and then opens the wizard form. When the user selects an image in the wizard, the form's *Picture* property is stored in the *strPicture* variable and then the form's picture is set to the picture value stored in the variable. The *PicturePicker* function is shown below.

```
Public Function PicturePicker(strFormName As String, _
strCtlName As String, strCurrentValue As String) As Variant
'Selects a background picture for a form

On Error GoTo PicturePickerError

   strPicture = strCurrentValue
   DoCmd.OpenForm FormName:="fdlgPicturePicker", windowmode:=acDialog
   PicturePicker = strPicture

PicturePickerExit:
   Exit Function

PicturePickerError:
   MsgBox "Error No:  " & Err.Number & "; error message:  " _
   & Err.Description
   Resume PicturePickerExit

End Function

Public Function ChangePicture() As String

On Error GoTo ChangePictureError

   Dim strWinDir As String
   Dim strBitmapsDir As String
   Dim intPicture As Integer
   Dim strPicture As String
   Dim ctlPicture As Control
   Dim objWord As Object

   Set objWord = CreateObject("Word.Application")
   Set frm = Screen.ActiveForm
   intPicture = frm![grpPicture]
   Set ctlPicture = frm![imgBackground]

   'Get Windows directory from the registry.
   strWinDir = objWord.System.PrivateProfileString("", _
     "HKEY_LOCAL_MACHINE\SOFTWARE\Microsoft\Windows\CurrentVersion\Setup", _
     "WinDir") & "\"

   'Get Access directory from the SysCmd function.
   strBitmapsDir = SysCmd(acSysCmdAccessDir) & _
   "Bitmaps\Styles\"
```

```
    Select Case intPicture

        Case 1
            strPicture = strBitmapsDir & "Clouds.wmf"

        Case 2
            strPicture = strBitmapsDir & "Sea_dusk.wmf"

        Case 3
            strPicture = strBitmapsDir & "Globe.wmf"

        Case 4
            strPicture = strBitmapsDir & "Stone.bmp"

        Case 5
            strPicture = strBitmapsDir & "Flax.bmp"

        Case 6
            strPicture = strWinDir & "Setup.bmp"

        Case 7
            strPicture = strBitmapsDir & "Pattern.bmp"

    End Select

    ctlPicture.Picture = strPicture
    ChangePicture = strPicture

ChangePictureExit:
    Exit Function

ChangePictureError:
    MsgBox "Error No: " & Err.Number & "; Description: " _
    & Err.Description
    Resume ChangePictureExit

End Function
```

The LNC Rename Add-In

The LNC Rename add-in (a library database containing several menu add-ins and property builders) was a much more ambitious project than the three small add-ins discussed earlier. This add-in applies the Leszynski Naming Convention (LNC) to database objects and controls on forms and reports and corrects all references to renamed database objects. An excellent Access add-in named Find And Replace (FAR) is already available. The FAR add-in does find-and-replace in properties, SQL statements, and other places where references might need to be changed, as well as in VBA code. To avoid extra work (and with the permission of that add-in's author, Rick Fisher), my LNC Rename add-in calls certain functions in the FAR add-in to do the work of fixing references to database objects with changed names.

InsideOut

An Access 2000 add-in will work with both Access 2000 and Access 2002 databases, whereas an Access 2002 add-in (that is, an MDA database created as an Access 2002 database) will work only with Access 2002 databases. Therefore, so that the same add-in can be used with both Access 2000 and Access 2002, I recommend creating the MDA database as an Access 2000 database. (To do this, choose Tools, Options, and select Access 2000 as the Default File Format on the Advanced tab of the Options dialog box before creating the database).

The LNC Rename add-in includes three menu add-ins for renaming database objects, form controls, and report controls, as well as two property builders, one for renaming the current control and one for renaming all controls on the current form or report. The USysRegInfo table rows needed for these add-ins are shown in Table 21-7.

Table 21-7. USysRegInfo rows for the LNC Rename add-in

Subkey	Type	ValName	Value
HKEY_CURRENT_ACCESS_PROFILE Menu Add-ins\Rename &Form Controls	0		
HKEY_CURRENT_ACCESS_PROFILE \Menu Add-ins\Rename &Form Controls	1	Library	lACCDIR\LNC Rename.mda
HKEY_CURRENT_ACCESS_PROFILE \Menu Add-ins\Rename &Form Controls	1	Expression	=GenerateForms Table( )
HKEY_CURRENT_ACCESS_PROFILE \Menu Add-ins\Rename &Report Controls	0		
HKEY_CURRENT_ACCESS_PROFILE \Menu Add-ins\Rename &Report Controls	1	Library	lACCDIR\LNC Rename.mda
HKEY_CURRENT_ACCESS_PROFILE \Menu Add-ins\Rename &Report Controls	1	Expression	=GenerateReports Table( )
HKEY_CURRENT_ACCESS_PROFILE \Menu Add-ins\Rename Database &Objects	0		

Subkey	Type	ValName	Value
HKEY_CURRENT_ACCESS_PROFILE \Menu Add-ins\Rename Database &Objects	1	Library	lACCDIR\LNC Rename.mda
HKEY_CURRENT_ACCESS_PROFILE \MenuAdd-ins\Rename Database &Objects	1	Expression	=Rename DatabaseObjects( )
HKEY_CURRENT_ACCESS_PROFILE \Wizards\Property Wizards\Name\ LNC Builder	0		
HKEY_CURRENT_ACCESS_PROFILE \Wizards\Property Wizards\Name\ LNC Builder	1	Description	LNC Rename Current Control
HKEY_CURRENT_ACCESS_PROFILE \Wizards\Property Wizards\Name \LNC Builder	4	Can Edit	1
HKEY_CURRENT_ACCESS_PROFILE \Wizards\Property Wizards\Name \LNC Builder	1	Library	lACCDIR\LNC Rename.mda
HKEY_CURRENT_ACCESS_PROFILE \Wizards\Property Wizards\Name \LNC Builder	1	Function	LNCBuilder
HKEY_CURRENT_ACCESS_PROFILE \Wizards\Property Wizards\Name \LNC Builder All	0		
HKEY_CURRENT_ACCESS_PROFILE \Wizards\Property Wizards\Name \LNC Builder All	1	Description	LNC Rename All Controls
HKEY_CURRENT_ACCESS_PROFILE \Wizards\Property Wizards\Name \LNC Builder All	4	Can Edit	1
HKEY_CURRENT_ACCESS_PROFILE \Wizards\Property Wizards\Name \LNC Builder All	1	Library	lACCDIR\LNC Rename.mda
HKEY_CURRENT_ACCESS_PROFILE \Wizards\Property Wizards\Name \LNC Builder All	1	Function	LNCBuilderAll

Figure 21-17 shows the Add-Ins menu with the three LNC Rename menu add-ins.

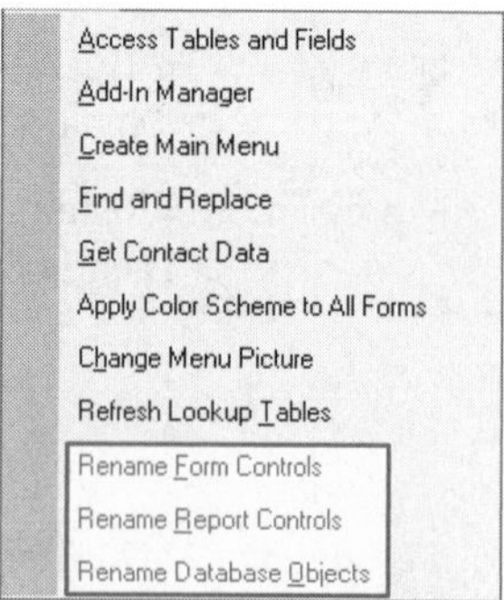

Figure 21-17. The Add-Ins menu in an Access database lists the three LNC Rename menu add-ins.

A brief description of these add-ins follows; for a more detailed discussion of how to use the LNC Rename add-in to rename database objects, see Chapter 15, "Using Add-Ins to Expand Access Functionality."

Rename Database Objects Menu Add-In

The Rename Database Objects menu add-in renames top-level database objects: tables, queries, forms, reports, macros, and modules. It uses an option group on a form for selecting one type of database object to rename rather than renaming all database objects in one pass. The first reason for this is that sometimes (usually, in fact) it isn't necessary to rename all types of database objects. You might have only one macro, AutoKeys, and a few modules that already have the *bas* tag. In that case, you don't need to process macros or modules.

note You must have the Find And Replace add-in installed before you can use the Rename Database Objects menu add-in. See Chapter 15, "Using Add-Ins to Expand Functionality" for instruction on installing this add-in.

Another reason for selecting database object types for separate processing is that it's helpful to break up the renaming task into segments, especially if you're renaming database objects in a large database. The process of renaming objects can be mind numbing. Taking a break between object types can help clear your mind.

Finally, processing each type of database object separately allows the use of different criteria for each type of object that's renamed. Access creates temporary filters and other objects behind the scenes, which should be screened out of the list of objects to be renamed. (See Figure 21-18, which shows some of these objects as they appear in the MSysObjects system table.)

MSysObjects : Table

Name	Owner	ParentId
Sales by Employee		-2147483645
Sales by Event Type		-2147483645
~sq_cEvents~sq_cEmployeeID		251658241
~sq_cEvents~sq_cEventTypeID		251658241
~sq_cFee Schedules~sq_cEventID		251658241
~sq_cPayments~sq_cPaymentMethodID		251658241
~sq_cRegistration~sq_cEmployeeID		251658241
~sq_cRegistration~sq_cEventID		251658241
~sq_cRegistration~sq_cFeeScheduleID		251658241
~sq_fAttendees		251658241
~sq_fAttendees Subform		251658241
~sq_fEmployees		251658241
~sq_fEvent Fee Schedule Subform		251658241
~sq_fEvent Types		251658241
~sq_fEvents		251658241
~sq_fEvents Subform		251658241
~sq_fFee Schedules		251658241
~sq_fMy Company Information		251658241
~sq_fPayment Methods		251658241
~sq_fPayments		251658241

Record: 1 of 92

Figure 21-18. Temporary objects are listed in the MSysObjects table.

Also, some database objects might already have appropriate tags. They should also be excluded from the list of objects to rename.

Figure 21-19 shows a diagram of the functions called and forms opened by the Rename Database Objects menu add-in.

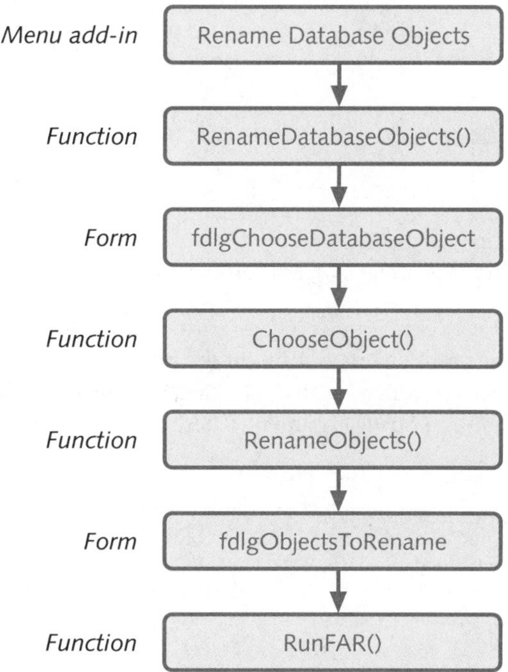

Figure 21-19. The Rename Database Objects menu add-in uses various functions and forms.

Chapter 21

When you select the Rename Database Objects add-in, it calls the *RenameDatabase-Objects* function, which opens the fdlgChooseDatabaseObject wizard form.

```
Public Function RenameDatabaseObjects()
'Called from USysRegInfo (menu add-in)
On Error GoTo RenameDatabaseObjectsError

   strForm = "fdlgChooseDatabaseObject"
   DoCmd.OpenForm FormName:=strForm, view:=acNormal, _
   windowmode:=acDialog

RenameDatabaseObjectsExit:
   Exit Function
RenameDatabaseObjectsError:
   MsgBox "Error No: " & Err.Number & "; Description: " _
   & Err.Description
   Resume RenameDatabaseObjectsExit

End Function
```

The wizard form for renaming database objects is shown in Figure 21-20. This form lets the user select the type of database object to rename (only one at a time, for the reasons discussed earlier).

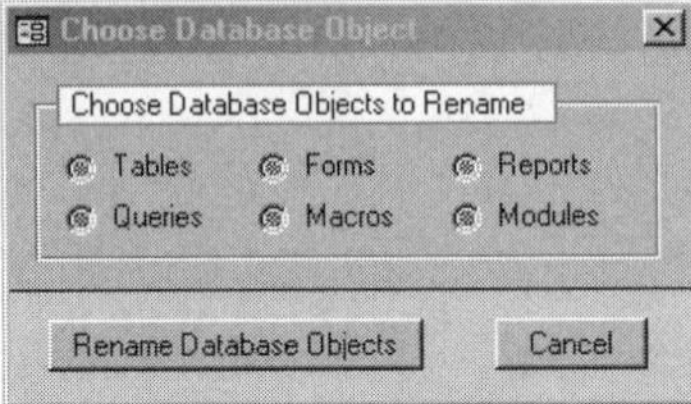

Figure 21-20. The Choose Database Object wizard form lets you select the type of database object to rename.

The *Click* event procedure of the cmdRename button on the fdlgChooseDatabaseObject form calls the *ChooseObject* function, which in turn calls the *RenameObjects* function with the appropriate object name as a *String* argument. These functions are shown below.

```
Public Function ChooseObject()
'Called from cmdRename on fdlgChooseDatabaseObject

On Error GoTo ChooseObjectError

   Dim intChoice As Integer

   intChoice = _
   Nz(Forms![fdlgChooseDatabaseObject]![fraChooseDBObject])
```

```
  Select Case intChoice

     Case 1
        Call RenameObjects("Table")
        Exit Function
     Case 2
        Call RenameObjects("Query")
        Exit Function
     Case 3
        Call RenameObjects("Form")
        Exit Function
     Case 4
        Call RenameObjects("Report")
        Exit Function
     Case 5
        Call RenameObjects("Macro")
        Exit Function
     Case 6
        Call RenameObjects("Module")
        Exit Function
     Case Else
        MsgBox "Please select an option"
        Exit Function
  End Select
  DoCmd.Close

ChooseObjectExit:
  Exit Function

ChooseObjectError:
  MsgBox "Error No: " & Err.Number & "; Description: " _
  & Err.Description
  Resume ChooseObjectExit

End Function

Public Function RenameObjects(strObjectType)
'Called from ChooseObjects function in this module

On Error GoTo RenameObjectsError

  Dim strCallingSystemTable As String
  Dim strSystemTable As String
  Dim strChooseForm As String
  Dim strChooseObject As String

  strCallingSystemTable = "MSysObjects"
  strSystemTable = "zLNCtblSysObjects"
  strObjectsTable = "zLNCtblObjectsToRename"
```

(continued)

```
strForm = "fdlgObjectsToRename"
strSubform = "fsubObjectsToRename"
strChooseForm = "fdlgChooseDatabaseObject"
strCodeDB = CodeDb.Name
strCallingDB = CurrentDb.Name
strQuery = "zLNCqappCheck" & strObjectType
strChooseObject = "fdlgChooseDatabaseObject"

DoCmd.SetWarnings False

'Delete old tables.
ClearCodeSystemTable
ClearCodeObjectsTable
ClearCurrentSystemTable
ClearCurrentObjectsTable

'Create system objects table in calling database.
strSQL = "CREATE TABLE " & strSystemTable & " _
          (Name TEXT (255), Type INTEGER);"
DoCmd.RunSQL strSQL

'Fill system table from MSysObjects table.
strSQL = "INSERT INTO " & strSystemTable & _
    "(Name, Type) SELECT MSysObjects.Name, " & _
    "MSysObjects.Type FROM MSysObjects;"
DoCmd.RunSQL strSQL

'Copy filled system table to code database.
DoCmd.CopyObject strCodeDB, , acTable, strSystemTable

'Generate table of objects to rename in calling database.
strSQL = "CREATE TABLE " & strObjectsTable & _
   "(ObjectName TEXT (100), NewName TEXT (100), Use YESNO);"
DoCmd.SetWarnings False
DoCmd.RunSQL strSQL

'Copy blank objects table in calling
'database to code database
'so that it will be available as the form's record source.
DoCmd.CopyObject strCodeDB, , acTable, strObjectsTable

'Run query to append rows from system table to objects table
'in code database.
DoCmd.OpenQuery strQuery

'Count number of objects to rename.
Set dbs = CodeDb
Set rst = dbs.OpenRecordset(strObjectsTable)
intCount = rst.RecordCount
rst.Close
```

```
    If intCount = 0 Then
       MsgBox "No " & Plural(strObjectType) & " to rename"
       DoCmd.Close acForm, strChooseForm
       Call RenameDatabaseObjects
    Else
       'Open dialog box where user can select objects to
          'rename, and modify the suggested name if desired.
       DoCmd.OpenForm strSubform, acDesign
       Set frmSub = Forms(strSubform)
       frmSub![lblObjectName].Caption = "Old " & _
          strObjectType & " Name"
       frmSub![lblNewName].Caption = "New " & _
          strObjectType & " Name"
       DoCmd.Close acForm, frmSub.Name, acSaveYes
       DoCmd.OpenForm strForm, acDesign
       Set frm = Forms(strForm)
       frm.Caption = Plural(strObjectType) & " to Rename"
       frm![cmdRename].Caption = "Rename Checked " & _
         Plural(strObjectType)
       DoCmd.OpenForm FormName:=strForm, _
         view:=acNormal, windowmode:=acDialog
    End If

RenameObjectsExit:
    Exit Function

RenameObjectsError:
    MsgBox "Error No: " & Err.Number & "; Description: " & _
       Err.Description
    'Delete or clear old tables
    ClearCodeSystemTable
    ClearCodeObjectsTable
    ClearCurrentSystemTable
    ClearCurrentObjectsTable
    Resume RenameObjectsExit

End Function
```

The *RenameObjects* function clears old tables of object names and creates new ones in the calling database, filling them from the MSysObjects table in the calling database. After the tables have been created, they're copied to the code database so that they can be used as record sources for the next wizard form to be displayed. Finally, the fdlgObjectsToRename form is opened, with its subform bound to the table of objects just created. The form's caption (and the command button's caption) are set to the appropriate form type, so the same generic form can be used for all types of database objects. Figure 21-21 shows the fdlgObjectsToRename form as it appears if the user has selected Forms To Rename on the fdlgChooseDatabaseObject form.

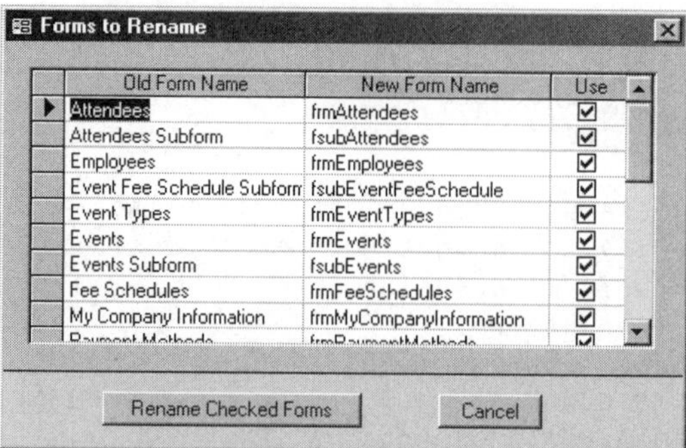

Figure 21-21. The Forms To Rename dialog box suggests new names using LNC tags.

This form displays the suggested new names for the database objects, with a Use column for unchecking selected forms. When cmdRename on the form is clicked, its *Click* event procedure calls the *RunFAR* function, which opens the FAR add-in dialog box, prepopulated with information about old and new form names from the wizard form. FAR then proceeds to locate all the references to the old object names in the database so that you can accept or reject the proposed changes.

Rename Form Controls Menu Add-In

After all the database objects have been renamed, the next step is to rename controls on forms and reports. Figure 21-22 shows a flow chart of the functions and forms called by the Rename Form Controls menu add-in.

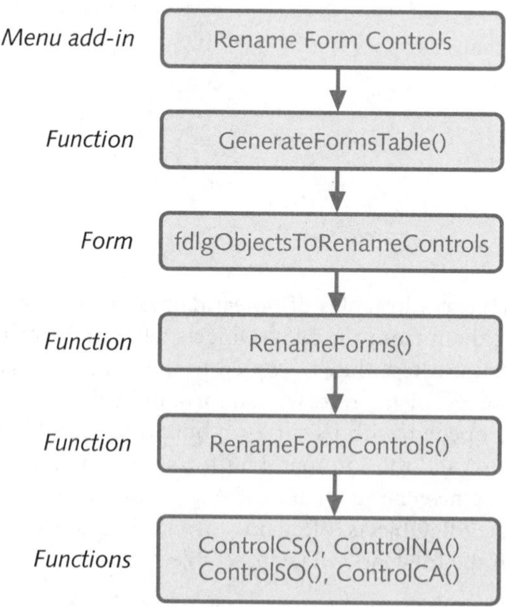

Figure 21-22. The Rename Form Controls menu add-in uses various functions and forms.

The Rename Form Controls menu add-in, which renames controls on forms, runs the *GenerateFormsTable* function, shown here.

```
Public Function GenerateFormsTable()
'Called from USysRegInfo (menu add-in)

On Error GoTo GenerateFormsTableError

   strObjectType = "Form"
   strObjectsTable = "zLNCtblObjectsToRename"
   strForm = "fdlgObjectsToRenameControls"
   strSubform = "fsubObjectsToRenameControls"
   strCodeDB = CodeDb.Name

   'Delete or clear old tables.
   ClearCodeSystemTable
   ClearCodeObjectsTable
   ClearCurrentSystemTable
   ClearCurrentObjectsTable

   'Generate table of forms to rename in calling database.
   strSQL = "CREATE TABLE " & strObjectsTable & _
      "(ObjectName TEXT (100), Use YESNO);"
   DoCmd.SetWarnings False
   DoCmd.RunSQL strSQL

   'Fill table with form names.
   strSQL = "INSERT INTO " & strObjectsTable _
        & "(ObjectName, Use) " _
        & "SELECT MSysObjects.Name, -1 AS " _
        & UseIt FROM MSysObjects " _
        & "WHERE MSysObjects.Type=-32768 " _
        & "ORDER BY MSysObjects.Name;"
   DoCmd.RunSQL strSQL

   'Copy table in calling database to code database
   'so that it will be available as the form's record source.
   DoCmd.CopyObject strCodeDB, , acTable, strObjectsTable

   'Generate table of control types to use in renaming controls
   '(if it doesn't already exist).
   CreateCTTable

   'Open form displaying data from table just created for
   'user selection of forms to rename.
   DoCmd.OpenForm strSubform, acDesign
   Set frmSub = Forms(strSubform)
   frmSub![lblObjectName].Caption = strObjectType & " Name"
```

(continued)

Chapter 21

```
    DoCmd.Close acForm, frmSub.Name, acSaveYes
    DoCmd.OpenForm strForm, acDesign
    Set frm = Forms(strForm)
    frm.Tag = strObjectType
    frm.Caption = strObjectType & "s to Rename"
    frm![cmdRename].Caption = "Rename Controls on Checked " _
         & strObjectType & "s"
    DoCmd.OpenForm strForm, acNormal

GenerateFormsTableExit:
    Exit Function

GenerateFormsTableError:
    MsgBox "Error No: " & Err.Number & "; Description: " _
         & Err.Description
    Resume GenerateFormsTableExit

End Function
```


This function starts by calling functions (*ClearCodeSystemTable*, *ClearCodeObjectsTable*, *ClearCurrentSystemTable*, and *ClearCurrentObjectsTable*) that delete several tables used in the add-in (if they exist in the calling database). Next the function creates a SQL statement and then runs it to create the table of form names.

note Curiously (and inconsistently), the *RunSQL* method of the *DoCmd* object, when run from a library database, works on tables in the calling database, whereas the *OpenQuery* method works on tables in the code database.

The SQL statement includes the Data Definition Language (DDL) CREATE TABLE statement to create an initial blank table to be filled with form names.

tip The CREATE TABLE statement creates a table in the current database. If you need to create a table in the code database, use the Data Access Objects (DAO) *CreateTableDef* method, specifying *CodeDb* as the database in which to create the table.

The second SQL statement in the function appends the names of all forms from the MSysObjects system table to the newly created table. The table is then copied to the code database so that it will be available as the wizard form's data source. Next the *CreateCTTable* function is called to create a table of standard control types, which is filled with the numeric codes and descriptions of the control types most commonly used in Access forms and reports. This table is used in determining the control type for renaming in later functions.

Finally, the function opens the wizard form fdlgObjectsToRenameControls with its form and command button captions set with appropriate text. This form is also used for renaming reports, with appropriate captions. The form allows the user to select the forms whose controls should be renamed. It has the newly created table of form names as its subform's record source.

When the cmdRename button on fdlgObjectsToRenameControls is clicked, the *RenameForms* function is run.

```
Public Function RenameForms()
'Called from cmdRename on fdlgObjectsToRenameControls

On Error GoTo RenameFormsError

   'Set reference to add-in library database.
   Set dbs = CodeDb
   Set rst = dbs.OpenRecordset _
       ("zLNCtblObjectsToRename", dbOpenTable)
   Set frm = Forms![fdlgObjectsToRenameControls]
   intCount = rst.RecordCount
   rst.Close

   If intCount = 0 Then
      intReturn = MsgBox("Do you want to select any forms " _
        & "for control renaming?", vbYesNo + vbQuestion _
        + vbDefaultButton1, "No forms selected")
      If intReturn = vbYes Then
         frm![subObjectsToRename].SetFocus
      ElseIf intReturn = vbNo Then
         DoCmd.Close acForm, frm.Name
         Exit Function
      End If
   ElseIf intCount > 0 Then
      DoCmd.Close acForm, frm.Name
      intReturn = RenameFormControls()
   End If

RenameFormsExit:
   Exit Function

RenameFormsError:
   MsgBox "Error No: " & Err.Number & "; Description: " _
   & Err.Description
   Resume RenameFormsExit

End Function
```

Chapter 21

The *RenameForms* function checks whether any forms have been selected. If none have been selected, the function displays a message box asking whether the user wants to select any forms; a negative answer closes the dialog box, and a positive answer returns the user to the wizard form, where he or she can select some forms. After at least one form has been selected, the function calls the *RenameFormControls* function.

```
Public Function RenameFormControls() As Integer
'Called from RenameForms in this module

On Error GoTo RenameFormControlsError

   Dim fTag As Integer
   Dim fUnbound As Integer
   Dim intTag As Integer
   Dim strFormName As String
   Dim strPrefix As String
   Dim strControlName As String
   Dim strControlSource As String
   Dim strCaption As String
   Dim i As Integer

   'Determine whether original control names should be
   'stored in Tag property.
   strMessage = "When processing forms, should the " _
        & "original control name be saved to the " _
        & "control's Tag property?"
   intTag = MsgBox(strMessage, vbYesNo + vbQuestion + _
      vbDefaultButton2, "Control Name Backup")

   If intTag = vbYes Then
      fTag = True
   Else
      fTag = False
   End If

   'Pick up form name from table just created
   '(using CodeDb to get table from add-in library database).
   Set dbs = CodeDb
   Set rst = dbs.OpenRecordset("zLNCtblObjectsToRename", _
        dbOpenDynaset)
    Do Until rst.EOF
      strFormName = rst![ObjectName]
      If rst![Use] = True Then
         'Process this form.
         DoCmd.OpenForm strFormName, acDesign
         Set frm = Forms(strFormName)
         For Each ctl In frm.Controls
            strControlName = ctl.Name
            lngControlType = ctl.ControlType
            fUnbound = False
```

```
Select Case lngControlType
    'Controls with control source
    Case acTextBox
        strPrefix = "txt"
        Call ControlCS(ctl, strPrefix, fTag)

    Case acComboBox
        strPrefix = "cbo"
        Call ControlCS(ctl, strPrefix, fTag)

    Case acCheckBox
        strPrefix = "chk"
        strControlSource = ctl.ControlSource
        If fUnbound = False Then
            Call ControlCS(ctl, strPrefix, fTag)
        Else
            Call ControlNA(ctl, strPrefix, fTag)
        End If

    Case acBoundObjectFrame
        strPrefix = "frb"
        Call ControlCS(ctl, strPrefix, fTag)

    Case acListBox
        strPrefix = "lst"
        Call ControlCS(ctl, strPrefix, fTag)

    Case acOptionGroup
        strPrefix = "fra"
        Call ControlCS(ctl, strPrefix, fTag)

    Case acOptionButton
        strPrefix = "opt"
        strControlSource = ctl.ControlSource
        If fUnbound = False Then
            Call ControlCS(ctl, strPrefix, fTag)
        Else
            Call ControlNA(ctl, strPrefix, fTag)
        End If

    'Controls with caption only
    Case acToggleButton
        strPrefix = "tgl"
        Call ControlCA(ctl, strPrefix, fTag)

    Case acLabel
        strPrefix = "lbl"
        Call ControlCA(ctl, strPrefix, fTag)
```

(continued)

```
                Case acCommandButton
                   strPrefix = "cmd"
                   Call ControlCA(ctl, strPrefix, fTag)

                'Controls with source object only
                Case acSubform
                   strPrefix = "sub"
                   Call ControlSO(ctl, strPrefix, fTag)

                'Controls with none of the above
                Case acObjectFrame
                   strPrefix = "fru"
                   Call ControlNA(ctl, strPrefix, fTag)

                Case acImage
                   strPrefix = "img"
                   Call ControlNA(ctl, strPrefix, fTag)

                Case acTabCtl
                   strPrefix = "tab"
                   Call ControlNA(ctl, strPrefix, fTag)

                Case acLine
                   strPrefix = "lin"
                   Call ControlNA(ctl, strPrefix, fTag)

                Case acPage
                   strPrefix = "pge"
                   Call ControlNA(ctl, strPrefix, fTag)

                Case acPageBreak
                   strPrefix = "brk"
                   Call ControlNA(ctl, strPrefix, fTag)

                Case acRectangle
                   strPrefix = "shp"
                   Call ControlNA(ctl, strPrefix, fTag)

             End Select

SkipToHere:
         Next ctl
         intReturn = MsgBox("Save and close this form?", _
            vbYesNoCancel + vbQuestion + vbDefaultButton1, _
               "Form Controls Renamed")
         If intReturn = vbYes Then
            DoCmd.Close acForm, strFormName, acSaveYes
```

```
            ElseIf intReturn = vbNo Then
               'Leave this form open in Design view without saving it.
            ElseIf intReturn = vbCancel Then
               Exit Function
            End If
         End If
         rst.MoveNext
      Loop
      rst.Close

      MsgBox "All forms processed!"

   RenameFormControlsExit:
      'Delete old tables (no longer needed).
      ClearCodeSystemTable
      ClearCodeObjectsTable
      ClearCurrentSystemTable
      ClearCurrentObjectsTable
      Exit Function

   RenameFormControlsError:
      'If an option button or check box is unbound, set
      'fUnbound to True so that the code uses the NA function instead of CS.
      If Err.Number = 2455 Then
         fUnbound = True
         Resume Next
      Else
         MsgBox "Error No: " & Err.Number & "; Description: " _
         & Err.Description
         Resume RenameFormControlsExit
      End If

   End Function
```

The *RenameFormControls* function first displays a message box asking whether the original control name should be stored in the control's *Tag* property. It then cycles through the forms in the zLNCtblObjectsToRename table (the record source of the fdlgObjectsToRenameControls form's subform) using a DAO recordset. If the form has its *Use* property set to True (indicating that it was selected on the wizard form), the form opens and the code cycles through its *Controls* collection. For each control, the control name and control type are saved to variables; a *Select Case* statement processes each control type in turn, using Access named constants from the *AcControlType* enum to identify the control type.

Instead of writing a separate function to handle each control type, I streamlined the code by writing several functions to process groups of controls with similar characteristics. These functions (and the control types they handle) are listed in Table 21-8.

Table 21-8. **Functions for renaming controls**

Function	Description	Control types
ControlCS	Renames controls with control sources	Text Box Combo Box Bound Check Box Bound Object Frame ListBox Option Group Bound Option Button
ControlCA	Renames controls with captions	Toggle Button Label Command Button
ControlSO	Renames controls with source objects	Subform/Subreport
ControlNA	Renames controls with none of the above characteristics	Object Frame Image Tab Line Page Page Break Rectangle

The *ControlCS* function takes the control, the standard LNC tag, and a flag variable as arguments. First it stores the control's control source and name to variables, and then it checks whether the control already has the correct tag and handles a few special cases. If the control source isn't empty, it's used as the new control name's base name component (stripped of spaces and other characters by the *StripNonAlphaNumericChars* function). The proposed new control name consists of the LNC tag plus the base name.

If the control source is empty, the old control name is used as the base name. Another special case takes care of a control on reports created by the Database Wizard. Finally, a message box is displayed to show the user the original control name, the control type, the control source, and the proposed new control name. A *Do While…Loop* structure is set up to suggest a new name until the user accepts the proposed name, and it meets the LNC specifications for that control type.

The function's error handler takes care of the common case (especially on reports) of several controls having the same control source or caption. When this occurs, a *1* is added to the end of the proposed control name, with an explanatory message.

```
Public Function ControlCS(ctl As Control, _
   strPrefix As String, fTag As Integer) As Integer
'Called from RenameFormControls and RenameReportControls in this module
'Does group renaming of all controls with control sources
'on a form or report

On Error GoTo ControlCSError

   Dim strControlSource As String

   strControlSource = Nz(ctl.ControlSource)
   strOldCtlName = ctl.ControlName

   'Check whether control is already correctly named and also special case
   'for controls whose original name starts with "Option" or "Frame"
   '(same first three letters as prefix).
   If left(strOldCtlName, 3) = strPrefix And _
      left(strOldCtlName, 6) _
      <> "Option" And left(strOldCtlName, 3) = strPrefix And _
      left(strOldCtlName, 5) <> "Frame" Then
      Exit Function

   'If the control source isn't empty, use it.
   ElseIf strControlSource <> "" Then
      strNewCtlName = strPrefix & _
        StripNonAlphaNumericChars(strControlSource)
   'Otherwise, use the original control name.
   Else
      strNewCtlName = strPrefix & _
        StripNonAlphaNumericChars(strOldCtlName)
   End If

   'Fix name of "Page x of y" text box controls
   'on Database Wizard reports.
   If strNewCtlName = "txtPagePageofPages" Then
      strNewCtlName = "txtPages"
   End If

   'Show the user
   '  - the original control name
   '  - the control type
   '  - the control source
   '  - the proposed new name
   'and ask whether the new name is acceptable.
   intRenameFail = True
   Do While intRenameFail
      intRenameFail = False
```

(continued)

```
        intReturn = MsgBox( _
          "Rename " & _
          DLookup("[ControlTypeName]", "zLNCtblControlType", _
          "[ControlType] = " & ctl.ControlType) _
          & " control currently named " _
          & strOldCtlName & vbCrLf & _
          "(control source: " & strControlSource & ") " & _
          "to" & vbCrLf & strNewCtlName & "?", _
          vbYesNo + vbQuestion + vbDefaultButton1, _
          "Rename control")

        'If the user clicks the Yes button, rename the control.
        If intReturn = vbYes Then
           If fTag = True Then
              ctl.Tag = ctl.ControlName
           End If
           ctl.ControlName = strNewCtlName

           'Otherwise, display an input box for editing the name.
        ElseIf intReturn = vbNo Then
           strNewCtlName = _
              InputBox("Modify new control name", _
              "Rename control", strNewCtlName)
              ctl.ControlName = strNewCtlName
        End If
     Loop

ControlCSExit:
     Exit Function
ControlCSError:
     'If the proposed control name is already in use,
     'return to the renaming dialog box.
     intRenameFail = True
     If Err.Number = 2104 Then
        MsgBox "There is another control named " & _
           strNewCtlName & "; please try again", , _
           "Control Name Used"
        strNewCtlName = strNewCtlName & "1"
     Else
        MsgBox ("Error No:  " & Err & "; error message:  " & Error(Err))
     End If

     Resume Next

End Function
```

The *ControlCA* function differs only in a few respects from the *ControlCS* function: It stores the control's caption rather than its control source, and it uses the caption to create the new control's base name.

```
Public Function ControlCA(ctl As Control, _
strPrefix As String, fTag As Integer) As Integer
'Called from RenameFormControls and
'RenameReportControls in this module
'Does group renaming of all controls with
'captions on a form or report

On Error GoTo ControlCAError

   Dim strCaption As String

   strOldCtlName = ctl.ControlName
   strCaption = ctl.Caption

   If left(strOldCtlName, 3) = strPrefix Then
      Exit Function
   ElseIf strCaption <> "" Then
      If left(strCaption, 3) = "frm" Then
         strNewCtlName = strPrefix & _
            Mid(StripNonAlphaNumericChars(strCaption), 4)
      ElseIf left(strCaption, 4) = "fsub" Then
         strNewCtlName = strPrefix & _
            Mid(StripNonAlphaNumericChars(strCaption), 5)
      Else
         strNewCtlName = strPrefix & _
            StripNonAlphaNumericChars(strCaption)
      End If
   ElseIf strCaption = "" Then
      If left(strOldCtlName, 3) = "frm" Then
         strNewCtlName = strPrefix & _
            Mid(StripNonAlphaNumericChars(strOldCtlName), 4)
      ElseIf left(strOldCtlName, 4) = "fsub" Then
         strNewCtlName = strPrefix & _
            Mid(StripNonAlphaNumericChars(strOldCtlName), 5)
      Else
         strNewCtlName = strPrefix & _
            StripNonAlphaNumericChars(strOldCtlName)
      End If
   End If

   If Right(strNewCtlName, 12) = "SubformLabel" Then
      strNewCtlName = left(strNewCtlName, _
      Len(strNewCtlName) - 12)
   ElseIf Right(strNewCtlName, 5) = "Label" Then
      strNewCtlName = left(strNewCtlName, _
      Len(strNewCtlName) - 5)
   End If
```

(continued)

```
   intRenameFail = True
   Do While intRenameFail
      intRenameFail = False
      intReturn = MsgBox("Rename " _
         & DLookup("[ControlTypeName]", _
         "zLNCtblControlType", "[ControlType] = " _
         & ctl.ControlType) _
         & " control currently named " & strOldCtlName _
         & vbCrLf & _
         "(caption: " & strCaption & ") to" & vbCrLf & _
         strNewCtlName & "?", vbYesNo + vbQuestion + _
         vbDefaultButton1, "Rename control")
      If intReturn = vbYes Then
         If fTag = True Then ctl.Tag = ctl.ControlName
         ctl.ControlName = strNewCtlName
      ElseIf intReturn = vbNo Then
         strNewCtlName = InputBox("Modify new control name", _
            "Rename control", strNewCtlName)
         ctl.ControlName = strNewCtlName
      End If
   Loop

ControlCAExit:
   Exit Function

ControlCAError:
   'If the proposed control name is already in use,
   'return to the renaming dialog box.
   intRenameFail = True
   If Err.Number = 2104 Then
      MsgBox "There is another control named " & _
         strNewCtlName & "; please try again", , _
         "Control Name Used"
      strNewCtlName = strNewCtlName & "1"
   Else
      MsgBox ("Error No:  " & Err & "; error message:  " _
            & Error(Err))
   End If

   Resume Next

End Function
```

The *ControlSO* function stores the *SourceObject* property of the control and uses it to create the new control base name. It has a number of special cases to deal with subform/subreport names created by various Access wizards.

```
Public Function ControlSO(ctl As Control, _
strPrefix As String, fTag As Integer) As Integer
'Called from RenameFormControls and RenameReportControls in this module
'Does group renaming of all controls with source objects on a form or report

On Error GoTo ControlSOError

   strOldCtlName = ctl.ControlName
   strSourceObject = Nz(ctl.SourceObject)

   If left(strOldCtlName, 3) = strPrefix Then
      Exit Function
   ElseIf strSourceObject <> "" Then
      If left(strSourceObject, 3) = "frm" Then
         strNewCtlName = strPrefix & _
            Mid(StripNonAlphaNumericChars(strSourceObject), 4)
      ElseIf left(strSourceObject, 4) = "fsub" Then
         strNewCtlName = strPrefix & _
            Mid(StripNonAlphaNumericChars(strSourceObject), 5)
      Else
         strNewCtlName = strPrefix & _
            StripNonAlphaNumericChars(strSourceObject)
      End If
   ElseIf strSourceObject = "" Then
      If left(strOldCtlName, 3) = "frm" Then
         strNewCtlName = strPrefix & _
            Mid(StripNonAlphaNumericChars(strOldCtlName), 4)
      ElseIf left(strOldCtlName, 4) = "fsub" Then
         strNewCtlName = strPrefix & _
            Mid(StripNonAlphaNumericChars(strOldCtlName), 5)
      Else
         strNewCtlName = strPrefix & _
            StripNonAlphaNumericChars(strOldCtlName)
      End If
   Else
      strNewCtlName = strPrefix & _
         StripNonAlphaNumericChars(strOldCtlName)
   End If

   If Right(strNewCtlName, 7) = "Subform" Then
      strNewCtlName = left(strNewCtlName, _
                      Len(strNewCtlName) - 7)
   End If

   intRenameFail = True
   Do While intRenameFail
      intRenameFail = False
      intReturn = MsgBox("Rename " _
         & DLookup("[ControlTypeName]", _
```

(continued)

```
            "zLNCtblControlType", "[ControlType] = " _
            & ctl.ControlType) _
            & " control currently named " & strOldCtlName _
            & vbCrLf & _
            "(source object: " & strSourceObject & ") to" _
            & vbCrLf & _
            strNewCtlName & "?", vbYesNo + vbQuestion _
            + vbDefaultButton1, _
            "Rename control")
         If intReturn = vbYes Then
            If fTag = True Then ctl.Tag = ctl.ControlName
            ctl.ControlName = strNewCtlName
         ElseIf intReturn = vbNo Then
            strNewCtlName = InputBox("Modify new control name", _
               "Rename control", strNewCtlName)
            ctl.ControlName = strNewCtlName
         End If
      Loop

   ControlSOExit:
      Exit Function

   ControlSOError:
      'If the proposed control name is already in use,
      'return to the renaming dialog box.
      intRenameFail = True
      If Err.Number = 2104 Then
         MsgBox "There is another control named " & _
            strNewCtlName & "; please try again", , _
            "Control Name Used"
         strNewCtlName = strNewCtlName & "1"
      Else
         MsgBox ("Error No:  " & Err & "; error message:  " _
                & Error(Err))
      End If
      Resume ControlSOExit

   End Function
```

The catch-all *ControlNA* function, after dealing with some special cases, proposes a new control name composed of the LNC tag and the old control name (stripped of nonalphanumeric characters).

```
Public Function ControlNA(ctl As Control, _
strPrefix As String, fTag As Integer) As Integer
'Called from RenameFormControls and RenameReportControls
'in this module
'Does group renaming of all controls that do not fit the
'other categories on a form or report
```

```
On Error GoTo ControlNAError

   strOldCtlName = ctl.ControlName

   'Special case for lines whose default name is "Line"
   'or "Option" (same first three letters as the
   'standard prefix)
   If left(strOldCtlName, 3) = strPrefix And _
        left(strOldCtlName, 6) <> "Option" And _
        left(strOldCtlName, 4) <> "Line" Then
      Exit Function
   Else
      strNewCtlName = strPrefix & _
         StripNonAlphaNumericChars(strOldCtlName)
   End If

   intRenameFail = True
   Do While intRenameFail
      intRenameFail = False
      intReturn = MsgBox("Rename " _
         & DLookup("[ControlTypeName]", _
         "zLNCtblControlType", "[ControlType] = " _
         & ctl.ControlType) & _
         " control currently named " & strOldCtlName & " to" _
         & vbCrLf _
         & strNewCtlName & "?", vbYesNo + vbQuestion + _
         vbDefaultButton1, _
         "Rename control")
      If intReturn = vbYes Then
         If fTag = True Then ctl.Tag = ctl.ControlName
         ctl.ControlName = strNewCtlName
      ElseIf intReturn = vbNo Then
         strNewCtlName = InputBox("Modify new control name", _
            "Rename control", strNewCtlName)
         ctl.ControlName = strNewCtlName
      End If
   Loop

ControlNAExit:
   Exit Function

ControlNAError:
   'If the proposed control name is already in use,
   'return to the renaming dialog box.
   intRenameFail = True
   If Err.Number = 2104 Then
      MsgBox "There is another control named " & _
         strNewCtlName & "; please try again", , _
         "Control Name Used"
      strNewCtlName = strNewCtlName & "1"
```

(continued)

```
    Else
        MsgBox ("Error No:  " & Err & "; error message:  " _
            & Error(Err))
    End If
    Resume ControlNAExit

End Function
```

The *StripNonAlphaNumericChars* function is shown in the section "Creating COM Add-Ins," page 931.

After all the controls on a form have been processed, the *RenameFormControls* function proceeds to the next form, and so on, until all the forms in the database have had their controls renamed.

Rename Report Controls Menu Add-In

The third menu add-in, Rename Report Controls, works the same as Rename Form Controls except it processes controls on reports rather than on forms. (See Figure 21-23.) A different add-in is required because opening reports requires a different syntax than opening forms.

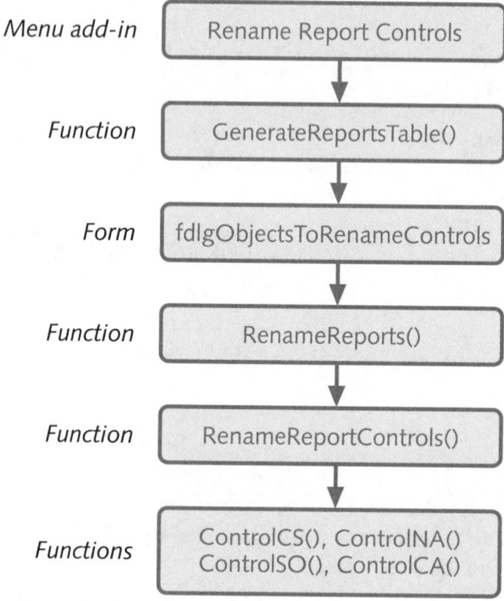

Figure 21-23. The Rename Report Controls menu add-in uses various functions and forms.

LNC Builder

The LNC Builder is a Property Wizard; it hooks on to the *Name* property of a control and is used to rename an individual control in design view. A function called from a Property Builder has three required arguments, which represent the object name (the form or report name for the LNC Builders), the control name, and the current value of the property (the *Name* property for these builders).

Clicking the Build button to the right of the *Name* property in a control's properties sheet (as shown in Figure 21-24) opens a Choose Builder dialog box, which lists the two LNC builders.

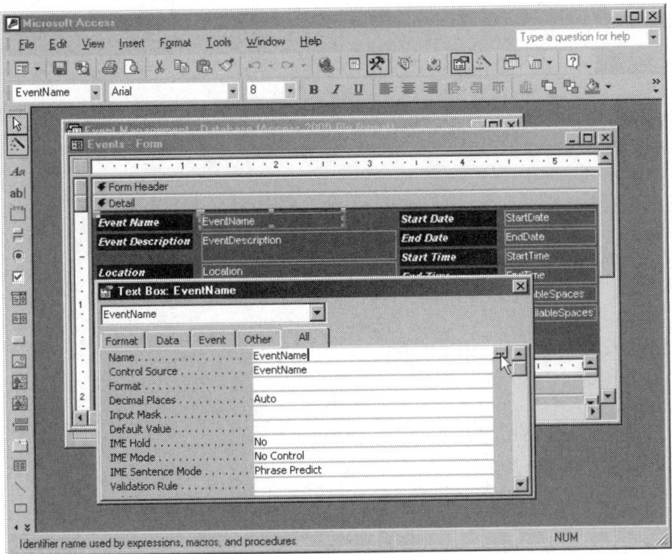

Figure 21-24. You click the Build button to open the LNC Builder for renaming a control.

The LNC Rename Current Control option is selected by default in the dialog box (as shown in Figure 21-25).

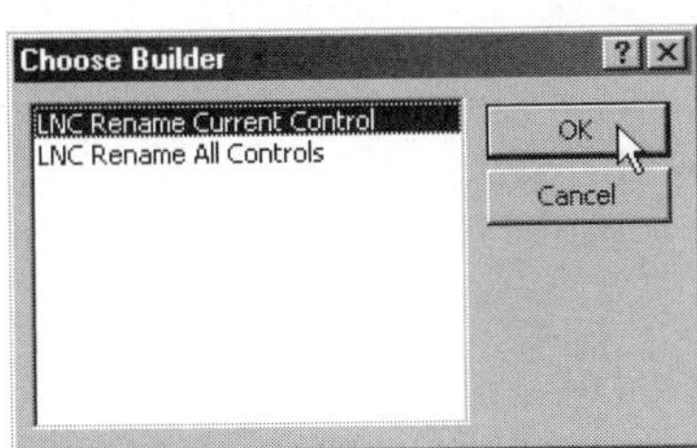

Figure 21-25. The LNC Rename Current Control item is selected by default.

When you select this builder, it runs the *LNCBuilder* function, shown below. The *LNCBuilder* function picks up the name of the current form or report, the name of the control, and the *Name* property's current value from the control that invokes it. These arguments are then used in the function's code. The function clears old tables in the calling database, runs *CreateCTTable* to create a table of control types, determines whether the current object is a form or report, and then goes to the appropriate segment of code to set a reference to either a form control or a report control. Next the code jumps to the *DetermineControlType* label, where a message box appears asking whether the old control name should be saved to the *Tag* property, and then a *Select Case* statement (similar to the one in the *RenameFormControls* function) is set up to rename the control according to its type.

```
Public Function LNCBuilder(strObjectName As String, _
strCtlName As String, strCurrentValue As String) As Variant
'Called from USysRegInfo (Property Wizard)
'A Property Builder that renames an individual control
'on a form or report

On Error GoTo LNCBuilderError

   Dim fTag As Integer
   Dim strPrefix As String
   Dim fUnbound As Boolean
   Dim strControlSource As String
   Dim strCaption As String

   'Delete old tables in calling database.
   ClearCurrentSystemTable
   ClearCurrentObjectsTable

   'Generate table of control types to use in renaming controls
   '(if it doesn't already exist).
   CreateCTTable

   strOldCtlName = strCurrentValue

   'Determine whether current object is a form or a report.
   For Each frm In Forms
      If frm.Name = strObjectName Then
         GoTo ObjectIsForm
      End If
   Next frm

   'strObjectName not found in forms; check whether
   'it is a report.
   For Each rpt In Reports
      If rpt.Name = strObjectName Then
         GoTo ObjectIsReport
      End If
```

Chapter 21

```
   Next rpt

   MsgBox "Current object isn't a form or a report; exiting"
   Exit Function

ObjectIsForm:
   Set frm = Forms(strObjectName)
   Set ctl = frm(strCtlName)
   GoTo DetermineControlType

ObjectIsReport:
   Set rpt = Reports(strObjectName)
   Set ctl = rpt(strCtlName)

DetermineControlType:
   lngControlType = ctl.ControlType

   'Determine whether the Tag property has a value.
   strMessage = "Save the original control name to " _
                & "the control's Tag property?"

   'Set fTag to save control name to Tag only if Tag is empty.
   If IsNull(ctl.Tag) = True Or ctl.Tag = "" Then
      fTag = True
   Else
      fTag = False
   End If

   'Run code to create suggested control name
   'based on control type.
   fUnbound = False

   Select Case lngControlType
      'Control with control source
      Case acTextBox
         strPrefix = "txt"
         strNewCtlName = ControlCS(ctl, strPrefix, fTag)

      Case acComboBox
         strPrefix = "cbo"
         strNewCtlName = ControlCS(ctl, strPrefix, fTag)

      Case acCheckBox
         strPrefix = "chk"
         strControlSource = ctl.ControlSource
         If fUnbound = False Then
            strNewCtlName = ControlCS(ctl, strPrefix, fTag)
```

(continued)

```
      Else
         strNewCtlName = ControlNA(ctl, strPrefix, fTag)
      End If

   Case acBoundObjectFrame
      strPrefix = "frb"
      strNewCtlName = ControlCS(ctl, strPrefix, fTag)

   Case acListBox
      strPrefix = "lst"
      strNewCtlName = ControlCS(ctl, strPrefix, fTag)

   Case acOptionGroup
      strPrefix = "fra"
      strNewCtlName = ControlCS(ctl, strPrefix, fTag)

   Case acOptionButton
      strPrefix = "opt"
      strControlSource = ctl.ControlSource
      If fUnbound = False Then
         strNewCtlName = ControlCS(ctl, strPrefix, fTag)
      Else
         strNewCtlName = ControlNA(ctl, strPrefix, fTag)
      End If

   'Control with caption only
   Case acToggleButton
      strPrefix = "tgl"
      strNewCtlName = ControlCA(ctl, strPrefix, fTag)

   Case acLabel
      strPrefix = "lbl"
      strNewCtlName = ControlCA(ctl, strPrefix, fTag)

   Case acCommandButton
      strPrefix = "cmd"
      strNewCtlName = ControlCA(ctl, strPrefix, fTag)

   'Control with source object only
   Case acSubform
      strPrefix = "sub"
      strNewCtlName = ControlSO(ctl, strPrefix, fTag)

   'Control with none of the above
   Case acObjectFrame
      strPrefix = "fru"
      strNewCtlName = ControlNA(ctl, strPrefix, fTag)
```

```
        Case acImage
            strPrefix = "img"
            strNewCtlName = ControlNA(ctl, strPrefix, fTag)

        Case acTabCtl
            strPrefix = "tab"
            strNewCtlName = ControlNA(ctl, strPrefix, fTag)

        Case acLine
            strPrefix = "lin"
            strNewCtlName = ControlNA(ctl, strPrefix, fTag)

        Case acPage
            strPrefix = "pge"
            strNewCtlName = ControlNA(ctl, strPrefix, fTag)

        Case acPageBreak
            strPrefix = "brk"
            strNewCtlName = ControlNA(ctl, strPrefix, fTag)

        Case acRectangle
            strPrefix = "shp"
            strNewCtlName = ControlNA(ctl, strPrefix, fTag)

    End Select

LNCBuilderExit:
    'Delete old tables in calling database.
    ClearCurrentSystemTable
    ClearCurrentObjectsTable
    Exit Function

LNCBuilderError:
    'If an option button or check box is unbound, set
    'fUnbound to True so that the code uses the NA function instead of CS.
    Select Case Err.Number
        Case 2455
            fUnbound = True
            Resume Next
        Case 2465
            MsgBox "You can't rename a single control " _
                & "from the Detail section"
            Resume LNCBuilderExit
        Case Else
            MsgBox "Error No: " & Err.Number & "; Description: " _
                & Err.Description
            Resume LNCBuilderExit
    End Select

End Function
```

When the new control name has been determined, it is presented in a Rename Control message box. (A typical one is shown in Figure 21-26.) This is the same message box that's used in the Rename Form Controls and Rename Report Controls menu add-ins.

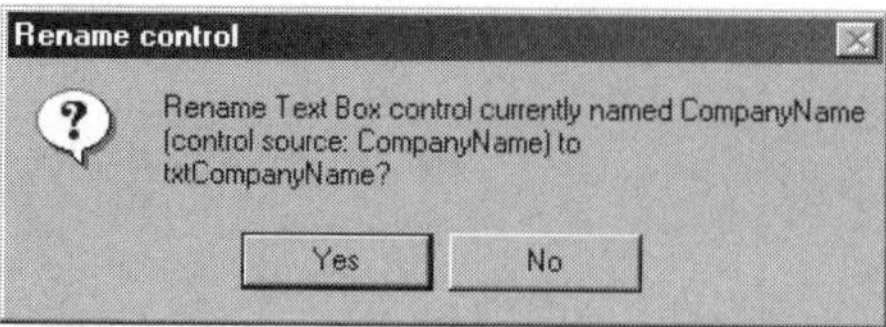

Figure 21-26. The Rename Control message box proposes a new name for a text box control.

LNC Builder All

The LNC Builder All Property Builder (listed as a wizard in the registry) also runs from the *Name* property, but this builder runs only from the *Name* property of a form or report's detail section. Selecting the LNC Rename All Controls item in the Choose Builder dialog box runs the *LNCBuilderAll* function, which cycles through all the controls on the current form or report, displaying a Rename Control message box for each (as shown in Figure 21-26).

```
Public Function LNCBuilderAll(strObjectName As String, _
   strCtlName As String, strCurrentValue As String) As Variant
'Called from USysRegInfo (property wizard)
'A Property Builder that renames all the controls on a form
'or report

On Error GoTo LNCBuilderAllError

   Dim i As Integer
   Dim fTag As Integer
   Dim intTag As Integer
   Dim strPrefix As String
   Dim fUnbound As Boolean
   Dim strControlSource As String
   Dim strCaption As String

   'Delete old tables in calling database.
   ClearCurrentSystemTable
   ClearCurrentObjectsTable

   'Generate table of control types to use in renaming controls
   '(if it doesn't already exist).
   CreateCTTable
```

```
   strOldCtlName = strCurrentValue

   'Determine whether original control names should
   'be stored in Tag property.
   strMessage = "When processing controls, should the " _
        & "original control name be saved to the " _
        & "control's Tag property?"
   intTag = MsgBox(strMessage, vbYesNo + vbQuestion + _
      vbDefaultButton2, "Control Name Backup")

   If intTag = vbYes Then
      fTag = True
   Else
      fTag = False
   End If

   'Determine whether current object is a form or a report.
   For Each frm In Forms
      If frm.Name = strObjectName Then
         GoTo ObjectIsForm
      End If
   Next frm

   'strObjectName not found in forms; check whether
   'it is a report.
   For Each rpt In Reports
      If rpt.Name = strObjectName Then
         GoTo ObjectIsReport
      End If
   Next rpt

   MsgBox "Current object isn't a form or a report; exiting"
   Exit Function

ObjectIsForm:
   Set frm = Forms(strObjectName)
   For Each ctl In frm.Controls
      strCtlName = ctl.Name
      lngControlType = ctl.ControlType
      fUnbound = False

      Select Case lngControlType
         'Controls with control source
         Case acTextBox
            strPrefix = "txt"
            Call ControlCS(ctl, strPrefix, fTag)
```

(continued)

```
Case acComboBox
   strPrefix = "cbo"
   Call ControlCS(ctl, strPrefix, fTag)

Case acCheckBox
   strPrefix = "chk"
   strControlSource = ctl.ControlSource
   If fUnbound = False Then
      Call ControlCS(ctl, strPrefix, fTag)
   Else
      Call ControlNA(ctl, strPrefix, fTag)
   End If

Case acBoundObjectFrame
   strPrefix = "frb"
   Call ControlCS(ctl, strPrefix, fTag)

Case acListBox
   strPrefix = "lst"
   Call ControlCS(ctl, strPrefix, fTag)

Case acOptionGroup
   strPrefix = "fra"
   Call ControlCS(ctl, strPrefix, fTag)

Case acOptionButton
   strPrefix = "opt"
   strControlSource = ctl.ControlSource
   If fUnbound = False Then
      Call ControlCS(ctl, strPrefix, fTag)
   Else
      Call ControlNA(ctl, strPrefix, fTag)
   End If

'Controls with caption only
Case acToggleButton
   strPrefix = "tgl"
   Call ControlCA(ctl, strPrefix, fTag)

Case acLabel
   strPrefix = "lbl"
   Call ControlCA(ctl, strPrefix, fTag)

Case acCommandButton
   strPrefix = "cmd"
   Call ControlCA(ctl, strPrefix, fTag)
```

```
         'Controls with source object only
         Case acSubform
            strPrefix = "sub"
            Call ControlSO(ctl, strPrefix, fTag)

         'Controls with none of the above
         Case acObjectFrame
            strPrefix = "fru"
            Call ControlNA(ctl, strPrefix, fTag)

         Case acImage
            strPrefix = "img"
            Call ControlNA(ctl, strPrefix, fTag)

         Case acTabCtl
            strPrefix = "tab"
            Call ControlNA(ctl, strPrefix, fTag)

         Case acLine
            strPrefix = "lin"
            Call ControlNA(ctl, strPrefix, fTag)

         Case acPage
            strPrefix = "pge"
            Call ControlNA(ctl, strPrefix, fTag)

         Case acPageBreak
            strPrefix = "brk"
            Call ControlNA(ctl, strPrefix, fTag)

         Case acRectangle
            strPrefix = "shp"
            Call ControlNA(ctl, strPrefix, fTag)

      End Select

SkipToHereForm:
   Next ctl
   GoTo Success

ObjectIsReport:
   Set rpt = Reports(strObjectName)
   For Each ctl In rpt.Controls
      strCtlName = ctl.Name
      lngControlType = ctl.ControlType
      fUnbound = False
```

(continued)

```
Select Case lngControlType
   'Controls with control source
   Case acTextBox
      strPrefix = "txt"
      Call ControlCS(ctl, strPrefix, fTag)

   Case acComboBox
      strPrefix = "cbo"
      Call ControlCS(ctl, strPrefix, fTag)

   Case acCheckBox
      strPrefix = "chk"
      strControlSource = ctl.ControlSource
      If fUnbound = False Then
         Call ControlCS(ctl, strPrefix, fTag)
      Else
         Call ControlNA(ctl, strPrefix, fTag)
      End If

   Case acBoundObjectFrame
      strPrefix = "frb"
      Call ControlCS(ctl, strPrefix, fTag)

   Case acListBox
      strPrefix = "lst"
      Call ControlCS(ctl, strPrefix, fTag)

   Case acOptionGroup
      strPrefix = "fra"
      Call ControlCS(ctl, strPrefix, fTag)

   Case acOptionButton
      strPrefix = "opt"
      strControlSource = ctl.ControlSource
      If fUnbound = False Then
         Call ControlCS(ctl, strPrefix, fTag)
      Else
         Call ControlNA(ctl, strPrefix, fTag)
      End If

   'Controls with caption only
   Case acToggleButton
      strPrefix = "tgl"
      Call ControlCA(ctl, strPrefix, fTag)

   Case acLabel
      strPrefix = "lbl"
      Call ControlCA(ctl, strPrefix, fTag)
```

```
            Case acCommandButton
                strPrefix = "cmd"
                Call ControlCA(ctl, strPrefix, fTag)

            'Controls with source object only
            Case acSubform
                strPrefix = "sub"
                Call ControlSO(ctl, strPrefix, fTag)

            'Controls with none of the above
            Case acObjectFrame
                strPrefix = "fru"
                Call ControlNA(ctl, strPrefix, fTag)

            Case acImage
                strPrefix = "img"
                Call ControlNA(ctl, strPrefix, fTag)

            Case acTabCtl
                strPrefix = "tab"
                Call ControlNA(ctl, strPrefix, fTag)

            Case acLine
                strPrefix = "lin"
                Call ControlNA(ctl, strPrefix, fTag)

            Case acPage
                strPrefix = "pge"
                Call ControlNA(ctl, strPrefix, fTag)

            Case acPageBreak
                strPrefix = "brk"
                Call ControlNA(ctl, strPrefix, fTag)

            Case acRectangle
                strPrefix = "shp"
                Call ControlNA(ctl, strPrefix, fTag)

        End Select

SkipToHereReport:
    Next ctl

Success:
    MsgBox "All controls renamed!"

LNCBuilderAllExit:
    'Delete old tables in calling database.
    ClearCurrentSystemTable
```

(continued)

```
    ClearCurrentObjectsTable
    Exit Function

LNCBuilderAllError:
    'If an option button or check box is unbound, set
    'fUnbound to True so that the code uses the NA function instead of CS.
    If Err.Number = 2455 Then
        fUnbound = True
        Resume Next
    Else
        MsgBox "Error No: " & Err.Number & "; Description: " _
            & Err.Description
        Resume LNCBuilderAllExit
    End If

End Function
```


Preventing Problems with Access Add-Ins

The following suggestions will make it easier to debug your add-in projects:

- To verify that your add-in has been installed properly, write a simple function to display a message box and enter it as the function to run in the USysRegInfo table's Function line. After you have verified that the add-in was installed correctly (the message box appears when you run the add-in), replace this test function with the add-in's main function in the USysRegInfo table.
- When you need to make a change to an add-in, first uninstall it in the Add-In Manager (in a regular database), then close the database, and then open the add-in database for editing. Otherwise, you might get an error message about the database being in use as a library database, and you won't be able to open it for modifications. After making the changes, compile the add-in's VBA code, save and close it, and then reinstall it from a regular database using the Add-In Manager.
- Occasionally, after making changes to an add-in database, you might find that the latest changes aren't visible when you run the add-in. In that case, uninstall the add-in, and then reinstall it to force the latest version of the add-in to run. (You can do this in a single session in the Add-In Manager dialog box.)
- While working on an add-in, if you make copies of the add-in database from time to time (definitely a good idea), place the copies in another folder (not the working folder or the Add-Ins folder). Otherwise, you'll see duplicate entries in the Add-In Manager dialog box, with no way to tell which is the latest version of the add-in.

Troubleshooting

When I try to run an add-in, I get the following message: *The wizard you need may be missing from the Libraries key of the Microsoft Access section of the Windows Registry*

This error has several possible causes. One is an error in the USysRegInfo table—either the wrong registry key or a typo in the add-in name or a function name. Another possible cause is an uncompiled database. Check the USysRegInfo table to make sure all the information in it is correct, and then compile the add-in database, close it, and try again.

Creating COM Add-Ins

COM add-ins were introduced in Office 2000; they significantly extend the functionality of add-ins because they're available to all Office applications and can also be run from the Visual Basic Editor window. A COM add-in is a dynamic-link library (DLL) that's registered so that it works with Office applications (or, in some cases, an ActiveX EXE file). You can create COM add-ins using Microsoft Visual C++, Microsoft Visual J++, Microsoft Visual Basic 5.0 or later, or VBA 6.0 or later. To create a COM add-in with VBA, you need Office XP Developer, which includes the special tools you need to create these add-ins.

With a COM add-in, there's no USysRegInfo table and no add-in database. Instead, you create a VBA project (VBA file), and when the project is complete, you create a DLL file, which is placed in the add-ins folder and installed by means of the COM Add-Ins menu (not the regular Add-Ins menu). COM add-ins can create menu commands (on any menu) and toolbar buttons, which gives them more flexibility than regular Access add-ins.

The COM Add-Ins menu isn't displayed by default; to make it visible, open the Customize dialog box by right-clicking on the gray background of a toolbar. Locate COM Add-Ins at the bottom of the list of commands in the Tools category on the Commands tab (as shown in Figure 21-27), and drag it to the desired toolbar location.

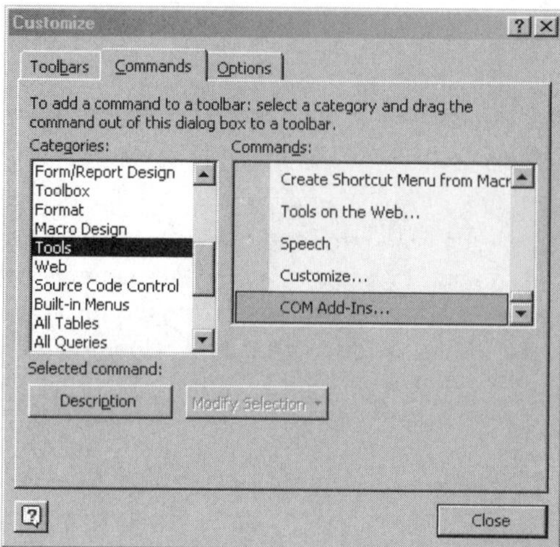

Figure 21-27. You can find the COM Add-Ins selection in the Customize dialog box.

Creating the LNC Rename COM Add-In

Unlike with regular add-ins, you can't write COM add-ins in the regular version of Access—you must have Office XP Developer or another programming language that supports creating COM add-ins, such as Visual Basic or Visual C++. Creating COM add-ins in VBA is slightly different from creating them in Visual Basic, so some of the screen shots and code might differ between the two. This section describes creating COM add-ins in VBA, using the tools that are part of Office XP Developer.

If you have Office XP Developer installed, switch to the Visual Basic Editor and choose File, New Project. Select Add-In Project in the New Project dialog box, as shown in Figure 21-28.

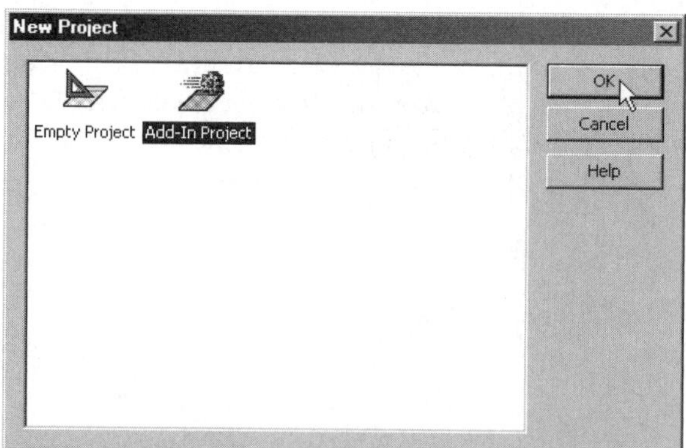

Figure 21-28. You create a new COM add-in project by selecting Add-In Project in the New Project dialog box.

The new COM add-in project is initially called AddInProject1, but you can rename it to something more meaningful. Under the new project is a Designers folder, with a new designer, named AddInDesigner1 by default. If you're writing a COM add-in for multiple Office applications, you need a designer for each one because designers are application- and version-specific.

Renaming a Project

To rename the project (or designer), highlight its *Name* property in the project (or designer) properties sheet and modify it as desired, as shown in Figure 21-29. Project and designer names can't contain spaces, and it's best to stick with all-alphanumeric names.

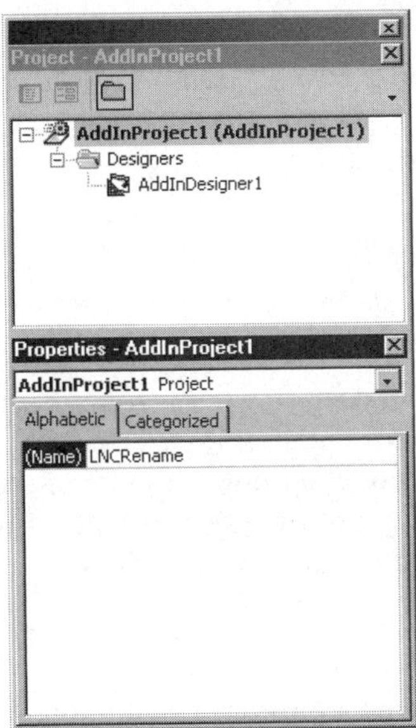

Figure 21-29. You can give a project a more meaningful name in its properties sheet.

The new designer's properties sheet is then displayed; you can fill it in with general project information. (Figure 21-30 shows the properties sheet filled in for the LNC Rename COM add-in project.) The *Addin Display Name* property is the name of the COM add-in as displayed in the COM Add-Ins dialog box (the dialog box that appears when you click the COM Add-Ins toolbar button or menu command). The *Addin Description* property gives more information about the COM add-in's functionality. Curiously, the description isn't visible in the COM Add-Ins dialog box, but you can read it using the *COMAddIn* object's *Description* property in VBA.

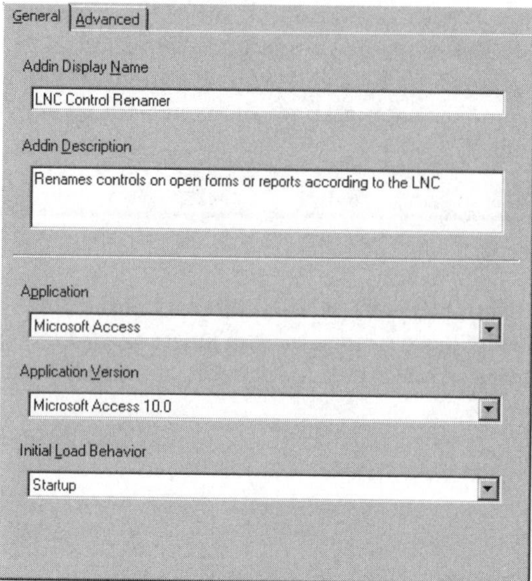

Figure 21-30. You can use the LNC Rename COM Add-In project designer's properties sheet to specify some of its properties.

In the Application drop-down list, you can select the Office application in which the COM add-in will run. In the Application Version drop-down list, you can select the version of that application. It doesn't offer a choice, however—only the current version is available for selection. The Initial Load Behavior drop-down list offers several alternatives for loading the COM add-in; the Startup option is generally the most useful. A final properties sheet selection, Add-In Is Command-Line Safe (does not put up any UI) isn't relevant to Office add-ins; it will disappear from the properties sheet after an Office application is selected.

After you fill in the properties sheet, you can save the project. The proposed save name will be AddInProject1.vba even if you gave the project a more meaningful name. You should override the suggested file name with a more meaningful name, which will then be the suggested save name for the DLL you create later on.

The next step is to create the code (and possibly a form) for the COM add-in. Although you use a different process for creating the COM add-in than for a regular Access add-in and the interface is also different, the core code can be the same, so I decided to recycle some of the code I used in my LNC Rename add-in for a COM add-in to rename controls on forms and reports.

As you'll recall, the LNC Rename Access add-in consists of several menu add-ins and two Property Builders. For the COM add-in, I decided to create a set of toolbar buttons to rename controls on all open forms or all open reports (an option between the Access menu add-ins that rename all form or report controls and the Property Builder that renames all controls on just the current form or report).

The designer has its own class module, which is accessible through the View Code command on the designer's shortcut menu. To work with the host application, the COM add-in works with events that fire when the add-in is loaded or unloaded or when the host application starts or shuts down. These events are implemented via the IDTExtensibility2 library within the designer's class module. To implement this functionality, you add the following line to the Declarations section of the designer's class module:

```
Implements IDTExtensibility2
```

After you add this line, you can select the IDTExtensibility2 library in the Object box in the Visual Basic Editor window and then select the five event procedures in the Procedure box, creating code stubs for each event. The designer's class module must have code stubs for all five procedures, even if you don't need code in all of them. You can put a comment in the procedures that don't need functional code.

COM add-ins are typically implemented as toolbar buttons or menu commands that can be placed on any toolbar or menu in the host application. If you're going to use a toolbar button or menu command as the COM add-in's interface, you must also add two (or more) statements to the module's Declarations section. Specifically, you need to declare one or more *CommandBarButton* objects using the *WithEvents* keyword so that you can write code for their *Click* event(s).

Because a designer is application-specific, any code that applies specifically to an individual Office application should be located in the designer class module; code that applies to all Office applications should be located in a standard module so that it can be called from any or all designers. The AccessDesigner module code is shown here. This code contains the *IDTExtensibility2* event procedures, the functions to create (and remove) the add-in's toolbar buttons, functions that handle the renaming of Access controls, and an error handler function.

```
Implements IDTExtensibility2

Private WithEvents pctlFormButton As Office.CommandBarButton
Private WithEvents pctlReportButton As Office.CommandBarButton

'Global variable to store reference to host application
Public gobjAppInstance As Object

'Regular variables for creating toolbar buttons
Dim cbrMenu As Office.CommandBar
Dim ctlBtnAddIn As Office.CommandBarButton

'Global variables for handling renaming
Public gctl As Access.Control
Public gdbs As DAO.Database
Public gfrm As Access.Form
```

(continued)

```
Public gintRenameFail As Integer
Public gintReturn As Integer
Public glngControlType As Long
Public grpt As Access.Report
Public grst As DAO.Recordset
Public gstrMessage As String
Public gstrNewCtlName As String
Public gstrOldCtlName As String
Public gstrSQL As String
Public gstrSourceObject As String

'Regular variables for handling renaming
Dim i As Integer
Dim blnTag As Boolean
Dim intTag As Integer
Dim strPrefix As String
Dim blnUnbound As Boolean
Dim strControlSource As String
Dim strCaption As String
Dim strObjectName As String
Dim strCtlName As String

'Constants for characters surrounding ProgID
Const PROG_ID_START As String = "!<"
Const PROG_ID_END As String = ">"


Sub AddInErr(errX As ErrObject)
'Displays message box with error information

   Dim strMsg As String

   strMsg = "An error occurred in the LNC " _
       & "Renaming COM add-in " _
       & vbCrLf & "Error #:" & errX.Number _
       & vbCrLf & "Description: " & errX.Description
   MsgBox strMsg, , "Error!"

End Sub

Private Sub IDTExtensibility2_OnAddInsUpdate(custom() _
   As Variant)

On Error GoTo ErrorHandler

   'No code needed, but must have the event stub.

ErrorHandlerExit:
   Exit Sub
```

```
ErrorHandler:
   AddInErr Err
   Resume ErrorHandlerExit

End Sub

Private Sub IDTExtensibility2_OnBeginShutdown(custom() _
   As Variant)

On Error GoTo ErrorHandler

   'No code needed, but must have the event stub.

ErrorHandlerExit:
   Exit Sub

ErrorHandler:
   AddInErr Err
   Resume ErrorHandlerExit

End Sub

Private Sub IDTExtensibility2_OnConnection(ByVal Application _
    As Object, ByVal ConnectMode As _
    AddInDesignerObjects.ext_ConnectMode, ByVal AddInInst _
    As Object, custom() As Variant)
'Calls shared code to create a new command bar button
'to rename controls on a form or report

On Error GoTo ErrorHandler

   Set pctlFormButton = CreateFormCommandBarButton _
         (Application, ConnectMode, AddInInst)
   Set pctlReportButton = CreateReportCommandBarButton _
         (Application, ConnectMode, AddInInst)

ErrorHandlerExit:
   Exit Sub

ErrorHandler:
   AddInErr Err
   Resume ErrorHandlerExit

End Sub

Private Sub IDTExtensibility2_OnDisconnection _
(ByVal RemoveMode As AddInDesignerObjects.ext_DisconnectMode, _
   custom() As Variant)
```

(continued)

```
On Error GoTo ErrorHandler

   'Call common procedure to disconnect add-in.
   RemoveAddInCommandBarButton RemoveMode

ErrorHandlerExit:
   Exit Sub

ErrorHandler:
   AddInErr Err
   Resume ErrorHandlerExit

End Sub

Private Sub IDTExtensibility2_OnStartupComplete(custom() _
   As Variant)

On Error GoTo ErrorHandler

   'No code needed, but must have the event stub.

ErrorHandlerExit:
   Exit Sub

ErrorHandler:
   AddInErr Err
   Resume ErrorHandlerExit

End Sub

Private Sub pctlFormButton_Click(ByVal ctl As _
   Office.CommandBarButton, CancelDefault As Boolean)

   Call LNCRenameFormControls

End Sub

Private Sub pctlReportButton_Click(ByVal ctl As _
   Office.CommandBarButton, CancelDefault As Boolean)

   Call LNCRenameReportControls

End Sub

Public Function CreateFormCommandBarButton _
   (ByVal Application As Object, _
   ByVal ConnectMode As AddInDesignerObjects.ext_ConnectMode, _
   ByVal AddInInst As Object) As Office.CommandBarButton
```

```
On Error GoTo ErrorHandler

   'Store reference to Application object in a public variable
   'so that other procedures in the add-in can use it.
   Set gobjAppInstance = Application

   'Return reference to command bar.
   Set cbrMenu = gobjAppInstance.CommandBars("Form Design")

   'Add button to call add-in from command bar, if it doesn't
   'already exist.
   'Look for button on command bar.
   Set ctlBtnAddIn = cbrMenu.FindControl _
      (Tag:="Rename Form Controls")
   If ctlBtnAddIn Is Nothing Then
      'Add new button.
      Set ctlBtnAddIn = _
      cbrMenu.Controls.Add(Type:=msoControlButton, _
      Parameter:="Rename Form Controls")
      'Set button's Caption, Tag, Style,
      'and OnAction properties.
      With ctlBtnAddIn
         Caption = "&Rename Controls"
         .Tag = "Rename Form Controls"
         .Style = msoButtonCaption
         'Run main add-in function.
         .OnAction = PROG_ID_START & AddInInst.ProgId _
            & PROG_ID_END
      End With
   End If
   'Return reference to new command bar buttons.
   Set CreateFormCommandBarButton = ctlBtnAddIn

ErrorHandlerExit:
   Exit Function

ErrorHandler:
   AddInErr Err
   Resume ErrorHandlerExit

End Function

Public Function CreateReportCommandBarButton _
  (ByVal Application As Object, _
   ByVal ConnectMode As AddInDesignerObjects.ext_ConnectMode, _
   ByVal AddInInst As Object) As Office.CommandBarButton
```

(continued)

Chapter 21

```
On Error GoTo ErrorHandler

    'Store reference to Application object in a public variable
    'so that other procedures in the add-in can use it.
    Set gobjAppInstance = Application

    'Return reference to command bar.
    Set cbrMenu = gobjAppInstance.CommandBars("Report Design")

    'Add button to call add-in from command bar, if it doesn't
    'already exist.
    'Look for button on command bar.
    Set ctlBtnAddIn = cbrMenu.FindControl _
                (Tag:="Rename Report Controls")
    If ctlBtnAddIn Is Nothing Then
        'Add new button.
        Set ctlBtnAddIn = cbrMenu.Controls.Add _
           (Type:=msoControlButton, _
            Parameter:="Rename Report Controls")
        'Set button's Caption, Tag, Style,
        'and OnAction properties.
        With ctlBtnAddIn
            .Caption = "&Rename Controls"
            .Tag = "Rename Report Controls"
            .Style = msoButtonCaption
            'Run main add-in function
            .OnAction = PROG_ID_START & AddInInst.ProgId _
                & PROG_ID_END
        End With
    End If

    'Return reference to new command bar button.
    Set CreateReportCommandBarButton = ctlBtnAddIn

ErrorHandlerExit:
   Exit Function

ErrorHandler:
   AddInErr Err
   Resume ErrorHandlerExit

End Function

Function RemoveAddInCommandBarButton(ByVal _
    RemoveMode As AddInDesignerObjects.ext_DisconnectMode)
'This procedure removes the command bar buttons for
'the add-in if the user disconnected it.
```

```
On Error GoTo ErrorHandler

    'If user unloaded add-in, remove button.
    'Otherwise, add-in is being unloaded because
    'application is closing; in that case,
    'leave button as is.
    If RemoveMode = ext_dm_UserClosed Then
        On Error Resume Next
        'Delete custom command bar button.
        gobjAppInstance.CommandBars("Form Design").Controls _
            ("Rename Form Controls").Delete
        gobjAppInstance.CommandBars("Report Design").Controls _
            ("Rename Report Controls").Delete
        On Error GoTo ErrorHandlerExit
    End If

ErrorHandlerExit:
   Exit Function

ErrorHandler:
   AddInErr Err
   Resume ErrorHandlerExit

End Function

Public Function LNCRenameFormControls() As Variant
'Renames all the controls on open forms

   'Generate table of control types to use in renaming controls
   '(if it doesn't already exist).
   CreateCTTable

On Error GoTo ErrorHandler

   'Determine whether any forms are open, and exit if not.
   If Forms.Count = 0 Then
      MsgBox "No forms are open; exiting"
      GoTo ErrorHandlerExit
   End If

   'Determine whether original control names
   'should be stored in Tag property.
   gstrMessage = "When form processing controls, " _
         & "should the original control name be saved to " _
         & "the control's Tag property?"
   intTag = MsgBox(gstrMessage, vbYesNo + vbQuestion + _
      vbDefaultButton2, "Control Name Backup")
```

(continued)

```
If intTag = vbYes Then
   blnTag = True
Else
   blnTag = False
End If

'Process open forms.
For Each gfrm In Forms

   For Each gctl In gfrm.Controls
      strCtlName = gctl.Name
      glngControlType = gctl.ControlType
      blnUnbound = False

      Select Case glngControlType
         'Controls with control source
         Case acTextBox
            strPrefix = "txt"
            i = ControlCS(gctl, strPrefix, blnTag)

         Case acComboBox
            strPrefix = "cbo"
            i = ControlCS(gctl, strPrefix, blnTag)

         Case acCheckBox
            strPrefix = "chk"
            strControlSource = gctl.ControlSource
            If blnUnbound = False Then
               i = ControlCS(gctl, strPrefix, blnTag)
            Else
               i = ControlNA(gctl, strPrefix, blnTag)
            End If

         Case acBoundObjectFrame
            strPrefix = "frb"
            i = ControlCS(gctl, strPrefix, blnTag)

         Case acListBox
            strPrefix = "lst"
            i = ControlCS(gctl, strPrefix, blnTag)

         Case acOptionGroup
            strPrefix = "fra"
            i = ControlCS(gctl, strPrefix, blnTag)

         Case acOptionButton
            strPrefix = "opt"
            strControlSource = gctl.ControlSource
            If blnUnbound = False Then
               i = ControlCS(gctl, strPrefix, blnTag)
```

```
   Else
      i = ControlNA(gctl, strPrefix, blnTag)
   End If

'Controls with caption only
Case acToggleButton
   strPrefix = "tgl"
   i = ControlCA(gctl, strPrefix, blnTag)

Case acLabel
   strPrefix = "lbl"
   i = ControlCA(gctl, strPrefix, blnTag)

Case acCommandButton
   strPrefix = "cmd"
   i = ControlCA(gctl, strPrefix, blnTag)

'Controls with source object only
Case acSubform
   strPrefix = "sub"
   i = ControlSO(gctl, strPrefix, blnTag)

'Controls with none of the above
Case acObjectFrame
   strPrefix = "fru"
   i = ControlNA(gctl, strPrefix, blnTag)

Case acImage
   strPrefix = "img"
   i = ControlNA(gctl, strPrefix, blnTag)

Case acTabCtl
   strPrefix = "tab"
   i = ControlNA(gctl, strPrefix, blnTag)

Case acLine
   strPrefix = "lin"
   i = ControlNA(gctl, strPrefix, blnTag)

Case acPage
   strPrefix = "pge"
   i = ControlNA(gctl, strPrefix, blnTag)

Case acPageBreak
   strPrefix = "brk"
   i = ControlNA(gctl, strPrefix, blnTag)

Case acRectangle
   strPrefix = "shp"
   i = ControlNA(gctl, strPrefix, blnTag)
```

(continued)

```
            End Select
         Next gctl
      Next gfrm
      Call MsgBox("All form controls renamed!", vbOKOnly, "Done")

   ErrorHandlerExit:
      Exit Function

   ErrorHandler:
      'If an option button or a check box is unbound, set
      'blnUnbound to True so that the code uses the NA function instead of CS.
      If Err.Number = 2455 Then
         blnUnbound = True
         Resume Next
      Else
         AddInErr Err
         Resume ErrorHandlerExit
      End If

   End Function

   Public Function LNCRenameReportControls() As Variant
   'Renames all the controls on open reports

      'Generate table of control types to use in renaming controls
      '(if it doesn't already exist).
      CreateCTTable

   On Error GoTo ErrorHandler

      'Determine whether any reports are open, and exit if not.
      If Reports.Count = 0 Then
         MsgBox "No reports are open; exiting"
         GoTo ErrorHandlerExit
      End If

      'Determine whether original control names
      'should be stored in Tag property.
      gstrMessage = "When processing report controls, should " _
           & "the  original control name be saved to the " _
           & "control's Tag property?"
      intTag = MsgBox(gstrMessage, vbYesNo + vbQuestion + _
         vbDefaultButton2, "Control Name Backup")

      If intTag = vbYes Then
         blnTag = True
      Else
         blnTag = False
      End If
```

```
'Process open reports.
For Each grpt In Reports

   For Each gctl In grpt.Controls
      strCtlName = gctl.Name
      glngControlType = gctl.ControlType
      blnUnbound = False

      Select Case glngControlType
         'Controls with control source
         Case acTextBox
            strPrefix = "txt"
            i = ControlCS(gctl, strPrefix, blnTag)

         Case acComboBox
            strPrefix = "cbo"
            i = ControlCS(gctl, strPrefix, blnTag)

         Case acCheckBox
            strPrefix = "chk"
            strControlSource = gctl.ControlSource
            If blnUnbound = False Then
               i = ControlCS(gctl, strPrefix, blnTag)
            Else
               i = ControlNA(gctl, strPrefix, blnTag)
            End If

         Case acBoundObjectFrame
            strPrefix = "frb"
            i = ControlCS(gctl, strPrefix, blnTag)

         Case acListBox
            strPrefix = "lst"
            i = ControlCS(gctl, strPrefix, blnTag)

         Case acOptionGroup
            strPrefix = "fra"
            i = ControlCS(gctl, strPrefix, blnTag)

         Case acOptionButton
            strPrefix = "opt"
            strControlSource = gctl.ControlSource
            If blnUnbound = False Then
               i = ControlCS(gctl, strPrefix, blnTag)
            Else
               i = ControlNA(gctl, strPrefix, blnTag)
            End If
```

(continued)

```
            'Controls with caption only
            Case acToggleButton
               strPrefix = "tgl"
               i = ControlCA(gctl, strPrefix, blnTag)

            Case acLabel
               strPrefix = "lbl"
               i = ControlCA(gctl, strPrefix, blnTag)

            Case acCommandButton
               strPrefix = "cmd"
               i = ControlCA(gctl, strPrefix, blnTag)

            'Controls with source object only
            Case acSubform
               strPrefix = "sub"
               i = ControlSO(gctl, strPrefix, blnTag)

            'Controls with none of the above
            Case acObjectFrame
               strPrefix = "fru"
               i = ControlNA(gctl, strPrefix, blnTag)

            Case acImage
               strPrefix = "img"
               i = ControlNA(gctl, strPrefix, blnTag)

            Case acTabCtl
               strPrefix = "tab"
               i = ControlNA(gctl, strPrefix, blnTag)

            Case acLine
               strPrefix = "lin"
               i = ControlNA(gctl, strPrefix, blnTag)

            Case acPage
               strPrefix = "pge"
               i = ControlNA(gctl, strPrefix, blnTag)

            Case acPageBreak
               strPrefix = "brk"
               i = ControlNA(gctl, strPrefix, blnTag)

            Case acRectangle
               strPrefix = "shp"
               i = ControlNA(gctl, strPrefix, blnTag)

         End Select
      Next gctl
   Next grpt
```

```
   Call MsgBox("All report controls renamed!", _
            vbOKOnly, "Done")

ErrorHandlerExit:
   Exit Function

ErrorHandler:
   'If an option button or a check box is unbound, set
   'blnUnbound to True so that the code uses the NA
   'function instead of CS.
   If Err.Number = 2455 Then
      blnUnbound = True
      Resume Next
   Else
      AddInErr Err
      Resume ErrorHandlerExit
   End If

End Function

Public Function ControlCS(ctl As Control, _
strPrefix As String, blnTag As Boolean) As Integer
'Does group renaming of all controls with control sources
'on a form or report

On Error GoTo ErrorHandler

   Dim strControlSource As String

   strControlSource = Nz(ctl.ControlSource)
   gstrOldCtlName = ctl.ControlName

   'Check whether control is already correctly
   'named and also special case for
   'controls whose original name starts
   'with "Option" or "Frame"
   '(same first three letters as prefix).
   If Left(gstrOldCtlName, 3) = strPrefix And _
      Left(gstrOldCtlName, 6) _
      <> "Option" And Left(gstrOldCtlName, 3) = strPrefix And _
      Left(gstrOldCtlName, 5) <> "Frame" Then
      Exit Function

   'If the control source isn't empty, use it.
   ElseIf strControlSource <> "" Then
      gstrNewCtlName = strPrefix & _
        StripNonAlphaNumericChars(strControlSource)
   'Otherwise, use the original control name.
```

(continued)

```
    Else
       gstrNewCtlName = strPrefix & _
         StripNonAlphaNumericChars(gstrOldCtlName)
    End If

    'Fix name of "Page x of y" text box controls
    'on Database Wizard reports.
    If gstrNewCtlName = "txtPagePageofPages" Then
       gstrNewCtlName = "txtPages"
    End If

    'Show the user
    '  - the original control name
    '  - the control type
    '  - the control source
    '  - the proposed new name
    'and ask whether the new name is acceptable.
    gintRenameFail = True
    Do While gintRenameFail
       gintRenameFail = False
       gintReturn = MsgBox( _
           "Rename " & _
           DLookup("[ControlTypeName]", "zLNCtblControlType", _
           "[ControlType] = " & ctl.ControlType) _
           & " control currently named " _
           & gstrOldCtlName & vbCrLf & _
           "(control source: " & strControlSource & ") " & _
           "to" & vbCrLf & gstrNewCtlName & "?", _
           vbYesNo + vbQuestion + vbDefaultButton1, _
           "Rename control")

       'If the user clicks the Yes button, rename the control.
       If gintReturn = vbYes Then
          If blnTag = True Then
             ctl.Tag = ctl.ControlName
          End If
          ctl.ControlName = gstrNewCtlName

          'Otherwise, display an input box for editing the name.
       ElseIf gintReturn = vbNo Then
          gstrNewCtlName = _
             InputBox("Modify new control name", _
             "Rename control", gstrNewCtlName)
             ctl.ControlName = gstrNewCtlName
       End If
    Loop

ErrorHandlerExit:
   Exit Function
```

Chapter 21

```
ErrorHandler:
   'If the proposed control name is already in use,
   'return to the renaming dialog box.
   gintRenameFail = True
   If Err.Number = 2104 Then
      MsgBox "There is another control named " & _
         gstrNewCtlName & "; please try again", , _
         "Control Name Used"
      gstrNewCtlName = gstrNewCtlName & "1"
   Else
      AddInErr Err
      Resume ErrorHandlerExit
   End If

   Resume Next

End Function

Public Function ControlCA(ctl As Control, _
strPrefix As String, blnTag As Boolean) As Integer

'Does group renaming of all controls with
'captions on a form or report

On Error GoTo ErrorHandler

   Dim strCaption As String

   gstrOldCtlName = ctl.ControlName
   strCaption = ctl.Caption

   If Left(gstrOldCtlName, 3) = strPrefix Then
      Exit Function
   ElseIf strCaption <> "" Then
      If Left(strCaption, 3) = "frm" Then
         gstrNewCtlName = strPrefix & _
            Mid(StripNonAlphaNumericChars(strCaption), 4)
      ElseIf Left(strCaption, 4) = "fsub" Then
         gstrNewCtlName = strPrefix & _
            Mid(StripNonAlphaNumericChars(strCaption), 5)
      Else
         gstrNewCtlName = strPrefix & _
            StripNonAlphaNumericChars(strCaption)
      End If
   ElseIf strCaption = "" Then
      If Left(gstrOldCtlName, 3) = "frm" Then
         gstrNewCtlName = strPrefix & _
            Mid(StripNonAlphaNumericChars(gstrOldCtlName), 4)
      ElseIf Left(gstrOldCtlName, 4) = "fsub" Then
```

(continued)

```
            gstrNewCtlName = strPrefix & _
               Mid(StripNonAlphaNumericChars(gstrOldCtlName), 5)
         Else
            gstrNewCtlName = strPrefix & _
               StripNonAlphaNumericChars(gstrOldCtlName)
         End If
      End If

      If Right(gstrNewCtlName, 12) = "SubformLabel" Then
         gstrNewCtlName = Left(gstrNewCtlName, _
               Len(gstrNewCtlName) - 12)
      ElseIf Right(gstrNewCtlName, 5) = "Label" Then
         gstrNewCtlName = Left(gstrNewCtlName, _
               Len(gstrNewCtlName) - 5)
      End If

      gintRenameFail = True
      Do While gintRenameFail
         gintRenameFail = False
         gintReturn = MsgBox("Rename " _
            & DLookup("[ControlTypeName]", _
            "zLNCtblControlType", "[ControlType] = " _
            & ctl.ControlType) _
            & " control currently named " & gstrOldCtlName _
            & vbCrLf & _
            "(caption: " & strCaption & ") to" & vbCrLf & _
            gstrNewCtlName & "?", vbYesNo + vbQuestion + _
            vbDefaultButton1, "Rename control")
         If gintReturn = vbYes Then
            If blnTag = True Then ctl.Tag = ctl.ControlName
            ctl.ControlName = gstrNewCtlName
         ElseIf gintReturn = vbNo Then
            gstrNewCtlName = InputBox("Modify new control name", _
               "Rename control", gstrNewCtlName)
            ctl.ControlName = gstrNewCtlName
         End If
      Loop

ErrorHandlerExit:
   Exit Function

ErrorHandler:
   'If the proposed control name is already in use,
   'return to the renaming dialog box.
   gintRenameFail = True
   If Err.Number = 2104 Then
      MsgBox "There is another control named " & _
         gstrNewCtlName & "; please try again", , _
         "Control Name Used"
      gstrNewCtlName = gstrNewCtlName & "1"
```

```
   Else
      AddInErr Err
      Resume ErrorHandlerExit
   End If

   Resume Next

End Function

Public Function ControlSO(ctl As Control, _
strPrefix As String, blnTag As Boolean) As Integer
'Does group renaming of all controls with source objects on a form
'or report Called from RenameFormControls and RenameReportControls in
'this module

On Error GoTo ErrorHandler

   gstrOldCtlName = ctl.ControlName
   gstrSourceObject = Nz(ctl.SourceObject)

   If Left(gstrOldCtlName, 3) = strPrefix Then
      Exit Function
   ElseIf gstrSourceObject <> "" Then
      If Left(gstrSourceObject, 3) = "frm" Then
         gstrNewCtlName = strPrefix & _
            Mid(StripNonAlphaNumericChars(gstrSourceObject), 4)
      ElseIf Left(gstrSourceObject, 4) = "fsub" Then
         gstrNewCtlName = strPrefix & _
            Mid(StripNonAlphaNumericChars(gstrSourceObject), 5)
      Else
         gstrNewCtlName = strPrefix & _
            StripNonAlphaNumericChars(gstrSourceObject)
      End If
   ElseIf gstrSourceObject = "" Then
      If Left(gstrOldCtlName, 3) = "frm" Then
         gstrNewCtlName = strPrefix & _
            Mid(StripNonAlphaNumericChars(gstrOldCtlName), 4)
      ElseIf Left(gstrOldCtlName, 4) = "fsub" Then
         gstrNewCtlName = strPrefix & _
            Mid(StripNonAlphaNumericChars(gstrOldCtlName), 5)
      Else
         gstrNewCtlName = strPrefix & _
            StripNonAlphaNumericChars(gstrOldCtlName)
      End If
   Else
      gstrNewCtlName = strPrefix & _
         StripNonAlphaNumericChars(gstrOldCtlName)
   End If
```

(continued)

```
    If Right(gstrNewCtlName, 7) = "Subform" Then
       gstrNewCtlName = Left(gstrNewCtlName, _
            Len(gstrNewCtlName) - 7)
    End If

    gintRenameFail = True
    Do While gintRenameFail
       gintRenameFail = False
       gintReturn = MsgBox("Rename " & _
          DLookup("[ControlTypeName]", _
          "zLNCtblControlType", "[ControlType] = " & _
          ctl.ControlType) _
          & " control currently named " & _
          gstrOldCtlName & vbCrLf & _
          "(source object: " & gstrSourceObject & ") to" _
          & vbCrLf & _
          gstrNewCtlName & "?", vbYesNo + _
          vbQuestion + vbDefaultButton1, _
          "Rename control")
       If gintReturn = vbYes Then
          If blnTag = True Then ctl.Tag = ctl.ControlName
          ctl.ControlName = gstrNewCtlName
       ElseIf gintReturn = vbNo Then
          gstrNewCtlName = InputBox("Modify new control name", _
             "Rename control", gstrNewCtlName)
          ctl.ControlName = gstrNewCtlName
       End If
    Loop

ErrorHandlerExit:
   Exit Function

ErrorHandler:
   'If the proposed control name is already in use,
   'return to the renaming dialog box.
   gintRenameFail = True
   If Err.Number = 2104 Then
      MsgBox "There is another control named " & _
         gstrNewCtlName & "; please try again", , _
         "Control Name Used"
      gstrNewCtlName = gstrNewCtlName & "1"
   Else
      AddInErr Err
      Resume ErrorHandlerExit
   End If
   Resume ErrorHandlerExit

End Function
```

```
Public Function ControlNA(ctl As Control, _
   strPrefix As String, blnTag As Boolean) As Integer
'Called from RenameFormControls and RenameReportControls
'in this module
'Does group renaming of all controls not fitting the
'other categories on a form or report

On Error GoTo ErrorHandler

   gstrOldCtlName = ctl.ControlName

   'Special case for lines whose default name is "Line"
   'or "Option" (same first three letters
   'as the standard prefix)
   If Left(gstrOldCtlName, 3) = strPrefix And _
      Left(gstrOldCtlName, 6) <> "Option" And _
      Left(gstrOldCtlName, 4) <> "Line" Then
      Exit Function
   Else
      gstrNewCtlName = strPrefix & _
          StripNonAlphaNumericChars(gstrOldCtlName)
   End If

   gintRenameFail = True
   Do While gintRenameFail
      gintRenameFail = False
      gintReturn = MsgBox("Rename " & _
         DLookup("[ControlTypeName]", _
         "zLNCtblControlType", "[ControlType] = " & _
         ctl.ControlType) & _
         " control currently named " & gstrOldCtlName _
         & " to" & vbCrLf _
         & gstrNewCtlName & "?", _
         vbYesNo + vbQuestion + vbDefaultButton1, _
         "Rename control")
      If gintReturn = vbYes Then
         If blnTag = True Then ctl.Tag = ctl.ControlName
         ctl.ControlName = gstrNewCtlName
      ElseIf gintReturn = vbNo Then
         gstrNewCtlName = InputBox("Modify new control name", _
            "Rename control", gstrNewCtlName)
         ctl.ControlName = gstrNewCtlName
      End If
   Loop

ErrorHandlerExit:
   Exit Function
```

(continued)

```
ErrorHandler:
   'If the proposed control name is already in use,
   'return to the renaming dialog box.
   gintRenameFail = True
   If Err.Number = 2104 Then
      MsgBox "There is another control named " & _
         gstrNewCtlName & "; please try again", , _
         "Control Name Used"
      gstrNewCtlName = gstrNewCtlName & "1"
   Else
      AddInErr Err
   End If
   Resume ErrorHandlerExit

End Function

Public Function CreateCTTable()
'Called from LNCRenameFormControls and
'LNCRenameReportControls function
'in this module

   Dim strCTTable As String

   strCTTable = "zLNCtblControlType"

   'Delete old table, if there is one.
   Set gdbs = CurrentDb
   strCTTable = "zLNCtblControlType"
   On Error Resume Next
   gdbs.TableDefs.Delete strCTTable

On Error GoTo ErrorHandler
   'Generate table of control types to use
   'in renaming controls.
   'If there is a "table not found" error, exit function.
   gstrSQL = "CREATE TABLE " & strCTTable & _
      "(ControlType LONG, ControlTypeName TEXT (50));"
   DoCmd.RunSQL gstrSQL

   'Append data to table of control types.
   Set gdbs = CurrentDb
   Set grst = gdbs.OpenRecordset(strCTTable, dbOpenTable)
   With grst
      .AddNew
      !ControlType = 100
      !ControlTypeName = "Label"
      .Update
      .AddNew
      !ControlType = 101
```

```
!ControlTypeName = "Rectangle"
.Update
.AddNew
!ControlType = 102
!ControlTypeName = "Line"
.Update
.AddNew
!ControlType = 103
!ControlTypeName = "Image"
.Update
.AddNew
!ControlType = 104
!ControlTypeName = "Command Button"
.Update
.AddNew
!ControlType = 105
!ControlTypeName = "Option Button"
.Update
.AddNew
!ControlType = 106
!ControlTypeName = "Check Box"
.Update
.AddNew
!ControlType = 107
!ControlTypeName = "Option Group"
.Update
.AddNew
!ControlType = 108
!ControlTypeName = "Bound Object Frame"
.Update
.AddNew
!ControlType = 109
!ControlTypeName = "Text Box"
.Update
.AddNew
!ControlType = 110
!ControlTypeName = "List Box"
.Update
.AddNew
!ControlType = 111
!ControlTypeName = "Combo Box"
.Update
.AddNew
!ControlType = 112
!ControlTypeName = "Subform/Subreport"
.Update
.AddNew
!ControlType = 114
!ControlTypeName = "Object Frame"
.Update
```

(continued)

```
      .AddNew
      !ControlType = 118
      !ControlTypeName = "Page Break"
      .Update
      .AddNew
      !ControlType = 122
      !ControlTypeName = "Toggle Button"
      .Update
      .AddNew
      !ControlType = 123
      !ControlTypeName = "Tab Control"
      .Update
      .AddNew
      !ControlType = 124
      !ControlTypeName = "Page"
      .Update
      .Close
   End With

ErrorHandlerExit:
   Exit Function

ErrorHandler:
   If Err.Number = 3010 Then
      'Control types table already exists
      Exit Function
   Else
      AddInErr Err
      Resume ErrorHandlerExit
   End If

End Function
```

The *Declarations* section of this module declares two command bar buttons (pctlFormButton and pctlReportButton), using the *WithEvents* keyword. These buttons will be used to run the LNC Rename code for renaming form or report control buttons. The buttons are created on specific Access toolbars, so their code must be in the Designer module even though CommandBars and CommandBarButtons belong to the Office object model. The *OnAddInsUpdate*, *OnBeginShutdown*, and *OnStartupComplete* events don't need any code in this add-in.

The *Declarations* section of this module also declares several groups of global and regular variables—a global variable to reference the host application, global variables to rename controls, regular variables for creating the toolbar buttons and for handling renaming, and two constants for the special characters needed to surround the ProgId used for setting the command bar buttons' *OnAction* property.

The *OnConnection* event procedure sets the command bar button variables. It uses the *CreateFormCommandBarButton* and *CreateReportCommandBarButton* functions to create these buttons on the appropriate Access toolbars.

The *OnDisconnection* event procedure runs a function (also included in this module) to remove the two command bar buttons when the add-in is disconnected. The buttons aren't removed when the host application is closed—only when the add-in is unloaded in the COM Add-Ins dialog box. The last two functions in this module are the *Click* event procedures for the two command bar buttons. They run the *LNCRenameFormControls* and *LNCRenameReportControls* functions, which rename form controls and report controls.

See Chapter 13, "Customizing Access Toolbars and Menus (Command Bars)," for more details on creating command bar buttons.

The module's first procedure is a custom error handler function that's called by the other functions in the module. After the *IDTExtensibility2* event procedures, there are two *Click* event procedures to run the *LNCRenameFormControls* and *LNCRenameReportsControls* functions (also in this module).

The *CreateFormCommandBarButton* function creates the toolbar button for renaming controls on open forms. This function first sets the *gobjAppInstance* global variable to the Access *Application* object, and then it sets a reference to the Form Design toolbar (the toolbar where the button will be created). The code looks for the button on this toolbar (so as not to create a duplicate button) using its *Tag* property; if it doesn't find the button, it creates one.

Normally, a command bar button's *OnAction* property is set to the name of a macro (a *Sub* procedure with no arguments) that's run when the button is clicked. However, for buttons used in COM add-ins, a special syntax is used, which sets the *OnAction* property to the ProgId of the COM add-in. (The button's *Click* event is handled by the *Click* event procedure.)

note A COM add-in's ProgID (programmatic identifier) is the subkey created for the add-in in the registry. It consists of the name of the project followed by the name of the designer, separated by a period.

The *CreateReportCommandBarButton* function is similar; it creates a button for the Report Design toolbar. The *RemoveAddInCommandBarButton* function removes the add-in's command buttons; it's called by the *OnDisconnection* event procedure.

The *LNCRenameFormControls* and *LNCRenameReportControls* functions are based on code used in the Access LNC Rename add-in, so I won't address them in detail here. The significant differences are that each of these functions deals with one type of database object (forms or reports) and cycles through the open forms (or reports) only. (The Rename Form Controls and Rename Report Controls menu add-ins rename controls on all forms or reports, regardless of whether they're open.) This provides an intermediate step between renaming controls on all forms (or reports) and renaming only the controls on the current form (or report). The user can open only the forms or reports that need their controls renamed and then click the Rename Controls button on the form or report design toolbar.

The *LNCRenameFormControls* and *LNCRenameReportControls* functions call the same functions for renaming of various controls that are used in the Access add-in.

Troubleshooting

When I try to compile my COM add-in, I get the message *Compile error: User-defined type not defined*

This error (which can occur in a regular Access database, an Access add-in, or a COM add-in) most likely results from a missing or wrong version reference. To fix the broken reference, follow these steps:

1. If necessary, reset the code by clicking the Reset button or by choosing Run, Reset.
2. Uninstall the add-in from the Add-Ins (or COM Add-Ins) dialog box in an Access database.
3. Close the database.
4. Open the add-in (if it's an Access add-in), or follow the steps in the sidebar "Reopening a COM Add-In for Editing," page 961, to open a COM add-in.
5. Choose Tools, References in the Visual Basic Editor window, and look for any references that are marked *MISSING*. Uncheck them, and then look for the correct version of the object library (such as Microsoft DAO 3.6 Object Library) and check it.

If your code uses DAO database or recordset objects, you need a reference to the DAO object library. This reference isn't included in a new Access 2000 or Access 2002 database—you have to add it manually. After checking all the references you need, compile the add-in (or database). (If it's a COM add-in, save it as a DLL again.) After that the code should run.

The LNC Rename COM add-in also has a supporting code module, a standard module named basSharedCode. This module contains all the generic Office code that can be used for other designers if I decide to extend this add-in to support other Office applications. (This module currently includes only the *StripNonAlphaNumericChars* function and the *AddInErr* error handler function.) The basSharedCode module's code is shown here.

```
Option Explicit

Public Function StripNonAlphaNumericChars(strText As String) As String
'Strips a variety of nonalphanumeric characters from a text string
```

```
On Error GoTo ErrorHandler

   Dim strTestString As String
   Dim strTestChar As String
   Dim lngFound As Long
   Dim i As Integer
   Dim strStripChars As String

   strStripChars = " `~!@#$%^&*()-_=+[{]};:',<.>/?" _
   & Chr$(34) & Chr$(13) & Chr$(10)
   strTestString = strText

   i = 1
   Do While i <= Len(strTestString)
     'Find a strippable character.
     strTestChar = Mid$(strTestString, i, 1)
     lngFound = InStr(strStripChars, strTestChar)
     If lngFound > 0 Then
       strTestString = Left(strTestString, i - 1) _
   & Mid(strTestString, i + 1)
     Else
       i = i + 1
     End If
   Loop

   StripNonAlphaNumericChars = strTestString

ErrorHandlerExit:
   Exit Function

ErrorHandler:
   AddInErr Err
   Resume ErrorHandlerExit

End Function
```

Installing a COM Add-In

When you create a DLL for a COM add-in (by choosing File, Make *ProjectName*.DLL), the add-in is automatically installed on that computer. To install it on another computer, copy the DLL file to that computer's add-ins folder (C:\Documents and Settings*User Name*\Application Data\Microsoft\AddIns for Windows 2000, or C:\Windows\Application Data\Microsoft\Addins for Windows Me), open an Access database, and then open the COM Add-Ins dialog box from its toolbar button.

If the add-in appears in the list of available add-ins, just select it; otherwise, click the Add button, as shown in Figure 21-31, and select the DLL file from its folder.

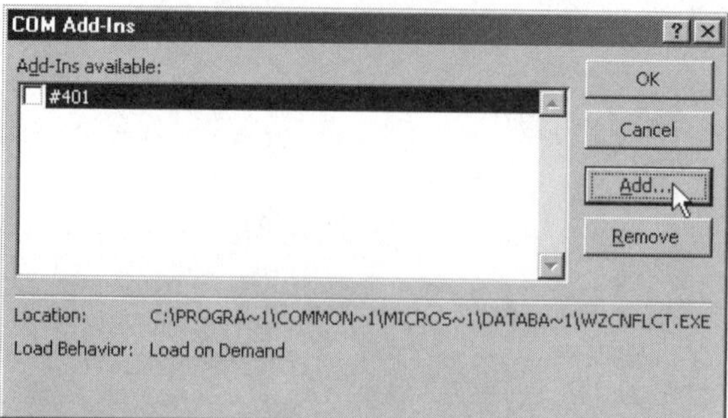

Figure 21-31. You install a new COM add-in in the COM Add-Ins dialog box.

In the Add Add-In dialog box that appears, you can select the DLL file to install, as shown in Figure 21-32.

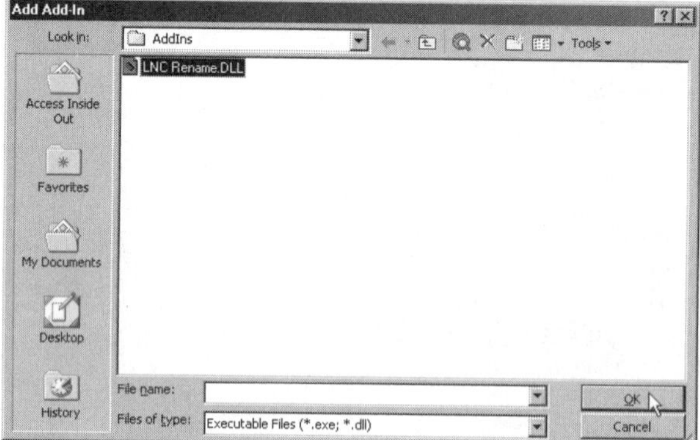

Figure 21-32. You select the COM DLL file to install from the Add Add-In dialog box.

The COM add-in now appears in the COM Add-Ins dialog box, selected, as shown in Figure 21-33. You can clear its check box to temporarily unload it, or you can select it and click the Remove button to completely remove it. It's a good idea to remove the add-in before modifying its design; you then reinstall it after creating the new DLL file.

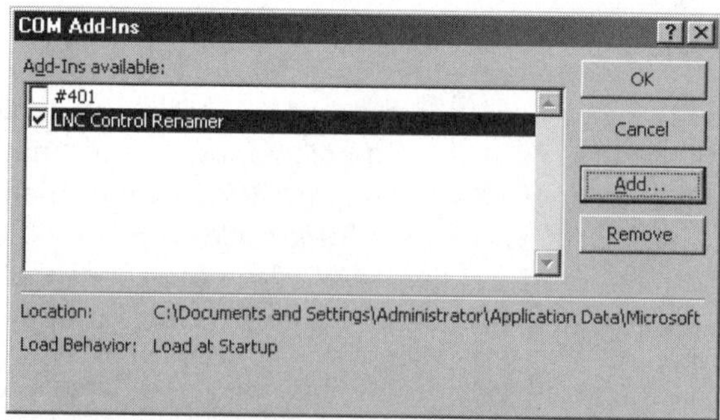

Figure 21-33. The LNC Control Renamer add-in is listed as an installed COM add-in.

Chapter 21

Reopening a COM Add-In for Editing

It's easy to reopen an Access add-in for editing. Just open the MDA file as you would open any database. However, COM add-ins are prepared as VBA files and then saved as DLL files, and thus they can't be opened directly (unless you have Visual Basic installed, in which case double-clicking a VBA file will open it in Visual Basic, which isn't what you want when working with a COM add-in project file created with VBA).

To reopen a COM add-in project for editing, follow these steps:

1. Open an Access database.
2. Uninstall the COM add-in from the COM Add-Ins dialog box.
3. In an Access window without any database opened, press Alt+F11 to open the Visual Basic Editor window.
4. Choose File, Open Project, and navigate to the folder in which you saved the COM add-in project (probably the standard add-ins folder: C:\Documents and Settings*User Name*\Application Data\Microsoft\AddIns folder for Windows 2000, or C:\Windows\Application Data\Microsoft\Addins for Windows Me). Select the project, and click Open, as shown in Figure 21-34.

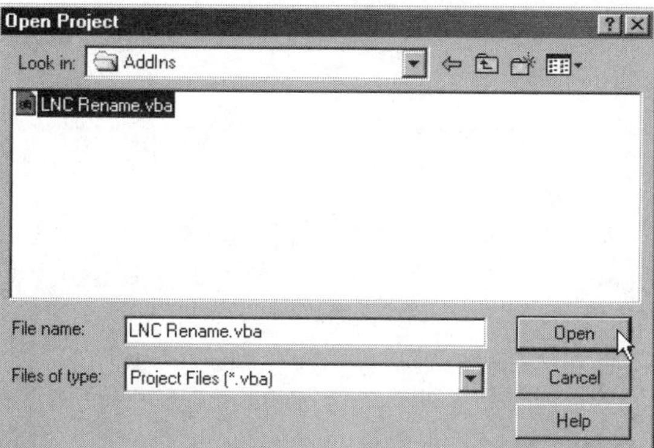

Figure 21-34. Open the COM add-in's saved VBA project to edit the add-in.

The project opens in the Project Explorer, and you can edit it as needed. When you've finished, recompile the project by choosing Debug, Compile *ProjectName*, and then create an updated DLL file by choosing File, Make *ProjectName*.DLL.

Click OK, and you'll see a Rename Controls button on the Form Design and Report Design toolbars. Figure 21-35 shows this button on the Form Design toolbar, in the upper right corner.

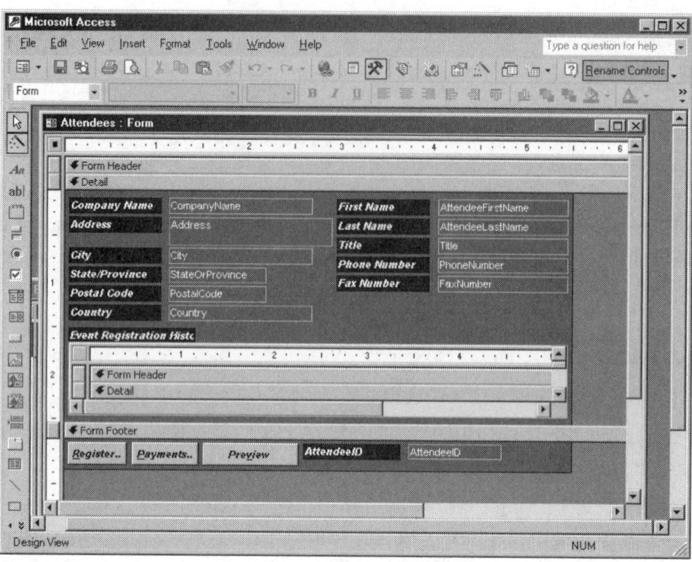

Figure 21-35. The Rename Controls button on the Form Design toolbar lets you run the add-in quickly.

For information about using the LNC Control Renamer add-in, see Chapter 15, "Using Add-Ins to Expand Access Functionality."

InsideOut

When you add a control to a command bar (toolbar or menu bar) in a COM add-in, you need to know the command bar's name—the name used to reference it in VBA code. But the names on the View menu's Toolbars submenu and in the Customize dialog box's Toolbars list might not be the same as those used in code. You can see the command bar names by iterating through the application's *CommandBars* collection, which displays the *Name* property of each command bar in the Immediate window.

on the CD After running the *ListCommandBars* function (located in basUtilities in the Test Access 2002 database), you'll see a list of command bar names in the Immediate window. Simply select the name of the command bar you want to reference in code, copy it with Ctrl+C, and then paste it into your VBA code with Ctrl+V, to ensure that you are using the correct name for the command bar .

Although my sample COM add-in doesn't use a form, COM add-ins in general can include *UserForm* objects. (You're probably familiar with UserForms from Word, Excel, or Outlook.) By default, UserForms aren't available in Access because Access has its own forms, which are much more useful for displaying Access data. (UserForms and controls on UserForms can't be bound to data.) This means that you can't use a UserForm in the Access Designer portion of a COM add-in, at least if you create the COM add-in in the Access Visual Basic Editor window.

Part 7

Appendixes

Appendix A
Setup and Installation

Most users don't need to install more than one version of Microsoft Office, but if you develop applications for other users, you probably need to have two or even three different versions of Office installed. The "Installing Office XP" section of this appendix deals with installing Office XP, and the "Working with Multiple Versions of Access" section describes some techniques you can use to make it easier to work in more than one version of Microsoft Access, including the creation of multiple boot partitions so that each version of Office can be installed in its own partition.

Definitions of Terms

- **Partition.** A partition is a portion of a hard drive used to store programs or data. A partition has a letter designation (starting with C). You can create partitions with the old DOS FDISK utility, or with a utility such as PartitionMagic.
- **Boot Partition.** A boot partition is a partition with a bootable operating system installed. With a utility such as BootMagic or System Commander, you can select which operating system to use when you restart your computer.

Installing Office XP

Before you install Office XP you need to make sure you have the right operating system and enough RAM on your computer, and you also need to decide whether you are going to do a clean install of Office XP or install over an existing installation of Office. The following sections will guide you in these considerations.

System Requirements

To install Office XP, you need one of the following operating systems:

- Windows 98, Second Edition
- Windows Millennium Edition (Me)
- Windows NT 4.0 with Service Pack 6 or greater
- Windows 2000 (recommended)
- Windows XP

The RAM requirements for Office XP differ according to the operating system. The following requirements are for Office XP itself; add 8 MB of RAM for each Office application running simultaneously:

- Windows 98, Second Edition: 24 MB
- Windows Me: 32 MB
- Windows NT 4.0: 32 MB
- Windows 2000: 64 MB
- Windows XP: 128 MB

Clean Install vs. Installing over a Previous Version of Office

If you are installing Office XP on a new computer, or in a boot partition that has no version of Office installed, you are doing a clean install. You can do a clean installation of Office XP on a computer that has a previous version of Office if you are willing to reformat the computer (or the boot partition) before you install Office XP.

A clean installation prevents you from carrying over any possible problems from the previous installation of Office, and also ensures that all the supporting files for Office XP are the correct versions. However, if you have a previous version of Office installed, and everything is working fine (and you don't need to preserve the older version as a separate installation), you are probably better off installing Office XP over your previous installation, as described in the next section.

If you are installing to a computer (or boot partition) on which a previous version of Office is installed, you will be prompted to remove the previous version during the Office XP setup. The removal will happen automatically, but your Office settings will be preserved, so you don't have to reselect them.

Running Office XP Setup

Before you install Office XP, close down any running programs (including the Office Shortcut Bar), and move the shortcuts in the Startup group to the desktop to make the numerous restarts go faster. (To move the Startup shortcuts, right-click the taskbar and select Properties from the shortcut menu. In the Taskbar And Start Menu Properties dialog box, select the Advanced tab and click the Advanced button. In the Windows Explorer window that opens, navigate to the Startup folder under the Programs folder, select all items in the Startup folder, and drag them to the desktop.)

The following steps explain specifically how to install Office XP over Office 97, SR-2, on a boot partition with Windows 98, Second Edition, but the process is similar for other combinations of operating system and Office versions.

Appendix A: Setup and Installation

1 Insert the Office XP CD and run Setup. The first screen to appear is the Office Component Updates screen, shown in Figure A-1.

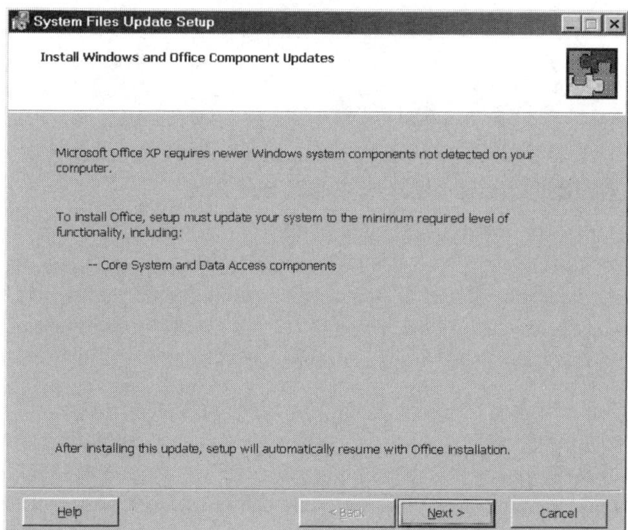

Figure A-1. Start your installation on the Office Component Updates screen.

2 Click Next to install the updates.

3 Select the I Accept The Terms In The License Agreement check box (see Figure A-2) to make the Install button available.

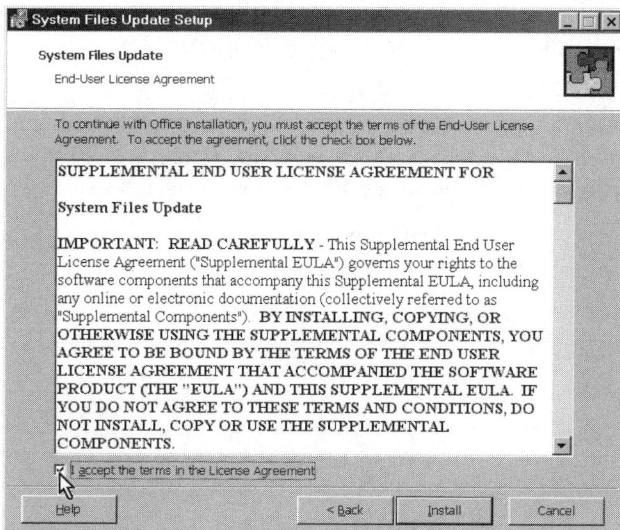

Figure A-2. You must agree to the terms in the end-user license to continue with the install.

A System Files Update screen appears next, showing progress as the system files are updated for the older operating system, as shown in Figure A-3.

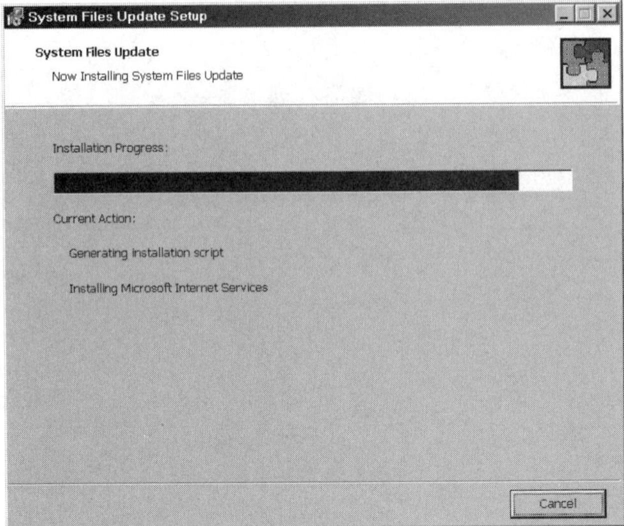

Figure A-3. This screen shows the progress of the System Files Update installation.

A message box appears, advising that you need to restart your computer.

4 Click Yes to restart your computer.

> **note** If you have a multiboot setup, select the same operating system partition after restarting Windows to resume setup where it left off.

5 When you are back in Windows, you will see another message advising you that the Windows installer was updated, and that you need to restart Windows again. Click OK to restart Windows a second time.

   If Setup does not resume on its own, re-insert the Office XP CD or run Setup.exe from the CD.

6 In the User Information screen that appears next (see Figure A-4), enter your name, initials, and (optionally) organization, and the Product Key from the back of the CD case. Click Next.

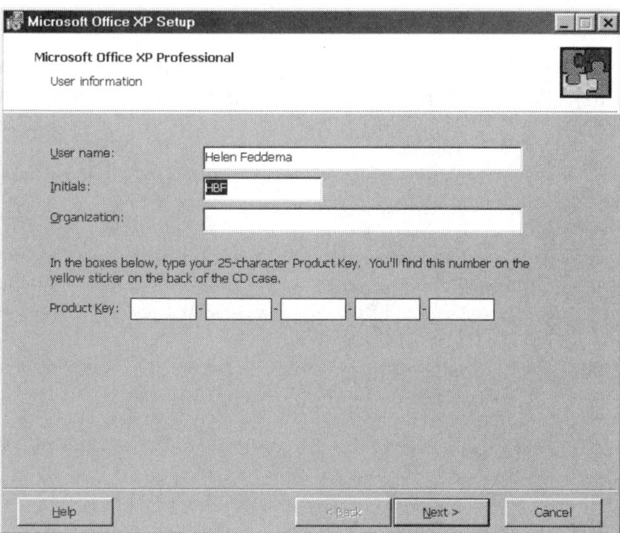

Figure A-4. Enter the requested information in the User Information screen.

7 Select the I Accept The Terms In The License Agreement check box and click Next.

The main Setup screen appears. From here you have several options:

- **Upgrade Now.** Upgrades your current Office installation, installing the most commonly used Office XP components in the same folder as the older version of Office. This can be misleading if your old Office folder had a name that included the version. (See Figure A-5.)

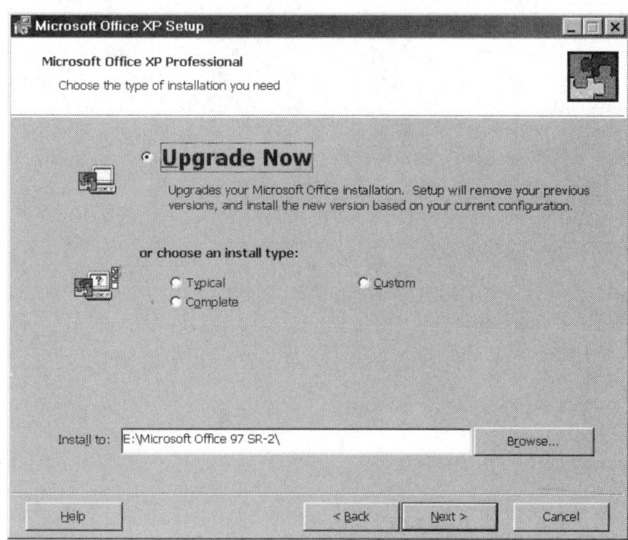

Figure A-5. The main Setup screen offers several installation options.

The other install type options let you select three types of installation:

- **Custom.** Allows you to select from a list of all the Office XP components, select a different location, and decide whether you want to keep your previous Office version.
- **Complete.** Installs all Office XP components. This is the recommended option if you have the space.
- **Typical.** This option, which is only available if there is an existing Office installation, ignores your current configuration and installs Office XP with the most commonly used files.

Independently of the install option, you can click Browse next to the Install To box to select (or create) the install folder for Office XP.

8 After you select the options you prefer (and browse to create a nondefault install folder if you want), click Next.

9 Select which previous Office components to uninstall, as shown in Figure A-6. The default option is to remove all previous versions.

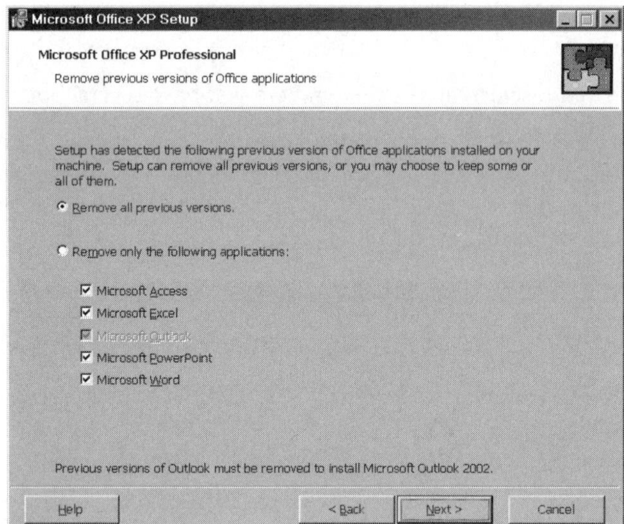

Figure A-6. You have several options for removing previous Office components.

Although I chose to remove the previous version of Office when I installed Office XP, I checked afterward and found the Office 97 installation was still in its folder, with all of its files intact, as far as I could see. If you really want to remove the previous version of Office, it's best to uninstall it and then delete its folder before starting the installation of Office XP.

The next screen has a summary of the Office XP components to install, as shown in Figure A-7.

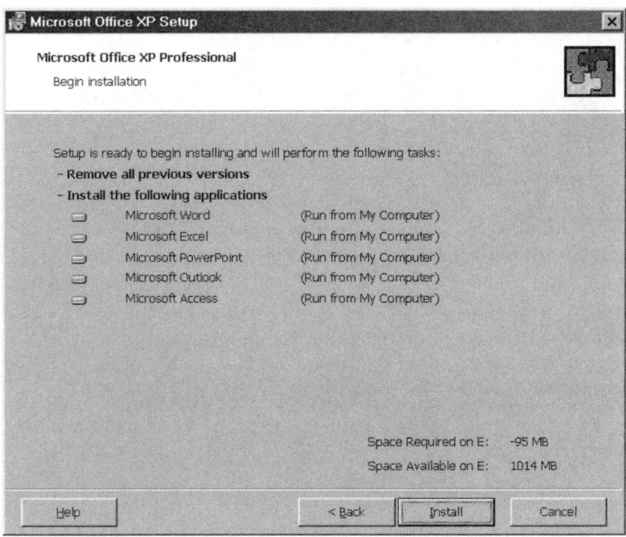

Figure A-7. The Begin Installation screen summarizes the Office XP components to install.

10 Click Install to start installing Office XP. You will get a progress screen showing the progress of various phases of installation, as shown in Figure A-8.

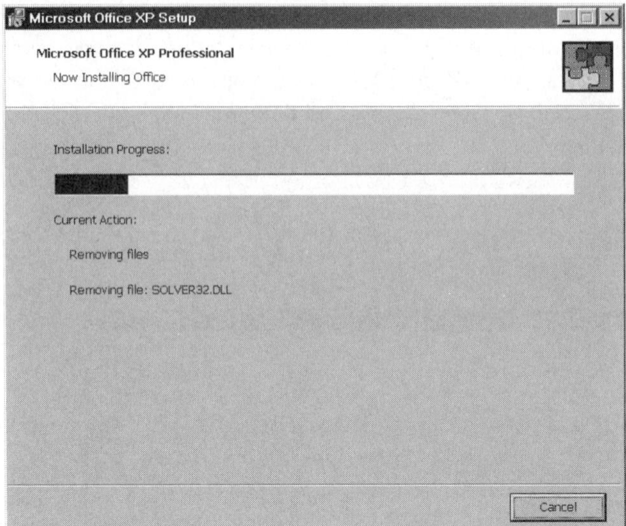

Figure A-8. The Installation Progress screen lets you know what stage the installation is in.

A final Restart message appears next. (See Figure A-9.)

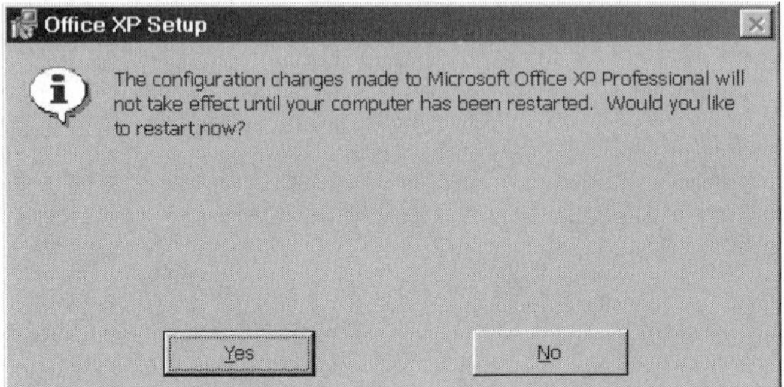

Figure A-9. The final Restart message looks like this.

You now have two new items on your Start menu—New Office Document and Open Office Document. You'll find the main Office applications at the bottom of the Programs folder, as shown in Figure A-10.

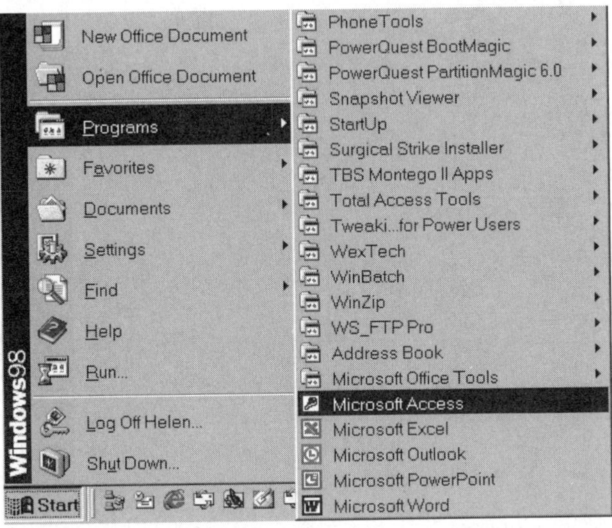

Figure A-10. Office XP shortcuts are conveniently located on the Start menu.

11 If you moved shortcuts from the Startup folder to the desktop, move them back now, omitting shortcuts from the previous version of Office. (New ones will be created for Office XP.)

> **tip** To turn on the Office Shortcut Bar, double-click the Msoffice.exe file in the Microsoft Office\Office10 folder.

Activation

The first time you run an Office XP application (or at any rate, some time before the fiftieth use), you have to activate Office.

To activate Office, follow these steps:

1 Open any Office application. The Activation Wizard opens, offering you a choice of activating Office XP by the Internet or by phone, as shown in Figure A-11.

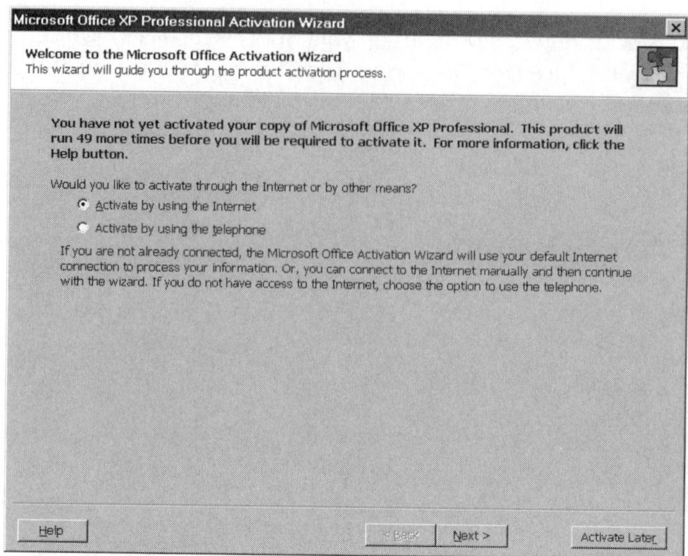

Figure A-11. The first screen of the Activation Wizard offers two options for activation.

If you select the Internet option, you will get the Dial-Up Connection dialog box unless you are already connected. After a connection is made, the Privacy Policy screen appears, as shown in Figure A-12.

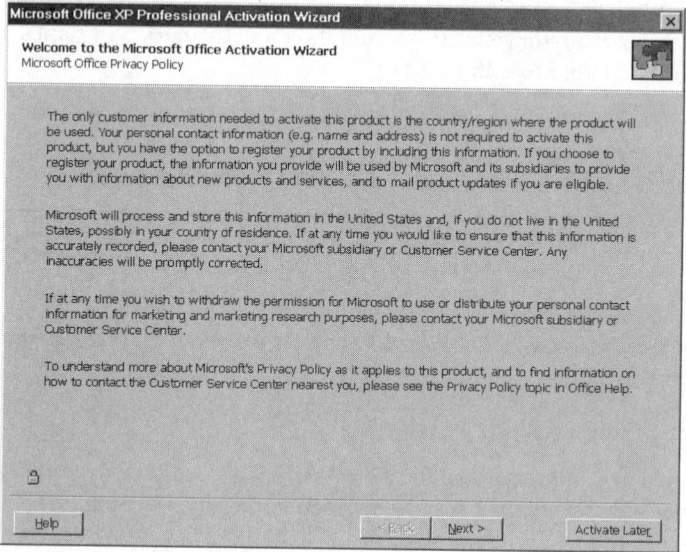

Figure A-12. The Privacy Policy screen of the Activation Wizard looks like this.

2 In the Customer Information screen that appears next (see Figure A-13), enter your personal information. If you don't want to transmit personal data, you can simply select your Country/Region. Click Next.

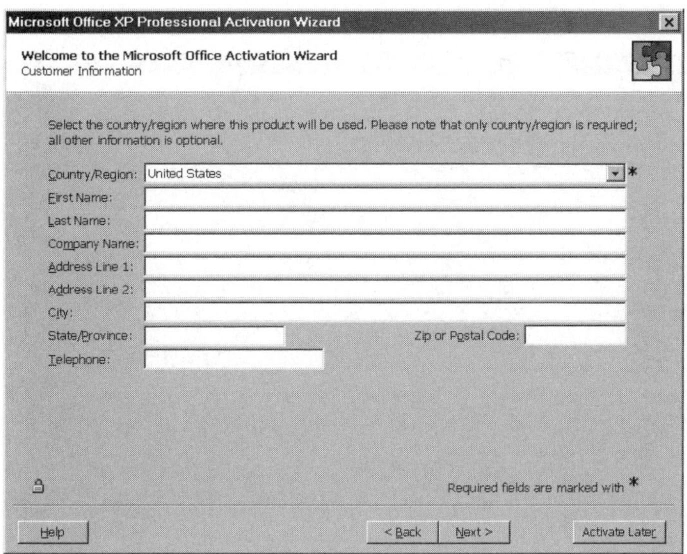

Figure A-13. Enter your personal information on the Customer Information screen of the Activation Wizard.

3 On the Special Offers screen (shown in Figure A-14), you can select several check boxes if you want to receive information or newsletters. Enter your e-mail address if you select any of the check boxes.

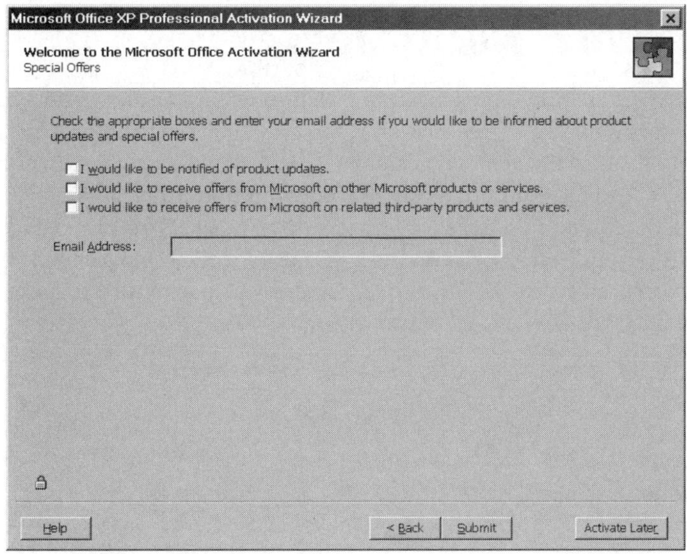

Figure A-14. The Special Offers screen of the Activation Wizard allows you to receive newsletters and other information that might be of interest.

4 Click Submit to activate Office.

When activation is completed, the Activation Complete screen appears, as shown in Figure A-15.

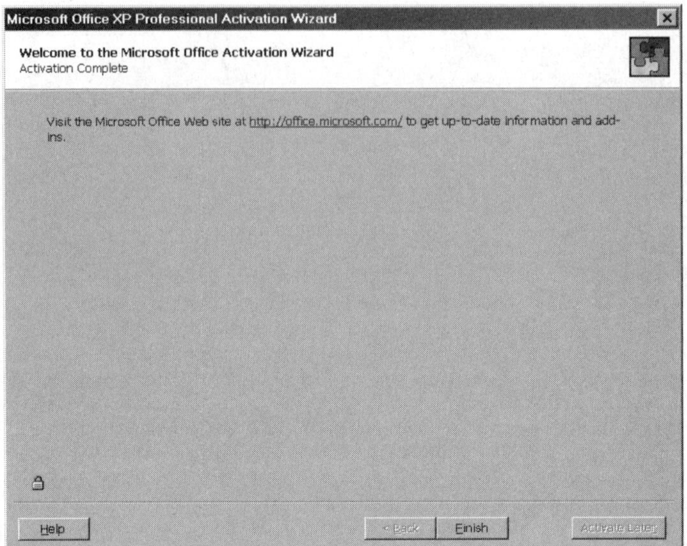

Figure A-15. The Activation Complete screen of the Activation Wizard lets you know you've successfully activated Office.

5 Click Finish to quit the Activation Wizard.

Working with Multiple Versions of Access

Access 2002 offers users more flexibility than ever for working with Access databases in different versions. You can work with an Access 2000 database in Access 2002 without converting the database, and you can save an Access 2002 database in either Access 2000 or Access 97 format. Additionally, you can connect an Access 2002 or Access 2000 front-end database to an Access 97 back-end database. You can even set up multiple front ends (say, in Access 2002, Access 2000, and Access 97) to allow users with different versions of Access to work with the same Access 97 back-end database.

The Two Native Formats of Access 2002

As Access has progressed from version to version, each version has had a new format, thereby requiring you to convert older databases to the new version of Access to get full read-write functionality. Conversion was a one-way trip: After you converted a database to the newer version, the older version of Access couldn't read the converted database. Until Access 2000, Access (unlike Word and Excel) had no provision for saving an Access database in an older Access format.

Access 2002 has two native formats with full read-write functionality: Access 2002 and Access 2000. You can open an Access 2000 database in Access 2002, without getting a message asking if you want to convert it, and work with it much as you would in Access 2000. You can even select Access 2000 as the default file format for new databases, by choosing Tools, Options, Advanced, as shown in Figure A-16.

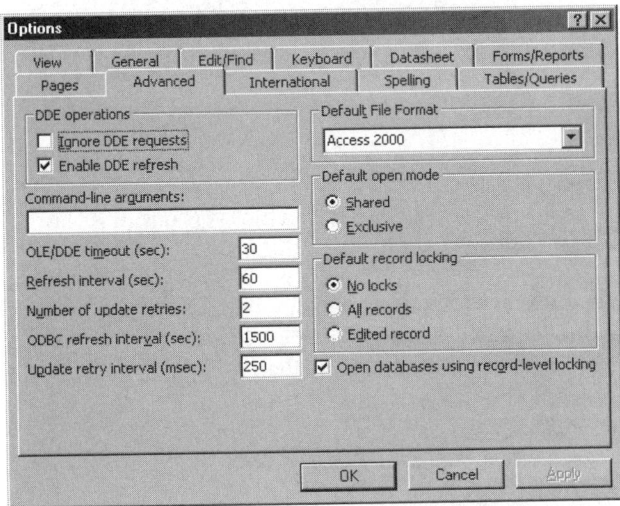

Figure A-16. You can select Access 2000 as the database format for new databases.

This option is handy if you are working in Access 2002 with databases intended for use by Access 2000 users. With Access 2000 selected as the default file format, every new database you create in Access 2002 will be an Access 2000 database.

If you are working with an Access 2002 database in Access 2000, you won't be able to use the new features of Access 2002, such as PivotTables and PivotCharts, and you might have problems with data access pages, since data access pages have been greatly enhanced in Access 2002. However, if you need to maintain a database for use by persons working in multiple versions of Access, this is not a serious limitation.

Converting Databases to Other Versions of Access

Access 2000 for the first time included a utility for saving an Access 2000 database in Access 97 format. Access 2002 extended this utility—now you can save an Access 2002 database in either Access 2000 or Access 97 format, and you can save an Access 2000 database (opened in Access 2002) in Access 97 or Access 2002 format. Figure A-17 shows the Convert Database submenu for an Access 2002 database, with three selections. Depending on the database type, two selections of the three will be available.

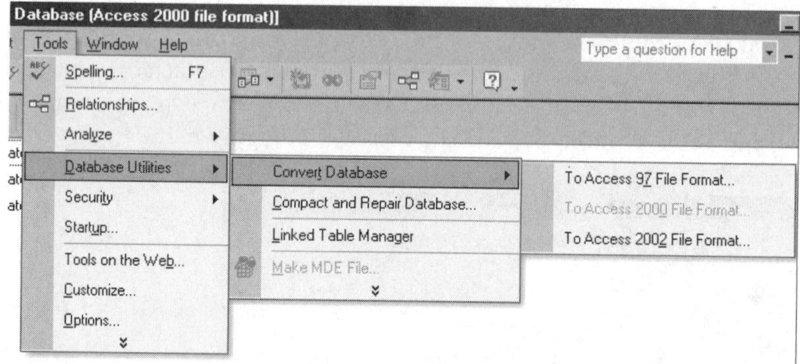

Figure A-17. You can save an Access database to other versions of Access.

If you open an Access 97 database in Access 2002, you will get the message shown in Figure A-18, with options either to convert the database to the currently selected database format (the one set in the Options dialog box's Advanced tab) or to open the database in a mode that doesn't allow design changes.

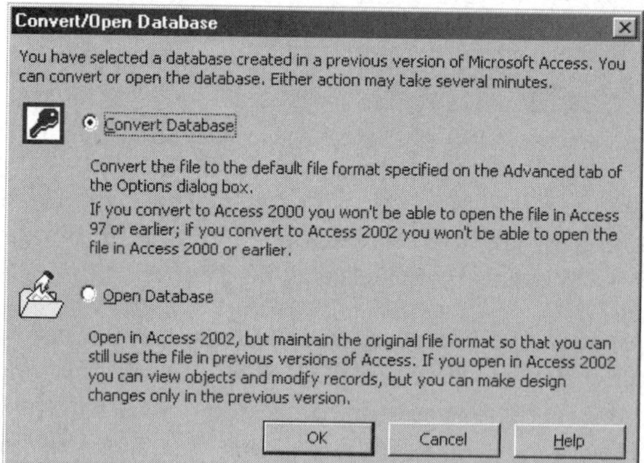

Figure A-18. The Convert/Open message appears when you open an Access 97 database in Access 2002.

If all you need to do is modify data, opening the Access 97 database is a reasonable option, but if you need to change the structure of any database objects, you will need to convert the database. After conversion, you won't be able to open the database in Access 97.

Working with Access 97 and Access 2000 Databases in Access 2002

While Access 2002 allows you to work with databases in Access 2000 and (with some limitations) Access 97 formats, sometimes you might need more than this functionality. Suppose you have a situation in which Access 97, Access 2000, and Access 2002 users all need to work with a specific Access database in its native format. You can accomplish this goal this by following these steps:

note These instructions assume that you are starting with an Access 2000 single-file database and that you have Access 97, Access 2000, and Access 2002 installed separately. (This would be a requirement in any case, to support users of all three Access versions.)

See "Installing Multiple Versions of Access in Different Boot Partitions" later in this appendix for information on installing multiple versions of Access on the same computer.

1. Split the database into a front-end database and a back-end database. You can either do this manually or by using the Database Splitter utility. (See Figure A-19.)

For more details on using the Database Splitter utility, see Chapter 15, "Using Add-Ins to Expand Access Functionality."

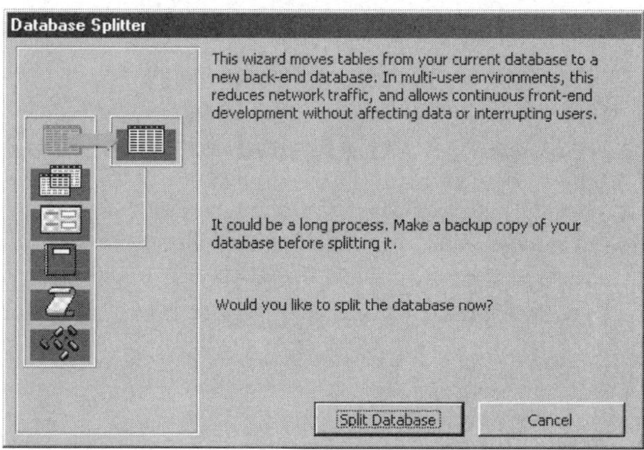

Figure A-19. Use the Database Splitter utility to split the database into a front end and a back end.

2. Open the back-end database, and save it to Access 97 format by choosing Tools, Database Utilities, Convert Database, To Access 97 File Format.
3. Open the front-end database, and (if necessary) remove any features that won't work in Access 97, such as subdatasheets, use of the ADO object model in VBA code, and data access pages.
4. Close the front-end database and rename it, including **2000** in the name to indicate that it is the Access 2000 front-end. This database will be used by Access 2000 and Access 2002 users.
5. Convert the front-end database to Access 97 format, giving it a name that includes **97** to identify it as the Access 97 front end.
6. Open the Access 2000 front end database in Access 2000, open the Visual Basic Editor window, and compile and save the database. Check that its tables are correctly linked to the Access 97 back-end database; if they're not, relink them.
7. Open the Access 97 front-end database in Access 97, open the Visual Basic Editor window, and compile and save the database. Check that its tables are correctly linked to the Access 97 back-end database; if they're not, relink them.

Now you have an Access 97 back-end database containing the data, and two front-end databases (one in Access 97 format and one in Access 2000 format). Access 97 users can use the Access 97 front-end database; Access 2000 and Access 2002 users can use the Access 2000 front-end database.

note You can have a back-end database as old as Access 2.0, with front ends from Access 2.0 and up. However, so many changes have been made from Access version 2.0 to Access 2002 that you will have to sacrifice a lot of functionality to work with all versions from Access 2.0 to Access 2002.

Working with Access 97, Access 2000, and Access 2002

If you need to maintain separate installations of multiple versions of Access, such as Access 97, Access 2000, and Access 2002, you can install different versions of Office (or even just the Access component of Office) on the same computer. You can either install them in the same boot partition (or the only boot partition), or install them in separate boot partitions.

Installing Multiple Versions of Access in the Same Boot Partition

You can install multiple versions of Office (or Access) in the same boot partition, but if you do, you are likely to have some problems. Because different versions of Office use different versions of common controls and DLLs, installing two versions of Office on the same computer can lead to problems in the following areas (unless you install the Office versions in separate boot partitions, as described in the next section):

- Wizards
- Database templates
- Add-ins
- Importing and exporting
- Automation code

Installing Multiple Versions of Access in Different Boot Partitions

To avoid problems with wizards, database templates, add-ins, import/export, and Automation code, your best bet is to install each version of Office in a separate boot partition, using an application such as System Commander (see the V Communications, or VCOM, Web site, *http://www.v-com.com*, for information on this product), or BootMagic, which is included with PartitionMagic. (See the PowerQuest Web site, *http://www.powerquest.com*, for information on these products.)

System Commander and BootMagic both allow you to set up multiple boot partitions and run different versions of Office in each partition. You can also take advantage of multiple boot partitions to install different operating systems in each boot partition, such as Windows 98, Second Edition, Windows Me, and Windows 2000. Office installations in different boot partitions can (and for convenience, should) share the same Documents folder, located on the D (or higher) drive so that it will be available to all operating system partitions.

Setting Up a Boot Partition for Running Office XP on Windows Me

To set up a separate boot partition for installing Office XP, running on Windows Me, using PartitionMagic/BootMagic v. 6.0, follow these steps:

1. Prepare a startup disk from an existing installation of Windows Me by choosing Start, Settings, Control Panel, Add/Remove Programs, selecting the Startup Disk tab in the Add/Remove Programs dialog box, and clicking the Create Disk button, as shown in Figure A-20.

> **note** At the time of writing, PowerQuest had just released PartitionMagic 7.0. If you are using this new version, some of the steps here might be different.

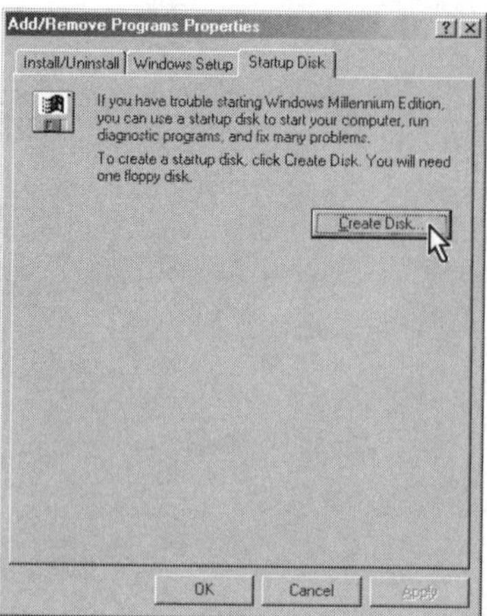

Figure A-20. Begin setting up a boot partition by preparing a Windows Me startup disk.

2 When the Insert Disk dialog box appears, insert a disk and click OK to start copying files.

3 Create a BootMagic rescue disk if you don't already have one. (It should have been created during the installation of BootMagic.) Use the Create BootMagic Diskette selection in the PowerQuest BootMagic program group, as shown in Figure A-21, and follow the steps for creating a BootMagic rescue disk.

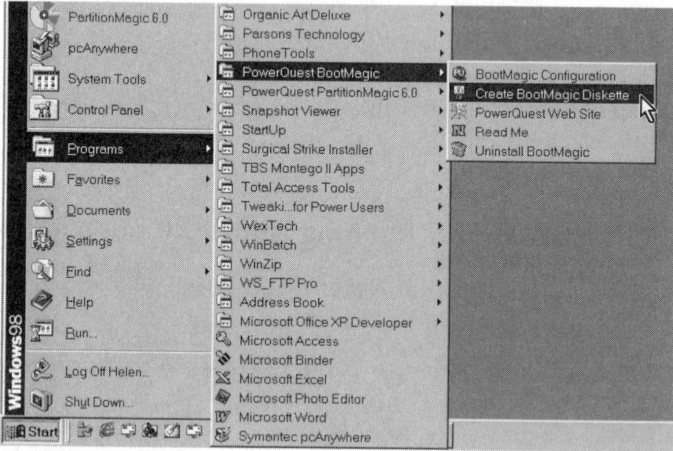

Figure A-21. Create a BootMagic rescue disk if you don't already have one.

4 Open PartitionMagic and click Create New Partition, as shown in Figure A-22. The Create New Partition Wizard opens.

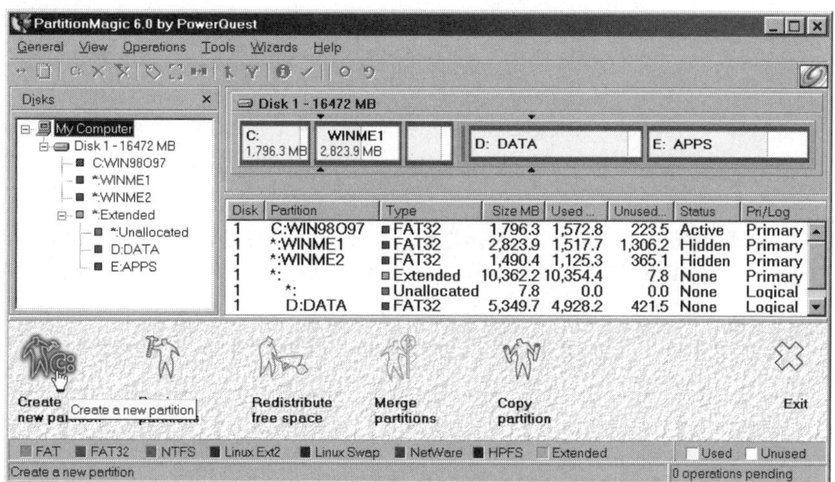

Figure A-22. Create a new partition by using PartitionMagic 6.0.

5 Click Next, as shown in Figure A-23.

Figure A-23. The Create New Partition Wizard helps you create a boot partition.

6. Proceed through the steps of the Create New Partition Wizard, selecting Disk 1 (if you have multiple disks), and selecting the option for using the new partition for an operating system.
7. On the screen where you selected the operating system, select Windows 95/98 (because Windows Me is not an available option).
8. After you complete the steps of the Create New Partition Wizard, select the new partition in the PartitionMagic window, right-click it to open its shortcut menu, select Advanced, and then select Set Active from the Advanced submenu.
9. After you set the new partition as the active partition, restart the computer. Put the Windows Me startup disk in Drive A before doing so.
10. After you reboot to Windows Me from the startup disk, the new, empty partition is active, and is labeled as Drive C. Place the Windows Me CD in the CD drive and install it to the new partition.
11. After you install Windows Me, install Office XP to the new partition.
12. After you install Office XP, insert the BootMagic rescue disk and restart Windows.
13. When the BootMagic menu appears, click Add to add a new operating system. Select the new operating system. It will probably be labeled Windows95/98, not Windows Me.

    You now have two (or more) selections on your BootMagic menu, so you can select which partition to use every time you restart your computer.

InsideOut

I like to keep all my operating systems on Drive C, my data on Drive D, and my applications on Drive E (except for applications that are specific to an operating system). This prevents data and applications from being wiped out when I need to reformat a partition—for example, if I want to remove all traces of a beta application before installing a new version of Office.

Some Common Problems with Using an Access Database in Multiple Versions of Access

Here are some of the most common problems you might encounter when working with an Access database across different versions of Access:

- **Problem:** You get a compile error when opening an Access 2000 database in Access 2002.

  Solution: Compile and save the database in Access 2000. If there are any errors, you might need to modify the code so it will run in Access 2000.

- **Problem:** An Access 2000 database runs more slowly after you save the changes in Access 2002.

  Solution: After you make changes to an Access 2000 database in Access 2002, the version of the Visual Basic project is incremented, which prevents Access 2000 from loading the compiled version of the project. Compile and save the database in Access 2000 to allow the compiled project to be loaded.

- **Problem:** A form, report, combo box, or list box shows the correct data in Access 2002, but incorrect data in Access 2000.

  Solution: This might be the result of the higher length limit on SQL statements used as record sources and row sources in Access 2002 (32,750 characters, as opposed to 2,000 characters in Access 2000). You might need to replace the SQL statement with a saved query if you can't make the SQL statement short enough.

- **Problem:** A macro that works in Access 2002 doesn't work in Access 2000.

  Solution: Several new macro actions were added in Access 2002. Check the macro in Access 2000 and remove any actions labeled as "Macro action from newer Access version" in the Comment column.

- **Problem:** After you open an Access 2000 file in Access 2002, data access pages aren't usable in Access 2000.

  Solution: When you open an Access 2000 database in Access 2002, data access pages are converted so that they can use the latest versions of the Office Web components (PivotTables, PivotCharts, and Office Spreadsheets). The original data access page is saved as a backup, which you can open in Access 2000.

- **Problem:** An Access 2000 database can't be saved as an MDE or ADE file in Access 2002.

  Solution: You must either save the Access 2000 file as an MDE or ADE file in Access 2000, or convert the file to Access 2002, and then save it as an MDE or ADE file in Access 2002.

Troubleshooting

I have an Access 2000 database that I use in both Access 2000 and Access 2002. When I open the database in Access 2000 after working on it in Access 2002, I get a compile error.

When you open an Access 2000 database in Access 2002, all the references to Office 2000 (in the References dialog box, version 9.0) Office components are automatically upgraded to version 10.0 for Office XP. However, when you later reopen the same database in Access 2000, some references (particularly those to the Word or Outlook object library) aren't downgraded to version 9.0, which causes errors.

If you need to work with the Word or Outlook object model (say, to create Word documents or Outlook tasks from Access data), follow the steps below to prevent this problem. (Thanks to Alan Taylor for this solution.)

1. Ensure that your Office 2000 object libraries are in a location available to you when you are working in Office XP. (This might involve copying them to a folder on the D or higher drive if you have Office 2000 and Office XP installed in different boot partitions.) The version 9.0 object libraries are located in the Microsoft Office\Office folder for Office 2000; the names of the major object libraries are listed below:

Excel	Excel9.olb
Outlook	msoutl9.olb
PowerPoint	msppt9.olb
Word	msword9.olb

2. Open the Access 2000 database in Access 2002, and press Alt+F11 to open the Visual Basic Editor window; then choose Tools, References to open the References dialog box.
3. Clear the check marks for any of the above-listed object libraries you use in your VBA code.
4. Use the Browse button to select the Office 2000 versions of the object libraries you need to use.
5. Figure A-24 shows the References dialog box for an Access 2000 database open in Access 2002, with the Word and Outlook version 9.0 object libraries selected (among others). There is no need to select the Access 9.0 object library; it upgrades and downgrades between versions 9.0 and 10.0 automatically.

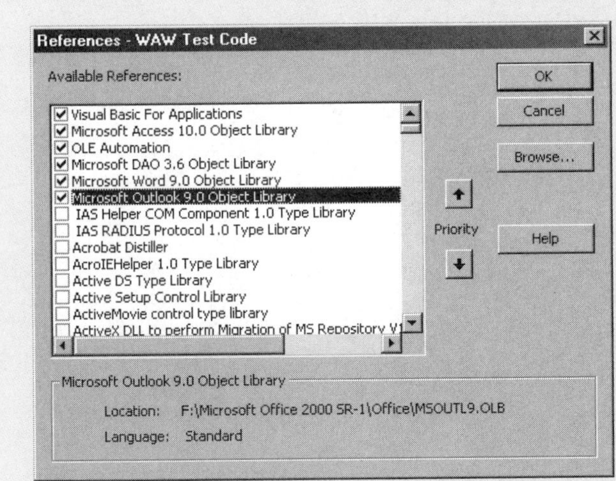

Figure A-24. Use this dialog box to select the object libraries you need.

6. Choose Debug, Compile Databasename to compile the database's code, and then close the database.

The database will now work correctly (without reference errors), whether you open it in Access 2000 or Access 2002.

Appendix B
Distributing Access Applications

When you create a Microsoft Access application, you may want to install it on computers where Access is not installed. If you have Microsoft Office XP Developer, you can use one of its components to prepare a set of files to distribute to the individuals who will be using your database, including a run-time version of Access, which lets Access databases be installed and run by users who don't have the full version of Access.

The Packaging Wizard component of Office XP Developer allows you to prepare a package of all the files that your application needs, making it easy to distribute the application to users. When you need to distribute an Access application to individuals who don't have Access, you can include a run-time version of Access in your distribution package so that users can run the application even if they don't have Access installed.

While the run-time feature is the main reason to use the Packaging Wizard, you may also want to prepare a package of files to distribute to users (even those who have Access installed), in order to guarantee that they have the correct versions of any ActiveX controls you use in the application. Because the lack of an ActiveX control on a user's computer (or the wrong version of the control) can cause cryptic errors in an application, preparing a distribution package is a good idea if you use any ActiveX controls in your application.

See "Working with ActiveX Controls" in Chapter 6, "Working with Form Controls," for more information on ActiveX controls.

The Packaging Wizard doesn't create a single executable file the way Microsoft Visual Basic does. Instead, it creates a set (perhaps quite a large set) of CAB files, which you can distribute to users on a CD or over a network. The distribution package includes a Setup program (similar to the one used by many Microsoft programs) that makes it easy for users to install the application. In this appendix, you'll learn how to prepare a set of distribution files to distribute to users, so that they can install and use your application, with all the components the application needs to run properly.

note If you have used the Setup Wizard for previous versions of Office XP Developer (or its predecessor, Office Developer Edition, or ODE), you may have prepared setup packages to be distributed on floppy disks. The floppy disk option is not available in Office XP Developer—probably just as well because of the size of the distribution files.

Appendix B

Installing the Packaging Wizard

When you install Office XP Developer, the Packaging Wizard is installed by default, although you can deselect the Packaging Wizard while installing Office XP Developer. To check whether this MOD component has been installed, open the Visual Basic Editor window in an Access 2002 database by pressing Alt+F11 and then choosing Add-Ins, Add-In Manager. If the Packaging Wizard appears in the list of available add-ins, as shown in Figure B-1, it is installed and ready to use.

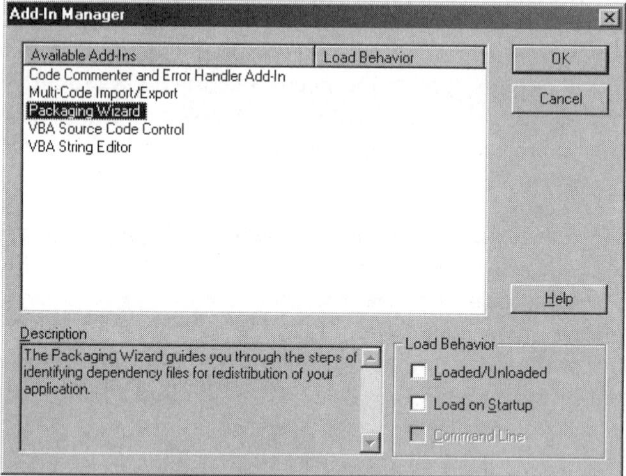

Figure B-1. Check for the Packaging Wizard in the Add-In Manager.

If you don't see any add-ins listed, Office XP Developer has probably not been installed. If other add-ins are listed but the Packaging Wizard is not, Office XP Developer might have been installed with the Packaging Wizard component deselected.

In either case, in order to install (or reinstall) Office XP Developer with the Packaging Wizard component, follow these steps:

1. Insert the CD labeled "Microsoft Office XP Developer." The Office XP Developer Setup screen appears, as shown in Figure B-2.
2. If it is highlighted (and it probably will be), click the Windows Component Update link to start installing the Windows components needed by Office XP Developer .

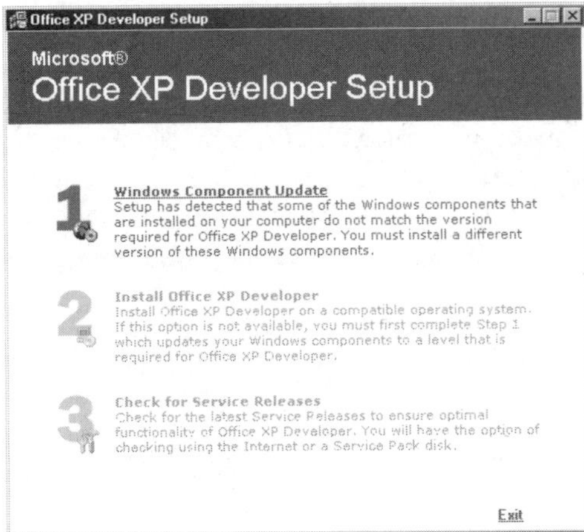

Figure B-2. The Office XP Developer Setup screen looks like this.

3. The End User License Agreement appears next; click I Accept The Agreement and click Continue.
4. Click Install Now! to start installing the components shown on the screen. You'll see a progress bar that displays installation progress.

   Next, a Restart Windows message box appears. Depending on which components need to be installed on your system, you might have to restart Windows several times. After the last restart, you will see the Congratulations screen.
5. On the Office XP Developer Setup screen, click Install Office XP Developer to start installing Office XP Developer. After a brief delay while loading installation components, you will get the Setup Start page.
6. Click Continue to go to the Options screen, where you can choose to deselect some Office XP Developer components. However, you're better off installing them all if you have the room.
7. If you don't want to install Office XP Developer to the default location, click Browse to select a non-default location for the Office XP Developer files. After selecting the components you want to install, and perhaps creating a new installation path, click Install Now!

   The Install screen appears next, with a progress bar indicating installation progress. After a final restart, Office XP Developer is installed, and you are ready to use the Packaging Wizard and other components.

Using the Packaging Wizard

To demonstrate the Packaging Wizard, this section includes a small sample application, Address Book 2002, with several forms that use special ActiveX controls: the CommonDialog control, the Calendar control, and the DateTimePicker control. When you run the Packaging Wizard, it analyzes the application and gathers together all the files needed to support these special controls, along with the standard Access support files.

To prepare a set of distribution files for an Access application, follow these steps (using Address Book 2002 as an example):

1. Open the Address Book 2002 database and press Alt+F11 to open the VBE window.
2. Choose Add-Ins, Add-In Manager in the Visual Basic Editor window.

> **caution** The Add-Ins command in the Visual Basic Editor window gives you different selections than the Add-Ins command in the Access database window. Make sure you are opening the Add-Ins Manager from the Visual Basic Editor window so that you can use the Office XP Developer components.

3. The Add-In Manager dialog box opens, as shown in Figure B-3.

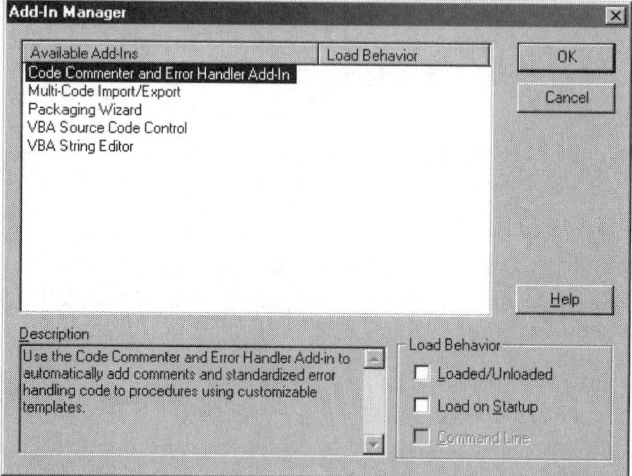

Figure B-3. The Add-In Manager dialog box helps determine which Office XP Developer components are loaded on startup.

You can set the Load behavior separately for each component, and also determine whether that component is loaded on startup.

4 Because the Packaging Wizard is used infrequently, it is probably not set to load on startup. Select it, and then check the Loaded/Unloaded check box to load it now.

5 Click OK to close the Add-In Manager, and then choose Add-Ins, Packaging Wizard in the Visual Basic Editor window.

6 Select Check This Box To Hide This Screen In The Future on the first page of the wizard if you don't want to see this page again, and click Next.

7 Select the application you want to package and the package you want to build. As shown in Figure B-4, the current database is pre-loaded as the main file, and a package name is suggested, based on the database name. You can also copy, rename, or delete existing distribution packages on this screen. Click Next when you've made your selections.

> **tip** Click Help on any Packaging Wizard page to get more information on the page's options.

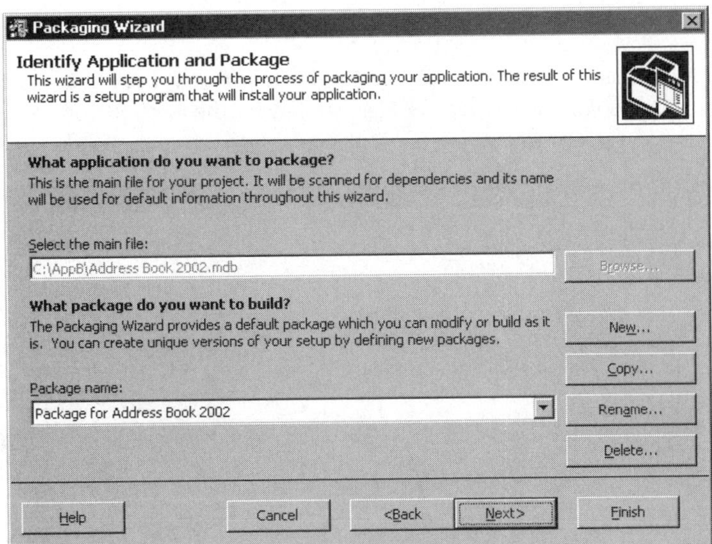

Figure B-4. This page of the Packaging Wizard allows you to identify the application you want to package and select the package to build for it.

8 Enter (or accept) the application title, company name, version, and setup language, as shown in Figure B-5. Click Next.

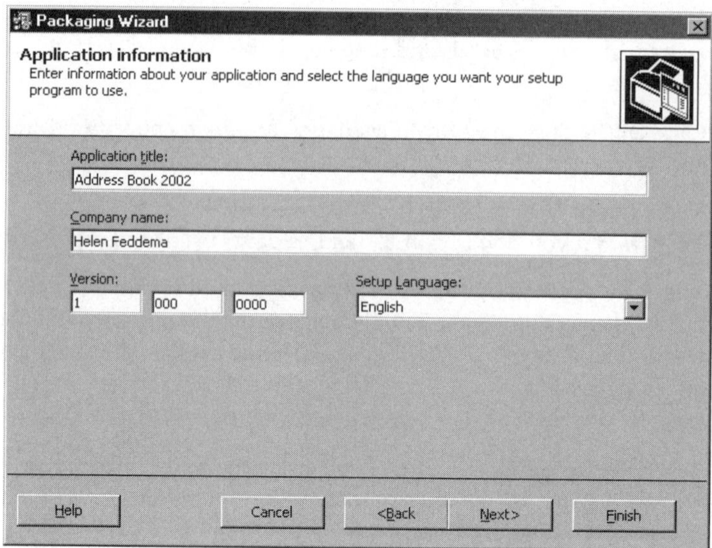

Figure B-5. Enter the relevant package information on the Application Information page.

9 The Dependencies screen (shown in Figure B-6) lists the package's components, including various supporting files needed for the ActiveX controls used in the sample application.

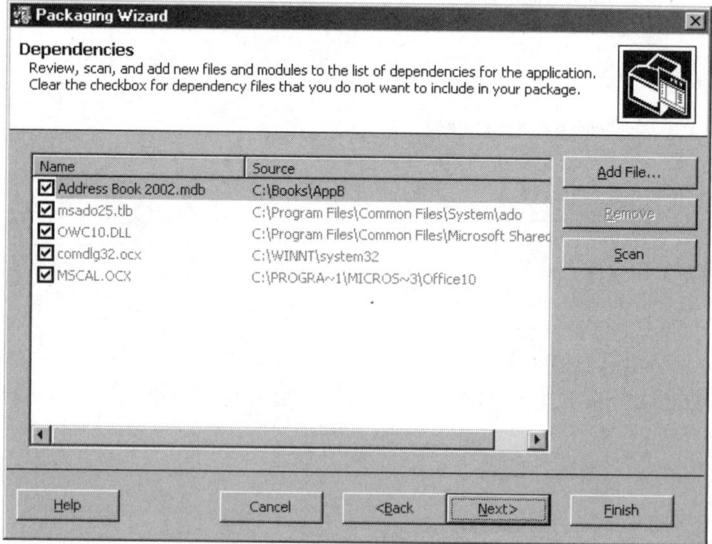

Figure B-6. The Dependencies screen of the Packaging Wizard allows you to choose files and modules for the application.

caution You may see some components you don't recognize in the list prepared by the Packaging Wizard. It's advisable to leave them in the package; they are probably support files needed by some application component, and if you delete a file your application needs, the users will have problems running the application.

To add an icon for the application, click Add File to open a standard File Open dialog box to select the icon. The new icon will appear at the bottom of the Dependencies screen. Click Next.

10 The Modify Installation Locations screen (see Figure B-7) shows where each component will be installed. The suggested locations for standard components should generally not be changed; if you need to add components manually, you will have to select the appropriate location for them. Click Next.

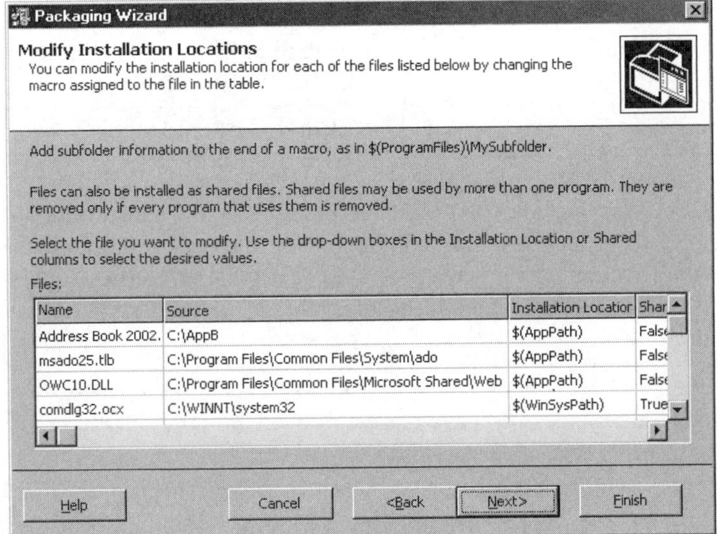

Figure B-7. Generally, you should leave the suggested locations for components as is.

Table B-1 lists the available choices.

Table B-1. Standard installation locations for the Packaging Wizard

Installation location options	Example
$(AppPath)	C:\Program Files*ApplicationName*
$(WinPath)	C:\Windows
$(WinSysPath)	C:\Windows\System
$(WinSysPathSysFile)	C:\Windows\System32
$(CommonFiles)	C:\Program Files\Common Files
$(CommonFilesSys)	C:\Program Files\Common Files\System
$(ProgramFiles)	C:\Program Files
$(MSDAOPath)	C:\Program Files\Common Files\ Microsoft Shared\DAO
$(Font)	C:\Windows\Fonts

11 Check Yes, Include The Access Runtime if your users might not have Access installed. Check Yes, Include System Files to ensure that your application will run, in case it uses any of these files. Select Install Internet Explorer 5.1 only if your application requires this program. Select the install language from the drop-down list. Click Next.

tip If the application's users do have Access installed, be sure to leave the Access Runtime checkbox unchecked — the run-time files are very large.

12 Check the two check boxes on the next screen if you want to include the Microsoft SQL Server 2000 Desktop Engine (MSDE)—which you might need if you are packaging a project (ADP file) rather than a database (MDB file)—and the Replication Manager, needed if your application uses replication. Click Next.

13 Create Start menu shortcuts as needed. (See Figure B-8.)

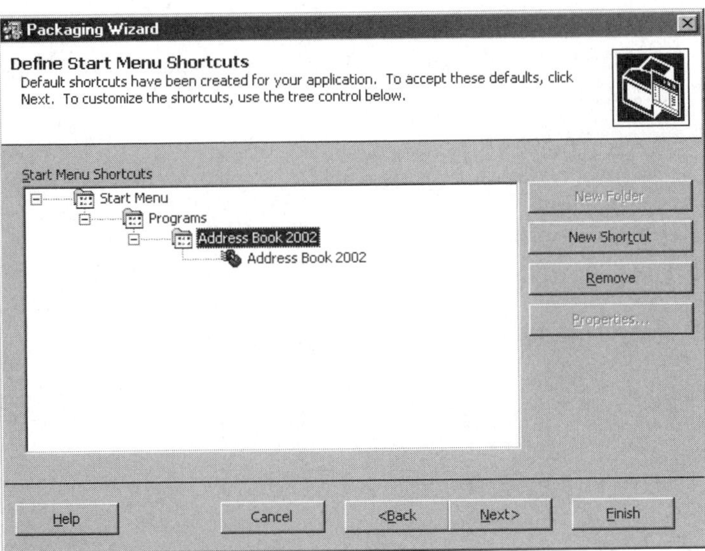

Figure B-8. The Define Start Menu Shortcuts screen of the Packaging Wizard allows you to create a shortcut to your application.

14 To assign a custom icon to the application (the icon file must have been included in the set of distribution files, as described earlier), select the Address Book 2002 shortcut and click Properties.

15 In the Icon drop-down list of the properties sheet, select the icon you added to the distribution set, and click OK.

16 To create a shortcut to compact the database, click the application program group (Address Book 2002 in this case) and then click New Shortcut.

A new shortcut appears in the program group.

17 Select the new shortcut and click Properties. In the properties sheet, enter a name and description for the shortcut, and (for a Compact shortcut) select the Specify Custom Command Line check box and add **/compact** to the end of the standard wizard-generated command line, as shown in Figure B-9. Click OK.

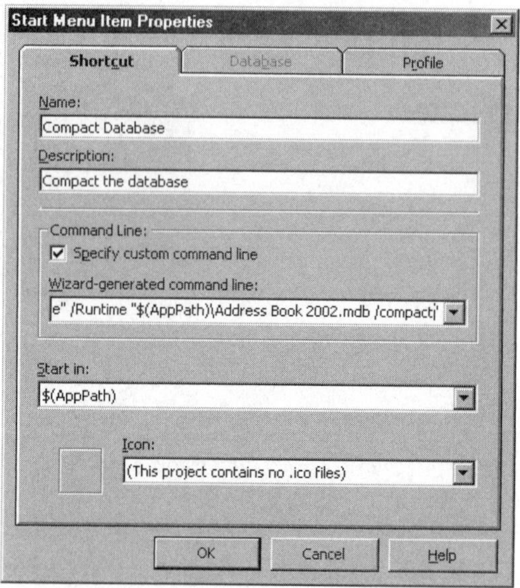

Figure B-9. You can create a shortcut to compact the database.

You can also select an icon for the shortcut, if one was included in the package of files.

> **tip** For a list of command-line switches to use in shortcuts, open the Startup Command-Line Options Help topic.

After clicking the OK button on the properties sheet, the new shortcut is now listed as Compact Database. Click Next.

18 Specify a command to run after the application is installed, such as an MS-DOS batch file or a Script Host file (or leave blank if you don't need to run a command). (See Figure B-10.) Click Next.

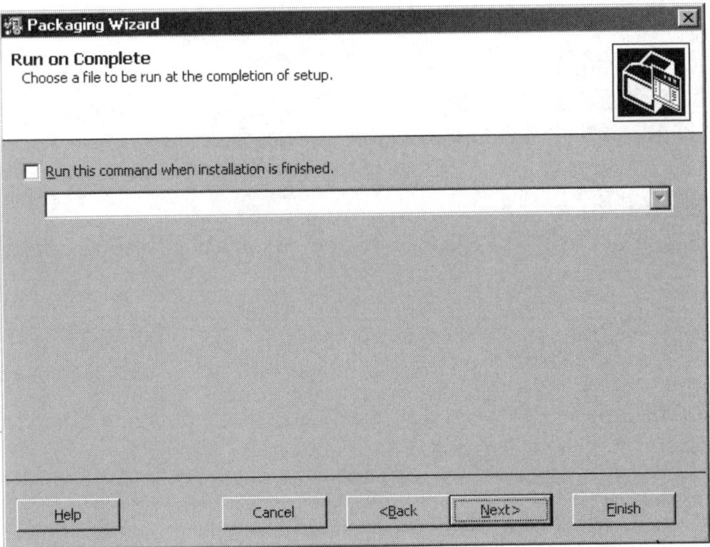

Figure B-10. The Run On Complete screen of the Packaging Wizard allows you to specify a command to run at the end of installation.

19 Choose to create your application package immediately or save the setup script for later use. Click Finish.

If you choose to save the package script without building, the wizard will close when you click Finish. You can run the wizard again later, select the saved script, and generate the set of distribution files.

If you choose to build the setup program, when you click Finish, the Browse For Folder dialog box appears. Select (or create) the folder to hold the package files. The default folder is called Package; it's located under the folder containing the application database. Click OK.

The first time you run the wizard, you will get the message shown in Figure B-11. This message appears when there is no disk image of standard Access components to use when preparing distribution packages.

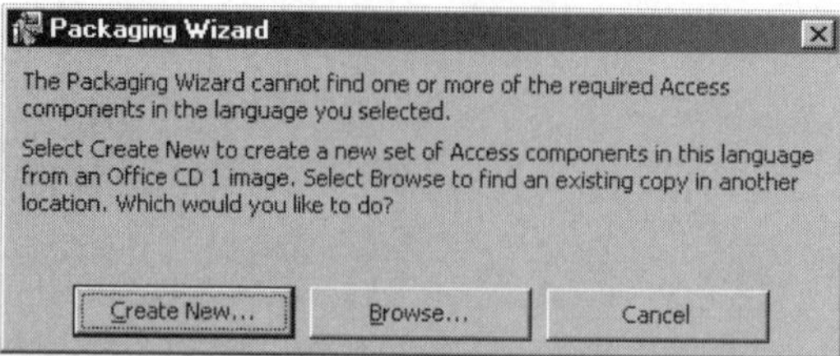

Figure B-11. The Packaging Wizard displays this message if it can't find the standard Access components.

20 To create the set of Access components, insert the Office XP CD (the regular Office CD, not the Office XP Developer CD), and click Create New.

21 In the Browse For Folder dialog box, accept the default location for the Access files or select another location.

22 Select your CD drive in the same dialog box, and click OK. The files are copied from the CD to the new folder, without any progress bar or dialog box. However, you can see the lights flickering on your CD drive and computer hard drive during the copying process. When all the files are copied, the Create Package screen appears again, and the progress bar will start moving. The package will be created. When it is done, the Package Complete! screen appears.

To distribute the packaged files, copy them to a CD. When the user inserts the CD, the Setup program will start automatically.

note A patch for the Microsoft Office XP Developer Packaging Wizard was posted to the Office Developer page of the Microsoft Web site on October 17, 2001. The patch can be downloaded from *http://msdn.microsoft.com/downloads/*.

Appendix C
Security

If you are creating databases for your own use, or you don't need to restrict access to your databases in any way, you might not need this chapter. However, when you develop databases for use by others (particularly in a corporate environment), you often need to limit the access of certain users to an application, or to specific application components. For example, you might need to restrict access to sensitive employee data (such as salaries) to employees in the Payroll department, or limit access to forms and reports in Design view to users in the MIS department.

Microsoft Access offers a variety of ways to restrict user access to database components. Some of these methods are quick and easy to apply; others are complex and the steps to implement those methods lengthy. This chapter describes some of the ways you can protect an Access database (or specific database components) against unwanted inspection or modification.

Hiding Database Objects

One of the simplest ways to limit access to certain database objects is to hide them. For example, to hide a lookup table so that users can't see it (and therefore can't modify it), right-click the table in the database window and then select Properties. Check the Hidden check box in the properties sheet to hide the table, as shown in Figure C-1.

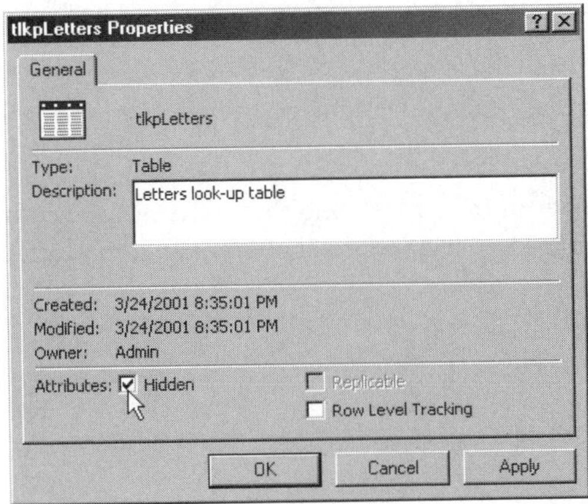

Figure C-1. Hide a table if you don't want users to see it.

caution You might think that you can hide a database object by selecting it in the database window and then selecting Hide from the Window menu. However, this action hides the entire database window, not just the selected object.

It is easy to hide a database object so that users can't see it. (The database object will remain available for use by other database components, and in VBA code.) However, a knowledgeable user won't have much trouble finding that object. All the user needs to do is select the Hidden Objects check box on the View page of the Options dialog box, rendering hidden objects visible in the database window (though their icons are dimmed), and then open the hidden object's properties sheet and clear the Hidden check box.

Because of the ease with which users can uncover hidden objects, this method does not offer any real security against users viewing or modifying objects. Use this technique primarily when you want to conceal system tables, forms under development, or other database objects that might be confusing to users or just clutter up the database window.

Encryption

Encrypting a database offers another kind of protection: The database will be unintelligible when viewed by using a utility program or a word processor.

To encrypt a database, you must be either the database's owner or (if the database is secured) a member of the Admins group of the workgroup information file used to secure the database. You must also be able to open the database in exclusive mode. If you can meet these conditions, choose Tools, Security, Encrypt/Decrypt Database to encrypt the database. (See Figure C-2.)

An Encrypt Database As window appears, in which you can specify the name and path of the encrypted database.

After you click Save, a progress bar in the status pane shows the progress of creating the encrypted database. (The original, unencrypted database remains unaffected.)

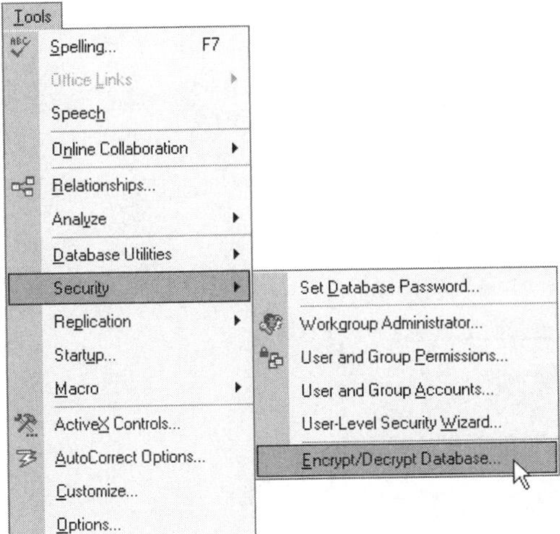

Figure C-2. Encrypting a database provides more security than simply hiding it.

You can view any database object in an encrypted database, and you can also switch to Design view and look at the code. Thus, encrypting a database won't protect database objects against viewing or modification. However, encryption does prevent examination of the database by someone using a utility program or word processor, and thus it can provide protection when transmitting a database electronically or storing it on various media.

Password-Protecting VBA Code

If you are primarily interested in protecting your VBA code from viewing or modification (either because you don't want the database's functionality to be modified or destroyed, or it is a commercial product that you are selling and you don't want to give away the code that makes it work), you can use a password to secure only the code.

To set a VBA code password, follow these steps:

1. Switch to the Visual Basic Editor window by pressing Alt+F11 or choosing Tools, Macro, Visual Basic Editor.
2. Choose Tools, *Databasename* Properties to open the Project Properties dialog box.
3. Click the Protection tab, select the Lock Project For Viewing check box, and then enter a password in both text boxes, as shown in Figure C-3.

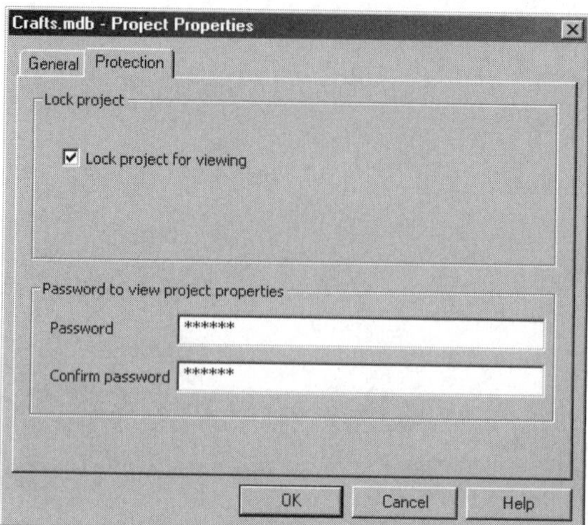

Figure C-3. Set a password to protect a database's VBA code.

After you close and reopen the database, the *Databasename* Password dialog box will appear when you attempt to open a module. You must enter the password to view or modify the VBA code in the database.

Saving as an MDE File

An even more secure method of preventing user access to VBA code is to save a database as an MDE file. This technique compiles all modules, removes all editable code, and compacts the database into an MDE file. To save a database as an MDE file, choose Tools, Database Utilities, Make MDE File, as shown in Figure C-4.

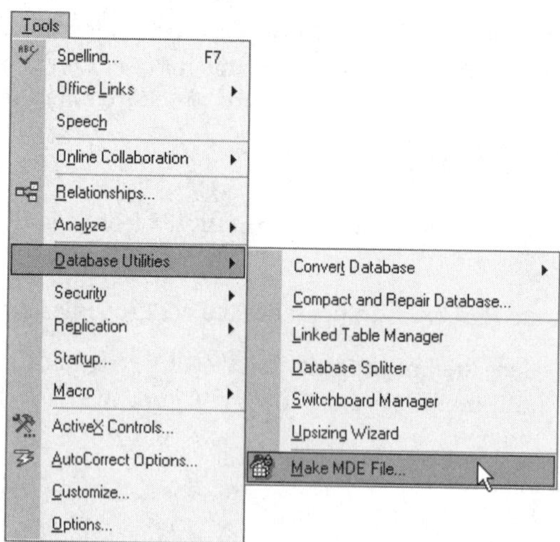

Figure C-4. Save a database as an MDE file for an even more secure method of protecting your VBA code.

A Save MDE As dialog box appears, in which you can specify the path and name of the MDE file.

An MDE file is smaller than an MDA file and might have better performance. Compared to an MDA file, an MDE file has the following characteristics:

- Doesn't allow viewing or modification of forms, reports, or modules in Design view
- Doesn't allow adding, deleting, or changing references to object libraries or databases
- Doesn't allow changing of code (MDE files don't contain any code)
- Doesn't allow importing or exporting of forms, reports, or modules

caution Converting an MDA file to an MDE file is a one-way trip. If you lose the original MDA file, you won't be able to re-create it from the MDE file.

Startup Options

The Startup dialog box (opened by choosing Tools, Startup) offers several options for restricting user access to various parts of a database, in particular the Display Database Window, Allow Full Menus, and Use Access Special Keys check boxes. If you clear all three of these check boxes (see Figure C-5), users won't be able to see the database window and won't be able to restore it by using the F11 hot key or the Unhide command on the Window menu. Of course, you need to have a main menu form set as the Display Form/Page or the database will open to a blank window.

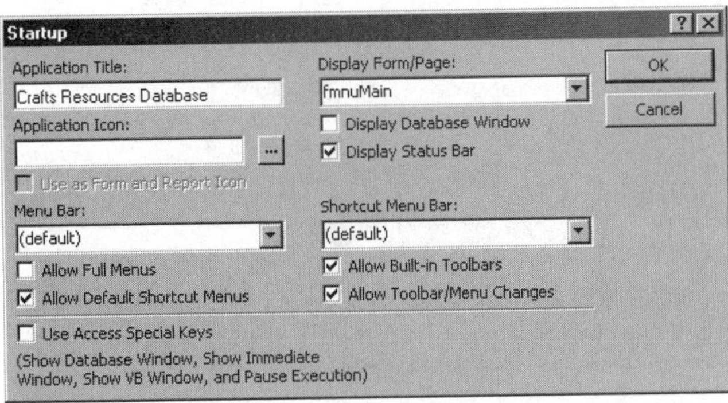

Figure C-5. You can turn off access to the database window in the Startup dialog box.

This option is a good way to restrict users to working with a database through the menus and other interface elements you have designed. However, it does not totally prevent access to the database window, as users can still bypass the startup settings by holding down the Shift key while opening the database.

Database Password

Suppose you want to restrict access to a database to certain individuals (say, coworkers, and not casual passers-by). You can set a database password to restrict access to the database to people who know the password. After you set a database password, users who try to open the database will be asked to enter a password into a Password Required dialog box.

Only users who have the password can open the database. After the user enters the password and opens the database, no further restrictions are imposed on access to database objects, so this method is primarily useful for preventing casual access to databases by anyone with access to a computer. (Unless you keep the password on a sticky note attached to the monitor.)

To set a database password, follow these steps:

1. Choose File, Open.
2. In the Open dialog box, select the database for which you want to set a password, click the down arrow next to the Open button, and select the Open Exclusive option, as shown in Figure C-6.

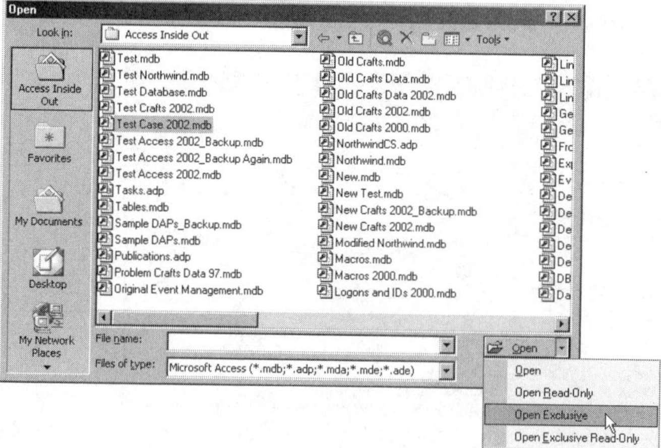

Figure C-6. Open a database in exclusive mode.

3 Choose Tools, Security, Set Database Password.

4 The Set Database Password dialog box opens, as shown in Figure C-7. Enter the password twice, and click OK.

Figure C-7. Enter the password twice.

After you close and reopen the database, the Password Required dialog box appears.

> **tip** To remove a database password, first open the database in exclusive mode. Then choose Tools, Security, Unset Database Password.

User-Level Security

The most sophisticated type of security (and not surprisingly, the most complicated and difficult to implement) is user-level security, which is implemented by means of a workgroup (a group of users who need to share data). User-level security allows you to grant different levels of access to specific database objects to different groups of users, a more sophisticated and flexible method of restricting access to database components than a database password's all-or-nothing approach.

User-level security is complex, but the User-Level Security Wizard walks you through the process of implementing a standard user-level security scheme. (If you need a customized scheme, you will still have to work through the selections on the Security submenu.)

To set up security with the User-Level Security Wizard, follow these steps:

1 Open the database you want to secure in shared mode (this is the default mode).

2 Choose Tools, Security, User-Level Security Wizard.

Appendix C

Joining the Admin Group

If you get the message shown in Figure C-8, you have to do some preparatory work in the Security submenu before running the wizard.

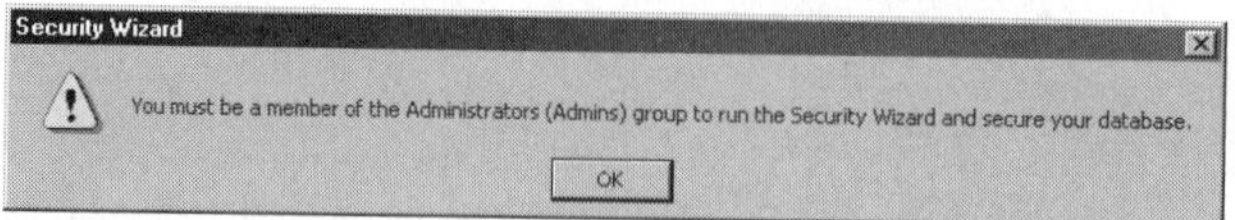

Figure C-8. If this error message appears when you first run the User-Level Security Wizard, you need to do a little extra work first.

Normally, all you need to do is choose Tools, Security, Workgroup Administrator, and then click Join in the Workgroup Administrator dialog box, as shown in Figure C-9.

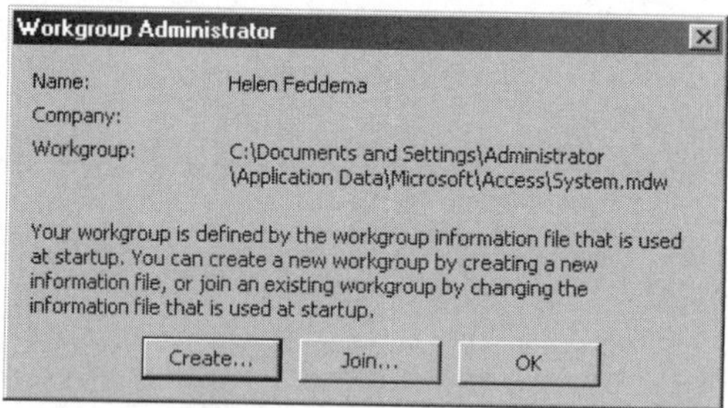

Figure C-9. Join the default workgroup.

The Workgroup Information File dialog box appears next, as shown in Figure C-10. Click OK to join the default workgroup, or browse for another workgroup.

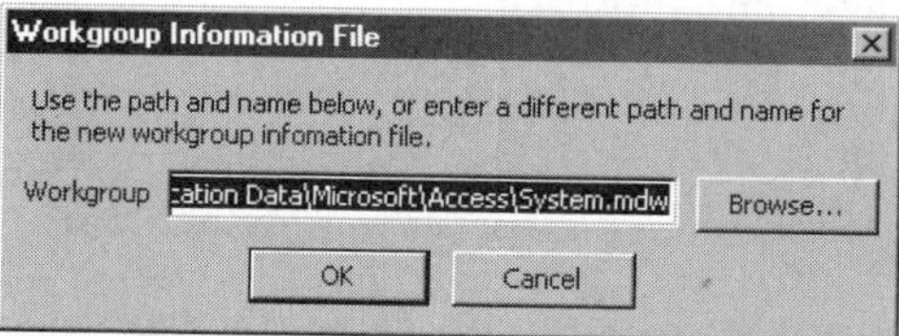

Figure C-10. Select the default workgroup to join.

Click OK in the success message box, and then click OK again in the Workgroup Administrator dialog box.

Now you're ready to use the User-Level Security Wizard.

The first screen of the wizard appears, as shown in Figure C-11.

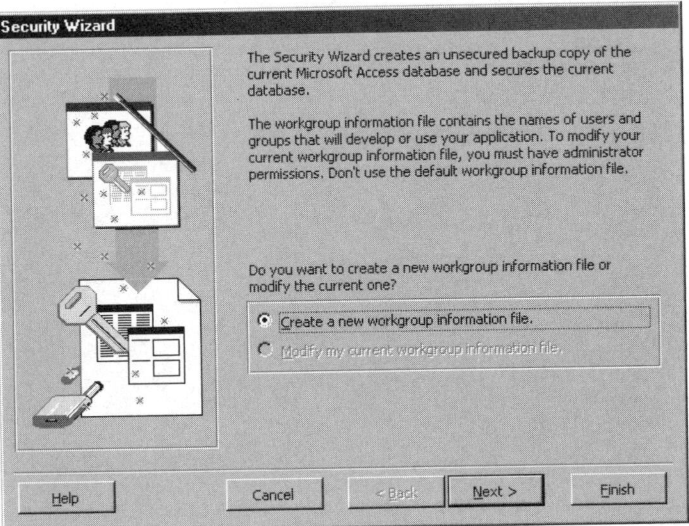

Figure C-11. The first screen of the User-Level Security Wizard looks like this.

tip For more information on user-level security, click Help on the wizard screen.

3. Click Next to create a new workgroup information file.
4. Specify the name and location of the new workgroup, its ID (WID), and your name and company. The last two fields are optional. (See Figure C-12.) In the option group at the bottom of the screen, choose between using the new workgroup as the default one or making a shortcut to open the secured database. (The latter option is recommended.) Click Next.

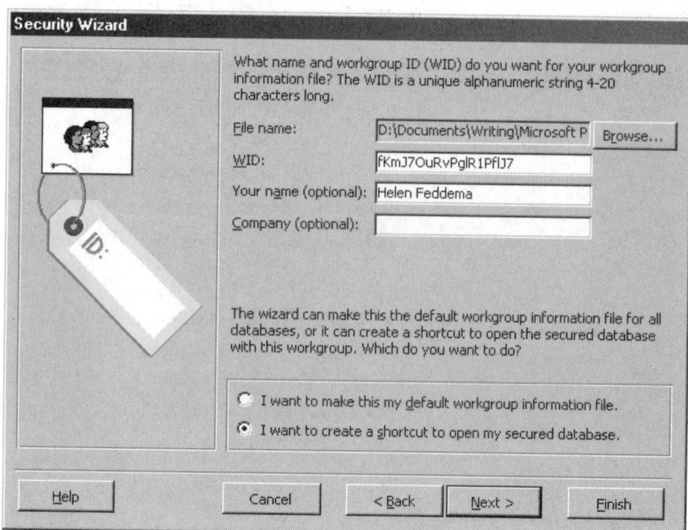

Figure C-12. Specify various settings for the new workgroup information file.

5 Specify which objects to secure. (See Figure C-13.) By default, all database objects are selected, which is generally desirable. Click Next.

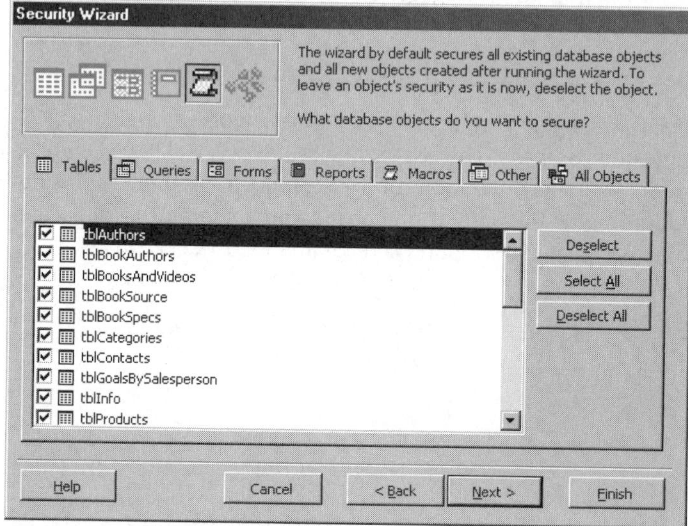

Figure C-13. Select the database objects you want to secure.

caution If you ever worked with user-level security in Access 97 or earlier, you might remember that modules could be secured. Since Access 2000, modules can't be secured with user-level security; you must either password-protect your VBA code or save the database as an MDE file.

6 As shown in Figure C-14, you can optionally create a variety of different user groups with preset permissions. Click Next.

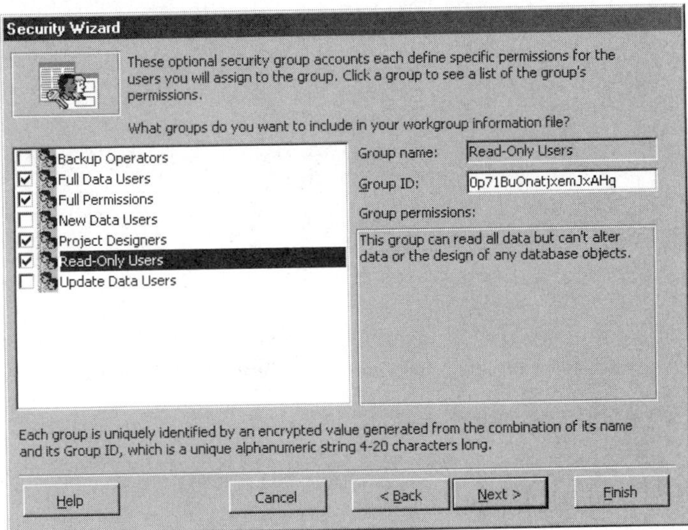

Figure C-14. Select standard user groups for the workgroup information file.

7 You now can assign permissions to the Users group, as shown in Figure C-15. (All users belong to this group.) However, it is generally best to leave this option at the default (No, The Users Group Should Not Have Any Permissions) to ensure that permissions are acquired only through specific group membership. Click Next.

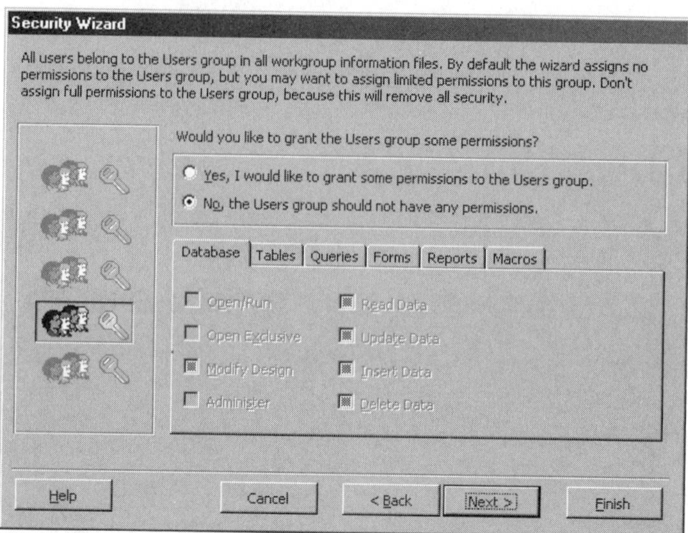

Figure C-15. Set permissions for the Users group.

8 Add users to the workgroup file, as shown in Figure C-16. (You can add more users later on from the Security submenu.) Click Next.

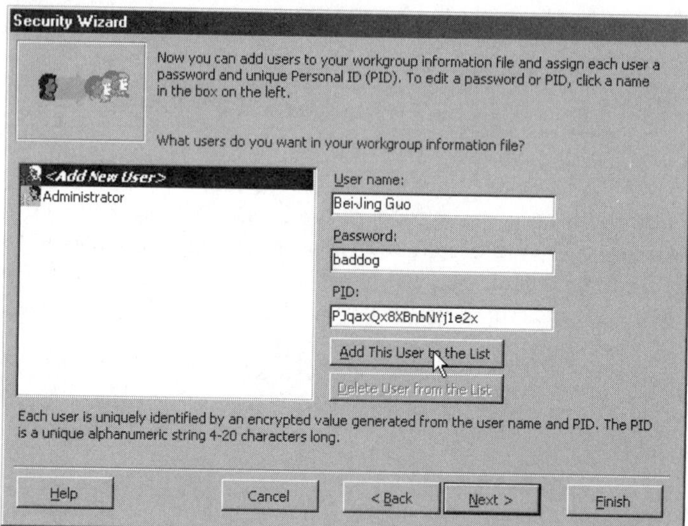

Figure C-16. Add a user to the workgroup information file.

9 Assign users to groups or select a group and assign users to it, as shown in Figure C-17. Click Next.

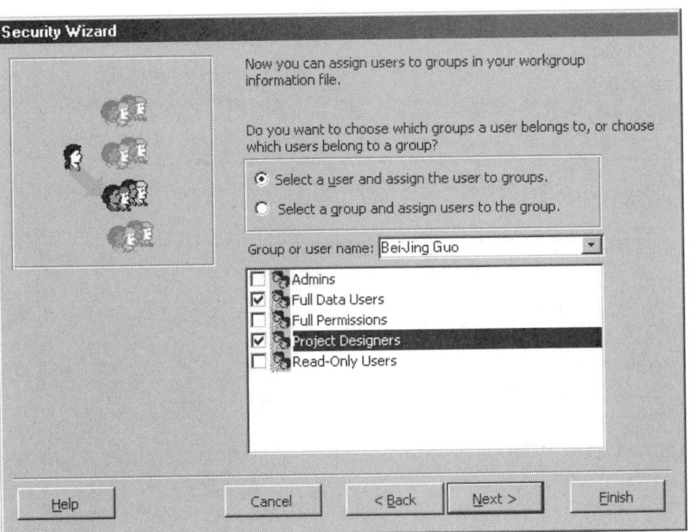

Figure C-17. Assign users to groups.

10 Specify the name of the backup (unsecured) database copy (see Figure C-18). You can choose to display Help on customizing security. Click Finish.

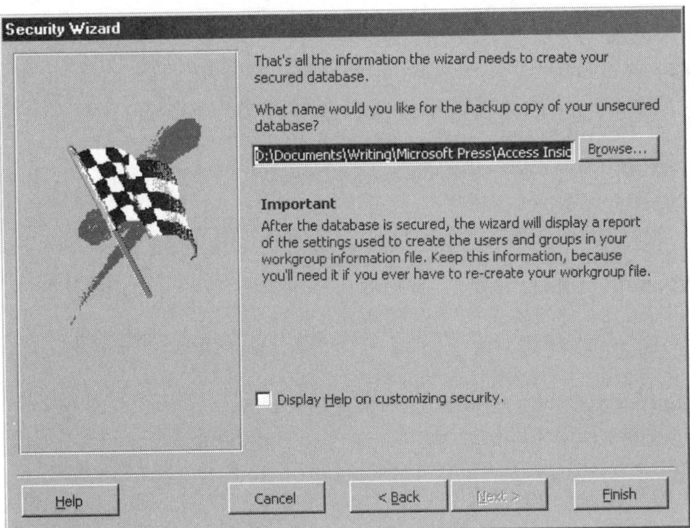

Figure C-18. Save the backup (unsecured) database.

You'll see a progress bar indicating that security is being applied to the database objects. When the wizard finishes, the Security Wizard report appears in print preview. Figure C-19 shows a portion of this report.

One-step Security Wizard Report

This report contains the information you need to re-create your workgroup file and regain access to your secured database in case of corruption. It is highly recommended that you print or export this report and keep it somewhere secure.

Unsecured Database:

D:\Documents\Writing\Microsoft Press\Access Inside Out\Test Case 2002.bak

Secured Database:

D:\Documents\Writing\Microsoft Press\Access Inside Out\Test Case 2002.mdb

Workgroup Information File:

D:\Documents\Writing\Microsoft Press\Access Inside Out\Secured.mdw

User Name:

Helen Feddema

Company:

Workgroup ID:

fKmJ7OuRvPglR1PflJ7

Secured Objects:

Figure C-19. The One-Step Security Wizard report looks like this.

As noted in the report header, you should print the report or export it to a file (by clicking Publish It To Microsoft Word on the toolbar) so that you will have a record of the settings used to create the workgroup information file and the secured database. Whether or not you publish the report to Word, upon closing the report you will get a message asking if you want to save the report as a snapshot. If you click Yes in this dialog box, the report will be saved as a snapshot (.snp) file.

After you close the snapshot file, you will get a message that the Security Wizard has encrypted your database, and that you must close Access and then reopen it to use the secured database. The shortcut requested in step 4 of the wizard is located on your desktop. If you open the shortcut's properties sheet, you will see its *Target* property is set as shown in the following code. (The exact paths will depend on the location of Office XP, the database, and the workgroup file.)

```
"F:\Microsoft Office XP\Office10\MSACCESS.EXE"
"D:\Documents\Writing\Microsoft Press\Access Inside Out\
    Test Case 2002.mdb" /WRKGRP
"D:\Documents\Writing\Microsoft Press\Access Inside Out\Secured.mdw"
```

This lengthy target expression specifies the Access executable, the secured database, and the workgroup information file to use with the database. When the database is opened by using this shortcut, the Logon dialog box appears. (See Figure C-20.) After someone enters a user name and that user's password, the secured database opens, with access to the database objects set according to the group (or groups) to which that user belongs.

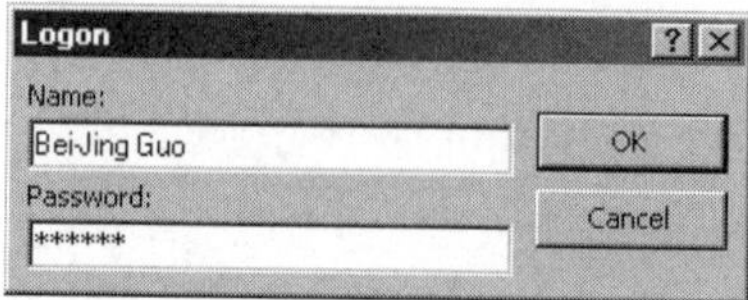

Figure C-20. The Logon dialog box for a secured database looks like this.

Appendix D
Replication

Database replication lets users in multiple locations update data in an application while allowing design changes only in a single copy of the database. This ensures that the integrity of the database design is preserved. When a database is replicated, two or more copies of the database are created; one is the Design Master, which is the only database in which design changes can be made, and any others are replicas. You can create as many replicas as you want. The Design Master and the replicas together form a replica set, which has a unique replica set identifier.

Replicas and Synchronization

Several techniques are available for synchronizing data in Microsoft Access databases, as described in the following list. Note that database synchronization is useful only when the users of the Design Master and all the replicas are connected to the same network (at least some of the time).

Briefcase replication You can use the Windows Briefcase component to keep a database up-to-date. This approach is used primarily in single-user situations in which data is taken off line on a laptop and later synchronized with the desktop database.

Database replication You can use commands on the Tools menu in Access to create and synchronize database replicas.

Replication Manager This component of Microsoft Office XP Developer is a full-featured tool for managing replicas, setting synchronization schedules, and viewing members of replica sets.

Programmatic replication Using components of the Jet and Replication Objects (JRO) object model, you can write code to compact databases, refresh data from the cache, and create and maintain replicated databases.

SQL Server replication Using a project with a SQL Server back end, the SQL Server administrator can set up replication. Users can work on data access pages off line and later synchronize them with the SQL Server database.

Replicating a Database

To replicate a database, follow these steps:

1 Open the database to be replicated.

2 In a multiuser situation, be sure that all users have closed the database.

3 If the database has a database password, remove it. (See the upcoming sidebar.)

4 Choose Tools, Replication, Create Replica.

5 In the warning dialog box that appears (Figure D-1), click Yes.

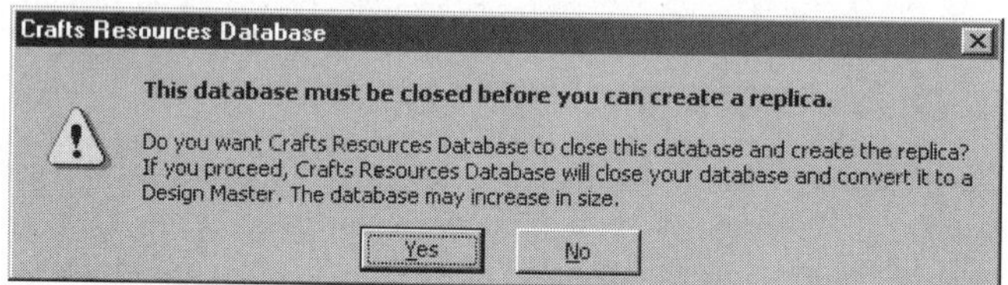

Figure D-1. Close the database to be replicated.

6 You'll see a dialog box that asks whether you want to make a backup copy of your database before converting it to a Design Master (as shown in Figure D-2). It's a good idea to click Yes if you haven't already created a backup of the database.

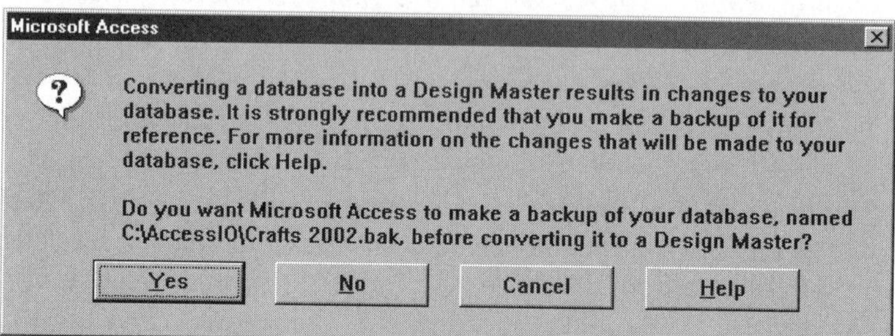

Figure D-2. Create a backup before converting a database to a Design Master.

7 In the Location Of New Replica dialog box that appears next, you can browse for the location to which you want to save the first replica in the replica set. By default, the first replica's name is "Replica of Databasename.mdb," but you can change it to something more meaningful, such as "Boston replica of *Databasename*.mdb."

8 Click the Priority button to set the priority for the replica. The priority can be set to a value from 0 through 100. (If there is a conflict during synchronization, the replica with the highest priority takes precedence.) To prevent users from deleting records in the replica, check the Prevent Deletes check box. Figure D-3 shows the replica being saved in a network folder under the name "Boston replica of Crafts 2002.mdb."

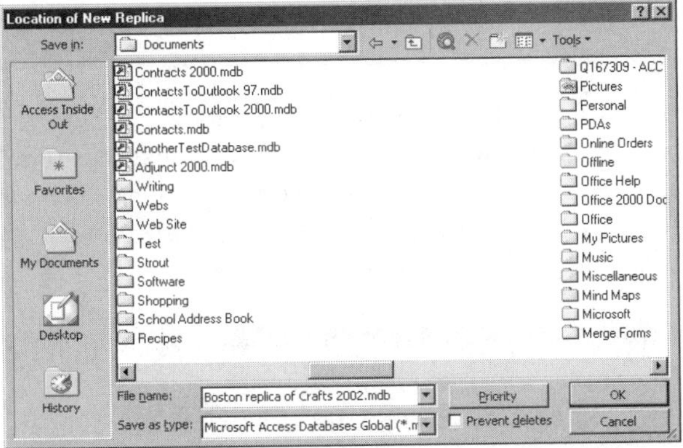

Figure D-3. Save the first replica in the replica set.

9 Click OK. You'll see a progress bar and then a success message, as shown in Figure D-4 .

Figure D-4. This message will appear after you create a replica.

Removing a Database Password

To remove a database password, follow these steps:

1. Choose File, Open.
2. Select the file you want to open, click the arrow next to the Open button, and select Open Exclusive from the drop-down list.
3. In the Password Required dialog box, type the database password and then click OK. (Passwords are case sensitive.)
4. Choose Tools, Security, and then select Unset Database Password.
5. Type your current password in the Unset Database Password dialog box and click OK.

The original database is now a Design Master. If you look at the database objects, you'll see that the original objects all have new icons, indicating that they're replicated objects. You'll also see several new replication tables. (See the "Replication Reference" section later in this chapter for information on these tables.) Figure D-5 shows the Tables tab of the Crafts 2002 database Design Master.

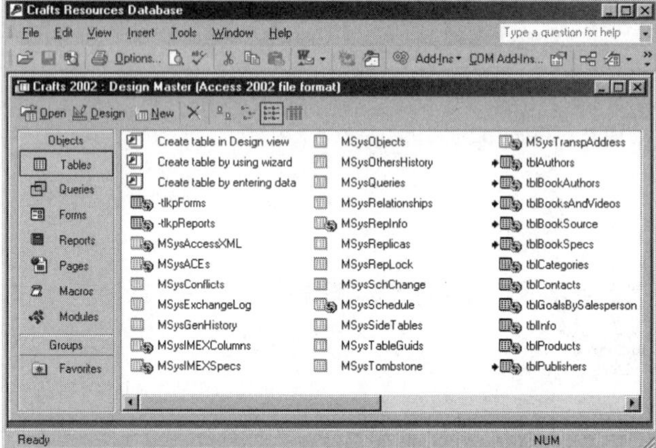

Figure D-5. Here's a Design Master of the Crafts 2002 database with new replication tables.

> **note** Design Masters and replicas have the same icon as regular Access databases, so before you make any changes, check the name of the database to make sure you're working with the correct one.

After replicating a database, when you create a new object in that database, the Save As dialog box will have a Make Replicable check box (as shown in Figure D-6). Check the check box to make the new object replicable (so it will be replicated to the replicas); leave it cleared to keep the object local to the Design Master database.

Figure D-6. Save a new table in a Design Master database.

Working with a Replicated Database

You can make design changes (such as adding, deleting, or modifying database objects) only in the Design Master of a replica set; you can modify data either in the Design Master or in the replicas. As users add, change, or modify data or as the database designer changes database objects, the Design Master and the various replicas in the replica set will get out of synch.

To synchronize a database, follow these steps:

1. Choose Tools, Replication, Synchronize Now.
2. If any objects are open in the database, a dialog box will inform you that all open objects must be closed (as shown in Figure D-7). Click Yes to close the open databases.

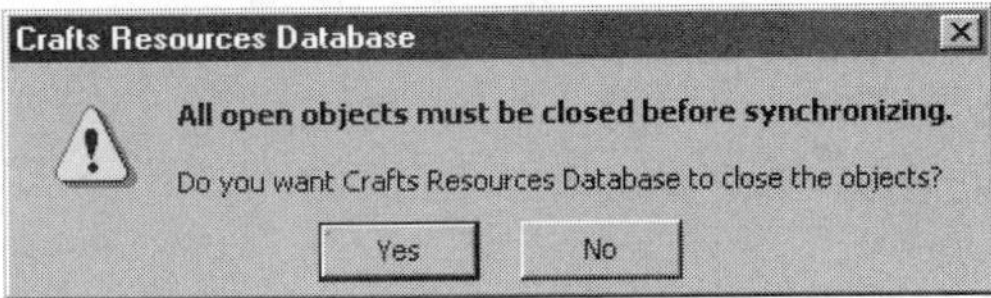

Figure D-7. Close open databases before synchronization.

3 The Synchronize dialog box will appear next (as shown in Figure D-8), with the name of the single replica in this replica set selected. You can use the Browse button to select another replica if the replica set has more than one replica.

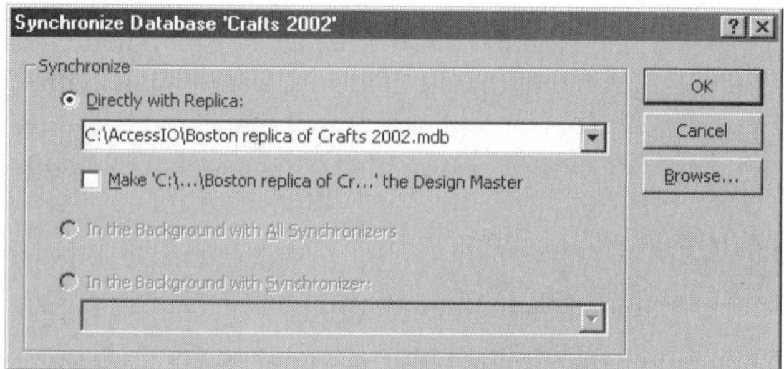

Figure D-8. Select a replica for synchronization.

4 Click OK to start synchronizing. A dialog box will appear warning you that the database must be closed prior to synchronization; click Yes to close the database and continue.

5 You'll see a progress bar indicating the progress of the synchronization, and then you should see the success message shown in Figure D-9.

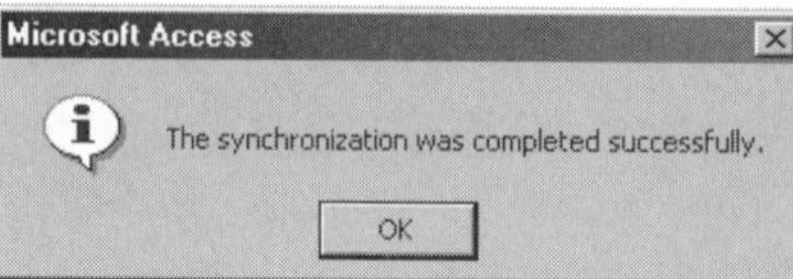

Figure D-9. This message should appear after you synchronize a replica.

Most of the time, Access will successfully resolve replication conflicts using the priority numbers assigned to members of the replica set. However, if you don't receive the success message shown in the figure, you should check for synchronization errors to find out what went wrong. To check for synchronization errors, choose Tools, Replication, Resolve Conflicts to open the Conflict Viewer.

Replication Reference

When you replicate an Access database, a number of changes are made to the database. These changes are visible only if you've checked the System Objects check box on the View tab in the Options dialog box. The fields listed in Table D-1 are added to the tables, and the tables listed in Table D-2 are added to the database. The properties listed in Table D-3 might also be added to the database.

Table D-1. New replication fields

Field	Description
s_GUID	A globally unique identifier (GUID) for each record
s_Lineage	A binary field that contains information about the history of changes to each record
s_ColLineage	A binary field that contains information about the history of changes to each field
s_Generation	A field that stores information regarding groups of changes

The information in these fields can't be changed.

An additional field named *Gen*_Fieldname will be added for each Memo or OLE Object field in the database.

A number of tables are added to a database when it is replicated. The most significant of these tables are listed in Table D-2.

Table D-2. Replication tables

Table	Description
MSysSideTables	A table used to store information about conflicts between the user's replica and another replica in the replica set. This table isn't replicated. It's supplied for information only, and its contents can be modified or deleted by custom conflict-resolution routines or by the user. All side tables are named *table*_conflict, where *table* is the original name of the table. (This table exists only if conflicts have occurred.)
MSysSchemaProb	A table that is present only when an error has occurred while the design of a replica is being updated. It provides additional details about the cause of the error. This is a local table and isn't replicated.
MSysReplicas	A table that stores details, such as the Replica ID and path, of all known replicas in the replica set. This table appears in all members of the replica set, but it is not replicated.
MSysTranspAddress	A table that stores addressing information for the Synchronizer and defines the set of synchronizers known to this replica set. This replicated table appears in all members of the replica set.
MSysTombstone	A table that stores information about deleted records and allows deletions to be dispersed to other replicas during the synchronization process. This table appears in all members of the replica set, but it is not a replicated table.
MSysRepInfo	A table that stores information about the entire replica set, including the identity (GUID) of the Design Master. The table contains a single record. This replicated table appears in all members of the replica set.
MSysExchangeLog	A table that stores information about replica synchronizations that have taken place. It is a local table and isn't replicated.

The information in these tables (except for MSysSideTables) can't be changed.

Table D-3. **Replication properties**

Property	Description
Replicable or *ReplicableBool*	A database or object property. When the property is set to *T* (or to *True* for *ReplicableBool*), the database, table, or query is replicable. The *Replicable* and *ReplicableBool* properties can be used interchangeably.
KeepLocal	A property appended to a table or query. When the property is set to *T*, the object should not be replicated when the database is replicated. An object that is already replicated can't have its *KeepLocal* property set to *T*.
ReplicaID	A property that provides each member of the replica set with unique identification. This property is read-only and is stored in the MSysReplicas system table.
DesignMasterID	The *ReplicaID* of the Design Master. It is stored in the MSysRepInfo system table as *SchemaMaster*.
ColumnLevelTracking	A database or table property. When the property is set to *True* (the default), conflicts are tracked at the column level of a table.

note The *Replicable* and *KeepLocal* properties apply only to tables and queries. This is because other database objects (such as forms, reports, macros, and modules) are either all replicated or all local. Only tables and queries can be set to replicable or local individually.

When a database is replicated, any incremental *AutoNumber* fields in the tables will be changed to random numbering. Existing records will keep their values, but new records will have random *AutoNumber* values.

Appendix E

Upsizing to SQL Server

At some point you might want to upgrade your Microsoft Access database to SQL Server, either because of its size or so that you can run it as a client-server database. You can use the Upsizing Wizard to partially automate this task. The Upsizing Wizard will do the basic conversion of the Access (MDB file) database into a SQL Server database with a project (ADP file) front end. The wizard will also convert most queries into stored procedures and views. You will still have some work to do to make your new SQL Server application more efficient, but the wizard does a good part of the basic work for you.

Why Upsize?

There are several reasons to upgrade an Access database to SQL Server:

Size Access databases have a size limit of 2 GB; SQL Server databases can be as large as a terabyte.

Reliability SQL Server offers better performance than Access in many situations. When you run SQL Server on Microsoft Windows 2000, it can process queries in parallel, using multiple threads, minimizing additional memory requirements when more users are added.

Availability You can back up a SQL Server database while it is running, allowing the database to be available all the time.

Security With a trusted connection, SQL Server integrates with the Windows 2000 system security to provide a single secured access to the network and the database.

Recoverability SQL Server has a recovery feature that automatically recovers a database to the last state of consistency in the event of a crash or power outage.

Reliable distributed data and batch transactions SQL Server supports atomic transactions with transaction logging, guaranteeing that all changes in a transaction are either committed or rolled back.

Server-based processing SQL was designed from the beginning as a client-server database, with data and indexes residing on a single server for more efficient processing.

Using the Upsizing Wizard

Before you run the Upsizing Wizard, back up your database and ensure that you have enough disk space for the new SQL Server database—you'll need at least twice the size of the Access database, preferably more. Make sure that each table has a unique index: SQL Server can upsize an existing index, but it can't create one, and a table without a unique index won't be updatable in SQL Server. If you have hidden tables that you want to upsize, make them visible, because hidden tables aren't upsized.

note **Make a hidden table visible**

To make a hidden table visible, select Tools, Options and check the Hidden objects check box on the View page; this lets you see hidden tables in the Database window (though their icons appear dimmed). Then right-click the hidden table to be made visible, open its properties sheet, and clear the Hidden check box.

tip See the Help topic "About Upsizing a Microsoft Access Database" for further considerations in upsizing secured Access databases.

To convert the Northwind sample database to SQL Server, follow these steps:

1 Copy Northwind to another folder.

2 Open the Northwind copy, and select Tools, Database Utilities, Upsizing Wizard, as shown in Figure E-1.

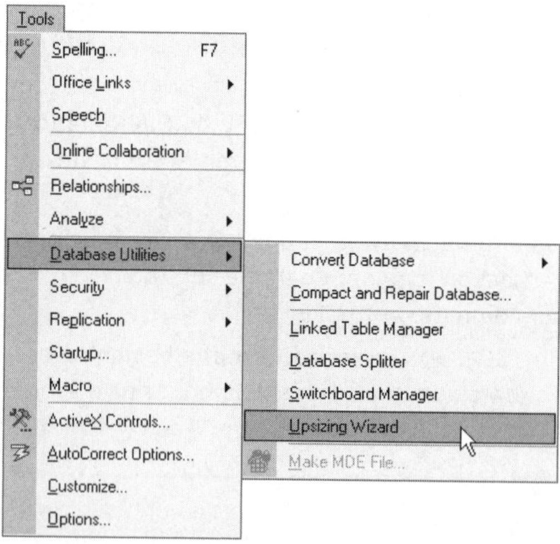

Figure E-1. Start the Upsizing Wizard.

3 Choose to use an existing SQL Server database or create a new one, as shown in Figure E-2. Click Next.

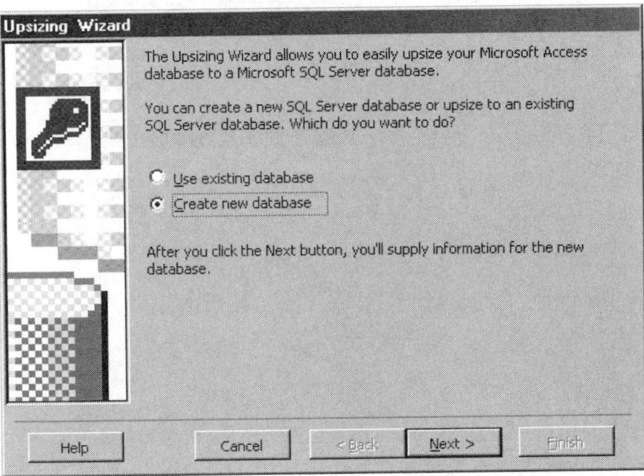

Figure E-2. Choose whether to use an existing SQL Server database or create a new one.

4 Choose a server for the new SQL Server database, and give the database a name, as shown in Figure E-3. Click Next.

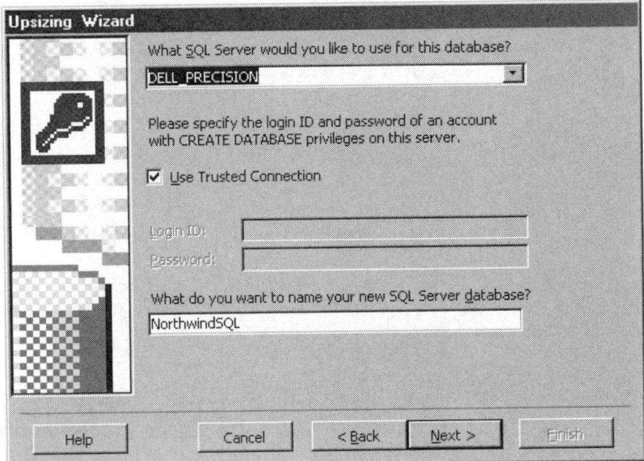

Figure E-3. Specify the server and database name for the new SQL Server database.

You can also set up an explicit connection by clearing the Use Trusted Connection check box and entering the login ID and password for a connection.

5 Select the tables to export to SQL Server, as shown in Figure E-4. Click Next.

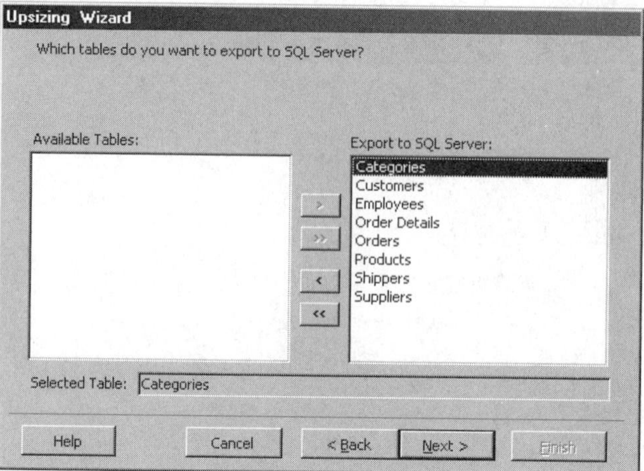

Figure E-4. Select the tables to export.

6 Select which table attributes to upsize, as shown in Figure E-5. You also have several options for adding timestamp fields to tables. Click Next.

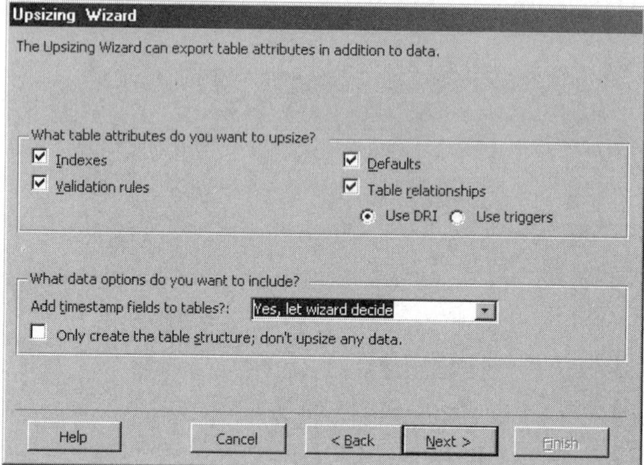

Figure E-5. You have several choices for table attributes to export to SQL Server tables.

Appendix E

note The Help button on the screens of the Upsizing Wizard doesn't open Help topics appropriate for this wizard; it opens a Help topic about the Link Table Wizard.

7 Choose to create a new Access client/server application (an Access project with a SQL Server back end), link SQL Server tables to an existing application, or make no application changes, as shown in Figure E-6. Click Next.

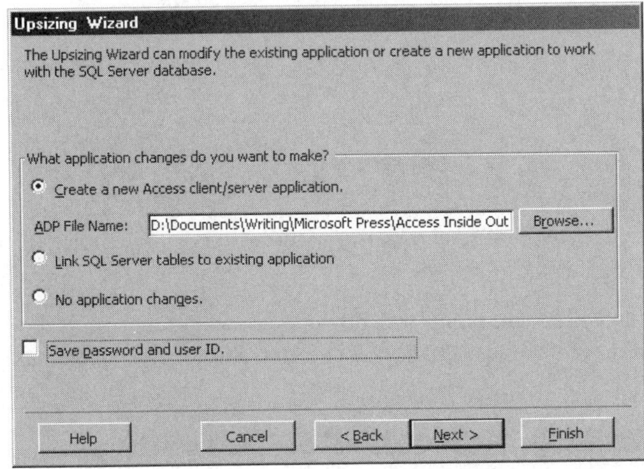

Figure E-6. Choose to create a new application or link to an existing application.

8 Before the wizard finishes, you can choose to open the new ADP file or return to the MDB file, as shown in Figure E-7. Click Finish.

tip **Download SQL Server Books Online**

SQL Server Books Online documents SQL Server extensively; it is installed with SQL Server 2000. If you don't have either of these programs, you can download this Help file from the SQL Server Books Online Web site at *http://www.microsoft.com/SQL/techinfo/productdoc/2000/books.asp*. Alternatively, you can purchase the SQL Server 2000 180-day trial CD; it also installs this useful information resource for SQL Server.

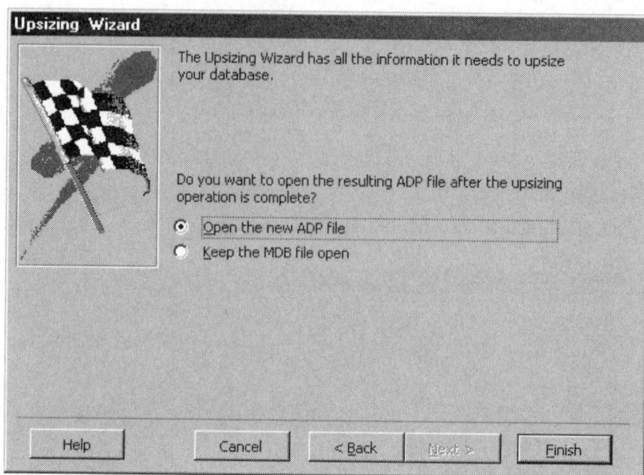

Figure E-7. The final screen of the wizard offers you a choice of opening the ADP or staying in the MDB.

After you click Finish, a progress dialog box appears, showing the progress of the creation of the new SQL Server database and Access project, as shown in Figure E-8.

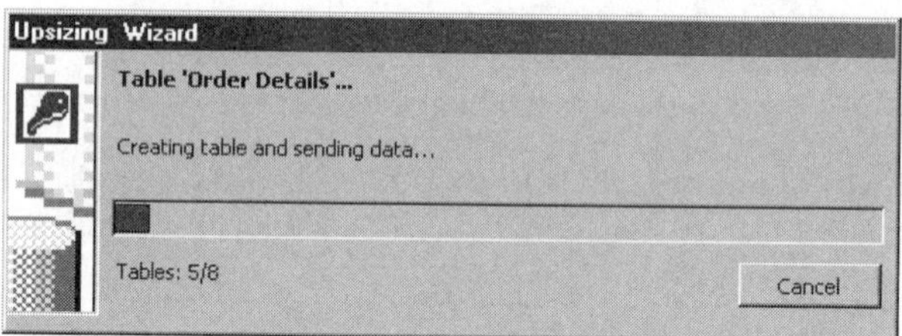

Figure E-8. The Upsizing Wizard dialog box shows the progress of creating the new SQL Server database and Access project front end.

When the process is complete, an Upsizing Wizard report opens in print preview, as shown in Figure E-9.

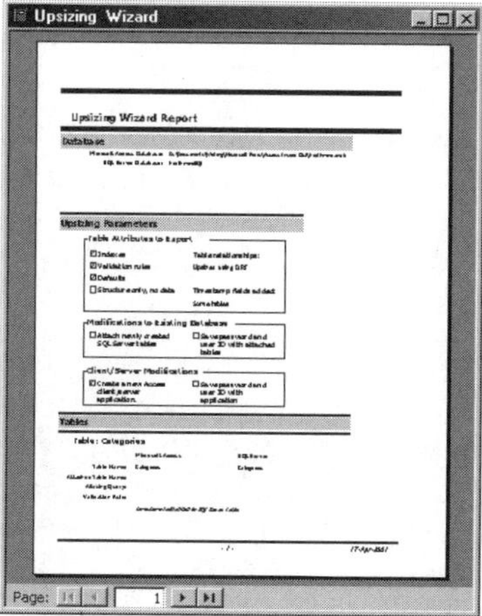

Figure E-9. The Upsizing Wizard report looks like this in print preview.

The report gives full details about the conversion, down to the data type of each field in each SQL Server table. Any problems will be reported in this document. Figure E-10 shows that some of the Northwind queries could not be upsized because they were DISTINCTROW queries.

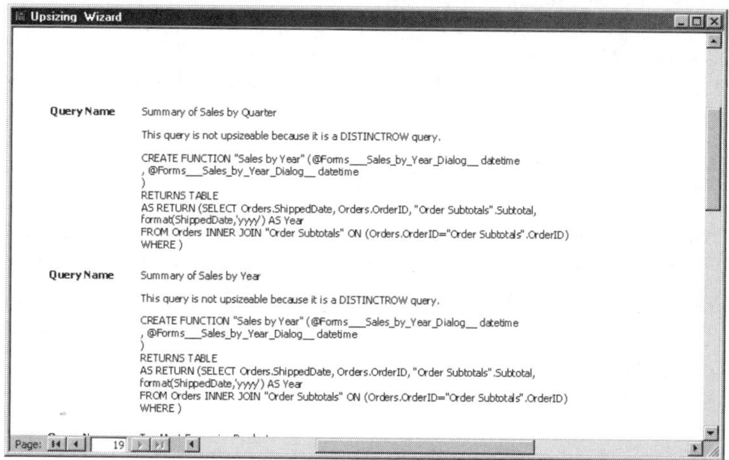

Figure E-10. Problems upsizing DISTINCTROW queries appear in the Upsizing Wizard report.

note Even though you select opening the ADP on the final wizard screen, you may be returned to the Access (MDB) database. In that case, just close the database, and open the project (ADP) file.

The project front end looks much like the Access database (see Figure E-11); however, all the tables are actually SQL Server tables, linked to the ADP front end.

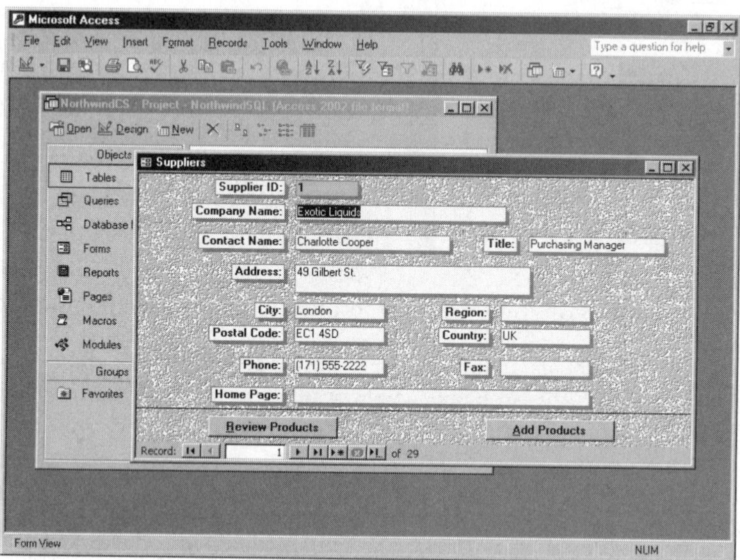

Figure E-11. The Suppliers form in the new Access project (ADP) file looks like this.

Fine-Tuning After Upsizing

While generally the Upsizing Wizard does a good job of upsizing Access tables to SQL Server tables, you might encounter problems, particularly with tables that don't have a unique index. (They will be omitted.) Certain field properties that aren't supported in SQL Server will be dropped (such as *AllowZeroLength*, *InputMask*, and *Format*), and hidden tables will be skipped.

Queries are more likely to cause problems when upsizing. Some Access query types don't have corresponding views or stored procedures in projects, and others are changed in various ways. In the preceding example, the Northwind Quarterly Orders by Product crosstab query wasn't converted at all, with an error message "Crosstab queries cannot be upsized." The Sales By Year query failed to upsize because a function (*Format*) was used in a column expression. However, the union query Customers And Suppliers By City was upsized correctly (something the Access 2000 Upsizing Wizard couldn't handle).

After you upsize a database, check all the database objects and make any needed changes, including recreating the queries that didn't make it and modifying forms and reports as needed for efficient functioning in a project. A full discussion of optimizing projects with SQL Server back ends is beyond the scope of this book; for more details on working with projects and SQL Server tables, you might want to look at a book such as *Inside Microsoft SQL Server 2000*, by Kalen Delaney, based on the first edition by Ron Soukup (Microsoft Press, 2000).

Appendix F
Control Properties

Following is a list of control properties and the controls they apply to. A few properties are available only in VBA code; they are indicated by "VBA only" after the property name or control name. For more information about a control property (including some of the more obscure properties not described in this book), position the insertion point in the property box of the properties sheet and press F1 to open context-specific Help.

Access control properties

Property	Applies to
Action	VBA only
AllowAutoCorrect	Combo Box Text Box
AutoActivate	Bound Object Frame Unbound Object Frame
AutoExpand	Combo Box
AutoRepeat	Command Button
AutoTab	Text Box
BackColor	Bound Object Frame Combo Box Image Label List Box Option Group Rectangle Text Box Unbound Object Frame

(continued)

Appendix F

(continued)

Property	Applies to
BackStyle	Bound Object Frame Combo Box Image Label Option Group Rectangle Tab Control Text Box Unbound Object Frame
BorderColor	Bound Object Frame Check Box Combo Box Image Label Line List Box Option Button Option Group Rectangle Subform Text Box Unbound Object Frame
BorderLineStyle	VBA only
BorderStyle	Bound Object Frame Check Box Combo Box Image Label Line List Box Option Button Option Group Rectangle Subform Text Box Unbound Object Frame

Appendix F: Control Properties

Property	Applies to
BorderWidth	Bound Object Frame Check Box Combo Box Image Label Line List Box Option Button Option Group Subform Rectangle Text Box Unbound Object Frame
BottomMargin	Label Text Box
BoundColumn	Combo Box List Box
Cancel	Command Button
CanGrow	Text Box Subform
CanShrink	Text Box Subform
Caption	Command Button Label Toggle Button
Class	VBA only
ColumnCount	Combo Box List Box Unbound Object Frame

(continued)

(continued)

Property	Applies to
ColumnHeads	Combo Box List Box Unbound Object Frame (VBA only)
ColumnHidden	VBA only
ColumnOrder	VBA only
ColumnWidth	VBA only
ColumnWidths	Combo Box List Box
ConditionalFormat	Combo Box Text Box
ControlSource	Bound Object Frame Check Box Combo Box List Box Option Group Text Box Toggle Button
ControlTipText	Bound Object Frame Check Box Combo Box Command Button Image Label List Box Option Button Option Group Text Box Toggle Button Unbound Object Frame

Property	Applies to
ControlType	VBA only
DecimalPlaces	Combo Box Text Box
Default	VBA only
DefaultValue	Check Box Combo Box List Box Option Group Text Box Toggle Button
DisplayType	Bound Object Frame Unbound Object Frame
DisplayWhen	Bound Object Frame Check Box Combo Box Command Button Image Label Line List Box Option Button Option Group Rectangle Subform Tab Control Text Box Toggle Button Unbound Object Frame

(continued)

(continued)

Property	Applies to
Enabled	Bound Object Frame Check Box Combo Box Command Button List Box Option Button Option Group Subform Tab Control Text Box Toggle Button Unbound Object Frame
EnterKeyBehavior	Text Box
EventProcPrefix	VBA only
FilterLookup	Text Box
FontBold	VBA only (set through *Font Weight* property in the interface)
FontItalic	Combo Box Command Button Label List Box Tab Control Text Box Toggle Button
FontName	Combo Box Command Button Label List Box Tab Control Text Box Toggle Button

Property	Applies to
FontSize	Combo Box Command Button Label List Box Tab Control Text Box Toggle Button
FontUnderline	Combo Box Command Button Label List Box Tab Control Text Box Toggle Button
FontWeight	Combo Box Command Button Label List Box Tab Control Text Box Toggle Button
ForeColor	Combo Box Command Button Label List Box Text Box Toggle Button
Format	Combo Box Text Box

(continued)

(continued)

Property	Applies to
Height	Bound Object Frame Check Box Combo Box Command Button Image Label Line List Box Option Button Option Group Rectangle Tab Control Subform Text Box Toggle Button Unbound Object Frame
HelpContextId	Bound Object Frame Check Box Combo Box Command Button Image Label List Box Option Button Option Group Tab Control Text Box Toggle Button Unbound Object Frame

Property	Applies to
HyperlinkAddress	Command Button Image
HyperlinkSubAddress	Command Button Image
ImageHeight	Image
ImageWidth	Image
IMEHold	Combo Box List Box Text Box
IMEMode	Combo Box List Box Text Box
IMESentenceMode	Combo Box List Box Text Box
InputMask	Combo Box Text Box
InSelection	VBA only
IsHyperlink	Combo Box Text Box
Item	VBA only
KeyboardLanguage	Combo Box Text Box

(continued)

(continued)

Property	Applies to
Left	Bound Object Frame Check Box Combo Box Command Button Image Label Line List Box Option Button Option Group Page Break Subform Rectangle Tab Control Text Box Toggle Button Unbound Object Frame
LeftMargin	Label Text Box
LimitToList	Combo Box
LineSlant	Line
LineSpacing	Label Text Box
LinkChildFields	Subform Unbound Object Frame
LinkMasterFields	Subform Unbound Object Frame
ListCount	VBA only
ListIndex	VBA only

Property	Applies to
ListRows	Combo Box
ListWidth	Combo Box
Locked	Bound Object Frame Check Box Combo Box List Box Option Button Option Group Subform Text Box Toggle Button Unbound Object Frame
LpOleObject	VBA only
MultiRow	Tab Control
MultiSelect	List Box
Name	Bound Object Frame Check Box Combo Box Command Button Image Label Line List Box Option Button Option Group Page Break Rectangle Subform Tab Control Text Box Toggle Button Unbound Object Frame

(continued)

(continued)

Property	Applies to
NumeralShapes	Combo Box Label List Box Text Box
ObjectPalette	VBA only
ObjectVerbsCount	VBA only
OldBorderStyle	VBA only
OLEClass	Unbound Object Frame
OLEType	Bound Object Frame Unbound Object Frame
OLETypeAllowed	Bound Object Frame Unbound Object Frame
OptionValue	Option Button
Picture	Command Button Image Toggle Button
PictureAlignment	Image
PictureData	VBA only
PictureTiling	Image
PictureType	Command Button Image Toggle Button
ReadingOrder	Check Box Combo Box Command Button Label List Box Option Button Text Box Toggle Button

Appendix F: Control Properties

Property	Applies to
RightMargin	Label Text Box
RowSource	Combo Box List Box Unbound Object Frame
RowSourceType	Combo Box List Box Unbound Object Frame
ScrollBarAlign	Combo Box List Box Text Box
ScrollBars	Text Box
Section	VBA only
SelLength	Combo Box Text Box
SelStart	Combo Box Text Box
SelText	Combo Box Text Box
ShortcutMenuBar	Bound Object Frame Check Box Combo Box Command Button Image List Box Option Button Option Group Tab Control Text Box Toggle Button Unbound Object Frame

(continued)

(continued)

Property	Applies to
SizeMode	Bound Object Frame Image Unbound Object Frame
SourceDoc	Bound Object Frame Unbound Object Frame
SourceItem	Bound Object Frame Unbound Object Frame
SourceObject	Subform Unbound Object Frame (VBA only)
SpecialEffect	Bound Object Frame Check Box Combo Box Image Label Line List Box Option Button Option Group Rectangle Subform Text Box Unbound Object Frame
StatusBarText	Bound Object Frame Check Box Combo Box Command Button List Box Option Button Option Group Subform Tab Control Text Box Toggle Button Unbound Object Frame

Property	Applies to
Style	Tab Control
TabFixedHeight	Tab Control
TabFixedWidth	Tab Control
TabIndex	Bound Object Frame Check Box Combo Box Command Button List Box Option Group Subform Tab Control Text Box Toggle Button Unbound Object Frame
TabStop	Bound Object Frame Check Box Combo Box Command Button List Box Option Group Subform Tab Control Text Box Toggle Button Unbound Object Frame

(continued)

(continued)

Property	Applies to
Tag	Bound Object Frame Check Box Combo Box Command Button Image Label Line List Box Option Button Option Group Page Break Rectangle Subform Tab Control Text Box Toggle Button Unbound Object Frame
Text	VBA only
TextAlign	Combo Box Label Text Box
TextFontCharSet	VBA only

Property	Applies to
Top	Bound Object Frame Check Box Combo Box Command Button Image Label Line List Box Option Button Option Group Page Break Rectangle Subform Tab Control Text Box Toggle Button Unbound Object Frame
TopMargin	Label Text Box
Transparent	Command Button
TripleState	Check Box Toggle Button
UpdateOptions	Bound Object Frame Unbound Object Frame

(continued)

(continued)

Property	Applies to
ValidationRule	Check Box Combo Box List Box Option Group Text Box Toggle Button
ValidationText	Check Box Combo Box List Box Option Group Text Box Toggle Button
Verb	Bound Object Frame Unbound Object Frame
Vertical	Label Text Box
Visible	Bound Object Frame Check Box Combo Box Command Button Image Label Line List Box Option Button Option Group Page Break Rectangle Subform Tab Control Text Box Toggle Button Unbound Object Frame

Property	Applies to
Width	Bound Object Frame
	Check Box
	Combo Box
	Command Button
	Image
	Label
	Line
	List Box
	Option Button
	Option Group
	Rectangle
	Subform
	Tab Control
	Text Box
	Toggle Button
	Unbound Object Frame

Index to Troubleshooting Topics

Index

Symbols and Numbers

A

D

G

P

V

W

About the Author

Helen Feddema grew up in New York City. She was ready for computers when she was 12, but computers were not yet ready for her. So she earned a degree in philosophy from Columbia University and a master's in theological studies from Harvard Divinity School while working at various office jobs. It was at HDS that she acquired her first computer, an Osborne, and soon computers were her primary interest. She started with word processing and spreadsheets, went on to learn dBASE, and did dBASE development for several years, part of this time as a corporate developer. After being laid off in a flurry of corporate downsizing, she started doing independent consulting and development, using dBASE, ObjectVision, WordPerfect, and Paradox.

Always on the lookout for something new and better, Helen beta tested Access 1.0 and soon recognized that this was the database she'd been expecting ever since Windows 3.0 was introduced and she had perceived the gap waiting to be filled by a great Windows database. Since then she has worked as a developer of Microsoft Office applications, specializing in Access, Outlook, and Word.

Helen has been a prolific author and coauthor of Access-related books and publications, cowriting *Inside Microsoft Access* (New Riders, 1992), *Access How-Tos* (Waite Group Press, 1995), and *MCSD: Access 95 Study Guide* (Sybex, 1998), and authoring *DAO Object Model: The Definitive Reference* (O'Reilly, 2000) and two books within the "The Pros Talk Access" series—*Power Forms* and *Power Reports* (Pinnacle, 1994). Other Office-related books include *Teach Yourself Project (*Que, 1998) and *Special Edition: Using Microsoft Outlook 2000* (Que, 1999), among others.

She has also been a regular contributor to Pinnacle's *Smart Access* and *Office Developer* journals, edits Woody's *Access Watch* e-zine, and writes its "Access Archon" column. Helen maintains a Web page (*http://www.helenfeddema.com*) with a large selection of code samples that focus on connecting Access, Outlook, Word, and Excel (including several Access add-ins). The site includes all of her "Access Archon" articles.

She is a big-time beta tester, sometimes having seven or eight betas running at once (mostly Microsoft). She has participated in every Access beta from 1.0 to 2002 and is a member of the Access Insiders group.

Helen lives in the mid-Hudson Valley area of New York State, with three cats and three computers.

The manuscript for this book was prepared and galleyed using Microsoft Word 2002. Pages were composed by Microsoft Press using Adobe PageMaker 6.52 for Windows, with text in Minion and display type in Syntax. Composed pages were delivered to the printer as electronic prepress files.

coverdesigner
GIRVIN/Strategic Branding & Design

coverillustrator
Todd Daman

interiorgraphicdesigner
James D. Kramer

interiorartist
Rob Nance

principalcopyeditor
Shawn Peck

indexer
Shane-Armstrong Information Systems

for Stepping Stone Graphics

compositor
Barbara Levy

proofreader
Marilyn Orozco

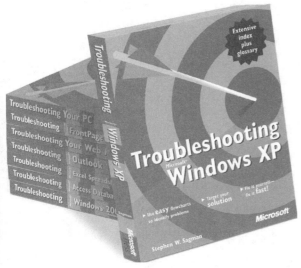

Get a **Free**
e-mail newsletter, updates, special offers, links to related books, and more when you

register on line!

Register your Microsoft Press® title on our Web site and you'll get a FREE subscription to our e-mail newsletter, *Microsoft Press Book Connections.* You'll find out about newly released and upcoming books and learning tools, online events, software downloads, special offers and coupons for Microsoft Press customers, and information about major Microsoft® product releases. You can also read useful additional information about all the titles we publish, such as detailed book descriptions, tables of contents and indexes, sample chapters, links to related books and book series, author biographies, and reviews by other customers.

Registration is easy. Just visit this Web page and fill in your information:

http://www.microsoft.com/mspress/register

Microsoft

Proof of Purchase

Use this page as proof of purchase if participating in a promotion or rebate offer on this title. Proof of purchase must be used in conjunction with other proof(s) of payment such as your dated sales receipt—see offer details.

Microsoft® Access Version 2002 Inside Out

0-7356-1283-8

CUSTOMER NAME

Microsoft Press, PO Box 97017, Redmond, WA 98073-9830

MICROSOFT LICENSE AGREEMENT

Book Companion CD

IMPORTANT—READ CAREFULLY: This Microsoft End-User License Agreement ("EULA") is a legal agreement between you (either an individual or an entity) and Microsoft Corporation for the Microsoft product identified above, which includes computer software and may include associated media, printed materials, and "online" or electronic documentation ("SOFTWARE PRODUCT"). Any component included within the SOFTWARE PRODUCT that is accompanied by a separate End-User License Agreement shall be governed by such agreement and not the terms set forth below. By installing, copying, or otherwise using the SOFTWARE PRODUCT, you agree to be bound by the terms of this EULA. If you do not agree to the terms of this EULA, you are not authorized to install, copy, or otherwise use the SOFTWARE PRODUCT; you may, however, return the SOFTWARE PRODUCT, along with all printed materials and other items that form a part of the Microsoft product that includes the SOFTWARE PRODUCT, to the place you obtained them for a full refund.

SOFTWARE PRODUCT LICENSE

The SOFTWARE PRODUCT is protected by United States copyright laws and international copyright treaties, as well as other intellectual property laws and treaties. The SOFTWARE PRODUCT is licensed, not sold.

1. **GRANT OF LICENSE.** This EULA grants you the following rights:
   a. **Software Product.** You may install and use one copy of the SOFTWARE PRODUCT on a single computer. The primary user of the computer on which the SOFTWARE PRODUCT is installed may make a second copy for his or her exclusive use on a portable computer.

   b. **Storage/Network Use.** You may also store or install a copy of the SOFTWARE PRODUCT on a storage device, such as a network server, used only to install or run the SOFTWARE PRODUCT on your other computers over an internal network; however, you must acquire and dedicate a license for each separate computer on which the SOFTWARE PRODUCT is installed or run from the storage device. A license for the SOFTWARE PRODUCT may not be shared or used concurrently on different computers.

   c. **License Pak.** If you have acquired this EULA in a Microsoft License Pak, you may make the number of additional copies of the computer software portion of the SOFTWARE PRODUCT authorized on the printed copy of this EULA, and you may use each copy in the manner specified above. You are also entitled to make a corresponding number of secondary copies for portable computer use as specified above.

   d. **Sample Code.** Solely with respect to portions, if any, of the SOFTWARE PRODUCT that are identified within the SOFTWARE PRODUCT as sample code (the "SAMPLE CODE"):

      i. **Use and Modification.** Microsoft grants you the right to use and modify the source code version of the SAMPLE CODE, *provided* you comply with subsection (d)(iii) below. You may not distribute the SAMPLE CODE, or any modified version of the SAMPLE CODE, in source code form.

      ii. **Redistributable Files.** Provided you comply with subsection (d)(iii) below, Microsoft grants you a nonexclusive, royalty-free right to reproduce and distribute the object code version of the SAMPLE CODE and of any modified SAMPLE CODE, other than SAMPLE CODE, or any modified version thereof, designated as not redistributable in the Readme file that forms a part of the SOFTWARE PRODUCT (the "Non-Redistributable Sample Code"). All SAMPLE CODE other than the Non-Redistributable Sample Code is collectively referred to as the "REDISTRIBUTABLES."

      iii. **Redistribution Requirements.** If you redistribute the REDISTRIBUTABLES, you agree to: (i) distribute the REDISTRIBUTABLES in object code form only in conjunction with and as a part of your software application product; (ii) not use Microsoft's name, logo, or trademarks to market your software application product; (iii) include a valid copyright notice on your software application product; (iv) indemnify, hold harmless, and defend Microsoft from and against any claims or lawsuits, including attorney's fees, that arise or result from the use or distribution of your software application product; and (v) not permit further distribution of the REDISTRIBUTABLES by your end user. Contact Microsoft for the applicable royalties due and other licensing terms for all other uses and/or distribution of the REDISTRIBUTABLES.

2. **DESCRIPTION OF OTHER RIGHTS AND LIMITATIONS.**
   - **Limitations on Reverse Engineering, Decompilation, and Disassembly.** You may not reverse engineer, decompile, or disassemble the SOFTWARE PRODUCT, except and only to the extent that such activity is expressly permitted by applicable law notwithstanding this limitation.
   - **Separation of Components.** The SOFTWARE PRODUCT is licensed as a single product. Its component parts may not be separated for use on more than one computer.
   - **Rental.** You may not rent, lease, or lend the SOFTWARE PRODUCT.
   - **Support Services.** Microsoft may, but is not obligated to, provide you with support services related to the SOFTWARE PRODUCT ("Support Services"). Use of Support Services is governed by the Microsoft policies and programs described in the

user manual, in "online" documentation, and/or in other Microsoft-provided materials. Any supplemental software code provided to you as part of the Support Services shall be considered part of the SOFTWARE PRODUCT and subject to the terms and conditions of this EULA. With respect to technical information you provide to Microsoft as part of the Support Services, Microsoft may use such information for its business purposes, including for product support and development. Microsoft will not utilize such technical information in a form that personally identifies you.

- **EULA Rights Transfer.** You may permanently transfer all of your rights under this EULA, provided you retain no copies, you transfer all of the SOFTWARE PRODUCT (including all component parts, the media and printed materials, any upgrades, this EULA, and, if applicable, the Certificate of Authenticity), **and** the recipient agrees to the terms of this EULA.
- **Termination.** Without prejudice to any other rights, Microsoft may terminate this EULA if you fail to comply with the terms and conditions of this EULA. In such event, you must destroy all copies of the SOFTWARE PRODUCT and all of its component parts.

3. **COPYRIGHT.** All title and copyrights in and to the SOFTWARE PRODUCT (including but not limited to any images, photographs, animations, video, audio, music, text, SAMPLE CODE, REDISTRIBUTABLES, and "applets" incorporated into the SOFTWARE PRODUCT) and any copies of the SOFTWARE PRODUCT are owned by Microsoft or its suppliers. The SOFTWARE PRODUCT is protected by copyright laws and international treaty provisions. Therefore, you must treat the SOFTWARE PRODUCT like any other copyrighted material **except** that you may install the SOFTWARE PRODUCT on a single computer provided you keep the original solely for backup or archival purposes. You may not copy the printed materials accompanying the SOFTWARE PRODUCT.

4. **U.S. GOVERNMENT RESTRICTED RIGHTS.** The SOFTWARE PRODUCT and documentation are provided with RESTRICTED RIGHTS. Use, duplication, or disclosure by the Government is subject to restrictions as set forth in subparagraph (c)(1)(ii) of the Rights in Technical Data and Computer Software clause at DFARS 252.227-7013 or subparagraphs (c)(1) and (2) of the Commercial Computer Software—Restricted Rights at 48 CFR 52.227-19, as applicable. Manufacturer is Microsoft Corporation/One Microsoft Way/Redmond, WA 98052-6399.

5. **EXPORT RESTRICTIONS.** You agree that you will not export or re-export the SOFTWARE PRODUCT, any part thereof, or any process or service that is the direct product of the SOFTWARE PRODUCT (the foregoing collectively referred to as the "Restricted Components"), to any country, person, entity, or end user subject to U.S. export restrictions. You specifically agree not to export or re-export any of the Restricted Components (i) to any country to which the U.S. has embargoed or restricted the export of goods or services, which currently include, but are not necessarily limited to, Cuba, Iran, Iraq, Libya, North Korea, Sudan, and Syria, or to any national of any such country, wherever located, who intends to transmit or transport the Restricted Components back to such country; (ii) to any end user who you know or have reason to know will utilize the Restricted Components in the design, development, or production of nuclear, chemical, or biological weapons; or (iii) to any end user who has been prohibited from participating in U.S. export transactions by any federal agency of the U.S. government. You warrant and represent that neither the BXA nor any other U.S. federal agency has suspended, revoked, or denied your export privileges.

DISCLAIMER OF WARRANTY

NO WARRANTIES OR CONDITIONS. MICROSOFT EXPRESSLY DISCLAIMS ANY WARRANTY OR CONDITION FOR THE SOFTWARE PRODUCT. THE SOFTWARE PRODUCT AND ANY RELATED DOCUMENTATION ARE PROVIDED "AS IS" WITHOUT WARRANTY OR CONDITION OF ANY KIND, EITHER EXPRESS OR IMPLIED, INCLUDING, WITHOUT LIMITATION, THE IMPLIED WARRANTIES OF MERCHANTABILITY, FITNESS FOR A PARTICULAR PURPOSE, OR NONINFRINGEMENT. THE ENTIRE RISK ARISING OUT OF USE OR PERFORMANCE OF THE SOFTWARE PRODUCT REMAINS WITH YOU.

LIMITATION OF LIABILITY. TO THE MAXIMUM EXTENT PERMITTED BY APPLICABLE LAW, IN NO EVENT SHALL MICROSOFT OR ITS SUPPLIERS BE LIABLE FOR ANY SPECIAL, INCIDENTAL, INDIRECT, OR CONSEQUENTIAL DAMAGES WHATSOEVER (INCLUDING, WITHOUT LIMITATION, DAMAGES FOR LOSS OF BUSINESS PROFITS, BUSINESS INTERRUPTION, LOSS OF BUSINESS INFORMATION, OR ANY OTHER PECUNIARY LOSS) ARISING OUT OF THE USE OF OR INABILITY TO USE THE SOFTWARE PRODUCT OR THE PROVISION OF OR FAILURE TO PROVIDE SUPPORT SERVICES, EVEN IF MICROSOFT HAS BEEN ADVISED OF THE POSSIBILITY OF SUCH DAMAGES. IN ANY CASE, MICROSOFT'S ENTIRE LIABILITY UNDER ANY PROVISION OF THIS EULA SHALL BE LIMITED TO THE GREATER OF THE AMOUNT ACTUALLY PAID BY YOU FOR THE SOFTWARE PRODUCT OR US$5.00; PROVIDED, HOWEVER, IF YOU HAVE ENTERED INTO A MICROSOFT SUPPORT SERVICES AGREEMENT, MICROSOFT'S ENTIRE LIABILITY REGARDING SUPPORT SERVICES SHALL BE GOVERNED BY THE TERMS OF THAT AGREEMENT. BECAUSE SOME STATES AND JURISDICTIONS DO NOT ALLOW THE EXCLUSION OR LIMITATION OF LIABILITY, THE ABOVE LIMITATION MAY NOT APPLY TO YOU.

MISCELLANEOUS

This EULA is governed by the laws of the State of Washington USA, except and only to the extent that applicable law mandates governing law of a different jurisdiction.

Should you have any questions concerning this EULA, or if you desire to contact Microsoft for any reason, please contact the Microsoft subsidiary serving your country, or write: Microsoft Sales Information Center/One Microsoft Way/Redmond, WA 98052-6399.

PN [illegible]96